THE
EXPOSITOR'S
BIBLE
COMMENTARY

THE
EXPOSITOR'S BIBLE COMMENTARY

with
The New International Version
of
The Holy Bible

IN TWELVE VOLUMES

VOLUME 4

(1 KINGS–JOB)

Regency
Reference Library
Zondervan Publishing House
Grand Rapids, Michigan

THE EXPOSITOR'S BIBLE COMMENTARY, VOLUME 4

Copyright © 1988 by The Zondervan Corporation
Grand Rapids, Michigan

Regency Reference Library is an imprint of Zondervan
Publishing House, 1415 Lake Drive, S.E.,
Grand Rapids, Michigan 49506

Library of Congress Cataloging in Publication Data
(Revised for vol. 4)

The Expositor's Bible commentary.

Includes bibliographies.
Contents: v. 1. Introductory articles.— v. 4. I Kings–
Job.—[etc.]—v. 12. Hebrews–Revelation.
1. Bible—Commentaries. I. Gaebelein, Frank Ely, 1899– .
II. Douglas, J. D. (James Dixon) III. Bible. English. New
International. 1976.
BS491.2.E96   220.7'7   76-41334
ISBN 0-310-36460-4 (v. 4)

Printed in the United States of America

91 92 93 94 95 / DH / 10 9 8 7 6 5

This edition is printed on acid-free paper and meets the
American National Standards Institute Z39.48 standard.

CONTENTS

CONTRIBUTORS TO VOLUME 4

1 and 2 Kings: R. D. Patterson

B.A., Wheaton College; M.Div., Los Angeles Baptist Seminary; Th.M., Talbot Seminary; M.A., Ph.D., U.C.L.A.

Dean of Graduate Studies; Chairman, Department of Biblical Studies, Liberty Baptist Theological Seminary

and Hermann J. Austel

B.S., M.A., Ph.D., U.C.L.A.; M.Div., Los Angeles Baptist Seminary

Dean and Professor of Old Testament, Northwest Baptist Seminary

1 and 2 Chronicles: J. Barton Payne

A.B., M.A., University of California; B.D., San Francisco Theological Seminary; Th.M., Ph.D., Princeton Theological Seminary

Former Professor of Old Testament, Covenant Theological Seminary

Ezra, Nehemiah: Edwin Yamauchi

B.A., Shelton College; M.A., Ph.D., Brandeis University

Professor of History, Miami University (Ohio)

Esther: F. B. Huey, Jr.

B.B.A., University of Texas, Austin; M.Div., Ph.D., Southwestern Baptist Theological Seminary

Professor of Old Testament, Southwest Baptist Theological Seminary

Job: Elmer B. Smick

B.A., The King's College; Th.B., S.T.M., Faith Theological Seminary; Ph.D. Dropsie College

Professor of Old Testament Languages and Literature, Gordon-Conwell Theological Seminary

PREFACE

The title of this work defines its purpose. Written primarily by expositors for expositors, it aims to provide preachers, teachers, and students of the Bible with a new and comprehensive commentary on the books of the Old and New Testaments. Its stance is that of a scholarly evangelicalism committed to the divine inspiration, complete trustworthiness, and full authority of the Bible. Its seventy-eight contributors come from the United States, Canada, England, Scotland, Australia, New Zealand, and Switzerland, and from various religious groups, including Anglican, Baptist, Brethren, Free, Independent, Methodist, Nazarene, Presbyterian, and Reformed churches. Most of them teach at colleges, universities, or theological seminaries.

No book has been more closely studied over a longer period of time than the Bible. From the Midrashic commentaries going back to the period of Ezra, through parts of the Dead Sea Scrolls and the Patristic literature, and on to the present, the Scriptures have been expounded. Indeed, there have been times when, as in the Reformation and on occasions since then, exposition has been at the cutting edge of Christian advance. Luther was a powerful exegete, and Calvin is still called "the prince of expositors."

Their successors have been many. And now, when the outburst of new translations and their unparalleled circulation have expanded the readership of the Bible, the need for exposition takes on fresh urgency.

Not that God's Word can ever become captive to its expositors. Among all other books, it stands first in its combination of perspicuity and profundity. Though a child can be made "wise for salvation" by believing its witness to Christ, the greatest mind cannot plumb the depths of its truth (2 Tim. 3:15; Rom. 11:33). As Gregory the Great said, "Holy Scripture is a stream of running water, where alike the elephant may swim, and the lamb walk." So, because of the inexhaustible nature of Scripture, the task of opening up its meaning is still a perennial obligation of biblical scholarship.

How that task is done inevitably reflects the outlook of those engaged in it. Every Bible scholar has presuppositions. To this neither the editors of these volumes nor the contributors to them are exceptions. They share a common commitment to the supernatural Christianity set forth in the inspired Word. Their purpose is not to supplant the many valuable commentaries that have preceded this work and from which both the editors and contributors have learned. It is rather to draw on the resources of contemporary evangelical scholarship in producing a new reference work for understanding the Scriptures.

A commentary that will continue to be useful through the years should handle contemporary trends in biblical studies in such a way as to avoid becoming outdated when critical fashions change. Biblical criticism is not in itself inadmissable, as some have mistakenly thought. When scholars investigate the authorship, date, literary characteristics, and purpose of a biblical document, they are practicing biblical criticism. So also when, in order to ascertain as nearly as possible the original form of the text, they deal with variant readings, scribal errors, emendations, and other phenomena in the manuscripts. To do these things is essential to responsible exegesis and exposition. And always there is the need to distinguish hypothesis from fact, conjecture from truth.

The chief principle of interpretation followed in this commentary is the grammatico-historical one—namely, that the primary aim of the exegete is to make clear the meaning of the text at the time and in the circumstances of its writing. This endeavor to understand what in the first instance the inspired writers actually said must not be confused with an inflexible literalism. Scripture makes lavish use of symbols and figures of speech; great portions of it are poetical. Yet when it speaks in this way, it speaks no less truly than it does in its historical and doctrinal portions. To understand its message requires attention to matters of grammar and syntax, word meanings, idioms, and literary forms—all in relation to the historical and cultural setting of the text.

The contributors to this work necessarily reflect varying convictions. In certain controversial matters the policy is that of clear statement of the contributors' own views followed by fair presentation of other ones. The treatment of eschatology, though it reflects differences of interpretation, is consistent with a general premillennial position. (Not all contributors, however, are premillennial.) But prophecy is more than prediction, and so this commentary gives due recognition to the major lode of godly social concern in the prophetic writings.

THE EXPOSITOR'S BIBLE COMMENTARY is presented as a scholarly work, though not primarily one of technical criticism. In its main portion, the Exposition, and in Volume 1 (General and Special Articles), all Semitic and Greek words are transliterated and the English equivalents given. As for the Notes, here Semitic and Greek characters are used but always with transliterations and English meanings, so that this portion of the commentary will be as accessible as possible to readers unacquainted with the original languages.

It is the conviction of the general editor, shared by his colleagues in the Zondervan editorial department, that in writing about the Bible, lucidity is not incompatible with scholarship. They are therefore endeavoring to make this a clear and understandable work.

The translation used in it is the New International Version (North American Edition). To the International Bible Society thanks are due for permission to use this most recent of the major Bible translations. It was chosen because of the clarity and beauty of its style and its faithfulness to the original texts.

To the associate editor, Richard P. Polcyn, and to the contributing editors— Dr. Walter C. Kaiser, Jr., Dr. Bruce K. Waltke, and Dr. Ralph H. Alexander for the Old Testament, and Dr. James Montgomery Boice and Dr. Merrill C. Tenney for the New Testament—the general editor expresses his gratitude for their unfailing cooperation and their generosity in advising him out of their expert scholarship. And to the many other contributors he is indebted for their invaluable part in this work. Finally, he owes a special debt of gratitude to Dr. Robert K. DeVries, publisher, The Zondervan Corporation, and Miss Elizabeth Brown, secretary, for their assistance and encouragement.

Whatever else it is—the greatest and most beautiful of books, the primary source of law and morality, the fountain of wisdom, and the infallible guide to life—the Bible is above all the inspired witness to Jesus Christ. May this work fulfill its function of expounding the Scriptures with grace and clarity, so that its users may find that both Old and New Testaments do indeed lead to our Lord Jesus Christ, who alone could say, "I have come that they may have life, and have it to the full" (John 10:10).

FRANK E. GAEBELEIN

ABBREVIATIONS

A. General Abbreviations

A	Codex Alexandrinus	Nestle	Nestle (ed.) *Novum*
Akkad.	Akkadian		*Testamentum Graece*
א	Codex Sinaiticus	no.	number
Ap. Lit.	Apocalyptic Literature	NT	New Testament
Apoc.	Apocrypha	obs.	obsolete
Aq.	Aquila's Greek Translation	OL	Old Latin
	of the Old Testament	OS	Old Syriac
Arab.	Arabic	OT	Old Testament
Aram.	Aramaic	p., pp.	page, pages
b	Babylonian Gemara	par.	paragraph
B	Codex Vaticanus	Pers.	Persian
C	Codex Ephraemi Syri	Pesh.	Peshitta
c.	*circa*, about	Phoen.	Phoenician
cf.	*confer*, compare	pl.	plural
ch., chs.	chapter, chapters	Pseudep.	Pseudepigrapha
cod., codd.	codex, codices	Q	Quelle ("Sayings" source
D	Codex Bezae		in the Gospels)
DSS	Dead Sea Scrolls (see E.)	qt.	quoted by
ed., edd.	edited, edition, editor; editions	q.v.	*quod vide*, which see
e.g.	*exempli gratia*, for example	R	Rabbah
Egyp.	Egyptian	rev.	revised, reviser, revision
et al.	*et alii*, and others	Rom.	Roman
EV	English Versions of the Bible	RVm	Revised Version margin
fem.	feminine	Samar.	Samaritan recension
ff.	following (verses, pages, etc.)	SCM	Student Christian Movement Press
fl.	flourished	Sem.	Semitic
ft.	foot, feet	sing.	singular
gen.	genitive	SPCK	Society for the Promotion
Gr.	Greek		of Christian Knowledge
Heb.	Hebrew	Sumer.	Sumerian
Hitt.	Hittite	s.v.	*sub verbo*, under the word
ibid.	*ibidem*, in the same place	Syr.	Syriac
id.	*idem*, the same	Symm.	Symmachus
i.e.	*id est*, that is	T	Talmud
impf.	imperfect	Targ.	Targum
infra.	below	Theod.	Theodotion
in loc.	*in loco*, in the place cited	TR	Textus Receptus
j	Jerusalem or	tr.	translation, translator,
	Palestinian Gemara		translated
Lat.	Latin	UBS	Tha United Bible Societies'
LL.	Late Latin		Greek Text
LXX	Septuagint	Ugar.	Ugaritic
M	Mishnah	u.s.	*ut supra*, as above
masc.	masculine	v., vv.	verse, verses
mg.	margin	viz.	*videlicet*, namely
Mid	Midrash	vol.	volume
MS(S)	manuscript(s)	vs.	versus
MT	Masoretic text	Vul.	Vulgate
n.	note	WH	Westcott and Hort, *The*
n.d.	no date		*New Testament in Greek*

B. Abbreviations for Modern Translations and Paraphrases

AmT	Smith and Goodspeed, *The Complete Bible, An American Translation*	Mof	J. Moffatt, *A New Translation of the Bible*
ASV	American Standard Version, American Revised Version (1901)	NAB	The New American Bible
		NASB	New American Standard Bible
		NEB	The New English Bible
		NIV	The New International Version
Beck	Beck, *The New Testament in the Language of Today*	Ph	J. B. Phillips *The New Testament in Modern English*
BV	Berkeley Version (The Modern Language Bible)	RSV	Revised Standard Version
		RV	Revised Version — 1881–1885
JB	The Jerusalem Bible	TCNT	Twentieth Century New Testament
JPS	*Jewish Publication Society Version of the Old Testament*	TEV	Today's English Version
KJV	King James Version	Wey	*Weymouth's New Testament in Modern Speech*
Knox	R.G. Knox, *The Holy Bible: A Translation from the Latin Vulgate in the Light of the Hebrew and Greek Original*	Wms	C. B. Williams, *The New Testament: A Translation in the Language of the People*
LB	The Living Bible		

C. Abbreviations for Periodicals and Reference Works

AASOR	*Annual of the American Schools of Oriental Research*	BASOR	*Bulletin of the American Schools of Oriental Research*
AB	*Anchor Bible*	BC	Foakes-Jackson and Lake: *The Beginnings of Christianity*
AIs	de Vaux: *Ancient Israel*		
AJA	*American Journal of Archaeology*	BDB	Brown, Driver, and Briggs: *Hebrew-English Lexicon of the Old Testament*
AJSL	*American Journal of Semitic Languages and Literatures*	BDF	Blass, Debrunner, and Funk: *A Greek Grammar of the New Testament and Other Early Christian Literature*
AJT	*American Journal of Theology*		
Alf	Alford: *Greek Testament Commentary*	BDT	Harrison: *Baker's Dictionary of Theology*
ANEA	*Ancient Near Eastern Archaeology*	Beng.	Bengel's *Gnomon*
ANEP	Pritchard: *Ancient Near Eastern Pictures*	BETS	*Bulletin of the Evangelical Theological Society*
ANET	Pritchard· *Ancient Near Eastern Texts*	BH	*Biblia Hebraica*
		BHS	*Biblia Hebraica Stuttgartensia*
ANF	Roberts and Donaldson: *The Ante-Nicene Fathers*	BJRL	*Bulletin of the John Rylands Library*
A-S	Abbot-Smith: *Manual Greek Lexicon of the New Testament*	BS	*Bibliotheca Sacra*
		BT	*Babylonian Talmud*
AThR	*Anglican Theological Review*	BTh	*Biblical Theology*
BA	*Biblical Archaeologist*	BW	*Biblical World*
BAG	Bauer, Arndt, and Gingrich: *Greek-English Lexicon of the New Testament*	CAH	*Cambridge Ancient History*
		CanJTh	*Canadian Journal of Theology*
		CBQ	*Catholic Biblical Quarterly*
BAGD	Bauer, Arndt, Gingrich, and Danker: *Greek-English Lexicon of the New Testament* 2nd edition	CBSC	*Cambridge Bible for Schools and Colleges*
		CE	*Catholic Encyclopedia*
		CGT	*Cambridge Greek Testament*

CHS	Lange: *Commentary on the Holy Scriptures*	IDB	*The Interpreter's Dictionary of the Bible*
ChT	*Christianity Today*	IEJ	*Israel Exploration Journal*
DDB	*Davis' Dictionary of the Bible*	Int	*Interpretation*
Deiss BS	Deissmann: *Bible Studies*	INT	E. Harrison: *Introduction to the New Testament*
Deiss LAE	Deissmann: *Light From the Ancient East*	IOT	R. K. Harrison: *Introduction to the Old Testament*
DNTT	*Dictionary of New Testament Theology*	ISBE	*The International Standard Bible Encyclopedia*
EBC	*The Expositor's Bible Commentary*	ITQ	*Irish Theological Quarterly*
EBi	*Encyclopaedia Biblica*	JAAR	*Journal of American Academy of Religion*
EBr	*Encyclopaedia Britannica*		
EDB	*Encyclopedic Dictionary of the Bible*	JAOS	*Journal of American Oriental Society*
EGT	Nicoll: *Expositor's Greek Testament*	JBL	*Journal of Biblical Literature*
EQ	*Evangelical Quarterly*	JE	*Jewish Encyclopedia*
ET	*Evangelische Theologie*	JETS	*Journal of Evangelical Theological Society*
ExB	*The Expositor's Bible*		
Exp	*The Expositor*	JFB	Jamieson, Fausset, and Brown: *Commentary on the Old and New Testament*
ExpT	*The Expository Times*		
FLAP	Finegan: *Light From the Ancient Past*		
GKC	Gesenius, Kautzsch, Cowley, *Hebrew Grammar*, 2nd Eng. ed.	JNES	*Journal of Near Eastern Studies*
		Jos. Antiq.	Josephus: *The Antiquities of the Jews*
GR	*Gordon Review*	Jos. War	Josephus: *The Jewish War*
HBD	*Harper's Bible Dictionary*	JQR	*Jewish Quarterly Review*
HDAC	Hastings: *Dictionary of the Apostolic Church*	JR	*Journal of Religion*
		JSJ	*Journal for the Study of Judaism in the Persian, Hellenistic and Roman Periods*
HDB	Hastings: *Dictionary of the Bible*		
HDBrev.	Hastings: *Dictionary of the Bible*, one-vol. rev. by Grant and Rowley	JSOR	*Journal of the Society of Oriental Research*
		JSS	*Journal of Semitic Studies*
HDCG	Hastings: *Dictionary of Christ and the Gospels*	JT	*Jerusalem Talmud*
		JTS	*Journal of Theological Studies*
HERE	Hastings: *Encyclopedia of Religion and Ethics*	KAHL	Kenyon: *Archaeology in the Holy Land*
HGEOTP	Heidel: *The Gilgamesh Epic and Old Testament Parallels*	KB	Koehler-Baumgartner: *Lexicon in Veteris Testament Libros*
HJP	Schurer: *A History of the Jewish People in the Time of Christ*	KD	Keil and Delitzsch: *Commentary on the Old Testament*
		LSJ	Liddell, Scott, Jones: *Greek-English Lexicon*
HR	Hatch and Redpath: *Concordance to the Septuagint*	LTJM	Edersheim: *The Life and Times of Jesus the Messiah*
HTR	*Harvard Theological Review*	MM	Moulton and Milligan: *The Vocabulary of the Greek Testament*
HUCA	*Hebrew Union College Annual*		
IB	*The Interpreter's Bible*		
ICC	*International Critical Commentary*	MNT	Moffatt: *New Testament Commentary*

MST	McClintock and Strong: *Cyclopedia of Biblical, Theological, and Ecclesiastical Literature*	SJT	*Scottish Journal of Theology*
NBC	Davidson, Kevan, and Stibbs: *The New Bible Commentary*, 1st ed.	SOT	Girdlestone: *Synonyms of Old Testament*
NBCrev.	Guthrie and Motyer: *The New Bible Commentary*, rev. ed.	SOTI	Archer: *A Survey of Old Testament Introduction*
		ST	*Studia Theologica*
NBD	J. D. Douglas: *The New Bible Dictionary*	TCERK	Loetscher: *The Twentieth Century Encyclopedia of Religious Knowledge*
NCB	*New Century Bible*	TDNT	Kittel: *Theological Dictionary of the New Testament*
NCE	*New Catholic Encyclopedia*	TDOT	*Theological Dictionary of the Old Testament*
NIC	*New International Commentary*		
NIDCC	Douglas: *The New International Dictionary of the Christian Church*	THAT	*Theologisches Handbuch zum Alten Testament*
NovTest	*Novum Testamentum*	ThT	*Theology Today*
NSI	Cooke: *Handbook of North Semitic Inscriptions*	TNTC	*Tyndale New Testament Commentaries*
NTS	*New Testament Studies*	Trench	Trench: *Synonyms of the New Testament*
ODCC	*The Oxford Dictionary of the Christian Church*, rev. ed.	TWOT	*Theological Wordbook of the Old Testament*
Peake	Black and Rowley: *Peake's Commentary on the Bible*	UBD	*Unger's Bible Dictionary*
PEQ	*Palestine Exploration Quarterly*	UT	Gordon: *Ugaritic Textbook*
PNFl	P. Schaff: *The Nicene and Post-Nicene Fathers* (1st series)	VB	Allmen: *Vocabulary of the Bible*
		VetTest	*Vetus Testamentum*
PNF2	P. Schaff and H. Wace: *The Nicene and Post-Nicene Fathers* (2nd series)	Vincent	Vincent: *Word-Pictures in the New Testament*
PTR	*Princeton Theological Review*	WBC	*Wycliffe Bible Commentary*
RB	*Revue Biblique*	WBE	*Wycliffe Bible Encyclopedia*
RHG	Robertson's *Grammar of the Greek New Testament in the Light of Historical Research*	WC	*Westminster Commentaries*
		WesBC	*Wesleyan Bible Commentaries*
		WTJ	*Westminster Theological Journal*
RTWB	Richardson: *A Theological Wordbook of the Bible*	ZAW	*Zeitschrift für die alttestamentliche Wissenschaft*
SBK	Strack and Billerbeck: *Kommentar zum Neuen Testament aus Talmud und Midrash*	ZNW	*Zeitschrift für die neutestamentliche Wissenschaft*
		ZPBD	*The Zondervan Pictorial Bible Dictionary*
		ZPEB	*The Zondervan Pictorial Encyclopedia of the Bible*
SHERK	*The New Schaff-Herzog Encyclopedia of Religious Knowledge*	ZWT	*Zeitschrift für wissenschaftliche Theologie*

D. Abbreviations for Books of the Bible, the Apocrypha, and the Pseudepigrapha

OLD TESTAMENT

Gen	2 Chron	Dan
Exod	Ezra	Hos
Lev	Neh	Joel
Num	Esth	Amos
Deut	Job	Obad
Josh	Ps(Pss)	Jonah
Judg	Prov	Mic
Ruth	Eccl	Nah
1 Sam	S of Songs	Hab
2 Sam	Isa	Zeph
1 Kings	Jer	Hag
2 Kings	Lam	Zech
1 Chron	Ezek	Mal

NEW TESTAMENT

Matt	1 Tim
Mark	2 Tim
Luke	Titus
John	Philem
Acts	Heb
Rom	James
1 Cor	1 Peter
2 Cor	2 Peter
Gal	1 John
Eph	2 John
Phil	3 John
Col	Jude
1 Thess	Rev
2 Thess	

APOCRYPHA

1 Esd	1 Esdras	Ep Jer	Epistle of Jeremy
2 Esd	2 Esdras	S Th Ch	Song of the Three Child.
Tobit	Tobit		(or Young Men)
Jud	Judith	Sus	Susanna
Add Esth	Additions to Esther	Bel	Bel and the Dragon
Wisd Sol	Wisdom of Solomon	Pr Man	Prayer of Manasseh
Ecclus	Ecclesiasticus (Wisdom of	1 Macc	1 Maccabees
	Jesus the Son of Sirach)	2 Macc	2 Maccabees
Baruch	Baruch		

PSEUDEPIGRAPHA

As Moses	Assumption of Moses	Pirke Aboth	Pirke Aboth
2 Baruch	Syriac Apocalypse of Baruch	Ps 151	Psalm 151
3 Baruch	Greek Apocalypse of Baruch	Pss Sol	Psalms of Solomon
1 Enoch	Ethiopic Book of Enoch	Sib Oracles	Sibylline Oracles
2 Enoch	Slavonic Book of Enoch	Story Ah	Story of Ahikar
3 Enoch	Hebrew Book of Enoch	T Abram	Testament of Abraham
4 Ezra	4 Ezra	T Adam	Testament of Adam
JA	Joseph and Asenath	T Benjamin	Testament of Benjamin
Jub	Book of Jubilees	T Dan	Testament of Dan
L Aristeas	Letter of Aristeas	T Gad	Testament of Gad
Life AE	Life of Adam and Eve	T Job	Testament of Job
Liv Proph	Lives of the Prophets	T Jos	Testament of Joseph
MA Isa	Martyrdom and Ascension	T Levi	Testament of Levi
	of Isaiah	T Naph	Testament of Naphtali
3 Macc	3 Maccabees	T 12 Pat	Testaments of the Twe
4 Macc	4 Maccabees		Patriarchs
Odes Sol	Odes of Solomon	Zad Frag	Zadokite Fragments
P Jer	Paralipomena of Jeremiah		

E. Abbreviations of Names of Dead Sea Scrolls and Related Texts

CD	Cairo (Genizah text of the) Damascus (Document)	1QSa	Appendix A (Rule of the Congregation) to 1Qs
DSS	Dead Sea Scrolls	1QSb	Appendix B (Blessings) to 1QS
Hev	Nahal Hever texts	3Q15	Copper Scroll from Qumran Cave 3
Mas	Masada Texts		
Mird	Khirbet mird texts	4QExod a	Exodus Scroll, exemplar "a" from Qumran Cave 4
Mur	Wadi Murabba'at texts		
P	Pesher (commentary)	4QFlor	Florilegium (or Eschatological Midrashim) from Qumran Cave 4
Q	Qumran		
1Q, 2Q, etc.	Numbered caves of Qumran, yielding written material; followed by abbreviation of biblical or apocryphal book.	4Qmess ar	Aramaic "Messianic" text from Qumran Cave 4
QL	Qumran Literature	4QpNah	Pesher on portions of Nahum from Qumran Cave 4
1QapGen	Genesis Apocryphon of Qumran Cave 1	4QPrNab	Prayer of Nabonidus from Qumran Cave 4
1QH	*Hodayot* (Thanksgiving Hymns) from Qumran Cave 1	4QpPs37	Pesher on portions of Psalm 37 from Qumran Cave 4
1QIsa a,b	First or second copy of Isaiah from Qumran Cave 1	4QTest	Testimonia text from Qumran Cave 4
1QpHab	Pesher on Habakkuk from Qumran Cave 1	4QTLevi	Testament of Levi from Qumran Cave 4
1QM	*Milhamah* (War Scroll)	4QPhyl	Phylacteries from Qumran Cave 4
1QpMic	Pesher on portions of Micah from Qumran Cave 1	11QMelch	Melchizedek text from Qumran Cave 11
1QS	*Serek Hayyahad* (Rule of the Community, Manual of Discipline)	11QtgJob	Targum of Job from Qumran Cave 11

TRANSLITERATIONS

Hebrew

א = '		ד = $\underline{d}$		י = y		ס = s		ר = r
ב = b		ה = h		כ = k		ע = '		שׁ = $\acute{s}$
ב = $\underline{b}$		ו = w		ך כ = $\underline{k}$		פ = p		שׁ = $š$
ג = g		ז = z		ל = l		ף פ = $\underline{p}$		תּ = t
ג = $\underline{g}$		ח = ḥ		ם מ = m		ץ צ = ṣ		ת = $\underline{t}$
ד = d		ט = ṭ		ן נ = n		ק = q		

(ה) ָ = $\hat{a}$ (h)		ָ = $\bar{a}$		ַ = a		ֳ = ^{a}
ֵי = $\hat{e}$		ֵ = $\bar{e}$		ֶ = e		ֱ = ^{e}
ִי = $\hat{\imath}$		ֹ = $\bar{o}$		ִ = i		ְ = ^{e} (if vocal)
וֹ = $\hat{o}$				ָ = o		ֳ = ^{o}
וּ = $\hat{u}$				ֻ = u		

Aramaic

$' \; b \; g \; d \; h \; w \; z \; \underline{h} \; \underline{t} \; y \; k \; l \; m \; n \; s \; ' \; p \; \underline{s} \; q \; r \; \acute{s} \; š \; t$

Arabic

$' \; b \; t \; \underline{t} \; \check{g} \; \underline{h} \; \underline{\underline{h}} \; d \; \underline{d} \; r \; z \; s \; \check{s} \; \underline{s} \; \underline{d} \; \underline{t} \; \underline{z} \; ' \; \acute{g} \; f \; q \; k \; l \; m \; n \; h \; w \; y$

Ugaritic

$' \; b \; g \; d \; \underline{d} \; h \; w \; z \; \underline{h} \; \underline{\underline{h}} \; \underline{t} \; \underline{z} \; y \; k \; l \; m \; n \; s \; \grave{s} \; ' \; \acute{g} \; \underline{p} \; \underline{s} \; q \; r \; š \; t \; \underline{t}$

xv

Greek

α	—	a	π	—	p	αι	—	ai
β	—	b	ρ	—	r	αὐ	—	au
γ	—	g	σ,ς	—	s	ει	—	ei
δ	—	d	τ	—	t	εὐ	—	eu
ε	—	e	υ	—	y	ηὐ	—	ēu
ζ	—	z	φ	—	ph	οι	—	oi
η	—	ē	χ	—	ch	οὐ	—	ou
θ	—	th	ψ	—	ps	υι	—	hui
ι	—	i	ω	—	ō			
κ	—	k				ῥ	—	rh
λ	—	l	γγ	—	ng	ʽ	—	h
μ	—	m	γκ	—	nk			
ν	—	n	γξ	—	nx	ᾳ	—	ā
ξ	—	x	γχ	—	nch	ῃ	—	ē
ο	—	o				ῳ	—	ō

xvi

1, 2 KINGS

Richard D. Patterson and Hermann J. Austel

1, 2 KINGS

Introduction

1. Historical Background

The events of Israel's history from the latter days of King David till the capture of Jerusalem are selectively recounted in the two books of Kings, to which two short footnotes are appended, one concerning an incident in the early days of the Exile (2 Kings 25:22–26), the other concerning the release of the captured Judean king Jehoiachin after the death of Nebuchadnezzar (2 Kings 25:27–30). The historical details span 971 to 562 B.C.

The involved period moves from the politically powerful and luxurious days at the close of the united kingdom under Solomon to the division of the kingdom under Rehoboam and then traces the fortunes of the northern and southern kingdoms to their demise in 722 B.C. and 586 B.C., respectively. Numerous references to the external political powers and peoples of the times—e.g., the Egyptians, Philistines, Phoenicians, Arameans, Ammonites, Moabites, Edomites, Assyrians, and Chaldeans—are integrated into the inspired record. In particular the Israelites were to experience the Aramean threats and Assyrian pressures of the ninth century B.C., the great Assyrian invasions of the eighth century B.C., together with the resultant *pax Assyriaca* in the seventh century B.C., and the fall of the Neo-Assyrian Empire at the hands of the rising power of the Chaldeans under their brilliant king Nebuchadnezzar II.

Numerous archaeological discoveries have confirmed, illuminated, or supplemented the biblical record, many of which will be noted in the comments and notes that follow. Particularly important to the understanding of the Bible is the recovered inscriptional material from Assyria and Babylonia. The careful collation of these writings (supplemented by other epigraphic finds) with the biblical narrative has brought greater clarity to the understanding of the Near East during the early and middle segments of the first millennium B.C.

Kings is, however, more than an account of the political and social history of this period. It records Israel's spiritual response to God who had taken her into covenant relationship with himself (2 Kings 17:7–23), and who had bestowed great privileges to her through the promise made to David (1 Kings 2:2–4). Accordingly, within its pages is found a detailed summary of the spiritual experiences of her people—particularly her kings, prophets, and priests, whose activities largely point to the need for the advent of the one who would combine the intended ideal of these three offices in himself.

2. Unity, Authorship, and Date

The inclusion of the material on but one scroll shows that the Hebrews considered the books of Kings to be one book (see Canonicity). Thematically the continuity of the Elijah narrative (1 Kings 17–2 Kings 2), itself part of the prophetic section dominating 1 Kings 16:29–2 Kings 9:37, and the recurring phrase "to this day" (1 Kings 9:13; 10:12 [NIV, "since that day"]; 2 Kings 2:22; 10:27; 14:7; 16:6; 17:23, 34, 41; 21:15) clearly indicate that the two books of Kings form a single literary unit.

The problem of the history of the compilation of the book is more pressing. The author of the book mentions using several source documents, three specifically: (1) "the book of the annals of Solomon" (1 Kings 11:41), drawn from biographical, annalistic, and archival material contemporary with the details of 1 Kings 1–11; (2) "the book of the annals of the kings of Israel," mentioned some seventeen times in 1 Kings 14:29–2 Kings 15:31 and drawn largely from the official records of the northern kingdom that were kept by the court recorder (cf. 2 Sam 8:16; 20:24; 1 Kings 4:3; 2 Kings 18:18, 37; 2 Chron 34:8); and (3) "the book of the annals of the kings of Judah," mentioned fifteen times (1 Kings 14:29–2 Kings 24:5), being a record of the events of the reigns of the kings of the southern kingdom from Rehoboam to Jehoiakim.

Other unnamed sources may likewise have been drawn on for the book's final composition, such as the court memoirs of David (1 Kings 1:1–2:11), a cycle involving the house of Ahab and the prophets Elijah and Elisha (1 Kings 16:29–2 Kings 9:37), the records of the prophet Isaiah (Isa 36–39), and two concluding historical abstracts (2 Kings 25:22–26, 27–30).

The use of source material and the great time span involved have occasioned numerous suggestions as to the unity, authorship, and date of Kings. Whereas older liberal critical theory tended to find three redactors of Kings, current opinion tends to isolate two strata: a preexilic source that reached its compilation by 598/597 B.C. and an exilic redactor who completed his work about 550 B.C. Both redactions were part of a "Deuteronomic School" whose chief interests revolved around the principles of (1) cultic orthodoxy as centered in the temple, (2) prophetic fulfillment of the Word of God, and (3) divine retribution for Israel's failure to maintain its orthodoxy as epitomized in the Book of Deuteronomy.

Kings is thus seen to be one of the major products of this "Deuteronomic School" whose literary output included the Deuteronomic laws together with their subsequent historical framework and the bulk of the former prophets. This literary activity originated in the late eighth or seventh century B.C., reached its peak in the Josianic reform, and was completed by an exilic compiler within the same tradition.

This critical scheme, best represented by Noth, has not, however, gained universal acceptance even among liberal scholars.[1] Thus some liberal scholars have stressed the artificiality of the resultant break between Numbers and Joshua and an increased appreciation of the complexity of the structure of the "Deuteronomic History" as reasons for rejecting or reevaluating Noth's simplistic hypothesis.

Most conservative scholars have rejected Noth's hypothesis altogether, noting that the disagreement among critical scholars as to both the origin and the extent of the "Deuteronomic History" casts doubt on the validity of the method itself. Indeed the term "Deuteronomic" is somewhat of a misnomer, for it unwarrantedly assumes that someone associated with the compilation of Deuteronomy was also associated in the production of Kings.

Quite the contrary, there is no solid proof that such is the case. Rather there is growing evidence that Deuteronomy in its entirety is authentically reflective of its time-honored Late Bronze dating.[2]

While it is true that there is much in common between Deuteronomy and Joshua-Kings (cf., e.g., Deut 28; Josh 23; 2 Kings 17:18–23), W. Kaiser, Jr., demonstrates that the basic theological viewpoint of Kings is precisely that which has flowed unswervingly down from Moses.[3] As K. Kitchen remarks, "In fact, a careful reading of the Old Testament at large may simply indicate that much of what is attributed to the Deuteronomic viewpoint is but the common ground of Hebrew mainstream belief (orthodoxy if one will), with rather little that is absolutely distinctive. Hence, 'covenantal' (or, 'mainstream' rather than 'orthodox'?) would be a fairer label than 'Deuteronomic,' if label be needed."[4]

Despite Kings's reflection of mainstream orthodoxy, the point of view and emphases are somewhat different. Whereas Deuteronomy's presentation of the covenant relationship was prescriptive and narrative, that of Kings is narrative and evaluative. This, coupled with differences of internal detail and the newly established disallowance of a late date for Deuteronomy, makes any discussion of a "Deuteronomic School" of history to be, at best, most tenuous. As R.K. Harrison (IOT, p. 732) points out, "There is, . . . a significant difference of emphasis in the two works, and this fact alone should be sufficient to deter the casual ascription of the epithet 'Deuteronomic' to the work of the author of Kings."[5]

Everywhere except in the two appendices Kings bears the impress of being a unified book expressing the viewpoint of a single author who has woven together his historical data in accordance with a single purpose and with a uniform literary style. Jewish tradition (*Baba Bathra* 15a) identifies that author as Jeremiah. Since, however, OT narrative literature was usually anonymous, scholars have frequently attributed the authorship of Kings to some prophet who "was nevertheless a man likeminded with Jeremiah and almost certainly a contemporary who lived and wrote under the same influences."[6]

Although little is actually gained by such a position except to avoid the categorical

---

[1]See A.N. Radjawane, "Das deuteronomistische Geschichtswerk," *Theologische Rundschau* 38 (1973–74): 177–216.

[2]See M. Kline, *The Structure of Biblical Authority* (Grand Rapids: Eerdmans, 1972), pp. 131–53.

[3]*Toward an Old Testament Theology* (Grand Rapids: Zondervan, 1978), pp. 63–66.

[4]"Ancient Orient, 'Deuteronism,' and the Old Testament," *New Perspectives on the Old Testament*, ed. J.B. Payne (Waco: Word, 1970), p. 17.

[5]See further P.C. Craigie, *The Book of Deuteronomy* (Grand Rapids: Eerdmans, 1976), p. 49.

[6]G.R. Driver, *An Introduction to the Literature of the Old Testament* (Edinburgh: T. & T. Clark, 1902), p. 199.

assertion that Jeremiah was the author, it must be admitted that the author's failure to use the familiar names for the kings of Judah as employed by Jeremiah (see Notes on 2 Kings 24:8) argues for caution in too readily following the traditional identification of Jeremiah as the author. However the distinction in the employment of royal names between the books of Jeremiah and Kings may be one of formality, the official names being deemed more proper for an objective history.

At least the majority of the book bears the impress of being the product of one author, who, as an eyewitness of the Jewish nation's final demise, was concerned to show the divine reasons for that fall. In so doing he utilized many sources, weaving the details together into an integrated whole that graphically portrayed Israel's covenant failure. Despite the lack of dogmatic certainty, a reasonable case can be made for Jeremianic authorship (cf. G. Archer, SOTI rev., p. 289). S.J. Schultz ("Kings," ZPEB, 3:812) affirms the likelihood that "the prophets kept the records throughout the generations of the Hebrew Kingdoms." Since he was descended from the priestly line of Abiathar, and since in all probability his father, Hilkiah, was active in communicating both the traditional facts and the teaching of Israel's past, it is very likely that Jeremiah had access to historical and theological source materials. Furthermore he would have had more ready entrée to the royal annals than any other prophet. Certainly no other prophet was so intimately involved in the final stages of Judah's history. If so, Jeremiah may have been active in composing the greater part of the history of the Book of Kings (1 Kings 14–2 Kings 23:30) during the so-called silent years of his prophetic ministry after his call in 627 B.C., during the long reign of the godly Josiah. Certainly the contents of all but the last appendix (2 Kings 25:27 –30) could have been written by Jeremiah. Perhaps this was added by Baruch or one of the prophets within the Jeremianic tradition; 2 Kings 25:22–26, which was drawn from Jeremiah 40–44, possibly also was written by the same writer as a bridge to the later historical notice concerning Jehoiachin.

3. Origin, Occasion, and Purpose

If the conclusions reached in the preceding section are correct, a distinction must be made between the place of origin of the author's sources and that of the book's final edition. Thus some of the sources would originate in the archives of the royal court (e.g., 1 Kings 4; 9–11) or the temple (1 Kings 5–8). Thiele (*Mysterious Numbers*, pp. 174–91) makes a strong case for the separate incidents in the book being kept in various prophetic centers throughout the northern and southern kingdoms. Such prophetic records are cited as source material for Chronicles (e.g., 1 Chron 29:29; 2 Chron 9:29; 12:15; 13:22; 26:22). Again the origin of 2 Kings 18:9–20:19 in the writings of Isaiah (36–39) has been well demonstrated by E.J. Young.[7] If all this is allowed, the author would have a considerable body of spiritually evaluative material at his disposal. The two exilic appendices could have originated in Jerusalem or, more probably, in Babylon.

The origin of the basic collection itself would clearly be Jerusalem. The book gives the impression of having been written by an eyewitness to those climactic events closing the checkered histories of Israel and Judah, those dramatic affairs providing

---

[7]*The Book of Isaiah* (Grand Rapids: Eerdmans, 1974), 2:556–65.

the occasion and purpose of the book. Contemplating the tragedy taking place before his very eyes, the author sets forth an accurate record of the events of his own day and those that had transpired since the glorious days of the Solomonic Era. As such Kings forms a sequel to Samuel.

Kings is, however, more than a chronicle of events. Masterly selecting his sources and utilizing his own experiential knowledge, the author writes to demonstrate conclusively to his readers both the necessity of the believer's keeping his covenantal obligations before God and the history of those most responsible for leading God's people in their stewardship of the divine economy: Israel's kings and prophets. Hence Kings everywhere bears the twin marks of redemptive history and personal accountability. Key verses include 1 Kings 2:2–5; 8:20, 23–26, 66; 9:4–9; 11:36–39; 2 Kings 8:19; 17:7–23; 21:10–15; 24:1–4, 20. It should be noted, however, that even though the author wrote with a basic philosophy of history, the resultant presentation is not necessarily so interpretative as to diminish the verity of the events and details he narrates. The credibility of the content of both the sources and the author's interpretative use of them are guaranteed by divine inspiration.[8]

4. Literary Form

The nature of the theme and subject matter of Kings makes any discussion of literary style difficult. Nevertheless, certain stylistic features are observable.

The author tended to write thematically, occasionally leaving his presentation out of chronological order. Notable examples include (1) Solomon's organization of his kingdom (1 Kings 4), which is appended to the discussion of his wisdom in chapter 3 even though the majority of the details belong to a later period; (2) the full details relative to Solomon's building activities (1 Kings 5:1–7:12), which are included before discussing the vessels of the temple and the dedicatory service (1 Kings 7:12–8:66), all of which are recounted before any discussion of the Solomonic politico-socio-economic situation (1 Kings 9–11); (3) a discussion of later happenings at Jeroboam's newly erected altar (1 Kings 13) followed by other incidents in Jeroboam's life (1 Kings 14:1–20) immediately after a notice of the building of the rival cult center (1 Kings 12:25–33) but before the author returns to Rehoboam (1 Kings 12:1–24; 14:21–31); (4) the placing together of the bulk of the material relative to the prophetic ministries of Elijah and Elisha into two major groups (1 Kings 17–19; 2 Kings 1:1–8:15); (5) a discussion of later happenings in Samaria appended to the account of its fall (2 Kings 17); (6) the detailing of the most outstanding example of Hezekiah's trust in God (2 Kings 18:7b–19:37) before discussing the details relative to Hezekiah's sickness and recovery and the visit of Merodach-Baladan's embassy (2 Kings 20); and including (7) the details relative to the death of Sennacherib (2 Kings 19:36–37) with the discussion of Sennacherib's western campaign in Judah (2 Kings 18:13–19:36).

When it comes to the presentation of the historical data relative to the history of the divided kingdom, the author rather consistently used the following order: (1) an

---

[8]See further, R.E. Clements, *One Hundred Years of Old Testament Interpretation* (Philadelphia: Westminster, 1976), pp. 47–48; and W. Barclay, ed., *The Bible and History* (Nashville: Abingdon, 1968), pp. 13–15.

introductory statement concerning the accession of the king is given, this normally being synchronized with the reign of the corresponding king in the other kingdom; (2) then follows the biographical details—for the kings of the southern kingdom this includes a statement of the age of the king at his accession, the length of his reign, the name of the queen mother, and a spiritual evaluation of his reign; for the northern kingdom this involves a statement as to the capital city of the king, the length of his reign, and an indication as to his character—(3) then a selective record of the king's reign is presented, followed by a concluding formula that includes a source where further facts regarding the king's reign may be found, a statement of his death and burial, and an indication of his successor. Outstanding examples of the full-blown formula are Jehoahaz of Israel (2 Kings 13:1–9) and Azariah of Judah (2 Kings 15:1–7).

Variations, of course, do occur, such as the modification or omission of the notice of the king's death and/or burial, as in the case of Joash, Hezekiah, and Jehoiachin. Other notable omissions include (1) the introductory statement as to the age of Jehu, (2) the name of the queen mother with Jehoram I and Nadab, (3) the capital city of Jeroboam I and Nadab, and (4) the name of the king's successor in the case of usurpation.

Arising from the basic intention of the author to attempt to recount the history of the two kingdoms simultaneously (see chart 2, page 17), the record is arranged so as to give the full account of one king or dynasty before rehearsing the story of the contemporary activities in the corresponding kingdom.

Within this general framework, the author attempts to faithfully relate the facts as he has learned them in a basically annalistic format. In accordance with the source material, however, he often reproduces prophetic pronouncements (nearly every chapter from 1 Kings 11 to 2 Kings 22 contains prophetic material), poetic utterances (e.g., 1 Kings 22:17; 2 Kings 19:21–28), and proverbial wisdom (e.g., 1 Kings 3:16–28; 20:11; 2 Kings 14:9). The total work is marked by a lively narrative style often interspersed with sparkling dialogue.

By way of contrast with the other two books covering the historical details of the united and divided kingdoms, one might say that whereas Samuel's author uses a biographical style and Chronicles is written from a theological standpoint, the author of Kings employs a largely narrative-annalistic approach.

Thematically whereas the author of Samuel writes from the standpoint of a special interest in the prophetic unfolding of the kingdom of Israel, especially as centered in the emergence, triumph, and struggles within the house of David (whose centrality to Israelite history was guaranteed by divine covenant [2 Sam 7]), and the Chronicler writes from the particular viewpoint of divine evaluation of how Israel (and particularly Judah) responded to the revealed standards of the sovereign God, the author of Kings attempts to give a balanced account of the general activities that characterized the outworking of the divine covenant in Israel's first kingdom period.

5. Theological Values

That Kings chronicles Israel's spiritual odyssey enables us to glean something of the author's theological outlook. The main theological interest is the relationship of a sovereign God to a responsible people, Israel. In striking such a balance, the author of Kings draws particular attention to the Mosaic and Davidic covenants. Indeed, the redemptive history and theological perspective of Kings are largely developed through David and Israel's appropriation of God's blessing in accordance with her compliance with the standards of the Torah (cf. 1 Kings 2:4–5).

From the first chapter to the last, God is seen in sovereign control of the world governments. He alone is the living God (1 Kings 8:60; 17:1, 12; 18:15, 39; 22:14; 2 Kings 2:6, 14; 5:16; 19:15–19) who is the Creator (2 Kings 19:15) and Provider of life (1 Kings 17:3–24; 19:1–8). Both transcendent (1 Kings 8:27; 2 Kings 2:1–12; 19:15) and immanent (1 Kings 9:3), he is the omnipresent (1 Kings 8:27), omnipotent (1 Kings 8:42; 18:38; 2 Kings 17:36), and omniscient God (1 Kings 3:9, 28; 4:29–34; 5:7, 12; 10:24; 2 Kings 19:27) to whom the angels minister (1 Kings 13:18; 19:5; 22:19–23; 2 Kings 1:15; 19:15) and with whom all the world has to do (1 Kings 8:41–43; 2 Kings 19:19). A God of love (1 Kings 10:9) and goodness (1 Kings 8:66; 2 Kings 20:19), he is also a God of justice and righteousness (1 Kings 2:32–33, 44; 8:31–53; 9:6–9; 10:9; 11:11–13; 13:21–32; 15:29–30; 16:1–4, 12–13, 18–19; 21:19–29; 2 Kings 17:18–23; 21:10–15; 24:1–4).

Although men are sinners (1 Kings 8:46; 11:4; 2 Kings 17:14–18), God is the author of redemption (1 Kings 8:51) and graciously forgives those who humble themselves before him (1 Kings 8:33–40, 46–50; 21:27–29; 2 Kings 22:11, 19–20). Moreover he hears and answers prayer (1 Kings 8:28–30, 44–53; 13:6; 17:20–22; 18:36–38; 2 Kings 2:14; 4:33–37; 6:17–20; 13:4–5; 19:14–19; 20:2–6) and faithfully keeps his promises (1 Kings 8:20, 23–26, 56; 11:12–13, 32, 34; 16:34; 17:14–16; 2 Kings 1:17; 7:16–20; 8:19; 9:36–37; 10:10, 17; 13:23; 15:12; 24:13). Man ought to worship him (1 Kings 3:15; 8:12–66; 9:25; 2 Kings 17:28) and follow him completely (1 Kings 13:8–26; 2 Kings 5:15–16; 11:17; 17:35–39; 20:3). Accordingly great prominence is given to the temple and its institutions (1 Kings 6–8; 2 Kings 12:4–16; 21:7; 22:3–7; 23:1–3, 21–23; 24:13; 25:13–17). The believer should make God's inviolable Word and standards (1 Kings 16:34; 21:3–4; 2 Kings 14:6; 18:12) the center of his life (1 Kings 2:3–4; 6:11–13; 8:58; 9:4; 11:10–11, 38; 2 Kings 8:2; 17:37–39; 18:5–6; 21:8; 22:11; 23:1–25) and live so as to be concerned for God's sacred reputation (1 Kings 8:60; 2 Kings 2:23–25; 5:8; 19:19).

God has revealed himself in many ways (1 Kings 3:5–15; 8:10–12; 9:2–9; 11:11–13), but especially to Israel (1 Kings 8:51–53, 66; 2 Kings 17:35–39; 21:8–9), that nation he had granted great covenant promises to (2 Kings 13:23), especially through David, his servant (1 Kings 2:33, 45; 3:6, 14; 6:12–13; 8:20, 23–26, 66; 11:32–39; 15:4–5; 2 Kings 8:19; 19:20–37). Although God has redeemed Israel (1 Kings 8:51; 2 Kings 17:7) and patiently guided, cared, and borne with his people, they had rejected him despite his repeated warnings (2 Kings 17:7–23; 21:10–15).

Because of Israel's unique relationship to God, the sin of idolatry is severely denounced (1 Kings 11:4–2 Kings 24:19 *passim*). On the positive side, great place is accorded to prophecy (1 Kings 11:29–39; 12:22–24; 13:1–14:20; 16:1–4, 7, 12–13; 20:22, 28, 35–43; 22:7–38; 2 Kings 1:1–2:11, 19–25; 3:11–20; 8:7–15; 9:6–10; 13:14 –21; 14:25–27; 17:13, 23; 19:20–37; 20:1–21; 21:10–15; 22:14–20).

Thus Kings is not only history but redemptive and teleological history built around the twin themes of divine sovereignty and human responsibility, particularly as they were operative through God's covenant people, Israel. In this regard comparison may again be drawn between Kings, Samuel, and Chronicles. Whereas Samuel features human responsibility in the stewardship of the divine economy and

Chronicles emphasizes the divine sovereignty, Kings attempts to effect a balance between the two.[9]

6. Canonicity

The canonicity of Kings has never been questioned. It was regarded from the first by the Hebrews as canonical and, because it was considered to be written by Jeremiah, was placed among the former prophets. Moreover, it was always valued as being foundational for the messages of the canonical prophets.

Due to its length, Kings appears in the LXX as two books called the "Third" and "Fourth" books of "Kingdoms," being the sequel to Samuel, whose books are entitled "First" and "Second Kingdoms." The LXX arrangement was followed by the Latin Vulgate, which entitled Kings *Liber Regum Tertius et Quartus*. Josephus's limitation of the Hebrew canon to twenty-four books (*Contra Apion* 1.8) would seem to verify the traditional scheme of canonical arrangement with Lamentations perhaps included with Jeremiah and Ruth with Judges. If so, Kings was clearly recognized as canonical by the first century A.D. Its authoritative recognition and employment by Jesus and the NT writers renders any doubt concerning its canonical status by that date out of the question.

7. Text

The Hebrew text of Kings has long been of scholarly interest, particularly the relation of the MT to the LXX. It has generally been conceded that numerous textual difficulties exist in the MT and that the LXX is a valuable tool in ascertaining the correct Hebrew text. The fragments of Kings from Qumran that have thus far been published tend to corroborate both the existence of Hebrew texts that were closer to the LXX than the MT and the high value of the LXX for the purposes of textual criticism in Kings.[10]

8. Chronology

Because the OT writers utilized only relative reference points in affixing their time-sequence structure, an absolute dating of a given event on the basis of purely OT data is largely impossible. Moreover the complexity of methodology and lack of uniformity in determining dated events greatly hampers the quest for precision. Thus in some eras Israel began its new year in the fall; in others, in the spring. In some cases the nonaccession-year system, by which the remaining days of a calendar year in which a king was crowned were counted as that king's first year, was used; in others, the accession-year reckoning was employed, in which case the king's first year would begin with the first day of the calendar year following his inauguration.

---

[9]See further W.C. Kaiser, Jr., *The Old Testament in Contemporary Preaching* (Grand Rapids: Baker, 1973), pp. 88–91; R.I. McNeely, *First and Second Kings* (Chicago: Moody, 1978), pp. 9–11; Schultz, "Kings," ZPEB, 3:822–23.

[10]See further F.M. Cross, *The Ancient Library of Qumran* (Garden City: Doubleday, 1961), pp. 180ff.; cf. Shenkel.

Still further an adding of the reign of years of all the Jewish kings yields too high a total for the period between Solomon and the Fall of Jerusalem.

Accordingly recourse must be made to secular dates in the ancient Near East that have been established with greater precision. The Canon of Ptolemy (the Greek geographer and astronomer of Egypt, c. A.D. 70–161) has been particularly helpful. Ptolemy made a list of the rulers of Babylon from 747 B.C. until his own day. As well the finding of the ancient Assyrian *limmu*, or eponym, lists, by which a given year was named for the person who occupied the office of *limmu*, has also been of great importance. These lists also often mention important historical or astronomical details, such as an eclipse of the moon or sun. One such solar eclipse has been scientifically computed to have occurred on 15 June 763 B.C. The dating of the whole list can therefore be affixed, resulting in a reliable series of dates for the period 892–648 B.C. Interestingly enough the accession year of Sargon II of Assyria as king over Babylon in both the eponym lists and the Ptolemaic Canon comes out to 709 B.C., providing a cross-check on the reliability of these two external sources. Dates for the period before 892 B.C. must be sought from Mesopotamian data drawn from the various Assyrian and Babylonian lists and synchronous histories (detailing contacts between Assyrian and Babylonian kings) and from Egyptian sources. Dates for the period after 648 B.C. can be gleaned both from Ptolemy's Canon and from the annals of the later Babylonian kings. This latter source, which has been made available through the efforts of Wiseman (*Chronicles*), yields a series of precise dates within the period of 626–566 B.C.

These sources provide a fairly accurate time sequence for dating the events of the ancient Near East, particularly so for the period represented by Kings (971–566 B.C.). Therefore where OT events are actually mentioned in external records, they may be assigned precise dates. Since several events are common both to Kings and the external sources, the general time framework of much of the period from Solomon to the Fall of Jerusalem can be acknowledged as rather well established.

Nevertheless several problems still remain, difficulties that have been resolved in various ways by OT scholars, depending largely on their point of view with regard to harmonizing the biblical dates with the external sources. Some scholars (e.g., Jules Oppert) have attempted to harmonize the Assyrian chronology with the biblical data.[11] Oppert claimed to have discovered a forty-seven-year gap in the Assyrian record that he felt accounted for the variation between the Assyrian and biblical dates. Unfortunately the data he based his claim on have not stood the test of historical verification.

Other scholars have aimed at the harmonization of the biblical events with the established Assyrian dates. This method usually accounts for the seemingly longer period in the OT by assuming a number of coregencies, the overlapping reigns thus reducing considerably the total number of years for the whole series in Kings to a figure that is in line with the Assyrian total. Although this position has generally prevailed among biblical scholars of all theological persuasions, it has yielded varying results; and a number of competing systems have appeared. German scholars have followed largely the system worked out by Begrich as modified by Jepsen,[12]

---

[11]Cited in O.T. Allis, *The Old Testament, Its Claims and Its Critics* (Grand Rapids: Baker, 1972), pp. 399–400, 481, n. 60).

[12]Joachim Begrich, *Die Chronologie der Könige von Israel und die Quellen des Rahmens der Königsbücher* (Tübingen: University Press, 1929); A. Jepsen and R. Hanhart, *Untersuchungen zur israelitisch-jüudischen Chronologie* (Berlin: Walter de Gruyter, 1964).

which arrives at its dates by presuming a shift in the month of the new year in Israel and a change from the nonaccession year to the accession-year system when the Jewish states became Assyrian vassals. Andersen (followed with variations by S. Hermann), however, holds that the calendar year always began in the fall, that the nonaccession-year system was consistently employed by both Israel and Judah, and that coregencies and rival kingdoms were not included in reckoning a king's total years.[13]

English writers usually reflect either the system of Thiele or Albright. The former achieves his dates by a complicated process of calendrical change, variation in the employment of accession-year versus nonaccession-year systems between and within the Jewish states, overlapping coregencies, and, where necessary, outright emendation of the biblical text. Albright, who was progressively impressed by the importance of the Lucianic recension of the LXX for determining the chronology of Kings, arrives at his conclusions through still freer use of minor revision of the MT.

Still others (e.g., George Smith) have decided that a correlation between the Assyrian and Hebrew dates is unnecessary, each being viewed as "correct" according to its own system. Smith suggests that there may be errors in the Assyrian annalistic accounts and that often incorrect and needless reconciliations between Assyrian and biblical events have been made.[14] Thus he denies that the Ahabu and Iaua mentioned in the Assyrian records have anything to do with Ahab and Jehu and that Israel had any connection either with the famous Battle of Qarqar (853 B.C.) or with Assyria at all until the time of Menahem and Tiglath-pileser in the late eighth century B.C. Smith's suggestion allows the number of years allotted to a given king in the Hebrew account to be taken more literally without recourse to any compressed total of years as represented by the coregency theories. However the problem of too many years for the period covered by Kings remains for this theory; and new difficulties arise such as the the need for finding two Hazaels in Syria (if the biblical data are to square with known dates for Syrian kings) and the postulation of errors in the otherwise usually accurate Assyrian records (e.g., in the case of Menahem) in order to deny seemingly obvious historical correlations. The theory has not found many adherents.[15]

The position taken here follows basically that of J. Barton Payne,[16] which, though a modification of the coregency theory, maintains a high regard for the MT and refuses to resort to conjectural emendations. Payne affirms that the nonaccession-dating system was used in the northern kingdom (by which the year of a king's enthronement is considered as both his first year and the last year of his predecessor) and that the new year always began in the fall. The southern kingdom, however, began its year in the fall and used the accession-year system until 848 B.C., when, under the influence of Athaliah, Jotham changed Judah to the nonaccession system. However both kingdoms utilized the accession-year system from the early eighth century B.C., probably under the influence of Assyria.

---

[13]K.T. Andersen, "Die Chronologie der Könige von Israel und Juda," ST 23 (1969): 67–112.

[14]George Adam Smith, *The Assyrian Eponym Canon* (London: Harper & Bros., 1875).

[15]A notable exception is Allis, *Old Testament*, pp. 398–430. For the problem of the identification of Jehu with Iaua, see the objections of P.K. McCarter, "Yaw, Son of Omri: A Philological Note on Israelite Chronology," BASOR 216 (1974): 5–7, and the answers of M. Weippert, "Jau(a) mārHumri—Joram odor Jehu von Israel?" VetTest 28 (1978): 113–18. Note the mediating position of E.R. Thiele, "An Additional Note on 'Yau, Son of Omri,'" BASOR 222 (1976): 19–23.

[16]"Chronology of the Old Testament," ZPEB, 1:829–45.

Payne supplies the following guidelines in computing the regnal years of the kings: "The following interpretative bases concern coregencies . . . during the divided kingdom period. (a) The years of coregency are regularly included in the totals for the respective reigns. . . . (b) The Book of Kings records each ruler in a sequence determined by the beginning of sole reign rather than of co-regency. . . . (c) 'Coregencies commence with the first rather than accession years.' "[17]

Admittedly several difficulties remain, notably in the last half of the eighth century B.C. On the whole, however, the conclusions reached by Payne seem satisfactory and best able to account for the various historical and chronological data; hence it will be followed with but slight modification. The resultant dates for the kings of Israel and Judah follow:

NORTHERN KINGDOM		SOUTHERN KINGDOM	
First Dynasty			
Jeroboam I	931–910	Rehoboam	931–914
Nadab	910–909	Abijah	913–910
Second Dynasty			
Baasha	909–886	Asa	909–868
Elah	886–885		
[Zimri]	885		
Third Dynasty			
Omri	885–874		
Ahab	874–853	*Jehoshaphat	872–847
Ahaziah	853–852	*Jehoram	852–841
Joram	852–841	Ahaziah	841
		Athaliah	841–835
Fourth Dynasty			
Jehu	841–814	Joash	835–796
Jehoahaz	814–798		
*Jehoash	798–782	*Amaziah	796–767
*Jeroboam II	793–753	*Azariah	791–739
Zechariah	753		
Concluding Kings			
Shallum	752	*Jotham	752–736
Menahem	751–742		
Pekahiah	741–740	*Ahaz	(743)
Pekah	740–732		736–720
Hoshea	732/1–722	*Hezekiah	729/8–699
		Manasseh	698–643
		Amon	642–640
		Josiah	640–609
		Jehoahaz	609
		Jehoiakim	609–598
		Jehoiachin	598
		Zedekiah	597–586

* = coregency

For further details see the helpful bibliographies given by Hayes and Miller, pp. 678–83; Payne (ZPEB, 1:845); K.A. Kitchen and T.C. Mitchell, "Chronology of the Old Testament," NBD, pp. 217–23; and S.J. DeVries, "Old Testament Chronology," IDB Supplementary vol., p. 64.

---

[17]Ibid., p. 838.

DATE	ISRAEL	SYRIA	JUDAH	PROPHETS	ASSYRIA	EGYPT
931	Jeroboam I		Rehoboam			
913			Abijah			
911			Asa		Adad Nirari II	
910	Nadab					
909	(2) Baasha					
890					Tukulti Ninurta II	
886	Elab					
885	Zimri Tibni (3) Omri					
884					Assur Nasir Pal II	
881		Ben Hadad I				
874	Ahab		Jehoshaphat	Elijah		
860		Ben Hadad II				
859					Shalmaneser III	
853	Ahaziah	BATTLE	OF	QARQAR		
852	Joram					
848			Jehoram	Elisha		
841	(4) Jehu	Hazael	Ahaziah Athaliah			
835			Joash			
823					Shamshi-Adad V	
814	Jehoahaz					
811					Adad Nirari III (811–783)	
802		Ben Hadad III				
798	Jehoash					
796			Amaziah			
792	Jeroboam II		Uzziah	Hosea (770–725) Joel (770) Amos (770–755) Obadiah (760) Jonah (760–755)	(3 Weak	
760	Zechariah				Kings)	
752	Shallum Menahem					

745	Pekahiah			
742	Pekah			
740		Jotham	Tiglath Pileser III	Isaiah (740–685?)
735		Ahaz		Micah (735–725)
732	Hoshea			
730				End of 22nd dynasty by Tefnekht (24th dynasty) End of 23rd dyn. by Piankhy (752–715, 25th dynasty)
727			Shalmaneser V	
722	Fall of N.K.		Sargon II	

DATE	JUDAH	PROPHETS	ASSYRIA	EGYPT	BABYLON
720				Bakenrenef (24th dyn., 720–715)	
716	Hezekiah (coreg. 729)			Shabaku (25th dyn. 716–701, defeats 24th dyn.)	
705			Sennacherib		
701	BATTLE		OF	EL TEKEH Shebitku (701–690)	
698	Manasseh				
690	(Samaritans)			Taharqa (690–664)	
681			Esarhaddon		
671				Fall of Memphis	
668			Assurbanipal		
664				Tanutamun (664–653)	
663				Fall of Thebes	
660		Nahum (660–655)			
642	Amon				
640	Josiah	Habakkuk (665–650)			
630		Zephaniah (635–630)		26th dyn.:	
626		Jeremiah (626–580)	Assur Etil Ilani (et al.)	Psamtik I (665–609)	Nabupolassar
612			Fall of Nineveh		
609	Jehoahaz		Battle of Haran	Neco II (609–594)	
608	Jehoiakim				
605	1st Deportation	Daniel (606–535)	Battle of Charchemish		Nebuchadnezzar
598	Jehoiachin 2nd Deportation Zedekiah	Ezekiel (598–570)			
594				Psamtik II (594–588)	
588				Apries (588–568)	
586	FALL OF JERUSALEM				
568	3rd Deportation			Amasis (568–526)	

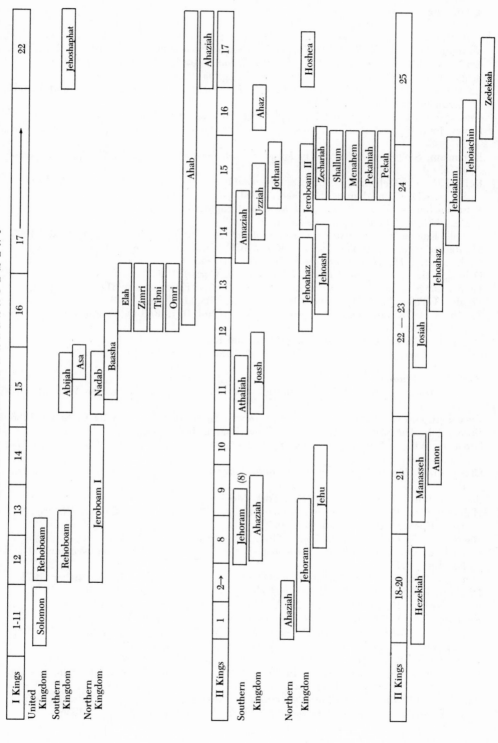

KINGS : CHAPTER ARRANGEMENT

I Kings

| 1-11 | 12 | 13 | 14 | 15 | 16 | 17 ———→ | 22 |

United Kingdom: Solomon

Southern Kingdom: Rehoboam | Rehoboam | Abijah | Asa | Jehoshaphat

Northern Kingdom: Jeroboam I | Nadab | Baasha | Elah | Zimri | Tibni | Omri | Ahab | Ahaziah

II Kings

| 1 | 2→ | 8 | 9 (8) | 10 | 11 | 12 | 13 | 14 | 15 | 16 | 17 |

Southern Kingdom: Jehoram | Ahaziah | Athaliah | Joash | Amaziah | Uzziah | Jotham | Ahaz

Northern Kingdom: Ahaziah | Jehoram | Jehu | Jehoahaz | Jehoash | Jeroboam II | Zechariah | Shallum | Menahem | Pekahiah | Pekah | Hoshea

II Kings

| 18-20 | 21 | 22 — 23 | 24 | 25 |

Hezekiah | Manasseh | Amon | Josiah | Jehoahaz | Jehoiakim | Jehoiachin | Zedekiah

9. Bibliography

Commentaries and Histories
Albright, W.F. *The Biblical Period from Abraham to Ezra*. New York: Harper & Row, 1963.
Avi-Yonah, Michael, ed. *A History of the Holy Land*. Toronto: MacMillan, 1969.
Bright, John. *A History of Israel*. 3d ed. Philadelphia: Westminster, 1981.
Edersheim, Alfred. *The Bible History, Old Testament*. 7 vols. in 2 vols. Grand Rapids: Eerdmans, 1956.
Gray, John. *I & II Kings*. 2d ed. Philadelphia: Westminster, 1970.
Hayes, John H., and Miller, J. Maxwell, eds. *Israelite and Judean History*. London: SCM, 1977.
Herrmann, Siegfried. *A History of Israel in Old Testament Times*. Philadelphia: Fortress, 1975.
Keil, C.F., and Delitzsch, F. *Biblical Commentary on the Old Testament: The Books of the Kings*. KD. Grand Rapids: Eerdmans, 1954.
Krummacher, F.W. *Elijah the Tishbite*. Grand Rapids: Baker, 1977.
_____. *Elisha*. Grand Rapids: Baker, 1976.
Merrill, Eugene H. *An Historical Survey of the Old Testament*. Nutley, N.J.: Craig, 1969.
Montgomery, James A. *The Books of Kings*. ICC. Edinburgh: T. & T. Clark, 1967.
Noth, Martin. *The History of Israel*. New York: Harper & Row, 1960.
Orlinsky, Harry M. *Ancient Israel*. 2d ed. Ithaca: Cornell University Press, 1960.
Payne, David F. *Kingdoms of the Lord*. Grand Rapids: Eerdmans, 1981.
Pfeiffer, Charles F. *Old Testament History*. Grand Rapids: Baker, 1973.
Snaith, N.H. "Kings." *The Interpreter's Bible*. IB. Vol. 3. Edited by George Buttrick. New York: Abingdon, 1956.
Wood, Leon J. *Israel's United Monarchy*. Grand Rapids: Baker, 1979.
_____. *A Survey of Israel's History*. rev. ed. Grand Rapids: Zondervan, 1986.

Background Studies
Aharoni, Yohanan, and Avi-Yonah, Michael. *The MacMillan Bible Atlas*. New York: MacMillan, 1968.
Buccellati, Giorgio. *Cities and Nations of Ancient Syria*. Rome: Universita Di Roma, 1966.
Bronner, L. *The Stories of Elijah and Elisha*. Leiden: Brill, 1968.
Crockett, William Day. *A Harmony of the Books of Samuel, Kings, and Chronicles*. Grand Rapids: Baker, 1951.
Cross, Frank Moore. *Canaanite Myth and Hebrew Epic*. Cambridge: Harvard University Press, 1973.
de Vaux, Roland. *Ancient Israel*. New York: McGraw-Hill, 1961.
Hallo, William W., and Simpson, William Kelly. *The Ancient Near East: A History*. New York: Harcourt Brace Jovanovich, 1971.
Harrison, R.K. *Old Testament Times*. Grand Rapids: Eerdmans, 1970.
Herzog, Chaim, and Gichon, Mordechai. *Battles of the Bible*. London: Weidenfeld and Nicolson, 1978.
Hindson, Edward E. *The Philistines and the Old Testament*. Grand Rapids: Baker, 1971.
Hopkins, I.W.J. *Jerusalem: A Study in Urban Geography*. Grand Rapids: Baker, 1970.
Jones, Gwilym H. *1 and 2 Kings*. 2 vols. Grand Rapids: Eerdmans, 1984.
Kitchen, K.A. *Ancient Orient and Old Testament*. Chicago: Inter-Varsity, 1966.
_____. *The Third Intermediate Period in Egypt*. Warminster: Aris & Phillips, 1973.
_____. *The Bible in Its World*. Downers Grove: Inter-Varsity, 1977.
Larue, Gerald A. *Babylon and the Bible*. Grand Rapids: Baker, 1969.
Luckenbill, Daniel David. *Ancient Records of Assyria and Babylonia*. 2 vols. Chicago: University of Chicago Press, 1926–27.
Parrot, André. *Nineveh and the Old Testament*. New York: Philosophical Library, 1955.
_____. *Babylon and the Old Testament*. New York: Philosophical Library, 1956.

Saggs, H.W.F. *The Greatness That Was Babylon*. New York: Hawthorne, 1962.
———. *Assyriology and the Study of the Old Testament*. Cardiff: University of Wales Press, 1969.
Shenkel, James Donald. *Chronology and Recensional Development in the Greek Text of Kings*. Cambridge: Harvard University Press, 1968.
Thiele, Edwin R. *The Mysterious Numbers of the Hebrew Kings*. Grand Rapids: Eerdmans, 1965.
Thompson, J.A. *The Bible and Archaeology*. 3d ed. Grand Rapids: Eerdmans, 1982.
Unger, Merrill F. *Israel and the Aramaeans of Damascus*. Grand Rapids: Baker, 1957.
———. *Archaeology and the Old Testament*. 4th ed. Grand Rapids: Zondervan, 1960.
Van Der Meer, P. *The Chronology of Ancient Western Asia and Egypt*. 2d ed. Leiden: Brill, 1963.
Wiseman, D.J. *Chronicles of Chaldaean Kings*. London: British Museum, 1956.
———, ed. *Peoples of Old Testament Times*. Oxford: Clarendon, 1973.
Wright, G. Ernest, ed. *The Bible and the Ancient Near East*. Garden City: Doubleday, 1961.
Yamauchi, Edwin M. *The Stones and the Scriptures*. Philadelphia: Lippincott, 1972.
———. *Foes from the Northern Frontier*. Grand Rapids: Baker, 1982.

Articles

Aberbach, Moses, and Smolar, Leivy. "Jeroboam and Solomon: Rabbinic Interpretations." *Jewish Quarterly Review* 59 (1968): 118–31.
———. "Jeroboam's Rise to Power." *Journal of Biblical Literature* 88 (1969): 69–72.
Ackroyd, P.R. "I and II Kings." *Interpreter's Dictionary of the Bible*. Supplementary volume. Edited by K. Crim. Nashville: Abingdon, 1976.
Allen, R.B. "Elijah the Broken Prophet." *Journal of the Evangelical Theological Society* 22 (1979): 193–202.
Astour, Michael C. "841 B.C.: The First Assyrian Invasion of Israel." *Journal of the American Oriental Society* 91 (1971): 383–89.
Berkowitz, Louis. "Has the U.S. Geological Survey Found King Solomon's Gold Mines?" *Biblical Archaeology Review* 3 (1977): 28–33.
Burrows, Millar. "The Conduit of the Upper Pool." *Zeitschrift für die alttestamentliche Wissenschaft* 70 (1958): 221–27.
Dennison, James T., Jr. "Elijah the Tishbite: A Note on I Kings 17:1." *Westminster Theological Journal* 41 (1978): 124–26.
Freedman, D.N. "The Babylonian Chronicle." *Biblical Archaeologist* 19 (1956): 50–60.
Geyer, J.B. "2 Kings XVIII 14–16 and the Annals of Sennacherib." *Vetus Testamentum* 21 (1971): 604–6.
Gooding, D.W. "Jeroboam's Rise to Power: A Rejoinder." *Journal of Biblical Literature* 91 (1972): 529–33.
Grayson, A.K. "Studies in Neo-Assyrian History." *Bibliotheca Orientalis* 23 (1976): 134–45.
Hallo, W.W. "From Qarqar to Carchemish: Assyria and Israel in the Light of New Discoveries." *Biblical Archaeologist Reader, 2*. Edited by D.N. Freedman and E.F. Campbell, Jr. Garden City: Doubleday, 1964.
Haran, Manahem. "The Rise and Decline of the Empire of Jeroboam ben Joash." *Vetus Testamentum* 17 (1967): 266–97.
Jenkins, A.K. "Hezekiah's Fourteenth Year." *Vetus Testamentum* 26 (1976): 284–98.
Klein, R.W. "Jeroboam's Rise to Power." *Journal of Biblical Literature* 89 (1970): 217–18.
———. "Once More: 'Jeroboam's Rise to Power.'" *Journal of Biblical Literature* 92 (1973): 582–84.
MacDonald, J. "The Status and Role of the NA'AR in Israelite Society." *Journal of Near Eastern Studies* 35 (1976): 147–70.
Malamat, A. "The Kingdom of David and Solomon in Its Contact with Egypt and Aram Naharaim." *Biblical Archaeologist* 21 (1958): 96–102.

Mazar, A. " 'The Bull Site'—An Iron Age I Open Cult Place." *Bulletin of the American Schools of Oriental Research* 247 (1982): 27–42.

Mazar, B. "The Aramean Empire and Its Relations with Israel." *Biblical Archaeologist* 25 (1962): 97–120.

McCarter, P.K. "Yaw, Son of Omri." *Bulletin of the American Schools of Oriental Research* 216 (1974): 5–7.

Miller, J.M. "The Fall of the House of Ahab." *Vetus Testamentum* 17 (1967): 319–24.

Morgenstern, J. "The Festival of Jerobeam I." *Journal of Biblical Literature* 83 (1964): 109–17.

Na'aman, Nadav. "Two Notes on the Monolith Inscription of Shalmaneser III from Kurkh." *Tel Aviv* 3 (1976): 89–106.

———. "The Brook of Egypt and Assyrian Policy on the Border of Egypt." *Tel Aviv* 6 (1979): 68–90.

Oswalt, J.N. "Chronology of the OT." *The International Standard Bible Encyclopedia*. Revised Edition. ISBE rev. Vol. 1. Edited by G.W. Bromiley. Grand Rapids: Eerdmans, 1979.

Payne, J.B. "Chronology of the Old Testament." *Zondervan Pictorial Encyclopedia of the Bible*. ZPEB. Vol. 1. Edited by M.C. Tenney. Grand Rapids: Zondervan, 1975.

Redford, Donald B. "Studies in Relations Between Palestine and Egypt During the First Millennium B.C." *Journal of the American Oriental Society* 93 (1973): 3–17.

Schultz, H.G. "The Interphased Chronology of Jotham, Ahaz, Hezekiah and Hoshea." *Journal of the Evangelical Theological Society* 8 (1966): 81–90.

Tadmor, H. "The Campaigns of Sargon II of Ashur: A Chronological-Historical Study." *Journal of Cuneiform Studies* 12 (1958): 22–40, 77–100.

Van Beek, G.W. "Frankincense and Myrrh." *Biblical Archaeologist* 23 (1960): 69–95.

Weinfeld, M. "The Counsel of the 'Elders' to Rehoboam and Its Implications." *Maarav* 3 (1982): 27–53.

Wood, B.G. "Water Systems of Ancient Jerusalem." *Bible and Spade* (1975): 42–56.

Wright, G.E. "The Temple in Palestine-Syria." *The Biblical Archaeologist Reader*. Edited by G.E. Wright and D.N. Freedman. Garden City: Doubleday, 1961.

Zuidhof, A. "King Solomon's Molten Sea and (π)." *Biblical Archaeologist* 45 (1982): 179–84.

10. Outline

6. The reign of Amaziah in the southern kingdom (14:1–22)
7. The reign of Jeroboam II in the northern kingdom (14:23–29)
8. The reign of Uzziah in the southern kingdom (15:1–7)
9. The reign of Zechariah in the northern kingdom (15:8–12)
D. The Era of the Decline and Fall of the Northern Kingdom (15:13–17:41)
1. The reign of Shallum in the northern kingdom (15:13–15)
2. The reign of Menahem in the northern kingdom (15:16–22)
3. The reign of Pekahiah in the northern kingdom (15:23–26)
4. The reign of Pekah in the northern kingdom (15:27–31)
5. The reign of Jotham in the southern kingdom (15:32–38)
6. The reign of Ahaz in the southern kingdom (16:1–20)
7. The reign of Hoshea in the northern kingdom (17:1–23)
8. The repopulation of Samaria (17:24–41).
III. The Southern Kingdom (18:1–25:30)
A. The Reign of Hezekiah (18:1–20:21)
1. Hezekiah's accession and early deeds (18:1–12)
2. The Assyrian invasion (18:13–37)
3. The continued siege of Jerusalem (19:1–13)
4. The delivery of Jerusalem (19:14–37)
5. Hezekiah's miraculous recovery (20:1–11)
6. Hezekiah and Merodach-Baladan (20:12–21)
B. The Reign of Manasseh (21:1–18)
C. The Reign of Amon (21:19–26)
D. The Reign of Josiah (22:1–23:30)
1. Accession and early reforms (22:1–7)
2. The Book of the Law (22:8–13)
3. The advice of Huldah (22:14–20)
4. Further reforms (23:1–23)
5. Latter days (23:24–30)
E. The Last Days of Judah (23:31–25:21)
1. The reign of Jehoahaz (23:31–33)
2. The reign of Jehoiakim (23:34–24:7)
3. The reign of Jehoiachin (24:8–16)
4. The reign of Zedekiah (24:17–25:21)
F. Historical Appendixes (25:22–30)
1. Judah in exile (25:22–26)
2. The later history of Jehoiachin (25:27–30)

Text and Exposition

I. The United Kingdom (1 Kings 1:11–11:43)

A. Solomon's Exaltation as King (1:1–2:11)

1. Adonijah's plot to seize the crown (1:1–10)

The Book of Kings begins with the rather sad circumstances surrounding the accession of Solomon to the throne of his father, David. Two primary factors are involved: (1) David's feebleness and apparent laissez faire attitude toward government in his later years, and (2) Adonijah's self-willed ambition to succeed his father, based on the fact that he was the oldest of David's surviving sons. In this ambition he was supported by some influential members of David's government, despite David's clearly expressed designation of Solomon (cf. Notes).

a. David's feebleness

1:1–4

> ¹When King David was old and well advanced in years, he could not keep warm even when they put covers over him. ²So his servants said to him, "Let us look for a young virgin to attend the king and take care of him. She can lie beside him so that our lord the king may keep warm."
> ³Then they searched throughout Israel for a beautiful girl and found Abishag, a Shunammite, and brought her to the king. ⁴The girl was very beautiful; she took care of the king and waited on him, but the king had no intimate relations with her.

1 This brief account of David's feebleness and apparent inability to act decisively is given as the backdrop to Adonijah's attempted coup. It is somewhat startling to see the once so vigorous king now, at scarcely seventy years of age (cf. 2 Sam 5:4–5), in such a state of debilitation. The reason for this is generally sought in the rigors of his years of exile followed by the severe demands of establishing his mastery, not only over Judah and all Israel, but also over the surrounding nations as well.

It would seem, however, that the one thing that did more than anything else to sap David's strength and will to govern decisively in his latter years was the series of disasters let loose on him and his family following his disgraceful act of adultery with Bathsheba and the indirect murder he committed in an attempt to cover up his sin. This shattering chain of events included Amnon's rape of his half-sister Tamar; Amnon's subsequent murder by Absalom, Tamar's full brother; Absalom's revolt with its severe disruptions, followed by his death, with its great emotional impact on David (2 Sam 18:32–19:8); David's ill-judged census with the resultant plague; and then Shibni's brief revolt. There can be no doubt that these terrible experiences coupled with his knowledge of moral lapse, though forgiven, did much to rob David of his earlier physical and spiritual élan.

2–4 The suggestion made by David's ministers conforms to a type of diatherapy attested in later literature. A virgin was chosen because she had the status of a concubine though in actual fact she served David as a nurse. The whole point of the paragraph is to show (1) how David's feebleness encouraged Adonijah to believe he could successfully force David's hand in his favor, and (2) why Adonijah's later request to Solomon brought about such severe consequences (cf. comments on 2:13–25).

Notes

For a discussion of the "Succession Narrative" view of 2 Sam 9–20 and 1 Kings 1–2, see the note on 2:13.

2 The expression "to attend the king" (lit., "to stand before the king") is usually used of the activity of a servant or court minister before a master or king or of a priest before God (S. Amsler, "עָמַד ['āmaḏ]," *Theologisches Handwörterbuch zum Alten Testament*, ed. E. Jenni and C. Westermann [Munich: Chr. Kaiser Verlag, 1978]).

W.F. Albright ("The Seal of Eliakim and the Latest Preexilic History of Judah, With Some Observations on Ezekiel," JBL 51 [1932]: 79f.) lists a number of contemporary seals of court officials using the title עֶבֶד (*ʿeḇeḏ*, "servant"), which may be translated "minister" (of the king).

The suggested diatherapy is described by Josephus (Antiq. VII, 343 [xiv.3]) as a medical prescription. Galen (*Methus medicus* 8.7, cited by Montgomery, pp. 71f.) confirms it as a practice in Greek medicine. There are similarities in modern emergency procedures for treating hypothermia, in which, among other things, the body heat of a healthy person is used to help warm the afflicted victim.

b. *Adonijah's attempted coup d'état*

1:5–10

⁵Now Adonijah, whose mother was Haggith, put himself forward and said, "I will be king." So he got chariots and horses ready, with fifty men to run ahead of him. ⁶(His father had never interfered with him by asking, "Why do you behave as you do?" He was also very handsome and was born next after Absalom.)

⁷Adonijah conferred with Joab son of Zeruiah and with Abiathar the priest, and they gave him their support. ⁸But Zadok the priest, Benaiah son of Jehoiada, Nathan the prophet, Shimei and Rei and David's special guard did not join Adonijah.

⁹Adonijah then sacrificed sheep, cattle and fattened calves at the Stone of Zoheleth near En Rogel. He invited all his brothers, the king's sons, and all the men of Judah who were royal officials, ¹⁰but he did not invite Nathan the prophet or Benaiah or the special guard or his brother Solomon.

5–6 Adonijah, encouraged by David's feebleness and aided and abetted strongly by Joab, David's military chief of staff, and by Abiathar, one of the two high priests, thought he could force David's hand by presenting David and the people with a *fait accompli*. Adonijah no doubt felt justified in his claim to the throne in that he seems to have been the oldest surviving son, thus putting him in the succession (though no normal succession patterns had as yet been established in Israel). He surely knew that this attempt was in direct contravention of God's will and David's explicit wishes (2 Sam 12:24–25; 1 Chron 22:9–10; 1 Chron 28:4–7). Adonijah, however, was like Absalom, his brother, in being willful and self-centered, though a naturally attractive person and a born leader. Verse 6 notes David's failure in the matter of disciplining Adonijah as a boy. One wonders how much of this failure was due to the loss of his own moral credibility because of the Bathsheba affair. Amnon and Absalom showed a similar willfulness.

7 Joab, the most powerful of Adonijah's supporters, had always been fiercely loyal to David, but not to David's wishes (see at 2:5). In supporting Adonijah's pretentions to the throne, Joab was acting characteristically. It is very likely that the planning and execution of the attempted coup was as much Joab's doing as Adonijah's. He was not consciously disloyal to David, but he opposed David's (and God's) choice of Solomon as David's successor and did his best to frustrate David's will.

Abiathar, the other named active supporter of Adonijah, had been the only survivor of Saul's massacre of Ahimelech the high priest and his family. He fled to David at Keilah, bringing the ephod with him (1 Sam 22:20–22; 23:6, 9). He served as high priest during David's reign and seems to have been senior to Zadok (1 Kings 2:26–27; Mark 2:26). It seems, though, that at least from the time that David returned the ark to Jerusalem, Zadok gained in prominence since he presided as priest in the tabernacle at Gibeon (1 Chron 16:39). This statement in Chronicles suggests that Abiathar served as high priest in Jerusalem where the ark was located. But since Gibeon was the site of the tabernacle and the chief place of worship (1 Kings 3:4–15) until such time as the temple should be built, it would seem likely that Zadok was commonly regarded as de facto high priest. Whether or not a professional jealousy developed that then resulted in Abiathar's taking a political position opposite to that of Zadok must remain a moot point. It is tragic and disappointing to see one who had been with David in his difficult years, and who had, like Joab, remained faithful, now opposing what he knew to be David's—and more importantly God's—wishes.

8–10 There were those, however, who did not support Adonijah. Zadok was the son of Ahitub (2 Sam 8:17), a descendant of Eleazar, the third son of Aaron. In 1 Chronicles 12:26–28 he is listed as a warrior of the house of Levi and one of those who came to David at Hebron to offer him the rulership over all Israel. He is cited in eight passages as serving along with Abiathar as chief priest under David's rule (see, e.g., 1 Chron 15:11). After the ark was restored to Jerusalem, Zadok is described in 1 Chronicles 16:39 as serving at Gibeon, where the tabernacle was situated. Later, when David was forced to flee Jerusalem before his son Absalom, it was Zadok who had charge of the ark (2 Sam 15:24–25). Both he and Abiathar were loyal supporters of David.

Benaiah of Kabzeel, son of Jehoiada, was renowned as one of the greatest of David's thirty mighty men (2 Sam 23:20–23; 1 Chron 11:22–25). David put him in charge of his bodyguard, the Kerethites and Pelethites (2 Sam 8:18; 20:23; 23:23).

Nathan was a "non-writing" prophet who played an important role in David's reign. David had gone to him to indicate his desire to build a temple unto the Lord, and it was through Nathan that God responded with the Davidic covenant (2 Sam 7). Later God sent Nathan to deal with David over the matter of his sin with Bathsheba (2 Sam 12). Nathan was also sent by God to David on the occasion of Solomon's birth to declare God's special love for Solomon (2 Sam 12:24–25). Solomon is here shown to be a symbol of God's forgiving grace (that David recognized this is seen in the choice of the name Solomon ["peace"]—i.e., the rift between God and David was healed—as well as in the appellation Jedidiah). But the passage also clearly implies God's choice of Solomon as David's successor.

Notice God's words in 2 Samuel 7:15: "My love [*ḥeseḏ*] will never be taken away from him" (cf. also Ps 89:24 [25 MT], 28 [29 MT]). Though 2 Samuel 12:24–25 uses *'āhaḇ* ("love") and *yᵉḏiḏ* ("beloved"), the connection would seem to be a valid one. Keil (p. 18) notes from 2 Samuel 7:12–16 that God "did not ensure the establishment of the throne to any one of his existing sons, but to him that would come out of his loins (*i.e.* to Solomon, who was not yet born)." Nathan apparently had David's full confidence as God's spokesman, and he demonstrated here again his sensitivity to God's will as well as to David's wishes regarding the succession to the throne.

Shimei and Rei are otherwise unknown, though Shimei may well be the Shimei, son of Ela (4:18), who was appointed by Solomon as one of twelve district governors (4:7).

Also absent was David's "special guard [*gibbôrîm*]" (vv.8, 10). The exact composition of this group is not clear. Second Samuel 23:8–39 describes the *gibbôrîm* as thirty-seven "mighty men" (officers?) who were renowned for their faithfulness and deeds of valor. Benaiah was one of these. It is highly probably that this "special guard" was composed of mercenary soldiers such as the Kerethites and Pelethites as well as Gittites. These were not under the authority of Joab and are mentioned in 2 Samuel 15:15–18 as being loyal to David during Absalom's rebellion.

Adonijah's attempted usurpation of the throne began with a ceremonial gathering of his supporters. Absalom had begun his coup in a similar manner (2 Sam 15:11–12). The participation of Abiathar and Joab in the ritual sacrifice and communal meal lent an aura of legitimacy to the occasion.

En Rogel (modern Bir Ayyub ["Job's well"]) was located slightly southeast of Jerusalem, near the confluence of the Hinnom and Kidron valleys. This place was farther removed from the palace than Gihon, the normal place for such festivities. As such it was ideally located for Adonijah's purpose of presenting David with a *fait accompli*, counting on David's illness to render him incapable of overturning Adonijah's plans.

Notes

5 Despite the assertion of many (e.g., Gray, *Kings*, p. 87) that it was Solomon and his supporters who were guilty of intrigue, it seems clear it was Adonijah who was thus guilty. Second Sam 12:24–25; 1 Chron 22:9–10; and 1 Chron 28:4–7 clearly show that Solomon was God's choice as well as David's. That Adonijah and his followers were fully aware of this can be seen from the fact that Solomon and his supporters were not invited (nor was David informed, for that matter!). Those who see Solomon as the ambitious opportunist can do so only by making the gratuitous assumption that the passages quoted above are an editorial apologetic for the Solomonic succession.

Adonijah certainly had the right of it from the normal human perspective. He was the oldest surviving son, and he had considerable personal appeal. In Joab he acquired a powerful supporter. As for Solomon, those who supported him had only God's and David's clearly expressed will as a basis for such support. He did not have the natural claims that Adonijah had. Those who supported Solomon must have done so from the conviction that he was God's choice. David's choice of Solomon cannot truly be explained as being the result of the influence of Bathsheba as a favorite wife. His genuine and heartfelt repentance over his tragic sin against God in connection with Bathsehba and Uriah makes it impossible to accept the fact that he would, as a matter of personal preference, select the son of Bathsheba as his successor. Only the conviction that (1) his sin was truly forgiven and (2) that God himself saw fit to select Bathsheba's son as a token of his forgiving grace could cause David to select Solomon. When Bathsheba and Nathan approached David, they didn't plead for a change in plans, only that David should follow through on his previous promises. Note also that in 1 Chron 22, David is seen as making substantial preparations for the building of the temple in order to help Solomon as much as possible, saying that "Solomon my son is young and inexperienced." The clandestine nature of the attempted coronation affords further proof.

The order of David's first four sons was Amnon, Kileab, Absalom, and Adonijah, these and two others having been born in Hebron (2 Sam 3:2–5). Kileab, the second, must have died as a child; for no further mention is made of him. Amnon was slain by Absalom, ostensibly as an act of vengeance for Amnon's forcible seduction of Absalom's sister Tamar (2 Sam 13); but Absalom's later actions make it appear very likely that his aspirations to the throne had more to do with the slaying than the desire to avenge his sister.

---

2. The counterplan of Nathan and Bathsheba

1:11–31

¹¹Then Nathan asked Bathsheba, Solomon's mother, "Have you not heard that Adonijah, the son of Haggith, has become king without our lord David's knowing it? ¹²Now then, let me advise you how you can save your own life and the life of your son Solomon. ¹³Go in to King David and say to him, 'My lord the king, did you not swear to me your servant: "Surely Solomon your son shall be king after me, and he will sit on my throne"? Why then has Adonijah become king?' ¹⁴While you are still there talking to the king, I will come in and confirm what you have said."

¹⁵So Bathsheba went to see the aged king in his room, where Abishag the Shunammite was attending him. ¹⁶Bathsheba bowed low and knelt before the king.

"What is it you want?" the king asked.

¹⁷She said to him, "My lord, you yourself swore to me your servant by the LORD your God: 'Solomon your son shall be king after me, and he will sit on my throne.' ¹⁸But now Adonijah has become king, and you, my lord the king, do not know about it. ¹⁹He has sacrificed great numbers of cattle, fattened calves, and sheep, and has invited all the king's sons, Abiathar the priest and Joab the commander of the army, but he has not invited Solomon your servant. ²⁰My lord the king, the eyes of all Israel are on you, to learn from you who will sit on the throne of my lord the king after him. ²¹Otherwise, as soon as my lord the king is laid to rest with his fathers, I and my son Solomon will be treated as criminals."

²²While she was still speaking with the king, Nathan the prophet arrived. ²³And they told the king, "Nathan the prophet is here." So he went before the king and bowed with his face to the ground.

²⁴Nathan said, "Have you, my lord the king, declared that Adonijah shall be king after you, and that he will sit on your throne? ²⁵Today he has gone down and sacrificed great numbers of cattle, fattened calves, and sheep. He has invited all the king's sons, the commanders of the army and Abiathar the priest. Right now they are eating and drinking with him and saying, 'Long live King Adonijah!' ²⁶But me your servant, and Zadok the priest, and Benaiah son of Jehoiada, and your servant Solomon he did not invite. ²⁷Is this something my lord the king has done without letting his servants know who should sit on the throne of my lord the king after him?"

²⁸Then King David said, "Call in Bathsheba." So she came into the king's presence and stood before him.

²⁹The king then took an oath: "As surely as the Lord lives, who has delivered me out of every trouble, ³⁰I will surely carry out today what I swore to you by the Lord, the God of Israel: Solomon your son shall be king after me, and he will sit on my throne in my place."

³¹Then Bathsheba bowed low with her face to the ground and, kneeling before the king, said, "May my lord King David live forever!"

Nathan's prompt and decisive action foiled Adonijah's plot by rousing David to take the steps necessary to insure the public proclamation of Solomon as king. By so doing Nathan not only worked out God's will but also saved Solomon's life. Despite the urgency of the situation, however, Nathan displayed once again the ability to act tactfully and judiciously, just as he had done when he brought to David's attention the enormity of his sin in connection with Bathsheba and Uriah.

11–31 Nathan proposed to send Bathsheba in first. Her status as favored wife would ensure a quick hearing, and immediate action was indeed necessary (vv.1–14). Her role was to rouse David to action by asking him how he could allow Adonijah to become king when he had solemnly sworn that Solomon should reign after him (vv.13, 17). Nathan would then confirm her statements and tactfully urge David to act (v.14).

The validity of Solomon's claim to the throne was not in question here. Both Bathsheba and Nathan knew David's disposition in the matter. The danger was that Adonijah would succeed to the throne through David's inaction. Thus they made three points:

1. Adonijah was making a determined bid for the throne (vv.18–19).

2. "The eyes of all Israel are on you, to learn from you who will sit on the throne of my lord the king after him" (v.20).

3. If Adonijah should become king, the life of Solomon and Bathsheba would become forfeit (v.21).

David responded vigorously and promised to carry out that very day the oath he had made with regard to Solomon (vv.29–30).

Notes

11 Gray (*Kings*, p. 87) points out that "the omission of Solomon and his supporters from Adonijah's ceremonial meal at En Rogel was more than discourtesy or willful neglect. There were already two rival parties in Jerusalem, and Adonijah was not going to grant his rivals immunity by eating a communal meal with them." The normal practice was for the successful claimant to the throne to execute the unsuccessful rival. See Judg 9:5; 1 Kings 15:29; 2 Kings 10:6–14; 11:1.

3. *Solomon's anointing*

1:32–40

³²King David said, "Call in Zadok the priest, Nathan the prophet and Benaiah son of Jehoiada." When they came before the king, ³³he said to them: "Take your

lord's servants with you and set Solomon my son on my own mule and take him down to Gihon. ³⁴There have Zadok the priest and Nathan the prophet anoint him king over Israel. Blow the trumpet and shout, 'Long live King Solomon!' ³⁵Then you are to go up with him, and he is to come and sit on my throne and reign in my place. I have appointed him ruler over Israel and Judah."

³⁶Benaiah son of Jehoiada answered the king, "Amen! May the LORD, the God of my lord the king, so declare it. ³⁷ As the LORD was with my lord the king, so may he be with Solomon to make his throne even greater than the throne of my lord King David!"

³⁸So Zadok the priest, Nathan the prophet, Benaiah son of Jehoiada, the Kerethites and the Pelethites went down and put Solomon on King David's mule and escorted him to Gihon. ³⁹Zadok the priest took the horn of oil from the sacred tent and anointed Solomon. Then they sounded the trumpet and all the people shouted, "Long live King Solomon!" ⁴⁰And all the people went up after him, playing flutes and rejoicing greatly, so that the ground shook with the sound.

32–40 The men that David called to carry out the public anointing of Solomon were Benaiah (v.32), the commander of David's special guard; Zadok (v.34), the priest; and Nathan, the prophet. The servants referred to in v.33 are identified in v.38 as the guard composed of Kerethites and Pelethites.

Gihon (v.33), the site of the anointing, was just outside the city in the Kidron Valley, on the east bank of Ophel. It was at that time Jerusalem's major source of water and was therefore a natural gathering place of the populace.

The fact that Solomon was mounted on David's royal mule demonstrated to the populace that this anointing had David's blessing. Thus there could be no doubt whatever in the public mind as to David's wishes in the matter of the succession (v.39). Had David not acted with decision, the people might well have supported Adonijah's claims. As it was, they followed David and supported Solomon with great spontaneous rejoicing.

Notes

33 The mule—פִּרְדָּה (pirdāh, "female mule")—was a recent innovation in Israel and seems at this time to have been used primarily by the royal court and the aristocracy. It was imported (1 Kings 10:25; Ezek 27:14), due to the prohibition of Lev 19:19 with regard to the crossbreeding of animals. In 2 Sam 13:29 (the first mention) they were ridden by David's sons. In 2 Sam 18:9, Absalom was riding a mule at the time of his death. Somewhat later mules seemed to be more common and were used as burden bearers (2 Kings 5:17; 1 Chron 12:40; Ezra 2:66; cf. W.S. McCullough, IDB, s.v.).

34 The situation here described is that of a coregency. E. Ball ("The Coregency of David and Solomon," VetTest 27 [1977]: 268–79) has shown that there is a strong precedent for such a coregency in Egyptian practice, giving examples from the sixth through the twenty-third dynasties.

35 The correlation of this event with 1 Chron 23:1—"When David was old and full of years, he made his son Solomon king over Israel"—is not perfectly clear. Edersheim (7:55–56) and H.L. Ellison (NBCrev., pp. 382f.) seem to have the best view, that the 1 Chron 23:1 statement is a compact account of 1 King 1:28–40, especially vv.38–40. The coronation was then further confirmed at the great assembly of leaders as described in 1 Chron 28–

29. First Chron 29:22 describes a second confirmatory anointing as was experienced by Saul and David in 1 Sam 11:15 and 2 Sam 2:4; 5:3 (the latter passage a third anointing, this time to be king over the ten northern tribes as well).

---

4. Adonijah's submission

1:41–53

> [41] Adonijah and all the guests who were with him heard it as they were finishing their feast. On hearing the sound of the trumpet, Joab asked, "What's the meaning of all the noise in the city?"
> [42] Even as he was speaking, Jonathan son of Abiathar the priest arrived. Adonijah said, "Come in. A worthy man like you must be bringing good news."
> [43] "Not at all!" Jonathan answered. "Our lord King David has made Solomon king. [44] The king has sent with him Zadok the priest, Nathan the prophet, Benaiah son of Jehoiada, the Kerethites and the Pelethites, and they have put him on the king's mule, [45] and Zadok the priest and Nathan the prophet have anointed him king at Gihon. From there they have gone up cheering, and the city resounds with it. That's the noise you hear. [46] Moreover, Solomon has taken his seat on the royal throne. [47] Also, the royal officials have come to congratulate our lord King David, saying, 'May your God make Solomon's name more famous than yours and his throne greater than yours!' And the king bowed in worship on his bed [48] and said, 'Praise be to the LORD, the God of Israel, who has allowed my eyes to see a successor on my throne today.' "
> [49] At this, all Adonijah's guests rose in alarm and dispersed. [50] But Adonijah, in fear of Solomon, went and took hold of the horns of the altar. [51] Then Solomon was told, "Adonijah is afraid of King Solomon and is clinging to the horns of the altar. He says, 'Let King Solomon swear to me today that he will not put his servant to death with the sword.' "
> [52] Solomon replied, "If he shows himself to be a worthy man, not a hair of his head will fall to the ground; but if evil is found in him, he will die." [53] Then King Solomon sent men, and they brought him down from the altar. And Adonijah came and bowed down to King Solomon, and Solomon said, "Go to your home."

41–53 David's response to the coronation (vv.47–48) is both touching and typical of him. David saw in this event the beginning of the fulfillment of God's promise to him as described in 2 Samuel 7, and he was profoundly grateful to a gracious and loving God. The kingdom would not be removed from David at his death as was the case with Saul. Rather in Solomon there began the long line of David's descendants that would ultimately lead to the promised Messiah, who was both the son of David and the Son of God.

The swelling sound of the public rejoicing and of the instruments reached the ears of Adonijah's supporters at En Rogel (v.41). Their initial puzzlement soon turned to alarm as they learned from Jonathan, son of Abiathar, that Solomon had been publicly proclaimed king and that this had been received with great enthusiasm (vv.42–48). This effectively put an end to Adonijah's plot as the participants quickly scattered (v.49).

Adonijah's response was to seek asylum by grasping the horns of the altar (v.50). He expected Solomon to execute the rival claimant to the throne, as he himself would have done had he been successful in gaining the throne. Solomon was more gracious, however, guaranteeing Adonijah's safety as long as he conducted himself properly (v.51). To be a "worthy man" in this context simply means that Adonijah would renounce any claims to the throne, that he would avoid seditious intrigue and support Solomon's rights with regard to the kingship over Israel.

Notice that Solomon as coregent acted here with the full authority of kingship.

Notes

50 This method of seeking sanctuary was a time-honored custom. In Israel the grasping of the horns of the altar did not provide sanctuary for all types of criminals—only those guilty of the unintentional slaying of another. "In the horns of the altar, as symbols of power and strength, there was concentrated the true significance of the altar as a divine place, from which there emanated both life and health. . . . By grasping the horns of the altar the culprit placed himself under the protection of the saving and helping grace of God, which wipes away sin, and thereby abolishes punishment" (Keil, p. 25). The horns were the projections at the corners of the altar on which the blood of sacrifice was smeared.

The location of the altar is not mentioned, though it was most likely in the tent that David had erected in Jerusalem to house the ark of the covenant.

5. David's charge to Solomon

2:1–11

¹When the time drew near for David to die, he gave a charge to Solomon his son.
²"I am about to go the way of all the earth," he said. "So be strong, show yourself a man, ³and observe what the LORD your God requires: Walk in his ways, and keep his decrees and commands, his laws and requirements, as written in the Law of Moses, so that you may prosper in all you do and wherever you go, ⁴and that the LORD may keep his promise to me: 'If your descendants watch how they live, and if they walk faithfully before me with all their heart and soul, you will never fail to have a man on the throne of Israel.'
⁵"Now you yourself know what Joab son of Zeruiah did to me—what he did to the two commanders of Israel's armies, Abner son of Ner and Amasa son of Jether. He killed them, shedding their blood in peacetime as if in battle, and with that blood stained the belt around his waist and the sandals on his feet. ⁶Deal with him according to your wisdom, but do not let his gray head go down to the grave in peace.
⁷"But show kindness to the sons of Barzillai of Gilead and let them be among those who eat at your table. They stood by me when I fled from your brother Absalom.
⁸"And remember, you have with you Shimei son of Gera, the Benjamite from Bahurim, who called down bitter curses on me the day I went to Mahanaim. When he came down to meet me at the Jordan, I swore to him by the LORD: 'I will not put you to death by the sword.' ⁹But now, do not consider him innocent. You are a man of wisdom; you will know what to do to him. Bring his gray head down to the grave in blood."
¹⁰Then David rested with his fathers and was buried in the City of David. ¹¹He had reigned forty years over Israel—seven years in Hebron and thirty-three in Jerusalem.

1 David's last charge to Solomon is in two parts. The first has to do with Solomon's spiritual life (vv.2–4), the second gives instruction concerning the disposition of matters pertaining to Joab, to the sons of Barzillai, and to Shimei (vv.5–12).

There can be no doubt that much of Solomon's early spiritual vitality and dedication to God may be attributed to David's deep personal relationship to his Lord and his desire to honor him. Proverbs 4:3–9 indicates (see Introduction to Proverbs, this series, for the question of the authorship of Prov 1–9) that David spent time with Solomon as he was growing up, teaching and admonishing him from the Word of God. It is not clear just how strongly David instructed his other sons, though v.6 indicates that David did not properly discipline Adonijah. It is probable that since David knew from the time of Solomon's birth that he was to be his successor, he gave him special instruction to prepare him for kingship.

It is clear from 1 Chronicles 22–29 that David did everything in his power to smooth the way for Solomon to follow him as king, not only in drawing up the plans (cf. 1 Chron 28:11–19) for the temple, amassing the necessary materials and funds (cf., e.g., 1 Chron 22:14–16) and soliciting the help and cooperation of Israel's leadership (cf., e.g., 1 Chron 22:17–19), but also in admonishing and encouraging Solomon to carry out faithfully the task committed to him (cf. 1 Chron 22:6–13; 28:9 –20). In Solomon, David found a responsive and humble heart. Amnon, Absalom, and Adonijah, Solomon's three older brothers, were spiritually and morally deficient; but Solomon had a heart prepared by God, and he responded willingly to David's instruction.

David's legacy to Solomon was thus much more than a great kingdom with secure borders, tributary nations, and considerable wealth and prestige. Far more importantly he instilled in Solomon a love for God and his Word. He gave to Solomon a proper orientation to life and leadership and was himself an outstanding role model, despite his failures, of a man whose heart truly beat for God.

2–3 David's final words of admonition echo those of God to Joshua (Josh 1:6–9) as the latter was about to begin in his role as commander of the hosts of Israel (cf. also Deut 31:6–8, 23). The basic injunction was that Solomon should conduct himself in his personal life, and in his role as leader of God's people, in accordance with God's Word (cf. also Deut 17:18–20). Solomon was to be strong and show himself to be a man. The same expression was used by the Philistines in 1 Samuel 4:9 as they encouraged one another in their battle against what they assumed to be insurmountable odds.

In Joshua 1:6–9 the words "strong and courageous" (h^azak $we^{\prime e}m\bar{a}s$) encouraged Joshua in respect to the carrying out of his commission to lead Israel into her inheritance in the face of hostile Canaanites. Here as well Solomon as the new leader was told to face courageously the various tasks, difficulties, and dangers he would face as king. For both Joshua and Solomon, courage had its source in God. Its direction, the way it is to be exercised, is based on the Word of God, which also guarantees success. As Solomon steeped himself in and obeyed the Word, he would have both the knowledge and courage to act in accordance with God's will.

4 These words hark back to 2 Samuel 7:12–13 and point to Solomon's responsibilities in the matter of the Davidic covenant. This involves primarily a mental and spiritual attitude in which there is a wholehearted devotion to God. Though the covenant is unconditional with respect to its ultimate goal of bringing in the Messiah

from the line of David, each individual king must heed God's Word from the heart if he would experience the blessing of God.

5–6 The second part of David's last words left Solomon with some matters that he considered to be unfinished business. First was Joab, the commander of David's armies. Joab had been a mixed blessing to David, fiercely loyal, but not always faithful in carrying out his wishes. On the good side it can be said for Joab that he was an outstanding general, an example of his ability being the initial capture of Jerusalem for David (1 Chron 11:6, 8). He never wavered in his loyalty to David's kingship. He also had occasional flashes of spiritual insight, opposing the census (1 Chron 21:3–4) that brought grief to David.

On the other hand there were many problems that Joab created for David. He had a repeated history of taking matters into his own hands, oftentimes creating embarrassing situations for David, often forcing his hand. Joab had killed Absalom against David's express command. In 2 Samuel 3:22–27 he killed Abner in an act of treachery.

After the revolt of Absalom, David appointed Amasa (Absalom's field commander) to muster the men of Judah in order to track down Sheba who had led ten tribes in a secessionist move (2 Sam 20). When Amasa failed to meet the appointed deadline, David turned to Abishai, Joab's brother, to lead the punitive expedition. But Joab took matters into his own hands and treacherously killed Amasa (who had come belatedly) and then took command of the armies. Now once again Joab tried to force David's hand, supporting Adonijah's attempted usurpation of the succession to the throne.

Why had not David dealt with Joab before this? The answer is probably to be found in the fact that David felt under obligation to Joab, and though David was certainly not lacking in courage, he was not able to cope with the mixture of Joab's loyalty and his misdeeds. Yet he realized that Joab's murder of Abner and Amasa, at least, must not go unpunished. Solomon was the natural one to deal with the matter, since Joab had been guilty of sedition in attempting to forestall the succession to the throne of the man of David's choice.

7 In the matter of the sons of Barzillai, David was simply asking Solomon to continue to carry out his own promise to Barzillai as a reward for his loyal support during David's brief exile during Absalom's revolt (2 Sam 19:31–39).

8–9 The matter of Shimei was more difficult. He had clearly acted in a death-deserving way during David's flight from Absalom (2 Sam 16:5–14). Yet on his return to Jerusalem, David had pardoned Shimei (2 Sam 19:18–23). Perhaps David felt the pardon had been rash. At any rate he knew that Shimei's "repentance" was not a sincere one and that he was a potential troublemaker. David now left the matter in Solomon's hands, trusting in Solomon's wisdom to deal properly with the situation.

10–11 Having made all the preparations possible for a successful reign for his son, David died, having ruled a total of forty years, including the first seven years at Hebron over Judah alone. Just how long the coregency lasted cannot be stated with any degree of certainty. Estimates range from two to three months (because of the extreme senility described in 1:1–4) to several years.

Notes

2–4 Montgomery, Gray et al. consider this passage to be a Deuteronomistic insertion. Such a view reflects the totally gratuitous assumptions of source criticism with its unfounded reconstructions of Israelite history. That David should base his final admonition to the young king on God's words to Joshua is entirely in character for one who penned the words of Ps 19:7–14.

B. *Solomon's establishment of the kingdom (2:12–3:28)*

1. *The assumption of the throne*

> 2:12

> > [12]So Solomon sat on the throne of his father David, and his rule was firmly established.

12 However long or short the coregency was, v.12 states that when David died, Solomon's rule was firmly established. There was no question in any one's mind who was king, and Solomon had firm control over the kingdom.

One matter that is usually lost sight of is that during Adonijah's attempt to preempt the throne, Solomon himself did not indulge in plotting to make the throne certain for himself. He exercised remarkable restraint. But once he was formally declared to be king, he acted firmly and with decision and dispatch.

2. Adonijah's further plot and execution

> 2:13–25

> > [13]Now Adonijah, the son of Haggith, went to Bathsheba, Solomon's mother. Bathsheba asked him, "Do you come peacefully?"
> > He answered, "Yes, peacefully." [14]Then he added, "I have something to say to you."
> > "You may say it," she replied.
> > [15]"As you know," he said, "the kingdom was mine. All Israel looked to me as their king. But things changed, and the kingdom has gone to my brother; for it has come to him from the LORD. [16]Now I have one request to make of you. Do not refuse me."
> > "You may make it," she said.
> > [17]So he continued, "Please ask King Solomon—he will not refuse you—to give me Abishag the Shunammite as my wife."
> > [18]"Very well," Bathsheba replied, "I will speak to the king for you."
> > [19]When Bathsheba went to King Solomon to speak to him for Adonijah, the king stood up to meet her, bowed down to her and sat down on his throne. He had a throne brought for the king's mother, and she sat down at his right hand.
> > [20]"I have one small request to make of you," she said. "Do not refuse me."
> > The king replied, "Make it, my mother; I will not refuse you."
> > [21]So she said, "Let Abishag the Shunammite be given in marriage to your brother Adonijah."

²²King Solomon answered his mother, "Why do you request Abishag the Shunammite for Adonijah? You might as well request the kingdom for him—after all, he is my older brother—yes, for him and for Abiathar the priest and Joab son of Zeruiah!"

²³Then King Solomon swore by the LORD: "May God deal with me, be it ever so severely, if Adonijah does not pay with his life for this request! ²⁴And now, as surely as the LORD lives—he who has established me securely on the throne of my father David and has founded a dynasty for me as he promised—Adonijah shall be put to death today!" ²⁵So King Solomon gave orders to Benaiah son of Jehoiada, and he struck down Adonijah and he died.

13-17 That Adonijah was ambitious and not yet done with his hopes for securing the throne for himself is seen in this section. (For an opposing view of this interpretation, see the note on v.13.) In asking for the hand of Abishag (v.17), he was almost certainly not pursuing romantic interests but trying to secure for himself a claim to the throne. De Vaux (pp. 116-17) notes that

> from some passages it appears that the king's harem, at least in the early days of the monarchy, used to pass to his successor. In 2 Sam 12:8 Nathan says that it was Yahweh himself who, by establishing David as king of Israel, had given him the wives of his master Saul. Absalom publicly approached the concubines whom David had left in Jerusalem; it was a way of asserting that he was now king (2 Sam 16:21-22), for possession of the harem was a title to the throne. Ishbosheth's anger against Abner, who had taken one of Saul's concubines (2 Sam 3:7 -8), is easy to explain if she had passed by inheritance to Ishbosheth, for Abner's action would imply that he was disputing the power with him.

According to Herodotus (3.68), the custom existed among the Persians. The ancient Arabs had a similar practice.

Although 1:4 states clearly that David had no marital relations with Abishag, her function being a therapeutic one, she was officially regarded as being one of David's wives. As such she would provide an additional argument for Adonijah's royal pretensions. He informed Bathsheba that the kingdom had been as good as his and that all Israel had regarded him as king, thus clearly indicating that his aspirations were not really dead.

18-22 Bathsheba, realizing Abishag's true status, saw no harm in the request and went to Solomon to intercede for Adonijah. But Solomon saw through the scheme and, probably startling his mother considerably, spoke rather vehemently: "You might as well request the kingdom for him" (v.20)!

23-25 Solomon reacted swiftly to Adonijah's ploy and ordered Benaiah to execute him. Though this may seem harsh, it was clearly necessary since Adonijah was evidently still hoping to establish himself on the throne. To leave him alive with such ambitions would leave a festering sore in the kingdom.

It should be noted that Solomon was not acting out of vindictiveness. No mention is made of any punitive actions toward the other brothers, who had at least tacitly supported Adonijah (1:9).

Notes

13 First Kings 1–2 is frequently joined with 2 Sam 9–20 and called the Succession Narrative. This view was formulated by Leonhard Rost ("Die Überlieferung von der Thronnachfolge Davids," *Beiträge zur Wissenschaft vom Alten Testament und Neuen Testament* [Stuttgart, 1926], 3.6). In brief this view holds that this portion of Scripture was compiled by an apologist for Solomon. The seeming harshness with which he dealt with Adonijah, Joab, Shimei, and Abiathar is supposed to be vindicated by the long history of rebelliousness against the throne of David (i.e., Absalom, Shimei, Sheba) and by the unfitness to rule of Solomon's older brothers—Amnon rapes his sister and is murdered; Absalom rebels against David and publicly enters his father's harem as a claim to the throne; then Adonijah wants to take Abishag, technically David's concubine, as his wife, thus strengthening his claims to the throne. Only Solomon is truly worthy to rule.

This view, with occasional modifications, has generally been a part of "critical orthodoxy." P. Kyle McCarter, Jr. ("The Succession Narrative as Court Apologetic," Int 35 [1981]: 355–67) modifies the prevailing view with the observation that only 1 Kings 1–2 really has to do with Solomon, that 2 Sam 9–20 really has to do with David's reign, and that the Solomonic apologist did not compose those chapters but used them to support the actual "succession narrative"—1 Kings 1–2.

In the same issue of *Interpretation* (35 [1981]), Peter Ackroyd ("The Succession Narrative so-called," pp. 383–96) takes exception to the idea of a "succession narrative" written by an apologist for Solomon. He holds that 2 Samuel 9–20 and 1 Kings 1–2 do not comprise a self-contained narrative. Nor is it possible to support a rigid single purpose view of the narrative without highlighting some portions and ignoring or explaining away other portions. There are, in his view, enough uncomplimentary assessments of both David and Solomon in this material to make one question their use in a pro-Solomonic apologetic. Though he does not accept the true historicity of this narrative, he yet maintains that "any attempt at mere historical reconstruction is out" and that it is best to read the material "straight," as it has been for centuries.

In the view of those who see a Solomonic apologetic in the first two chapters of 1 Kings, Solomon is the usurper rather than Adonijah. The latter is to be pitied, especially in having his romantic aspirations toward Abishag so unjustly and cruelly thwarted.

The difficulties and inconsistencies in adopting such a view are considerable and can only be maintained by resorting to unfounded presuppositions and historical reconstructions that compound the uncertainties and problems. On the other hand, there is a clear and consistent testimony in the narrative as it stands to the grace and sovereign purpose of God in choosing David and Solomon, with all their shortcomings and failures, to be kings and forerunners of the Messiah who would be provided by God for his people, Israel, and for the world.

3. The deposition of Abiathar

2:26–27

26To Abiathar the priest the king said, "Go back to your fields in Anathoth. You deserve to die, but I will not put you to death now, because you carried the ark of the Sovereign Lᴏʀᴅ before my father David and shared all my father's hardships." 27So Solomon removed Abiathar from the priesthood of the Lᴏʀᴅ, fulfilling the word the Lᴏʀᴅ had spoken at Shiloh about the house of Eli.

26 Abiathar was banished to his home in Anathoth (c. three and a half miles north of Jerusalem). (The prophet Jeremiah came from priestly stock at Anathoth.) He deserved to die because he opposed not only David's will but also God's will in the matter of succession. But since he had served faithfully, having been loyal to David in his hard times and having borne the ark (2 Sam 15:24, 29; 1 Chron 15:11-15) in his capacity as high priest, Solomon allowed him to live. Notice the words "I will not put you to death now." The reprieve from execution was dependent on continued good behavior.

27 The removal of Abiathar from the active priesthood and the sole tenancy of Zadok as high priest was a fulfillment of God's word to Eli (1 Sam 2:30-33).

4. The execution of Joab

2:28-34

> 28When the news reached Joab, who had conspired with Adonijah though not with Absalom, he fled to the tent of the LORD and took hold of the horns of the altar. 29King Solomon was told that Joab had fled to the tent of the LORD and was beside the altar. Then Solomon ordered Benaiah son of Jehoiada, "Go, strike him down!"
> 30So Benaiah entered the tent of the LORD and said to Joab, "The king says, 'Come out!'"
> But he answered, "No, I will die here."
> Benaiah reported to the king, "This is how Joab answered me."
> 31Then the king commanded Benaiah, "Do as he says. Strike him down and bury him, and so clear me and my father's house of the guilt of the innocent blood that Joab shed. 32The LORD will repay him for the blood he shed, because without the knowledge of my father David he attacked two men and killed them with the sword. Both of them—Abner son of Ner, commander of Israel's army, and Amasa son of Jether, commander of Judah's army—were better men and more upright than he. 33May the guilt of their blood rest on the head of Joab and his descendants forever. But on David and his descendants, his house and his throne, may there be the LORD's peace forever."
> 34So Benaiah son of Jehoiada went up and struck down Joab and killed him, and he was buried on his own land in the desert.

28-29 Solomon now began to carry out David's injunctions with regard to his own "unfinished business." Having heard of Solomon's actions with regard to Adonijah and Abiathar, Joab knew that judgment would not be long in coming. In seeking sanctuary by grasping the horns of the altar, he no doubt was thinking only of his involvement with Adonijah's plot. It would be in keeping with Joab's character to have dismissed from his mind any thought of blame, much less punishment, in regard to the two murders. In any case Joab's act of seeking sanctuary would put Solomon's execution order in as bad a light as possible by making him appear to be violating a commonly accepted sanctuary. Solomon would have to contend with strong emotions on the part of many of the people.

30-33 Joab's refusal to leave frustrated Benaiah's mission since he hesitated to touch Joab while he clung to the altar (v.30). When Solomon sent Benaiah back to execute Joab at the altar, he justified the order as an act of justice to remove bloodguiltiness from David and his descendants (v.31). This was not "specious reasoning" (Gray,

Kings, p. 109). Solomon was carrying out David's wishes (v.32). This matter was of great importance to David's conscience and the integrity of his reign because the murders were not a private matter (v.33). One might term Joab's murders as political assassinations. The national interest and conscience were involved.

34 Benaiah carried out Solomon's order. No public outcry is recorded. On the contrary, the last sentence in the chapter states that "the kingdom was now firmly established in Solomon's hands" (v.46).

Notes

28 The horns of the altar provided sanctuary for those guilty of involuntary manslaughter, but not for those guilty of premeditated or intentional murder.

5. *The elevation of Benaiah and Zadok*

2:35

35The king put Benaiah son of Jehoiada over the army in Joab's position and replaced Abiathar with Zadok the priest.

35 The two chief conspirators as well as Adonijah were now removed. It should be clearly understood that though Solomon's actions strengthened his hand and fixed him firmly in the rulership, his acts were not acts of personal vengeance or political expediency. These men had actively and with deliberate forethought opposed the divine will. It must also be made clear to all the people that Joab's willful acts could not be condoned, even though they were perpetrated in the name of David's government. Joab and Abiathar were now replaced by Benaiah and Zadok.

Notes

35 Ezekiel restricts the eschatological priesthood to the Zadokites since they alone were innocent of apostasy (Ezek 44:15–16). They retained the priesthood till 171 B.C. when Antiochus conferred it on Menelaus. The Essenes at Qumran were at odds with the priests of the day and awaited the restoration of the Zadokites, whom they looked on as the only legitimate priestly family.

6. *The execution of Shimei*

2:36–46

36Then the king sent for Shimei and said to him, "Build yourself a house in Jerusalem and live there, but do not go anywhere else. 37The day you leave and cross the Kidron Valley, you can be sure you will die; your blood will be on your own head."

³⁸Shimei answered the king, "What you say is good. Your servant will do as my lord the king has said." And Shimei stayed in Jerusalem for a long time.

³⁹But three years later, two of Shimei's slaves ran off to Achish son of Maacah, king of Gath, and Shimei was told, "Your slaves are in Gath." ⁴⁰At this, he saddled his donkey and went to Achish at Gath in search of his slaves. So Shimei went away and brought the slaves back from Gath.

⁴¹When Solomon was told that Shimei had gone from Jerusalem to Gath and had returned, ⁴²the king summoned Shimei and said to him, "Did I not make you swear by the LORD and warn you, 'On the day you leave to go anywhere else, you can be sure you will die'? At that time you said to me, 'What you say is good. I will obey.' ⁴³Why then did you not keep your oath to the LORD and obey the command I gave you?"

⁴⁴The king also said to Shimei, "You know in your heart all the wrong you did to my father David. Now the LORD will repay you for your wrongdoing. ⁴⁵But King Solomon will be blessed, and David's throne will remain secure before the LORD forever."

⁴⁶Then the king gave the order to Benaiah son of Jehoiada, and he went out and struck Shimei down and killed him.

The kingdom was now firmly established in Solomon's hands.

36 Shimei was not one of the conspirators with Adonijah, but he had considerable potential for stirring up opposition to the house of David. His attitude toward the latter is seen in 2 Samuel 16:5–13. In a gesture of generosity, David forgave him for his cursings and acts of hatred. Yet David no doubt realized the insincerity of Shimei's repentance and the very real probability of a return on Shimei's part to active hostility at the earliest sign of weakness. But he also felt that justice had not been served. Shimei was a scoundrel and needed to be dealt with. David was powerless because of his promise. It was up to Solomon to see to it.

37 Solomon's wisdom and ability to govern is demonstrated at the very outset of his reign. By forbidding Shimei to cross the Kidron Valley on pain of death, Solomon kept him "isolated from his kinsmen of Benjamin, who had been the spearhead of the revolt against David under Sheba (2 Sam 20)" (Gray, *Kings*, p. 111).

38–40 For three years Shimei obeyed the restriction of the king (v.38); but when two of his slaves fled to Achish of Gath, he violated his parole and went after his slaves personally (vv.39–40). Had Shimei taken the conditions of his confinement seriously and been an honest man, he should have gone to Solomon and requested either that the latter regain his slaves for him or else allow him to make the trip.

41–43 Solomon calls Shimei to account for his breach of an oath to God. He had already been the recipient of a gracious pardon from David. But now Solomon was going to mete out justice on the exact terms of the oath. Shimei had taken grace lightly and demonstrated his unrepentant heart. For this he would die in strict accord with the terms of their agreement. He was unworthy of another pardon.

44 With Shimei's execution justice was fully served; yet Solomon astutely allowed Shimei to condemn himself.

45-46 The last opponent of the Davidic dynasty was now gone, and David's throne had been securely established. David had his detractors; but God caused him to prevail, not only in his own rule, but in seeing his son Solomon sitting on his throne as God had promised. The Davidic covenant was now on its way toward fulfillment. Solomon—granted by God's grace a kingdom of peace and prosperity—is, in this and in his extraordinary insight, a type of the coming Son of David, the Messiah.

Notes

40 Montgomery (pp. 96ff.) gives examples of extradition practices of fugitives in the second millennium. In addition to the Hittite and Akkadian documents pertaining to fugitives, the Aramaic vassal treaties also contain provisions on this matter.

7. *The spiritual condition of Solomon's kingdom*

3:1-3

> ¹Solomon made an alliance with Pharaoh king of Egypt and married his daughter. He brought her to the City of David until he finished building his palace and the temple of the LORD, and the wall around Jerusalem. ²The people, however, were still sacrificing at the high places, because a temple had not yet been built for the Name of the LORD. ³Solomon showed his love for the LORD by walking according to the statutes of his father David, except that he offered sacrifices and burned incense on the high places.

1 Solomon's marriage to Pharaoh's daughter was the seal of a political alliance with Egypt. That such a marriage came about gives some indication of the importance of the kingdom Solomon inherited from his father as well as the decline of Egyptian power at this time. Formerly Egyptian Pharaohs consistently refused to allow their daughters to marry even the most important and powerful foreign kings. In this instance it appears that Pharaoh felt it to be advantageous to ally himself with Solomon, giving him not only his daughter but also Gezer as a wedding gift. This would give him clear trade routes through Palestine. Solomon, on the other hand, could by this means secure his southern border.

The rendering "made an alliance with Pharaoh" reflects accurately the literal Hebrew: "became Pharaoh's son-in-law," which stresses the relationship between father-in-law and bridegroom rather than that between the bride and the bridegroom. This was a rather common practice as a means of cementing and maintaining international agreements and securing a nation's borders.

Edersheim's (5:63) comments on this marriage are typical of most writers:

> Such a union was not forbidden by the law [which only forbade alliance with the Canaanites (Exod 34:16; Deut 7:3)], nor was the daughter of Pharaoh apparently implicated in the charge brought against Solomon's other foreign wives of having led him into idolatry (1 Kings xi.1–7). In fact, according to Jewish tradition, the daughter of Pharaoh actually became a Jewish proselyte. Still, Solomon seems to have felt the incongruity of bringing her into the palace of David, within the

bounds of which "the Ark of the Lord" appears to have been located (2 Chron viii.11), and she occupied a temporary abode "in the city of David," until the new palace of Solomon was ready for her reception.

The city of David was located on the southern portion of the eastern ridge of Jerusalem (cf. Aharoni/Avi-Yonah, map 114). This lies between the Kidron Valley on the east and the (now nonexistent) Tyropoeon Valley on the west. It slopes down into the Valley of Hinnom at the point where it joins the Kidron Valley. This was the site of Jebusite Jerusalem and David's Jerusalem. Solomon extended the city to the north, where he also built the temple.

Solomon kept Pharaoh's daughter in the older city of David until he had completed his building projects. Then he built a palace for her (1 Kings 7:8; 9:24; 2 Chron 8:11), presumably as part of his palace complex. Second Chronicles 8:11 indicates that Pharaoh's daughter was not housed in David's palace. She was not to live in David's palace "because the places the ark of the LORD has entered are holy." According to Keil the tent housing the ark of the covenant was placed in David's palace complex. Thus, though Pharaoh's daughter temporarily resided in the city of David, it would not have been in the palace itself.

2 The "however" (raq, which also appears in v.3; NIV, "except") is intended to point out that, though conditions generally were very good, there was one matter that needed correcting, the practice of sacrificing at the "high places" (bāmôt). These latter were open-air sanctuaries that were mostly found on hill tops (1 Kings 11:7; 2 Kings 16:4), but also in towns (1 Kings 13:32) and in valleys (Jer 7:31; Ezek 6:3). De Vaux (pp. 284–88) points out that they were mounds or knolls, places of eminence for purposes of worship. The simplest ones had merely an altar, but they might also be more elaborate as in the case of the one at Gibeon (v.4).

The high places were a constant sore point in Israel, and the prophets of God frequently spoke out against them. There were two basic problems with them: (1) they detracted from the principle of the central sanctuary (Deut 12:1–14); and (2) since worship at high places was a Canaanite custom, syncretism was not only a very real danger but an all too common occurrence. Israel was specifically forbidden to utilize pagan high places and altars (Deut 12:2–4, 13), and as soon as God had established his people in the Land of Promise, they were to worship at a sanctuary in the place appointed by God.

The latter half of the verse gives the reasons for the common use of various "high places" for worship: the temple had not yet been built. Before Eli's time the tabernacle had been at Shiloh; but with the Philistines' capture of the ark, Shiloh lost its significance as the place of God's presence among his people. Even after the ark was returned by the Philistines, it remained for years in the house of Abinadab (1 Sam 7:1), until David removed it to Jerusalem (2 Sam 6) to a tent he had prepared for it there (v.17). In the meantime the tabernacle was removed from Shiloh after the capture of the ark.

The ark next appears at Nob (1 Sam 21), where it remained until Saul massacred the priests there (1 Sam 22). At some point after this event, it was moved to Gibeon where it is mentioned in connection with Zadok's high priestly ministry (1 Chron 16:39–40). There were then, in effect, two tabernacles during David's reign. The one in Gibeon was without the ark; the one in Jerusalem had the ark but not the original trappings of the tabernacle (2 Chron 1:3–5). This state of affairs matched that of the double priesthood of Zadok and Abiathar.

At this point the concept of the central sanctuary was, so to speak, in limbo. As a result it was common for even godly people to worship in various high places.

One might well ask why David did not reunite the ark with the tabernacle. There seem to be several reasons.

1. Jerusalem was the designated site of the future temple. Placing the ark at Gibeon would easily have jeopardized this plan.

2. It seems that the tabernacle was only moved after some disaster had befallen (as at Shiloh and Nob). Public sentiment probably would otherwise have been opposed to a move.

3. David had it in his heart to build a permanent house of the Lord and thus no doubt considered the situation as temporary. There was thus doubtless a greater need felt for building the temple.

3 High commendation is here given Solomon. He loved the Lord and showed it in his walk. He truly feared the Lord and obeyed David's instruction with regard to his walk before God. David himself had loved God from the heart and was deeply aware of the grace of God at work in his life (Pss 18; 31:19, 23; 34:8–10). Solomon, the son of Bathsheba, as the least likely candidate to be God's choice as David's successor, must have been very conscious of God's gracious hand in his life.

What seems to be a qualification in respect to Solomon's godliness—"except that he offered sacrifices . . ."—may in actuality not be intended to detract from his character. It may well be that both here and in v.2 the statement concerning worshiping in various high places is an allusion to a state of incompleteness that did not end until the temple was completed. Pharaoh's daughter resided temporarily in the city of David until the palace and the temple were built. Just so was the worship of the Lord conducted at the high places until the temple was built.

Notice that Samuel brought offerings at various high places (cf. 1 Sam 9:11–25). These sacrifices were apparently supplementary to the official services connected with the tabernacle. This practice was legitimate at this time as long as the high places had no associations whatsoever with Canaanite religions. After the building of the temple, the high places were no longer legitimate.

Notes

1 This was not Solomon's first marriage. Comparing his son Rehoboam's age (forty-one) at the time of his succeeding to the throne (14:21) with the length of Solomon's reign (forty years; cf. 11:42–43), it is clear that he had already married Naamah the Ammonitess before he himself became king.

It is commonly thought that the Egyptian princess was of the relatively weak Twenty-First Dynasty (cf. Wood, *Survey*, p. 293; Gray, *Kings*, pp. 118–20). A. Malamat ("Aspects of the Foreign Policies of David and Solomon," JNES 22 [1963]: 12ff.) identifies the Pharaoh as Siamun, second to the last of the Twenty-First Dynasty.

8. Solomon's sacrifice at Gibeon

3:4

⁴The king went to Gibeon to offer sacrifices, for that was the most important high place, and Solomon offered a thousand burnt offerings on that altar.

4 According to 2 Chronicles 1:2–3, the entire leadership of the nation went with Solomon to Gibeon to bring a great offering to God. One thousand burnt offerings were brought, indicating that this was an especially important occasion. The purpose was clearly to bring thanksgiving for establishing him in the kingdom and also to seek God's blessing on his reign.

9. Solomon's dream and prayer for wisdom

3:5–15

⁵At Gibeon the Lord appeared to Solomon during the night in a dream, and God said, "Ask for whatever you want me to give you."

⁶Solomon answered, "You have shown great kindness to your servant, my father David, because he was faithful to you and righteous and upright in heart. You have continued this great kindness to him and have given him a son to sit on his throne this very day.

⁷"Now, O Lord my God, you have made your servant king in place of my father David. But I am only a little child and do not know how to carry out my duties. ⁸Your servant is here among the people you have chosen, a great people, too numerous to count or number. ⁹So give your servant a discerning heart to govern your people and to distinguish between right and wrong. For who is able to govern this great people of yours?"

¹⁰The Lord was pleased that Solomon had asked for this. ¹¹So God said to him, "Since you have asked for this and not for long life or wealth for yourself, nor have asked for the death of your enemies but for discernment in administering justice, ¹²I will do what you have asked. I will give you a wise and discerning heart, so that there will never have been anyone like you, nor will there ever be. ¹³Moreover, I will give you what you have not asked for—both riches and honor—so that in your lifetime you will have no equal among kings. ¹⁴And if you walk in my ways and obey my statutes and commands as David your father did, I will give you a long life." ¹⁵Then Solomon awoke—and he realized it had been a dream.

He returned to Jerusalem, stood before the ark of the Lord's covenant and sacrificed burnt offerings and fellowship offerings. Then he gave a feast for all his court.

5 God's appearance to Solomon in a dream was an auspicious beginning for him and indicated clearly that God had not only graciously received the sacrifices but was prepared to do great things for Solomon and his people. Solomon was later once again favored with an appearance of God (1 Kings 9:1–9). That God had in such a remarkable way declared himself willing to pour out his blessing on Solomon and his work makes him all the more culpable in his later apostasy (cf. 1 Kings 11:9). With great privilege comes great responsibility.

6 Solomon responded to God's gracious offer by a heartfelt expression of gratitude for God's great kindness demonstrated toward David during his lifetime and now also after his death in providing David a son as successor, the first in the line from which Messiah would come. God was able to exercise kindness and express his love toward David because of his responsiveness in seeking God and walking in his ways. The emphasis is on God's kindness rather than on David's righteousness.

7 Solomon's declaration here showed his true humility before God, as God's pleased response demonstrates. The term "little child," or young lad, relates both to his relative youth and to his inexperience in government.

8 The responsibilities facing Solomon were all the greater in that Israel was God's chosen nation. She had to be governed in accordance with God's precepts if the people were to experience his blessing. A wisdom that God alone could give was needed here.

Another item of thankfulness and praise is added here—the faithfulness of God in respect to the Abrahamic covenant. The words "too numerous to count or number" reflect the words of God to Abraham in Genesis 13:16. God had greatly blessed and increased Abraham's people in stature and in numbers.

9 Notice that it was not speculative wisdom that Solomon was concerned about. What he asked for was an understanding or discerning heart so that he might be able to govern God's people justly. This quality of a government administration in which truth and justice are paramount and where a life in which the fear of God is at the core is seen fully developed in Isaiah 11:2–5. Here Messiah is depicted as the ideal ruler. Solomon, in seeing the need for these qualities and in seeking them for himself, is in so much a type of the Messiah, the Son of David *par excellence*.

10–13 Matthew 6:33 is well illustrated here. Solomon bypassed the kind of request that most men would commonly make—prosperity, a long life, victory over enemies, etc. He sought the more essential thing, and because of this God promised him the wisdom that he sought in such measure that he would stand alone among men (vv. 10–12). In addition God granted him what he had not requested—wealth and honor unequaled in his lifetime (v. 13).

In granting Solomon "a wise and discerning heart" (*lēb ḥākām weⁿābôn*, v. 12), God gave him the ability to judge and rule well. But God here also went beyond Solomon's request and opened up his understanding in areas beyond those having to do with rulership. First Kings 4:29–34 and 10:1–25 sum up his fame and the vast extent of his insight and learning.

14 Here God reminds Solomon of his continued responsibility to walk righteously before God as David had done and as David had enjoined him to do. God's faithfulness to the Davidic covenant remained fixed; but if Solomon wished to enjoy God's fullest blessing, he must walk in accordance with God's will.

15 When Solomon awoke, very much aware that God had spoken to him in a dream, he returned to Jerusalem and brought burnt offerings and fellowship offerings. By so doing Solomon was expressing his thanks for God's goodness. He brought all his officials together for a feast so that they also might rejoice in thanksgiving at this renewed manifestation of God's grace toward Israel and the house of David.

Notes

6 The exact meaning of the important word חֶסֶד (*ḥesed*, "kindness") is much debated. The traditional translation was "lovingkindness" (KJV), "mercy," or "love." The most frequent word used by the LXX is ἔλεος (*eleos*, "mercy"). The Targums are not perfectly consistent but usually use a derivative of טָב (*ṭāḇ*, "good") (H. Stoebe, "חֶסֶד [*ḥesed*] *Theologisches Handwörterbuch zum Alten Testament*). Since the publication in 1927 of N. Glueck's doctoral dissertation (tr. into Eng. as "Ḥesed in the Bible"), the prevailing scholarly opinion on the meaning of the word became something like "covenant loyalty." BDB (1917) and W. Gesenius and F. Buhl (*Hebräisches und Aramäisches Handwörterbuch über das Alte Testament*, 1915, reprint [Berlin: Springer, 1954]) have the traditional renderings. But KB describes it as the "mutual liability of those . . . belonging together." The 1967 edition has moved back toward the more traditional position in those passages dealing with God's dealings with man: "*Treue, Güte, Huld*" ("faithfulness, goodness, grace or favor").

Glueck's view was that *ḥesed* did not basically involve mercy or love but primarily a strict loyalty and faithfulness to covenant obligations. In 1951 H. Stoebe, in his doctoral dissertation, differed with Glueck and came back to the more traditional rendering of "kindness" or "goodheartedness." This view is reflected in his article on *ḥesed* (see above). Katherine Sakenfeld (*The Meaning of Ḥesed in the Hebrew Bible* [Missoula, Mont.: Scholars, 1978]) has also modified Glueck's view, seeing the theological usage as (1) deliverance exercised toward the needy who are obedient and (2) forgiveness toward the penitent. This is an expression of God's faithfulness to his covenant people.

Ḥesed involves both activity and attitude, the attitude basically reflecting the goodness and love of God, the activity being the outworking of this love as God works on behalf of one who is in need. The outworking of God's love is on the basis of a previously established relationship. But behind this relationship is the eternal *ḥesed* or goodness of God. This kindness is not exercised indiscriminately but in accordance with principles that God himself has established. He is gracious (exercises *ḥesed*) to Israel in Exodus 34:6–7 for two reasons: (1) his promise made to their father Abraham and (2) their repentant faith. In the present passage God's exercise of lovingkindness was made possible by David's response of faith-inspired obedience. Solomon's succession to the throne was the visible evidence of God's gracious establishment of the Davidic dynasty.

15 Many make at least part of this verse—"He returned to Jerusalem, stood before the ark of the Lord's covenant"—to be a later addition, either to emphasize the primacy of Jerusalem (Montgomery) or to "redeem the orthodox reputation of the builder of the Temple" (Gray, *Kings*, pp. 126f.). This view is not based on objective evidence and is typical of many similar efforts to distinguish between historical fact and Deuteronomistic insertions. There is a considerable lack of consistency in the identification of these so-called later insertions due to the subjective nature of these views.

W.S. LaSor (NBCrev., p. 327) questions the presence of the ark in Jerusalem at this time, but there is no reason at all to doubt the accuracy of the text (cf. K.A. Kitchen, "Ark" [NBD, s.v.]; P. Feinberg, "Tabernacle" [WBC]; and W. Lotz et al., "Ark of the Covenant" [ISBErev., 1:294]).

10. *Solomon's wisdom: the smothered baby*

3:16–28

[16]Now two prostitutes came to the king and stood before him. [17]One of them said, "My lord, this woman and I live in the same house. I had a baby while she

was there with me. [18]The third day after my child was born, this woman also had a baby. We were alone; there was no one in the house but the two of us.

[19]"During the night this woman's son died because she lay on him. [20]So she got up in the middle of the night and took my son from my side while I your servant was asleep. She put him by her breast and put her dead son by my breast. [21]The next morning, I got up to nurse my son—and he was dead! But when I looked at him closely in the morning light, I saw that it wasn't the son I had borne."

[22]The other woman said, "No! The living one is my son; the dead one is yours."

But the first one insisted, "No! The dead one is yours; the living one is mine." And so they argued before the king.

[23]The king said, "This one says, 'My son is alive and your son is dead,' while that one says, 'No! Your son is dead and mine is alive.'"

[24]Then the king said, "Bring me a sword." So they brought a sword for the king. [25]He then gave an order: "Cut the living child in two and give half to one and half to the other."

[26]The woman whose son was alive was filled with compassion for her son and said to the king, "Please, my lord, give her the living baby! Don't kill him!"

But the other said, "Neither I nor you shall have him. Cut him in two!"

[27]Then the king gave his ruling: "Give the living baby to the first woman. Do not kill him; she is his mother."

[28]When all Israel heard the verdict the king had given, they held the king in awe, because they saw that he had wisdom from God to administer justice.

16–27 This incident is given to illustrate the unusual sagacity of Solomon. Here was a case where there were no witnesses; so it was impossible to prove by conventional means which of the litigants had a just case. Solomon displayed his extraordinary insight into human nature as well as shocking boldness of action in exposing fraud.

The mother of the dead baby wanted a baby of her own. This desire for a baby to mother was stronger than her grief and love for her dead baby. In trying to attach to herself the other woman's baby, she was motivated equally strongly by her envy of the other woman who still had her baby. It was this underlying motive that was the target of Solomon's startling edict: "Cut the living child in two" (v.25). Thus the Gordian knot was cut and true justice was done.

28 Solomon's verdict and the way it was achieved soon became common knowledge, and the people held him in great awe. Here was clear evidence to an unusual degree of a God-given ability to rule wisely and justly.

C. Solomon's Organization of the Kingdom (4:1–34)

1. His officials

4:1–19

[1]So King Solomon ruled over all Israel. [2]And these were his chief officials:

Azariah son of Zadok—the priest;
[3]Elihoreph and Ahijah, sons of Shisha—secretaries;
Jehoshaphat son of Ahilud—recorder;
[4]Benaiah son of Jehoiada—commander in chief;
Zadok and Abiathar—priests;
[5]Azariah son of Nathan—in charge of the district officers;
Zabud son of Nathan—a priest and personal adviser to the king;
[6]Ahishar—in charge of the palace;

Adoniram son of Abda—in charge of forced labor.

⁷Solomon also had twelve district governors over all Israel, who supplied provisions for the king and the royal household. Each one had to provide supplies for one month in the year. ⁸These are their names:

Ben-Hur—in the hill country of Ephraim;

⁹Ben-Deker—in Makaz, Shaalbim, Beth Shemesh and Elon Bethhanan;

¹⁰Ben-Hesed—in Arubboth (Socoh and all the land of Hepher were his);

¹¹Ben-Abinadab—in Naphoth Dor (he was married to Taphath daughter of Solomon);

¹²Baana son of Ahilud—in Taanach and Megiddo, and in all of Beth Shan next to Zarethan below Jezreel, from Beth Shan to Abel Meholah across to Jokmeam;

¹³Ben-Geber—in Ramoth Gilead (the settlements of Jair son of Manasseh in Gilead were his, as well as the district of Argob in Bashan and its sixty large walled cities with bronze gate bars);

¹⁴Ahinadab son of Iddo—in Mahanaim;

¹⁵Ahimaaz—in Naphtali (he had married Basemath daughter of Solomon);

¹⁶Baana son of Hushai—in Asher and in Aloth;

¹⁷Jehoshaphat son of Paruah—in Issachar;

¹⁸Shimei son of Ela—in Benjamin;

¹⁹Geber son of Uri—in Gilead (the country of Sihon king of the Amorites and the country of Og king of Bashan). He was the only governor over the district.

1 This passage (vv.1–19) gives an indication of the organizational development of the kingdom under Solomon. There had already been considerable changes made in Israel during the reigns of the previous two kings. When Saul became king, there was a loose confederacy, something akin to an amphictyony, among the tribes. Through his early victories he welded the nation into a kingdom. But his governmental style was modest and simple. He made no great demands on the people. There was no great central bureaucracy and no lavish court. There is no record of any system of taxation.

David developed a kingdom in a truer sense. His rule was much stronger than Saul's, and he had far greater and more lasting success in defeating Israel's enemies. When he died he had established a great and powerful empire, extending Israel's borders and exercising control over vassal states from the Gulf of Aqaba and the River of Egypt to the northwestern part of the Euphrates. He captured Jerusalem from the Jebusites and made it a strong and permanent capital. His court, though not lavish, was far more extensive than Saul's. His chief officials were almost as numerous as Solomon's. David seems to have had some system of internal taxation, and he certainly received tribute from his various vassal states. One matter of organizational development that was particularly dear to David's heart was that of the temple ministry. He laid the groundwork for an elaborate worship service, including music, in preparation for the time when the temple would be built.

Solomon inherited a great kingdom. His role was one of consolidation and increased internal strengthening. He established a well-organized and strong central government, much stronger than ever before. He developed a system of taxation and forced labor to support a much admired and elaborate governmental structure and his great building projects, foremost being the temple and the palace.

Verses 2–19 list Solomon's officials. Verses 2–6 list his chief administrators, vv.7–19 his district governors. Verses 11, 15 indicate this list was compiled at about the midpoint of Solomon's reign, since two of the officials are sons-in-law of Solomon. In addition the names of especially prominent men who served in the earlier part of Solomon's reign are included. This is certainly true of Abiathar (v.4), who was deposed almost immediately, and probably of Zadok (v.4), who had already served at length under David and most likely didn't live overlong into Solomon's reign. In Abiathar's case it is of course possible that he still carried the title of priest even though he was no longer permitted to function as such—a de facto exile.

2 Various suggestions have been made with regard to Azariah and the office held by him. The best view appears to be that this Azariah was the grandson of Zadok (1 Chron 6:8–9) and became the high priest after the death or incapacitation of Zadok. (The designation "son" for "grandson" is common OT usage.) Ahimaaz, Azariah's father, had apparently died or else could not serve for some reason. That Azariah is here designated as high priest can be seen from the following reasons:

1. The expression "the priest" is the usual way of designating the high priest (de Vaux, p. 378).

2. In a reign in which the construction of a magnificent temple is one of the chief accomplishments, the high priestly office would properly be listed first among the officials.

3. There is no persuasive evidence (with one possible exception, 2 Sam 8:18) that the word *kôhēn* ("priest") is ever used of a secular office (so Keil et al.). Such a secular usage is not recognized by either BDB or KB, and most commentators reject it.

4. Zadok, who had served for many years under David, was surely an elderly man when Solomon became king and would not have lived overly long into Solomon's reign, necessitating a successor.

5. To make the sentence say, "Azariah, son of Zadok the priest, (and) Elihoreph and Ahaziah—secretaries" is contrary to the structure of the context: "x son of y— (office)."

3 The two "secretaries" (*sōpᵉrîm*) served as private secretaries as well as secretary of state. Their father had served in the same office under David. De Vaux (p. 131) states that the secretary played a considerable part in public affairs, ranking just below the master of the palace.

The "recorder" (*mazkîr*) was also a very high official. De Vaux calls him the "royal herald." The Hebrew means literally "the one who calls, names, reminds, reports." He was in charge of palace ceremonies, the chief of protocol. He reported public needs to the king and in turn was the king's spokesman (de Vaux, p. 132).

4 Benaiah, formerly commander of David's special guard, now became the "commander-in-chief" of all the armies.

As stated earlier, Zadok probably did not serve long under Solomon, being elderly at Solomon's succession to the throne. Abiathar was almost immediately deposed. They are listed here because of the outstanding roles they had played in the kingdom.

5 Azariah son of Nathan was in charge of the twelve district governors named in vv.7 –19.

Zabud was another son of Nathan. His function as priest may have been to assist the king in the exercise of his spiritual and ceremonial concerns. He was also called the "friend" of David. This seems to have been a title of honor and distinction and indicated one who was a close and trusted personal adviser. Hushai (2 Sam 15:37) was so designated.

6 Ahishar was "in charge of the palace." De Vaux calls him the "master of the palace." Under Solomon his functions were apparently restricted to that of chief steward of the palace, but his office gradually gained in importance until it was comparable to the office of the Egyptian vizier, the first minister of state (cf. de Vaux, pp. 129–31). A good example of the importance this office took on is found in Isaiah 22:15–24, in which Shebna, the one "in charge of the palace," is to be deposed because he had misused his power in self-aggrandizement. His replacement would "be a father . . . to the house of Judah" (v.21). He would have the key of the house of David on his shoulder. "What he opens no one can shut, and what he shuts no one can open" (v.22). In Revelation 3:7 the Lord Jesus describes his own authority in the same terms. He is God's anointed and the one fully empowered to speak and act for him.

Adoniram was in charge of the forced labor or corvée. This system was widely practiced in the ancient Near East as a means of carrying out public building projects. Samuel (1 Sam 8:12–17) warned that this would be one of the evils of instituting a monarchy. Its extensive use by Solomon, even though there seem to have been lighter demands made on Israelites than on foreign subjects and vassals, eventually created great bitterness and dissatisfaction. This was one of the major reasons given by the northern ten tribes for their secession from the kingdom.

7 The responsibility of these governors was to supply provisions for the royal court. Each of the twelve was responsible for these provisions for one month out of the year. The twelve divisions coincided only in part with the old tribal divisions. In only six instances are tribal names mentioned.

The twelve officers were under the general supervision of Azariah (v.5). De Vaux holds that, though the raising of revenue was the avowed object of this system of district governors, these men held wider responsibilities in the administration of area affairs.

8–19 Keil (p. 46) suggests that the order of the districts is most likely the order in which supplies were to be sent. The territory of Judah is not explicitly mentioned. De Vaux (pp. 135ff.) and others hold that v.19b should be translated "there was one governor over the land." "The land" would refer to Judah, which had an unnamed governor, perhaps because he was part of the court itself (i.e., perhaps the Azariah of v.5). This view is based on the Assyrian custom of referring to the central province of the empire as *mātu,* "the land." The NIV, NASB, and KJV rendering—"he [i.e., Geber] was the only governor over the district"—reflects the interpretation that, despite the size of the district governed by Geber, there was only one governor.

In either case it would appear that Judah may have received special privileges, which would tend to foster resentment on the part of the other tribes.

Notes

2 Several views differing from that given in the exposition follow:

1. The description "priest" refers to Zadok, not to Azariah (so Vul., Syr., KJV, ISBE [1915, 1979]).

2. The term כֹּהֵן (kōhēn, "priest") here refers to a secular office, namely "minister," "privy counsellor" (Keil, pp. 44f.; Bähr, *The Books of the Kings*, CHS, p. 47; Edersheim, 5:67, n.1). This view is based chiefly on 2 Sam 8:18 where David's sons were "royal advisers" (NIV), "chief rulers" (KJV), "chief ministers" (NASB). Kōhēn is regularly translated "priest." The JB and NEB also translate "priest" here. S.R. Driver (*Notes on the Hebrew Text and Topography of the Books of Samuel* [Oxford: Clarendon, 1913], in loc.) maintains that the word must be translated "priest," that there is "no trace of any secular office" here. Seemingly supporting Keil's contention is the fact that the parallel passage in 1 Chron 18:17 designates David's sons as "chief officials at the king's side." Notice also that the LXX translates 2 Sam 8:18 αὐλάρχαι ("chief of the court"). The latter passage does afford some difficulty if khn is translated "priest"; and just in what way David's sons could have functioned as priests is unclear, though de Vaux (p. 361) cites examples of non-Levites such as Samuel who performed certain priestly functions.

3. Montgomery (pp. 112–16) (followed by the NEB) emends the text so that the Elihoreph of v.3 reads ʿal-haḥōrep ("over the autumn"), referring to the beginning of the year. He holds that this has reference to the Assyrian *limmu* official by whom the year was designated. There are no valid grounds for such an emendation, which requires yet another to support it: the plural "sons of Shishu" would have to be emended to the singular. Furthermore it would leave an awkward conjunction "and" before Ahijah, one which would not fit the structural pattern of the rest of the passage. It ought to be noticed that many writers take the view adopted in the exposition but combine it with the view that the mention of Zadok and Abiathar as priests ought to be deleted (cf. de Vaux, p. 128; Hermann, pp. 180, 183 n.41; E.W. Heaton, *Solomon's New Men* [New York: Pica, 1974], pp. 50, 184 n.19).

19 Aharoni/Avi-Yonah (map 73) describe the boundaries of these twelve divisions. The fact that the boundaries did not coincide with the tribal boundaries has led some to suggest that Solomon did this deliberately in order to lessen tribal consciousness and solidarity. Whether this was his purpose or whether it was an attempt to make the territories as equal as possible in size and/or wealth cannot be stated with any degree of assurance. Whatever the motives might have been, the result was a general weakening of tribal boundaries, with the most notable exception of Judah.

2. His kingly splendor

4:20–28

20The people of Judah and Israel were as numerous as the sand on the seashore; they ate, they drank and they were happy. 21And Solomon ruled over all the kingdoms from the River to the land of the Philistines, as far as the border of Egypt. These countries brought tribute and were Solomon's subjects all his life.
22Solomon's daily provisions were thirty cors of fine flour and sixty cors of meal, 23ten head of stall-fed cattle, twenty of pasture-fed cattle and a hundred sheep and goats, as well as deer, gazelles, roebucks and choice fowl. 24For he ruled over all the kingdoms west of the River, from Tiphsah to Gaza, and had peace on all sides. 25During Solomon's lifetime Judah and Israel, from Dan to Beersheba, lived in safety, each man under his own vine and fig tree.

²⁶Solomon had four thousand stalls for chariot horses, and twelve thousand horses.
²⁷The district officers, each in his month, supplied provisions for King Solomon and all who came to the king's table. They saw to it that nothing was lacking. ²⁸They also brought to the proper place their quotas of barley and straw for the chariot horses and the other horses.

20 This and the following verse hark back to the Abrahamic covenant and give testimony to the faithfulness of God in carrying out his promises. The growth of the nation, numerically and territorially, the prosperity of the people, and their happiness all attest to the blessing of God. Solomon's kingdom in its broad outlines and at the acme of its greatness was a foretaste, a type of the yet future and far greater fulfillment of God's promise in the millennial reign of Christ. Essential to this type is the rulership of both David and Solomon. David in his passionate love for the Lord, in his great victories over the enemies of God's people, and in his establishment of a great kingdom is a type of the coming Messiah. Solomon also is such a type, in his wisdom and reign of peace.

21 The countries that David had conquered remained subject to Solomon and brought him tribute throughout his reign. This was one of the noteworthy signs of God's blessing in keeping with the Davidic covenant. The usual experience of ancient empire builders was that when the old king died, the subject nations would withhold tribute and challenge the new king in rebellion. This necessitated repeated punitive expeditions to reinforce the former king's terms and to prove the ability of the new king to enforce his will. Solomon did not have to do this. God granted him a peaceful reign in which he could focus his energies on the temple and other building projects. He was also able to devote himself to administrative matters, to the building up of extensive and expanding foreign trade, and to his pursuit of wisdom and knowledge.

22 This and the following verses give an indication of the size and splendor of the court of Solomon. This magnificent court as well as the fabled wisdom of Solomon stirred great interest throughout the surrounding world (cf. v.34; 10:1-9). The provisions noted here were *daily* requirements.

The "cor" was a large measure of capacity. It was equivalent to the *ḥōmer* ("a donkey load"). Estimates vary considerably as to the exact amount involved. O.R. Sellers ("Weights and Measures," IDB) estimates about fifty-five gallons but recognizes that this is not certain. D.J. Wiseman and D.H. Wheaton ("Weights and Measures," NBD) estimate forty-eight gallons; KB estimates one hundred gallons.

The daily requirement of fine flour amounted to between 150 and 280 bushels, that of coarse flour or meal, 300 to 560 bushels. Thenius (cited by Keil, p. 53) calculates that this amount of flour would produce 28,000 pounds of bread, sufficient for fourteen thousand people. (Montgomery [pp. 127ff.] holds that four thousand to five thousand is a more reasonable figure.)

23 In addition to the large numbers of domesticated animals, game animals were also brought in. The exact identity of the "choice fowl" (*barbur*) is not clear. Gray (*Kings*, p. 143) suggests geese as a possibility, while G.R. Driver (cited in Gray, *Kings*, p. 143) suggests "young hens" and KB a type of cuckoo.

24-25 Solomon's kingdom was a peaceful and prosperous one (v.24). With control over all the kingdoms west of the Euphrates, Solomon was able to provide peace and security for his people. The statement that "each man [sat] under his own vine and fig tree" (v.25) speaks of undisturbed prosperity and became a favorite catch phrase used by the prophets to indicate the ideal conditions prevailing in Messiah's kingdom (Mic 4:4; Zech 3:10). The fact that a man could enjoy the fruit of the vine and the fig tree meant that there was a complete absence of warfare and economic disruption.

26-28 The reading "four thousand" reflects the parallel passage in 2 Chronicles 9:25 and some Greek MSS. The MT reads "forty thousand" and is considered an old copyist's error. (Because of early systems of numerical abbreviation, transmission errors with numbers were more likely than in other portions of the text.) Keil (p. 53) holds that the 1,400 chariots ascribed to Solomon's court would make 4,000 a suitable figure, with 2 horses per chariot and one in reserve.

The 12,000 horses (*pārāšîm*) may also indicate horsemen (so LXX and NASB). Possibly the horse and rider as a unit is in view.

Notes

21 This verse begins chapter 5 in the MT.

3. *His superior wisdom*

4:29-34

> [29]God gave Solomon wisdom and very great insight, and a breadth of understanding as measureless as the sand on the seashore. [30]Solomon's wisdom was greater than the wisdom of all the men of the East, and greater than all the wisdom of Egypt. [31]He was wiser than any other man, including Ethan the Ezrahite—wiser than Heman, Calcol and Darda, the sons of Mahol. And his fame spread to all the surrounding nations. [32]He spoke three thousand proverbs and his songs numbered a thousand and five. [33]He described plant life, from the cedar of Lebanon to the hyssop that grows out of walls. He also taught about animals and birds, reptiles and fish. [34]Men of all nations came to listen to Solomon's wisdom, sent by all the kings of the world, who had heard of his wisdom.

The one attribute most characteristic of Solomon is wisdom. Interest in wisdom (*hokmāh*) was widespread in the ancient world. In the Gentile world wisdom was primarily associated with the ability to be successful. It was not a speculative discipline but intensely practical. It pertained to all walks of life: priests (re proper practice in ritual), magicians (re skill in the practice of their arts), craftsmen of all sorts (re skillful workmanship), and administrators (re good management) etc. It did not usually deal with pure moral values. Though frequently associated with religious activity, its concern had to do with ritual and magical skills.

In the OT *hokmāh* is frequently used in the broad sense of skill in craftsmanship or administration, etc. An outstanding example is Exodus 31:3, in which the two craftsmen appointed to make the tabernacle were given wisdom (NIV "skill") in carrying out their work. This kind of practical wisdom is applied to life as a whole— the art of being successful, i.e., how best to make one's way through life. Wise men were those who had unusual insight into human nature and in the problems of life in general. Thus they were sought as advisers to kings and rulers. At the very heart, however, of the concept of wisdom in the OT lies the recognition that God is the Author and End of life and that a meaningful or successful life is one that has its focus in God. This finds typical expression in the statement "The fear of the Lord— that is wisdom" (Job 28:28). He who fears the Lord receives wisdom from him, the ability to see things from God's perspective. Thus true wisdom gives discernment in spiritual and moral matters. It also enables man to discriminate between that which is helpful and that which is harmful. Every aspect of human endeavor is included: the spiritual, intellectual, secular, and practical. It covers man's relationship to God as well as his relationship to other men.

29 The expression "breadth of understanding" means a comprehensive understanding (Keil) and is illustrated by the numerous areas of knowledge in which Solomon was at home (vv.32–33).

30 The "East" here probably refers to Mesopotamia generally, which was commonly regarded as a major seat of culture and learning (cf. Isa 2:6). It produced a great body of literature, most of it mythological, but also much wisdom material. Egypt also was a prolific producer of literature dealing with wisdom.

31 Solomon's wisdom was recognized to be greater than that of any other man. He is compared in particular with four men noted for their wisdom as expressed in proverbs and songs. Ethan is the author of Psalm 89, Heman of Psalm 88. Calcol and Darda, apart from their appearance with Ethan and Heman in the genealogical list in 1 Chronicles 2:6, are otherwise unknown. Mahol is treated in most translations as a proper name. It seems to be more likely, however, that the expression "sons of Mahol" is a designation of membership in a guild or profession, i.e., "singers" (*māḥôl* is literally "dance," but sacred dance and song were closely related).

32 Many of Solomon's proverbs are preserved in the Book of Proverbs. These were not only unusually sagacious but were inspired of the Holy Spirit. Besides the Song of Solomon, two songs or psalms are similarly preserved in Scripture (Pss 72, 127).

33 Solomon was skilled and learned in many areas. He was an astute observer of life and nature and from his careful observations was able to illustrate various facets of human nature and activity. God had granted Solomon great insight and a great thirst for knowledge.

34 The name Solomon soon became synonymous with a superior wisdom, so much so that kings of distant nations sent representatives to Jerusalem. This involved more than curiosity. It was a mark of respect and perhaps in many instances a desire to profit from his wisdom and learning. First Kings 10 gives a concrete example in the visit of the queen of Sheba.

Notes

---

30 Gray (*Kings*, p. 146) notes that *qedem* may denote time as well as place; so כָּל־בְּנֵי־קֶדֶם (*kol-bᵉnê-qedem*, "all the men of the East") might be translated "all the men of old," i.e., the ancients. This understanding is unlikely, however, in view of the fact that the other comparison is geographical. Some feel that Edom is meant rather than Mesopotamia, since it was the home of Job's comforters.

33 Bruce Waltke suggests (personal communication) that by naming everything Solomon brought it under his rule.

D. *Solomon's building program (5:1–8:66)*

1. *Preparations for building the temple (5:1–18)*

a. *The league with Hiram of Tyre*

5:1–12

¹When Hiram king of Tyre heard that Solomon had been anointed king to succeed his father David, he sent his envoys to Solomon, because he had always been on friendly terms with David. ²Solomon sent back this message to Hiram:

³"You know that because of the wars waged against my father David from all sides, he could not build a temple for the Name of the Lord his God until the Lord put his enemies under his feet. ⁴But now the Lord my God has given me rest on every side, and there is no adversary or disaster. ⁵I intend, therefore, to build a temple for the Name of the Lord my God, as the Lord told my father David, when he said, 'Your son whom I will put on the throne in your place will build the temple for my Name.'

⁶"So give orders that cedars of Lebanon be cut for me. My men will work with yours, and I will pay you for your men whatever wages you set. You know that we have no one so skilled in felling timber as the Sidonians."

⁷When Hiram heard Solomon's message, he was greatly pleased and said, "Praise be to the Lord today, for he has given David a wise son to rule over this great nation."

⁸So Hiram sent word to Solomon:

"I have received the message you sent me and will do all you want in providing the cedar and pine logs. ⁹My men will haul them down from Lebanon to the sea, and I will float them in rafts by sea to the place you specify. There I will separate them and you can take them away. And you are to grant my wish by providing food for my royal household."

¹⁰In this way Hiram kept Solomon supplied with all the cedar and pine logs he wanted, ¹¹and Solomon gave Hiram twenty thousand cors of wheat as food for his household, in addition to twenty thousand baths of pressed olive oil. Solomon continued to do this for Hiram year after year. ¹²The Lord gave Solomon wisdom, just as he had promised him. There were peaceful relations between Hiram and Solomon, and the two of them made a treaty.

After he had firmly established himself and his administration, Solomon began laying the groundwork for the carrying out of what was perhaps the major achievement of his reign—the building of the temple and palace complexes. The planning and oversight of the construction program of a project of such magnitude required considerable managerial skill, and Solomon demonstrated here again the unusual gifts granted him by God. It should be noted that Assyrian and Babylonian kings prided themselves in large building projects that they considered to be monuments to their wisdom, power, and glory (cf. Nebuchadnezzar in Dan 4:30).

1 Hiram of Tyre, who had made peace with David and was his best friend, now sent an embassy to extend his best wishes to Solomon on his accession to the throne. Here is another example of the benefits accruing to Solomon because of his father, David. The latter had been on good terms with Hiram, who now offered Solomon a continuation of friendly relations.

2 Solomon responded in kind and in a preliminary to a trade agreement disclosed to Hiram his intentions with regard to the building project.

3 "You know" is a good indication that Hiram's relationship to David was more than one of peaceful coexistence or even of healthy commercial relations. David had let Hiram know what his intentions had been in regard to the building of the temple.

The building of the temple had been a matter very much on David's heart (2 Sam 7:1–17; 1 Chron 17:1–15). It is one of the outstanding examples of the mentality of this "man after God's own heart." He loved God with all his being and sincerely wanted to honor him. He felt it to be inappropriate that he should live in a fine palace when God's "house" was in reality a tent. Even after he was told that he would not be allowed to build the temple (and was given instead the great promise of the Davidic covenant), he did all he could in the planning and preparation for the temple (1 Chron 22; 29) to give Solomon as much help as possible.

4–5 God firmly established Solomon in the kingdom. There was peace within the kingdom, and there were no threats from the outside. Solomon was prepared to carry out his father's wishes. David's injunctions to Solomon with regard to the temple are recorded in 1 Chronicles 22:11–16 and 1 Chronicles 28:9–21. Solomon could not help but be impressed by David's intensity and sense of purpose in this.

Solomon was very much aware of his great responsibility, both toward God and toward his father. This is made quite clear by his quoting God's word to David (v.5b). What is also evident in this is his conviction that God would do his part in enabling him to complete the task: "Your son . . . will build the temple for my name."

6 Solomon now asked Hiram for a trade agreement similar to the one that had existed between David and Hiram, but on a much larger scale (cf. 2 Sam 5:11; 1 Chron 22:4). The Cedars of Lebanon were famed for their beauty and were greatly desired by rulers of Mesopotamia, Egypt, and Syro-Palestine for their building projects. Hiram's work force, skilled in felling and transporting timber, would be supplemented by labor sent by Solomon. The payment for goods and services was to be set by Hiram.

7 On receiving Solomon's message, Hiram acted enthusiastically. Solomon's request would initiate a major trade agreement beneficial to both parties.

8–9 Hiram agreed to Solomon's proposal and stated that he would be responsible for shipping the timbers by log rafts to the port that Solomon would designate. From that point they would be Solomon's responsibility. In return Solomon was to provide Hiram with provisions for his court.

10-11 There was an ample supply of timber for Solomon. In return he provided Hiram with wheat and olive oil, commodities not found in abundance in mountainous Phoenicia, whose economy was primarily based on an extensive shipping trade and export of timber.

12 The quality of wisdom is once again attributed to Solomon, seen here as a fulfillment of God's promise. The aspect of wisdom referred to here is that of managerial and diplomatic prowess. Solomon in 1 Kings 3 humbly recognized his deficiencies, and God granted him an abundant measure of wisdom so that he might be able to deal successfully with the various problems that might arise from the large undertaking before him.

Notes

3 Hiram had already assisted David in supplying for him many of the materials that he was stockpiling for the future temple (1 Chron 22:4).
5 The "Name" of God signifies "the active presence in the fulness of the revealed character" (Motyer, NBD, p. 863; cf. Kaiser, "Name," ZPEB, 4:360–66).
6 The fact that Hiram, king of Tyre, was asked to supply timber and skilled lumbermen indicates that his authority and sphere of influence extended well beyond Tyre (where no cedars grew). Notice that the lumbermen, whom Hiram would use, are called Sidonians, indicating Tyrian influence over Sidon (though it is possible that the name Sidonian may have been used to designate people generally of what was later called Phoenicia, since Sidon was the oldest Phoenician city). Wiseman (NBD, p. 992) states that when the "Sea peoples" invaded the Phoenician coast (c. 1200 B.C.), the Sidonians fled to Tyre, which then became the principle port.
8-9 Montgomery (p. 135) cites an inscription of Nebuchadnezzar's found in Lebanon: "What no former king had accomplished, I cleaved high mountains, lime-stone I broke off, I opened. I cut a road for the cedars, and before Marduk my king (I brought) massive, tall, strong cedars, of wonderful beauty, whose dark appearance was impressive, the mighty product of the Lebanon." In a special purchase of wood for Egypt, Wen-amon (c. 1000 B.C.) relates how three hundred men and three hundred oxen were sent to fell the trees, which lay in the forest over the winter; then in the "third month of summer they were dragged to the shore" (ibid.).
11 On the unit of capacity, see the note on 4:22.

b. *The levy on the people*

5:13–18

¹³King Solomon conscripted laborers from all Israel—thirty thousand men. ¹⁴He sent them off to Lebanon in shifts of ten thousand a month, so that they spent one month in Lebanon and two months at home. Adoniram was in charge of the forced labor. ¹⁵Solomon had seventy thousand carriers and eighty thou-

sand stonecutters in the hills, ¹⁶as well as thirty-three hundred foremen who supervised the project and directed the workmen. ¹⁷At the king's command they removed from the quarry large blocks of quality stone to provide a foundation of dressed stone for the temple. ¹⁸The craftsmen of Solomon and Hiram and the men of Gebal cut and prepared the timber and stone for the building of the temple.

13–14 The following verses give information on the labor force that Solomon raised to carry out the great task of gathering materials and then building the temple. The thirty thousand conscripted laborers were taken from all the tribes of Israel and sent in shifts of ten thousand to help the Phoenicians in the felling and transporting of the timbers from Lebanon. Each shift stayed one month at a time, so that each man worked for Solomon four months per year. The other eight months he worked on his own fields. This method of providing labor (called corvée) for large public projects was common in the ancient world but a fairly new innovation in Israel. In the list of David's officials, Adoniram is said to be over the forced labor. This would indicate that David used the corvée system to a limited degree, but nothing further is said about it. Solomon, however, used it extensively. The more splendid the royal court, the greater the demand on the people.

15–16 The 70,000 carriers and 80,000 stonecutters were non-Israelites (2 Chron 2:17–18). They constituted a permanent "slave labor force" (1 Kings 9:22), with the more onerous tasks to perform. Gray (*Kings*, in loc.) notes that the verb *ḥāṣab*, from which the word "stonecutter" is derived, "denotes the splitting of blocks from the living rock rather than the more skilled operation of hewing or dressing (*pāsal*)." The dressing of the stones was done by Israelite and Phoenician craftsmen. The stone was quarried in Israel, probably much of it in Jerusalem itself. A large quarry "called 'Solomon's quarries', lies directly under the city of Jerusalem" (Wood, *United Monarchy*, p. 313). The 3,300 foremen and overseers here were mostly Canaanites, with a smaller group of Israelites acting as higher supervisors.

17 The "large blocks of quality stone" for the foundation of the temple were squared off so that each stone would fit perfectly. According to 6:7 these large ashlar blocks were cut and squared at the quarry.

18 Other stones were prepared along with wood beams by skilled craftsmen, some from Israel, but most from Phoenicia. The city Gebal (Byblos) is particularly mentioned as providing a large part of these artisans. Again, according to 6:7, these men performed their craft at a place apart from the building site itself. This required careful planning and measuring and illustrates how well organized the whole program was and how skillfully the work was done.

Notes

---

14 First Chronicles 19:1–9 describes David's efforts to gather materials for the temple. Mentioned are gold, silver, bronze, iron, wood, onyx, turquoise, various other gems, and marble. These materials were utilized for the finish work, including plating and overlay work, and for the furniture.

15 The non-Israelite forced laborers in 9:20–21 are called מַס־עֹבֵד (*mas-ʿōbēd,* "slave labor force"). These constituted a permanent body of forced laborers. This is to be contrasted with the Israelite work force. Of the Israelites, 9:22 states that they were not made slaves (*ʿōbĕdîm*). They were made to work, but only for one-third of the year, and were considered free men. Verses 22–23 describe the kind of obligations required of the Israelites. They were chiefly used in the armed services, in skilled and supervisory positions, etc.

16 The numbers of supervisors as given here (3,300) and in 9:23 (550) does not seem to agree with the numbers given in 2 Chron 2:17 (3,600) and 2 Chron 8:10 (250). Keil (pp. 63f.), following Michaelis, suggests a reasonable solution, noting that the two sets of numbers agree when added: Kings—3,300 + 550 = 3,850; Chron—3,600 + 250 = 3,850. The differences in the figures arise from the fact that the two authors use a "different method of classification," i.e., Chronicles distinguishes the Canaanite overseers (3,600) from the Israelite (250), while Kings distinguishes between classes of overseers; 3,300 lower and 550 higher overseers. Of the latter, 250 were Israelites and 300 Canaanites.

---

2. The building of the temple (6:1–38)

a. Introduction

6:1

¹In the four hundred and eightieth year after the Israelites had come out of Egypt, in the fourth year of Solomon's reign over Israel, in the month of Ziv, the second month, he began to build the temple of the LORD.

The temple was in reality a permanent tabernacle as far as its symbolism and typology are concerned. It is basically the dwelling place of God with his people. There is a spiritual and symbolic continuity that transcends the structure itself. Whether it be (1) a tent in the wilderness, (2) the splendid, awe-inspiring structure Solomon built, (3) the relatively simple building erected by the returned exiles, (4) the lavish and ornate edifice it became through Herod's efforts, or (5) its future millennial form, it is the house of God, where God condescends to meet his people. This is seen, for example, in the exchange between David and God in 2 Samuel 7, in which God is described as living among his people in a tent, moving with them from place to place. Later David's son would build a house for God's name. From God's perspective there is no essential difference, whether the house be a tent or a splendid structure of stone and cedar. Perhaps even clearer is Haggai 2:3, 7, 9. Solomon's temple had been destroyed. Now, seventy years later, a new building had been put up—two different buildings; yet in v.3 both together are referred to as "this house." Verse 9 also sees one house, with its "latter glory . . . greater than the former" (NASB). God's house had had great glory in Solomon's time. In Haggai's time it was poor by comparison, but Haggai stated that the time would come when its glory would far outshine the former.

When Hebrews 9 compares the earthly sanctuary (v.1) with the perfect, heavenly one (v.11), it is the tabernacle that is discussed in terms of its symbolism and typology. This is because it is in connection with the tabernacle, for which Moses received specific construction specifications from the Lord, that the proper procedure for sacrifice and worship is given. Since the tabernacle is the forerunner of the temple, the same manner of sacrifice and ritual procedure pertained to both.

Basically the tabernacle was a *miškān* ("dwelling place"). This obviously does not mean that God depends on man to put a roof over his head. What it does mean is that God condescends to identify himself with his people, a graciously intimate association in which God makes it possible for men to approach him. This latter aspect is emphasized in the second appellation—*'ōhel mōʿēd* ("Tent of Meeting"). God has made provision for a meeting between God and man. This coming together is clearly seen as taking place by God's appointment, at the place and time of his designation, and in a manner prescribed by him. It is the one place where formal approach to God is to be made.

A third designation—*'ōhel hāʿēdût* ("tent of the testimony")—is an ever-present testimony to the covenant God had made with his people. It reminded them of the privileges and promises as well as their responsibilities relating to that covenant.

The fourth frequently found name is the *miqdāš* ("sanctuary," "Holy Place"). This points to the majesty and the separateness of God as contrasted to the sinfulness and unworthiness of man. It is to be remembered that, though God is indeed gracious, it is not a light thing to come into his presence. It can only be possible by the God-appointed means of sacrifice and cleansing, and that with a sincere heart, not carelessly or frivolously.

The general symbolism of the temple as the place that God indwells is continued in the church age in the temple that is the individual believer's body and in the temple that is the corporate body of believers, the church.

The basic plan of the temple proper was the same as that of the tabernacle, except that the dimensions of the sanctuary were doubled. Notice that according to 1 Chronicles 28:11–12, it was David who drew up the plans for the temple as "the Spirit had put in his mind."

1 Solomon began the actual building of the temple in the fourth year of his reign. Since this event is linked to the Exodus of Israel from Egypt, this verse is one of the major pieces of internal evidence for the dating of the Exodus. Thiele's date (p. 205) for the end of Solomon's reign is 931/932 B.C. This puts the beginning of his forty-year reign at 971/970 and the fourth year at 967/966 and the date of the Exodus at 1447/1446. This date accords well with other biblical evidence (Judg 11:26 and the length of the time of the Judges) as with external historical evidence (for a good summary treatment, see Wood, *Survey*, pp. 88–109; G.A. Archer, *Encyclopedia of Bible Difficulties* [Grand Rapids: Zondervan, 1982], pp. 223–34; and Bruce Waltke, "Palestinian Artifactual Evidence Supporting the Early Date of the Exodus," BS 129 [1972]: 33–47).

The site of the building of the temple is not given here, but 2 Chronicles 3:1 states that it was "on Mount Moriah, where the LORD had appeared to his father David. It was on the threshing floor of Araunah the Jebusite, the place provided by David." This was also the site of the (aborted) sacrifice of Isaac by Abraham (Gen 22:2). It lay on the rocky platform just to the north of the city of David on the eastern ridge of Jerusalem, "on an eminence appropriate to its character" (H.G. Stigers, "Temple," ZPEB, 5:622–66).

Notes

Critical orthodoxy has held that the tabernacle was an invention of the priestly school writing during or after the Exile. By this view it was the temple of Solomon that was the original model for the tabernacle rather than the reverse (cf., e.g., de Vaux, *Ancient Israel*, p. 314). But recently the priority of the tabernacle has been defended by F.M. Cross in a paper delivered at a colloquium held in Jerusalem on 14 March 1977 (reported by Valerie Fargo in "Temples and High Places: A Colloquium," BA 40 [1977]: 55). He holds this view because of similarities in the description of the tabernacle to ancient Canaanite descriptions of the tent of the assembly of the gods. Richard Friedman ("The Tabernacle in the Temple," BA 40 [1981]: 161–70), a student of Cross, supports the priority of the tabernacle by giving biblical and extrabiblical evidence that it was actually housed in the temple of Solomon. To make the tabernacle a late priestly fabrication involves insurmountable difficulties.

1 If one is willing to accept Scripture as accurate and authoritative and yet is unwilling to accept the early date of the Exodus, then the figure 480 must be understood as an indefinite number indicating a time span of twelve generations, figuring forty years per generation as a literary device. Since in reality a generation might have been a little over twenty years, the real time span would have been much shorter than 480 years. But this is not at all a satisfactory view, since there is nothing in this verse or the context that would lead one to make such an assumption.

The month Ziv, the second month, corresponds to our April/May.

On the location of the temple, see the fine article by Stigers (ZPEB, 5:622-66). More recently A.S. Kaufman ("Where the Ancient Temple of Jerusalem Stood," *Biblical Archaeology Review*, vol. 9, no. 2 [1983]: 42) states that the temple stood approximately 330 feet to the northwest of the present Dome of the Rock, rather than on the site of the Dome itself, as has been usually assumed. Kaufman's site is recognized as an alternative location in The Pictorial Archive's *Student Map Manual, a Historical Geography* (Grand Rapids: Zondervan, 1979), section 14-2.

b. *The outer structure*

6:2–14

[2]The temple that King Solomon built for the LORD was sixty cubits long, twenty wide and thirty high. [3]The portico at the front of the main hall of the temple extended the width of the temple, that is twenty cubits, and projected ten cubits from the front of the temple. [4]He made narrow clerestory windows in the temple. [5]Against the walls of the main hall and inner sanctuary he built a structure around the building, in which there were side rooms. [6]The lowest floor was five cubits wide, the middle floor six cubits and the third floor seven. He made offset ledges around the outside of the temple so that nothing would be inserted into the temple walls.

[7]In building the temple, only blocks dressed at the quarry were used, and no hammer, chisel or any other iron tool was heard at the temple site while it was being built.

[8]The entrance to the lowest floor was on the south side of the temple; a stairway led up to the middle level and from there to the third. [9]So he built the temple and completed it, roofing it with beams and cedar planks. [10]And he built the side rooms all along the temple. The height of each was five cubits, and they were attached to the temple by beams of cedar.

[11]The word of the LORD came to Solomon: [12]"As for this temple you are building, if you follow my decrees, carry out my regulations and keep all my commands

and obey them, I will fulfill through you the promise I gave to David your father. ¹³And I will live among the Israelites and will not abandon my people Israel." ¹⁴So Solomon built the temple and completed it.

2 Verses 2–10 give the general dimensions of the temple. These are inside measurements and do not include the thickness of the walls. The temple (lit., "house") is here the main, central structure of the temple complex. Its dimensions were sixty cubits long by twenty wide by thirty high. (The cubit varied somewhat but may for most general purposes be considered to be approximately eighteen inches in length; see Notes.) This was exactly twice the size of the tabernacle proper.

3 There was a portico (or porch, vestibule—ʾûlām) attached to the front of the "main hall of the temple" (hêkal habbayit; hêkal may refer to a palace or a temple or, as in this passage, the main room of the temple, distinct from the debîr, "Most Holy Place"). It measured ten by twenty cubits, its long side going along the breadth of the temple proper.

4 The "clerestory windows" (ḥallônê šequpîm) were probably on the side walls above the side chambers (cf. v.5). The exact nature of the windows is not known. Some have suggested slatted or latticed windows. Others, following the Targums ("open inside and closed outside") and Aquila ("broad within and narrow without"), suggest windows narrower outside than in.

5–6 Against the outside walls of the temple proper (main hall and inner sanctuary), Solomon built a three-tiered structure divided into an unspecified number of rooms (Ezekiel's temple [Ezek 41:5–11], which also has three tiers of side rooms, has thirty rooms per level). Verse 10 gives the height of these rooms as five cubits each. At each level of the side rooms, the thickness of the wall was decreased by a half cubit on the outside wall and similarly on the inside wall so that the floor beam rested on the resulting offset ledge. Thus the width of each successive story increased by one cubit. By this means the beams had supports without being "inserted" or bonded into the inner temple wall. They were not structurally a part of the temple.

7 It is not necessary to see here, with Gray (Kings, p. 165), a concession to the "long-standing taboo in the religion of Israel" against using iron in the construction of the altar (Exod 20:25), since iron was indeed used at the quarries. It does indicate excellent organization and planning. The erection of the temple could go much faster and with far less confusion by utilizing precut and prefitted materials. In addition the relative quiet would be consistent with the sacredness of the undertaking.

8 The entrance to the side room was on the right (south) side, probably in the middle (cf. Notes). Access to the second and third levels is most often understood to have been by means of a spiral staircase (lûlîm) that led through the middle story to the third floor.

9 Apart from the statement that the roof was constructed of beams and cedar planks, no details are given. Stigers ("Temple," ZPEB, 5:628) states that the wooden planks formed "a bed on which clay was packed and covered with a pulverized limestone marl, rolled flat, smooth, and hard, providing a cementlike surface which was practically impervious to water."

10 The use to which these rooms were put is not mentioned, but they were undoubtedly intended for storage purposes.

11 First Kings 9:2 states that after the dedication of the temple, the Lord appeared to Solomon a second time (the first time being at Gibeon, 1 Kings 3), referring to direct personal appearances of the Lord. In the present passage God evidently spoke to Solomon through a prophet.

12–13 These are encouraging words, putting God's blessing on the building of the temple. God was indeed with Solomon in this massive undertaking, and he would indeed recognize the temple as his dwelling place among his people. This promise takes in two aspects of the Davidic covenant. First, God established for David a lasting dynasty (lit., "house") and declared that his son Solomon would be the one to build the house for the Name of the Lord that David had desired to build. Second, Solomon, in order to experience the blessings of the Davidic covenant (see Notes), must exhibit the faith and obedience of David toward the Word of God. (This is perhaps one of the reasons why succeeding generations of kings were compared to David as to their godliness or lack thereof.) The same holds true for each generation of the people Israel. Thus the temple in all its splendor and ritual is by itself not sufficient. God requires obedient hearts. In this matter alone there stands a great gulf between the faith of Israel and the cultic ritual of the surrounding Gentile nations. The call of God issued through Isaiah (ch. 55) was echoed by generations of godly prophets, and v.3 of that chapter is pertinent to this passage: "Give ear and come to me. . . . I will make an everlasting covenant with you, my faithful love promised to David."

14 This concludes the exterior structure. The next verses describe the work done in the interior.

Notes

2 The cubit is the measure of the distance between the elbow and the tip of the middle finger. Since this length varies somewhat from person to person, the exact length had to be standardized for building projects. Bible dictionaries generally give the length of the common cubit to be seventeen and one-half inches. This has been determined by comparing the length of Hezekiah's tunnel (1,749 ft.) with the statement in the Siloam inscription that it was 1,200 cubits long (a round figure?), thus resulting in a cubit length of 17.5 inches. (The calculations based on the volume of Solomon's "molten sea" [7:23–26] can only yield approximate results, since the determination of the liquid measure "bath" depends partly on the length of the cubit.)

There was also a longer cubit in use, estimated to be about 20.5 inches in length. Kaufman ("Ancient Temple," pp. 48f.) points out that the Mishnah speaks of three types of medium cubits, the old cubit of Moses (2 Chron 3:3), used in Solomon's temple; the small cubit, reserved for holy structures (used in Herod's temple); and the standard cubit for profane use. They differed from one another by one-half a finger breadth.

In the same article Kaufman has measured a number of archaeological remains on the temple mount. Those associated with Herod's temple are 43.7 cm or multiples thereof. Those associated with Solomon's temple are 42.8 cm or multiples thereof, one-half finger-breadth shorter. The remains of a Herodian boundary wall measure four cubits of 44.5 cm in width, one-half handbreath longer. These measurements accord remarkably well with the Mishnaic statement. The cubit, then, used for the Solomonic temple was 16.9 inches. The Herodian sacred cubit was 17.2 inches and the common cubit, 17.5 inches. This last agrees with the figure obtained from the measurement of Hezekiah's tunnel.

3 Our passage says nothing about the height of the portico, but 2 Chron 3:4 says that it was 120 cubits (c. 180 ft.) high (NIV mg.). The NIV follows some Greek and Syriac MSS and reads twenty cubits. Stigers (ZPEB, 5:633f.) holds that the great height of 120 cubits reflects the later dimensions of the temple, since Josephus (Antiq. IX, 236–37 [xi.2]) speaks of additions and embellishments that Jotham made to the porticos and gateways. Keil (p. 68) regards the statement in Chronicles to be a transmissional error, that the height was either twenty cubits or, more likely, thirty cubits to match the height of the temple proper. On the whole Stigers's solution seems preferable.

5 The word translated "structure"—יָצִיעַ (yāṣîaʿ, Qere), יָצוּעַ (yāṣûaʿ, Kethiv)—is uncertain. Yāṣûaʿ means "bed," "couch." Thus it has been suggested that the rendering here ought to be "foundation" or "platform." Ezekiel 41:8 is adduced as support for this, since in that passage there is clearly a support platform built for the three levels of side chambers. Keil (p. 70) suggests "outwork" (lit., "stratum"), "here, the lower building or outwork erected against the rooms mentioned." Montgomery (p. 148) similarly suggests a basic meaning of "layer," then "side-wing." NASB has "stories."

7 The stone that was quarried was white limestone and famous for its beauty (called the "royal stone" by the Arabs). It is reduced to lime when exposed to a hot fire. Thus when the temple burned (2 Kings 25:9), it was not only the wood that burned, but the stones themselves were reduced to a lime powder.

8 The NIV, with other modern versions (NASB, NEB, JB), follows the LXX and the Targums in reading "the entrance to the lowest [הַתַּחְתֹנָה, hattahtōnāh] floor." This is an attractive possibility with some strong support in the Targums and a similar passage in Ezek 41:7. Yet the MT deserves serious consideration. It reads הַתִּיכֹנָה (hattîkōnāh, "the middle"). "The middle" then refers to the middle of the wing rather than to the middle floor. In this case the word צֵלָע (ṣēlāʿ, "floor") is not to be understood in the collective sense "side rooms" but as a single side room. The translation then is "The entrance was at the middle side chamber on the south wing." The lower floor is not specifically mentioned because that would be the obvious place for the door.

The rendering "spiral staircase" for לוּלִים (lûlîm) is suggested by the LXX, Targums, and the Vulgate. The remains of such a staircase have been found in a palace of the eighteenth century B.C. at Achana. Other suggestions have been made such as a series of ladderlike steps, a flying wing, or stairs with landings.

12 "I will fulfill through you" is probably better rendered "I will fulfill with regard to you my promise that I made with David your father" (cf. also NASB, NEB, JB). There is more involved here than the fulfillment of promise in the completion of the temple. There is also the matter of the conditions on which God could bless Solomon.

c. *The inner structure*

6:15–35

> ¹⁵He lined its interior walls with cedar boards, paneling them from the floor of the temple to the ceiling, and covered the floor of the temple with planks of pine. ¹⁶He partitioned off twenty cubits at the rear of the temple with cedar boards from floor to ceiling to form within the temple an inner sanctuary, the Most Holy Place. ¹⁷The main hall in front of this room was forty cubits long. ¹⁸The inside of the temple was cedar, carved with gourds and open flowers. Everything was cedar; no stone was to be seen.
>
> ¹⁹He prepared the inner sanctuary within the temple to set the ark of the covenant of the Lord there. ²⁰The inner sanctuary was twenty cubits long, twenty wide and twenty high. He overlaid the inside with pure gold, and he also overlaid the altar of cedar. ²¹Solomon covered the inside of the temple with pure gold, and he extended gold chains across the front of the inner sanctuary, which was overlaid with gold. ²²So he overlaid the whole interior with gold. He also overlaid with gold the altar that belonged to the inner sanctuary.
>
> ²³In the inner sanctuary he made a pair of cherubim of olive wood, each ten cubits high. ²⁴One wing of the first cherub was five cubits long, and the other wing five cubits—ten cubits from wing tip to wing tip. ²⁵The second cherub also measured ten cubits, for the two cherubim were identical in size and shape. ²⁶The height of each cherub was ten cubits. ²⁷He placed the cherubim inside the innermost room of the temple, with their wings spread out. The wing of one cherub touched one wall, while the wing of the other touched the other wall, and their wings touched each other in the middle of the room. ²⁸He overlaid the cherubim with gold.
>
> ²⁹On the walls all around the temple, in both the inner and outer rooms, he carved cherubim, palm trees and open flowers. ³⁰He also covered the floors of both the inner and outer rooms of the temple with gold.
>
> ³¹For the entrance of the inner sanctuary he made doors of olive wood with five-sided jambs. ³²And on the two olive wood doors he carved cherubim, palm trees and open flowers, and overlaid the cherubim and palm trees with beaten gold. ³³In the same way he made four-sided jambs of olive wood for the entrance to the main hall. ³⁴He also made two pine doors, each having two leaves that turned in sockets. ³⁵He carved cherubim, palm trees and open flowers on them and overlaid them with gold hammered evenly over the carvings.

15 When the exterior structure was complete, Solomon lined the interior walls with cedar planks from floor to ceiling. The floors were also covered with wood, in this case pine or fir. Whatever the exact identity of this wood, it was often used together with cedar. The two were highly regarded and became a symbol of luxuriousness and stateliness. From this and the following verses in this chapter, and in chapter 7, it is quite evident that Solomon was sparing no expense in building the temple, using the finest and costliest materials available. His prayer in chapter 8 makes it clear that in doing this Solomon was giving expression to his sincere love for and devotion to God. Though God could not be enriched, Solomon was demonstrating in a practical way that nothing but the best is good enough for God. This is an abiding principle for believers of all ages and ought to find expression in every area of life.

16–18 The inner sanctuary or "Most Holy Place" was partitioned off from the main hall by cedar planks (v.16). The dimensions were twice those of the inner sanctuary of the tabernacle. This left forty cubits for the main hall (v.17), likewise twice as large as those of the Holy Place in the tabernacle.

No stone was visible anywhere in the temple (v.18). Not only was everything lined with cedar, but the wood paneling was covered with fine, delicate carvings.

19 The inner sanctuary (*dᵉḇîr*) was the Most Holy Place or Holy of Holies because it housed the ark of the covenant, a symbol of the presence of God. First Samuel 4:4 and 2 Samuel 6:2 speak of God as being enthroned between the cherubim. In Exodus 25:21–22 God told Moses that he would meet with him there and give him all his commands for the Israelites. The top of the ark could be called "the mercy seat" or "place of propitiation" in view of the annual sprinkling by the high priest of the blood of atonement. It was from between the cherubim that the glory of the Lord began his departure from the temple in Ezekiel 10:4. Thus the ark in the Most Holy Place is the focal point of the temple and its ritual, not as an object of worship or superstitious awe, but as the place where God manifested his presence in his converse with his people. Thus in this and the following verses everything is designed to express the awesome dignity, splendor, and holiness of God's presence.

20–22 The room was a perfect cube, overlaid in its entirety with gold, as was the cedar altar of incense (cf. v.22). This altar was physically placed in the main hall or Holy Place directly before the entrance into the Most Holy Place (Exod 30:6), but functionally and symbolically it was associated with the Most Holy Place. Thus v.22 notes that it "belonged to the inner sanctuary" (cf. also Heb 9:4). By means of this altar, the priest could daily burn incense in the worship of God who was symbolically enthroned between the cherubim in the inner sanctuary.

Not only the inner sanctuary, but all the inside walls of the temple were overlaid with gold. The gold chains, stretched across the front of the inner sanctuary, served to strengthen the concept of the inacessibility of this Most Holy Place.

23–28 Two cherubim made of olive wood and covered with gold were placed in the inner chamber (vv.23, 28). Each had a wingspan of ten cubits (vv.24–26). They were so placed that they faced the door (2 Chron 3:13). Thus their combined wingspan reached from one wall to the other (v.27). (Notice that the two cherubim on the ark faced each other.) These composite figures (cf. Ezek 1:4–14) represented the cherubim associated with the throne and government of God (Ezek 1:22–28). They are also the guardians of the way to God (Gen 3:24). The impact to the beholder of these representations of the cherubim would be to impress on him the awesomeness of God's holiness. Approaching God is not a light or frivolous matter and must be undertaken in the exact way he has prescribed—through the blood.

29–35 Doors of olivewood were made for the entry to the inner sanctuary and larger, double-leaved doors of pine or fir for the entry to the main hall. Second Chronicles 3:14 does not mention the doors but mentions the veil that was hung between the two chambers. The jambs for both sets of doors were of olive wood. The doors as well as the walls (vv.20–22) and even the floors were covered with gold (v.30), with gold hammered into the carvings on the door (v.32). The covering of the floors with gold has often been scoffed at as being preposterous; yet it is in keeping with Solomon's desire to show forth in the temple, as much as humanly possible, the glory of God. It was his testimony to the greatness of God, and indeed the fame of this temple was spread far and wide so that honor and glory accrued to God as a result (10:9).

Notes

20 The fact that the Most Holy Place was twenty cubits high when the Holy Place or main hall was thirty cubits high has occasioned some discussion. The best evidence suggests that the floor level was the same for both rooms and that there was an attic above the Most Holy Place (Stigers, ZPEB, 5:633).

31 The translation "five-sided jambs" expresses the generally current view of a Hebrew phrase that has occasioned some difficulty. חֲמִשִׁית (ḥᵃmišît) may be rendered "one-fifth" or "five-sided" (KB). The KJV renders "the lintel (and) side parts (were) a fifth part (of the wall)." But this seems unlikely when v.33 is taken into account (the מֵאֵת [mēᵓēt] is difficult to account for in the parallel rendering "one-fourth part"). Gray (Kings, p. 173) suggests that the door posts together with a gabled lintel, forming a pentagon, may be in view here. Montgomery (pp. 159f.) regards the word "jambs" as a gloss and sees a reference here to a projecting framework (porch) of the doorway and translates: "He made doors of oleaster wood, the portal a pentagon." On the whole a rendering similar to the NIV, NASB, JB, and NEB seems most satisfactory.

34 Each door had two foldable (or turnable) leaves, forming smaller doors within the larger, probably for convenience in ordinary entry.

d. The court

6:36

36And he built the inner courtyard of three courses of dressed stone and one course of trimmed cedar beams.

36 An inner court, called in 2 Chronicles 4:9 the court of the priests, was built with three courses of dressed stone and then one layer of trimmed cedar beams. Ezra 6:4 describes the same construction method. This type of construction is attested at Ras Shamra, Cnossus, Mycenae, and other ancient cities. "This may have been a precaution against earthquake damage" (Gray, Kings, p. 175). First Kings 7:9–12 describes another court that enclosed the whole temple and palace complex.

e. Conclusion

6:37–38

37The foundation of the temple of the LORD was laid in the fourth year, in the month of Ziv. 38In the eleventh year in the month of Bul, the eighth month, the temple was finished in all its details according to its specifications. He had spent seven years building it.

37–38 Seven years were required to complete the temple. An enormous amount of man hours and a lavish expenditure of funds were involved. All the plans and specifications of David were carried out. It must have been a moment of great satisfaction to Solomon to see the fulfillment of his father's dream; and when God acknowledged the temple by filling it with his glory, Solomon's joy knew no bounds.

3. Solomon's other buildings

7:1–12

¹It took Solomon thirteen years, however, to complete the construction of his palace. ²He built the Palace of the Forest of Lebanon a hundred cubits long, fifty wide and thirty high, with four rows of cedar columns supporting trimmed cedar beams. ³It was roofed with cedar above the beams that rested on the columns— forty-five beams, fifteen to a row. ⁴Its windows were placed high in sets of three, facing each other. ⁵All the doorways had rectangular frames; they were in the front part in sets of three, facing each other.

⁶He made a colonnade fifty cubits long and thirty wide. In front of it was a portico, and in front of that were pillars and an overhanging roof.

⁷He built the throne hall, the Hall of Justice, where he was to judge, and he covered it with cedar from floor to ceiling. ⁸And the palace in which he was to live, set farther back, was similar in design. Solomon also made a palace like this hall for Pharaoh's daughter, whom he had married.

⁹All these structures, from the outside to the great courtyard and from foundation to eaves, were made of blocks of high-grade stone cut to size and trimmed with a saw on their inner and outer faces. ¹⁰The foundations were laid with large stones of good quality, some measuring ten cubits and some eight. ¹¹Above were high-grade stones, cut to size, and cedar beams. ¹²The great courtyard was surrounded by a wall of three courses of dressed stone and one course of trimmed cedar beams, as was the inner courtyard of the temple of the LORD with its portico.

1 It took Solomon almost twice as long to build his palace complex as to build the temple. This was due to the numerous public and private building units that were constructed, six of which are briefly described in this passage. Also to be considered is the fact that in the case of the temple, there had been extensive advanced planning and acquisition of materials. This was not the case with the palace.

It should be noted that the temple and the palace were included in one large complex and were enclosed within one courtyard (v.12). This was no doubt intended to give visual expression to the fact that the king was to act on behalf of God. He himself was to walk in God's ways and, as shepherd of the people, lead them and direct them to God. As such he was a type of Christ, the Son of David, who will rule the earth from Jerusalem and who even now is seated at the right hand of God.

The description of the various parts of the palace are extremely sketchy; so it is difficult to make an accurate reconstruction. No remains have been found, but the unearthing of two Solomonic "palaces" at Megiddo may furnish some indications of the basic plan. David Ussishkin ("King Solomon's Palaces," BA 36 [1973]: 78–105) summarizes the general conclusions that have been drawn from comparative archaeological data. The "palaces" at Megiddo were built on the plan of the "Bît-ḫilāni," an architectural style in use in northern Syria and southern Anatolia. The term was probably originally employed to designate a magnificent style of porticoed entry hall, a long room entered on the broad side through a portico with several pillars. Then it came to include the whole complex of rooms served by this entry hall. The throne room was considerably larger than the entry and was also entered on the broad side.

In addition to these two major halls, there were a number of smaller rooms and also apparently one or more courtyards. There was also at least one upper story. The two Megiddo "palaces" follow this plan, as do four bît-ḫilānis found in the Acropolis of Zinjirli (ancient Samal, an Aramean city of northern Syria). These buildings were constructed in the tenth through the eighth centuries B.C. Verses 6–9 seem to suggest a similar style of construction. This may mean that all the buildings except the Palace of the Forest of Lebanon were part of one massive structure, but this is by no means certain. In any case the Palace of the Forest of Lebanon was a separate building.

2–5 The Palace of the Forest of Lebanon was so named because of its cedar construction. It was an imposing structure one hundred cubits long, fifty cubits wide, and thirty cubits high. Its exact function is not perfectly clear, though it is referred to in 10:17 as the repository of three hundred shields of gold. Isaiah 22:8 also speaks of armor placed in the "Palace of the Forest." This latter passage is in a context of warfare; so real weapons, not ceremonial shields, are involved. This indicates that the building was at least in part an armory.

6 As indicated above, the five building units described in vv.6–9 may have been part of one grand structure. The colonnade was a magnificent porticoed entry hall, through which one entered the Hall of Justice (v.7).

7 The throne hall or royal audience chamber also served as the Hall of Justice, where the king personally heard complaints and meted out justice in cases that could not be handled by lesser officials (cf. 3:16–28).

The layout of this throne room was most likely similar to that of contemporaneous throne rooms in Syria and Assyria. "Thus, almost certainly it was a rectangular hall with the official entrance in its long side. The throne was placed on a rectangular dais or raised base, constructed at the far side of the hall adjacent to its short wall and centrally placed" (Ussishkin, "Solomon's Palaces," p. 90). Usually the throne was placed at the end of the hall left of the entry. The throne itself is described in 10:18–20.

8 As to the private residence of Solomon as well as that for Pharaoh's daughter, nothing is said except that they were similar in design and set away from the public building.

9–12 The stones used in the palace complex were high quality stones, precisely cut, and trimmed on both inner and outer faces (v.9). The foundation stones were quite large, measuring twelve to fifteen feet in length (v.10). Similar ashlar stones have been found above the foundations of the southern "palace" in Megiddo.

The large outer court "enclosed both the Temple and the palace works of Solomon" (Stigers, ZPEB, 5:531). The construction, three layers of stone and one of cedar beams (v.12), was the same as for the wall of the inner court. This typically Phoenician construction style is represented at Megiddo in the Solomonic gate as well as in the gate of the court to the southern palace (Ussishkin, "Solomon's Palaces," p. 105).

Notes

1 That the thirteen years are to be understood of the palace alone, apart from the construction of the temple, is seen from 9:10, where twenty years is given as the total building time.

2–5 Wiseman (NBD, p. 917) refers to the Palace of the Forest of Lebanon as "a hypostyle entrance hall." Wood (*United Monarchy*, p. 291 n.17) suggests that this may be the name of the palace itself and that the other buildings named in the following verses "may refer to sections of the total palace."

---

4. The vessels of the temple (7:13–51)

a. Hiram the craftsman

7:13–14

¹³King Solomon sent to Tyre and brought Huram, ¹⁴whose mother was a widow from the tribe of Naphtali and whose father was a man of Tyre and a craftsman in bronze. Huram was highly skilled and experienced in all kinds of bronze work. He came to King Solomon and did all the work assigned to him.

13–14 Hiram (NIV "Huram"; so also in 2 Chron 2:13; 4:11) was an outstanding master craftsman brought in from Tyre. He is obviously to be distinguished from the king of the same name. He was half Phoenician and half Israelite, his mother being from the tribe of Naphtali. Our text describes him as being skilled in bronze work. Second Chronicles 2:14 adds that he was likewise skilled in working with gold, silver, iron, stone, wood, and various dyes and fine linen. This is strongly reminiscent of the skills of Bezalel the craftsman who was chosen by God to make the tabernacle (Exod 31:2–3; 35:30–31).

Hiram was "highly skilled and experienced." More literally "he was filled with wisdom [*ḥokmāh*] and understanding [*tebûnāh*] and knowledge [*da'at*] in doing every kind of bronze work." This illustrates the broad semantic range of the words "wisdom" and "understanding." Hiram's wisdom consisted in his practical skills. Notice that Solomon not only utilized the finest materials, but he also spared no expense in hiring the finest workmen. Since Hiram's skills are so similar to those of Bezalel, who is described in Exodus 31:3 as being especially prepared and enabled by God for the task of building the tabernacle, it is not inappropriate to see in Hiram one also prepared and enabled by God for this special project, though it is not expressly stated. It ought also to be noted that Hiram was the son of a widow. This was a considerable handicap in the ancient world. That he should achieve such renown in his craftsmanship attests not only to his diligence but also to the grace of God.

Notes

---

14 In 2 Chron 2:14 Hiram the king says that the mother of Hiram the craftsman is from Dan. This apparent contradiction has a ready solution if one considers that the city Dan and its territories were by Solomon's time part of the general region of Napthali (cf. Aharoni/Avi-Yonah, map 113). Thus Hiram's mother could easily be of the tribe of Napthali yet have lived in Dan.

---

b. The two bronze pillars

7:15–22

15He cast two bronze pillars, each eighteen cubits high and twelve cubits around, by line. 16He also made two capitals of cast bronze to set on the tops of the pillars; each capital was five cubits high. 17A network of interwoven chains festooned the capitals on top of the pillars, seven for each capital. 18He made pomegranates in two rows encircling each network to decorate the capitals on top of the pillars. He did the same for each capital. 19The capitals on top of the pillars in the portico were in the shape of lilies, four cubits high. 20On the capitals of both pillars, above the bowl-shaped part next to the network, were the two hundred pomegranates in rows all around. 21He erected the pillars at the portico of the temple. The pillar to the south he named Jakin and the one to the north Boaz. 22The capitals on top were in the shape of lilies. And so the work on the pillars was completed.

15 These two ornamented bronze pillars are the first of the objects made by Hiram for the temple. Every indication is that they were not structurally part of the temple but were freestanding. They were placed "at" or "near" the portico (v.21; 2 Chron 3:17 has "in the front of"). The fact that they are described here rather than in chapter 6 tends to confirm their structural independence. Numerous examples have been found of similar pairs of freestanding pillars in the ancient Near East, from Egypt, Assyria, Phoenicia, and Cyprus. These pillars were quite large, eighteen cubits high with a circumference of twelve cubits. They were hollow, four finger-breadths thick (Jer 52:21), and were cast in molds (v.46).

16–20 The capitals, also bronze, were cast separately and were five cubits in length (v.16). They were bowl shaped (v.42; 2 Chron 4:12–13) and were adorned with pomegranates, lily petals, and a network of interwoven chains (vv.17–20). D.J. Wiseman and C.J. Davey (Illustrated Bible Dictionary [Wheaton: Tyndale House, 1980], 2:726) suggest that "the capital had four opened and inverted lotus petals (šûšan, RSV 'lily-work') four cubits in width . . . and above this an inverted bowl (gullāh)." This view is based on evidence from the text and from the known examples of the period. If this picture is correct, then the chain network fringed with the two hundred pomegranates encircled the bowl above the inverted lily (see Wiseman, NBD, p. 593, fig. 116, for a reconstruction of the pillar according to the model suggested above).

21–22 The pillar placed on the right or south side of the entrance to the portico was named Jakin. The other, on the left or north side, was named Boaz. Gray (Kings, p. 187) suggests appropriately that these names "may reflect the relationship of God and king, Jachin ('he established') referring to the initiative of God, and Boaz ('by him is he mighty') expressing the dependence of the king." These twin pillars may well have been a memorial in which David (the planner) and Solomon (the executor) give humble testimony to the grace of God in establishing (Heb. root kûn, Hiphil; the same as for "Jakin") for David a perpetual dynasty and an acknowledgement as well of the king's dependence on God for a successful reign.

In practical terms the pillars were to be an ever-present reminder to each successive king of the fact that he was ruling by God's appointment and by his grace, and that in God lay his strength. Just so ought believers today to be ever mindful of God's grace in their lives and of their utter dependence on him.

Notes

15 Second Chron 3:15 states: "In front of the temple he made two pillars, which [together] were thirty-five cubits long." The insertion of the word "together" reflects the view held by many conservatives (e.g., Stigers, ZPEB, 5:629; Wiseman and Davey, *Dictionary*, 2:726) that this figure is the combined length of the two columns (shaft length). "The additional cubit of length most likely was a separate cast base" (Stigers, ZPEB, 5:629). Others (e.g., Keil, p. 97) hold that the Chronicles passage reflects a scribal error. Second Kings 25:17 and Jer 52:21 both give the length as eighteen cubits.

16 The height of the capitals is given in 2 Kings 25:17 as three cubits. The apparent discrepancy has been explained by some as an error in textual transmission, by others as being due to the fact that the capitals may have been reduced in size during a renovation of the temple during the reign of Joash (2 Kings 12:6-14), and by still others as involving a different point of measurement that "would refer to the upper portion of the capital, leaving two cubits for the height of the lily work" (Stigers, ZPEB, 5:629). This last suggestion appears most tenable, particularly since the passage that is largely parallel to 2 Kings 25:17, namely Jer 52:22, reads five cubits (ruling out the idea of a shortening of the capital).

17 The details are difficult to reconstruct with any great deal of assurance because of the sketchy description given in the text. Alternative suggestions include Keil's (pp. 97f.), that "the lily work occupied the top portion of the capitals"; the chain network encircled the capital below the lily work, with one row of pomegranates above and one below the chain. Montgomery (p. 171) suggests that there were two strings of pomegranates suspended, ninety-six each in suspension and four attached at the four quarters. This is an attempt to account for Jer 52:23, which says that there was a total of one hundred pomegranates with ninety-six "on the sides" (NIV; *rûḥôt*, i.e., "wind [directions]"). Montgomery (p. 171) understands it to mean "pendant" (i.e., in the air). Karl Chr.W.F. Bähr (*The Books of the Kings*, CHS, pp. 84f.) suggests that the ninety-six pomegranates were turned to the four quarters in some way. The expression "seven for each capital" may refer to the components of each network or, with Keil (pp. 87f.), "seven twists arranged as festoons, which were hung round the capitals."

18 The MT rendered literally is "he made pillars . . . capitals on top of the pomegranates" (fifty Heb. MSS read "pillars" instead of "pomegranates"). The NIV rendering reflects a textual change suggested by most commentators. It is assumed that the words "pillars" and "pomegranates" were somehow switched. This seems to be confirmed by v.19. The NASB renders the MT as it stands. The KJV retains the MT but ignores the Masoretic punctuation in making a more understandable rendering: "He made the pillars, and two rows . . . to cover the chapiters that were upon the top, with pomegranates."

21 R.B.Y. Scott ("The Pillars Jachin and Boaz," JBL 58 [1939]: 143-47) has suggested that the names Jakin and Boaz are the initial words of a dedicatory inscription of the type found on a pillar east of Gudea's temple in Lagash that records Enlil's choice of King Gudea as his high priest. He suggests that the full inscription might have read something like "He (Yahweh) will establish the throne of David, and his kingdom to his seed forever," and "In the strength of (revocalizing *bōaz* to *b^eōz*) Yahweh shall the king rejoice." This suggestion is adopted by Wiseman (NBD, p. 593).

Other suggestions have been made with regard to the significance of these pillars. Kimchi (cited in Keil, pp. 102f.) interprets the first name as "Let this temple stand forever," and the second, "Solomon desired that God would give it strength and endurance" (i.e., Boaz is taken to mean "in it is strength"). The pillars are then regarded to be "symbols of the stability and strength . . . of the kingdom of God in Israel as embodied in the Temple."

S. Yeivin ("Yachin and Boaz," PEQ 91 [1959]: 6-22) suggests that the pillars are reminiscent of the pillars of fire and smoke during the Exodus and are thus symbols of the divine presence. This latter view has been taken up by many who have adopted the view that the pillars were giant incense stands or cressets where the fat of sacrifices was burnt (cf. W.F. Albright, "Two Cressets from Marisa and the Pillars of Jachin and Boaz," BASOR 85 [1942]: 18-27; and H.G. May, "The Two Pillars Before the Temple of Solomon," BASOR 88 [1942]: 19-27). By this view the fire and smoke ascending from the pillars were visible representations of the presence of God in the fire and smoke during Israel's wilderness journey. In objection to this latter view it might be said that (1) there is absolutely no indication that these pillars were cressets; (2) the archaeological evidence is not compelling; and (3) the names of the pillars are not appropriate to this suggested symbolism.

---

c. The bronze Sea

7:23-26

23He made the Sea of cast metal, circular in shape, measuring ten cubits from rim to rim and five cubits high. It took a line of thirty cubits to measure around it. 24Below the rim, gourds encircled it—ten to a cubit. The gourds were cast in two rows in one piece with the Sea.

25The Sea stood on twelve bulls, three facing north, three facing west, three facing south and three facing east. The Sea rested on top of them, and their hindquarters were toward the center. 26It was a handbreadth in thickness, and its rim was like the rim of a cup, like a lily blossom. It held two thousand baths.

23-26 The great Sea, made of cast bronze, was another marvelous example of the superb craftsmanship of Hiram. It was cast in one piece, including the lilylike rim and the two rows of gourds below the rim (v.24). The bronze bulls were cast separately, since they were later removed by Ahaz and replaced with a stone base (2 Kings 16:17). The exact shape is not known. Calculations attempting to determine the exact relationship between the measure of volume, the bath, and the cubit are marred by this lack of information. Some have assumed it to be cylindrical; others, hemispherical in shape. Something approaching a hemisphere is indicated by the fact that it required a support (2 Kings 16:17).

The statement regarding the circumference of thirty cubits has been much discussed and criticized, since it yields a value for π of three (rather than 3.14). Various solutions have been suggested, involving different means of taking the measurements. The simplest solution is also the most obvious and most likely, that the figures are not intended to be mathematically precise to three or four significant figures, but only to one, yielding a value for π of three.

The Sea, together with the ten movable basins, served as the laver had in the tabernacle, for ceremonial cleansing. Second Chronicles 4:6 informs us that the Sea was used by the priests for their washing, while the basins were used for the rinsing of the burnt offerings. The ceremonial stipulations for the priesthood with regard to the cleansing required in connection with their ministry and approach to God (Exod 30:18-21) were intended to teach a truth that transcends mere ritualism, namely, that he who would approach God and serve him needs to be cleansed from the pollution of the world. In that great passage speaking of a conversion of Israel, Ezekiel (Ezek 36:25-28) speaks of the cleansing that God will perform for Israel, removing all filthiness and idolatry from them, giving them a new heart and causing them to live in the land of God's appointment.

Notes

---

25 It has often been claimed that the combination of the bulls and the Sea is related to the pagan myths involving the divine creative activity in overcoming the sea. Actually the word בָּקָר (*bāqār,* "bull") is the generic term for cattle generally and may indicate oxen as well as cows. The distinctive word for "bull" (*šôr*) is not used here. It would be incredible for David and Solomon to try to bring about a syncretization of faith in the Lord with pagan mythology. When occasionally religious forms and terms overlapped with those of the world at large, it was not because biblical revelation adopted pagan superstition. The terms and forms were clearly defined so there could be no mistaking the uniqueness of God's revelation of himself and of the God-ordained way of man's approach to God.

26 The volume of the Sea was 2,000 baths, generally calculated to be about 11,500 gallons. A difficulty arises with reference to the statement in 2 Chron 4:5, which says that the value was 3,000 baths (c. 17,500 gallons). It has been suggested that the discrepancy was occasioned by the type of transmissional error susceptible to numbers given in shorthand form (cf. Keil, p. 104).

Another solution is suggested by C.C. Wylie ("On King Solomon's Molten Sea," BA 12 [1949]: 86-90), that the figure 2,000 given in Kings is calculated on the assumption that the Sea is a hemisphere, while in Chronicles the Sea is assumed to be a cylinder, yielding the figure 3,000. He uses the rabbinical formula that gives the ratio of one bath to eight cubic cubits. A third solution is suggested by J.L. Mihelic (IDB, 4:253), that both figures are later scribal traditions. A fourth suggestion, which seems quite probable and is advanced by G. Goldworthy (ZPEB, 5:318) as a possibility, is that different standards of measurement were used for cubit or bath.

---

d. The ten bronze basins and their stands

7:27-39

[27]He also made ten movable stands of bronze; each was four cubits long, four wide and three high. [28]This is how the stands were made: They had side panels attached to uprights. [29]On the panels between the uprights were lions, bulls and cherubim—and on the uprights as well. Above and below the lions and bulls were wreaths of hammered work. [30]Each stand had four bronze wheels with bronze axles, and each had a basin resting on four supports, cast with wreaths on each side. [31]On the inside of the stand there was an opening that had a circular frame one cubit deep. This opening was round, and with its basework it measured a cubit and a half. Around its opening there was engraving. The panels of the stands were square, not round. [32]The four wheels were under the panels, and the axles of the wheels were attached to the stand. The diameter of each wheel was

a cubit and a half. [33]The wheels were made like chariot wheels; the axles, rims, spokes and hubs were all of cast metal.

[34]Each stand had four handles, one on each corner, projecting from the stand. [35]At the top of the stand there was a circular band half a cubit deep. The supports and panels were attached to the top of the stand. [36]He engraved cherubim, lions and palm trees on the surfaces of the supports and on the panels, in every available space, with wreaths all around. [37]This is the way he made the ten stands. They were all cast in the same molds and were identical in size and shape.

[38]He then made ten bronze basins, each holding forty baths and measuring four cubits across, one basin to go on each of the ten stands. [39]He placed five of the stands on the south side of the temple and five on the north. He placed the Sea on the south side, at the southeast corner of the temple.

27–37 Ten mobile stands were constructed in order to carry the lavers or basins. They were four cubits square and three cubits high. There were lavishly engraved panels all around the stands, every available space being utilized in depicting cherubim, lions, and palm trees (v.36; cf. the picture of a similar bronze cart from Cyprus c. 1150 B.C., NBD, fig. 205, p. 1244). The wheels were like chariot wheels. In v.34 the word "handles" is probably better rendered "supports" (*k**ṭēpôṭ*) with NASB. The axles went through the bottom of these supports (v.32). These stands were mobile so that the basins could be moved to wherever they were needed.

38–39 The basins were also bronze, each holding forty baths (c. 230 gallons) and measuring four cubits (c. six feet). Though they were mobile, their normal placement was in the main hall of the temple, five on the right side and five on the left. Their purpose was to supply water for rinsing the burnt offerings (2 Chron 4:6).

The Sea was placed at the southeast corner of the temple. Notice that in Ezekiel's temple the river flows from the southeast corner of the temple (Ezek 47:1–2).

e. *Summary of Hiram's bronze work*

7:40–47

[40]He also made the basins and shovels and sprinkling bowls.

So Huram finished all the work he had undertaken for King Solomon in the temple of the LORD:

[41]the two pillars;
  the two bowl-shaped capitals on top of the pillars;
  the two sets of network decorating the two bowl-shaped capitals on top of the pillars;
[42]the four hundred pomegranates for the two sets of network (two rows of pomegranates for each network, decorating the bowl-shaped capitals on top of the pillars);
[43]the ten stands with their ten basins;
[44]the Sea and the twelve bulls under it;
[45]the pots, shovels and sprinkling bowls.

All these objects that Huram made for King Solomon for the temple of the LORD were of burnished bronze. [46]The king had them cast in clay molds in the plain of the Jordan between Succoth and Zarethan. [47]Solomon left all these things unweighed, because there were so many; the weight of the bronze was not determined.

40a The small bronze implements are listed starting here. The basins (*kîyyōrôt*) here are small vessels used for carrying away the ashes from the altar. In 2 Kings 25:14 and 2 Chronicles 4:11 they are called pots (*sîrōt*). The shovels were for the actual removal of the ashes from the altar, and the sprinkling bowls (*mizrāqôt*) were large bowls used at the altar of burnt offering, probably for the catching of the blood.

40b–45 A summary of the items of bronze fashioned by Hiram begins at this point. Our account does not mention the bronze altar (2 Chron 4:1).

46–47 The casting of the bronze was done in the lower Jordan Valley. Succoth was on the east side of the Jordan on the Jabbok River as it comes into the Jordan Valley. Zarethan is not as certainly located but is placed by Aharoni/Avi-Yonah (map 112) downstream from Zarethan on the Jabbok River, closer to the Jordan, south by southwest of Succoth. This general area shows abundant evidence of having been an active center of metallurgy during the period of the Hebrew monarchy. There is an abundance of good clay; and with available wood for charcoal and a prevalent north wind, this area was an ideal center for metalsmiths.

The casting method used by Hiram was the *cire perdue* or lost-wax process, used from 2500 B.C. in Egypt until the Middle Ages. It is still often used for high quality sculptures. First a clay core is made, then covered with wax to the desired thickness. The wax is molded according to the intended design, then overlaid with specially prepared clay. The whole mold is then evenly baked for a period of time, possibly several days. During this time the wax is withdrawn through the outer mold through vents. Then molten bronze is poured into the same vents. Huge furnaces must have been used by Hiram and great skill required to ensure a uniform flow and distribution of molten metal and proper escape of gases (cf. EB, 1976, 11:1093, 1095f.; 16:430). Only a master craftsman could have successfully carried out so huge an undertaking as was required here.

f. The furnishings of the temple

7:48–50

⁴⁸Solomon also made all the furnishings that were in the Lord's temple:

the golden altar;
the golden table on which was the bread of the Presence;
⁴⁹the lampstands of pure gold (five on the right and five on the left, in front of the inner sanctuary);
the gold floral work and lamps and tongs;
⁵⁰the pure gold basins, wick trimmers, sprinkling bowls, dishes and censers; and the gold sockets for the doors of the innermost room, the Most Holy Place, and also for the doors of the main hall of the temple.

48 A list of golden furnishings and implements begins here. On the golden altar, see Exodus 30:1–4. On the table of the bread of the Presence, see Exodus 25:23–30. The present passage does not mention the number of tables, but 2 Chronicles 4:8 informs us that there were ten tables of the Presence. Later, in 2 Chronicles 29:18, after Hezekiah had the temple purified, the priests reported to him that the "table for setting out the consecrated bread, with all its articles" had been purified. It would seem from these accounts that, though there were actually ten tables, they were often considered as a unit (one table in ten parts, so to speak), which they were as far as their function and symbolism were concerned.

49 On the golden lampstands, see Exodus 25:31–40. Here again, as with the table of the Presence, the one lampstand of the tabernacle became ten; yet so far as their function and symbolism were concerned, they were one unit. Note again that the symbolism of the earthly sanctuary as described in Hebrews 9 is based on the OT descriptions of the tabernacle, which served as the basic model for the temple.

50 It is noted that even the sockets of the doors of the Most Holy Place and of the main hall were of gold.

g. *The treasures of the temple*

7:51

> ⁵¹When all the work King Solomon had done for the temple of the LORD was finished, he brought in the things his father David had dedicated—the silver and gold and the furnishings—and he placed them in the treasuries of the LORD's temple.

51 With the completion of the temple, Solomon brought into the treasury (possibly the sidechambers of ch.6) the great wealth of gifts David had dedicated to the Lord (1 Chron 29). David had, in his great love for the Lord, given freely and gladly his "personal treasures of gold and silver for the temple" of his God, "over and above everything" he had provided for the temple (1 Chron 29:3). His love for God and great enthusiasm encouraged his officials to give in a commensurate way. David's infectious joy affected the whole nation. His praying in 1 Chronicles 29:10–20 is a model that is difficult to surpass, of joyous thanksgiving for the privilege of being allowed to give to the Lord. His prayer that God might give Solomon the whole-hearted devotion to keep God's commands and to build the temple had now been answered. One cannot help but feel that, just as David's officials caught the joy of giving, so did Solomon catch the enthusiasm of carrying out the great program of building the temple. This is an excellent illustration of one of the great principles of leadership.

5. *The dedication of the temple (8:1–66)*

a. *Moving the ark and the tabernacle to the temple*

8:1–11

> ¹Then King Solomon summoned into his presence at Jerusalem the elders of Israel, all the heads of the tribes and the chiefs of the Israelite families, to bring up the ark of the LORD's covenant from Zion, the City of David. ²All the men of Israel came together to King Solomon at the time of the festival in the month of Ethanim, the seventh month.
> ³When all the elders of Israel had arrived, the priests took up the ark, ⁴and they brought up the ark of the LORD and the Tent of Meeting and all the sacred furnishings in it. The priests and Levites carried them up, ⁵and King Solomon and the entire assembly of Israel that had gathered about him were before the ark, sacrificing so many sheep and cattle that they could not be recorded or counted.

⁶The priests then brought the ark of the Lord's covenant to its place in the inner sanctuary of the temple, the Most Holy Place, and put it beneath the wings of the cherubim. ⁷The cherubim spread their wings over the place of the ark and overshadowed the ark and its carrying poles. ⁸These poles were so long that their ends could be seen from the Holy Place in front of the inner sanctuary, but not from outside the Holy Place; and they are still there today. ⁹There was nothing in the ark except the two stone tablets that Moses had placed in it at Horeb, where the Lord made a covenant with the Israelites after they came out of Egypt.

¹⁰When the priests withdrew from the Holy Place, the cloud filled the temple of the Lord. ¹¹And the priests could not perform their service because of the cloud, for the glory of the Lord filled his temple.

1–2 With the completion of the temple and with all the furniture in place, the crowning event was about to take place, the placement of the ark into its permanent home. For Israel it marked the beginning of a new era: Now, more than ever before, there was a feeling of permanence. The ark was no longer housed in a temporary shelter in Jerusalem; the dichotomy in the sanctuary, with the ark in Jerusalem and the tabernacle at Gibeon, was ended.

To mark this great occasion with the dignity and solemnity it deserved, Solomon assembled all the elders of Israel with the tribal and family chiefs. As God's anointed shepherd, he involved all Israel through its elders and chiefs in the moving of the ark and the dedication of the temple. This involved more than mere pomp and ceremony. Solomon was very much in earnest about the spiritual significance of this occasion; and he desired that the heart of all Israel be knit together in the dedication of the temple and, more importantly, in the dedication of their hearts to God.

Reference to 6:38, noting the completion of the temple in the eighth month, makes it clear that there was a time lapse between the completion and the dedication of the temple, since the latter was accomplished on the seventh month (the year is not given). The view held by Ewald and others that the dedication was held a month before the completion is denied by 7:51, which states that the furnishings were put in place after the completion. The view of Keil (p. 118), that Solomon waited thirteen years, until his palace was completed, is based on 1 Kings 9, in which God seems to be responding to Solomon's dedicatory prayer (v.3) only after the completion of the palace, thirteen years later.

It is difficult, however, to believe that Solomon would wait so long before bringing the ark to the temple. Then, too, the time note in 9:1 is most naturally understood to indicate that what is given in chapter 9 took place at a time different from the events of chapter 8. The most satisfactory view is that Solomon waited eleven months before the dedication. Some have suggested that during this time some of the furnishings might have been completed and installed. But much more to the point is the suggestion that Solomon waited until the seventh month because of its symbolic importance, for it is in the seventh month that the Feast of Booths was celebrated.

The Feast of Booths was the last in the series of yearly feasts and was also known as the Feast of Ingathering. It was a harvest feast; but, more importantly, it celebrated the end of the wilderness wanderings and the fact that God had brought his people home into the Land of Promise, i.e., had given them rest (Deut 12:8–11). Zechariah 14:16–21 singles out this feast as mandatory for surviving Gentiles as well as redeemed Israel in the Messianic Age. This is consistent with the understanding that it celebrates the fulfillment of God's promise, the establishment of Israel in the land under God's Messiah.

For Solomon the completion of the temple betokened the fulfillment of God's promise, not only to establish Israel, but also to dwell in their midst and be their God (cf. Rev 21:3). This latter aspect is often lost sight of. Without God's presence Israel's possession of the land would be an empty blessing. This was recognized by Moses in Exodus 33:12-16. It is God's presence that makes Israel uniquely blessed among all nations. Another passage that may have a bearing on Solomon's timing is Deuteronomy 31:10-11, in which God makes provision for a renewal of the covenant every seven years (the year of remission [of debt]) at the time of the Feast of Booths. Though there is no indication in our passage that this was one of those occasions, it is nonetheless of interest that the two stone tablets of the covenant are mentioned as being contained in the ark. It is surely true that Solomon had in his heart and mind the thought of a covenant renewal, a personal and national rededication to God. It is not the ritual that is emphasized but the outpouring of Solomon's heart to God. What could have been merely a ritual dedication is transformed into a genuine expression of praise and desire to serve the Lord.

3-5 It was the priests who took up the ark in the prescribed manner. Before the ark was a great procession of the assembled chiefs and elders led by Solomon. In keeping with the solemnity of the occasion, sheep and cattle were sacrificed in such numbers that no one could keep track. The Hebrew participial form "sacrificing" (*mᵉzabbᵉhîm*, v.5) would indicate that the sacrifices were being made as the ark progressed the short distance from the city of David to the temple. This view is strengthened by the precedent set by David when he brought the ark to Jerusalem (2 Sam 6:13). With each six steps taken by the priests carrying the ark, David sacrificed a bull and a fattened calf.

Notice that the Tent of Meeting (traditionally called the tabernacle) was also brought up. This was the original tent that had been at Gibeon. It, with its furnishings, was evidently stored somewhere in the temple.

6-8 The priests, who alone were permitted in the temple proper, placed the ark in its appointed place, under the outstretched wings of the golden cherubim (v.6), the representations of those highly exalted angelic beings associated with the throne of God and his rule (see comments on 6:23-28). The ark was placed crosswise to the door, in a north-south alignment. The staves, which were extended lengthwise along the ark according to Josephus (Antiq. III, 136 [vi.5]), were also aligned in the same direction, crosswise to the door. This accounts for the statement that the wings of the cherubim, which stretched north to south, overshadowed the ark and its staves (v.7). These staves, or carrying poles, were so long that the ends could only be seen if one were to look into the Most Holy Place from a place near the opening (i.e., the staves extended considerably beyond the doorway) (v.8). The statement about the staves shows that Exodus 25:15 was complied with, that the staves were not to be removed from the ark. Even though the ark was now in its permanent home, the staves remained in place, a reminder of its journeys at the head of God's people. Though all the other furnishings had been newly made, the ark, representing the ruling presence of God, was still the same as that made while Israel was encamped at Sinai.

9 The ark had in it only the two stone tablets from Horeb, the witness of the covenant God had made with his people. It was for this reason that the ark was called the "ark of the covenant of the Lord" and also the "ark of the testimony." Here was the abiding witness to God's solemn purpose with regard to Israel, to make it a "kingdom of priests and a holy nation" (Exod 19:6). It was also a sobering reminder to Israel of her responsibilities before God. With regard to this latter aspect of the ark of the testimony or witness, it must be remembered that were it not for the blood of the atonement, the ark must of necessity be a throne of holy and terrible judgment, for "there is no one righteous, not even one" (Rom 3:10; cf. vv.9 –20; cf. Ps 14:1: "There is no one who does good"). But by God's gracious provision, the ark became a throne of mercy for the one who by faith approached in God's appointed way.

Thus while the ark was too holy for even the priests to touch, and while it spoke of the awesome holiness and majesty of a sovereign God, it became through the atoning blood a witness to the forgiving, protecting, and comforting presence of God for the believer.

10–11 When the priests had placed the ark in the Most Holy Place and had withdrawn, the cloud of the glory of God descended and filled the temple, just as had been the case at the inauguration of the tabernacle (Exod 40:34–35). God was thereby graciously acknowledging Solomon's handiwork and indicating his intention of dwelling with his people. The glory cloud was the visible manifestation of the presence of God. The rabbinic designation was "the Shekinah Glory," from the Hebrew root meaning "to dwell." The concept of the manifested glory of God is a pervasive and important theme in the OT and extends into the NT (see EBC 7:265–66).

Notes

2 The "time of the festival" is the Feast of Booths, celebrated for seven days from the fifteenth day of the seventh month. Ethanim ("perennial," signifying the onset of the fall or "early" rains) was the older designation for the seventh month. In later times it became known by the Babylonian name Tishri ("beginning"—i.e., the start of the civil year), thus moving the author to explain that Ethanim was the seventh month.

3 See R. Friedman, "The Tabernacle in the Temple," BA 40 (1981): 161–70, for evidence of the fact that Solomon's temple contained the Tent of Meeting.

8 The KJV rendering of this verse is indicative of a commonly held view with regard to the staves: "and they drew out the staves, that the ends of the staves were seen out in the holy place before the oracle." By this view "the staves were drawn so far forward that their ends touched the veil of the most holy place, and caused visible protrusions on the outside" (Bähr, *The Books of the Kings*, CHS, p. 96, explaining the rabbinic interpretation [which he does not hold]). The Hiphil of the verb אָרַךְ ('ārak) may mean "to draw out, lengthen," as the KJV renders it. It may also be used intransitively, i.e., "be long" (KB), as must be the case here since הַבַּדִּים (habbaddîm, "the staves") is clearly subject and not object. In reference to the rabbinic view that the tips of the staves so touched the veil that they caused visible protrusions, it is difficult to explain how this might be visible within the Holy Place, but not from the portico. It also does not account well for the statement in v.7 that the staves as well as the ark were overshadowed by the wings of the cherubim.

9 Hebrews 9:4 says of the ark that it "contained the gold jar of manna, Aaron's staff that had budded, and the stone tablets of the covenant." Although the problem of relating this statement to 1 Kings 8:9 has been addressed in various ways, it may be reasonable to suggest a solution similar to the one applied to the incense altar that is sometimes described as being in the (outer) sanctuary (see comment on 6:22), namely that this altar was *physically* in the outer sanctuary, just outside the entrance to the inner sanctuary; yet *functionally* it belonged to the latter. Just so the pot of manna and the staff of Aaron, though not actually inside the ark of the testimony, nonetheless formed part of the witness during the days of Moses and perhaps Joshua, reminding Israel of their rebellious spirit and lack of trust in God. These were concrete examples of sinful behavior, but the testimony of the two tablets of stone had a more lasting function.

10 There is a parallel to this event in Acts 2:1–4 in which God marks the inception of the church as the temple of the Holy Spirit by making his presence known through the sound of a mighty rushing wind and by filling those present with the Holy Spirit.

---

b. *Solomon's address*

8:12–21

¹²Then Solomon said, "The Lord has said that he would dwell in a dark cloud; ¹³I have indeed built a magnificent temple for you, a place for you to dwell forever."

¹⁴While the whole assembly of Israel was standing there, the king turned around and blessed them. ¹⁵Then he said:

"Praise be to the Lord, the God of Israel, who with his own hand has fulfilled what he promised with his own mouth to my father David. For he said, ¹⁶'Since the day I brought my people Israel out of Egypt, I have not chosen a city in any tribe of Israel to have a temple built for my Name to be there, but I have chosen David to rule my people Israel.'

¹⁷"My father David had it in his heart to build a temple for the Name of the Lord, the God of Israel. ¹⁸But the Lord said to my father David, 'Because it was in your heart to build a temple for my Name, you did well to have this in your heart. ¹⁹Nevertheless, you are not the one to build the temple, but your son, who is your own flesh and blood—he is the one who will build the temple for my Name.'

²⁰"The Lord has kept the promise he made: I have succeeded David my father and now I sit on the throne of Israel, just as the Lord promised, and I have built the temple for the Name of the Lord, the God of Israel. ²¹I have provided a place there for the ark, in which is the covenant of the Lord that he made with our fathers when he brought them out of Egypt."

12–13 Solomon recognized the glory cloud for what it was and saw in it God's approval and promised presence. When he said, "The Lord has said that he would dwell in a dark cloud [lit., 'thick darkness']," he was referring, as Keil (p. 123) correctly points out, "to the utterances of God in the Pentateuch concerning the manifestation of his gracious presence among his people" (cf. Exod 19:9; 20:21; Lev 16:2).

God said that he would "dwell" in thick darkness. This is not his normal, regular habitation, but he manifested himself in this form for Israel's sake. Solomon's response to this gracious manifestation was that he had built a "magnificent [lit., 'princely'] temple" for the Lord so that he might sit enthroned in regal splendor as befits his majesty. It is clear from vv. 27–28 that Solomon was under no illusions, as though God needed the temple for his own sake. But just as God is enthroned in heaven, so he has seen fit to use Solomon's temple as his throne on earth. By using the word "forever" (v.13), Solomon no doubt has reference both to the contrast with the impermanent tabernacle and the permanent relationship that God had seen fit to establish between himself and Israel, this relationship taking on new meaning and impetus in the Davidic covenant.

14 Solomon had been speaking to God. He now turned to the people and blessed them. As king and shepherd, Solomon was to be both the civil leader and the spiritual leader. Solomon, having been graciously put on the throne by God, having been allowed to carry out the great task of building the temple, and having experienced the entering of the glory cloud into the temple, blessed the people. He did so on God's authority, as his representative.

15–21 The blessing takes the form of praise to God for fulfilling his promise to David (v.15; cf. 2 Sam 7). Notice the expressions "with his own hand" and "with his own mouth." What God has promised he has also carried out. The hand is the biblical symbol for sovereignty. There are two aspects mentioned by Solomon: (1) God has raised up Solomon to sit on David's throne, as he had promised, and (2) God has allowed Solomon to build the temple (v.20). Since the Davidic covenant implied benefit to Israel through God-appointed leadership and ultimately the coming Messiah, God had clearly begun the fulfillment of the covenant; and Israel could expect to receive the bounty of God's blessings if the people walked in his ways. Notice that the blessing begins and ends with the statement that God brought his people (Israel) out of Egypt (vv.16, 21).

c. Solomon's sevenfold prayer of dedication (8:22–53)

1) The theme of the prayer

8:22–30

> [22]Then Solomon stood before the altar of the LORD in front of the whole assembly of Israel, spread out his hands toward heaven [23]and said:
>
> "O LORD, God of Israel, there is no God like you in heaven above or on earth below—you who keep your covenant of love with your servants who continue wholeheartedly in your way. [24]You have kept your promise to your servant David my father; with your mouth you have promised and with your hand you have fulfilled it—as it is today.
>
> [25]"Now LORD, God of Israel, keep for your servant David my father the promises you made to him when you said, 'You shall never fail to have a man to sit before me on the throne of Israel, if only your sons are careful in all they do to walk before me as you have done.' [26]And now, O God of Israel, let your word that you promised your servant David my father come true.
>
> [27]"But will God really dwell on earth? The heavens, even the highest heaven, cannot contain you. How much less this temple I have built! [28]Yet give attention to your servant's prayer and his plea for mercy, O LORD my God. Hear the cry and the prayer that your servant is praying in your presence this day. [29]May your eyes be open toward this temple night and day, this place of which you said, 'My Name shall be there,' so that you will hear the prayer your servant prays toward this place. [30]Hear the supplication of your servant and of your people Israel when they pray toward this place. Hear from heaven, your dwelling place, and when you hear, forgive.

The theme of Solomon's dedicatory prayer is that as God had seen fit to honor his word up to that time, he would continue to do so in accepting the prayers of his people and in granting forgiveness. These prayers are seen as being directed to God through the temple. Solomon was praying, in effect, that God might always recognize the temple as the way for sinful man to approach a holy God.

22 Solomon stood before the whole assembly. Second Chronicles 6:13 notes that he had made a three-cubits-high bronze platform. He stood facing the assembly with his hands outstretched in prayer. This was a common attitude in prayer in the ancient world, the supplicant standing with outstretched and opened hands (cf. Isa 1:15). Solomon stood as the representative and shepherd of his people, leading them in public worship and acting as intercessor. His prayer stands as one of the great public prayers of Scripture (cf. Ezra 9:5).

23–24 One of the great dangers in analyzing a prayer such as this one is to either reduce it to its theological bones or to treat it in liturgical terms and thus take the heart out, losing the warmth, passion, concern, and love for God. When Solomon opened with that great confession: "O LORD, God of Israel, there is no God like you in heaven above or on earth below" (v.23), this was not liturgy; nor was it merely a statement of theological fact. Solomon was greatly moved on this occasion. It was a day of fulfilled desires and prayers, a day in which God had graciously manifested himself in the glory cloud, a day of bright hope for Israel and the house of David in their covenant relationship with God. When he extolled the greatness and uniqueness of the Lord, it was with a full and overflowing heart. So it was with Israel after they had just experienced the unforgettable crossing of the Red Sea (Exod 15:11). This glad confession is one of the grand themes of the Psalms. Even Nebuchadnezzar, after his third humbling encounter with God, had a similar confession (Dan 4:3, 34–35).

What particularly moved Solomon on this occasion was the faithfulness of God in carrying out his promise (v.24). One of the great self-affirmations of God in the OT is that he is a God of love (*ḥeseḏ*) and is faithful to his word. Two key passages that give expression to this are Exodus 34:6–7 and Deuteronomy 7:9–10. *Ḥeseḏ* occurs in both, as does the word "faithfulness" (*'emeṯ* in the first and *ne'emān* in the second passage). Exodus 34:6–7 is God's self-revelatory response to Moses after he had interceded for a people that had sinned terribly against God. The emphasis is on God's faithful and forgiving love for the repentant sinner. This has its counterpart in the surety of judgment for the one who is unrepentant. In Deuteronomy 7:9–10 the situation is different. There is a covenant renewal in progress, and Moses is admonishing Israel to love God and keep his commands. They are to know that God is faithful to his covenant and to his love for those whose hearts are right toward him. For those who reject him, there is once again the surety of judgment.

Both passages are frequently quoted and alluded to, the first when the need for forgiveness is in the forefront (notable is Num 14:17–20), the second when men are encouraged to love God and walk in his ways, or when in prayer this attribute of God is the reason for praise or petition. This is the case in the present passage (cf. also Dan 9:4, where Daniel indeed confessed the sin of his people but where the major point of his prayer was to ask God to carry out his promise to bring Israel back to the land).

In citing the faithfulness of God in maintaining his covenant and his love, Solomon did not lose sight of man's responsibility to respond to God and to love him whole-heartedly. In this he faithfully reflects the thought of Deuteronomy 7:9–10.

Notice also that Solomon here repeats the thought of v.15, namely, that what God has promised with his mouth, he has fulfilled with his hand. With his sovereign power he is able to fully carry out whatever he has promised.

25 Solomon's confidence in praying was bolstered by previously answered prayer. Answered prayer is today also a strong basis for confidence in prayer. A second ground of confidence is God's own promise. His servants frequently claimed his promises when they prayed, and God honored these requests (cf. Exod 32:13; Dan 9:1–18). In making this petition, Solomon recognized his own responsibility and tacitly rededicated himself to walking after God.

26 The major point, however, of these verses is a plea that God, who had so far been faithful in every way to his covenant with David (as evidenced in the completion of the temple and the rulership of Solomon), might always accept this temple and condescend to dwell there, receiving those who approach him by way of the temple.

27 This verse is parenthetical, as can be seen from the fact that v.28 is grammatically connected to v.26 (cf. comments and note on v.28).

By means of the rhetorical question, Solomon made it very clear that he was under no illusions as to the meaning of the temple, nor was it properly speaking a home for God. It would be utterly impossible to build a house that could even begin to be commensurate with, or adequate to, the majesty of the Lord. God does not need the temple, but the temple needs God! God does not need Israel, but Israel needs God!

28 Verse 28 is grammatically connected to v.26, and they literally read: "And let your word . . . come true. . . . in giving attention to your servant's prayer." In making this great request, Solomon realized that on the actual merits of the case, he would have no right to pray as he did were it nor for God's own promise given by his grace. The only claim Solomon had on the Lord was God's own word, freely given; but God's word is a bond that cannot be broken, so that Solomon was able to pray with assurance and confidence. This privilege is the portion of believers of all ages.

29 The expression "have the eye fixed on" (NIV "open toward") an object is a common and graphic way of signifying care and attentiveness (cf. Pss 31:22; 34:15; 101:6). This verse forms the core of the whole prayer. God had condescended to allow a temple to be built for his name (5:5). He had by this means identified himself with his people. This means that God had through the temple provided a place of contact between man and God, a way for sinful man to approach a holy God, to have his sins forgiven, and to live in fellowship with him. Solomon prayed that God might continue to acknowledge the temple and the one who comes to him by way of the temple as he had promised.

30 Solomon next made a general, practical application of the request of v.29: he anticipated various situations in which a sinful people, suffering calamity because of God's judgment, would repent and pray. Solomon's earnest request was that God would not close his ears to repentant and believing prayer directed to God by way of the temple. Notice that God's dwelling place, or place of enthronement (*yāšaḇ*), is in heaven. The temple, as the place where God's name is enthroned, is a type of the true heaven and at the same time the way of approach to God.

Notes

22 From 2 Chron 6:13 we learn the additional fact that Solomon first stood, then knelt down, still with his hands outstretched. This is confirmed in 1 Kings 8:54.

2) Seven specific requests

8:31–53

31"When a man wrongs his neighbor and is required to take an oath and he comes and swears the oath before your altar in this temple, 32then hear from heaven and act. Judge between your servants, condemning the guilty and bringing down on his own head what he has done. Declare the innocent not guilty, and so establish his innocence.

33"When your people Israel have been defeated by an enemy because they have sinned against you, and when they turn back to you and confess your name, praying and making supplication to you in this temple, 34then hear from heaven and forgive the sin of your people Israel and bring them back to the land you gave to their fathers.

35"When the heavens are shut up and there is no rain because your people have sinned against you, and when they pray toward this place and confess your name and turn from their sin because you have afflicted them, 36then hear from heaven and forgive the sin of your servants, your people Israel. Teach them the right way to live, and send rain on the land you gave your people for an inheritance.

37"When famine or plague comes to the land, or blight or mildew, locusts or grasshoppers, or when an enemy besieges them in any of their cities, whatever disaster or disease may come, 38and when a prayer or plea is made by any of your people Israel—each one aware of the afflictions of his own heart, and spreading out his hands toward this temple—39then hear from heaven, your dwelling place. Forgive and act; deal with each man according to all he does, since you know his heart (for you alone know the hearts of all men), 40so that they will fear you all the time they live in the land you gave our fathers.

41"As for the foreigner who does not belong to your people Israel but has come from a distant land because of your name—42for men will hear of your great name and your mighty hand and your outstretched arm—when he comes and prays toward this temple, 43then hear from heaven, your dwelling place, and do whatever the foreigner asks of you, so that all the peoples of the earth may know your name and fear you, as do your own people Israel, and may know that this house I have built bears your Name.

44"When your people go to war against their enemies, wherever you send them, and when they pray to the LORD toward the city you have chosen and the temple I have built for your Name, 45then hear from heaven their prayer and their plea, and uphold their cause.

46"When they sin against you—for there is no one who does not sin—and you become angry with them and give them over to the enemy, who takes them captive to his own land, far away or near; 47and if they have a change of heart in the land where they are held captive, and repent and plead with you in the land of their conquerors and say, 'We have sinned, we have done wrong, we have acted wickedly'; [48]and if they turn back to you with all their heart and soul in the land of their enemies who took them captive, and pray to you toward the land you gave their fathers, toward the city you have chosen and the temple I have built for your Name; [49]then from heaven, your dwelling place, hear their prayer and their plea, and uphold their cause. [50]And forgive your people, who have sinned against you; forgive all the offenses they have committed against you, and cause their conquerors to show them mercy; [51]for they are your people and your inheritance, whom you brought out of Egypt, out of that iron-smelting furnace.

[52]"May your eyes be open to your servant's plea and to the plea of your people Israel, and may you listen to them whenever they cry out to you. [53]For you singled them out from all the nations of the world to be your own inheritance, just as you declared through your servant Moses when you, O Sovereign LORD, brought our fathers out of Egypt."

The background to most of the various calamities described in the following verses is found in Leviticus 26 and Deuteronomy 28–30. Both passages begin with the description of the blessing that will be Israel's portion if she walks in God's ways. The bulk of the material describes the curses in the form of various calamities that will befall the people if they do not obey God. Leviticus 26 particularly describes an escalating intensity or seriousness of difficulties, an ever-worsening series of events that will come on a disobedient people. Each calamity is designed to bring them to repentance; but if they still will not repent, then worse will come. In both passages the final blow is exile from the Land of Promise. But in Leviticus 26:40–45 and Deuteronomy 30:1–10, God promises that when they are cast out of the land, if they will then take to heart what has befallen them and repent, that God will listen to their prayer and restore them to the land.

In asking that God should hear the prayers of a repentant people, whatever may have befallen them, Solomon was once again basing his request on the word of God himself. Thus Solomon could pray with assurance and expectancy.

31–32 Solomon's first request involves cases in which an oath is brought before the Lord in attesting to the truth of a claim (cf. Exod 22:11), cases in which there are no human witnesses (e.g., Exod 22:6–12; Lev 6:1–5). These have to do with damage or loss of property entrusted to another, dispute over whether a piece of property has been found by another, or when fraud of some sort has been perpetrated. Solomon prayed that when an oath is brought before the Lord in such a case, that he will judge between the guilty and the innocent, judging the one and establishing the innocence of the other. Solomon's concern was not only for upholding justice, but perhaps chiefly for the sanctity of an oath brought before God, so that his holiness might not be taken lightly.

33–34 Solomon's second request involves prayer for forgiveness after a defeat by the enemy (cf. Lev 26:17; Deut 28:25). This defeat was caused by sin and the repeated refusal to listen to God's admonitions. It entailed subjugation by the enemy with considerable hardship and the taking of prisoners (not here a mass removal of population). The conditions of restoration are here given as (1) turning back to God (repenting), (2) confessing God's name (i.e., acknowledging his lordship), and (3) prayer in the temple. This last element implies a coming to God in the way prescribed by him. The answer looked for is the forgiveness of sin and restoration of the captives to the land.

35–36 Solomon's third request concerns the drought brought on the land by the sin of the people (cf. Lev 26:19; Deut 28:23). Israel's crops depended on good and well-timed fall and spring rains. The Canaanites thought to ensure for themselves fertility for their land and abundant rains by worshiping Baal, the supposed god of the storm. The Israelites were very much prone to emulate their neighbors in the licentious worship of this idol. As a consequence God withheld the rain (cf., e.g., chs. 17–18) so that they might realize that the Lord alone is the provider of all blessing. This passage gives the same three conditions of restoration as v.33. Restoration here involved answered prayer in the forgiveness of sin and the restoration of rain. In addition Solomon prayed that God might teach Israel how to walk before him so that they might enjoy the fullness of God's blessing.

37–40 Solomon's fourth request deals with famine, various kinds of plagues, and enemy incursions that bring about severe economic disruptions (cf. Lev 26:16, 19–26; Deut 28:22–23, 38, 59–61). The emphasis is on individual recognition and acknowledgment of sin. It puts the stress on personal and individual responsibility before God; first, in each man recognizing his own guilt and responsibility; and, second, in turning to God in sincere prayer. Notice the emphasis on the heart, that is, the inner man, rather than ritual alone. God, who knows the heart, will respond to man's prayer in accordance with the reality of his repentance. The object is that men will fear God.

41–43 Solomon's fifth request recognizes God's wider purpose in his dealings with Israel, namely, that as Gentiles see God working in and through Israel, they might desire to know Israel's God. Solomon prayed that as the foreigner approached God through the temple, God might hear him so that he too would truly come to fear God.

44–45 Solomon's sixth request involves situations where the people do not have access to the temple because they are in a foreign country. In this instance it involves soldiers sent to battle in distant places. Under these circumstances they were to pray *to the Lord,* toward the temple. It was not the temple per se that rendered prayer effective; it was the Lord who saw fit to dwell there who answered prayer.

46–51 Solomon's seventh request deals with the last in the series of calamities God promised to bring on Israel if the people persisted in disobedience (Lev 26:27–39; Deut 28:45–68). But just as God provided hope for a repentant Israel in Leviticus 26:40–45 and Deuteronomy 30:1–10, so did Solomon, on the basis of these passages, pray that God would continue to show himself a faithful and forgiving God. A mass deportation of the nation as a whole, with resultant scattering through many nations, would normally spell the end of the nation. In Israel's case, however, God would use calamity and distress to bring her to an awareness of her sin so that she would turn to God and receive forgiveness and be restored. Notice the conditions of restoration: a change of heart, i.e., a repentant spirit that leads to confession of sin; a turning back to God with all her heart and soul; and a praying toward the land of her fathers and the temple (trusting in God's promise; cf. Dan 6:10).

For those who respond as indicated, there will be complete restoration and vindication (v.49, "uphold their cause"). God, who loved his people enough and was strong enough to bring them out of the iron-smelting furnace of Egypt, will also bring about his full and sovereign purposes with his people.

52–53 Here is the conclusion to this magnificent example of believing intercessory prayer. Notice that though throughout his prayer Solomon put great stress on the centrality of the temple, this was not for reasons of vainglory, as being his special accomplishment. His basic concern was for his people: "May you listen to them whenever they cry out to you" (v.52). God had singled them out from all nations to be his special inheritance, and he had delivered them from Egypt (v.53). May he continue to care for his people until his complete purpose is fulfilled!

Notes

31 Leviticus 26 and Deut 28–30 give a preview of Israelite history, including their sinful disobedience, dispersion, and restoration. The restoration from the Babylonian exile is a foreshadowing of Israel's final conversion and restoration as detailed in the Prophets.
42 The arm of God, outstretched or bared, is a frequent term used to signify the unlimited power of God in his dealings with men. Thus he redeemed Israel out of Egypt (Deut 4:34; 5:15 et al.; Isa 52:10). The mighty hand of God has a similar meaning but stresses more the sovereignty of God, his ability to do whatever he sets out to do.

d. Solomon's benediction

8:54–61

> 54When Solomon had finished all these prayers and supplications to the LORD, he rose from before the altar of the LORD, where he had been kneeling with his hands spread out toward heaven. 55He stood and blessed the whole assembly of Israel in a loud voice, saying:
>
> 56"Praise be to the LORD, who has given rest to his people Israel just as he promised. Not one word has failed of all the good promises he gave through his servant Moses. 57May the LORD our God be with us as he was with our fathers; may he never leave us nor forsake us. 58May he turn our hearts to him, to walk in all his ways and to keep the commands, decrees and regulations he gave our fathers. 59And may these words of mine, which I have prayed before the LORD, be near to the LORD our God day and night, that he may uphold the cause of his servant and the cause of his people Israel according to each day's need, 60so that all the peoples of the earth may know that the LORD is God and that there is no other. 61But your hearts must be fully committed to the LORD our God, to live by his decrees and obey his commands, as at this time."

54–56 As Solomon stood before the people to bless them, his heart was filled with praise; and once again he spoke of God's faithfulness in fulfilling all his promises. The key word here is "rest" (v.56), which has important soteriological connotations. In Deuteronomy 12:9–10 "rest" is described as Israel's living in security in the Land of Promise. In the following verses, Israel is told to bring her sacrifices to the place (temple) where God will cause his name to dwell. Then will the people rejoice before the Lord (Deut 9:12). There can be no doubt that Solomon saw the temple as the completion of the picture of rest as portrayed in Deuteronomy 12. Not only was Israel living in peace and security, enjoying the fruitfulness of the land, but God was formally dwelling in their midst. This made everything complete. Solomon, at this high point of his life, saw with Moses and other great men of God that peace, security, and material prosperity are empty unless God is at the center of things. Solomon's kingdom, with God's "residence" in the center, foreshadows the messianic kingdom with its rest.

The rest enjoyed by Solomon and his generation was not complete, nor was it final. Psalm 95:7b-11 gives sad expression to the fact that Israel had not entered God's true rest because of unbelief and rebellion. Hebrews 3-4 expatiates on this theme and admonishes the Jewish reader not to repeat the mistake of his forefathers but to trust God and his Messiah. "There remains, then, a Sabbath-rest for the people of God" (Heb 4:9). That true and eternal rest is found in Christ and in him alone.

57-61 This passage expresses a twofold wish with a twofold purpose. The first wish and purpose is contained in vv.57-58: May the Lord always be with us and never forsake us so that (infinitive construct of purpose or result) he may turn our hearts to him. The second is found in vv.59-60: May the Lord always remember to uphold our cause so that all peoples may know that the Lord is God. The first speaks of a continued internal working of God to make his people conformable to his will. The second speaks of a continued external working of God to bring about a change in the Gentiles, that they too may come to a saving knowledge of God.

These verses also illustrate the balance between God's work in the human heart and life on the one hand (vv.57, 59) and man's responsibility on the other (v.61). Verse 58 recognizes that the ultimate motivation and enabling for a godly life come from God. Verse 61 emphasizes human initiative.

Notes

54 Second Chron 7:1-3 adds here that at the conclusion of Solomon's prayer, "fire came down from heaven and consumed the burnt offering and the sacrifices, and the glory of the Lord filled the temple."

57-58 Verse 57 is more than a request for God's help in times of difficulty. It extends to the desire that God's Spirit may never stop working to bring his people to an obedient walk before the Lord. Verse 58 shows that obeying God's commandments, etc., is basically an affair of the heart.

59 עָשָׂה מִשְׁפָּט (ʿāśāh mišpāṭ, "uphold the cause") is literally "do or provide justice," which means to do right by someone, to see that he is fairly treated, and, in some instances, to vindicate someone who has been wronged. In this context it undoubtedly means that God should champion the cause of Israel in the face of all kinds of adversity. It is of course self-evident that God's ability to do this depends on the extent to which Israel's cause is in keeping with the will of God.

The expression דְּבַר־יוֹם בְּיוֹמוֹ (deḇar-yôm beyômô, "according to each day's need") is reminiscent of other well-loved passages of Scripture: Exod 16:16-30: God provided enough manna for each day, no more and no less; Deut 33:25: "Your strength will equal your days"; Matt 6:11: "Give us today our daily bread" (KJV); John 1:16: "Of his fulness [i.e., of his grace] we have all received. . ., grace upon grace" (NASB), i.e., with each new need, God has supplied the needed grace.

61 The expression שָׁלֵם (*šālēm*, "fully committed"; lit., "be complete, whole, entire") is more than just an emotional attachment. It finds expression in an appropriate lifestyle, "to live by his decrees" and "to obey his commands." The words "to live" and "to obey" are explanatory infinitives.

The words "as at this time" are a reminder that at the time of the dedication of the temple, enthusiasm was running high. Solomon's prayer was that his people might not slacken in their desire to please God but might continue to walk wholeheartedly in his ways. It is sad that Solomon himself failed in this.

---

e. Solomon's dedicatory sacrifice

8:62–66

> [62]Then the king and all Israel with him offered sacrifices before the LORD. [63]Solomon offered a sacrifice of fellowship offerings to the LORD: twenty-two thousand cattle and a hundred and twenty thousand sheep and goats. So the king and all the Israelites dedicated the temple of the LORD.
>
> [64]On that same day the king consecrated the middle part of the courtyard in front of the temple of the LORD, and there he offered burnt offerings, grain offerings and the fat of the fellowship offerings, because the bronze altar before the LORD was too small to hold the burnt offerings, the grain offerings and the fat of the fellowship offerings.
>
> [65]So Solomon observed the festival at that time, and all Israel with him—a vast assembly, people from Lebo Hamath to the Wadi of Egypt. They celebrated it before the LORD our God for seven days and seven days more, fourteen days in all. [66]On the following day he sent the people away. They blessed the king and then went home, joyful and glad in heart for all the good things the LORD had done for his servant David and his people Israel.

62–63 All Israel joined Solomon in bringing sacrifices on this grand occasion. The large number (22,000 cattle and 120,000 sheep and goats) was appropriate both to the occasion and to the number of people present to participate in the fellowship offerings. For these offerings the fat, blood, and entrails belonged to the Lord; and the flesh was eaten by the offerer. These offerings were brought over a period of fourteen days, since according to v.65 the normal period of seven days for the Feast of Tabernacles was extended by another seven days. The fellowship offering was a voluntary act of worship and was intended to testify to the fellowship between God and the man whose sin had been forgiven. After those portions belonging to God had been offered, a communal or fellowship meal was held for the offerer and his family and for the Levites.

64–66 To accommodate the large numbers of sacrifices, the whole middle part of the court in front of the temple was consecrated. The large number of sacrifices and the involvement of the people attest to the unity of purpose and the wholehearted-ness of the devotion of people and king.

The Feast of Booths was in itself a grand occasion for rejoicing and for an enhanced spirit of community among all Israelites. The dedication of the temple made this occasion all the more joyful and memorable, and the time of celebration was suitably extended. When the people left, they went home rejoicing and with a great feeling of satisfaction in the realization that God's blessing was on the king and on the nation as a whole. This was indeed a memorable and significant occasion.

Notes

63 חָנַךְ (*ḥānak*, "dedicated") is used to refer to inaugural activities such as with a new home (Deut 20:5). It is the root from which the word Hanukkah (the feast commemorating the rededication of the temple after the desecrations of Antiochus Epiphanes) is derived and means basically "to begin, initiate, inaugurate."

E. *The Activities of the Solomonic Era (9:1–11:43)*

1. *The Lord's second appearance to Solomon*

9:1–9

¹When Solomon had finished building the temple of the Lᴏʀᴅ and the royal palace, and had achieved all he had desired to do, ²the Lᴏʀᴅ appeared to him a second time, as he had appeared to him at Gibeon. ³The Lᴏʀᴅ said to him:

"I have heard the prayer and plea you have made before me; I have consecrated this temple, which you have built, by putting my Name there forever. My eyes and my heart will always be there.

⁴"As for you, if you walk before me in integrity of heart and uprightness, as David your father did, and do all I command and observe my decrees and laws, ⁵I will establish your royal throne over Israel forever, as I promised David your father when I said, 'You shall never fail to have a man on the throne of Israel.'

⁶"But if you or your sons turn away from me and do not observe the commands and decrees I have given you and go off to serve other gods and worship them, ⁷then I will cut off Israel from the land I have given them and will reject this temple I have consecrated for my Name. Israel will then become a byword and an object of ridicule among all peoples. ⁸And though this temple is now imposing, all who pass by will be appalled and will scoff and say, 'Why has the Lᴏʀᴅ done such a thing to this land and to this temple?' ⁹People will answer, 'Because they have forsaken the Lᴏʀᴅ their God, who brought their fathers out of Egypt, and have embraced other gods, worshiping and serving them—that is why the Lᴏʀᴅ brought all this disaster on them.' "

1–2 God had already signally honored Solomon by appearing to him at Gibeon. Now once again God appeared to him to encourage him to remain faithful and to walk in God's ways. This made Solomon's later declension all the more reprehensible (cf. 11:9–10). The time of this appearance was after the completion of Solomon's major building projects—the temple and palace complexes. It is often felt that this appearance most naturally coincided with the ceremonies dedicating the temple; yet there are some difficulties with that view (see comment on 8:1). Though it might seem strange that the Lord waited thirteen years after Solomon's prayer of dedication to reply, there are three considerations (besides those discussed in 8:1) that make this entirely feasible.

First, God did indeed respond immediately to Solomon's prayer. Second Chronicles 7:1–7 records the consuming of the sacrifices by fire sent from heaven immediately after Solomon's prayer. This was followed by the filling of the temple once again with the glory cloud. This must certainly be considered as both an answer by God and a very clear endorsement of the temple and of Solomon's dedicatory prayer as well. At this point no other answer was really necessary.

Second, there is no reason why there could not have been an unreported message through a prophet. This would have gone unrecorded because of the much more momentous appearance of God himself with essentially the same message. The recording of this appearance was important because of 11:9–10.

The third consideration seeks to provide an answer to the question of the reason for the Lord's appearance to Solomon at this point in time if it was not in direct response to his dedicatory prayer. The answer may lie in the fact that Solomon had come to a spiritual crossroads. This is suggested first by the fact that the year in which he completed the palace (his twenty-fourth year, twenty years after he began the temple) is mentioned three times (7:1; 9:1, 10). Apart from the notations on the year that he began building (6:1) and finished building the temple (6:38), this is the only event linked to his regnal calendar. There were other significant accomplishments (e.g., the fortification of Jerusalem, Hazor, Megiddo, and Gezer, 9:15–19), but they are reported almost in passing.

A second matter that points to a crossroads at this time is the remark in 11:4, that as Solomon grew older he began to follow after other gods, despite God's two appearances to him (11:9). This declension obviously began after his twenty-fourth year, since God does not condemn him in chapter 9. It was certainly a gradual thing that began in the heart and only slowly began to appear openly. It would be in keeping with the character of God to speak forcefully and urgently to Solomon, warning him against turning from his walk with God (cf. vv.6–9).

3 God acknowledged the temple, consecrating it by putting his name there. Neither the ritual nor the splendor of the building made it the dwelling place of God. It was God's sovereign and gracious choice to thus dwell among his people and to acknowledge them as his own. Solomon had asked (8:29) that God's eyes might be on the temple. God replied that not only his his eyes but also his heart would be there. The following verses state the conditions.

4–5 These words reiterate the responsibilities of those who come after David. Again it is emphasized that more than ritual observances are in view. It is the integrity of the heart, the wholehearted walk before God, that he demands. Unfortunately this was where Solomon failed later in life. It was not that he rejected God, but his heart became divided in his loyalties (11:4) so that the passion for God that characterized his father and Solomon himself in his younger years was no longer there.

6–9 These verses give dire warning as to the disastrous consequences that result from apostasy. Solomon's history (ch. 11) shows that this warning was needed and particularly at this time in his life. This appearance of God was an act of grace and was intended as an urgent reminder to Solomon to guard his heart. A second thing to note here is that the consequences of disobedience are far-reaching. As kings, Solomon and his successors were responsible for the whole nation. Failure on the king's part affected all the people. Israel's subsequent history amply illustrates this principle. As the king went, so went the people. In Jeremiah 23 and Ezekiel 34 the prophets excoriated the bad shepherds (the kings) who did not feed the flock and who led the sheep astray.

There are two interrelated consequences that would result from disobedience. The one is the exile of the people (v.7) and the other God's rejection of the temple, leading to its destruction (vv.8-9). This state of affairs would lead in turn to a twofold reaction on the part of Gentile observers: (1) ridicule of Israel and (2) questions as to the reasons for such a disaster (vv.7, 9).

The seriousness of the threatened disasters is seen from the following considerations.

1. The word "cut off" (*kārat*, v.7) is frequently used in situations where a person is cut off or excluded from the fellowship of God's people (e.g., Lev 17:4, 9; Num 19:20). It is a drastic measure reserved for one who has committed a serious offense against God.

2. The word "reject" (*šillaḥ*, v.7), used in connection with the temple, is the word used of a man divorcing his wife. As such it speaks of a far more serious matter than the terminating of a business arrangement. Strong emotions and grief are involved (this is also the figure used frequently by the prophets of God, as the husband putting away Israel, the unfaithful wife).

3. Israel will become a "byword" (*māšāl*) and an "object of ridicule" (*šenînāh*). These words are "expressive of extraordinary calamity" (Gray, *Kings*, p. 238) and are found also in Deuteronomy 28:37 (where *māšāl* is rendered "object of scorn" in the NIV) and Jeremiah 24:9. The first of these words (*māšāl*) is usually rendered "a proverb." The second word (*šenînāh*) is related to the word "tooth" (*šēn*) and "make sharp" (*šānan*) and speaks of sharp, cutting taunts (cf. Ps 64:3: "They sharpen their tongues like swords").

Verses 8-9 describe the lesson to be learned from this by the Gentiles as they ask one another why this destruction has come about. The destroyed temple will become an object lesson in disobedience. When the answer is given as to the reason for this destruction, namely, that it is because Israel has forsaken God and turned to idols, there is implied in that answer amazement at the fact that a people could be so foolish as to reject the God who had taken them out of bondage and made them into a great nation, proving himself in the process with great and mighty deeds. Jeremiah (Jer 2) notes that even the Gentiles do not forsake their own gods (who are in reality powerless nothings) to turn after foreign gods.

Notes

1 The expression "all he had desired to do" may be rendered more literally "every deep desire that he wished to carry out." חֵשֶׁק (*ḥēšeq*, "deep desire") involves strong emotional attachment, a passion. The verb is used of a man's strong desire for a woman (Gen 34:8; Deut 21:11), of God's strong love for Israel (Deut 7:7; 10:15), and of man's longing for God (Ps 91:14). It speaks here (and in v.19) of the passion with which Solomon carried out his building projects—they were dear to his heart. Second Chron 7:11 restricts the object of his desire here to the temple and the palace.

5 On the unconditional aspects of the Davidic covenant, see the comment on 2:4.

6 Jeremiah 34 and Ezek 34 not only point out the failure of the past and current kings, however. They promise the coming of the true Shepherd, who will truly care for the sheep and lead them in the ways of God (cf. Jer 23:5-6).

8 NIV's "though this temple is now imposing," which is similar in thought to the KJV—
"(which) is high"—and JB—"as for this exalted Temple"—is an attempt to deal with the
Hebrew text without emendations and at the same time take into account the text of 2
Chron 7:21. The Hebrew in our passage reads וְהַבַּיִת הַזֶּה יִהְיֶה עֶלְיוֹן (wᵉhabbayit hazzeh
yihyeh ʿelyôn), which is most naturally rendered "and this house will be high." Second
Chron 7:21 reads אֲשֶׁר הָיָה עֶלְיוֹן (ᵃšer hāyāh ʿelyôn), which is normally rendered "which
was high." The NIV takes the Chronicles passage to be normative and renders Kings
accordingly. Critics generally emend the ʿelyôn to either לְעִיִּים (lᵉʿîyyîm) or לְעִיִּין (lᵉʿîyyîn),
so that the translations become "this house will become a ruin" (Kings) and "this house has
become a ruin" (Chron). Keil's solution (p. 139), adopted in the commentary, is to render
Kings, "this house will be high" (i.e., will stand as a high example for all to see) and Chron,
"this house stands (has become) high."

---

2. The business relation between Solomon and Hiram

9:10–14

> ¹⁰At the end of twenty years, during which Solomon built these two buildings—
> the temple of the LORD and the royal palace—¹¹King Solomon gave twenty towns
> in Galilee to Hiram king of Tyre, because Hiram had supplied him with all the
> cedar and pine and gold he wanted. ¹²But when Hiram went from Tyre to see the
> towns that Solomon had given him, he was not pleased with them. ¹³"What kind
> of towns are these you have given me, my brother?" he asked. And he called
> them the Land of Cabul, a name they have to this day. ¹⁴Now Hiram had sent to
> the king 120 talents of gold.

10–14 This paragraph relates a business transaction between Solomon and Hiram
involving the transfer of twenty border towns. These towns were in Galilee in the
western part of the territory of Asher. They lay generally east and southeast of the
city of Acco. A town named Cabul has been identified in this area.

In the arrangements made in chapter 5, Solomon traded wheat and oil (v.11) for
timber. We read here (vv.11, 14) that Hiram also sent 120 talents of gold (equivalent
to about four and one-half tons) to Solomon. Apparently more payment was required
than what Solomon could provide in grain and oil; so he ceded these border towns
(v.13). Hiram, after inspecting the area, was not happy with the towns and, according to 2 Chronicles 8:2, returned them to Solomon (presumably in favor of payment
of a different kind), who then rebuilt the towns and settled Israelites in them.

The name "Cabul" (v.14) has been traditionally rendered "as nothing." Others
suggest the meaning "border territory."

3. The levy of forced labor and urban development

9:15–24

> ¹⁵Here is the account of the forced labor King Solomon conscripted to build the
> LORD's temple, his own palace, the supporting terraces, the wall of Jerusalem, and
> Hazor, Megiddo and Gezer. ¹⁶(Pharaoh king of Egypt had attacked and captured
> Gezer. He had set it on fire. He killed its Canaanite inhabitants and then gave it
> as a wedding gift to his daughter, Solomon's wife. ¹⁷And Solomon rebuilt Gezer.)
> He built up Lower Beth Horon, ¹⁸Baalath, and Tadmor in the desert, within his
> land, ¹⁹as well as all his store cities and the towns for his chariots and for his
> horses—whatever he desired to build in Jerusalem, in Lebanon and throughout
> all the territory he ruled.

²⁰All the people left from the Amorites, Hittites, Perizzites, Hivites and Jebusites (these peoples were not Israelites), ²¹that is, their descendants remaining in the land, whom the Israelites could not exterminate—these Solomon conscripted for his slave labor force, as it is to this day. ²²But Solomon did not make slaves of any of the Israelites; they were his fighting men, his government officials, his officers, his captains, and the commanders of his chariots and charioteers. ²³They were also the chief officials in charge of Solomon's projects—550 officials supervising the men who did the work.

²⁴After Pharaoh's daughter had come up from the City of David to the palace Solomon had built for her, he constructed the supporting terraces.

15 The description of the forced labor is given in vv.20–23. In the intervening passage there is a brief description of Solomon's various building projects.

"Supporting terraces" (v.15) is traditionally and generally known by the name "Millo," which is basically a transliteration from the Hebrew *millô'*. The nature of the structure involved has been much debated, as has its location. Perhaps the most widely held view currently—and that adopted by the NIV—is that it consisted of architectural terracing and buttressing along the northeastern slope of the east hill of Jerusalem, the city of David. This would have filled a considerable depression between the city of David and the temple and palace complex to the north. The purpose would have been to allow the construction of more buildings in the area and, perhaps more importantly, adequate fortifications as near to the water supply as possible. Its construction was a major undertaking (cf. 11:27), ranking in importance with the fortification projects of Jerusalem, Hazor, Megiddo, and Gezer.

On the "wall of Jerusalem," nothing much can be said except that the fortifications of Jerusalem had to be extended considerably so as to include the temple and new palace.

In addition to the expanding and strengthening of Jerusalem, three key cities were selected for rebuilding, as was the case with Gezer, or for enlargement and strengthening of fortifications. Recent work has demonstrated that these three cities had certain characteristics in common with regard particularly to their fortifications attributable to the Solomonic era. Noteworthy are distinctive casemate walls with the outer wall measuring five feet and the inner wall four feet thick. The interior chambers are seven feet wide (similar walls of the Solomonic era have been found in numerous cities throughout Israel).

Most distinctive are the gate complexes, which are identical in plan and virtually of the same dimensions in all three cities. These gates feature a four-entry, six-chamber inner gate with twin towers at the first entry. Most of the gate extends inward from the casemate wall, with only the twin towers extending out from the wall. At both Megiddo and Gezer an outer double-entry gate has been found (the appropriate area has not as yet been excavated at Hazor). At Gezer the entry through the outer gate was from the right at an angle of approximately forty-five degrees. At Megiddo the approach was from the left, the gate being set at approximately seventy-five degrees. The direction and angle of approach was no doubt dictated by the topography.

Hazor was strategically placed in the north (c. three miles north of the Sea of Galilee), being situated at the juncture of the two major highways approaching from the north. It became Israel's chief bulwark against northern invaders until it was destroyed in the eighth century by Tiglath-pileser III.

Megiddo was the great fortress that controlled one of the major passes from the Plain of Sharon on the coast into the Valley of Jezreel through the Carmel range. It figures in prophecy as the staging area for the last great battle (Armageddon) in which Christ will defeat the forces of the Antichrist.

16 Gezer, on the road from Joppa to Jerusalem, had been a powerful Canaanite city. Though it was included in the tribal territory of Ephraim, it was not occupied by the Israelites until the time of Solomon. Then it was given to Solomon as a wedding gift by Pharaoh to his daughter. He had burned the city and killed its inhabitants, giving it to Solomon to rebuild and inhabit with Israelites.

17 Upper and Lower Beth Horon were strategically placed, controlling the access to the highlands of Judea from the coastal plain through the Valley of Aijalon. The lower city, being about one and one-half miles farther west, was fortified by Solomon to guard against enemy approach from its vulnerable western side.

18 Baalath was the designation of several cities in Canaan. The one in question here is most likely the city also known as Kiriath Jearim, where the ark was kept for some time after its return from the Philistines. This assumes that the names Baalath and Baalah (by which name Kiriath Jearim was also known) are interchangeable. This would then be a fortress guarding another of the western approaches to Jerusalem.

"Tadmor" is the Qere reading, which the Masoretes preferred to the Kethiv, which reads "Tamar." Second Chronicles 8:4 reads "Tadmor." Wood (*United Monarchy*, p. 292) considers the fortification of Tadmor in Syria to be part of the one instance of conquest ascribed to Solomon (2 Chron 8:3). He first conquered Hamath Zobah, then fortified Tadmor.

19 Solomon built up an extensive network of supply centers and towns to house his chariotry. These places are not specified but certainly included the cities just mentioned in addition to other strategic locations throughout the kingdom. Though he was a man of peace, Solomon was well prepared militarily to defend his kingdom.

20–23 On the forced labor or corvée, see 4:6 and comment on 5:13–18.

24 On Pharaoh's daughter, see the comment on 3:1. It seems likely since the work on the Millo, or "supporting terraces," was not begun until after the queen had been moved, that the Millo must be located near or in the city of David and that the construction activities would have been at or near the site of her temporary home. It also appears likely that existing structures may have been razed to allow the construction over a large area of this buttressing work.

Notes

15 The word "Millo" has the root מָלֵא (*mālēʾ*, "to fill"). The Akkadian *tamlu* is a terrace or artificial mound. The term is used in Judg 9:6, 20 in "the house of Millo," apparently a type of fortification. Its principal use, however, is in connection with the fortifications of Jerusalem. T.C. Mitchell (NBD, p. 823) holds to a common view, that it is a solid tower or a bastion filling some weak point in the walls (cf. also Wood, *United Monarchy*, pp. 230f.). Aharoni/Avi-Yonah (map 114) shows the Millo to be a fortification between the city of David and Ophel.

After the excavations of K. Kenyon in Jerusalem during the years 1961–67, the view expressed in the commentary has been widely held (cf. Kenyon's *Jerusalem* [New York: McGraw-Hill, 1967], pp. 50–51, and plates 29–30). This seems to be a reasonable view, whether or not Kenyon has found the actual remains of the Millo. (L. Stager, "The Archaeology of the East Slope of Jerusalem and the Terraces of Kidron," JNES vol. 41, no. 2 [1982]: 111–21, while agreeing with Kenyon's concept of the type of structure involved, disputes the fact that the terraces she found were part of the Millo.) It accords well with the Hebrew root of the word; it explains the massive nature of the undertaking; and it also explains why occasional repairs were necessary. See also on v.24.

In 1980 Yigal Shiloh ("The City of David Archeological Project: The 3rd Season," BA 40 [1981]: 169) tentatively identified a massive stepped-stone structure as having been built in the tenth century B.C., the time of Solomon. This structure, which includes a well-built buttress, has not as yet been fully excavated; but Shiloh holds that it may well be "a portion of the defence system belonging to the royal precinct of Jerusalem—the upper city of monarchic times." One of the aims of the next season's excavation was to clarify if possible the relationship of this and other structures in the area to the Millo. Unfortunately the excavation was halted by a dispute over rabbinic laws relating to burial sites.

Some recent treatments of the walls and gates of these three cities are (1) Y. Yadin, *Hazor*, Schweich Lectures, 1970 (London: Oxford University Press, 1972; see particularly pp. 135–38, 147–61. In the latter section Yadin compares the walls and gates of all three cities); (2) Y. Yadin, "New Light on Solomon's Megiddo," BA 23 (1960): 62–68; (3) William Dever et al., "Further Excavations at Gezer, 1967–71," BA 34 (1971): 94–132 (see particularly the plan of excavated Gezer [p. 96] and pp. 112–16 on the Solomonic gateway); and (4) Heaton, *Solomon's New Men*, pp. 66–72.

In "Was the 'Solomonic' City Gate at Megiddo Built by King Solomon?" BASOR 239 (1980): 1–18, D. Ussishkin challenges the identification of the Megiddo gates as Solomonic. Yadin has a rejoinder in the same issue (pp. 19–23). The identification of these gates as Solomonic is supported by V.M. Fargo in "Is the Solomonic City Gate at Megiddo Really Solomonic?" *Biblical Archaeology Review* 9 (1983): 16–18.

---

4. Solomon's religious activities

9:25

25Three times a year Solomon sacrificed burnt offerings and fellowship offerings on the altar he had built for the LORD, burning incense before the LORD along with them, and so fulfilled the temple obligations.

25 This note is added, as Keil suggests, to show that once the temple had been built, Solomon's practice of sacrificing at the various high places (3:2–4) ceased. Presumably the people followed him in this. As king he led the people, as on the day of dedication, in bringing before the Lord the burnt offerings and peace (or fellowship) offerings on the three great feast days.

5. Solomon's commercial activities

9:26–28

> [26]King Solomon also built ships at Ezion Geber, which is near Elath in Edom, on the shore of the Red Sea. [27]And Hiram sent his men—sailors who knew the sea—to serve in the fleet with Solomon's men. [28]They sailed to Ophir and brought back 420 talents of gold, which they delivered to King Solomon.

26–27 A completely new approach to international trade began here as far as Israel was concerned. Phoenicia was the major shipping power in the Mediterranean, while Israel controlled the major inland trade routes in the Levant. With Israel newly exercising control of the Negev as far as the Gulf of Aqaba, new possibilities opened up. Solomon made a treaty with Hiram of Tyre that was apparently mutually attractive. Both kings would be able to conduct extensive trade throughout the Red Sea area. In this venture Hiram supplied the seamen and shipping and ship-building skills, and Solomon gave Tyre access to the Red Sea and probably undertook a major share of the financing.

28 Ophir was fabled for its fine gold (Job 22:24) and as a center for the obtaining of exotic goods. It provided a rich source of revenue for Solomon and Hiram. Its location is still debated.

Notes

28 Ophir may have been as near as southwest Arabia, in which case the three-year journey was due to extensive coastal trade on the way and long layovers due to wind and weather conditions. Ophir was itself a major trading center, accounting for the appearance in 10:22 of some commodities (such as apes) that were not indigenous to Arabia.

Some have suggested that Ophir was in East Africa; still others favor Supara near Bombay, India. If correct, this would account for the length of the voyages. The fact that all the commodities mentioned in 10:22 were well-known in ancient India would lend some support to this view.

6. Solomon and the queen of Sheba

10:1–13

> [1]When the queen of Sheba heard about the fame of Solomon and his relation to the name of the LORD, she came to test him with hard questions. [2]Arriving at Jerusalem with a very great caravan—with camels carrying spices, large quantities of gold, and precious stones—she came to Solomon and talked with him about all that she had on her mind. [3]Solomon answered all her questions; nothing was too hard for the king to explain to her. [4]When the queen of Sheba saw all the wisdom of Solomon and the palace he had built, [5]the food on his table, the seating of his officials, the attending servants in their robes, his cupbearers, and the burnt offerings he made at the temple of the LORD, she was overwhelmed.

⁶She said to the king, "The report I heard in my own country about your achievements and your wisdom is true. ⁷But I did not believe these things until I came and saw with my own eyes. Indeed, not even half was told me; in wisdom and wealth you have far exceeded the report I heard. ⁸How happy your men must be! How happy your officials, who continually stand before you and hear your wisdom! ⁹Praise be to the LORD your God, who has delighted in you and placed you on the throne of Israel. Because of the LORD's eternal love for Israel, he has made you king, to maintain justice and righteousness."

¹⁰And she gave the king 120 talents of gold, large quantities of spices, and precious stones. Never again were so many spices brought in as those the queen of Sheba gave to King Solomon.

¹¹(Hiram's ships brought gold from Ophir; and from there they brought great cargoes of almugwood and precious stones. ¹²The king used the almugwood to make supports for the temple of the LORD and for the royal palace, and to make harps and lyres for the musicians. So much almugwood has never been imported or seen since that day.)

¹³King Solomon gave the queen of Sheba all she desired and asked for, besides what he had given her out of his royal bounty. Then she left and returned with her retinue to her own country.

The visit of the queen of Sheba is a graphic illustration of the fame of Solomon and of the awe that the reports of his wisdom and splendor inspired. The many legends and highly embellished accounts that have grown around this visit among Arabs, Jews, and Abyssinians attest to the widespread knowledge of the event and to the interest it created.

1 Sheba was in southwest Arabia, present-day Yemen. It is the best-watered and most fertile area of Arabia. By employing an extensive irrigation system, it developed a strong agricultural economy. But its chief strength lay in its being a center of trade. Its location kept it fairly secure from the power struggles in the Fertile Crescent and at the same time enabled it to be a convenient trade depot for traffic involving Africa, India, and the Mediterranean countries. It was famous for its trade in perfumes, incense, gold, and gem stones.

Solomon's fame reached the queen, probably through the caravan traders that regularly passed through Israel on their way to Damascus or to Gaza. It should be noted that his fame was associated with the name of the Lord. It was well-known that he was an enthusiastic and faithful servant of the Lord and that he humbly attributed his wisdom and success to the Lord. It has been suggested that surely the real reason for the queen's going to Solomon was for purposes of making trade agreements, but this is not stated. Undoubtedly business was transacted under the polite fiction of an exchange of gifts (cf. vv.2, 10–13). Our passage makes it clear, however, that she did come to see for herself whether the glowing reports had been exaggerated or not.

The Lord Jesus (Matt 12:42) used this incident along with the repentance of the Ninevites to castigate the scribes and Pharisees for their obstinate refusal to give him a fair hearing, when Gentiles, with far less reason to listen, responded. The queen of Sheba is commended for her interest and her willingness to travel a great distance to try to discover the truth of the report about Solomon. Yet the scribes, who should by their acquaintance with messianic Scripture have been interested in learning whether the claims of Christ were true, refused to listen—and Christ is far greater than Solomon.

"Hard questions" (ḥîḏôṯ) is generally translated "riddles," which were enigmatic sayings or questions that cloaked a deeper philosophical, practical, or theological truth. Arabic literature abounds in riddles and proverbs. They were a favorite sport and a way to test one's mettle. It would appear from the following verses that the "riddles" or "hard questions" posed by the queen were not mere frivolous tests of mental quickness but a genuine seeking for truths hidden in some of the enigmatic sayings known to her.

2 The queen came with a large caravan of camels carrying the trade goods for which Sheba was noted. Spices (Arabian balm) were native to South Arabia and were thus perhaps the most valued item in the whole inventory. Notice that v.10 mentions the 120 talents (four and one-half tons) of gold and many precious stones, but the spices are singled out for special comment. Never again were so many spices brought in as on that occasion. When she arrived, she put before Solomon all the questions on her mind.

3-5 Solomon's wisdom was not exaggerated. The queen was not disappointed in his ability nor in the wisdom he displayed. Not only his wisdom, but the splendor of his court and the manner of the temple ceremonies overwhelmed her. This last is literally "there was no more spirit left in her," which indicates extremely strong emotion. It is used in Joshua 2:11 and 5:1 of the dismay and consternation experienced by the Canaanites at the coming of Israel, not because of the strength of Israel's army, but because of the very evident miraculous working of God on their behalf. "Dismay" would not be correct here; but she was totally undone, "out of her wits" (NIV, "overwhelmed"), with amazement.

6-7 The queen had thought the reports about Solomon to be exaggerated, that no man could be as great as he was reputed to be. Yet now she freely confessed that his fame had not even begun to do him justice.

8 "How happy your men must be!" is the word 'ašrê, found so often in the Psalms (cf. Ps 1:1 et al.) translated "Blessed!" It stresses the subjective appreciation of a great favor or blessing, an experience to be enjoyed, savored to its fullness. It is quite possible that Solomon's servants had begun to take for granted all that they were experiencing in Solomon's presence. But the queen, seeing all this for the first time, was overwhelmed with wonder.

9 A wise and good king is a blessing to his people, and God's choice of Solomon as king was a mark of his love and favor for Israel.

10 See the comment on v.2.

11-12 The wealth of precious materials brought to Solomon from Sheba caused the historian to insert at this point the mention in particular of a very precious wood that was imported in unheard of quantities (just as with the spice or balsam that had just come from Sheba). The identity of this almugwood is not known today. Traditionally it has been thought to be a type of sandalwood, but there is no certainty on the matter. It was known and used in Ras Shamra, and it is mentioned in the Alalakh tablets as being used for fine furniture. Solomon used it for supports (or steps?) in the temple and palace and for musical instruments.

13 Solomon gave the queen all she asked for (in trade for the items she had brought?). In addition he bestowed lavish gifts on her in keeping with his majesty.

Notes

1 The letter שׁ (š) in the word "Sheba" (שְׁבָא, šᵉḇāʾ) was equivalent to the south Arabic s, so that the people were also known as Sabeans.

Arab queens from northern Arabia are mentioned in Assyrian records, and Tiglath-pileser IV lists tribute coming from an Arabian queen.

Keil (p. 158) suggests that לְשֵׁם יהוה (lᵉšēm yhwh, lit., "with regard to the name of the LORD") speaks of "the fame which Solomon had acquired through the name of the Lord, or through the fact that the Lord had so glorified himself in him."

Since Sabean merchants regularly traveled through Israel, certain agreements and financial arrangements were certainly already in effect. The fact that Solomon had now put a merchant fleet into the Red Sea and possibly the Indian Ocean might easily have affected Sheba's strong position in the caravan trade. It has therefore been suggested that this was her primary motive in seeing Solomon, especially since the passage is preceded by the account of Solomon's fleet (9:26–28), and since vv.11–12 are brought into the narrative parenthetically. But this is only speculation. It is possible to explain the whole passage from 9:26 through chapter 10 as an account of the various sources of Solomon's wealth, including Sheba. This is not to say that there was no talk of business (v.13 certainly implies that trading had been done), but probably not as a major motive. Compare vv.23–24, which indicate that many others sought an audience with Solomon simply because of his fabled wisdom.

10 The Jewish romantic legend that the queen desired and received a son fathered by Solomon is unsubstantiated, as is the Ethiopic tradition that the royal Abyssinian line was founded by the offspring of Solomon and the queen of Sheba.

---

7. The wonders of the Solomonic era

10:14–29

[14]The weight of the gold that Solomon received yearly was 666 talents, [15]not including the revenues from merchants and traders and from all the Arabian kings and the governors of the land.

[16]King Solomon made two hundred large shields of hammered gold; six hundred bekas of gold went into each shield. [17]He also made three hundred small shields of hammered gold, with three minas of gold in each shield. The king put them in the Palace of the Forest of Lebanon.

[18]Then the king made a great throne inlaid with ivory and overlaid with fine gold. [19]The throne had six steps, and its back had a rounded top. On both sides of the seat were armrests, with a lion standing beside each of them. [20]Twelve lions stood on the six steps, one at either end of each step. Nothing like it had ever been made for any other kingdom. [21]All King Solomon's goblets were gold, and all the household articles in the Palace of the Forest of Lebanon were pure gold. Nothing was made of silver, because silver was considered of little value in Solomon's days. [22]The king had a fleet of trading ships at sea along with the ships of Hiram. Once every three years it returned, carrying gold, silver and ivory, and apes and baboons.

[23]King Solomon was greater in riches and wisdom than all the other kings of the earth. [24]The whole world sought audience with Solomon to hear the wisdom

God had put in his heart. ²⁵Year after year, everyone who came brought a gift—articles of silver and gold, robes, weapons and spices, and horses and mules.

²⁶Solomon accumulated chariots and horses; he had fourteen hundred chariots and twelve thousand horses, which he kept in the chariot cities and also with him in Jerusalem. ²⁷The king made silver as common in Jerusalem as stones, and cedar as plentiful as sycamore-fig trees in the foothills. ²⁸Solomon's horses were imported from Egypt and from Kue—the royal merchants purchased them from Kue. ²⁹They imported a chariot from Egypt for six hundred shekels of silver, and a horse for a hundred and fifty. They also exported them to all the kings of the Hittites and of the Arameans.

This section continues to describe the glories and the splendor of Solomon's reign, as begun in 9:26.

14–15 The 666 talents (twenty-five tons) represents Solomon's yearly income in gold from all sources, including commerce and taxes. In addition there was an unspecified amount of income from tolls or tariffs from the various merchants and business agents that traveled through the land, as well as tribute from conquered kings. The "Arabian kings" of v.15 were tribal chiefs of miscellaneous peoples living in the desert to the south and to the east. The governors were probably the district governors (4:7–19).

16–17 These verses describe the ceremonial shields that Solomon kept in the Palace of the Forest of Lebanon. "These shields, like all the shields of the ancients, were made of wood or basket-work, and covered with gold plate instead of leather" (Keil, p. 162). The large shield "was adapted to cover the whole body, being either oval or rectangular like a door. This was carried by the heavy-armed infantry (2 Chron 14:8)" (J. Charley, NBD, p. 82). The small shield was carried by archers (2 Chron 14:8). Each large shield in this case was covered with six hundred bekas (or one-half shekels), the small shield with three minas (= three hundred bekas). The weights per shield were about seven and one-half and three and three-fourths pounds respectively.

18–21 The ivory throne, overlaid with finest gold (v.18), was a large and imposing object, in keeping with the symbolism of the seat of justice and rulership of a great kingdom. The armrests were flanked by lions, as were each of the six steps (vv.19–20). Verse 21 well illustrates the wealth of Solomon's kingdom.

22 The trading ships are literally "ships of Tarshish." Most likely this name referred to large merchant ships designed to carry ore. They were seaworthy enough to travel long distances under difficult weather conditions. These ships came to be used for other types of cargo as well.

There is abundant evidence of the existence in Solomonic times of copper refineries, though the large installation at Ezion-geber is now recognized to be a fortress and storehouse and not a copper smelter as was first thought (cf. Bright, *Israel*, pp. 211f.). It is likely that refined metals were shipped out of Ezion-geber in return for the exotic items listed in our passage. Compare Ezekiel 27:12 in which Tarshish "exchanged silver, iron, tin and lead for your [i.e., Tyrian] merchandise." In vv.24–25 the ships of Tarshish are described as carrying beautiful garments and rugs, etc.

23–25 To the statement in 4:29–34 extolling the breadth of wisdom and knowledge of Solomon, this passage adds, first, that he was wealthier than any king on earth (v.23) and, second, that "the whole world sought audience with Solomon to hear the wisdom God had put in his heart" (v.24). This is in accordance with God's promise of 3:13.

26 On the ratio of horses to chariots, Gray (*Kings*, p. 268) says, "Since three horses (a pair and a led one) were reckoned to a chariot team in Canaan on the evidence of the Ras Shamra texts (UT Krt, 128f), 12,000 horses would number stud-stock and reserves, as well as horses in breaking and trained animals."

This passage brings to mind the three prohibitions of Deuteronomy 17:16–17 for the anticipated kings: (1) he must not acquire great numbers of horses, (2) he must not take numerous wives, and (3) he must not amass for himself great amounts of gold and silver. For his failure in the second prohibition, Solomon is taken to task in chapter 11. He is not taken to task for either his many horses or his wealth.

In the matter of horses, there seem to be two concerns: (1) the false reliance on chariotry (the most potent weaponry of the day) as a means of preserving and/or expanding the kingdom and (2) making Israelites go back to Egypt for the horses. Craigie (*Deuteronomy*, pp. 255f.) suggests that this latter concern may have to do with diplomatic or trade relationships, resulting in large scale importation of horses, or perhaps the trading of men (as mercenaries?—so G. von Rad, *Studies in Deuteronomy* [London: SCM, 1966], p. 119, who suggests that this may account for the Israelite military colony at Elephantine) for horses.

Isaiah 31:1–3 warns against going to Egypt for help, relying on her chariots and horses (cf. also Isa 30:2). This latter passage suggests that what is in view is not trade agreements but rather a defense alliance in which Israel puts herself under the protective umbrella of Egypt and makes herself dependent on Egypt, under her control, thus effectively losing the freedom God had given Israel from Egypt.

On the amassing of personal wealth, one must remember that wealth was one of the bonuses God had promised Solomon (3:13). It was God's gift, and he should not be criticized for it. No doubt the prohibition in Deuteronomy has to do with motivation and priorities, in which personal gain is the issue (cf. Jer 22, in which Judah's kings are more concerned for personal luxury than in the welfare of the nation).

27 That which is considered a "precious" metal, silver, became a "common" metal because of its abundance. Cedar, which had to be imported from Lebanon, became as common (in buildings) as the indigenous sycamore-fig trees.

28–29 Solomon not only acquired chariots and horses, he became a trader in these items. They were imported from Kue (probably Cilicia) and Egypt. The Cilicians had been known for some time as breeders of fine horses. Solomon's agents were active in seeking out the best horses and values available.

Questions have been raised on the reading *miṣrayim* ("Egypt"), since Egypt was not known at this time as a source for horse purchases. Consequently it is suggested that in place of Egypt, *muṣrî* ought to be read. The latter was supposedly a region just north of the Taurus mountains and was noted for its fine horses. The same emendation is suggested for v.29. This suggestion must be rejected for the following reasons.

1. A scriptural statement ought not to be held suspect until confirmed by a secular source. This is especially true when there are no contradictory statements involved.

One must guard against the mentality that says, "Solomon is said to have imported horses from Egypt. But there is no confirmation in secular literature of horses being purchased from Egypt. Therefore this statement is doubtful."

2. Second Chronicles 9:28 says that Solomon's horses were imported from Egypt and "from all other countries." This latter statement indicates that the Kings passage might mean that horses were purchased from as far away as Cilicia in the north to Egypt in the south—wherever the best buys became available.

3. To deny the purchase of horses from Egypt makes Deuteronomy 17:16 meaningless. One of the main points is that men ought not to be bartered (as mercenaries? laborers?) to Egypt for horses. That would completely undo God's work of redemption. To make the word Egypt there anything else makes nonsense out of the verse. (Isaiah 31:1-3, though three centuries later, is certainly clear on the strength of Egyptian chariotry.)

4. A look at a map (cf. Aharoni/Avi-Yonah, map 115) will make one wonder why it is that the Hittite kings (v.29) who are practically next door to Cilicia (and Musri), at least much closer than Israel, would go through Israel as a middleman? It does not seem reasonable. If, however, the horses that they purchased from Solomon came originally from Egypt, it makes sense. Apparently Egyptian horses had qualities different from Cilician horses. The Hittite kings could purchase Cilician horses for themselves, but the Egyptian horses they bought through Solomon. As for Solomon (v.28), he bought his own horses from both Egypt and Cilicia.

Notes

---

15 The word "Arabian" (kings) is הָעֶרֶב (hā'ereb), which means "a mixed, miscellaneous people" (the "mixed multitude" of Exod 12:38). In Jer 25:24 they are described as people who live in the desert (possibly equated with the Arabs mentioned in the same verse). The word "Arab" (עֲרַב, 'arab) has the same consonants, differing only in the Masoretic vocalization. This latter vocalization appears in 2 Chron 9:14.

16-17 The figures given with the large shields (in both Kings and Chronicles) are not specified as to the units of weight intended (i.e., simply "600"). Normally "shekels" is to be supplied in such situations. For the small shield, v.17 specifies three mina (= 150 shekels) while Chronicles reads 300 (unspecified). A comparison of the last two figures leads to the conclusion that the unspecified weights are to be understood as *temple* shekels that are one-half the weight of the ordinary shekel. The beka (בֶּקַע (beqa', "split (shekel)"]) is its equivalent. Thus the NIV reading of 600 and 300 bekas (temple shekels) is justified.

19 The "round top" renders עָגֹל ('āgōl). The word has been revocalized by some to read עֵגֶל ('ēgel, "calf"), to agree with the LXX "heads of calves." They see in this reflexes of the Baal cult, whose symbol was the bull. Gray (*Kings*, p. 266) admits that "this motif is not attested on any of the thrones of the ancient Near East known in sculpture." The reading of the LXX is not sufficient to warrant revocalizing the MT. It is more probable that the "rounded top," on the other hand, is to be thought of as being similar to the top of the seat-back of the throne of King Ahiram of Byblos as depicted on the latter's sarcophagus (cf. Ussishkin, "Solomon's Palaces," p. 91, fig. 7). On this throne the top of the throne is folded over the back and downward in an inverted U shape. The top could very well be described as "rounded."

22 For a discussion of the location of Tarshish, see the note on 22:48-49.

תֻּכִּיִּים (tukkîyîm, "baboons") was traditionally rendered "peacocks" (so KJV, NASB). KB sees it as an onomatopoeic word imitating the sound of a hen, citing Kurdish *dik*, Sanskrit *çikhi*, and Arabic *daḥdaḥ*, all meaning "hen." W.F. Albright (*Archaeology and the Religion of Israel* [Baltimore: Penguin, 1956], p. 212), on the other hand, equates it with the Egyptian *t.ky*, "ape." (The t is the feminine article.) Montgomery (p. 224) and Gray (*Kings,* p. 262) concur with Albright. JB translates "baboons" and NEB, "monkeys."

28 Since the discovery of the place name "Kue" (קֻה, *qeweh*) in the ZKR inscription from Syria, eighth and ninth century B.C., the rendering "from Kue" has been accepted as correct. Kue is almost certainly Cilicia.

On the substitution of Musri for Egypt, see the note on 2 Kings 19:24.

---

8. Solomon's many wives

11:1–13

> ¹King Solomon, however, loved many foreign women besides Pharaoh's daughter—Moabites, Ammonites, Edomites, Sidonians and Hittites. ²They were from nations about which the LORD had told the Israelites, "You must not intermarry with them, because they will surely turn your hearts after their gods." Nevertheless, Solomon held fast to them in love. ³He had seven hundred wives of royal birth and three hundred concubines, and his wives led him astray. ⁴As Solomon grew old, his wives turned his heart after other gods, and his heart was not fully devoted to the LORD his God, as the heart of David his father had been. ⁵He followed Ashtoreth the goddess of the Sidonians, and Molech the detestable god of the Ammonites. ⁶So Solomon did evil in the eyes of the LORD; he did not follow the LORD completely, as David his father had done.
>
> ⁷On a hill east of Jerusalem, Solomon built a high place for Chemosh the detestable god of Moab, and for Molech the detestable god of the Ammonites. ⁸He did the same for all his foreign wives, who burned incense and offered sacrifices to their gods.
>
> ⁹The LORD became angry with Solomon because his heart had turned away from the LORD, the God of Israel, who had appeared to him twice. ¹⁰Although he had forbidden Solomon to follow other gods, Solomon did not keep the LORD's command. ¹¹So the LORD said to Solomon, "Since this is your attitude and you have not kept my covenant and my decrees, which I commanded you, I will most certainly tear the kingdom away from you and give it to one of your subordinates. ¹²Nevertheless, for the sake of David your father, I will not do it during your lifetime. I will tear it out of the hand of your son. ¹³Yet I will not tear the whole kingdom from him, but will give him one tribe for the sake of David my servant and for the sake of Jerusalem, which I have chosen."

When one considers the grand heights of Solomon's spiritual fervor and the great wisdom granted him by God, it seems impossible that he could have been so foolish as to succumb to idolatry. Yet it did happen, not overnight, but by slow degrees. First it was tolerated in his household. Once he became accustomed to it and comfortable with it, he also began to participate in idolatry with his wives. Solomon never renounced the Lord, but his heart was not entirely devoted to the Lord either. The syncretism that he began to display was a curse that plagued Israel through the years and ultimately led to the destruction of Jerusalem and the temple and to the exile of the people.

Solomon's life stands as a solemn warning against ungodly alliances and relationships that can only destroy the believer's spiritual vitality (cf. Neh 13:26).

1–3 Solomon was a great man, but he had feet of clay. He was spiritually unable to survive his disobedience to God's prohibition in Deuteronomy 17:16–17 on taking more than one wife (see comments on 10:26–29). In the Pentateuch God frequently warned Israel against intermingling and intermarrying with the Canaanites. Part of the reason was the extreme moral degeneracy of the Canaanites (Gen 19; Lev 18:1 –30 [esp. vv.24–30]; Deut 9:5; 12:29–31). Intermarriage inevitably led to toleration and finally observance of Canaanite religious practices (Exod 34:12–17; Deut 7:1–5). Another danger lay in the fact that there was great similarity in some of the religious terminology; and though the theology behind the terms was radically different, it was very easy to adopt by degrees a comfortable syncretism and ultimately to forget the Lord and to serve idols.

If anyone should take these warnings seriously, it should be the king, who leads by example. Yet Solomon apparently considered himself above the law and paid a bitter price. Though many marriages may originally have been entered into for the cementing of diplomatic alliances and others merely for the purpose of increasing the royal harem to add to the splendor of the king, vv.1–2 point out that Solomon "loved" many foreign women. Verse 2 adds that he "held fast to them in love." This speaks of strong emotional attachment, which is normal and desirable in a husband. But because Solomon was attached to the wrong women, he was led astray. The seven hundred wives and three hundred concubines, though perhaps adding to the splendor of Solomon's kingdom, were his downfall.

4 As Solomon grew older, his resistance wore down; and he became increasingly vulnerable. His service to the Lord became more and more perfunctory. Notice that his love for the Lord is measured by the standards of David, who, with all his faults, loved God with a passion throughout his lifetime.

5–8 "Ashtoreth" (v.5) is a deliberate distortion of Ashtart, the Canaanite fertility goddess. The revocalization is based on the word for "shame" (*bōšet*). "Molech" (or "Milcom," as the text reads here; both spellings refer to the same god) is a deliberate distortion of the word *melek* ("king"; see the note on 2 Kings 16:3). The worship of Ashtoreth involved fertility rites. In not only allowing these practices in his own household but participating in them to some degree, Solomon sinned grievously against the Lord (v.6). Apparently Solomon showed no favoritism but treated all the gods alike, even to the honoring of "Chemosh," the Moabite equivalent of the Ammonite Molech or Milcom (vv.7–8).

9–10 Solomon's sin was all the greater because of the special privileges he had enjoyed. Two are specifically named, one here (v.9), the other in v.11. God had singled Solomon out by appearing to him twice (see on ch. 9). Solomon lacked neither proof nor evidence of God's love and power. He had abundantly tasted God's love (1) by being chosen, contrary to custom and expectation, as David's successor; (2) in being given the special, personal name "Jedidiah" (i.e., "loved by the Lord"); (3) in receiving every benefit imaginable; and (4) in being visited by God twice for encouragement and admonition. He had also abundantly seen the power of God in that (1) he was put on the throne in the face of the power and influence of Adonijah's followers (Joab in particular), (2) he was granted unchallenged power and prestige as king, and (3) he was given success in his endeavors beyond all expectation. This should have created in Solomon a lifelong love and devotion of the deepest kind.

11–13 The second special privilege that was Solomon's was his relationship to David and the covenant God had made with him. He had not earned it; he was born into it. He had also been thoroughly instructed and trained by David (and possibly Nathan) in preparation for the high calling that was his (see on 2:2). As much as he could, David had poured into him his own love and passion for the Lord and his dreams for the house that would reflect the glory of the Lord. Solomon threw aside all these privileges when he followed after idols. He frittered away the continued joy and fellowship with God that could have been his for life. The punishment would be in accordance with the terms of the covenant with David. Yet even there God exercised mercy for David's sake. The kingdom was not taken from Solomon during his lifetime, nor was the kingdom to be totally removed from the line of David. One tribe would remain to fulfill God's promise to David (see Notes).

Notes

13 That one tribe was given to David and ten would be torn away (vv.31, 35) has created some difficulty in understanding. The most satisfactory view is that represented by Leon Wood ("Simeon, the Tenth Tribe of Judah," JETS 19 [1971]: 221-25; id., *United Monarchy*, p. 333). Notice first that according to 12:20 "only the tribe of Judah remained loyal to the house of David." Yet v.21 says that Rehoboam "mustered the whole house of Judah and the tribe of Benjamin." Possibly the contrast between "whole house of Judah" and "the tribe of Benjamin" is a hint that Benjamin's loyalties were divided. This is in fact what Wood suggests, that the northern portion of Benjamin, including Bethel, Ramah, and Jericho, became part of the northern nation. Thus, though most of Benjamin joined Judah, it was not counted as a full tribe (i.e., "whole house"). Simeon, which had originally received certain cities scattered throughout Judah as its inheritance, seems to have migrated to the north at some time before the division since in both 2 Chron 15:9 and 34:6 Simeon is listed with Ephraim and Manasseh in such a way that it seems necessary to include it with the north (cf. also J. Oswalt, ZPEB, 5:439f.) If this is correct, then Simeon was counted as part of the northern ten tribes, while Benjamin was not counted as a full tribe. However La Sor (NBC, p. 335) suggests that Simeon was absorbed into the tribe of Judah, thus not being counted as a separate tribe.

9. Solomon's adversaries (11:14–40)

a. Hadad the Edomite

11:14–22

[14]Then the LORD raised up against Solomon an adversary, Hadad the Edomite, from the royal line of Edom. [15]Earlier when David was fighting with Edom, Joab the commander of the army, who had gone up to bury the dead, had struck down all the men in Edom. [16]Joab and all the Israelites stayed there for six months, until they had destroyed all the men in Edom. [17]But Hadad, still only a boy, fled to Egypt with some Edomite officials who had served his father. [18]They set out from Midian and went to Paran. Then taking men from Paran with them, they went to

Egypt, to Pharaoh king of Egypt, who gave Hadad a house and land and provided him with food.

[19]Pharaoh was so pleased with Hadad that he gave him a sister of his own wife, Queen Tahpenes, in marriage. [20]The sister of Tahpenes bore him a son named Genubath, whom Tahpenes brought up in the royal palace. There Genubath lived with Pharaoh's own children.

[21]While he was in Egypt, Hadad heard that David rested with his fathers and that Joab the commander of the army was also dead. Then Hadad said to Pharaoh, "Let me go, that I may return to my own country."

[22]"What have you lacked here that you want to go back to your own country?" Pharaoh asked.

"Nothing," Hadad replied, "but do let me go!"

14–22 Hadad was the first of three men raised up by God to be adversaries against Solomon. It appears that as his reign drew to a close, these three men became increasingly worrisome to him. Hadad was of Edom's royal family (v.14), the only survivor of a severe slaughter when David's army under Abishai, son of Zeruiah, defeated the Edomites with a slaughter of eighteen thousand men (2 Sam 8:13–14; 1 Chron 18:12–13). This slaughter seems to have taken place over a period of six months when for some unknown reason Joab sought to destroy the Edomite army (vv.15–16). Hadad managed to escape and found his way to Egypt with a number of servants (v.17). There he was given Pharaoh's sister-in-law as his wife (v.19). He continued in Pharaoh's favor, and Hadad's son was raised with the royal household (v.20). Hadad, however, continued to harbor strong bitterness against Israel; and the moment the news came that David and Joab had died, Hadad returned to Edom (vv.21–22). There, in some unspecified way, he created trouble for Solomon, presumably not being very effective until Solomon's later years.

b. Rezon of Damascus

11:23–25

[23]And God raised up against Solomon another adversary, Rezon son of Eliada, who had fled from his master, Hadadezer king of Zobah. [24]He gathered men around him and became the leader of a band of rebels when David destroyed the forces ‚of Zobah‚; the rebels went to Damascus, where they settled and took control. [25]Rezon was Israel's adversary as long as Solomon lived, adding to the trouble caused by Hadad. So Rezon ruled in Aram and was hostile toward Israel.

23–25 The second adversary was Rezon, who had served under Hadadezer, king of Zobah. After David defeated Hadadezer (2 Sam 8:3–9), Rezon, who had escaped, formed a group of raiders and bandits who ultimately gained control of Damascus (v.24). Since David had thoroughly defeated Zobah and Damascus both, put garrisons in the latter city (2 Sam 8:6), and had reduced it to a tributary, it seems likely that Rezon's seizing of Damascus did not take place until later in Solomon's reign. At some point, probably after he had finished his palace, Solomon defeated Zobah and Hamath and went as far as Tadmor, making it a fortified outpost. Thus it is unlikely that Rezon made his move into Damascus until Solomon's declining years. However that may be, he was Solomon's troublemaker in the north while Hadad caused problems in the south (v.25).

Notes

23 שָׂטָן (śāṭān, "adversary") is the word from which the name of the great adversary of men is derived.

c. Jeroboam

11:26–40

26Also, Jeroboam son of Nebat rebelled against the king. He was one of Solomon's officials, an Ephraimite from Zeredah, and his mother was a widow named Zeruah.

27Here is the account of how he rebelled against the king: Solomon had built the supporting terraces and had filled in the gap in the wall of the city of David his father. 28Now Jeroboam was a man of standing, and when Solomon saw how well the young man did his work, he put him in charge of the whole labor force of the house of Joseph.

29About that time Jeroboam was going out of Jerusalem, and Ahijah the prophet of Shiloh met him on the way, wearing a new cloak. The two of them were alone out in the country, 30and Ahijah took hold of the new cloak he was wearing and tore it into twelve pieces. 31Then he said to Jeroboam, "Take ten pieces for yourself, for this is what the LORD, the God of Israel, says: 'See, I am going to tear the kingdom out of Solomon's hand and give you ten tribes. 32But for the sake of my servant David and the city of Jerusalem, which I have chosen out of all the tribes of Israel, he will have one tribe. 33I will do this because they have forsaken me and worshiped Ashtoreth the goddess of the Sidonians, Chemosh the god of the Moabites, and Molech the god of the Ammonites, and have not walked in my ways, nor done what is right in my eyes, nor kept my statutes and laws as David, Solomon's father, did.

34" 'But I will not take the whole kingdom out of Solomon's hand; I have made him ruler all the days of his life for the sake of David my servant, whom I chose and who observed my commands and statutes. 35I will take the kingdom from his son's hands and give you ten tribes. 36I will give one tribe to his son so that David my servant may always have a lamp before me in Jerusalem, the city where I chose to put my Name. 37However, as for you, I will take you, and you will rule over all that your heart desires; you will be king over Israel. 38If you do whatever I command you and walk in my ways and do what is right in my eyes by keeping my statutes and commands, as David my servant did, I will be with you. I will build you a dynasty as enduring as the one I built for David and will give Israel to you. 39I will humble David's descendants because of this, but not forever.' "

40Solomon tried to kill Jeroboam, but Jeroboam fled to Egypt, to Shishak the king, and stayed there until Solomon's death.

26–28 The third and by far most serious problem for Solomon in his latter years was Jeroboam, an Ephraimite of considerable ability and energy. The story of his rebellion, or the "lifting his hand against the king," starts with v.27. He was part of the Ephraimite labor force working on the Millo (see on 9:15) and a breach in the wall of the city of David. Jeroboam did his work so well that he attracted Solomon's attention and was put in charge of the contingent from Ephraim and Manasseh (v.28). He was evidently a charismatic leader.

29–32 About this time, while still overseeing this construction project (which took place sometime after Solomon's twenty-fourth year [9:10–15]), Jeroboam met Ahijah the prophet from Shiloh (v.29). This of course was a planned meeting on Ahijah's part. When they were alone in the open country, Ahijah symbolically told Jeroboam what God's plans were for him and Solomon. He tore his own new cloak into twelve pieces (v.30), told Jeroboam to take ten (v.31), and then explained the meaning of the prophecy.

33–35 See the comments on vv.7–13.

36 With the words "that David my servant may always have a lamp before me in Jerusalem," God expresses the unconditional aspect of the Davidic covenant: God will at some future time reestablish the throne of David in full glory—in the person of the Messiah, the Anointed One. Keil (p. 181) notes the reoccurrence of this expression in 15:4; 2 Kings 8:19; and 2 Chronicles 21:7. He suggests that it is explained in 2 Samuel 21:17, "where David's regal rule is called the light which God's grace had kindled for Israel, and affirms that David was never to want a successor upon the throne." Gray (*Kings*, p. 297) says that the "light . . . symbolizes the living representative of the house of the founder David (cf. 2 Sam 14:7)." The symbolism is striking and beautiful. It ought to be noted in addition that not only is the line of David perpetuated as a light is kept burning, but this light is in Jerusalem, the city where God chose to put his name. There is in view, then, a future for God's city, Jerusalem.

37–38 God gave Jeroboam the grand opportunity of establishing a lasting dynasty. The conditions were the same as those imposed on the sons of David. The standard of the godly walk is once again David. Unfortunately Jeroboam was an extremely able but unworthy man. He proved to be an ambitious and greedy opportunist. Chapter 12 shows that he had the ability of playing on men's emotions to achieve his ends. All his subsequent actions demonstrate the mentality of a man who was determined to achieve his own ends, ignoring God and his ways in the process.

39 Here is both a reaffirmation of the enduring nature of God's promise to David and a clear statement to Jeroboam and his successors that the house of David will win in the end. Starting with Rehoboam's loss, first, of the ten tribes, then the deprivations of Shishak (ch. 14), Judah became both the smaller and generally the weaker kingdom. It was indeed a shock for Rehoboam and the tribe of Judah to be reduced overnight from the most powerful tribe in an illustrious and world-renowned kingdom to a small state that was soon stripped of what wealth it had left. But God said that it would not always be thus. There seems to be an implication here, as it is explicitly stated in the prophets, that in the future the tribes will all once again be under the leadership of Judah.

40 At some point after the prophecy of Ahijah, the attempt at rebellion spoken of in v.26 took place. No details are given. It can however be reasonably assumed that Jeroboam was busily fanning the flames of dissatisfaction on the part of the northern tribes with the leadership of the house of David and, in particular, the oppressive requirements imposed on them to maintain the splendid style of Solomon's government. Notice the contrast here between Jeroboam and David, both of whom became a king after a disobedient king. David waited on God, but Jeroboam took matters into his own hands. Solomon, also, was disappointing. Rather than bowing humbly before the will of God as David had under God's chastening hand, Solomon reacted in the manner of Saul, causing Jeroboam to flee into exile.

Notes

28 "Man of standing" is a possible rendering of גִּבּוֹר חָיִל (*gibbôr ḥāyil*), but probably not the most accurate in this context. The traditional rendering has been "mighty man of valor." Gray (*Kings,* p. 82) says, "Under Saul it comes to mean one able in virtue of his property to equip himself, and possibly also followers, for war." H. Kosmala (TDOT, 2:374) takes a more balanced view: "It can mean strength (general, of a warrior, of military forces), ability (in war and in some vocation), or wealth (possessions), but the meaning must be determined by the context. Thus a *gibbor chayil* can be . . . an able man in any aspect, especially with regard to work (Jeroboam I, 1 K. 11:28)." Kosmala is surely correct, since Jeroboam is further described as an industrious or energetic man.
29 Ahijah, the prophet from Shiloh, appears again in chapter 14, and is also listed in 2 Chronicles 9:29 as having recorded his prophecy concerning Solomon.
30-31 The symbolic tearing of the coat is reminiscent of Samuel's action in 1 Samuel 15: 27-31, with a similar significance.

10. Solomon's death

11:41-43

[41]As for the other events of Solomon's reign—all he did and the wisdom he displayed—are they not written in the book of the annals of Solomon? [42]Solomon reigned in Jerusalem over all Israel forty years. [43]Then he rested with his fathers and was buried in the city of David his father. And Rehoboam his son succeeded him as king.

41-43 The royal annals of Solomon contained a more complete record of the events surrounding his administration, but the account recorded in Scripture is God's inspired message, given for the instruction and benefit of the reader.

Solomon left a big mark in history. His memory and fame live on. He represents the first stage in the fulfillment of the Davidic covenant; and, despite his faults, he foreshadows the coming Christ, the true Son of David. In addition his inspired words of wisdom as recorded in Scripture have challenged, taught, and inspired men throughout the ages.

II. The Divided Kingdom (1 Kings 12:1-2 Kings 17:41)

A. *The Division and Early Kings (1 Kings 12:1-16:14)*

1. *The accession of Rehoboam and secession of the Ten Tribes*

12:1-24

[1]Rehoboam went to Shechem, for all the Israelites had gone there to make him king. [2]When Jeroboam son of Nebat heard this (he was still in Egypt, where he

had fled from King Solomon), he returned from Egypt. [3]So they sent for Jeroboam, and he and the whole assembly of Israel went to Rehoboam and said to him: [4]"Your father put a heavy yoke on us, but now lighten the harsh labor and the heavy yoke he put on us, and we will serve you."

[5]Rehoboam answered, "Go away for three days and then come back to me." So the people went away.

[6]Then King Rehoboam consulted the elders who had served his father Solomon during his lifetime. "How would you advise me to answer these people?" he asked.

[7]They replied, "If today you will be a servant to these people and serve them and give them a favorable answer, they will always be your servants."

[8]But Rehoboam rejected the advice the elders gave him and consulted the young men who had grown up with him and were serving him. [9]He asked them, "What is your advice? How should we answer these people who say to me, 'Lighten the yoke your father put on us'?"

[10]The young men who had grown up with him replied, "Tell these people who have said to you, 'Your father put a heavy yoke on us, but make our yoke lighter' —tell them, 'My little finger is thicker than my father's waist. [11]My father laid on you a heavy yoke; I will make it even heavier. My father scourged you with whips; I will scourge you with scorpions.'"

[12]Three days later Jeroboam and all the people returned to Rehoboam, as the king had said, "Come back to me in three days." [13]The king answered the people harshly. Rejecting the advice given him by the elders, [14]he followed the advice of the young men and said, "My father made your yoke heavy; I will make it even heavier. My father scourged you with whips; I will scourge you with scorpions." [15]So the king did not listen to the people, for this turn of events was from the LORD, to fulfill the word the LORD had spoken to Jeroboam son of Nebat through Ahijah the Shilonite.

[16]When all Israel saw that the king refused to listen to them, they answered the king:

> "What share do we have in David,
>   what part in Jesse's son?
> To your tents, O Israel!
>   Look after your own house, O David!"

So the Israelites went home. [17]But as for the Israelites who were living in the towns of Judah, Rehoboam still ruled over them.

[18]King Rehoboam sent out Adoniram, who was in charge of forced labor, but all Israel stoned him to death. King Rehoboam, however, managed to get into his chariot and escape to Jerusalem. [19]So Israel has been in rebellion against the house of David to this day.

[20]When all the Israelites heard that Jeroboam had returned, they sent and called him to the assembly and made him king over all Israel. Only the tribe of Judah remained loyal to the house of David.

[21]When Rehoboam arrived in Jerusalem, he mustered the whole house of Judah and the tribe of Benjamin—a hundred and eighty thousand fighting men—to make war against the house of Israel and to regain the kingdom for Rehoboam son of Solomon.

[22]But this word of God came to Shemaiah the man of God: [23]"Say to Rehoboam son of Solomon king of Judah, to the whole house of Judah and Benjamin, and to the rest of the people, [24]'This is what the LORD says: Do not go up to fight against your brothers, the Israelites. Go home, every one of you, for this is my doing.'" So they obeyed the word of the LORD and went home again, as the LORD had ordered.

1–2 "All the Israelites" (v.1) manifestly refers to the representatives of the northern tribes. It may be that even during the years of the united monarchy, the "structure of a double crown, one of Judah and the other of Israel, was maintained," as J. Myers (AB, *II Chronicles*, p. 65) suggests. Bright (*History*, p. 210) theorizes that Solomon may likewise have gone to Shechem for official recognition by the northern confederacy. The basic differences between the northern and southern tribes had never been fully resolved even in the strong administrative periods of David and Solomon. That Rehoboam consented to go to Shechem for the inaugural ceremonies underscores the critical nature of the times and the insecurity of his position on the throne.

Jeroboam, mindful of his previous anointing (cf. 11:26–40) and confident that the time was ripe for him to make a move toward securing the throne, returned to lend his weight to the negotiations (v.2). Many Jewish commentators suggest that the Ten Tribes had actually gathered at Shechem expressly to make Jeroboam their king.

3–5 Jeroboam was well received by the delegation and accompanied them to the meeting with Rehoboam where their demands for social reform were voiced (vv.3–4). Particularly burdensome were the corvée, or compulsory service (over which, interestingly enough, Jeroboam had been appointed by Solomon [see 11:28]), and the taxation that Rehoboam's father levied on the land. Both lay on the people like a heavy yoke. After hearing the northern demands, Rehoboam obtained a three-day period for considering the terms of their requests (v.5).

6–11 Calling in the elder counselors who had served through the difficult Solomonic years, Rehoboam was advised to grant the demands of the northern kingdom so as to gain their loyalty (vv.6–7). Next Rehoboam turned to his own contemporaries for advice (vv.8–9). This group may have served as an administrative advisory body, perhaps concerned with national preparedness. The young men gave Rehoboam the counsel he wished to hear. They advised him to follow a harsh line (vv.10–11). Was Solomon too hard on them? He would be tougher. His little finger would be thicker than Solomon's loins!

12–15 When the northern delegation returned on the prescribed day (v.12), Rehoboam followed the advice of the younger men implicitly, delivering the harsh ultimatum (vv.13–14). The author of Kings interrupts the narrative (v.15) to point out that the decision of Rehoboam and his counselors was in accordance with a turn of affairs arranged by God's sovereign disposition, as prophesied previously by Ahijah (cf. 2 Chron 10:15).

16–17 After Rehoboam's unfavorable reply to their request, the delegation delivered its formal note of secession (v.16). That the delegates were prepared for the worst seems obvious from their carefully composed poetic reply. The reply itself is drawn largely from the traitorous words of Sheba, who led an unsuccessful rebellion in the days of David (2 Sam 20). The long-standing jealousy between the tribes, coupled with the hostility of the northern tribes to the Davidic covenant (2 Sam 7), comes to the surface in all its ugliness and fateful consequences.

Consequently the kingdom was divided. Rehoboam retained the rule only over Judah and Benjamin (v.17), which Rehoboam's forces managed to occupy as a much needed buffer zone between Jerusalem and the north.

18–24 Rehoboam quickly tested the decision of the delegates by sending Adoniram, his chief tax collector, to gather the taxes; he gathered only stones for his effort. With Adoniram dead and the people gathered into a bitter mob, Rehoboam fled for his life (v.18). There remained only the formal invitation to Jeroboam to become king of the northern tribes, followed by the coronation ceremony before the assembled multitude. The schism was complete and was to be permanent (v.19), despite a long period of incessant warfare between the two states.

Having failed to acquire the north's willing subservience, Rehoboam decided on an outright invasion of the new kingdom and so gathered a large army (v.21; cf. 2 Chron 11:1–4). However Shemaiah the prophet warned Rehoboam not to attempt to undo what God had decreed (vv.22–24); Rehoboam wisely abandoned the attack.

Notes

1 Several etymologies have been proposed for the name Rehoboam. Two suggestions are the most common: (1) "the divine kinsman is extended" or (2) "the people are/is extended."

G.E. Wright ("Shechem and Tribal League Shrines," VetTest 21 [1971]: 572–603) points out that in the light of historical research it would not be unreasonable "to suggest that . . . for 500 years or so (1700–1200 B.C.) Shechem was a 'Holy City' whose political relations were arranged by compact." Since Shechem had thus had a long and important history as a political and religious center, it is small wonder that, with the death of Solomon and in the midst of troubled times, Shechem would again come into prominence.

2 The MT's וַיֵּשֶׁב (wayyēšeḇ, "and he dwelt") should be pointed wayyāšoḇ ("and he returned") with A, the Syriac version of the Hexapla, the Vulgate, and 2 Chron 10:2. בְּמִצְרַיִם (bᵉmiṣrayim, "in Egypt") is to be understood here as "from Egypt," as read in 2 Chron 10:2.

It has been suggested that the name Jeroboam ("let the people be great") may be a throne name, deliberately chosen to be provocative to Rehoboam; for details see Albright, *Abraham to Ezra*, pp. 30f. Some (e.g., Bright, *History*, p. 210, and Klein, "Jeroboam's Rise," pp. 217f.) suggest that Jeroboam was not personally present at the meeting with Rehoboam, but that he returned only after the talks between the north and the south had ended. It could be, of course, that Jeroboam simply made his influence felt through the delegates (so J. Liver, "The Book of the Acts of Solomon," *Biblica* 46 [1967]: 96ff.). The plain reading of the text, however, seems to preclude either of the latter alternatives. The order appears to be (1) Jeroboam hears of the death of Solomon and of the disgruntled feelings of the north; (2) Jeroboam returns to capitalize on the situation and to make himself available; (3) having been summoned by the "official party" of the northern kingdom, he takes the lead in the negotiations; and (4) when the demands of the north are refused, Jeroboam is proclaimed king in a solemn assembly at Shechem.

6–7 Weinfeld (pp. 27–53), by subjecting the terminology of v.7 to a thorough study of both the biblical and extrabiblical evidence, conclusively demonstrates the legal aspects of the northern kingdom's request for exemption from the corvée and the heavy taxes imposed on them. For the existence of a council of elders and young arms-bearing men, see "Gilgamesh and Agga," ANET, p. 45; cf. 1 Kings 21:11.

10 קָטָנִּי (qāṭānnî, "my littlest part") is usually understood as in the Vulgate: *minimus digitus*

meus ("my little finger"); but since the compared member is lesser, KB (p. 835) may be correct in viewing the phrase euphemistically.

11 עֲקְרַבִּים (*ʿaqrabbîm*, "scorpions") were many-tailed whips armed with barbed points or hooks that, when lashed against the intended victim, felt like a scorpion's sting (cf. 1 Macc 6:51).

18 הִתְאַמֵּץ (*hitʾammēṣ*, "managed") means literally "to strengthen oneself," "summon all one's strength."

19 The verb translated "rebellion"—פָּשַׁע (*pāšaʿ*)—carries the idea of deliberate sinning, in this case against the will of God.

22 Shemaiah is associated only with this incident (cf. 2 Chron 11:2–4; 12:5–8). He may be identical with the Shemaiah who, with Iddo the seer, wrote a history of the reign of Rehoboam (2 Chron 12:15). According to the LXX, Shemaiah was the prophet who figured in the incident of the tearing of Jeroboam's mantle (11:29–40), an event that it includes after 12:24. Indeed at this point the LXX gives an extended discussion of Jeroboam's origin and rise to power.

---

2. The reign of Jeroboam in the northern kingdom (12:25–14:20)

a. The condemnation of Jeroboam's religion

12:25–13:34

²⁵Then Jeroboam fortified Shechem in the hill country of Ephraim and lived there. From there he went out and built up Peniel.

²⁶Jeroboam thought to himself, "The kingdom will now likely revert to the house of David. ²⁷If these people go up to offer sacrifices at the temple of the LORD in Jerusalem, they will again give their allegiance to their lord, Rehoboam king of Judah. They will kill me and return to King Rehoboam."

²⁸After seeking advice, the king made two golden calves. He said to the people, "It is too much for you to go up to Jerusalem. Here are your gods, O Israel, who brought you up out of Egypt." ²⁹One he set up in Bethel, and the other in Dan. ³⁰And this thing became a sin; the people went even as far as Dan to worship the one there.

³¹Jeroboam built shrines on high places and appointed priests from all sorts of people, even though they were not Levites. ³²He instituted a festival on the fifteenth day of the eighth month, like the festival held in Judah, and offered sacrifices on the altar. This he did in Bethel, sacrificing to the calves he had made. And at Bethel he also installed priests at the high places he had made. ³³On the fifteenth day of the eighth month, a month of his own choosing, he offered sacrifices on the altar he had built at Bethel. So he instituted the festival for the Israelites and went up to the altar to make offerings.

¹³:¹By the word of the LORD a man of God came from Judah to Bethel, as Jeroboam was standing by the altar to make an offering. ²He cried out against the altar by the word of the LORD: "O altar, altar! This is what the LORD says: 'A son named Josiah will be born to the house of David. On you he will sacrifice the priests of the high places who now make offerings here, and human bones will be burned on you.'" ³That same day the man of God gave a sign: "This is the sign the LORD has declared: The altar will be split apart and the ashes on it will be poured out."

⁴When King Jeroboam heard what the man of God cried out against the altar at Bethel, he stretched out his hand from the altar and said, "Seize him!" But the hand he stretched out toward the man shriveled up, so that he could not pull it back. ⁵Also, the altar was split apart and its ashes poured out according to the sign given by the man of God by the word of the LORD.

⁶Then the king said to the man of God, "Intercede with the LORD your God and

pray for me that my hand may be restored." So the man of God interceded with the LORD, and the king's hand was restored and became as it was before.

⁷The king said to the man of God, "Come home with me and have something to eat, and I will give you a gift."

⁸But the man of God answered the king, "Even if you were to give me half your possessions, I would not go with you, nor would I eat bread or drink water here. ⁹For I was commanded by the word of the LORD: 'You must not eat bread or drink water or return by the way you came.' " ¹⁰So he took another road and did not return by the way he had come to Bethel.

¹¹Now there was a certain old prophet living in Bethel, whose sons came and told him all that the man of God had done there that day. They also told their father what he had said to the king. ¹²Their father asked them, "Which way did he go?" And his sons showed him which road the man of God from Judah had taken. ¹³So he said to his sons, "Saddle the donkey for me." And when they had saddled the donkey for him, he mounted it ¹⁴and rode after the man of God. He found him sitting under an oak tree and asked, "Are you the man of God who came from Judah?"

"I am," he replied.

¹⁵So the prophet said to him, "Come home with me and eat."

¹⁶The man of God said, "I cannot turn back and go with you, nor can I eat bread or drink water with you in this place. ¹⁷I have been told by the word of the LORD: 'You must not eat bread or drink water there or return by the way you came.' "

¹⁸The old prophet answered, "I too am a prophet, as you are. And an angel said to me by the word of the LORD: 'Bring him back with you to your house so that he may eat bread and drink water.' " (But he was lying to him.) ¹⁹So the man of God returned with him and ate and drank in his house.

²⁰While they were sitting at the table, the word of the LORD came to the old prophet who had brought him back. ²¹He cried out to the man of God who had come from Judah, "This is what the LORD says: 'You have defied the word of the LORD and have not kept the command the LORD your God gave you. ²²You came back and ate bread and drank water in the place where he told you not to eat or drink. Therefore your body will not be buried in the tomb of your fathers.' "

²³When the man of God had finished eating and drinking, the prophet who had brought him back saddled his donkey for him. ²⁴As he went on his way, a lion met him on the road and killed him, and his body was thrown down on the road, with both the donkey and the lion standing beside it. ²⁵Some people who passed by saw the body thrown down there, with the lion standing beside the body, and they went and reported it in the city where the old prophet lived.

²⁶When the prophet who had brought him back from his journey heard of it, he said, "It is the man of God who defied the word of the LORD. The LORD has given him over to the lion, which has mauled him and killed him, as the word of the LORD had warned him."

²⁷The prophet said to his sons, "Saddle the donkey for me," and they did so. ²⁸Then he went out and found the body thrown down on the road, with the donkey and the lion standing beside it. The lion had neither eaten the body nor mauled the donkey. ²⁹So the prophet picked up the body of the man of God, laid it on the donkey, and brought it back to his own city to mourn for him and bury him. ³⁰Then he laid the body in his own tomb, and they mourned over him and said, "Oh, my brother!"

³¹After burying him, he said to his sons, "When I die, bury me in the grave where the man of God is buried; lay my bones beside his bones. ³²For the message he declared by the word of the LORD against the altar in Bethel and against all the shrines on the high places in the towns of Samaria will certainly come true."

³³Even after this, Jeroboam did not change his evil ways, but once more appointed priests for the high places from all sorts of people. Anyone who wanted to become a priest he consecrated for the high places. ³⁴This was the sin of the house of Jeroboam that led to its downfall and to its destruction from the face of the earth.

25–30 Jeroboam's plans for the administration of the new kingdom are now detailed. It was imperative that he act wisely, lest the people become dissatisfied and return their allegiance to Rehoboam (vv.26–27). No doubt much of the administrative machinery (minus the hated corvée established by David and Solomon) was utilized. His years serving Solomon in a responsible position probably aided Jeroboam's leadership in this area. Shechem was refurbished and made the capital. Peniel received his attention also and may have served subsequently as an alternate royal residence (cf. Jos. Antiq. VIII, 225 [viii.4]).

The people, however, must be cared for not only administratively but also religiously. Here Jeroboam miscalculated and substituted human wisdom for divine direction. Although God may have allowed the kingdom to be divided politically, he intended no theological schism. Fearing that a continued adherence to the established faith with its center of worship in Jerusalem might bring about a return to the south in the people's affection, Jeroboam established an alternate and more convenient religious experience. Rather than making the long trip to Jerusalem, the people of the north could now select one of the two more accessible worship centers: Dan, in the northern sector of the northern kingdom, or Bethel, in the extreme south, both of which had long-standing traditions as religious cities. Bethel was to be especially prominent throughout the rest of the history of the northern kingdom (cf. Amos 7:13).

At each cult center Jeroboam erected a temple, probably to house the sacred image and altar. The golden calves he caused to be erected (vv.28–29) were probably not intended to be construed as pagan images per se but representations of animals on whose back stood the invisible god, unseen by the eye of the worshiper. Similar practices involving the worship of the Canaanite god Baal Hadad are well documented in the literature and art of Ugarit. It was inevitable that religious confusion and apostasy would soon set in (cf. 14:9; Hos 8:6).

31–33 To further his religious goals, Jeroboam instituted a new religious order drawn from non-Levitical sources (vv.31–32). Indeed the Levitical priests refused to have any share in such unscriptural procedures, choosing rather to leave their homes and go over to Rehoboam and the southern kingdom where the true faith was retained (2 Chron 11:13–17). In this they were followed by many other believers from the north.

Completing his religious innovations, Jeroboam instituted an annual feast on the fifteenth day of the eighth month (v.33), no doubt rivaling the Feast of Tabernacles in the seventh month in Jerusalem.

13:1–3 God sent his prophet out of Judah to rebuke Jeroboam and his apostate religion (v.1). How tragic that no prophet could be found in the north that could speak for God's cause! The man of God came to the altar where Jeroboam was leading in the false sacrifices and prophesied by the authority and power of the word of the Lord that a coming prince of the house of David, Josiah by name, would one day burn the bones of Jeroboam's priests on that altar, thereby defiling it forever (v.2; cf. 2 Kings 23:15–20).

In confirmation of his prophecy, the prophet gave a sign: the altar would be split apart and its ashes poured out (v.3). According to the Levitical regulations, the ashes were to be carried off carefully to a clean place for disposal (Lev 1:16; 4:12;

118

6:10–11). Their pouring out, together with the destruction of the altar, would signify God's invalidating of the sacrificial service being held at Bethel.

4–6 Infuriated, Jeroboam pointed his hand at the prophet and gave orders that he be seized. But the very hand, stretched out in condemnation, was itself rebuked by being instantly withered (v.4). The king who would himself "take a hand" in the religious ceremony of his people found that strong hand totally impotent. Moreover the prophesied sign descended on the altar with a lightninglike stroke (v.5). Terrified and humbled Jeroboam pled with the man of God that his hand be restored; whereupon the prophet interceded with God, and the king's hand was restored to its former condition (v.6). Another miracle had occurred!

7 Finally Jeroboam was convinced by the twin miracles of the altar's destruction and the restoration of his withered hand that the prophet was indeed from the Lord, hence a man whose authority and power were to be reckoned with; so he invited the prophet to dine with him (v.7). Whether Jeroboam intended the dining hall of the sanctuary or that of his own home in Bethel is not certain. Whether or not Jeroboam hoped to win such a holy man over to his side, he clearly intended to try both to mollify the prophet's stand and to save face before the multitude.

8–10 The man of God, however, would not be so easily manipulated (v.8). He refused most stringently. Nothing the king could offer enticed him. God had laid on him three rules of conduct for the road: he was neither to eat nor to drink nor even to return by the way he had come (v.9). So holy was his mission that the very way he had traveled had been rendered sacred (cf. Matt 2:12; James 2:25). Rejecting the king and his offer, he departed by another road (v.10).

11–22 Learning of the incident in Bethel from his sons and recognizing that the man of God must be a true prophet, an aged prophet of Bethel set out to overtake the man of God (vv.11–14). Probably the old prophet hoped for fellowship and encouragement. When he at last overcame Jeroboam's rebuker, he invited the man of God to dine with him, assuring him that his previous instructions against eating and drinking had been superceded by a subsequent revelation (vv.15–17). Was not he also a prophet (v.18)?

The prophet from Judah was too easily convinced by the old man's deception. Perhaps a fundamental flaw in his character can herein be detected: his carrying out of God's charge may have been sheerly from command, not conviction. At any rate he went with the prophet of Bethel (v.19). While they were dining, the word of the Lord truly did come to the old prophet (v.20). (So important was the message that it is specially set off in the Hebrew text.) Because the man of God had disobeyed the full counsel of God, he would not be buried in the tomb of his father; this meant that he would meet a violent death along the way home (vv.21–22).

23–30 As soon as the meal had ended and the man of God had taken his leave, a lion met him on the road, killed him, and stood over his fallen body (vv.23–24). Eventually the news of the tragedy reached the aged prophet (v.25). Surmising that the events were the fulfillment of the Lord's prophetic judgment, he went and found that all was as it had been reported: the body of the man of God lay on the road with the lion yet standing guard beside it. The body had not been eaten, nor had the prophet's donkey, which stood beside his fallen master. It could only be the judgment of God (v.26)! Striding past the sentrylike lion, the prophet tenderly picked up the body of the man of God; brought it back to town; and, after proper mourning, laid it to rest in his own tomb (vv.28–30).

31–32 After the burial, the old prophet gave instructions that when he died he should be laid to rest beside the man of God (v.31). So powerful an effect had the whole series of events produced on him, and so assured was he that all the man of God had predicted would surely come to pass, that the old prophet longed, at least in death, to be united with this holy man. The LXX and Old Latin versions curiously suggest that the prophet of Bethel's chief desire was that both his bones and those of the man of God escape the certain doom of the coming judgment on the area. The prophecy was to be fulfilled minutely in the reform of Josiah (2 Kings 23:15–18).

33–34 One would think that the foregoing events would have influenced Jeroboam to turn to God. Such was not to be the case. Having had his hand restored and being rid of the irksome prophet from Judah, Jeroboam only intensified his apostate religious policy, a program that was to become the ruin of the northern kingdom and for which his name was to live in infamy. Thus it was to be repeatedly said of the wicked kings of the northern kingdom: "He walked in the ways of Jeroboam, the son of Nebat, who made Israel to sin."

Notes

---

28 For illustrations of similar cultic practices at Ugarit, see J.B. Pritchard, ed., *The Ancient Near East in Pictures Relating to the Old Testament* (Princeton, N.J.: Princeton University Press, 1954), figures 500, 501, 522, 534, and 537.

Eva Danelius, "The Sins of Jeroboam Ben-Nabat," JQR 58 (1961): 95–114, suggests that Jeroboam's golden calves were in reality representations of the Egyptian cow-goddess Hathor.

31 Jeroboam's "high places" were centers of cult worship that further rivaled the temple in Jerusalem.

מִקְצוֹת הָעָם (*miqṣôt hā ʿām,* "from all sorts of people") indicates that Jeroboam appointed priests from all levels and segments of society except the Levites.

33 It may be that the change of months is in keeping with agricultural festival observances—based primarily on calendrical considerations—previously held in Canaan; see J. Morgenstern, "The Festival of Jeroboam I," JBL 83 (1964): 109–18. If so, Jeroboam thereby gave an aura of traditional legitimacy to his bold move for religious independence from the established religion at Jerusalem.

On the whole question of Jeroboam's religious reforms, see R. de Vaux, *The Bible and the Ancient Near East* (Garden City: Doubleday, 1971), pp. 97–110.

13:1 אִישׁ אֱלֹהִים (*ʾîš ʾelōhîm,* "man of God") is a general term for a prophet, laying stress on the fact of his divine ministry. Other terms for prophet emphasize his call—נָבִיא (*nābîʾ,* "prophet"), his reception of the divine communication—רֹאֶה (*rōʾeh,* "seer") and חֹזֶה (*hōzeh,* "seer"), the relation between God and his prophet—עֶבֶד יהוה (*ʿebed yhwh,* "servant of Yahweh"), or his position before the world as he carried out his God-appointed task—מַלְאַךְ יהוה (*malʾak yhwh,* "the messenger of Yahweh").

If Josephus's suggestion (Antiq. VIII, 240–41 [ix.1]) that the prophet's name was Yadon is accepted, he may perhaps be connected with the Iddo mentioned as a chronicler of the events of Abijah's day (2 Chron 13:22).

2 While Edersheim (5:140–41) suggests that the name Josiah is a later insertion by the writer of Kings, and Keil (pp. 202–3) suggests that the name is a mere appellative ("he whom Yahweh supports") that was fulfilled to the very name, there is no a priori reason why God could not record the actual name of the individual involved centuries beforehand (cf. Isa 44:28; 45:1). See also Mic 5:2, where the name of the birthplace of Messiah is given several centuries before Christ's birth.

3 מוֹפֵת (*môpēt*, "sign," "wonder") denotes a miracle. The word is used particularly in connection with God's miraculous doings through his messengers in Egypt (Exod 4:21; 7:3, 9; 11:9–10; Deut 4:34; 6:22; 7:19; 26:8; 29:3 [2 MT]; 34:11; Pss 78:43; 105:27; 135:9; Jer 32:20–21). It appears frequently in parallel with its synonym אוֹת (*'ôt*, "sign"; e.g., Exod 7:3; Deut 6:22; Ps 78:43). Whereas the latter term emphasizes the intended purpose of God's miraculous doings, the former (cf. נִפְלָאָה [*niplā'āh*, "wonder"]) records the effect that the miracle produced on those who beheld it.

4 וַתִּיבַשׁ יָדוֹ (*wattîbaš yāḏô*, "but the hand . . . shriveled up") signifies a "drying up" or "shriveling" as the consequence of the loss of vital energy.

6 חָלָה (*ḥālāh*, "intercede") is often used of the intercession of the godly before their Lord (cf., Exod 32:11; Ps 119:58; Jer 26:19; Dan 9:13; Zech 8:21–22; Mal 1:9).

22 קֶבֶר (*qeḇer*, "grave") refers here to the family sepulcher, hence NIV's "the tomb of your father." Such tombs, if belonging to the wealthy, could be hewn out of soft limestone and consist of an antechamber and an inner cave where the bodies were laid in niches. The entrance to the sepulcher was guarded by a stone (see Edersheim, 5:141). For the average man more modest tombs were cut out of the soft limestone in some wadi near the deceased man's home.

24 Montgomery (p. 265) suggests that מָצָא (*māṣā'*, "met") here is perhaps to be understood as in Aramaic-Syriac מְטִי (*mᵉṭî*, "chance upon"). For Ugaritic *mṣ'/mġy* ("reach"), see UT, p. 436.

אַרְיֵה (*'aryēh*, "lion") is used forty-two times in the OT of a small type of African lion known in Palestine and the Near East in ancient times. For further details see TDOT, 1:374–88.

32 The mention of the "towns of Samaria" before the founding of the city of Samaria by Omri (16:24) or before the political territory known as Samaria came into being in the Sargonid Period (721–705 B.C.) (2 Kings 17:29) suggests that the words of the old prophet of Bethel have been updated by the author of Kings.

---

b. *The consequences of Jeroboam's religion*

14:1–20

¹At that time Abijah son of Jeroboam became ill, ²and Jeroboam said to his wife, "Go, disguise yourself, so you won't be recognized as the wife of Jeroboam. Then go to Shiloh. Ahijah the prophet is there—the one who told me I would be king over this people. ³Take ten loaves of bread with you, some cakes and a jar of honey, and go to him. He will tell you what will happen to the boy." ⁴So Jeroboam's wife did what he said and went to Ahijah's house in Shiloh.

Now Ahijah could not see; his sight was gone because of his age. ⁵But the Lord had told Ahijah, "Jeroboam's wife is coming to ask you about her son, for he is ill, and you are to give her such and such an answer. When she arrives, she will pretend to be someone else."

⁶So when Ahijah heard the sound of her footsteps at the door, he said, "Come in, wife of Jeroboam. Why this pretense? I have been sent to you with bad news. ⁷Go, tell Jeroboam that this is what the Lord, the God of Israel, says: 'I raised you up from among the people and made you a leader over my people Israel. ⁸I tore the kingdom away from the house of David and gave it to you, but you have not been like my servant David, who kept my commands and followed me with all his

heart, doing only what was right in my eyes. ⁹You have done more evil than all who lived before you. You have made for yourself other gods, idols made of metal; you have provoked me to anger and thrust me behind your back.

¹⁰" 'Because of this, I am going to bring disaster on the house of Jeroboam. I will cut off from Jeroboam every last male in Israel—slave or free. I will burn up the house of Jeroboam as one burns dung, until it is all gone. ¹¹Dogs will eat those belonging to Jeroboam who die in the city, and the birds of the air will feed on those who die in the country. The LORD has spoken!'

¹²"As for you, go back home. When you set foot in your city, the boy will die. ¹³All Israel will mourn for him and bury him. He is the only one belonging to Jeroboam who will be buried, because he is the only one in the house of Jeroboam in whom the LORD, the God of Israel, has found anything good.

¹⁴"The LORD will raise up for himself a king over Israel who will cut off the family of Jeroboam. This is the day! What? Yes, even now. ¹⁵And the LORD will strike Israel, so that it will be like a reed swaying in the water. He will uproot Israel from this good land that he gave to their forefathers and scatter them beyond the River, because they provoked the LORD to anger by making Asherah poles. ¹⁶And he will give Israel up because of the sins Jeroboam has committed and has caused Israel to commit."

¹⁷Then Jeroboam's wife got up and left and went to Tirzah. As soon as she stepped over the threshold of the house, the boy died. ¹⁸They buried him, and all Israel mourned for him, as the LORD had said through his servant the prophet Ahijah.

¹⁹The other events of Jeroboam's reign, his wars and how he ruled, are written in the book of the annals of the kings of Israel. ²⁰He reigned for twenty-two years and then rested with his fathers. And Nadab his son succeeded him as king.

1–3 When Jeroboam's son fell critically ill (v.1), the king sent his wife in disguise to Ahijah to learn whether the prince would recover (vv.2–3). Since Ahijah had successfully predicted his kingship (11:29–39), Jeroboam doubtless hoped that the old prophet might once again have good news. Perhaps he sent his wife because he himself felt convicted that he had not heeded Ahijah's admonitions (11:38).

4–16 Since Ahijah was now aged and blind (v.4), there was every hope that the subterfuge might succeed. But God had disclosed Jeroboam's hypocrisy to Ahijah (v.5) so that with her first footstep he greeted her instantly as Jeroboam's wife and delivered to her God's dire message of rebuke (vv.6–16). Despite God's goodness to him, Jeroboam had utterly despised God and committed gross sin. Jeroboam's contemptuous attitude is emphasized by the phrase "thrust me behind your back" (v.9; cf. Ezek 23:35).

Ahijah added a further message: not only would Jeroboam's dynasty quickly be cut off, but because the sin condition initiated by Jeroboam would permeate all Israel, the kingdom itself would one day fail, and its people would be scattered abroad (vv.14–16).

17–18 As soon as Jeroboam's wife reached Tirzah, true to Ahijah's prophecies, the lad died (v.17). A period of great mourning followed (v.18). Those with spiritual insight who knew the circumstances probably realized that the lad's death served as a guarantee of the full completion of all that Ahijah had prophesied.

19–20 The history of Jeroboam I concludes with the summary of his reign in accordance with the usual stylized formula.

Notes

1 Here the LXX departs from the MT and resumes at v.21, the material contained in the MT of vv.1–18 being represented variously in the LXX of 12:24^{g-n}.

2 הִשְׁתַּנִּית (hištannît, "disguise yourself") comes from the root שָׁנָה (šānāh, "alter oneself"). In her disguise the king's wife took along the gifts prescribed for a prophet to be given by one of humble status (cf. 1 Sam 9:8). The LXX identifies Jeroboam's wife as Ano, daughter of Pharaoh Shishak, perhaps confusing the situation with that of Hadad of Edom (cf. 11:14 –20).

3 For נִקֻּדִים (niqqudîm, "[crumbled] bread"), some have suggested a relationship with the Arabian naqada ("prick out," hence "cakes with perforations"). Others compare the word with נָקֹד (nāqôd, "speckled"; cf. Gen 30:32; cf. also Arab. naqqaṭa ["be speckled," II stem]), Ethiopic naqwᵉṭ ("point") and suggest that these were "speckled cakes," like the sweet bread with seeds on a crust still found in the Near East today. The Targum suggests "sweet meats"; the LXX translates it "raisin cakes."

בַּקְבֻּק (baqbuq, "jar") is onomatopoeic, emulating the sound of liquid leaving the jar. דְּבַשׁ (dᵉbaš, "honey") is probably to be retained despite Gray's suggestion (Kings, in loc.) that it might be a liquid prepared from grape juice. The two words are properly rendered by NIV, "jar of honey." Beehive-shaped jugs are well attested in the archaeological artifacts of ancient Palestine; see A. Honeyman, "The Pottery Vessels of the Old Testament," PEQ (1939): 76–90; J. Patch, "Honey," ISBE, 3:1418–19.

7 When God made Jeroboam the נָגִיד (nāgîd, "[spiritual] leader"), his intention for Jeroboam differed from Jeroboam's plans. He was more interested in being a מֶלֶךְ (melek, "king").

9 For details on מַסֵּכוֹת (massēkôt, "molten images"), see Gray, Kings, p. 337; id., "Idol," IDB, 2:673–75; F.B. Huey, Jr., "Idolatry," ZPEB, 3:242–48.

10 The use of לָכֵן הִנְנִי (lākēn hinnî, "therefore behold me") followed by the participle is a normal means for introducing a prophetic threat for the imminent future.

מַשְׁתִּין בְּקִיר (maštîn bᵉqîr, "every last male") means literally "he who urinates against the wall" (cf. KJV). The Hebrew verb form is doubtless composed with an infixed t, as in both Akkadian šiānu(m) and Ugaritic tyn ("urinate"). For further examples of "infixed t" in Hebrew, see B.W.W. Dombrowski, "Some Remarks on the Hebrew Hithpaʿel and Inversative -t in the Semitic Languages," JNES 21 (1962): 220–23; M. Dahood, Psalms, 3:388-89.

NIV is perhaps as reasonable as any of the many attempts to understand עָצוּר וְעָזוּב (ʿāṣûr wᵉʿāzûb, "slave," "free"), which has become symbolic of "all kinds and classes" (cf. Deut 32:36; 1 Kings 21:21; 2 Kings 9:8; 14:26).

11 Unlike their counterparts in the west, dogs were often the scourge of the ancient Near East. Unfed, they became scavengers, always ready to eat anything (cf. 16:4; 21:24; Pss 22:16; 59:6, 14–15; Jer 15:3). That Ahijah's prophetic threats are presented under the figures of defilement and detested images emphasizes the heinousness of Jeroboam's religion and the awful judgment that results from such practices. Vicious sin begets vigorous judgment. See also the notes on 21:23 and 2 Kings 8:13.

13 The death of Jeroboam's child may well bear on the problem of God's gracious dealing with young children (cf. 2 Sam 12:23).

14 The phrase זֶה הַיּוֹם וּמֶה גַּם־עָתָּה (zeh hayyôm ûmeh gam-ʿattāh, "this is the day! What? Yes, even now") is difficult and has occasioned much discussion. It seems to emphasize what should happen today and immediately afterward. Not only would Jeroboam's son die that very day; but because of a settled heart condition and predisposition towards sin, God had already set into operation those forces that would ultimately destroy the nation.

15 The אֲשֵׁרִים (ᵃšērîm, "Asherah poles"), sacred to the worship of the goddess Asherah, became a besetting sin in the northern kingdom and even spread to the south until the

reign of Josiah (2 Kings 23). This goddess figures prominently in the ancient Canaanite literature and is known from the cultus of other cultures in the ancient Near East as well. Her worship enters the OT in an advanced form in which Asherah has already been fused with other fertility goddesses. The goddess was customarily worshiped in association with sacred trees or poles that were symbolic of life and fertility. For details see J.C. deMoor, TDOT, 1:438–44, and the helpful remarks of A. Lemaire, "Who or What was Yahweh's Asherah?" *Biblical Archaeology Review* 10 (1984): 42–51.

17 Tirzah, now rather confidently identified with Tell el-Farʿah in the northern portion of Mount Ephraim on the strategic road from Shechem to Bethshan, was noted for its great beauty (S of Songs 6:4). The capital of the northern kingdom was soon to be shifted from Shechem to Tirzah, remaining there through the second dynasty. The events of the short-lived reign of Zimri took place in Tirzah (16:15–20). After reigning there six years, Omri, the founder of the third dynasty, moved the capital to Samaria (16:23–24), which was to remain the northern capital until its fall in 722 B.C.

19–20 For the "book of the annals of the kings of Israel," see the Introduction, p. 4.

---

3. The reign of Rehoboam in the southern kingdom

14:21–31

> ²¹Rehoboam son of Solomon was king in Judah. He was forty-one years old when he became king, and he reigned seventeen years in Jerusalem, the city the LORD had chosen out of all the tribes of Israel in which to put his Name. His mother's name was Naamah; she was an Ammonite.
>
> ²²Judah did evil in the eyes of the LORD. By the sins they committed they stirred up his jealous anger more than their fathers had done. ²³They also set up for themselves high places, sacred stones and Asherah poles on every high hill and under every spreading tree. ²⁴There were even male shrine prostitutes in the land; the people engaged in all the detestable practices of the nations the LORD had driven out before the Israelites.
>
> ²⁵In the fifth year of King Rehoboam, Shishak king of Egypt attacked Jerusalem. ²⁶He carried off the treasures of the temple of the LORD and the treasures of the royal palace. He took everything, including all the gold shields Solomon had made. ²⁷So King Rehoboam made bronze shields to replace them and assigned these to the commanders of the guard on duty at the entrance to the royal palace. ²⁸Whenever the king went to the LORD's temple, the guards bore the shields, and afterward they returned them to the guardroom.
>
> ²⁹As for the other events of Rehoboam's reign, and all he did, are they not written in the book of the annals of the kings of Judah? ³⁰There was continual warfare between Rehoboam and Jeroboam. ³¹And Rehoboam rested with his fathers and was buried with them in the City of David. His mother's name was Naamah; she was an Ammonite. And Abijah his son succeeded him as king.

21–25 The notices of Rehoboam's reign in Judah begin with a spiritual evaluation (vv.21–22; cf. 2 Chron 12:14). Tragically Rehoboam's record was little better than Jeroboam's. He, too, allowed rival worship centers and pagan fertility practices to spread throughout the land (vv.23–24). While Rehoboam seems to have begun his reign well (cf. 2 Chron 11:5–17, 23), he soon abandoned the law of the Lord (2 Chron 12:1). As a result, in Rehoboam's fifth year (926 B.C.), God sent punishment in the form of an invasion by Shishak I, the Egyptian Pharaoh.

Shishak had an interesting history. Toward the end of Egypt's weak and divided Twenty-First Dynasty, mention is made of a Lybian who through marriage and favorable dealings with the high priest finally gained control of the government, founding the Twenty-Second Dynasty as Sheshonq I (biblical Shishak). Sheshonq was able to reunify the country and restore a certain amount of stability to the crown. Egypt could now once again look beyond her borders. Having renewed the old ties with Byblos and having regained economic supremacy in Nubia, Sheshonq saw an opportunity to deal with Palestine. Probably he had advised Jeroboam— whom he had harbored for many years awaiting the demise of Solomon—in his quest for the northern throne. So, perhaps through some border incident, pretext was found for a full invasion.

26–28 On the basis of the biblical account and the archaeological data from ancient Egypt, it is clear that Sheshonq swept through much of both Israel and Judah, taking heavy spoil (v.26). Sheshonq lists 150 cities he took in the campaign.

The Chronicler records that Jerusalem itself was severely looted; only the repentance of Rehoboam and his leaders at God's rebuke through Shemaiah, the prophet, saved the land and people from total destruction. Significant among the spoil treasures were Solomon's golden shields (v.26; see 10:16–17), kept in the Palace of the Forest of Lebanon (see 7:2). To replace the shields that were used at state ceremonial functions, Rehoboam had bronze shields made and entrusted them to the commander of his royal bodyguard who now stored them in the guardhouse (vv.27–28).

29–31 The chapter closes with the additional notice of strained relations between the northern and southern kingdoms throughout Rehoboam's reign (v.30). Since Rehoboam had complied with the divine prohibition against overt warfare (cf. 12:21–24), more than likely the reference is to a "cold war" or to occasional border skirmishes. Rehoboam was succeeded by his son Abijah (v.31).

Notes

21 Gray (*Kings*, pp. 341–42) suggests that the fact that Rehoboam's mother was an Ammonitess may have political implications, such as an early placating of Ammon by Solomon.

Because the name of the queen mother is regularly given with the assumption of the new king, some have suggested that a matriarchate may have existed in Judah, with inheritance counted through the female line (see Harrison, pp. 187–89). All that such notices show, however, is the identity of the reigning queen mother who held an official court status (15:13) and played a powerful role in Judean politics. She is often mentioned alongside the king (Jer 22:26; 29:2) and apparently even wore a crown emblematic of her position (Jer 13:18). The prominence of the position doubtless facilitated Athaliah's usurpation of the royal throne itself (2 Kings 11:1–3).

24 קָדֵשׁ (*qādēš*, "[male] shrine prostitute") is used at times in distinction to the feminine form (Deut 23:18). Shrine prostitutes appear among the lists of cultic personnel in ancient Ugarit. See W.F. Albright, *Archaeology and Religion of Israel* (Garden City: Doubleday, 1969), pp. 153–54. However Montgomery (p. 273) may be right in suggesting that both sexes may be intended (so NIV), the masculine singular being deliberately derogatory and portraying such individuals as little better than beasts. Cultic prostitution was symptomatic of Judah's basic spiritual harlotry that was to plague it throughout the years of its existence.

25 Sheshonq's ascendency and triumph were meteoric; Egypt's new-found star, however, fell as quickly as it rose. The Pharaoh died suddenly, and the kingdom was left in the hands of those of lesser ability. Egypt's hopes of greatness soon expired. See further Redford, pp. 10–16.

For a good discussion of Sheshonq's campaign in Palestine, see B. Mazar, "The Campaign of Pharaoh Shishak to Palestine," VetTest Supplements 4 (1957): 57–66; for Shishak himself, see Kitchen, *Third Intermediate Period,* pp. 85–88, 109–16, 287–302.

26 According to the LXX, the weapons David had dedicated as a result of his campaign against the Aramean Hadadezer (cf. 2 Sam 8:7) were all carried away. See the note on 2 Kings 11:10.

28 The term רָצִים (*rāṣîm,* "guards") refers to an ancient and well-known class of professional soldiers. The name means literally "runners" and was used of a class of royal escorts who ran before the king (2 Sam 15:1; 1 Kings 1:5; cf. Akkad. *rēdû,* "runner"; see the remarks of G.R. Driver and J.C. Miles, *The Babylonian Laws* [Oxford: Clarendon, 1960], 2:161). The term also designates the royal bodyguard that constantly protected the king and assisted him in crucial matters (1 Sam 22:17; 2 Kings 10:25). Here it appears that their duties also included keeping watch over the various portions of the palace and temple complex. On the use of prisoners of war as royal bodyguards, see I.J. Gelb, "Prisoners of War in Early Mesopotamia," JNES 32 (1973): 92ff.

31 The information that Rehoboam was buried with his fathers is omitted in 2 Chron 12:16, the Chronicler possibly viewing Rehoboam as unworthy of being mentioned alongside David and Solomon. He also makes no reference to Rehoboam's pagan mother.

אֲבִיָּם (*ᵃḇiyyām,* "Abijam") is read by the MT. At least ten MSS and the Hebrew edition of Kennicott and DeRossi read "Abijah" (cf. LXX, Αβιου, *Abiou*). Montgomery (p. 273) suggests that Abijam was a popular designation of the king, the *am* being hypocoristic as in the case of the name found at Tell Ta'annak—Aḥiyami; see also C. Gordon, UT, p. 349. Doubtless the king's name was Abijah ("Yahweh is my father"), as befitting a king of the southern kingdom.

---

4. The reign of Abijah in the southern kingdom

15:1–8

> [1]In the eighteenth year of the reign of Jeroboam son of Nebat, Abijah became king of Judah, [2]and he reigned in Jerusalem three years. His mother's name was Maacah daughter of Abishalom.
>
> [3]He committed all the sins his father had done before him; his heart was not fully devoted to the LORD his God, as the heart of David his forefather had been. [4]Nevertheless, for David's sake the LORD his God gave him a lamp in Jerusalem by raising up a son to succeed him and by making Jerusalem strong. [5]For David had done what was right in the eyes of the LORD and had not failed to keep any of the LORD's commands all the days of his life—except in the case of Uriah the Hittite.
>
> [6]There was war between Rehoboam and Jeroboam throughout ₊Abijah's₎ lifetime. [7]As for the other events of Abijah's reign, and all he did, are they not written in the book of the annals of the kings of Judah? There was war between Abijah and Jeroboam. [8]And Abijah rested with his fathers and was buried in the City of David. And Asa his son succeeded him as king.

1–5 Attention is focused on the short-lived reign of Abijah (v.1) in but few details: (1) the continuing prominence of the dowager queen Maacah (v.2), (2) the continuance of apostasy in the southern kingdom (v.3), and (3) the continuing war with the north (v.6).

Maacah (v.2) was apparently the daughter of Uriel of Gibeah (2 Chron 13:2) and Tamar (2 Sam 14:27), hence the granddaughter of Absalom, David's rebellious son. The favorite of Rehoboam's eighteen wives, she was the mother of Abijah and the grandmother of Asa (vv.9–10). Her continued prominence testifies to her strong personality.

Rehoboam's spiritual example was reflected in his son (v.4). How careful the believer must be to leave a spiritual legacy to his family (1 Chron 22:7–19; 2 Chron 1:8–10; 1 Cor 4:15–16; 11:1; Phil 4:8–9)! Abijah's imitation of his father's religion (v.3) stands in bold contrast to that of his forefather David (v.5), with whom God had entered into covenant relationship (2 Sam 7:4–17). Although Abijah was a poor representative of the house of David (cf. 11:4), yet he who remains faithful (2 Tim 2:13) would honor the man after his own heart in preserving his heir (cf. 1 Sam 13:14; Ps 89:19–29; Acts 13:22). Further God was to take a hand in turning the religious situation in Judah around—he would raise up a godly son to the throne of Judah.

6–8 Abijah inherited his father's continued friction with Jeroboam and the northern kingdom, only now it took the form of open warfare between the two Hebrew states. Fortunately for Judah, Abijah's underlying faith could rise to the surface in times of crisis. Second Chronicles 13:3–22 (q.v.) relates one such instance. In a major battle between the two antagonists, Abijah and his few troops were delivered from certain defeat when the Lord intervened for them on behalf of Abijah's prayer.

Notes

2 "Three years" is the correct reading here, not the six years of the LXX[b1]. As Rehoboam was already forty-one years old at his ascension and reigned twenty-seven years, Abijah was probably himself of mature years when he ascended the throne. It is little wonder, then, that it could be said of him that he had known nothing but war in his lifetime (v.6).

3 שָׁלֵם (šālēm, "fully devoted") means literally "be at peace with."
Here David is called אָבִיו (ʾābîw, "his father"), the term, as with other biblical terms for relationship (e.g., "son"), being used imprecisely. NIV is correct in translating "his forefather."

4 נִיר (nîr, "lamp") is used figuratively in the OT of man's posterity. A man's life and work were not extinguished if he had progeny (11:36 [see note in loc.]; 2 Kings 8:19; 2 Chron 21:7).
On the significance of "covenant" in the OT, see R. Clements, *Genesis 15 and Its Meaning for Israelite Tradition* (Naperville: Allenson, n.d.), pp. 79–88; W.J. Beecher, *The Prophets and the Promise* (Grand Rapids: Baker, 1975); John Bright, *Covenant and Promise* (Philadelphia: Westminster, 1976); and W.J. Kaiser, Jr., "The Blessing of David: The Charter for Humanity," *The Law and the Prophets*, ed. J.H. Skilton (Philadelphia: Presbyterian and Reformed, 1974), pp. 298–318.

5. The reign of Asa in the southern kingdom

15:9–24

⁹In the twentieth year of Jeroboam king of Israel, Asa became king of Judah, ¹⁰and he reigned in Jerusalem forty-one years. His grandmother's name was Maacah daughter of Abishalom.

¹¹Asa did what was right in the eyes of the LORD, as his father David had done. ¹²He expelled the male shrine prostitutes from the land and got rid of all the idols his fathers had made. ¹³He even deposed his grandmother Maacah from her position as queen mother, because she had made a repulsive Asherah pole. Asa cut the pole down and burned it in the Kidron Valley. ¹⁴Although he did not remove the high places, Asa's heart was fully committed to the LORD all his life. ¹⁵He brought into the temple of the LORD the silver and gold and the articles that he and his father had dedicated.

¹⁶There was war between Asa and Baasha king of Israel throughout their reigns. ¹⁷Baasha king of Israel went up against Judah and fortified Ramah to prevent anyone from leaving or entering the territory of Asa king of Judah.

¹⁸Asa then took all the silver and gold that was left in the treasuries of the LORD's temple and of his own palace. He entrusted it to his officials and sent them to Ben-Hadad son of Tabrimmon, the son of Hezion, the king of Aram, who was ruling in Damascus. ¹⁹"Let there be a treaty between me and you," he said, "as there was between my father and your father. See, I am sending you a gift of silver and gold. Now break your treaty with Baasha king of Israel so he will withdraw from me."

²⁰Ben-Hadad agreed with King Asa and sent the commanders of his forces against the towns of Israel. He conquered Ijon, Dan, Abel Beth Maacah and all Kinnereth in addition to Naphtali. ²¹When Baasha heard this, he stopped building Ramah and withdrew to Tirzah. ²²Then King Asa issued an order to all Judah—no one was exempt—and they carried away from Ramah the stones and timber Baasha had been using there. With them King Asa built up Geba in Benjamin, and also Mizpah.

²³As for all the other events of Asa's reign, all his achievements, all he did and the cities he built, are they not written in the book of the annals of the kings of Judah? In his old age, however, his feet became diseased. ²⁴Then Asa rested with his fathers and was buried with them in the city of his father David. And Jehoshaphat his son succeeded him as king.

9–15 When Asa assumed the kingly office in the twentieth year of Jeroboam's reign (910 B.C.), the influence of Maacah, his grandmother and the dowager queen, was still pronounced (vv.9–10). Although Asa's long forty-one year reign was to be eventful, during his first ten years he enjoyed a time of peace (cf. 2 Chron 14:1), perhaps the benefit of Abijah's victory over the north.

Asa used these ten years wisely, expunging idolatry and enforcing the observance of true religion, securing the defenses of the country and strengthening the armed forces (vv.11–13; 2 Chron 14:2–8). In all this "he did what was right in the eyes of the LORD" (v.11). His piety and wise preparations would put the country in good stead, for shortly after this period he faced and defeated an invasion led by Zerah, the Ethiopian (2 Chron 14:9–15), probably a commander of the Egyptian Pharaoh Osorkon I (914–874 B.C.).

In the third month of the fifteenth year of his reign, Asa, encouraged by the prophet Azariah (2 Chron 15:1–7), convened an assembly in which all true Israelites were invited to renew the covenant with the Lord. The meeting was attended with great praise and joy (2 Chron 15:9–15). At the same time Asa instituted stringent spiritual reforms, aimed at removing the remaining vestiges of idolatry and fertility rites (2 Chron 15:8). Even the politically and religiously powerful Maacah was able to be disposed of once and for all (v. 13). No doubt she had used the outbreak of the war as an occasion to reintroduce the public worship of Asherah (v. 13; cf. 2 Chron 15:16). While Asa stopped short of a total cleansing of the land, he was a god-fearing man who led the way for his people in public dedication to God (vv. 14–15; cf. 2 Chron 15:17–18).

16–17 Meanwhile in the northern kingdom Jeroboam had died and was succeeded by Nadab, his son (vv. 25–32). Nadab reigned only two years before he was assassinated by Baasha, who instituted the short-lived second Israelite dynasty. Baasha's ascension year was the third year of Asa's reign. Throughout Asa's early years, Baasha had been occupied with securing the throne and other internal affairs. However he had probably looked on disapprovingly at the turn of events in Judah. But with a victorious and strengthened Judah whose renewed vitality had succeeded even in drawing away many of his citizens, Baasha could no longer remain inactive.

Moving swiftly into Judah, Baasha seized Ramah, only four miles north of Jerusalem itself (v. 17). This action not only stopped the further drawing away of Baasha's subjects, but also cut off the main road north out of Jerusalem, thus shutting down all communications between Judah and Israel. This gave Baasha control of the trade routes.

18–19 Asa's reaction was singularly strange. Despite God's great deliverance from Zerah and Asa's own religious reforms, Asa turned suddenly to human devices to deal with the new crisis. Perhaps his own forces had suffered heavy losses in the past war. Perhaps the many years of success had encouraged him to rely on himself in political affairs while trusting God for spiritual matters. Asa did not even bother to pose the problem to God as Rehoboam had done (cf. 12:22–24). Too often a dichotomy exists between the believer's spiritual life and his daily duties. Stripping the temple and palace of treasures, Asa sent a delegation to the Aramean king Ben-Hadad, proposing that he break his treaty with the northern kingdom and put military pressure on it so that the Israelite incursion into Judah would be recalled.

A long-standing hostility had existed between the Arameans and the Hebrews. David had subdued the chief Aramean tribes, occupying the main area of Syria itself (cf. 2 Sam 8:3–12; 1 Chron 18:3–11); and although these regions largely remained subservient to Solomon, already in Solomon's day Rezon ben Eliada had managed to establish himself in Damascus, being "Israel's adversary as long as Solomon lived" (11:23–25).

Apparently a new dynasty had gained control in Damascus and, with the division of the united monarchy, had supported the northern kingdom. Ben-Hadad, who first appears here in history and is to play a major role in the affairs of the Near East in subsequent years, had a treaty alliance with Baasha. But seeing Asa's treasure and sensing the gain that was to be had from a new league with Judah and from a military venture against Israel, Ben-Hadad was only too happy to help (v. 19). He may have followed Asa's suggestion of appealing to a prior treaty between Damascus and Jerusalem as a pretext for coming to Judah's aid against Baasha.

20–22 Moving swiftly Ben-Hadad ravaged Baasha's northern sector, not only gaining for himself access to the international caravan routes that led from Egypt through Phoenicia and on to Damascus, but giving Asa the desired relief in Judah (v.20). For in order to meet the new emergency on his northern flank, Baasha was forced to abandon his operations at Ramah (v.21).

Asa, for his part, quickly mobilized Judah's forces and retook Ramah, dismantling Baasha's fortifications and using the building material to fortify Mizpah and Geba (v.22), thus providing strongholds for his reestablished control in Benjamin.

Needless to say Asa's actions did not solve the relations with the north, but they did give him respite from further invasions throughout the rest of his reign. Although we hear of no more wars in Asa's day, it was a time of spiritual defeat. His self-assertedness took its toll. The Chronicler reports that when God sent his prophet Hanani to rebuke him for having forsaken God to trust in man in the war, Asa both threw that seer into prison and dealt harshly with any who dissented with state policy. Thus begins a long and checkered history of the persecution of God's prophets (2 Chron. 16:7–10; cf. 2 Kings 17:13–14).

23–24 The parting notices concerning Asa deal with the loathsome disease in his feet (v.23) that served only to harden his heart. For his funerary observance Asa had the air filled with sweet spices (2 Chron 16:12–14); but no amount of manmade perfume can hide the noxious stench of the life of a believer alienated from God! How far he had fallen and from what great spiritual heights! Asa's life remains as an exemplary admonition to the believer to abide humbly in Christ, lest his life become totally unproductive for God (cf. John 15:5–6; 1 Cor 9:27).

Notes

10 Since the MT calls Maacah Asa's mother, some have suggested that Abijah and Asa were brothers. Others have suggested that Maacah was the name of two different women, one of whom bore Abijah and the other, Asa. The NIV takes the simpler view that the mother of Abijah and Asa's grandmother were one and the same person. This seems the obvious intent of the passage.

Other notable dowagers include the biblical queen Athaliah (2 Kings 11), the Egyptian queen Hatshepsut (1504–1483 B.C.), and the Assyrian queen Sammuramat (811–808 B.C.), perhaps the original queen behind the legendary Greek Semiramis. On the importance and position of the dowager, see the comments of Gray, *Kings*, p. 106, and S.W. Baur, "Queen Mother," ISBE, 4:25:13–14.

12 The author of Kings has telescoped Asa's early and later religious reforms into one summary account. For details as to the chronology of events of Asa's reign, see Thiele, pp. 59–62; Kitchen, *Third Intermediate Period*, p. 309; Crockett, pp. 210–16.

It has been suggested that etymologically גִּלֻּלִים (*gillulîm*, "idols") means "forms in the round," whether sculptured or an object in the natural world. In the OT it is used synonymously with שִׁקּוּצִים (*šiqqûṣîm*, "detested thing," "idol"). Some have suggested a relationship to גֵּל (*gēl*, "dung pellet"), hence "filthy thing," "idol." Still others suggest a relationship to the Arabic *galîl* ("venerated object"). At any rate, throughout the OT it is always used disdainfully (e.g., Lev 26:30).

13 מִפְלֶצֶת (*mipleṣet*, "horrible, repulsive thing") is from the verb פָּלַץ (*pālaṣ*, "shudder," used of an earthquake in Job 9:6). The emphasis is on the terrible shock the detestable Asherah worship ought to have produced in the heart of the believer.

The Kidron Valley, the deep depression east of Jerusalem between the temple heights and the Mount of Olives, became from Asa's time onward the place where reformer kings destroyed all idolatrous cult objects (cf. 2 Kings 23:4–15; 2 Chron 29:16; 30:14).

15 The dedicated articles may have included material from the local shrines outside Jerusalem, spoils from the war with Zerah, or even Rehoboam's bronze shields made to replace the gold shields taken by Sheshonq.

17 Ramah is to be identified with the present-day Arab village of Ar-ram, five and one-half miles north of Jerusalem. It lay on the main north-south commercial artery and was of strategic military importance since it controlled access to the foothills of Ephraim and the Mediterranean coast.

19 Was Asa's referral to an existing treaty between Judah and Damascus a fact or a manufactured wish? Gray (*Kings*, p. 352) opts for the former idea and suggests that this possibly explains why Abijah was so successful against Jeroboam. Snaith (pp. 135f.) decides for the latter possibility so that Asa was suggesting a renewal of an old covenant that had perhaps been allowed to lapse. The simplest solution seems to be that Asa suggested that a treaty had tacitly existed since the days of the united monarchy. The phrase "between my father and your father" need indicate nothing more than a general reference to existing relations between these Aramean and Jewish heads of state. Asa appears to be finding legal grounds for Ben-Hadad to justify his violation of the Aramean treaty with Israel.

23 Various suggestions have been made as to the nature of Asa's diseased feet. The Talmud decides for gout, and Montgomery (p. 278) for dropsy. Snaith (p. 136) suggests that "feet" is a euphemism for the reproductive organ; hence Asa had venereal disease.

---

6. *The reign of Nadab in the northern kingdom*

15:25–31

> 25Nadab son of Jeroboam became king of Israel in the second year of Asa king of Judah, and he reigned over Israel two years. 26He did evil in the eyes of the LORD, walking in the ways of his father and in his sin, which he had caused Israel to commit.
>
> 27Baasha son of Ahijah of the house of Issachar plotted against him, and he struck him down at Gibbethon, a Philistine town, while Nadab and all Israel were besieging it. 28Baasha killed Nadab in the third year of Asa king of Judah and succeeded him as king.
>
> 29As soon as he began to reign, he killed Jeroboam's whole family. He did not leave Jeroboam anyone that breathed, but destroyed them all, according to the word of the LORD given through his servant Ahijah the Shilonite— 30because of the sins Jeroboam had committed and had caused Israel to commit, and because he provoked the LORD, the God of Israel, to anger.
>
> 31As for the other events of Nadab's reign, and all he did, are they not written in the book of the annals of the kings of Israel?

25–31 Jeroboam's son Nadab succeeded him, reigning in Tirzah (v.25). In his second year Nadab attempted to capture the important Philistine city of Gibbethon (cf. 16:15–17). However in the midst of the siege he was assassinated by Baasha (probably one of his military officers), who seized the throne (vv.27–28). Baasha immediately liquidated all the royal house (v.29), thus confirming Ahijah's prediction that God would judge the sins of the house of Jeroboam (v.30; cf. 14:9–16).

7. The second dynasty in Israel (15:32–16:14)

a. Baasha

15:32–16:7

> [32]There was war between Asa and Baasha king of Israel throughout their reigns.
> [33]In the third year of Asa king of Judah, Baasha son of Ahijah became king of all Israel in Tirzah, and he reigned twenty-four years. [34]He did evil in the eyes of the LORD, walking in the ways of Jeroboam and in his sin, which he had caused Israel to commit.
> [16:1]Then the word of the LORD came to Jehu son of Hanani against Baasha: [2]"I lifted you up from the dust and made you leader of my people Israel, but you walked in the ways of Jeroboam and caused my people Israel to sin and to provoke me to anger by their sins. [3]So I am about to consume Baasha and his house, and I will make your house like that of Jeroboam son of Nebat. [4]Dogs will eat those belonging to Baasha who die in the city, and the birds of the air will feed on those who die in the country."
> [5]As for the other events of Baasha's reign, what he did and his achievements, are they not written in the book of the annals of the kings of Israel? [6]Baasha rested with his fathers and was buried in Tirzah. And Elah his son succeeded him as king.
> [7]Moreover, the word of the LORD came through the prophet Jehu son of Hanani to Baasha and his house, because of all the evil he had done in the eyes of the LORD, provoking him to anger by the things he did, and becoming like the house of Jeroboam—and also because he destroyed it.

32–34 Political change did not signal a change in spiritual outlook. The founder of the second dynasty proved to be as wicked as Jeroboam and Nadab before him. Baasha compounded his murder of Nadab and the remainder of the first dynasty by walking in the spiritual harlotry that Jeroboam had introduced.

16:1–4 Accordingly God sent Jehu the prophet to reprimand Baasha and announce his demise. Jehu told him that although God had exalted Baasha to be king (though not sanctioning Baasha's means of getting there), hoping for a change in the spiritual climate of Israel, Baasha had sought only his own ends and had perpetuated the persistent sins of his predecessors (v.2). Therefore he and his house would fall like that of Jeroboam, and beasts and birds of prey would feed on their fallen bodies (vv.3–4).

5–7 Baasha had come from lowly origins. Except for his war with Asa (15:32), little is heard of him; and the scriptural account quickly passes on to Elah, his son (v.6). God's denunciation of Baasha adds further explanation to the subsequent condemnation of Asa for not leaving his war with Baasha in God's hands.

Notes

1 Jehu son of Hanani (cf. 2 Chron 20:34) is known also as the author of a history that was included in "the book of the kings of Israel" (see Introduction, p. 4). He was also to be

active in the reign of Jehoshaphat of Judah (cf. 2 Chron 19:2–3). For additional details on the reign of Baasha, see Josephus (Antiq. VIII, 298–308 [xii.3–4]).

2 The words "exalted from the dust" emphasize the lowly origin of Baasha.

For נָגִיד (*nāgîd,* "leader"), see the note on 14:7. God was still looking for a leader of strong spiritual conviction. Note also God's tender reminder that Israel was yet "my people." The term was used again and again by the prophets of the eighth century in delivering God's pleadings to an unrepentant Israel.

3 מַבְעִיר (*mabʿîr,* "consume") means literally "reduce to ashes." For the dogs see the note on 14:11.

7 Two problems have perplexed the expositors about the phrase "And also because he destroyed it." First, the antecedent of "it" and, second, the precise understanding of the compound Hebrew particle עַל אֲשֶׁר (*ʿal ʾašer,* "also because"). As for the former problem, most English translations render the Hebrew pronoun "it" and understand the antecedent to be "the house of Jeroboam." On the whole this is the simplest solution. The Hebrew particle is usually translated as in the NIV ("because"). Thus God condemned Baasha for becoming an imitator of Jeroboam's sinful house and that in spite of the very fact that Baasha had himself been raised up of God to put an end to Jeroboam and his line. Implicit in the statement is the condemnation of Baasha's murder of Jeroboam's line. It is one thing to displace a rival; it is quite another to murder his family! Although he had raised Baasha up in spite of his murderous intention, God had in no way condoned Baasha's deeds.

---

b. *Elah*

16:8–14

> [8]In the twenty-sixth year of Asa king of Judah, Elah son of Baasha became king of Israel, and he reigned in Tirzah two years.
>
> [9]Zimri, one of his officials, who had command of half his chariots, plotted against him. Elah was in Tirzah at the time, getting drunk in the home of Arza, the man in charge of the palace at Tirzah. [10]Zimri came in, struck him down and killed him in the twenty-seventh year of Asa king of Judah. Then he succeeded him as king.
>
> [11]As soon as he began to reign and was seated on the throne, he killed off Baasha's whole family. He did not spare a single male, whether relative or friend. [12]So Zimri destroyed the whole family of Baasha, in accordance with the word of the LORD spoken against Baasha through the prophet Jehu—[13]because of all the sins Baasha and his son Elah had committed and had caused Israel to commit, so that they provoked the LORD, the God of Israel, to anger by their worthless idols.
>
> [14]As for the other events of Elah's reign, and all he did, are they not written in the book of the annals of the kings of Israel?

8–14 As in the case of Jeroboam's son, so Baasha's son, Elah, reigned but two years (v.8), and was also assassinated. Like Nadab, Elah was interested in Gibbethon and had sent his army commander, Omri, to put it under siege. He himself remained behind in Tirzah. During a drinking bout at the house of Arza, Elah's official, Zimri, a military officer, killed him (vv.9–10). Zimri thereupon assumed the kingship, subsequently murdered all Elah's descendants, and finished the second dynasty, as Jehu had prophesied (vv.11–12). The Lord's judgment on the house of Baasha had come quickly (v.13).

Notes

8 For "the twenty-sixth year," 2 Chron 16:1 has "the thirty-sixth year," which is probably a copyist's error (see Gleason Archer, *Encyclopedia of Bible Difficulties* [Grand Rapids: Zondervan, 1982], pp. 225–26).

11 For מַשְׁתִּין (*maštîn*, "a single male"), see the note on 14:10.

The גֹּאֲלָיו (*gōʾălāyw*, lit., "his relatives") were those charged with restoring the dead man's property and the avenging of his death (cf. Josh 20:3; 2 Sam 14:11; see also TDOT, 2:350–52).

B. *The Era of the Third Dynasty (1 Kings 16:15–2 Kings 9:37)*

1. *Interregnum: Zimri and Tibni*

    16:15–22

    ¹⁵In the twenty-seventh year of Asa king of Judah, Zimri reigned in Tirzah seven days. The army was encamped near Gibbethon, a Philistine town. ¹⁶When the Israelites in the camp heard that Zimri had plotted against the king and murdered him, they proclaimed Omri, the commander of the army, king over Israel that very day there in the camp. ¹⁷Then Omri and all the Israelites with him withdrew from Gibbethon and laid siege to Tirzah. ¹⁸When Zimri saw that the city was taken, he went into the citadel of the royal palace and set the palace on fire around him. So he died, ¹⁹because of the sins he had committed, doing evil in the eyes of the LORD and walking in the ways of Jeroboam and in the sin he had committed and had caused Israel to commit.

    ²⁰As for the other events of Zimri's reign, and the rebellion he carried out, are they not written in the book of the annals of the kings of Israel?

    ²¹Then the people of Israel were split into two factions; half supported Tibni son of Ginath for king, and the other half supported Omri. ²²But Omri's followers proved stronger than those of Tibni son of Ginath. So Tibni died and Omri became king.

15–20 Zimri's fiery ambitions were to go up in flame. As soon as the encamped army at Gibbethon heard of the coup d'état, they proclaimed their commander, Omri, king and marched on Tirzah (vv. 15–17). Having retreated to the inner recesses of the palace citadel, Zimri set fire to it, burning himself to death (v. 18). The author notes that Zimri's spiritual condition had been no different than those leaders who had preceded him (v. 19).

21–22 In the wake of Zimri's unsuccessful rebellion, loyalties in Israel remained divided, half supporting Omri and half supporting a certain man named Tibni.

Notes

---

18 For Omri see the note on v.21

19 Notice again the divine sentence due to sin. While Zimri was an instrument of God's judgment, he was not God's choice as king.

21 Tibni, son of Binath, is otherwise unknown in the OT. The name itself may be paralleled in the Akkadian Tabni-Ea ("may Ea give a son") and the Phoenician Tabnit. The LXX and Josephus render his name Tabni. Ginath could indicate a place name. Gina is mentioned in the Amarna Tablets, possibly the OT En Gannim (Josh 19:21), modern Jenin on the southern edge of the Plain of Esdraelon. The LXX reports that Tibni was aided by his brother Joram, and Josephus (Antiq. VIII, 311 [xii.5]) says that Omri's followers killed Tibni.

Montgomery (p. 290) suggests that Omri's name is of Arabic origin (cf. Omar), being frequently attested in South Arabia. It seems possible that Omri may have been a foreigner who had risen to prominence in the military. The close relationship of the third dynasty with Phoenicia may point to his Canaanite extraction, while the choice of Jezreel may indicate Omri's affinity with the tribe of Issachar.

Although the Scriptures dispose of Omri's accomplishments in a few verses (see also Mic 6:16, which indicates that Omri enacted some statutes of lasting spiritual damage), secular history indicates that Omri was a man of international importance.

The Moabite Stone (ANET, pp. 320f.) relates that Omri had conquered the fertile and strategic Moabite Plains north of the Arnon River. His stature is further attested by the fact that the Assyrian kings uniformly designate Israel by the name *Bît Ḥumri(a)* ("House of Omri"). The fact that he married his son Ahab to Jezebel, the Phoenician princess, while possibly for economic benefits, had political overtones as well, geared to offset the rising power of Ben-Hadad of Damascus, whom Ahab was to face throughout his reign.

---

2. The reign of Omri in the northern kingdom

16:23-28

> [23] In the thirty-first year of Asa king of Judah, Omri became king of Israel, and he reigned twelve years, six of them in Tirzah. [24] He bought the hill of Samaria from Shemer for two talents of silver and built a city on the hill, calling it Samaria, after Shemer, the name of the former owner of the hill.
>
> [25] But Omri did evil in the eyes of the LORD and sinned more than all those before him. [26] He walked in all the ways of Jeroboam son of Nebat and in his sin, which he had caused Israel to commit, so that they provoked the LORD, the God of Israel, to anger by their worthless idols.
>
> [27] As for the other events of Omri's reign, what he did and the things he achieved, are they not written in the book of the annals of the kings of Israel? [28] Omri rested with his fathers and was buried in Samaria. And Ahab his son succeeded him as king.

23-24 After a four-year struggle (cf. v.15 with v.23), Omri succeeded in gaining control of all the northern kingdom (v.23). He immediately undertook the building of a new capital that would lie in neutral ground (as David had done in selecting Jerusalem) and would be militarily defensible (v.24). He selected a strategic and centrally located hill site overlooking the chief commercial routes of the Esdraelon Plain. There he built his new capital city and named it Samaria, after Shemer, its former owner.

25-28 Despite Omri's forward-looking vision for restoring Israel's strength and his many accomplishments, spiritually he was more destitute than all his predecessors (vv.25–26). Not only did he perpetuate the spiritual sins of Jeroboam, but his ties with Phoenicia were to unleash on Israel the common pagan social and religious practices known to the ancient world. Therefore the scriptural record concerning Omri is both brief and condemnatory.

3. The reign of Ahab in the northern kingdom (16:29–22:40)

a. The accession of Ahab

16:29–34

> ²⁹In the thirty-eighth year of Asa king of Judah, Ahab son of Omri became king of Israel, and he reigned in Samaria over Israel twenty-two years. ³⁰Ahab son of Omri did more evil in the eyes of the LORD than any of those before him. ³¹He not only considered it trivial to commit the sins of Jeroboam son of Nebat, but he also married Jezebel daughter of Ethbaal king of the Sidonians, and began to serve Baal and worship him. ³²He set up an altar for Baal in the temple of Baal that he built in Samaria. ³³Ahab also made an Asherah pole and did more to provoke the LORD, the God of Israel, to anger than did all the kings of Israel before him.
>
> ³⁴In Ahab's time, Hiel of Bethel rebuilt Jericho. He laid its foundations at the cost of his firstborn son Abiram, and he set up its gates at the cost of his youngest son Segub, in accordance with the word of the LORD spoken by Joshua son of Nun.

29–30 Ahab's twenty-two year reign (v.29) marked the depths of spiritual decline in Israel. No more notorious husband and wife team is known in all the sacred Scriptures (cf. 21:25–26). Ahab built on his father's foundation, not only in bringing Israel into the arena of international conflict, but causing it to serve and worship Baal (v.30).

31–32 Ahab was a man of complex character. The remainder of this chapter makes it clear that he was unconcerned with true, vital faith (cf. 21:20). Not only did he participate personally in the sins of Jeroboam, but having willingly married Jezebel, he followed her in the worship of Baal-Melqart, officially instituting and propogating Baal worship throughout his kingdom.

34 An example of his spiritual infidelity is seen as he granted to Hiel of Bethel the authority to rebuild Jericho as a fortified town, despite Joshua's long-standing curse. The undertaking was to cost Hiel the lives of his eldest and youngest sons, in accordance with Joshua's prophetic pronouncement (Josh 6:26).

The subsequent chapters of 1 Kings show that Ahab was selfish and sullen (20:43; 21:4–5), cruel (22:27), morally weak (21:1–16), and concerned with luxuries of this world (22:39). Though he could display real bravery (ch. 20; 22:1–39) and at times even heeded God's word (18:16–46; 20:13–17, 22, 28–30; 21:27–29; 22:30), nevertheless he was basically a compromiser as far as the will of God was concerned (20:31 –34, 42–43; 22:8, 18, 26–28). The divine estimation of his character stands as a tragic epitaph: "There was never a man like Ahab, who sold himself to do evil in the eyes of the LORD" (21:25; cf. 16:33; 21:20; see also the note on 2 Kings 10:18).

Notes

31 Although Montgomery (p. 291) disallows it, the name אִיזֶבֶל (*'izebel*, "Jezebel") is probably derived from the Semitic *'ayya* ("Where [is] 'zebūl, the prince"). Names with *'ayya* are common enough (cf. *'ayya abu*, "Job," i.e., "Where is the father?" see H.B. Huffmon, *Amorite Personal Names in the Mari Texts* [Baltimore: Johns Hopkins Press, 1965], pp. 102f., 161), and *Zebul* was a standard title for Baal at Ugarit. Indeed the separate parts of the name were actually recited in the cultic ceremony: "Where is Baal the Mighty, Where is the Prince, Lord of the Earth?" (Gordon, UT, p. 49). A relation to the old east Semitic deity Ayya (see J.J.M. Roberts, *The Earliest Semitic Pantheon* [Baltimore: Johns Hopkins Press, 1976], pp. 19–21) is unlikely. It is possible that the scribes saw in the name an obvious pun, since אִי (*'î*) can under certain conditions be understood as "no" (hence "no prince"), or Zebul can be read *Zibl* ("dung"; hence "Where is the dung?"). See further the note on 2 Kings 1:2.

Ethbaal, Jezebel's father, was not only king of the Sidonians but, according to Josephus (*Contra Apion*, I, 123 [18]), a priest of Astarte when he gained the throne by murdering the last of the descendants of Hiram I of Tyre. Ethbaal's dynasty endured for at least a century. Thus, as Josephus (Antiq., VIII, 317 [xiii.1]) reports, he was king of Tyre and Sidon. The fact that Ben-Hadad I erected a stele to Baal-Melqart may well indicate that a treaty existed between Phoenicia and Israel.

32 Ahab's altar in the temple in Samaria doubtless was patterned after its prototype in Tyre, which Hiram had built and in which he set a golden pillar (Jos. Antiq. VIII, 145 [v.iii]).

34 While it is true that Joshua appointed Jericho to the territory of Benjamin (Josh 18:12), and that there is evidence of habitation there subsequent to Joshua's curse and prior to Hiel's rebuilding activities (cf. Judg 3:13; 2 Sam 10:5), there is neither scriptural nor archaeological indication of any building of a permanently fortified place. Whether Hiel deliberately sacrificed his sons as foundation offerings (as the Targ. explains), a practice fairly well documented in the ancient Near East (see R.A. Macalister, *The Excavations of Gezer* [London: J. Murray, 1912], 2:428; but see Montgomery [pp. 287–88]), or whether his building activities were attended by the accidental deaths of his two sons, Joshua's predictive curse was completely fulfilled.

Ahab himself was possibly behind the building activities, considering Jericho important to his military problems with Moab (cf. 22:39; 2 Kings 1:1; 3:5 with the Moabite Stone, lines 6–9; ANET, p. 320).

---

b. *The prophetic ministry of Elijah (17:1–19:21)*

1) *Elijah's call*

17:1–6

> ¹Now Elijah the Tishbite, from Tishbe in Gilead, said to Ahab, "As the LORD, the God of Israel, lives, whom I serve, there will be neither dew nor rain in the next few years except at my word."
> ²Then the word of the LORD came to Elijah: ³"Leave here, turn eastward and hide in the Kerith Ravine, east of the Jordan. ⁴You will drink from the brook, and I have ordered the ravens to feed you there."
> ⁵So he did what the LORD had told him. He went to the Kerith Ravine, east of the Jordan, and stayed there. ⁶The ravens brought him bread and meat in the morning and bread and meat in the evening, and he drank from the brook.

1 In those dark times God raised up a light, the prophet Elijah. Reared in rugged Gilead, Elijah was a rugged individualist, a man of stern character and countenance, zealous for the Lord. Elijah sought Ahab and delivered the Lord's pronouncement. In contrast to those who were not gods, whose idols Ahab ignorantly worshiped, the living Lord, who was truly Israel's God, would withhold both dew and rain for the next several years.

Already the drought had lain on the land some six months (cf. Luke 4:25; James 5:17 with 1 Kings 18:1); now the reason for it all was to be revealed to Israel's apostate leadership. The message was clear: Israel had broken the pledge of its covenantal relationship with God (Deut 11:16–17; 28:23–24; cf. Lev 26:19; 1 Kings 8:35). Therefore God was demonstrating his concern for both his people's infidelity and their folly in trusting in false fertility gods like Baal. No rain! There would not even be dew until God's authentic messenger would give the word! Unknown to Ahab, Elijah had agonized over the sin of his people and had prayed to the Lord for corrective measures to be levied on his people. Accordingly Elijah was God's logical choice.

2–6 To impress the message and its deep spiritual implications further on Ahab and all Israel, God sent Elijah into seclusion. Not only would Ahab's frantic search for the prophet be thwarted, but Elijah's very absence would be living testimony of a divine displeasure (cf. Ps 74:1, 9). Moreover Elijah himself had much to learn, and the time of solitude would furnish needed moments of divine instruction.

Obeying God's directions implicitly, Elijah walked the fifteen miles from Jezreel eastward to the Jordan River (v.5). There in Kerith, one of the Jordan's many narrow gorges, Elijah took up his residence. Alone and relying solely on divine provision, Elijah was nourished by the available water of Kerith and by ravens sent from God (v.6).

Notes

---

1 The name Elijah means "Yah is my God." The designation "the Tishbite" is uncertain. The NIV, following the RSV (cf. LXX), interprets it as a place name in Gilead. Since Byzantine times Listib, eight miles north of the Jabbok River, in the area of the shore of Mar Ilyas, has been suggested as Elijah's town. A Thisbe/Tisbeh in Naphtali is known from the apocryphal story of Tobit. This latter identification seems more likely since the MT (followed by the Vul.) literally reads that Elijah was merely one of the "settlers" in Gilead. Thus Elijah had probably come from Tisbeh in Naphtali and had taken up residence among the settlers in Gilead. Dennison (pp. 124–26) suggests plausibly that Elijah's family had been displaced to Gilead during the Aramean Wars of Baasha's time.

The phrase "neither dew nor rain" is reminiscent of David's lament over Saul and Jonathan (2 Sam 1:21). The importance of these words to the reputation of Baal can be seen in Danel's lament over Aqhat in the Ugaritic literature (see ANET, p. 153).

By "rain" was meant the regular early and latter rain of October/November and March/April. Their loss would be a mark of God's disfavor (see EBC, 2:253–54). The dew (often falling as heavy as drizzle in some regions of Palestine) was also a sign of God's favor to his covenant people (Deut 33:28; Prov 19:12). However it could be withdrawn from a thankless and apostate people (Hos 14:5; Hag 1:10). How good and pleasant it is when a grateful and obedient people willingly serve God in oneness of heart. Such service becomes as refreshing to God as the dew (Pss 110:3; 133:1, 3).

4 Various suggestions repoint the MT's עֹרְבִים (*'ōrᵉḇîm,* "ravens") in some other way so as to yield something like "merchants" or "Arabs"; all are needless concessions to antisupernaturalism. God's miracles do not need to be buttressed with rationalistic façade.

---

2) *Elijah and the widow at Zarephath*

17:7–24

> [7]Some time later the brook dried up because there had been no rain in the land. [8]Then the word of the Lord came to him: [9]"Go at once to Zarephath of Sidon and stay there. I have commanded a widow in that place to supply you with food."
> [10]So he went to Zarephath. When he came to the town gate, a widow was there gathering sticks. He called to her and asked, "Would you bring me a little water in a jar so I may have a drink?" [11]As she was going to get it, he called, "And bring me, please, a piece of bread."
> [12]"As surely as the Lord your God lives," she replied, "I don't have any bread—only a handful of flour in a jar and a little oil in a jug. I am gathering a few sticks to take home and make a meal for myself and my son, that we may eat it—and die."
> [13]Elijah said to her, "Don't be afraid. Go home and do as you have said. But first make a small cake of bread for me from what you have and bring it to me, and then make something for yourself and your son. [14]For this is what the Lord, the God of Israel, says: 'The jar of flour will not be used up and the jug of oil will not run dry until the day the Lord gives rain on the land.'"
> [15]She went away and did as Elijah had told her. So there was food every day for Elijah and for the woman and her family. [16]For the jar of flour was not used up and the jug of oil did not run dry, in keeping with the word of the Lord spoken by Elijah.
> [17]Some time later the son of the woman who owned the house became ill. He grew worse and worse, and finally stopped breathing. [18]She said to Elijah, "What do you have against me, man of God? Did you come to remind me of my sin and kill my son?"
> [19]"Give me your son," Elijah replied. He took him from her arms, carried him to the upper room where he was staying, and laid him on his bed. [20]Then he cried out to the Lord, "O Lord my God, have you brought tragedy also upon this widow I am staying with, by causing her son to die?" [21]Then he stretched himself out on the boy three times and cried to the Lord, "O Lord my God, let this boy's life return to him!"
> [22]The Lord heard Elijah's cry, and the boy's life returned to him, and he lived. [23]Elijah picked up the child and carried him down from the room into the house. He gave him to his mother and said, "Look, your son is alive!"
> [24]Then the woman said to Elijah, "Now I know that you are a man of God and that the word of the Lord from your mouth is the truth."

7–16 When the heavy rains of late autumn and early winter, which were needed to prepare the earth for cultivation, failed to materialize (v.7), God set the second stage of caring for his prophet into operation (v.8). He sent him to a certain widow of Zarephath in Phoenician Sidon, Jezebel's very own homeland (v.9). On arriving there, Elijah was led to the widow whom God had mentioned (v.10). The prophet put a severe test before her (vv.11–14). If she would first bake a small loaf for Elijah before seeing to her family's needs, God would honor her faith with a supply of flour and oil so long as the drought should last. Taking the prophet at his word, she obeyed; and all came to pass even as he had promised (vv.15–16).

The incident must have served not only as a source of great comfort for the simple, godly non-Jewish woman (cf. Deut 10:18–19), but also as a strengthening to Elijah's faith in God's providence (cf. Ps 37:3–4; Isa 41:10). The episode also stands impressed in the pages of history as a lasting memorial to the availability of God's full provision to all who believe, whether Jew or Gentile (Matt 10:41–42; Luke 4:25 –26).

17–24 With the passing of time, the widow's little lad who had been thus rescued from death through Elijah's miracle fell fatally ill (v.17). Gently taking the lad from his mother's arms, the prophet carried him up to his own quarters (v.19). Elijah was puzzled as to the Lord's purpose in all this. Pleading with the Lord for the lad's life, he followed prayer with active faith, stretching himself out on the boy three times (vv.20–21). Perhaps the widow had already experienced some hope in giving the body of the boy to the prophet. Elijah, too, was confident that God would yet do another miracle. Their expectation was rewarded. Life returned to the lad, and Elijah returned him to the widow's arms (vv.22–23). God's purpose was now evident. Her sin was not at issue (cf. John 9:3), but the testing had come in order that her newly found faith might be brought to settled maturity. Yahweh ("the LORD") was not only the God of the Jews (v.24) but of all those who believe (cf. Rom 3:29); he was not only the God of the living but the God of resurrection (cf. Luke 20:38; John 11:25–26).

Notes

9 Zarephath (cf. Akkad. *ṣarpitu*, Egyp. *ḏarpata*, Gr. *sarepta*) is modern Ras Ṣarafand, seven miles south of Sidon. The widow's position was most precarious. Although the institution of Levirate marriage (cf. Deut 25:5–10) offered some hope for the widow without a son, widows such as this one were largely dependent on charity. Many, such as this widow, were very poor. For Elijah to seem to make himself dependent on such a one would provoke a dramatic test of faith in God's provision. See R. Patterson, "The Widow, the Orphan and the Poor," BS 130 (1973): 223–34.

12 מָעוֹג (*mā῾ôg*, "cake," "bread") is usually derived from the Arabic *῾a῾ waju* ("curved," hence "round cake/bread"). It differs from the more usual word עֻגָּה (*῾uggāh*, "cake of [bread]") found in v.13. Note that the denominative verb עוּג (*῾ûg*, "bake [a cake]") was used of baking on stones (cf. 19:6) heated with dry dung rather than charcoal for fuel (cf. Ezek 4:12).

15–16 The miracle had continued application as Elijah stayed on with the widow, the prophet lodging in the separate quarters on the roof (v.19). The jar of flour did not come to an end, nor did she lack oil. There is no indication of a massive supply, simply that the ingredients were always on hand as they were needed. Each use of the flour and oil would require faith that God would meet daily need (cf. Matt 6:11). Thus both Elijah and the widow learned to put their continued faith and trust in the Provider rather than in the provision.

18 For the expression מַה־לִּי וָלָךְ (*mah-llî wālāk*, "What do you have against me?"), see the note on 2 Kings 3:13 (cf. Judg 11:12; 2 Sam 16:10; John 2:4). The woman felt that some forgotten sin on her part occasioned her son's death. She believed that such sin could not

go unrequited in the presence of a man in whom the Spirit of God abode (cf. Mark 1:24; Luke 5:8).

19 עֲלִיָּה (*ʿăliyyāh*, "upper room") refers to a temporary shelter or room on the roof, accessible from outside the house. Such structures are common in the Near East. This arrangement would allow the widow not only her needed privacy but would safeguard her reputation.

20 גַּם (*gam*, "also") indicates that Elijah wondered whether the death of the lad and the widow's previous plight were not divinely caused. Perhaps the Lord's further purpose might be to restore the child for the widow's good and God's glory.

21 Elijah's stretching himself on the lad's body three times while calling on God was to bring forth the full power of the thrice holy God (cf. Num 6:24–26; Isa 6:3). There is no certain indication that he used the same technique that Elisha would later use with the Shunammite's dead lad (cf. 2 Kings 4:34), though that is possible. (Paul was prepared to perform a similar symbolic act in the case of Eutychus [Acts 20:10; cf. Acts 9:36–43].)

24 Whether in the prophet's life or his mouth, the Lord's word was אֱמֶת (*ʾemet*, "truth"). The Syriac translation, followed by Jerome, that the lad was the prophet Jonah is totally unsatisfactory and historically impossible (cf. 2 Kings 14:25).

---

3) *Elijah and Obadiah*

18:1–15

¹After a long time, in the third year, the word of the LORD came to Elijah: "Go and present yourself to Ahab, and I will send rain on the land." ²So Elijah went to present himself to Ahab.

Now the famine was severe in Samaria, ³and Ahab had summoned Obadiah, who was in charge of his palace. (Obadiah was a devout believer in the LORD. ⁴While Jezebel was killing off the LORD's prophets, Obadiah had taken a hundred prophets and hidden them in two caves, fifty in each, and had supplied them with food and water.) ⁵Ahab had said to Obadiah, "Go through the land to all the springs and valleys. Maybe we can find some grass to keep the horses and mules alive so we will not have to kill any of our animals." ⁶So they divided the land they were to cover, Ahab going in one direction and Obadiah in another.

⁷As Obadiah was walking along, Elijah met him. Obadiah recognized him, bowed down to the ground, and said, "Is it really you, my lord Elijah?"

⁸"Yes," he replied. "Go tell your master, 'Elijah is here.' "

⁹"What have I done wrong," asked Obadiah, "that you are handing your servant over to Ahab to be put to death? ¹⁰As surely as the LORD your God lives, there is not a nation or kingdom where my master has not sent someone to look for you. And whenever a nation or kingdom claimed you were not there, he made them swear they could not find you. ¹¹But now you tell me to go to my master and say, 'Elijah is here.' ¹²I don't know where the Spirit of the LORD may carry you when I leave you. If I go and tell Ahab and he doesn't find you, he will kill me. Yet I your servant have worshiped the LORD since my youth. ¹³Haven't you heard, my lord, what I did while Jezebel was killing the prophets of the LORD? I hid a hundred of the LORD's prophets in two caves, fifty in each, and supplied them with food and water. ¹⁴And now you tell me to go to my master and say, 'Elijah is here.' He will kill me!"

¹⁵Elijah said, "As the LORD Almighty lives, whom I serve, I will surely present myself to Ahab today."

1–6 During the third year of Elijah's stay in Zarephath, God commanded Elijah to present himself before Ahab; he, not Baal, would send rain on the land (v.1).

By now the effects of the drought were severe. A heavy famine lay on the land (v.2). Ahab then summoned Obadiah (v.3), the royal chamberlain, and revealed his plans for a sweeping survey of the land to see whether there would be any fodder available at all for the animals (v.5). Presumably Ahab would take one route and Obadiah another (v.6).

7 Obadiah was a believer. He had even risked his life to hide and sustain one hundred of the Lord's prophets from Jezebel's purge. As Obadiah proceeded on the king's commission, Elijah met him. Though he could scarcely believe his eyes, Obadiah recognized Elijah and bowed respectfully to God's great prophet.

8–15 Elijah gave Obadiah a higher commission: he was to inform Ahab that Elijah was back and wanted an audience with the king (v.8). Obadiah protested that such a mission might cost him his life (v.9). Since Ahab had scrupulously sought Elijah everywhere, and since God might conceivably send Elijah off at a moment's notice, should Obadiah report to Ahab that he had found Elijah? For if he should come and not find the prophet, Ahab's wrath might be vented on the faithful Obadiah (vv.10 –14). After Elijah had assured him that he would surely remain to meet Ahab (v.15), Obadiah sought the king.

Notes

3 Obadiah ("servant of the Lord") has been identified in Jewish tradition with the minor prophet of the same name, but such an identification is unlikely. His office apparently involved being the king's personal representative and the bearer of the royal seal.

4 For this association of prophets that met and possibly lived together for study, prophesying and spiritual edification, and service, see 1 Sam 10:5; 2 Kings 2:3–7; 6:1–2. La Sor (NBC, p. 343) wisely cautions against ascribing too much prominence to the school of prophets as is sometimes done (cf., e.g., C.F. Whitley, *The Prophetic Achievement* [Leiden: Brill, 1963], pp. 3–4; R.B.Y. Scott, *The Relevance of the Prophets*, rev. ed. [New York: MacMillan, 1968], pp. 45–47). Certainly the OT says little about them. For further details see H. Freeman, *Introduction to the Old Testament Prophets* (Chicago: Moody, 1971), pp. 30–34. That Obadiah would have little difficulty in finding caves for the sons of the prophets can be seen in that over two thousand caves have been counted in the Mount Carmel area. NIV's "fifty in each" is probably the correct understanding as read in thirteen Hebrew MSS and as comparison with v.13 indicates. The LXX reads "by fifties" (cf. RSV, NASB). One "fifty" seems to have been omitted in the transmission of the MT here.

5 The importance of horses to Ahab is reflected in the records of Shalmaneser III of Assyria (859–824 B.C.), who mentioned that two thousand chariots were furnished by Ahab to the Syrian coalition that opposed him at Qarqar (see ANET, p. 279).

9–10 "Your God" lays stress on the close relation between Elijah and God; it need not imply that Obadiah was an unbeliever, apostate, or a compromising believer.

12 For the transporting of a prophet via the Spirit of the Lord, see Ezek 3:14; 8:3; 11:1, 24; 37:1; 43:5; Acts 8:39; Rev 17:3; 21:10. Should he not be able to produce Elijah, Obadiah's situation could be a desperate one, as attested by the use of the Hebrew construction waw plus the suffixed conjugation after a previous clause containing a prefixed conjugation (or nonindicative mood) verb to indicate likely or actual result.

15 The NIV rightly translates יהוה צְבָאוֹת (*yhwh ṣeḇāʾôt*, "Yahweh of hosts") as "LORD Almighty," discerning that the divine name cannot stand in the construct state. Accordingly Byzantine and Medieval writers preferred to translate the term by κύριος παντοκράτωρ

(*kyrios pantokratōr*, "Lord Almighty"), found frequently in the LXX (cf. 2 Cor 6:18). The form is probably an abbreviation of some longer term, such as "The Lord YHWH, the God of hosts" (Amos 3:13). Theologically it signifies that the Lord stands as a mighty ruler at the head of a vast retinue of heavenly powers that are ready to act at his command. See further G. Vos, *Biblical Theology* (Grand Rapids: Eerdmans, 1954), pp. 258–63, and C.K. Lehman, *Biblical Theology* (Scottdale: Herald, 1971), 1:222–30.

---

4) Elijah and the prophets of Baal

18:16-46

[16]So Obadiah went to meet Ahab and told him, and Ahab went to meet Elijah. [17]When he saw Elijah, he said to him, "Is that you, you troubler of Israel?"

[18]"I have not made trouble for Israel," Elijah replied. "But you and your father's family have. You have abandoned the LORD's commands and have followed the Baals. [19]Now summon the people from all over Israel to meet me on Mount Carmel. And bring the four hundred and fifty prophets of Baal and the four hundred prophets of Asherah, who eat at Jezebel's table."

[20]So Ahab sent word throughout all Israel and assembled the prophets on Mount Carmel. [21]Elijah went before the people and said, "How long will you waver between two opinions? If the LORD is God, follow him; but if Baal is God, follow him."

But the people said nothing.

[22]Then Elijah said to them, "I am the only one of the LORD's prophets left, but Baal has four hundred and fifty prophets. [23]Get two bulls for us. Let them choose one for themselves, and let them cut it into pieces and put it on the wood but not set fire to it. I will prepare the other bull and put it on the wood but not set fire to it. [24]Then you call on the name of your god, and I will call on the name of the LORD. The god who answers by fire—he is God."

Then all the people said, "What you say is good."

[25]Elijah said to the prophets of Baal, "Choose one of the bulls and prepare it first, since there are so many of you. Call on the name of your god, but do not light the fire." [26]So they took the bull given them and prepared it.

Then they called on the name of Baal from morning till noon. "O Baal, answer us!" they shouted. But there was no response; no one answered. And they danced around the altar they had made.

[27]At noon Elijah began to taunt them. "Shout louder!" he said. "Surely he is a god! Perhaps he is deep in thought, or busy, or traveling. Maybe he is sleeping and must be awakened." [28]So they shouted louder and slashed themselves with swords and spears, as was their custom, until their blood flowed. [29]Midday passed, and they continued their frantic prophesying until the time for the evening sacrifice. But there was no response, no one answered, no one paid attention.

[30]Then Elijah said to all the people, "Come here to me." They came to him, and he repaired the altar of the LORD, which was in ruins. [31]Elijah took twelve stones, one for each of the tribes descended from Jacob, to whom the word of the LORD had come, saying, "Your name shall be Israel." [32]With the stones he built an altar in the name of the LORD, and he dug a trench around it large enough to hold two seahs of seed. [33]He arranged the wood, cut the bull into pieces and laid it on the wood. Then he said to them, "Fill four large jars with water and pour it on the offering and on the wood."

[34]"Do it again," he said, and they did it again.

"Do it a third time," he ordered, and they did it the third time. [35]The water ran down around the altar and even filled the trench.

[36]At the time of sacrifice, the prophet Elijah stepped forward and prayed: "O LORD, God of Abraham, Isaac and Israel, let it be known today that you are God in Israel and that I am your servant and have done all these things at your com-

³⁷Answer me, O Lᴏʀᴅ, answer me, so these people will know that you, O Lᴏʀᴅ, are God, and that you are turning their hearts back again."

³⁸Then the fire of the Lᴏʀᴅ fell and burned up the sacrifice, the wood, the stones and the soil, and also licked up the water in the trench.

³⁹When all the people saw this, they fell prostrate and cried, "The Lᴏʀᴅ—he is God! The Lᴏʀᴅ—he is God!"

⁴⁰Then Elijah commanded them, "Seize the prophets of Baal. Don't let anyone get away!" They seized them, and Elijah had them brought down to the Kishon Valley and slaughtered there.

⁴¹And Elijah said to Ahab, "Go, eat and drink, for there is the sound of a heavy rain." ⁴²So Ahab went off to eat and drink, but Elijah climbed to the top of Carmel, bent down to the ground and put his face between his knees.

⁴³"Go and look toward the sea," he told his servant. And he went up and looked.

"There is nothing there," he said.

Seven times Elijah said, "Go back."

⁴⁴The seventh time the servant reported, "A cloud as small as a man's hand is rising from the sea."

So Elijah said, "Go and tell Ahab, 'Hitch up your chariot and go down before the rain stops you.' "

⁴⁵Meanwhile, the sky grew black with clouds, the wind rose, a heavy rain came on and Ahab rode off to Jezreel. ⁴⁶The power of the Lᴏʀᴅ came upon Elijah and, tucking his cloak into his belt, he ran ahead of Ahab all the way to Jezreel.

16–19 Ahab, hoping to deal with Elijah from a position of strength, greeted him with the charge of being a troublemaker in Israel (vv.16–17). Possibly the king was implying that the famine was all Elijah's fault; because of Elijah's hostile attitude, Baal had become angered and so had withheld rain for the past three years. Elijah's reply is particularly instructive. Not he, but Ahab and his family were the real troublers, because they had made Baal worship the state religion (v.18). Did Baal have the power to withhold and bring rain? Let the priests of Baal and Asherah (Baal's consort) be brought together at Mount Carmel, Baal's very stronghold (v.19). Let it be seen once and for all who truly is God!

20–21 When Ahab had assembled the priests of Baal on Mount Carmel to confront Yahweh's prophet (v.20), Elijah addressed the many people who had gathered to see the contest (v.21). Joshua's choice (Josh 24:15) was theirs: Serve God or serve another (cf. Matt 6:24). But unlike Joshua's people, Elijah's audience held its peace.

22–24 To this hesitant multitude Elijah proposed a test in accordance with the scriptural precedent established by Aaron (Lev 9). The 450 prophets of Baal were to choose two bulls, one for their offering and the other for Elijah, who would oppose them by himself (vv.22–23). After each adversary had prepared his respective altar, each would wait for his god to ignite the wood under the sacrifice. The multitude agreed to this (v.24).

25–29 Elijah deferred the first opportunity to Baal's prophets (v.25). Despite all their plaintive wailing and ecstatic dancing, when morning gave way to noon and still Baal had failed to provide the necessary fire, Elijah began to taunt his antagonists (vv.26–27). Was Baal not a god? Perhaps he was lost in deep thought or preoccupied with his many cares or had gone to care for his many commercial interests. All these activities were characteristic of the duties attributed to the pagan gods. Perhaps, like many of the gods of the ancient Near East, he was asleep and needed to be awakened by cultic ritual.

The prophets of Baal became more frantic (v.28). In renewed frenzy they lacerated themselves with swords and spears, the blood flowing freely down their perspiration-soaked bodies. The ritual went on and on at an increasingly feverished pitch. As the time for the evening sacrifice came, there was still no response (v.29).

30–32 Turning from Baal's prophets, Elijah called the people to an altar of the Lord that was in ruins (v.30). Selecting twelve stones according to the number of the tribes of Israel (a fact that underscored the divine displeasure concerning Jeroboam's schism), Elijah rebuilt the altar and then dug a spacious trench around it (vv.31–32).

33–35 When the wood had been arranged on the altar and the sacrifice cut and placed on the wood, Elijah amazed his audience by commanding that four large jars of water be filled and poured on the offering and wood (v.33). He had this done a second and a third time (v.34) so that not only the altar but the sacrifice and the wood were thoroughly drenched, and water filled the surrounding trench (v.35).

36–38 At the precise moment when all hope of igniting the wood seemed totally lost, Elijah stepped forward and called on God (v.36). He pled with the covenant God of Israel to validate that he alone was still God in Israel and this Elijah, who had prophesied the drought and was now calling for a miracle, was truly his servant. He asked God to answer him so that all would know that the Lord was ever anxious for their repentance and return to him (v.37). Striking with lightninglike power, God answered; and such an answer! Heavenly fire fell and consumed not only the wood and sacrifice, but the stones, the soil, and even the surrounding water (v.38). What a contrast! The prophets of Baal had kept up their wailing and wild ritual for the better part of a day and met with dead silence. Elijah's petition had lasted less than a minute but produced spectacular results. The difference lay in the One addressed.

39–40 The people responded in true belief and worship (v.39). Falling to the ground, they confessed that truly Yahweh alone is God! But Elijah wanted total commitment from those who were gathered there. He commanded that these prophets of Baal be seized and executed (v.40). Their wicked crimes against man and God demanded the death penalty (cf. Deut 7:2–6; 13:13–15; 17:2–5). The people reacted instantaneously; they took Baal's prophets in charge to the Kidron Valley and executed them there. Elijah himself remained behind; the people would see to the execution.

41 Then Elijah sought a private audience with the king, for he had an important message to deliver. Ahab could break from the fast of the day and take nourishment, for God would soon send the long withheld rain.

42–46 While the king went away rejoicing to eat and drink, Elijah climbed farther up the mountain to pray and observe God's working (v.42). While Elijah buried his head between his knees in full and reverential concourse with God, he sent his servant to the mountain's peak to herald the approaching rain (v.43). The servant, however, quickly brought back the report "no rain in sight." Again and again as Elijah persevered in heartfelt prayer, the servant was sent to the summit. On the seventh trip he returned with the good news (v.44). A small cloud, the size of a man's hand, could be seen on the distant horizon.

Elijah did not hesitate. He sent word to Ahab that he should leave now lest a torrential rain overtake him on the way (v.44). Nor did Ahab tarry. As he made haste for Jezreel and Jezebel, the sky grew black with heavy clouds, and strong winds began to blow (v.45). As he rode along, the downpour fell on him.

What a momentous day it had been for the king! How his head must have reeled with the thoughts of the contest: the pitiful screams of Baal's helpless priests, the calm yet awe-inspiring petition of Elijah, the terrifying and spectacular holocaust that followed, the repentance of the people, and the execution of the pagan prophets! As Ahab rode along through the gathering downpour, the spirit-empowered prophet through whom God had effected his great triumph ran ahead of the royal chariot like a specter (v.46).

Notes

18 By "Baals" is intended local shrines where Baal was worshiped.

19 Mount Carmel is part of the Carmel Ridge that divides the coastal plain of Palestine into the Plain of Acco to the north and the plains of Sharon and Philistia to the south. To this day a Carmelite Monastery, dedicated to the remembrance of Elijah, exists at the end of the northwestern part of the mountain. The actual scene of Elijah's contest, however, may well be sought on the eastern side among Carmel's taller peaks at El Muḥraqa.

Note that the four hundred prophets of Asherah, who were included in Elijah's challenge, were not present for the contest (cf. vv.22, 40).

21 The verb פָּסַח (pāsaḥ, "waver") means literally "be lame" (cf. Akkad. pessû ["lame"]). In the Piel it means "limp," as in the case of Mephibosheth (2 Sam 9:13). Elijah obviously intends a wordplay, comparing the people's indecision with the frenzied ritualistic dance of the prophets of Baal. See de Vaux, "The Prophets of Baal on Mt. Carmel," in The Bible, pp. 240–43.

27 Elijah's irony bordered on sarcasm (cf. 22:15). שִׂיחַ (śîaḥ, "deep in thought") and שִׂיג (śîg, "busy"; probably a biform of סִיג/סוּג, [sûg/sîg, "move," "turn back"]) occur together also in Ecclus 13:26, where they are rendered by the LXX χρηματίζειν (chrē matizein, "to be engaged in business"). Hence de Vaux (The Bible, pp. 243–46) suggests that they are synonymous and typical of Baal-Melqart's commercial activities. G.R. Driver ("Problems of Interpretation in the Heptateuch," Mélanges bibliques rédigés en l'honneur de André Robert [Paris: Bloud & Gay, 1957], pp. 66–68) likewise considers them synonymous, equating the former word with שִׂיחַ/שׂוּחַ (śîaḥ/śûaḥ, "to defecate"). He concludes that the whole phrase is euphemistic.

On the whole it may be safest to follow the NIV here in separating all three ideas of the verse, relating them to the known activities of the great gods of the ancient Near East. On the awakening of the gods, see de Vaux, The Bible, pp. 246–50.

29 The time of the evening sacrifice when the chief daily service would be observed (Jos. Antiq. XIV, 65 [iv.3]) was about three P.M. (see A. Edersheim, The Temple [Grand Rapids: Eerdmans, 1972], p. 143).

30 The availability of a fallen altar to Yahweh here may have provided an additional reason for selecting Mount Carmel as the contest place.

33–35 The threefold application of the water points to the full reliance of Elijah on the omnipotence of God. How carefully God had prepared his prophet at Zarephath for this precise moment (cf. 17:21)!

36 The use of the familiar motif of the "God of Abraham, Isaac and Jacob/Israel" was a reminder to Elijah's hearers that the covenant God of Israel is ever faithful to his people and longs to be their provider and only God in the fullest sense (cf. Deut 29:12–13; 30:19 –20).

37 For a similar figure, see the comments on Joel 2:12–14. For the "fire of the LORD/God," see Lev 9:24; Num 11:1–3; 2 Kings 1:10–12; 1 Chron 21:26; 2 Chron 7:1. Fire was a symbol of the divine presence (Exod 3:2; 19:17–18; Deut 5:4), especially in God's purifying and sanctifying influences (Ezek 1:13; Mal 3:2–3).

38 Several scholars have suggested that the "fire" was a lightning stroke; if so, it heralded the onset of the soon-coming storm. L. Bronner (*The Stories of Elijah and Elisha* [Leiden: Brill, 1968], pp. 54–77) demonstrates that Yahweh's command over fire, water, and rain is a deliberate repudiation of Baalism.

41 הֶמוֹן (*hᵃmôn*, "sound") is an onomatopoeic word. The excitement of those dramatic events is further heightened by a word that signals the onset of the coming storm.

42 The bowing of the head in humble reverence is familiar in the Ugaritic texts and in the Egyptian Tale of Sinuhe (cf. also Luke 18:13).

44 M.W. Tippetts, a scientifically trained Christian teacher living in Saugus, California, who has special ability in mathematics, estimates that the cumulonimbus clouds seen by Elijah would have been about thirty thousand feet high and probably moved in from the Mediterranean Sea at a rate of about twenty to twenty-five miles per hour.

45 עָבִים (*ᵃḇîm*, "clouds") refers to a thick, dark, rainy cloud mass (cf. Judg 5:4; 2 Sam 23:4).

Ahab's need for haste in the face of the oncoming cloudburst can be appreciated when one realizes that his chariot must travel seventeen miles to Jezreel through the accumulating mud and across the quickly swelling dry wadis.

46 Jezreel, modern Zen'in, lay at the foot of Mount Gilboa, midway between Megiddo and Bethshan.

The fact that Elijah ran ahead of Ahab's chariot contains several points of interest.

1. That Elijah could have made such a run is assured in that Arab runners could easily cover one hundred miles in two days (see Montgomery, p. 307).

2. Elijah's motive in running before Ahab may well have been a mark of humility. Certainly the position as an outrunner for the king was a privileged one in the ancient Near East (see the "Barrakab Inscription," ANET, p. 655; cf. Esth 6:9, 11).

3. Elijah's concern for Ahab's spiritual welfare when he would face Jezebel with the news of the events of this day probably also weighed heavily on Elijah. Elijah himself would come to wicked Jezebel as a herald of the truth (cf. Jonah 1:2; 3:2; 1 Tim 2:7; 2 Tim 1:11; 2 Peter 2:5).

4. The motif of the "out-stretched hand of God" on behalf of his own is a familiar one in the OT (see, e.g., Exod 6:6–7; 7:5; Deut 5:15; 26:5–9; Jer 32:16–22). The prophets used it also to remind Israel and Judah that that same divine hand could be stretched out in judgment against his own when sinful disobedience entered their lives (Isa 5:25–26; 9:12–17; 10:4; Jer 21:5; Ezek 14:13; 16:27).

---

5) Elijah and Jezebel

19:1–9a

> ¹Now Ahab told Jezebel everything Elijah had done and how he had killed all the prophets with the sword. ²So Jezebel sent a messenger to Elijah to say, "May the gods deal with me, be it ever so severely, if by this time tomorrow I do not make your life like that of one of them."

³Elijah was afraid and ran for his life. When he came to Beersheba in Judah, he left his servant there, ⁴while he himself went a day's journey into the desert. He came to a broom tree, sat down under it and prayed that he might die. "I have had enough, Lᴏʀᴅ," he said. "Take my life; I am no better than my ancestors." ⁵Then he lay down under the tree and fell asleep.

All at once an angel touched him and said, "Get up and eat." ⁶He looked around, and there by his head was a cake of bread baked over hot coals, and a jar of water. He ate and drank and then lay down again.

⁷The angel of the Lᴏʀᴅ came back a second time and touched him and said, "Get up and eat, for the journey is too much for you." ⁸So he got up and ate and drank. Strengthened by that food, he traveled forty days and forty nights until he reached Horeb, the mountain of God. ⁹There he went into a cave and spent the night.

1–3a On his arrival at Jezreel, Ahab recounted to Jezebel all that Elijah had done. The words are significant (v.1). Although Ahab had witnessed God's power in the famine and in the consuming of the sacrifice and the sending of the rain, before the imposing presence of Jezebel he could but attribute it all to Elijah, even blaming him for the death of the prophets of Baal. Her reaction was predictable. She sent a message to Elijah, giving him twenty-four hours to leave Jezreel or be killed (v.2). The threat was effective; Elijah ran for his life (v.3a).

Probably Elijah had played into Jezebel's hand. Had she really wanted Elijah dead, she surely would have seized him without warning and slain him. What she desired was that Elijah and his God be discredited before the new converts who had aided Elijah by executing the prophets of Baal. Without a leader revolutionary movements usually stumble and fall away. Just when God needed him the most, the divinely trained prophet was to prove a notable failure.

It has often been asked how a man could experience such divine provision, perform such great miracles, singlehandedly withstand 450 pagan prophets and the king himself, and yet cower before feminine threats. It must be remembered, of course, that Jezebel was anything but a "mere woman." She was of royal blood and every bit a queen. She could be ruthless in pursuing her goals (21:11–15). Her personality was so forceful that even Ahab feared her and was corrupted by her (16:31; 21:25). Both the northern kingdom (16:32–33) and the southern kingdom, through the marriage of her (step) daughter Athaliah to the royal house of Judah (2 Kings 8:16–19; 11:1–20; 2 Chron 21:5–7; Ps 45), experienced moral degredation and spiritual degeneracy through her corrupting influence.

Yet Elijah was not without blame. God's subsequent tender dealings with his prophet were to bring his spiritual problem to light. His God-given successes had fostered an inordinate pride (cf. vv.4, 10, 14) that had made him take his own importance too seriously. Moreover Elijah had come to bask in the glow of the spectacular. He may have fully expected that because of what had been accomplished at Mount Carmel, Jezebel would capitulate and pagan worship would come to an end in Israel—all through his influence!

Whereas the great spectacle had failed to melt Jezebel's icy heart and, worse, she would take his life, his pride was shattered; and he became a broken man. What Elijah needed to learn, God would soon show him (vv.11–12). God does not always move in the realm of the extraordinary. To live always seeking one "high experience" after another is to have a misdirected zeal. The majority of life's service is in quiet, routine, humble obedience to God's will.

3–9 When the fleeing prophet had reached Beersheba some ninety miles to the south, he dismissed his servant (v.36). There was no need to jeopardize his life further. In his extreme dejection, Elijah wished only to be alone. Nor, for that matter, could he be safe in Beersheba, for Jezebel's influence could reach even this southernmost city. Accordingly Elijah turned still further southward, journeying out into the desert (v.4).

Taking refuge under the scant shade of a broom tree, Elijah prayed for death (cf. Job 10:18–22). He, the mighty prophet, had stood for God as boldly as any of those who had gone before him. Yet here he was, alone and seemingly deserted in this desert wasteland, the very symbol of a wasted life. Yet God would tenderly nourish and lead his prophet to a place where he would get some much needed instruction (cf. Moses, Exod 2:15–3:22; Paul, Gal 1:15–17). After a forty-day trek, Elijah found that he had been drawn by divine providence to Mount Sinai, the sacred place of God's self-disclosure (v.8).

After arriving at Mount Sinai, Elijah located a cave and fell fast asleep (v.9). He may have been in a spot more sacred then he realized. The Hebrew text says, "He came there to *the* cave," possibly the very "cleft of the rock" where God had placed Moses as his glory passed by (Exod 33:21–23).

Notes

3 Most modern commentaries and versions follow the lead of the ancient versions in pointing the Hebrew phrase וַיִּרָא (*wayyirā'*, "and he was afraid") rather than reading the MT's וַיַּרְא (*wayyar'*, "and he saw"). Allen, however, ably demonstrates the defensibility of the MT. He rightly contends (p. 202) that Elijah fled, not in fear, but as a prophet broken by Jezebel's unrepentant paganism and continuing power over the nation and its destiny.

4 רֹתֶם (*rōtem*, "broom bush"), a shrub found in abundance in southern Palestine, has long slender branches with small leaves and fragrant, delicate blossoms. Common among the wadis, they often reach a height of ten feet (cf. *Fauna and Flora of the Old Testament* [London: United Bible Societies, 1972], pp. 100-101).

7 For the "angel of the LORD," see the note on 2 Kings 1:3.

8 Horeb (i.e., Mount Sinai) is called "the mountain of God," as in Exod 3:1; see also Exod 4:27; 18:5; Deut 5:2. On the spiritual significance of Sinai, see TWOT, 2:622–23.

Elijah's forty-day journey is not without significance. Indeed a straight trip from Beersheba would require little more than a quarter of that time. Therefore the period is designedly symbolic. As the children of Israel had a notable spiritual failure and so were to wander forty years in the wilderness, so a defeated Elijah was to spend forty days in the desert (cf. Num 14:26–35). As Moses had spent forty days on the mountain without bread and water, sustained only by God while he awaited a new phase of service (Exod 34:28), so Elijah was to spend forty days thrown on the divine enablement as he prepared for a recommissioning by God (cf. Matt 4:1–2). As Moses was to see the presence of God (Exod 33:12–23), so Elijah was to find God, though in a different way than he could ever imagine.

---

6) *Elijah and the Lord*

19:9b–18

And the word of the LORD came to him: "What are you doing here, Elijah?"
¹⁰He replied, "I have been very zealous for the LORD God Almighty. The Israel-

ites have rejected your covenant, broken down your altars, and put your prophets to death with the sword. I am the only one left, and now they are trying to kill me too."

^{11}The LORD said, "Go out and stand on the mountain in the presence of the LORD, for the LORD is about to pass by."

Then a great and powerful wind tore the mountains apart and shattered the rocks before the LORD, but the LORD was not in the wind. After the wind there was an earthquake, but the LORD was not in the earthquake. ^{12}After the earthquake came a fire, but the LORD was not in the fire. And after the fire came a gentle whisper. ^{13}When Elijah heard it, he pulled his cloak over his face and went out and stood at the mouth of the cave.

Then a voice said to him, "What are you doing here, Elijah?"

^{14}He replied, "I have been very zealous for the LORD God Almighty. The Israelites have rejected your covenant, broken down your altars, and put your prophets to death with the sword. I am the only one left, and now they are trying to kill me too."

^{15}The LORD said to him, "Go back the way you came, and go to the Desert of Damascus. When you get there, anoint Hazael king over Aram. ^{16}Also, anoint Jehu son of Nimshi king over Israel, and anoint Elisha son of Shaphat from Abel Meholah to succeed you as prophet. ^{17}Jehu will put to death any who escape the sword of Hazael, and Elisha will put to death any who escape the sword of Jehu. ^{18}Yet I reserve seven thousand in Israel—all whose knees have not bowed down to Baal and all whose mouths have not kissed him."

9b–10 At length the word of the Lord aroused Elijah. The penetrating interrogation called for minute self-evaluation (v.9b; cf. Gen 3:9). Did Elijah yet understand his failure and God's gracious guidance in bringing him to this place? Elijah's reply indicated that he did not. Like Phineas of old, he alone had been very zealous for the Lord in the midst of gross idolatry (v.10; cf. Num 25:7–13). His soul was somewhat bitter at having served God so earnestly and spectacularly and yet having experienced rejection and solitary exile.

11–14 The Lord did not comment on Elijah's self-justification but offered instruction. He was to come out of the cave and stand before the Lord, for he would soon pass by (v.11). Suddenly a rock-shattering tempest smote the mountain around Elijah. Surely this would announce the divine presence. But the Lord was not in the wind. There followed a fearful earthquake, but still God was not there. A sudden fire followed (v.12); yet God had not come. All these physical phenomena were known to be often precursors of God's coming (Exod 19:16, 18; Judg 5:4–5; 2 Sam 22:8–16; Pss 18:7–15; 68:8; Heb 12:18). There followed a faint whisper, a voice quiet, hushed, and low. Elijah knew it instantly (v.13a). It was God! What a lesson for Elijah! Even God did not always operate in the realm of the spectacular!

Pulling his prophet's cloak over his face, Elijah made his way reverently out of the cave (v.13b; cf. Exod 3:6; 33:20; Isa 6:2–3). Again came the divine question: "What are you doing here, Elijah?" Elijah's reply was the same (v.14; cf. v.10). How slow he was to learn! Yet much of what he said was true. Though he had failed at the last, he had been faithful; and truly persecution was rampant in Israel. It was understandable why he would feel quite alone.

15–18 God again dealt graciously with his prophet. He was to go back to the northern kingdom (v.15), the place where he had veered off the track with God in his spiritual life (cf. Abram, Gen 13:3–4; John Mark, Acts 15:39). Elijah still had work to accomplish for God. That task was threefold: (1) in the realm of international politics, he was to anoint Hazael to succeed Ben-Hadad, Israel's perennial adversary in Damascus; (2) in national affairs, Jehu was to be anointed as the next king (v.16); and (3) in the spiritual realm, Elisha was to be commissioned as his own successor (cf. God's instruction to Moses in Num 27:18–23).

The threefold commission was singularly interrelated (v.17). Jehu's work would supplement that of Hazael, that is, any who fell to Israel to escape Hazael's purge would be dealt with by Jehu. In turn those who survived Jehu's slaughter must face the spiritual judgment of Elisha. To encourage his restored prophet further, God set the record straight: there were yet seven thousand true believers in Israel (v.18).

Notes

15 For Hazael see the comment on 2 Kings 8:8; for Jehu, see 2 Kings 9–10.

7) *Elijah and the call of Elisha*

19:19–21

> [19] So Elijah went from there and found Elisha son of Shaphat. He was plowing with twelve yoke of oxen, and he himself was driving the twelfth pair. Elijah went up to him and threw his cloak around him. [20] Elisha then left his oxen and ran after Elijah. "Let me kiss my father and mother good-by," he said, "and then I will come with you."
>
> "Go back," Elijah replied. "What have I done to you?"
>
> [21] So Elisha left him and went back. He took his yoke of oxen and slaughtered them. He burned the plowing equipment to cook the meat and gave it to the people, and they ate. Then he set out to follow Elijah and became his attendant.

19–20 Since the key figure in Elijah's threefold commission was Elisha, Elijah sought him out first. He found Elisha busily engaged in plowing (v.19). Coming on him suddenly, Elijah threw his mantle over Elisha, a symbol of Elisha's call to the prophetic office. Elijah himself continued on without a word. When Elisha was able to collect his wits, he ran after Elijah, asking only that he be allowed to take leave of his family (v.20). Elijah's reply indicates that he himself had not called Elisha; it was God's call. Whether Elisha would follow that call was his own decision.

21 Elisha meant business for God. Taking his leave of Elijah, Elisha returned home to enjoy a farewell meal with his family and friends. The meat was cooked over Elisha's own plowing equipment. Thus he had burned his past behind him. Henceforth he would serve God. However this first meant learning more of him through Elijah.

Notes

21 Elisha's genuine break with the past stands in bold contrast with those false disciples who wished only to appear pious before Jesus (Matt 8:18–22; Luke 9:57–62). Elisha begins a period of humble service and training at the side of the master prophet, much as Joshua served under Moses (cf. Exod 24:13–18; Num 27:18–23; Deut 1:38; 3:21–22, 27–28; 31: 7–23; 34:9).

---

c. Ahab and the campaign for Samaria (20:1–43)

1) The Aramean crisis

20:1–12

> ¹Now Ben-Hadad king of Aram mustered his entire army. Accompanied by thirty-two kings with their horses and chariots, he went up and besieged Samaria and attacked it. ²He sent messengers into the city to Ahab king of Israel, saying, "This is what Ben-Hadad says: ³'Your silver and gold are mine, and the best of your wives and children are mine.'"
>
> ⁴The king of Israel answered, "Just as you say, my lord the king. I and all I have are yours."
>
> ⁵The messengers came again and said, "This is what Ben-Hadad says: 'I sent to demand your silver and gold, your wives and your children. ⁶But about this time tomorrow I am going to send my officials to search your palace and the houses of your officials. They will seize everything you value and carry it away.'"
>
> ⁷The king of Israel summoned all the elders of the land and said to them, "See how this man is looking for trouble! When he sent for my wives and my children, my silver and my gold, I did not refuse him."
>
> ⁸The elders and the people all answered, "Don't listen to him or agree to his demands."
>
> ⁹So he replied to Ben-Hadad's messengers, "Tell my lord the king, 'Your servant will do all you demanded the first time, but this demand I cannot meet.'" They left and took the answer back to Ben-Hadad.
>
> ¹⁰Then Ben-Hadad sent another message to Ahab: "May the gods deal with me, be it ever so severely, if enough dust remains in Samaria to give each of my men a handful."
>
> ¹¹The king of Israel answered, "Tell him: 'One who puts on his armor should not boast like one who takes it off.'"
>
> ¹²Ben-Hadad heard this message while he and the kings were drinking in their tents, and he ordered his men: "Prepare to attack." So they prepared to attack the city.

1–6 Ben-Hadad, king of Israel's perennial enemy around Damascus, saw his opportunity to eliminate a famine-weakened Israel. Gathering a coalition of some thirty-two kings, he swept southward, quickly putting Samaria itself under siege (v.1). To humiliate Ahab further, he sent messengers demanding silver and gold and the choicest of his wives and children (vv.2–3). When Ahab agreed to his terms readily, Ben-Hadad demanded the additional right to unlimited search of the palace and the houses of Ahab's officials so as to carry away anything of value (vv.4–6).

7–12 Ahab was alarmed at this demand and convened his council of elders (v.7). Advised by the elders not to capitulate (v.8), Ahab sent back a refusal to Ben-Hadad (v.9). The Aramean king sent a third note to Ahab, threatening to destroy Samaria so thoroughly that there would not be enough left of it to make a handful of dust for each of his men (v.10). Ahab's proverbial reply is a classic illustration of Near Eastern colloquial wisdom: "Let not one who girds on his armor boast like one who takes it off" (cf. v.11). Ben-Hadad "got the message." Infuriated he gave orders to prepare for the attack (v.12).

Notes

1 The identity of this king has been the subject of much scholarly debate. Some scholars (e.g., Albright, Bright, Montgomery, Unger) decide that this king is still Ben-Hadad I, assigning to him a reign that spanned most of the ninth century. Others (e.g., Edwards, Keil, Kitchen, Malamat, Wood), on the basis of v.34, which appears to differentiate the king of this chapter from the one who invaded the northern kingdom previously in the days of Baasha, suggest that Ben-Hadad I died somewhere about 860 B.C., and that he had been succeeded by his son, Ben-Hadad II (c. 860–843 B.C.).

On the whole the second interpretation seems to fit the historical details adequately and allows the most natural interpretation of 1 Kings 20:34. The Annals of Shalmaneser III of Assyria (858–824 B.C.) give his name as (Ḥ)adad-Ezer, possibly a throne name. Accordingly the identity and dates of the Aramean kings adopted here are as follows: Ben-Hadad I (c. 885–860), son of Tabrimmon (1 Kings 15:18); Ben-Hadad II (c. 860–842); Hazael (c. 841–802); and Ben-Hadad III (c. 802–780?). F.M. Cross, "The Stele Dedicated to Melcarth by Ben-Hadad of Damascus," BASOR 205 (1972): 36–42, postulates four kings named Ben-Hadad: I (885–870); II (870–842); III (845–842), and IV (806–770), the latter being the son of Hazael (841–806). For an evaluation and criticism of Cross's view and the whole problem, see W. Shea, "The Kings of the Melqart Stela," *Maarav* 1 (1979): 159–76. See further the note on 2 Kings 13:3.

Confederations of kings were common in the ancient Near East. Shalmaneser III mentions that this same Ḥadad-Ezer was part of a coalition of twelve kings that withstood him at the Battle of Qarqar (see ANET, pp. 278–79). The Zakir Stele mentions a coalition of seven kings headed by Ben-Hadad III (see ANET, pp. 655–56).

Several motives may be suggested for Ben-Hadad's attack late in Ahab's reign. Perhaps Ben-Hadad wanted Ahab to join his anti-Assyrian coalition (as Ahab later did). Perhaps it was due to the long-standing commercial rivalry and political enmity that had festered since Baasha's days, coupled with the fear that Ahab might become an ally of the Assyrian king. At any rate the effects of the drought and famine had created an opportunity to eliminate further difficulty from his southern frontier.

3 Ben-Hadad's demands were a virtual call for Ahab to be reduced to vassal status. One is reminded of Xerxes' later demands for submission on the part of the Greeks by presenting the token demands of earth and water (Herodotus *Persian Wars* 5.17ff., 73; 7.133, 174). The fact that Ahab willingly acquiesced to Ben-Hadad's initial demands indicates Israel's desperate condition.

10 Ben-Hadad's boast was that not only had he the striking force to reduce Samaria to dust, but he had the manpower to carry that dust away by the handful. Aquila's text is even more dramatic: "by pinches." Another Greek variant suggests that there would not be enough dust left to make a foxhole.

2) *The Israelite triumph*

20:13-34

¹³Meanwhile a prophet came to Ahab king of Israel and announced, "This is what the LORD says: 'Do you see this vast army? I will give it into your hand today, and then you will know that I am the LORD.'"

¹⁴"But who will do this?" asked Ahab.

The prophet replied, "This is what the LORD says: 'The young officers of the provincial commanders will do it.'"

"And who will start the battle?" he asked.

The prophet answered, "You will."

¹⁵So Ahab summoned the young officers of the provincial commanders, 232 men. Then he assembled the rest of the Israelites, 7,000 in all. ¹⁶They set out at noon while Ben-Hadad and the 32 kings allied with him were in their tents getting drunk. ¹⁷The young officers of the provincial commanders went out first.

Now Ben-Hadad had dispatched scouts, who reported, "Men are advancing from Samaria."

¹⁸He said, "If they have come out for peace, take them alive; if they have come out for war, take them alive."

¹⁹The young officers of the provincial commanders marched out of the city with the army behind them ²⁰and each one struck down his opponent. At that, the Arameans fled, with the Israelites in pursuit. But Ben-Hadad king of Aram escaped on horseback with some of his horsemen. ²¹The king of Israel advanced and overpowered the horses and chariots and inflicted heavy losses on the Arameans.

²²Afterward, the prophet came to the king of Israel and said, "Strengthen your position and see what must be done, because next spring the king of Aram will attack you again."

²³Meanwhile, the officials of the king of Aram advised him, "Their gods are gods of the hills. That is why they were too strong for us. But if we fight them on the plains, surely we will be stronger than they. ²⁴Do this: Remove all the kings from their commands and replace them with other officers. ²⁵You must also raise an army like the one you lost—horse for horse and chariot for chariot—so we can fight Israel on the plains. Then surely we will be stronger than they." He agreed with them and acted accordingly.

²⁶The next spring Ben-Hadad mustered the Arameans and went up to Aphek to fight against Israel. ²⁷When the Israelites were also mustered and given provisions, they marched out to meet them. The Israelites camped opposite them like two small flocks of goats, while the Arameans covered the countryside.

²⁸The man of God came up and told the king of Israel, "This is what the LORD says: 'Because the Arameans think the LORD is a god of the hills and not a god of the valleys, I will deliver this vast army into your hands, and you will know that I am the LORD.'"

²⁹For seven days they camped opposite each other, and on the seventh day the battle was joined. The Israelites inflicted a hundred thousand casualties on the Aramean foot soldiers in one day. ³⁰The rest of them escaped to the city of Aphek, where the wall collapsed on twenty-seven thousand of them. And Ben-Hadad fled to the city and hid in an inner room.

³¹His officials said to him, "Look, we have heard that the kings of the house of Israel are merciful. Let us go to the king of Israel with sackcloth around our waists and ropes around our heads. Perhaps he will spare your life."

³²Wearing sackcloth around their waists and ropes around their heads, they went to the king of Israel and said, "Your servant Ben-Hadad says: 'Please let me live.'"

The king answered, "Is he still alive? He is my brother."

³³The men took this as a good sign and were quick to pick up his word. "Yes, your brother Ben-Hadad!" they said.

"Go and get him," the king said. When Ben-Hadad came out, Ahab had him come up into his chariot.

³⁴"I will return the cities my father took from your father," Ben-Hadad offered. "You may set up your own market areas in Damascus, as my father did in Samaria."

Ahab said, "On the basis of a treaty I will set you free." So he made a treaty with him, and let him go.

13–14 While Ben-Hadad and his men reinforced their courage with strong drink, Ahab received a divine messenger (v.13). An unknown prophet of God advised the king that if he would call on the select officers of his provincial commanders to lead the attack, God would give him the victory (v.14).

15–21 Setting out at noon with the young officers in the lead, the Syrian forces were, in accordance with the prophecy, easily routed. The Arameans suffered heavy losses of men and material, Ben-Hadad himself barely escaping with his life (vv.15 –21). Surely such a divine deliverance against impossible odds should have convinced Ahab of God's continuing concern for him and the people of Israel. But this was not the case.

22–25 After Ahab's victory, the prophet returned to warn the king to strengthen his defenses for Ben-Hadad would surely return next year (v.22). The warning was well-taken, for even then Ben-Hadad's counselors were advising him that since Israel's gods were mountain gods, Israel could be defeated in the plains (v.23). Ben-Hadad only needed to replace the defeated officers with new commanders, raise another army, and choose a battle site in the plains (vv.24–25).

26–31 Following their respective counselors' advice, both kings faced each other in battle in the valley before Aphek (v.26). Although the Israelite forces were vastly outnumbered (v.27), God promised Ahab through his prophet that because the Arameans considered his power to be limited to the mountains, he would see to their defeat (v.28).

In the ensuing fray, Ben-Hadad's army suffered almost total annihilation. Even most of those who escaped the battlefield died under the collapsing walls of Aphek (vv.29–30). Within the citadel of Aphek, where Ben-Hadad and his counselors had taken refuge, the king was advised of a new plan. Since the Israelite kings were reputed to be tender-hearted, if the royal party put on garments of repentance and approached Ahab, perhaps he would be merciful (v.31).

32–34 Accordingly Ben-Hadad's counselors went to Ahab with pleas of mercy (v.32). They were not disappointed, for Ahab commanded that Ben-Hadad be summoned for conciliation (v.33). When Ben-Hadad offered to return the Israelite territory that his father had previously taken (cf. 15:20) and establish new trade concessions, Ahab effected a treaty with Ben-Hadad and released him (v.34). In so doing Ahab was trusting in his own appraisal of his needs and the world situation rather than in God who had given him the miraculous victory.

Notes

13 According to Josephus (Antiq. VIII, 389 [xiv.5]) and the rabbinic interpreters, the prophet was Micaiah Ben Imlah (cf. 22:8); but this is merely a guess.

14–15 The נְעָרִים (na'ªrîm, "young officers") probably comprised a mobile unit of professional soldiers. Like the following term—שָׂרֵי הַמְּדִינוֹת (śārê hammeedînôt, "provincial commanders"; cf. Esth 1:3)—it is a technical military designation. See further J. MacDonald, "NA'AR in Israelite Society"; B. Cutler and J. MacDonald, "The Identification of the NA'AR in the Ugaritic Texts," *Ugarit-Forschungen* 8 (1976): 27–35.

15 By בְּנֵי יִשְׂרָאֵל (beenê yiśrā'ēl, "Israelites") is intended either a select group of Israelites whose status and substance obliged them to support the military program of the realm or simply the total number of Ahab's soldiers quartered at Samaria.

17–22 The battle strategy appears to have been to send out the small but well-trained advance party who could perhaps draw near to the Syrians without arousing too much alarm and then, at a given signal, initiate a charge that, joined by Ahab's main striking force, would both catch the drunken Arameans off guard and throw them into confusion. The plan was more successful than Ahab dared to imagine.

22 לִתְשׁוּבַת הַשָּׁנָה (litšûbat haššānāh, "at the turn of the year") is taken by the NIV to be "next spring," i.e., the time for battle (cf. 2 Sam 11:1). Late spring and early summer was one of two regular seasons for military expedition, when grass was readily available for the cattle.

24–25 פַּחוֹת (paḥôt, "officers"; cf. Akkad. bēl pīḫani ["prefect"]). The counselors advised Ben-Hadad to dispense with the calling of individual units that left him with an army of heterogeneous parts and to form an integrated whole that would comprise a disciplined fighting force.

Undisciplined noncohesive units can easily quit fighting in the midst of the battle's heat (cf. Antony's difficulties in Greece in his fighting with Octavian) or get sidetracked by stopping for plunder (as did the army of Thutmose III before Megiddo).

30 חֶדֶר בְּחָדֶר (ḥeder beḥāder, "inner room") is found in 22:25 and 2 Kings 9:2, where a similar meaning is demanded. The phrase could also signify that the king fled "from room to room."

31 On חֶסֶד (ḥesed, "merciful"), see the note on 3:6.

While Ben-Hadad's counselors undoubtedly hoped for generosity from Ahab, Gray (*Kings*, p. 429) may be right in suggesting that the Syrians were counting on the Israelites' known reputation for being covenant makers and keepers.

32 The counselors' sackcloth was symbolic of mourning and penitence. The rope around the head was a sign of supplication, the figure being that of the porter at the wheel of the victor's chariot (see Sennacherib's third campaign, ANET, p. 287).

33 The force of the verbal aspect of נָחַשׁ (nāḥaš, "take as a good sign") indicates that Ben-Hadad's embassy came looking for a favorable omen in Ahab's speech or attitude.

חָלַט (ḥālaṭ, "pick up") is a hapax legomenon (occurs only here in the OT). The etymology could lie in Aramaic, the language of the counselors. Aramaic/Syrian חְלַט (heelaṭ, "to mix") might be appropriate here, the wily counselors seizing on Ahab's reply and quickly mixing his words into the directions for delivering Ben-Hadad.

Ben-Hadad may well have come and put his shoulder to Ahab's chariot, thereby giving a symbolic act of submission (see the Barrakab Inscription, ANET, p. 655).

34 It would appear that Ahab and Ben-Hadad were rearranging the terms of a previously existing treaty, perhaps enacted as a result of the action detailed in 15:18–20 (q.v.). Here, of course, the stipulations are somewhat reversed: the lost Israelite districts are restored, and the trade concessions in Damascus previously held by Ben-Hadad in Samaria are granted to Ahab. See further the note on v.1.

By חוּצוֹת (ḥûṣôt, "streets," "outside places") is meant bazaars set up in a foreign land (cf. Neh 13:16), hence NIV's "market areas." For details of similar treaty stipulations, see the vassal treaties of Mati'ilu of Arpad with the Assyrian king Ashurnirari V (ANET, pp. 532–33) and with Barga'yah of *Ktk* (see ANET, pp. 659–61).

The reason for Ahab's leniency toward Ben-Hadad may lie in his appraisal of the troublesome political situation of those days. Already Shalmaneser III was on the move against the Aramean tribes. Ahab doubtless preferred to have a restored and friendly Ben-Hadad with his ability to deliver a sizeable force of chariots and infantry between himself and Shalmaneser. In this regard notice M. Elat, "The Campaigns of Shalmaneser III Against Aram and Israel," IEJ 25 (1975): 25–35. The two allies, along with several other Aramean kings, were soon to face Shalmaneser head-on in the famous Battle of Qarqar in 853 B.C. See Hallo, "Qarqar," pp. 158–61.

---

3) *The prophet's rebuke*

20:35–43

35By the word of the Lord one of the sons of the prophets said to his companion, "Strike me with your weapon," but the man refused.
36So the prophet said, "Because you have not obeyed the Lord, as soon as you leave me a lion will kill you." And after the man went away, a lion found him and killed him.
37The prophet found another man and said, "Strike me, please." So the man struck him and wounded him. 38Then the prophet went and stood by the road waiting for the king. He disguised himself with his headband down over his eyes. 39As the king passed by, the prophet called out to him, "Your servant went into the thick of the battle, and someone came to me with a captive and said, 'Guard this man. If he is missing, it will be your life for his life, or you must pay a talent of silver.' 40While your servant was busy here and there, the man disappeared."

"That is your sentence," the king of Israel said. "You have pronounced it yourself."
41Then the prophet quickly removed the headband from his eyes, and the king of Israel recognized him as one of the prophets. 42He said to the king, "This is what the Lord says: 'You have set free a man I had determined should die. Therefore it is your life for his life, your people for his people.'" 43Sullen and angry, the king of Israel went to his palace in Samaria.

35–40a Ahab's leniency toward Ben-Hadad and self-trust were not to go without divine rebuke. God again raised up a prophet to deal with Ahab. This prophet, by divine command, asked one of his companions to smite him (v.35). Because the second prophet refused to obey the divine direction, he was immediately killed by a lion (v.36). The first prophet then got another man to strike him (v.37). Thus wounded he waited in a disguise for Ahab (v.38). When the king passed by, the prophet represented himself as a soldier who had been wounded in battle and to whom had been assigned a prisoner on penalty of his life or the payment of a large sum of money (v.39). Unfortunately he had inadvertently allowed his prisoner to escape (v.40a).

40b–43 Merciless Ahab confirmed the sentence (v.40b). At that point the prophet revealed himself to the king (v.41). The prophet's action had been symbolic. Ahab was that one who had allowed the prisoner to escape; therefore, as he himself had judged to be right, the king would pay with his life and Israel should suffer loss (v.42). It was a sullen and angry Ahab who returned in triumph from the battle to his palace in Samaria (v.43).

Notes

35 This is the first mention of "the sons of the prophets," though that prophetic band had existed at least since the days of Samuel (1 Sam 10). See further the note on 1 Kings 18:4.

36 It is tacitly implied that the first prophet had made it clear to the second prophet that his strange command was from the Lord. For the killing of a disobedient prophet by a lion, see 13:14–30.

37 The smiting and wounding of the prophet not only gave an authentic tone to the prophet's tale but would signify to Ahab what he might expect because of his folly in releasing Ben-Hadad.

39 The principle of making payment or restitution for the loss of an entrusted item was already established in the Law (cf. Exod 22:7–15). The silver payment, however, was an exorbitant one, one hundred times that of the price of a slave (Exod 21:32).

42 As a spoil of holy warfare in which God clearly had given the victory, Ben-Hadad should have been devoted to destruction (cf. Lev 27:29; Josh 6:17–21; 1 Sam 15:7–10, 18–23).

43 סַר (sar, "sullen") comes from the root sārar ("be stubborn"; cf. Akkad. sarāru, "be unstable, obstinate"). It often portrays Israel, which, like Ahab, walked in its own stubborn way (cf. Neh 9:29; Ps 78:8; Isa 1:23; 65:2; Jer 5:23; 6:28; Zech 7:11).

d. Ahab and the conscription of Naboth's vineyard

21:1–29

¹Some time later there was an incident involving a vineyard belonging to Naboth the Jezreelite. The vineyard was in Jezreel, close to the palace of Ahab king of Samaria. ²Ahab said to Naboth, "Let me have your vineyard to use for a vegetable garden, since it is close to my palace. In exchange I will give you a better vineyard or, if you prefer, I will pay you whatever it is worth."

³But Naboth replied, "The LORD forbid that I should give you the inheritance of my fathers."

⁴So Ahab went home, sullen and angry because Naboth the Jezreelite had said, "I will not give you the inheritance of my fathers." He lay on his bed sulking and refused to eat.

⁵His wife Jezebel came in and asked him, "Why are you so sullen? Why won't you eat?"

⁶He answered her, "Because I said to Naboth the Jezreelite, 'Sell me your vineyard; or if you prefer, I will give you another vineyard in its place.' But he said, 'I will not give you my vineyard.'"

⁷Jezebel his wife said, "Is this how you act as king over Israel? Get up and eat! Cheer up. I'll get you the vineyard of Naboth the Jezreelite."

⁸So she wrote letters in Ahab's name, placed his seal on them, and sent them to the elders and nobles who lived in Naboth's city with him. ⁹In those letters she wrote:

"Proclaim a day of fasting and seat Naboth in a prominent place among the people. ¹⁰But seat two scoundrels opposite him and have them testify that he has cursed both God and the king. Then take him out and stone him to death."

¹¹So the elders and nobles who lived in Naboth's city did as Jezebel directed in the letters she had written to them. ¹²They proclaimed a fast and seated Naboth in a prominent place among the people. ¹³Then two scoundrels came and sat opposite him and brought charges against Naboth before the people, saying, "Naboth has cursed both God and the king." So they took him outside the city and stoned him to death. ¹⁴Then they sent word to Jezebel: "Naboth has been stoned and is dead."

¹⁵As soon as Jezebel heard that Naboth had been stoned to death, she said to Ahab, "Get up and take possession of the vineyard of Naboth the Jezreelite that he refused to sell you. He is no longer alive, but dead." ¹⁶When Ahab heard that Naboth was dead, he got up and went down to take possession of Naboth's vineyard.

¹⁷Then the word of the LORD came to Elijah the Tishbite: ¹⁸"Go down to meet Ahab king of Israel, who rules in Samaria. He is now in Naboth's vineyard, where he has gone to take possession of it. ¹⁹Say to him, 'This is what the LORD says: Have you not murdered a man and seized his property?' Then say to him, 'This is what the LORD says: In the place where dogs licked up Naboth's blood, dogs will lick up your blood—yes, yours!' "

²⁰Ahab said to Elijah, "So you have found me, my enemy!"

"I have found you," he answered, "because you have sold yourself to do evil in the eyes of the LORD. ²¹'I am going to bring disaster on you. I will consume your descendants and cut off from Ahab every last male in Israel—slave or free. ²²I will make your house like that of Jeroboam son of Nebat and that of Baasha son of Ahijah, because you have provoked me to anger and have caused Israel to sin.'

²³"And also concerning Jezebel the LORD says: 'Dogs will devour Jezebel by the wall of Jezreel.'

²⁴"Dogs will eat those belonging to Ahab who die in the city, and the birds of the air will feed on those who die in the country."

²⁵(There was never a man like Ahab, who sold himself to do evil in the eyes of the LORD, urged on by Jezebel his wife. ²⁶He behaved in the vilest manner by going after idols, like the Amorites the LORD drove out before Israel.)

²⁷When Ahab heard these words, he tore his clothes, put on sackcloth and fasted. He lay in sackcloth and went around meekly.

²⁸Then the word of the LORD came to Elijah the Tishbite: ²⁹"Have you noticed how Ahab has humbled himself before me? Because he has humbled himself, I will not bring this disaster in his day, but I will bring it on his house in the days of his son."

1–5 Ahab's covetous eye became enamored with a choice vineyard that lay next to his palatial retreat in Jezreel (v.1). He desired to turn this vineyard into a vegetable garden; so he offered to buy it from its owner, Naboth, or give him another in exchange for it (v.2). When Naboth declined to part with his paternal inheritance (v.3), Ahab returned indignantly to the palace (v.4). There Jezebel found him sulking in bed with his face turned to the wall and refusing to eat (v.5).

6–8 Jezebel's inquiry revealed Naboth's refusal to grant Ahab's wishes (v.6). Having assured him that she knew how to handle such situations, even if the king did not, Jezebel had letters sent in Ahab's name to the elders of Naboth's village, in a conspiracy against him (vv.7–8).

9–10 On a given day the elders and nobles, who comprised a sort of local senate (cf. Deut 16:18), were to call an assembly for solemn fasting (v.9), as though the city had committed some great sin (cf. 1 Sam 7:6) whose penalty needed averting (cf. Lev

4:13–21; Deut 21:1–9; 2 Chron 20:2–4; Joel 1:14–15). Naboth was to be given a conspicuous place so that the two accusers could easily single him out (v.10; cf. Num 35:30; Deut 17:6; 19:15; cf. Matt 18:16; 26:60; 2 Cor 13:1). It may be that Naboth was an influential person anyway; so his prominent position at the meeting would not arouse suspicion.

The charge against Naboth was twofold: he had blasphemed both God and the king. The penalty for such action was death by stoning (Deut 13:10–11; 17:5), outside the city (Lev 24:14; Deut 22:24). Proper procedure called for the witnesses to lay their hands on the accused (Lev 24:14) and cast the first stones (cf. John 8:7). Since death by stoning was the responsibility of the whole community, the rest of the people were to take up the stoning.

11–16 The queen's directive was duly carried out, and word was taken to Jezebel that Naboth was dead (vv.11–14). Ahab immediately took possession of the property (v.16). Tragically the Scriptures do not indicate that Ahab was concerned enough to ask how Naboth had died or how the property was suddenly available for royal claim.

17–20a Once more Elijah was summoned by God to confront Ahab (vv.17–18). Ahab no longer called Elijah "the troubler of Israel" but "my enemy" (v.20a). Doubtless his guilt weighed so heavily on his own conscience that he knew Elijah was there to condemn him.

20b–24 Elijah gave God's message plainly: because Ahab had sold himself to do only evil, God's sure judgment would come on him (v.21). In the very place where the dogs had licked up Naboth's blood, they would do likewise to Ahab (v.19). Yes, Ahab and his house would be cut off like those of the first two dynasties, his spiritual predecessors in idolatry (vv.21–22). The divine sentence envisioned a terrible slaughter and carnage (v.24). Nor would Jezebel escape; the dogs would eat her flesh by the wall of Jezreel (v.23).

25–26 The divine estimation of Ahab is clearly rendered: Ahab was the vilest of all the Israelite kings. Completely under the domination of his wicked, pagan wife, he was unmatched in evil and spiritual harlotry in Israel.

27–29 Ahab reacted strongly to the Lord's rebuke, clothed himself in sackcloth, and fasted (v.27). Therefore God again sent Elijah word concerning the king: because he had humbled himself, the threatened punishment would be delayed until the lifetime of his son (vv.28–29). However no stay of execution would be granted for the villainous Jezebel.

The king's remorse was sincere; paradoxically Ahab could be influenced for good by the divine message (cf. 1 Kings 17 and see the note on 2 Kings 10:18). Therefore the Lord in his longsuffering bore with the king yet further. There is little indication, however, that Ahab's basic character was altered so as to produce that godly repentance and genuine faith that lead to a real conversion experience. To the contrary, there is no indication that he changed his idolatrous ways, much less restored the ill-gotten vineyard. How gracious is an everloving God who deals in boundless mercy even with a thankless and thoughtless generation (cf. 2 Peter 3:9)!

Notes

1 The phrase "some time later" is omitted in the LXX, since it inverts chapters 20 and 21. It may, however, refer back to the incidents of chapter 19, during which time the events of chapter 20 took place. Yet chapter 20 has set the background for chapter 22; but the final contest between Elijah, who has returned to Samaria, and Ahab must first be told.

הֵיכַל (hēkāl, "palace") first occurs here in Kings in this sense. Previously it was used of Solomon's temple (6:3–38). Both meanings are allowable. The word is of Mesopotamian origin (Sumerian E. GAL; Akkad. êkallu, "big house," "palace"; cf. also Egyp. pr⁽⁾, "big house," and only later "Pharaoh"; see A. Gardiner, Egyptian Grammar, 3d ed. [London: Oxford University Press, 1957], p. 75).

The title "king of Samaria" (cf. 2 Kings 1:3) locates the base of power for the Omride Dynasty.

3 Naboth's refusal indicates that such a course of action would be profane in the eyes of God, being expressly forbidden by the law (Lev 25:23–28; Num 36:7–12).

7 The independent personal pronoun "you," in an emphatic position in the MT, probably indicates a touch of sarcasm: " Are you not the one who exercises kingship over Israel?"

8 Written by the royal scribe, ancient סְפָרִים (sᵉpārîm, "letters") were chiefly in the form of a scroll written in columns (occasionally on both sides) and sealed in clay or wax with the sender's personal sign. Such seals have been frequently found in the excavations of Palestine (cf. TWOT, 2:632–34).

9 For assemblies for solemn fastings, see the comments on Joel 1:14–18.

10 The two witnesses are called literally "sons of Belial" (i.e., "sons of worthlessness"; cf. Prov 19:28). The term is used of utter reprobates (hence NIV's "scoundrels," cf. Judg 19:22; 1 Sam 10:27) and came to be applied by Jewish writers and the writers of the NT to Satan (cf. 2 Cor 6:15).

בֵּרַכְתָּ (bēraktā) is literally "thou has blessed." Because it was considered blasphemy even to mention the cursing of God (cf. Job 1:5; 2:5, 9; Ps 10:3), the Jews employed a euphemism in mentioning the practice. The NIV puts the message into indirect discourse and gives the sense intended: "cursed." F.I. Andersen ("The Socio-Juridical Background of the Naboth Incident," JBL 85 [1966]: 46–55) suggests that the charge against Naboth was that he defaulted on his promise to sell his land to the king, a charge that would provide grounds for Ahab's seizure of Naboth's property in accordance with the legal codes of the ancient Near East. If, in addition, he had taken a formal oath in the presence of God and king as to his rightful ownership of the property or as to his refusal to sell and he was convicted of wrongdoing, such blasphemous conduct would demand his death.

14 According to 2 Kings 9:26, Naboth's sons were also put to death at the same time. Since there was no male heir and because the crime was blasphemy, Near Eastern custom dictated that the king could lay a claim against the property. But such confiscation was against the spirit of the law (Deut 13:12–16; 17:14–17).

19 R. Jamieson (JFB, 2:365) points out that since dogs were allowed to run wild in packs in the ancient world, it was common to speak of giving the carcass of an enemy or a scoundrel to the dogs (cf. Ps 68:23 and Achilles' treatment of Hector in Homer's Iliad, book 22). The fact that the prophecy was not literally fulfilled is conditioned by vv.27–29; the modified prophecy was fulfilled in Jehu's slaughter of Ahab's sons (2 Kings 9:26) and in the licking of Ahab's blood by dogs at the pool in Samaria (1 Kings 22:37–38).

23 The threat was literally fulfilled (see 2 Kings 9:30–37). Jezebel was thrown from the window of her house, which may have been on the city wall. The fact that 2 Kings 9:10, 36–37 uses the phrase חֵלֶק יִזְרְעֶאל (hēleq yizrᵉᶜeᵉl, "the portion of Jezreel") need not mean that one must insert this here in v.23 as do the Vulgate, Syriac, Targum, and nine Hebrew MSS. These probably corrected v.23 in accordance with the later fulfillment statement in 2 Kings 9:36.

25–26 The divine evaluation of Ahab at this point may indicate an editorial comment by the author of Kings, which he places between the two source documents he was utilizing.

27 The rending of garments was a common expression of grief or terror in the face of great personal or national calamity (Gen 37:29, 34; 44:13; Num 14:6; Josh 7:6; Judg 11:35; 2 Sam 1:2; 3:31; 2 Kings 5:7–8; 11:14; 19:1; 22:11; Ezra 9:3; Esth 4:1; Job 2:12).

---

e. Ahab and the campaign for Ramoth Gilead (22:1–40)

1) The prophetic declarations

22:1–28

¹For three years there was no war between Aram and Israel. ²But in the third year Jehoshaphat king of Judah went down to see the king of Israel. ³The king of Israel had said to his officials, "Don't you know that Ramoth Gilead belongs to us and yet we are doing nothing to retake it from the king of Aram?"

⁴So he asked Jehoshaphat, "Will you go with me to fight against Ramoth Gilead?"

Jehoshaphat replied to the king of Israel, "I am as you are, my people as your people, my horses as your horses." ⁵But Jehoshaphat also said to the king of Israel, "First seek the counsel of the LORD."

⁶So the king of Israel brought together the prophets—about four hundred men —and asked them, "Shall I go to war against Ramoth Gilead, or shall I refrain?"

"Go," they answered, "for the Lord will give it into the king's hand."

⁷But Jehoshaphat asked, "Is there not a prophet of the LORD here whom we can inquire of?"

⁸The king of Israel answered Jehoshaphat, "There is still one man through whom we can inquire of the LORD, but I hate him because he never prophesies anything good about me, but always bad. He is Micaiah son of Imlah."

"The king should not say that," Jehoshaphat replied.

⁹So the king of Israel called one of his officials and said, "Bring Micaiah son of Imlah at once."

¹⁰Dressed in their royal robes, the king of Israel and Jehoshaphat king of Judah were sitting on their thrones at the threshing floor by the entrance of the gate of Samaria, with all the prophets prophesying before them. ¹¹Now Zedekiah son of Kenaanah had made iron horns and he declared, "This is what the LORD says: 'With these you will gore the Arameans until they are destroyed.'"

¹²All the other prophets were prophesying the same thing. "Attack Ramoth Gilead and be victorious," they said, "for the LORD will give it into the king's hand."

¹³The messenger who had gone to summon Micaiah said to him, "Look, as one man the other prophets are predicting success for the king. Let your word agree with theirs, and speak favorably."

¹⁴But Micaiah said, "As surely as the LORD lives, I can tell him only what the LORD tells me."

¹⁵When he arrived, the king asked him, "Micaiah, shall we go to war against Ramoth Gilead, or shall I refrain?"

"Attack and be victorious," he answered, "for the LORD will give it into the king's hand."

¹⁶The king said to him, "How many times must I make you swear to tell me nothing but the truth in the name of the LORD?"

¹⁷Then Micaiah answered, "I saw all Israel scattered on the hills like sheep without a shepherd, and the LORD said, 'These people have no master. Let each one go home in peace.'"

¹⁸The king of Israel said to Jehoshaphat, "Didn't I tell you that he never prophesies anything good about me, but only bad?"

¹⁹Micaiah continued, "Therefore hear the word of the LORD: I saw the LORD

sitting on his throne with all the host of heaven standing around him on his right and on his left. 20And the LORD said, 'Who will entice Ahab into attacking Ramoth Gilead and going to his death there?'

"One suggested this, and another that. 21Finally, a spirit came forward, stood before the LORD and said, 'I will entice him.'

22" 'By what means?' the LORD asked.

" 'I will go out and be a lying spirit in the mouths of all his prophets,' he said.

" 'You will succeed in enticing him,' said the LORD. 'Go and do it.'

23"So now the LORD has put a lying spirit in the mouths of all these prophets of yours. The LORD has decreed disaster for you."

24Then Zedekiah son of Kenaanah went up and slapped Micaiah in the face. "Which way did the spirit from the LORD go when he went from me to speak to you?" he asked.

25Micaiah replied, "You will find out on the day you go to hide in an inner room."

26The king of Israel then ordered, "Take Micaiah and send him back to Amon the ruler of the city and to Joash the king's son 27and say, 'This is what the king says: Put this fellow in prison and give him nothing but bread and water until I return safely.' "

28Micaiah declared, "If you ever return safely, the LORD has not spoken through me." Then he added, "Mark my words, all you people!"

---

1 Some three years after the last Syrian war (1 Kings 20), probably late in the same year that the combined Aramean and Hebrew forces had withstood Shalmaneser III at Qarqar (853 B.C.), Ahab became concerned for the recovery of Ramoth Gilead to the east of the Jordan. Although the territory had been ceded over to Israel by Ben-Hadad in his submission to Ahab, the affair with Assyria had probably kept the Israelites from reoccupying the territory. With the threat of hostilities somewhat relaxed, however, and with Ben-Hadad once again flexing his military muscles, the strategic importance of Ramoth Gilead, with its key fortress at the eastern end of the Plain of Jezreel that barred access to the very heart of Israel, became all too apparent.

2–5 When Jehoshaphat of Judah arrived in the north to visit his brother-in-law Ahab (v.2), possibly to evaluate the international situation now that Qarqar was past, he found a concerned Ahab. Having shared his worries concerning Ramoth Gilead with his official staff, Ahab asked Jehoshaphat whether he would join him in a campaign to reoccupy the area (v.4). Jehoshaphat instantly put himself and his forces and supplies at Ahab's disposal, but quickly added that he would like to have the Lord's mind as to the venture (v.5).

6–14 Accordingly Ahab called in his prophets (v.6). He had gathered another four hundred prophets, probably belonging to the state religion established by Jeroboam. These all prophesied victory for Ahab in the projected campaign (v.12). One of them, a certain Zedekiah son of Kenaanah, had even cast a pair of iron horns to symbolize that the allied Israelite forces would surely gore the Arameans to death at Ramoth Gilead (v.11). Jehoshaphat, however, failed to be assured by these pseudo-prophets of an unlawful cult and asked whether a prophet of Yahweh were available for consultation (v.7). Ahab could produce only one—a certain Micaiah son of Imlah, whom he hated because he seemed always to prophesy evil against the king (v.8). Nevertheless, at Jehoshaphat's insistence Micaiah was summoned (v.9).

As Micaiah was brought to the waiting kings, he was informed that the "other prophets" had all given a favorable prognostication and so was warned to be agreeable (v. 13). Micaiah, being a true prophet of the Lord, replied that he could speak only what the Lord told him to say (v. 14).

15–23 At first Micaiah told Ahab to "attack and be victorious" (v. 15). Ahab sensed the sarcasm and demanded the truth (v. 16). Micaiah answered with two parabolic visions. In the first Israel was likened to shepherdless sheep scattered on the mountains, which must find their own way home (v. 17). In the second Micaiah described a heavenly scene in which the Lord and his hosts discussed the best way to get Ahab to Ramoth Gilead so that he might fall in battle (vv. 19–23). It was decided that false prophets, possessed by a lying spirit, would feed Ahab's ego by assuring him of victory in the projected battle.

24–25 Micaiah's message was clear: Ahab's prophets were wrong; Ahab would go up to defeat and death. At this point Zedekiah son of Kenaanah decided on a face-saving measure: he slapped Micaiah on the face, inquiring as to how the Spirit of the Lord had gone from himself to go to Micaiah (v. 24). Micaiah had a prophecy for Zedekiah, also. Zedekiah would understand Micaiah's prophecy fully in that day when he would hide himself from the enemy in an inner room (v. 25).

26–28 Ahab demanded that Micaiah be put in prison on minimum rations until the king should return (vv. 26–27). Micaiah had one last word for the king and all the assembled people: If Ahab returned at all, then the Lord had not spoken through Micaiah (v. 28)!

Notes

1 The exact location of Ramoth Gilead is debated, at least three sites being strongly suggested. Famed as the home of Jephthah (Judg 11:34) and as a key administrative center in the Solomonic era (1 Kings 4:13), it had been lost to Israel when Ben-Hadad took it from Omri (cf. Jos. Antiq. VIII, 398–99 [xv.3]). It was to figure greatly in the fall of the Omride Dynasty (cf. 2 Kings 9:1–15; 2 Chron 22:2–6).

   That Ahab's daughter was married to Jehoshaphat's son probably indicates that at least a loose alliance existed between the two kingdoms. See Malamat, pp. 90–93.

   By "horses" Jehoshaphat probably meant his war chariots (cf. Exod 15:19). The parallel account in 2 Chron 18:3 does not read these words but does give Jehoshaphat's promise to join Ahab in war.

5 דָּרַשׁ (dāraš, "seek") is the usual word for consulting an oracle. The kings of the ancient Near East commonly sought the will of the god before entering into battle. See for example the Zakir Inscription (ANET, p. 655) and the Moabite Stone (ANET, pp. 320f.). The Assyrian kings regularly consulted an oracle before battle (see the various annalistic reports in ANET, pp. 274–301). For consulting the Lord before battle, see Judg 20:27–28; 1 Sam 23:2–4; 30:8; 2 Sam 5:19–25.

6 Cyrus Gordon (*The Ancient Near East*, 3d rev. ed. [New Castle: Norton, n.d.], p 202) calls such false prophets "a variety of court flatterers."

8 One wonders as to Ahab's failure to mention Elijah. Perhaps he was absent, leaving only Micaiah available for consultation. Even he had to be brought out from prison.

9 סָרִיס (sārîs, "[court] official") comes from the Akkadian ša rēši (šarri) ("the one of the

[king's] head"). Its frequent translation by "eunuch" comes from the ancient practice of using such men in key positions in the court (cf. Esth 2:3–15; 4:4–5; see further TWOT, 2:634–35).

10 Threshing floors were often places of spiritual significance (cf. Judg 6:36–40). Thus Joseph mourned for Jacob at a threshing floor (Gen 50:10), and David built an altar and Solomon the temple at the famous threshing floor of Araunah (2 Sam 24:18–25; 1 Chron 21:15–22:1; 2 Chron 3:1). In Canaanite tradition the threshing floor became the scene where court was held at a place near the city gate (see ANET, pp. 144–45, 151, 153). Gordon (UT, p. 381) compares the word to the Akkadian *maqrattu* found at Nuzu that depicts a place where a court of justice was held.

11 Zedekiah attempted to reinforce his use of symbolic magic with Scripture (Deut 33:17). For the image of the goring horn, see Dan 8; Mic 4:13; Zech 1:18–19. Sennacherib, on his fifth campaign, reported that he led his men like a wild ox (see R. Borger, *Babylonisch-Assyrische Lesestücke* [Rome: Pontificum Institutum Biblicum, 1963], 3:47). Ashurbanipal reported that his enemies were gored by the goddess Ninlil's horns (see ANET, p. 300). Pharaoh could also be represented as a goring bull, as already on the Narmer Palette (see Seton Lloyd, *The Art of the Ancient Near East* [New York: Praeger, 1961], pp. 32–33, ill. 14).

15–16 Ahab, emboldened by the prophets' unanimous prediction and by Zedekiah's prophetic dramatization, may have thought that he saw in Micaiah's sarcastic agreement some weakness. Perhaps Micaiah had no message at all?

17 Edersheim (*History*, 6:65–67) correctly interprets Micaiah's twofold reply as a parabolic vision by which God reveals to Micaiah what would surely happen, even though the specific details in the framework of the occasion did not actually happen. Presented in dramatic form (in answer to Zedekiah's dramatic enactment), the twofold divine message would more forcefully impress the divine interpretation on the assembled crowd.

The motif of the shepherd and the sheep is a familiar one. God himself was shepherd to Israel, his flock (Isa 40:11; Jer 31:10; Ezek 34:12; cf. Gen 48:15; 49:24; Pss 23:1; 80:1). Israel's leaders were charged with caring for the people as a shepherd watched over his flock (Num 27:17). The later prophets were to address Israel's leaders as false shepherds (Jer 2:8; 10:21; 23; 25:32–38; Ezek 34; Zech 10:2–3; 11:4–17). Ultimately the Messiah would be the great (Heb 13:20) and Good Shepherd who lays down his life for the sheep (Zech 13:7; John 10:11–18; 1 Peter 2:25). For the smitten shepherd and the scattered sheep, see Zech 13:7; Matt 26:31; Mark 14:27.

19 The concept of a parabolic vision obviates any need to resort to explaining this passage in terms of any supposed cultic mythological concept of a supreme god and his royal court, as is so frequently done; see, for example, W.F. Albright, *Yahweh and the Gods of Canaan* (Garden City: Doubleday, 1969), pp. 191ff.

That the angels do form a heavenly assemblage is stated elsewhere in the Scriptures (Job 1:6; 2:1; Pss 82:1; 89:6–7; 103:19–20; 148:1–2; Zech 6:5–8; cf. 1 Tim 5:21; Heb 1:6; 12:22; Rev 5:11–12; 7:11–12; 14:10), though this in no way need be construed that they meet to counsel God or to intercede for those on earth.

20 The "lying spirit" is as Keil (pp. 276f.) and Montgomery (p. 339) correctly maintain, the personified spirit of prophecy (cf. 1 Sam 10:10–12; 19:23–24; Zech 13:2; 1 John 4:6) that works in accordance with the sovereign will of God. That the prophets were under evil influence is true; but their delusive prophecies only fed the king's own self-destructive ends. The Lord used all these conditions to effect his will in the situation.

24–25 The fulfillment of Micaiah's prophecy regarding Zedekiah is not recorded but likely took place when Jehu seized the palace (2 Kings 10:17–27).

26 The "king's son" probably refers here to an important state official who was of royal blood. See A.F. Rainey, "The Prince and the Pauper," *Ugarit-Furschungen* 7 (1975): 427–32.

28 Micaiah put forward the test of external verification and held all assembled as witnesses.

2) *The Israelite defeat*

22:29–40

²⁹So the king of Israel and Jehoshaphat king of Judah went up to Ramoth Gilead. ³⁰The king of Israel said to Jehoshaphat, "I will enter the battle in disguise, but you wear your royal robes." So the king of Israel disguised himself and went into battle.

³¹Now the king of Aram had ordered his thirty-two chariot commanders, "Do not fight with anyone, small or great, except the king of Israel." ³²When the chariot commanders saw Jehoshaphat, they thought, "Surely this is the king of Israel." So they turned to attack him, but when Jehoshaphat cried out, ³³the chariot commanders saw that he was not the king of Israel and stopped pursuing him.

³⁴But someone drew his bow at random and hit the king of Israel between the sections of his armor. The king told his chariot driver, "Wheel around and get me out of the fighting. I've been wounded." ³⁵All day long the battle raged, and the king was propped up in his chariot facing the Arameans. The blood from his wound ran onto the floor of the chariot, and that evening he died. ³⁶As the sun was setting, a cry spread through the army: "Every man to his town; everyone to his land!"

³⁷So the king died and was brought to Samaria, and they buried him there. ³⁸They washed the chariot at a pool in Samaria (where the prostitutes bathed), and the dogs licked up his blood, as the word of the LORD had declared.

³⁹As for the other events of Ahab's reign, including all he did, the palace he built and inlaid with ivory, and the cities he fortified, are they not written in the book of the annals of the kings of Israel? ⁴⁰Ahab rested with his fathers. And Ahaziah his son succeeded him as king.

29–33 Despite Micaiah's warning, Jehoshaphat accompanied Ahab to the battle (v.29). Although he disdained Micaiah's prophecy, Ahab obviously did not take it lightly; for though Jehoshaphat went into battle in full royal regalia, Ahab disguised himself (v.30). Jehoshaphat's compliance with Ahab's plan nearly cost him his life, for Ben-Hadad had given strict orders to his commanders to search out the king of Israel (v.31). Thus he repaid Ahab's leniency (cf. 20:34, 42). Mistaking Jehoshaphat for Ahab, Ben-Hadad's men were on the verge of killing the Judean king when his cry convinced them that they were pursuing the wrong man (vv.32–33).

34–36 Ahab was not to escape the prophecy, however. A "random" arrow found its mark, inflicting a mortal wound so that Ahab was wheeled out of the battle (v.34). Although he had many shortcomings, cowardice in battle was not one of them. So that the soldiers would not become discouraged by his death, Ahab had his dying body propped up in his chariot (v.35). As the sun set on the day's battle, Ahab's life blood gave out. When it was known that the king was dead, as Ahab had feared and as Micaiah had predicted, the army scattered (v.36).

37–40 The dead king's body was returned to Samaria and buried (v.37). While his blood-stained chariot was being washed at a pool frequented by harlots, true to the various prophecies (20:42; 21:19; 22:17, 20), dogs licked up his blood (v.38). Thus did notorious Ahab leave his famed ivory palace behind him; he was succeeded by Ahaziah, his son (v.40).

Notes

29 Although Jehoshaphat promised Ahab full support in the campaign, Ben-Hadad's instructions to his commanders and the sparing of Jehoshaphat's life, as well as the failure to mention any Judean army either in battle or on the return from the fray, may indicate that Jehoshaphat had perhaps led only a token force. At any rate his presence at Ramoth Gilead was severely denounced by God's prophet (2 Chron 19:1–3).

31–32 God's hand was at work in the entire episode. Ben-Hadad's orders were intended to cut the battle short and so save many lives, so that there might be adequate manpower in the event of any renewed hostilities with Shalmaneser III. Indeed the Aramean-led coalition was to face Shalmaneser again in 849, 845, and 841 B.C. But Ben-Hadad's very orders were arranged by God to effect Ahab's demise, as well as God's superintending intercession in behalf of Jehoshaphat (2 Chron 18:31).

32 On אָמְרוּ (*āmᵉrû*, "they thought"), see the note on 2 Kings 5:11.

34 The emphasis of the phrase "at random" turns on the bowman's skill, not his understanding that he was aiming at Ahab. The arrow struck Ahab between one of the strips of armor consisting of movable joints that joined the solid breastplate and the lower armor. Such armor has been found in several places throughout the Near East. See W.H. Mare, "Armor, Arms," ZPEB, 1:312–20.

38 The alternate NIV reading "cleaned the weapons" depends on changing זֹנוֹת (*zōnōt*, "harlots") to זְיָנוֹת (*zᵉyānōt*), taking it from the Aramaic sense of "armor" (cf. KJV; Syr., "they cleaned his armor").

The reference to harlots is not without its point. That pool where Ahab's blood flowed may, as Edersheim (*History*, 6:72) suggests, have been a sacred one erected for the lustration rites of the priestesses of the very cult Ahab and Jezebel introduced into Israel. Such "priestesses" are called by the sacred writer for what they were: "harlots." Thus did the pool of spiritual harlotry engulf its paramours beneath its enticing surface. The LXX is even more emphatic: "The swine and the dogs licked up the blood and the harlots bathed in the blood."

39 Ahab's palace (cf. Amos 3:15), unearthed in the excavations at Samaria, could be described as an "ivory house" for three reasons: (1) the outside of the building was covered with a polished white limestone that would give an ivorylike appearance in the gleaming sun, (2) the internal wall panels were made of inlaid ivory, and (3) the furniture was lavishly decorated with inlaid ivory.

---

4. The reign of Jehoshaphat in the southern kingdom

22:41–50

⁴¹Jehoshaphat son of Asa became king of Judah in the fourth year of Ahab king of Israel. ⁴²Jehoshaphat was thirty-five years old when he became king, and he reigned in Jerusalem twenty-five years. His mother's name was Azubah daughter of Shilhi. ⁴³In everything he walked in the ways of his father Asa and did not stray from them; he did what was right in the eyes of the LORD. The high places, however, were not removed, and the people continued to offer sacrifices and burn incense there. ⁴⁴Jehoshaphat was also at peace with the king of Israel.

⁴⁵As for the other events of Jehoshaphat's reign, the things he achieved and his military exploits, are they not written in the book of the annals of the kings of Judah? ⁴⁶He rid the land of the rest of the male shrine prostitutes who remained there even after the reign of his father Asa. ⁴⁷There was then no king in Edom; a deputy ruled.

⁴⁸Now Jehoshaphat built a fleet of trading ships to go to Ophir for gold, but they

never set sail—they were wrecked at Ezion Geber. ⁴⁹At that time Ahaziah son of Ahab said to Jehoshaphat, "Let my men sail with your men," but Jehoshaphat refused.

⁵⁰Then Jehoshaphat rested with his fathers and was buried with them in the city of David his father. And Jehoram his son succeeded him.

41–42 Jehoshaphat, who had ruled three years as coregent with his father, Asa, came into independent rule in the fourth year of Ahab of Israel (874–853 B.C.) or 870 B.C. (v.41). His total reign was some twenty-five years (873–848 B.C.) (v.42). The record of Jehoshaphat's reign is greatly abbreviated by the author of Kings, containing only a short sketch of his lengthy reign, a brief evaluation of his spiritual condition and activities, and a few notices of international events before recording his death. A fuller discussion of the events of Jehoshaphat's reign can be found in 2 Chronicles 17:1–21:1 (q.v.).

43–46 Jehoshaphat's spiritual condition was basically sound and largely commended by God (v.43a; cf. 2 Chron 17:3–4; 19:4–7; 20:3–13, 32). His concern for spiritual things (2 Chron 17:7–9) manifested itself in religious and social reforms (v.46; cf. 2 Chron 17:6; 19:3–11). Accordingly God blessed his reign (2 Chron 17:1–6, 12–18:1) and gave him respite and respect with all the lands round about (v.44; 2 Chron 17:10 –11; 20:28–30). He did, however, stop short of a full purging of idolatry (v.43b; 2 Chron 20:33); and the marriage of his son Jehoram to Athaliah, Ahab's daughter, was to bring about a tragic condition in Judah (2 Kings 8:18–19; 11:1–3; 2 Chron 21:6– 7, 11).

Three other tragic areas are singled out in the divine record: (1) Jehoshaphat went with Ahab to the battle of Ramoth Gilead, despite Micaiah's warning (cf. 2 Chron 18:28–19:3); (2) he subsequently entered into an ill-fated commercial venture with Ahaziah (vv.48–49; 2 Chron 20:35–37); and (3) still later he went with Jehoram on his Transjordanian expedition (2 Kings 3:6–27).

47–49 The historical notice in v.47 is probably intended to explain how it was that Jehoshaphat could have renewed commercial activities in Ezion Geber. The Edomite weakness may be attributable to Jehoshaphat's victory over the Transjordanian coalition, as detailed in 2 Chronicles 20. Jehoshaphat's commercial alliance with Ahaziah (v.48) was denounced by the Lord through his prophet Eliezer (2 Chron 20:36–37). Because Ahaziah was an apostate, God had sent a storm to destroy the fleet before it could set sail. Evidently Jehoshaphat was wise enough to refuse a second trading proposal put forward by Ahaziah (v.49).

50 The notice of Jehoshaphat's passing is amplified by the fact that his further life and history were recorded in the historical records of Jehu son of Hanani (cf. 2 Chron 20:34).

Notes

41 The LXX omits vv.41–50 here, though the full account is given after 16:28. Jehoshaphat ("Yahweh has judged") is the second Judean king with the *YAH* element in his name; most of the subsequent kings would have it.

45 Jehoshaphat's exploits and military achievements include the strengthening of his border by establishing permanent garrison cities along the northern frontier (2 Chron 17:1–2, 12), the training and equipping of a sizeable army (2 Chron 17:14–19) that was able to quell a Transjordanian invasion (2 Chron 20:1–30), and the placing of Edom under Judean control, thereby controlling the important caravan route to the south (2 Kings 3:8–27; 2 Chron 20:36). His political successes inaugurated an era of peace and cooperation with Israel, with whom Judah had been constantly at war (v.44; 2 Kings 3; 2 Chron 18:1–19:3). Jehoshaphat was also an able administrator, effecting some important judicial (2 Chron 19:5–11) and religious reforms (2 Chron 17:3–9).

46 For male shrine-prostitutes see the note on 14:24.

47 Edom's continued dependence on Judah can be seen in the fact that it joined with Israel and Judah in their later Moabite expedition (2 Kings 3:9–27).

48–49 The original location of Tarshish has not been established with absolute certainty. Some have linked it with Tartessus in Spain (BDB, p. 1076) or with Numidian Africa (E.J. Young, *The Book of Isaiah* [Grand Rapids: Eerdmans, 1974], 1:128). The inscriptions of Esarhaddon of Assyria (681–668 B.C.) equate it with a Phoenician land at the west end of the Mediterranean Sea (cf. Jonah 1:3), and an inscription from Nora on Sardinia links that Phoenician trading center with Tarshish (see M. Unger, *Archaeology and the Old Testament* [Grand Rapids: Zondervan, 1954], pp. 225f.). Isaiah (23:1) seems to connect Tarshish with Greek maritime activity (cf. Gen 10:4; Isa 66:19). W.F. Albright, "New Light on the Early History of Phoenician Colonization," BASOR 83 (1941): 21, points out the relation of Tarshish with Akkadian *taršišu* ("smelting plant," "refinery"), suggesting that Jehoshaphat's Tarshish ships were a refinery fleet that transported smelted ore.

While Tarshish apparently lay in the western Mediterranean, possibly on Sardinia, it could be reached via Ezion Geber (10:22; 2 Chron 20:36). Accordingly Cyrus Gordon (*Before Columbus* [New York: Crown, 1971], pp. 113f.; 136f.) boldly suggests an Atlantic port, possibly even a new world site, such as Mexico!

Not only metal ores, but various precious and exotic commodities are tied in with Tarshish fleets (e.g., gold, silver, iron, tin, lead, ivory products, and peacocks; cf. 10:22; 2 Chron 9:21; Jer 10:9; Ezek 27:12). The trade in these luxury items from distant lands may have transferred the original significance into a general term for a distant and exotic land reached by "Tarshish ships."

---

5. *The reign of Ahaziah in the northern kingdom*

22:51–1:18

[51]Ahaziah son of Ahab became king of Israel in Samaria in the seventeenth year of Jehoshaphat king of Judah, and he reigned over Israel two years. [52]He did evil in the eyes of the Lord, because he walked in the ways of his father and mother and in the ways of Jeroboam son of Nebat, who caused Israel to sin. [53]He served and worshiped Baal and provoked the Lord, the God of Israel, to anger, just as his father had done.

[1]After Ahab's death, Moab rebelled against Israel. [2]Now Ahaziah had fallen through the lattice of his upper room in Samaria and injured himself. So he sent messengers, saying to them, "Go and consult Baal-Zebub, the god of Ekron, to see if I will recover from this injury." [3]But the angel of the Lord said to Elijah the Tishbite, "Go up and meet the messengers of the king of Samaria and ask them, 'Is it because there is no God in Israel that you are going off to consult Baal-Zebub, the god of Ekron?' [4]Therefore this is what the Lord says: 'You will not leave the bed you are lying on. You will certainly die!'" So Elijah went.

⁵When the messengers returned to the king, he asked them, "Why have you come back?"

⁶"A man came to meet us," they replied. "And he said to us, 'Go back to the king who sent you and tell him, "This is what the LORD says: Is it because there is no God in Israel that you are sending men to consult Baal-Zebub, the god of Ekron? Therefore you will not leave the bed you are lying on. You will certainly die!" ' "

⁷The king asked them, "What kind of man was it who came to meet you and told you this?"

⁸They replied, "He was a man with a garment of hair and with a leather belt around his waist."

The king said, "That was Elijah the Tishbite."

⁹Then he sent to Elijah a captain with his company of fifty men. The captain went up to Elijah, who was sitting on the top of a hill, and said to him, "Man of God, the king says, 'Come down!' "

¹⁰Elijah answered the captain, "If I am a man of God, may fire come down from heaven and consume you and your fifty men!" Then fire fell from heaven and consumed the captain and his men.

¹¹At this the king sent to Elijah another captain with his fifty men. The captain said to him, "Man of God, this is what the king says, 'Come down at once!' "

¹²"If I am a man of God," Elijah replied, "may fire come down from heaven and consume you and your fifty men!" Then the fire of God fell from heaven and consumed him and his fifty men.

¹³So the king sent a third captain with his fifty men. This third captain went up and fell on his knees before Elijah. "Man of God," he begged, "please have respect for my life and the lives of these fifty men, your servants! ¹⁴See, fire has fallen from heaven and consumed the first two captains and all their men. But now have respect for my life!"

¹⁵The angel of the LORD said to Elijah, "Go down with him; do not be afraid of him." So Elijah got up and went down with him to the king.

¹⁶He told the king, "This is what the LORD says: Is it because there is no God in Israel for you to consult that you have sent messengers to consult Baal-Zebub, the god of Ekron? Because you have done this, you will never leave the bed you are lying on. You will certainly die!" ¹⁷So he died, according to the word of the LORD that Elijah had spoken.

Because Ahaziah had no son, Joram succeeded him as king in the second year of Jehoram son of Jehoshaphat king of Judah. ¹⁸As for all the other events of Ahaziah's reign, and what he did, are they not written in the book of the annals of the kings of Israel?

51–53 The chapter closes with a notice of the accession of Ahab's son, Ahaziah, and a note that he "provoked the LORD, the God of Israel, to anger, just as his father had done."

1–4 Ahab's son Ahaziah (853–852 B.C.) perpetuated his father's wickedness incurring God's judicial anger (1 Kings 22:51–53). The divine judgment took numerous forms: (1) *politically*, Moab found in the death of Ahab occasion to rebel against Israel (v.1); (2) *economically*, God thwarted Ahaziah's attempted commercial enterprise with Jehoshaphat (1 Kings 22:47–48; 2 Chron 20:36–37); (3) *personally*, the circumstances of Ahaziah's life were allowed to proceed in such a way that Israel's new king suffered a serious fall through the latticework of the upper chamber to the courtyard below (v.2).

Ahaziah was aware of the seriousness of his physical condition. In such circumstances a man's basic spiritual temperament will often surface. Immersed in the Baalism of his father, Ahaziah naturally sent messengers to inquire of the oracle at Ekron whether he would recover from his injuries (v.2). Scarcely had they begun their mission when suddenly an austere-appearing man, dressed in a rough animal-hide garment girded at the waist with a leather belt (v.8), interrupted them. Before they could gather their composure, this man sternly announced the answer to their message (v.4), together with a denunciation of the whole mission. The king had erred in seeking information from the false god of the Philistines; and he was wrong in hoping that he might recover, for surely he would die in his wickedness.

5–8 The fearful appearance and awful message caused the messengers to return instantly to the king (v.5), where they reported to Ahaziah the whole episode (v.6). The king recognized at once that the stern rebuke was from none other than Elijah the Tishbite (v.8). In at least this he was correct, for God had caused Elijah to meet the king's messengers and deliver the divine sentence. The secret mission and the hidden desires of the royal chambers were not unknown to the true King of the universe. What an awesome realization that must have been for Ahaziah! Yet there is no hint in the scriptural record that Ahaziah repented in the least. Rather all that follows speaks of an obdurately stubborn and sinful heart.

9–10 It seems that Ahaziah knew well the whereabouts of Elijah and immediately sent off a contingent of soldiers to bring him (by force if necessary) to the king (v.9). Ahaziah apparently picked a commander and squad that shared his insolent godliness; for on arriving where Elijah was located, they demanded the prophet's surrender. Elijah seized on the aptness of the prophetic title "man of God"; he was indeed God's man! Since that was so, such ungodliness—even in the line of duty—would be judged. Instantly, at Elijah's bidding, heavenly fire consumed the commander and all his men (v.10).

11–14 When the captain and his fifty men did not return, Ahaziah sent a still more arrogant commander together with his fifty-man squad, who met the very same judgment (vv.11–12). Doubtless word of the fate of those soldiers had by now become known to the king so that as he selected a third commander and his fifty, his selection was of a man of greater wisdom (v.13). As this commander and his men dutifully placed themselves before Elijah, they respectfully petitioned him both for their lives (v.14) and for the prophet to kindly consent to accompany them back to Samaria and to the king.

15–18 In accordance with God's instructions, Elijah went with the commander to Ahaziah where he repeated clearly in the king's ear the divine sentence. Ahaziah's case was settled. Because of his stubborn disbelief and settled wickedness, the king would surely die (v.16). And so it was to come to pass, his brother Joram succeeding the childless Ahaziah in what was the second year of the reign of Jehoshaphat's son, also named Jehoram (852 B.C.), of the southern kingdom (v.17).

Notes

51–53 For Ahaziah's relations with Moab and his injury and death, see 2 Kings 1:1–18; 3:5.

1 The notice concerning the Moabite rebellion provides the historical framework for events after the passing of Ahab. The author will return to the Moabite problem again in ch. 3.

2 On the upper room see the note on 9:30. The typical Syrian upper balcony was enclosed with a jointed wood lattice-work that, while suitable for privacy, could easily be broken. For legislation concerning protective parapets to minimize the danger of someone falling from domestic houses, see Deut 22:8.

The exact name and distinct nature of בַּעַל זְבוּב (*Baʿal zᵉbûb*, "Baal-Zebub"), the local god of Ekron, have been much discussed (cf. Matt 12:24). The more original cognate may be Baal Zebûl ("Baal is prince"; see the note on 1 Kings 16:31).

Although Hebrew scribes may have deliberately perpetuated the inherent confusion in the names with pejorative intent so that "Prince Baal" became Baal Zebel ("lord of dung") and Baal Zebûb ("lord of flies"), the presence of the form Baal Zebûb here, reflected fully in the Syriac and the Vulgate traditions, may indicate some more originally positive designation. The existence in Ugaritic of the cognate term 'il ḏbb (ANET, p. 137) may, as J.J.M. Roberts (*The Earliest Semitic Pantheon* [Baltimore: Johns Hopkins Press, 1972], p. 119) suggests, make it "impossible to simply dismiss *zᵉbub* as a vulgarization for *zᵉbūl*." Moreover the uncertainties inherent in Ugaritic ḏ (see UT, pp. 26f.) complicate the entire picture so that perhaps the original signification will never be known. Indeed since the term is uniquely associated with a Philistine setting, conceivably a non-Semitic origin may well be demanded.

The question naturally arises as to why Ahaziah should send away to foreign soil to inquire of Baal, since Baalism permeated the Israelite kingdom. The answer may be threefold.

1. Politically, as was so often true in Israel and the ancient Near East, the young king may well have had his political rivals and enemies. Ahaziah may have wished to keep the knowledge of his true condition secret from them.

2. Religiously, Baal seems to have been particularly the cult-god of Ekron (e.g., as opposed to Dagon at Ashdod). Moreover the Philistines and possibly the Baal of Ekron had a well-known reputation for divination and soothsaying (1 Sam 6:2; Isa 2:6).

3. Geographically, Ekron lay near at hand, being located just a few miles from the confluence of Israel's southwestern border with Judah and Philistia.

3 The term מַלְאַךְ יהוה (*malʾak yhwh*, "the angel of the LORD") occurs in Kings only in this setting (cf. v.15) and in 1 Kings 19:7 and 2 Kings 19:35. In none of these cases does the term appear to refer to a Christophany. Both here and in 1 Kings 19 (note esp. v.5), the angel in question is Yahweh's messenger (angel) in contradistinction to that of the wicked royalty. In 2 Kings 19:35 (q.v.) God's death angel is in view.

The title "king of Samaria" reflects a frequent biblical custom of designating a king by his capital city (cf. 1 Kings 21:1; Jonah 3:6). It is by no means a mark of late editorialism, as often charged.

Concerning לִדְרֹשׁ בְּבַעַל זְבוּב (*lidrōš bᵉbaʿal zᵉbûb*, "to consult Baal-Zebub"), the OT normally uses the verb דָּרַשׁ (*dāraš*, "consult") with the simple accusative when the mind of the true God is sought (e.g., 1 Kings 22:8; 2 Kings 3:11; 8:8; 22:13, 18); but when a false deity is involved, the preposition בְּ (*b*, "in," "from") is frequently employed as is the case here (cf. 1 Sam 28:7; 1 Chron 10:13).

8 בַּעַל שֵׂעָר (*baʿal śēʿār*, lit., "possessor of hair") has been understood in two ways: (1) "a hairy man" (so the ancient vers., KJV, NASB); (2) "a garment of hair" (so NIV, RSV, and the majority of modern commentators). Not only the syntax, which stresses the appearance of Elijah as one who wore a hairy garment girded at the waist with a leather belt, but the prophetic garb itself (cf. Zech 13:4) and the typical role of Elijah ascribed to John the Baptist (Matt 3:4) favor the latter view.

9 The term שַׂר־חֲמִשִּׁים (*śar-ḥᵃmiššîm*, "captain of fifty") indicates something of the organization of Israel's standing army (see further de Vaux, *Ancient Israel*, pp. 214–28). The similar title occurs in the Akkadian *rab ḥamšû*. The hill on which Elijah sat has been identified by many as one of the peaks of Carmel.

9–10 For the term "man of God," see the note on 13:1.

11–14 Each captain of fifty approached Elijah differently. The first went boldly up the hill before Elijah in person; the second presented his deeds still more harshly but at a distance; the third again climbed the hill but with all due respect and in great fear.

13–14 The third captain was, apparently, of finer spiritual fiber than the preceding two and the king himself. He struck the fine balance of doing his duty, but not without recourse to God as the higher power (cf. Matt 22:21; 1 Peter 2:17).

17 The chronological note with regard to Jehoram of Israel's ascending to the throne takes its point of departure as the second year of Jehoram of Judah, due to the fact that Jehoram would rule Judah for the greater part of the time that Israel's Jehoram was ruling in the north.

	Israel	*Judah*
2 Kings 1:17	Jehoram's first year	= Jehoram's second year (cf. his coregency) = 852 B.C.
2 Kings 3:1	Jehoram's first year	= Jehoshaphat's eighteenth year (since his independent reign, which began in 870/869) = 852 B.C.
2 Kings 8:16	Jehoram's fifth year	= Jehoram's first year (of independent rule) = 848 B.C.

Accordingly Jehoram of the northern kingdom reigned 852–841 B.C., Jehoram of the southern kingdom, 853 (coregent; 848, full power)–841 B.C., Jehoshaphat, southern kingdom, 872 (coregent; 870/869, full power)–848 B.C.

---

6. The eras of Jehoram of the northern kingdom and Jehoram and Ahaziah of the southern kingdom (2:1–9:37)

a. Prophetic transition: Elijah and Elisha

2:1–25

¹When the LORD was about to take Elijah up to heaven in a whirlwind, Elijah and Elisha were on their way from Gilgal. ²Elijah said to Elisha, "Stay here; the LORD has sent me to Bethel."

But Elisha said, "As surely as the LORD lives and as you live, I will not leave you." So they went down to Bethel.

³The company of the prophets at Bethel came out to Elisha and asked, "Do you know that the LORD is going to take your master from you today?"

"Yes, I know," Elisha replied, "but do not speak of it."

⁴Then Elijah said to him, "Stay here, Elisha; the LORD has sent me to Jericho."

And he replied, "As surely as the LORD lives and as you live, I will not leave you." So they went to Jericho.

⁵The company of the prophets at Jericho went up to Elisha and asked him, "Do you know that the LORD is going to take your master from you today?"

"Yes, I know," he replied, "but do not speak of it."

⁶Then Elijah said to him, "Stay here; the Lᴏʀᴅ has sent me to the Jordan." And he replied, "As surely as the Lᴏʀᴅ lives and as you live, I will not leave you." So the two of them walked on.

⁷Fifty men of the company of the prophets went and stood at a distance, facing the place where Elijah and Elisha had stopped at the Jordan. ⁸Elijah took his cloak, rolled it up and struck the water with it. The water divided to the right and to the left, and the two of them crossed over on dry ground.

⁹When they had crossed, Elijah said to Elisha, "Tell me, what can I do for you before I am taken from you?"

"Let me inherit a double portion of your spirit," Elisha replied.

¹⁰"You have asked a difficult thing," Elijah said, "yet if you see me when I am taken from you, it will be yours—otherwise not."

¹¹As they were walking along and talking together, suddenly a chariot of fire and horses of fire appeared and separated the two of them, and Elijah went up to heaven in a whirlwind. ¹²Elisha saw this and cried out, "My father! My father! The chariots and horsemen of Israel!" And Elisha saw him no more. Then he took hold of his own clothes and tore them apart.

¹³He picked up the cloak that had fallen from Elijah and went back and stood on the bank of the Jordan. ¹⁴Then he took the cloak that had fallen from him and struck the water with it. "Where now is the Lᴏʀᴅ, the God of Elijah?" he asked. When he struck the water, it divided to the right and to the left, and he crossed over.

¹⁵The company of the prophets from Jericho, who were watching, said, "The spirit of Elijah is resting on Elisha." And they went to meet him and bowed to the ground before him. ¹⁶"Look," they said, "we your servants have fifty able men. Let them go and look for your master. Perhaps the Spirit of the Lᴏʀᴅ has picked him up and set him down on some mountain or in some valley."

"No," Elisha replied, "do not send them."

¹⁷But they persisted until he was too ashamed to refuse. So he said, "Send them." And they sent fifty men, who searched for three days but did not find him. ¹⁸When they returned to Elisha, who was staying in Jericho, he said to them, "Didn't I tell you not to go?"

¹⁹The men of the city said to Elisha, "Look, our lord, this town is well situated, as you can see, but the water is bad and the land is unproductive."

²⁰"Bring me a new bowl," he said, "and put salt in it." So they brought it to him. ²¹Then he went out to the spring and threw the salt into it, saying, "This is what the Lᴏʀᴅ says: 'I have healed this water. Never again will it cause death or make the land unproductive.' " ²²And the water has remained wholesome to this day, according to the word Elisha had spoken.

²³From there Elisha went up to Bethel. As he was walking along the road, some youths came out of the town and jeered at him. "Go on up, you baldhead!" they said. "Go on up, you baldhead!" ²⁴He turned around, looked at them and called down a curse on them in the name of the Lᴏʀᴅ. Then two bears came out of the woods and mauled forty-two of the youths. ²⁵And he went on to Mount Carmel and from there returned to Samaria.

1–2 The account of Elijah's last journey on earth begins with the aged prophet walking with his trusty aid, Elisha (v.1). The two departed from a certain Gilgal, probably not the well-known Gilgal of Joshua's day, but one located some eight miles north of Bethel in the hill country on the way to Shiloh. As they proceeded southward toward Bethel, Elijah indicated to Elisha that the Lord wanted him to go all the way to Bethel to visit his prophetic school there and so urged Elisha to stay on in Gilgal (v.2). The polite form of Elijah's command indicates that the prophet's words were permissive rather than prohibitive.

The reason for the command is not explicatively stated. Elijah no doubt knew that this was the day God would take him to be with himself (cf. vv.1, 10) and that he would leave his work to others—especially to Elisha (1 Kings 19:16). Perhaps he sought an assurance of the Lord's will with regard to that succession by putting Elisha to the test. More likely the test was primarily for the strengthening of Elisha's faith. It would appear from the narrative that Elijah had disclosed to his various students that his ministry was nearing a close and that one day soon he would pass by for the last time.

Elisha either knew from separate divine communication or strongly suspected that this day might be Elijah's last. Strongly desirous of God's will for his life and concerned that he would indeed succeed Elijah as the Lord's prophet to Israel, Elisha was determined to be with his tutor until the last. Accordingly he would not be dissuaded; he would go where Elijah went.

Notice that even though Elijah knew this was to be his last day on earth, his life was so ordered that he humbly would be about his normal duties when the Lord would take him. Moreover it would appear that his last concern was that the Lord's work would continue after his passing; so he wanted to assure himself of the progress of his "seminary students."

3 When Elijah and Elisha reached Bethel, the company of prophetic students perhaps wondered whether this would be the expected day. Not wishing to impose themselves on Elijah, they delicately drew Elisha aside to inquire of Elijah whether this was that day. Elisha was convinced of it and indicated as much to them but commanded them strongly not to speak of it. Elijah would have no self-gratifying show of form toward himself. Whatever glory would occur on that day would be to God, not to his prophet. Nor would there be tears of sorrow, for it would be a day of joyous triumph for the Lord. Elijah's wish was for God's work to go on uninterrupted, with or without his presence.

4 As Elijah prepared to leave for the school at Jericho, about fourteen miles to the southeast, he again gave permission to Elisha to remain behind. Once more Elisha steadfastly refused.

5–7 The scene at Bethel was replayed at Jericho. Again the members of the prophetical school asked Elisha about Elijah's departure; again Elisha demanded their silence; again Elijah instructed Elisha to stay behind, this time as he headed for the Jordan River, some five miles away (vv.5–6). Once more Elisha averred that he would not leave Elijah's side. Three times Elijah had tested his successor; thrice Elisha stood the test (cf. Matt 4:1–11; Luke 22:31–62; John 21:15–27). When the two prophets left for the Jordan, fifty of the prophetical students followed at a distance, anxiously awaiting the Lord's dealing with Elijah (v.7). What a contrast these fifty spiritually concerned young men formed with the squads of fifty that Ahaziah had recently sent to Elijah (cf. ch. 1)!

8 The two great prophets, master and successor, stood at the banks of the Jordan. Taking his prophet's mantle and rolling it up rodlike—as did Moses of old at the Red Sea (cf. Exod 14:16–28)—Elijah smote the river. Immediately the waters on one side piled up in a heap, the waters on the other side running off towards the Dead Sea. As had happened so long ago, the Jordan again parted; and the two passed through on dry ground (cf. Exod 14:21–22; 15:8; Josh 2:10; 3:14–17; 4:22–24; Ps 114:3–5). Only here the order is reversed. Whereas Israel had crossed into Canaan

175

to take possession of its God-appointed earthly heritage and Elisha, too, must return there to the place of his appointment, Elijah passed out of Canaan through the boundary waters of Jordan to his heavenly service, there to await his future renewed earthly appearance (cf. Mal 4:5; Matt 17:4; Mark 9:5; Luke 9:33; Rev 11:6). In this regard his ministry anticipated that of his Messiah who came incarnately to an earthly service (John 1:12) and subsequently as resurrected Savior ascended again into heaven, there to await his triumphant, glorious second advent (cf. Zech 14:3, 9; Matt 24:30; Acts 1:9–11; 1 Tim 3:16; Rev 19:11–17).

9 Elijah, sensing the imminency of his departure, asked what further thing he could do for his successor. To the very end he remained concerned for others and for the continuance of God's work.

Elisha's reply suggests that he caught the intent of his master's question. He asked for a double portion of Elijah's spirit. Undoubtedly Elisha did not ask this simply for the privilege of being Elijah's successor in terms of the Deuteronomic legislation concerning the eldest son's inheritance (Deut 21:17), for such both he and Elijah knew him to be (cf. 1 Kings 19:16–21). Nor was this simply to give some confirmatory sign for Elisha's appearance, for this is scarcely a "difficult thing" (v.10). Rather, the enormity of the loss of Elijah, that spirit-filled and empowered prophet, must have so gripped the humble Elisha that, claiming his position as first born, he asked for the firstborn's "double portion"—that is, for especially granted spiritual power far beyond his own capabilities to meet the responsibilities of the awesome task that lay before him. He wished, virtually, that Elijah's mighty prowess might continue to live through him.

10 All this lay beyond Elijah's power to grant. Nonetheless it was not beyond the divine prerogative. Indeed, doubtless by divine direction, Elijah told Elisha that if God so chose to allow Elisha to see Elijah's translation, then (and only then) would the full force of Elisha's request be granted. The sign would indicate to Elisha that God, who alone could grant such a request, had done so.

11–12 And so it would be! Suddenly, as the two walked and talked together, a fiery chariot swooped between them and took Elijah along in its terrific wind up into heaven (v.11). It was over in an instant. Elisha could but cry out in amazed tribute to his departed master (v.12). Elijah was gone. One era had ended; another had begun.

13–14 In joy mixed with sorrow, Elisha turned from viewing the heavenly spectacle that had assured him of his request to Elijah and saw yet a further sign—Elijah's fallen mantle lay at Elisha's feet. The younger prophet had once had that mantle symbolically laid on his shoulders (1 Kings 19:19); now it would rest there permanently. All he need do was pick it up. As he did so, "he picked up" as well the load of service that Elijah had left for him to do. With that very same mantle, he retraced his steps and reached the Jordan (v.13). Repeating Elijah's actions, he cried out for divine intervention on his behalf (v.14). Once again the Jordan parted, bringing not only full confirmation of his prophetic office to Elisha, but divine accreditation for him before the eyes of the fifty students who had witnessed the entire event.

15–18 The fifty instantly recognized the transferal of prophetic prominence to Elisha and accepted his leadership. The matter of Elijah's actual translation to heaven without seeing death was more difficult to comprehend, as was, indeed, the mysterious doings of the Spirit of God with man (cf. 1 Kings 18:12). To their repeated insistence that they be allowed to search the existing countryside to be sure that Elijah was truly no longer in the vicinity, Elisha at last gave in (vv.15-17). When they were fully satisfied that Elijah was nowhere to be found, they returned to Elisha, doubtless with greater resolve to listen to their new leader (v.18).

19-22 The chapter closes with two miracles of Elisha. These immediately established the character of his ministry—his would be a helping ministry to those in need, but one that would brook no disrespect for God and his earthly representatives. In the case of Jericho, though the city had been rebuilt (with difficulty) in the days of Ahab (1 Kings 16:34, q.v.), it had remained unproductive. Apparently the water still lay under Joshua's curse (cf. Josh 6:26), so that both citizenry and land suffered greatly (v.19). Elisha's miracle fully removed the age-old judgment, thus allowing a new era to dawn on this area (vv.20-22). Interestingly Elisha wrought the cure through means supplied by the people of Jericho so that their faith might be strengthened through submission and active participation in God's cleansing work.

23-25 Elisha's sweet memories of Jericho received a souring touch at Bethel (v.23). The public insult against Elisha was aimed ultimately at the God whom he represented. Indeed Elisha's whole prophetic ministry was in jeopardy; therefore the taunt had to be dealt with decisively. The sudden arrival of the two bears who mauled forty-two youths to death would serve as both an awful sentence on unbelievers—and thus, too, on Jeroboam's cult city—and a published reminder that blasphemy against the true God and his program would be met with swift and certain consequences (v.24). With these two miracles Elisha's position as successor to Elijah as God's chief prophet to Israel was assured.

Notes

1 The definite article in בַּסְּעָרָה (*bas*^e*'ārāh*, lit., "in the whirlwind") lays stress on the well-known whirlwind by which Elijah was translated into heaven without seeing death. It does not guarantee that Elijah knew the precise method of his departure from this life. The plain implication of this text is that he knew beforehand that this was the day of his change and, doubtless, Elijah expected something extraordinary.
2 For the existence of prophetic schools in ancient Israel, see Krummacher, *Elijah the Tishbite*, pp. 328-29; L.J. Wood, *The Prophets of Israel* (Grand Rapids: Baker, 1979), pp. 164-66.

Sadly Gilgal and Bethel were to be condemned by prophets in the next century as centers of pagan idolatry (Hos 4:15; 9:15; 12:11; Amos 4:4; 5:5). The mention of fifty prophets from Jericho in v.7 does not, as F.W. Meyer (*Elijah and the Secret of His Power* [Chicago: Moody, 1976], p. 154) maintains, demand that the schools were always formed into groups of fifty young men (cf., e.g., 4:43). Rather all that is stated is that fifty of their number were present. Doubtless the three prophetic schools were in some way dependent on Elijah's leadership.
3 The same verb לֹקֵחַ (*lōqēaḥ*, "is going to take") is used of Enoch's translation (Gen 5:24).
9 The "double portion" has been widely discussed. The position taken here avoids the

extremes of holding that nothing more than the right of succession is requested by Elisha (Montgomery) and the view that Elisha is asking for a double measure of Elijah's Holy Spirit (Luther), an idea often fortified by noting that Elisha performed "double" the miracles that Elijah had done (see, e.g., J.P. Free, *Archaeology and Bible History* [Wheaton: Scripture, 1962], pp. 184–85).

Spiritual comparisons between Elijah and Christ are abundant. Certainly the desire of each to prepare his disciples adequately for events after his departure is most evident (cf. Luke 24:44–48; John 14–16; see also the apostles' concern for their readers, 2 Tim 4:1–8; 2 Peter 1:12–15).

11 Edersheim (*History*, 6:99) appropriately points out that Elijah went to heaven, not in a fiery chariot as often popularly held, but in the whirlwind that accompanied the theophany. For the divine presence in the fire, chariots, and whirlwind, see Isa 66:15.

12 Elisha's cry was one of tribute to Elijah. The translated prophet had been a spiritual father to Israel and as such, spiritually, her foremost defense. Elisha would doubtless be pleased at the same testimony given to him at his death (2 Kings 13:14). The cry is one of personal sorrow and loss as well, as his rending of his clothes indicates (cf. Joel 2:13; see that note on 1 Kings 21:27).

17 Concerning עַד־בֹּשׁ (ʿaḏ-bōš, "until he was ashamed to refuse"), whether Elisha's shame was felt for his disciples in their adamant refusal to be dissuaded in the search for Elijah or was born of his own insensitivity to their incredulity is uncertain. It is instructive that Elisha's prohibitive command "do not send them" (v.16) is softened on their return to the vetitive "Did I not tell you, you ought not to go?"

20–21 The use of salt from a new bowl symbolized the cleansing of the waters so that they would take on new properties. For the ritual use of salt in purification, see Lev 2:13; Num 18:19; Ezek 43:24.

23 Baldness, regarded as a disgrace, was here an epithet of scorn (cf. Isa 3:17, 24).

24 Montgomery (p. 366) notes that bears were common enough in ancient Israel. The *Ursus Syriacus* was noted for its ferocity. The awfulness of the sentence has caused many to brand the account as unhistorical and incompatible with genuine piety. But the identification of the number of youths (forty-two) and the crucial nature of the challenge—the youth's taunting "Go on up" was doubtless a mocking caricature of Elijah's own "going up" into heaven—argue for its factualness. Accounts such as this and the execution of the Canaanites, while difficult to understand from the purely human ethical standpoint, must be left ultimately with the divine sovereignty and to the justice of an all-righteous God who does not act capriciously. Certainly in each case the vileness and corruption of the Canaanite religion and its danger to Israel are to be underscored. Moreover D. Bailey (*God and History in the Old Testament* [New York: Harper and Row, 1976], p. 94) remarks that God's messengers were "to be approached with reverence and circumspection, and without mockery or abuse, because that which had expressed itself through them is not to be mocked or abused."

---

b. *Jehoram and the Moabite campaign*

3:1–27

¹Joram son of Ahab became king of Israel in Samaria in the eighteenth year of Jehoshaphat king of Judah, and he reigned twelve years. ²He did evil in the eyes of the LORD, but not as his father and mother had done. He got rid of the sacred stone of Baal that his father had made. ³Nevertheless he clung to the sins of Jeroboam son of Nebat, which he had caused Israel to commit; he did not turn away from them.

⁴Now Mesha king of Moab raised sheep, and he had to supply the king of Israel with a hundred thousand lambs and with the wool of a hundred thousand rams.

⁵But after Ahab died, the king of Moab rebelled against the king of Israel. ⁶So at that time King Joram set out from Samaria and mobilized all Israel. ⁷He also sent this message to Jehoshaphat king of Judah: "The king of Moab has rebelled against me. Will you go with me to fight against Moab?"

"I will go with you," he replied. "I am as you are, my people as your people, my horses as your horses."

⁸"By what route shall we attack?" he asked.

"Through the Desert of Edom," he answered.

⁹So the king of Israel set out with the king of Judah and the king of Edom. After a roundabout march of seven days, the army had no more water for themselves or for the animals with them.

¹⁰"What!" exclaimed the king of Israel. "Has the Lord called us three kings together only to hand us over to Moab?"

¹¹But Jehoshaphat asked, "Is there no prophet of the Lord here, that we may inquire of the Lord through him?"

An officer of the king of Israel answered, "Elisha son of Shaphat is here. He used to pour water on the hands of Elijah."

¹²Jehoshaphat said, "The word of the Lord is with him." So the king of Israel and Jehoshaphat and the king of Edom went down to him.

¹³Elisha said to the king of Israel, "What do we have to do with each other? Go to the prophets of your father and the prophets of your mother."

"No," the king of Israel answered, "because it was the Lord who called us three kings together to hand us over to Moab."

¹⁴Elisha said, "As surely as the Lord Almighty lives, whom I serve, if I did not have respect for the presence of Jehoshaphat king of Judah, I would not look at you or even notice you. ¹⁵But now bring me a harpist."

While the harpist was playing, the hand of the Lord came upon Elisha ¹⁶and he said, "This is what the Lord says: Make this valley full of ditches. ¹⁷For this is what the Lord says: You will see neither wind nor rain, yet this valley will be filled with water, and you, your cattle and your other animals will drink. ¹⁸This is an easy thing in the eyes of the Lord; he will also hand Moab over to you. ¹⁹You will overthrow every fortified city and every major town. You will cut down every good tree, stop up all the springs, and ruin every good field with stones."

²⁰The next morning, about the time for offering the sacrifice, there it was— water flowing from the direction of Edom! And the land was filled with water.

²¹Now all the Moabites had heard that the kings had come to fight against them; so every man, young and old, who could bear arms was called up and stationed on the border. ²²When they got up early in the morning, the sun was shining on the water. To the Moabites across the way, the water looked red—like blood. ²³"That's blood!" they said. "Those kings must have fought and slaughtered each other. Now to the plunder, Moab!"

²⁴But when the Moabites came to the camp of Israel, the Israelites rose up and fought them until they fled. And the Israelites invaded the land and slaughtered the Moabites. ²⁵They destroyed the towns, and each man threw a stone on every good field until it was covered. They stopped up all the springs and cut down every good tree. Only Kir Hareseth was left with its stones in place, but men armed with slings surrounded it and attacked it as well.

²⁶When the king of Moab saw that the battle had gone against him, he took with him seven hundred swordsmen to break through to the king of Edom, but they failed. ²⁷Then he took his firstborn son, who was to succeed him as king, and offered him as a sacrifice on the city wall. The fury against Israel was great; they withdrew and returned to their own land.

1–5 The notice of Jehoram's (Joram's) accession over Israel is accompanied by a spiritual evaluation (v.1). Although he had torn down the stele to Baal that Ahab and Jezebel had erected (v.2), his perpetuation of the state cult of the golden calves that Jeroboam had established was condemnable (v.3). Thus he led Israel in continued apostasy. Within a few years of the beginning of Jehoram's twelve-year reign (852–841 B.C.), Mesha, the Moabite king, refused to send the required tribute of wool and rebelled against Israel (vv.4–5).

6–9 Quickly mobilizing his forces (v.6), Jehoram also enlisted Jehoshaphat of Judah to join with him in the expedition against the Moabites (v.7). Jehoshaphat remained a relative of Jehoram of Israel; for his son (and coregent), also named Jehoram, was married to the Jehoram of Israel's aunt, Athaliah. Jehoshaphat quickly agreed. Moreover he probably felt that he had a score to settle with Moab for the previous Moabite-Judean war (2 Chron 20:1–29). In that campaign Judah had regained mastery over previously held Ezion Geber and apparently had control over Edom itself; for when Jehoram asked his advice in planning the expedition, Jehoshaphat immediately proposed a route through Edom (v.8). Not only would this have the element of surprise to commend it, but it would gain the allied help of the Edomite forces. Moreover it would insure the invaders not only protection for the rear, but the advantage of avoiding a head-on assault across the Arnon River and into the Moabite strength that a northern invasion would necessitate. Nevertheless a week's trek through the eastern Edomite watershed nearly accomplished what the Moabites' desired: the wasting of the total armed forces of the allies together with their water supply (v.9). The allies seemed at the point of extinction.

10–14 The king of Israel was terrified, seeing only certain doom (v.10). Jehoshaphat, whatever his short comings, was concerned with spiritual things (cf. the remarks on 1 Kings 22:41–53); and, as on another occasion (1 Kings 22:7), he asked for a true prophet of the Lord (v.11). One of Jehoram's attendants reported that the prophet Elisha was available. Recognizing that God's presence was with Elisha, Jehoshaphat led the other two kings to God's prophet (v.12). At their approach Elisha addressed Jehoram—whose war with the Moabites the campaign really was—with words of strong rebuke (v.13). Why had Jehoram come to God's prophet and not to those of Baal whom Israel's royal house served? But for Jehoshaphat's sake, Elisha promised the kings that he would seek God's mind in the situation (v.14).

15–19 Having called for a harpist, Elisha went to prayer (v.15). God's answer came: there would be ample water for the physical needs (vv.16–17); moreover the Lord would give them victory over the Moabites (vv.18–19). The revelation included directions for human response. The kings' men were to dig ditches; for though they would see no storm, yet the Lord would send water in abundance. And so it came about.

20–25 At the time of the morning sacrifice, the area was filled to overflowing with water that ran down out of the mountains of Edom (v.20). God had sent necessary life-giving water. But these waters were to spell death for the Moabites (v.21). Viewing that same water, reddened by the soil and gleaming all the redder in the rising eastern sun, the enemy mistook it for blood (v.22) and, surmising that the three former antagonists had had a falling out that had led to their near mutual extermination, they rushed to the Israelite camp intent on plunder (v.23). Too late they realized their mistake. The disorganized Moabite soldiers were met by the well-stationed allies who not only turned them back but, in turn, invaded Moab, effecting a great destruction (v.24). The Moabites fell back in disarray as far as Kir Hareseth, where they determined to make a final stand (v.25).

26–27 As the desperate struggle of the siege of Kir Hareseth continued, the frenzied Moabite king sacrificed his firstborn son and heir to the throne so that the anger of his gods might be appeased and the city delivered. While Moab's god could never deliver the king and the city, the act had the desired effect. Sickened by the maddened spectacle of senseless human sacrifice, the allies lifted the siege and returned to their homes. As Krummacher (*Elisha*, p. 45) remarks, "The object of the campaign had been attained; the power of Moab was broken, the rebellion suppressed, and the country again placed under the sceptre of the king of Israel."

Notes

4 נֹקֵד (*nōqēd*, lit., "sheepmaster") is a term also applied to Amos (1:1). Gray (*Kings*, pp. 484 –85) suggests that since the term is also applied to one of the chief priests at Ugarit and is related to an Akkadian verbal cognate used in divination through animal livers, Mesha himself may have been a hepatoscopist. Although there can be no certainty in the matter, support for this view may arise from the reported "revelations" to Mesha and in the sacrifice of his own son to accomplish the deliverance of Moab.

4–5 The discovery of the Moabite Stone of King Mesha brings the affairs of Israel's Omride Dynasty into close relationship with Moab (cf. the note on 1 Kings 16:21 and see ANET, pp. 320–21).

While the precise historical details and correspondences are difficult to trace, apparently Omri had defeated northern Moab (southern Moab seems to have remained free of Israelite domination, cf. 2 Chron 20), a subjugation that was to continue for some forty years, i.e., through his reign (885–874 B.C.) and that of Ahab (874–853 B.C.), Ahaziah (853–852 B.C.), and the first part of Jehoram (852–841 B.C.). The domination of Moab would thus be by Omri and Ahab, the insurrection against Israel occurring after the death of Ahab (1:1; 3:5) and partially through the reign of Omri's grandson Jehoram. Since Jehoshaphat had accompanied Ahab to the battle of Ramoth Gilead (1 Kings 22:1–38) in 853 B.C. and had turned back decisively an invasion of combined Transjordanian armies (2 Chron 20:1–29), circumstances allowed him to enter into a maritime enterprise with Ahaziah based at Ezion Geber in 852. The events of this chapter, therefore, probably are to be dated shortly before Jeshoshaphat's death in 848 B.C. See further J.R. Bartlett, "The Moabites and Edomites," in Wiseman, *Peoples*, pp. 229–58.

12 Elisha's own reputation and past relationship with Elijah are evidently well-known to Jehoshaphat. Whether Elisha was by divine direction traveling with the army, as diviners-prophets often did in the ancient Near East (cf. C.F. Jean, *Archives royales de Mari*, A. Parrot and G. Dossin, edd. [Paris: Imprimerie Nationale, 1950ff.], 2, letter 22, lines 28–31), or simply was ministering in the area is uncertain.

13 The Hebrew idiom מַה־לִּי וָלָךְ (*māh-llî wālāk*, "What do we have to do with each other?") is commonly employed to express emphatic denial (cf. 2 Sam 16:10) or differences of opinion between the persons involved (cf. John 2:4).

15 Elisha's call for a minstrel has often been cited as evidence that Israel's prophets were ecstatics. But, as L.J. Wood (*The Holy Spirit in the Old Testament* [Grand Rapids: Zondervan, 1976], p. 118) points out, "It is more likely amid these calamitous circumstances Elisha simply wanted soothing music played so that he might be quieted before God and thus to be brought to a mood conducive for God to reveal to him his will."

17 Flash flooding in otherwise dry wadis is common enough in arid portions of the world. Not only the timing of the heaven-sent waters, but the total effect of their arrival bespeak the miraculous fulfillment of Elisha's prophetic message. Seemingly barren and harmless riverbeds can become perilous places for those unfortunate enough to become trapped there in torrential waters born from distant storm-soaked mountains.

19 The wartime measures depicted here are severe and, in the case of the despoiling of the fruit trees, even beyond the normal limitation of battle (cf. Deut 20:19–20). The biblical indication of Moab's numerous fortified cities has been demonstrated to be accurate by the archaeological investigations of Nelson Glueck, "Explorations in Eastern Palestine," AASOR 3 (1939): 60ff.; 4 (1951): 371ff.

21–23 Verse 21 is past perfect in prospect. When news of the approaching allied invasion force had reached Mesha, he mobilized Moab and brought his troops to the Edomite frontier. There they were in a position to see the miraculous waters. In accordance with their understanding of previous relations between the three former antagonists, the Moabites made the improper inductive leap that the kings, due to their desperate circumstances, had had a falling out that had led to severe bloodshed. That such disaffection between allied kings did happen can be illustrated by the case of Graeco-Egyptian campaign against the Persian holdings in Phoenicia in 360 B.C. (see A.H. Gardner, *Egypt of the Pharaohs* [Oxford: Clarendon, 1961], p. 376; Diodorus 15.90ff.).

26 The Moabite king's choice to cut through the Edomite forces was probably made as the easiest possible route to escape and, as well, an attempt to even the score with his former ally whom Mesha most surely considered a traitor. No evidence exists for the conjecture to read Aram for Edom, so that the Moabite king was attempting to make his way in safety to friendly Aramean territory.

27 The account of Mesha's sacrifice of his firstborn son is a case of the Scriptures providing supplementary information to details of secular history. Montgomery (p. 363) reports that Mesha's desperate action is amply paralleled in the literature of the ancient Near East. The mention of great—קֶצֶף (*qesep*)—"fury" against Israel is difficult. Keil (in loc.) suggests that God's fury was against Israel because of the lengths to which their pressure had driven the Moabite king. Most commentators suggest that the word is to be understood in the sense of Israel's personal indignation and sickening of heart at the gruesome scene.

---

c. Elisha's miracles (4:1–6:7)

1) The replenishing of the widow's oil

4:1–7

[1]The wife of a man from the company of the prophets cried out to Elisha, "Your servant my husband is dead, and you know that he revered the Lord. But now his creditor is coming to take my two boys as his slaves."

[2]Elisha replied to her, "How can I help you? Tell me, what do you have in your house?"

"Your servant has nothing there at all," she said, "except a little oil."

[3]Elisha said, "Go around and ask all your neighbors for empty jars. Don't ask for just a few. [4]Then go inside and shut the door behind you and your sons. Pour oil into all the jars, and as each is filled, put it to one side."

[5]She left him and afterward shut the door behind her and her sons. They brought the jars to her and she kept pouring. [6]When all the jars were full, she said to her son, "Bring me another one."

But he replied, "There is not a jar left." Then the oil stopped flowing.

[7]She went and told the man of God, and he said, "Go, sell the oil and pay your debts. You and your sons can live on what is left."

1 Chapters 4 through 7 make up the heart of what is frequently known as the Elisha cycle (chs. 2–13), being a collection of Elisha's miraculous deeds and ministry. The first of these records the special case of a widow who, because her husband had been a prophet, came to Elisha for aid (v.1). The death of her husband had brought on desperate circumstances: an outstanding indebtedness she was unable to meet had occasioned her creditor's insistence that her two children be taken as slaves to work off the debt. However inhumane this might seem, the creditor was within his rights; for Mosaic Law allowed him to enslave the debtor and his children as far as the Year of Jubilee in order to work off a debt (Exod 21:2–4; Lev 25:39; Neh 5:5; Isa 50:1; Amos 2:6; 8:6; cf. Matt 18:25).

2–4 Having learned from the woman that she had nothing that could provide sustenance for the family except a small flask of oil (for anointing the body), Elisha instructed her to borrow utensils from her neighbors and, having done so, to shut herself up in her house and fill them with the oil that would come from the flask (vv.2–4). She could thus repay her creditor and use the overabundance for her family's needs.

5–7 The woman responded in faith and, miraculously, all came to pass as Elisha had promised (vv.5–6). The fact that she herself was to act in faith would enlarge her faith; the fact that Elisha would not be there when the miracle took place would display the power of God alone and thus encourage her to still greater faith. Devout obedience can produce brimful spiritual blessings!

Notes

1 Josephus (*Antiq.* IX, 47 [iv.2]) and some rabbis assert that the widow's husband was the righteous Obadiah who had aided the persecuted prophets during Ahab's reign (1 Kings 18:4), a work carried on by the widow herself after his demise, to her financial ruin. Support for this suggestion has been found in the widow's plea that her husband, like Obadiah, was one who revered the Lord (cf. 1 Kings 18:12).

2 The enslavement of family members in lieu of payment of debt was also known in the extrabiblical ancient Near East (cf. Code of Hammurabi, par. 117).

אָסוּךְ (*'āsûk*, lit., "flask [anointing] of oil," from סוּךְ (*sûk*, "anoint")) is a hapax legomenon. Some have suggested that the widow had used up the oil to support her family and the prophets and that now she was down to her very last bit of oil for one last use for herself. Such, however, is mere conjecture. Rather it would appear that she had used up all her husband's estate and that God's provision consisted not only in meeting her indebtedness but in providing for her a means of future support (cf. v.7).

The command to fill the jars behind closed doors delivers the miracle from a mere spectacle; it was a private need, privately met by a sovereign and loving God (cf. Matt 6:6). The order contained in Elisha's instructions was significant: the meeting of one's just debts was a matter of prime importance, casting reflection on the God whom the widow served.

2) *The revivification of the Shunammite's son*

4:8–37

⁸One day Elisha went to Shunem. And a well-to-do woman was there, who urged him to stay for a meal. So whenever he came by, he stopped there to eat. ⁹She said to her husband, "I know that this man who often comes our way is a holy man of God. ¹⁰Let's make a small room on the roof and put in it a bed and a table, a chair and a lamp for him. Then he can stay there whenever he comes to us."

¹¹One day when Elisha came, he went up to his room and lay down there. ¹²He said to his servant Gehazi, "Call the Shunammite." So he called her, and she stood before him. ¹³Elisha said to him, "Tell her, 'You have gone to all this trouble for us. Now what can be done for you? Can we speak on your behalf to the king or the commander of the army?' "

She replied, "I have a home among my own people."

¹⁴"What can be done for her?" Elisha asked.

Gehazi said, "Well, she has no son and her husband is old."

¹⁵Then Elisha said, "Call her." So he called her, and she stood in the doorway. ¹⁶"About this time next year," Elisha said, "you will hold a son in your arms."

"No, my lord," she objected. "Don't mislead your servant, O man of God!"

¹⁷But the woman became pregnant, and the next year about that same time she gave birth to a son, just as Elisha had told her.

¹⁸The child grew, and one day he went out to his father, who was with the reapers. ¹⁹"My head! My head!" he said to his father.

His father told a servant, "Carry him to his mother." ²⁰After the servant had lifted him up and carried him to his mother, the boy sat on her lap until noon, and then he died. ²¹She went up and laid him on the bed of the man of God, then shut the door and went out.

²²She called her husband and said, "Please send me one of the servants and a donkey so I can go to the man of God quickly and return."

²³"Why go to him today?" he asked. "It's not the New Moon or the Sabbath."

"It's all right," she said.

²⁴She saddled the donkey and said to her servant, "Lead on; don't slow down for me unless I tell you." ²⁵So she set out and came to the man of God at Mount Carmel.

When he saw her in the distance, the man of God said to his servant Gehazi, "Look! There's the Shunammite! ²⁶Run to meet her and ask her, 'Are you all right? Is your husband all right? Is your child all right?' "

"Everything is all right," she said.

²⁷When she reached the man of God at the mountain, she took hold of his feet. Gehazi came over to push her away, but the man of God said, "Leave her alone! She is in bitter distress, but the LORD has hidden it from me and has not told me why."

²⁸"Did I ask you for a son, my lord?" she said. "Didn't I tell you, 'Don't raise my hopes'?"

²⁹Elisha said to Gehazi, "Tuck your cloak into your belt, take my staff in your hand and run. If you meet anyone, do not greet him, and if anyone greets you, do not answer. Lay my staff on the boy's face."

³⁰But the child's mother said, "As surely as the LORD lives and as you live, I will not leave you." So he got up and followed her.

³¹Gehazi went on ahead and laid the staff on the boy's face, but there was no sound or response. So Gehazi went back to meet Elisha and told him, "The boy has not awakened."

³²When Elisha reached the house, there was the boy lying dead on his couch. ³³He went in, shut the door on the two of them and prayed to the LORD. ³⁴Then he got on the bed and lay upon the boy, mouth to mouth, eyes to eyes, hands to hands. As he stretched himself out upon him, the boy's body grew warm. ³⁵Elisha turned away and walked back and forth in the room and then got on the bed and

stretched out upon him once more. The boy sneezed seven times and opened his eyes.
³⁶Elisha summoned Gehazi and said, "Call the Shunammite." And he did. When she came, he said, "Take your son." ³⁷She came in, fell at his feet and bowed to the ground. Then she took her son and went out.

8–14 The course of Elisha's ministry often took him through Shunem, where certain kind friends lived (v.8). Accordingly, at the wife's suggestion, the husband prepared special quarters for Elisha wherein he might rest (vv.9–10). On one such journey Elisha wondered how he might repay the Shunammite woman's many kindnesses to him (vv.1–13). When she indicated that she dwelled comfortably among her own people and had no special needs, Gehazi, Elisha's attendant, pointed out that the couple was childless; and, since the husband was old, the woman's longing for a child seemed hopeless (v.14). Jewish tradition asserts that Gehazi's motives were engendered by lust. Certainly the suggestion may have been innocent enough; but as the story unfolds, it does appear that the woman surely did not trust Gehazi.

15–28 Under divine direction Elisha acted at Gehazi's suggestion and informed the Shunammite woman that in the next year she would give birth to a son (vv.15–16). So it came to pass, at the appointed time the child was born and in time grew into a young lad (v.17). One day as he helped his father in the field, the lad was taken suddenly critically ill and died (vv.18–20). After placing the lad's body on the bed in the chamber of the prophet who had first announced his life, the Shunammite lady immediately set out for Mount Carmel where Elisha was ministering (vv.21–25). Her faith convinced her that somehow Elisha could be instrumental in again doing the seemingly impossible. He had previously announced life for her who had no hope of producing life; perhaps he could once more give life to her son. Bypassing Gehazi whom Elisha had sent to meet her, she made directly for Elisha; and grasping tightly his feet, she poured out the details of the tragedy (vv.26–28).

29–30 Elisha quickly sent Gehazi ahead with instructions to lay the prophet's staff on the dead lad (v.29). The woman, who apparently had never trusted Gehazi, would entrust neither herself nor the final disposition of her son to him but rather stayed with Elisha until he could reach Shunem (v.30). Her faith and concern for her son's cure were totally centered in God's approved prophet.

31–37 As Elisha and the mother approached the city, Gehazi reported that, though he had carried out Elisha's bidding, nothing at all had happened (v.31). Perhaps Gehazi had expected something extraordinary. But the merely routine fulfilling of one's duties will never effect successful spiritual results. Elisha went straight to the dead lad and, putting all others out and shutting the door, besought the Lord for the lad's life (vv.32–33). His prayers were followed with prophetic symbolic actions, doubtless learned from his teacher Elijah's experience with the widow of Zarephath (cf. 1 Kings 17:17–22). Elisha stretched his body on the lad's so that his mouth, eyes, and hands correspondingly met those of the lad; and the boy's body grew warm again (v.34). After rising and walking about in continued prayer, he repeated the symbolic action (v.35). This time the lad sneezed seven times and opened his eyes. Having sent Gehazi for the mother, Elisha delivered the recovered lad to her (v.36). The woman gratefully thanked the the prophet and joyfully took up her son and went out (v.37).

As in the case of Elijah and the widow of Zarephath, both Elisha and the Shunammite woman had seen their faith successfully tested; and they were rewarded with the desires of their hearts and corresponding increase in their faith.

Notes

8 The Shunammite's wife was אִשָּׁה גְדוֹלָה (*'iššāh gᵉdôlāh*, "a well-to-do," lit., "a great woman") whose economic and social prominence would necessitate no normal favors from the prophet (v.13). Being a pious woman, her concern for the prophet was purely spontaneous and bears the impress of a genuinely godly sense of hospitality.

12 Gehazi is called Elisha's נַעַר (*na'ar*, "lad," "servant"). For the same word as a social-military term, see the note on 1 Kings 20:14–15. For the use of the word to connote special concern, see H. Bariligo, "The Case of the *nᵉ'ārîn*," *Beth Mikra* 27 (1981–82): 151 –80. Probably Gehazi is the unnamed (chief) attendant in v.43, the term שָׁרַת (*šārat*, "serve," "attend") being used of Elisha's own relation to Elijah (1 Kings 19:21). Despite his privileged position and personal worth to Elisha, Gehazi seems to have resented his secondary status, identifying himself as Elisha's "servant" or "slave" (cf. 2 Kings 5:25).

16 The woman's astonished reaction is filled with deep emotion and to the point of poignancy. Such a seemingly unattainable hope was to cherish a promise too precious for disappointment.

23 The reply of the Shunammite's husband that it was neither New Moon nor Sabbath held twofold significance: (1) only on such days would the prophet most likely be expected to be available for teaching; (2) it was a work day, when one ordinarily attended to his business. The father's remarks were full of apprehension—was the child, then, critically ill? Her reply—"It is well"—was designed to alleviate his fears without plainly telling him that she was going to Elisha so that he might restore their dead son.

26–27 The Shunammite's reply to Gehazi is deliberately ambiguous. It may be taken as a polite greeting and as a tacit assertion of her faith: everything would turn out well once she had reached Elisha! Her distrust of Gehazi is well taken, as his subsequent actions display. For the grasping of the feet in humiliation and veneration, see Matt 28:9.

28 The mother's deep bitterness of sorrow is shown in her pointed rhetorical question. She had not asked for a son; it was Elisha that had promised her one. Was now her great gift from God to be snatched from her and so to leave her in a worse state than before? It would have been better never to have a son than to have such joy taken away so quickly!

29 Elisha's further command to Gehazi to greet no one in the way underscores the urgency of the situation. His mission must not be slowed down with idle greetings or compromised with common business (cf. Luke 10:4).

Although the author of Kings assigns no reason at all for Elisha's instructions and actions, Elisha surely did not send Gehazi on a hopeless mission. Because he was young, Gehazi could cover the distance to Shunem quickly; and it was imperative that a representative of God arrive there as soon as possible. Very likely Gehazi's task was preparatory and symbolic of the soon arrival of Elisha himself. For one thing, placing Elisha's staff on the boy's body would, as Bronner (*Stories*, p. 105) suggests, prevent its premature burial. Further the staff as the symbol of God-given prophetic power (cf. Exod 4:1–4; 17:8 –13) signified Elisha's faith that God would stay further physical degeneration until he could come.

32–35 Elisha's faith was evidenced not only by fervent prayer but in carrying out, on his part, known prophetic symbolism (cf. 1 Kings 17:21; Acts 20:9–10). (For NT raisings of the dead, see Mark 5:39–42; Luke 7:13–15; John 11:43–44; Acts 9:36–43.)

36 Throughout the narrative Elisha contacts the Shunammite woman through Gehazi (cf. vv.11–13, 15, 25, 29). This is not merely to mark his prophetic status and prestige but to involve Gehazi in the ministry so that he might have opportunity to mature in the faith.

---

3) *The rectification of dinner problems*

4:38–44

³⁸Elisha returned to Gilgal and there was a famine in that region. While the company of the prophets was meeting with him, he said to his servant, "Put on the large pot and cook some stew for these men."

³⁹One of them went out into the fields to gather herbs and found a wild vine. He gathered some of its gourds and filled the fold of his cloak. When he returned, he cut them up into the pot of stew, though no one knew what they were. ⁴⁰The stew was poured out for the men, but as they began to eat it, they cried out, "O man of God, there is death in the pot!" And they could not eat it.

⁴¹Elisha said, "Get some flour." He put it into the pot and said, "Serve it to the people to eat." And there was nothing harmful in the pot.

⁴²A man came from Baal Shalishah, bringing the man of God twenty loaves of barley bread baked from the first ripe grain, along with some heads of new grain. "Give it to the people to eat," Elisha said.

⁴³"How can I set this before a hundred men?" his servant asked.

But Elisha answered, "Give it to the people to eat. For this is what the LORD says: 'They will eat and have some left over.' " ⁴⁴Then he set it before them, and they ate and had some left over, according to the word of the LORD.

38–41 The chapter closes with two incidents relative to Elisha's miraculous help in food matters in the prophetic school at Gilgal. In the first instance, a student who had been sent to gather wild vegetables brought an unknown type to them and cut the gatherings into the stew (vv.38–39). Its bitter taste convinced the diners that the stew was poisoned; so immediately they cried out to Elisha (v.40). He called for meal to be brought; and when he had stirred it into the pot, the stew was found to be both tasteful and safe (v.41). Elisha's faith effected a miraculous cure. As had been the case with Elijah his teacher, Elisha had used flour to demonstrate the concern of God for man's daily provisions (cf. 1 Kings 17:14–16).

42–43 The second case involves the multiplication of a score of small loaves of fresh barley bread and some ears of new grain. These had been brought to Elisha as firstfruits (v.42). Normally these portions were reserved for God (Lev 23:20) and the Levitical priests (Num 18:13; Deut 18:4–5). Because the religion in the northern kingdom was apostate, the loaves had been brought by their owner to one whom he considered to be the true repository of godly religion in Israel. Elisha did not hesitate. He ordered them distributed to the young prophets, despite the protest of his servant (probably Gehazi) who realized that, humanly speaking, the gift was insufficient to feed everyone (v.43). Nevertheless Elisha ordered their distribution, telling his servant that there would surely be sufficient for all—in fact, some would be left over.

44 As Elisha had promised, so it came to pass. Elisha's faith in the miracle-working

God had again been rewarded; and he, on whom the believer is to wait for his daily bread, had supplied richly (cf. Matt 6:21).

Notes

---

38 For the location of this Gilgal, see the comments on 2:1. Like Elijah, Elisha ministered to men's needs in days of famine (cf. 1 Kings 18:2).

Elisha, as titular head of the prophets, duly acted as host at the communal meal. This anticipated the divine Host who so often freely and abundantly provided for his disciples (cf. Matt 15:29–39; Mark 14:12–25; Luke 24:28–31; John 6:1–13; 21:9–13; 1 Cor 11:23–25).

43–44 The multiplication of the loaves in accordance with the word of the Lord through his prophet anticipates the messianic ministry of the Living Word himself (cf. Matt 14:16–20; 15:36–37; John 6:11–13). C.S. Lewis (*Miracles* [New York: MacMillan, 1953], pp. 16f.) calls such cases "miracles of the old creation" involving "miracles of fertility," i.e., those in which man sees in extraordinary fashion that which God alone has produced customarily in nature. While far beyond man's ability, they are routine for the Lord of the impossible.

---

4) *The restoration of Naaman*

5:1–27

¹Now Naaman was commander of the army of the king of Aram. He was a great man in the sight of his master and highly regarded, because through him the LORD had given victory to Aram. He was a valiant soldier, but he had leprosy.

²Now bands from Aram had gone out and had taken captive a young girl from Israel, and she served Naaman's wife. ³She said to her mistress, "If only my master would see the prophet who is in Samaria! He would cure him of his leprosy."

⁴Naaman went to his master and told him what the girl from Israel had said. ⁵"By all means, go," the king of Aram replied. "I will send a letter to the king of Israel." So Naaman left, taking with him ten talents of silver, six thousand shekels of gold and ten sets of clothing. ⁶The letter that he took to the king of Israel read: "With this letter I am sending my servant Naaman to you so that you may cure him of his leprosy."

⁷As soon as the king of Israel read the letter, he tore his robes and said, "Am I God? Can I kill and bring back to life? Why does this fellow send someone to me to be cured of his leprosy? See how he is trying to pick a quarrel with me!"

⁸When Elisha the man of God heard that the king of Israel had torn his robes, he sent him this message: "Why have you torn your robes? Have the man come to me and he will know that there is a prophet in Israel." ⁹So Naaman went with his horses and chariots and stopped at the door of Elisha's house. ¹⁰Elisha sent a messenger to say to him, "Go, wash yourself seven times in the Jordan, and your flesh will be restored and you will be cleansed."

¹¹But Naaman went away angry and said, "I thought that he would surely come out to me and stand and call on the name of the LORD his God, wave his hand over the spot and cure me of my leprosy. ¹²Are not Abana and Pharpar, the rivers of Damascus, better than any of the waters of Israel? Couldn't I wash in them and be cleansed?" So he turned and went off in a rage.

¹³Naaman's servants went to him and said, "My father, if the prophet had told you to do some great thing, would you not have done it? How much more, then,

when he tells you, 'Wash and be cleansed'!" ¹⁴So he went down and dipped himself in the Jordan seven times, as the man of God had told him, and his flesh was restored and became clean like that of a young boy.

¹⁵Then Naaman and all his attendants went back to the man of God. He stood before him and said, "Now I know that there is no God in all the world except in Israel. Please accept now a gift from your servant."

¹⁶The prophet answered, "As surely as the LORD lives, whom I serve, I will not accept a thing." And even though Naaman urged him, he refused.

¹⁷"If you will not," said Naaman, "please let me, your servant, be given as much earth as a pair of mules can carry, for your servant will never again make burnt offerings and sacrifices to any other god but the LORD. ¹⁸But may the LORD forgive your servant for this one thing: When my master enters the temple of Rimmon to bow down and he is leaning on my arm and I bow there also—when I bow down in the temple of Rimmon, may the LORD forgive your servant for this."

¹⁹"Go in peace," Elisha said.

After Naaman had traveled some distance, ²⁰Gehazi, the servant of Elisha the man of God, said to himself, "My master was too easy on Naaman, this Aramean, by not accepting from him what he brought. As surely as the LORD lives, I will run after him and get something from him."

²¹So Gehazi hurried after Naaman. When Naaman saw him running toward him, he got down from the chariot to meet him. "Is everything all right?" he asked.

²²"Everything is all right," Gehazi answered. "My master sent me to say, 'Two young men from the company of the prophets have just come to me from the hill country of Ephraim. Please give them a talent of silver and two sets of clothing.' "

²³"By all means, take two talents," said Naaman. He urged Gehazi to accept them, and then tied up the two talents of silver in two bags, with two sets of clothing. He gave them to two of his servants, and they carried them ahead of Gehazi. ²⁴When Gehazi came to the hill, he took the things from the servants and put them away in the house. He sent the men away and they left. ²⁵Then he went in and stood before his master Elisha.

"Where have you been, Gehazi?" Elisha asked.

"Your servant didn't go anywhere," Gehazi answered.

²⁶But Elisha said to him, "Was not my spirit with you when the man got down from his chariot to meet you? Is this the time to take money, or to accept clothes, olive groves, vineyards, flocks, herds, or menservants and maidservants? ²⁷Naaman's leprosy will cling to you and to your descendants forever." Then Gehazi went from Elisha's presence and he was leprous, as white as snow.

1–7 The latter days of the reign of Israel's king Jehoram were marked by hostilities with the Aramean king Ben-Hadad II. Probably due to Israel's failure to participate in the continued Syro-Assyrian confrontation that marked most of the sixth decade of the ninth century B.C., the Arameans continually chastened the northern kingdom with systematic raids (cf. 2 Kings 6:8), culminating in an all-out military excursion into Israel (cf. 2 Kings 6:24–7:20).

During the course of one such raid, an Israelite maiden had fallen into the hands of Ben-Hadad's field marshall, Naaman (vv.1–2). Although Naaman was a brilliant commanding officer, he suffered from a serious and incurable skin disease. On one occasion when Naaman was home from fighting and relations were stabilized somewhat between Damascus and Israel, the Israelite servant girl informed her Aramean master that there was a prophet in Israel who could effect Naaman's cure (v.3). When Naaman was advised of such a hope, he spoke to Ben-Hadad who, in turn, sent Naaman with rich gifts and a letter of introduction to Jehoram so that the Syrian general might be healed (vv.4–6). Jehoram, believing the situation to be impossible, thought that Ben-Hadad was seeking an occasion for renewed warfare (v.7). Evidently no mention was made of Israel's prophet in the correspondence, so that Jehoram was unaware of the context of the request.

8–14 News of the whole affair reached Elisha, who sent word to Jehoram that God was still at work in Israel and could work through his authoritative prophet (v.8). Accordingly Naaman was sent to Elisha who, rather than receiving him, sent his servant to meet Naaman (vv.9–10a). He must understand that Elisha served a greater king than did the Syrian general. However Elisha's message through Gehazi was one of great hope. If he would but wash himself seven times in the Jordan, he would be cleansed (v.10b). Naaman, angered by his poor reception and thinking Elisha was a quack, strode away angrily (vv.11–12). Yet God was at work in the proud, self-reliant Gentile's life (v.3); he used Naaman's own Aramean aide who suggested that since Elisha's instructions were simple enough, they ought to be tested (v.13). What did he have to lose? Naaman followed the advice and was instantly cured (v.14).

15–19 Gratefully Naaman returned to Elisha and offered him rich gifts (v.15). Although Naaman urged them on him insistently, the prophet refused (v.16). Naaman had become convinced that Yahweh alone was God. Naaman asked Elisha whether two mule loads of Israelite soil might be taken with him back to Syria so that whenever circumstances forced him to bow ceremonially to the Aramean gods with his king, he might in reality be placing his knees in the soil of the true God of Israel (vv.17–18). Thus he might be a true though secret believer. His request granted, Naaman set out for home (v.19).

20–21 The story next focuses on Gehazi who saw an opportunity to gain some of the proffered commodities for himself (v.20). Slipping away stealthily, he overtook the Syrian general (v.21). What a contrast can be seen in the meeting between Naaman and Gehazi! Naaman's descent from his chariot to meet Elisha's servant is a mark of his being a changed man. No longer a proud, arrogant person (vv.9–12), the grateful (v.15), reverent (v.17), and humble (v.18) Aramean came down from his honored place to meet a prophet's servant. He who had been a fallen, hopeless sinner displayed the true believer's grace. Contrariwise Gehazi, who had enjoyed all the privileges of his master's grace, was about to abuse them and fall from that favor.

22–26 Having convinced Naaman that Elisha had experienced an unexpected need, he extracted from the grateful Syrian commander a handsome sum of gifts, which he subsequently concealed until he could have opportunity to retrieve them (vv.22–24). He then attempted to steal back to Elisha's house unnoticed—only to be confronted by the prophet (v.25). His master knew all that had transpired (v.26)! Gehazi's lies only worsened the situation (v.25).

27 Accordingly Elisha announced Gehazi's punishment: Naaman's leprosy would become Gehazi's. Elisha's privileged aide was banished in disgrace, for he had misused his favored position in an attempt to acquire wealth to himself. Gehazi needed to learn that the ministry has no place for those who would make merchandise of it. The moral and spiritual flaws in his character that one senses in the previous record have surfaced. His basic spiritual insensitivity had betrayed him in the time of testing so that rather than his character being refined his work was refused (cf. 1 Peter 1:6–7).

Notes

1 While שַׂר־צָבָא (śar-ṣᵉḇā᾽, "commander of the army") is not the only term used of an army's highest-ranking officer, such is its clear intention in the case of Phicol (Gen 21:22), Sisera (1 Sam 12:9), and Joab (1 Chron 27:34; cf. also the theophany in Josh 5:14–15). Doubtless Naaman held such an honor with the Aramean king, who must have been Ben-Hadad II. Naaman's epithets are instructive: אִישׁ גָּדוֹל (᾽îš gāḏôl, "a great man"), a man of high social standing and importance whose influence reached to the king himself; נְשָׂא פָנִים (nᵉśu᾽ pānîm, "highly regarded," lit., "lifted up of face"), a term reminiscent of his being dubbed with the king's scepter (cf. Esth 8:3–4); גִּבּוֹר חַיִל (gibbôr ḥayil, "valiant soldier"), i.e., a man of landed property whose wealth, bearing, and personal valor destined him for high military service. A man of unusual stature and potential, Naaman's successes were effected by the Lord himself so that both this Gentile officer and Elisha's servant, Gehazi, might know the Lord's correction.

Because מְצֹרָע (mᵉṣōrā᾽, "leper") was translated by the LXX word λέπρα (lepra, "leprosy") (though true leprosy was normally designated by ἐλεφαντίασις [elephantiasis]), ancient (e.g., Vul., leprosus, "leprous") and modern translations have uniformly followed its lead. Obviously the term is of wider dimension, being used not only of true leprosy (e.g., of Azariah, 15:5 q.v.), but of serious skin conditions (Lev 13:1–46) and of fungi in clothing (Lev 13:47–56) and houses (Lev 14:33–59). Naaman's social participation makes it doubtful that he suffered from Hanson's disease. See further the comments of G.J. Wenham, *The Book of Leviticus* (Grand Rapids: Eerdmans, 1979), pp. 189–214.

3 Elisha was called by the internationally known term "prophet." But Elisha was more; he was the prophet *par excellence* of Israel. While Samaria, as the chief and capital city, may denote Israel as such, probably Elisha was actually residing there at the time (cf. 6:32). For the various OT terms for prophet, see the note on 1 Kings 13:1.

The maiden's confident assertion that Elisha could "cure him [Naaman] of his leprosy" is reminiscent of Miriam who, too, was received back into camp after her healing from leprosy. The Hebrew verb is the same in both cases: אָסַף (᾽āsap, "gather," "receive").

5–6 Montgomery (p. 374) notes instances of medical courtesy in the literature of the ancient Near East. Letters of introduction such as that sent by the Aramean king were, of course, very common (cf. 2 Cor 3:1). For correspondence in the ancient Near East, see Saggs, *Greatness*, pp. 244–47; A.L. Oppenheim, *Letters from Mesopotamia* (Chicago: University Press, 1967).

7 Jehoram's reaction at what he considered a letter of provocation is reminiscent of the comments between the Hyksos king Apophis and the Egyptian Pharaoh Seqnen-Re at Thebes (ANET, pp. 231f.). For a biblical example, see 1 Kings 20:1–11; cf. 2 Kings 14:8 –10.

8 For the tearing of robes in grief and agitation, see the note on 11:14.

11 אָמַר (᾽āmar) normally is used of "speaking," but occasionally some of the wider usages attested in this common Semitic root (e.g., Akkad. "see," Geez "show," Tigre "know") are at times felt in the OT. The Hebrew idiom "to say in one's heart" (i.e., "think") is a kindred idea (Deut 8:17; 1 Kings 12:26), so that the use of the verb independently with a similar nuance is a natural development (cf. Gen 20:11; 26:9; Num 24:11; Ruth 4:4; 1 Sam 20:26; 2 Sam 5:6; 12:22; 1 Kings 22:32). See further Cohen, *Dictionnaire*, 1:23–24; TDOT, 1:328–45.

The position of the prepositional phrase "unto me" is emphatic: "(I thought)—unto me he would surely come out!" Naaman was incensed. Here was a person whom he considered to be both ethnically and socially inferior to himself who failed to receive him. Furthermore he certainly was not acting like any of the "prophets" Naaman knew.

13 Since he called his master "father," the term may indicate something of the warmness that the servant felt for Naaman (cf. 2:12). Suggested emendations (see the critical notes in

current Hebrew editions of the Bible) are quite unnecessary. For washing and cleansing, see Ps 51:2; Isa 1:16.

14 The prophet (cf. v.3) is here termed "man of God"; see the note on 1 Kings 13:1.

15 Naaman could in no sense be allowed to think that God's favor was to be purchased or that the prophet served God only for the desire of personal gain. Moreover a soul for whom God was concerned was at stake. God's blessing had been designed for Naaman's response in repentance and faith (cf. Rom 2:4), Gentile though he was (cf. Luke 4:27).

17 Montgomery (p. 377) reports that the transporting of holy soil was a widespread custom. Naaman's faith was yet untaught; and with his personal need to follow publicly the state cults, Elisha may have felt that available Israelite soil may have afforded Naaman with some tangible reminder of his cleansing and new relationship to God.

18 The name of the Aramean god Rimmon probably contains a scribal parody of the Syrian storm god Hadad, whom the Assyrians called *Ramānu* ("the thunderer"). The father of Ben-Hadad I was named Tabrimmon (1 Kings 15:18); so the equation of Rimmon with Hadad as the god of the royal house of Damascus seems certain. Both gods are often integrated with the Canaanite Baal. In typical Jewish fashion the Aramean god is given a new vowel pointing, here that of the Hebrew word for pomegranate.

20 כִּי־אִם־רַצְתִּי (*kî-'im-raṣtî*, "I will run") contains an extremely emphatic resolve (cf. 1 Sam 25:34). Gehazi will most certainly correct Elisha's light treatment of this foreigner by going after him and relieving him of some of the "blessing."

24 More than likely the definite article with הָעֹפֶל (*hā'ōpel*, "the hill") designates the well-known hill before the city. Gehazi would want to dismiss the Syrian general's guards before reaching the crest of the hill and coming into full view of the citizens of Samaria and Elisha in particular.

26 To Elisha's question "Where have you been?" Gehazi implies that he had not gone anywhere. Elisha exposed Gehazi's lie by reporting that not only had he gone, but Elisha's heart-spirit had gone with him through the whole sorry affair!

---

5) *The recovery of the ax head*

6:1-7

> ¹The company of the prophets said to Elisha, "Look, the place where we meet with you is too small for us. ²Let us go to the Jordan, where each of us can get a pole; and let us build a place there for us to live."
>
> And he said, "Go."
>
> ³Then one of them said, "Won't you please come with your servants?"
>
> "I will," Elisha replied. ⁴And he went with them.
>
> They went to the Jordan and began to cut down trees. ⁵As one of them was cutting down a tree, the iron axhead fell into the water. "Oh, my lord," he cried out, "it was borrowed!"
>
> ⁶The man of God asked, "Where did it fall?" When he showed him the place, Elisha cut a stick and threw it there, and made the iron float. ⁷"Lift it out," he said. Then the man reached out his hand and took it.

1-7 In contrast to Gehazi who had received the reward of his unfaithfulness, the account unfolded here is a demonstration of the reward of faithful labor. During the evil days of Jehoram's reign and Elisha's prophetic ministry, a certain meeting place for the sons of the prophet's instruction proved too small for their assembly (v.1). This school apparently was located in Jericho near the Jordan (vv.2, 4), a known center of prophetic instruction (cf. ch. 2). Accordingly Elisha acceded to the request to build larger quarters and even went with them to the work (v.3). In the course of their labor, one student lost the iron ax head of his borrowed ax and cried out to Elisha (v.5). In the power of God, Elisha then caused the submerged ax head to surface and instructed the pupil to retrieve the ax; thus he would personally participate in the miracle (vv.6–7). Attempts to explain fully or explain away the miracle are fruitless. The miracle only needs to be accepted in accordance with the simple statement of the written report.

d. Elisha's ministry (6:8–8:15)

1) Prelude to war: the Aramean incursion

6:8–23

8Now the king of Aram was at war with Israel. After conferring with his officers, he said, "I will set up my camp in such and such a place."

9The man of God sent word to the king of Israel: "Beware of passing that place, because the Arameans are going down there." 10So the king of Israel checked on the place indicated by the man of God. Time and again Elisha warned the king, so that he was on his guard in such places.

11This enraged the king of Aram. He summoned his officers and demanded of them, "Will you not tell me which of us is on the side of the king of Israel?"

12"None of us, my lord the king," said one of his officers, "but Elisha, the prophet who is in Israel, tells the king of Israel the very words you speak in your bedroom."

13"Go, find out where he is," the king ordered, "so I can send men and capture him." The report came back: "He is in Dothan." 14Then he sent horses and chariots and a strong force there. They went by night and surrounded the city.

15When the servant of the man of God got up and went out early the next morning, an army with horses and chariots had surrounded the city. "Oh, my lord, what shall we do?" the servant asked.

16"Don't be afraid," the prophet answered. "Those who are with us are more than those who are with them."

17And Elisha prayed, "O LORD, open his eyes so he may see." Then the LORD opened the servant's eyes, and he looked and saw the hills full of horses and chariots of fire all around Elisha.

18As the enemy came down toward him, Elisha prayed to the LORD, "Strike these people with blindness." So he struck them with blindness, as Elisha had asked.

19Elisha told them, "This is not the road and this is not the city. Follow me, and I will lead you to the man you are looking for." And he led them to Samaria.

20After they entered the city, Elisha said, "LORD, open the eyes of these men so they can see." Then the LORD opened their eyes and they looked, and there they were, inside Samaria.

21When the king of Israel saw them, he asked Elisha, "Shall I kill them, my father? Shall I kill them?"

22"Do not kill them," he answered. "Would you kill men you have captured with your own sword or bow? Set food and water before them so that they may eat and drink and then go back to their master." 23So he prepared a great feast for them, and after they had finished eating and drinking, he sent them away, and they returned to their master. So the bands from Aram stopped raiding Israel's territory.

8–12 The account now returns to the intermittent warfare between the Arameans and Israelites. Time after time the Israelite king and his forces were delivered from ambush because of Elisha's warning, for by divine revelation Elisha was party to the

Aramean king's secret plans (vv.8–9). Elisha's aid to Jehoram became common knowledge and was duly reported to the Aramean king, who had suspected a traitor within his own court (vv.10–12).

13–20 Accordingly, having learned that Elisha had gone to Dothan, the Arameans surrounded the city by night in order to take Elisha by force (vv.13–14). Doubtless Elisha knew about all this, too, but allowed himself to be trapped so that the subsequent entrapment of the Arameans might work to God's glory and for his good (v.15). When Elisha's servant awakened and saw the great Aramean force, he cried out in dismay to Elisha. Elisha, however, assured him that the forces of God outnumbered the forces of the enemy. In accordance with Elisha's prayer, the servant's eyes were enabled to behold the company of an innumerable angelic host that stood ready to intercede for Elisha (v.17). However this incident would not be one of protracted battle but another case of miraculous deliverance. In accordance with Elisha's prayer, the enemy army became totally blind and was led away by Elisha to Samaria, about ten miles away (vv.18–19). Once inside the city, the army discovered that instead of taking Elisha captive, they were prisoners of Jehoram (v.20).

21–23 At Elisha's directions, rather than killing their enemies (v.21), the Israelites treated them to a sumptuous feast (v.22) and, having given them provisions for the journey home to Syria, sent them away (v.23). Elisha's intercession and instructions proved ultimately to be the divine remedy for the momentary ills of Israel: the Arameans reported Israel's kindness, and their guerrilla raids ceased.

Notes

10 NIV's "time and again" is an appropriate rendering of the Hebrew "not once or twice." Truly the innermost secrets of men lie open to the omniscient God (cf. Dan 2:22).

15 If the events of the chapter follow chronologically after those of ch. 5, Elisha's servant cannot be Gehazi.

16 Elisha's word of assurance to this servant has become a source of comfort to many subsequent servants of God who have faced seemingly overwhelming adversity.

17 The spectacular sight that the servant was enabled to see was like the double army of angels encamped around Jacob (Gen 32:1–2). The Lord's promise to "encamp around those who fear him" (Ps 34:7; cf. Pss 55:18; 91) had become a visible reality to Elisha's servant. The whole episode underscores the power of prayer (cf. James 5:16). For divine revelation to men and of the activities of the unseen world, see Ezek 10–11; Dan 10; cf. Num 12:6.

18 Keil (in loc.) explains Elisha's deception as a *ruse de guerre*. Yet in a sense his words are true; the city where Elisha would ultimately be found would be Samaria, not Dothan.

2) The siege of Samaria

6:24–7:20

²⁴Some time later, Ben-Hadad king of Aram mobilized his entire army and marched up and laid siege to Samaria. ²⁵There was a great famine in the city; the

siege lasted so long that a donkey's head sold for eighty shekels of silver, and a fourth of a cab of seed pods for five shekels.

²⁶As the king of Israel was passing by on the wall, a woman cried to him, "Help me, my lord the king!"

²⁷The king replied, "If the LORD does not help you, where can I get help for you? From the threshing floor? From the winepress?" ²⁸Then he asked her, "What's the matter?"

She answered, "This woman said to me, 'Give up your son so we may eat him today, and tomorrow we'll eat my son.' ²⁹So we cooked my son and ate him. The next day I said to her, 'Give up your son so we may eat him,' but she had hidden him."

³⁰When the king heard the woman's words, he tore his robes. As he went along the wall, the people looked, and there, underneath, he had sackcloth on his body. ³¹He said, "May God deal with me, be it ever so severely, if the head of Elisha son of Shaphat remains on his shoulders today!"

³²Now Elisha was sitting in his house, and the elders were sitting with him. The king sent a messenger ahead, but before he arrived, Elisha said to the elders, "Don't you see how this murderer is sending someone to cut off my head? Look, when the messenger comes, shut the door and hold it shut against him. Is not the sound of his master's footsteps behind him?"

³³While he was still talking to them, the messenger came down to him. And the king said, "This disaster is from the LORD. Why should I wait for the LORD any longer?"

^{7:1}Elisha said, "Hear the word of the LORD. This is what the LORD says: About this time tomorrow, a seah of flour will sell for a shekel and two seahs of barley for a shekel at the gate of Samaria."

²The officer on whose arm the king was leaning said to the man of God, "Look, even if the LORD should open the floodgates of the heavens, could this happen?"

"You will see it with your own eyes," answered Elisha, "but you will not eat any of it!"

³Now there were four men with leprosy at the entrance of the city gate. They said to each other, "Why stay here until we die? ⁴If we say, 'We'll go into the city'—the famine is there, and we will die. And if we stay here, we will die. So let's go over to the camp of the Arameans and surrender. If they spare us, we live; if they kill us, then we die."

⁵At dusk they got up and went to the camp of the Arameans. When they reached the edge of the camp, not a man was there, ⁶for the Lord had caused the Arameans to hear the sound of chariots and horses and a great army, so that they said to one another, "Look, the king of Israel has hired the Hittite and Egyptian kings to attack us!" ⁷So they got up and fled in the dusk and abandoned their tents and their horses and donkeys. They left the camp as it was and ran for their lives.

⁸The men who had leprosy reached the edge of the camp and entered one of the tents. They ate and drank, and carried away silver, gold and clothes, and went off and hid them. They returned and entered another tent and took some things from it and hid them also.

⁹Then they said to each other, "We're not doing right. This is a day of good news and we are keeping it to ourselves. If we wait until daylight, punishment will overtake us. Let's go at once and report this to the royal palace."

¹⁰So they went and called out to the city gatekeepers and told them, "We went into the Aramean camp and not a man was there—not a sound of anyone—only tethered horses and donkeys, and the tents left just as they were." ¹¹The gatekeepers shouted the news, and it was reported within the palace.

¹²The king got up in the night and said to his officers, "I will tell you what the Arameans have done to us. They know we are starving; so they have left the camp to hide in the countryside, thinking, 'They will surely come out, and then we will take them alive and get into the city.'"

¹³One of his officers answered, "Have some men take five of the horses that are left in the city. Their plight will be like that of all the Israelites left here—yes,

they will only be like all these Israelites who are doomed. So let us send them to find out what happened."

¹⁴So they selected two chariots with their horses, and the king sent them after the Aramean army. He commanded the drivers, "Go and find out what has happened." ¹⁵They followed them as far as the Jordan, and they found the whole road strewn with the clothing and equipment the Arameans had thrown away in their headlong flight. So the messengers returned and reported to the king. ¹⁶Then the people went out and plundered the camp of the Arameans. So a seah of flour sold for a shekel, and two seahs of barley sold for a shekel, as the Lord had said.

¹⁷Now the king had put the officer on whose arm he leaned in charge of the gate, and the people trampled him in the gateway, and he died, just as the man of God had foretold when the king came down to his house. ¹⁸It happened as the man of God had said to the king: "About this time tomorrow, a seah of flour will sell for a shekel and two seahs of barley for a shekel at the gate of Samaria."

¹⁹The officer had said to the man of God, "Look, even if the Lord should open the floodgates of the heavens, could this happen?" The man of God had replied, "You will see it with your own eyes, but you will not eat any of it!" ²⁰And that is exactly what happened to him, for the people trampled him in the gateway, and he died.

24 Yet at a later date war broke out again between Ben-Hadad II and Jehoram (v.24). Perhaps the miraculously arranged temporary lull had been divinely designed to teach Israel God's abiding love and concern for his people, to whom he had sent his duly authenticated prophet, Elisha. But with no evidence of repentance by Israel, God withdrew his protective hand; and Israel faced a full-scale Syrian invasion. The Arameans were eminently successful, penetrating to the very gates of Samaria itself, and putting the city under a dire siege.

25–29 The lengthy besiegement evoked a severe famine that, in turn, produced highly inflated prices for the humblest commodities. So scarce had food become that one day as the king was on a tour about the embattled city's wall, he stumbled on a case of cannibalism (v.26). By agreement two women had eaten the son of one of them (v.28); but when it came time for the second woman to surrender her son to the fire, she had hidden him, thus occasioning the first woman's complaint to the king (v.29).

30–33 Jehoram's reaction was one of anguished horror. He tore his robes, revealing his sackcloth garments of grief underneath. Enraged and blaming Elisha for the whole affair, he dispatched a messenger to seize and behead Elisha (v.31). When he had come to himself, however, he ran after his messenger, hoping to stay his hand. By divine insight Elisha knew the details of the whole episode and instructed certain elders who were with him to bar the door of the house until Jehoram could overtake his executioners (v.32). When the king arrived, he was admitted into the house (v.33). Convinced that the Lord had pronounced the doom of the city, Jehoram had all but given up any hope of the Lord's deliverance. Yet perhaps his realization that all that had transpired was from the Lord carried with it the faintest hope that God would yet miraculously intervene. The restraint of the messenger and the king's words hint at the faint hope of divine consolation. Such comfort Elisha would proceed to give.

7:1–2 Elisha seized on the king's last glimmer of hope (v.1). By the next day conditions would so improve that good products would be available again, even though at a substantial price. Jehoram's chief aide found such a statement preposterous (v.2). Even if the Lord should open the windows of heaven and pour down a flood of flour and grain, so dire had the famine been that even this would not suffice to effect Elisha's prediction.

The aide's words are filled with ridicule and heaped with sarcasm, as if to say, "Oh sure, Yahweh is even now making windows in heaven! So what? Could this word of yours still come to pass?" Whether the aide thought of the biblical phrase (Gen 7:11) or of the heavenly windows of the Baal fertility cult is uncertain. In any case he was skeptical of the whole thing.

The prophet assured Jehoram's aide that not only would the prophecy come true, but the officer would see it with his own eyes. However he would not eat any of it! His faithless incredulity would cause him to miss God's blessing on the people.

3–5 God moves mysteriously. His means of effecting the fulfillment of Elisha's prophecy were perhaps no less amazing than the aide's taunts. Four leprous men who lived outside the city gate knew that their situation was desperate (v.3). Accordingly they resolved to surrender to the Arameans (v.4). Death already stared them in the face; they had nothing to lose by going over to the Syrians. Slipping away at twilight they traveled circumlocutiously to the far end of the besieger's encampment. As they moved cautiously into the camp, to their surprise they met not one man—the camp was totally deserted (v.5).

6–7 The author of Kings explains that the Lord had miraculously caused the Arameans to hear what seemed to them the approach of a great army to liberate the besieged Israelites (v.6). Throwing caution to the wind, they had abandoned the camp with its supplies, running for fear of their lives (v.7). Precisely how the Lord produced the desired effect is not stated; but whatever the method, the Lord had once again miraculously intervened for his undeserving people.

8–14 The four rushed about eating and drinking their fill, gathering and hiding their booty (v.8). When the exhilaration of the moment had worn off, they realized that as Israelites it was their duty to tell the good news to others (v.9). Accordingly they hurried on the shortest way to the city and informed the gatekeepers that the Arameans had suddenly left (v.10). The good news reverberated throughout the city, reaching even the ears of the sleeping king (v.11). A cautious Jehoram was not so certain of the state of affairs (v.12). Perhaps the Arameans had withdrawn a bit to lure the Israelites into the camp so as to fall on them unawares and thus gain entrance into Samaria. Acting on the advice of his officers, he sent two chariot teams to scout out the whereabouts of the Arameans (vv.13–14). While Jehoram could scarcely spare them, yet if they were overtaken by the enemy, their plight would be little worse than what seemed inevitable should they remain in Samaria.

15 The scouting party soon returned with the staggering news. It was all true. For some reason the Arameans had fled in panic, leaving the road strewn with equipment and clothing as far as the Jordan River.

16–20 The king commanded the people to go to the Aramean camp and despoil it.

By day's end Elisha's amazing prophecy stood fulfilled, including the portion that dealt with Jehoram's aide. For in their mad rush for spoil, the people trampled him to death in the gateway he had been assigned to guard.

Notes

25 The written consonants of the MT's חריונים have been divided in some translations into חֲרֵי יוֹנִים (ḥārê yônîm, "dove's dung"; so NASB, KJV, RSV). The NIV apparently follows Gray (p. 518) and others in adopting an often-suggested emendation to חֲרוּבִים (ḥᵃrûbîm, "[carob] seed pods"). The pointing of the MT חֲרֵייוֹנִים (ḥiryyônîm) comes from the reading of a few MSS and the Qere: דִּבְיוֹנִים (dibyônîm, "doves'/pigeons' droppings"). If dove's dung is not the popular name for some common food or was not simply to be used as fuel for fire or as a substitute for salt (so Jos. Antiq. IX, 62 [iv.4]), the reduction of the people to eating dung may be paralleled by a similar incident at the siege of Jerusalem (see Jos. War, V, 571 [xiii.7]).

27–29 Cannibalism in time of siege was the prophetic threat for Israel's disobedience (Lev 26:29; Deut 28:53, 57; Ezek 5:10). It was to befall Jerusalem both in OT times (Lam 2:20; 4:10) and in NT times (cf. Jos. War, VI, 201–13 [iii.4]). For extrabiblical cases see A. Leo Oppenheim, "Siege Documents from Nippur," Iraq 17 (1955): 68–89.

7:1 Public business was carried on at the gate of the city (cf. Gen 19:1; Ruth 4:1; 2 Sam 15:1–5).

2 For שָׁלִישׁ (šālîš, "officer"), see the note on 9:25.

3 For leprosy in the OT, see the note on 5:1. The men apparently lived in some temporary shelter outside the city wall and had been left by the invaders to their eventual fate.

4 The term נִפְּלָה (nippᵉlāh, "let us go over"; lit., "fall away to," i.e., "desert") is a technical one.

5 קְצֵה מַחֲנֵה (qᵉṣēh maḥᵃneh, "the edge of the camp") we take to mean, not the outskirts of the encampment nearest the city's walls, but, in accordance with the natural meaning of the words, the camp's farthermost end. This is demanded for several reasons.

1. A direct approach to the camp would probably incur instant death; it was better to surrender to the least fortified position.

2. It would allow the possibility that the men might find a spot where they could slip unawares into camp for their needs and creep away without discovery. Even though they had decided to desert to the Arameans, this could be viewed as only a final course of action to be taken when worse might come to worst.

3. It allows sufficient time for the miraculous flight of the Arameans before the arrival of the lepers and while they were traveling out of sight of the camp itself.

4. It may provide the occasion for the miracle itself; perhaps the Lord had in some way magnified the stumbling footsteps of the men as they made their way around the camp's opposite end.

6 Since Egypt was in decline at this time, some scholars have suggested that a Cilician kingdom known as Musri, whose spelling in Semitic would have been the same first three consonants (msr) as the Hebrew word for Egypt, was intended (see Gray, Kings, pp. 524f.; Montgomery, p. 387). But since the Akkadian spelling for Egypt was uniformly muṣir throughout the first millennium B.C., the very existence of such a kingdom is conjectural at best. There can be little doubt that the MT intends Egypt; see further the note on 19:24.

9 עָוֹן (ʿāwôn) means primarily "iniquity," then the "guilt" that stems from iniquity, and thus the consequences of it all—"punishment." Accordingly what the lepers feared was not that the Arameans might return and do them in but that a greedy failure to share in

the available bounty would make them culpable and hence deserving of divine chastisement.

12 Jehoram seems not to have entertained the possibility that the reported good news might be connected with Elisha's prophecy.

13 The verse is a well-known crux, the MT being generally regarded as corrupt (see Gray, *Kings*, pp. 520f.). Certainly the redundant phraseology makes the syntax awkward at best. But the report of impassioned speech with its broken diction makes an accurate recording very difficult. The NIV has paraphrased well the intent of the MT. The whole emphasizes the hopeless situation in which Israel found herself.

---

3) *Postscript to war: the restitution of the Shunammite's land and the coup d'état of Hazael*

8:1–15

¹Now Elisha had said to the woman whose son he had restored to life, "Go away with your family and stay for a while wherever you can, because the LORD has decreed a famine in the land that will last seven years." ²The woman proceeded to do as the man of God said. She and her family went away and stayed in the land of the Philistines seven years.

³At the end of the seven years she came back from the land of the Philistines and went to the king to beg for her house and land. ⁴The king was talking to Gehazi, the servant of the man of God, and had said, "Tell me about all the great things Elisha has done." ⁵Just as Gehazi was telling the king how Elisha had restored the dead to life, the woman whose son Elisha had brought back to life came to beg the king for her house and land.

Gehazi said, "This is the woman, my lord the king, and this is her son whom Elisha restored to life." ⁶The king asked the woman about it, and she told him.

Then he assigned an official to her case and said to him, "Give back everything that belonged to her, including all the income from her land from the day she left the country until now."

⁷Elisha went to Damascus, and Ben-Hadad king of Aram was ill. When the king was told, "The man of God has come all the way up here," ⁸he said to Hazael, "Take a gift with you and go to meet the man of God. Consult the LORD through him; ask him, 'Will I recover from this illness?'"

⁹Hazael went to meet Elisha, taking with him as a gift forty camel-loads of all the finest wares of Damascus. He went in and stood before him, and said, "Your son Ben-Hadad king of Aram has sent me to ask, 'Will I recover from this illness?'"

¹⁰Elisha answered, "Go and say to him, 'You will certainly recover'; but the LORD has revealed to me that he will in fact die." ¹¹He stared at him with a fixed gaze until Hazael felt ashamed. Then the man of God began to weep.

¹²"Why is my lord weeping?" asked Hazael.

"Because I know the harm you will do to the Israelites," he answered. "You will set fire to their fortified places, kill their young men with the sword, dash their little children to the ground, and rip open their pregnant women."

¹³Hazael said, "How could your servant, a mere dog, accomplish such a feat?"

"The LORD has shown me that you will become king of Aram," answered Elisha.

¹⁴Then Hazael left Elisha and returned to his master. When Ben-Hadad asked, "What did Elisha say to you?" Hazael replied, "He told me that you would certainly recover." ¹⁵But the next day he took a thick cloth, soaked it in water and spread it over the king's face, so that he died. Then Hazael succeeded him as king.

1–6 Chapter 8 opens with a last glimpse of Elisha's former servant, Gehazi. Apparently King Jehoram of Israel had summoned Gehazi to learn from a reliable source something of the great prophet whose miraculous prediction had just come to pass. The wise deployment of divine providence is also in evidence; for the Shunammite woman (probably widowed by this time) had just returned after the seven-year famine she had fled from at Elisha's warning, only to find her property had been appropriated (vv.1-3).

A woman of strong resolve, she immediately determined to take her case directly to the king, to whom she was going when she happened on Jehoram talking with Gehazi (v.4). God has so arranged the details of life that Gehazi could identify the woman and so aid in the verification of her claim; and she, in turn, would be living proof of Gehazi's account to the king of Elisha's mighty deeds (v.5).

The time of the encounter has been much debated, many suggesting that the meeting must have taken place before Gehazi had contracted leprosy. If, however, neither Naaman nor Gehazi, who received Naaman's affliction, had leprosy proper (see the note on 5:1), such need not be the case. Furthermore royal prerogative often sets aside all other enactments. If the text is in chronological order, one may have reason to conjecture that Gehazi had repented of his sins and had been restored to a place of usefulness for God, despite his forfeiture of position with Elisha.

7-8 The next incident from the Elisha cycle both closes the wars with Ben-Hadad II and initiates the critical circumstances that will culminate in the crucial events of 841 B.C. (see ch. 9). Ben-Hadad II, the Aramean king (860-842 B.C.), lay ill (v.7). News reached him that his old antagonist, Elisha, was at that very moment traveling in the area. Feeling that Elisha's arrival might be fortuitous, he sent Hazael, one of his trusted officials, with an appropriate royal escort to inquire of Elisha whether or not he would recover from his sickness (v.8). He could not know, of course, that Elisha had come to carry out the Lord's instructions to Elijah relative to dynastic change, both in Damascus and in Samaria (1 Kings 19:15-17, q.v.).

9-11a Hazael dutifully carried out his master's instructions (v.9). Elisha's reply to Hazael was an enigmatic one: the answer to the king's question was both yes and no (v.10). Yes: if left to normal circumstances of healing, the king would recover; and no: Elisha, who was at that moment anointing Hazael as king, knew that this treacherous man would use the king's illness to effect his coup d'état. Accordingly Hazael could testify truthfully to the king. The illness was not a fatal one of itself. Elisha's reply and icy stare indicate that Hazael had already plotted the king's demise through the situation and that Elisha knew his secret thoughts. Hazael blushed in shame (v.11a).

11b-13 Elisha's stares soon turned to weeping (v.11b). In answer to Hazael's question, Elisha indicated that he wept for the great barbarity that Hazael, as Aram's next king, would inflict on Israel (v.12). Despite Hazael's protests to the contrary (v.13), such would indeed be the case (cf. 10:32-33; 13:3).

14-15 Doubtless Elisha's assurances to Hazael that he would be the next king of Damascus gave pretext to him that he had a mandate to be carried out. When he returned to the palace, he told his master the good news: the king would surely recover (v.14). However the next day opportunity came to carry out the long-standing purpose. Having smothered the king, he assumed the throne (v.15).

Notes

1–3 Seven-year famines were not unknown in the ancient Near East (cf. Gen 41:29–32; see also ANET, p. 31).

1 The verb גּוּרִי (*gûrî*, "stay for awhile") indicates that the Shunammite woman was only to become a resident alien in a foreign land, with full intention of returning to her own land. Her return within seven years may have aided her legal claim to her property (cf. Exod 21:2; 23:10–11; Lev 25:1–7; Deut 15:1–6; Ruth 1:1, 22; 4:3–4).

4 For OT leprosy see the note on 5:1.

6 For סָרִיס (*sārîs*, "official") see the notes on 1 Kings 22:9 and 2 Kings 18:17. The instruction of the king to return to the plaintiff not only her property but its back income for the period of her Philistine sojourn shows the impression the incident made on the king.

9 The words "your son" are terms of spiritual protocol, underscoring the humility of the supplicant.

11 A touch of pathos is evident in the scriptural notice "Then the man of God began to weep" (cf. Gen 42:24; 43:30; Matt 26:75; Luke 22:62; John 11:35).

12 For the barbaric picture described here, see the note on 15:16.

13 For the dog as a figure of abasement, see the note on 1 Kings 14:11.

15 Hazael is often mentioned in the records of Shalmaneser III. Hazael's usurpation is duly noted in that Hazael is called "son of a nobody"; see further Luckenbill, *Ancient Records*, 1:246; S. Barabas, "Hazael," ZPEB, 3:49.

---

e. *The reign of Jehoram of the southern kingdom*

8:16–24

> [16]In the fifth year of Joram son of Ahab king of Israel, when Jehoshaphat was king of Judah, Jehoram son of Jehoshaphat began his reign as king of Judah. [17]He was thirty-two years old when he became king, and he reigned in Jerusalem eight years. [18]He walked in the ways of the kings of Israel, as the house of Ahab had done, for he married a daughter of Ahab. He did evil in the eyes of the LORD. [19]Nevertheless, for the sake of his servant David, the LORD was not willing to destroy Judah. He had promised to maintain a lamp for David and his descendants forever.
>
> [20]In the time of Jehoram, Edom rebelled against Judah and set up its own king. [21]So Jehoram went to Zair with all his chariots. The Edomites surrounded him and his chariot commanders, but he rose up and broke through by night; his army, however, fled back home. [22]To this day Edom has been in rebellion against Judah. Libnah revolted at the same time.
>
> [23]As for the other events of Jehoram's reign, and all he did, are they not written in the book of the annals of the kings of Judah? [24]Jehoram rested with his fathers and was buried with them in the City of David. And Ahaziah his son succeeded him as king.

16–18 The author of Kings shifts his attention to the southern kingdom and to the two sons of Jehoshaphat. The synchronism of v.16 records the year of Jehoram's assumption of full power of state (see note on 1:17). Jehoram's ungodly character is noted along with the primary factor in the spiritual apostasy: his marriage to Ahab's daughter (v.18; cf. ch. 11). The Chronicler (2 Chron 21:11) adds that Jehoram made all Judah to sin according to the religion of the Canaanites.

19–24 The perverse nature of Jehoram is further evidenced in that after his father's death he slew all his brothers and any possible claimant to the throne (2 Chron 21:2 –4). Despite Jehoram's spiritual and moral bankruptcy, God honored the covenant with the house of David (v.19; cf. 2 Chron 21:7) and did not destroy the kingdom. Nevertheless Jehoram and Judah did experience judgment in the form of three military engagements (cf. 2 Chron 21:10): (1) Edom revolted successfully, a rebellion that nearly cost Jehoram his life in attempting to suppress it (vv.20–22a; cf. 2 Chron 21:8–10a); (2) simultaneously Libnah revolted (v.22b; cf. 2 Chron 21:10b); and (3) the Philistines and Arabians launched a massive attack that reached Jerusalem itself and cost the king all his sons except Ahaziah (cf. 2 Chron 21:16–17 with 2 Chron 22:1). Judah and its kings were smitten with the plague (2 Chron 21:12–15), Jehoram himself succumbing eventually with an incurable disease in the bowels (2 Chron 21:15, 18–19). Thus an unfortunate period of Judah's history, in the form of a wicked and apostate son of the house of David, passed, wicked Jehoram himself being excluded from the royal sepulcher (vv.23–24; 2 Chron 21:20b).

Notes

---

18 The royal marriage of the two houses of Israel and Judah was to spell catastrophe for Judah. Already Athaliah's influence was felt in Jehoram's murder of the royal house (cf. 11:1) and the subsequent introduction of Baal worship (1 Kings 16:29–33; 2 Kings 11:17 –18; 2 Chron 24:7). Both Jehoram and Ahab, his father-in-law, were dominated by strong-willed *femme fatales*, by whom they would fall, both spiritually and physically (cf. 1 Kings 21:25–26; see Jos. *Antiq*. IX, 96 [v.1]).

19 לָתֵת לוֹ נִיר (*lātēt lô nîr*, lit., "to give a lamp to him," i.e., in accordance with the Davidic covenant) shows that God would yet maintain David's line as a light of testimony to divine faithfulness, despite the individual faithlessness of some members of the Davidic line (see Ps 89:19–37). The full covenant promise itself remains to be fulfilled in the greater David (Ps 110; Matt 27:64; Luke 1:68–75; 20:41–44; Acts 2:29–36; Rev 5:5–14; 19:11–21). See further the comment on 1 Kings 11:36.

22 Due to the economic importance of established trade routes, Judean clashes with Edom usually triggered Philistine and Arabic military activities with Judah (2 Chron 21:16; 26: 6–7; 28:17–19; cf. Joel 3:4–8, 19; Amos 1:6–8; Obad 11–14?). It is not certain whether the Philistine-Arab attack of 2 Chron 21:16–17 occurred precisely at the time of Libnah's revolt, but the two events most certainly were related to each other and to the Edomite rebellion.

23 Second Chron 21:12–15 (q.v.) records a letter of divine judgment from Elijah the prophet to King Jehoram. Archer (*Encyclopedia*, pp. 226–27) argues persuasively that Elijah may actually not have been yet translated into heaven before the accession of Jehoram of Judah.

24 For Jehoram's death from an incurable disease, see 2 Chron 21:15–19.

---

f. *The reign of Ahaziah of the southern kingdom*

  8:25–29

   ²⁵In the twelfth year of Joram son of Ahab king of Israel, Ahaziah son of Jehoram king of Judah began to reign. ²⁶Ahaziah was twenty-two years old when he

became king, and he reigned in Jerusalem one year. His mother's name was Athaliah, a granddaughter of Omri king of Israel. [27]He walked in the ways of the house of Ahab and did evil in the eyes of the LORD, as the house of Ahab had done, for he was related by marriage to Ahab's family.

[28]Ahaziah went with Joram son of Ahab to war against Hazael king of Aram at Ramoth Gilead. The Arameans wounded Joram; [29]so King Joram returned to Jezreel to recover from the wounds the Arameans had inflicted on him at Ramoth in his battle with Hazael king of Aram.

Then Ahaziah son of Jehoram king of Judah went down to Jezreel to see Joram son of Ahab, because he had been wounded.

25–26a Ahaziah succeeded his father, Jehoram, in the critical year 841 B.C. He was not to survive the momentous waves of political events that were to inundate the ancient Near East in that year. Indeed in 841 B.C. Shalmaneser III of Assyria (859 –824 B.C.) at last was able to break the coalition of western allies with whom he had previously fought a long series of battles (853, 848, 845). While all these complex details were part of God's teleological processes in the government of the nations and his dealing with Israel, doubtless the long-standing controversy and the growing specter of Assyrian power could be felt in the political intrigues that brought about the death of Ben-Hadad II of Damascus and the downfall of the Omride Dynasty in Israel. Before 841 had ended Hazael would be master of Damascus (where Shalmaneser had set him up after having defeated him in battle), the pro-Assyrian Jehu would initiate the fourth dynasty in Israel (chs. 9–10), and the wicked Athaliah would sit as usurper on the throne of Judah (ch. 11).

26b–29 Ahaziah, too, was under the paganistic spell of wicked Athaliah (v.26b; cf. 2 Chron 22:3–5) and perpetuated the Baalism that his father had fostered (v.27). Likewise, at the first opportunity he joined in with Ahab's son Jehoram in renewed hostilities with the Arameans in Ramoth Gilead (v.28; 1 Kings 22:1–40). Once more the battle went badly for Israel and Judah, for in that battle King Jehoram was sorely wounded and returned to Jezreel for rest and recovery from his wounds (v.29; cf. 9:14–16). The chapter ends with a concerned Ahaziah going to visit Jehoram in Jezreel. He would not return to Jerusalem alive (cf. 9:16, 24–29).

Notes

25 For details as to political relations between Shalmaneser III of Assyria and Syro-Palestine, see Hallo, "Qarqar," pp. 157–62; Astour, pp. 383–89; A.R. Green, "Sua and Jehu, The Boundaries of Shalmaneser's Conquest," PEQ (1979): 35–39. See also the note on 10: 30–32.

26 Ahaziah doubtless was twenty-two when he began to reign, not forty-two as 2 Chron 22:2 affirms, a reading that preserves an ancient scribal slip. Note the similar problem in 2 Kings 24:8 (cf. 2 Chron 36:9–10).

The NIV correctly translates בַּת־עָמְרִי (baṯ-ʿomrî) "the granddaughter of Omri" (cf v.18), her patrilineage being traced back to the founder of Israel's third dynasty. The Hebrew words for son (בֵּן, bēn) and daughter (בַּת, baṯ) often have nuances such as grandson (e.g., Gen 31:28) and granddaughter (as here). See further the discussion in TDOT, 2:149–53, 333–36. The precise relationship of Athaliah to Ahab and Jezebel has been variously debated by scholars, with differing conclusions being drawn, such as Athaliah's being (1) the daughter of Omri (Gray), (2) the daughter of Ahab and Jezebel (Keil), or (3) simply the daughter of Ahab (but not of Jezebel, Bright). For details see G.H. Jones, *1 & 2 Kings*, New Century Bible Commentary, 2 Parts (Grand Rapids: Eerdmans, 1984), 2:446 –47.

28–29 God's judgment against Jehoram and Ahaziah would be accomplished as a corollary to the fulfillment of Elisha's sentence against the house of Ahab (cf. 1 Kings 21:21–24; 2 Kings 9:36–37). Both were brought about under God's sovereign supervision of the complex international events that culminated in 841 B.C. (cf. Job 24:22–24; Rom 11:33).

---

g. The reign of Jehoram of the northern kingdom

9:1–37

¹The prophet Elisha summoned a man from the company of the prophets and said to him, "Tuck your cloak into your belt, take this flask of oil with you and go to Ramoth Gilead. ²When you get there, look for Jehu son of Jehoshaphat, the son of Nimshi. Go to him, get him away from his companions and take him into an inner room. ³Then take the flask and pour the oil on his head and declare, 'This is what the LORD says: I anoint you king over Israel.' Then open the door and run; don't delay!"

⁴So the young man, the prophet, went to Ramoth Gilead. ⁵When he arrived, he found the army officers sitting together. "I have a message for you, commander," he said.

"For which of us?" asked Jehu.

"For you, commander," he replied.

⁶Jehu got up and went into the house. Then the prophet poured the oil on Jehu's head and declared, "This is what the LORD, the God of Israel, says: 'I anoint you king over the LORD's people Israel. ⁷You are to destroy the house of Ahab your master, and I will avenge the blood of my servants the prophets and the blood of all the LORD's servants shed by Jezebel. ⁸The whole house of Ahab will perish. I will cut off from Ahab every last male in Israel—slave or free. ⁹I will make the house of Ahab like the house of Jeroboam son of Nebat and like the house of Baasha son of Ahijah. ¹⁰As for Jezebel, dogs will devour her on the plot of ground at Jezreel, and no one will bury her.' " Then he opened the door and ran.

¹¹When Jehu went out to his fellow officers, one of them asked him, "Is everything all right? Why did this madman come to you?"

"You know the man and the sort of things he says," Jehu replied.

¹²"That's not true!" they said. "Tell us."

Jehu said, "Here is what he told me: 'This is what the LORD says: I anoint you king over Israel.' "

¹³They hurried and took their cloaks and spread them under him on the bare steps. Then they blew the trumpet and shouted, "Jehu is king!"

¹⁴So Jehu son of Jehoshaphat, the son of Nimshi, conspired against Joram. (Now Joram and all Israel had been defending Ramoth Gilead against Hazael king of Aram, ¹⁵but King Joram had returned to Jezreel to recover from the wounds the Arameans had inflicted on him in the battle with Hazael king of Aram.) Jehu said, "If this is the way you feel, don't let anyone slip out of the city to go and tell the news in Jezreel." ¹⁶Then he got into his chariot and rode to Jezreel, because Joram was resting there and Ahaziah king of Judah had gone down to see him.

¹⁷When the lookout standing on the tower in Jezreel saw Jehu's troops approaching, he called out, "I see some troops coming."

"Get a horseman," Joram ordered. "Send him to meet them and ask, 'Do you come in peace?' "

18The horseman rode off to meet Jehu and said, "This is what the king says: 'Do you come in peace?' "

"What do you have to do with peace?" Jehu replied. "Fall in behind me."

The lookout reported, "The messenger has reached them, but he isn't coming back."

19So the king sent out a second horseman. When he came to them he said, "This is what the king says: 'Do you come in peace?' "

Jehu replied, "What do you have to do with peace? Fall in behind me."

20The lookout reported, "He has reached them, but he isn't coming back either. The driving is like that of Jehu son of Nimshi—he drives like a madman."

21"Hitch up my chariot," Joram ordered. And when it was hitched up, Joram king of Israel and Ahaziah king of Judah rode out, each in his own chariot, to meet Jehu. They met him at the plot of ground that had belonged to Naboth the Jezreelite. 22When Joram saw Jehu he asked, "Have you come in peace, Jehu?"

"How can there be peace," Jehu replied, "as long as all the idolatry and witchcraft of your mother Jezebel abound?"

23Joram turned about and fled, calling out to Ahaziah, "Treachery, Ahaziah!"

24Then Jehu drew his bow and shot Joram between the shoulders. The arrow pierced his heart and he slumped down in his chariot. 25Jehu said to Bidkar, his chariot officer, "Pick him up and throw him on the field that belonged to Naboth the Jezreelite. Remember how you and I were riding together in chariots behind Ahab his father when the LORD made this prophecy about him: 26'Yesterday I saw the blood of Naboth and the blood of his sons, declares the LORD, and I will surely make you pay for it on this plot of ground, declares the LORD.' Now then, pick him up and throw him on that plot, in accordance with the word of the LORD."

27When Ahaziah king of Judah saw what had happened, he fled up the road to Beth Haggan. Jehu chased him, shouting, "Kill him too!" They wounded him in his chariot on the way up to Gur near Ibleam, but he escaped to Megiddo and died there. 28His servants took him by chariot to Jerusalem and buried him with his fathers in his tomb in the City of David. 29(In the eleventh year of Joram son of Ahab, Ahaziah had become king of Judah.)

30Then Jehu went to Jezreel. When Jezebel heard about it, she painted her eyes, arranged her hair and looked out of a window. 31As Jehu entered the gate, she asked, "Have you come in peace, Zimri, you murderer of your master?"

32He looked up at the window and called out, "Who is on my side? Who?" Two or three eunuchs looked down at him. 33"Throw her down!" Jehu said. So they threw her down, and some of her blood spattered the wall and the horses as they trampled her underfoot.

34Jehu went in and ate and drank. "Take care of that cursed woman," he said, "and bury her, for she was a king's daughter." 35But when they went out to bury her, they found nothing except her skull, her feet and her hands. 36They went back and told Jehu, who said, "This is the word of the LORD that he spoke through his servant Elijah the Tishbite: On the plot of ground at Jezreel dogs will devour Jezebel's flesh. 37Jezebel's body will be like refuse on the ground in the plot at Jezreel, so that no one will be able to say, 'This is Jezebel.' "

1 In those critical days when King Jehoram remained at the royal retreat in Jezreel recuperating from his wounds suffered in the battle against the Arameans at Ramoth Gilead (8:28–29; 9:14), Elisha summoned his trusty attendant, who was one of the "company of the prophets," in order to send him with a commission to anoint the next king of Israel. The scene of this anointing would be that same Ramoth Gilead where the Israelite troops remained stationed in prolonged confrontation with the Damascene Arameans.

2–3 Once there the young prophet was to single out Jehu, the ranking army commander, take him aside privately into a room, pour a flask of oil on his head, and pronounce that God had anointed him as the next king of Israel. Having accomplished his task, the prophet was immediately to hasten from the house so as to avoid any diminishing of the act itself. God's work is often best done and left to have its own impact.

4–10 The young prophet duly did as he was instructed (v.4). Arriving in Ramoth Gilead, he sought out Jehu (v.5); and, having brought him into the house, he anointed his head and delivered God's solemn words to him (v.6). Jehu's divine commission was twofold: (1) he was to annihilate all the wicked and apostate house of Ahab (2) so as to avenge the blood of God's own who had been martyred for their faithfulness (v.7). In this Jehu was to be God's instrument of divine vengeance against Jezebel's bloody persecutions. When he had finished these words, in obedience to his orders, he literally ran from the house (v.10).

11–13 After the young prophet had fled, Jehu went out to the court where his fellow officers were sitting. They, of course, wanted to know what had occasioned the arrival of "this madman" (v.11). The term betrays the low spiritual condition of the soldiers and carries with it their contempt for God's prophets. When Jehu replied rather nonchalantly that this sort of character was liable to say anything, the officers, suspecting something important had occurred, pressed him all the harder (v.12). Jehu then revealed the gist of what had happened: God had sent the prophet to anoint him as king! Perhaps recalling the similar past anointings of Saul and David and assuredly sporting for insurrection, the officers responded immediately, spreading their cloaks under Jehu as a sign of submission (v.13). Having blown the trumpet, they proclaimed to all the army that Jehu was the next king of Israel.

14–16 The enthusiastic response to the prophet's pronouncement by his men prompted Jehu to take an active lead in a formal coup d'état (v.14). Having doubtless left a security force to continue the defense of Ramoth Gilead and having given instructions that none be allowed to slip out of the city and go with a warning to Jehoram in Jezreel, Jehu took a select group of troops and set out for Jezreel and the recuperating Jehoram (vv.15–16). In God's providence (cf. 2 Chron 22:7), Ahaziah of Judah was at Jezreel visiting his ailing relative (cf. 8:29).

17–21 The scene switches to Jezreel. As Jehu rode swiftly toward the city, the watchman announced the approach of troops (v.17). Jehoram sent a messenger on horseback to intercept the column and inquire as to its mission. When the horseman reached Jehu and asked him whether all was well, Jehu bid him to fall in with his troops, which he did (v.18). When the watchman reported all this to Jehoram, a second horseman was sent out—with the same result (vv.19–20). When the watchman next reported that the approach of the chariot looked like the wild driving of Jehu, Jehoram and Ahaziah rode their chariots out to meet him (v.21). Significantly they met Jehu at the plot of ground that Ahab had purloined from Naboth.

22–24 A third time Jehu was asked whether he had come in peace (v.22). The royal query was greeted in a still rougher manner than the preceding two. Jehoram's espousal of the idolatry and witchcraft instituted by Jezebel had rendered any talk of "peace" impossible. Jehoram realized that Jehu's reply meant that a coup d'état was taking place (v.23). Having warned Ahaziah of the treachery, Jehoram attempted to flee but was struck dead in his chariot by Jehu's well-aimed arrow (v.24).

25–29 In fulfillment of Elijah's prophetic threat (cf. 1 Kings 21:19–24), which apparently Jehu and his chariot officers had heard, Jehu instructed his aide to throw Jehoram's fallen body onto Naboth's field (vv.25–26). Ahaziah's attempt to escape Jehu was also abortive (v.27). Sorely wounded he managed to gain his flight as far as Megiddo where in the confused events that followed (see Notes) he ultimately died. Afterwards his servant took his body to Jerusalem for burial in the royal tombs (v.28).

30–34a News of all this had no doubt reached Jezebel. Sensing her own imminent demise, she arranged herself in queenly fashion and went to the window to await Jehu's arrival (v.30). As Jehu entered the gate below, she called tauntingly to him with words calculated to cut Jehu down to size (v.31). Jehu is called a "Zimri," a name Buccellatti (p. 203) notes had become synonymous with "traitor," the implication being that usurpers usually do not last too long themselves. Jehu was fully up to the occasion. Looking up to the window where Jezebel was, he called out for anyone who would stand with him (v.32). When some of the eunuchs responded to Jehu's bidding, Jezebel was thrown to the courtyard below (v.33). Jehu subsequently rode over the fallen body and went in to dine in the banquet hall of his predecessor (v.34a).

34b–37 Later, on thinking over the events that had recently transpired, Jehu gave instructions that Jezebel's body be given a proper burial, since she had been a king's daughter (v.34b). But his second thoughts were too late. The servant found precious little of Jezebel's remains (v.35). When this was reported to Jehu, he recognized immediately the full force of Elijah's awful prophecy (vv.36–37; cf. 1 Kings 21:23).

Notes

4 For the more technical applications of the term נַעַר (na'ar, "young man," "servant"), see the note on 1 Kings 20:14–15.
   For the general organization of the Israelite armies, see AIs, 1:213–28.
5 While Jehu's reply implies that he was no more of a high officer than any other man with whom he sat in council, the fact that he was the one who replied to the prophet argues for the fact that Jehu was moderating the staff meeting, hence was its ranking officer.
6 The phrase עַם יהוה ('am yhwh, "the LORD's people") reminded Jehu that though God had chastened his people, he had not yet cast them off. Jehu's call was to serve in God's authority before his covenant nation, Israel.
8 Verses 8–10 in large measure repeat the prophetic threat of 1 Kings 21:21–23 (q.v.). For the enigmatic "slave or free," see the note on 1 Kings 14:10.
10 The accusative noun "Jezebel" stands first here so as to capture the emphatic prediction of 1 Kings 21:23.
11 The word מְשֻׁגָּע (mešuggā', "madman") is a strong one, being used of madness in general (Deut 28:34), of David's feigned madness at Gath (1 Sam 21:12–15), of false prophets (Hos 9:7), and even of Shemaiah's contempt for Jeremiah (Jer 29:24–28). As Gray (Kings, p. 542) points out, this passage is often cited along with such passages as Jer 29:26, where

the denominative verb הִתְנַבֵּא (hiṯnabbēʾ) is used of madness, in support of the theory that ecstasy was an essential feature of Hebrew prophecy. This theory is often utilized to reduce the OT prophet to the level of the wicked excesses of heathen diviners. Freeman (*Old Testament Prophets*, p. 60), however, concludes: "At times the behavior of the prophet was unusual or abnormal but a careful consideration of each of these instances will reveal some divine purpose or spiritual significance . . . the symbolic acts of some of the prophets were not ordinary or normal behavior."

12 The word שֶׁקֶר (šeqer, "that's not true") means a desperate lie but was probably used hyperbolically and in good sport by Jehu's fellow officers who, though having little use for God or his prophets, nonetheless wanted to know what really happened in there. One is reminded of the question put to Alexander after his consultation with the oracle at Siwah (see U. Wilcken, *Alexander the Great* [New York: Norton, 1967], pp. 121–29).

13 The officers' cloaks were doubtless laid for Jehu, the steps of the house serving as a makeshift throne, with Jehu probably sitting on the top ones. The strewing of garments was a mark of homage (cf. Matt 21:8). For the blowing of the trumpet and the shouting of "long live the king," see 1 Kings 1:34 (cf. 2 Kings 11:12).

17 Although the battle had been severe, so that Israel's king had been wounded (cf. 8:24–25), nevertheless Israel must have been holding its own against Hazael at this stage; for Jehu was able to leave sufficient troops at the front and still effect a coup d'état in Israel. For future relations between Hazael and Israel, see the note on 10:30–32.

18 מַה־לְּךָ וּלְשָׁלוֹם (mah-lleḵā ûlešālôm, "what do you have to do with peace") is literally "What (is) to you and to peace?" i.e., "Do not worry about peace." D.J. Wiseman (" 'Is it peace?'—Covenant and Diplomacy," VetTest 32 [1982]: 319–21) suggests that the whole incident from Elisha's anointing to Jehoram's questions reflects terminology drawn from international protocol and negotiations. For Jehoram the negotiations failed.

20 The word בְּשִׁגָּעוֹן (bešiggāʾôn, "like a madman") is derived from the same root as the word used for madness in v.11. The phrase has caused great problems so that the versions have rendered it variously, LXX with the idea of a peculiar alternating motion, the Vulgate with a word meaning an (hostile) approach, and the Peshitta with a word meaning "hastily." Interestingly the Targum translates it "quietly" (a concept found also in Jos. *Antiq*. IX, 177 [vi.3]), hence "marched slowly and in good order."

22 זְנוּנִים (zenûnîm, "idolatry"; lit., "harlotries") and כְּשָׁפִים (kešāpîm, "witchcraft," "sorceries"; cf. Akkad. kišpu ["witchcraft," "sorcery"] from kašāpu ["to bewitch," "cast a spell"]) designate the heinous nature of Jezebel's reign. Spiritual whoredom had allured Israel's religious devotees into demonic practices.

25 "Bidkar" was Jehu's שָׁלִישׁ (šālîš, "chief" or "chariot officer"), the third man in the chariot (besides the driver and warrior) whose task it was to hold the shield and arms of the warrior. Eventually the term was applied to a high-ranking official (cf. 7:2).

The phrase רֹכְבִים צְמָדִים (rōḵebîm ṣemāḏîm, "riding together in chariots") is ambiguous. It may mean, as Kimchi (Keil, in loc.) suggests, that Jehu and Bidkar rode together in one chariot as part of the chariot team; or it may mean that as young men each was manning his own chariot behind Ahab but close enough to hear the prophecy.

26 The variance between this verse and 1 Kings 21:19, 21–24 is to be accounted for by noting that Jehu was merely repeating the substance of Elijah's words in such a way as to accredit himself as God's avenging agent.

27 The circumstances of Ahaziah's flight, capture, death, and burial have been much discussed. Taken at face value, the Kings account seems to say that Ahaziah was wounded on the ascent to Gur and died in Megiddo, from which his body was taken to Jerusalem for burial. Second Chron 22:8–9 seems to indicate that Ahaziah was overtaken in Samaria where he had sought refuge with relatives and was brought to Jehu and executed, his body being interred with honor by Jehu's men. One possibility of reconciling the problem is to suggest that although Ahaziah was wounded at the ascent to Gur, he was apprehended by Jehu's men in Samaria (where he lay recovering from his wounds) and then taken to Megiddo where he was put to death, his body being given to his servants who

took him to Jerusalem for burial in the royal tomb (v.28; cf. 2 Chron 22:9). Whereas the author of Kings emphasized Ahaziah's flight and eventual execution in Megiddo, the Chronicler laid stress on his arrest. The accounts, therefore, are supplementary, not contradictory.

29 For the apparent discrepancy in the details relative to Ahaziah's ascension, see the note on 8:26 and the remarks of Archer, *Encyclopedia*, p. 206.

30 Doubtless Jezebel's adornment was intended to create a queenly appearance in the face of impending death and served as a royal burial preparation.

Jezebel was in her "upper chamber," the whole upper story doubtless forming the royal quarters, much in the style of the Syrian *bit Ḥillāni* ("house with windows"), which had attached balconies with lattice-work screens. See further the note on 1:2 and the remarks in the note on 1 Kings 17:19. For the figure of the woman at the window, cf. Judg 5:28; see also Aharoni/Avi Yonah, p. 85, and R. Patterson, "The Song of Deborah," *Tradition and Testament*, edd. John and Paul Feinberg (Chicago: Moody, 1981), p. 141.

31 The words הַשָׁלוֹם (*haš̌ālôm*, "Have you come in peace?") are in mockery of the question already asked three times.

34 Jehu sat at the king's table, not "as if nothing untoward had happened" (Montgomery, p. 403), but as attesting his right to the royal domain and as a mark of communion between the local officials and the new king. Hermann (p. 221) points out: "But in occupying Jezreel Jehu has not yet finished his work. Jezreel was a secondary residence, perhaps a royal family lived there, as did the aristocratic upper class, and there was a real risk that they might organize resistance."

The particle attached to the imperative פִּקְדוּ־נָא (*piqdû-nā*, "take care of") may represent a softened attitude on Jehu's part. Jehu's reason for Jezebel's burial—that she was "the daughter of a king"—pays service to her royalty while tacitly denying that she properly was queen of Israel. Although a Phoenician princess, since she was an idolatress who was under God's curse, she could not rightly be considered Israel's queen.

C. *The Era of the Fourth Dynasty (10:1–15:12)*

1. *The reign of Jehu in the northern kingdom*

10:1–36

¹Now there were in Samaria seventy sons of the house of Ahab. So Jehu wrote letters and sent them to Samaria: to the officials of Jezreel, to the elders and to the guardians of Ahab's children. He said, ²"As soon as this letter reaches you, since your master's sons are with you and you have chariots and horses, a fortified city and weapons, ³choose the best and most worthy of your master's sons and set him on his father's throne. Then fight for your master's house."

⁴But they were terrified and said, "If two kings could not resist him, how can we?"

⁵So the palace administrator, the city governor, the elders and the guardians sent this message to Jehu: "We are your servants and we will do anything you say. We will not appoint anyone as king; you do whatever you think best."

⁶Then Jehu wrote them a second letter, saying, "If you are on my side and will obey me, take the heads of your master's sons and come to me in Jezreel by this time tomorrow."

Now the royal princes, seventy of them, were with the leading men of the city, who were rearing them. ⁷When the letter arrived, these men took the princes and slaughtered all seventy of them. They put their heads in baskets and sent them to Jehu in Jezreel. ⁸When the messenger arrived, he told Jehu, "They have brought the heads of the princes."

209

Then Jehu ordered, "Put them in two piles at the entrance of the city gate until morning."

⁹The next morning Jehu went out. He stood before all the people and said, "You are innocent. It was I who conspired against my master and killed him, but who killed all these? ¹⁰Know then, that not a word the LORD has spoken against the house of Ahab will fail. The LORD has done what he promised through his servant Elijah." ¹¹So Jehu killed everyone in Jezreel who remained of the house of Ahab, as well as all his chief men, his close friends and his priests, leaving him no survivor.

¹²Jehu then set out and went toward Samaria. At Beth Eked of the Shepherds, ¹³he met some relatives of Ahaziah king of Judah and asked, "Who are you?"

They said, "We are relatives of Ahaziah, and we have come down to greet the families of the king and of the queen mother."

¹⁴"Take them alive!" he ordered. So they took them alive and slaughtered them by the well of Beth Eked—forty-two men. He left no survivor.

¹⁵After he left there, he came upon Jehonadab son of Recab, who was on his way to meet him. Jehu greeted him and said, "Are you in accord with me, as I am with you?"

"I am," Jehonadab answered.

"If so," said Jehu, "give me your hand." So he did, and Jehu helped him up into the chariot. ¹⁶Jehu said, "Come with me and see my zeal for the LORD." Then he had him ride along in his chariot.

¹⁷When Jehu came to Samaria, he killed all who were left there of Ahab's family; he destroyed them, according to the word of the LORD spoken to Elijah.

¹⁸Then Jehu brought all the people together and said to them, "Ahab served Baal a little; Jehu will serve him much. ¹⁹Now summon all the prophets of Baal, all his ministers and all his priests. See that no one is missing, because I am going to hold a great sacrifice for Baal. Anyone who fails to come will no longer live." But Jehu was acting deceptively in order to destroy the ministers of Baal.

²⁰Jehu said, "Call an assembly in honor of Baal." So they proclaimed it. ²¹Then he sent word throughout Israel, and all the ministers of Baal came; not one stayed away. They crowded into the temple of Baal until it was full from one end to the other. ²²And Jehu said to the keeper of the wardrobe, "Bring robes for all the ministers of Baal." So he brought out robes for them.

²³Then Jehu and Jehonadab son of Recab went into the temple of Baal. Jehu said to the ministers of Baal, "Look around and see that no servants of the LORD are here with you—only ministers of Baal." ²⁴So they went in to make sacrifices and burnt offerings. Now Jehu had posted eighty men outside with this warning: "If one of you lets any of the men I am placing in your hands escape, it will be your life for his life."

²⁵As soon as Jehu had finished making the burnt offering, he ordered the guards and officers: "Go in and kill them; let no one escape." So they cut them down with the sword. The guards and officers threw the bodies out and then entered the inner shrine of the temple of Baal. ²⁶They brought the sacred stone out of the temple of Baal and burned it. ²⁷They demolished the sacred stone of Baal and tore down the temple of Baal, and people have used it for a latrine to this day.

²⁸So Jehu destroyed Baal worship in Israel. ²⁹However, he did not turn away from the sins of Jeroboam son of Nebat, which he had caused Israel to commit—the worship of the golden calves at Bethel and Dan.

³⁰The LORD said to Jehu, "Because you have done well in accomplishing what is right in my eyes and have done to the house of Ahab all I had in mind to do, your descendants will sit on the throne of Israel to the fourth generation." ³¹Yet Jehu was not careful to keep the law of the LORD, the God of Israel, with all his heart. He did not turn away from the sins of Jeroboam, which he had caused Israel to commit.

³²In those days the LORD began to reduce the size of Israel. Hazael overpowered the Israelites throughout their territory ³³east of the Jordan in all the land of Gilead (the region of Gad, Reuben and Manasseh), from Aroer by the Arnon Gorge through Gilead to Bashan.

³⁴As for the other events of Jehu's reign, all he did, and all his achievements, are they not written in the book of the annals of the kings of Israel?
³⁵Jehu rested with his fathers and was buried in Samaria. And Jehoahaz his son succeeded him as king. ³⁶The time that Jehu reigned over Israel in Samaria was twenty-eight years.

1–8 With the deaths of Jehoram (9:24–26), Ahaziah and his attendants (2 Chron 22:8 –9), and Jezebel (2 Kings 9:32–33), Jehu next moved to eliminate any competitive threat to his newly won crown from the surviving members of the royal family who had taken refuge in Samaria, the capital city (v.1). He warned those officials who cared for them to prepare for battle (vv.2–3). The heads of state in Samaria felt that resistance was futile and sent Jehu a letter of submission (vv.4–5). With this concession in hand, Jehu sent a second letter, demanding that the heads of Jehoram's surviving heirs be brought to him in Jezreel (v.6). Again the officials complied and sent the severed heads to Jehu, who then had them placed in two piles before the gate of Jezreel (vv.7–8).

9–11 On the next day Jehu addressed the assembled people, absolved them of any guilt, and again proclaimed his divine mission (vv.9–10). While it was true that he had slain his master, the heads of the slain sons of the house of Ahab had come there through other (divine) means and so were a further sign that all of Elijah's prophetic threats were coming to pass. Having said that, Jehu ordered the seizure and execution of any who might yet remain of Ahab's descendants in Jezreel, as well as any of Jehoram's officials, aides, and friends (v.11). Even the state priests who served them were put to death.

12–14 With affairs settled to his liking in Jezreel, acting on the favorable response of the leaders of Samaria, Jehu set out for Israel's capital city (v.12). As he traveled southward, he met a party of forty-two of Ahaziah's relatives who were coming to pay their respects to the royal family of Israel and Samaria (v.13). They would fare no better than the deceased Judean king. Jehu ordered their instant seizure and execution (v.14). As ordered, there were no survivors. Jehu's reason for this mass murder is not given. Perhaps it was intended to be further evidence of his goal to stamp out Baalism everywhere. Perhaps he even held wild hopes of some day being able to lay some claim against Judah as well. As Herrmann (p. 222) remarks, "We do not know what was in Jehu's mind. But by now the royal house of David, too, had suffered great losses at his hands." Jehu, however, was taking no chances. Since the two royal houses were related (cf. 8:16–18), no possible claimant would be allowed to live. Furthermore their demise might pose some question as to proper succession to the Judean throne.

15 On leaving yet another bloody scene, Jehu encountered a mysterious figure, one Jehonadab the Recabite, who, having heard of Jehu's anti-Baal crusade, had apparently come to meet the new Israelite king. Jeremiah (ch. 35) records that Jehonadab was the leader of an aesthetic group that lived an austere, nomadic life in the desert, drinking no wine and depending solely on the Lord for their sustenance. Separatist to the core and strong patriots, they lived in protest to the materialism and religious compromise in Israel. Accordingly Jehonadab was extremely interested in Jehu's reputed desire to purge the nation of its heathenism. Perhaps he hoped that in Jehu a sense of national repentance and longing for Yahweh would now take place.

16–17 Jehu recognized Jehonadab immediately and, having greeted him with the usual blessing, inquired whether he was in agreement with him. When Jehonadab replied that he was, Jehu gave him his hand, both in friendship and to receive him into his chariot so that he might witness Jehu's further zeal for the Lord (v.16). One wonders what Jehonadab must have felt when, on their entrance into Samaria, Jehu's first order of business was the execution of any who might be in any way related to the house of the preceding dynasty. Nevertheless he continued with Jehu in his further purgation (v.17). With the death of the "sons of Ahab," the divine sentence had been carried out to the fullest (1 Kings 21:21).

18–24 Jehu's continued purge of Baalism in Israel next took the form of deception. Feigning that he himself was a devotee of Baal, he ordered a great assembly for sacrifice to be held in Samaria and ordered all the priests and ministers of Baal to come, on penalty of death (vv.18–19). On the day set for the feast, the various ministers arrived. To readily identify them as Baal's faithful, each was given a special robe (vv.20–22). With the temple of Baal crowded with Baal's priests, and with the temple guarded securely by eighty selected guards, Jehu and Jehonadab entered the temple to see the opening sacrifices (vv.23–24).

25–27 When the ceremonies had begun, Jehu and Jehonadab stepped outside; then Jehu gave the prearranged signal for the guards to enter the temple and slay the worshipers (v.25). This they did, penetrating even into the ruined shrine of the temple. None escaped. After the execution had been accomplished, the wooden images and stone statues of Baal were carried outside and demolished; then the temple itself was torn down and burned (vv.26–27a). To desecrate the site and mark the contempt attendant to it, Jehu converted it into a place for public convenience (v.27b).

28–36 Jehu had exterminated the worship of Baal in Israel (v.28). For this the Lord commended him and promised him a royal succession to the fourth generation (v.30). Yet Jehu was to prove a disappointment to God; for his reform was soon seen to be political and selfish rather than born of any deep concern for God (v.31). Not only did he not keep the law in his heart, but he perpetuated the state cultus of the golden calf established by Jeroboam I (v.29). Therefore God allowed the Arameans to plunder and reduce systematically the size of Israel, beginning with the loss of Israel's Transjordanian holdings (vv.32–33). Despite his cometlike beginning, spiritually speaking, Jehu was a falling star; so his reign is largely passed over in silence.

Notes

1 Ahaziah's flight to Samaria was a reminder to Jehu that there was still a source of possible intrigue and insurrection there. If one retains the reading of the MT—שָׂרֵי יִזְרְעֶאל (śārê yizrᵉ'e'l, "the officials of Jezreel")—it could indicate that before Jehu had come from Megiddo to Jezreel, those officials in Jezreel entrusted with the care of the royal children

had taken their wards and fled to Samaria. The letters thus addressed per se to "the officials of Jezreel" (i.e., the place where they often served and from which they had just come) would be intended for all the officials of Samaria (cf. v.5). Such an address would make the leaders of Samaria aware that Jehu meant business and yet indicate that their lives were not in jeopardy—Jehu simply wanted the royal survivors. Thus construed Jezreel would not necessarily be viewed as "manifestly a clerical error" (Edersheim, *History*, 6:206; cf. Keil, p. 346).

More usually, however, "Jezreel" is emended to "Israel"; or the phrase is altered so as to read "to the officials of the city, to the elders, etc." This latter suggestion has the support of some ancient MSS and versions and appears to be demanded by the reply in v.5. The difficulty of preserving the sense of the MT may argue for the alternative reading. Moreover those addressed in v.1 are those who reply in v.5.

The problem is further complicated by the word סְפָרִים (*sᵉpārîm*, "letters"). While one may argue for the sending of just one letter (the *m* of the MT being viewed as an enclitic *m*, as does Montgomery, p. 408; cf. LXX), most versions follow the MT in reading "letters." Josephus (*Antiq*. IX, 125 [vi.5]) suggests that Jehu wrote two letters, one to those who cared for the children and one to the officials of Samaria.

The seventy sons of Ahab are his surviving grandchildren.

הַזְּקֵנִים (*hazzᵉqēnîm*, "the elders") held positions of state, not just within Samaria.

הָאֹמְנִים (*hāʾōmᵉnîm*, "the guardians") would consist of those appointed to be the custodians of the royal children; the term perhaps is to be understood as "foster-parents" (cf. Ruth 4:16).

2 וְעַתָּה (*wᵉʿattāh*, "and now") is the usual means in ancient correspondence for introducing the demands or decision of the writer. Obviously the contents of the letter are greatly abbreviated. The author of Kings records only the barest essential data necessary to his account. Accordingly the elaborate attempts of A. Alt ("Der Stadtstaat Samaria," *Kleine Schriften zum Geschichte des Volkes Israel* [Munich: Beck, 1959], 3:285–88; see further G. Buccellati, *Cities and Nations of Ancient Syria* [Rome: Universita di Roma, 1966], pp. 187–91), who relies heavily on the three diplomatic letters of exchange here, to detect a distinction between the city-state and the kingdom of Israel with the capital at Jezreel is, at best, most tentative.

5 On אֲשֶׁר־עַל־הַבַּיִת (*ᵃšer-ʿal-habbayit*, "palace administrator"), see the note on 15:5.

On אֲשֶׁר עַל־הָעִיר (*ᵃšer ʿal-hāʿîr*, "city governor"), compare the Akkadian *bēl āli* ("city ruler").

8 This gruesome deed was often practiced in the ancient Near East, as reflected in the annals of the Assyrian kings. Thus, for example, Shalmaneser III reports in his famous Monolith Inscription:

> From Hubushkia I departed [to] Sugunia, the royal city of Arame, the Urartian (Armenian), I drew near. The city I stormed (and) captured. Multitudes of his warriors I slew. His booty I carried off. A pyramid (pillar) of heads I reared in front of his city. —Luckenbill, *Ancient Records*, 1:213

Such grisly acts knew no bounds. On one occasion Ashurbanipal severed the head of his fallen enemy and reports:

> I did not give his body to be buried. I made him more dead than he was before. I cut off his head and hung it on the back of Nabû-kâtâ-sabat, (his) twin brother (?). —Ibid., 2:312

Ashur Nasir-pal was particularly vicious in his treatment of the captured enemy. The events of one occasion form a macabre parallel to the account here in 2 Kings:

> To the city of Sûru of Bit-Halupê I drew near, and the terror of the splendor of Assur, my lord, overwhelmed them. The chief men and the elders of the city, to save their lives, came forth into my presence and embraced my feet, saying: "If it is thy pleasure, slay! If it is thy pleasure, let live! That which thy heart desireth, do!" Ahiababa, the son of nobody, whom they had brought from Bit-Adini, I took captive. In the valor of my heart and with the fury of my weapons I stormed the city. All the

rebels they seized and delivered them up. Azi-ilu I set over them as my own governor. I built a pillar over against his city gate, and I flayed all the chief men who had revolted, and I covered the pillar with their skins; some I walled up within the pillar, some I impaled upon the pillar on the stakes, and others I bound to stakes round about the pillar; many within the border of my own land I flayed, and I spread their skins upon the walls; and I cut off the limbs of the officers, of the royal officers who had rebelled. Ahiababa I took to Nineveh, I flayed him, I spread his skin upon the wall of Nineveh. My power and might I established over the land of Lakê.

—Ibid., 1:144–45

According to Josephus (Antiq. IX, 127 [vi.5]), the men bearing the severed heads arrived while Jehu and his friends were eating supper! If so, one is reminded of the Assyrian relief showing the king feasting with his queen while the head of his vanquished enemy hangs in a nearby tree (Pritchard, *Pictures*, p. 156, plate 451).

12 Since those whom Ahaziah's relatives had come to see lived (according to v.1) in Samaria, the uninformed travelers must have come up the coast to Megiddo and turned eastward to the Jezreel-Samaria road, intending to make their way southward to the Israelite capital.

13 Perhaps the sense of מָצָא (māṣā', "he met"; lit., "found," "come upon") is that of Jehu's actually reaching the Judean party, i.e., "overtaking them" on the way (cf. UT, p. 436). Since the brothers of Ahaziah had been previously carried off and killed by Jehoram (cf. 2 Chron 21:17), the term here must have the broader sense of Ahaziah's relatives (stepbrothers, nephews, cousins, etc.).

15 The term בֶּן־רֵכָב (ben-rēkāb, "son of Recab") became a tribal designation for the aesthetic-minded Recabites (Jer 35:1–16). So faithful had the later Recabites been to the precepts laid down by Jehonadab that Jeremiah could announce that they would be exempted from the Chaldean invasion (Jer 35:17–19).

According to 1 Chron 2:55, Recab came from a Kenite clan. Because Hobab, the father-in-law of Moses, was also a Kenite (Num 10:29), Keil (p. 349) has suggested that "the Recabites were probably descendants of Hobab, since the Kenites the sons of Hobab had gone with the Israelites from the Arabian desert to Canaan, and had there carried on their nomad life (Judg. i. 16, iv. 11, 1 Sam xv. 6)." Although this has recently been challenged (see F.S. Frich, "The Rechabites Reconsidered," JBL 90 [1971]: 279–87), traditional biblical scholarship has held that the Recabites were noted not only for their abilities in metalworking and crafts but for their orthodoxy as well. As craftsmen and tradesmen the nomadic Kenites were known in the monarchy period to have lived extensively in southern Judah, though the events in Judg 4–5 demonstrate that some of them had previously migrated northwest into Galilee, a fact that authenticates Jehonadab's more northerly connections.

Edersheim (*History*, 6:209f.) theorizes that Jehonadab and the Recabites had probably been greatly influenced by the ministry of Elisha so that with Elijah's words being dramatically fulfilled before their eyes, like John the Baptist of the NT, Jehonadab had a kind of kingdom hope that in Jehu the fortunes of Israel would soon be restored.

18 The note that "Ahab served Baal a little" is probably not totally at variance with the scriptural denunciation of his actions, recorded in 1 Kings 16:29–33; for it will be remembered that (1) he was completely dominated by his wife, Jezebel (1 Kings 21:25–26), (2) he could repent when challenged by divine rebuke (1 Kings 21:28), and (3) his own children bore names compounded with Yahweh, perhaps indicating that more than state policy was involved in the choice of these names. Probably Ahab really cared little about spiritual matters or affairs; Ahab's weak character justly was condemned, for it allowed Israel to plummet to the depths of spiritual degradation.

25 Whether Jehu himself offered the heathen sacrifice (so Gray, Montgomery) or merely saw to its offering by the designated priests (Keil) is uncertain.

For רָצִים (rāṣîm, "guards"; lit., "runners") and שָׁלִשִׁים (šālešîm, "officers"), see the notes on 1 Kings 14:28 and 2 Kings 9:25.

28–32 Jehu is commended and rewarded for his faithfulness in carrying out Elijah's prophecies against Ahab's wicked house. God's promise was literally kept; Jehu's descendants—Jehoahaz, Joash, Jeroboam II, and Zechariah—succeeded him in turn in Israel's fourth dynasty. While there is acceptance of the effects of the deed, the man and his motives did not necessarily win divine approval. Jehu's true heart may be seen both in his half-hearted observance of the law and in his espousal of Jeroboam's apostate state religion. Accordingly there is no contradiction in the Lord's condemnation of Jehu as delivered by Hosea (1:4).

Jehu's manipulation of any and all circumstances for his desired selfish ends is amply illustrated by his submission to Shalmaneser II, as recorded by the Assyrian king on his famous Black Oblisk: "The tribute of Jehu, son of Omri; I received"; for details see Unger, *Archaeology,* p. 246; for the problem of the identification of the correct Hebrew king, see McCarter, pp. 1–7; Weippert, pp. 114–18.

32–33 Although defeated by Shalmaneser III of Assyria in 841 B.C., the Aramean king Hazael managed to retain his independence and, since his former ally Israel now was ruled by a pro-Assyrian king, he looked menacingly southward. Hazael took advantage of Shalmaneser's primary occupation with affairs in the east during the years 839–828 B.C. and his final six years of revolution at home (827–822) to afflict Jehu (841–814) and his son Jehoahaz (814–798) severely. Not only was Israelite Transjordania lost to Hazael's forces, but the Aramean king, on the death of Jehu, was able to march unchecked into Israel and Judah (cf. 12:18). How appropriately Elisha had wept (8:11–12)!

Only the appearance of a new strong Assyrian king (Adad Nirari III, 841–783 B.C.) would check Hazael's relentless surge. See the note on 13:4–5. For the historical background of the late eighth century in Israel, see Hallo and Simpson, *A History,* pp. 128f.

---

2. *The reign of Athaliah in the southern kingdom*

11:1–16

¹When Athaliah the mother of Ahaziah saw that her son was dead, she proceeded to destroy the whole royal family. ²But Jehosheba, the daughter of King Jehoram and sister of Ahaziah, took Joash son of Ahaziah and stole him away from among the royal princes, who were about to be murdered. She put him and his nurse in a bedroom to hide him from Athaliah; so he was not killed. ³He remained hidden with his nurse at the temple of the LORD for six years while Athaliah ruled the land.

⁴In the seventh year Jehoiada sent for the commanders of units of a hundred, the Carites and the guards and had them brought to him at the temple of the LORD. He made a covenant with them and put them under oath at the temple of the LORD. Then he showed them the king's son. ⁵He commanded them, saying, "This is what you are to do: You who are in the three companies that are going on duty on the Sabbath—a third of you guarding the royal palace, ⁶a third at the Sur Gate, and a third at the gate behind the guard, who take turns guarding the temple—⁷and you who are in the other two companies that normally go off Sabbath duty are all to guard the temple for the king. ⁸Station yourselves around the king, each man with his weapon in his hand. Anyone who approaches your ranks must be put to death. Stay close to the king wherever he goes."

⁹The commanders of units of a hundred did just as Jehoiada the priest ordered. Each one took his men—those who were going on duty on the Sabbath and those who were going off duty—and came to Jehoiada the priest. ¹⁰Then he gave the commanders the spears and shields that had belonged to King David and that were in the temple of the LORD. ¹¹The guards, each with his weapon in his hand, stationed themselves around the king—near the altar and the temple, from the south side to the north side of the temple.

¹²Jehoiada brought out the king's son and put the crown on him; he presented him with a copy of the covenant and proclaimed him king. They anointed him, and the people clapped their hands and shouted, "Long live the king!"
¹³When Athaliah heard the noise made by the guards and the people, she went to the people at the temple of the LORD. ¹⁴She looked and there was the king, standing by the pillar, as the custom was. The officers and the trumpeters were beside the king, and all the people of the land were rejoicing and blowing trumpets. Then Athaliah tore her robes and called out, "Treason! Treason!"
¹⁵Jehoiada the priest ordered the commanders of units of a hundred, who were in charge of the troops: "Bring her out between the ranks and put to the sword anyone who follows her." For the priest had said, "She must not be put to death in the temple of the LORD." ¹⁶So they seized her as she reached the place where the horses enter the palace grounds, and there she was put to death.

1 On the news of the death of her son Ahaziah, Athaliah, the dowager queen, took whatever measures were necessary to seize the throne for herself, including the murder of her own grandchildren and all that remained of the royal family. With all natural heirs put out of the way, she ascended the throne, inaugurating a seven-year reign.

2-3 As in other desperate times, a godly woman would be used of God to stem the tide of apostasy. This ninth century "Jochebed" was named Jehosheba (v.2). A princess in her own right—being the daughter of Jehoram and sister of Ahaziah—she was also the wife of the high priest Jehoiada (2 Chron 22:11). Conspiring with her nurse (and doubtless the high priest as well), Jehosheba hid the baby, at first in one of the palace chambers, then subsequently smuggled him into her temple quarters where she managed to conceal him for six full years (v.3).

4-12 In the seventh year, with the child now older, Jehoiada mustered his courage (2 Chron 23:1) and laid plans to dislodge the usurping queen from her ill-gotten throne (v.4). First, he secured the allegiance of the military officials and temple personnel. Second, he summoned the Levites and heads of families throughout the southern kingdom to Jerusalem and swore them to loyalty to the true king (cf. 2 Chron 23:2). Third, on a set day he had the temple personnel seal off the temple area at the changing of the guard and had trusted guards deployed in strategic fashion (vv.5-8).

Edersheim (*History*, 7:16) describes the process as follows:

> As each of the "courses" into which the priesthood was divided relieved the other at the beginning of every Sabbath, so apparently also the royal bodyguard. The plan now agreed upon was, that the guard which was relieved should instead of returning to their homes or barracks, march into the Temple, where the high-priest would furnish them with weapons from those that had formerly belonged to David, and which, no doubt, according to sacred custom, had been deposited in the sanctuary. The sole object of that guard (2 Kings xi.7, 11) was in two divisions to surround the new king on either side, with orders to cut down any one who should try to penetrate their ranks, and to close around the person of the king in all his movements. Thus far for the guard that had been relieved. On the other hand, the relieving guard was to be arranged in three divisions. One of these was to form, as usual, the guard of the royal palace, so that the

suspicions of Athaliah should not be aroused. The second division was to occupy the gate Sur, also called the "gate of the foundation" (2 Chron xxiii. 5); while the third division was to be massed in "the gate behind the guard," the same as "the gate of the guard" (2 Kings xi. 19), and which probably formed the principal access from the palace into the Temple. The object of all this was to guard the palace—not only to disarm suspicion, but for defence (2 Kings xi. 5), and to ward off or bar any attempt on the part of adherents of Athaliah to possess themselves of the royal residence.

Fourth, with everyone in place, Jehoiada led the king to the appointed spot, perhaps in the innermost court between the temple and the altar, and anointed him as king, to the shouts of acclamation of the gathered throng (v.12).

13–16 When the clamor of the people reached the ears of Athaliah, she made her way to the scene of jubilation (v.13). The sight that greeted her eyes doubtless made her heart sink (v.14). There, on the royal dias at the eastern gate of the inner court to the temple, stood a newly crowned king, surrounded by the high officials both in the religious order and in the military, amid great fanfare and the joyous shouts of the people. She shrieked out her condemnation: it was treason. But her cry was to have as little effect as that of Israel's Jehoram to Athaliah's son Ahaziah (9:23). At Jehoiada's command she was seized and escorted to the gate used for the palace horses and put to death by the sword (vv.15–16). Thus Athaliah, the most infamous queen of Judah, died at the hands of her executioners, much as did her mother, Jezebel, queen of Israel (9:27–37).

Notes

---

2 According to Josephus (*Antiq*. IX, 141 [vii.1]), Jehosheba (Jehoshabeath, 2 Chron 22:11) was Ahaziah's half-sister, born to Jehoram by another woman. This may also have been the case with the royal infant, Joash, whose mother was one Zibiah of Beersheba (2 Chron 24:1). If so, this could account for the reason why the infant was missed in Athaliah's massacre; perhaps even his birth was unnoticed by the queen mother. Interestingly Jehoiada had his young ward, Joash, marry two wives (2 Chron 24:3), to whom were born sons and daughters.

The חֲדַר הַמִּטּוֹת (*haḏar hammiṭṭôṯ*, "bedroom") was more properly a storeroom where bedding was kept.

4–20 The difference in detail and emphases between the account here and that in 2 Chron 23:1–11 that have led scholars to postulate contradictions between the two are clearly overdrawn. Both accounts are merely summary statements of the essential details, the account in Kings emphasizing the part played by the military in defense of the king and palace, and that in Chronicles, the role of the Levites in making the temple secure. The two, then, are supplementary, not contradictory.

4 The "Carites" are mentioned only here and in 2 Sam 20:23 (q.v.), where they are associated with the Pelethites, who appear as bodyguards of the king. In that passage the LXX reads "Kerethites," the more usual term associated with the Pelethites (cf. 1 Kings 1:38). Both terms are connected with the Aegean World, the former Crete, the latter more specifically with the Philistines (see J. Greenfield, "Cherethites and Pelethites," IDB, 1:577). While some see a distinction in origin between the Carites (Siclia) and Kerethites (Crete), the alternations between the two in 2 Sam 20:23 argues for their identity.

For "guards" (lit., "runners") see the note on 1 Kings 14:28. In 2 Chron 23:1–2 the names of the five captains of hundreds are given together with information regarding their gathering of the Levites and family heads.

7 Although scholars disagree as to the precise reconstruction of the details, it is generally conceded that the Sabbath changeover provided an ideal time for Jehoiada to utilize all the guards in effecting his plan. See further G.H. Jones, *1 and 2 Kings* (NCBC; Grand Rapids: Eerdmans, 1984), 2:478–80, and G. Robinson, "Is II Kings XI:6 a Gloss?" VetTest 27 (1977): 56–61.

8 According to 2 Chron 23:7, the Levites formed a further circle around the king that was especially charged with the security of the temple. As Edersheim (*History,* 7:18) remarks:

> We therefore conclude that this division of Levites was to form an outer circle not only around the king, but also around his military guard. This also explains the difference in the directions given in 2 Kings xi. 8 to the military guards to kill those who penetrated their "ranks," and in 2 Chron. xxiii. 7 to the Levites, to kill those who penetrated into the Temple. In other words, the Levites were to stand beyond the guards, and to prevent a hostile entrance into the Temple buildings; and if any gained their way through them to the ranks of the military, they were to be cut down by the guards. Thus the king was really surrounded by a double cordon—the military occupying the inner court around his person, while the Levites held the outer court and the gates.

10 These weapons were originally dedicated by David from his campaign against the Aramean Hadadezer (2 Sam 8:7). According to the LXX on 1 Kings 14:26, these were carried away in Shishak's campaign, though the MT does not specifically say so. This passage may indicate that David's weapons were not surrendered at that time together with "all the treasures" or simply that the replaced weaponry continued to be known as "King David's."

12 הָעֵדוּת (hāʿēḏûṯ, "copy of the covenant") basically means "testimony," "statute," and is used of the law, especially the Ten Commandments (Exod 31:18), but also of the whole law of God (Ps 119:88). Although the situation is not without difficulty, according to Deut 17:18 a copy of the law was to be made by the king himself from one given to him by the priests and was to be kept with the king always so that it became the rule for all his life. Thus by putting the crown on the young king's head and a copy of the law in his hand, Jehoiada was acting in accordance with the ancient scriptural precedent, a move calculated to strengthen the hand of the supporters of the rightful king of the people.

עֵדוּת (ʿēḏûṯ) is also a treaty term (cf. the related Akkad. *adû,* "formal agreement"), being used in contexts dealing with covenants, especially with the Davidic covenant (see M. Weinfeld, "Berith," TDOT, 2:257, 259). Not only because of ancient scriptural warrant, then, but in affirmation of obedience to God's covenant with David, Jehoiada proclaimed this renewal of the promise given to the house of David. This was further evidence for the deposing of Athaliah. The NIV's "copy of the covenant" is, therefore, doubly meaningful. The copy of the law in his hand would be a visible symbol of the pledge to so live as to make the promise of God's covenant grant to David and his house fully applicable to Joash's reign. For the Deuteronomic provision for kingship and its relation to the Davidic covenant, see Kaiser, *OT Theology,* pp. 143–68.

14 The NIV follows the usual understanding of הָעַמּוּד (hāʿammûḏ, "the pillar"), as do most modern versions and commentaries. The word, however, can signify a raised platform, tribunal, or step (cf. Vul. on 2 Chron 23:13: *gradum,* "step," "post"; *tribunal,* 2 Kings 11:14). In the parallel account in 2 Chron 23:13, the LXX reads "in his place," a translation certainly allowable for the MT there and in the similar circumstances regarding Josiah (2 Chron 34:31). Accordingly Keil (p. 362) may be correct in suggesting that the

king's platform was placed "at the eastern gate of the inner court . . . where he visited the temple on festive occasions (cf. ch xxiii.3), and it was most probably identical with the brazen scaffold . . . mentioned in 2 Chron. vi.13."

---

3. The reign of Joash in the southern kingdom

11:17–12:21

[17]Jehoiada then made a covenant between the LORD and the king and people that they would be the LORD's people. He also made a covenant between the king and the people. [18]All the people of the land went to the temple of Baal and tore it down. They smashed the altars and idols to pieces and killed Mattan the priest of Baal in front of the altars.

Then Jehoiada the priest posted guards at the temple of the LORD. [19]He took with him the commanders of hundreds, the Carites, the guards and all the people of the land, and together they brought the king down from the temple of the LORD and went into the palace, entering by way of the gate of the guards. The king then took his place on the royal throne, [20]and all the people of the land rejoiced. And the city was quiet, because Athaliah had been slain with the sword at the palace. [21]Joash was seven years old when he began to reign.

[12:1]In the seventh year of Jehu, Joash became king, and he reigned in Jerusalem forty years. His mother's name was Zibiah; she was from Beersheba. [2]Joash did what was right in the eyes of the LORD all the years Jehoiada the priest instructed him. [3]The high places, however, were not removed; the people continued to offer sacrifices and burn incense there.

[4]Joash said to the priests, "Collect all the money that is brought as sacred offerings to the temple of the LORD—the money collected in the census, the money received from personal vows and the money brought voluntarily to the temple. [5]Let every priest receive the money from one of the treasurers, and let it be used to repair whatever damage is found in the temple."

[6]But by the twenty-third year of King Joash the priests still had not repaired the temple. [7]Therefore King Joash summoned Jehoiada the priest and the other priests and asked them, "Why aren't you repairing the damage done to the temple? Take no more money from your treasurers, but hand it over for repairing the temple." [8]The priests agreed that they would not collect any more money from the people and that they would not repair the temple themselves.

[9]Jehoiada the priest took a chest and bored a hole in its lid. He placed it beside the altar, on the right side as one enters the temple of the LORD. The priests who guarded the entrance put into the chest all the money that was brought to the temple of the LORD. [10]Whenever they saw that there was a large amount of money in the chest, the royal secretary and the high priest came, counted the money that had been brought into the temple of the LORD and put it into bags. [11]When the amount had been determined, they gave the money to the men appointed to supervise the work on the temple. With it they paid those who worked on the temple of the LORD—the carpenters and builders, [12]the masons and stonecutters. They purchased timber and dressed stone for the repair of the temple of the LORD, and met all the other expenses of restoring the temple.

[13]The money brought into the temple was not spent for making silver basins, wick trimmers, sprinkling bowls, trumpets or any other articles of gold or silver for the temple of the LORD; [14]it was paid to the workmen, who used it to repair the temple. [15]They did not require an accounting from those to whom they gave the money to pay the workers, because they acted with complete honesty. [16]The money from the guilt offerings and sin offerings was not brought into the temple of the LORD; it belonged to the priests.

[17]About this time Hazael king of Aram went up and attacked Gath and captured it. Then he turned to attack Jerusalem. [18]But Joash king of Judah took all the

sacred objects dedicated by his fathers—Jehoshaphat, Jehoram and Ahaziah, the kings of Judah—and the gifts he himself had dedicated and all the gold found in the treasuries of the temple of the LORD and of the royal palace, and he sent them to Hazael king of Aram, who then withdrew from Jerusalem.

¹⁹As for the other events of the reign of Joash, and all he did, are they not written in the book of the annals of the kings of Judah? ²⁰His officials conspired against him and assassinated him at Beth Millo, on the road down to Silla. ²¹The officials who murdered him were Jozabad son of Shimeath and Jehozabad son of Shomer. He died and was buried with his fathers in the City of David. And Amaziah his son succeeded him as king.

17–21 After the departure of the deposed Athaliah, Jehoiada led the king and the people in a twofold ceremony of covenant renewal: on the one hand, the king and the people swore their unswerving allegiance to God; on the other, the people affirmed their unfailing support of the reconstituted Davidic line (v.17). In attestation to their vows, a thorough cleansing of the land followed (v.18). Baal's temple was torn down, his priest Mattan slain before the images, and the altar thoroughly pulverized (2 Chron 23:17). Not only was the pagan worship of Baal put away, but a reorganization of the temple worship followed that was in accordance with the law of Moses and that followed the order instituted by David.

That day was capped with a thrilling scene. With Jehoiada in the lead, the royal bodyguard escorted the young king toward the palace, followed by the high officials representing the military, civil, and religious orders, with the joyous people bringing up the rear (v.19). From the eastern temple the ecstatic entourage swept majestically out the inner temple court and, moving southward through the middle court, entered through the upper gate into the palace. Eventually the throng reached the throne room, where the king was duly enthroned. It had been a memorable day—a day when Jerusalem and Judah ascended to the spiritual heights (v.20). Yet while the fire of spiritual reforms had been ignited and was to burn brightly for a time, in the very dependence of the king on others could be seen a flicker that would one day cause the fiery zeal for the Lord to sputter before the chilling winds of apostasy. This same Joash and many of the same officials would, on another day, bring Judah down to the dregs of the degraded Canaanite religion that they had just rendered dormant. Merely programmed religion is perilous; genuine faith must be personal.

12:1–6 Chapter 12 begins with a notice of Joash's matrilineage. Then follows a favorable evaluation of his earlier years as king, together with the notice that nevertheless worship at the various high places continued (vv.1–3). Next is an account (vv.4–16) of the preparations for and repair of the temple. Joash's first edict in this regard (doubtless made early in his reign; cf. 2 Chron 24:5) called for the setting aside of money collected as a result of the payment of special religious taxes and voluntary offerings (v.4). The Chronicler adds that the Levites were to gather such funds personally, collecting them from the cities of Judah (v.5). Although all haste was bidden in the matter, yet by the twenty-third year (v.6) the Levites delayed (2 Chron 24:5). No formal reasons are cited for this seeming lack of effort by the Levites. Whatever the problem was, the system was not working.

7–16 Accordingly Joash decided to take matters into his own hands and decreed that a chest be set outside the wall to the inner court at the southern gate on the right side of the entrance into the temple, so that everyone who passed through might cast his contribution in for the temple's repair (vv.2–9; cf. 2 Chron 24:8). Joash also had a proclamation read throughout Judah as to the need and intent of the box, urging all citizens to participate willingly in accordance with Moses' ancient institution (cf. Exod 25:2–3; 30:12–16; Lev 27:2–8 with 2 Chron 24:9). The response was tremendous (v.10; cf. 2 Chron 24:10). Soon there was ample money to begin the work and the workmen were commissioned (vv.11–12; cf. 2 Chron 24:11–13). A comparison of v.13 with 2 Chronicles 24:14 indicates that no monies were used for making the sacred vessels so long as the repairs of the temple proceeded. So successful had been the king's program and so well did all concerned carry out their duties that there was even money left over for the provision of sacred vessels for the sanctuary service (2 Chron 24:14).

17–21 The narrative quickly shifts in time, noting that the Aramean king Hazael had renewed his pressure against Israel and Judah, penetrating down the coast as far as Philistia and turning then inland to make a direct attack against Jerusalem (v.17). A siege of Jerusalem was averted only when Joash stripped the royal treasury and the wealth of the temple as payment to Hazael (v.18).

The reason for this drastic turn of events can be gleaned from the supporting details in 2 Chronicles 24:14–22. Regular temple worship had continued throughout the days of Jehoiada; but after the death of the godly high priest, Joash fell into the hands of godless advisors who turned his heart to Canaanite practices. Although the Lord continually warned the king and his confidants, his pleadings fell on deaf ears. Indeed in one instance the king and his staff went so far as to stone Jehoiada's son Zechariah for delivering the Lord's pronouncement against them.

Accordingly, when God's patience had run full course, he delivered Joash and Judah into the hands of the Arameans. The plight of the northern kingdom (cf. 2 Kings 13:1–3) also descended on the south. Hazael, though equipped with an inferior army, was under God's direction immediately successful, defeating Judah suddenly and sending much booty back to Damascus (2 Chron 24:23–24). The campaign brought death to many in Judah. Even the king was sorely wounded (2 Chron 24:25). The narrative in Kings joins the historical report at this point. With total defeat imminent, Joash bribed Hazael and so delivered Jerusalem (v.18).

Nothing, however, is recorded of any repentance on Joash's part. So obdurate did he remain in his sin that he was to die in a palace intrigue (vv.20–21). So blood guilty was he that, though he was interred in Jerusalem, he was excluded from burial in the royal sepulcher (2 Chron 24:25).

Notes

17 For further instances of the instituting of a covenant renewal, see Deut 27–30, Josh 24, and 2 Kings 23:1–3. The covenant renewal was particularly necessary after the unholy interruption represented by Athaliah's usurpation of the crown.

12:1 The EV's 11:21 is 12:1 in the MT, each succeeding verse in the MT being one number larger than the EV.

2 The notice that Joash conducted himself circumspectly while Jehoiada yet lived is ominous in tone (cf. 2 Chron 24:17–22) and a reminder of the need for personal faith.

5 The noun מַכָּרוֹ (makkārô, "treasurers"; lit., "his assessor") comes from the Semitic root that means "do business" (so, e.g., Akkad.; cf. Heb. מָכַר [mākar, "sell"]; hence, e.g., Akkad. makkāru ["trader"]; Ugar. mkr ["merchant"]; cf. Egyp. mkr ["merchant"]). Here the term must refer to a type of temple personnel who, perhaps, as Gray suggests (Kings, p. 586), assisted the priests with the evaluation of sacrifices and offerings brought to the temple. The term is also used of the temple personnel and of tax assessors at Ugarit. Traditionally the noun has been misunderstood as coming from the Heb. נָכַר (nākar, "be acquainted with," hence "acquaintance" (cf. NASB, KJV, RSV).

6–8 The failure of the early measures to accomplish the needed repairs caused the king to take away from the priests' control the supervision of the task and to take more decisive action. The prestige of the royal office would thus be lent to the project.

9 At first sight a discrepancy seems to exist between the details in Kings and those in Chronicles. Whereas this verse locates Joash's chest "beside the altar, on the right side" (cf. Jos. Antiq. IX, 163 [viii.2]), 2 Chron 24:8 places it without "at the gate of the temple." Actually the chest could not have been placed beside the altar per se, for this would contravene Levitical stipulation. The intent of the text of Kings is simply that the chest was set against the altar wall at the entrance that lay to the right side of the altar, or the southern entrance to the middle court. So understood, the texts of Kings and Chronicles are in natural agreement.

10–16 The accounts in Kings and Chronicles are again supplementary. The officers who collected the money from the full chest were two: (1) the royal scribe and (2) the chief priest's designated official. Having been brought to the royal office, the money would be weighed and then distributed to the supervisors of the building operations. The men involved were so trustworthy that no accounting was demanded of them. The word אֱמוּנָה ('emûnāh, "faithful," "completely honest") underscores the complete integrity of those involved.

17 The date of the Aramean invasion mentioned here probably occurred soon after the death of Šamši-Adad V of Assyria in 811 B.C. The death of the king in the ancient Near East customarily signaled an occasion for military activity. Moreover in Assyria Queen Semiramis ruled as regent for the young Adad-Nirari III (811–783 B.C.) for the first few years. Accordingly Hazael seized the opportunity to march inland against the recently crowned Joash, following this up with a full strike into Philistia and Judea. Hazael's victorious moves brought him much booty and left many dead behind him; even Joash was wounded in the campaign. This need not imply, however, as some have suggested, that Joash was assassinated as he lay recovering from his wounds. Actually the details of the Aramean campaign and Joash's death may be separated by nearly a decade, with Joash's death not until 798 B.C. In the OT details are often telescoped, with events of cause and effect brought together, though separated by many years and other events. The point of the biblical account is simply that Joash remained in settled apostasy and growing degeneracy until the citizenry could stand it no longer and put him to death. The royal bed often became a death bed in the ancient Near East (cf., e.g., the account of the assassination of the Egyp. king Amenemhet, ANET, p. 418–19).

21 The variation Zabad of 2 Chron 24:26 and the Jozabad here may simply be one of a shortened form much like that between Joash and Jehoash.

The variation between Jehozabad's apparent mother Shomer (Kings) and Shimrith (Chron) may be accounted for in terms of difference between feminine names ending in āh (here shortened further in MT) and t. It is also possible that the Shomer of Kings was the father of Shimrith (Chron), mother of Jehozabad. It is singularly strange that both men may have had the same name and both mothers were Transjordanians.

4. *The reign of Jehoahaz in the northern kingdom*

13:1–9

¹In the twenty-third year of Joash son of Ahaziah king of Judah, Jehoahaz son of Jehu became king of Israel in Samaria, and he reigned seventeen years. ²He did evil in the eyes of the LORD by following the sins of Jeroboam son of Nebat, which he had caused Israel to commit, and he did not turn away from them. ³So the LORD's anger burned against Israel, and for a long time he kept them under the power of Hazael king of Aram and Ben-Hadad his son.

⁴Then Jehoahaz sought the LORD's favor, and the LORD listened to him, for he saw how severely the king of Aram was oppressing Israel. ⁵The LORD provided a deliverer for Israel, and they escaped from the power of Aram. So the Israelites lived in their own homes as they had before. ⁶But they did not turn away from the sins of the house of Jeroboam, which he had caused Israel to commit; they continued in them. Also, the Asherah pole remained standing in Samaria.

⁷Nothing had been left of the army of Jehoahaz except fifty horsemen, ten chariots and ten thousand foot soldiers, for the king of Aram had destroyed the rest and made them like the dust at threshing time.

⁸As for the other events of the reign of Jehoahaz, all he did and his achievements, are they not written in the book of the annals of the kings of Israel? ⁹Jehoahaz rested with his fathers and was buried in Samaria. And Jehoash his son succeeded him as king.

1–9 In the very year that Joash launched his campaign to repair the temple, Jehoahaz, son of Jehu (10:35), ascended the throne in the northern kingdom. He was to reign sixteen years (814–798 B.C.). Because Jehoahaz perpetuated the sins of his father in following the long-standing state religion instituted by Jeroboam I, God allowed the Aramean king Hazael (843–798 B.C.) to afflict the northern kingdom directly (vv.2–3; see further the note on 12:17). Hazael's affliction of Israel was to trouble Jehoahaz throughout his reign, though, apparently, the earlier part of Jehoahaz's rule was most severely affected (cf. v.22). So sore had the Aramean encroachment been that the northern kingdom was at one point left with but fifty horses, ten chariots, and ten thousand infantry (v.7)—a far cry from the time when Ahab alone could muster two thousand chariots for the allied forces at Qarqar.

In such lowly circumstances Jehoahaz at last sought the Lord's favor (v.4). While his repentance was seemingly genuine, the state religion of the golden calves was allowed to remain, as was the cultus connected with the Asherah pole in Samaria (v.6). Nevertheless God in his covenant mercy (v.23) did so arrange the circumstances as to send relief to Israel with the result that the closing years of Jehoahaz's reign were free of Aramean intervention (v.5).

Little else is reported of Jehoahaz's reign, Jehu's son going to his reward in 798 B.C. and being succeeded by his son, Jehoash (v.9).

Notes

3 The chronological understanding of the details of vv.4–7 and vv.22–24 turns on two items: (1) comparison of the details of the scriptural account with the recorded history of the ancient Near East, and (2) a recognition that Ben-Hadad is not here called king but merely the son of Hazael. With regard to the latter point, Keil (pp. 375–76) is probably correct in suggesting that Ben-Hadad's activity lay in his service as a commanding officer in his father's army. As to the former point, it seems clear that Hazael's chief military activity fell in the early periods surrounding the death of Šamši-Adad V in 811 B.C., during the one-half decade that followed while Semiramis was regent for the young Adad-Nirari III (811–783 B.C.); see the note on 12:17. Since Aramean fortunes were always linked to the Assyrians who traditionally sought an access to the Mediterranean, Hazael's ability to move effectively against Israel-Judah was contingent on Assyria's intervention. Accordingly, when Adad-Nirari III was at last able to rule in his own right, he turned his attention immediately to the Aramean problem in a series of western thrusts (805–802 B.C.), the last of which saw the capture of Damascus and the submission of the western states. It may be that dynastic change occurred in Syria at this time, with Hazael's son Ben-Hadad III assuming the throne. Certainly Hazael seems to have been on the throne in 805, being simply designated "the Lord," perhaps a shortened form of a title known from Arslan Tash (ancient Ḥadatu, the Assyrian provincial capital of the west) reading "Belonging to our Lord, Hazael." This (so R. Bowman, "Hazael," IDB, 2:538) may well be part of the booty carried off by Adad-Nirari in his strikes against Syria.

Since nothing is heard of Hazael beyond the Fall of Damascus and since shortly after that Ben-Hadad III is known to be occupying the throne (though in a far reduced capacity as the Melqart Stele demonstrates; see the note on 1 Kings 20), we may provisionally assign the date of these two Aramean kings as follows: Hazael, c. 841–802; Ben-Hadad III, 802–780.

The strong position of Assyria after 805 would seem to call for the attack described here in ch. 13 to have occurred between the period 814–806, before the revived Assyrian presence in great power in the west. After this Israel had respite from the Aramean menace.

4–5 The "deliverer" has been variously identified as Zakir of Hamath (E. Yamauchi, "Documents from Old Testament Times: A Survey of Recent Discoveries," WTJ 41 [1978]: 26–27; S. Cook, CAH, 3:363), Jehoash and Jeroboam II of the northern kingdom (Keil, p. 375; Edersheim, 7:38), Elisha (J. Gray, p. 595), and Adad-Nirari III of Assyria (J.B. Payne, *The Theology of the Older Testament* [Grand Rapids: Zondervan, 1962], p. 132; Hallo, "Qarqar," p. 42). In the light of the historical records noted above, this last suggestion is perhaps the simplest, Adad-Nirari III being Israel's "savior-deliverer" much as later Cyrus would be God's "shepherd" (Isa 44:28–45:1).

---

5. *The reign of Jehoash in the northern kingdom*

13:10–25

¹⁰In the thirty-seventh year of Joash king of Judah, Jehoash son of Jehoahaz became king of Israel in Samaria, and he reigned sixteen years. ¹¹He did evil in the eyes of the LORD and did not turn away from any of the sins of Jeroboam son of Nebat, which he had caused Israel to commit; he continued in them.

¹²As for the other events of the reign of Jehoash, all he did and his achievements, including his war against Amaziah king of Judah, are they not written in the book of the annals of the kings of Israel? ¹³Jehoash rested with his fathers, and Jeroboam succeeded him on the throne. Jehoash was buried in Samaria with the kings of Israel.

¹⁴Now Elisha was suffering from the illness from which he died. Jehoash king of Israel went down to see him and wept over him. "My father! My father!" he cried. "The chariots and horsemen of Israel!"

¹⁵Elisha said, "Get a bow and some arrows," and he did so. ¹⁶"Take the bow in your hands," he said to the king of Israel. When he had taken it, Elisha put his hands on the king's hands.

¹⁷"Open the east window," he said, and he opened it. "Shoot!" Elisha said, and

he shot. "The LORD's arrow of victory, the arrow of victory over Aram!" Elisha declared. "You will completely destroy the Arameans at Aphek."

¹⁸Then he said, "Take the arrows," and the king took them. Elisha told him, "Strike the ground." He struck it three times and stopped. ¹⁹The man of God was angry with him and said, "You should have struck the ground five or six times; then you would have defeated Aram and completely destroyed it. But now you will defeat it only three times."

²⁰Elisha died and was buried.

Now Moabite raiders used to enter the country every spring. ²¹Once while some Israelites were burying a man, suddenly they saw a band of raiders; so they threw the man's body into Elisha's tomb. When the body touched Elisha's bones, the man came to life and stood up on his feet.

²²Hazael king of Aram oppressed Israel throughout the reign of Jehoahaz. ²³But the LORD was gracious to them and had compassion and showed concern for them because of his covenant with Abraham, Isaac and Jacob. To this day he has been unwilling to destroy them or banish them from his presence.

²⁴Hazael king of Aram died, and Ben-Hadad his son succeeded him as king. ²⁵Then Jehoash son of Jehoahaz recaptured from Ben-Hadad son of Hazael the towns he had taken in battle from his father Jehoahaz. Three times Jehoash defeated him, and so he recovered the Israelite towns.

10–13 The account of the sixteen-year reign of Jehoash of Israel begins with a typical notice of character (evil), a mention of the most important event in his reign (his war with Amaziah), and a statement as to his demise. A record of an incident in which Jehoash met with the dying Elisha follows.

14 Jehoash addressed Elisha with words reminiscent of the venerable prophet's own testimony at Elijah's translation (cf. 2:12 and note in loc.). While they were full of respect, the words were less than full of faith. Yet because of the very fact that Jehoash had at least come to Elisha and had addressed him courteously, the Lord was to use the occasion to attempt to increase Jehoash's slim faith.

15–20a Elisha instructed Israel's king to pick up his bow (v.15). When he had done so, the prophet placed his own hands on those of the king, thereby indicating that what he was about to do would be full of spiritual symbolism (v.16). That act was the shooting of an arrow out the east window—toward Aram. Elisha explained the deed: Jehoash would win a total victory at Aphek against Arameans (v.17). But the divine promise was to be augmented by personal participation. Accordingly Jehoash was told next to shoot arrows into the ground; obviously victory at Aphek was to be followed by subsequent victories over the hated Arameans. Jehoash obediently complied but with his own reasoning powers. He struck the ground three times with his arrows rather than using the five or six arrows that he had with him (vv.18–19). Elisha was justifiably angry with the king. Had he used all his arrows, the Arameans would have been completely vanquished. Now Jehoash would gain but three victories. With this pronouncement the aged prophet had finished his earthly course (v.20a).

20b–21 One last miracle would attend God's faithful prophet. In those last dark days before stability was restored to the area by Adad-Nirari III, bands of Moabite marauders would ravish the land at the beginning of the harvest season (v.20b). Evidently Elisha had died at such a time. On one occasion, as a funeral procession made its way to the burial place, a looting party swooped down on them (v.21). In their need for swift flight, the members of the procession quickly halted and hastily placed the body of the dead man in the first available tomb—which happened to be Elisha's. When the burial party lowered the linen-wrapped body of the dead man into the tomb, it came into contact with the remains of Elisha. Instantly the man was revived. The juxtaposition of this event with the account that precedes makes it clear that herein was another divinely intended sign for Jehoash and Israel: God was the God of the living, not the dead (cf. Luke 20:38), not only for Elisha and the man who had been restored to life, but for Israel as well. Israel could yet "live" if she would but appropriate the eternally living God as her own. The entire episode was, further, a corroborative sign that what Elisha had prophesied would certainly come to pass. Only a living God could guarantee such a thing (cf. Isa 44).

22–25 The chapter closes with some historical notices concerning the strained Aramean-Israelite relations during the reign of Jehoahaz and Jehoash. Conditions improved during Jehoash's reign as the Israelite king, in accordance with Elisha's prophecy, defeated the Aramean king Ben-Hadad III, son of Hazael, three times. This record is a further indication of the inviolability of God's Word and God's continued faithfulness to the basic covenant made with the patriarchs.

Notes

10 The notice that Jehoash succeeded to Israel's throne in the thirty-seventh year of Joash of Judah's reign appears to be at variance with the note on 13:1, that Jehoahaz became king in Joash's twenty-third year. Since Jehoahaz reigned seventeen years, one would expect something like the thirty-ninth or fortieth year of Joash's reign to be the point of correlation, a figure actually supported by the LXX^g.

Perhaps the simplest solution is to follow Thiele (*Mysterious Numbers*, p. 72), who points out that the synchronism between Jehoash of Israel and Joash of Judah

> is of considerable interest and importance, for it is a synchronism of a king of Israel with a king of Judah, not according to the nonaccession-year system which has thus far been employed in Israel since the beginning of its history but which is here impossible, but according to the accession-year system. . . . The employment of such a synchronism for a king of Israel, on the accession-year basis, would indicate a shift from nonaccession- to accession-year reckoning. . . . all the reigns of the kings of Israel until the end of that nation are henceforth reckoned according to the accession-year system. The date of the accession of Jehoash of Israel can therefore be established at sometime between Nisan and Tishri, 798.

14 For Jehoash's cry relative to Elisha, see the note on 2:12.

16 The prophet offered Jehoash the opportunity to assume the position of spiritual leadership that Elisha was about to vacate. Such would not be the case; his faith was scant, and the divine evaluation of his character (v.11) is not favorable.

18 Jehoash missed God's intention when he shot the arrows only "three times." Incomplete faith would gain but partial victory.

20 Keil (p. 378) estimates that Elisha had "held his prophetical office for at least fifty years." The MT's בָּא שָׁנָה (bāʾ šānāh, "every spring"; lit., "[when] a year had come/gone") is ambiguous at best.

The planned war campaigning in the ancient Near East could take place anywhere between April and the late fall (see de Vaux, AIs, p. 251). The type of razzia, or plundering foray, envisioned here, however, need not be structured quite so closely, though the text indicates that the Moabite raids were regularly carried out about the same time each year.

22–25 For the historical reconstruction of the period of Israelite-Aramean relations, see the note on v.3. A recently found early eighth century B.C. inscription of Adad-Nirari III at tell Er Rimah mentions the tribute of "Iu'asu (Jehoash) the Samaritan." The growing preoccupation of Adad-Nirari III with the affairs in the east and Joash's treaty link with him, along with the growing weakness of Aram in the days of Ben-Hadad III, who was being pressed by Zakir of Hamath and Luash, provided the historical framework for the outworking of Elisha's prophecy. See further A. Malmat, "The Arameans," in Wiseman, *Peoples*, pp. 145f., 152f.; D.W. Thomas, *Documents from Old Testament Times* (New York: Harper & Row, 1961), pp. 242–50.

---

6. The reign of Amaziah in the southern kingdom

14:1–22

¹In the second year of Jehoash son of Jehoahaz king of Israel, Amaziah son of Joash king of Judah began to reign. ²He was twenty-five years old when he became king, and he reigned in Jerusalem twenty-nine years. His mother's name was Jehoaddin; she was from Jerusalem. ³He did what was right in the eyes of the LORD, but not as his father David had done. In everything he followed the example of his father Joash. ⁴The high places, however, were not removed; the people continued to offer sacrifices and burn incense there.

⁵After the kingdom was firmly in his grasp, he executed the officials who had murdered his father the king. ⁶Yet he did not put the sons of the assassins to death, in accordance with what is written in the Book of the Law of Moses where the LORD commanded: "Fathers shall not be put to death for their children, nor children put to death for their fathers; each is to die for his own sins."

⁷He was the one who defeated ten thousand Edomites in the Valley of Salt and captured Sela in battle, calling it Joktheel, the name it has to this day.

⁸Then Amaziah sent messengers to Jehoash son of Jehoahaz, the son of Jehu, king of Israel, with the challenge: "Come, meet me face to face."

⁹But Jehoash king of Israel replied to Amaziah king of Judah: "A thistle in Lebanon sent a message to a cedar in Lebanon, 'Give your daughter to my son in marriage.' Then a wild beast in Lebanon came along and trampled the thistle underfoot. ¹⁰You have indeed defeated Edom and now you are arrogant. Glory in your victory, but stay at home! Why ask for trouble and cause your own downfall and that of Judah also?"

¹¹Amaziah, however, would not listen, so Jehoash king of Israel attacked. He and Amaziah king of Judah faced each other at Beth Shemesh in Judah. ¹²Judah was routed by Israel, and every man fled to his home. ¹³Jehoash king of Israel captured Amaziah king of Judah, the son of Joash, the son of Ahaziah, at Beth Shemesh. Then Jehoash went to Jerusalem and broke down the wall of Jerusalem from the Ephraim Gate to the Corner Gate—a section about six hundred feet long. ¹⁴He took all the gold and silver and all the articles found in the temple of the LORD and in the treasuries of the royal palace. He also took hostages and returned to Samaria.

¹⁵As for the other events of the reign of Jehoash, what he did and his achievements, including his war against Amaziah king of Judah, are they not written in the book of the annals of the kings of Israel? ¹⁶Jehoash rested with his fathers and was buried in Samaria with the kings of Israel. And Jeroboam his son succeeded him as king.

¹⁷Amaziah son of Joash king of Judah lived for fifteen years after the death of Jehoash son of Jehoahaz king of Israel. ¹⁸As for the other events of Amaziah's reign, are they not written in the book of the annals of the kings of Judah?

¹⁹They conspired against him in Jerusalem, and he fled to Lachish, but they

sent men after him to Lachish and killed him there. [20]He was brought back by horse and was buried in Jerusalem with his fathers, in the City of David.

[21]Then all the people of Judah took Azariah, who was sixteen years old, and made him king in place of his father Amaziah. [22]He was the one who rebuilt Elath and restored it to Judah after Amaziah rested with his fathers.

1–7 If those who conspired against Joash, Judah's eighth king, had hoped for a dramatic change in governmental leadership, they were to be disappointed. Amaziah did indeed carry out his office in accordance with the demands of orthodoxy, as witnessed by his stringent treatment of the sons of his father's assassin (vv.5–6). Yet the Scriptures record that he did not serve God "wholeheartedly" (2 Chron 25:2). Certainly he was no David; rather he was another Joash; for he perpetuated the state policy of allowing sacrifice and offerings in the high places (vv.3–4).

Two dramatic events were to mark Amaziah's reign: (1) his God-given victory over Edom and (2) his self-inflicted loss to Israel. The first is dismissed in a single verse (v.7) but receives expanded treatment in 2 Chronicles (25:5–15), where the basic weakness in Amaziah's character is readily shown.

According to the Chronicler, Amaziah laid careful plans for the reconquest of Edom (lost in the days of Jehoram [8:20–22]). He began with a general census and conscription of able-bodied men twenty years of age and upward (2 Chron 25:5). He added to the three-thousand-man army by raising another one hundred thousand mercenaries from Israel (2 Chron 25:6), which, however, he subsequently dismissed when rebuked by one of the Lord's prophets (2 Chron 25:7–10, 13). Thus encouraged that his cause was just and that God would give him the victory, Amaziah invaded Edom and inflicted a crushing defeat.

Life's successes are not, however, always the victories they seem to be. A notable defeat for Amaziah occurred here (2 Chron 25:14–16). Having vanquished Edom and carried off booty and captives, he foolishly worshiped their captive gods. For this the man of God again rebuked Amaziah. This time, however, Amaziah no longer "needed God"; for he considered that he himself had won the battle. So he threatened the prophet and sent him away. Yet before he left that prophet announced Amaziah's doom for his spiritual callousness and self-will.

8–10 This knowledge of Amaziah's character and the information that the dismissed and disgruntled Israelite mercenaries had looted the northernmost Judean cities on their way home to Israel (2 Chron 25:13) set the background for the second major event of Amaziah's time—the contest with Jehoash of Israel (vv.8–14; cf. 2 Chron 25:17–24). Still irked by the strong prophetic rebuke, Amaziah sought the advice of those who would indulge his self-will (2 Chron 25:17). Angry over the conduct of the Israelite mercenaries, he used their actions as a provocation for war. Moreover, having defeated Edom with ease, Amaziah overestimated his own abilities and reasoned that he would have little trouble with his northern brother (v.10; cf. 2 Chron 25:19).

To Amaziah's arrogant battle challenge, Jehoash returned a reply couched in parabolic fable. For Amaziah to presume to challenge Jehoash was like a lowly thistle making pretentious demands against a great Lebanese cedar, only to be trampled under foot by a passing animal. How empty the boasting of such a puny antagonist! Similarly Amaziah ought not to let success over a tiny nation go to his head. In locking horns with Jehoash, the renowned victor over the Arameans, Amaziah was inviting personal and national disaster.

11–16 Amaziah's headstrong ambitions nevertheless knew no bounds. Throwing caution to the wind, he moved his troops to a confrontation with Jehoash at Judean Beth Shemesh. In that battle Jehoash emerged the victor, routing Amaziah's army (2 Chron 25:22) and taking Judah's king captive (v.12). Jehoash followed up his triumph with a thrust against Jerusalem that resulted in the loss of some six hundred feet of city wall, the confiscation of the temple furnishings and palace treasures, and the taking of many prisoners of war (vv.13–14). Amaziah's lesson in self-will had cost his nation dearly. The Chronicler (2 Chron 25:20) reports that behind it all lay the wise hand of Providence arranging the details of the lives of all concerned to teach Amaziah and Judah the folly of trusting in foreign gods.

17–22 The account of Amaziah's life closes with a further note that he outlived Jehoash of the northern kingdom by some fifteen years (v.17) and apparently was then released to return home by Israel's next king, Jeroboam II. Such a move would cause an unsettling factionalism, for Judah would now have two kings: Azariah, whom Amaziah had made coregent before his battle with Jehoash, and the restored Amaziah. Amaziah's apostasy had already brought him many adversaries; his return only aroused old antagonisms and, doubtless, new political enemies. The tension of having two kings was resolved in a conspiracy against Amaziah that first caused his flight and then ended with his death in Lachish.

Notes

5–6 Amaziah acted in accordance with the legal precedences contained in Deut 24:16 and that before the supposed D code had been discovered! See further the note on 22:8.

7 The seizure of Sela was a remarkable feat. Sela lay amid the seemingly impregnable rocks and cliffs of the Wadi Musa and has traditionally been identified with the place where the Nabataean stronghold of Petra would be erected. See further J. Lawlor, *The Nabataeans in Historical Perspective* (Grand Rapids: Baker, 1974), pp. 127–39; D. Baly, *The Geography of the Bible* (New York: Harper & Row, 1974), pp. 236–40; A. Negev, "Petra," *Encyclopedia of Archaeological Excavations in the Holy Land,* ed. M. Avi Yonah, 4 vols. (Englewood Cliffs, N.J.: Prentice-Hall, 1975), 4:943–58.

According to 2 Chron 25:11–12, the capture of Sela was preceded by an overwhelming victory in the Salt Valley below in which ten thousand Edomites lost their lives and an equal number were subsequently cast from one of Sela's heights to the jagged valley below.

That Amaziah's campaign was not of the nature of a permanent invasion is seen in that Edom's continued hostility toward Judah forced Azariah to reassert his control over it (v.22; cf. Joel 3:19; Amos 1:11–12; see further the remarks to the Introduction of Joel, EBC, 7:229–30).

9 With this fable compare that of Jotham in Judg 9:7–15. For the Hebrew fable itself, see R.J. Williams, "The Fable in the Ancient Near East," in *A Stubborn Faith,* ed. E.C. Hobbs (Dallas: SMU Press, 1956), pp. 3–26.

13–17 The rehearsal of Amaziah's patrilineage here is unusual. It may be a reminder of the legitimacy of his claim to the Judean crown, even in exile.

Wood (*Survey*, p. 351) is probably correct in affirming that Amaziah was taken to Samaria along with the hostages, his release and subsequent fifteen-year reign (v.15) occurring only at Jehoash's death. Certainly the MT says nothing about Amaziah's release. Moreover the notice of the fifteen-year reign of Amaziah after Jehoash's death has little force if Amaziah was freed at the time of the capture of Jerusalem. Also the data of Uzziah's years of rule fit well with the idea that Amaziah was not present. See further Thiele, *Mysterious Numbers*, pp. 83–87.

13–14 The breaching of Jerusalem's walls and the carrying off of the treasures by Jehoash may occasion part of Obadiah's charges against Edom (see esp. Obad vv.6–7, 11–14). The Corner Gate was located in the northwestern corner of the city's walls. It was Jerusalem's most vulnerable (cf. 18:27).

19–20 Lachish would again play a vital role in the latter days of Hezekiah and in Judah's final demise (Jer 34:7), as attested by the famous Lachish Letters. See the note on 25:22.

The return of Amaziah's body by horse-drawn chariot may indicate either a stately funeral cortège (Šanda) or simply that the very royal chariot by which Amaziah thought to make his escape was used to carry his dead body back to Jerusalem (Edersheim) or perhaps that his own chariot formed the hearse for the procession. The scriptural presentation does not always (cf. 15:3) cast Amaziah in a particularly good light, his entire reign being viewed as an aspect of the era of Jehoash of Israel (13:10–14:16). Even his final fifteen years are discussed in relation to Jehoash's death (14:17–22).

21 Though the wording is clumsy and confusing, Azariah's (Uzziah's) age must be that at which he had first been instituted as coregent תחת (*tahat*) "beside" or "under (the authority of)" (for this use of the preposition, see Gen 41:35; Num 5:19) his father (cf. 15:1–2; 2 Chron 26:1–3). For a decade he had reigned in his father's stead while he was imprisoned in the northern kingdom (792/791–782 B.C.). For fifteen years he ruled conjointly with Amaziah, who had been released from captivity (782–767). He would yet reign twenty-seven more years as king in his own right, or for a total of fifty-two years.

22 The mention of Uzziah's restoration of Edomite Elath marks the first significant act of Uzziah's independent rule and largely sets a historical peg for the entrance of the king into his period of greatness (cf. 2 Chron 26:3–15).

---

7. The reign of Jeroboam II in the northern kingdom

14:23–29

> [23] In the fifteenth year of Amaziah son of Joash king of Judah, Jeroboam son of Jehoash king of Israel became king in Samaria, and he reigned forty-one years. [24] He did evil in the eyes of the LORD and did not turn away from any of the sins of Jeroboam son of Nebat, which he had caused Israel to commit. [25] He was the one who restored the boundaries of Israel from Lebo Hamath to the Sea of the Arabah, in accordance with the word of the LORD, the God of Israel, spoken through his servant Jonah son of Amittai, the prophet from Gath Hepher.
>
> [26] The LORD had seen how bitterly everyone in Israel, whether slave or free, was suffering; there was no one to help them. [27] And since the LORD had not said he would blot out the name of Israel from under heaven, he saved them by the hand of Jeroboam son of Jehoash.
>
> [28] As for the other events of Jeroboam's reign, all he did, and his military achievements, including how he recovered for Israel both Damascus and Hamath, which had belonged to Yaudi, are they not written in the book of the annals of the kings of Israel? [29] Jeroboam rested with his fathers, the kings of Israel. And Zechariah his son succeeded him as king.

23–29 The chapter closes with a brief notice of the forty-one year reign of Jeroboam II (793–752 B.C.) (v.23). The era of Jeroboam (northern kingdom) and Azariah (southern kingdom) would mark a significant change in the fortunes of God's people. These would be days of unparalleled prosperity for the twin kingdoms, both economically (as attested by the Samaria Ostraca) and politically. Indeed together they would acquire nearly the same territorial dimensions as in the days of the united monarchy (v.25). However God's blessings are too often taken for granted. And so it proved to be in Israel-Judah of the eighth century B.C. (cf. Hos 13:6; Joel 1:1–2:27; Amos 6:1–8). Spiritually the lives of God's people degenerated into open sin in the northern kingdom (cf. Hosea, Amos) and into an empty formalism in the south (cf. Joel). In such an era God therefore raised up the great writing prophets, one of whom, Jonah, is mentioned here (v.25).

Great responsibility for Israel's spiritual problem lay with her leadership. Jeroboam II, while a capable administrator and military leader, had no concern for vital religion (v.24; cf. 1 Chron 5:11–17; Hos 4:6–5:7; 7:5). He simply carried out the ritual of the standard state religion begun by Jeroboam I.

Nonetheless Jeroboam's external accomplishments were many. In accordance with an unrecorded prophecy of Jonah, Jeroboam restored fully the borders of Israel so that they extended from the entrance of Hamath (located in the great Beqa' Valley amid the Lebanese Mountains south of Hamath) to the Sea of Arabah (or Dead Sea). Apparently even Hamath and Damascus came under Israelite superiority (v.28). Amos (6:13–14) indicates that the Transjordanian territories were probably also recovered at this time.

In all this the faithfulness of God, despite Israel's unfaithfulness (cf. Hos 2:2–3:5; 11:1–14:8; Amos 3:1–15), is evident. Because Israel had fallen into such desperate spiritual conditions (vv.26–27), a merciful God had acted on behalf of his people. As he had granted them deliverance from external pressures by sending Adad-Nirari III of Assyria against the Arameans (cf. 13:5, 22–23) initiating a period of recovery under Jehoash (13:25; 14:14–15), so now in a grander way he culminated that deliverance with full victory over the Arameans, one that included Israel's recovery of its former boundaries (vv.27–28).

When Jeroboam II died in 752 B.C., he left behind a strong kingdom but, unfortunately, one whose core foundation was so spiritually rotten that the edifice of state would not long withstand the rising tides of international intrigue and pressure.

Notes

23 Jeroboam II's assumption of power in the fifteenth year of Amaziah (782–781 B.C.) indicates the time of his independent reign. His forty-one-year reign reckons from 793, the time of his appointment as coregent with his father, Jehoash. The juxtaposition of the two coregencies of Jeroboam II in the northern kingdom and Uzziah in the southern kingdom is not without vital historical significance and is crucial for the establishment of the correct chronology of the eighth-century kings. In this regard see Thiele, *Mysterious Numbers,* pp. 83–87.

25 The first word of לְבוֹא חֲמָת (*lᵉḇôʾ ḥᵃmāṯ,* "Lebo Hamath") may form part of the geographic name (NIV) or be translated "entrance to Hamath."

The Sea of the Arabah may well be equated with "the valley of the Arabah" of Amos 6:14, which, in turn, may be the same as Isaiah's (15:7) "Ravine of the Poplars" at the southern end of the Dead Sea across the Jordan. If so, Jeroboam's Transjordanian conquest was a total one. In all this it would appear that Uzziah and Jeroboam and the twin kingdoms lived in essential harmony and cooperation.

The mention of the prophet Jonah here gives historical and chronological orientation to the famous prophet from Gath Hepher.

26 For the phrase "slave or free," see the note on 1 Kings 14:10.

28 Among the "other events" of Jeroboam II was his attention to the economy and the agricultural needs of the country. Verification of Israel's prosperity comes from the recovery of the famous Samaria Ostraca, dating from this general period. These are bills of lading for delivery of fine oil and barley sent to Samaria from the royal estates. The prevalence of the names of Canaanite deities among the personal names mentioned in the receipts attests to the loss of vital religion at this time. See further Hermann, pp. 237–39; Harrison, pp. 220–27. But note also the views of W.H. Shea, "The Date and Significance of the Samaritan Ostraca," IEJ 17 (1977): 16–27.

For the texts themselves, see J. Gibson, *Syrian Semitic Inscriptions* (Oxford: Clarendon, 1973), pp. 5–15. On the great inner corruption of Israelite society in the eighth century B.C., see Bright, *History*, pp. 241–48.

The NIV (cf. Montgomery, p. 446), sensing the difficulty of retaining the MT's לִיהוּדָה (*lîhûdāh*, "for Judah") in the light of the known history of the era, repoints the MT to read "to Yaudi," so as to equate the name with that of an ancient city in northern Syria (cf. ANET, p. 654), better known in the Assyrian inscriptions as Samal, which seems for a period of time to have established relations with this area (cf. W. Beyerlin, *Near Eastern Religious Texts Relating to the Old Testament* [Philadelphia: Westminster, 1975], p. 260).

The distinction between "the entrance to Hamath" (v.25) and Hamath and Damascus here is an accurate one. "Damascus" and "Hamath" must refer to the kingdoms represented by the capital cities, since Hamath lay outside the boundaries of ideal Israel (cf. Num 34:8) and never had been captured by David as such. While Damascus had fallen to Israel in the days of the united kingdom (1 Kings 11:24), there is no reason to assume the case is different with Hamath, especially since the Assyrian Adad-Nirari III had taken Damascus shortly before (802 B.C.). Even Adad-Nirari's weak successors had campaigned in the area five times in the era from 773–754 B.C. For light on these events and campaigns during this period in Syria from the Assyrian annals of the eighth century B.C., see Luckenbill, *Ancient Records*, pp. 260–68.

---

8. The reign of Uzziah in the southern kingdom

15:1-7

> [1]In the twenty-seventh year of Jeroboam king of Israel, Azariah son of Amaziah king of Judah began to reign. [2]He was sixteen years old when he became king, and he reigned in Jerusalem fifty-two years. His mother's name was Jecoliah; she was from Jerusalem. [3]He did what was right in the eyes of the LORD, just as his father Amaziah had done. [4]The high places, however, were not removed; the people continued to offer sacrifices and burn incense there.
>
> [5]The LORD afflicted the king with leprosy until the day he died, and he lived in a separate house. Jotham the king's son had charge of the palace and governed the people of the land.
>
> [6]As for the other events of Azariah's reign, and all he did, are they not written in the book of the annals of the kings of Judah? [7]Azariah rested with his fathers and was buried near them in the City of David. And Jotham his son succeeded him as king.

1–4 Judah's tenth king was Azariah ("Yahweh has helped"), known also as Uzziah ("Yahweh is my strength"), the latter name possibly being assumed on the occasion of his independent reign (v.1). Azariah had been made coregent at the time of Amaziah's ill-conceived campaign against Jehoash (14:8–14; 2 Chron 25:17–24). After Amaziah's release at the death of Jehoash in 782 B.C. and subsequent assassination in 767, Azariah took the throne in his own right and ruled until 740. Thus, counting his coregencies, Azariah ruled some fifty-two years.

Several reasons may be found for such a lengthy reign besides the longevity of the king. First, Israel's perennial enemy, Assyria, was in a state of severe decline. After the death of the vigorous king Adad-Nirari III (810–783), Assyria was ruled by three weak kings—Shalmaneser IV (782–774), Aššur Dan III (773–756), and Aššur Nirari V (755–746)—who strove desperately to maintain themselves against the advance of their hostile northern neighbors, Urartu, and campaigned mainly to the south and east. Moreover Assyria was rocked internally by plagues in 765 and 759 and by internal revolts (763–759).

Second, relations between Jeroboam II of Israel and Azariah remained cordial so that together the two nations were able eventually to acquire nearly the same territorial dimension as in the days of the united monarchy. Indeed the Chronicler makes it clear that the era of the early eighth century B.C. was one of great expansion militarily, administratively, commercially, and economically, a period whose prosperity was second only to that of Solomon (2 Chron 26:1–15).

Third, and more basically, Azariah was noted as a man who utilized well the spiritual heritage that he had gained from his father (v.3; cf. 2 Chron 26:4–5). Accordingly God's abundant blessing was shed on him (2 Chron 26:6–15) so that his fame spread throughout the Near Eastern world (2 Chron 26:8, 15).

The mention of the continued worship at the "high places" (v.4) indicates a state policy of noninterference with competing religious forms that had been in force since at least the time of Joash (cf. 12:3; 14:3–4). The apparent compromise is indicative of a basic spiritual shallowness that was to surface in the prophecies of the great writing prophets of the eighth century B.C.

Times of plenty and ease too often lead to spiritual lethargy. God's abundant blessings can all too readily be taken for granted and become commonplace. In such circumstances a people's religious experience can degenerate into an empty formalism or, worse, erupt into open apostasy and moral decadence. So it was in eighth century Israel. Hosea (775–725 B.C.) warned of the misuse of wealth and the twin dangers of apostasy and loose morality. Joel (770–765) cried out against Judah's superficial religion. Amos (765–755) spoke a similar message, while also emphasizing Israel's moral and social corruption. Obadiah (765) and Jonah (760) were called primarily to give messages of judgment against foreign powers; but they, too, reflect something of the social upheaval and spiritual barrenness of a self-gratifying people. The collective prophetic challenge to repentance and a return to making God primary in the believers' lives reflects the low spiritual tone of the times.

5–7 Great earthly success is seldom well-managed to spiritual benefit. As with Solomon before him, Azariah's successes proved to be his undoing. His great power fostered such pride and haughtiness that about 750 B.C. he sought to add to his vast power by usurping the prerogatives of the sacred priesthood. Challenged to his face by the priests as he attempted to make an offering at the altar of incense, he was also instantaneously judged by God, who smote him with leprosy (v.5). Driven from the temple forever, Azariah remained a leper thereafter, dwelling in isolation until his death (2 Chron 26:16–21). During Azariah's last decade, due to his leprosy, his son Jotham was made coregent and public officiator, though doubtless Azariah remained the real power behind the throne.

Notes

1–2 Verse 1 indicates the occasion of Uzziah's independent reign; v.2 relates his age at the time of his coregency and the total number of years that he ruled either as coregent or in his own right.

5 בֵּית הַחָפְשִׁית (*bêt haḥopšît*, "separate house") involves the idea of the king occupying a place where he was free from the routine responsibilities of royalty (cf. Heb. 1 Sam 17:25). The term is a difficult one and receives varying treatment in the ancient versions, being rendered by the Peshitta "in a house hidden away" and by the Vulgate "in a free house, separately." The LXX simply transliterates the term. A. Guillaume ("Hebrew and Arabic Lexicography, A Comparative Study," *Abr-Nahrain* 4 [1965]: 6) suggests a relation with the Arabic *ḥaffaša* ("he stayed in his tent," i.e., "he dwelt in his house without leaving it"). That Azariah remained the dominant figure behind the throne is certain if he can be identified with the "Azriyau" mentioned as the leader of a coalition that opposed Tiglath-pileser III in his first western campaign. For details see Thiele, *Mysterious Numbers,* pp. 93–94; D. Luckenbill, "Azariah of Judah," AJSL 41 (1925): 217–32; contrariwise, see Montgomery, pp. 446–47.

The title עַל־הַבַּיִת (ʿal-habbayit, "over the palace"; lit., "over the house") doubtless deals with the management of the myriad of complex details relative to the smooth functioning of palace life. The title was previously ascribed to Solomon's chamberlain Ahishar (1 Kings 4:6) and later was to be held by Eliakim, Hezekiah's official (18:18; Isa 36:3). The title is known from a clay seal impression from Lachish bearing the name Gedaliah, probably the one whom the Babylonians appointed governor after the Fall of Jerusalem (25:22).

Josephus (*Antiq.* IX, 225 [x.4]) connects the events of Uzziah's leprous condition with the earthquake recorded in Amos 1:1. For a discussion of leprosy in the Bible, see the note on 5:1.

6 Although Azariah was buried in the city of David and in the royal burial field, his body was excluded from the royal tombs (cf. 2 Chron 26:22–23). An ossuary has been discovered by E.L. Sukenik ("Funerary Tablet of Uzziah, King of Judah," PEQ 63 [1931]: 217–21) with the Aramaic inscription "Hitherto were brought the bones of Uzziah, king of Judah. Do not open."

9. The reign of Zechariah in the northern kingdom

15:8–12

8In the thirty-eighth year of Azariah king of Judah, Zechariah son of Jeroboam became king of Israel in Samaria, and he reigned six months. 9He did evil in the eyes of the LORD, as his fathers had done. He did not turn away from the sins of Jeroboam son of Nebat, which he had caused Israel to commit.

10Shallum son of Jabesh conspired against Zechariah. He attacked him in front of the people, assassinated him and succeeded him as king. 11The other events of Zechariah's reign are written in the book of the annals of the kings of Israel. 12So the word of the LORD spoken to Jehu was fulfilled: "Your descendants will sit on the throne of Israel to the fourth generation."

8–12 Little is recorded of Zechariah, the fourth descendant of Jehu to assume the throne of Israel, except the familiar evaluation that he did evil in perpetuating the idolatrous sins of Jeroboam I and that he died in an assassination plot. With the passing of Zechariah, the Lord's prophetic promise to Jehu (10:30) stood fulfilled (cf. Amos 7:9).

The shortness of Zechariah's reign and that of Shallum, his murderous successor, doubtless points up the great contrast in their abilities with those of Jeroboam II and underscores the weakness of the northern kingdom. The openness of Shallum's deed is expressive of Israel's social degradation.

Notes

10 The MT's reading קָבָל־עָם (*qāḇāl-ʿām*, "in front of the people," i.e., in public view) is emended in the Lucianic Recension of the LXX to read "In Ibleʿam" (cf. NIV mg.), making Zechariah's death near where Jehu had massacred Judah's royal house (9:27; 10:12 –14), perhaps a touch of poetic justice. If this reading is allowed, Shallum may have been a citizen of the Esdraelon Plain. Shallum's nonroyal status is indicated in the Assyrian annals that take note of his usurpation by calling him "the son of nobody" (cf. 2 Kings 8:15).

D. *The Era of the Decline and Fall of the Northern Kingdom (15:13–17:41)*

1. *The reign of Shallum in the northern kingdom*

15:13–15

> [13]Shallum son of Jabesh became king in the thirty-ninth year of Uzziah king of Judah, and he reigned in Samaria one month. [14]Then Menahem son of Gadi went from Tirzah up to Samaria. He attacked Shallum son of Jabesh in Samaria, assassinated him and succeeded him as king.
>
> [15]The other events of Shallum's reign, and the conspiracy he led, are written in the book of the annals of the kings of Israel.

13–15 Shallum's designation "son of Jabesh" may mark either a clan name or indicate that he was the leader of a Gileadite reaction against the crown. His minimal reign of but one month was terminated by a retaliatory raid by Menahem, who, in turn, usurped the throne.

Menahem, who may have been a military commander under Zechariah, brought his forces against Shallum in Samaria from Tirzah, an ancient Canaanite city important for its strategic commercial location and noted for its surpassing beauty (S of Songs 6:4). Tirzah had served as a royal retreat (1 Kings 14:17) and as a national capital (1 Kings 16:8–10) and had remained an important city.

From Tirzah Menahem launched a savage campaign against Tiphsah for its failure to open its gates to him. This latter city, whose exact location remains uncertain, may have withstood Menahem and Shallum or may have contested Menahem's attempt to reassert Israelite strength in the area. Although Tiphsah is otherwise insignificant in OT history, its importance to Menahem lay in its attitude toward him at a time when he must allow no rebellion to his authority if his quest for the throne was to be carried out smoothly. Menahem thus served notice that he would brook no resistance from any quarter.

Notes

14 The name Menahem ("comforting") may indicate that the new king's parents were well advanced in years or that his parents found comfort in his birth due to the death of an earlier child.

2. *The reign of Menahem in the northern kingdom*

15:16–22

> 16At that time Menahem, starting out from Tirzah, attacked Tiphsah and every-one in the city and its vicinity, because they refused to open their gates. He sacked Tiphsah and ripped open all the pregnant women.
> 17In the thirty-ninth year of Azariah king of Judah, Menahem son of Gadi be-came king of Israel, and he reigned in Samaria ten years. 18He did evil in the eyes of the LORD. During his entire reign he did not turn away from the sins of Jeroboam son of Nebat, which he had caused Israel to commit.
> 19Then Pul king of Assyria invaded the land, and Menahem gave him a thou-sand talents of silver to gain his support and strengthen his own hold on the kingdom. 20Menahem exacted this money from Israel. Every wealthy man had to contribute fifty shekels of silver to be given to the king of Assyria. So the king of Assyria withdrew and stayed in the land no longer.
> 21As for the other events of Menahem's reign, and all he did, are they not written in the book of the annals of the kings of Israel? 22Menahem rested with his fathers. And Pekahiah his son succeeded him as king.

16–22 Menahem's decade of rule is characterized as one of total sinfulness. In addition to further prostituting Israel's religious experience, he compromised her independence by becoming a vassal to Pul (or, more properly, Tiglath-pileser III, 745–727 B.C.) of Assyria. His motive in doing so was not one of patriotic concern for Israel's survival. Rather he hoped that the Assyrian alliance would solidify his hold on the throne of Israel. In order to gain the Assyrian king's backing, he levied a tax of fifty shekels of silver on the wealthy men of the realm so that the assessed levy of one thousand talents of silver might be gathered (vv.19–20). Since a talent then weighed about seventy-five pounds, this was obviously a tremendous sum.

Nevertheless the sum was fully met, and Tiglath-pileser "withdrew and stayed in the land no longer" (v.20). While Menahem thus bought the crown for himself and respite from Assyria, the hard stipulations were to cause further internal friction that was to ignite the fires of insurrection soon after his son, Pekahiah, succeeded him. Although Menahem had thought to buy time, perhaps even Israel's independence, his policy was to spell out the beginning of the end. A totally apostate Israel was to reap the harvest of her spiritual wickedness at the hands of the very ones whom Menahem had trusted for deliverance.

To understand the complex events of the late eighth century B.C., a word must be said concerning the Assyrians. After nearly a half century of decline, Assyria reawakened with the usurpation of the throne by Tiglath-pileser III in 745 B.C. Indeed he and his successors in the Neo-Assyrian Empire were to effect a drastic change in the balance of power in the ancient Near East. Having solidified the kingdom in the east, Tiglath-pileser turned his attention to the west in 743. Although the exact course of his western campaign is difficult to follow, it seems clear that all of Syro-Palestine submitted to the Assyrian yoke. Among those nations and kings whose tribute is recorded in his annals is the name Menahem of Israel, thus confirming the biblical account.

Notes

16 Identified with Tell el Far'ah, Tirzah remains one of the most striking confirmations of biblical details turned up by the archaeologist's spade. See E.G. Wright, "The Excavation of Tell el Far'ah," BA 12 (1949): 66–68.

"The ripping open" of the expectant women would be a visible, though ghastly, reminder of the city's failure to "open up" unto Menahem's demands. For the mention of this heathen practice, see 8:12; Hos 13:16; Amos 1:13.

19 That the MT's Pul and the Assyrian Tiglath-pileser were one and the same (cf. 1 Chron 5:26) is abundantly clear from the fact that Assyrian kings frequently had two names, a throne name for Assyria and one for Babylonia. Thus the Tiglath-pileser of Assyria was known as Pul(u) much as Shalmaneser V was known as Ululaia in Babylon. For details see CAH, 3:32. For information regarding Tiglath-pileser III's western campaign, see CAH, 3:33–35, and Hallo, "Qarqar," pp. 169–71.

20 Possible reference to these events in Menahem's dealings with Tiglath-pileser III may be reflected in Hosea's oracle (8:8–10), though J.B. Payne, *Encyclopedia of Biblical Prophecy* (New York: Harper & Row, 1973), p. 404, prefers to associate Hosea's warning with the events of that Assyrian king's second western campaign.

3. *The reign of Pekahiah in the northern kingdom*

15:23–26

[23]In the fiftieth year of Azariah king of Judah, Pekahiah son of Menahem became king of Israel in Samaria, and he reigned two years. [24]Pekahiah did evil in the eyes of the LORD. He did not turn away from the sins of Jeroboam son of Nebat, which he had caused Israel to commit. [25]One of his chief officers, Pekah son of Remaliah, conspired against him. Taking fifty men of Gilead with him, he assassinated Pekahiah, along with Argob and Arieh, in the citadel of the royal palace at Samaria. So Pekah killed Pekahiah and succeeded him as king.

[26]The other events of Pekahiah's reign, and all he did, are written in the book of the annals of the kings of Israel.

23–26 Few details are recorded of the two year reign of Menahem's son Pekahiah except the notice of his evil spiritual condition and the coup d'état that took his life. The insurrection originated with the king's own personal bodyguard. While two of the chief officers (Argob and Arieh) remained loyal to the king, even laying down their lives for him, the third, Pekah (apparently an influential Gileadite), found an occasion to trap the king in the citadel of the royal palace. Having slain him, Pekah seized the throne.

The usurpation and troubled times that were to follow make it clear that there was an anti-Assyrian party that had remained submerged during the rule of the fiery Menahem. Indeed the notice of a twenty-year reign for Pekah (v.27) would seem to indicate that this Gileadite strong man had laid claim to the crown some twelve years earlier and had been prevented from taking the throne only by Menahem's swift action in those unsettled times during Shallum's conspiracy. Pekahiah's appointment of Pekah to be a chief officer among his bodyguards may thus have been an attempt to placate the rival party.

Notes

---

25 The enigmatic "Argob and Arieh" (lit., "eagle and lion") has been taken by M.J. Geller, "A New Translation for 2 Kings XV 25," VetTest 26 (1976): 374–77, as a compound phrase referring to a sphinxlike statue that symbolically guarded the gate, much as the colossal *aladlammû* figures that protected the gates of the Neo-Assyrian kings.

---

4. The reign of Pekah in the northern kingdom

15:27–31

> [27]In the fifty-second year of Azariah king of Judah, Pekah son of Remaliah became king of Israel in Samaria, and he reigned twenty years. [28]He did evil in the eyes of the LORD. He did not turn away from the sins of Jeroboam son of Nebat, which he had caused Israel to commit.
>
> [29]In the time of Pekah king of Israel, Tiglath-Pileser king of Assyria came and took Ijon, Abel Beth Maacah, Janoah, Kedesh and Hazor. He took Gilead and Galilee, including all the land of Naphtali, and deported the people to Assyria. [30]Then Hoshea son of Elah conspired against Pekah son of Remaliah. He attacked and assassinated him, and then succeeded him as king in the twentieth year of Jotham son of Uzziah.
>
> [31]As for the other events of Pekah's reign, and all he did, are they not written in the book of the annals of the kings of Israel?

27–31 The chronology of Pekah's time is beset with serious problems. To Pekah is attributed a twenty-year reign, beginning with the end of the fifty-two-year reign of Azariah of Judah. Further v.30 indicates that his reign was terminated by Hoshea's conspiracy in the twentieth year of Jotham's rule. Verse 33, however, indicates that Jotham reigned but sixteen years. Moreover v.32 notes that Jotham himself began to rule in Pekah's second year. Further synchronisms occur in v.8, where the thirty-eighth year of Azariah is marked as Zechariah's accession year; in 16:1, where the seventeenth year of Pekah and the accession year of Ahaz are equated; and in 17:1, where the twelfth year of Ahaz is given as the first of Hoshea's nine years.

Because the Fall of Samaria can be assigned confidently to 722 B.C. on the basis of both biblical and secular history, and because Azariah's fifty-second year can be shown to be 740 B.C., it would appear that there is no room for a twenty-year reign for Pekah, particularly in that due allowance must be made for the reigns of Zechariah (six months), Shallum (one month), Menahem (ten years), Pekahiah (two years), and Hoshea (nine years) in the same interval of time.

The resolution of these data, while difficult, is not impossible. Probably because Pekah carried out a consistent anti-Assyrian policy, the chronicles of the southern kingdom gave full credit to Pekah's regnal claims. It would seen that already at the death of Zechariah in 752 B.C., Pekah had claimed the kingship and was recognized as king in Transjordanian Gilead. However the swift action of the Israelite military forces through Menahem prevented Pekah from furthering his aspirations for the next decade. In 742, when the powerful Menahem died, the problem of Pekah again surfaced, Pekahiah solving the problem by bringing Pekah into a position of prominence within his own bodyguard. After two years Pekah was able to find an opportunity to dispose of Pekahiah and rule in his own right over all Israel until the troublesome international events associated with Tiglath-pileser III's second western campaign (743–732) forced his demise at the hands of a pro-Assyrian faction led by Hoshea (732).

Allowing for the differing accession systems in Israel and Judah, the various dates and data can be harmonized as follows:

753/752	Azariah's thirty-eighth year (including coregency), the year of Shallum's usurpation and of Menahem's seizing the throne of Israel, the year of Pekah's "rule" in Gilead.
742	The death of Menaham, the accession of Pekahiah
740/739	The assassination of Pekahiah and the accession of Pekah, the death of Azariah in Judah and the accession of Jotham (already a coregent since 752/751) in the "second year" of Pekah's independent rule.
736	The year Jotham gave the reigns of government over to Ahaz (= Pekah's "seventeenth year").
732/731	Hoshea seizes power; = Pekah's "twentieth year" and the twelfth year of Ahaz (who apparently had been appointed crown prince and heir designate by his father in the crisis during Tiglath-pileser III's first western compaign in 744).
732/731	Jotham's twentieth year (Jotham had apparently lived for four years beyond the relinquishment of his throne to Ahaz).

Pekah's stormy beginning was to characterize his short independent rule. In 734 Tiglath-pileser III swept out of Assyria on a second western campaign that was to break the anti-Assyrian coalition headed by the Aramean king Rezin and Pekah of Israel. By 732 the alliance was thoroughly broken and Damascus had fallen. All the western Fertile Crescent, from the Taurus Mountains on the north to the border of Egypt on the south, lay in Assyrian hands. The Syrian states were divided into five provinces, Israel into three.

The battle against Israel centered in Galilee: Ijon, Abel Beth Maacah, Janoah,

Kedesh, and Hazor all being known Galilean cities (v.29). The text also adds significantly that Tiglath-pileser III swept into Pekah's center of power, Gilead (cf. 1 Chron 5:25–26). Because the cities lay in a general north-south direction, the biblical account may well preserve the Assyrian king's line of march. The mention of Janoah may indicate that after the victory over Kadesh, Tiglath-pileser divided his forces, half proceeding southward against Hazor and on to Gilead, and the other half moving southwest to Janoah and then on to Phoenicia.

With the loss of Galilee and Gilead and with the presence of Assyrian troops all along Israel's western frontier, it seemed evident that Pekah's anti-Assyrian policy had brought Israel to the point of extinction. Accordingly, while Tiglath-pileser was concluding the siege of Damascus in 732, a pro-Assyrian party, led by Hoshea, succeeded in defeating and displacing Pekah, an insurrection that cost the controversial Gileadite his life (v.30). By dispatching Pekah and submitting to Tiglath-pileser, the ultimate demise of Israel was postponed for a decade. But her end was sure, for her corruption was total, permeating all levels of society. In vain God's prophets had plead with an unrepentant and apostate people (cf. Isa 1–5; Mic 1–3; 6–7).

Notes

27 For details relative to the intricate chronological problems of this period, see H. Stigers, "Chronology," pp. 81ff.; id., "Pekah," ZPEB, 4:669ff.; Tadmor, pp. 22–40, 77–100; Thiele, *Mysterious Numbers*, pp. 77–140; J.B. Payne, "Chronology of the Old Testament," ZPEB, 1:839–42.

29 For information relative to Tiglath-pileser III's second western campaign, see Hallo, "Qarqar," pp. 171–74; Aharoni/Avi Yonah, pp. 94–95. It is, of course, possible that the biblical record simply summarizes the account of Tiglath-pileser III's campaign against Israel, with no conclusions drawn as to the order of his plan of attack. Bright (*History*, p. 217) suggests a coastal attack in 734, the Syro-Israelite thrust in 733, and the taking of Damascus in 732. For the Assyrian text, see ANET, pp. 283ff.

30 Tiglath-pileser III claims that the Israelites "overthrew their king Pekah and I placed Hoshea as king over them" (ANET, p. 284). He goes on to record Israel's tribute to him. Evidently by submitting to Tiglath-pileser, the pro-Assyrian party in Israel sought immediate recognition of its government and confirmation of Hoshea as king. See further the note at 17:1.

5. *The reign of Jotham in the southern kingdom*

15:32–38

³²In the second year of Pekah son of Remaliah king of Israel, Jotham son of Uzziah king of Judah began to reign. ³³He was twenty-five years old when he became king, and he reigned in Jerusalem sixteen years. His mother's name was Jerusha daughter of Zadok. ³⁴He did what was right in the eyes of the LORD, just as his father Uzziah had done. ³⁵The high places, however, were not removed; the people continued to offer sacrifices and burn incense there. Jotham rebuilt the Upper Gate of the temple of the LORD.

³⁶As for the other events of Jotham's reign, and what he did, are they not written in the book of the annals of the kings of Judah? ³⁷(In those days the LORD began to send Rezin king of Aram and Pekah son of Remaliah against Judah.) ³⁸Jotham rested with his fathers and was buried with them in the City of David, the city of his father. And Ahaz his son succeeded him as king.

32-33 The reign of Jotham was a continuation of that of his father, Uzziah. Already coregent for at least a decade, political and religious conditions remained largely as they were in Azariah's day; the country's prosperity continued as well (2 Chron 27:1 -4). Regrettably that prosperity was to lead, as it so often does, to spiritual neglect (cf. Isa 1-5), a condition that was to make Judah ripe for open apostasy in Ahaz's day. Although the Chronicler (2 Chron 27:6) gives Jotham a clear record, one cannot but wonder at the extent of the effect that Azariah's sin had had on Jotham and that, in turn, on the young Ahaz.

34-35 Jotham turned his attention to his country's internal needs. He rebuilt the Upper Gate at the northern entrance of the temple (v.35) and extended the wall of Ophel (2 Chron 27:3; cf. 2 Chron 26:9). He also turned his attention to urban planning, constructing cities in the highlands of Judah that, together with a system of towers and fortification in the wooded areas, could serve both economic and military purposes.

At the onset of his reign, the Ammonites, from whom Azariah had exacted tribute (2 Chron 26:8), refused to acknowledge Jotham's overlordship. This occasioned successful campaigns against the Ammonites so that they once again paid their tribute (2 Chron 27:5). The notice that this tribute continued into the second and third year may correlate with the probability that Jotham had turned over the reigns of government to his coregent son, Ahaz, about the year 736, possibly due to some failure in health, or due to rising international tensions.

36-38 Toward the end of Jotham's days, political storm clouds began to appear on the international horizon. The Chronicler speaks of "all his wars" (2 Chron 27:7); and the author of Kings notes that Rezin, the Aramean king, and Pekah, Israel's king, began their incursions into Judah (v.37). The issue was designed by the Lord to test the young Ahaz in spiritual things, but there would be no repentance in this third generation.

Notes

35 Second Chron 27 reports that Jotham was a powerful warrior (vv.5-7) and that, in addition to his work on the Upper Gate of the temple, he "did extensive work on the wall at the hill of Ophel"; and, having built towns in the Judean hills, he constructed "forts and towers in the wooded areas" (vv.3b-4). For confirmation of the latter details, see E. Oren, "ZIQLAG—A biblical city on the edge of the NEGEV," BA 45 (1982): 177-78.

6. *The reign of Ahaz in the southern kingdom*

16:1–20

¹In the seventeenth year of Pekah son of Remaliah, Ahaz son of Jotham king of Judah began to reign. ²Ahaz was twenty years old when he became king, and he reigned in Jerusalem sixteen years. Unlike David his father, he did not do what was right in the eyes of the LORD his God. ³He walked in the ways of the kings of Israel and even sacrificed his son in the fire, following the detestable ways of the nations the LORD had driven out before the Israelites. ⁴He offered sacrifices and burned incense at the high places, on the hilltops and under every spreading tree.

⁵Then Rezin king of Aram and Pekah son of Remaliah king of Israel marched up to fight against Jerusalem and besieged Ahaz, but they could not overpower him. ⁶At that time, Rezin king of Aram recovered Elath for Aram by driving out the men of Judah. Edomites then moved into Elath and have lived there to this day.

⁷Ahaz sent messengers to say to Tiglath-Pileser king of Assyria, "I am your servant and vassal. Come up and save me out of the hand of the king of Aram and of the king of Israel, who are attacking me." ⁸And Ahaz took the silver and gold found in the temple of the LORD and in the treasuries of the royal palace and sent it as a gift to the king of Assyria. ⁹The king of Assyria complied by attacking Damascus and capturing it. He deported its inhabitants to Kir and put Rezin to death.

¹⁰Then King Ahaz went to Damascus to meet Tiglath-Pileser king of Assyria. He saw an altar in Damascus and sent to Uriah the priest a sketch of the altar, with detailed plans for its construction. ¹¹So Uriah the priest built an altar in accordance with all the plans that King Ahaz had sent from Damascus and finished it before King Ahaz returned. ¹²When the king came back from Damascus and saw the altar, he approached it and presented offerings on it. ¹³He offered up his burnt offering and grain offering, poured out his drink offering, and sprinkled the blood of his fellowship offerings on the altar. ¹⁴The bronze altar that stood before the LORD he brought from the front of the temple—from between the new altar and the temple of the LORD—and put it on the north side of the new altar.

¹⁵King Ahaz then gave these orders to Uriah the priest: "On the large new altar, offer the morning burnt offering and the evening grain offering, the king's burnt offering and his grain offering, and the burnt offering of all the people of the land, and their grain offering and their drink offering. Sprinkle on the altar all the blood of the burnt offerings and sacrifices. But I will use the bronze altar for seeking guidance." ¹⁶And Uriah the priest did just as King Ahaz had ordered.

¹⁷King Ahaz took away the side panels and removed the basins from the movable stands. He removed the Sea from the bronze bulls that supported it and set it on a stone base. ¹⁸He took away the Sabbath canopy that had been built at the temple and removed the royal entryway outside the temple of the LORD, in deference to the king of Assyria.

¹⁹As for the other events of the reign of Ahaz, and what he did, are they not written in the book of the annals of the kings of Judah? ²⁰Ahaz rested with his fathers and was buried with them in the City of David. And Hezekiah his son succeeded him as king.

1–2 The account of Ahaz's wicked reign as given by the author of Kings centers around three main subjects: (1) his character (vv. 1–4), (2) his war with Rezin and Pekah (vv. 5–9), and (3) his further apostasy as consequence of his reliance on Tiglath-pileser III (vv. 10–18). Supplemental details concerning his life and times (cf. vv. 19–20) are to be found in 2 Chronicles 28 and Isaiah 7–12.

Ahaz's reign forms a stark contrast with that of his father and grandfather, and yet they had sown the seeds of the apostasy that would fructify in Ahaz's day. The luxury and ease of the time of Uzziah and Jotham had produced a spiritual indolence in Judah that would allow Ahaz's open sin to flourish.

3-4 Not content to continue the standing state policies of limited religious compromise (see the remarks on 15:5-7), Ahaz transgressed the bounds of propriety by imitating the idolatrous heathen practices of Israel. Most nefarious of all was his participation in the debased Molech rites, even going so far as to send his own son through the sacrificial fires (v.3; cf. Lev 18:21; 20:1-5; Deut 12:31; 2 Kings 21:6). These rites took place at the confluence of the Hinnom and Kidron valleys in a sacred enclosure known as Topheth (cf. 23:10; Isa 30:33; Jer 7:31). The exact nature of the sacrifices and the divinities involved have been the subject of much discussion. The finding, however, of the same type of sacred place with the same name in the transplanted Phoenician colony of Carthage, where the sacrificial offering was called by a name made up of the same Semitic consonants (MLK) contained in the name "Molech," would seem to argue that there was no deity named Molech to whom the Judeans sacrificed. Rather the real god involved was the old Canaanite deity Baal, with human sacrifice made to him called *mlk* (cf. Jer 19:5; 32:35). The rites were heinous and a total defilement of the God-given sacrificial service. The later spiritual reformation of Josiah was to bring an end to these sinister proceedings, a judgment Jeremiah utilized in picturing God's coming judgment on his sinful people (Jer 2:23; 7:30-33; 19:5-6).

The valley's reputation for extreme wickedness gave rise to the employment of its name as a term for the eschatological place for punishment of the wicked (1 Enoch 27:1ff.; 54:1ff.; 56:3f.; 90:26), a designation confirmed by Christ himself (Matt 5:22; 10:28; 13:42, 50; 18:9; 23:15, 33; 25:41).

5-6 The causes of Ahaz's war with Israel and Syria were at least fourfold.

1. On the human level, Rezin of Syria and Pekah of Israel were doubtless desirous of Judah's support in their planned insurrection against Tiglath-pileser III of Assyria.

2. As Edersheim (*History*, 7:96ff.) notes, the two leaders may have had a personal dislike for Ahaz.

3. On the spiritual plain, the whole affair seems to be a concentrated satanic effort to put an end to the Davidic line on the throne in Jerusalem (cf. Isa 7:5-7).

4. God was superintending the whole complex undertaking. He would deal with an apostate Israel (cf. 17:5-18; 18:11-12), thwart the satanically inspired plans against the house of Israel by bringing defeat to Rezin and Pekah (Isa 7:5-16), and bring chastisement to a spiritually bankrupt Ahaz (2 Chron 28:5, 19).

The full details of the complex international situation must be gleaned not only from chapter 16 but also from 15:37; 2 Chronicles 28; and Isaiah 7:1-16. These sources show that the Syro-Israelite alliance had been operative against Judah already in Jotham's day (15:37). The allied attack against Judah was two-pronged. Rezin came along the eastern portion of Judah, driving down to the key seaport of Elath and taking it (v.6; 2 Chron 28:5). Pekah launched an effective general campaign against northern Judah that resulted in the death of thousands of Judeans and the capture of hundreds of others (though the captives were later granted their freedom and returned to Jericho through the intercession of the prophet Obed; cf. 2 Chron 28:6-15). Moreover the newly liberated Edom took the opportunity to strike back, carrying away some Judeans into captivity (2 Chron 28:17). As well the Philistines found the time ripe to make renewed incursions into the western Shephelah and take captive certain cities in southern Judah.

Then a new attack, aimed at taking Jerusalem itself and installing a client king on the throne, took place (Isa 7:2–6). Surrounded by hostile enemies on all sides, Ahaz received God's prophet Isaiah. He assured Ahaz that the enemy would fail; God himself would see to that. Ahaz could ask any confirmatory sign that he wished, and it would be granted (Isa 7:7–11). Ahaz, with a flare of piety, refused Isaiah's words (Isa 7:12), preferring to rely on his own resourcefulness. (Notice that God did nevertheless give Ahaz a sign, the prophecy associated with the virgin birth of the Messiah, Isa 7:13–16; cf. Matt. 1:22–23.)

7–9 Ahaz sent away to Tiglath-pileser III and hired his deliverance from what seemed certain defeat (vv.7–9; cf. 2 Chron 28:16, 21). Tiglath-pileser complied all too readily, eventually thoroughly subduing the Arameans, taking Damascus and deporting its inhabitants, and executing Rezin (v.9). Israel was spared only through Hoshea's coup d'état and swift submission to Assyria, a takeover that cost Pekah his life (15:29–30).

God's message through Isaiah (Isa 7:7–9, 16) had come true, though the total picture was not in accordance with God's desires for Ahaz. Accordingly, Judah, far from being actually delivered, would also soon feel the heel of the oppressor marching through her land and streets (cf. Isa 7:17–20). What had been an opportunity for spiritual victory had become a first step into a quicksand bog that would ultimately swallow Judah in defeat and deportation.

10–11 After Tiglath-pileser III had secured Damascus, he apparently summoned his new vassals there to receive their tokens of submission, among whom was Ahaz. While at Damascus Ahaz was much impressed with a type of altar in use there and sent back instructions to Uriah, the priest, for its construction, a task duly completed before the king's return.

12–13 When Ahaz returned he had his daily offerings presented on this new altar, thereby dedicating the altar's use to the Lord. The offerings that were made were all of the sweet savor type, expressing the maintenance of the believer's communion with God: the burnt and meal offerings symbolizing dedication and service, the fellowship (peace) offering symbolizing fellowship, and the drink offering emphasizing the joy of life poured out to God in Spirit-led obedience (v.13). What a parody of piety! He who knew nothing of genuine godliness would fain his devotion to God and that via an alien altar!

14–16 The following verses catalog Ahaz's further religious innovations, all of which speak clearly of his deepening apostasy. The prescribed brazen altar was transferred from facing the sanctuary entrance to the northside (v.14). Accordingly all future offerings would be made on the recently dedicated Damascene altar (v.15). The brazen altar would henceforth be used by Ahaz in connection with his divination practices, indicating Ahaz's involvement in Assyrian cultic rites.

17 Ahaz went even further. The high stands holding the altar were appropriated by him for their brass. Likewise he lowered the molten sea by taking away the brass bulls that supported it and placed it on a low stone pedestal.

18 Not content with these "reforms" in the ceremonial furnishings, Ahaz went still further. The king's own covered stand that opened into the inner court, together with his private entrance to that place, were removed "in deference to the king of Assyria." The exact impact of these words is difficult to ascertain. Whether Tiglath-pileser wanted less prestige to be held by his new vassal or felt that such a special royal place might indicate too close a tie to an established religion that might later foster a spirit of independence against Assyria is uncertain. At any rate the whole-sale changes were either made at the Assyrian king's suggestion or were done to gain his pleasure.

19–20 Ahaz went yet further in his apostasy. According to 2 Chronicles 28:24–25, he went so far as to mutilate the temple furniture and close the temple itself so that the services within the Holy Place were discontinued. "Worship services" would henceforth be held only in connection with the new altar or at one of the several altars erected throughout Jerusalem or at the high places dedicated to the various gods that were established throughout Judah by royal edict (v.4). All this not only speaks of Ahaz's depraved spiritual condition but was probably carried out as an expression of his good will toward Tiglath-pileser. Officially nothing offensive to the Assyrian king would henceforth be practiced. Thus did Ahaz go to his reward, clothed, spiritually speaking, in an Assyrian mantle (cf. Josh 7:21).

Notes

1 The name Ahaz is a shortened form of Jehoahaz ("Whom Yahu has possessed"; cf. the similar name Ahaziah), as the appearance of his name in the tribute lists of Tiglath-pileser III (i.e., *Yauḥazi*) makes clear.

2 The notice that Ahaz was but twenty years old at his accession and that he ruled sixteen years has occasioned no little difficulty, particularly since, according to 2 Chron 29:1, his son Hezekiah was already twenty-five when he succeeded his father. Some MSS of the ancient Greek and Syriac versions at 2 Chron 28:1 record Ahaz's age at his accession as twenty-five. While this reading would have the advantage of making Ahaz sixteen rather than eleven at the time of his son's birth, the MT's lower figure is not impossible in the light of Near Eastern marriage practices.

If a sixteen-year-independent reign (732–716 B.C.) for Ahaz is not primarily in view here, the answer to this knotty problem is to be sought in the tangled chronology of the late eighth century B.C. Ahaz may have lived four years after handing over the reigns of government to Hezekiah in 720 B.C., an event that may be related to the Assyrian-Philistine wars of 720 and 716 B.C. Accordingly, the Chronicler's note as to Hezekiah's accession is reckoned from the sole reign of Hezekiah in 716 B.C. Ahaz was born in 756 and died in 716; and Hezekiah was born in 741–740, when Ahaz was fifteen or sixteen, a possibility that may account for the reading of the Greek and Syriac texts for 2 Chron 28:1.

3 The Molech problem is a complex one. That literal human sacrifice was involved (contra N.H. Snaith, "The Cult of Molech," VetTest 16 [1966]: 123f.) is abundantly shown in the Canaanite literary texts and is elsewhere implied or stated in the OT.

In some cases Molech appears to refer to a personal god (see Lev 20:1–5, though this is by no means certain). Those who take the word as a deity differ as to his identity. Some equate him with Milcolm, the national god of Ammon (1 Kings 11:7), a name that itself is a deliberate scribal misvocalization of the name based on the Semitic word *mlk*. (For a recent discussion of the nature and function of Milcolm, see W.H. Shea, "Milkom as the

Architect of Rabbath-Ammon's Natural Defences in the Ammon Citadel Inscription," PEQ 111 [1978]: 17–25.) But 2 Kings 23:10, 13 appears to differentiate between the worship of Milcolm and "Molech." (Some suggest that Molech likewise is a scribal corruption, the vowels for the consonants *mlk* being supplied from the Heb. בֹּשֶׁת (*bōšet*, "shame"].) Others consider Molech to be Melek Athtar, a well-known astral deity in the ancient Near East of whom several deities (e.g., Milcolm and Chemosh) are local expressions; see IDB, 3:422f.; cf. Amos 5:26–27; Acts 7:43.

The name Molech more than likely originates in the ancient Semitic term *mālik*, being the absolute state of a noun meaning "king." Thus the word was at first an epithet of a deity. Significantly the first reference to God as "king" is in the mouth of the pagan diviner Balaam (Num 23:21), as R.B. Allen, "The Theology of the Balaam Oracles," *Tradition and Testament*, John and Paul Feinberg, edd. (Chicago: Moody, 1981), pp. 103, 118, aptly points out. J.J.M. Roberts, *The Earliest Semitic Pantheon* (Baltimore: Johns Hopkins Press, 1972), pp. 42–43, 105–6, decides that the original deity with whom the term was combined was Dagan. In time the term split off and became used independently. As such the name was widely utilized throughout the Semitic world. (See further J. Ebach, "ADRMLK, Moloch und BAʿALADR: Eine Notiz zum Problem der Moloch-Verehrung im alten Israel," *Ugarit-Forschungen* 11 [1979]: 211–26.)

However, though the evidence renders it certain that the term *mālik* enjoyed widespread use as a divine name, the issue is whether an independent deity by that name is intended in the OT and more specifically in eighth/seventh century Judah. Although George C. Herder (*The Cult of Molek* [Sheffield: JSOT, 1985]) argues forcibly for a chthonic deity whose worship was especially observed in Jerusalem, the linguistic and archaeological data as harmonized with the biblical data (cf. 23:10 with Jer 7:31; 19:5–6; 32:35) best favor the idea that *mlk* refers to a type of sacrifice made to Baal in a sacred enclosure known as a tophet. (Notice, however, that in Syriac "tophet" means "fire pit.") For further details see B.H. Warmington, *Carthage* (Baltimore: Penguin, 1964), pp. 158ff.; L.E. Stager and S.R. Wolff, "Child Sacrifice at Carthage," *Biblical Archaeology Review* 10 (1984): 30–47.

7 Notice that in the short excerpt given of Ahaz's letter to Tiglath-pileser, Ahaz already acknowledged his vassal status.

10 The prototype of Ahaz's new altar has been often disputed, with some deciding for an Assyrian style altar (e.g., Gray, Gressman, Kittel, Montgomery, T.H. Robinson) and others (e.g., Šanda, de Vaux) favoring an Aramean one. Although it is possible that the Assyrian state cultus would be initiated at Damascus as the official religion, there is no reason to assume that an existing Syrian altar could not have been used. Such syncretistic elements are well known. Moreover Ahaz was known to be a devotee of Syro-Palestinian worship practices (vv.2–4; 2 Chron 28:23). See further the helpful remarks of Saggs, *Assyriology*, pp. 21–22.

דְּמוּת (*demût*, "likeness") and תַּבְנִית (*tabnît*, "shape," "pattern") are well rendered by NIV's "sketch" and "detailed plans." The former word gives the altar's outward appearance and may indicate an artist's sketch; the latter suggests an architect's drawing.

12–13 The verbs here should be given indirect force, with Uriah actually officiating in the service at the king's command.

15 Although לְבַקֵּר (*lebaqqēr*, "for seeking guidance") bears many nuances, the context suggests the idea of consulting a diviner.

17 For the Solomonic basins and movable stands and the molten sea, see 1 Kings 7:23, 27. Ahaz's appropriation of the panels and bases from the sacred furniture does not seem to be for the purpose of sending a further gift to Tiglath-pileser but rather for deemphasizing their importance in the worship services. Perhaps he planned to reuse them in some other decorative way. At any rate death overtook him before his attention could be turned to them. They are mentioned among the several items that were carried away in the later Babylonian despoiling of Jerusalem (25:13–14; Jer 27:19–20; 52:17–23).

מַרְצֶפֶת אֲבָנִים (*marṣepet ʾabānîm*, "stone base") refers not to the stone pavement of the court as the Vulgate suggests, but, as Keil (p. 407) decides, to a pedestal made of stones (cf. LXX: βάσις λιθίνη, [*basis lithinē*, "stone base"]).

---

7. The reign of Hoshea in the northern kingdom

17:1–23

[1]In the twelfth year of Ahaz king of Judah, Hoshea son of Elah became king of Israel in Samaria, and he reigned nine years. [2]He did evil in the eyes of the LORD, but not like the kings of Israel who preceded him.

[3]Shalmaneser king of Assyria came up to attack Hoshea, who had been Shalmaneser's vassal and had paid him tribute. [4]But the king of Assyria discovered that Hoshea was a traitor, for he had sent envoys to So king of Egypt, and he no longer paid tribute to the king of Assyria, as he had done year by year. Therefore Shalmaneser seized him and put him in prison. [5]The king of Assyria invaded the entire land, marched against Samaria and laid siege to it for three years. [6]In the ninth year of Hoshea, the king of Assyria captured Samaria and deported the Israelites to Assyria. He settled them in Halah, in Gozan on the Habor River and in the towns of the Medes.

[7]All this took place because the Israelites had sinned against the LORD their God, who had brought them up out of Egypt from under the power of Pharaoh king of Egypt. They worshiped other gods [8]and followed the practices of the nations the LORD had driven out before them, as well as the practices that the kings of Israel had introduced. [9]The Israelites secretly did things against the LORD their God that were not right. From watchtower to fortified city they built themselves high places in all their towns. [10]They set up sacred stones and Asherah poles on every high hill and under every spreading tree. [11]At every high place they burned incense, as the nations whom the LORD had driven out before them had done. They did wicked things that provoked the LORD to anger. [12]They worshiped idols, though the LORD had said, "You shall not do this." [13]The LORD warned Israel and Judah through all his prophets and seers: "Turn from your evil ways. Observe my commands and decrees, in accordance with the entire Law that I commanded your fathers to obey and that I delivered to you through my servants the prophets."

[14]But they would not listen and were as stiff-necked as their fathers, who did not trust in the LORD their God. [15]They rejected his decrees and the covenant he had made with their fathers and the warnings he had given them. They followed worthless idols and themselves became worthless. They imitated the nations around them although the LORD had ordered them, "Do not do as they do," and they did the things the LORD had forbidden them to do.

[16]They forsook all the commands of the LORD their God and made for themselves two idols cast in the shape of calves, and an Asherah pole. They bowed down to all the starry hosts, and they worshiped Baal. [17]They sacrificed their sons and daughters in the fire. They practiced divination and sorcery and sold themselves to do evil in the eyes of the LORD, provoking him to anger.

[18]So the LORD was very angry with Israel and removed them from his presence. Only the tribe of Judah was left, [19]and even Judah did not keep the commands of the LORD their God. They followed the practices Israel had introduced. [20]Therefore the LORD rejected all the people of Israel; he afflicted them and gave them into the hands of plunderers, until he thrust them from his presence.

[21]When he tore Israel away from the house of David, they made Jeroboam son of Nebat their king. Jeroboam enticed Israel away from following the LORD and caused them to commit a great sin. [22]The Israelites persisted in all the sins of Jeroboam and did not turn away from them [23]until the LORD removed them from his presence, as he had warned through all his servants the prophets. So the people of Israel were taken from their homeland into exile in Assyria, and they are still there.

1–3 Hoshea had been granted the throne by the military in a purge that was largely a placating move toward Assyria. That such was the case can be seen in that when the opportunity presented itself, Hoshea quickly attempted to throw off the Assyrian yoke by entering into an anti-Assyrian coalition. That effort, however, failed, a failure that would seal the fate of the northern kingdom.

When Tiglath-pileser III died in 727 B.C. and was succeeded by his son Shalmaneser V (727–722), the time seemed ripe for certain western states to renounce their vassal status. Moreover a seemingly important ally lay southward in the delta of Egypt, one Tefnekht, the Pharaoh of the Twenty-Fourth Dynasty. Tefnekht had succeeded in bringing the decadent Twenty-Second Dynasty to an end and was even then vying for prominence in Egypt with Piankhy, the Pharaoh of the Ethiopian based Twenty-Fifth Dynasty (which had dispatched the Theban Twenty-Third Dynasty).

4 The mention of "So king of Egypt" in v.4 has occasioned a good deal of controversy, for there is no known Egyptian king by that name. Attempts have been made to identify this "So" with Osorkon of the Twenty-Third Dynasty or with Shabako of the Twenty-Fifth Dynasty, or to assign to him merely a field commander's status. The simplest answer lies with the suggestion of H. Goedicke ("The End of So, King of Egypt," BASOR 171 [1963]: 64–66), who has pointed out that Sais (lit., *sa'w*), the Egyptian capital of the Twenty-Fourth Dynasty, would be pronounced *sā* in Akkadian (the lingua franca of the ancient Near East) but *sô* in Hebrew. Thus understood v.4 would read "he had sent envoys to Sais (even unto) the king of Egypt" (see NIV mg.).

5–6 Hoshea (as well as Judah, 18:21) was to learn that Egypt was indeed "a splintered reed." Tefnekht could not even survive Egypt's internal struggle. Nor was Hoshea to succeed against Shalmaneser. The Assyrian monarch marched quickly into Israel, secured its submission, and imprisoned Hoshea himself (v.5). Subsequently he again invaded the land, devastating its length and breadth, and placed Samaria under siege in the year 725 B.C. Ultimately the Israelite capital fell (722), and its surviving inhabitants were deported to Mesopotamia and Media.

The natural reading of the biblical record would seem to be that Shalmaneser is to be identified with "the king of Assyria" (vv.5–6). Sargon (Shalmaneser's successor), however, claimed that he had captured Samaria. The problem may possibly be resolved by holding that though Shalmaneser was still king, he was not personally present at Samaria's fall, the culmination of the campaign being accomplished by his general Sargon.

7–8 The author rehearses the causes that necessitated the divine punishment. His indictment of Israel begins with a reminder that God alone had released the Israelites from their oppression and bondage in Egypt and had brought them to the Promised Land. Their historical foundation was essentially a spiritual one. Having brought Israel from bondage to glorious freedom, God had every right to expect them to walk in newness of life, as befitting a redeemed people (cf. Deut 5–6; 10:12 –11:32).

9–17 The opposite, however, had been the case. The shameful record of Israel's spiritual harlotry is catalogued (cf. Isa 5; Mic 6:3–5, 9–16). Against the clear prohibitions of God (Exod 20:2-6; Lev 18:4-5, 26; 20:22-23; Deut 5:6-10), the people had entered into the worship patterns of the pagan nations that God had driven out of the land. This apostasy had been formally initiated by Israel's own kings, and all Israel had followed their devious plan to pretend to worship God in the official state religion.

Matters had grown even worse. The external rites had become more openly false. Israel's worship included setting up sacred shrines and Asherah poles, the following of pagan incense customs, worshiping at cultic high places, and even open idolatry. Although God had driven the nations that practiced these abominations out of the land, Israel still corrupted herself with them, despite the fact that God had sent prophets to warn the people to turn from this wickedness. Israel, who had associated herself with the abominations of the Canaanites, also appropriated their punishment. Just as God had driven out the Canaanites, so he would drive Israel out (vv. 18-20, 23), into exile (v. 23).

It was all to no avail. Obdurately set in their own ways, the Israelites refused to acknowledge God's commands and warnings. Like the surrounding nations, they followed worthless idols and became useless to God. Every sort of idolatry had been tried, from the calves of Jeroboam to the Asherah pole, from the worship of the heavenly hosts to that of Baal and the loathsome practice of human sacrifice. Divination and deliberate sorcery had further corrupted their spiritual experience. Most basic of all, they had not only denied God's covenant with them, but had refused the God of the covenant, rejecting his rightful sovereignty over them.

18-23 The inevitable result was that Israel aroused God's righteous wrath (vv. 18-19). In accordance with the set terms of the inviolable covenant, God must punish her. This he did, by allowing Israel to fall into the hands of the Assyrian invader (vv. 20-23). Judah had been left to ponder her own spiritual condition before God. Unfortunately she would not learn from the lesson of Israel.

Notes

1 A comparison with 15:30 makes it certain that the last year of Pekah, the first year of Hoshea, the twelfth year of Ahaz, and the twentieth year of Jotham are one and the same, that is, 732 B.C.

6 Sargon's claim to have taken Samaria does not surface until much later in his reign, and then at a time when considerable official writing was devoted to portraying his greatness. For details see Tadmor, pp. 22-40, 77-100; Hallo, "Qarqar," pp. 175f.

The list of cities the deportees were relocated to probably reflects a straight line of march. According to Sargon's annals, he deported some 27,290 inhabitants of Samaria, while relocating others in Israel and reorganizing the area as an Assyrian province. For details see Luckenbill, *Ancient Records*, 2:2, 26-27.

9 וַיְחַפְּאוּ (wayᵉḥappᵉʾû, "[the Israelites] secretly did") reveals that Israel's motives were blatantly perverse, feigning worship of God while secretly doing things contrary to his clear instructions.

10 For the religious practices of Jeroboam, see the note on 1 Kings 14:15.

12 For גִּלֻּלִים (gillulîm, "idols"; lit., "images in the round"), see the note on 1 Kings 15:12.

13 For God's pleading with Israel to turn from her wicked ways and back to God, see the remarks on Joel 2:12-14. For שׁוּב (šûḇ, "turn," "return"), see W.L. Holladay, *The Root šûbh in the Old Testament* (Leiden: Brill, 1958).

The conjunction "and" does not appear in the final phrase in the MT; so it may be best to translate the phrase with the LXX: "through all his prophets, every seer." God had sent every type of prophet.

14 The "stiff-necked fathers" were disbelieving Israelites in Moses' day (cf. Deut 10:16). Their descendants also had not trusted God. The verb אָמַן (*'āman,* "be firm"), used here in the Hiphil stem, connotes the idea of a belief that brings true reliance (i.e., genuine biblical faith; cf. Isa 53:1). The derived noun אֱמוּנָה (*'emûnāh,* "faithfulness") lays stress on an outward condition that gives full attestation to an inward reality (cf. Isa 7:9; see also TDOT, 1:293–309).

15–17 The people's willing adherence to Jeroboam's great sin of deliberately initiating a pseudoreligion into Israel's experience stands as a major issue in God's case against his people. How great the responsibility of those whom God places in a position of trust (cf. Luke 12:48; Heb 13:17)!

For Asherah see the note on 1 Kings 14:15. For the passing of children through fire, see the note on 2 Kings 16:3. The origin of Astral worship in Israel is obscure but was attested as early as the eighth century B.C. (Amos 5:26). It may have gained official sanction in the northern kingdom due to the subjection of Menahem and Hoshea to Assyria and then been introduced into Judah under similar conditions by Ahaz (cf. 23:12). The practice thrived in the days of Manasseh (21:5) but was abolished by Josiah (23:4–5, 12). Such worship was specifically forbidden in the law (Deut 4:19; 17:3).

18–10 The syntax of the MT here is most expressive. The writer proceeds asyndetically, exclaiming poignantly, "Only the tribe of Judah was left." Yet even they did not keep the Lord's commands but walked in the practices that Israel had observed. Knowing the outcome of Judah's history, the writer was so overcome that he had to add these words parenthetically to Israel's history. One can almost feel his inner grief. How could Judah be so stupid? How could she have failed to heed the lessons of God's dealing with the northern kingdom? Ultimately God had to reject all Israel.

21–23 The rehearsal of Israel's sin in following the perversity of Jeroboam closes with a note that Israel was yet in exile in the days of the author of Kings. This statement makes any postexilic date for this section of Kings most difficult.

---

8. *The repopulation of Samaria*

17:24–41

[24]The king of Assyria brought people from Babylon, Cuthah, Avva, Hamath and Sepharvaim and settled them in the towns of Samaria to replace the Israelites. They took over Samaria and lived in its towns. [25]When they first lived there, they did not worship the LORD; so he sent lions among them and they killed some of the people. [26]It was reported to the king of Assyria: "The people you deported and resettled in the towns of Samaria do not know what the god of that country requires. He has sent lions among them, which are killing them off, because the people do not know what he requires."

[27]Then the king of Assyria gave this order: "Have one of the priests you took captive from Samaria go back to live there and teach the people what the god of the land requires." [28]So one of the priests who had been exiled from Samaria came to live in Bethel and taught them how to worship the LORD.

[29]Nevertheless, each national group made its own gods in the several towns where they settled, and set them up in the shrines the people of Samaria had made at the high places. [30]The men from Babylon made Succoth Benoth, the men from Cuthah made Nergal, and the men from Hamath made Ashima; [31]the Avvites made Nibhaz and Tartak, and the Sepharvites burned their children in the fire as sacrifices to Adrammelech and Anammelech, the gods of Sepharvaim.

³²They worshiped the LORD, but they also appointed all sorts of their own people to officiate for them as priests in the shrines at the high places. ³³They worshiped the LORD, but they also served their own gods in accordance with the customs of the nations from which they had been brought.

³⁴To this day they persist in their former practices. They neither worship the LORD nor adhere to the decrees and ordinances, the laws and commands that the LORD gave the descendants of Jacob, whom he named Israel. ³⁵When the LORD made a covenant with the Israelites, he commanded them: "Do not worship any other gods or bow down to them, serve them or sacrifice to them. ³⁶But the LORD, who brought you up out of Egypt with mighty power and outstretched arm, is the one you must worship. To him you shall bow down and to him offer sacrifices. ³⁷You must always be careful to keep the decrees and ordinances, the laws and commands he wrote for you. Do not worship other gods. ³⁸Do not forget the covenant I have made with you, and do not worship other gods. ³⁹Rather, worship the LORD your God; it is he who will deliver you from the hand of all your enemies."

⁴⁰They would not listen, however, but persisted in their former practices. ⁴¹Even while these people were worshiping the LORD, they were serving their idols. To this day their children and grandchildren continue to do as their fathers did.

24 To the demise of Israel and her indictment, a historical note is appended. In accordance with the deportation system used so fully by Tiglath-pileser III and followed by his successors, a vast transplantation of populaces occurred. Israelites were sent to Mesopotamia and even beyond; Babylonians and Arameans were transferred to Israel. Not only did the Assyrian monarchs hope to make the repopulated and reconstituted districts more manageable, but they hoped to train and encourage the citizenry to transfer their loyalties to the Assyrian Empire.

25–27 The new settlers in Samaria, however, soon encountered difficulties. Perhaps because many unburied bodies still remained after the bloody warfare and due to the depopulating of the land, voracious lions began to roam freely through the area (v.25). When the immigrants arrived, they faced this menace. Many of them lost their lives. They immediately suspected that "the god of the land" (v.27) was punishing them because of their failure to worship him. Therefore they sent a report to the Assyrian king for some religious leadership (v.26). There was some truth to their evaluation of things. Although God had sent his people into exile because of their failure to live up to the stipulations of the covenant with God, he would not leave the land without any witness to himself. The lions were a reminder of the broken covenant and of God's claim on the land (Lev 18:24–30).

28 The Assyrian king granted the request. Accordingly one of Israel's exiled priests returned to the land and reinstituted the worship of the Lord at Bethel, the traditional cult center of the northern kingdom. The religion, however, that such a priest would teach would be the false worship instituted by Jeroboam. The result was a mixture of truth combined with the corrupted experience of Israel (now deepened by two centuries of growing apostasy) and the pagan rites brought by the new settlers.

29–31 Moreover the various immigrants continued the worship of their own gods in the places where they settled (v.29). Those from Babylonia worshiped Succoth Benoth (v.30), probably a deliberate scribal pun on the Babylonian *Ṣarpanitu,* Marduk's wife. Those from Cuth continued their worship of Nergal, the great chthonic deity and god of pestilence.

Those from Syrian backgrounds worshiped the deities associated with their cults. The Syrian gods that are recorded here are likely all deliberate misspellings. Ashima is possibly an abbreviated form of the goddess Malkat Shemayin or the Canaanite Asherah (cf. Amos 8:14 NIV mg.). Some have suggested a connection with the late Syrian goddess Sima or with the well-known Phoenician god Eshmun. Nibhaz (v.31) is otherwise unknown, the most usual conjecture being that it is a corruption of the word for altar, now deified. Tartak is possibly a miswriting of Atargatis, the familiar Syrian goddess. Adrammelech and Anammelech are similar corrupt names probably representing Canaanite forms of the important Phoenician deities Baal and 'an, the masculine form of Anat, known from Phoenician and Ugaritic names.

32–41 Thus this Samarian worship from the onset was syncretistic. While the various people observed the worship of the Lord (in its Jeroboamic corrupt form), they also continued their own religious practices (vv.32–33). The author of Kings evaluates the situation as being one of total confusion (v.34). Above all he makes it clear that the new Samarian worship did not represent the true faith; not only was it syncretistic (vv.34, 40–41), but it violated the clear commands and stipulations contained in Israel's covenant with God (vv.34–40).

With this summation the divine case against Israel has been made. Despite all that the great Redeemer had done for his people, their thankless, hardened, and apostate hearts had led them into spiritual, moral, and social corruption and thus to their own demise. Israel's checkered history should have provided a lesson for Judah; it remains an example for the church (cf. 1 Cor 10:11–13).

Notes

24 The order in which the cities are mentioned may indicate the sequence of making up the train of relocated personnel; up from Babylon, past Cuthah, westward along the Euphrates River to Hamath, and then southward through Syria and Phoenicia into Israel. For the Assyrian practice of deportation, see the remarks in CAH, 3:41f. Notice that Samaria now names the new Assyrian province, the name being drawn from Tiglath-pileser III's former designation of Israel as Samerina (see Luckenbill, *Ancient Records*, 1:276, 279; 2:134).

25 The time of the deportees' arrival has been much discussed. Since Sargon records the quellings of a revolt in southern Mesopotamia in his first year and the deporting of people to "Hatti Land" (i.e., Palestine) and speaks of suppressing similar revolts in Syria and Arabia in his second and seventh years, doubtless the repopulation of Samaria began almost immediately (see Luckenbill, *Ancient Records*, 2:3, 6–8). Later Assyrian kings added substantially to Samaria's members (Ezra 4:2).

27 The author apparently had access to the official correspondence and excerpted what was important to his narrative—the king's order. The passage has the ring of authenticity. For insight into Akkadian epistolary style, see R. Patterson, *Old Babylonian Parataxis* (Ann Arbor: University Microfilms, 1970), pp. 100–105. That Sargon would have sent such a priest to care for an internal religious problem can no longer be doubted. See S.M. Paul, "Sargon's Administrative Dictum in 2 Ki 17:17," JBL 88 (1969): 73–74.

30–31 As it stands in the MT, the Babylonian deity means "booth of girls," a nonsense form. The precise Babylonian deity involved is difficult to ascertain. Hebrew scribes frequently altered the names of pagan deities, thereby refusing to acknowledge their existence (e.g., the "Babylonian" names of the three Hebrew children [Dan 1:7; cf. Matt 12:24–27]). Similarly the names of the Syrian deities of v.31 are likely all deliberate misspellings.

41 Some Samarians, however, worshiped the true God (cf. 2 Chron 30:10–19). For the later features of the Samaritan religion and the Jewish hatred of the Samaritans, see John 4:9; 8:48; A. Edersheim, *History of the Jewish Nations* (Grand Rapids: Baker, n.d.), p. 249; id., LTJM, 1:396–403.

III. The Southern Kingdom (18:1–25:30)

A. *The Reign of Hezekiah (18:1–20:21)*

1. *Hezekiah's accession and early deeds*

18:1–12

> ¹In the third year of Hoshea son of Elah king of Israel, Hezekiah son of Ahaz king of Judah began to reign. ²He was twenty-five years old when he became king, and he reigned in Jerusalem twenty-nine years. His mother's name was Abijah daughter of Zechariah. ³He did what was right in the eyes of the LORD, just as his father David had done. ⁴He removed the high places, smashed the sacred stones and cut down the Asherah poles. He broke into pieces the bronze snake Moses had made, for up to that time the Israelites had been burning incense to it. (It was called Nehushtan.)
>
> ⁵Hezekiah trusted in the LORD, the God of Israel. There was no one like him among all the kings of Judah, either before him or after him. ⁶He held fast to the LORD and did not cease to follow him; he kept the commands the LORD had given Moses. ⁷And the LORD was with him; he was successful in whatever he undertook. He rebelled against the king of Assyria and did not serve him. ⁸From watchtower to fortified city, he defeated the Philistines, as far as Gaza and its territory.
>
> ⁹In King Hezekiah's fourth year, which was the seventh year of Hoshea son of Elah king of Israel, Shalmaneser king of Assyria marched against Samaria and laid siege to it. ¹⁰At the end of three years the Assyrians took it. So Samaria was captured in Hezekiah's sixth year, which was the ninth year of Hoshea king of Israel. ¹¹The king of Assyria deported Israel to Assyria and settled them in Halah, in Gozan on the Habor River and in towns of the Medes. ¹²This happened because they had not obeyed the LORD their God, but had violated his covenant—all that Moses the servant of the LORD commanded. They neither listened to the commands nor carried them out.

1–2 Perhaps the knottiest of all scriptural chronological problems occurs in this chapter. The data are these: the third year of Hoshea is the accession year of Hezekiah's twenty-nine-year reign (cf. v.1 with 2 Chron 29:1); v.9 equates Hoshea's seventh year with Hezekiah's fourth year, and v.10 places Hoshea's ninth year in juxtaposition with Hezekiah's sixth year. Thus the dating of the early years of Hezekiah's reign is inextricably tied with Hoshea's rule. Since Hoshea came to the throne in 732/731 B.C., Hezekiah would appear to have begun his rule in 729/728.

Verse 12, however, records the invasion of Sennacherib that led to the famous Battle of El Tekeh as being in Hezekiah's fourteenth year. Since that date can be accurately determined as being 701 B.C., this verse would seem to place Hezekiah's accession date at 716/715 (cf. Isa 36:1). Adding to the difficulties is the scriptural notice in 16:1–2 that Ahaz reigned sixteen years after Pekah's seventeenth year (736/735), making Ahaz's final date to be 720/719.

Despite the many ingenious attempts to resolve these difficulties, the harmonization of these data remains a thorny problem. Obviously we are not yet able to grasp fully the details and principles that the Hebrew writers utilized in making these chronological correlations. While definite resolution of the details cannot be made presently, it may be simplest to view 729/728 as Hezekiah's first year as coregent with Ahaz, a joint rule that he was to share until 720/719. After Ahaz's death in 716, Hezekiah would then have ruled independently from 715 onward, or fourteen years before the Assyrian campaign of 701. Since the commencement of Hezekiah's independent rule began only in 715 and Ahaz's reign must have terminated in 720/719, the actual reins of government must have passed to Hezekiah some three or four years before Ahaz's death, just as Jotham lived on until 732 after committing governmental control to Ahaz in 736 (see the note on 16:2).

3–4 Hezekiah's godly character is sketched at the onset of things. He was concerned about the things of God, following in the footsteps of David his forefather in performing righteous deeds (v.3). This took the form early in his reign of a thorough reformation of the idolatrous practices of Ahaz (v.4). Not only did Hezekiah take away the high places and destroy the cultic stone pillars and Asherah poles, but his iconoclastic purge singled out Moses' bronze serpent (cf. Num 21) that had lately become an object of veneration.

5–7 The divine evaluation is a favorable one: (1) there was none who equaled Hezekiah in his trust of the Lord (v.5); (2) he followed the Lord faithfully (v.6a); and (3) he obeyed implicitly the law of God (v.6b). Hence God was with him and blessed him with success (v.7). Hezekiah's character stands as a reminder that living for God's glory is for the believer's good also (cf. v.7 with 2 Chron 31:20–21).

While the writer of Kings concentrates on the political events of Hezekiah's reign, the author of Chronicles gives supplemental information as to Hezekiah's continuing reformation. Hezekiah's spiritual concern brought about a cleansing of the temple, thus undoing the evil deeds of Ahaz (2 Chron 29:3–19). This was followed by a reconstruction and rededication of the temple (2 Chron 29:20–36), accomplished with proper sacrifices (vv.20–24), with sincere worship (vv.25–30), and with glad service to God (vv.31–36). Hezekiah's further reforms included the reinstitution of the Passover (2 Chron 30), an observation performed with careful forethought (vv.1 –12) and in accordance with the divine command, tempered with mercy (vv.13–22) and with protracted festivity (vv.23–27). The author of Chronicles tells of still later iconoclastic purges in which all the people of Israel participated (2 Chron 31:1) and of Hezekiah's further attention to spiritual details and provisions (2 Chron 31:2–19), closing with the notice that Hezekiah characteristically lived out his life in utter devotion to God and so was successful in all that he did (2 Chron 31:20–21).

8–12 After the writer of Kings has familiarized his readers with Hezekiah's godly faculties, qualities undergirding him in the many crises of his life, he immediately turns his attention to one of the most critical episodes of Hezekiah's existence and that of the southern kingdom as well. As an example of his godly concern and good success, he points out that Hezekiah rebelled against the king of Assyria. Not only that, but he turned against "the great king's" vassal, Philistia, defeating it from one end to the other. All Hezekiah's deeds, even his military accomplishments, thereby stand in stark contrast to the example of fearful Israel that perished because of unbelief and disobedience.

The time of Hezekiah's rebellion and occupation of Philistia must lie late in his reign, probably near the middle of the last quarter of the eighth century B.C. Hezekiah's early years were doubtless devoted to religion and internal affairs. Indeed Sargon's western expeditions in 717/716 and again in 712, the latter of which was centered in Philistia and involved military action against Egypt and Transjordania, would make any military move by Hezekiah most unlikely until much later. However Sargon's last half-decade (710–705) was occupied with troubles nearer home. Restless Arameans applied constant pressure in southern Mesopotamia; there was also the ever-present menace of Merodach-Baladan (cf. 20:12–13), the perennial king of Bit-Yakin and claimant to the throne of Babylon. Accordingly Hezekiah's growing boldness and military operations must fall within Sargon's last years, probably occurring at his death in 705, the usual occasion for such actions.

Notes

1–2 While the solutions proposed here are beset with difficulties (cf. J.B. Payne, "Chronology," ZPEB, 1:842–44), they are, for the most part, the simplest. See further Stigers, "Chronology," pp. 81–90; Wood, *Survey*, p. 317 n. Certainly those views that would seek to solve the difficulties by deliberately emending the text (for which there is no warrant in the ancient versions or MSS, see Young, *Isaiah*, 1:541–42) or would cast doubt on the infallibility of the MT (e.g., Thiele, "Note on 'Yaw,'" pp. 19–23) must be rejected. For criticism of the views of Wellhausen and Thiele and a further discussion of the whole problem, see Allis, *Old Testament*, pp. 407–16.

4 The worship and bringing of incense associated with the bronze serpent, the ancient symbol of personal deliverance, may well have been connected with the Asherah cultus, such practices being well documented in the Canaanite artifacts. Grammatically the name Nehushtan may indicate a play on words, נְחַשׁ הַנְּחֹשֶׁת (*neḥaš hanneḥōšet*, "the bronze serpent") contemptuously being called by Hezekiah נְחֻשְׁתָּן (*neḥuštān*, "thing of brass"), or it may be understood as the name given by the devotees to the cult object.

8 For discussion of the reign of Sargon, see Hallo, "Qarqar," pp. 176–82.

---

2. *The Assyrian invasion*

18:13–37

> [13]In the fourteenth year of King Hezekiah's reign, Sennacherib king of Assyria attacked all the fortified cities of Judah and captured them. [14]So Hezekiah king of Judah sent this message to the king of Assyria at Lachish: "I have done wrong. Withdraw from me, and I will pay whatever you demand of me." The king of Assyria exacted from Hezekiah king of Judah three hundred talents of silver and thirty talents of gold. [15]So Hezekiah gave him all the silver that was found in the temple of the LORD and in the treasuries of the royal palace.
>
> [16]At this time Hezekiah king of Judah stripped off the gold with which he had covered the doors and doorposts of the temple of the LORD, and gave it to the king of Assyria.
>
> [17]The king of Assyria sent his supreme commander, his chief officer and his field commander with a large army, from Lachish to King Hezekiah at Jerusalem.

They came up to Jerusalem and stopped at the aqueduct of the Upper Pool, on the road to the Washerman's Field. [18]They called for the king; and Eliakim son of Hilkiah the palace administrator, Shebna the secretary, and Joah son of Asaph the recorder went out to them.

[19]The field commander said to them, "Tell Hezekiah:

" 'This is what the great king, the king of Assyria, says: On what are you basing this confidence of yours? [20]You say you have strategy and military strength—but you speak only empty words. On whom are you depending, that you rebel against me? [21]Look now, you are depending on Egypt, that splintered reed of a staff, which pierces a man's hand and wounds him if he leans on it! Such is Pharaoh king of Egypt to all who depend on him. [22]And if you say to me, "We are depending on the LORD our God"—isn't he the one whose high places and altars Hezekiah removed, saying to Judah and Jerusalem, "You must worship before this altar in Jerusalem"?

[23]" 'Come now, make a bargain with my master, the king of Assyria: I will give you two thousand horses—if you can put riders on them! [24]How can you repulse one officer of the least of my master's officials, even though you are depending on Egypt for chariots and horsemen? [25]Furthermore, have I come to attack and destroy this place without word from the LORD? The LORD himself told me to march against this country and destroy it.' "

[26]Then Eliakim son of Hilkiah, and Shebna and Joah said to the field commander, "Please speak to your servants in Aramaic, since we understand it. Don't speak to us in Hebrew in the hearing of the people on the wall."

[27]But the commander replied, "Was it only to your master and you that my master sent me to say these things, and not to the men sitting on the wall—who, like you, will have to eat their own filth and drink their own urine?"

[28]Then the commander stood and called out in Hebrew: "Hear the word of the great king, the king of Assyria! [29]This is what the king says: Do not let Hezekiah deceive you. He cannot deliver you from my hand. [30]Do not let Hezekiah persuade you to trust in the LORD when he says, 'The LORD will surely deliver us; this city will not be given into the hand of the king of Assyria.'

[31]"Do not listen to Hezekiah. This is what the king of Assyria says: Make peace with me and come out to me. Then every one of you will eat from his own vine and fig tree and drink water from his own cistern, [32]until I come and take you to a land like your own, a land of grain and new wine, a land of bread and vineyards, a land of olive trees and honey. Choose life and not death!

"Do not listen to Hezekiah, for he is misleading you when he says, 'The LORD will deliver us.' [33]Has the god of any nation ever delivered his land from the hand of the king of Assyria? [34]Where are the gods of Hamath and Arpad? Where are the gods of Sepharvaim, Hena and Ivvah? Have they rescued Samaria from my hand? [35]Who of all the gods of these countries has been able to save his land from me? How then can the LORD deliver Jerusalem from my hand?"

[36]But the people remained silent and said nothing in reply, because the king had commanded, "Do not answer him."

[37]Then Eliakim son of Hilkiah the palace administrator, Shebna the secretary and Joah son of Asaph the recorder went to Hezekiah, with their clothes torn, and told him what the field commander had said.

13 The date of Sennacherib's campaign must be calculated from the time of Hezekiah's independent rule in 715, a date that harmonizes well with the data from Assyrian sources. Sennacherib (705–681 B.C.) was at first occupied with affairs close to home and so was not free to deal with Hezekiah. His first two campaigns were launched against the nearer menace, the continuing presence of Merodach-Baladan and the pesky Arameans, problems he inherited from his father. But having secured things in the south and east, Sennacherib was free to deal with the west, against which he launched his famous third campaign. His annals (see Luckenbill, *Ancient Records*, pp. 118-21) record the might of his all-out attack. Swooping down from the north, Sennacherib quickly dispatched the Phoenician cities and then unleashed his fury against Philisitia. He notes that the citizens of Ekron had thrown in their lot with the Egyptians and Hezekiah of Judah, even going so far as to deliver their king (and Sennacherib's vassal) into the hands of Hezekiah for confinement. Apparently by-passing Ekron for the moment, Sennacherib marched down the Philistine coast as far as Ashkelon. Having secured the submission of that key city and having deported its king to Assyria, Sennacherib turned his attention inland in a thrust that would not only secure the key city of Judean Lachish but would effectively separate the remaining Philistines and Judeans from Egyptian help.

14-16 Verse 14 joins Sennacherib's campaign at this point. Sennacherib has taken Lachish and is busily engaged in mopping up the nearby fortified cities of Judah. With Phoenicia and most of Philistia laid waste, and with Sennacherib's forces already in the land, Hezekiah sensed the enormity of his impending doom. Overwhelmed by a sense of certain tragedy, he acted out of human propriety and sent a letter of submission to Sennacherib, indicating that he would agree to whatever terms of tribute Sennacherib would demand. In meeting Sennacherib's levy, Hezekiah went beyond the terms, emptying the coffers of both temple and palace and even stripping off the gold from the doors and door posts of the temple (vv.15-16).

17-18 Hezekiah's generosity served only to whet Sennacherib's appetite. Doubtless he reasoned that these could only be a token payment; surely immense stores of wealth must lie hidden within the fortified walls of Jerusalem. Accordingly, as he continued operations in the Lachish area and laid plans for the capture of Ekron, Sennacherib sent a strong contingent under the direction of senior members of his staff to place Jerusalem under siege.

The Assyrian delegation came to the aqueduct of the Upper Pool, on the road to the Washerman's Field (cf. Isa 7:3). There they sent for Hezekiah, who, rather than appearing himself (probably considering it improper protocol to do so), sent three chief officials to deal with the three Assyrian delegates: Eliakim, son of Hilkiah, the palace administrator (cf. Isa 22:20-21), Shebna, the scribe, and Joash, son of Asaph, the king's herald (v.18).

The location of the meeting place of the two delegations has been much discussed. Similarly the precise identification of the various pools mentioned in connection with the Assyrian menace (cf. 20:20; 2 Chron 32:4, 30; Isa 22:9, 11; 36:2) and Hezekiah's plans for the defense of Jerusalem (2 Chron 32:1-8; Isa 22:8-11) have been subjects of much controversy.

The available data seem to point to a northwest Jerusalem location for the meeting place, at a spot where the enemy might easily enjoy a commanding view of the city. Confirmation of this may be forthcoming from Josephus (*War* V, 303 [vii.3]; 504 [xii.2]), who speaks of this area as "the camp of the Assyrians." If so, the Upper Pool of v.17 and the pool of 20:20 (q.v.; cf. 2 Chron 32:30; Isa 8:5-8) are to be differentiated. Certainly Hezekiah would have taken steps to insure the security of both pools, as well as the cutting off of all the water sources available to Sennacherib's army (cf. 2 Chron 32:3-4; Isa 22:9-12). Further evidence for differentiation between the pools of v.17 and 20:20 comes from the scriptural indication that the area was in existence before Hezekiah's siege preparations, being the scene of Isaiah's earlier meeting with Ahaz. What a contrast in circumstances this spot was witness-ing! Here Isaiah had carried the encouraging message of the God of the universe to a godless king; now the emissaries of "the great king" bore a distressing dispatch to the God-fearing Hezekiah.

19–25 The message to Hezekiah was couched in terms of brilliant psychological warfare. Sennacherib's warning is given in two stages: in vv.19–22 he points out that Hezekiah's tactics and trust are ill conceived; in vv.23–25 he suggests that Hezekiah's supposed strengths are really weaknesses.

Thus Sennacherib cautioned Hezekiah that his military preparations and faith in Egypt's power to deliver Jerusalem were doomed to failure. Relying on Pharaoh, as a matter of fact, is like trusting one's weight to a splintered staff! Even Hezekiah's professed confidence in God was ill-taken, since Hezekiah's iconoclastic purge had destroyed many opportunities of additional divine help. Surely the Judean king's insistence on worshiping only one God at one altar in Jerusalem was sheer bigotry!

Beginning with v.23 the Rab Shakeh (field commander) reiterates the folly of Hezekiah's course of action. Did Hezekiah trust in military strength? What real strength did he have? Sennacherib had the resources to put two thousand horses at Jerusalem's disposal, but there would not be enough trained horsemen in Judah to ride them! The implication is that wars are won with the chariotry, the point where Hezekiah was lamentably weak. How, then, could Hezekiah have thought to re-pulse even the least of Sennacherib's officials? Any reliance on puny Egypt for chariots was nonsense. Further, as for Hezekiah's reputation for trusting in the Lord for deliverance, this again was folly; for it was Yahweh himself who had told Sen-nacherib to attack and destroy Judah!

26–27 The answer of Hezekiah's embassy was scarcely one of strength. Fearing the effect of the Assyrian official's words on the populace that lived on the wall, he requested that the Rab Shakeh switch his speech to Aramaic (v.26). The Assyrian's haughty retort was that those on the wall had a stake in all this, as well as Hezekiah (v.27). After all, when the Assyrians really placed the city under heavy siege, the common Jerusalemites would take the brunt of the attack. So great would be the hunger and so scarce the provisions that Jerusalem's citizenry would be reduced to consuming their own bodily issues. They had a right to hear!

28–32 As the Rab Shakeh continued his remarks, he shouted all the louder (v.28). He told the people that Hezekiah was not to be trusted (v.29). Hezekiah could not deliver them from the Assyrians, and Yahweh would not do so (v.30). The Assyrian official lashed out at Hezekiah's previous words of encouragement and categorically denied their truthfulness (cf. 2 Chron 32:7–8). Rather than believing their king, they should align themselves with the rising star of Sennacherib (v.31). They should conclude a peace treaty with "the great king" by surrendering and coming out to him. Then they could enjoy the fine things of their own land in abundance. Further-more the Assyrian king would even take them to a new and better life in another land, which he had especially set aside for them (v.32). Rather than the grim pros-pects that faced them, theirs could be a life of peace and plenty, of life and not death.

The Rab Shakeh's words were carefully chosen and highly emotive. By their acquiesence to the Assyrian king's demands, the Judeans would thereby conclude an agreement with him that would effect blessed conditions for all concerned.

33–35 Having urged the people to reject Hezekiah's promises and choose those of Sennacherib, the Rab Shakeh gave the people incentives for doing so by citing the evidence of Sennacherib's victories. Hezekiah was only misleading them with his talk of deliverance by Yahweh. None of the gods of the many leaders that had opposed Sennacherib had delivered his people (vv.33–35). Could they expect to fare better?

The Assyrian official viewed all gods alike. The proof of their capability was in their power to deliver their people. This they had not done, neither the gods of the Arameans nor those of Jerusalem's sister, Samaria. The implication was clear: Yahweh, like the other gods, had not been able to stop Sennacherib previously, nor could he now.

36–37 The Rab Shakeh's words were not received in the way that he had hoped. Faithful to Hezekiah's instructions, his delegates remained stonily silent. They came back sadly to the king, however, and told him of the enemy's words.

Notes

13 Notice that 18:13, 17–20:17 is very closely reproduced in Isa 36:1–38:8; 39:1–8. The writer of 2 Chron 32:9–19 has restructured and stylized the material of 2 Kings 18:19–38; 19:10–13. Jenkin's suggestion (pp. 284–98) that the details of this section are to be connected with Sargon's suppression of the revolt headed by Ashdod in 714–712 B.C. but later reinterpreted in the light of Sennacherib's campaign of 701 is foundationless.

14 חָטָאתִי (ḥāṭāʾtî, "I have done wrong [lit., 'sinned']") shows Hezekiah's use here of known diplomatic parlance. From an Assyrian point of view, a "sin" against the crown meant any offense that involved the failure to recognize Assyrian sovereignty. Similarly the verbs נָתַן (nātan, "give," "place") and נָשָׂא nāśāʾ, "lift up," "bear") are terms of vassalage, hence the NIV's "pay" and "demand." Note a similar plea by the king of Lydia to Ashurbanipal after a frightful Cimmerian invasion. "Your father cursed my father and so evil came upon him. As for me, I am your slave who fears you. Be gracious unto me and I will pull your yoke" (N.J. Lau and S. Langdon, *The Annals of Ashurbanipal* [Leiden: Brill, 1903], plate 8, lines 124–25). Although Hezekiah might not have intended subservience to Sennacherib, the incident breathes the air of diplomatic negotiations. See D.J. Wiseman, "Is it peace—Covenant and Diplomacy?" VetTest 32 (1982): 316–17.

Hezekiah's tribute is strikingly confirmed by Sennacherib's own account (see Luckenbill, *Ancient Records*, 2:120–21).

17 The nouns involved are not personal names, as implied in the KJV, but known Assyrian military titles. The first term—תַּרְתָּן (tartān "supreme commander")—stands for the Assyrian turtannu ("second in command," i.e., to the king, or "supreme field commander"; cf. Isa 20:1). The second term—רַב־סָרִיס (rab-sārîs, "chief officer"; lit., "chief eunuch")—is the title of a senior military officer, taken by some to be the equivalent of the Assyrian rabû ša rēši ("chief of the head"). In either case the idea is given properly in the NIV (cf. Jer 39:3, 13). The third officer—רַב־שָׁקֵה (rab-šāqēh, "chief aide")—is the Akkadian rab šaqû ("chief cupbearer," "commandant").

For further details as to the problem of the location of this consultation and of the Jerusalemite pools mentioned in connection with Hezekiah, see Gray, *Kings*, pp. 679–82,

703–4; Burrows, pp. 221–27; for a brief discussion of Jerusalem's water supply, see Yagal Shiloh, "The Rediscovery of Warren's Shaft," *Biblical Archaeology Review* 7 (1981): 24–39; id., "The City of David Archaeological Project The Third Season–1980," BA 44 (1981): 161–71; and Hopkins, pp. 45–47. For Hezekiah's siege preparations, see B. Mazar and G. Cornfield, *The Mountain of the Lord* (Garden City: Doubleday, 1975), pp. 175ff. For a consideration of the accurate recording of the Rab Shakeh's speech, see H. Wildberger, "Die Rede des Rabsake vor Jerusalem," *Theologische Zeitschrift* 35 (1979): 35–47.

Although Sennacherib's annals do not mention the conquest of Lachish in connection with his third campaign, an inscription on a relic in the British Museum indicates that Sennacherib did indeed take the city along with much booty. See further J.B. Pritchard, *Archaeology and the Old Testament* (Princeton: University Press, 1958), pp. 19ff.

18 Eliakim and Shebna are mentioned also in Isa 22, where Shebna was yet the royal chamberlain. Isaiah prophesied that he would be replaced by Eliakim. Such apparently had come to pass, but Shebna still held the important post of secretary.

19 "The great king" was the standard designation appropriated by all the neo-Assyrian kings and followed by the neo-Babylonian and Persian monarchs. In time past it was reserved for those kings who had achieved international recognition as heads of "super powers." Thus the Hittite king Ḫattushilish III rebuked the Assyrian king Adad-Nirari I in his bid for the right to bear this title. Although Adad-Nirari had achieved great things, he had not yet become a "great king." For details see the discussion in CAH, 2.2:258f., 278.

21 The figure of Egypt as a splintered reed is appropriate. The Nile River was rich in the reeds that were so important to Egyptian life. In this respect Sennacherib's evaluation of Egypt was in harmony with the prophecies of Isaiah (Isa 20; 30:3–5; 31:1–3). How seldom man learns the lessons of history! Ezekiel was to deliver a similar oracle in the days of neo-Babylonian crisis (Ezek 29:6–7).

23 The verb הִתְעָרֶב (*hiṯʿārebb̲*, "make a bargain") carries the idea of exchanging pledges or entering into a common enterprise with someone. The Rab Shakeh's words are a mere taunt, designed to show that the Hebrews were neither trained nor equipped with the necessary components of "modern warfare."

25 Rab Shakeh's pronouncement was designed to strike terror into the hearts of the Jerusalemites (cf. 2 Chron 32:18). Even God was against them!

26 Aramaic became the diplomatic lingua franca of the Near East in the neo-Assyrian period. That a well-educated member of Sennacherib's staff could speak both Hebrew and Aramaic as well as Akkadian need no longer be doubted. Saggs (*Assyriology*, pp. 17–18) notes that the Assyrians frequently sent a token contingent to effect the surrender of a city, bringing in a full striking force only after a negative reply. Saggs also points out a close parallel between the conduct of the Assyrian officers at Jerusalem with that of certain officers who sent a report to the Assyrian king during the siege of Babylon, in which they, too, addressed their remarks to the native populace, hoping to draw their support over to the Assyrians.

27 For the words "dung" and "urine," the Masoretes euphemistically substituted "their going forth" and "the water of their feet." The written text, however, preserves the Assyrian language of the street, words no doubt chosen to dramatize the horror of the coming siege. The Assyrians were not above the use of crude speech for dramatic effect. Thus Sennacherib reports in his eighth campaign that the terrified enemy charioteers "passed hot urine and left their excrement in their chariots" (personal tr. from the original Assyrian; cf. R. Borger, *Babylonisch-Assyrische Lesestücke* [Rome: Pontificium Institutum Biblicum, 1963], vol. 3, table 50).

31 The phrase עֲשׂוּ־אִתִּי בְרָכָה (*ʿăśû-ʾittî b̲erāk̲āh*, "make peace with me"; lit., "make me a blessing") is difficult. The idea seems to be that in surrendering to Sennacherib, the Judeans would actually be helping him fulfill his God-given task of bringing conditions of blessing throughout the world.

The vine and the fig tree were well-known symbols of God's blessing on his people (cf.

Joel 1:7), and "water from the well" (NIV, "water from his own cistern") signified refreshment and abundance of life.

The Rab Shakeh's (field commander) words also frankly admit that the Jerusalemites would have their lands and possessions taken from them, but the words are skillfully chosen so as to paint a rosy picture of their prospective life in exile. It would be life as they had known it, only better. Yea, blessing would rest on them all.

32 The verb יַסִּית (yassît, "he is misleading")—as opposed to the synonymous פָּתָה (pittāh, "deceive")—carries with it the idea of cunningness. Rab Shakeh almost implied that Hezekiah was deceitful; though he encouraged the people with talk of divine intervention, he really knew better.

37 The torn clothes of Hezekiah's ambassadors was a sign of both grief and shame that God's name had been blasphemed (cf. 19:4).

---

3. The continued siege of Jerusalem

19:1–13

¹When King Hezekiah heard this, he tore his clothes and put on sackcloth and went into the temple of the LORD. ²He sent Eliakim the palace administrator, Shebna the secretary and the leading priests, all wearing sackcloth, to the prophet Isaiah son of Amoz. ³They told him, "This is what Hezekiah says: This day is a day of distress and rebuke and disgrace, as when children come to the point of birth and there is no strength to deliver them. ⁴It may be that the LORD your God will hear all the words of the field commander, whom his master, the king of Assyria, has sent to ridicule the living God, and that he will rebuke him for the words the LORD your God has heard. Therefore pray for the remnant that still survives."

⁵When King Hezekiah's officials came to Isaiah, ⁶Isaiah said to them, "Tell your master, 'This is what the LORD says: Do not be afraid of what you have heard—those words with which the underlings of the king of Assyria have blasphemed me. ⁷Listen! I am going to put such a spirit in him that when he hears a certain report, he will return to his own country, and there I will have him cut down with the sword.' "

⁸When the field commander heard that the king of Assyria had left Lachish, he withdrew and found the king fighting against Libnah.

⁹Now Sennacherib received a report that Tirhakah, the Cushite king of Egypt, was marching out to fight against him. So he again sent messengers to Hezekiah with this word: ¹⁰"Say to Hezekiah king of Judah: Do not let the god you depend on deceive you when he says, 'Jerusalem will not be handed over to the king of Assyria.' ¹¹Surely you have heard what the kings of Assyria have done to all the countries, destroying them completely. And will you be delivered? ¹²Did the gods of the nations that were destroyed by my forefathers deliver them: the gods of Gozan, Haran, Rezeph and the people of Eden who were in Tel Assar? ¹³Where is the king of Hamath, the king of Arpad, the king of the city of Sepharvaim, or of Hena or Ivvah?"

1–2 When Hezekiah heard the report of his delegation, he was filled with grief (v. 1). Tearing his clothes and donning sackcloth (traditional symbols of mourning; cf. Esth 4:1–3; Joel 1:13), he went with heavy heart to the temple to pour out his soul before God. God's very name and reputation were at stake in this time of national crisis! Desiring to do all that was within his power to know God's will, he sent Eliakim, Shebna, and the leading priests, all dressed in sackcloth, to meet with Isaiah so that he might hear God's word through his prophet (v.2; cf. Deut 18:18).

3 In briefing Isaiah as to the present emergency, the king's delegation also explained Hezekiah's deep concern in the matter. It was a day of "distress." The word connotes not only the idea of trouble because of the Assyrian menace, but the anguish of heart that every true Israelite must have felt. Furthermore it was a day of rebuke and correction; Hezekiah sensed that the Lord was even now chastising his people (Hos 5:9–15). As well it was a day of disgrace or contempt; perhaps God was even now about to reject and cast off his people completely (cf. Deut 32:18–43; Jer 14:12; Lam 2:6).

4 It is to Hezekiah's credit that he realized the deeper spiritual issues involved in the crisis. It was not enough to bring the stated services and religious practices up to standard; God must be a living reality in every believer's life. Despite his zeal for holiness, perhaps he had erred in the way he, as king, had led the people in the realm of international politics. Had he perpetuated the policies of Ahaz in depending on his own wisdom and the strength of others in dealing with national affairs rather than depending on God? Far greater than the danger of the Assyrian at the walls was divine displeasure. Hezekiah must have God's mind.

Hezekiah realized that God was the living God in contradistinction to any of the so-called gods that the Rab Shakeh had mentioned. Moreover Hezekiah knew that God was jealous for his own name and would intervene on behalf of a people whose heart was right toward him (cf. Joel 2:12–17). Further he was "your God," that is, Isaiah was his personal spokesman. Hezekiah therefore urged Isaiah to join him in prayer for the remnant of God's people.

5–7 Hezekiah's trust in God and confidence in Isaiah were not misplaced. Isaiah indeed did have a message for the repentant Hezekiah. He was not to fear the blasphemous words of Sennacherib's underlings—nor of Sennacherib himself (v.6). Indeed "the great king," rather than adding Jerusalem to his list of conquests, would himself be given a spirit of fearfulness, so that when distressing news came to him out of Assyria, he would give up the siege and head for home immediately (v.7). Once there he would be killed. God assured Hezekiah that he was in the entire situation, superintending the details in accordance with his purposes.

God did not disclose to Hezekiah how all this would come about. It was enough for him to know and to believe that God would deal with the Assyrian threat. Thus Hezekiah's faith could mature as he continued to pray and wait for God to effect his plan. What a wondrous experience awaits those who trust in God completely!

While the Scriptures do not say so, Hezekiah obviously returned a negative reply to Sennacherib's demands. Accordingly the Rab Shakeh set out to deliver Hezekiah's refusal to his master.

8–9 Learning that Sennacherib had moved on to join his siege forces at Libnah, the Rab Shakeh joined him there with his report (v.8). The reason for Sennacherib's removal follows in v.9: it had been reported to him that the Egyptian army under Tirhakah was even now advancing through the Philistine coast to aid the Philistine city of Ekron. Apparently by-passing Ekron, the Assyrian king was able to bring his forces safely to El Tekeh, where he met and defeated the Egyptian troops. After the victory at El Tekeh, Sennacherib turned back inland to capture Timnah and then Ekron itself (see Luckenbill, *Ancient Records*, 2:120).

While Sennacherib was thus engaged in fighting, he sent a siege contingent to

Jerusalem so that Hezekiah could not attack from the rear. As well he sent the Rab Shakeh back to Jerusalem with a message for Hezekiah designed to continue the psychological warfare.

10–13 Understanding clearly that Hezekiah's previous reply indicated a firm belief that Yahweh would deliver Jerusalem and his people from the Assyrian king, Sennacherib concentrated his message on the absurdity of such a belief (v. 10). Assuredly Hezekiah knew that Assyria had destroyed all those countries that had opposed him, and none of their gods had been able to deliver them (vv. 11–12). To make Hezekiah take even more notice and fear, he added that the kings of those countries had paid the price of oblivion (v. 13). Hezekiah had better take care!

Notes

3 The latter part of the verse evidently contains a well-known proverb that emphasized the need for superior strength to intervene in a time of overwhelming danger (cf. Hos 13:13).
6 The word נַעַר (naʿar, "underling") is usually translated "lad" or "servant." However MacDonald (pp. 147–70) has argued forcefully that in military contexts those designated by this term are young men of good birth who spend their lives in the service of the king. MacDonald prefers the term "squire." If so, the Lord's words need not be taken in so derogatory fashion as is usually assumed but may be a reflection of their social status. These are merely professional soldiers, carrying out the words of the king. There is, however, a greater King here who will deal personally and finally with "the great king" of Assyria. See the note on 20:14.
7 The report Sennacherib was to hear probably does not refer to the news of the destruction of his army (v.35), for Sennacherib himself would be at Jerusalem. Nor could it refer to the report of Tirhakah's advance (v.9), for he responded with force to that. Rather it refers to upsetting news from the Assyrian homeland. Coupled with the God-implanted spirit of fear and the destruction of his army, it would be sufficient to send Sennacherib rushing home.

The closing words need not imply that Sennacherib would die immediately on his return to Assyria, but simply that he would not again come back to Judah and that eventually he would be assassinated (cf. vv.36–37).
9 While reconciliation of the details of Sennacherib's campaign with the data of 2 Kings 18:13 –19:37 remains difficult, it is by no means impossible. Some scholars see in the scriptural passage two parallel accounts of Sennacherib's delegations to Hezekiah: (1) 18:13–19:7 and (2) 19:8–37. They are divided, however, as to whether 19:36–37 belongs to the second or the first account and as to whether 19:8–9a belongs with the second account or forms a bridge between the two. Actually there is no need to see any parallel account in 19:8–37 at all, the latter portion being a continuance of the psychological warfare already initiated. Moreover it chiefly relates details that are not contained in the earlier portion.

Some scholars who maintain the integrity of the MT argue that a harmonization between the scriptural record and Sennacherib's annals can be made only by postulating that after the Battle of El Tekeh (reflected in 18:13–16), Sennacherib returned many years later to fight a second campaign against Jerusalem (18:17–19:37). See, for instance, Crockett, pp. 322-30, and especially the excursus of Bright, *History*, pp. 282–87. The mention of the coming of Tirhakah to do battle with Sennacherib seems to support the idea that this section of the text must refer to a second campaign unmentioned in Sennacherib's annals that took place between the onset of Tirhakah's reign in 690 B.C. and the death of Sennacherib in 681. Further certain studies by Egyptologists purported to show that Tirhakah was a mere nine or ten years old in 701 and hence could not have been at El Tekah.

Unfortunately for the two campaign hypothesis, while Sennacherib mentioned five other subsequent campaigns, there is no mention of any renewed engagement in the west or with Judah. This seems strange if indeed he had fought a subsequent campaign against Jerusalem. Moreover the mention of Tirhakah as being Pharaoh, when at El Tekeh he would not yet have been the king, is a simple example of an author writing after the event and proleptically giving to an individual his eventual title. Kitchen (*Ancient Orient*, pp. 82 –83) demonstrates that Tirhakah's own stele does precisely the same thing: "His Majesty [Tirhakah] was in Nubia, as a goodly youth . . . amidst the goodly youths whom His Majesty King Shebitku had summoned from Nubia." Furthermore recent studies have demonstrated that Tirhakah was at least twenty or twenty-one years old in 701 B.C. and possibly even older than that, hence well able to lead his brother Shebitku's forces. For full details see Kitchen, *Third Intermediate Period*, pp. 154–72, 383–86; and A.F. Rainey, "Taharqa and Syntax," *Tel Aviv* 3 (1976): 38–41.

Still further B. Geiger ("2 Kings XVIII 14–16 and The Annals of Sennacherib," VetTest 21 [1971]: 604–6) has demonstrated that it is impossible to harmonize the details of 18:14 –16 with the account of Sennacherib's third campaign as required by the two campaign theorists. Finally it is questionable that Hezekiah actually lived into the second decade of the seventh century B.C. as necessitated by this thesis.

Actually only one campaign, just as recorded by Sennacherib, is demanded by the biblical account if one accepts the primacy of the scriptural order of events rather than the face-saving boasts of Sennacherib, whose report is laid out geographically and thematically in his annals. See further N. Na'aman, "Sennacherib's 'Letter to God' on His Campaigns to Judah," BASOR 214 (1974): 25–39 (cf. his "Sennacherib's Campaign to Judah and the Date of the LMLK Stamps," VetTest 29 [1979]: 61–86).

---

4. *The delivery of Jerusalem*

19:14–37

¹⁴Hezekiah received the letter from the messengers and read it. Then he went up to the temple of the Lord and spread it out before the Lord. ¹⁵And Hezekiah prayed to the Lord: "O Lord, God of Israel, enthroned between the cherubim, you alone are God over all the kingdoms of the earth. You have made heaven and earth. ¹⁶Give ear, O Lord, and hear; open your eyes, O Lord, and see; listen to the words Sennacherib has sent to insult the living God.

¹⁷"It is true, O Lord, that the Assyrian kings have laid waste these nations and their lands. ¹⁸They have thrown their gods into the fire and destroyed them, for they were not gods but only wood and stone, fashioned by men's hands. ¹⁹Now, O Lord our God, deliver us from his hand, so that all kingdoms on earth may know that you alone, O Lord, are God."

²⁰Then Isaiah son of Amoz sent a message to Hezekiah: "This is what the Lord, the God of Israel, says: I have heard your prayer concerning Sennacherib king of Assyria. ²¹This is the word that the Lord has spoken against him:

" 'The Virgin Daughter of Zion
  despises you and mocks you.
The Daughter of Jerusalem
  tosses her head as you flee.
²²Who is it you have insulted and blasphemed?
  Against whom have you raised your voice
and lifted your eyes in pride?
  Against the Holy One of Israel!
²³By your messengers
  you have heaped insults on the Lord.

And you have said,
    "With my many chariots
I have ascended the heights of the mountains,
    the utmost heights of Lebanon.
I have cut down its tallest cedars,
    the choicest of its pines.
I have reached its remotest parts,
    the finest of its forests.
24 I have dug wells in foreign lands
    and drunk the water there.
With the soles of my feet
    I have dried up all the streams of Egypt."

25 " 'Have you not heard?
    Long ago I ordained it.
In days of old I planned it;
    now I have brought it to pass,
that you have turned fortified cities
    into piles of stone.
26 Their people, drained of power,
    are dismayed and put to shame.
They are like plants in the field,
    like tender green shoots,
like grass sprouting on the roof,
    scorched before it grows up.

27 " 'But I know where you stay
    and when you come and go
    and how you rage against me.
28 Because you rage against me
    and your insolence has reached my ears,
I will put my hook in your nose
    and my bit in your mouth,
and I will make you return
    by the way you came.'

29 "This will be the sign for you, O Hezekiah:

    "This year you will eat what grows by itself,
        and the second year what springs from that.
    But in the third year sow and reap,
        plant vineyards and eat their fruit.
30 Once more a remnant of the house of Judah
    will take root below and bear fruit above.
31 For out of Jerusalem will come a remnant,
    and out of Mount Zion a band of survivors.

The zeal of the LORD Almighty will accomplish this.

32 "Therefore this is what the LORD says concerning the king of Assyria:

    "He will not enter this city
        or shoot an arrow here.
    He will not come before it with shield
        or build a siege ramp against it.
33 By the way that he came he will return;
    he will not enter this city,

                            declares the LORD.
34 I will defend this city and save it,
    for my sake and for the sake of David my servant."

35 That night the angel of the LORD went out and put to death a hundred and eighty-five thousand men in the Assyrian camp. When the people got up the next

morning—there were all the dead bodies! [36]So Sennacherib king of Assyria broke camp and withdrew. He returned to Nineveh and stayed there.

[37]One day, while he was worshiping in the temple of his god Nisroch, his sons Adrammelech and Sharezer cut him down with the sword, and they escaped to the land of Ararat. And Esarhaddon his son succeeded him as king.

14–15 Sennacherib's letter was duly delivered and reached Hezekiah's hands. When he had read it, he took it along with him to the temple and spread it out before the Lord (v.14; cf. 2 Chron 32:17). Hezekiah's action was one of simple faith that God still planned to intervene even as he had promised. As a child bringing his broken toy to his father for repair, so Hezekiah laid the issues in God's sight for resolution. Hezekiah then poured out his soul's concern to his heavenly Father. He addressed God as the personal God of Israel who was his possession and the one who in infinite mercy meets with his people from his dwelling place between the cherubim above the ark of the covenant (v.15). While he is Israel's God, he is also the only true God who sovereignly controls the destinies of all nations. He is nothing less than the Creator—and Consummator—of all things.

16 Hezekiah next pleaded with God to take notice of the way Sennacherib had blasphemed him. The figures are full of intensity. A person who wishes to hear more distinctly turns one ear toward the source of the sound (cf. Ps 45:10). Those who desire to see more clearly must open both eyes (cf. Zech 12:4). The prayer, like that of Daniel (Dan 9:17–19), is concerned most of all about the reputation of the living God.

17–18 Yet Hezekiah understood not only the truth but also the limits of Sennacherib's remarks. To be sure the Assyrian king had laid waste the aforementioned nations together with their lands (v.7). Certainly he had destroyed the powerless gods of those nations (v.18). But they were mere idols—not gods at all! None of that proved anything, for Sennacherib now stood in the presence of the only true God.

19 Having assured God that he understood the issues at hand, Hezekiah closed his prayer with a plea for God's deliverance of Israel so that all people might know that Yahweh alone is God. The true believer is concerned in every situation that the character and reputation of God not be brought into disrepute; rather he longs that God be glorified for who he is as well as for what he has done.

20 The Lord's answer was not long in coming. Isaiah sent a message from God to Hezekiah, assuring him that his prayer had been heard. The major portion of that message is composed within a threefold poetic utterance: (1) for Sennacherib there is a reply to his misguided boasting (vv.21–28); (2) for Hezekiah God gives a sign that he would deal with Sennacherib and deliver his people (vv.29–31); and (3) for all there is a prophetic declaration that Sennacherib would not even begin the battle of Jerusalem let alone conquer it (vv.32–34).

21 The first of the utterances is given in the ancient taunt-song form, designed so as to humiliate Sennacherib by casting his own words in his teeth, thus showing him how ridiculous they sounded. Did Sennacherib despise and degrade all nations and their worship? Jerusalem, in turn, would disdain him, tossing her head at him (cf.

Job 16:4; Pss 22:7; 109:25; Jer 18:16) as he fled in cowardice. The term "virgin" emphasizes that Jerusalem would not be violated by Sennacherib. By the use of a rhetorical question, God points out that Sennacherib had not wisely considered his course of action. His pride and arrogance had caused him to insult the Holy One of Israel. God's own holiness had been manifested clearly through his chosen people Israel (Ps 89:18), however much they may have failed him or poorly represented him (cf. Ps 78:41). What Sennacherib needed to understand was that a holy God would not countenance sin, whether in his own people (cf. Isa 1:4–31) or in those nations whose destinies he controls (Jer 50:29).

22–24 God next dealt with Sennacherib's many boasts, in which he took such pride and on the basis of which he considered himself above man or God. Sennacherib had many chariots in which he had personally scaled rugged and previously inaccessible mountain passes. He had felled the finest timbers of Lebanon (v.23). On the one hand, he had dug wells in foreign soil; on the other, he had dried up the streams of Egypt (v.24).

The language here is highly figurative, the point being that in Sennacherib's mind no obstacle of man or nature was sufficient to withstand him. The words repeat Sennacherib's inner musings, ideas known only to himself, or so he thought. But God knows the innermost intents of all men (Ps 44:21), and his word penetrates man's deepest being (Heb 4:12). The revelation of these hidden desires ought to have struck terror into Sennacherib's heart, convincing him that Yahweh was truly God (cf. Dan 2:47).

On his second campaign Sennacherib had scaled hitherto inaccessible mountain passes and would do so again in his subsequent campaign. The other deeds had been accomplished only in his own mind. Like the greatest of Mesopotamian kings, he would penetrate Lebanon to secure its cedar. He saw himself drinking water from the wells he would dig in arid places. Contrariwise Egypt's delta would be dried up by the soles of his feet.

25–26 God then confronted Sennacherib with that which he had apparently not considered: Sennacherib's successes were foreordained by God (v.25). Moreover God's purposes had not been done in secret; he had proclaimed them through his prophets of all ages and even then was bringing them to pass. The result had been that Sennacherib had been able to wreak havoc on people who were totally powerless and as helpless as tender herbage and plants before the blasts of the Sirocco (v.26). No, Sennacherib should not boast as though what he had done was either self-generated or self-accomplished. It was God's divine government that was at work; Sennacherib was but God's instrument of correction for Israel and the nations.

27–28 Having revealed to Sennacherib that he knew his innermost thoughts and desires and that in his sovereign administration of the flow of history he had ordained Sennacherib's past successes, God then informed Sennacherib that he was aware of his every action, including his blasphemous insolence. Sennacherib had enjoyed God-given success; now he would learn of defeat. He would be subdued like an animal and returned to his own land.

29–31 God next turned to Hezekiah with a reassuring sign (v.29). God had similarly offered Hezekiah's father, Ahaz, a sign (Isa 7:11), which, when refused, was given to the people. The sign would be one of extreme importance to besieged Jerusalem. In what remained of the present year, there would be food enough from that which had been spilled accidentally in the sowing and had sprung up by itself as an after-growth. Since military campaigns were regularly planned to coincide with the harvest so that the armies might live off the land, and since Israel's year began in early fall, there would be little left of "this year." Accordingly as the new year dawned, due to the extent of the devastation, they would again largely depend on grain that came up of its own accord in random fashion.

For the third year, however, there was a direct divine command: "Sow and reap, plant vineyards and eat fruit." Here was direct assurance that the people might resume normal agriculture activities with full expectation of eating the fruits of their labor. When in the harvest of the third year the people ate in abundance, they would know assuredly that God had been in the entire crisis. He had allowed the Assyrians to chastise his people for their own good. But because of Judah's godly leadership, he had delivered them, as a testimony both to the godless Sennacherib and to his spiritually slack nation. From this they should learn their lesson that God was dealing with a backsliding people. The experience should serve as a further sign of that future remnant that the Messiah will deliver at his coming (vv.30–31; cf. Joel 3:9–17; Zech 12:3–9; 14:1–15).

32–34 God closed his utterance with a final message to the Assyrian king. Sennacherib would not only not enter Jerusalem but would not even lay a full scale siege against it (v.32). No arrow would fall into the city; neither shield nor siege ramp would appear before it. Quite the contrary, Sennacherib would turn around and go home (v.33); for God himself was defending and would deliver Jerusalem, not only for his own name's sake (vv.4, 19), but on the basis of his standing promise to David (v.34; cf. 2 Sam 7; 1 Kings 11:13, 34–39; 2 Kings 8:19).

That Sennacherib failed in his attempt to take Jerusalem is apparent from the annals of his third campaign. Although he claimed the capture and despoiling of some forty-six Judean cities, when it came to Jerusalem, he could only report: "Himself [Hezekiah] I made a prisoner in Jerusalem, his royal residence, like a bird in a cage" (ANET, p. 288). The only validity to Sennacherib's face-saving words can be seen when he surrounded Jerusalem during his protracted campaigning in Judah and Philistia.

35–36 That very night the prophetic utterance was fulfilled. As the Assyrian army slept, the angel of the Lord slew 185,000 of the soldiers (v.35). When Sennacherib and those who survived arose the next morning, they were greeted by a veritable graveyard. All around them lay bodies, dead bodies! Having already just received alarming news from home (cf. v.7) and with his army now decisively depleted, Sennacherib broke camp and returned to Nineveh (v.36). Though he would yet fight another five campaigns, he would never again return to Judah. The Israelite's God was the living God!

37 Some twenty years later (681 B.C.), two of Sennacherib's own sons assassinated him and successfully escaped to Urartu. Another son, Esarhaddon (681–686), succeeded Sennacherib as king. The last vestige of the divine prophecy stood complete. While God's program may seem to tarry (cf. 2 Peter 3:4–9), it will be accomplished. The mills of God grind slowly but exceedingly fine.

Notes

21 For the use of the taunt song in the ancient Near East, see P.C. Craigie, "The Song of Deborah and the Epic of Tukultininurta," JBL 88 (1969): 161f.

The term (בַּת) בְּתוּלַת (*bᵉtûlat [bat]*, "virgin [daughter of]") is a stereotyped phrase with civil or national emphasis; for example: virgin (daughter) of Sidon (Isa 23:12), Zion (Isa 37:22; Lam 2:13), Babylon (Isa 47:1), Egypt (Jer 46:11), Judah (Lam 1:15), Israel (Jer 18:13; 31:21; Amos 5:2), my people (Jer 14:17). This emphasis may be one feature in Isaiah's selection of a different Hebrew word for "virgin" in Isa 7:14.

23 For Sennacherib's mountain campaign, see Luckenbill, *Ancient Records*, 2:161f. The penetration of Lebanon's forest is a frequent boast of the Mesopotamian kings from Gilgamesh onward; see A. Heidel, *The Gilgamesh Epic and Old Testament Parallels* (Chicago: University Press, 1963), pp. 6–7.

24 The digging of wells was common in the ancient Near East and extremely important (e.g., Gen 26:18–22). Sennacherib often reported his concern with water, especially in association with the traditional Mesopotamian royal duty of the digging of canals (e.g., Luckenbill, *Ancient Records*, 2:149f.). Although Sennacherib's traversing of formidable streams is frequently reported (ibid., pp. 123, 144), he did not reach the Nile River in Egypt.

יְאֹרֵי מָצוֹר (*yᵉʾōrē̆ māṣôr*, "streams of Egypt") is literally "the rivers of besieged/fortified places" (cf. KJV). The noun *māṣôr* is commonly used in martial contexts. Note that the besiegers' diversion of water supplies of protected cities was a common battle tactic; see Cyrus's actions at Babylon as recorded by Herodotus (*Persian Wars* 1.190–91). In some places (e.g., Isa 19:6; 37:25; Ezek 27:7; Mic 7:12), however, it has been taken as an alternate spelling for Egypt (cf. Akkad. *muṣur/muṣri* ["Egypt"]; see Luckenbill, *Ancient Records*, 2:298). The NIV reflects this idea here. However such is by no means certain. Of the four contexts mentioned, Ezek 27:7 rests purely on a conjectural emendation. Micah 7:12 can be understood as "fortified cities" (cf. KJV), though the text at this point is difficult and some wordplay seems clearly demanded. Moreover the parallel with "Assyria" seems to call for a place name, hence Egypt (though "Tyre" could conceivably be read). In Isa 19:6 there is no warrant for reading "streams of Egypt" since the usual spelling for Egypt occurs throughout the context, unless it be that the combination with יְאֹר (*yᵉʾōr*, "river"), as here and in Isa 37:25, has become a stereotyped phrase meaning "streams of Egypt."

The Assyrian plans of conquest included Egypt, since it was to her that the western nations looked for support. However the goal was not to be reached until the days of Esarhaddon (671 B.C.) and Ashurbanipal (667, 663). Interestingly the flood waters of the Nile did serve as a veritable fortress for the late Egyptian Pharaoh Nectanebo I (378–361 B.C.) in his defense against the invading Persians in 373 B.C.

Others have suggested a still different solution to the problem, namely, that there was a land called by the Assyrians *muṣur/muṣri*, assumedly located north of the Taurus Mountains in Asia Minor (see Luckenbill, *Ancient Records*, 1:223; cf. Gray, *Kings*, pp. 268–69). Accordingly some have suggested that the normal spelling for Egypt—מִצְרַיִם (*miṣrayim*)—can at times be confused with *muṣri*. Proposed examples include 1 Kings 10:28–29 and 2 Kings 7:6, but neither case is at all certain. On the problem of *muṣur/muṣri*, see H. Tadmor, "Que and Muṣri," IEJ 11 (1961): 423–32.

Recently Hayim Tawil, "The Historicity of 2 Kings 19:24 (= Isa 37:25): The Problem of *Yeʾōrê Māsor*," JNES 41 (1982): 195–206, has conjectured that the much-debated term refers to the streams of (Mount) Muṣri (modern Jebel Bashiqah) whose headwaters were utilized by Sennacherib to bring water to Nineveh in 702 and 609 B.C. (Tawil argues for the latter date.) While he makes an admirable case for such an identification here, his proposal to read *muṣri* twice in Mic 7:12 struggles a great deal more and fails completely in Isa 19:6.

The whole matter is far from settled; the contrast with the parallel member suggests something like "savage/overflowing [from the root *sārar*] rivers," an image that suits Isa 19:6 admirably as well. The play on the twice-occurring *māṣôr* of Mic 7:12, while presently obscure, may yield something like "in that day people will come to you from Assyria with its *fortified* cities, yea from [its] territory [borders, as in Akkad. *miṣru*] as far as the Euphrates."

25 Sennacherib often boasted of his thorough devastation of enemy cities; see Luckenbill, *Ancient Records*, 2:117.

26 For the scriptural representation of mankind as grass, see Pss 37:2; 90:5–6; 103:15–16; Isa 40:6–8; 1 Peter 1:24. The image of the Sirocco, suggested here, is made explicit in the Dead Sea Isaiah Scroll, which reads in Isa 37:27: "scorched before the east wind."

27 The phrase "going out and coming in" is used in the OT of the totality of man's activity (e.g., Deut 28:6; Ps 121:8).

28 The figures of the hook in the nose and the bit in the mouth are used in the OT of restraining animals (e.g., Ps 32:9; Ezek 19:4). Used in reference to Sennacherib's activities, the figures are doubly fitting. Not only did he need to be restrained like a wild animal (cf. Isa 30:28), but the Assyrians frequently thus treated their captured prisoners (see Luckenbill, *Ancient Records*, 2:314–15, 319). The Assyrian drawings often depict the leading of bound prisoners of war (cf. Pritchard, *Pictures*, vol. 1, fig. 121).

29 In the regulations for the sabbatical year (Lev 25:5, 11), סָפִיחַ (*sāpîaḥ*, "what grows by itself"; e.g., grain that grows from seed that was spilled unintentionally in the sowing) designated grain left untouched by plowing that grew up of its own accord. Hence some have suggested that 701 B.C. was a sabbatical year, and the next year would be a fiftieth or jubilee year in which no sowing could take place (Lev 25:11–12). Unfortunately this cannot be proven conclusively. If such were the case, however, then the events of the whole crisis could be viewed as divinely timed so as to coincide with the Levitical stipulations in order that Judah would be forced doubly to place her full trust in God alone.

סָחִישׁ (*sāḥîš*, "random growth") is probably a by-form of שָׂחִיס (*šāḥîs*, "random growth"). The possibility of the divine superintendence even as to the timing of these events to concur with the sabbatical year and the year of jubilee, followed by a third year of newness of life's activities, gains force if it can be shown to be related to the use of the numeral three in specialized contexts. The motif of the third day/year (etc.) can be employed (1) to emphasize decisiveness of action or the resolution of problems (Gen 34:25; 40:18–20; 42:18; 1 Sam 20:12; 1 Kings 12:12; Esth 5:1); (2) to set aside a day of specialized activity (Exod 19:1, 15; Num 19:12, 19; 31:19; 2 Kings 20:5, 8); (3) to do spiritual service for God (Ezra 6:15); and (4) to observe spiritual sacrifice and communion in newness of walk with God (Lev 7:17; Luke 13:32; 24:5b–7, 21, 44–49; Acts 10:40; 1 Cor 15:4).

31 For the remnant see the note on Joel 2:32.

32 A parallel to Sennacherib's boast can be found in the well-known Apology of the Hittite king Ḫattusilis III, who reports that the goddess Ishtar shut up his nephew and rival Urhitesupas in the city of Samuhas "like a pig in a sty" (E.H. Sturtevant and G. Bechtel, *A Hittite Chrestomathy* [Philadelphia: Linguistic Society of America, 1935], p. 81).

34 The previous satanic attempt to unseat illegally the house of David in the days of Hezekiah's father, Ahaz, had been overruled by God (Isa 7:1–16). Sennacherib's efforts to unseat the godly Hezekiah would fare no better. When it would be time for a sinful Jerusalem to fall, it would be at the divine direction (2 Chron 36:14–17); and even then the house of David would be sovereignly sustained until the coming of the Messiah (Isa 7:1–9:7; Matt 1; Luke 1:26–37, 67–69; 2:4–11).

35 For the destroying angel of the Lord, see Exod 12:12–13, 23; 2 Sam 24:15–16; for the angelic destruction of armies, see Rev 9:13–18; for the divine deliverance of Israel, see Isa 26:20–21; Joel 3:16–17; Zech 12:6–9; 13:8–9.

Herodotus (*Persian Wars* 2.141) preserves an Egyptian tradition that in answer to the prayers of Sethos, the god Vulcan delivered the Egyptians from Sennacherib at Pelusium by sending field mice through the Assyrian camp to eat up the Assyrians' quivers and bow strings and the leather straps on their shields. Weaponless the major portion of the Assyrian army barely escaped with its life.

37 Nisroch is an intentional scribal corruption, probably of Marduk. For Adrammelech see the note on 17:31. Sharezer is a hypocoristic form (cf. Belshazzar [Dan 5:1] and Daniel's "Babylonian" name Belteshazzar [Dan 1:7]).

---

5. Hezekiah's miraculous recovery

20:1-11

¹In those days Hezekiah became ill and was at the point of death. The prophet Isaiah son of Amoz went to him and said, "This is what the LORD says: Put your house in order, because you are going to die; you will not recover."

²Hezekiah turned his face to the wall and prayed to the LORD, ³"Remember, O LORD, how I have walked before you faithfully and with wholehearted devotion and have done what is good in your eyes." And Hezekiah wept bitterly.

⁴Before Isaiah had left the middle court, the word of the LORD came to him: ⁵"Go back and tell Hezekiah, the leader of my people, 'This is what the LORD, the God of your father David, says: I have heard your prayer and seen your tears; I will heal you. On the third day from now you will go up to the temple of the LORD. ⁶I will add fifteen years to your life. And I will deliver you and this city from the hand of the king of Assyria. I will defend this city for my sake and for the sake of my servant David.'"

⁷Then Isaiah said, "Prepare a poultice of figs." They did so and applied it to the boil, and he recovered.

⁸Hezekiah had asked Isaiah, "What will be the sign that the LORD will heal me and that I will go up to the temple of the LORD on the third day from now?"

⁹Isaiah answered, "This is the LORD's sign to you that the LORD will do what he has promised: Shall the shadow go forward ten steps, or shall it go back ten steps?"

¹⁰"It is a simple matter for the shadow to go forward ten steps," said Hezekiah. "Rather, have it go back ten steps."

¹¹Then the prophet Isaiah called upon the LORD, and the LORD made the shadow go back the ten steps it had gone down on the stairway of Ahaz.

1 Taken at face value, the opening phrase—"in those days" (v.1)—seems to place the events of this chapter near the time of Sennacherib's invasion in 701 B.C. Several problems stand in the way, however, of so simple a solution.

1. Because Hezekiah was granted fifteen additional years of life, this would take his years beyond the accession date of his son Manasseh in 698. While a coregency is possible, and there is the option that Hezekiah gave the crown to Manasseh, neither alternative commends itself, especially in the light of Manasseh's demonstrated wickedness (cf. ch. 21). It is possible, of course, that Manasseh's ungodly character only surfaced after his father's death, much as Nero was at his worst only after the death of Seneca his teacher.

2. Hezekiah's sickness must be coordinated with Merodach-Baladan's embassy. Merodach-Baladan enjoyed two periods of rule in Babylon that coincide with Hezekiah's reign: 721–710 B.C., a period ending when Sargon drove him back to his tribal position in Bit Yakin, and a short period in 703, when Merodach-Baladan succeeded in retaking the throne of Babylon from the popular favorite Marduk Zakir

Shumi. This short-lived latter rule was terminated when Sennacherib invaded Babylon, sending the wily Merodach-Baladan scurrying for safety once more.

The shortness of Merodach-Baladan's later rule tends to favor a date in his earlier reign for the events of chapter 20. If Hezekiah died around 698 B.C., then the illness of Hezekiah would be placed at 713/712, with Merodach-Baladan's embassy arriving shortly afterward. Because Merodach-Baladan had lived at peace with Sargon since 721, the news of the renewed Babylon intrigue could have given occasion for Sargon's attack against him in 710. These data may also tie in with Sargon's campaign against the Egyptian and Philistine alliance, leading to the battle for Ashdod in 712, and may indicate something of the general nature of the anti-Assyrian international intrigues. Sargon mentioned that Judah had been invited by the allies to join them in the rebellion.

3. The remembrance of Hezekiah's wealth, strength, and friendship may have been a contributing factor to the timing of Merodach-Baladan's later rebellion after the death of Sargon.

In the light of chronological difficulties, it therefore seems best to take the phrase "in those days" to be a general statement referring to some time in the reign of Hezekiah. If so, the events of chapter 20 (cf. Isa 38–39) probably belong chronologically before those of 18:7b–19:37), these latter verses being recorded beforehand simply as the example *par excellence* of Hezekiah's trust in God (cf. 18:7a). If Young (*Isaiah*, 2:457f., 507, 556–65) is correct, that Isaiah's prophecy in chapters 36–39 forms the basis for the text in Kings, and that the events of Isaiah 36–37 (cf. 2 Kings 18:7b–19:37), though occurring later, are given first to round off his discussion dealing with the Assyrian period of his ministry before moving on to the Babylonian period (Isa 40–66, introduced by chs. 38–39), then the author of Kings may be following the thematic order of Isaiah. If so, there is a double reason for the present order in Kings, neither of which is caused by chronological considerations.

In those critical days, then, when Sargon was moving toward Ashdod to deal with the western rebels (among whom Hezekiah himself had been somewhat implicated), Isaiah delivered God's message to a sick Hezekiah. It was time for Hezekiah to put his house in order; for as things stood, he would surely die. Hezekiah needed to be certain that not only were the affairs of state in order, but that he and his house were on proper terms with God.

2–3 Hezekiah was a man of faith. Turning his face to the wall, thereby both dismissing Isaiah and entering into solitary communion with God, Hezekiah poured out his heart to his Lord. Hezekiah reminded God of his faithfulness, both in his personal conduct and in his righteous deeds, and of his wholehearted devotion to God. Hezekiah then wept bitterly. God knew the yearning of his heart that he did not express. In accordance with God's own promises, Hezekiah had a right to expect a longer life than that which appeared to be forthcoming (cf. Exod 20:12; Deut 5:29; 30:16). So much was true. But Hezekiah's concerns were deeper than any personal desire for added years. This is clear from the Lord's answer to Hezekiah's prayer (vv.5–6). What would become of that nation? His reforms were barely yet in progress. What would become of Judah? There was so much more to be done. Deeper still, he would die without a male heir, for no son had yet been born to him. What, then, would become of the house of David? The program and person of God were at stake, and Hezekiah believed that somehow he was vitally involved in them. How could it end like this?

4–6 Isaiah had not yet cleared the palace when God sent him back with a message for Hezekiah (v.4): the Lord God of his father David had heard Hezekiah's righteous prayer and justifiable concern and had seen his tears (v.5). Therefore God would heal him and give him fifteen additional years of service (v.6). Moreover, for his own name's sake and because of the promise made to David, God would deliver Jerusalem throughout Hezekiah's lifetime. The mention of Hezekiah's going into the temple on the third day is both a recognition of his godly habit of life and a reminder of his obligations to render thanks to the Lord for his healing.

7 Not only did Isaiah have spiritual news and instructions for Hezekiah, he also had directions for the king's physical recovery. In accordance with those orders, a poultice of figs was mixed and applied to Hezekiah's ulcerated sore, and he recovered. Although God chose to work through the accepted medical standards of the day, it is certain that ultimately the healing was effected by the divine word.

8–11 Hezekiah asked for a confirmatory sign that all that Isaiah had said was true (v.8). How different his attitude from that of Ahaz who refused any divine sign (Isa 7:12)! Isaiah asked Hezekiah whether the sun's shadow should go forward or return ten places (v.9). Hezekiah reasoned that going backward would be the greater sign, since that would contradict the natural processes (v.10). In accordance with Hezekiah's choice, Isaiah prayed to the Lord, and so it came to pass (v.11).

By whatever means the deed was accomplished, it was a miracle effected by the sovereign power of God alone and intended to be a sign to Hezekiah that he would recover and serve his Redeemer yet another fifteen years. What a comfort this knowledge ought to have been to Hezekiah throughout his remaining years! Yet the author of Chronicles records that Hezekiah did not fully respond to God's kindness toward him. Rather he became proud so that God's wrath came on him and his people, a judgment that was averted only when Hezekiah humbled himself and repented (2 Chron 32:25–26). This would appear to refer to the subsequent crisis brought on by his rashness as detailed in 2 Kings 18–19.

Notes

1 For data relative to the earlier date for Hezekiah's illness and Merodach-Baladan's embassy, see J.B. Payne, "Chronology," ZPEB, 1:843–44; Young, *Isaiah*, pp. 212–13.

For a discussion favoring the 703 B.C. date, see Bright, *History*, p. 267; and Saggs, *Greatness*, pp. 118f.

Still a third position is favored by Thiele (*Mysterious Numbers*, p. 159; cf., p. 465), who holds that Hezekiah's sickness and Merodach-Baladan's embassy came after the Battle of El Tekeh and subsequent to the withdrawal of Sennacherib in 701 B.C. According to this theory Merodach-Baladan, who was reduced to fighting guerrilla warfare in his exiled status, hoped to find in Hezekiah a new ally for a renewed bid for a wide-ranging anti-Assyrian coalition (cf. Jos. *Antiq*. X, 10 [ii.1]). In addition to the grave chronological problems his theory encounters, it must also face the problem of how Hezekiah could have shown Merodach-Baladan's embassy much in the way of treasury (cf. vv.13, 15) when he had previously stripped away everything to give tribute to Sennacherib (18:14–16). Moreover since Sennacherib hunted Merodach-Baladan unmercifully after 703 B.C., it is doubtful that he was in much of a position to send an embassy to Hezekiah.

3–5 J.C. Whitcomb, Jr. (*Solomon to the Exile* [Grand Rapids: Baker, 1971], pp. 125ff.) suggests on the basis of 2 Chron 32:25–26 that God intended to punish Hezekiah's pride. But Hezekiah's pride is better connected with his actions in the reception of Merodach-Baladan's envoys (cf. vv.12–18), the Chronicler's observations forming part of his final evaluation concerning Hezekiah's eventual character.

Nor did God punish Hezekiah by giving him the full measure of his "wrongful prayer" as some have suggested. Indeed selfish, misdirected prayer (James 4:3) and petitions that are contrary to God's will are not granted (cf. Deut 3:23–26; 2 Cor 12:8 with 2 Chron 7:14; John 15:7).

Hezekiah plainly attested that his devotion was unfeigned, being לֵבָב שָׁלֵם (*lēbāb šālēm*, "wholehearted"), a claim vindicated on his recovery, when he praised God in humble gratitude (Isa 38:9–20).

Hezekiah's concern stands in contrast to the sentiment found in the inscription of the Eshmunʿazar Sarcophagus: "I have been snatched away before my time, the son of a number of restricted days." For the translation see ANET, p. 662; for commentary see H. Donner and W. Röllig, *Kanaanäische und Aramäische Inschriften* (Wiesbaden: Harrassowitz, 1964), 2:21. Interesting parallels occur (1) in the inscription of Agbar the priest and (2) in the Apology of Ḥattusilis: (1) "Because of my righteousness before him, he gave me a good name and prolonged my days" (ANET, p. 661); (2) "For Ḥattusilis, the years (are) short. . . . Now give him to me and let him be my priest. Then he (shall be) alive" (Sturtevant and Bechtel, *Hittite Chrestomathy*, p. 66).

The pledge of divine protection and deliverance was to be effective, not only in the Sargonid era, but into the great crisis of Sennacherib's day as well.

7 The use of figs to draw an ulcerated sore is ancient, attested as early as the Ras Shamra Tablets. Pliny (*Natural History* 22.7) mentions such a remedy. See Keil, pp. 462–63.

9 מַעֲלוֹת (*maʿᵃlôt*, "steps") has been variously understood. Some have suggested by the term "steps of Ahaz" is meant both a sundial and the degrees of shadow registered on it (so Targ., Jerome, Symm.; cf. KJV; Keil, p. 464). Current scholarship tends to take the phrase literally of a flight of stairs by which time was told in accordance with the sun's shadow cast on it, apparently by some physical object. Young (*Isaiah*, 2:515) has perhaps the best suggestion:

> It is thought that the device consisted of two sets of steps each facing a wall whose shadow fell upon the steps. As the sun rose, the eastern steps would be in the wall's shadow, which as the day advanced, would grow shorter. On the other hand, during the afternoon, the steps facing west would more and more be in the shadow. According to IQ, the steps were of the עֲלִיּוֹת (upper chamber) of Ahaz. Possibly it was midday when Isaiah spoke. The shadow had just descended the eastern steps and now was ready to ascend the western steps. Instead, however, the shadow again ascended the eastern steps ("Behold, I am causing to return [i.e., to ascend] the shadow of the steps which had gone down [during the morning] on the steps of Ahaz, namely, the sun, etc.").

The miracle itself has been much debated. Certainly there is no need to postulate any reversal of the earth's rotation or receding of the sun. The fact that the miracle was felt only "in the land" (i.e., Judah; cf. 2 Chron 32:31) makes such solutions most dubious. Similarly reports of a supposed lost astronomical day rest on specious grounds. Rather a simple localized refraction of the sun's rays would be sufficient to account for the phenomenon. Keil (p. 465) reports that such a case was noted in A.D. 1703. Whitcomb (*Solomon*, pp. 127–29) is probably right in terming it a "geographically localized miracle."

6. Hezekiah and Merodach-Baladan

20:12-21

¹²At that time Merodach-Baladan son of Baladan king of Babylon sent Hezekiah letters and a gift, because he had heard of Hezekiah's illness. ¹³Hezekiah received the messengers and showed them all that was in his storehouses—the silver, the gold, the spices and the fine oil—his armory and everything found among his treasures. There was nothing in his palace or in all his kingdom that Hezekiah did not show them.

¹⁴Then Isaiah the prophet went to King Hezekiah and asked, "What did those men say, and where did they come from?"

"From a distant land," Hezekiah replied. "They came from Babylon."

¹⁵The prophet asked, "What did they see in your palace?"

"They saw everything in my palace," Hezekiah said. "There is nothing among my treasures that I did not show them."

¹⁶Then Isaiah said to Hezekiah, "Hear the word of the LORD: ¹⁷The time will surely come when everything in your palace, and all that your fathers have stored up until this day, will be carried off to Babylon. Nothing will be left, says the LORD. ¹⁸And some of your descendants, your own flesh and blood, that will be born to you, will be taken away, and they will become eunuchs in the palace of the king of Babylon."

¹⁹"The word of the LORD you have spoken is good," Hezekiah replied. For he thought, "Will there not be peace and security in my lifetime?"

²⁰As for the other events of Hezekiah's reign, all his achievements and how he made the pool and the tunnel by which he brought water into the city, are they not written in the book of the annals of the kings of Judah? ²¹Hezekiah rested with his fathers. And Manasseh his son succeeded him as king.

12 During his newly acquired years, God soon allowed Hezekiah's intentions to be put to the test (cf. 2 Chron 32:31). The Babylonian king, Merodach-Baladan, hearing of Hezekiah's miraculous recovery together with the supernatural sign, sent an embassy to Hezekiah, ostensibly to deliver a message of congratulations and a gift to him. The checkered career of Merodach-Baladan, however, makes it clear that his motives were politically engendered, hoping to find in Hezekiah a new ally in his struggles against Assyria.

13 Hezekiah received the messengers warmly. Doubtless he told them the whole story of his healing and the remarkable incident of the retreating of the sun's shadow. But he went beyond this. To impress his guests still further, he showed them the vast store of riches contained in the palace complex.

14–18 When the Babylonian embassy had left, Isaiah immediately confronted Hezekiah (v.14), who was still dazzled by the fact that he could have been so well-known in distant Babylon. He freely told Isaiah all that had transpired (v.15). Rather than earning the prophet's commendation, Hezekiah drew his condemnation. Hezekiah had been foolish. Not only would the extent of Jerusalem's wealth now be known and desired by all (cf. Sennacherib's demands in 18:13–16), but one day this same Babylon would invade the land and carry off its populace and all its treasures (v.17). Yes, even Hezekiah's own descendants would be taken captive and employed in the service of a Babylonian king (v.18; cf. 24:12–16; 2 Chron 33:11; Dan 1:3–5). Quite out of keeping with his righteous character, Hezekiah's folly would prove to be a contributing factor in the fulfillment of the ancient prophecies (Lev 26:33; Deut

28:64–67; 30:3). Hezekiah's experience remains a stern warning to all the perils of pride (cf. Prov 16:5, 18; 28:25–26; 29:23).

19 Hezekiah responded with humility and genuine godliness, acknowledging the propriety of Isaiah's God-given message. Hezekiah's last words contain a touch of pathos. While he was thankful that God would keep his promise not to surrender Judah and Jerusalem in his day (cf. v.6), yet he realized that his own actions had put his nation and his posterity in danger.

20 The chapter closes with a notice of Hezekiah's many achievements. The extent of his success is enlarged on by the author of Chronicles, from whom we also learn that the water conduit mentioned in 2 Kings dealt with the water of Gihon (2 Chron 32:27–31). These waters were directed within Jerusalem's walls via a specially constructed tunnel leading to a reservoir, known as the Pool of Siloam. The completion of this 1,777-foot tunnel made the waters of Gihon inaccessible to an enemy but readily available to a besieged population.

Archaeological confirmation of Hezekiah's architectural feat came with the recovery of the Siloam inscription that told of the excitement of Hezekiah's workmen who were approaching each other from opposite ends of the rock-hewn conduit from Gihon to Siloam (see ANET, p. 321).

21 Thus passed the king who was unsurpassed in his trust of the Lord (cf. 18:5). Second Chronicles 32:33 adds that he was buried with full honors by the citizenry of Jerusalem in the upper section of the tombs of the sons of David.

Notes

---

12 The MT's Berodach-Baladan should be read as in Isa 39:1, Merodach-Baladan being the Hebraic representation of the Akkad. Marduk Apal Iddina ("Marduk has given a son").

13 בְּשָׂמִים (beśāmîm, "spices") were widely used as fragrances, in cosmetics, and in worship and funerary rites. Highly prized, they were included in the presents brought by the queen of Sheba to Solomon (1 Kings 10:2, 10). Probably frankincense and myrrh made up the chief spices. For the commercial importance of spices, see Van Beek, pp. 99–126.

By the armory is probably meant "the Palace of the Forest of Lebanon" (cf. 1 Kings 7:2–5; Isa 22:8).

14 Notice that it was Isaiah *the* prophet who came to Hezekiah in his official capacity as God's chosen spokesman. His use of the Socratic method in bringing rebuke to the king helped Hezekiah to see the vaingloriousness in his conduct, thus bringing him to desire God's will for his life (v.19).

16 Isaiah 39:5 reads more forcefully: "Hear the word of the LORD Almighty." Rather than permitting himself to be entangled with other nations in cases of political turmoil as did his father, Ahaz, it would have been better for Hezekiah to seek the one who alone could fight Israel's battles. Hezekiah was to remember the lesson (cf. 19:14–19).

17 Although Isaiah's prophecy began to be fulfilled already in the days of Hezekiah's son, Manasseh (2 Chron 33:11), its full realization came only with the Fall of Jerusalem in 586 B.C. (2 Chron 36:18), more than a full century later. The mention of Jerusalem's fall to Babylon at a time when Assyria was the dominant power and immediate threat is clear evidence of the inspiration of Scripture and the trustworthiness of biblical prophecy (cf. Isa 41:21–23; 44:7–8; Rev 1:1, 19).

18 Although Isaiah's words are condemnatory, Hezekiah did at least receive assurance that one concern in his prayer to God would be answered—he would have a son! For סָרִיס (*sārîs*, "eunuch"), see the note on 18:17.

B. *The Reign of Manasseh*

21:1–18

¹Manasseh was twelve years old when he became king, and he reigned in Jerusalem fifty-five years. His mother's name was Hephzibah. ²He did evil in the eyes of the LORD, following the detestable practices of the nations the LORD had driven out before the Israelites. ³He rebuilt the high places his father Hezekiah had destroyed; he also erected altars to Baal and made an Asherah pole, as Ahab king of Israel had done. He bowed down to all the starry hosts and worshiped them. ⁴He built altars in the temple of the LORD, of which the LORD had said, "In Jerusalem I will put my Name." ⁵In both courts of the temple of the LORD, he built altars to all the starry hosts. ⁶He sacrificed his own son in the fire, practiced sorcery and divination, and consulted mediums and spiritists. He did much evil in the eyes of the LORD, provoking him to anger.

⁷He took the carved Asherah pole he had made and put it in the temple, of which the LORD had said to David and to his son Solomon, "In this temple and in Jerusalem, which I have chosen out of all the tribes of Israel, I will put my Name forever. ⁸I will not again make the feet of the Israelites wander from the land I gave their forefathers, if only they will be careful to do everything I commanded them and will keep the whole Law that my servant Moses gave them." ⁹But the people did not listen. Manasseh led them astray, so that they did more evil than the nations the LORD had destroyed before the Israelites.

¹⁰The LORD said through his servants the prophets: ¹¹"Manasseh king of Judah has committed these detestable sins. He has done more evil than the Amorites who preceded him and has led Judah into sin with his idols. ¹²Therefore this is what the LORD, the God of Israel, says: I am going to bring such disaster on Jerusalem and Judah that the ears of everyone who hears of it will tingle. ¹³I will stretch out over Jerusalem the measuring line used against Samaria and the plumb line used against the house of Ahab. I will wipe out Jerusalem as one wipes a dish, wiping it and turning it upside down. ¹⁴I will forsake the remnant of my inheritance and hand them over to their enemies. They will be looted and plundered by all their foes, ¹⁵because they have done evil in my eyes and have provoked me to anger from the day their forefathers came out of Egypt until this day."

¹⁶Moreover, Manasseh also shed so much innocent blood that he filled Jerusalem from end to end—besides the sin that he had caused Judah to commit, so that they did evil in the eyes of the LORD.

¹⁷As for the other events of Manasseh's reign, and all he did, including the sin he committed, are they not written in the book of the annals of the kings of Judah? ¹⁸Manasseh rested with his fathers and was buried in his palace garden, the garden of Uzza. And Amon his son succeeded him as king.

1–6 Manasseh came to the throne of Judah at the age of twelve, reigning for some fifty-five years (698/697–642 B.C.), the longest reign in Judah's history (v.1). Born soon after the Sargonid crisis, Manasseh must have seen God's great deliverance at Jerusalem. Nevertheless with his father's death, he soon plunged into every manner of spiritual wickedness (v.2). The high places Hezekiah had destroyed were rebuilt, the Canaanite religious practices relative to Baal and Asherah were reintroduced, and he established and participated in a state astral cult (v.3). So far did his spiritual harlotry take him that Manasseh introduced pagan altars in both the outer and the priest's courts and even in the temple itself (vv.4–5). Ultimately the hated Asherah pole was placed in the temple, the very abode of the sacred name. Moreover he went so far as to involve his own son in the loathsome and detestable rites of infant sacrifice; he practiced sorcery and divination and consulted purveyors of demonic activity (v.6).

7–9 Manasseh's great evil provoked the Lord to anger. Placing the Asherah pole within the temple was especially offensive (v.7). God had promised to dwell in peace among his people forever (cf. 2 Sam 7:13; 1 Kings 8:16; 9:3), if they would but serve him in righteousness (v.8; cf. 2 Sam 7:10; 1 Kings 9:6–9). But the people indulged themselves with the lustful Manasseh rather than harken to their Redeemer (v.9). Accordingly Manasseh's Judah exceeded in spiritual degradation the original Canaanites whom God had driven out before Israel (cf. Amos 2:9–10). What a tragedy! How superficial had been the nation's compliance with Hezekiah's reforms! Without a strong spiritual leader, the sinful people quickly turned to their own evil machinations. The judgment of God could not be far away.

10–11 Throughout Manasseh's wicked reign God warned of the grave consequences of the king's sin, sending repeated warnings to his prophets. Yet neither king nor people paid any attention to God's denunciations (cf. 2 Chron 33:10).

12–13 God therefore set in motion those forces that would bring destruction on Jerusalem and Judah (cf. Jer 15:1–4). In rehearsing the coming judgment, God used three well-known literary figures: (1) the tingling ears, (2) the measuring and plumb lines, and (3) the dish wiped clean. By the first he emphasized the severity of the judgment: it would be of such untold dimension that it would strike terror into the hearts of all who heard of its execution (cf. 1 Sam 3:11; Jer 19:3–9). By the second God used a figure often associated with building (cf. Zech 1:16) but employed also of the measuring of destruction (Isa 34:11; Amos 7:7–9). Just as God had taken the measure of Samaria so as to destroy it, so Jerusalem would fall. Even as the Lord had plumbed the house of Ahab in order to exterminate it, so the people of Jerusalem would be executed. By the third the complete destruction of Jerusalem was emphasized. As one wipes a dish clean, turning it over so that no drop is left, so Jerusalem's destruction would be total. None would remain.

14–16 Because Israel had forsaken God and provoked him to wrath time without end since he had redeemed them from Egypt, he would forsake wicked Judah, the last vestige of his inheritance. He would give them over for a prey to be looted and plundered (cf. Deut 28:49–68; Isa 42:22; Jer 30:16; Hab 1:5–11). The wicked reign of Manasseh had become the capstone of the wall of sin that Israel had built between herself and God (v.16). God now had taken its measure and marked it for destruction.

17–18 The writer of Kings brings Manasseh's history to a close by indicating further source material for the details of his infamous life and noting that at his death he was buried in his private garden called "The Garden of Uzza." The picture thus presented by our author is bleak, portraying the dominant themes of the vast majority of

Manasseh's long reign. This critical evaluation is a proper one. Manasseh's personal example and leadership in sin was to have a permanent effect, bringing on Judah's certain demise despite the temporary reforms of Josiah.

The author of Chronicles records that the Lord had humbled Manasseh by allowing him to fall into the hands of the king of Assyria, an event that brought about Manasseh's repentance and a short period of religious reformation (2 Chron 33:11–17). Although the time of Manasseh's capture, release, and repentance is nowhere indicated, the fact that Kings presents such a uniform description of Manasseh's bad character tends to suggest that this experience must have occurred late in his reign.

The widespread revolts during the reign of Ashurbanipal, which occurred from 652–648 B.C., may provide the occasion for Manasseh's summons to Babylon and imprisonment. If so, his subsequent release and reform were apparently far too late to have much of an effect on the obdurately backslidden populace.

Notes

1 The era of the reigns of Manasseh and Amon (698/697–640 B.C.) was to be an eventful one. When Sennacherib died, he left an Assyrian kingdom that comprised nearly all the ancient Fertile Crescent, exclusive of Egypt. It was a strong kingdom, one ruled through a well-established bureaucracy that had inherited and built on the time-honored techniques of Mesopotamian administrative procedure.

Accordingly, though the annals of Esarhaddon (681–668 B.C.) and Ashurbanipal (668–626) record numerous campaigns that were to advance Assyrian territory from Persia and Arabia on the east and south to Egypt as far up the Nile as Thebes on the southwest, still, the times were largely peaceful and prosperous. They are often designated the *Pax Assyriaca*. Thus Esarhaddon and Ashurbanipal were largely able to enjoy the fruits of the earlier Sargonid kings' labor and could turn their attention to great building projects, religious pursuits, and the cultivation of the Assyrian *beaux arts* and *belles-lettres*. Layard's discovery of the library of Ashurbanipal at Nineveh calls attention to the Assyrian concern for the cultivation of the Mesopotamian literary tradition.

3 Manasseh's renewed introduction of astral worship was strictly against the scriptural injunctions (Deut 4:19; 17:2–7). Such practices had already been condemned by the eighth-century prophets (e.g., Isa 47:13; Amos 5:26). The effects of Manasseh's evil were to continue beyond his days, as the denunciations of the seventh-century prophets testify (e.g., Jer 8:2; 19:13; Zeph 1:5).

7 For the Asherah pole see the note on 1 Kings 14:15.

10 The names of God's prophets are not given here. Certainly Isaiah's later ministry extended until Manasseh's time. The evils of Manasseh's day may be reflected in Habakkuk's scathing denunciations (e.g., Hab 1:2–4). Nahum's prophecy against Assyria may have been misappropriated by Manasseh in such a way as to encourage his waywardness both toward God and Assyria, thereby further deepening the wrath of both.

16 Manasseh's shedding of "innocent blood" refers not only to human sacrifice, but probably to the martyrdom of God's holy prophets. Josephus (*Antiq.* X, 37 [iii.1]) affirms that Manasseh not only slew all the righteous men of Judah but especially the prophets he slew daily until Jerusalem "was overflowing with blood." Uniform Jewish and Christian tradition holds that Manasseh had Isaiah sawn asunder (cf. Heb 11:37).

17 Additional source material for information on Manasseh is included in 2 Chron 33:18–19 (q.v.).

18 Some scholars suggest that Manasseh's captivity occurred during the reign of Esarhaddon

(681–668 B.C.), who mentioned the summoning of Manasseh along with other rulers to Nineveh (see ANET, p. 291). Certainly Esarhaddon had many vassals (for details see D.J. Wiseman, "The Vassal Treaties of Esarhaddon," *Iraq* 20 [1958]: 1–99). While Esarhaddon did often summon his vassals to himself, his time seems much too early to be harmonized with the scriptural record.

Moreover the Bible indicates that Manasseh was called to Babylon, not Nineveh. Babylon became virtually a second capital of the realm in Ashurbanipal's day. Ashurbanipal also mentioned Manasseh among the kings who accompanied him on his first Egyptian campaign in 668 B.C. (see ANET, p. 294), but here (as in the case of Esarhaddon's inscription) Manasseh did not seem to be in the king's disfavor.

In favor of a later date (c. 650–648 B.C.) is the fact that the revolts of that time involved sizeable opposition in the west, including such time-honored Judean allies as Phoenicia and Egypt. The whole affair revolved around Ashurbanipal's seditious brother Shamash-shum-ukin and the city of Babylon. Since Ashurbanipal himself then occupied the throne of Babylon for a year (648–647), it would afford a logical time for Manasseh's summons to Babylon in order to determine his degree of participation in the revolt. Manasseh's eventual acquittal and return to Judah would allow little time for his newly found faith to have a permanent effect.

C. *The Reign of Amon*

21:19–26

¹⁹Amon was twenty-two years old when he became king, and he reigned in Jerusalem two years. His mother's name was Meshullemeth daughter of Haruz; she was from Jotbah. ²⁰He did evil in the eyes of the Lord, as his father Manasseh had done. ²¹He walked in all the ways of his father; he worshiped the idols his father had worshiped, and bowed down to them. ²²He forsook the Lord, the God of his fathers, and did not walk in the way of the Lord.

²³Amon's officials conspired against him and assassinated the king in his palace. ²⁴Then the people of the land killed all who had plotted against King Amon, and they made Josiah his son king in his place.

²⁵As for the other events of Amon's reign, and what he did, are they not written in the book of the annals of the kings of Judah? ²⁶He was buried in his grave in the garden of Uzza. And Josiah his son succeeded him as king.

19–22 The short reign of Amon was a replay of the earlier period of his father, Manasseh. The author of Kings notes simply that he was as evil as his father and so perpetuated all of Manasseh's earlier idolatry (vv.20–21). The author of Chronicles (2 Chron 33:21–23) adds that Amon failed to humble himself but rather "increased his guilt."

23–26 In the year of 640 B.C., the wicked Amon was assassinated by his own officials who, in turn, were executed by the populace (vv.23–24). Amon's son Josiah was established as the next king (v.26). Although the Scriptures give no reason for the conspiracy, its cause may lie within the tangled web of revolts that Ashurbanipal suppressed from 642–639 and that caused him to turn his attention to the west. Certainly his menacing advance took him as far as Phoenicia. At this time, too, he may have resettled newly deported elements in Samaria (cf. Ezra 4:9–10). Amon's death may thus reflect a power struggle between those who wished to remain loyal to the Assyrian crown and those who aspired to link Judah's fortunes to the rising star of Psammetik I (664–609) of Egypt's Twenty-Sixth Dynasty.

At any rate, in 640 B.C. Amon's body was interred in the Garden of Uzza; and his eight-year-old son, Josiah, acceded to the Judean throne.

D. *The Reign of Josiah (22:1–23:30)*

1. *Accension and early reforms*

22:1–7

> ¹Josiah was eight years old when he became king, and he reigned in Jerusalem thirty-one years. His mother's name was Jedidah daughter of Adaiah; she was from Bozkath. ²He did what was right in the eyes of the LORD and walked in all the ways of his father David, not turning aside to the right or to the left.
>
> ³In the eighteenth year of his reign, King Josiah sent the secretary, Shaphan son of Azaliah, the son of Meshullam, to the temple of the LORD. He said: ⁴"Go up to Hilkiah the high priest and have him get ready the money that has been brought into the temple of the LORD, which the doorkeepers have collected from the people. ⁵Have them entrust it to the men appointed to supervise the work on the temple. And have these men pay the workers who repair the temple of the LORD—⁶the carpenters, the builders and the masons. Also have them purchase timber and dressed stone to repair the temple. ⁷But they need not account for the money entrusted to them, because they are acting faithfully."

1–2 A mere lad of eight years old when he came to the throne, Josiah probably owed much of his spiritual concern to his mother, Jedidah, and probably to the guidance of pious men in prominent positions. He quickly demonstrated himself to be one who followed his forefather David in godliness, walking circumspectly before God and men.

3–7 The author of Kings quickly moves to the most outstanding example of Josiah's godly fidelity: his repair of the temple in his eighteenth year (622 B.C.). According to 2 Chronicles 34:3–7, however, this example of piety was preceded by a time of definite committal to the Lord at the age of sixteen and, beginning some four years later, by a thorough iconoclastic purge in which he not only attacked the idolatry of Judah but eventually took it on himself to extend his efforts to Israel as well. Accordingly Josiah's action here in his eighteenth year was quite in keeping with his true spiritual character.

At this time Josiah sent his secretary Shaphan to Hilkiah the high priest with a royal command to utilize the freewill offerings of the people for the appropriation of supplies and the paying of the laborers so as to begin the repair of the temple.

Notes

---

1 The description of Josiah as "not turning aside to the right or to the left" from God's standards for man is apparently drawn from Deut 17:11, 20; 28:14. The right hand-left hand motif, which frequently expresses completeness or full participation on the part of the persons involved (cf. Ezek 39:3; Dan 12:7; Jonah 4:11; Matt 6:3; 2 Cor 6:7), here stresses Josiah's singlehearted devotion to God's approved course of conduct for his life (cf. 23:25).

2 Josiah's growing hunger for the Lord may have been fed by the ministry of the prophet Zephaniah (635–625 B.C.). That his reformation, begun in 628, could actually spill over into the north is easily understood when one recalls the decaying conditions within Assyria in those last years preceding Ashurbanipal's death in 626.

4 Second Chron 34:8 mentions two other men who made up the king's commission: Maaseiah and Joah, son of Joahaz, the royal herald. It was an important task; accordingly Josiah sent trusted officials to see to it. Josiah's choice of Shaphan to head the royal commission was a wise one; for his godly influence was to be felt not only in his own time but in that of his sons Ahikam (Jer 26:24), Elasah (Jer 29:3), and Gemariah (Jer 36:10, 25), and his grandson Gedaliah (Jer 39:14).

Probably a chest had been placed at the entrance of the temple for the receiving of the freewill offerings of the people, as in the days of Joash (12:10). According to 2 Chronicles 34:9, this constituted money that had been contributed even by believing Israelites who resided in the northern kingdom.

---

2. The Book of the Law

22:8-13

> [8]Hilkiah the high priest said to Shaphan the secretary, "I have found the Book of the Law in the temple of the LORD." He gave it to Shaphan, who read it. [9]Then Shaphan the secretary went to the king and reported to him: "Your officials have paid out the money that was in the temple of the LORD and have entrusted it to the workers and supervisors at the temple." [10]Then Shaphan the secretary informed the king, "Hilkiah the priest has given me a book." And Shaphan read from it in the presence of the king.
>
> [11]When the king heard the words of the Book of the Law, he tore his robes. [12]He gave these orders to Hilkiah the priest, Ahikam son of Shaphan, Acbor son of Micaiah, Shaphan the secretary and Asaiah the king's attendant: [13]"Go and inquire of the LORD for me and for the people and for all Judah about what is written in this book that has been found. Great is the LORD's anger that burns against us because our fathers have not obeyed the words of this book; they have not acted in accordance with all that is written there concerning us."

8–10 When the royal commission arrived, Hilkiah also had news for them: he had found a copy of the Book of the Law (v.8). Although scholars have often argued as to the contents of that manuscript, the king's later reaction when he heard the law read (vv.11–13) and the subsequent further reforms (23:4–20) and religious observances (2 Chron 35:1–19) indicate that it included at least key portions, if not the whole, of Deuteronomy (e.g., Deut 28–30).

The royal commission stayed long enough to be assured that the king's wishes had been carried out (2 Chron 34:10–13), during which time Shaphan had an opportunity to examine the new scroll. When the commission returned, Shaphan reported to the king. His orders had been carried out and the work begun (v.9). He also told the king about the exciting new discovery that he had brought back with him and proceeded to read selected portions of it to the king (v.10).

11–13 The king's reaction at the reading of the law was one of immediate contrition, as expressed in the sign of lamentation and grief, the tearing of his robes (v.11). The basis of his grief was twofold: Judah's guilt and her judgment. The nation had sinned grievously in breaking God's covenant in both its idolatry and its social injustices;

therefore, in accordance with the terms of that violated covenant, judgment must come. With repentant and sorrowful heart, Josiah sent a commission made up of trusted officials and the high priest Hilkiah to the prophetess Huldah, who lived in the second district of Jerusalem (cf. Zeph 1:10), to inquire as to the Lord's present intention regarding Judah (vv. 12–13).

Notes

8 Some scholars suggest that the newly found scroll was a testimonium of covenantal material. Keil (p. 478) opts for the whole Pentateuch, deposited by the side of the ark of the covenant.

9 The names of the trusted officials who supervised the repair project are recorded in 2 Chron 34:12.

12 Joining Shaphan and his son Ahikam on the commission were Asaiah and Achbor. Achbor (called Abdon in 2 Chron 34:20) was the father of Elnathan, one of Jehoiachin's advisors (Jer 26:22; 36:25). Second Chron 34:21 indicates that Josiah's concern was for Israel as well as for Judah.

3. The advice of Huldah

22:14–20

14Hilkiah the priest, Ahikam, Acbor, Shaphan and Asaiah went to speak to the prophetess Huldah, who was the wife of Shallum son of Tikvah, the son of Harhas, keeper of the wardrobe. She lived in Jerusalem, in the Second District.

15She said to them, "This is what the LORD, the God of Israel, says: Tell the man who sent you to me, 16·This is what the LORD says: I am going to bring disaster on this place and its people, according to everything written in the book the king of Judah has read. 17Because they have forsaken me and burned incense to other gods and provoked me to anger by all the idols their hands have made, my anger will burn against this place and will not be quenched.' 18Tell the king of Judah, who sent you to inquire of the LORD, 'This is what the LORD, the God of Israel, says concerning the words you heard: 19Because your heart was responsive and you humbled yourself before the LORD when you heard what I have spoken against this place and its people, that they would become accursed and laid waste, and because you tore your robes and wept in my presence, I have heard you, declares the LORD. 20Therefore I will gather you to your fathers, and you will be buried in peace. Your eyes will not see all the disaster I am going to bring on this place.'"

So they took her answer back to the king.

14–20 Huldah faithfully rendered the Lord's message for the people (vv. 15–17) and Josiah (vv. 18–20). Because Judah had persisted in its idolatry and wickedness, the sentence of judgment recorded in God's Word, which the king had just heard, would surely come to pass. As for the king himself, because he had responded to God's Word and humbled himself, and because he had grieved over Judah's sinful conditions, he would be spared the anguish of seeing God's devastating judgment carried out.

At first sight the promise seems to be at variance with the fact that Josiah died in battle (23:29–30). However, though the words in v.20 might be construed as indicating peaceful death, such need not be the case. The phrase "be gathered to one's fathers" simply points to the fact that men die and are buried, not to the manner of their death (cf. Gen 25:8, 17; 35:29; 49:29, 33; Num 20:24–29; 27:13; 31:2; Deut 32:50; Judg 2:10; Job 27:19; Jer 8:2; 25:33). The point here is that Josiah would die at peace with God before his awful sentence would descend on his people.

Notes

14 Huldah the prophetess is otherwise unknown in the OT. The fact that Zephaniah was not consulted may indicate that his prophetic ministry had ceased by this time. Although Jeremiah had certainly begun prophesying (cf. Jer 1:1), it may be that his early ministry (Jer 1–6) had been completed and, having contributed to Josiah's early spiritual concern, he was presently at Anathoth. It has been suggested that Huldah's husband, Shallum (son of Tokhath, son of Hasrah [2 Chron 34:22]), may have been related to Jeremiah (Jer 32:7 –12); but this is not certain.

The second district was so named because it formed the first addition to the old city. Its location is probably to be sought west of the temple complex in the upper Tyropoeon Valley, in the commercial quarter. If so, this may indicate the humble circumstances of the faithful prophetess and her husband.

20 Josiah's being buried "in peace" reflects his state of well-being with God. The phrase is drawn from ancient diplomatic parlance, as shown by D.J. Wiseman, "Is it peace—Covenant and Diplomacy," VetTest 32 (1982): 323–25.

"To be gathered to one's fathers" may also contain an underlying hint of an OT hope for life after death. That the reality of a conscious afterlife existed in OT times may be seen from Gen 22:5; Job 14:14–15; 19:25–27; Pss 16:9–11; 22:22–24; 49:14–15; 73:23–26; Isa 25:8; 26:19; Dan 12:2–3; Hos 13:14.

4. Further reforms

23:1–23

¹Then the king called together all the elders of Judah and Jerusalem. ²He went up to the temple of the LORD with the men of Judah, the people of Jerusalem, the priests and the prophets—all the people from the least to the greatest. He read in their hearing all the words of the Book of the Covenant, which had been found in the temple of the LORD. ³The king stood by the pillar and renewed the covenant in the presence of the LORD—to follow the LORD and keep his commands, regulations and decrees with all his heart and all his soul, thus confirming the words of the covenant written in this book. Then all the people pledged themselves to the covenant.

⁴The king ordered Hilkiah the high priest, the priests next in rank and the doorkeepers to remove from the temple of the LORD all the articles made for Baal and Asherah and all the starry hosts. He burned them outside Jerusalem in the fields of the Kidron Valley and took the ashes to Bethel. ⁵He did away with the pagan priests appointed by the kings of Judah to burn incense on the high places of the towns of Judah and on those around Jerusalem—those who burned incense to Baal, to the sun and moon, to the constellations and to all the starry hosts. ⁶He

took the Asherah pole from the temple of the LORD to the Kidron Valley outside Jerusalem and burned it there. He ground it to powder and scattered the dust over the graves of the common people. ⁷He also tore down the quarters of the male shrine prostitutes, which were in the temple of the LORD and where women did weaving for Asherah.

⁸Josiah brought all the priests from the towns of Judah and desecrated the high places, from Geba to Beersheba, where the priests had burned incense. He broke down the shrines at the gates—at the entrance to the Gate of Joshua, the city governor, which is on the left of the city gate. ⁹Although the priests of the high places did not serve at the altar of the LORD in Jerusalem, they ate unleavened bread with their fellow priests.

¹⁰He desecrated Topheth, which was in the Valley of Ben Hinnom, so no one could use it to sacrifice his son or daughter in the fire to Molech. ¹¹He removed from the entrance to the temple of the LORD the horses that the kings of Judah had dedicated to the sun. They were in the court near the room of an official named Nathan-Melech. Josiah then burned the chariots dedicated to the sun.

¹²He pulled down the altars the kings of Judah had erected on the roof near the upper room of Ahaz, and the altars Manasseh had built in the two courts of the temple of the LORD. He removed them from there, smashed them to pieces and threw the rubble into the Kidron Valley. ¹³The king also desecrated the high places that were east of Jerusalem on the south of the Hill of Corruption—the ones Solomon king of Israel had built for Ashtoreth the vile goddess of the Sidonians, for Chemosh the vile god of Moab, and for Molech the detestable god of the people of Ammon. ¹⁴Josiah smashed the sacred stones and cut down the Asherah poles and covered the sites with human bones.

¹⁵Even the altar at Bethel, the high place made by Jeroboam son of Nebat, who had caused Israel to sin—even that altar and high place he demolished. He burned the high place and ground it to powder, and burned the Asherah pole also. ¹⁶Then Josiah looked around, and when he saw the tombs that were there on the hillside, he had the bones removed from them and burned on the altar to defile it, in accordance with the word of the LORD proclaimed by the man of God who foretold these things.

¹⁷The king asked, "What is that tombstone I see?"

The men of the city said, "It marks the tomb of the man of God who came from Judah and pronounced against the altar of Bethel the very things you have done to it."

¹⁸"Leave it alone," he said. "Don't let anyone disturb his bones." So they spared his bones and those of the prophet who had come from Samaria.

¹⁹Just as he had done at Bethel, Josiah removed and defiled all the shrines at the high places that the kings of Israel had built in the towns of Samaria that had provoked the LORD to anger. ²⁰Josiah slaughtered all the priests of those high places on the altars and burned human bones on them. Then he went back to Jerusalem.

²¹The king gave this order to all the people: "Celebrate the Passover to the LORD your God, as it is written in this Book of the Covenant." ²²Not since the days of the judges who led Israel, nor throughout the days of the kings of Israel and the kings of Judah, had any such Passover been observed. ²³But in the eighteenth year of King Josiah, this Passover was celebrated to the LORD in Jerusalem.

1–3 On receiving Huldah's answer, the king convened his elders for consultation (v.1). As a result of that meeting, all levels of Judean society were called together in public assembly so that they might hear a reading from the newly found scroll (v.2). When that had been accomplished, the king led his people in a ceremony of covenant renewal wherein they pledged themselves to follow the Lord and his commands unswervingly (v.3). Like Moses and Joshua of old, Josiah took his place as a virtual meditator of the covenant between his people and their sovereign.

4–7 The covenant renewal was followed by renewed religious reforms. In accordance with the royal command, the priests conducted a thorough search of the temple to remove anything that spoke of heathen worship. In accordance with the scriptural standards, the pagan cult articles were taken outside Jerusalem to the Kidron Valley and burned, their ashes subsequently taken to Bethel, where paganism first had its official sanction in Israel (v.4). In taking the detested pagan abominations to the Kidron (v.6), Josiah followed the lead of the earlier royal reformers Asa (1 Kings 15:13) and Hezekiah (2 Chron 29:16; 30:14). The removal of the ashes to Bethel constituted a public denunciation of the place.

8–9 Josiah also recalled all the Levitical priests from their duties at the various high places throughout Judah (v.8). While those priests were admitted to the fellowship, their previous service had rendered them ineligible to officiate in the temple services (v.9); hence they were put on a status with those priests who had bodily defects (Lev 21:17–23). The high places were then desecrated so that those spurious centers of worship might no longer be maintained. Likewise the altar at the high place that was situated at one of Jerusalem's own gates was torn down.

10–12 Josiah's reforms were thoroughgoing. Topheth, the sacred precinct in the Valley of Hinnom, sacred to the Molech rites, was desecrated (v.10). The horses dedicated to the sun, which were quartered at the very entrance to the temple, were disposed of and their chariots burned (v.11). His reforms likewise turned to the altars used in astral worship located on the roof of the upper room built by Ahaz (v.12). These doubtless had been restored by Manasseh and Amon, along with the construction of the pagan altars (cf. 21:5). The pulverized debris from these objects was cast into the Kidron Valley.

13–18 Even those cult places that had enjoyed a long existence, having escaped the thoroughgoing reforms of Hezekiah, were now dismantled and desecrated (v.13). The pagan altars near Jerusalem had been built by Solomon himself. The altar at Bethel, which Josiah's reform also reached, had been established by Jeroboam at Solomon's death; but in the course of time a purely Canaanite worship had apparently replaced the earlier worship of the golden calf. In the former cases Josiah defiled those cult places by filling them with human bones (vv.14–15; cf. Num 19:16). In the latter instance, not content with destroying the high place and burning the Asherah pole, he exhumed the human bones from the graves situated on the mountain and burned them on the altar, thus defiling it forever. This action fulfilled the words of the unknown prophet of Judah of old (1 Kings 13:26–32). The remains of that prophet, along with those of the misguided prophet of Bethel (1 Kings 13:11ff.), however, were left undisturbed (vv.17–18).

19–20 Indeed, not only Bethel, but all the high places of the former northern kingdom were to feel the wrath of Josiah's purge (v.19). The various high places were destroyed and the priests of those illicit rites were slaughtered on their altars, which were further desecrated by the burning of human bones on them (v.20; cf. 2 Chron 34:6–7).

21–23 Josiah's attitude toward spiritual reform was not purely negative. He also gave instructions that the Passover be held as soon as it could be done in strict accordance with the law (v.21). Accordingly, in the eighteenth year of his reign, the Passover was celebrated in Jerusalem (v.23), the likes of which had not been seen since the days of Samuel (v.22). Not only was it observed as the law prescribed (2 Chron 35:1–19), but it was celebrated by all Judah and Israel (2 Chron 35:18).

Notes

2 By the term "the Book of the Covenant" may be intended that Josiah had those portions of the law read that dealt with Israel's basic covenant with God (e.g., Lev 26; Deut 28; see the note on 1 Kings 8:31).

4 This passage is strikingly similar to Jer 31:40 (Qere; N.B. Kethib = שְׁרֵמוֹת [šᵉrēmôt, lit., "cut off," "isolated places"]), where in describing the extent of the restored Jerusalem the words "all the terraces out to the Kidron Valley" are met. Since Jeremiah's designation of the renewed city appears to circumscribe the city, going from northeast to northwest, then down the west and across from southwest to southeast, then up the east side to the Horse Gate, the fields would appear to lie in the lower portion of the Kidron Valley. Jeremiah indicates that dead bodies were cast there (cf. Jer 33:5) and that ashes of various types were taken there. Probably the sweepings of the temple and the refuse of the city were carried there as well. Situated near the detested and loathsome place known as Tophet in the Valley of Hinnom (cf. v.10; Jer 7:31; 19:5–6), the whole area was one of defilement. It just may be that Kings and Jeremiah refer to the same area and yield an apt description of the isolated and defiled place to which Josiah consigned the detestable and defiling cult objects.

6 Jeremiah 26:23 confirms that there was a burial ground in the Kidron Valley for the common people. The scattering of the ashes of the object of heathen idolatry may indicate that the burials there were likewise idolatrous.

7 Although הַקְּדֵשִׁים (haqqᵉdēšîm) denotes "the male shrine prostitutes," probably the term is used generically for prostitutes of both sexes who were employed in the heinous Canaanite fertility rites.

10 For Topheth and Molech, see the note on 16:3. The wickedness associated with the area and its later use as a dump for the burning of refuse gave rise to the use of the name גֵּי חִנֹּם (gê hinnōm, "Valley of Hinnom") for the place of final punishment–Gehenna (cf. Matt 10:28; Rev 19:20; 20:14–15).

11 The utilization of the horse in the solar cultus was widespread in the ancient Near East, being attested particularly in Assyrian and Aramean inscriptional and artifactual sources. Ezekiel reports that devotees of solar worship practiced their ritual within the inner court at the entrance to the temple, between the porch and the altar. Such worship probably came into Judah's religious experience with the abominations that Ahaz introduced (16:10 –16). Recent excavations at Jerusalem have uncovered a sacred shrine that included images of horses.

פַּרְוָר (parwār, "court") is a hapax legomenon, unless it is to be equated with פַּרְבָּר (parbār, lit., "pavilion"; 1 Chron 26:18). Unfortunately the exact meaning of this latter word is also uncertain. The NIV's "court" reflects a meaning well-known to late Hebrew. The sense of the passage here seems to demand a roofed area over the courtyard that was used for stabling the horses and chariots employed in the solar cultus.

12 The "upper room" was probably located in one of those buildings near the gate (cf. Jer 35:4). The OT attests to the use of the roof for astral worship (Jer 19:13; Zeph 1:5) and also for Baal worship (Jer 32:29). The latter case finds a parallel in the legend of King KRT (ANET, pp. 143–44).

13–20 This passage is instructive as to the severity and the extent of Josiah's reforms (cf. 2

Chron 34:33). The growing weakness of the Assyrian Empire probably gave Josiah the liberty to consider himself the rightful king of all Israel.

---

5. Latter days

23:24–30

24Furthermore, Josiah got rid of the mediums and spiritists, the household gods, the idols and all the other detestable things seen in Judah and Jerusalem. This he did to fulfill the requirements of the law written in the book that Hilkiah the priest had discovered in the temple of the LORD. 25Neither before nor after Josiah was there a king like him who turned to the LORD as he did—with all his heart and with all his soul and with all his strength, in accordance with all the Law of Moses.

26Nevertheless, the LORD did not turn away from the heat of his fierce anger, which burned against Judah because of all that Manasseh had done to provoke him to anger. 27So the LORD said, "I will remove Judah also from my presence as I removed Israel, and I will reject Jerusalem, the city I chose, and this temple, about which I said, 'There shall my Name be.' "

28As for the other events of Josiah's reign, and all he did, are they not written in the book of the annals of the kings of Judah?

29While Josiah was king, Pharaoh Neco king of Egypt went up to the Euphrates River to help the king of Assyria. King Josiah marched out to meet him in battle, but Neco faced him and killed him at Megiddo. 30Josiah's servants brought his body in a chariot from Megiddo to Jerusalem and buried him in his own tomb. And the people of the land took Jehoahaz son of Josiah and anointed him and made him king in place of his father.

24–25 The author of Kings approaches the end of Josiah's just reign. The thought of Josiah's strict piety in keeping the laws of the Passover leads to the further observation that he was ever consistent in his application of the law (v.24). As Josiah had meticulously fulfilled the requirements of the law relative to Israel's ceremonial worship with his many reforms, his repair of the temple, and his reinstitution of the Passover, so had he put away the evils of false personal religion. This included both those who dealt in spiritism and all sorts of objects of detestable idolatry. In summary it could be said of Josiah that none of the kings of Israel and Judah was his equal in zeal for the law (v.25). As Hezekiah had been unequaled in faith among the kings (18:5), so Josiah knew no rival in uncompromising adherence to the law of Moses.

26–28 The account of Josiah's godly life ends on a note of sadness. Despite all that he had done to remove Judah's idolatry, the effects of Manasseh's gross spiritual wickedness had had a permanent effect (v.26). Although Judah's outward worship experience had been set in order, the people's confession had been a mere externality. With the passing of Josiah, the internal condition of their obdurately apostate heart quickly surfaced (cf. Jer 5). Accordingly God's just wrath would yet reach his sinful people. If the prophets and righteous Josiah had not been able to turn the people from their wicked ways, only God's judgment could have the desired effect.

29–30 Josiah's death at Megiddo can be attributed to his part in the complex international events of the last quarter of the seventh century B.C. With the death of

Ashurbanipal in 626, the already decaying Neo-Assyrian Empire began to crumble quickly away. By 625 the Chaldean king Nabopolassar had been able to achieve independence for Babylon. From that point onward throughout the course of the next two decades, the Assyrian territory was systematically reduced, especially as Nabopolassar found common cause against Assyria, first with the Medes (616) and later with the Ummanmande (possibly a designation for the Scythians). In 614 the time-honored capital of Assyria, Asshur, fell to the Medes. In 612 Nineveh itself fell to the coalition of Chaldeans, Medes, and Ummanmande, the surviving Assyrian forces under Ashur-u-ballit fleeing to Haran.

In those critical times concerned with the rising power of the new Mesopotamian coalition, Egypt's Twenty-Sixth Dynasty Pharaoh, Neco, honored the previous diplomatic ties with Assyria. As Neco's predecessor, Psammetik I, had come to the aid of Assyria in 616 B.C., so Neco moved to join the surviving Assyrian forces under Ashur-u-ballit. It was to prevent this movement of Egyptian aid that Josiah deployed his forces in the Valley of Megiddo in 609. That action cost Josiah his life, though it did delay the Egyptian forces from linking with their Assyrian allies before Haran fell to the Chaldeans and Medes. A subsequent attempt to retake Haran failed completely; and the best Egypt could give the doomed Assyrians was a four-year standoff, the opposing armies facing each other at Carchemish, on the western Euphrates.

The Chronicler (2 Chron 35:20–25) reports that Josiah had refused Neco's attempts to avoid the affair at Megiddo and rather, having disguised himself, had personally fought against the Egyptians until he was mortally wounded. At that point Josiah was rushed back to Jerusalem where he was buried in his own tomb. Quite understandably he was lamented by all the people, including the prophet Jeremiah. Thus passed one of God's choicest saints and one of Judah's finest kings. Josiah's determined action had brought about his tragic death, but he was thereby spared the greater tragedy of seeing the ultimate death of his nation a scant twenty-three years later.

Notes

29–30 For further details as to political developments in the last quarter of the seventh century B.C., see Wiseman, *Chronicles,* pp. 5–31; Parrot, *Babylon,* pp. 80–88; id., *Nineveh,* pp. 76–87; and CAH, 3:126–31, 206–12. Note that a seal bearing the name of Pharaoh Psammetik I has been found in the recent excavations of Jerusalem; see G. Garner, "Diggings," *Buried History* 16 (1980): 9.

E. *The Last Days of Judah (23:31–25:21)*

1. *The reign of Jehoahaz*

23:31–33

> [31]Jehoahaz was twenty-three years old when he became king, and he reigned in Jerusalem three months. His mother's name was Hamutal daughter of Jeremi-

ah; she was from Libnah. ³²He did evil in the eyes of the LORD, just as his fathers
had done. ³³Pharaoh Neco put him in chains at Riblah in the land of Hamath so
that he might not reign in Jerusalem, and he imposed on Judah a levy of a
hundred talents of silver and a talent of gold.

31 At the death of the courageous and pious Josiah, the people of the land selected
his third surviving son, Shallum, who took the throne name Jehoahaz (cf. 1 Chron
3:15 with Jer 22:11–12), to be the next king. The selection of Jehoahaz is beset with
problems. According to 1 Chronicles 3:15, Johanan, not Jehoahaz (or Shallum), was
Josiah's eldest son. Because nothing further is known of Johanan, he probably had
died much earlier. Jehoiakim, the next eldest son, was passed over, the kingship
being conferred on Jehoahaz, who was two years younger (cf. v.36).

Just why Jehoahaz was selected instead of Jehoiakim is not certain, though the
reason may lie in the fact that they had different mothers, Jehoahaz being Josiah's
son by Hamutal, whereas Jehoiakim's mother was Zebudah. Perhaps Hamutal enjoyed a favored status.

32–33 Jehoahaz was no Josiah, however; nor, indeed, was any of his sons. His
deposition was swift in coming. Within three months Pharaoh Neco summoned
Jehoahaz to Riblah in Syria, his base of operations and staging area for the Assyrian
campaigns.

Notes

---

31 That Shallum/Jehoahaz was Josiah's third son, not his fourth as in the order in 1 Chron
3:15, is certain in that Zedekiah, who is listed third, was only twenty-one years old when
he became king in 597 B.C. (24:18). He would thus be only ten years old in 609, the year
of Jehoahaz's accession at twenty-three years of age. The names of Zedekiah and Jehoahaz
occurred together probably because they were from the same mother, Zedekiah's name
being listed before Jehoahaz's in deference to his longer reign. Since Jehoiakim preceded
Zedekiah as king, Jehoahaz's name became listed last.

Libnah's known dislike of Judah (cf. 8:22) may also account for the selection of Jehoahaz. Indeed Josiah's marriage to a girl from Libnah may have been politically motivated.
Thus by selecting the son whose mother came from a district that was often hostile to the
political center at Jerusalem, the people may have hoped that the new king would be
more acceptable to the Egyptian crown than Jehoiakim, his older brother, whose mother
came from Rumah (cf. v.36).

33 Neco (609–594 B.C.) was the second Pharaoh of Egypt's Twenty-Sixth or Saite Dynasty
(663–625), so named for the traditional home of its dynastic rulers in the Nile Delta. After
the withdrawal of the Assyrians in 663, Psammetik I (663–609), the founder of the dynasty, was soon able to reunite the country and, during those years when Ashurbanipal or
Assyria became increasingly preoccupied with affairs closer to home, was able to restore
much of Egypt's fortunes.

Noted for a cultural renaissance that emphasized a conscious reproduction of Egypt's
traditional intellectual and artistic achievements, the Saite Dynasty was nevertheless forward-looking in its political outlook. Indeed it was to display an inner solidarity that
would render it a force to be reckoned with by the competing powers of the late seventh
and early sixth centuries B.C. Its fall to the Persians in 525 would mark the passing of

Egypt's last prestigious dynasty. Although Egypt would know moments of independence later in her Twenty-Eighth, Twenty-Ninth, and Thirtieth dynasties (434–341 B.C.), a native dynasty would never again know greatness in the ancient Near Eastern world. For details as to the Saite Dynasty, see Kitchen, *Third Intermediate Period*, pp. 399–408; J.H. Breasted, *History of Egypt* (New York: Bantam, 1964), pp. 470–85.

---

2. The reign of Jehoiakim

23:34–24:7

³⁴Pharaoh Neco made Eliakim son of Josiah king in place of his father Josiah and changed Eliakim's name to Jehoiakim. But he took Jehoahaz and carried him off to Egypt, and there he died. ³⁵Jehoiakim paid Pharaoh Neco the silver and gold he demanded. In order to do so, he taxed the land and exacted the silver and gold from the people of the land according to their assessments.

³⁶Jehoiakim was twenty-five years old when he became king, and he reigned in Jerusalem eleven years. His mother's name was Zebidah daughter of Pedaiah; she was from Rumah. ³⁷And he did evil in the eyes of the Lord, just as his fathers had done.

²⁴:¹During Jehoiakim's reign, Nebuchadnezzar king of Babylon invaded the land, and Jehoiakim became his vassal for three years. But then he changed his mind and rebelled against Nebuchadnezzar. ²The Lord sent Babylonian, Aramean, Moabite and Ammonite raiders against him. He sent them to destroy Judah, in accordance with the word of the Lord proclaimed by his servants the prophets. ³Surely these things happened to Judah according to the Lord's command, in order to remove them from his presence because of the sins of Manasseh and all he had done, ⁴including the shedding of innocent blood. For he had filled Jerusalem with innocent blood, and the Lord was not willing to forgive.

⁵As for the other events of Jehoiakim's reign, and all he did, are they not written in the book of the annals of the kings of Judah? ⁶Jehoiakim rested with his fathers. And Jehoiachin his son succeeded him as king.

⁷The king of Egypt did not march out from his own country again, because the king of Babylon had taken all his territory, from the Wadi of Egypt to the Euphrates River.

34–37 Neco replaced Jehoahaz with Eliakim, Josiah's second son, giving him the throne name Jehoiakim (v.34; cf. 2 Chron 36:4). Neco took Jehoahaz as a captive as he returned to Egypt, where he remained until his death (cf. Jer 22:10–12; Ezek 19:1–4). Moreover Neco imposed a severe tribute on the new Judean king, a sum Jehoiakim raised by levying a heavy taxation on the citizenry (v.35). Judah had appeased her new overlord and she had a new king. A far cry from his godly father, Jehoiakim was to lead Judah into still deeper trouble spiritually and politically.

Jehoiakim's rule was like that of the wicked kings who preceded Josiah (cf. 2 Chron 36:5, 8). Jeremiah (Jer 22:17; 36:31) represents him as a monster who despoiled his own people (Jer 22:13–14); opposed the Lord's servants (Jer 26:20–23; 36:21–23); filled the land with violence, apostasy, and degradation (Jer 18:18–20; cf. 11:19); and led his people into open apostasy and degradation (Jer 8:4–12, 18–9:16; 10:1–9; 11:1–17; 12:10–12; 13:1–11; 17:21–23; 23:1–2, 9–40; 25:1–7).

24:1 Jehoiakim and Judah were soon to change masters. After the final defeat of the combined Assyrian and Egyptian forces at Carchemish, Nebuchadnezzar overtook the remaining Egyptian forces at Hamath. Those Egyptian troops that managed to escape fled to Egypt (cf. Jer 46:2ff.). Nebuchadnezzar boasted that he thus took "the whole land of Hatti" (i.e., Syro-Palestine); so doubtless our text is correct in reading that Judah and Jehoiakim became his vassal. This is further corroborated in Nebuchadnezzar's own chronicles when, after reporting his succession to the kingship in 605 B.C., he records for the following year the submission and tribute of "all the kings of Hatti."

Although Jehoiakim served Nebuchadnezzar for the next three years, he apparently awaited an opportunity to throw off the Babylonian yoke. When in 601 Neco turned back Nebuchadnezzar's forces at the Egyptian border, Jehoiakim assumed that his moment had arrived and so rebelled. Once again Judah would lean on the broken reed of Egypt.

2–7 War had cost both the Chaldeans and the Egyptians dearly so that Nebuchadnezzar was unable to mobilize the troops and equipment to deal with impudent Judah, now newly allied to his Egyptian adversary, Neco. Accordingly Nebuchadnezzar spent the next few years in rebuilding his armed might in anticipation of the time when he could deal with the insurgents. Meanwhile he moved against the Arameans and Arabians, thus strengthening his hold on Judah's Egyptian flank (v.2). This also put him in a position to utilize the Transjordanian tribes to send raiding parties into Judah. The author of Kings reports that that harassment found its ultimate origin in God's command to bring judgment to a wicked Judah that had followed in the train of Manasseh's wickedness, a judgment the prophets had repeatedly warned about (vv.3–4; cf., e.g., Jer 15:1–9; Hab 1:2–6; Zeph 1:4–13; 3:1–7).

In 598 B.C., Nebuchadnezzar was ready. Gathering his huge force, he set out for Jerusalem and the impenitent Jehoiakim. But Nebuchadnezzar was not to avenge himself on the Judean king personally; for even as he set out for Judah, Jehoiakim lay dead, succeeded by his son, Jehoiachin.

Notes

---

35 Jehoiakim's anxiety doubtless called for heavy-handed pressure tactics against the populace, since the royal coffers or temple funds could no longer supply the needed tribute (cf. 1 Kings 14:26; 15:18; 2 Kings 12:18; 14:14; 16:8). Indeed those reserves may never have been replenished after Hezekiah's big payment to Sennacherib (18:14–15).

36 Since Jehoiakim was twenty-five at his accession, he was older than both Jehoahaz who preceded him (v.31) and Zedekiah who succeeded him eleven years later at the age of twenty-one.

24:1 For further details on Nebuchadnezzar's victory at Carchemish and the subsequent events, see Jer 46:1–12; Wiseman, *Chronicles*, pp. 23–29; and Thiele, *Mysterious Numbers*, pp. 163–66.

Daniel and his three friends were among those who were deported to Babylon during this first movement of Nebuchadnezzar into Judah in 605 B.C. (Dan 1:1). Jehoiakim himself also may have been put in chains at this deportation, his captivity being avoided only by the substitution of Daniel and the princes and a suitable tribute (cf. 2 Chron 36:6–7; see further the note on v.11).

2 The term כַּשְׂדִּים (*kaśdîm*, "Babylonians," "Chaldeans") designates the inhabitants of a region in southern Babylonia. Beginning with Nabopolassar it is applied to the "Neo-

Babylonian" kingdom. After Nebuchadnezzar's subsequent subjugation of the Near East, "Chaldea" and "Chaldean" soon replaced "Babylonia" and "Babylonian" as the names of the country and populace who ruled the ancient Near Eastern world from their splendorous capital at Babylon.

After the fall of the Chaldean (or Neo-Babylonian) dynasty, the term "Chaldean" survived chiefly in the older more specialized technical sense of "soothsayer."

6 The cause of Jehoiakim's death is not given. Perhaps he was assassinated by those who wished to placate Nebuchadnezzar. See R. Green, "The Fate of Jehoiakim," *Andrews University Seminary Studies* 20 (1982): 103–9. A violent end for Jehoiakim seems probable on the basis of Jer 22:18–19; 36:30–31. See also the note on v.11.

7 Traditionally the Wadi of Egypt has been identified with Wadi el Arish, though N. Na'aman ("The Brook of Egypt and Assyrian Policy on the Border of Egypt," *Tel Aviv* 6 [1979]: 68–90) has argued convincingly for Nahal Besar.

---

3. The reign of Jehoiachin

24:8–16

8Jehoiachin was eighteen years old when he became king, and he reigned in Jerusalem three months. His mother's name was Nehushta daughter of Elnathan; she was from Jerusalem. 9He did evil in the eyes of the LORD, just as his father had done.

10At that time the officers of Nebuchadnezzar king of Babylon advanced on Jerusalem and laid siege to it, 11and Nebuchadnezzar himself came up to the city while his officers were besieging it. 12Jehoiachin king of Judah, his mother, his attendants, his nobles and his officials all surrendered to him.

In the eighth year of the reign of the king of Babylon, he took Jehoiachin prisoner. 13As the LORD had declared, Nebuchadnezzar removed all the treasures from the temple of the LORD and from the royal palace, and took away all the gold articles that Solomon king of Israel had made for the temple of the LORD. 14He carried into exile all Jerusalem: all the officers and fighting men, and all the craftsmen and artisans—a total of ten thousand. Only the poorest people of the land were left.

15Nebuchadnezzar took Jehoiachin captive to Babylon. He also took from Jerusalem to Babylon the king's mother, his wives, his officials and the leading men of the land. 16The king of Babylon also deported to Babylon the entire force of seven thousand fighting men, strong and fit for war, and a thousand craftsmen and artisans.

8–9 With his father dead, young Jehoiachin was faced with the awesome specter of the advancing armies of Nebuchadnezzar. Certainly he would get no help from Egypt, for Neco was in no position to challenge Nebuchadnezzar again (cf. v.7). Nor did the lad have the spiritual maturity to be able to utilize godly wisdom (v.9).

10–16 The armies of Nebuchadnezzar soon arrived and placed Jerusalem under a siege (v.10). At the appropriate time Nebuchadnezzar himself appeared before the beleaguered city, to whom Jehoiachin, the royal family, and the officials of state made their surrender (vv.11–12). Having taken his hostages in charge, Nebuchadnezzar stripped the royal palace and the temple of their treasures as spoils of war (v.13). Moreover he perpetuated the deportation system made famous by the Assyrians, seizing ten thousand of Jerusalem's leaders from every walk of life (vv. 14–16). With only the poor and unskilled people of the land remaining, it might be assumed that Jerusalem would cause no further trouble.

Notes

8 In 2 Chron 36:9 Jehoiachin's age is given as eight years old. Because Jehoiachin was married, it seems better to view that reading as a scribal slip and to follow the age recorded here in v. 8 and followed by the ancient versions—eighteen. Even a few Hebrew MSS read eighteen in the Chronicles passage. (See also the note on 8:26.)

Since Jehoiachin's name (cf. Yo-Yakin [Ezek 1:2]) is entered as Jeconiah in the genealogies (1 Chron 3:16–17), this was probably his original name. This harmonizes with the fact that Jeremiah, who at times used the personal names of the kings (e.g., Shallum, Jehoahaz [Jer 22:11]), usually rendered his name Jeconiah (Jer 24:1; 27:20; 28:4; 29:2), sometimes shortening it to Coniah (Jer 22:24, 28; 37:1). Jeconiah probably took the name Jehoiachin as his throne name, much as Shallum took the name Jehoahaz, Eliakim was given the throne name Jehoiakim, and Mattaniah was given the name Zedekiah.

11 Josephus (*Antiq.* X, 99–102 [vii.1]) gives an interesting account of Nebuchadnezzar's movements in 597 B.C. Josephus claims that Nebuchadnezzar personally had Jehoiakim executed, while placing Jehoiachin on the throne. Having left Jerusalem, it occurred to him that Jehoiachin might be a source of trouble to him because he had killed the young king's father. Accordingly he sent his army back to Jerusalem to take Jehoiachin and the elite of Jerusalem captive and installed Zedekiah on the throne.

Although Josephus's theory has the advantage of being easily reconciled with 2 Chron 36:6, 10, it squares neither with the facts of Nebuchadnezzar's chronicles nor with the biblical record here in vv. 5–17. Nor would it be logical for Nebuchadnezzar to have made Jehoiachin king rather than Zedekiah, for the very reasons suggested by Josephus.

12 The seeming discrepancy between the date of Jehoiachin's imprisonment, given here as the eighth year of Nebuchadnezzar's reign and in Jer 52:28 as his seventh year, is to be accounted for on the basis of the differing calendars used by the authors, the Jewish system utilized here and the Babylonian in Jeremiah. See further Thiele, *Mysterious Numbers*, pp. 167–72.

13 Nebuchadnezzar had previously taken part of Jerusalem's smaller treasures (2 Chron 36:7; Dan 1:2). This time his despoilment was a major one, with only a few smaller gold and silver items left behind (cf. 25:15), along with the larger brass vessels (cf. 25:13–17; Jer 27:18–22).

14–16 The statement as to the deportation of "all Jerusalem" begins with a general notice of the removal of the men in accordance with their military potential. This is followed by a further cataloging of Jerusalem's citizenry according to their social status: the king, the dowager, the king's wives, the royal officials, the active military, the craftsmen, and the artisans. The figure "ten thousand" is probably a round number of all types of deportees from Judah and Jerusalem including female captives. For a different reckoning, see the note on Jer 52:28 (EBC, 6:690).

חָרָשׁ (*ḥārāš*, "craftsman") and מַסְגֵּר (*masgēr*, "artisan") were important to both the economic and the military needs of the community. Their loss would have manifold ramifications for the city, for both its economy and its defense.

Only those who lacked status or professional skill were left behind. Among the leading Jerusalemites taken captive was the prophet Ezekiel (Ezek 1:2; 33:21).

4. *The reign of Zedekiah*

24:17–25:21

¹⁷He made Mattaniah, Jehoiachin's uncle, king in his place and changed his name to Zedekiah.

¹⁸Zedekiah was twenty-one years old when he became king, and he reigned in Jerusalem eleven years. His mother's name was Hamutal daughter of Jeremiah; she was from Libnah. ¹⁹He did evil in the eyes of the LORD, just as Jehoiakim had done. ²⁰It was because of the LORD's anger that all this happened to Jerusalem and Judah, and in the end he thrust them from his presence.

Now Zedekiah rebelled against the king of Babylon.

²⁵:¹So in the ninth year of Zedekiah's reign, on the tenth day of the tenth month, Nebuchadnezzar king of Babylon marched against Jerusalem with his whole army. He encamped outside the city and built siege works all around it. ²The city was kept under siege until the eleventh year of King Zedekiah. ³By the ninth day of the ₍fourth₎ month the famine in the city had become so severe that there was no food for the people to eat. ⁴Then the city wall was broken through, and the whole army fled at night through the gate between the two walls near the king's garden, though the Babylonians were surrounding the city. They fled toward the Arabah, ⁵but the Babylonian army pursued the king and overtook him in the plains of Jericho. All his soldiers were separated from him and scattered, ⁶and he was captured. He was taken to the king of Babylon at Riblah, where sentence was pronounced on him. ⁷They killed the sons of Zedekiah before his eyes. Then they put out his eyes, bound him with bronze shackles and took him to Babylon.

⁸On the seventh day of the fifth month, in the nineteenth year of Nebuchadnezzar king of Babylon, Nebuzaradan commander of the imperial guard, an official of the king of Babylon, came to Jerusalem. ⁹He set fire to the temple of the LORD, the royal palace and all the houses of Jerusalem. Every important building he burned down. ¹⁰The whole Babylonian army, under the commander of the imperial guard, broke down the walls around Jerusalem. ¹¹Nebuzaradan the commander of the guard carried into exile the people who remained in the city, along with the rest of the populace and those who had gone over to the king of Babylon. ¹²But the commander left behind some of the poorest people of the land to work the vineyards and fields.

¹³The Babylonians broke up the bronze pillars, the movable stands and the bronze Sea that were at the temple of the LORD and they carried the bronze to Babylon. ¹⁴They also took away the pots, shovels, wick trimmers, dishes and all the bronze articles used in the temple service. ¹⁵The commander of the imperial guard took away the censers and sprinkling bowls—all that were made of pure gold or silver.

¹⁶The bronze from the two pillars, the Sea and the movable stands, which Solomon had made for the temple of the LORD, was more than could be weighed. ¹⁷Each pillar was twenty-seven feet high. The bronze capital on top of one pillar was four and a half feet high and was decorated with a network and pomegranates of bronze all around. The other pillar, with its network, was similar.

¹⁸The commander of the guard took as prisoners Seraiah the chief priest, Zephaniah the priest next in rank and the three doorkeepers. ¹⁹Of those still in the city, he took the officer in charge of the fighting men and five royal advisers. He also took the secretary who was chief officer in charge of conscripting the people of the land and sixty of his men who were found in the city. ²⁰Nebuzaradan the commander took them all and brought them to the king of Babylon at Riblah. ²¹There at Riblah, in the land of Hamath, the king had them executed.

So Judah went into captivity, away from her land.

17–20 Nebuchadnezzar left the city standing; installed Josiah's remaining son, Mattaniah (whom he renamed Zedekiah), on the throne; and in due time returned to Babylon (v.17). While Jerusalem had been spared momentarily, its demise was certain. Not only was Zedekiah no better than the other descendants of Josiah (v.19), but even this latest judgment of God through the Chaldeans had had no effect on an obdurately apostate people. All that God had done both previously and currently to Judah and Jerusalem had been because of his settled wrath against their sin. Yet nothing had helped. Twice wicked Judah fought on against the divine chastisement (cf. Jer 37:1–2). The *coup mortel* would not be long in coming.

25:1–4 Late in the year 588 B.C., a Judean king once more was lured into the foolish mistake of rebelling against Babylon (v.1). Nebuchadnezzar immediately responded, this time sending the full weight of his mighty army. After setting up headquarters in Riblah, Jerusalem was placed under total siege (cf. Jer 39:1; 52:4; Ezek 24:2). With Jerusalem securely blockaded (cf. Jer 21:3–7), Nebuchadnezzar proceeded to reduce the Judean strongholds systematically (cf. Jer 34:7), thereby cutting off both military relief and economic replenishment. At one point Nebuchadnezzar's forces were forced to withdraw momentarily to deal with an Egyptian relief column under Apries (Jer 37:5), much to the joy of the misguided Jerusalemites, who prematurely assumed that they had been delivered from the siege (Jer 37:6–10). Nonetheless Jerusalem's beleaguered defenders were kept enclosed by the Chaldeans almost continuously until July of 586 B.C. (v.2). Finally, when strength and provisions were completely exhausted (v.3; cf. Jer 52:6; Lam 4:9–10; cf. Deut 28:53–55), the Neo-Babylonian troops breached the walls and poured into the city (v.4; cf. Jer 39:2–3). The prophesied tragedy had occurred (cf. Jer 19–20; 27–28; 37:8–10, 17; 38:17–23).

5–7 Still further prophetic details were to be realized; for when Zedekiah and the remaining Judean army attempted to gain their freedom and the safety of Ammon by slipping through a secluded gate near the king's garden, they were soon overtaken by their Chaldean pursuers (v.5; cf. Jer 32:5; 34:3; Ezek 12:12–13 with Jer 39:3 –5; 52:7–8). Zedekiah was taken captive to Nebuchadnezzar at Riblah. There, being forced to witness the execution of his own children so that the last thing he might remember seeing would be the end result of his foolish disobedience, his eyes were put out. He was then led away in bronze fetters to Babylon (vv.6–7), where he remained a prisoner until his death (cf. Jer 52:11).

8–12 About one month later, Nebuzaradan, the commander of Nebuchadnezzar's own imperial guard, arrived in Jerusalem to oversee its despoilation and destruction (v.8). Having set fire to all of Jerusalem's permanent buildings, including the temple and palace (cf. Jer 52:13), the Chaldeans demolished the city's walls (vv.9–10). Then they deported certain valued elements of the citizenry of Jerusalem and the populace of the surrounding countryside, some of whom apparently willingly defected to the invaders (v.11; cf. Jer 39:9; 52:15). Only the poorest of the people were left. These were to work the nearby fields and vineyards so that a stratum of inhabitants unlikely to cause further insurrection might be left to care for the basic needs of the remaining people of the land (v.12; cf. Jer 39:10; 52:16).

13–17 Particular notice is given to the temple furniture and furnishings that the Chaldeans carried away as spoils of war. Primary focus is on those heavy bronze items that had to be broken into smaller pieces to be removed: the pillars, the movable stands, and the Sea (v.13). Indeed the bronze gained from those items— together with the bronze bulls under the brazen Sea (cf. Jer 52:20)—was incalculable (v.16). A comparison of this account with the fuller inventory in Jeremiah 52:17 –23 reveals a thorough looting of all the gold, silver, and bronze temple utensils.

18–20 The disposition of the chief religious, military, and government officials as well as sixty of the notable men is given next. Among these were Seraiah the high priest, Zephaniah the next ranking priest, the commander-in-chief of Jerusalem's fighting men, and the secretary for the mobilization of Judah's citizenry (vv.18–19). All these prominent officials and people were taken to Riblah and executed (vv.20–21). Nebuchadnezzar would brook no further interference with the established order that Nebuzaradan had left behind. With the officialdom and leadership either put to death or taken captive into exile, it could be expected that the remaining populace would passively submit to their Chaldean overlords, especially since many of Judah's formerly landless people were now land holders.

Notes

17 Nebuchadnezzar's records concerned with his movements in this Judean campaign are spotty at best, mentioning only a skirmish in northern Syria in his eighth year and a movement to the Tigris in the following year, in which he also mentioned the suppression of some rebel, followed by a trip to Syria. The main Chaldean chronicles then end, having stated only that in his eleventh year Nebuchadnezzar mustered his army for an expedition to Syria. Unfortunately no Babylonian record of the campaign of 586 B.C. is extant.

One more glimpse of Nebuchadnezzar's further campaigning is afforded in one or two of the tablets that indicate he invaded Egypt in his thirty-seventh year (568/567 B.C.; cf. Jer 43:8–10; see Wiseman, *Chronicles,* pp. 94f.).

25:1 The circumstances of Zedekiah's rebellion, for which Nebuchadnezzar once more took the road to Jerusalem, are not further described; nor do we have details from the Babylonian sources. There seems little doubt, however, but that they were related to a renewed confidence in Egypt, on whom Israel and Judah had relied mistakenly so many times before.

After the death of Neco in 594 B.C., his son Psammetik II reigned for six years, leaving behind many monuments that attest to the vitality of his short-lived rule. In 588 his son Apries succeeded him to the throne with grandiose schemes of glory. Soon after his accession he appears to have influenced Zedekiah to revolt against Babylon (cf. Ezek 17:15–18). As evidence of his support for the beguiled Judean king, he attacked Phoenicia and subsequently came to his aid when the Babylonian king put Jerusalem under siege (cf. Jer 37:5, 11).

Zedekiah's confidence was ill-placed, however, for not only was Apries' help insufficient, but the Egyptian pharaoh possessed neither the strength nor the sagacity to merit such trust. His own life was to be marked by a series of difficulties, ending in a *coup d'état* and death in battle during a vain attempt to regain his throne.

דָּיֵק (*dāyēq,* "siege work"; cf. Jer 52:4) has been variously identified as a wall of circumvallation (Gray, Montgomery) or a siege tower (Keil; cf. GKC, pp. 197–98). Sennacherib mentions the use of earth ramps in his siege of Jerusalem, and the Assyrian kings often depicted the use of siege towers so that the attackers might fight on the same level as the defenders on the walls. The Hebrew term here probably signifies a tower that has been called into place atop the siege mound. For the similar mention of earth ramps and siege towers, see Ezek 21:22.

2 Details of Nebuchadnezzar's systematic reduction of the countryside are confirmed by the

Lachish Letters, which graphically portray the movement of the Babylonian forces in Judah (see ANET, pp. 321f.). Evidence for the Fall of Azekah (Letter IV), written soon after Jer 34:7, is particularly revealing. As well the report of Judah's sending of a high army official to Egypt (Letter III) and of the unrest in Jerusalem (Letter VI) are illuminating, as is the mention of "the prophet" (= Jeremiah? Letter VI).

4 The two walls near the king's garden between which Zedekiah and his army slipped out of Jerusalem probably lay at the extreme southeastern corner of the city, giving direct access to the Kidron Valley (cf. Neh 3:15). The NIV is probably correct in reading "toward the Arabah" (i.e., with the definite article). The Arabah commonly designated the great Jordan Rift Valley that extends throughout the length of the Holy Land from the Sea of Galilee to the Gulf of Aqabah. Zedekiah's apprehension in the plains that lay south of Jericho (v.5) confirms this identification.

6 Riblah, located on the right bank of the Orontes River in the Hamath district, lay on the main route along the western corridor of the Fertile Crescent. Because ample provision could be found nearby, it was, logistically speaking, ideally situated as a field headquarters for military expeditionary forces. Neco had thus used it (cf. 23:33), as had Nebuchadnezzar in his campaign against the Egyptians in 605 B.C.

7 The practice of putting out the eyes of prisoners is well-attested in the Assyrian annals; see Parrot, *Babylon,* p. 97; cf. Judg 16:21.

9 The phrase "all the houses" is probably qualified by "every important building" that follows.

18 From Ezra 7:1 we learn that Ezra the scribe would descend from Seriah. Interestingly Seriah's sons were not executed but merely deported (1 Chron 6:15). Zephaniah may be that same son of Maaseiah whom Jeremiah (Jer 21:1; 29:25) mentioned as a notable priest. The three "doorkeepers" were seemingly priests whose special duty was to superintend the security of the temple, hence were important officials.

19 The exact function of the royal advisors is unclear. The Hebrew text describes them as "five men from those who saw the king's face." Jeremiah (Jer 52:25) gives their number as seven. Both indicate that this was not the complete total of royal advisors but merely those "who were found in the city" (i.e., had not been able to make their escape).

21 Excavations in Judah and Jerusalem confirm the biblical indication of the complete destruction wrought by the Chaldean invaders. For details see Unger, *Archaeology,* pp. 291 –92.

F. Historical Appendixes (25:22–30)

1. Judah in exile

25:22–26

22Nebuchadnezzar king of Babylon appointed Gedaliah son of Ahikam, the son of Shaphan, to be over the people he had left behind in Judah. 23When all the army officers and their men heard that the king of Babylon had appointed Gedaliah as governor, they came to Gedaliah at Mizpah—Ishmael son of Nethaniah, Johanan son of Kareah, Seraiah son of Tanhumeth the Netophathite, Jaazaniah the son of the Maacathite, and their men. 24Gedaliah took an oath to reassure them and their men. "Do not be afraid of the Babylonian officials," he said. "Settle down in the land and serve the king of Babylon, and it will go well with you."

25In the seventh month, however, Ishmael son of Nethaniah, the son of Elishama, who was of royal blood, came with ten men and assassinated Gedaliah and also the men of Judah and the Babylonians who were with him at Mizpah. 26At this, all the people from the least to the greatest, together with the army officers, fled to Egypt for fear of the Babylonians.

22-24 The captivity of God's disobedient people, begun in 605 B.C., was completed: Seventy years would go by until the exiled Judeans would again see their homeland (2 Chron 36:15-21). To the history of the united and divided kingdoms is appended a note regarding the establishment of the new Judean vassal state. Fuller details are given in Jeremiah, from where these data are perhaps drawn. Of the prominent men of Jerusalem, only Jeremiah and Gedaliah were left behind (v.22; cf. Jer 39:11 -14). Jeremiah's stand on the Babylonian issue was doubtless well-known. Gedaliah's attitude was probably that of Ahikam, his father and a noted official (2 Chron 34:20), who had supported Jeremiah (Jer 26:24). Accordingly Gedaliah, who probably had the needed training, seemed the logical choice to be Babylon's governor designate over the newly formed district.

The choice was a popular one, and at first things went well (cf. Jer 40:1-12). Because of their confidence in Gedaliah, many of the surviving little guerrilla bands made their way back to Jerusalem to lay down their arms and take up residence there (vv.23-24), as did many of the Judeans who had fled to the Transjordanian lands (cf. Jer 40:11-12). Even Jeremiah at first went to Mizpah to lend his assistance to Gedaliah (Jer 40:6).

25-26 Trouble soon arose, however, in a conspiracy hatched by Baalis, the Ammonite king (Jer 40:13-15), and a young noble named Ishmael. Ishmael was successful in assassinating Gedaliah together with his invited banquet guests, both Jew and Babylonian (v.25; cf. Jer 41:1-3). Although Ishmael was dealt with severely by Johanan ben Kareah, he succeeded in making his escape to Ammon (Jer 41:11-15). Because the refugees feared reprisal for Gedaliah's murder, Johanan led a large contingent of them into Egypt, including Jeremiah whom the fleeing Jews took along with them despite his counsels and warnings (v.26; Jer 41:16-43:7).

Notes

22 Confirmation of the existence and importance of Gedaliah comes from a clay seal-impression from Lachish that reads "belonging to Gedaliah who is over the house." See J.M. Ward, "Gedaliah, " IDB, 3:360.

23 The four army officers mentioned here had apparently played prominent roles in Judah's latter days. Ishmael's murderous deeds and eventual escape are fully documented by Jeremiah (Jer 40:13-41:18), who reports that he was of royal blood (Jer 41:1). Likewise Jeremiah gave his full attention to Johanan's part in the formation of the new government, in the Ishmael affair, and in the subsequent flight to Egypt (Jer 40:7-43:7).

2. *The later history of Jehoiachin*

25:27-30

27In the thirty-seventh year of the exile of Jehoiachin king of Judah, in the year Evil-Merodach became king of Babylon, he released Jehoiachin from prison on the twenty-seventh day of the twelfth month. 28He spoke kindly to him and gave him a seat of honor higher than those of the other kings who were with him in Babylon. 29So Jehoiachin put aside his prison clothes and for the rest of his life

ate regularly at the king's table. ³⁰Day by day the king gave Jehoiachin a regular
allowance as long as he lived.

27–30 The account of the fortunes of the Judeans is brought to a close with a
postscript concerning the later lot of Jehoiachin, son of Jehoiakim. Since he was
seemingly considered by the Judeans the last legitimate king, news of his later
condition would be of great significance. After the death of Nebuchadnezzar in 561
B.C., his son and successor, Evil-Merodach (561–560), released the Judean king
from prison and accorded him due royal recognition. This included a place at the
king's table and regular allowance for the rest of his life (cf. Jer 52:31–34).

Thus the final curtain falls on the drama of the divided monarchy. What had been
a note of dark despair is illuminated by the light of God's gracious concern for his
own. Although God's people had been judged as they must, yet God would be with
them even in the midst of their sentence. Jehoiachin's release and renewed enjoyment of life thus stands as a harbinger of the further release and return of all the
nation, in accordance with God's promises (cf. Jer 31:18; Lam 5:21). The spiritually
minded believers perhaps would see in this incident an assurance of God's greater
redemption from bondage of those who looked forward to him who gives release and
eternal refreshment to all who love his appearing.

Notes

27 For details relative to the later life of Nebuchadnezzar, see Saggs, *Greatness*, pp. 142–44;
for Evil-Merodach, see K.L. Barker, "Evil-Merodach," ZPEB, 2:421.

28 Jehoiachin's renewed royal recognition is in harmony with the esteem he continued to be
held in in Judah. Jar handles found at Tell Beit Mirsim and Bethshemesh bearing the
stamp "Eliakim, steward of Yaukin" (= Jehoiachin) testify to the populace's continued
recognition of Jehoiachin as the rightful king of Judah.

29 Confirmation of this historical notice came with the discovery of ration tablets from the
reign of Nabonidus listing among the recipients "Yaukin, king of the land of Yahud [Ju-
dah]"; Jehoiachin was considered the rightful king of Judah even by the Chaldeans. For
details see Unger, *Archaeology*, p. 293.

30 The existence of the Jews in Egypt in the fifth century is now illustrated by the Elephantine Papyri. See B. Porten, *Archives from Elephantine* (Berkeley: University of California
Press, 1968).

1, 2 CHRONICLES

J. Barton Payne

1 CHRONICLES

Introduction

1. Title
2. Date and Authorship
3. Integrity and Validity
4. Sources

   a. Genealogies
   b. Documents
   c. Poems
   d. Prophecies
   e. Other Histories

5. Text
6. Canonicity
7. Occasion and Purpose
8. Theology
9. Theological Themes and Interests

   a. Promise of God
   b. Retribution
   c. Vocabulary
   d. Cultus
   e. Worship
   f. Kingdom
   g. History
   h. Omissions

10. Bibliography
11. Outline

God used the history of the ancient kingdom of Israel to reveal truths about himself and his relationship to men. But while he inspired the OT writers of the books of both Kings and Chronicles to interpret this history, their theological messages are distinct. If Kings, composed after the final collapse of the kingdom in 586 B.C., concentrates on how sin leads to defeat (2 Kings 17:15, 18), then Chronicles, coming after the two returns from exile in 537 and 458 B.C., recounts, from the same record, how "faith is the victory" (2 Chron 20:20, 22). Readers today may therefore find strength from God, knowing that his moral judgments (Kings) are balanced by his providential salvation (revealed in Chronicles).

1. Title

In Hebrew the biblical books of Chronicles are called *dibrê hayyāmîm* ("the words of the days"). Yet *dābār* may signify not only "word" but also "thing," "event," or "idea," so as to mean "The happenings of . . ."; and the plural of *yôm* ("day") may occasionally denote "years." Thus whether in the sense of "journal" (originally a daily account) or, more broadly, of "annals" (yearly accounts), the title suggested by the church father Jerome, in his *Prologus Galeatus*, viz., *Chronicon totius divinae historiae,* or "a chronicle of the whole of sacred history," was an appropriate rendering. It was later adopted by Luther and the EV.

This same phrase (*dibrê hayyāmîm*) occurs thirty-two times in 1–2 Kings, where it is consistently translated as "chronicles" (NIV). But these must refer to some Israelite court records rather than to our canonical Chronicles—not simply because Kings was composed a century before Chronicles had come into being, but also because these court records are appealed to as sources for events that are not mentioned in our books of Chronicles (cf. 1 Kings 14:19; 15:31).[1]

In the LXX the title of Chronicles is *paraleipomenōn*, which means "the things omitted." This title suggests that these books include the material excluded by 1 Samuel–2 Kings. While this view is partly correct, it is nevertheless inadequate for at least two reasons. First, Chronicles does more than supplement the earlier historical books of the "Former Prophets." Second, this view ignores the special material and unique distinctives of the author's account of the history of Israel. These unique features of Chronicles will be discussed below under "Theological Interests" and "Theology."

2. Date and Authorship

Current critical scholarship has been unable to achieve a consensus of thinking about many specific matters of introduction to Chronicles. As one has said, "The scope, purpose, date, and historical value of this work are all subject to violent debate . . . bordering on chaos" (Freedman, p. 436). But while Chronicles contains no direct statement about the circumstances of its own composition, still, for those who are willing to let the biblical data speak for itself, a fairly clear picture does emerge. The last recorded event in 2 Chronicles is the decree of Cyrus in 538 B.C., permitting the Jews to return from their exile in Babylon (36:22–23). One genealogy in 1 Chronicles (3:17–21) includes King Jehoiachin's grandson Zerubbabel, who led this return in the following year; and it goes on to name two of Zerubbabel's grandsons—Pelatiah and Jeshaiah—thus extending the time to about 500 B.C. The sons of four other men are then mentioned, but without indication of their place in the genealogy. The last of these is Shecaniah, whose line reaches down to seven great-great-grandchildren (3:24). So if Shecaniah belongs to the same general period as King Jehoiachin (born 616), these four additional generations would again suggest a time around 500 B.C. as the earliest possible date for Chronicles, according to the internal evidence.

Recent discoveries have produced external evidence by which the latest possible

---

[1]As a further demonstration, notice that *dibrê hayyāmîm* occurs similarly in Chronicles itself (cf. 1 Chron 27:24) in reference to earlier, and distinct, court records (here "the annals of King David").

date for the books may now be set. The discovery of fragments of an actual MS of Chronicles among the DSS at Qumran cave four "makes a third-century date difficult to maintain"; and Myers (*Chronicles*, 1:LXXXVII–LXXXVIII) says of the Chronicler that it is "imperative to place his activity in the Persian period (ca. 538–333 B.C.)." Such recognition becomes all the more significant when we realize that historical criticism had tended to relegate this work to the Greek period (down to 165 B.C.).[2] More specifically, if we accept the tradition that the OT canon was finalized during the general period of the Persian monarch Artaxerxes I (Longimanus)[3] (died 424 B.C.; cf. Neh 12:22, whose reference to Darius II—who was crowned in 423—is the last historical allusion to appear in the OT), then Chronicles would have to have been written before 420. If its composition, moreover, is associated with the work of Ezra, we must notice that the Aramaic language found in the book that bears Ezra's name matches that of the Elephantine papyri, which likewise belongs to the fifth century B.C.

Relationships between the books of Chronicles and Ezra provide the most important single clue for fixing the date and also the authorship of the former volume. Since Chronicles appears to be the work of an individual writer,[4] who was a Levitical leader,[5] some identification with Ezra the priest and scribe (Ezra 7:1–6) appears possible from the outset. This conclusion is furthered, moreover, by the personal qualities that the writer displays; for "the author . . . was an ecclesiastical official of knowledge, insight, wisdom, courage, organizing ability, and determination to put through his plan" (Myers, *Chronicles*, 1:LXXXVI).

The literary styles of the books are similar;[6] and their contents have much in common: the frequent lists and genealogies, their focus on ritual, and joint devotion to the law of Moses.[7] Most significant of all, the closing verses of 2 Chronicles (36:22 –23) are repeated as the opening verses of Ezra (1:1–3a).

Jewish tradition affirms that Ezra wrote Chronicles, along with the book that

---

[2]Though there has been much uncertainty: North ("Theology," p. 369) says, "The gamut of [recent] dates of composition includes no less than ten, from 165 B.C., favored by Lods, all the way back to 515." This last figure is the view of Freedman, for he feels that Chronicles must date back to Zerubbabel, in the century before Ezra. Other proposals include 400, Rudolph; 350 or at least pre-Hellenizing, de Vaux, Eissfeldt, Kittel; 300, Fohrer; early third century, Dentan (p. 12), because he assumes a four-volume work (1–2 Chron, Ezra, and Neh), with Jaddua (mentioned in Neh 12:11, 22) seen as contemporary with Alexander; or before 200 (pre-Seleucid), Noth, Pfeiffer, and Torrey. North ("The Chronicler," p. 404) favors a basic text that appeared in 400, but with "continuing adaptations from 400 to 170, or even later"; cf. S. Herrmann: "The work of the Chronicler was *not* begun during the Persian period, but . . . its preparation extended well into the second century" (*A History of Israel in Old Testament Times* [Philadelphia: Fortress, 1975], p. 321).

[3]Josephus, *Against Apion*, I.38 (8); cf. how the Apocrypha associates the close of the OT canon with Ezra and Nehemiah (2 Esd 14:45; 2 Macc 2:13) and R.L. Harris, *Inspiration and Canonicity of the Bible*, rev. ed. (Grand Rapids: Zondervan, 1969), p. 169.

[4]As summarized by Ackroyd ("The Theology," p. 103): "It may well be that we should think of the Chronicler as the representative of a particular school of thought . . . yet it is proper also to give credit to the creative thinking of a leading individual within such a group."

[5]Some would class him specifically as a temple singer (e.g., G. von Rad, *Old Testament Theology* [New York: Harper & Row, 1962], 1:352) rather than priest; see the recognition he bestows on the temple Levites (1 Chron 23:31–32, though see the commentary below; 2 Chron 30:16) and the comparative criticism of certain priests (2 Chron 29:34, though nothing would prevent a priest too from honestly reporting these facts, if such were indeed true).

[6]Francisco (3:298) represents a minority opinion, in claiming a more graphic style for Chronicles.

[7]This unity of aim is stressed by Rudolph ("Problems," p. 404).

bears his name; and in recent scholarship it was the archaeologist W.F. Albright who particularly reemphasized this conclusion.[8] North now states that "the unity of Ezra with Chronicles as the concept of a single author is today upheld by as unanimous a consensus as can be found anywhere in exegesis."[9]

For those, therefore, who accept the historicity of the events recorded in Ezra—from the decree of Cyrus in 538 down to Ezra's reform in 458–457 B.C.—and the validity of Ezra's autobiographical writing within the next few years, the date of composition for both books as one consecutive history must be about 450 B.C., and the place, Jerusalem.

The matter of the authorship of Chronicles is more complex and less clear-cut than the way my late colleague, J. Barton Payne, described it above. In recent academic circles there is a shift from the traditional view that Ezra wrote the work to the view that the author is unknown (cf. Eskenazi, Fensham, and Newsome).

The view of authorship by Ezra is logical for many reasons. First, according to Talmudic tradition (*Baba Bathra* 15a), Ezra wrote the work. Second, since the ending of 2 Chronicles (36:22–23) is practically identical to the beginning of Ezra (1:1–3a), the two books must belong together, coming from the same hand. Third, the works of Ezra seem to have distinctive features and vocabulary all their own. This unique style is all the more obvious when his historical account is contrasted with other historical accounts. Indeed one may find an impressive list of this distinctive vocabulary prepared by Driver[10] and supplemented by Curtis and Madsen (pp. 27–36).

The evidence supporting the traditional view has been challenged by both Evangelicals and non-Evangelicals. Two excellent critiques of Ezra's authorship are found in Japhet's penetrating article and in Williamson's investigations (*Israel*, pp. 37–59; *Chronicles*, pp. 5–17). Much of what follows reflects their views.

The linguistic evidence will be examined first. The vocabulary list initially seems impressive and decisive. The Ezra corpus (Chronicles, Ezra-Nehemiah) appears to have its own distinctive vocabulary and style, which easily contrasts with the rest of the OT. As a means for determining the extent of Ezra's authorship, first Japhet and then Williamson wanted to explore what would happen when this list is studied on its own in Chronicles and Ezra-Nehemiah, viz., whether the vocabulary list is shared by both sections of Ezra's work. The research can be found in Williamson (*Chronicles*, pp. 5–17). The conclusion does not point to the unity of authorship but rather in the other direction, to diversity of writers.

Differences between Chronicles and Ezra-Nehemiah are not limited to matters of style and vocabulary but include ideology. The problem of mixed marriages shows the contrast best. When this issue was faced after the return from the Exile, it was opposed by both Ezra the scribe and Nehemiah the governor. The latter's theological basis for resisting mixed marriages is given in Nehemiah 13:26: "Was it not because of marriages like these that Solomon king of Israel

---

[8]Albright ("Date and Personality") did, however, assign a late date to Ezra; and though he later shifted this from 397 B.C. to 428 ("A Brief History of Judah From the Days of Josiah to Alexander the Great," BA 9 [1946]: 13–14), he still located Ezra *after* Nehemiah (cf. Leeseberg, pp. 80, 86)—unnecessarily, since both dealt with the same situation of mixed marriages; see following on Ezra.

[9]"The Chronicler," p. 404; see also G. Fohrer, *Introduction to the Old Testament* (Nashville: Abingdon, 1968), p. 238.

[10]S.R. Driver, *An Introduction to the Literature of the Old Testament* (New York: Scribner, 1913), pp. 534–40.

sinned? Among the many nations there was no king like him. He was loved by his God, and God made him king over all Israel, but even he was led into sin by foreign women." Yet when checking the account of Solomon's reign in Chronicles, not a word is said about this matter; and no denunciation of him is pronounced!

Other differences in ideological outlook are also evident. First, Ezra and Nehemiah abound with stories of the conflict between the faithful Jews who are determined to rebuild Jerusalem and their Samaritan opponents who are eager to stop them. This conflict is absent in Chronicles; and, indeed, the faithful remnant of the northern kingdom regularly participates in the religious revivals of the southern kingdom. Second, the very important place of the Davidic covenant and dynasty for the restoration of Israel fills the pages of Chronicles; Ezra-Nehemiah, on the other hand, are practically silent on this subject. Third, Chronicles exhibits a highly developed philosophy of history that can be seen in the doctrine of retribution throughout the reigns of the various kings. This doctrine is of minimal importance to Ezra-Nehemiah. Some have questioned whether it is even there at all (Williamson, *Israel*, pp. 67–68)!

Finally there is the matter of the overlapping material at the end of Chronicles and the beginning of Ezra. In the Hebrew Scriptures Chronicles is placed at the end of the third division, "The Writings," as the last book in the OT. Ezra-Nehemiah come after Daniel and before Chronicles. If the traditional view about Ezra's authorship is correct, two difficulties are raised. First, why should only part of his corpus be admitted into the canon, rather than the whole work? Second, why should Chronicles *follow* Ezra-Nehemiah in the MT and not precede it, which would be more natural, given the sequence of the described events? Furthermore, if Ezra penned these works, would he not have wanted them to be read as a unit rather than as two sections in *reverse order*? The difficulties are there if one insists on Ezra's authorship of Chronicles, but they will vanish if someone else wrote the books.

The author of Chronicles is someone unknown, yet a lot like Ezra. He shared some interests with the great scribe but had his own distinct interests as well. Beyond this we cannot be too sure. (Samir B. Massouh)

3. Integrity and Validity

The uncertainties that characterize modern historical criticism continue to be displayed in reference to the unity (i.e., the textual integrity) that is to be found within Chronicles. Some say, "The work is pretty much as it was when it left the hands of the author."[11] Others speak of an "almost complete unanimity" in critical circles on "an inner core from some early postexilic date . . . near the time of Ezra and a substantial part dated nearer to the Maccabean uprising" (North, "Theology," p. 369).

Yet when it comes down to identifying just what these non-Ezran portions might be, the so-called unanimity seems unhappily to be at a premium. Von Rad held that the earliest versions of Chronicles lacked the present pervasive stress on Levitical singers, but Eissfeldt followed another tangent and viewed the additions by later editors as consisting especially of the genealogies.[12] Actually all of 1 and 2

---

[11]Myers, *Chronicles*, 1:LXIII, though "with possibly a few exceptions," 1:XVIII.

[12]O. Eissfeldt, *The Old Testament, an Introduction* (New York: Harper & Row, 1965), p. 540.

Chronicles and Ezra are so closely connected in language, ideas, and theological purpose that it would be difficult to account for them on a basis other than that of unity in authorship.

The separation of the Book of Ezra from Chronicles seems to date back to the fifth century and to the placement of these writings within the OT canon (see Canonicity). The Book of Chronicles, however, continued for a long time as a single volume. Its present division into two parts occurred when it was translated into Greek early in the second century B.C.; for this longer text could more easily be handled on two scrolls. The division now appears in all Bibles, including the printed Hebrew editions.

The validity, or historicity, of Chronicles—where its pages are simply reproducing material from some of the older OT books (see Sources)—has been more consistently questioned than perhaps any other historical portion of Scripture outside of Genesis. Writers earlier in this century, such as W.A.L. Elmslie, Robert H. Pfeiffer, or Adam C. Welsh, rejected the Chronicler's history out of hand as mere Levitical propaganda. Many later writers have concurred with Eissfeldt's dictum, that it "distorts the actual events . . . [which it] improperly interprets . . . with its ignoring of realities . . . [through] miraculous interventions by God,"[13] or with North's ("The Chronicler," p. 403), that its episodes are "created . . . as a kind of theological reasoning . . . [with] clear divergences from what has been proved by archaeology."[14] The book, it is thus claimed, presents not history but "what ought to have happened" (Elmslie, p. 341).

Much of this criticism, however, is subjective. Other commentators have insisted that "the Chronicler's story is accurate wherever it can be checked, though the method of presentation is homiletical" (Myers, *Chronicles*, 1:LXIII). Several archaeologists (e.g., Albright) have called attention to the many statements unique to Chronicles that are being confirmed by archaeological discoveries; and Fohrer acknowledges that "the data concerning military installations and battles, which go beyond the book of Kings and come from an unknown source, may be considered reliable and trustworthy."[15]

Attitudes toward 1 and 2 Chronicles, moreover, are largely preconditioned by what the individual critics may already have decided about the Pentateuch, whose priestly history and legislation is so consistently affirmed by Ezra's books. The date and authorship of the latter are thus involved in this same issue. "In other words," as Pfeiffer once said, "only scholars who reject the Wellhausen theory *in toto* could accept Albright's dating" for Chronicles.[16] Yet this indeed might be preferable to rejecting Ezra's testimony, especially since now excavations at ancient Ugarit have

---

[13]Ibid., p. 536; cf. Dentan's criticism (pp. 54–56) that Eissfeldt "introduces miraculous incidents where there were none in the original" (citing 2 Chron 7:1–3; cf. 1 Kings 8:54–56), since Dentan is unwilling to permit belief in fire from heaven, or in God's glory filling Solomon's temple.

[14]Though, strangely, North can also speak of it as "essentially accurate." The most some will say is that "what we learn from his additions to the narrative [of 2 Sam] has little value for understanding the reign of David, but it is of great importance for the light it casts on worship in the temple in the time of the Chronicler"(!) (Francisco, p. 297).

[15]*IOT*, p. 246; though he goes on to say, "The Chronicler's own material and the way in which he used his sources completely distorts the history of the monarchy" (p. 247).

[16]O. Pfeiffer, *Introduction to the Old Testament*, rev. ed. (New York: Harper, 1948), p. 812. For Chronicles depends on the whole Pentateuch, including "P," Wellhausen's supposedly latest stratum; cf. Snaith's evaluation (pp. 109–11).

confirmed the authenticity in Canaan of just such elaborate priestly rituals, and in the very century that Moses is known to have been leading Israel out of Egypt.[17]

A final particular element that relates to the Chronicler's validity has been stated as follows: "The only valid objection . . . could be his numbers which, by any interpretation, are impossibly high. This fact perhaps more than any other has made the Chronicler's work suspect" (Myers, *Chronicles*, 1:LXIII). Even in this area, however, his reliability has been confirmed.[18] Of the 629 specific numbers that occur in both books, only the figures in 1 Chronicles 22:14 and 29:4, 7, which list some of the precious metals offered for Solomon's temple, might suggest the need to resort to an explanation of special providence.[19] These along with such other numerical passages as may have raised question are dealt with in the body of the commentary that follows.

4. Sources

If Ezra the scribe is the man responsible for the present Book of Chronicles, his "scribism" may well account for the careful acknowledgment of historical sources that appears through the volume. These fall into the following categories.

a. *Genealogies*

For the tribe of Simeon, the author of Chronicles explains, "They kept a genealogical record" (1 Chron 4:33); and for Gad he identifies his sources even more closely: "These were entered in the genealogical records during the reigns of Jotham [751–736 B.C.] king of Judah and Jeroboam [II, 793–753] king of Israel" (5:17). He refers to similar official genealogical lists for Benjamin (7:9), Asher (7:40), "all Israel" (9:1), the Levitical gatekeepers (9:22), and the family of Rehoboam (2 Chron 12:15); and the very nature of his book suggests numerous others that just did not happen to be so mentioned. Many of the groupings, but not all, correspond to lists that appear in the Pentateuch or in subsequent historical books of the canon, from Joshua through 2 Kings (see the commentary for references).

b. *Documents*

Since the Chronicler not only describes how the Assyrian king Sennacherib "wrote letters" against Judah but then goes on to cite excerpts from them (2 Chron 32:17–20), these too seem to represent a literary source (cf. an immediately preceding message that is quoted as deriving from this same monarch, vv. 10–15). The book also concludes with a proclamation made by the Persian king Cyrus, which he "put in writing" (36:22–23), and which is of acknowledged authenticity (Leeseberg, pp. 82–83). Another kind of documentary source underlies the detailed descriptions

---

[17]Cf. H.P. Hahn, *The Old Testament in Modern Research* (Philadelphia: Muhlenberg, 1955), pp. 110–11. This takes on particular significance, when even conservative writers may be tempted to downplay the accuracy of Chronicles; cf. Clark Pinnock, in Jack Rogers, ed., *Biblical Authority* (Waco: Word, 1977), p. 72.

[18]E.J. Young, *An Introduction to the Old Testament*, rev. ed. (Grand Rapids: Eerdmans, 1960), pp. 420–21.

[19]J.B. Payne, "The Validity of the Numbers in Chronicles," BS 136 (1979): 109–28, 206–20; cf. also *Near East Archaeological Society Bulletin*, New Series 11 (1978):5–58.

of the Solomonic temple in Jerusalem, because references are made to the plans "of all that the Spirit had put in his [David's] mind" for it (1 Chron 28:11–12)—and not just in his mind, but " 'All this,' David said, 'I have in writing from the hand of the LORD upon me' " (v. 19). Other documents have been proposed as well.[20]

c. Poems

Second Chronicles 29:30 alludes to songs of praise in the words of David and Asaph (cf. the titles to Pss 50, 73–83) and 35:25 to laments for Josiah that were chanted by Jeremiah (not to be identified with his later, canonical Lamentations, over Jerusalem). Neither is actually quoted, though the allusions suggest the author's use of poetic sources (cf. David's reemployment of Pss 95:1–5; 96; and 106:1, 47–48, which Ezra did quote [in 1 Chron 16:8–36]).

d. Prophecies

Among its sources Chronicles refers to at least eleven different prophetic books: those by the earlier prophets Samuel, Gad (1 Chron 29:29), Nathan (1 Chron 29:29; 2 Chron 9:29), Ahijah (2 Chron 9:29), Shemaiah (12:15), and Iddo, including both the "visions of Iddo" (9:29) and his "annotations" (13:22); and those by the later prophets Jehu son of Hanani (20:34), Isaiah, including both his "vision" (the OT book, 32:32) and his last history of Uzziah (26:22), and Hozai (33:19 comment, perhaps meaning simply a book of "the seers"). Second Chronicles alludes (36:22) to the fulfillment of Jeremiah 29:10 and may quote from 29:13–14 (2 Chron 15:4, unless both are drawing on Deut 4:29).

e. Other Histories

Ezra's major reference work was "the book of the kings of Israel and Judah" (2 Chron 27:7; 35:27; 36:8; cf. slight variants in this title that appear in 16:11; 25:26; 28:26; 32:32, or abbreviations, in 1 Chron 9:1; 2 Chron 20:34; 33:18). He also refers at one point to the "annals of King David" (1 Chron 27:24, which may have been part of the same work) and to the "annotations on the book of the kings" (2 Chron 24:27). But though much material from the canonical books of 1 and 2 Kings does reappear in Chronicles, these cannot be the source here cited. For passages such as 1 Chronicles 9:1 and 2 Chronicles 27:7 refer to "the book of the kings" for additional data on genealogies and wars, about which nothing further actually occurs in our canonical books. So while Ezra did use this major reference work directly, it must have been some larger court record—authentic[21] but now lost—from which both Kings and Chronicles could draw.

Since this "larger court record" is known to have incorporated some of the prophetic writings that have been listed above (specifically, from Jehu's, 2 Chron 20:34, and Isaiah's, 32:32), some critics have proposed that this work may have been Ezra's

---

[20]In 2 Chron 35:4 Josiah spoke of Levitical divisions drawn up "according to the directions written by David . . . and Solomon." This might suggest the document (decree) that now occupies 1 Chron 23, but it might also refer to some other law of David on this subject that was reaffirmed by his son Solomon (cf. 2 Chron 8:14).

[21]It was specifically valuable for its cited events that are not recorded in Kings. Eissfeldt (*Old Testament*, p. 535), for example, concedes, "These passages . . . are to a large extent trustworthy and fill out, particularly in regards to the kings of Judah, the information given in Kings."

only source, that all the others he refers to were but "illusions, ghost sources."[22] Comparison, however, of Isaiah 36–39, when made with 2 Kings 18:13–20:19 and 2 Chronicles 32, illustrates how this particular prophetic writing came first to be incorporated into the major court record and then subsequently to be utilized by both of the latter books.

For the other sources then, there appears to be no valid reason for questioning their reality either; indeed, "the language of the author is too definite to assume otherwise" (Myers, *Chronicles*, 1:XLVII). All in all, 57.8 percent of the text of Chronicles exhibits verbal parallels with other portions of the OT.[23] These include especially the Pentateuch and Joshua for the genealogies and other such listings and 2 Samuel and 1–2 Kings for the history.

5. Text

Wherever the text of 1 Chronicles is paralleled by Samuel, and where the rabbinic Hebrew (MT) of Samuel is opposed by fragments from the major DSS (4QSam^a), Chronicles has been found to be closer to the latter; and it is frequently supported in such cases by the LXX version of Samuel. F.M. Cross thus deduces a Palestinian text of Samuel, which must have been used in 450 B.C. by Ezra for Chronicles and came to underlie both the Qumran text (Dead Sea) and the LXX (in Egypt) but was distinct from the Babylonian textual form that underlies the "short" or sometimes even "defective" MT of Samuel.[24]

The Hebrew text of Chronicles is in a fair state of preservation, perhaps because of its infrequent copying. This in turn must have been due to its date of composition (relatively late among the OT books: only Nehemiah, the final compilation of Psalms, and Malachi would seem to be younger, i.e., down to 420 B.C.), and to its less popular use.

This last factor, however, may have led to *more* textual errors, whether from lack of familiarity or from lack of care in its copying. In the eleven cases of disagreement over numbers that have arisen between the MTs of Chronicles and of Samuel/Kings because of copyists' errors, Chronicles is found to be correct in five cases, incorrect in five, and one remains uncertain.[25] The LXX translation of Chronicles, made about 200 B.C., is of aid in textual restorations at some points, because of its almost extreme literalness, but not at others, because of its own poor state of preservation (Curtis, pp. 37–41).

Nevertheless, despite some errors such as numerical data or geneological names, it can be confidently affirmed that "the Hebrew text of Chronicles has been transmitted reasonably well, and as a whole is considerably less corrupt than some of the other Old Testament canonical books" (R.K. Harrison, IOT, p. 1169)[ed.].

---

[22]Pfeiffer (*Introduction*, p. 805), who includes even the court record; so too Noth and Torrey. Eissfeldt (*Old Testament*, p. 533) claims that the prophetic sources "are likely to coincide, in part at least," with the court record, though conceding that "no proof can be offered."

[23]Eighteen hundred out of the 3,114 lines of the Chronicles text in Abba Bendavid's *Parallels in the Bible*, which are analyzed in greater detail in Payne, "Validity of Numbers," pp. 111ff.

[24]*Qumran and the History of the Biblical Text* (Cambridge, Mass.: Harvard University Press, 1975), pp. 311–12. Similarly the genealogies of 1 Chron 1–9, when opposing the MT of Genesis or Numbers, find support from the Samaritan Pentateuch.

[25]Payne, "Validity of Numbers," p. 126.

6. Canonicity

Within the OT canon, Chronicles follows Kings in the second, or historical, division. Despite its original unity with Chronicles, Ezra is placed after it as a separate book, according to the canon's oldest descriptions (cf. Jos. *Against Apion*, I. 38 [8]).[26] Moreover the incompleteness of form with which the decree of Cyrus appears —breaking off in the middle of the king's decree—at the close of 2 Chronicles, and with which Ezra opens, suggests that Chronicles was added to the canon after Ezra was already there.

A plausible explanation is as follows: when God inspired Ezra in 450 to write the total volume, he also inspired him to place the last part of it (= Ezra) within the OT canon, as the divinely authorized sequel to the historical record of Kings. Only subsequently, perhaps at the canon's final compilation shortly before 420, did God lead him to insert the rest (= Chron), as supplementary parallels to the materials found in Samuel and Kings.

The NT, while not specifically citing Chronicles, does occasionally quote from it (e.g., 1 Chron 16:35 in Acts 26:17; K. Aland's *The Greek New Testament*, UBS [New York: American Bible Society, 1966], p. 905, lists, indeed, sixty-eight quotations). Eventually the expanding Greek canon separated Ezra from Chronicles by its unhappy addition of the apocryphal Book of 1 Esdras. Last of all, at a point that cannot be documented prior to the fourth Christian century, rabbinic authorities combined the former and latter prophets and transferred some of the former prophets (the histories of Chron), some of the shorter scrolls, and one latter prophet (Daniel) to the third division, the Writings. This was probably for liturgical reasons. But though Chronicles, as a result, now stands at the very end of printed Hebrew Bibles, the English (and Greek) arrangement is the one that corresponds to the order of the canon in NT times.[27] For in Matthew 23:35 Christ spoke of all the martyrs from Abel in the first book (Gen) down to the last martyred minor prophet (Zechariah, who was "slain in the sanctuary";[28] Malachi is not known to have suffered martyrdom).

7. Occasion and Purpose

When Ezra returned from Babylon in 458 B.C., his heart was set on enthroning God's law in the postexile community of Judah (Ezra 7:10). He took immediate steps to restore temple worship (7:19–23, 27; 8:33–34) and to eliminate a number of mixed marriages that had arisen between certain Jews and their pagan neighbors

---

[26]In his total of thirteen "prophets after Moses," the eight former prophets seem to include Joshua, Judges-Ruth, Samuel, Kings, Chronicles, Ezra-Nehemiah, Esther, and Job.

[27]Uncritical acceptance of the rabbinic arrangement, as if it were original, has led to a number of unjustifiable insinuations against 1–2 Chronicles: that Judaism may have had "considerable discussion of their inclusion" and "hesitation on recognizing [their] canonicity" (Francisco, 3:297) or may even have "ignored" them, because they merely retold Kings "and in some details contradicted it" (Dentan, p. 154). Others suggest that the Alexandrian order of OT books implies that the Greek canon accepted them before the Hebrew did (A. Sundberg, "The OT in the Early Church," HTR 51 [1958]: 205–26). However, for a recent defense of the canonical order of the MT and of the view that the Zechariah referred to in Matt 23:35 was the son of Jehoiada mentioned in 2 Chron 24 (cf. The NIV Study Bible, p. 1477), see Roger Beckwith, *The Old Testament Canon of the New Testament Church* (Grand Rapids: Eerdmans, 1985), pp. 181–234 [ed.].

[28]Targum to Lam 2:20; cf. J.B. Payne, "Zachariah who Perished," *Grace Journal* 8 (1967): 34.

(chs. 9–10). Based on powers granted him by the Persian king (7:18–25), Ezra seems to have been the one who commenced the refortification of Jerusalem (4:16), though subsequently thwarted by bitter Samaritan opposition (vv.17–23; cf. Neh 1:3 –4). Not until 444, when Ezra was joined by Nehemiah, were the walls actually finished (Neh 6:15–16) and the law of Moses formally recognized by the community (ch. 8). Yet if Ezra was the Chronicler, as suggested above, then the appearance of his book about 450 becomes explainable as a concrete literary means to aid in the achievement of his purpose of rebuilding the theocracy.

Three major features appear, drawn from those parts of its contents that are distinct from the data found in the parallel books of Samuel and Kings.

1. Ezra's goal of maintaining Israel's racial and religious purity explains his stress on genealogical listings (e.g., as recorded in 1 Chron 1–9; cf. Ezra 2:62–63). Purity was needed for survival, as demonstrated by the continuing threats of religious syncretism and of possible absorption that continued through the following quarter century (Neh 13:23–25; Mal 2:10–16). The true Israel lay in Jerusalem and Judah (listed first among the tribes, 1 Chron 3–4), as supported also by Benjamin (Ezra 1:5, 10:9; cf. 2 Chron 31:1; 34:9). The greatest danger, on the other hand, was found among the Samaritan "people of the land" (Ezra 4:1–10; Neh 4:1–2); Chronicles thus avoids references to even the former Hebrew kingdom of Samaria,[29] though it does record with favor the participation within Judah of faithful Hebrews from the north (2 Chron 11:13–17; 30:1, 5–11; 34:6; 35:18; cf. Braun, "Reconsideration").

2. Ezra's zeal for worship according to the law and to its Levitical institutions explains his emphasis on the temple (1 Chron 22), the sacred ark (ch. 13), and its attendant Levitical priests and singers (chs. 15–16). The national tragedy, with which Chronicles' history concludes, demonstrated once and for all that worship was more important than the state, that God's sovereignty was more effectively achieved through David's care for the temple than through his empire (29:11–12). This accounts for the omission from Chronicles of certain royal biographical materials that are found in other OT books (cf. 1 Sam 9; 1 Kings 3:16–28) and also of extensive narratives about the prophets and their preaching of morality (1 Kings 17:1–22:40; 2 Kings 1:1–8; 15).[30]

The Chronicler's stress on David's rituals has led some to suggest that his purpose was to replace the Sinaitic covenant altogether, in popular esteem, with the Davidic[31]—clearly a misunderstanding: Ezra's intent was to write about the period of the kingdom, not that of Moses, to whose work he was thoroughly committed (1 Chron 6:49; 15:15). Similarly his stress on the nonpriestly Levites (as in 2 Chron 29:12–15), combined with some relatively unfavorable judgments on certain Levitical priests (29:34; 30:3; cf. later lapses of the priests, e.g., between Nehemiah's two governorships, Neh 13:6), must not be misunderstood as indicating an attempt to usurp functions from the priesthood. Ezra records how the Levites too were far from perfect (2 Chron 24:5; cf. 30:15, where both groups needed to

---

[29]von Rad (*Theology*, 1:348) traces out scholarly discussion on this subject.

[30]Though Chronicles too is concerned about prophets and the Word of God (1 Chron 10:13; 2 Chron 20:20) and about faith and repentance (2 Chron 7:14; 14:5).

[31]North (*Chronicles*, 1:404, 414) thus says he teaches "the superior definitiveness of the Davidic covenant over that of Sinai . . . [which is] no longer worth fostering as a vital force in the life of the people" (cf. statements in 1:402 and "Theology," p. 378, that Moses is "out of the picture," in favor of David).

313

repent). In matters of worship "he was in essence a reformer whose success may be judged by the fact that the Jewish community ever afterward . . . remained basically a religious community" (Myers, *Chronicles*, 1:LXXXVII).

3. Ezra's concern to encourage the exiles who had returned to Judah explains his rehearsals of the past glories of David [32] and the God-given victories of his dynasty (cf. 2 Chron 13; 17; 20; 25). Their disillusionment in the face of contemporary hardships accounts for his omission of David's initial lack of success (as found in 2 Sam 1–4), his subsequent sins and defeats (chs. 11–21), Solomon's failures (1 Kings 11), and the entire history of the apostate kingdom in northern Israel. What was needed among mid-fifth-century Palestinian Jews was not censure but morale building, through hope in the messianic house of David.[33]

This is not to say that the Chronicler denied the failures of the past; he assumed that his readers were aware of them (cf. 1 Chron 22:8; 28:3);[34] and he thus went on to emphasize, for example, the more encouraging second anointing of Solomon (1 Chron 29:22) or the more exemplary first ways of David (2 Chron 17:3). The judgments in Kings and the hopes in Chronicles are both prophetic; both are true, and both are necessary. The morality of the judgments is fundamental; however, to experience the redemption of the hopes is the more distinctive purpose of a Christian proclamation.

8. Theology

Even a preliminary survey of the Chronicler's theological perspective invalidates the modern criticism leveled against the book.[35] Ezra honors the transcendent majesty of God (1 Chron 29:11) and quotes statements from past history describing him as above all gods (2 Chron 2:5), dwelling in heaven (6:18; 7:14), and ruling all earth (20:6).[36] The Lord's presence must be mediated, therefore, by his "name" (which carries the force of his person, 12:13), especially in the temple (1 Chron 22:7; 29:16), and by his Spirit, especially for communications (1 Chron 12:18; 2 Chron 15:1; 24:20). Angels thus occupy a greater place in Chronicles than in the

---

[32]von Rad (*Theology*, 1:350) asks, "What does the Chronicler's account of history contain apart from David . . . a spotless holy king . . . not in Israel, but in the 'kingdom of Yahweh' (1 Chron 28:5)"; and he underlines the author's goal of guarding the OT's messianic traditions during a poor age (p. 351).

[33]A lesser emphasis on David in that part of his work that now makes up the Book of Ezra (though cf. Ezra 3:10; 8:20) has led Myers and others to assume for Chronicles an earlier source that was seeking to restore the Davidic dynasty, but that was toned down by a final editor, who aimed simply at continuity for the Jewish community (Myers, *Chronicles*, 1:XXXI; cf. von Rad, *Theology*, 1:351; Freedman, pp. 436 –42). Yet the postexilic part of Ezra's history seems simply to have had less occasion to speak of David; the hope in both parts is messianic and not immediately political.

[34]David's disputed rule at Hebron is not concealed (1 Chron 3:1; 11:1; cf. the recognition of its "seven" years in 29:27), nor are his flights to Adullam (11:15) and to Ziklag (12:1).

[35]E.g., "It is difficult to imagine any theological question asked in this generation on which the book of Chronicles is likely to shed any light" (J.L. McKenzie, *A Theology of the Old Testament* [Garden City, N.Y.: Doubleday, 1974], p. 27).

[36]God does not dwell on earth, in the sense of being "contained by it"; the temple exists primarily for worshiping him (2 Chron 2:6; though cf. a similar concept in 1 Kings 5:3–5, which speaks of "a house for his name").

corresponding parts of the other OT histories (1 Chron 21:12[37] or 21:18, 20, 27[38]), as does also the Lord's mediation through Satan (21:1).

Yet God can be imminent as well, intervening into history (1 Chron 12:18; cf. 2 Chron 20:13) in answer to men's prayers and songs (2 Chron 14:11; 18:31; 20:9–12). The continuity of his concern is emphasized by the phrase "God of [the] fathers," whether this is used in quotations (1 Chron 29:20; 2 Chron 20:6) or by the Chronicler himself (2 Chron 13:18; 15:12); and his covenant love for Israel (6:14) is recognized even by foreigners (2:11; 9:8). Yahweh is the God of revelation, who fulfills his predictions (10:15; 36:21) and keeps his promises (1 Chron 17:26; 2 Chron 1:9; 6:15). Prophets of God that appear in Chronicles (but not in Kings) include Iddo (2 Chron 13:22), Azariah son of Oded (15:1, 8), Eliezer (20:37), and Jeremiah (35:25; 36:12, 21 –22); and their writings receive a unique stress (sec. 4.d, above). Corresponding attention is given to the written Mosaic Law,[39] which is to be taught (17:9) and to be honored (31:4, 21; cf. Myers, *Chronicles*, 1:LXXV–LXXX).

An acceptable relationship of men with God depends on their approaching him in accordance with his own special revelation. Men are received through the instrumentality of sacrifice[40] and are to serve him in worship, with joy (1 Chron 29:21–22). Salvation comes particularly through the priesthood (typical of Jesus Christ), who ministered in the temple at Jerusalem (6:32; cf. v.10). Is then Ezra's stress on "the temple of the LORD in Jerusalem on Mount Moriah" (2 Chron 3:1; cf. 30:1) exclusivistic? Yes, in the sense of John 14:6—no one comes to the Father but by the Son—but no, in the sense of his being unduly narrow (cf. the latitude that is recorded in 2 Chron 30:18–20 for deviations in regard to ritual purification).

The Chronicler's emphasis on "all Israel" as the people of God (1 Chron 13:2; 2 Chron 11:13, and the note of appeal in 2 Chron 13:5; 30:8; cf. 30:18–19 and Ezra 6:21) is less exclusive in respect to the northern tribes than was Nehemiah's policy a few years later (cf. Williamson, *Israel*). He records how even foreigners could be used to communicate God's word (2 Chron 35:22; 36:22), though Ezra's postexilic situation left little room for outright appeals for their conversion.

Instead the Book of Chronicles stresses the doctrine of God's retribution on Israel, as follows:

Events in Kings	Explained in 2 Chronicles
Shishak's invasion (1 Kings 14:25)	due to Rehoboam's sin (12:1)
Asa's illness (15:23)	for distrust and oppression (16:7–10)
Uzziah's leprosy (2 Kings 15:5)	when invading the temple (26:16–21)
Manasseh's long reign (21:1)	explained (?)[41] by late conversion (33:12–16)

---

[37]They are mentioned in the very words of God (which do not include them in the parallel passage of 2 Sam 24:13, though the angelic presence is recognized, v.16).

[38]Not included in the parallel passages (2 Sam 24:18, 20, 25).

[39]This is whether the law is viewed in its totality, as in 1 Chron 22:12, or in its particular regulations, as in 16:40. Von Rad (*Theology*, 1:352) objects, unnecessarily, to what he conceives to be a shift away from the former (spiritual) stress to the latter (as legalistic).

[40]Ackroyd ("The Theology," pp. 106–7) can thus relate the Chronicler's doctrine of human salvation to his whole approach toward history, summed up in the idea of "disaster . . . as the preface to restoration": first, and less clearly, in the genealogies (1 Chron 1–9); then in the career of David (from Saul to God's choice of the temple, 10:1–22:1); and so on down through the divided kingdom to the temple's postexilic rebuilding (2 Chron 10–Ezra 6).

[41]Yet cf. Ezra's recognition of the inadequacy of this reform (33:17).

Such patterns of "short-range retribution" (North, "Theology," p. 36) are often dismissed by contemporary critics as being an attempt to relate God directly to each generation in a way that is "forced" and "unsatisfactory."[42] Their charge of fabrication, however, is neither provable nor plausible; for "the writer is not blind to reality but is simply relating material to prove his point. Only in this way will his readers be warned" (Francisco, 2:302–3).

Yet beyond the retribution lies hope. God himself was the true king of Israel, with the Davidic line serving as his deputies (1 Chron 29:23); and the messianic promise given through Nathan (17:14) remained continuously relevant (2 Chron 6:42; cf. North, "Theology," p. 379). A basic theme, therefore, in Chronicles is "rest": militarism, even David's, is criticized (1 Chron 22:8); and peace exists as an ideal, not simply when needed for building the temple (vv.9–10), but as the reward of God's grace (2 Chron 14:6; 20:30; cf. Braun, "Solomon, " pp. 582–86).[43] Was then Ezra's hope limited, as some claim,[44] to preserving postexilic Jewish society in its peaceful status quo? Hardly. The Davidic promises that he so faithfully recorded include anticipations that were not only dynastic (suggesting a revival of the throne, 7:18; 13:5), but also eschatological. The writer of Chronicles has been called "the guardian of the Messianic tradition";[45] that is to say, "Since the dynasty was not ruling in the Chronicler's day, he was surely thinking eschatologically of the new David . . . that would arise in God's good time" (Stinespring, p. 211).

9. Theological Themes and Interests[46]

Careful reading of Chronicles shows that the author has certain recurring theological interests that he promotes throughout his work.

a. *Promise of God*

First, unlike the Book of Esther, where God operates behind the scene, in Chronicles the Lord takes center stage and leaves no doubt as to who is in charge. Thus rather than giving political, sociological, military, or economic explanations—or stating immediate causes for events—the author presents God as the Lord of history and the cause of its events.

The prominence of God may be seen in several incidents. God put Saul to death and gave the kingdom to David (1 Chron 10:14); God routed the armies of Jeroboam when he attacked Abijah (2 Chron 13:13–16); God destroyed the mighty army of Zerah when it battled Asa and his smaller forces (2 Chron 14:12–13); the Lord established the kingdom of Jehoshaphat (2 Chron 17:5) and defeated a military alli-

---

[42]Von Rad, *Theology*, 1:349–50; he charges that "it raises the correspondence between guilt and punishment to the level of complete rational proof—no disaster without guilt, no sin without punishment" (1:348).

[43]Through God's providence, Israel would "not have to fight" (2 Chron 20:17)—though she still had to march out in the battle (v.16)!

[44]"The Chronicler . . . directly identifies the kingdom of God with the empiric post-exilic Israel," T.C. Vriezen, *An Outline of Old Testament Theology* (Newton, Mass.: C.T. Branford, 1960), p. 305; cf. Myers, *Chronicles*, 1:LXXXIV–V.

[45]Von Rad, *Theology*, 1:351.

[46]This section has been supplied by Samir B. Massouh.

ance of Moab, Ammon, and Mount Seir even before the Hebrew army began to fight (2 Chron 20:22–23).

Perhaps the finest example of God's direct divine intervention in history may be seen in the way he utterly destroyed the mighty army of Sennacherib when that proud Assyrian ruler dared to challenge the power of the Almighty and to compare him to the gods of the other nations (2 Chron 32:16–22).

b. *Retribution*

A second interest of the author is his doctrine of retribution (see Theology). The idea of sowing and reaping is hardly new to Chronicles. It is spelled out in some detail in Leviticus and Deuteronomy, where obedience results in blessings but disobedience brings about curses. While this basic doctrine is retained in Chronicles, it is modified in at least two ways. First, the burden of obedience lies primarily on the shoulder of the king of the nation. It is his response to God that seems to affect the direction of the nation as a whole. Some emphasis is placed on the obedience of ordinary citizens, but more attention is given to the disposition of the ruler. When the sovereign is faithful, he is often rewarded with military victory, secure kingdom, wealth, and honor. When he forsakes God, he often reaps defeats and diseases. The history of the southern kingdom abounds with illustrations of this doctrine of retribution, and the principle may be found in 1 Chronicles 10:13–14 and 28:8–9.

While Chronicles emphasizes the doctrine of retribution, especially in relationship to the sovereign's faithfulness, the principle of sowing and reaping does not work automatically or mechanically. The sovereign ruler is often warned by a prophetic word about the evils of abandoning God and is exhorted to seek him; hence the ruler can repent and, in doing so, avert a calamity or military defeat. Prophetic words are given to Asa and Jehoshaphat, just to mention two cases, and the principle is no where expressed more majestically than in God's response to Solomon's prayer at the dedication of the temple. These words (2 Chron 7:14) are probably the most popular and easily recognized passage in Chronicles.

c. *Vocabulary*

The author's third theological interest, closely related to the doctrine of retribution, is his constant use of standard vocabulary and expressions like "seeking God," "pure heart," "faithfulness," and "forsaking the LORD." Because seeking God and being faithful to him bring about his blessings, it is not surprising to find many exhortations and injunctions to do so. In his Psalm of Thanks, David exhorted the nation to seek the Lord (1 Chron 16:10–11) and, later on, exhorted the leaders to do the same as they helped Solomon build the temple (1 Chron 22:19). Solomon was told that he would find God if he sought him (1 Chron 28:9), and Azariah the son of Oded said the same thing to Asa (2 Chron 15:2).

At the dedication of the temple, God declared to the people the importance of seeking him (2 Chron 7:14); yet Rehoboam did evil because he did not seek God (2 Chron 12:14). The great reforms of Asa reached a zenith when the people made a covenant to seek God (2 Chron 15:12); yet the king himself was condemned for not seeking God's help against Baasha or healing of his diseased foot (2 Chron 16:9, 12). Jehoshaphat was condemned for going to the aid of Ahab but was not punished completely because he often sought the Lord (2 Chron 19:3). And finally, one of the most godly rulers of Judah, King Josiah, began his tremendous reform by first seeking God (2 Chron 34:3).

d. Cultus

A fourth interest of Chronicles can be seen in the emphasis given to the ark, the temple, and the priesthood. Large sections deal with these matters. Two chapters cover the transporting of the ark to Jerusalem; eight chapters deal with the preparation for building the temple. Three chapters describe the actual construction of the temple, and three more cover its dedication. Furthermore three chapters cover Josiah's reforms, with special emphasis on the restoration of the central sanctuary and its functions. These large blocks of material alone indicate how deeply concerned the author is with proper worship. This concern for details is due, in part, to the fact that the northern kingdom rejected Mount Zion as the central sanctuary and replaced it with the golden calves at Bethel and Dan.

e. Worship

A fifth interest of Chronicles is closely related to Israel's worship at the temple. The author is not just concerned with the right persons officiating at the right place in the right external manner. The Chronicler is concerned about the nature of true worship as opposed to correct ceremony. This concern for the right attitude of the heart may be traced in two ways. First, the word "heart" is used some thirty times in Chronicles. The expression "perfect heart" is used fifteen times in the OT, with the majority of cases, nine, being in Chronicles. So it is important to notice that the exhortations to seek God are often connected to seeking him with one's heart, or with a perfect heart. Thus the activity of seeking God should be accompanied with the right inner attitude.

A second way of tracing the Chronicler's concern for true worship may be seen from his treatment of Hezekiah's reform. When Hezekiah launched his great reform, many people, even from the northern kingdom, followed his lead. Yet the king found himself in an awkward situation. On one hand it was necessary to celebrate the Passover. One quick solution might have been to ask these people to wait a whole year till it was the correct time to celebrate the Passover. This Hezekiah chose not to do. Instead he celebrated the Passover *twice!* A rigid person who is only concerned with correct ritual would have condemned Hezekiah for violating the instructions about the Holy Days. The Chronicler does nothing of the sort. On the contrary, Hezekiah is portrayed as one of the godliest Judean kings.

f. Kingdom

A sixth interest of Chronicles is the kingship in Israel. Because large amounts of material deal with the ark and the temple, it would be easy to conclude that the priesthood is very important to the author, but the kingship is not. This is not the case, and the opposite is true. The kingship is very significant to the Chronicler, as can be seen in two ways.

First, the kingdom of God and the kingdom of Judah are often treated as if they are one and the same entity. How quickly the author can shift from one to the other, in the same breath, is illustrated by the following verses. David said about Solomon that God "has chosen my son Solomon to sit on the throne of the kingdom of the

LORD over Israel" (1 Chron 28:5). Later on it is reported that "Solomon sat on the throne of the LORD as king in place of his father David" (1 Chron 29:23).

Secondly, the kingdom is important as the guardian of the temple. It was King David who gathered the necessary material to build the temple. It was King David who captured Jerusalem, making it the home of the central sanctuary, and brought the ark of the covenant. It was King Solomon who built the temple and led in its dedication. While these large portions of Scripture deal with Israel's worship, the kings play the major role, while the priesthood stays in the periphery. After the division of Solomon's kingdom, the Judean kings regularly expressed their commitment to God in terms of religious reforms, as can be seen especially in the reigns of Hezekiah and Josiah.

True worship in Israel was not preserved by godly priesthood but by godly kingship. Indeed the only high priest of any importance in Chronicles is Jehoiada, due to his role in preserving Joash of the dynasty of David, after Queen Athaliah had succeeded in almost wiping out the whole royal family. The author, then, sees that the kingship is important for taking care of the temple and providing for it. Religious reforms, led by the kings, often result in the people turning to God and experiencing joy in worship. This sense of revival even reaches the northern kingdom, and its faithful remnant join the true believers in the South in seeking God with their heart. In all these activities it is the kings who lead the way.

g. History

A seventh interest of the Chronicler is seen from the way he records historical events. It is not enough that he should describe the building of the temple; he must go beyond that and point out the striking resemblance of this event to the construction of the tabernacle in the wilderness. Similarly it is not enough for him to say that Solomon succeeded David on the throne; the Chronicler goes on to show how this transition is practically identical to the one between Moses and Joshua. Thus Solomon is depicted as a second Joshua and David as a second Moses. The Chronicler's use of this typology will be discussed in more detail in the commentary.

h. Omissions

A final interest of Chronicles is unlike the other seven ones already mentioned above. It does not deal with themes that run throughout the Chronicler's work, but rather in the material that he chose to leave out and omit from his discussion of Israel's history. From the reign of David, he has deleted three main blocks of material. He has left out the events found at 1 Samuel 15–31, which cover David's life in the court of Saul and his fugitive days when pursued by his jealous father-in-law. Also deleted is the material found in 2 Samuel 1–4, which deals with competition between David and his followers in Hebron and Ish-Bosheth and his followers in the North. The third block of omitted material involves David's sin with Bathsheba and the problems that followed it: the murder of Uriah; the rape of Tamar; the assassination of Amnon; the escape, return, revolt, and death of Absalom; the revolt of Sheba; and the struggle between Solomon and Adonijah for the throne. In other words, most of the material in 2 Samuel 11–1 Kings 2, with the exception of the census, is omitted.

Concerning the reign of Solomon, Chronicles omits two blocks of material. First, as mentioned above, the struggle between Solomon and Adonijah for the throne, and the steps Solomon took to solidify his position: the killing of Adonijah, Joab, and Shimei, and the banishing of Abiathar to Anathoth are omitted. Second Chronicles deletes the material dealing with Solomon's many foreign wives, the resultant spread of idolatry, and God's punishment of the king for this sin (1 Kings 11).

After the division of Solomon's kingdom, Chronicles does not deal with the northern kingdom on its own terms and for its own intrinsic interest. Instead the Chronicler deals with it as it comes into contact with the kingdom of Judah, and especially as its citizens respond to the religious revivals in the South. This perhaps accounts for the omission of reference to the significant ministries of the great prophets Elijah and Elisha.

The Chronicler recorded a history of Israel in which he chose both to emphasize certain points and to delete some material, especially from the reigns of David and Solomon. The omissions should not cause the modern reader to conclude that the Chronicler was conspiring to hide the faults and sins of David and Solomon by presenting the two kings in better light than they deserve. There is no plot or attempt to suppress the truth. As pointed out above, the Chronicler often cited the sources he used. In doing so he identified the material he had and made it possible for his contemporaries to examine the same sources available to him. If one of these sources—perhaps the major one—is the canonical 1 Samuel–2 Kings, then the reader can find out for himself all about the failures and weaknesses of David and Solomon. Had the Chronicler desired to hide the facts, he would have avoided mentioning the books he used, thus blocking or hindering further investigation by interested readers.

Furthermore, from the way the Chronicler mentions his sources, he gives the impression that they are well known to everyone. In developing his theological commentary on the events of the past, he leaves out certain material that does not contribute to the point he is emphasizing. Those who want another perspective on history can read the former prophets or recite the facts that were well known to Israel.

10. Bibliography

Commentaries

Ackroyd, Peter R. *I and II Chronicles, Ezra, Nehemiah*. Torch Bible Commentaries. London: SCM, 1973.

Barnes, W.E. *The Books of the Chronicles*. CBSC. Cambridge: University Press, 1899.

Coggins, R.J. *The First and Second Books of the Chronicles*. The Cambridge Bible Commentary. Cambridge: Cambridge University Press, 1976.

Curtis, E.L., and Madsen, A.A. *A Critical and Exegetical Commentary on the Books of Chronicles*. ICC. New York: Scribner's, 1910.

Dentan, Robert C. *Kings-Chronicles*. The Layman's Bible Commentary. Richmond: John Knox, 1964.

Ellison, H.L. "I and II Chronicles." *New Bible Commentary: Revised*. Edited by D. Guthrie et al. Grand Rapids: Eerdmans, 1970.

Elmslie, W.L. "The First and Second Books of the Chronicles." *The Interpreters Bible*. Vol. 3. Edited by George Buttrick. New York: Abingdon, 1954.

Fensham, F.C. *The Books of Ezra and Nehemiah*. NICOT. Grand Rapids: Eerdmans, 1982.

Francisco, Clyde T. "1–2 Chronicles." *The Broadman Bible Commentary*. Vol. 3. Edited by C.J. Allen. Nashville: Broadman, 1969.

Harvey-Jellie, W.R. *Chronicles*. The Century Bible. Edinburg: T.C. and E.C. Jack, 1905.
Hebert, A. "I and II Chronicles." *Peake's Commentary on the Bible*. Edited by M.Black and H.H. Rowley. London: Thomas Nelson, 1962.
Keil, C.F. *The Books of the Chronicles*. KD. Grand Rapids: Eerdmans, 1950.
McConville, J.G. *I and II Chronicles*. The Daily Study Bible. Philadelphia: Westminster, 1984.
Myers, Jacob M. *I Chronicles. II Chronicles*. AB. New York: Doubleday, 1965.
North, Robert, "The Chronicler: 1–2 Chronicles, Ezra, Nehemiah." *The Jerome Biblical Commentary*. Vol. I. Edited by R.E. Brown, J.A. Fitzmyer, and R.E. Murphy. Englewood Cliffs, N.J.: Prentice-Hall, 1968.
Payne, J.B. "I Chronicles, II Chronicles." *The Wycliffe Bible Commentary*. Edited by C.F. Pfeiffer and E.F. Harrison. Chicago: Moody, 1962.
Rudolph, W. *Chronikbucher*. Handbuch zum Alten Testament. Tübingen: Mohr, 1955.
Sailhammer, John. *First and Second Chronicles*. Everyman's Bible Commentary. Chicago: Moody, 1983.
Sawyer, R.L. "I and II Chronicles." *Beacon Bible Commentary*. Vol. 2. Kansas City, Mo.: Beacon Hill, 1965.
Slotki, I.W. *Chronicles*. Soncino Books of the Bible. London: Soncino, 1952.
Williamson, H.G.M. *I and II Chronicles*. The New Century Bible Commentary. Grand Rapids: Eerdmans, 1982.
Zöckler, Otto. *The Book of Chronicles*. Lange's Commentary. New York: Scribner's, 1876.

Books
Allen, Leslie C. *The Greek Chronicles*. 2 vols. Leiden: Brill, 1975.
Noth, Martin. *Überlieferungsgeschichtliche Studien*. Tübingen: Neimeyer, 1957.
Rad, Gerhard von. *Das Geschichtsbild des chronistischen Werkes*. Stuttgard: Kohlhammer, 1930.
Snaith, N.H. "The Historical Books." *The Old Testament and Modern Study*, edited by H.H. Rowley. Oxford: University Press, 1951.
Torrey, C.C. *The Chronicler's History of Israel*. New Haven, Conn.: Yale University Press, 1954.
Welch, Adam C. *The Work of the Chronicler*. London: British Academy, 1939.
Williamson, H.G.M. *Israel and the Book of Chronicles*. Cambridge: University Press, 1977.

Articles
Ackroyd, Peter R. "History and Theology in the Writings of the Chronicler." *Concordia Theological Monthly* 38 (1967): 501–15.
––––––. "The Theology of the Chronicler." *Lexington Theological Quarterly* 8 (1973): 101–16.
Albright, W.F. "The Date and Personality of the Chronicler." *Journal of Biblical Literature* 40 (1921): 104–24.
Boyd, J. Oscar. "An Undesigned Coincidence." *Princeton Theological Review* 3 (1905): 299–303.
Braun, Roddy. "The Message of Chronicles: Rally Around the Temple." *Concordia Theological Monthly* 42 (1971): 502–14.
––––––. "Solomonic Apologetic in Chronicles." *Journal of Biblical Literature* 92 (1973): 503–16.
––––––. "Solomon, the Chosen Temple Builder: the Significance of I Chronicles 22, 28, and 29 for the Theology of Chronicles." *Journal of Biblical Literature* 95 (1976): 581–90.
––––––. "A Reconsideration of the Chronicler's Attitude Toward the North." *Journal of Biblical Literature* 96 (1977): 59–62.
Dillard, R.B. "The Reign of Asa (2 Chronicles 14–16): An Example of the Chronicler's Theological Method." *Journal of the Evangelical Theological Society* 23 (1980): 207–18.
––––––. "The Chronicler's Solomon." *Westminster Theological Journal* 43 (1981): 289–300.

Eskenazi, T.C. "The Chronicler and the Composition of 1 Esdras," *Catholic Biblical Quarterly* 48 (1986): 39–61.

Freedman, D.N. "The Chronicler's Purpose." *Catholic Biblical Quarterly* 23 (1961): 436–42.

Goldingay, John. "The Chronicler as a Theologian." *Biblical Theological Bulletin* 5 (1975): 99–126.

Japhet, Sara. "The Supposed Common Authorship of Chronicles and Ezra-Nehemiah Investigated Anew." *Vetus Testamentum* V, 18 (1968): 330–71.

Leeseberg, M.W. "Ezra and Nehemiah: a Review of the Return and Reform." *Concordia Theological Monthly* 33 (1962): 79–90.

Lemke, W.E. "The Synoptic Problem in Chronicles' History." *Harvard Theological Review* 58 (1965): 349–63.

Macmillan, Kerr D. "Concerning the Data of Chronicles." *The Presbyterian and Reformed Review* 11 (1900): 507–11.

Moriarty, F.L. "The Chronicler's Account of Hezekiah's Reform." *Catholic Biblical Quarterly* 27 (1965): 399–406.

Myers, J.M. "The *Kerygma* of the Chronicler." *Interpretation* 20 (1966): 259–73.

Newsome, James, Jr. "Toward a New Understanding of the Chronicler and His Purpose." *Journal of Biblical Literature* 94 (1975): 201–17.

North, Robert. "Theology of the Chronicler." *Journal of Biblical Literature* 82 (1963): 369–81.

Pfeiffer, Robert H. "I and II Chronicles." *Interpreter's Dictionary of the Bible*, edited by G. A. Buttrick. Nashville: Abingdon, 1962, 1:572–80.

Richardson, H.N. "The Historical Reliability of the Chronicler." *Journal of Bible and Religion* 26 (1958): 9–12.

Rudolph, W. "Problems of the Books of Chronicles." *Vetus Testamentum* 4 (1954): 401–9.

Schultz, S.J. "Books of Chronicles." *Zondervan Pictorial Encyclopedia of the Bible*, edited by M.C. Tenney. Grand Rapids: Zondervan, 1975, 1:809–15.

Stinespring, W.F. "Eschatology in Chronicles." *Journal of Biblical Literature* 80 (1961): 209–19.

Watson, W.G.E. "Archaic Elements in the Language of Chronicles." *Biblica* 53 (1972): 191–207.

Williamson, H.G.M. "The Accession of Solomon in the Book of Chronicles." *Vetus Testamentum* 26 (1976): 351–61.

———. "Eschatology in Chronicles." *Tyndale Bulletin* 28 (1977): 115–54.

———. "Sources and Redaction in the Chronicler's Genealogy of Judah." *Journal of Biblical Literature* 98 (1979): 351–59.

———. "'We are yours, O David': The Setting and Purpose of I Chronicles xii 1–23." *Oudtestamentische Studiën* 21 (1981): 164–76.

Zimmerman, F. "Chronicles as a Partially Translated Book." *Jewish Quarterly Review* 42 (1951–52): 387–412.

11. Outline

I. Genealogies (1 Chron 1:1–9:44)
   A. Patriarchs (1:1–54)
   B. Judah (2:1–4:23)
      1. The clan of Hezron (2:1–55)
      2. The family of David (3:1–24)
      3. Other clans of Judah (4:1–23)
   C. Simeon (4:24–43)
   D. Transjordan Tribes (5:1–26)
   E. Levi (6:1–81)
   F. Benjamin and Five Other Tribes (7:1–9:44)
      1. Summaries (7:1–40)
      2. Benjamin (8:1–40)
      3. Jerusalem's inhabitants (9:1–44)

II. The Reign of David (10:1–29:30)
   A. Background: the Death of Saul (10:1–14)
   B. David's Rise (11:1–20:8)
      1. David established in Jerusalem; his heroes (11:1–12:40)
      2. The ark sought (13:1–14)
      3. Independence from the Philistines (14:1–17)
      4. The ark brought to Jerusalem (15:1–16:43)
      5. Nathan's prophecy (17:1–27)
      6. Conquests and administration (18:1–17)
      7. Victories over Ammon (19:1–20:3)
      8. Philistine wars (20:4–8)
   C. David's Latter Days (21:1–29:30)
      1. The census (21:1–30)
      2. Temple preparations (22:1–19)
      3. Levitical organization (23:1–26:32)
      4. The civil organization (27:1–34)
      5. Final words (28:1–29:30)

III. The Reign of Solomon (2 Chron 1:1–9:31)
   A. Solomon's Inauguration (1:1–17)
   B. Solomon's Temple (2:1–7:22)
      1. Preparations (2:1–18)
      2. Construction (3:1–4:22)
      3. Dedication (5:1–7:22)
   C. Solomon's Kingdom (8:1–9:31)
      1. Its achievements (8:1–18)
      2. Its splendor (9:1–31)

IV. The Kingdom of Judah (10:1–36:23)
   A. The Division of the Kingdom (10:1–11:23)
   B. The Rulers of Judah (12:1–36:16)
      1. Rehoboam (12:1–16)
      2. Abijah (13:1–14:1a)
      3. Asa (14:1b–16:14)
      4. Jehoshaphat (17:1–20:37)
      5. Jehoram (21:1–20)

Text and Exposition

I. Genealogies (1:1–9:44)

A. Patriarchs

1:1–9:44

¹Adam, Seth, Enosh, ²Kenan, Mahalalel, Jared, ³Enoch, Methuselah, Lamech, Noah.

⁴The sons of Noah:
Shem, Ham and Japheth.

⁵The sons of Japheth:
Gomer, Magog, Madai, Javan, Tubal, Meshech and Tiras.
⁶The sons of Gomer:
Ashkenaz, Riphath and Togarmah.
⁷The sons of Javan:
Elishah, Tarshish, the Kittim and the Rodanim.

⁸The sons of Ham:
Cush, Mizraim, Put and Canaan.
⁹The sons of Cush:
Seba, Havilah, Sabta, Raamah and Sabteca.
The sons of Raamah:
Sheba and Dedan.
¹⁰Cush was the father of
Nimrod, who grew to be a mighty warrior on earth.
¹¹Mizraim was the father of
the Ludites, Anamites, Lehabites, Naphtuhites, ¹²Pathrusites, Casluhites (from whom the Philistines came) and Caphtorites.
¹³Canaan was the father of
Sidon his firstborn, and of the Hittites, ¹⁴Jebusites, Amorites, Girgashites, ¹⁵Hivites, Arkites, Sinites, ¹⁶Arvadites, Zemarites and Hamathites.

¹⁷The sons of Shem:
Elam, Asshur, Arphaxad, Lud and Aram.
The sons of Aram:
Uz, Hul, Gether and Meshech.
¹⁸Arphaxad was the father of Shelah,
and Shelah the father of Eber.
¹⁹Two sons were born to Eber:
One was named Peleg, because in his time the earth was divided; his brother was named Joktan.
²⁰Joktan was the father of
Almodad, Sheleph, Hazarmaveth, Jerah, ²¹Hadoram, Uzal, Diklah, ²²Obal, Abimael, Sheba, ²³Ophir, Havilah and Jobab. All these were sons of Joktan.

²⁴Shem, Arphaxad, Shelah,
²⁵Eber, Peleg, Reu,
²⁶Serug, Nahor, Terah
²⁷and Abram (that is, Abraham).

²⁸The sons of Abraham:
Isaac and Ishmael.
²⁹These were their descendants:
Nebaioth the firstborn of Ishmael, Kedar, Adbeel, Mibsam, ³⁰Mishma, Dumah, Massa, Hadad, Tema, ³¹Jetur, Naphish and Kedemah. These were the sons of Ishmael.

³² The sons born to Keturah, Abraham's concubine:
Zimran, Jokshan, Medan, Midian, Ishbak and Shuah.
The sons of Jokshan:
Sheba and Dedan.
³³ The sons of Midian:
Ephah, Epher, Hanoch, Abida and Eldaah.
All these were descendants of Keturah.

³⁴ Abraham was the father of Isaac.
The sons of Isaac:
Esau and Israel.
³⁵ The sons of Esau:
Eliphaz, Reuel, Jeush, Jalam and Korah.
³⁶ The sons of Eliphaz:
Teman, Omar, Zepho, Gatam and Kenaz;
by Timna: Amalek.
³⁷ The sons of Reuel:
Nahath, Zerah, Shammah and Mizzah.

³⁸ The sons of Seir:
Lotan, Shobal, Zibeon, Anah, Dishon, Ezer and Dishan.
³⁹ The sons of Lotan:
Hori and Homam. Timna was Lotan's sister.
⁴⁰ The sons of Shobal:
Alvan, Manahath, Ebal, Shepho and Onam.
The sons of Zibeon:
Aiah and Anah.
⁴¹ The son of Anah:
Dishon.
The sons of Dishon:
Hemdan, Eshban, Ithran and Keran.
⁴² The sons of Ezer:
Bilhan, Zaavan and Akan.
The sons of Dishan:
Uz and Aran.

⁴³ These were the kings who reigned in Edom before any Israelite king reigned:
Bela son of Beor, whose city was named Dinhabah.
⁴⁴ When Bela died, Jobab son of Zerah from Bozrah succeeded him as king.
⁴⁵ When Jobab died, Husham from the land of the Temanites succeeded him as king.
⁴⁶ When Husham died, Hadad son of Bedad, who defeated Midian in the country of Moab, succeeded him as king. His city was named Avith.
⁴⁷ When Hadad died, Samlah from Masrekah succeeded him as king.
⁴⁸ When Samlah died, Shaul from Rehoboth on the river succeeded him as king.
⁴⁹ When Shaul died, Baal-Hanan son of Acbor succeeded him as king.
⁵⁰ When Baal-Hanan died, Hadad succeeded him as king. His city was named Pau, and his wife's name was Mehetabel daughter of Matred, the daughter of Me-Zahab. ⁵¹ Hadad also died.

The chiefs of Edom were:
Timna, Alvah, Jetheth, ⁵²Oholibamah, Elah, Pinon, ⁵³Kenaz, Teman, Mibzar, ⁵⁴Magdiel and Iram. These were the chiefs of Edom.

Chronicles begins with nine chapters of genealogies. Their purpose is to show the place that the 450 B.C. postexilic community of Judah occupies within total history. Far from being merely dull lists to be passed over as rapidly as possible, they serve two practical functions. For the immediate situation, genealogies were important in providing the framework within which true Hebrews could establish their genealogical roots and by which religious purity could be maintained against outside groups and influences.

For the church's overall perspective, the genealogies reflect the providential design that marks the sweep of history from Eden onward. Particular names serve as reminders of God's dealings in the past; and the genealogies' focus on David and his dynasty embodies the OT hope for the future Messiah, with the meaningfulness that this provided for Ezra's generation.

Compare the similar genealogies that furnish a background for the NT Gospels (Matt 1; Luke 3). Their substance is drawn from the entire OT canon that precedes Chronicles (Gen–2 Kings), though supplemented by a few lists that have not otherwise been preserved.

Chapter 1 spans the centuries from Adam to the patriarch Jacob, who fathered the tribes of Israel. It corresponds roughly to Genesis in scope and, except for part of v.51, has that book wholly as its source. Branches of the human race rather remote from Israel are dismissed with little mention, while Ezra reproduces in greater detail those more closely related to his Jewish people.

1–4 Ezra's survey commences with Adam, not just Abraham the father of the Hebrews. This points to the unity of the race (Acts 17:26) and to the universality of God's redemptive program within history (Gen 3:15). Verses 1–4 are compiled from Genesis 5. Seth's brothers, Abel and Cain, with his line (Gen 4:17–25), are omitted as irrelevant, as without survivors.

5 Verses 5–23 are drawn from the "table of nations" in Genesis 10:2–29 (q.v.). The seven sons of Japheth founded the people of Europe and northern Asia (e.g., from Javan comes Greek Ionia; from Gomer, the ancient Cimmerians of the Russian plains; and from Madai, the Medes and Persians of Iran. Tubal and Meshech were ancestors of the eighth-century Tabali and Mushki who inhabited the Turkish plateau, according to contemporary Assyrian inscriptions).

7 Areas proposed for the first two Greek subgroups include Elishah (in south Greece; cf. KB, p. 54) and Sardinia; the latter two—"Kittim and Rodanim"—denote the islands of Cyprus and Rhodes.

8 The four sons of Ham founded ethnic groups in Africa and southwestern Asia (e.g., Put in Libya on the Mediterranean coast of Africa west of Egypt; and Cush, or "Ethiopia," in Nubia to its south).

9–11 Yet the five listed sons of Cush founded tribes that extended eastward from the coast of the Red Sea, across southern Arabia, to the Kassites in the Tigris-Euphrates Valley. The second river of Eden can thus be said to border Cush (Gen 2:13), and Babylon and Assyria pertain to the Cushite leader Nimrod (10:8–11).

12–16 The Hamitic Philistines were "sea peoples" before settling in Palestine, coming from the Casluhim, who were of Egyptian origin but are related to the Minoan culture of Caphtor (Crete) and the southern coast of Asia Minor (Amos 9:7).

17 The five sons of Shem produced the peoples who remained closest to mankind's original home in west-central Asia. Yet they ranged from Elam, north of the Persian Gulf, to Aram in Syria and Lud (Lydia) in central Turkey.

18 The name Eber forms the root of "Hebrew" (*'ibrî;* some have traced the name Ebrium/Ebrum of the Ebla tablets to the same root); but this patriarch was ancestor not only of Abraham (v.27), but also of a number of other unsettled people, known in ancient history as Ḥabiru or Apiru.

19–23 The only "dividing up" of the earth to which Genesis makes reference in its postdiluvian context is that which occurred at the confusion of languages at Babel (Gen 11:1–9). The name Peleg seems to have been derived from this event.

24–27 The list of names from Shem to Abram sums up the table of Genesis 11:10–26. Both men constitute significant reminders of God's special relations with his people: the first, as the initial example of the Lord's association with a particular part of humanity, i.e., the Semites (Gen 9:26: "the LORD [Yahweh] the God of Shem"), and Abraham as a climactic witness to divine election (12:2; 17:7). The latter's change of name is explained in Genesis 17:5.

28–34 The information on the families of Abraham and Isaac is identical with that found in Genesis 25:1–4, 9, and 13–16. Abraham's nomadic Arabian descendants through his two subordinate wives, Hagar and Keturah, are given first, before the biblical record focuses on Sarah's son, Isaac, who was the child of promise. Arabs became increasingly influential in Judah (cf. Neh 4:7–6:1) after occupying Ezion Geber at the northeast end of the Red Sea in 500 B.C. (IB, 6:858).

35 The remainder of chapter 1 summarizes the "table of Edom" in Genesis 36:4–5, 11–13, 20–28, 31–43—with few scribal corruptions in spelling (see Notes). The subject of the rest of 1–2 Chronicles is Jacob, or Israel, and the Twelve Tribes that descend from him; but before the record focuses on this younger of Isaac's twin sons, it lists the elder brother, Esau, and the Edomite tribes that he founded. They were Israel's closest "brothers" (Obad 10, 12) and near neighbors, after Arab pressure forced them into southern Judah fifty years prior to Ezra.

36 Timna, a daughter of Seir (v.39), became a subordinate wife of Esau's son Eliphaz (Gen 36:12), and was later honored by having her name bestowed on an Edomite chieftain and his district (36:40; cf. 1 Chron 1:51).

38 Seir belonged to a group called "Horites" (Gen 36:20), the ancient Hurrians, a major people of Mesopotamia (see H. Hoffner's discussion in D.J. Wiseman's *Peoples of Old Testament Times* [Oxford: Clarendon, 1973]). Some had settled in Edom (= Seir) before the coming of Esau (Deut 2:12, 22).

42 Uz gave the name to the home of the patriarch Job (Job 1:1), who may thus have been an early Edomite descendant of Esau (cf. Lam 4:21). Similarly Esau's son Eliphaz, the father of Teman, seems to have been in the ancestry of Job's friend Eliphaz the Temanite (Job 2:11).

51 The death of King Hadad is not mentioned in Ezra's biblical source (Gen 36:39), perhaps because Hadad II was still living when Moses authored this part of the Pentateuch, a thousand years before the inscripturation of Chronicles.

Notes

4 The latter two words of נֹחַ בְּנֵי נֹחַ (nōᵃḥ bᵉnê nōᵃḥ, "Noah. The sons of Noah") seem to have fallen out of the MT by scribal paraleipsis; and subsequent readers must simply have been expected to understand (from Gen 5:32) that the names of Shem, Ham, and Japheth that followed referred to brothers, not to three more successive generations (see KJV, NASB; cf. similar omissions of "the sons of Japheth," v.17 and "by" Timna, v.36).

17 מֶשֶׁךְ (mešek, "Meshech") is probably a scribal error (influenced by v.5) for מַשׁ (maš, "mash") as preserved in six MSS, the Syriac, and Gen 10:23.

22 עֵיבָל (ʿêḇāl, "Ebal") is probably a scribal error for עוֹבָל (ʿôḇāl, "Obal"), as preserved in nineteen MSS, the Syriac, and Gen 10:28.

34 Chronicles employs the covenant name Israel (cf. 1 Chron 2:1), never Jacob, except at 16:13, 17 (quoted from Ps 105, and even here in parallelism with Israel).

43 The marginal alternative—"before an Israelite king reigned over them"—is unlikely both grammatically and chronologically: Ezra's source (Gen 36:31) was written long before David's initial conquest of Edom, though Moses *did* anticipate the fact of Israelite kings (Gen 49:10; Deut 17:14).

בֶּלַע (belaʿ, "Bela"), son of Beor, is not to be confused with the later בִּלְעָם (bilʿām, "Balaam"), son of Beor (Num 22:5), living on the Euphrates.

B. Judah (2:1–4:23)

1. The clan of Hezron

2:1–55

¹These were the sons of Israel:
Reuben, Simeon, Levi, Judah, Issachar, Zebulun, ²Dan, Joseph, Benjamin, Naphtali, Gad and Asher.

³The sons of Judah:
Er, Onan and Shelah. These three were born to him by a Canaanite woman, the daughter of Shua. Er, Judah's firstborn, was wicked in the LORD's sight; so the LORD put him to death. ⁴Tamar, Judah's daughter-in-law, bore him Perez and Zerah. Judah had five sons in all.

⁵The sons of Perez:
Hezron and Hamul.

⁶The sons of Zerah:
Zimri, Ethan, Heman, Calcol and Darda—five in all.

⁷The son of Carmi:
Achar, who brought trouble on Israel by violating the ban on taking devoted things.

⁸The son of Ethan:
Azariah.

⁹The sons born to Hezron were:
Jerahmeel, Ram and Caleb.

¹⁰Ram was the father of
Amminadab, and Amminadab the father of Nahshon, the leader of the

people of Judah. [11]Nahshon was the father of Salmon, Salmon the father of Boaz, [12]Boaz the father of Obed and Obed the father of Jesse.

[13] Jesse was the father of
Eliab his firstborn; the second son was Abinadab, the third Shimea, [14]the fourth Nethanel, the fifth Raddai, [15]the sixth Ozem and the seventh David. [16]Their sisters were Zeruiah and Abigail. Zeruiah's three sons were Abishai, Joab and Asahel. [17]Abigail was the mother of Amasa, whose father was Jether the Ishmaelite.

[18] Caleb son of Hezron had children by his wife Azubah (and by Jerioth). These were her sons: Jesher, Shobab and Ardon. [19]When Azubah died, Caleb married Ephrath, who bore him Hur. [20]Hur was the father of Uri, and Uri the father of Bezalel.

[21] Later, Hezron lay with the daughter of Makir the father of Gilead (he had married her when he was sixty years old), and she bore him Segub. [22]Segub was the father of Jair, who controlled twenty-three towns in Gilead. [23](But Geshur and Aram captured Havvoth Jair, as well as Kenath with its surrounding settlements—sixty towns.) All these were descendants of Makir the father of Gilead.

[24] After Hezron died in Caleb Ephrathah, Abijah the wife of Hezron bore him Ashhur the father of Tekoa.

[25] The sons of Jerahmeel the firstborn of Hezron:
Ram his firstborn, Bunah, Oren, Ozem and Ahijah. [26]Jerahmeel had another wife, whose name was Atarah; she was the mother of Onam.

[27] The sons of Ram the firstborn of Jerahmeel:
Maaz, Jamin and Eker.

[28] The sons of Onam:
Shammai and Jada.
The sons of Shammai:
Nadab and Abishur.

[29] Abishur's wife was named Abihail, who bore him Ahban and Molid.

[30] The sons of Nadab:
Seled and Appaim. Seled died without children.

[31] The son of Appaim:
Ishi, who was the father of Sheshan.
Sheshan was the father of Ahlai.

[32] The sons of Jada, Shammai's brother:
Jether and Jonathan. Jether died without children.

[33] The sons of Jonathan:
Peleth and Zaza.
These were the descendants of Jerahmeel.

[34] Sheshan had no sons—only daughters.
He had an Egyptian servant named Jarha. [35]Sheshan gave his daughter in marriage to his servant Jarha, and she bore him Attai.

[36] Attai was the father of Nathan,
Nathan the father of Zabad,
[37] Zabad the father of Ephlal,
Ephlal the father of Obed,
[38] Obed the father of Jehu,
Jehu the father of Azariah,
[39] Azariah the father of Helez,
Helez the father of Eleasah,
[40] Eleasah the father of Sismai,
Sismai the father of Shallum,
[41] Shallum the father of Jekamiah,
and Jekamiah the father of Elishama.

[42] The sons of Caleb the brother of Jerahmeel:
Mesha his firstborn, who was the father of Ziph, and his son Mareshah, who was the father of Hebron.

⁴³The sons of Hebron:

Korah, Tappuah, Rekem and Shema. ⁴⁴Shema was the father of Raham, and Raham the father of Jorkeam. Rekem was the father of Shammai. ⁴⁵The son of Shammai was Maon, and Maon was the father of Beth Zur.
⁴⁶Caleb's concubine Ephah was the mother of Haran, Moza and Gazez. Haran was the father of Gazez.
⁴⁷The sons of Jahdai:

Regem, Jotham, Geshan, Pelet, Ephah and Shaaph.
⁴⁸Caleb's concubine Maacah was the mother of Sheber and Tirhanah. ⁴⁹She also gave birth to Shaaph the father of Madmannah and to Sheva the father of Macbenah and Gibea. Caleb's daughter was Acsah. ⁵⁰These were the descendants of Caleb.

The sons of Hur the firstborn of Ephrathah:

Shobal the father of Kiriath Jearim, ⁵¹Salma the father of Bethlehem, and Hareph the father of Beth Gader.
⁵²The descendants of Shobal the father of Kiriath Jearim were:

Haroeh, half the Manahathites, ⁵³and the clans of Kiriath Jearim: the Ithrites, Puthites, Shumathites and Mishraites. From these descended the Zorathites and Eshtaolites.
⁵⁴The descendants of Salma:

Bethlehem, the Netophathites, Atroth Beth Joab, half the Manahathites, the Zorites, ⁵⁵and the clans of scribes who lived at Jabez: the Tirathites, Shimeathites and Sucathites. These are the Kenites who came from Hammath, the father of the house of Recab.

Chapter 2 resumes the specific development of the nation of Israel. It continues from 1:34, where the two sons of Isaac had been introduced. Since the side line of the elder, Esau, was summarized in 1:35–54, Ezra can concentrate on the younger of the twins, Israel. But while our Chronicler lists all twelve of the sons of Israel-Jacob, his attention quickly focuses on Judah (2:3), the description of whose tribe occupies the next two and one-half chapters. Indeed after a supplement on those portions of the tribe of Simeon that remained as neighbors to southern Judah (4:24 –43), the genealogies of Chronicles devote themselves principally to Benjamin (chs. 8–9) and the priestly tribe of Levi (ch. 6). Only chapters 5 and 7 are left, for outlines, respectively, on the tribes of Transjordan and north Israel. For the land that was occupied by the Jews who returned from the Babylonian exile consisted primarily of the tribal territories of Judah and Benjamin. Also, the people who made up Ezra's community were largely from these same two tribes (Ezra 1:5; 10:9), which had composed the former southern kingdom. In his effort to maintain national purity, it was therefore natural that the Chronicler should concentrate on these particular genealogies. Judah was especially prominent (Ezra 4:4, 6): from it the very name "Jew" is derived.

Among the ten-listed grandsons of Judah (1 Chron 2:5–6; 4:21–22), the primary interest of this chapter (from 2:9 onward) rests on Hezron, the elder son of Perez, from whom were descended some of the leading elements of Judah's later population (see the charted genealogy of the tribe of Judah that follows).

Hezron's third son, Caleb, in his turn received major attention in two sections (vv. 18–20 and 42–55; cf. 4:1–4), though Hezron's second son, Ram, is presented first, because he embodies the messianic hope of Israel: from him comes the family of David (2:10–17).

1 Verses 1–2 are drawn from Genesis 35:22–26 and Exodus 1:1–5. All the passages list in first place Jacob's six sons by his wife Leah (from Reuben through Zebulun),

331

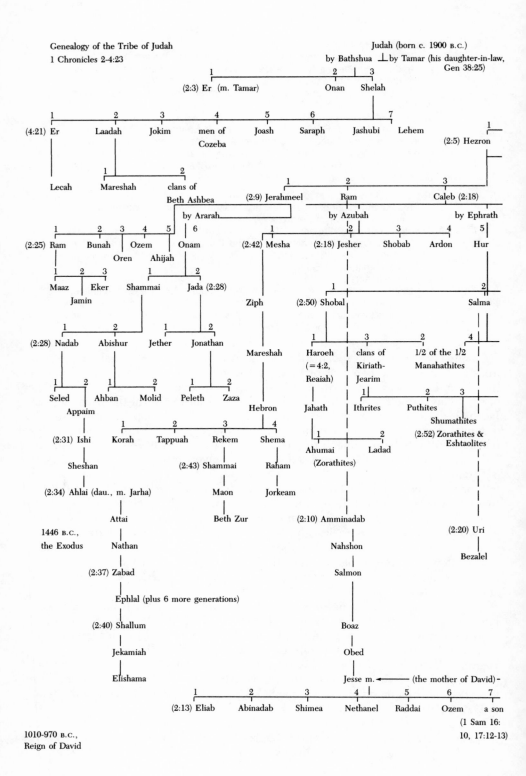

Genealogy of the Tribe of Judah
1 Chronicles 2-4:23

Judah (born c. 1900 B.C.)
by Bathshua ⊥ by Tamar (his daughter-in-law,
Gen 38:25)

1 (2:3) Er (m. Tamar)   2 Onan   3 Shelah

1 (4:21) Er   2 Laadah   3 Jokim   4 men of Cozeba   5 Joash   6 Saraph   7 Jashubi Lehem   1 (2:5) Hezron

Lecah   1 Mareshah   2 clans of Beth Ashbea

by Ararah   1 (2:9) Jerahmeel   2 Ram   3 Caleb (2:18)

by Azubah   by Ephrath

1 (2:25) Ram   2 Bunah   3 Ozem   Oren   4 Ahijah   5 Onam   6

1 (2:42) Mesha   2 (2:18) Jesher   3 Shobab   4 Ardon   5 Hur

1 Maaz   2 Eker   3 Shammai   Jamin   1 Jada (2:28)   2

Ziph   1 (2:50) Shobal   2 Salma

1 (2:28) Nadab   2 Abishur   1 Jether   2 Jonathan

Mareshah   1 Haroeh (= 4:2, Reaiah)   3 clans of Kiriath-Jearim   2 1/2 of the 1/2 Manahathites   4

1 Seled   2 Appaim   1 Ahban   2 Molid   1 Peleth   2 Zaza

Hebron   Jahath   1 Ithrites   2 Puthites   3   Shumathites

(2:31) Ishi   1 Korah   2 Tappuah   3 Rekem   4 Shema

1 Ahumai (Zorathites)   2 Ladad   (2:52) Zorathites & Eshtaolites

Sheshan   (2:43) Shammai   Raham

(2:34) Ahlai (dau., m. Jarha)   Maon   Jorkeam

Attai   Beth Zur   (2:10) Amminadab

(2:20) Uri

1446 B.C.,
the Exodus   Nathan

Nahshon

(2:37) Zabad   Salmon

Bezalel

Ephlal (plus 6 more generations)

(2:40) Shallum   Boaz

Jekamiah   Obed

Elishama   Jesse m. ◄——— (the mother of David)—

1 (2:13) Eliab   2 Abinadab   3 Shimea   4 Nethanel   5 Raddai   6 Ozem   7 a son

(1 Sam 16: 10, 17:12-13)

1010-970 B.C.,
Reign of David

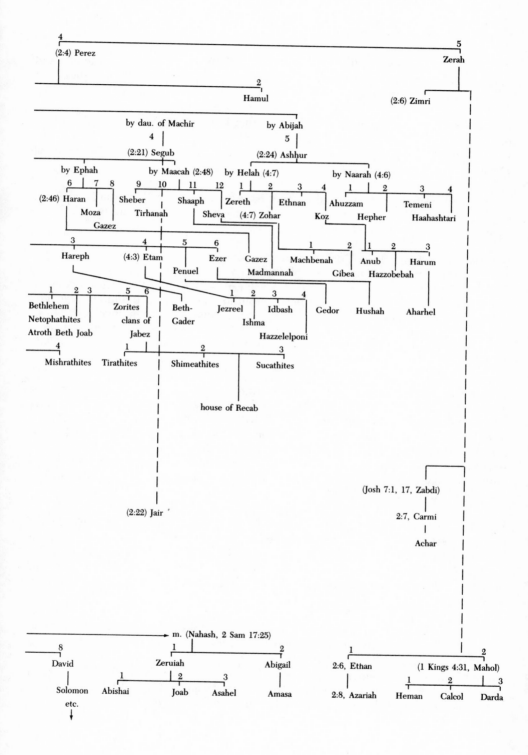

4
(2:4) Perez

5
Zerah

2
Hamul

(2:6) Zimri

by dau. of Machir
4
(2:21) Segub

by Abijah
5
(2:24) Ashhur

by Ephah
6   7   8
(2:46) Haran
Moza
Gazez

by Maacah (2:48)
9   10   11   12
Sheber   Shaaph
Tirhanah   Sheva

by Helah (4:7)
1   2   3   4
Zereth   Ethnan
(4:7) Zohar

by Naarah (4:6)
1   2   3   4
Ahuzzam   Temeni
Koz   Hepher   Haahashtari

3
Hareph

4
(4:3) Etam
Penuel

5   6
Ezer   Gazez
Madmannah

1   2   1   2   3
Machbenah   Anub   Harum
Gibea   Hazzobebah

1   2   3
Bethlehem
Netophathites
Atroth Beth Joab

5   6
Zorites
clans of
Jabez

Beth-
Gader

1   2   3   4
Jezreel   Idbash   Gedor   Hushah   Aharhel
Ishma
Hazzelelponi

4
Mishrathites

1
Tirathites

2
Shimeathites

3
Sucathites

house of Recab

(Josh 7:1, 17, Zabdi)

2:7, Carmi

Achar

(2:22) Jair

m. (Nahash, 2 Sam 17:25)

8
David

Solomon
etc.

1
Zeruiah

1   2   3
Abishai   Joab   Asahel

2
Abigail

Amasa

1
2:6, Ethan

2:8, Azariah

(1 Kings 4:31, Mahol)
2
1   2   3
Heman   Calcol   Darda

in the order of their birth; and the Pentateuchal sources place the four sons of the handmaids (Dan through Asher, in their order of birth) after Jacob's younger son by his wife Rachel, namely, Benjamin.

2 Chronicles, however, follows Genesis in placing Joseph before Benjamin; and before them both it puts Dan, following Zebulun, perhaps because both of these last receive no further treatment in Chronicles (see the note to 7:1).

3–4 These verses reflect the sordid dealings that Judah, his sons, and his Canaanite daughter-in-law Tamar had with each other, as recorded in Genesis 38 (q.v., esp. vv.2–7, 29–30; cf. 46:12). Yet God in his grace used a Tamar to be an ancestor of David and of Jesus Christ (Matt 1:3)!

5 Since Judah's first two sons died without issue, and since his third son is taken up in chapter 4 (vv.21–23), the present section focuses on the remaining two, as listed in Genesis 46:12 and Numbers 26:21.

6 Except for Zimri, these Zerahites can be identified from 1 Kings 4:31 as later descendants, not immediate "sons," of Zerah. Ezra singled them out as examples of God-given wisdom (cf. his reference to Bezalel in v.20) during the Solomonic period. Heman and Ethan, moreover, became authors of inspired psalmody (Pss 88–89), with which Ezra's concern for proper worship caused him to be involved. These authors must not, however, be confused with David's musicians, Heman, Asaph, and Ethan (1 Chron 15:19), who were from the tribe of Levi, not Judah (cf. 6:33–44).

7 Carmi is another Zerahite, identifiable from Joshua 7:1 as an immediate son of Zimri (Heb. Zabdi). While the latter has been equated with Zerah's son Zimri (Curtis, pp. 84, 86; Payne, "Chronicles," p. 370), he really appears (in Josh 7:17–18) to belong to the time of his direct grandson Achan (ʿākān). The last named is here called Achar (ʿākār, "disaster") because he was an ʿôkēr (a "bringer of disaster") on Israel. The name reminds us of his sin under Joshua at Jericho and how God's judgment may bring consequent disaster on his people (Josh 7:25; cf. 6:18 and the naming of the place as Achor in 7:26).

10 Verses 9–12 are drawn from Ruth 4:19–22. This passage furnishes the chief links in the ancestry of David, but it is by no means complete: three centuries elapse between Ram son of Hezron and Nahshon son of Amminadab, whose leadership "of the people of Judah" dates to the days of Moses in the wilderness (Exod 6:23; Num 1:7; 2:3) and whose son Salmon married Rahab the harlot after the Fall of Jericho (Matt. 1:5).

11 Another three centuries elapse before we reach Boaz the husband of Ruth, who were the grandparents of Jesse the father of David.

15 Verses 13–15 supplement 1 Samuel 16:6–9 on Jesse's family. Following his sixth son, Ozem, this source mentions another brother (1 Sam 16:10; 17:12) before David, but he is not named; he may have died soon after these events.

16–17 The genealogies of these four warriors, made famous under their half-uncle David (cf. 2 Sam 2:18–19; 19:13), are drawn from 2 Samuel 2:18 and 17:25; but apart from this latter passage, we would not have known that their mothers, Zeruiah and Abigail, were step-daughters of Jesse, born to David's mother by her presumably earlier marriage to Nahash.

18 The remainder of chapter 2 (vv.28–55) tabulates the descendants of the other sons of Hezron, through lists that have not been preserved elsewhere in Scripture. Some of the names that follow designate whole communities that sprang from his line; e.g., Tekoa (v.24), Beth Zur (v.45), Kiriath Jearim, Bethlehem, or Beth Gader (vv.50–54). Hezron's son Caleb is not to be confused with Moses' spy of the same name (4:15), who appeared three hundred years later.

20 Bezalel is recalled as the Calebite whose craftsmanship, given by the Spirit of God, equipped him to superintend construction for the Mosaic tabernacle (Exod 31:2–5; cf. 2 Chron 1:5). An interval of centuries seems again to separate his father, Uri, from their ancestors, Caleb's son Hur. The last named should thus be distinguished from their contemporary, the leader Hur who joined Aaron in upholding the hands of Moses (Exod 17:10, 12; cf. 24:14).

22 The Transjordanian conquests of Jair, a later descendant of Hezron's son Segub, also occurred under Moses. These are documented in Numbers 32:41 and Deuteronomy 3:14, where Jair is called a son of Manasseh, through Segub's mother, the daughter of Makir (vv.21, 23), rather than through his father, Hezron.

23 The total of sixty towns includes Jair's twenty-three plus a remaining thirty-seven at Kenath (Num 32:42); they may also be combined under Jair's name (Deut 3:4, 14; Josh 13:30; cf. Keil, p. 65, and Payne, "Validity," p. 127). Their loss to the Arameans may have occurred in the early ninth century, since by King Ahab's day (853 B.C.) Ramoth Gilead lay on the frontier (1 Kings 22:3).

25 The descendants of Jerahmeel (vv.25–41) came to occupy a broad area in the Negev of southern Judah. Some critics dismiss the Jerahmeelites as aliens; but while they can be mentioned with the Kenites (1 Sam 30:29), who had a truly foreign origin (see note on v.55), and can even be described in parallel with Judah (1 Sam 27:10), Jerahmeel himself is stated to be the firstborn son of Hezron, into whose clan foreign elements may subsequently have come to be incorporated.

35 Sheshan's daughter who married Jarha is probably the Ahlai mentioned in v.31.

41 The Elishama here named represents the twenty-third generation after Judah. With a lapse of some eight hundred years, this would bring us to about 1100 B.C., or to the generation of Jesse the father of David. Proposed identifications of Elishama with the priest of that name (2 Chron 17:8), in about 850 B.C., are thus unlikely chronologically and impossible because of the latter's tribe (Levi, not Judah).

42 The closing verses of the chapter revert to the family of Caleb. The line of descent shows that individuals are intended (Keil, pp. 68–70), though their associated groups did occupy such centers in Judah as Hebron, Mareshah, and Ziph.

47 The relationship of the six sons of Jahdai to Caleb is not given.

49 Caleb's "daughter" Acsah was only a distant descendant of Caleb the son of Hezron, though she was an immediate daughter of Caleb the son of Jephunneh, the faithful spy (listed in 4:15). She is remembered as the bride of Othniel, the first of the judges (Judg 3:9–11), having been promised to him for his conquest of Debir (Josh 15:15–19; Judg 1:11–15).

50 Ephrathah is a variant form for the name of Caleb's wife Ephrath (v.19).

55 The Kenites were originally a foreign people (Gen 15:19), some of whom, by marriage or by adoption, became incorporated into the tribe of Judah (cf. the instance of the family of Hobab, the brother-in-law of Moses, Num 10:29–32; Judg 1:16; 4:11). There is always room among the people of God for those who come to him by faith (Exod 12:38, 48; Eph 2:19).

The clan of Recab later included the reformer Jehonadab (2 Kings 10:15, 23), who preserved the purity of his descendants by retaining their primitive forms of nomadic life (Jer 35:6–10).

Notes

5 Hamul is sometimes equated with Mahol of 1 Kings 4:31, the father of three of the wise men listed in the next verse. These, however, are remote descendants of Hamul's brother Zerah (cf. Num 26:21); and "Mahol [is] the immediate father" (C.F. Burney, *Notes on the Hebrew Text of the Books of Kings* [Oxford: Clarendon, 1903], p. 51).

15 Alternatively the unnamed seventh son might be equated with "Elihu, a brother of David" (27:18); however, if he was thus well known, the omission of his name would be difficult to explain.

18 The verse literally reads "Azubah 'iššāh (אָשָּׁה, "wife"); and some, unnecessarily, go on to suggest that Caleb took his *father's* wife (North, "Chronicler," p. 406).

24 Myers (*Chronicles,* 1:10, 15) improperly identifies Ashhur with his nephew Hur (v.19), as though Caleb's marriage "to" (LXX, rather than "in," MT) was being repeated.

2. *The family of David*

3:1–24

¹These were the sons of David born to him in Hebron:

The firstborn was Amnon the son of Ahinoam of Jezreel;
the second, Daniel the son of Abigail of Carmel;
²the third, Absalom the son of Maacah daughter of Talmai king of Geshur;
the fourth, Adonijah the son of Haggith;
³the fifth, Shephatiah the son of Abital;
and the sixth, Ithream, by his wife Eglah.
⁴These six were born to David in Hebron, where he reigned seven years and six months.

David reigned in Jerusalem thirty-three years, ⁵and these were the children born to him there:

Shammua, Shobab, Nathan and Solomon. These four were by Bathsheba daughter of Ammiel. ⁶There were also Ibhar, Elishua, Eliphelet, ⁷Nogah, Nepheg, Japhia, ⁸Elishama, Eliada and Eliphelet—nine in all. ⁹All these were the sons of David, besides his sons by his concubines. And Tamar was their sister.

¹⁰Solomon's son was Rehoboam,
   Abijah his son,
   Asa his son,
   Jehoshaphat his son,
   ¹¹Jehoram his son,
   Ahaziah his son,
   Joash his son,
   ¹²Amaziah his son,
   Azariah his son,
   Jotham his son,
   ¹³Ahaz his son,
   Hezekiah his son,
   Manasseh his son,
   ¹⁴Amon his son,
   Josiah his son.
¹⁵The sons of Josiah:
   Johanan the firstborn,
   Jehoiakim the second son,
   Zedekiah the third,
   Shallum the fourth.
¹⁶The successors of Jehoiakim:
   Jehoiachin his son,
   and Zedekiah.

¹⁷The descendants of Jehoiachin the captive:
   Shealtiel his son, ¹⁸Malkiram, Pedaiah, Shenazzar, Jekamiah, Hoshama and Nedabiah.
¹⁹The sons of Pedaiah:
   Zerubbabel and Shimei.
   The sons of Zerubbabel:
   Meshullam and Hananiah.
   Shelomith was their sister.
   ²⁰There were also five others:
   Hashubah, Ohel, Berekiah, Hasadiah and Jushab-Hesed.
²¹The descendants of Hananiah:
   Pelatiah and Jeshaiah, and the sons of Rephaiah, of Arnan, of Obadiah and of Shecaniah.
²²The descendants of Shecaniah:
   Shemaiah and his sons:
   Hattush, Igal, Bariah, Neariah and Shaphat—six in all.
²³The sons of Neariah:
   Elioenai, Hizkiah and Azrikam—three in all.
²⁴The sons of Elioenai:
   Hodaviah, Eliashib, Pelaiah, Akkub, Johanan, Delaiah and Anani—seven in all.

This chapter chronologically follows 1 Chronicles 2, which had traced several of the branches of the tribe of Judah down to the time of Israel's united kingdom. At this point, however, the record restricts itself to the royal line of David (introduced in 2:15) and carries it through five centuries, to about 500 B.C. The prophecy of Jeremiah 22:30 in 597 had made it clear that no purely human descendant of his line could ever legitimately again occupy the throne; and when the Persians authorized the restoration of the Jewish community from Babylon in 538, they permitted no kingship.

Yet the Davidic family maintained its importance. It was represented in the return to Palestine, it supplied civic leaders for Judah (including her first two governors [see comment on v.19], down through 515 [Ezra 5:2, 15]), and Zechariah prophesied that it would continue to do so (Zech 12:7–10). This house held the ultimate hope of Israel. The Messiah would some day arise from it, that Son of David whom postexilic prophecy identified as more than human. He would be God's "fellow" (Zech 13:7, KJV), pierced as a man but acknowledged as deity (12:10). He would bring redemption from sin (13:1) and God's kingdom on earth (14:9).

1 The listing of David's children in verses 1–9 repeats and supplements 2 Samuel 3:2–5; 5:13–16; and 13:1. Daniel, his son by Abigail, is named, alternatively, Kileab in 2 Samuel 3:3.

5 The list of younger sons (vv.5–8) is repeated in 14:3–7. Solomon was chosen to succeed David (22:9) rather than one of his older brothers, at least three of whom were murdered in inner-family struggles.

6 The third son listed in this verse (omitted in 2 Sam) is Elpelet (cf. 14:5); his early death may account for David's choice of a longer form of this same name for his younger brother, Eliphelet (v.8; Keil, p. 78).

8 The next to last son was originally named Beeliada ($b^e{}^cely\bar{a}\underline{d}\bar{a}^c$, 14:7), meaning "The (divine) Master knows." But this was changed (both here and in 2 Sam 5:16) to Eliada (${}^>ely\bar{a}\underline{d}\bar{a}^c$, "God knows") to avoid the idolatrous implications of $b^e{}^cel$, which could be taken to mean Baal.

9 Second Samuel 13 reports the scandal of Tamar's rape by her half-brother Amnon and vengeance by her brother Absalom.

10 The remainder of the chapter lists the Davidic line of succession, first to the throne (vv.10–16, following the order in 1–2 Kings), and then, during the Exile and beyond, to such nonkingly leadership as they may have enjoyed (vv.17–24, which are new).

12 Azariah, as used here (and in 2 Kings), represents the throne name of Uzziah, as used elsewhere in Chronicles (cf. Isa 6:1; cf. J.A. Montgomery, *A Critical and Exegetical Commentary on the Books of Kings*, ICC [New York: Scribners, 1951], p. 446).

15 Similar is the name Shallum (as in Jer 22:11) for Jehoahaz (2 Chron 36:1–4; 2 Kings 23:31–34). Though younger than Jehoiakim, he was preferred to him for the throne, following Josiah's death in 609 B.C. (see 2 Chron 36:2 mg.); and though older in fact than Zedekiah (36:2, 11), he is here listed after him, probably because his reign was so much shorter.

Josiah's firstborn son, Johanan, is not mentioned elsewhere and may have died young.

16 The name Jeconiah (shortened to Coniah in mg. of Jer 22:24, 28; 37:1) means literally "Establishes (does) Yahweh"; but it usually has its elements transposed into Jehoiachin (2 Chron 36:9–10; 2 Kings 24:8–17), which means "Yahweh establishes."

17 Shealtiel was the physical son of Neri (Luke 3:27) but must have become the legal (adopted) son of Jeconiah soon after the latter's captivity in March 597 B.C., since five out of the seven sons are mentioned on a Babylonian ration receipt dated 592 (ANET, p. 308).

18 Shenazzar (*šn' ṣr*) has been equated with Sheshbazzar (*ššbṣr*, "prince of Judah," at the return in 538–537, Ezra 1:8); both seem to be shortened forms of the Akkadian Sin-aba-uṣur (*šn' b' ṣr*).

19 Shenazzar was succeeded as the first Persian governor of Judah (Ezra 5:4, 16) by his nephew Zerubbabel (2:2), physically the son of his next older brother Pedaiah, but reckoned as the legal son of the oldest brother, Shealtiel (Ezra 3:2, 8; Hag 1:1, 12; Matt 1:12; Luke 3:27). Shealtiel may have died without issue, so that his brother would have raised up seed to his name according to the custom of the levirate (Deut 25:5–10). The authenticity of many of the names that follow is confirmed by archaeological evidence from sixth and fifth centuries seals and letters (Myers, *Chronicles*, p. 21).

21 The Hebrew text does not have "and" to introduce "the sons of Rephaiah, of Arnan. . . ." These are *not* stated to be further grandsons of Zerubbabel but are presumably contemporaries of Jeconiah the captive whose relationship to him has not been preserved (see Introduction: Date).

22 Since only five names now appear in the list of Shemaiah's six sons, one must have fallen out.

Notes

5 The name Ammiel ("a kinsman [is] God") transposes into Eliam (2 Sam 11:3); cf. comment on v.16 above.

21 After Jeshaiah, the RSV reads with the LXX: "his son Rephaiah, his son Arnan . . . ," thus extending David's line for eight more generations (through v.24) beyond Zerubbabel's grandsons in 500 B.C. and implying an impossibly late date for the composition of Chronicles.

3. *Other clans of Judah*

4:1–23

¹The descendants of Judah:
    Perez, Hezron, Carmi, Hur and Shobal.
²Reaiah son of Shobal was the father of Jahath, and Jahath the father of Ahumai and Lahad. These were the clans of the Zorathites.

³These were the sons of Etam:

Jezreel, Ishma and Idbash. Their sister was named Hazzelelponi. ⁴Penuel was the father of Gedor, and Ezer the father of Hushah.

These were the descendants of Hur, the firstborn of Ephrathah and father of Bethlehem.

⁵Ashhur the father of Tekoa had two wives, Helah and Naarah.

⁶Naarah bore him Ahuzzam, Hepher, Temeni and Haahashtari. These were the descendants of Naarah.

⁷The sons of Helah:

Zereth, Zohar, Ethnan, ⁸and Koz, who was the father of Anub and Hazzobebah and of the clans of Aharhel son of Harum.

⁹Jabez was more honorable than his brothers. His mother had named him Jabez, saying, "I gave birth to him in pain." ¹⁰Jabez cried out to the God of Israel, "Oh, that you would bless me and enlarge my territory! Let your hand be with me, and keep me from harm so that I will be free from pain." And God granted his request.

¹¹Kelub, Shuhah's brother, was the father of Mehir, who was the father of Eshton. ¹²Eshton was the father of Beth Rapha, Paseah and Tehinnah the father of Ir Nahash. These were the men of Recah.

¹³The sons of Kenaz:

Othniel and Seraiah.

The sons of Othniel:

Hathath and Meonothai. ¹⁴Meonothai was the father of Ophrah.

Seraiah was the father of Joab,

the father of Ge Harashim. It was called this because its people were craftsmen.

¹⁵The sons of Caleb son of Jephunneh:

Iru, Elah and Naam.

The son of Elah:

Kenaz.

¹⁶The sons of Jehallelel:

Ziph, Ziphah, Tiria and Asarel.

¹⁷The sons of Ezrah:

Jether, Mered, Epher and Jalon. One of Mered's wives gave birth to Miriam, Shammai and Ishbah the father of Eshtemoa. ¹⁸(His Judean wife gave birth to Jered the father of Gedor, Heber the father of Soco, and Jekuthiel the father of Zanoah.) These were the children of Pharaoh's daughter Bithiah, whom Mered had married.

¹⁹The sons of Hodiah's wife, the sister of Naham:

the father of Keilah the Garmite, and Eshtemoa the Maacathite.

²⁰The sons of Shimon:

Amnon, Rinnah, Ben-Hanan and Tilon.

The descendants of Ishi:

Zoheth and Ben-Zoheth.

²¹The sons of Shelah son of Judah:

Er the father of Lecah, Laadah the father of Mareshah and the clans of the linen workers at Beth Ashbea, ²²Jokim, the men of Cozeba, and Joash and Saraph, who ruled in Moab and Jashubi Lehem. (These records are from ancient times.) ²³They were the potters who lived at Netaim and Gederah; they stayed there and worked for the king.

None of the genealogies of Judah recorded in 4:1–23 appear elsewhere in Scripture. Verses 1–8 supplement chapter 2 on the clan of Hezron, a son of Judah's fourth son Perez. In particular they concern four sons of Hur (cf. v.4), who were grandsons of Hezron's third son Caleb, and eight branches of his fifth son Ashhur. Verses 9–20 describe the situations of eight leaders in Judah: Jabez (v.9), Kelub

(v. 11), Kenaz (v. 13), Jehallelel (v. 16), Ezrah (v. 17), Hodiah (v. 19), Shimon, and Ishi (v. 20). However, while they too might be classified under Hezron, their exact relationship to him remains unknown, either because of gaps in Ezra's own sources or because of a lack of care in subsequent scribal transmission. Verses 21–23 outline the clan of Judah's third son Shelah (cf. 2:3).

1 Ezra expected his readers to recognize (from 2:5, 18, 50) that the five *descendants* of Judah, from Perez to Shobal, were not brothers but successive generations. "Carmi" must therefore be a scribal error (caused by 2:7?) for Caleb (Kelubai, cf. NIV mg. on 2:9; Curtis, p. 104).

2 This data supplements 2:52 on Hur's first son Shobal where Haroeh had appeared as a variant for Reaiah.

3–5 Similarly v. 3 on Hur's fourth son and v. 4 on his fifth and sixth supplement 2:19; and vv. 5–8, on the family of his uncle Ashhur, supplement 2:24.

6 "Haahashtari" is not a proper noun but is adjectival and designates "one descended from A(ha)shtar."

9 Jabez (*ya'bēṣ*), when read (by metathesis) as *ya'ṣēḇ*, means "he causes pain" (cf. the noun "pain" [*'ōṣeḇ*] at the end of the verse).

10 Yet Jabez's prayer of faith became an occasion of grace, so that God kept and blessed him, rather than *'oṣbî*, literally, "causing me pain."

12 Ir Nahash (cf. NIV mg., "city of copper," or "coppersmith") is Khirbet Nahas, on the west side of the Arabah, south of the Dead Sea (KB, p. 610).

13 Though originally a foreign Kenizzite (whether of Canaan, Gen 15:19, or of Edom, 36:42), Othniel was adopted into Israel's tribe of Judah and became the first of the judges (see above on 2:49 and 2:55). He who is adopted into the people of God can even become a leader.

15 Caleb was Othniel's brother; but he was sufficiently older (Judg 1:13; 3:9), having belonged to the previous wilderness generation among whom he was honored as one of the two faithful spies (Num 13–14).

16 The settlement of Jehallelel's descendants, with those of Calebite Mesha, at Ziph (cf. comments on 2:18, 42) in the southeastern part of Judah (Josh 15:24) confirms the preexilic authenticity of Ezra's source, since in his own day Judah's southern border failed to reach even to Hebron.

17 The wife of Mered here intended is Bithiah (v. 18). Her identification as a daughter of Pharaoh would locate this event during the early part of Israel's sojourn in Egypt (before 1800 B.C.), the union probably being made possible because of Joseph's prominence (cf. Keil, p. 92).

21 Mareshah, in southwest Judah, likewise experienced dual settlement (cf. comment on Ziph on v.16), both from these descendants of Judah's third son, Shelah, and from his fourth, Perez (2:4).

Over long periods Israel's genealogical clans could be associated with particular places, be organized into particular guilds—whether of linen workers (here), of potters (v.23), or of scribes (2:55)—or be maintained by particular royal patronage (4:23), a situation that has been confirmed archaeologically by the means of distinctive pottery marks (I. Mendelsohn, "Guilds in Ancient Palestine," BASOR 80 [1940]: 17–21).

Notes

15 For the suggestion that Othniel was Caleb's nephew, see L.J. Wood, "Othniel," ZPEB, 4:552–53.
21 In the seven sons of Shelah, some critics have claimed to find a variant history for the *five* sons of Judah himself (2:3–4), designed to eliminate "disedifying ancestors" (North, "The Chronicler," 1:406).

C. *Simeon*

4:24–43

[24] The descendants of Simeon:
Nemuel, Jamin, Jarib, Zerah and Shaul;
[25] Shallum was Shaul's son, Mibsam his son and Mishma his son.
[26] The descendants of Mishma:
Hammuel his son, Zaccur his son and Shimei his son.
[27] Shimei had sixteen sons and six daughters, but his brothers did not have many children; so their entire clan did not become as numerous as the people of Judah. [28] They lived in Beersheba, Moladah, Hazar Shual, [29] Bilhah, Ezem, Tolad, [30] Bethuel, Hormah, Ziklag, [31] Beth Marcaboth, Hazar Susim, Beth Biri and Shaaraim. These were their towns until the reign of David. [32] Their surrounding villages were Etam, Ain, Rimmon, Token and Ashan—five towns— [33] and all the villages around these towns as far as Baalath. These were their settlements. And they kept a genealogical record.

[34] Meshobab, Jamlech, Joshah son of Amaziah, [35] Joel, Jehu son of Joshibiah, the son of Seraiah, the son of Asiel, [36] also Elioenai, Jaakobah, Jeshohaiah, Asaiah, Adiel, Jesimiel, Benaiah, [37] and Ziza son of Shiphi, the son of Allon, the son of Jedaiah, the son of Shimri, the son of Shemaiah.

[38] The men listed above by name were leaders of their clans. Their families increased greatly, [39] and they went to the outskirts of Gedor to the east of the valley in search of pasture for their flocks. [40] They found rich, good pasture, and the land was spacious, peaceful and quiet. Some Hamites had lived there formerly.
[41] The men whose names were listed came in the days of Hezekiah king of Judah. They attacked the Hamites in their dwellings and also the Meunites who were there and completely destroyed them, as is evident to this day. Then they settled in their place, because there was pasture for their flocks. [42] And five hundred of these Simeonites, led by Pelatiah, Neariah, Rephaiah and Uzziel, the sons of Ishi, invaded the hill country of Seir. [43] They killed the remaining Amalekites who had escaped, and they have lived there to this day.

Because of their massacre of Shechem (Gen 34:24–30), the patriarchs Simeon and Levi were condemned to have their tribes scattered among Israel (49:5–7). The subsequent faithfulness of the Levites (Exod 32:27–29), moreover, converted their situation into one of blessing and of priestly leadership (Deut 33:8–11). But the Simeonites remained accursed (omitted altogether in the tribal blessings of Deut 33). Simeon was granted lands in Palestine only within the arid southwestern portions of Judah (Josh 19:1–9; cf. 15:26, 28–32, where these appear among territories that Joshua had previously assigned to Simeon's more favored neighbor; cf. F.M. Cross, Jr., and G. Ernest Wright, "The Boundary and Province Lists of the Kingdom of Judah," JBL 75 [1956]: 202–26); and it campaigned cooperatively with Judah in their conquest (Judg 1:3).

Chronicles records first the primary genealogy of Simeon (4:24–27), then its list of towns (vv.28–33), and finally a summary of two of its later migrations (vv.34–41; 42 –43). For after the division of Solomon's kingdom in 930 B.C., elements of Simeon either moved to the north or at least adopted its religious practices (cf. the inclusion of Beersheba along with the shrines of Ephraim that are condemned in Amos 5:5) so that they are counted among the northern tribes (2 Chron 15:9; 34:6; cf. L.J. Wood, "Simeon, the Tenth Tribe," JETS 14 [1971]: 221–25). Other Simeonites carried on in a seminomadic life in isolated areas that they could occupy, such as those noted at the close of this chapter (v.41 dates to Hezekiah, 726–697 B.C.).

24 This list of Simeon's sons comes from Numbers 26:12–13, which reflects Genesis 46:10 and Exodus 6:15, though with variations in spelling and with the omission of a third son, Ohad. The next son's name, Jarib, has been corrected by the Syriac to read Jachin, as in the other lists.

25–27 These verses constitute a supplement preserved only in Chronicles. Mibsam and his son Mishma should not be confused with Ishmaelites of the same names (1:29–30).

31 Beth Biri is the Chronicler's postexilic designation for Beth Lebaoth (Josh 19:6), and for Shaaraim we should read (with Josh 19:6) Sharuhen, a historically significant city located in this area.

39 The name Gedor has been emended, with the LXX, into Gerar, a city south of Gaza toward Philistia in the west (cf. 2 Chron 14:13–14 and Y. Aharoni, "The Land of Gerar," IEJ 6 [1956]: 26–32). Yet the presence of Meunites (see below on v.41) and the direction of Simeon's other recorded attack, toward Seir (vv.42–43), suggest a Gedor "overlooking the Dead Sea" to the east (NBD, p. 456).

40 In particular the Canaanites, as a branch of the Hamites (1:8), seem to be intended here.

41 The Meunites constitute an Edomite tribe; see the comment on 2 Chronicles 20:1 (cf. 26:7).

43 The phrase "remaining" Amalekites implies some previous avenging work, i.e., of Saul (1 Sam 14:48; 15:7) and of David (1 Sam 30:17; 2 Sam 8:12), against these ancient enemies of God's people (cf. Exod 17:8–13; Deut 25:17–19). Yet the tribe of

Simeon was motivated as well by economic factors of overpopulation (v.38) and shortage of pasture (vv.39, 41).

Notes

29 For "Bilhah" (בִּלְהָה, *bilhāh*) read with Josh 15:29, "Baalah" (בַּעֲלָה, *ba'ªlāh*; cf. LXX^A 6αλαα, *balaa*, and Josh 19:3; so IDB, "Baalah [3]"); and for "Tolad," with the Syriac and Josh 15:30; 19:4, "Eltolad."

31 Cross and Wright ("Lists," p. 213) accept this claim to pre-Davidic historicity but proceed to reject Joshua 15 as a later copying (p. 214), dating to the time of Jehoshaphat (p. 226).

D. *Transjordan Tribes*

5:1–26

¹The sons of Reuben the firstborn of Israel (he was the firstborn, but when he defiled his father's marriage bed, his rights as firstborn were given to the sons of Joseph son of Israel; so he could not be listed in the genealogical record in accordance with his birthright, ²and though Judah was the strongest of his brothers and a ruler came from him, the rights of the firstborn belonged to Joseph)—
³the sons of Reuben the firstborn of Israel:
Hanoch, Pallu, Hezron and Carmi.
⁴The descendants of Joel:
Shemaiah his son, Gog his son,
Shimei his son, ⁵Micah his son,
Reaiah his son, Baal his son,
⁶and Beerah his son, whom Tiglath-Pileser king of Assyria took into exile. Beerah was a leader of the Reubenites.
⁷Their relatives by clans, listed according to their genealogical records:
Jeiel the chief, Zechariah, ⁸and Bela son of Azaz, the son of Shema, the son of Joel. They settled in the area from Aroer to Nebo and Baal Meon.
⁹To the east they occupied the land up to the edge of the desert that extends to the Euphrates River, because their livestock had increased in Gilead.
¹⁰During Saul's reign they waged war against the Hagrites, who were defeated at their hands; they occupied the dwellings of the Hagrites throughout the entire region east of Gilead.

¹¹The Gadites lived next to them in Bashan, as far as Salecah:
¹²Joel was the chief, Shapham the second, then Janai and Shaphat, in Bashan.
¹³Their relatives, by families, were:
Michael, Meshullam, Sheba, Jorai, Jacan, Zia and Eber—seven in all.
¹⁴These were the sons of Abihail son of Huri, the son of Jaroah, the son of Gilead, the son of Michael, the son of Jeshishai, the son of Jahdo, the son of Buz.
¹⁵Ahi son of Abdiel, the son of Guni, was head of their family.
¹⁶The Gadites lived in Gilead, in Bashan and its outlying villages, and on all the pasturelands of Sharon as far as they extended.
¹⁷All these were entered in the genealogical records during the reigns of Jotham king of Judah and Jeroboam king of Israel.

¹⁸The Reubenites, the Gadites and the half-tribe of Manasseh had 44,760 men ready for military service—able-bodied men who could handle shield and sword,

who could use a bow, and who were trained for battle. ¹⁹They waged war against the Hagrites, Jetur, Naphish and Nodab. ²⁰They were helped in fighting them, and God handed the Hagrites and all their allies over to them, because they cried out to him during the battle. He answered their prayers, because they trusted in him. ²¹They seized the livestock of the Hagrites—fifty thousand camels, two hundred fifty thousand sheep and two thousand donkeys. They also took one hundred thousand people captive, ²²and many others fell slain, because the battle was God's. And they occupied the land until the exile.

²³The people of the half-tribe of Manasseh were numerous; they settled in the land from Bashan to Baal Hermon, that is, to Senir (Mount Hermon).

²⁴These were the heads of their families: Epher, Ishi, Eliel, Azriel, Jeremiah, Hodaviah and Jahdiel. They were brave warriors, famous men, and heads of their families. ²⁵But they were unfaithful to the God of their fathers and prostituted themselves to the gods of the peoples of the land, whom God had destroyed before them. ²⁶So the God of Israel stirred up the spirit of Pul king of Assyria (that is, Tiglath-Pileser king of Assyria), who took the Reubenites, the Gadites and the half-tribe of Manasseh into exile. He took them to Halah, Habor, Hara and the river of Gozan, where they are to this day.

Though the OT's postexilic restoration centered in Judah, the population included elements from all Twelve Tribes, whose identity the Chronicler was anxious to perpetuate (cf. Ezra 6:17; 8:35). Chapter 5 concerns those once settled east of the Jordan rift. Even prior to Joshua's conquest of Canaan in the west, Moses' people had suffered a series of unprovoked attacks from the kings in Transjordan (Num 21:21–23, 33). But all this had been of God (Deut 2:30) and resulted in the Israelites' acquisition of the whole territory from the Arnon (midway on the east shore of the Dead Sea) northward, and on through Gilead and Bashan. Moses then granted these areas (Num 32:33–42), respectively and at their own request, to Reuben (the subject of 1 Chron 5:1–10), Gad (vv.11–17), and half of the tribe of Manasseh (vv.23–24; cf. 7:14–19, on their western half).

The remaining verses of chapter 5 describe an early, joint military campaign (vv.18–22, elaborating v.10)—in which God rewarded their faith and their prayers with a great victory over the Ishmaelites—and their later deportation to Assyria (vv.25–26), as the result of collective apostasy.

1 Reuben's crime of incest with his father's subordinate wife Bilhah (Gen 35:22) cost him his rights of primogeniture (49:4), which involved a double portion of inheritance (Deut 21:17). This was transferred to Joseph, first son of Rachel, the wife whom Jacob-Israel loved (Gen 49:25–26; cf. 48:20–22, on Joseph's double-tribed status, through his sons Ephraim and Manasseh). Joseph's leadership was first exercised personally (Gen 50:21), then later through Joshua (an Ephraimite), and thus for three more centuries (cf. Judg 8:1–2; 12:1–6).

2 Yet Judah eventually became strongest: Jacob's prophecy of this tribe's preeminence over the other (Gen 49:8), and even of a scepter (v.10), was fulfilled in David's kingship (2 Sam 5:1–3; cf. 7:8), which entailed the effective rejection of Joseph (Ps 78:67–70), and was rendered eternal through David's greater son, who was also God's Son (2 Sam 7:14), Jesus the Messiah (Matt 1:1).

3 Reuben's four sons are listed just as in the Pentateuch (Gen 46:9; Exod 6:14; Num 26:5–6), but Ezra's data in the rest of the chapter is unique to Chronicles.

4 The text does not say from which of Reuben's sons Joel was descended.

6 The Assyrians exiled the Israelitish border tribes in 733 B.C. (vv.22, 26; 2 Kings 15:29).

8 The settlement in these areas (named also in Num 32:38) preceded 850 B.C., since they are claimed as Moabite in Mesha's inscription, as well as subsequently (Jer 48:1, 22; Ezek 25:9).

10 Saul himself fought in Transjordan (1 Sam 11:1–11), but with the Ammonites instead of the Hagrites, and at Jabesh Gilead, not far east of the river.

11 The plains of Bashan, extending from the gorge of the Yarmuk and thence north and east of Galilee, pertained to Manasseh (v.23). By wide scattering Gad's outposts reached them; but its major settlements lay in Gilead, south of the Yarmuk (cf. v.16).

14 The Gadite, Buz, is not otherwise known and is not to be confused with Abraham's nephew, Buz, the son of Nahor (Gen 22:21).

16 Sharon refers here, not to the coastal plain north of Philistia (Josh 12:18), but to broad pasturelands somewhere in Transjordan, mentioned as *srn* on line 13 of the Mesha inscription (cf. Notes).

17 The reigns of Jotham and Jeroboam (II) extended from 793 to 731 (to 753, for the latter, in Israel; and 750–731, for Jotham, in Judah).

19 Hagar was the mother of Ishmael, whose twelve sons, in turn, included Jetur (NT "Iturea," Luke 3:1) and Naphish (Gen 25:12, 15; cf. the presence of such Arab tribes with Moab in Ps 83:6). Though "the battle was God's" (v.22), his people still had to initiate it!

20 Further God's divine presence did not mean that his people would not have to cry out in the battle; but when they did, he vindicated the prayers of those who trusted in him.

21 The great numbers taken, including one hundred thousand people, shows this to have been no mere raid but a total, permanent occupation (cf. Payne, "Validity," p. 211).

23 Senir was the Amorite name for Mount Hermon (Deut 3:9).

26 Since Pul was the private name of Tiglath-pileser III prior to his accession in 745 B.C., the NIV has properly translated: "God stirred up the spirit of Pul, . . . that is, Tiglath-Pileser." The Lord used even Assyrians to accomplish his purposes (Isa 10:5 –6).

Notes

16 KB (p. 1011) here emends שָׁרוֹן (šārôn, "Sharon") to שִׂרְיֹן (śiryōn, "Sirion"), the Phoenician name for Mount Hermon (Deut 3:9; cf. comment on v.23); but this would be inappropriate in reference to Gad, in Gilead.

E. *Levi*

6:1–81

¹The sons of Levi:
Gershon, Kohath and Merari.
²The sons of Kohath:
Amram, Izhar, Hebron and Uzziel.
³The children of Amram:
Aaron, Moses and Miriam.
The sons of Aaron:
Nadab, Abihu, Eleazar and Ithamar.
⁴Eleazar was the father of Phinehas,
Phinehas the father of Abishua,
⁵Abishua the father of Bukki,
Bukki the father of Uzzi,
⁶Uzzi the father of Zerahiah,
Zerahiah the father of Meraioth,
⁷Meraioth the father of Amariah,
Amariah the father of Ahitub,
⁸Ahitub the father of Zadok,
Zadok the father of Ahimaaz,
⁹Ahimaaz the father of Azariah,
Azariah the father of Johanan,
¹⁰Johanan the father of Azariah (it was he who served as priest in the temple Solomon built in Jerusalem),
¹¹Azariah the father of Amariah,
Amariah the father of Ahitub,
¹²Ahitub the father of Zadok,
Zadok the father of Shallum,
¹³Shallum the father of Hilkiah,
Hilkiah the father of Azariah,
¹⁴Azariah the father of Seraiah,
and Seraiah the father of Jehozadak.
¹⁵Jehozadak was deported when the LORD sent Judah and Jerusalem into exile by the hand of Nebuchadnezzar.

¹⁶The sons of Levi:
Gershon, Kohath and Merari.
¹⁷These are the names of the sons of Gershon:
Libni and Shimei.
¹⁸The sons of Kohath:
Amram, Izhar, Hebron and Uzziel.
¹⁹The sons of Merari:
Mahli and Mushi.
These are the clans of the Levites listed according to their fathers:
²⁰Of Gershon:
Libni his son, Jehath his son,
Zimmah his son, ²¹Joah his son,
Iddo his son, Zerah his son

and Jeatherai his son.
²² The descendants of Kohath:
 Amminadab his son, Korah his son,
 Assir his son, ²³Elkanah his son,
 Ebiasaph his son, Assir his son,
 ²⁴ Tahath his son, Uriel his son,
 Uzziah his son and Shaul his son.
²⁵ The descendants of Elkanah:
 Amasai, Ahimoth,
 ²⁶ Elkanah his son, Zophai his son,
 Nahath his son, ²⁷Eliab his son,
 Jeroham his son, Elkanah his son
 and Samuel his son.
²⁸ The sons of Samuel:
 Joel the firstborn
 and Abijah the second son.
²⁹ The descendants of Merari:
 Mahli, Libni his son,
 Shimei his son, Uzzah his son,
 ³⁰ Shimea his son, Haggiah his son
 and Asaiah his son.

³¹These are the men David put in charge of the music in the house of the Lord after the ark came to rest there. ³²They ministered with music before the tabernacle, the Tent of Meeting, until Solomon built the temple of the Lord in Jerusalem. They performed their duties according to the regulations laid down for them.
 ³³Here are the men who served, together with their sons:
 From the Kohathites:
  Heman, the musician,
  the son of Joel, the son of Samuel,
  ³⁴ the son of Elkanah, the son of Jeroham,
  the son of Eliel, the son of Toah,
  ³⁵ the son of Zuph, the son of Elkanah,
  the son of Mahath, the son of Amasai,
  ³⁶ the son of Elkanah, the son of Joel,
  the son of Azariah, the son of Zephaniah,
  ³⁷ the son of Tahath, the son of Assir,
  the son of Ebiasaph, the son of Korah,
  ³⁸ the son of Izhar, the son of Kohath,
  the son of Levi, the son of Israel;
 ³⁹ and Heman's associate Asaph, who served at his right hand:
  Asaph son of Berekiah, the son of Shimea,
  ⁴⁰ the son of Michael, the son of Baaseiah,
  the son of Malkijah, ⁴¹the son of Ethni,
  the son of Zerah, the son of Adaiah,
  ⁴² the son of Ethan, the son of Zimmah,
  the son of Shimei, ⁴³the son of Jahath,
  the son of Gershon, the son of Levi;
 ⁴⁴ and from their associates, the Merarites, at his left hand:
  Ethan son of Kishi, the son of Abdi,
  the son of Malluch, ⁴⁵the son of Hashabiah,
  the son of Amaziah, the son of Hilkiah,
  ⁴⁶ the son of Amzi, the son of Bani,
  the son of Shemer, ⁴⁷the son of Mahli,
  the son of Mushi, the son of Merari,
  the son of Levi.

⁴⁸Their fellow Levites were assigned to all the other duties of the tabernacle, the house of God. ⁴⁹But Aaron and his descendants were the ones who presented offerings on the altar of burnt offering and on the altar of incense in connection

with all that was done in the Most Holy Place, making atonement for Israel, in accordance with all that Moses the servant of God had commanded.

⁵⁰ These were the descendants of Aaron:
  Eleazar his son, Phinehas his son,
  Abishua his son, ⁵¹Bukki his son,
  Uzzi his son, Zerahiah his son,
  ⁵² Meraioth his son, Amariah his son,
  Ahitub his son, ⁵³Zadok his son
  and Ahimaaz his son.

⁵⁴These were the locations of their settlements allotted as their territory (they were assigned to the descendants of Aaron who were from the Kohathite clan, because the first lot was for them): ⁵⁵They were given Hebron in Judah with its surrounding pasturelands. ⁵⁶But the fields and villages around the city were given to Caleb son of Jephunneh.

⁵⁷So the descendants of Aaron were given Hebron (a city of refuge), and Libnah, Jattir, Eshtemoa, ⁵⁸Hilen, Debir, ⁵⁹Ashan, Juttah and Beth Shemesh, together with their pasturelands. ⁶⁰And from the tribe of Benjamin they were given Gibeon, Geba, Alemeth and Anathoth, together with their pasturelands.

These towns, which were distributed among the Kohathite clans, were thirteen in all.

⁶¹The rest of Kohath's descendants were allotted ten towns from the clans of half the tribe of Manasseh.

⁶²The descendants of Gershon, clan by clan, were allotted thirteen towns from the tribes of Issachar, Asher and Naphtali, and from the part of the tribe of Manasseh that is in Bashan.

⁶³The descendants of Merari, clan by clan, were allotted twelve towns from the tribes of Reuben, Gad and Zebulun.

⁶⁴So the Israelites gave the Levites these towns and their pasturelands. ⁶⁵From the tribes of Judah, Simeon and Benjamin they allotted the previously named towns.

⁶⁶Some of the Kohathite clans were given as their territory towns from the tribe of Ephraim.

⁶⁷In the hill country of Ephraim they were given Shechem (a city of refuge), and Gezer, ⁶⁸Jokmeam, Beth Horon, ⁶⁹Aijalon and Gath Rimmon, together with their pasturelands.

⁷⁰And from half the tribe of Manasseh the Israelites gave Aner and Bileam, together with their pasturelands, to the rest of the Kohathite clans.

⁷¹ The Gershonites received the following:
  From the clan of the half-tribe of Manasseh
      they received Golan in Bashan and also Ashtaroth, together with their pasturelands;
⁷² from the tribe of Issachar
      they received Kedesh, Daberath, ⁷³Ramoth and Anem, together with their pasturelands;
⁷⁴ from the tribe of Asher
      they received Mashal, Abdon, ⁷⁵Hukok and Rehob, together with their pasturelands;
⁷⁶ and from the tribe of Naphtali
      they received Kedesh in Galilee, Hammon and Kiriathaim, together with their pasturelands.

  ⁷⁷The Merarites (the rest of the Levites) received the following:
  From the tribe of Zebulun
      they received Jokneam, Kartah, Rimmono and Tabor, together with their pasturelands;
⁷⁸ from the tribe of Reuben across the Jordan east of Jericho
      they received Bezer in the desert, Jahzah, ⁷⁹Kedemoth and Mephaath, together with their pasturelands;

⁸⁰ and from the tribe of Gad
they received Ramoth in Gilead, Mahanaim, ⁸¹Heshbon and Jazer, together with their pasturelands.

The tribe of Levi became Israel's hereditary religious leaders (cf. the introductory discussion to Simeon [4:24–43] above). Ezra took special pains to insure their presence within the second return, which he led back in 458 B.C. (Ezra 8:15–20); and from the start postexilic Judah depended on their proper service (1:5; 3:8; 6:18–20). Levi included the priesthood, so that Ezra himself was careful to present his Levitical credentials (7:1–5), going back to Aaron, Israel's initial high priest. Authentic genealogy, indeed, was essential for investiture (cf. 2:59–63)—hence the practical relevance of this chapter to the Chronicler's own day.

Yet a deeper and more abiding significance lies in the nature of Israel's priesthood as types. Their service in the sanctuary reflected a heavenly pattern (Exod 25:9, 40; Heb 8:2, 5); and the atoning acts performed by Aaron's descendants were but foreshadows of that ultimate sacrifice, accomplished by Jesus Christ, our Great High Priest, by the offering up of himself once and for all (Heb 9:14, 24–25).

Chapter 6 commences with Pentateuchal citations and concludes with territorial lists taken from Joshua, but it consists primarily of materials not found outside Chronicles. It takes up four major subjects: the line of the high priests (vv.3–15, 49 –53), the three clans of Levi (vv.16–30), the Levitical musicians (vv.31–48), and the cities that were assigned for the tribe's use (vv.54–81). The Levitical organization of David's day receives further treatment in chapters 23–26 (q.v.).

1 Levi's sons always appear in this order based on age (Gen 46:11; Exod 6:16; Num 3:17; 26:57).

2 Kohath is singled out (Exod 6:18; Num 3:19) as the ancestor of the priestly group.

3 This Amram is a family ancestor, separated by some 250 years and nine generations from the father of Moses and Aaron (cf. Exod 6:20; Num 26:59) and from about five thousand Amramites living in their day (cf. Num 26:62).

Of the sons of Aaron (derived from Exod 6:23; Lev 10:1; Num 3:2; 26:60), the first two died for their sacrilege (Lev 10:2; Num 26:61); and the succeeding line of priests is here traced only through Eleazar (cf. Exod 6:25; Num 25:7).

4 Some links have been omitted from the priestly genealogy: the twenty-one generations after Eleazar, down through Jehozadak at the Exile (v.15), span more than eight hundred years; and forty years per generation seems overly high. The list includes no descendants of Eleazar's younger brother, Ithamar, who held office during the last of the judges and the early kingdom—e.g., Eli, Phinehas III, Ahitub, Ahimelech I (= Ahijah ?), Abiathar, and Ahimelech II (1 Sam 14:3; 22:20; 2 Sam 8:17). Other preexilic high priests are not listed either: Amariah II (2 Chron 19:11), Jehoiada (22:11; 23:1; 24:15), his son Zechariah (24:20), Uriah (2 Kings 16:10), Azariah III (2 Chron 31:10), and Meraioth (1 Chron 9:11), son of Ahitub III (6:12) in the seventh century.

8 Serving under David in 1000 B.C. was Zadok (2 Sam 8:17; 15:24), son of Ahitub II (not to be confused with Ahitub I, noted above as the grandfather of David's other priest, Abiathar, who was of the Ithamar branch). Some critics tend to reject Zadok's Hebrew genealogy and label him a Jebusite, perhaps to be associated with Melchizedek (!) (e.g., H.H. Rowley, "Zadok and Nehushtan," JBL 58 [1939]: 113–41; but cf. C. Feinberg, "Priests and Levites," ZPEB, 4: 852–67, esp. pp. 859, 866–67).

9 Zadok's grandson Azariah I became high priest under Solomon, 970 B.C. (1 Kings 4:2).

10 Azariah II, "who served as priest in the temple Solomon built," would thus belong later and, allowing for gaps to include the long-lived Jehoiada (2 Chron 24:15; cf. KD, p. 118), could be the high priest who resisted Uzziah's trespass against the temple and its priesthood in 751 (26:17).

13 Hilkiah discovered the Book of the Law of the Lord given through Moses (2 Chron 34:14), the event that led to Josiah's reformation of 622.

15 Seraiah suffered martyrdom to the Babylonians in 586 (2 Kings 25:18); but his son Jehozadak was father of Jeshua, Judah's famous high priest of the return from captivity fifty years later (Ezra 3:2; 5:2; 10:18; Hag 1:1; Zech 3:1; 6:11).

17 The divisions of the three Levitical clans are those found in Exodus 6:17–19 and Numbers 3:18–20 (cf. Num 26:58).

22 Since Korah is known to have come from the clan-patriarch Kohath through the branch of Izhar (vv.37–38), Amminadab could possibly be an alternative name for it. Korah was the leader who rebelled against Moses and whom the earth swallowed (Num 16:32). Assir, Elkanah I (v.23), and Ebiasaph were then his sons (Exod 6:24) and not successive generations.

24 Uriel may be the Levite who led the entire Kohathite clan in David's day (15:5).

25 Comparisons with vv.35–36 show that this is not the Elkanah of v.23 but rather the great-great-great-great-grandson of his brother Ebiasaph, i.e., Elkanah II; see the charted genealogy of the tribe of Levi that follows.

26–27 Zophai, Nahath, and Eliab appear to be variant names for Zuph, Toah, and Eliel (vv. 34–35). The Levite Elkanah IV is the husband of Hannah and the father of Samuel the judge and prophet. Some critics tend to equate his Ephraimite residence (1 Sam 1:1) with tribal descent and then proceed to pervert the Chronicler's concern for Levitical authenticity into its very opposite, finding here a policy of fabricating Levitical pedigrees, to maintain a "theology of legitimacy" (North, "Theology," p. 371).

31 In his zeal for the proper worship of God, Ezra makes affirmations about the Davidic musicians (cf. Ezra 2:41) that have been questioned; but their historicity receives archaeological confirmation. W.F. Albright (*Archaeology and the Religion of Israel* [Baltimore: Johns Hopkins, 1942], p. 126) speaks even of pre-Davidic (Canaanite) guilds of singers.

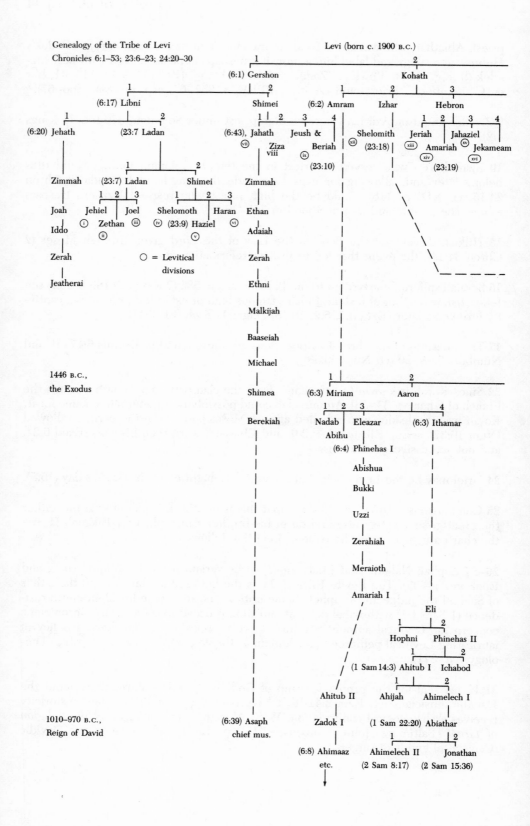

Genealogy of the Tribe of Levi
Chronicles 6:1–53; 23:6–23; 24:20–30

Levi (born c. 1900 B.C.)

1 (6:1) Gershon
2 Kohath

1 (6:17) Libni   2 Shimei
1 (6:2) Amram   2 Izhar   3 Hebron

1 (6:20) Jehath   2 (23:7 Ladan)
Shimei
1│2 3 4 (6:43), Jahath Jeush & Ziza viii Beriah (23:10)
Shelomith (23:18)
1 Jeriah 2 Amariah 3 Jahaziel 4 Jekameam
(xiii) (xiv) (xv) (xvi)
(23:19)

Zimmah
1 (23:7 Ladan)   2 Shimei
1 2 3 Jehiel Zethan Joel
(i) (ii) (iii)
1 2 3 Shelomoth (23:9 Haziel) Haran
(iv) (v) (vi)

Joah
Zimmah

Iddo
Ethan

Zerah
Adaiah

Jeatherai
Zerah

○ = Levitical divisions

Ethni

Malkijah

Baaseiah

Michael

1446 B.C.,
the Exodus
Shimea

1 (6:3) Miriam   2 Aaron

Berekiah
1 Nadab 2 Abihu 3 Eleazar 4 (6:3) Ithamar

(6:4) Phinehas I

Abishua

Bukki

Uzzi

Zerahiah

Meraioth

Amariah I

Eli
1 Hophni 2 Phinehas II

1 (1 Sam 14:3) Ahitub I 2 Ichabod

1 Ahijah 2 Ahimelech I

Ahitub II

(6:39) Asaph chief mus.

1010–970 B.C.,
Reign of David

Zadok I

(1 Sam 22:20) Abiathar
1 Ahimelech II 2 Jonathan
(2 Sam 8:17) (2 Sam 15:36)

(6:8) Ahimaaz
etc.

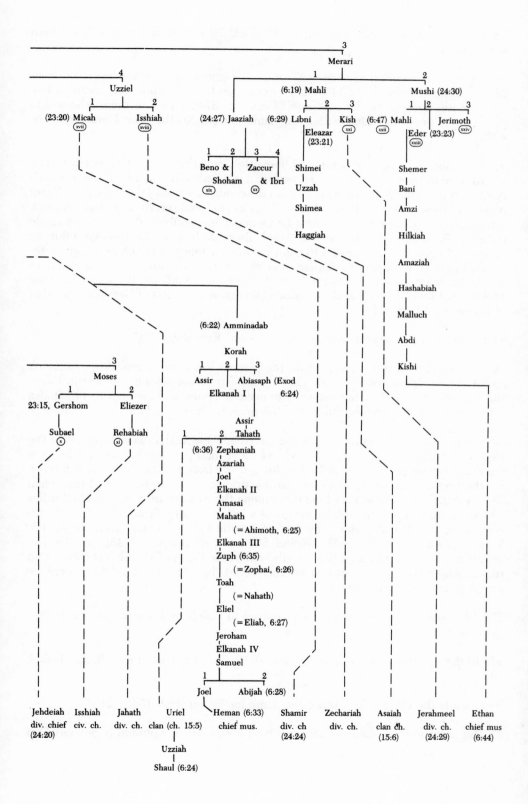

32 The tent was for God's *meeting* Israel (Exod 29:42–43), not primarily for men with each other!

33–37 David's musician Heman, 1000 B.C., is eighteen generations removed from Moses' adversary Korah, in 1445. This poses a problem for those advocating a late date for the Exodus, in the 1200's (NBCrev., p. 374), let alone those who would place Levi's grandson Izhar within the same period (North, "The Chronicler," p. 407).

42 The name of Asaph's ancestor Shimei, the immediate son of Gershon (v.17), seems here to have been transposed with that of Jahath (BH, p. 1336). The similarity then of five out of the six names of his descendants—from Jahath through Ethni (v.41)—to those of his brother Libni—Jehath to Jeatherai (vv.20–21)—has led some interpreters to assume that this must be an erroneous doublet, drawn from a single tradition, in which "the descent of Asaph fluctuated—whether through Libni or Shimei" (Curtis, p. 130). Yet 23:10 confirms the existence of Jahath as a legitimate, parallel branch of Gershon's younger son Shimei; and a deliberate reuse of names among brothers' sons is not infrequent (cf. the name Mahli, vv.19, 47, or how the Mahli of v.19 took for his child the name of this same older son of Gershon, i.e., that of his cousin Libni, v.29).

44 Ethan and Kishi appear also as Jeduthun and Kushaiah (15:17).

50–53 This section repeats vv.4–8 on the priestly line from Aaron, down to Zadok and Ahimaaz. It confirms that the Zadokite priests, alone among the Levitical divisions in David's day, had the authority to make a sacrificial atonement (v.49). It also furnishes a transition to the subject of the priestly cities that follows.

54 The remainder of chapter 6 lists the forty-eight towns that were assigned to the various branches of the tribe of Levi. As Jacob had predicted, they did become scattered among Israel (Gen 49:7). The list is taken from Joshua 21. Ezra's reference to "the first lot," which went to the Aaronic priests, confirms the record that when Joshua distributed the land in 1400 B.C. among the western nine and one-half tribes and Levi, he accomplished it by means of a lottery (Josh 4:2; 21:10). Albright (*Archaeology*, pp. 121–22, and "The List of Levitic Cities," *Louis Ginzberg Jubilee Volume* [New York: Jewish Theological Seminary of America, 1945], pp. 49–73), nevertheless, seeks to assign this distribution to the times of David. Yet there is no reason why all the towns had to be conquered (by David) before they could be assigned (and see Josh 13:1, 6).

56 The lands of Hebron had been promised to Caleb by both Moses and Joshua (Josh 14:6–15).

57 On the six cities of refuge, see Numbers 35, Deuteronomy 19:1–10, and Joshua 20.

58 Hilen is the Chronicler's postexilic name for Holon (Josh 15:51; 21:15).

61 The nonpriestly Kohathites also received towns out of Ephraim (v.66) and Dan

(Josh 21:5, specifically Eltekeh and Gibbethon, 21:23). The latter are required in v.68 to make up the subtotal of ten, where they are missing due to textual corruption.

68 Jokmeam is the Chronicler's postexilic name of Kibzaim (Josh 21:22).

Notes

70 Read "Taanach" (אֶת־תַּעְנַךְ, ʾeṯ-taʿnak), with Josh 21:25 (cf. Syr. ʿnt), for "Aner" (אֶת־עָנֵר, ʾeṯ-ʿānēr), a scribal corruption due to haplography of the ת (t), and substitute the alternate Hebrew reading "Ibleam" (יִבְלְעָם, yiḇlᵉʿām), with the LXX^AL and the Targum, for the shortened "Bileam" (בִּלְעָם, bilʿām).

72 Read "Kishion," with Josh 21:28 (cf. qsn, #37 in the list of Thutmose III), for "Kedesh."

73 Read "En-Gannim" (עֵין־גַּנִּים, ʿên-gannîm), with Josh 19:21, for "Anem" (עָנֵם, ʿānēm), due to haplography.

75 Read "Helkath," with Josh 19:25; 21:31, for "Hukok."

77 Read "Rimmon," with the LXX and Josh 19:13, for "Rimmono," a corruption due to dittography of a following ו (w).

F. Benjamin and Five Other Tribes (7:1-9:44)

1. Summaries

7:1-40

¹The sons of Issachar:
  Tola, Puah, Jashub and Shimron—four in all.
²The sons of Tola:
  Uzzi, Rephaiah, Jeriel, Jahmai, Ibsam and Samuel—heads of their families. During the reign of David, the descendants of Tola listed as fighting men in their genealogy numbered 22,600.
³The son of Uzzi:
  Izrahiah.
The sons of Izrahiah:
  Michael, Obadiah, Joel and Isshiah. All five of them were chiefs. ⁴According to their family genealogy, they had 36,000 men ready for battle, for they had many wives and children.
⁵The relatives who were fighting men belonging to all the clans of Issachar, as listed in their genealogy, were 87,000 in all.

⁶Three sons of Benjamin:
  Bela, Beker and Jediael.
⁷The sons of Bela:
  Ezbon, Uzzi, Uzziel, Jerimoth and Iri, heads of families—five in all. Their genealogical record listed 22,034 fighting men.
⁸The sons of Beker:
  Zemirah, Joash, Eliezer, Elioenai, Omri, Jeremoth, Abijah, Anathoth and Alemeth. All these were the sons of Beker. ⁹Their genealogical record listed the heads of families and 20,200 fighting men.
¹⁰The son of Jediael:
  Bilhan.

The sons of Bilhan:

Jeush, Benjamin, Ehud, Kenaanah, Zethan, Tarshish and Ahishahar. [11]All these sons of Jediael were heads of families. There were 17,200 fighting men ready to go out to war.

[12]The Shuppites and Huppites were the descendants of Ir, and the Hushites the descendants of Aher.

[13]The sons of Naphtali:

Jahziel, Guni, Jezer and Shillem—the descendants of Bilhah.

[14]The descendants of Manasseh:

Asriel was his descendant through his Aramean concubine. She gave birth to Makir the father of Gilead. [15]Makir took a wife from among the Huppites and Shuppites. His sister's name was Maacah.

Another descendant was named Zelophehad, who had only daughters.

[16]Makir's wife Maacah gave birth to a son and named him Peresh. His brother was named Sheresh, and his sons were Ulam and Rakem.

[17]The son of Ulam:

Bedan.

These were the sons of Gilead son of Makir, the son of Manasseh. [18]His sister Hammoleketh gave birth to Ishhod, Abiezer and Mahlah.

[19]The sons of Shemida were:

Ahian, Shechem, Likhi and Aniam.

[20]The descendants of Ephraim:

Shuthelah, Bered his son,
Tahath his son, Eleadah his son,
Tahath his son, [21]Zabad his son
and Shuthelah his son.

Ezer and Elead were killed by the native-born men of Gath, when they went down to seize their livestock. [22]Their father Ephraim mourned for them many days, and his relatives came to comfort him. [23]Then he lay with his wife again, and she became pregnant and gave birth to a son. He named him Beriah, because there had been misfortune in his family. [24]His daughter was Sheerah, who built Lower and Upper Beth Horon as well as Uzzen Sheerah.

[25]Rephah was his son, Resheph his son,
Telah his son, Tahan his son,
[26]Ladan his son, Ammihud his son,
Elishama his son, [27]Nun his son
and Joshua his son.

[28]Their lands and settlements included Bethel and its surrounding villages, Naaran to the east, Gezer and its villages to the west, and Shechem and its villages all the way to Ayyah and its villages. [29]Along the borders of Manasseh were Beth Shan, Taanach, Megiddo and Dor, together with their villages. The descendants of Joseph son of Israel lived in these towns.

[30]The sons of Asher:

Imnah, Ishvah, Ishvi and Beriah. Their sister was Serah.

[31]The sons of Beriah:

Heber and Malkiel, who was the father of Birzaith.

[32]Heber was the father of Japhlet, Shomer and Hotham and of their sister Shua.

[33]The sons of Japhlet:

Pasach, Bimhal and Ashvath.

These were Japhlet's sons.

[34]The sons of Shomer:

Ahi, Rohgah, Hubbah and Aram.

[35]The sons of his brother Helem:

Zophah, Imna, Shelesh and Amal.

356

³⁶ The sons of Zophah:

Suah, Harnepher, Shual, Beri, Imrah, ³⁷Bezer, Hod, Shamma, Shilshah, Ithran and Beera.

³⁸ The sons of Jether:

Jephunneh, Pispah and Ara.

³⁹ The sons of Ulla:

Arah, Hanniel and Rizia.

⁴⁰All these were descendants of Asher—heads of families, choice men, brave warriors and outstanding leaders. The number of men ready for battle, as listed in their genealogy, was 26,000.

Just as in the case of the two and one-half tribes of Transjordan (cf. the introductory discussion to 5:1–26), Ezra was concerned to perpetuate clan frameworks for other members of the former northern kingdom. Some representatives had associated themselves with Judah at the Fall of Samaria in 722 B.C. (cf. 2 Chron 30:1–2), or even previously (11:13–16); and Josiah's expansion a century later embraced many more (34:6; cf. 1 Chron 9:1). Others regained their place among God's people during the Exile of 586–538 (cf. Ezek 37:15–23) and were able to return to Judah under Zerubbabel or under Ezra himself (cf. the casual allusion in Luke 2:36 to Anna of the tribe of Asher, one of the "ten lost tribes"). In the buffer zone between north and south lay Benjamin, which could include even the northern religious center of Bethel (Josh 18:22). It is summarized in chapter 7, along with the Ephraimitic tribes, but is treated in greater detail in chapters 8 and 9 as Judah's major ally, both in the preexilic kingdom and postexilic restoration (1 Kings 12:21, or the "two-twelfths" implied in 11:30–31, and Ezra 4:1).

First Chronicles 7 outlines the clan structure that characterized Benjamin and five other tribes. Its sources are Genesis 46 and Numbers 26, but most of the later genealogies and other data lack biblical parallels. Chapter 7 describes Issachar (vv. 1–5), Benjamin (vv. 6–12), Naphtali (v. 13), the western half of Manasseh (vv. 14–19), Ephraim (vv. 20–29), and Asher (vv. 30–40). No mention is made of either Dan or Zebulun. Some interpreters have attempted to reconstruct their genealogies by a species of textual juggling, but these tribes may simply have had little influence or relevance among the Jews who made up Ezra's community.

1 The sons of Issachar appear as listed in Numbers 26:23–24, with Puah as a variation on Puvah (MT). Issachar's sons are also listed in Genesis 46:13, where, however, the MT reads "Job" for the "Jashub" read here and in Numbers 26:24 (doubtless a textual corruption since Jashub is reflected in the Genesis passage in the LXX and Samar.). Attempts to equate the well-known Job with Issachar's son rests, therefore, on tenuous textual and linquistic evidence.

2 Among the valiant descendants of Tola may have been the later judge who bore that clan name (Judg 10:1).

3–4 For Izrahiah and his four sons, even with "many wives," to have "36,000" warriors seems unlikely, as does the total (vv. 2–5) of 145,600 for just one tribe of the Twelve. This appears to be the first of nine passages in Chronicles (see Appendix B) where 'elep ("thousand") might better be interpreted as 'allûp ("chief"). Hence we should read in v.2: 22 *chiefs*, 600 (men); in v.3: 36 *chiefs;* and in v.5: 87 *chiefs* (cf. Payne, "Validity," p. 217).

6 Among the sons of Benjamin, Bela and Beker correspond to Genesis 46:21 (cf. Num 26:38). The third, Jediael, is not mentioned elsewhere. Other sons appear in 8:1–2.

7–11 The figures, as in v.3 (q.v.), should best be read: v.7, as 22 *chiefs*, 34 (men); v.9, as 20 *chiefs*, 200; and v.11, as 17 *chiefs*, 200.

12 Ir and Aher may be shortened forms for the names of Bela's youngest son Iri (v.7) and younger brother Aharah (8:1; cf. Num 26:38).

13 Naphtali's sons correspond to those listed in Genesis 46:24 and Numbers 26:48–49, with minor changes in spelling. The NIV's rendering of the concluding phrase is correct since Bilhah was the mother of Naphtali (Gen 30:3–8).

14 That Manasseh had an Aramean concubine may have reminded Ezra's readers of the racially mixed Samaritans in their own day (2 Kings 17:24, 29; Ezra 4:2–3). As appears from the more complete record of western Manasseh in Numbers 26:29–33, Asriel and Shemida (v.19) were the immediate sons of his grandson Gilead (cf. Josh 17:2).

15 Zelophehad came even three centuries later. His was the case raised by his daughters that prompted Moses' laws about female inheritance rights (Num 26:33; 27:1–11; 36:1–12).

20–21 Of Ephraim's four sons noted in vv.20–21, and 23, only Shuthelah had been recorded previously (Num 26:35); Ezer and Elead had probably joined the families of their grandfather Joseph's brothers, who had settled in Goshen, only to be slain there on the northeastern border of Egypt by Palestinian raiders who came down from their birthplace in Gath. (But see Keil [p. 139] et al., that Ezer and Elead were killed when they were involved in cattle rustling. The pronouns are ambiguous.)

25 Joshua is listed eight generations after Rephah. Taking Rephah's father as Ephraim's fourth son Beriah (v.23), we perceive Joshua's birth (c. 1500 B.C.; cf. Josh 24:29) to have been eleven generations after Joseph's, corroborating the approximately four-century interval that separated these two leaders.

30–31 The list of Asher's children plus two grandsons reproduces Genesis 46:17 (cf. Num 26:44–46).

35 Shomer's brother Helem appears in v.32 as Hotham.

39 Father-son sequences between verses suggest that Ulla (here) may be a variant name for Ara in the previous verse.

40 The numeral, as in v.3 (q.v.), should probably be read as 26 chiefs.

Notes

12 The NIV reading of v.13b would seem more appropriate if the latter part of v.12 were read, *The Hushites* were *the descendants of* "another [tribe]," i.e., of Dan, Jacob's other son by Bilhah (cf. Gen 46:23). Yet the phrase *his* (Jacob's?) *sons* (including Dan?) *by Bilhah* must remain suspect, when neither of these names appears elsewhere in the chapter.

21 Critical authors associate this event with some setback during the conquest under Joshua. W.F. Albright (*From the Stone Age to Christianity* [Baltimore: Johns Hopkins, 1946], p. 211; and even Keil, pp. 239–41) takes "Ephraim" (vv.22–23) as a later member of the tribe who had the same name as the patriarch.

2. *Benjamin*

8:1–40

[1]Benjamin was the father of Bela his firstborn,
Ashbel the second son, Aharah the third,
[2]Nohah the fourth and Rapha the fifth.
[3]The sons of Bela were:
Addar, Gera, Abihud, [4]Abishua, Naaman, Ahoah, [5]Gera, Shephuphan and Huram.
[6]These were the descendants of Ehud, who were heads of families of those living in Geba and were deported to Manahath:
[7]Naaman, Ahijah, and Gera, who deported them and who was the father of Uzza and Ahihud.
[8]Sons were born to Shaharaim in Moab after he had divorced his wives Hushim and Baara. [9]By his wife Hodesh he had Jobab, Zibia, Mesha, Malcam, [10]Jeuz, Sakia and Mirmah. These were his sons, heads of families. [11]By Hushim he had Abitub and Elpaal.
[12]The sons of Elpaal:
Eber, Misham, Shemed (who built Ono and Lod with its surrounding villages), [13]and Beriah and Shema, who were heads of families of those living in Aijalon and who drove out the inhabitants of Gath.
[14]Ahio, Shashak, Jeremoth, [15]Zebadiah, Arad, Eder, [16]Michael, Ishpah and Joha were the sons of Beriah.
[17]Zebadiah, Meshullam, Hizki, Heber, [18]Ishmerai, Izliah and Jobab were the sons of Elpaal.
[19]Jakim, Zicri, Zabdi, [20]Elienai, Zillethai, Eliel, [21]Adaiah, Beraiah and Shimrath were the sons of Shimei.
[22]Ishpan, Eber, Eliel, [23]Abdon, Zicri, Hanan, [24]Hananiah, Elam, Anthothijah, [25]Iphdeiah and Penuel were the sons of Shashak.
[26]Shamsherai, Shehariah, Athaliah, [27]Jaareshiah, Elijah and Zicri were the sons of Jeroham.
[28]All these were heads of families, chiefs as listed in their genealogy, and they lived in Jerusalem.

[29]Jeiel the father of Gibeon lived in Gibeon.
His wife's name was Maacah, [30]and his firstborn son was Abdon, followed by Zur, Kish, Baal, Ner, Nadab, [31]Gedor, Ahio, Zeker [32]and Mikloth, who was the father of Shimeah. They too lived near their relatives in Jerusalem.
[33]Ner was the father of Kish, Kish the father of Saul, and Saul the father of Jonathan, Malki-Shua, Abinadab and Esh-Baal.

34 The son of Jonathan:
   Merib-Baal, who was the father of Micah.
35 The sons of Micah:
   Pithon, Melech, Tarea and Ahaz.
   36 Ahaz was the father of Jehoaddah, Jehoaddah was the father of Alemeth, Azmaveth and Zimri, and Zimri was the father of Moza. 37Moza
   was the father of Binea; Raphah was his son, Eleasah his son and Azel
   his son.
38 Azel had six sons, and these were their names:
   Azrikam, Bokeru, Ishmael, Sheariah, Obadiah and Hanan. All these were
   the sons of Azel.
39 The sons of his brother Eshek:
   Ulam his firstborn, Jeush the second son and Eliphelet the third. 40The
   sons of Ulam were brave warriors who could handle the bow. They had
   many sons and grandsons—150 in all.
All these were the descendants of Benjamin.

First Chronicles 8 forms a major supplement to the summary of Benjamin given in 7:6–12. Its opening verses, however, on his first generations in Egypt are based on Numbers 26:38–40 (rather than on Gen 46:21, as in ch. 7). Verses 6–28 are almost without biblical parallel; they outline the genealogy of two family groups as these developed after the Hebrew conquest and resettlement of Canaan: the Benjamite household of Ehud, Israel's second judge (vv.6–7), and that of Shaharaim, some of whose great-grandchildren lived in the neighborhood of Jerusalem (v.28). The remainder of the chapter (vv.29–40) concerns the relatives who lived near them (v.32) and who formed the ancestry of Saul, part of whose descent had been given in 1 Samuel.

Chronicles elaborates this material, not simply because of the significance of King Saul and his family, as it continued a dozen generations after him, but primarily because of the importance of Benjamin as a tribe, which ranked second only to Judah in postexilic society, and because of the status it provided for many within its clan framework (cf. the introductory discussion on ch. 2, above, and Neh 11:4, 7, 31, 36).

1 The name of Benjamin's third son, Aharah (Aher, 7:12), corresponds to Ahiram in Numbers 26:38 (Ehi, in Gen 46:21), as do also those of the grandsons Addar (= Ard) and Naaman (v.3).

3 The second name in the list of Bela's sons (Gera) reappears as the seventh name (v.5); the former may have died prematurely.

6 Some five hundred years separate the latter Gera from his descendant Ehud, the left-handed Benjamite judge (Judg 3:15).

7 The nature of the civil rivalry that led Ehud's son Gera to deport his own clansmen remains unknown.

8 Though Shaharaim's movement to Moab seems to locate him in Palestine in Ehud's general period (cf. the Benjamite towns mentioned in vv.12–13), his exact ancestry is lacking. The divorce of his first two wives demonstrates even further the moral deterioration of Israel in c. 1300 B.C. (cf. the previous Benjamite outrages condemned in Judg 19:22–28; 20:12–14).

13 This victory over the men of Gath would precede their major Philistine reinforcement in 1200 B.C.

17 Meshullam, Heber, Ishmerai (v.18), and Shimei (v.21) seem to be variants for the names of Elpaal's sons Misham, Shemed, Eber, and Shema, as listed earlier (vv.12-13).

28 The phrase "all these" then identifies Beriah's and Shema's sons (vv.14–16, 19–21), brothers (vv.17–18), and grandsons (vv.22–27) as the ones living about Jerusalem (Keil, p. 149).

32 So when Mikloth and his son Shimeah are said to live not only (following the literal Heb.) "over against" (*neged*) their brothers (Mikloth's immediate family, in vv.30–31), but also "with" (*ʿim*) their relatives, we conclude that Mikloth's otherwise unidentified father Jeiel (cf. 1 Sam 9:1 and the variant form, Abiel) should be grouped with the sons of Beriah and Shema (see the charted genealogy of the tribe of Benjamin that follows).

33 Jeiel's fifth son, Ner, was the grandfather of Saul, the first king of Israel (1043–1010 B.C.; ZPEB, 1: 836), and also the father of Abner, Saul's military commander and uncle (1 Sam 14:50–51). Abinadab (1 Sam 31:2) appears elsewhere (1 Sam 14:49) as Ishvi (*yišwî*), perhaps a variant on *ʾišyô* ("man of Yahweh").

Abinadab's brother's name, Esh-Baal (meaning "man of the [divine] Master"), is changed throughout 2 Samuel (2:8–4:12) to Ish-Bosheth ("man of shame"); for the Hebrew word *baʿal* could be treated as a proper noun designating the shameful idol of that name (cf. the comment to 3:8, and Hos 2:16–17).

34 Similarly Merib-Baal ("warrior of the Master") appears in 2 Samuel (4:4–21:7) as Mephibosheth ("one who scatters [?] shame").

40 The warriors' "grandsons" represent the thirteenth generation after Mephibosheth, who was five at the death of Saul and Jonathan in 1010 B.C., which brings us to the Exile of 586.

Notes

---

36 Read "Jadah" (יַעְדָּה, *yaʿdāh*) with the LXX and 9:42 (q.v.) for "Jehoaddah" (יְהוֹעַדָּה, *yᵉhô-ʿaddāh*).

37 Read "Rephaiah" (רְפָיָה, *rᵉpāyāh*), with the LXX and 9:43, for "Raphah" (רָפָה, *rāpāh*).

---

3. *Jerusalem's inhabitants*

9:1–44

[1]All Israel was listed in the genealogies recorded in the book of the kings of Israel.

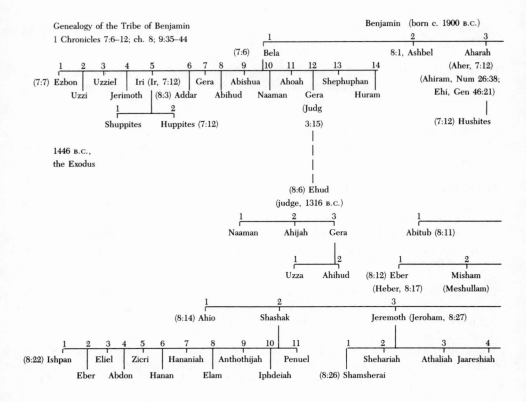

Genealogy of the Tribe of Benjamin
1 Chronicles 7:6–12; ch. 8; 9:35–44

Benjamin (born c. 1900 B.C.)

1446 B.C.,
the Exodus

1010–970 B.C.,
Reign of David

586 B.C., Exile

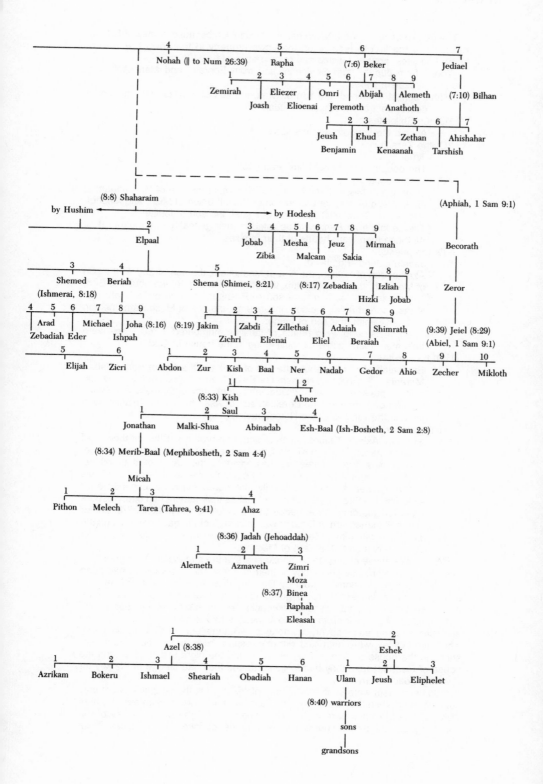

4   Nohah (∥ to Num 26:39)   5 Rapha   6 (7:6) Beker   7 Jediael

1 Zemirah   2 Eliezer   3 Omri   4 Abijah   5   6   7 Alemeth   8   9   (7:10) Bilhan
Joash   Elioenai   Jeremoth   Anathoth

1 Jeush   2 Ehud   3   4 Zethan   5   6 Ahishahar   7
Benjamin   Kenaanah   Tarshish

(8:8) Shaharaim   (Aphiah, 1 Sam 9:1)

by Hushim ◄————————————————► by Hodesh

  2 Elpaal   3 Jobab   4   5 Mesha   6   7 Jeuz   8   9 Mirmah   Becorath
Zibia   Malcam   Sakia

3 Shemed   4 Beriah   5 Shema (Shimei, 8:21)   6 (8:17) Zebadiah   7   8 Izliah   9   Zeror
(Ishmerai, 8:18)   Hizki   Jobab

4 Arad   5   6 Michael   7   8 Joha (8:16)   9   (8:19) 1 Jakim   2 Zabdi   3 Zillethai   4   5 Adaiah   6   7   8 Shimrath   9   (9:39) Jeiel (8:29)
Zebadiah   Eder   Ishpah   Zichri   Elienai   Eliel   Beraiah   (Abiel, 1 Sam 9:1)

5 Elijah   6 Zicri   1 Abdon   2 Zur   3 Kish   4 Baal   5 Ner   6 Nadab   7 Gedor   8 Ahio   9 Zecher   10 Mikloth

1 (8:33) Kish   2 Abner

1 Jonathan   2 Saul Malki-Shua   3 Abinadab   4 Esh-Baal (Ish-Bosheth, 2 Sam 2:8)

(8:34) Merib-Baal (Mephibosheth, 2 Sam 4:4)

Micah

1 Pithon   2 Melech   3 Tarea (Tahrea, 9:41)   4 Ahaz

(8:36) Jadah (Jehoaddah)

1 Alemeth   2 Azmaveth   3 Zimri
Moza
(8:37) Binea
Raphah
Eleasah

1 Azel (8:38)   2 Eshek

1 Azrikam   2 Bokeru   3 Ishmael   4 Sheariah   5 Obadiah   6 Hanan   1 Ulam   2 Jeush   3 Eliphelet

(8:40) warriors

sons

grandsons

The people of Judah were taken captive to Babylon because of their unfaithfulness. ²Now the first to resettle on their own property in their own towns were some Israelites, priests, Levites and temple servants.

³Those from Judah, from Benjamin, and from Ephraim and Manasseh who lived in Jerusalem were:

⁴Uthai son of Ammihud, the son of Omri, the son of Imri, the son of Bani, a descendant of Perez son of Judah.

⁵Of the Shilonites:

Asaiah the firstborn and his sons.

⁶Of the Zerahites:

Jeuel.

The people from Judah numbered 690.

⁷Of the Benjamites:

Sallu son of Meshullam, the son of Hodaviah, the son of Hassenuah;

⁸Ibneiah son of Jeroham; Elah son of Uzzi, the son of Micri; and Meshullam son of Shephatiah, the son of Reuel, the son of Ibnijah.

⁹The people from Benjamin, as listed in their genealogy, numbered 956. All these men were heads of their families.

¹⁰Of the priests:

Jedaiah; Jehoiarib; Jakin;

¹¹Azariah son of Hilkiah, the son of Meshullam, the son of Zadok, the son of Meraioth, the son of Ahitub, the official in charge of the house of God;

¹²Adaiah son of Jeroham, the son of Pashhur, the son of Malkijah; and Maasai son of Adiel, the son of Jahzerah, the son of Meshullam, the son of Meshillemith, the son of Immer.

¹³The priests, who were heads of families, numbered 1,760. They were able men, responsible for ministering in the house of God.

¹⁴Of the Levites:

Shemaiah son of Hasshub, the son of Azrikam, the son of Hashabiah, a Merarite; ¹⁵Bakbakkar, Heresh, Galal and Mattaniah son of Mica, the son of Zicri, the son of Asaph; ¹⁶Obadiah son of Shemaiah, the son of Galal, the son of Jeduthun; and Berekiah son of Asa, the son of Elkanah, who lived in the villages of the Netophathites.

¹⁷The gatekeepers:

Shallum, Akkub, Talmon, Ahiman and their brothers, Shallum their chief ¹⁸being stationed at the King's Gate on the east, up to the present time. These were the gatekeepers belonging to the camp of the Levites. ¹⁹Shallum son of Kore, the son of Ebiasaph, the son of Korah, and his fellow gatekeepers from his family (the Korahites) were responsible for guarding the thresholds of the Tent just as their fathers had been responsible for guarding the entrance to the dwelling of the LORD. ²⁰In earlier times Phinehas son of Eleazar was in charge of the gatekeepers, and the LORD was with him. ²¹Zechariah son of Meshelemiah was the gatekeeper at the entrance to the Tent of Meeting.

²²Altogether, those chosen to be gatekeepers at the thresholds numbered 212. They were registered by genealogy in their villages. The gatekeepers had been assigned to their positions of trust by David and Samuel the seer. ²³They and their descendants were in charge of guarding the gates of the house of the LORD—the house called the Tent. ²⁴The gatekeepers were on the four sides: east, west, north and south. ²⁵Their brothers in their villages had to come from time to time and share their duties for seven-day periods. ²⁶But the four principal gatekeepers, who were Levites, were entrusted with the responsibility for the rooms and treasuries in the house of God. ²⁷They would spend the night stationed around the house of God, because they had to guard it; and they had charge of the key for opening it each morning.

²⁸Some of them were in charge of the articles used in the temple service; they counted them when they were brought in and when they were taken out. ²⁹Others were assigned to take care of the furnishings and all the other articles of the sanctuary, as well as the flour and wine, and the oil, incense and spices. ³⁰But

some of the priests took care of mixing the spices. 31A Levite named Mattithiah, the firstborn son of Shallum the Korahite, was entrusted with the responsibility for baking the offering bread. 32Some of their Kohathite brothers were in charge of preparing for every Sabbath the bread set out on the table.

33Those who were musicians, heads of Levite families, stayed in the rooms of the temple and were exempt from other duties because they were responsible for the work day and night.

34All these were heads of Levite families, chiefs as listed in their genealogy, and they lived in Jerusalem.

35 Jeiel the father of Gibeon lived in Gibeon.

His wife's name was Maacah, 36and his firstborn son was Abdon, followed by Zur, Kish, Baal, Ner, Nadab, 37Gedor, Ahio, Zechariah and Mikloth. 38Mikloth was the father of Shimeam. They too lived near their relatives in Jerusalem.

39 Ner was the father of Kish, Kish the father of Saul, and Saul the father of Jonathan, Malki-Shua, Abinadab and Esh-Baal.

40 The son of Jonathan:

Merib-Baal, who was the father of Micah.

41 The sons of Micah:

Pithon, Melech, Tahrea and Ahaz.

42 Ahaz was the father of Jadah, Jadah was the father of Alemeth, Azmaveth and Zimri, and Zimri was the father of Moza. 43Moza was the father of Binea; Rephaiah was his son, Eleasah his son and Azel his son.

44 Azel had six sons, and these were their names:

Azrikam, Bokeru, Ishmael, Sheariah, Obadiah and Hanan. These were the sons of Azel.

Chapter 9 continues the Chronicler's discussion of preexilic Benjamin (begun in 7:6) by cataloging the family groups that lived in Jerusalem just prior to its capture and destruction in 586 B.C. In addition to Benjamin (vv.7–9), these included clans from Judah (vv.4–6) and especially from Levi because of its key functioning in the temple services: whether from among the priests (vv.10–13), the nonpriestly Levites in general (vv.14–16), or the more specialized gatekeepers (vv.17–19). This in turn leads into a description of their duties (vv.20–34). Jerusalem did, however, lie within the tribal boundaries of Benjamin (Josh 18:16, 28), and it had already received some discussion in the preceding chapter (8:28, 32); hence its inclusion at this point. Such information about former population groups and activities, in what was still the nation's capital city, was of prime importance to Ezra and his colleagues in their efforts to restore legitimate theocracy to Judah in their own postexilic situation.

Chapter 9 itself is sometimes assigned to the period of Persian restoration (though see comments to vv.2, 11) or even equated with a list of Nehemiah's during his own time (444 B.C.), of those who lived in Jerusalem and of those who resided outside (Neh 11:3–24). But while this latter document exhibits the same order in its categories (perhaps because based on 1 Chron 9), caution is advised. Thus even Myers (Chronicles, 1:67) admits: "The two lists are not so alike as sometimes supposed. . . . The MT has about eighty-one names for Nehemiah 11 and about seventy-one for Chronicles, of which only about thirty-five are the same or nearly so. Moreover some of these have a permanent relevance, e.g., names of priestly courses (vv.10, 12) or of genealogical ancestors (vv.11, 16), which are not subject to change in any event (cf. Keil's refutation of attempts to equate the two lists, pp. 153–56).

1 This transition verse shifts the reader's attention away from the tribal registers that

have gone before. "The book of the kings" designates a court record now lost (see Introduction: Sources).

2 The NIV's phrase "the first to resettle" represents words that are, literally, "the dwellers, the first ones" (cf. NASB, "the first who lived in"). In the present context the event that separates the Chronicler from "the first ones" is defined as the Babylonian captivity (v.1); hence the dwellers should probably be understood as the former, preexilic Jerusalemites (cf. the introduction to this chapter).

The "temple servants" (*neṭînîm*) were literally "given ones." They might consist of captives who had been spared but enslaved to temple service (cf. the *ytnm* in Ugar. texts coming shortly after Mosaic times). Early Hebrew examples include certain Midianite women (Num 31:35, 47) or the people of Gibeon (Josh 9:22–23), but their organization as a class is credited to David (Ezra 8:20).

3 Individual Jerusalemites who had come from Ephraim or other northern tribes receive no further mention, since the list that follows cites only major clan leaders.

5 For "Shilonites" read Shelanites, as in Numbers 26:20, since Perez (v.4), Shelah, and Zerah (v.6) make up the divisions of Judah (2:3–4).

10 Jedaiah, Jehoiarib, and Jakin, with Malkijah and Immer (v.12), are the names of the second, first, twenty-first, fifth, and sixteenth of the twenty-four priestly courses established by David (24:7–18), rather than names of individuals.

11 The fact that Azariah IV is the son of Hilkiah (see comment on 6:13) dates this listing to shortly after 622 B.C.

14 Shemaiah came from Merari, the third of the three Levitical clans.

15 Mattaniah belonged to the first, Gershon, through Asaph, one of David's chief musicians.

16 Obadiah was again of Merari, through the chief musician Jeduthun (= Ethan; cf. comment to 6:44), while Berekiah's ancestor Elkanah bears a frequently reappearing Kohathite name (cf. the chart of Levi, pp. 352–53).

18 Since the temple faced east, the "King's Gate" was the main gate (cf. Acts 3:2, in NT times), viz., the king's entrance (Ezek 46:1–2) and most honored station. Ezra's phrases "camp" of the Levites and God's "Tent" (v.19; cf. NIV mg.) recall how Levi once encamped on the four sides of the tabernacle (Num 3:25–38).

19 Though Korah had been slain (see comment on 6:22), his line continued. Coming from Kohath—the second clan but also that of Moses, Aaron, and the priests—the Korahites were even honored, by appointment as gatekeepers under Aaron's faithful grandson, Phinehas I, on whom God bestowed the Levitical covenant of peace (Num 25:11–13). Their status continued, through Kore, whether denoting Korah's immediate grandson of this name (1 Chron 26:1) or a later Kore in 725 B.C. (2 Chron 31:14), down to this Shallum a century later.

21 Since both Meshelemiah and Zechariah served under David (26:8–11), this "Tent of Meeting" (cf. comment on 6:32) would seem to refer to the curtained form of God's house (16:1; 17:1; cf. 22:1 and Ps 30 title) erected prior to Solomon's permanent temple (v.19 NIV mg.).

22 It was appropriate that Samuel, himself a Korahite (6:27 and comment) and one of the doorkeepers in his youth (1 Sam 3:15), should have anticipated David in their final organization (1 Chron 26). The way Israel could commit to them "their positions of trust" (*ʾemunāh*, also in v.31) indicates something of how the righteous live by faith, or trust, in God (Hab 2:4; Rom 1:17).

The number of their chiefs could vary: 94 under David (26:8–11); compare 139 among the first return (Ezra 2:42) and 172 under Nehemiah (Neh 11:19).

25 Twenty-four guard stations (26:17–18) and 216 chosen gatekeepers (212, v.22, plus the 4 leaders of vv.26–27, who stayed permanently in Jerusalem) works out exactly to 9 people for each post. If we assume eight-hour shifts, this would require 72 men on duty, one week out of every three; twelve-hour shifts would require 48 on a week's duty, once every four or five weeks.

30 Reference seems to be to spices used for the holy anointing oil, for those who mixed it were a closely restricted group (Exod 30:33, 38).

31 "The offering bread," more literally, "the things that were baked in pans" (NASB), refers to the flat cakes that were used in the meal, or cereal, offerings (Lev 2; 6:14–18; 7:9–10).

32 "The bread" refers to "the showbread" that was set out in rows on the golden table to symbolize the communion of redeemed men with God (Lev 24:5–6).

33 The musicians mentioned here are the leaders named in vv.14–16.

34 This verse then sums up all the Levitical inhabitants of Jerusalem (vv.10–33).

35–44 The rest of chapter 9 reverts to reproducing the lines of Benjamin that lived near Jerusalem (v.38). It virtually repeats 8:29–38 (q.v.) on the family of Saul; but its purpose here is to introduce the tragic conclusion to his reign (ch. 10).

Notes

20 The eldest son of the current high priest may regularly have had responsibility for the sanctuary; cf. the case of Phinehas's father, Eleazar (Num 3:2–3).

37 Read "Zeker," with the LXX^A and 8:31, for the fuller form "Zechariah."

38 Read "Shimeah" (שִׁמְאָה, *šimʾāh*), with the LXX and 8:32, for "Shimeam" (שִׁמְאָם, *šimʾām*).

II. The Reign of David (10:1–29:30)

A. *Background: the Death of Saul*

10:1–14

> ¹Now the Philistines fought against Israel; the Israelites fled before them, and many fell slain on Mount Gilboa. ²The Philistines pressed hard after Saul and his sons, and they killed his sons Jonathan, Abinadab and Malki-Shua. ³The fighting grew fierce around Saul, and when the archers overtook him, they wounded him.
> ⁴Saul said to his armor-bearer, "Draw your sword and run me through, or these uncircumcised fellows will come and abuse me."
> But his armor-bearer was terrified and would not do it; so Saul took his own sword and fell on it. ⁵When the armor-bearer saw that Saul was dead, he too fell on his sword and died. ⁶So Saul and his three sons died, and all his house died together.
> ⁷When all the Israelites in the valley saw that the army had fled and that Saul and his sons had died, they abandoned their towns and fled. And the Philistines came and occupied them.
> ⁸The next day, when the Philistines came to strip the dead, they found Saul and his sons fallen on Mount Gilboa. ⁹They stripped him and took his head and his armor, and sent messengers throughout the land of the Philistines to proclaim the news among their idols and their people. ¹⁰They put his armor in the temple of their gods and hung up his head in the temple of Dagon.
> ¹¹When all the inhabitants of Jabesh Gilead heard of everything the Philistines had done to Saul, ¹²all their valiant men went and took the bodies of Saul and his sons and brought them to Jabesh. Then they buried their bones under the great tree in Jabesh, and they fasted seven days.
> ¹³Saul died because he was unfaithful to the Lord; he did not keep the word of the Lord and even consulted a medium for guidance, ¹⁴and did not inquire of the Lord. So the Lord put him to death and turned the kingdom over to David son of Jesse.

Having established Israel's historical setting and ethnic bounds in the preceding genealogies (chs. 1–9), the Chronicler now enters on his main subject, the history of the Hebrew kingdom, with its theological conclusions. His central character is David, on whom the remainder of 1 Chronicles focuses (chs. 10–29). David's devotion led him to set up the institutions of public worship that Ezra was so eager to maintain. David's heroic personality exemplifies the success that God bestows on those who trust in him, whether in the Chronicler's time or any other. His posterity, moreover, constitutes the ruling dynasty of Judah throughout the rest of its independent history (the content of 2 Chron) and would bear its ultimate fruit in the eternal kingdom of Jesus the Messiah. Practical aims like these also explain why Ezra omitted the less edifying events of the reign of Saul; for he moves directly from the king's Benjamite genealogy (9:35–44) to his death (ch. 10), which precipitated David's rise to the throne (v.14). First Chronicles 10:1–12 derives directly from 1 Samuel 31, with slight differences in the choice of the details described; vv.13–14 then point up the chapter's negative doctrine, of the failure to which God condemns those who forsake him.

1 The Philistines were a Hamitic people, but of Minoan background rather than Canaanite (see on 1:12). Before the year 2000, some had settled on the southern coast of Palestine (Deut 2:23), the very name of which means "Philistine land," and encountered Abraham (Gen 21:32; cf. 26:14). They remained after Joshua's conquest in 1400 (Josh 13:2–3) and only temporarily lost certain of their cities to Judah (Judg

1:18). Shamgar's skirmish with them in 1250 (3:31) was successful but simultaneously demonstrates Israel's material disadvantage to their presence (cf. 1 Sam 13:19–22). With the Fall of Crete to widespread barbarian movements in 1200, the "remnant . . . of Caphtor" (Jer 47:4) reinforced the earlier Philistines on Asia's Canaanite mainland.

For a century, following a crushing defeat of the Peleset (generally conceded to be the Philistines) by Pharaoh Rameses III, the Philistines seemed content to consolidate their city-states; but then in three waves they almost overwhelmed Israel. The first extended for forty years, including Samson (Judg 10:7; 13:1; 1 Sam 4), but was broken in 1063 B.C. by Samuel at the second battle of Ebenezer (1 Sam 7:13); and the second wave, for perhaps ten years, by Saul at the battle of Micmash in 1041 (14:31). First Chronicles 10, which dates to 1010 B.C., marks the onset of the Philistines' last major advance and period of oppression, which would be broken some seven years later by David (1 Chron 14:10–16).

Mount Gilboa lay at the head of the great east-west Valley of Esdraelon, below Galilee, so that its loss by Israel enabled the Philistines to penetrate to the Jordan and even beyond (1 Sam 31:7).

2 On Saul's sons, see comment on 8:33.

4 Saul's fear of "abuse," if the Philistines should take him alive (cf. Judg 16:21), drove him to suicide, which was unprecedented in the OT (though cf. later occurrences in 2 Sam 17:23; 1 Kings 16:18). This testifies to the Philistine's cruelty despite material culture (cf. v.9 and today's use of "Philistine" as a byword for barbarism).

5 The context makes clear that Saul's death occurred at his own hands. Second Samuel 1:6–10 states only what an unscrupulous Amalekite reported. He seems in fact merely to have discovered the body, plundered it, and then lied in hopes of reward from David.

6 Those of Saul's house who stood with him ("all his men," 1 Sam 31:6) died together at Gilboa; others, however, both of his sons and troops, did survive (1 Chron 8:34 –40; 2 Sam 2:8; 21:8). Alternatively this might be the Chronicler's way of intimating the otherwise omitted data in 2 Samuel 1–4 on Ish-Bosheth.

10 First Samuel adds that the Philistines hung Saul's body on the walls of Beth Shan, a major city between Gilboa and the Jordan, and that the deity in whose temple they put his armor was Ashtoreth, goddess of sex and war (31:10). His head was placed in another's temple, that of the vegetation god Dagon (cf. 1 Sam 5:2–5). The validity of the two buildings has been attested archaeologically by the discovery of both temples in Beth Shan's ruins of this period (J. Finegan, *Light From the Ancient Past* [Princeton: University Press, 1931], p. 167).

11 The men of Jabesh Gilead in Transjordan remained faithful to Saul, their deliverer thirty years earlier (1 Sam 11:1-11).

13–14 Saul's unfaithfulness consisted of disobeying God's words through Samuel (1

Sam 13:8–9; 15:2–3) and of consulting the spiritist at Endor (28:7–13) instead of persevering—he had made some inquiry of him (v.6)—in prayer for divine grace.

Notes

12 אֵלָה (*ʾēlāh*, "great tree") refers simply to a large tree (KB, p. 50). First Sam 31:13, however, designates the species as that of a tamarisk (אֵשֶׁל, *ʾēšel*).

B. *David's Rise (11:1–20:8)*

1. *David established in Jerusalem; his heroes*

11:1–12:40

¹All Israel came together to David at Hebron and said, "We are your own flesh and blood. ²In the past, even while Saul was king, you were the one who led Israel on their military campaigns. And the LORD your God said to you, 'You will shepherd my people Israel, and you will become their ruler.' "

³When all the elders of Israel had come to King David at Hebron, he made a compact with them at Hebron before the LORD, and they anointed David king over Israel, as the LORD had promised through Samuel.

⁴David and all the Israelites marched to Jerusalem (that is, Jebus). The Jebusites who lived there ⁵said to David, "You will not get in here." Nevertheless, David captured the fortress of Zion, the City of David.

⁶David had said, "Whoever leads the attack on the Jebusites will become commander-in-chief." Joab son of Zeruiah went up first, and so he received the command.

⁷David then took up residence in the fortress, and so it was called the City of David. ⁸He built up the city around it, from the supporting terraces to the surrounding wall, while Joab restored the rest of the city. ⁹And David became more and more powerful, because the LORD Almighty was with him.

¹⁰These were the chiefs of David's mighty men—they, together with all Israel, gave his kingship strong support to extend it over the whole land, as the LORD had promised—¹¹this is the list of David's mighty men:

Jashobeam, a Hacmonite, was chief of the officers; he raised his spear against three hundred men, whom he killed in one encounter.

¹²Next to him was Eleazar son of Dodai the Ahohite, one of the three mighty men. ¹³He was with David at Pas Dammim when the Philistines gathered there for battle. At a place where there was a field full of barley, the troops fled from the Philistines. ¹⁴But they took their stand in the middle of the field. They defended it and struck the Philistines down, and the LORD brought about a great victory.

¹⁵Three of the thirty chiefs came down to David to the rock at the cave of Adullam, while a band of Philistines was encamped in the Valley of Rephaim. ¹⁶At that time David was in the stronghold, and the Philistine garrison was at Bethlehem. ¹⁷David longed for water and said, "Oh, that someone would get me a drink of water from the well near the gate of Bethlehem!" ¹⁸So the Three broke through the Philistine lines, drew water from the well near the gate of Bethlehem and carried it back to David. But he refused to drink it; instead, he poured it out before the LORD. ¹⁹"God forbid that I should do this!" he said. "Should I drink the blood of these men who went at the risk of their lives?" Because they risked their lives to bring it back, David would not drink it.

Such were the exploits of the three mighty men.

²⁰Abishai the brother of Joab was chief of the Three. He raised his spear

against three hundred men, whom he killed, and so he became as famous as the Three. 21He was doubly honored above the Three and became their commander, even though he was not included among them.

22Benaiah son of Jehoiada was a valiant fighter from Kabzeel, who performed great exploits. He struck down two of Moab's best men. He also went down into a pit on a snowy day and killed a lion. 23And he struck down an Egyptian who was seven and a half feet tall. Although the Egyptian had a spear like a weaver's rod in his hand, Benaiah went against him with a club. He snatched the spear from the Egyptian's hand and killed him with his own spear. 24Such were the exploits of Benaiah son of Jehoiada; he too was as famous as the three mighty men. 25He was held in greater honor than any of the Thirty, but he was not included among the Three. And David put him in charge of his bodyguard.

26The mighty men were:
Asahel the brother of Joab,
Elhanan son of Dodo from Bethlehem,
27Shammoth the Harorite,
Helez the Pelonite,
28Ira son of Ikkesh from Tekoa,
Abiezer from Anathoth,
29Sibbecai the Hushathite,
Ilai the Ahohite,
30Maharai the Netophathite,
Heled son of Baanah the Netophathite,
31Ithai son of Ribai from Gibeah in Benjamin,
Benaiah the Pirathonite,
32Hurai from the ravines of Gaash,
Abiel the Arbathite,
33Azmaveth the Baharumite,
Eliahba the Shaalbonite,
34the sons of Hashem the Gizonite,
Jonathan son of Shagee the Hararite,
35Ahiam son of Sacar the Hararite,
Eliphal son of Ur,
36Hepher the Mekerathite,
Ahijah the Pelonite,
37Hezro the Carmelite,
Naarai son of Ezbai,
38Joel the brother of Nathan,
Mibhar son of Hagri,
39Zelek the Ammonite,
Naharai the Berothite, the armor-bearer of Joab son of Zeruiah,
40Ira the Ithrite,
Gareb the Ithrite,
41Uriah the Hittite,
Zabad son of Ahlai,
42Adina son of Shiza the Reubenite, who was chief of the Reubenites, and the thirty with him,
43Hanan son of Maacah,
Joshaphat the Mithnite,
44Uzzia the Ashterathite,
Shama and Jeiel the sons of Hotham the Aroerite,
45Jediael son of Shimri,
his brother Joha the Tizite,
46Eliel the Mahavite,
Jeribai and Joshaviah the sons of Elnaam,
Ithmah the Moabite,
47Eliel, Obed and Jaasiel the Mezobaite.

12:1These were the men who came to David at Ziklag, while he was banished from the presence of Saul son of Kish (they were among the warriors who helped him in battle; [2]they were armed with bows and were able to shoot arrows or to sling stones right-handed or left-handed; they were kinsmen of Saul from the tribe of Benjamin):

[3]Ahiezer their chief and Joash the sons of Shemaah the Gibeathite; Jeziel and Pelet the sons of Azmaveth; Beracah, Jehu the Anathothite, [4]and Ishmaiah the Gibeonite, a mighty man among the Thirty, who was a leader of the Thirty; Jeremiah, Jahaziel, Johanan, Jozabad the Gederathite, [5]Eluzai, Jerimoth, Bealiah, Shemariah and Shephatiah the Haruphite; [6]Elkanah, Isshiah, Azarel, Joezer and Jashobeam the Korahites; [7]and Joelah and Zebadiah the sons of Jeroham from Gedor.

[8]Some Gadites defected to David at his stronghold in the desert. They were brave warriors, ready for battle and able to handle the shield and spear. Their faces were the faces of lions, and they were as swift as gazelles in the mountains.
  [9]Ezer was the chief,
    Obadiah the second in command, Eliab the third,
  [10]Mishmannah the fourth, Jeremiah the fifth,
  [11]Attai the sixth, Eliel the seventh,
  [12]Johanan the eighth, Elzabad the ninth,
  [13]Jeremiah the tenth and Macbannai the eleventh.
[14]These Gadites were army commanders; the least was a match for a hundred, and the greatest for a thousand. [15]It was they who crossed the Jordan in the first month when it was overflowing all its banks, and they put to flight everyone living in the valleys, to the east and to the west.

[16]Other Benjamites and some men from Judah also came to David in his stronghold. [17]David went out to meet them and said to them, "If you have come to me in peace, to help me, I am ready to have you unite with me. But if you have come to betray me to my enemies when my hands are free from violence, may the God of our fathers see it and judge you."

[18]Then the Spirit came upon Amasai, chief of the Thirty, and he said:

> "We are yours, O David!
>   We are with you, O son of Jesse!
> Success, success to you,
>   and success to those who help you,
>   for your God will help you."

So David received them and made them leaders of his raiding bands.

[19]Some of the men of Manasseh defected to David when he went with the Philistines to fight against Saul. (He and his men did not help the Philistines because, after consultation, their rulers sent him away. They said, "It will cost us our heads if he deserts to his master Saul.") [20]When David went to Ziklag, these were the men of Manasseh who defected to him: Adnah, Jozabad, Jediael, Michael, Jozabad, Elihu and Zillethai, leaders of units of a thousand in Manasseh. [21]They helped David against raiding bands, for all of them were brave warriors, and they were commanders in his army. [22]Day after day men came to help David, until he had a great army, like the army of God.

[23]These are the numbers of the men armed for battle who came to David at Hebron to turn Saul's kingdom over to him, as the LORD had said:
  [24]men of Judah, carrying shield and spear—6,800 armed for battle;
  [25]men of Simeon, warriors ready for battle—7,100;
  [26]men of Levi—4,600, [27]including Jehoiada, leader of the family of Aaron, with 3,700 men, [28]and Zadok, a brave young warrior, with 22 officers from his family;
  [29]men of Benjamin, Saul's kinsmen—3,000, most of whom had remained loyal to Saul's house until then;
  [30]men of Ephraim, brave warriors, famous in their own clans—20,800;
  [31]men of half the tribe of Manasseh, designated by name to come and make David king—18,000;

³²men of Issachar, who understood the times and knew what Israel should do—200 chiefs, with all their relatives under their command; ³³men of Zebulun, experienced soldiers prepared for battle with every type of weapon, to help David with undivided loyalty—50,000; ³⁴men of Naphtali—1,000 officers, together with 37,000 men carrying shields and spears; ³⁵men of Dan, ready for battle—28,600; ³⁶men of Asher, experienced soldiers prepared for battle—40,000; ³⁷and from east of the Jordan, men of Reuben, Gad and the half-tribe of Manasseh, armed with every type of weapon—120,000.

³⁸All these were fighting men who volunteered to serve in the ranks. They came to Hebron fully determined to make David king over all Israel. All the rest of the Israelites were also of one mind to make David king. ³⁹The men spent three days there with David, eating and drinking, for their families had supplied provisions for them. ⁴⁰Also, their neighbors from as far away as Issachar, Zebulun and Naphtali came bringing food on donkeys, camels, mules and oxen. There were plentiful supplies of flour, fig cakes, raisin cakes, wine, oil, cattle and sheep, for there was joy in Israel.

The next ten chapters in 1 Chronicles (11–20) cover the period between 1003 and about 995 B.C., during which David rose to the zenith of his power. The seven and one-half years of disputed succession, civil war, and Philistine domination (2 Sam 1 –4) that followed Saul's death in 1010 (cf. 2 Sam 5:5) are passed over. But they are not denied: Ezra's observation in the opening verse of the section (11:1), that Israel came to "Hebron" to anoint David, constitutes a tacit recognition of his initial installation there, but only by his own tribe of Judah (2 Sam 2:4, 10b); of the rejection of his appeal to the other tribes to the north and east (vv.5–6); and of their eventual choice of Saul's son Ish-Bosheth, 1005–1003 (vv.8–10a).

Instead Chronicles takes up and amplifies the record of 2 Samuel 5–10, which includes David's capture of Jerusalem and its establishment as a new political capital for him and his supporters (1 Chron 11–12); his achievement of independence from the Philistines (ch. 14); his return of the ark of the covenant, which made Jerusalem the religious capital of united Israel as well (chs. 13; 15–16); and the triumphant advance of his armies in every direction (chs. 18–20). Only the account of David's personal kindness to Jonathan's lame son Mephibosheth (2 Sam 9) is omitted.

The heart of this section is found in God's prophecy to David through Nathan (ch 17): "I have been with you wherever you have gone, and . . . I will subdue all your enemies" (vv.8, 10). The Lord's "great promises" (v.19) applied not only to David, but to "my people Israel" as a whole (v.9)—not only in the early tenth century B.C., but for "the future of the house of your servant" (v.17). Its assurances are applicable to Ezra's struggling postexilic community; to the present church of Jesus, whom David predicted, "He will be my son" (v.13; cf. Ps 110:1; Matt 22:42–45); and to that yet future kingdom of the Messiah, whose "throne will be established forever" (v.14).

The section's initial subdivision (1 Chron 11–12) documents David's ascendency. Following his consecration as king over a reunited Israel (11:1–3), one of his first acts was to capture and then to strengthen Jerusalem (vv.4–9). A parallel passage is found in 2 Samuel 5:1–10. The Chronicler then proceeds to describe David's heroes: "the Three" (vv.10–19), two of the major commanders (vv.20–25), and "the Thirty" (vv.26–47), with parallels occurring in 2 Samuel 23:8–39. A concluding list, however, is unique to 1 Chronicles (ch. 12). It describes the military leaders and tribal officers who came over to David before his final anointing and who played a primary role in his eventual elevation to the kingship (v.38). It suggests David's growing popular support beyond the four hundred men of 1 Samuel 22:2 (later six hundred, 27:2).

1 The phrase "all Israel" is characteristic of the Chronicler's concern for the unity of God's people. Emphasis here falls on the portions of Israel that had so far not recognized David's kingship.

2 The Lord's appointment of David dates back some twenty years to his first anointing, in the privacy of his family, by Samuel (1 Sam 15:28; 16:1–13). As David then demonstrated his ability for leadership (18:5, 16), he was increasingly recognized as standing in line for the throne (23:17; 25:30), even by Saul himself (24:20; 26:25). At Saul's death David had received a second anointing, over Judah (2 Sam 2:4); and Abner had started the preparation for his total rule (3:10).

3 This third anointing was preceded by a "compact" (*berît*, "covenant") before the Lord, by which both king and people acknowledged their mutual obligations under God. Such a "constitutional monarchy" was unique in the ancient Near East, for the only effective curb against despotism is one's personal belief in God and commitment to his higher kingship. Contrast the reputation for clemency and the religious scruples of even a weak Hebrew monarch like Ahab (1 Kings 20:31; 21:3–4, 27–29) with the natural (unrestrained) ruthlessness of his Canaanite wife, Jezebel (21:7–10).

4 Allusions to Jerusalem appear first in the Ebla tablets of 2400 B.C. The city is described as Salem in reference to Abraham in 2000 (Gen 14:18) and as Urusalim in the Egyptian Amarna letters, which confirm the Hebrew conquest in 1400. Jerusalem had led a southern Canaanite alliance against Joshua (Josh 10:1–5), who defeated its army and executed its king (10:10, 26; 11:7, 10). The tribe of Judah overran the defenses of the city itself (Judg 1:8), but the Jebusites soon reoccupied it. For almost four centuries Judah had been unable to win back Jerusalem and drive out its Canaanite inhabitants (Josh 15:63; Judg 1:21; 19:10–11), which helps explain the latter's overconfidence against David (1 Chron 11:5; 2 Sam 5:6). David had posted notice long before of his intention against the haughty city (1 Sam 17:54).

While 2 Samuel 5:6 identifies the attackers only as "David's men," Chronicles includes "all the Israelites" (cf. v.10 and 12:38, which concede the primary role exercised by David's particular followers).

6 The king's offer that whoever "leads the attack," i.e., first penetrated Jerusalem, would become commander over the armies of united Israel (omitted from 2 Samuel 5:8) may represent an attempt on his part to replace his effective but self-willed nephew Joab, who had been leading the forces of Judah up to this point (cf. 2 Sam 3:39). Joab nevertheless retained his post by bravely achieving the initial entrance, ascending a concealed watershaft from the Gihon spring so as to end up within the city walls (K.M. Kenyon, *Jerusalem: Excavating 3000 Years of History* [New York: McGraw-Hill, 1967], pp. 22, 30).

7 David's relocation to Jerusalem was a strategic move. It provided him not only with an impregnable citadel militarily, but also with a neutral site politically as a capital, lying as it did on the border between Judah and the northern tribes (cf. the similarly motivated choice of Washington D.C. in American history).

Near Eastern conquerors not infrequently named cities after themselves; e.g., Dur-Sharrukin ("the city of Sargon") in Assyria, or Alexandria, the result of the genius of Alexander the Great in Egypt.

8 Millo (NIV mg.) means "filling." These "terraces" had been built so that the city's eastern walls could extend far enough down the steep Kidron slope to encompass the Gihon watershaft, and they suffered a continuing need for repair (1 Kings 11:27; 2 Chron 32:5; Kenyon, *Jerusalem*, pp. 50–51, 79).

10 The remainder of the chapter is a catalog of David's mighty men, introduced at this point because of the significant role they played in his rise to the kingship and in his establishment at Jerusalem. Their listing, down through Uriah the Hittite (v.41), corresponds to one of the appendices in 2 Samuel (23:8–39), with minor variations, such as spelling. Twelve of their number reappear as commanders of the twelve corps into which David's troops were later organized (1 Chron 27).

11 The hero's sensational victory was actually over eight hundred men (2 Sam 23:8). Three hundred seems to be a scribal corruption, perhaps influenced by the number that appears in v.20 or by the nature of the numerical symbols employed. The situation would be similar to our reading a smudged VIII as III (see Appendix A and Payne, "Validity," p. 118).

12 David's greatest champions were "the Three," though the record of the third, Shammah (2 Sam 23:11), accidentally has been dropped.

13 After the words "the Philistines gathered there for battle," we should insert the material supplied in 2 Samuel 23:9 (following this clause) and on into v.11 (through a similar clause). It is an instance of scribal paraleipsis.

15 Next to "the Three" ranked the "the Thirty"—which was apparently the original number in this legion of honor among David's men. Second Samuel 23:24–39 actually lists thirty-seven, including the outstanding "Three" and the two commanders; and 1 Chronicles 11:41b–47 adds sixteen more, as new heroes were added to the group. Which ones of the "Thirty" performed the deed that follows is not stated.

The Valley of Rephaim, where the Philistines encamped, lies southwest of Jerusalem. Its mention connects this event with their first campaign against David (14:8–9), even before his capture of the city. David had thus retreated to his old outlaw stronghold at Adullam (1 Sam 22:1; 2 Sam 5:17). Its citation constitutes another allusion to David's difficult rise to power, which the Chronicler never seeks to conceal.

16–18 David poured out the water he had longed for as a libation offering to the Lord (Lev 23:37), showing both how precious he considered his men, who had risked their lives to get it, and how centrally he placed God in his own life.

19 David called the water their "blood," since life does depend on its presence (cf. Gen 9:4; Lev 17:14; Deut 12:23; and the Eng. phrase "lifeblood").

20–21 Abishai was David's half-nephew. His heroism was demonstrated by his having volunteered to go down at night with David into Saul's camp (1 Sam 26:6–7). He had also been a joint commander, with his brother Joab, against the forces of Ish-Bosheth and Abner (2 Sam 2:24). He was later to lead divisions in the wars against the Ammonites (10:10), Absalom (18:2), and Sheba (20:6). The locale of this incident has not been preserved, but it may have occurred when Abishai commanded an expedition against Edom (1 Chron 18:12).

22 The NIV phrase about Moab's "best men" reads in the Hebrew the *ᵃri'ēl* of Moab." "Ariel" must here be used, not in its impersonal sense of "the altar-hearth of God" (Isa 29:1–2, 7; = *har'ēl*, Ezek 43:15–16), but in its personal sense (Curtis), literally, "the lions of God," a superlative idiom, meaning that Benaiah overcame "the mighty lions (of Moab)" (KJV, "lionlike men").

23–25 When the spear of Benaiah's Egyptian opponent is said to be like "a weaver's rod," the reference is to the heavy shaft of a loom that holds the threads taut; i.e., this was a massive weapon. For such heroism he became commander of David's professional Cretan and Philistine troops (1 Chron 18:17) and later of Solomon's entire army (1 Kings 4:4).

26 The roster of the Thirty begins at this point and must have been first formulated some time before David became king of all Israel; for Asahel, the youngest of David's half-nephews, was killed pursuing Abner in his uncle's war against Ish-Bosheth (2 Sam 2:18–23).

This Elhanan, son of Dodo, should not be confused with Elhanan son of Jair, the hero who slew the brother of Goliath (20:5).

27 The qualifying phrase "the Harorite" (*hahᵃrôrî*) has shifted, by two easy scribal blunders, from *hahᵃrōḏî* (as in the LXX and 2 Sam 23:25), "the Harodite," meaning "a man from Harod," the pool near Mount Gilboa where Gideon tested his men (Judg 7:1–7). In vv.34–35, however, "the Hararite" is accurate.

But while the place names are subject to a measure of control, a number of the personal names (vv.27–38) differ from those found in the parallel list in 2 Samuel 23:25–36, perhaps partly because of later spelling patterns in Ezra's day, some 475 years after the writing of 2 Samuel.

31 Benaiah from Pirathon, in Ephraim, is not to be confused with Benaiah the commander (vv.22–25) from Kabzeel, near Beer Sheba, in the south.

36 For "Ahijah the Pelonite" read, with the LXX and 2 Samuel 23:34, "Eliam [= Ammiel, 1 Chron 3:5] the Gilonite," the father of Bathsheba and a son of David's counselor, Ahithophel (2 Sam 11:3), who did come from Giloh (15:12).

38 Here, as in so many of the other listings, read Joel the "son of" (rather than "brother of") Nathan, with the LXXᴮ and 2 Samuel 23:36.

12:1 Among those who supported David prior to his rise over all Israel (11:3), the first group listed in this chapter (12:1–7) are datable to the sixteen months just before Saul's death in 1010 B.C. They came to Ziklag, the town on the southwestern border of Judah, over which David had been appointed as a vassal ruler by Achish, the Philistine king of Gath (1 Sam 27:5–7).

2 The warriors were from Benjamin and were significant both for their individual prowess and for the fact that even though they were Saul's fellow tribesmen, they recognized David as God's appointed sovereign.

4 Though Ishmaiah is not listed among the Thirty, at one time he served as their commander (cf. also v.18 and 11:21).

6 The five Korahites were of Levi (see the comments on 6:22; 9:19) but probably lived in Benjamin.

8 Those listed from Gad (vv.8–15) joined David even earlier, while he was still in Judah in his desert stronghold, presumably the cave of Adullam (11:15; 12:16; cf. 1 Sam 22:1).

13 Jeremiah, the tenth Gadite leader, differs from the fifth (v.10) in that his Hebrew name has a longer form: *yirmᵉyāhû*.

14–15 During the first month (March/April), the Jordan is in its spring flood (cf. Josh 3:15; 4:18), which makes the Gadites' achievement all the more noteworthy.

18 The Holy Spirit literally "clothed himself with" Amasai. So inspired, his devotion to David as God's chosen servant is then expressed in Hebrew poetry, caught by BV as follows:

> We belong to you, O David;
>   We are with you, son of Jesse!
> Peace, yes perfect peace go with you;
>   Peace bless him who fights for you,
> Because your God does lend you aid.

19 The leaders from Manasseh (vv.19–23) arrived just before Saul's death at Gilboa, which lay in the western part of Manasseh's territory. David, however, was sent away from the actual battle, as explained in 1 Samuel 29. The Philistine commanders' mistrust and fear of David is stated clearly in 1 Samuel 29:4–5 (q.v.).

21 The Manassites' help against the raiders is explained in 1 Samuel 30.

22 The NIV rendering "like the army of God" reflects a Hebrew phrase that is literally "like the camp of God" (cf. comment on 11:22). It may be connected to the idea expressed in the divine name "LORD of hosts [= armies]" in 11:9 (NIV, "LORD Almighty"), which can refer to the armies of Israel. Here, however, David's multitude may be compared, poetically, with the heavenly hosts, whether of stars (Deut 4:19; Neh 9:6; Ps 33:6) or of angels (Gen 32:1–2; Ps 103:20–21).

23 The chapter concludes by enumerating the officers who came to Hebron seven and a half years later to turn over the whole nation to him (bringing us back to 11:1).

24 Although some have defended the accuracy of the large numbers given in these verses (e.g., Keil, pp. 189–93) or have suggested that they are deliberate hyperbole (R. Dillard, NIV Study Bible, p. 603), since these delegations are limited to specially equipped leaders—"famous in their own clans" (v.30; cf. v.25), presumably the same that are cited at the beginning of the next chapter as "commanders of thousands and commanders of hundreds" (13:1)—the numbers given should probably not be read as bare totals but, in this verse for example, as "six (commanders of) thousands, eight (commanders of) hundreds." There were, as we might say, 6 colonels and 8 captains, for a total of 14, not 6,800 (cf. J.W. Wenham, "Large Numbers in the Old Testament," *Tyndale Bulletin* 18 [1967]: 44–45). Notice what would otherwise be the incongruously small totals in v.28 with Zadok and 22 officers, or v.32, the apparently large delegation of 200 chiefs from Issachar. The number of officers assembled thus amounts to 398 (not 340,800 in Hebron at one time! cf. Payne, "Validity," p. 214).

27–28 Among the warriors from Levi, Jehoiada the priest seems to have been father of Benaiah, the major commander (11:22; 27:5), while Zadok, still young at this time, may be the Aaronite who became the colleague of Abiathar and later, under Solomon, his successor as high priest (29:22; 1 Kings 2:35; 4:4).

32 The men of Issachar "understood the times," and thus cast their lot with David rather than Saul.

39 The three-day feast at David's accession was an immediate, historic celebration; but it points to the doctrine of the future, messianic feast (Ps 22:29; Isa 25:6; Rev 19:7).

Notes

6 For various interpretations of the Hebrew word translated "watershaft" in 2 Sam 5:8, see P.K. McCarter, Jr., *II Samuel*, AB, pp. 139–40.

8 The expression that Joab "restored" (יְחַיֶּה, *yᵉḥayyeh*) the rest of the city means literally, "1, *preserve alive*, 2 [here], *bring to life*" (KB, p. 293; NASB, "repaired," mg.: "revived"). David repaired the citadel, but it was Joab (not mentioned in 2 Sam 5) who rebuilt the rest of the city.

11 In the direction of the NIV margin, "Jashobeam" (יָשְׁבְעָם, *yāšobʿām*) should be read as "Jishbaal" (יִשְׁבַּעַל, *yišbaʿal*), with the LXX; cf. 2 Sam 23:8, "Josheb-Basshebeth" (בַּשֶּׁבֶת יֹשֵׁב, *yōšēb baššebet*), for which the LXX suggests "Jishbosheth" (יִשְׁבֹּשֶׁת, *yišbōšet*; cf. comment on 1 Chron 8:33).

15 The word "band" represents מַחֲנֶה (*maḥᵃneh*), usually "camp" or "army." Here, however, it is not the entire army but a "band" corresponding (per Curtis, p. 189) to 2 Sam 23:13: חַיָּה (*ḥayyāh*) = חַוָּה, (*ḥawwāh*), "camp of tents."

27 "Shammoth" (שַׁמּוֹת, *šammôt*; LXXᴮ: σαμαωθ, *samaōth*) equals "Shamhuth" (שַׁמְהוּת, *šamhût*) in 27:8, where twelve of the heroes reappear as corps commanders.

12:1 Even some critical writers accept this material as a register of David's bodyguard vs. Saul (North, "The Chronicler," 1:409; "a source whose authenticity there is no reason to dispute," Myers, *Chronicles*, 1: LIII).

2. The ark sought

13:1–14

¹David conferred with each of his officers, the commanders of thousands and commanders of hundreds. ²He then said to the whole assembly of Israel, "If it seems good to you and if it is the will of the LORD our God, let us send word far and wide to the rest of our brothers throughout the territories of Israel, and also to the priests and Levites who are with them in their towns and pasturelands, to come and join us. ³Let us bring the ark of our God back to us, for we did not inquire of it during the reign of Saul." ⁴The whole assembly agreed to do this, because it seemed right to all the people.

⁵So David assembled all the Israelites, from the Shihor River in Egypt to Lebo Hamath, to bring the ark of God from Kiriath Jearim. ⁶David and all the Israelites with him went to Baalah of Judah (Kiriath Jearim) to bring up from there the ark of God the LORD, who is enthroned between the cherubim—the ark that is called by the Name.

⁷They moved the ark of God from Abinadab's house on a new cart, with Uzzah and Ahio guiding it. ⁸David and all the Israelites were celebrating with all their might before God, with songs and with harps, lyres, tambourines, cymbals and trumpets.

⁹When they came to the threshing floor of Kidon, Uzzah reached out his hand to steady the ark, because the oxen stumbled. ¹⁰The LORD's anger burned against Uzzah, and he struck him down because he had put his hand on the ark. So he died there before God.

¹¹Then David was angry because the LORD's wrath had broken out against Uzzah, and to this day that place is called Perez Uzzah.

¹²David was afraid of God that day and asked, "How can I ever bring the ark of God to me?" ¹³He did not take the ark to be with him in the City of David. Instead, he took it aside to the house of Obed-Edom the Gittite. ¹⁴The ark of God remained with the family of Obed-Edom in his house for three months, and the LORD blessed his household and everything he had.

First Chronicles 13 (esp. from v.6 onward) parallels the first part of 2 Samuel 6 (vv. 1–11). Chronologically the events that it describes followed David's wars with the Philistines (2 Sam 5:18–25), and perhaps the construction of his palace as well (5:11–12; cf. comment on 1 Chron 14:1). But to the Chronicler the account of David's search for the ark of God takes precedence over these other matters, to which he turns in the next chapter (14:1–2, 8–17). For logically in his mind, piety has greater significance than civil action. Ezra's primary concern was to lead the members of his postexilic Jewish community into an enthusiastic commitment to the faith and the practices enjoined in the law of Moses (Ezra 7:10). He therefore describes next the king's attempt to bring the ark of the covenant to Jerusalem, which illustrates a renewed desire on Israel's part to seek God (1 Chron 13:3) and to worship before him (v.8). Even the temporary suspension of David's attempt (vv.9 –13) became a demonstration of the necessity for exact conformity to the divine standards for worship, while the blessing that attended Obed-Edom's care for it (v.14) exemplified God's positive reward for devotion.

1 David consulted the military leaders, as in 2 Samuel 6:1.

2 But the Chronicler adds other details, whether of a more democratic character, i.e., calling in "the whole assembly" ("all the people," v.4), or of a more religious, including "priests and Levites," or more consecrated, specifically, to "the will of the LORD our God."

The phrase "the rest of our brothers" is literally "our brothers that are left." This may reflect something of the seriousness of the third major Philistine oppression against Israel, 1010–1003 B.C. (see commentary on 10:1), which David had just broken (2 Sam 5:20, 25).

3 The ark was a gold-covered chest, which contained among other items the stone tablets of the Decalogue (cf. Heb 9:4), which witnessed to God's covenant with his people. The ark was the most holy object in the whole system of Mosaic worship, for it served primarily as a sacramental symbol of the very presence of God, whose glory cloud was enthroned above it (v.6; Exod 25:22; cf. 1 Sam 4:7; J.B. Payne, *Theology of the Older Testament* [Grand Rapids: Zondervan, 1962], pp. 363–65). Israel, however, lapsed into a mechanical concept, that God was necessarily present with the ark. To overcome such superstitious notions about their having "God in a box," the Lord thus allowed his holy ark to be captured at the disastrous first battle of Ebenezer, about 1085 B.C. (1 Sam 4:10–11). But once this lesson had been absorbed, he resumed his manifestations of power from over its golden cover, the mercy seat.

Disrespect toward the holy object led to divine plagues, first against the pagan Philistines and then against the men of Judah at Beth Shemesh, who felt compelled to remove this fearful presence from their sight (1 Sam 6). For eighty years, therefore, it rested in the house of Abinadab at Kiriath Jearim (7:1), some eight miles west of Jerusalem on the border between Benjamin and Judah.

Characteristic of the religious insensitivity that marked the entire period of David's predecessor, the ark had not been sought in the days of Saul. One possible exception is noted in 1 Samuel 14:18; and even at this point the ark may not have been brought out but only asked for.

5 David assembled "all the Israelites" specified in 2 Samuel 6:1 as thirty thousand men. They gathered from Lebo Hamath in the north, in the valley between the Lebanons, to as far away as "the Shihor," traditionally understood as an Egyptian word meaning "pool [or 'stream'] of Horus," perhaps here identifying a watercourse in Egypt's eastern delta (cf. Notes).

6 "Baalah of Judah" (from 2 Sam 6:2)—or here, literally, "Baalath . . . that (belongs) to Judah"—is a Canaanite name for Kiriath Jearim (or Kiriath Baal, in Josh 18:14).

7 Uzzah and Ahio were sons, or descendants, of Abinadab (2 Sam 6:3).

9 The locations of "the threshing floor of Kidon" (called by the variant name "Nacon," 2 Sam 6:6) and of "Perez Uzzah" (v.11; cf. NIV mg.) remain unknown.

10 The severity of the divine judgment against Uzzah, even though his action had been well-intentioned, provided an illustration to all future generations of the necessity for reverence and for absolute conformity to God's directives concerning his holy objects. The transgression in this instance was twofold. First, the ark should not have been placed on a cart but carried by hand, as David himself later acknowledged (15:13). True, the Philistines had previously transported it on a wagon (1 Sam 6:11), but they had acted in heathen ignorance. Second, it should not have been touched. Even its authorized carriers, Levites of the clan of Kohath (cf. 15:2)—

which Abinadab may or may not have been—had long ago been warned against this by Moses, on pain of death (Num 4:15).

11 David's anger is psychologically explainable, if not ethically justifiable; for it was he who had the overall responsibility for the course of these events. But his anger rapidly turned to fear (v.12).

12 David's unwillingness, as he said, to "bring the ark of God *to me*," meant, in effect, that he did not want to bring it to his capital in Jerusalem, the city of David, that was so closely identified with himself.

13 Obed-Edom the Gittite (i.e., a resident of Gath) was indeed a Levite of the clan of Kohath, family of Korah (26:1, 4). As a Korahite gatekeeper (15:18, 24, and also a musician, v.21), he met the requirements of the law for service as a caretaker of the ark; and he was signally blessed.

Notes

5 Skeptics tend to limit Shihor to the Wadi el Arish, midway on the northern coast of Sinai between Israel and Egypt, and a natural dividing line. But in Isa 23:3 and Jer 2:18, Shihor is the Nile itself; and in Josh 13:3, at the least, a canal on the eastern edge of the Egyptian delta (KB, p. 965).

3. *Independence from the Philistines*

14:1–17

¹Now Hiram king of Tyre sent messengers to David, along with cedar logs, stonemasons and carpenters to build a palace for him. ²And David knew that the LORD had established him as king over Israel and that his kingdom had been highly exalted for the sake of his people Israel.

³In Jerusalem David took more wives and became the father of more sons and daughters. ⁴These are the names of the children born to him there: Shammua, Shobab, Nathan, Solomon, ⁵Ibhar, Elishua, Elpelet, ⁶Nogah, Nepheg, Japhia, ⁷Elishama, Beeliada and Eliphelet.

⁸When the Philistines heard that David had been anointed king over all Israel, they went up in full force to search for him, but David heard about it and went out to meet them. ⁹Now the Philistines had come and raided the Valley of Rephaim; ¹⁰so David inquired of God: "Shall I go and attack the Philistines? Will you hand them over to me?"

The LORD answered him, "Go, I will hand them over to you."

¹¹So David and his men went up to Baal Perazim, and there he defeated them. He said, "As waters break out, God has broken out against my enemies by my hand." So that place was called Baal Perazim. ¹²The Philistines had abandoned their gods there, and David gave orders to burn them in the fire.

¹³Once more the Philistines raided the valley; ¹⁴so David inquired of God again, and God answered him, "Do not go straight up, but circle around them and attack them in front of the balsam trees. ¹⁵As soon as you hear the sound of marching in the tops of the balsam trees, move out to battle, because that will mean God has gone out in front of you to strike the Philistine army." ¹⁶So David did as God

commanded him, and they struck down the Philistine army, all the way from Gibeon to Gezer.

[17]So David's fame spread throughout every land, and the LORD made all the nations fear him.

On the whole chapter 14 reflects its source in 2 Samuel 5:11–23, with a few additions. The events it describes do not seem to fit the three-month interval that elapsed between chapters 13 and 15, during which the ark remained with Obed-Edom (13:14; 15:25). They rather precede this (cf. the introductory discussion to ch. 13). After summarizing certain aspects of his family (vv.1–7), Ezra delineates the king's first international crisis, that of his confrontation with the Philistines (vv.8–17). For when David had finally fled from Saul's kingdom (in c. 1012 B.C.), he had become a Philistine vassal (1 Sam 27:1–28:2); and during his years at Hebron, which parallel the period of their third major oppression of the Hebrews (1010–1003; see comment on 10:1), the Philistines probably considered him as just another client king. Yet with his anointing as monarch over the reunited Israel, David became a threat they could no longer ignore (v.8). They attacked immediately, even before David had been able to occupy Jerusalem (11:7; see comment on 11:15). But because he looked to the Lord for his strength and for his strategy, he was able to beat back two Philistine offenses, to secure the independence of God's people, and to terminate forever the threat of Philistine conquest and oppression. The teaching of chapter 14 has a valid principle for Christian believers: "God has gone out in front of you to strike the Philistine army [i.e., your enemies]" (v.15).

1 William F. Albright has dated Hiram's kingship over Tyre to about 969–936 B.C., which is in the time of Solomon rather than of David (cf. Solomon's similar building contracts with Hiram, 2 Chron 2; cf. 8:18; 9:10, 21). Some commentators therefore prefer to date the construction of David's palace to a point late in his reign (John Bright, *A History of Israel* [Philadelphia: Westminster, 1959], p. 138).

2 Yet Chronicles (and 2 Sam 5:12) associates this project with David's being "established . . . as king" before the ark came to Jerusalem (15:1); so it may not be out of place to think of earlier dealings with Hiram of Tyre (who would subsequently become king) or even, as Myers (*Chronicles*, 1:106) has suggested, "that David had entered into some kind of relationship with Hiram's father Abibaal, which was renegotiated with Hiram and continued into the reign of Solomon." In any event this palace witnesses to how a pagan monarch may be used to serve the people of God (cf. Isa 23:18).

3 That David took "more wives" was a historical fact but a moral failure, directly contrary to the law (Deut 17:17; cf. the discussion of OT polygamy in Payne, *Theology*, pp. 317, 319, 331, 336, 344). This sin led to a whole series of disasters later on (2 Sam 11:27; cf. the implications of 13:4, 32, and even 1 Kings 1:5–6).

4–7 The list of David's younger sons has appeared also in 3:5–8 (q.v.).

8 The statement that David "went out to meet" the enemy summarizes several preceding events, including raids by the Philistines (v.9), his own initial retreat to the stronghold of Adullam (2 Sam 5:17), and the exploit of his heroes at the well of Bethlehem (1 Chron 11:15; see comment there).

9 The Valley of Rephaim lay southwest of Jerusalem and formed part of the boundary between Judah and Benjamin (Josh 15:8). It may correspond to the "Valley of Baca" (Ps 84:6; Heb. *bākā'*), due to the balsam trees that were there (vv.14–15). These are named, literally, "weepers" (*bᵉkā'îm*) because of their drops of milky sap (KB, p. 126).

10–12 Trusting in God's promise of victory, David completely routed the Philistines at Baal Perazim (cf. NIV mg.), so that he and his men took away their idols (2 Sam 5:21) and burned them, as required in the law (Deut 7:5, 25).

14–15 Against the Philistines' renewed invasion, the Lord guided David into an encircling movement. The signal for springing this ambush was a supernatural "sound of marching in the tops of the balsam trees," perhaps similar to the miracle recorded in 2 Kings 7:6.

16 David's striking the Philistines down "all the way . . . to Gezer," on the Philistine border, signified their total expulsion from Israelite territory.

4. *The ark brought to Jerusalem*

15:1–16:43

¹After David had constructed buildings for himself in the City of David, he prepared a place for the ark of God and pitched a tent for it. ²Then David said, "No one but the Levites may carry the ark of God, because the LORD chose them to carry the ark of the LORD and to minister before him forever."

³David assembled all Israel in Jerusalem to bring up the ark of the LORD to the place he had prepared for it. ⁴He called together the descendants of Aaron and the Levites:

⁵From the descendants of Kohath,
Uriel the leader and 120 relatives;
⁶from the descendants of Merari,
Asaiah the leader and 220 relatives;
⁷from the descendants of Gershon,
Joel the leader and 130 relatives;
⁸from the descendants of Elizaphan,
Shemaiah the leader and 200 relatives;
⁹from the descendants of Hebron,
Eliel the leader and 80 relatives;
¹⁰from the descendants of Uzziel,
Amminadab the leader and 112 relatives.

¹¹Then David summoned Zadok and Abiathar the priests, and Uriel, Asaiah, Joel, Shemaiah, Eliel and Amminadab the Levites. ¹²He said to them, "You are the heads of the Levitical families; you and your fellow Levites are to consecrate yourselves and bring up the ark of the LORD, the God of Israel, to the place I have prepared for it. ¹³It was because you, the Levites, did not bring it up the first time that the LORD our God broke out in anger against us. We did not inquire of him about how to do it in the prescribed way." ¹⁴So the priests and Levites consecrated themselves in order to bring up the ark of the LORD, the God of Israel. ¹⁵And the Levites carried the ark of God with the poles on their shoulders, as Moses had commanded in accordance with the word of the LORD.

¹⁶David told the leaders of the Levites to appoint their brothers as singers to

sing joyful songs, accompanied by musical instruments: lyres, harps and cymbals.

¹⁷So the Levites appointed Heman son of Joel; from his brothers, Asaph son of Berekiah; and from their brothers the Merarites, Ethan son of Kushaiah; ¹⁸and with them their brothers next in rank: Zechariah, Jaaziel, Shemiramoth, Jehiel, Unni, Eliab, Benaiah, Maaseiah, Mattithiah, Eliphelehu, Mikneiah, Obed-Edom and Jeiel, the gatekeepers.

¹⁹The musicians Heman, Asaph and Ethan were to sound the bronze cymbals; ²⁰Zechariah, Aziel, Shemiramoth, Jehiel, Unni, Eliab, Maaseiah and Benaiah were to play the lyres according to *alamoth,* ²¹and Mattithiah, Eliphelehu, Mikneiah, Obed-Edom, Jeiel and Azaziah were to play the harps, directing according to *sheminith.* ²²Kenaniah the head Levite was in charge of the singing; that was his responsibility because he was skillful at it.

²³Berekiah and Elkanah were to be doorkeepers for the ark. ²⁴Shebaniah, Joshaphat, Nethanel, Amasai, Zechariah, Benaiah and Eliezer the priests were to blow trumpets before the ark of God. Obed-Edom and Jehiah were also to be doorkeepers for the ark.

²⁵So David and the elders of Israel and the commanders of units of a thousand went to bring up the ark of the covenant of the LORD from the house of Obed-Edom, with rejoicing. ²⁶Because God had helped the Levites who were carrying the ark of the covenant of the LORD, seven bulls and seven rams were sacrificed. ²⁷Now David was clothed in a robe of fine linen, as were all the Levites who were carrying the ark, and as were the singers, and Kenaniah, who was in charge of the singing of the choirs. David also wore a linen ephod. ²⁸So all Israel brought up the ark of the covenant of the LORD with shouts, with the sounding of rams' horns and trumpets, and of cymbals, and the playing of lyres and harps.

²⁹As the ark of the covenant of the LORD was entering the City of David, Michal daughter of Saul watched from a window. And when she saw King David dancing and celebrating, she despised him in her heart.

¹⁶:¹They brought the ark of God and set it inside the tent that David had pitched for it, and they presented burnt offerings and fellowship offerings before God. ²After David had finished sacrificing the burnt offerings and fellowship offerings, he blessed the people in the name of the LORD. ³Then he gave a loaf of bread, a cake of dates and a cake of raisins to each Israelite man and woman.

⁴He appointed some of the Levites to minister before the ark of the LORD, to make petition, to give thanks, and to praise the LORD, the God of Israel: ⁵Asaph was the chief, Zechariah second, then Jeiel, Shemiramoth, Jehiel, Mattithiah, Eliab, Benaiah, Obed-Edom and Jeiel. They were to play the lyres and harps, Asaph was to sound the cymbals, ⁶and Benaiah and Jahaziel the priests were to blow the trumpets regularly before the ark of the covenant of God.

⁷That day David first committed to Asaph and his associates this psalm of thanks to the LORD:

⁸Give thanks to the LORD, call on his name;
  make known among the nations what he has done.
⁹Sing to him, sing praise to him;
  tell of all his wonderful acts.
¹⁰Glory in his holy name;
  let the hearts of those who seek the LORD rejoice.
¹¹Look to the LORD and his strength;
  seek his face always.
¹²Remember the wonders he has done,
  his miracles, and the judgments he pronounced,
¹³O descendants of Israel his servant,
  O sons of Jacob, his chosen ones.

¹⁴He is the LORD our God;
  his judgments are in all the earth.
¹⁵He remembers his covenant forever,
  the word he commanded, for a thousand generations,

16 the covenant he made with Abraham,
    the oath he swore to Isaac.
17 He confirmed it to Jacob as a decree,
    to Israel as an everlasting covenant:
18 "To you I will give the land of Canaan
    as the portion you will inherit."

19 When they were but few in number,
    few indeed, and strangers in it,
20 they wandered from nation to nation,
    from one kingdom to another.
21 He allowed no man to oppress them;
    for their sake he rebuked kings:
22 "Do not touch my anointed ones;
    do my prophets no harm."

23 Sing to the LORD, all the earth;
    proclaim his salvation day after day.
24 Declare his glory among the nations,
    his marvelous deeds among all peoples.
25 For great is the LORD and most worthy of praise;
    he is to be feared above all gods.
26 For all the gods of the nations are idols,
    but the LORD made the heavens.
27 Splendor and majesty are before him;
    strength and joy in his dwelling place.
28 Ascribe to the LORD, O families of nations,
    ascribe to the LORD glory and strength,
29   ascribe to the LORD the glory due his name.
  Bring an offering and come before him;
    worship the LORD in the splendor of his holiness.
30 Tremble before him, all the earth!
  The world is firmly established; it cannot be moved.
31 Let the heavens rejoice, let the earth be glad;
    let them say among the nations, "The LORD reigns!"
32 Let the sea resound, and all that is in it;
    let the fields be jubilant, and everything in them!
33 Then the trees of the forest will sing,
    they will sing for joy before the LORD,
    for he comes to judge the earth.

34 Give thanks to the LORD, for he is good;
    his love endures forever.
35 Cry out, "Save us, O God our Savior;
    gather us and deliver us from the nations,
  that we may give thanks to your holy name,
  that we may glory in your praise."
36 Praise be to the LORD, the God of Israel,
    from everlasting to everlasting.

Then all the people said "Amen" and "Praise the LORD."

37 David left Asaph and his associates before the ark of the covenant of the LORD to minister there regularly, according to each day's requirements. 38 He also left Obed-Edom and his sixty-eight associates to minister with them. Obed-Edom son of Jeduthun, and also Hosah, were gatekeepers.

39 David left Zadok the priest and his fellow priests before the tabernacle of the LORD at the high place in Gibeon 40 to present burnt offerings to the LORD on the altar of burnt offering regularly, morning and evening, in accordance with everything written in the Law of the LORD, which he had given Israel. 41 With them were Heman and Jeduthun and the rest of those chosen and designated by name to give thanks to the LORD, "for his love endures forever." 42 Heman and Jeduthun

were responsible for the sounding of the trumpets and cymbals and for the playing of the other instruments for sacred song. The sons of Jeduthun were stationed
at the gate.
⁴³Then all the people left, each for his own home, and David returned home to
bless his family.

While the transfer of the ark from Kiriath Jearim to Jerusalem occupies but one
chapter in 2 Samuel (6), it takes up three in 1 Chronicles: chapter 13, which carries
the account up to its turning aside to the house of Obed-Edom, and chapters 15–16,
on its final move into Jerusalem. This latter section parallels 2 Samuel 6:12–20, but
with a number of additions. These include David's elaborate preparations, both to
prevent any recurrence of the tragedy that had brought about Uzzah's death (15:1–
15), and also to insure an appropriate retinue of singers (vv. 16–24); his provision of
a model psalm of thanksgiving, that was used on the occasion of the ark's actual
installation into its new tent-abode (16:7–36); and his establishment of a permanent
Levitical organization to maintain regular services of worship before the ark in its
Jerusalem sanctuary (vv. 4–6, 37–42).

By the time of Ezra, Jerusalem had become more important religiously than
politically; and so it has remained, even up to the present. Our Chronicler therefore
resumes the narrative, begun in chapter 13, on how the ark came to be brought
inside the city; for it was this event that started the transformation of Jerusalem into
the religious capital of Israel. It remained only for an angelic revelation to David—
that Mount Moriah, on its north side, was to be the site for the altar of God (= "the
house of God," 22:1; 2 Chron 3:1)—to establish Yahweh's ultimate centralization of
Hebrew religion at this sanctuary. It became the fulfillment of what Moses had long
before predicted, that the Lord God would choose a place out of all their tribes for
his name to dwell; to his holy hill his people were to come for pilgrimage and for
sacrifice (Deut 12:5–7, 11–12).

1 It was the time needed for constructing these Davidic "buildings," clearly more
than the three months during which the ark remained with Obed-Edom (13:14),
that causes 14:1 to be dated before chapter 13 (cf. comments on 14:1 and 2).

At this point David "prepared . . . *a tent* for the ark" (cf. v. 12). His primary
reasons are given later (16:1–4). For it was not simply that reports had reached him
of God's blessing on the household of Obed-Edom (2 Sam 6:12)—indicating both
that the danger surrounding Uzzah had passed and that similar blessings might now
be anticipated for Jerusalem as well (!)—but he had a religious motivation, seeking
to establish a center of prayer and praise to the Lord (16:4).

2 Chapter 15 (here and in v. 13) gives a further explanation for Uzzah's disaster (cf.
comment on 13:10): the Levites should have carried the ark, as prescribed in
Deuteronomy 10:8.

4 So when David assembled Israel to bring the ark the rest of the way into Jerusalem (v. 3), he was careful to insure the presence of priests and Levites (as named in
v. 11). The latter are then particularly enumerated in vv. 5–10, along with the total
number of their followers, some 862 in all.

8 In addition to the three major clans of Levi—Gershon, Kohath, Merari (vv. 5–7;
cf. the genealogical chart, pp. 352–53)—there appear three subgroups within Ko-

hath: those of his third and fourth sons, Hebron and Uzziel (vv.9–10), and of Eliza-phan (here), who in particular was one of the three sons of Uzziel (Exod 6:22; Lev 10:4). With the passage of generations, these must have gained sufficiently in num-bers or in importance to warrant their separate representation.

12–15 David's order to the Levites to "consecrate themselves" (v.12) involved cer-tain prescribed ritual washings and the avoidance of any form of ceremonial defile-ment (Exod 19:10, 14–15; Lev 11:44).

16 The worship of God frequently takes the appropriate form of joyful song; and this occasion, on which the ark of the covenant was conducted into Jerusalem with a glad procession, marked the historical beginning of the ministry of the Levitical singers in Israel. Concerning the musical instruments specified, the second, the "harp" (*kinnôr*), was more of a zither (KB, p. 443); the third, "cymbals," has a qualifying participle, *mašmîʿîm* ("loud-sounding," NASB), but literally means "those which cause (men) to hear" (cf. v.19). Their function seems to be that of marking time, by sounding clearly and loudly. (On OT instruments in general, see ZPEB, 4:311–24.)

17 From the prominent clan of Kohath, Heman son of Joel, who was in turn a son of the prophet Samuel (6:28, 33; 1 Sam 8:2), was in first place among the musicians appointed for the occasion by the Levites themselves (also in v.19, but contrast 16:5 –7). With Heman were Asaph and Ethan son of Kushaiah (= Kishi, 6:44), from the other two clans, all three of whom continued on, serving as the chief musicians under David's subsequent permanent arrangements (16:37, 41–42).

20 Aziel is a shortened form of the name Jaaziel (v.18).
The phrase "according to *alamoth*" (cf. NIV mg.) occurs also in the title to Psalm 46. Since the noun means "maidens, virgins," such as are mentioned as beating tambourines in ceremonial processions of singers and other musicians (Ps 68:25), it may indicate music produced in a soprano register.

21 The phrase "according to *sheminith*" (again cf. NIV mg.) occurs also in the titles to Psalms 6 and 12. The word is derived from the root for "eight" and is usually thought to indicate music in a lower octave, in contrast to the preceding verse, though it might indicate an instrument that had eight strings (KB, p. 988).
Obed-Edom the Gittite was, in his hereditary position, a gatekeeper (v.18; KJV, "porter"; or doorkeeper, v.24). But in recognition of his faithful care for the ark during the preceding three months (13:14; cf. also the attendant risk, v.12), he was honored with a place among the zither players; and his post was subsequently made permanent (16:5, 38). Berekiah and Elkanah then took over some of the "keeping," and carrying, duty en route.

22 The position of Kenaniah is uncertain. Though not listed in v.11 with the Leviti-cal leaders, he is still designated "the head Levite." The NIV joins him with the preceding musicians (vv.19–21) as in charge of the singing (*maśśāʾ*, "a lifting up"). Yet the chief musicians have already been designated (v.17); and, since *maśśāʾ* no-where else means singing (though often "utterance," in the sense of a "lifting up" of the voice), it seems better here to join Kenaniah with the following "keepers" (vv.23 –24) and to take *maśśāʾ* in its basic sense of "burden" or "load" (KB, p. 569, for this passage; cf. v.27, "carrying the ark"). Verse 22 (and v.27) then says that Kenaniah was the head Levite in charge of the central task of transporting the ark; "he had to take the lead in the bearing because . . . he was instructed in that which was to be observed in it" (Keil, p. 205). The thought of 26:29—where Kenaniah was "assigned duties away from the temple," over external and material affairs rather than directing in worship—corresponds to this.

24 Seven priests are singled out as trumpeters (cf. 16:6). Blowing on silver trumpets was the one aspect of ceremonial music that had been legislated through Moses and was a function reserved for them (Num 10:8). (For a listing of archaeological illustrations on the use of trumpets in the ancient Near East, see Myers, *Chronicles*, 1:113.)

Jehiah is probably the gatekeeper Jeiel of vv.18, 21, and 16:5, though why he should be singled out for honor along with Obed-Edom is not explained.

25–26 The verb form stating that seven bulls and seven rams "were sacrificed" (v.26) is in fact a Qal active participle, possibly impersonal; but here more likely the simple idea is that "they sacrificed," i.e., the whole assembly, including the elders and commanders listed in v.25. David personally was responsible for the offering up of just one animal of each of these kinds, as recorded in 2 Samuel 6:13. God is said to have "helped the Levites," i.e., they were not struck down, as Uzzah had been (13:10).

27–29 The ephod was a surplice, or cape, worn in worship (Exod 28:6; 1 Sam 2:18). Beneath it David wore a robe of white linen—as did also the Levites—but in his enthusiastic devotion, dancing and celebrating with all his might before the Lord (v.29; 13:8, for the Chronicler was not trying to conceal a scandal, Keil, pp. 206–8; 2 Sam 6:14), he seems to have removed an outer garment and uncovered himself in a way that his wife Michal considered "unkingly" (2 Sam 6:20). David's uninhibited love for God stands in stark contrast to the rigid, unsympathetic attitude of this daughter of Saul (cf. 2 Sam 6:21–23).

An evidence preserved in writing of the "shouts" (v.28) with which the ark was brought up to Jerusalem may be found in Psalm 24. Composed by David, it could hardly have had a more fitting occasion for those cries of praise: "Lift up your heads, O you gates; . . . that the King of glory may come in" (v.7; cf. also Ps 132:8).

16:1 The statement that "they," i.e., the qualified Levites, "presented . . . offerings," just as "they" constitute the ones who "brought . . . and set" the ark in its place, provides background for clarifying the words in the next verse about "David . . . sacrificing" (see also in 2 Sam 6:13, 17). While each OT worshiper, according to the law of Moses, was expected to lead his own sheep to the sanctuary and slay it (Lev 1:3–5a; 3:2a), only the Aaronic priests were entitled to offer up the blood or other portions on the altar (1:5b; 3:2b, 5). Liberalism denies that Moses gave these laws or that they were in existence even in the time of the united kingdom; it claims rather that David served as his own officiating priest (Curtis, p. 218). Yet God's Word is clear: only the sons of Aaron had the divine authority to offer up sacrifices acceptable to God; only they were approved as legitimate types of Christ, the ultimate priest, who offered his precious blood that our sins might be forgiven (Heb 9:12, 14, 26, 28; cf. 2 Sam 8:18 NIV mg.).

In addition to burnt offerings, there were "fellowship offerings" (KJV, "peace offerings"). The latter not only symbolized atonement, as choice parts were burned in sacrifice on the altar, but also depicted the restored fellowship with God that comes as a result of the reconciliation. Most flesh from the peace offerings was eaten by the people themselves, sitting down, as it were, as guests of God's table, in a meal celebrating the restoration of their peace with him (Lev 7:15; cf. Exod 24:11 and the discussion of sacrifice and NT communion in Payne, *Theology*, pp. 383–87).

2 Though David's sacrifice was accomplished through the mediation of qualified priests (cf. preceding comment), he still invoked God's blessing on the people (cf. v.43 and Solomon's similar act in 1 Kings 8:55–60). Some of those matters that were often associated with priests—such as praying for blessings (Num 6:24–26) or wearing linen robes and ephods (cf. comment on 15:27)—were not necessarily restricted to the sons of Aaron.

3 The king's gifts to the people consisted of bread, *'ešpār*, and raisins. *'ešpār* occurs only here and in the parallel passage in 2 Samuel (6:19). It might mean, as in the NIV, "a cake of dates" (so KB, p. 95, based on a possible Arab. parallel); but the present contextual reference to the flesh of animals, as used in Israel's feasting (see comment on v.1), could favor, as in NASB, "a portion of meat" (so Myers, *Chronicles*, 1:114 n.).

4 David's appointment then of Levites to minister in music and praise to God marks a significant advance in the history of Israel's worship (cf. comment on 15:16). His previous arrangements for music (15:16–21, 24, 27–28) had been devised for just the one occasion; but now a continuing service is envisioned (cf. 16:37–42). The initial experiment must have proved to be eminently successful! But David acted on divine command, conveyed through the prophets Nathan and Gad (2 Chron 29:25). For with the ark permanently enshrined in Jerusalem (though cf. 2 Chron 35:3), those Levites who had formerly been charged with its transport could now be reassigned to other appropriate duties, such as gatekeepers; and in particular the "singers" came to assume a leading role in Judah's public devotion. Their presence constitutes a distinctive stress within Chronicles (see Introduction: Purpose, 2), which is now increasingly recognized—even in some critical circles—as "based on true tradition or material" (Myers, *Chronicles*, 1:LIV; cf. note to 15:16).

5 The king's elevation of Asaph to be the chief musician, confirmed in v.37, denotes a shift away from the Levites' own choice of Heman as the leader, up to this point (see comment on 15:17). No reason is given, though Asaph did represent the senior Levitical clan of Gershon (6:39–43). Personal ability may also have been a contributing factor, for Asaph and his descendants are listed as composers for twelve of the inspired OT psalms (Pss 50, 73–83).

The name "Jeiel," at its first mention, represents "Jaaziel" in the corresponding lists in chapter 15 (v.18; cf. comment on v.20).

6 Of the seven priestly trumpeters who participated in the procession into Jerusalem (15:24), only the sixth, Benaiah, to whom was added a Jahaziel, was permanently assigned to service before the ark; the others probably returned to their duties at the tabernacle, which remained still at Gibeon (see comment on v.39).

7 This verse introduces a model psalm of thanksgiving that has, with only slight modifications, been taken over from the OT Psalter of the period, as follows: vv.8–22 = Psalm 105:1–15; vv.23–33 = Psalm 96; and vv.34–36 = Psalm 106:1, 47–48. Are these extensive quotations, then, the words of David in about 1000 B.C. or of the Chronicler in about 450, illustrating liturgical usages in his own, postexilic time? We must distinguish between the phraseology of v.7 in itself and its function in the larger context of chapter 16.

Of the former W.T. Davison (HDB, 4:148) was correct when he said, "The psalm is not directly attributed to David, as the translation of v.7 ['David first committed to Asaph . . . this psalm of thanks to the Lord,' NIV] would imply." In reality all that the Hebrew says is "David assigned Asaph . . . to give thanks to the Lord" (NASB). Yet in light of the broader context, the NIV's rendering becomes justifiable. David's commission to Asaph (v.7) does function as the setting of the poem thus introduced (vv.8–36a); and the response of David's people (v.36b; see comment in loc.) is at the same time the conclusion of the quoted poetry, proving that it was in existence in 1000 B.C.

Davison (ibid.) himself goes on to concede as much, saying, "In ch. 16 . . . the writer puts a psalm in the mouth of David as appropriate to such an occasion." Yet if the words of this "writer" form a part of Scripture, inspired by the Holy Spirit, then the quoted verses must genuinely have been in the mouth of David. All three of the canonical psalms that he quoted are anonymous, "orphan psalms" (without title) in the OT Psalter; but on the basis of the king's use of them here, they should indeed be classed as his (cf. the NT's witness to his authorship of such similarly untitled poems as Ps 2, per Acts 4:25, or Ps 95, as affirmed in Heb 4:7).

The above-stated conclusion concerning Davidic authorship carries certain implications. On the one hand, the three quoted psalms—96, 105, and 106—are found not simply to derive wholly from Book IV of the Psalter (Pss 90–106), but the king's citation from the last named includes its verses of benediction, which mark the formal conclusion to this collection (cf. similar benedictions in the closing psalm for each of the preceding books: I, 41:13; II, 72:18–20; and III, 89:52). As a volume it must therefore have been available to the generation alive in 1000 B.C. (ZPEB, 4:926); and David would thus appear to be not only the author of Psalm 106 but also the compiler of Book IV. Since David also wrote Psalm 41 and compiled Book I (no chapter of which claims any other authorship), and since Solomon wrote Psalm 72 and compiled Book II (including a number of his father's compositions as well, 72:20), we are left only with Books III (Pss 73–89) and V (107–150) as stemming from later dates. Furthermore, it is a fact that all the clearly exilic psalms (as 79 or 137) or the postexilic ones (cf. 126:1–2 or, at the very end, 147:13) make their appearance within these latter collections (though cf. the note to 16:29 at the close of this section). On the other hand, the fact that David would reuse these three psalms that had been composed for other situations testifies to his awareness of their abiding worship.

That the king "committed" his poem "to Asaph" sheds light on the phrase found in so many of the psalm titles: "For the chief musician." What David composed, the Levitical musicians were directed to perform in worship.

8–12 After four introductory verses exhorting God's people to praise him, the call to "remember" (v.12) his "wonders" of old summarizes the message of Psalm 105. This Psalm, one of the OT's great historical surveys of the Lord's faithfulness, is a reminder that was particularly appropriate at this new turning point in Israel's history.

13 One of David's few changes in the text of Psalm 105 (v.6) occurs here, where he substitutes the name Israel for that of the grandfather, Abraham. He may have felt that his reference to the immediate ancestor of the twelve Hebrew tribes was more fitting on this national occasion.

14–17 The "covenant" ($b^e r\hat{\imath}t$, v.15) was God's legal instrument for the redemption of his people. Through it he graciously bequeathed an inheritance of reconciliation with himself to those who were its qualified heirs, those who met its condition of sincere faith in his promise (Gen 15:6; Heb 11:6). Though the instrument of redemption was first revealed in Eden to fallen Adam (Gen 3:15), it was confirmed to Noah (9:9) and to Abraham (1 Chron 16:16) and his chosen seed (Gen 17:7; Exod 19:5–6; Gal 3:29) for a "thousand generations." Its ultimate accomplishment depended on the death of Jesus Christ, the divine testator (Heb 9:15–17), an event symbolized under the anticipatory older testament by the shedding of sacrificial blood (Exod 24:6–8; Heb 9:18–22; cf. Payne, *Theology*, esp. pp. 71–95).

18–22 The Hebrew patriarchs wandered without a home of their own; for though they had been promised Palestine (v.18), it was in fact only their descendants who received it (Heb 11:9): David's contemporary audience.

The titles by which the patriarchs are described possess, at this early period, more generalized meanings than those they came to have later. They are called "anointed" (v.22), in the sense of being set apart by God's Spirit—a phrase elsewhere used specifically for prophets (1 Kings 19:16), priests (Exod 29:7), and kings (1 Sam 2:35), with whom the presence of the Spirit was symbolized by a visible anointing with oil, and ultimately for Jesus (Christ = Messiah = "anointed"; 1 Sam 2:10; Ps 2:2; Acts 10:38).

The patriarchs are also called "prophets," in the sense of being recipients of God's special revelation—a title later used specifically for those who proclaimed God's revealed will (cf. the definition implied in Exod 7:1–2). Abraham was thus designated a "prophet," at the time of God's special protection against Abimelech, the Philistine king of Gerar (Gen 20:7); others of the patriarchs did, however, make specific predictions (e.g., Jacob, Gen 48:19; 49:1). Psalm 105:16–45 then continues Israel's history on into the career of Joseph, the descent into Egypt, and the Lord's deliverance of the Hebrews in the Exodus, on the wilderness journey, and right up to the conquest of Canaan; but David now turns to another source.

23 With its appeal for "all the earth" to honor the Lord, Psalm 96 identifies itself as one of a series of six liturgical hymns (Pss 95–100) stressing the Creator's royal majesty. A recurring and key phrase, quoted in 1 Chronicles 16:31, is this: "The LORD reigns" (Ps 96:10, but also 97:1; 99:1). Such a theme was of course particularly relevant on this occasion, during which "the King of glory" (Ps 24:7–10) entered Jerusalem—and David quoted the entire psalm.

27 David's expression "in his [God's] dwelling place" ($bimq\bar{o}m\hat{o}$, "in his place") represents a change from the original phrase in Psalm 96:6, "in his sanctuary" (b^e-$miqd\bar{a}\check{s}\hat{o}$), appropriate enough for use before the tabernacle at Gibeon (1 Chron 16:39), but less so before the ark was in its new location at Jerusalem.

29 The idea of men coming "before him" took on fresh reality with the arrival of the ark, over which the cloud of God's presence rested (Num 7:89).

All people are told to worship the Lord in *ḥaḏraṯ-qōḏeš* (lit., "an adornment of holiness"). The KJV's "beauty of holiness" is familiar but imports a moral tone not originally intended (but cf. D. Kidner, *Psalms 1–72* [Downers Grove, Ill.: Inter-Varsity, 1973], p. 125). The NIV's "his holiness" adds an unwarranted pronoun and shifts the phrase into a characteristic of God rather than of his worshipers (cf. the alternative rendering in the NIV mg.), and it still seems to miss the concreteness usually associated with the noun "adornment" (KB, p. 226, though cf. its abstract use in Prov 14:28). The NASB's "holy array" fits the Hebrew and, if somewhat less exalted in content, still reminds us of the necessity of worshiping God with the best attire.

33 While earlier messianic prophecies had foretold our Lord's universal, millennial reign (Gen 49:10; Num 24:17; 1 Sam 2:10), these words—"he comes"—may be the first in all of written Scripture (Job 19:25 may well have been *spoken* earlier) to set forth the doctrine of the glorious second coming of Jesus Christ (J.B. Payne, *Encyclopedia of Biblical Prophecy* [New York: Harper & Row, 1973], p. 273).

34 Having quoted all of Psalm 96, David concluded his model hymn with the opening and closing verses of Psalm 106. Like 105, with which he began, 106 too is a historical psalm. It has less emphasis, however, on God's faithfulness and Israel's waywardness and its results, up through the period of the judges (106:34–47); truths still very much needed by those who had witnessed the fate of Uzzah.

35 The prayer "gather us and deliver us from the nations" was particularly fitting in light of the third Philistine oppression, just ended (cf. comments on 10:1; 13:2; 14:8, 16); this release many in fact account for David saying, "O God our Savior," when the original in Psalm 106:47 had been rather "O LORD our God." The same verse had said simply "gather us from the nations"; and some commentators proceed to assign it an exilic date (cf. note on v.29). Yet "there could have been no occasion from the entrance into Canaan onward when some Israelites were not held in alien slavery" (NBCrev., p. 517). Keil (p. 214) insists, "The words . . . do not presuppose that the people had been previously led away into the Chaldean exile, but only the dispersion of prisoners of war, led away captive into an enemy's land after a defeat. . . . It was just such cases Solomon had in view in his prayer, I Kings 8:46–50" (cf. vv.41–42 in Ps 106, that David did not quote, and the allusion, especially in v.46, to "all who held them captive").

36 Midway in the verse the quoted model hymn ceases and Ezra's narrative resumes, with the response of "all the people," those who were present then, at that time with David. Yet what they responded is itself a continuation of the quotation from Psalm 106:48, demonstrating that the quoted material belongs to the time of David and not simply to that of Ezra (cf. comment on v.7 and ZPEB, 4:926–27).

The people's first exclamation, "Amen," means literally "firm, steady." It could be rendered "True indeed!" Their second, "Praise the LORD" (*hallēl leyhwh*, in separate words), represents the familiar plural contracted form of Psalm 106's *halleluyāh*, i.e., "Hallelu Yah!"

37 A daily ministry, now before the ark, was fitting, since this holy object represented the continuing presence of God with his people. It was "the ark of the covenant," with its testamentary promise, "I am the LORD [Heb., Yahweh, 'the One who is present'; cf. Exod 3:12, 14] your God" (v.4; cf. comment on v.15, or Gen 17:7–8).

38 Hosah had not been mentioned previously. He was another doorkeeper, though of the clan of Merari (26:10–11), compared to Obed-Edom of Kohath (vv.1, 4). Obed-Edom's father is also named for the first time and is not to be confused with Jeduthun (alternate name for Ethan) the chief musician (vv.41–42), both because Ethan belonged to the clan of Merari, and because the name as given here in the consonantal text is really Jedithun. Obed-Edom continued in his double post of both musician (v.5) and doorkeeper (cf. comments on 15:21, though Keil, pp. 206, 219, raises the possibility of there being two different Obed-Edoms).

39 Zadok (see on 6:8), however, was sent back (cf. 15:11) to Gibeon to serve as high priest at the tabernacle, which continued to exist as Israel's primary sanctuary for sacrifice (v.40) till Solomon's construction of the Jerusalem temple (2 Chron 1:13; 5:5). Abiathar, on the other hand, seems to have remained at the capital (cf. 27:34), which may account for David's double high-priesthood (18:16).

41 God's "love" is here specified as his *ḥesed* (also in v.34), which refers to his loyalty to the provisions embodied in the covenantal relationship (see on 19:2; cf. Gen 21:23; Ps 136:10; and Payne, *Theology*, pp. 161–63).

Notes

16 Even among followers of the historical-critical method of interpreting Scripture, the historicity of David's originating the Levitical guilds of musicians in Jerusalem "is pretty well established in the tradition" (Myers, *Chronicles*, 1:111, citing W.F. Albright); it "seems to be authentic" (ibid., 1:112).

18 After "Jeiel" should probably be added, with the LXX (as referred to in the NIV mg.), the name of Azaziah (cf. v.21).

16:7 Keil strongly argues for the priority of the poem here over the view that it was compiled from the Psalms: "When we consider the contents of the whole hymn, it is manifest that it contains nothing which would be at all inconsistent with the belief that it was composed by David for the above-mentioned religious service" (p. 211).

29 Instead of David's exhortation at this point, "come before him," the king had originally written in Ps 96:8, "come into his courts," perhaps thinking of the tabernacle at Gibeon (cf. on vv.27 and 39). Yet because of such verbal changes, North and others would deny the authenticity of the psalms concerned (see comment to v.7). As opposed to Keil's (p. 211) assertion, that "the whole hymn . . . contains nothing which would be at all inconsistent with the belief that it was composed by David for the above-mentioned religious service," North ("The Chronicler," 1:410) claims, "References to the Temple and Diaspora are suppressed." Yet from Ps 105—whether we examine vv.1–15, which are quoted in 1 Chron 16:8–22, or for that matter any of the remaining verses (16–45), which are not—no such references are to be found; from Ps 96, see the comments on 1 Chron 16:27, 29, and from Ps 106, see comment on v.35.

5. Nathan's prophecy

17:1–27

¹After David was settled in his palace, he said to Nathan the prophet, "Here I am, living in a palace of cedar, while the ark of the covenant of the LORD is under a tent."

²Nathan replied to David, "Whatever you have in mind, do it, for God is with you."

³That night the word of God came to Nathan, saying:

⁴"Go and tell my servant David, 'This is what the LORD says: You are not the one to build me a house to dwell in. ⁵I have not dwelt in a house from the day I brought Israel up out of Egypt to this day. I have moved from one tent site to another, from one dwelling place to another. ⁶Wherever I have moved with all the Israelites, did I ever say to any of their leaders whom I commanded to shepherd my people, "Why have you not built me a house of cedar?"'

⁷"Now then, tell my servant David, 'This is what the LORD Almighty says: I took you from the pasture and from following the flock, to be ruler over my people Israel. ⁸I have been with you wherever you have gone, and I have cut off all your enemies from before you. Now I will make your name like the names of the greatest men of the earth. ⁹And I will provide a place for my people Israel and will plant them so that they can have a home of their own and no longer be disturbed. Wicked people will not oppress them anymore, as they did at the beginning ¹⁰and have done ever since the time I appointed leaders over my people Israel. I will also subdue all your enemies.

"'I declare to you that the LORD will build a house for you: ¹¹When your days are over and you go to be with your fathers, I will raise up your offspring to succeed you, one of your own sons, and I will establish his kingdom. ¹²He is the one who will build a house for me, and I will establish his throne forever. ¹³I will be his father, and he will be my son. I will never take my love away from him, as I took it away from your predecessor. ¹⁴I will set him over my house and my kingdom forever; his throne will be established forever.'"

¹⁵Nathan reported to David all the words of this entire revelation.

¹⁶Then King David went in and sat before the LORD, and he said:

"Who am I, O LORD God, and what is my family, that you have brought me this far? ¹⁷And as if this were not enough in your sight, O God, you have spoken about the future of the house of your servant. You have looked on me as though I were the most exalted of men, O LORD God.

¹⁸"What more can David say to you for honoring your servant? For you know your servant, ¹⁹O LORD. For the sake of your servant and according to your will, you have done this great thing and made known all these great promises.

²⁰"There is no one like you, O LORD, and there is no God but you, as we have heard with our own ears. ²¹And who is like your people Israel—the one nation on earth whose God went out to redeem a people for himself, and to make a name for yourself, and to perform great and awesome wonders by driving out nations from before your people, whom you redeemed from Egypt? ²²You made your people Israel your very own forever, and you, O LORD, have become their God.

²³"And now, LORD, let the promise you have made concerning your servant and his house be established forever. Do as you promised, ²⁴so that it will be established and that your name will be great forever. Then men will say, 'The LORD Almighty, the God over Israel, is Israel's God!' And the house of your servant David will be established before you.

²⁵"You, my God, have revealed to your servant that you will build a house for him. So your servant has found courage to pray to you. ²⁶O LORD, you are

God! You have promised these good things to your servant. ²⁷Now you have been pleased to bless the house of your servant, that it may continue forever in your sight; for you, O LORD, have blessed it, and it will be blessed forever."

As indicated in the introductory analysis of chapters 11–20, the heart of 1 Chronicles is to be found in chapter 17. Its substance is drawn from 2 Samuel 7 and largely corresponds to it, as it sets forth the abiding significance of the person and work of David. Chronologically chapter 17 came after the termination of the wars chronicled in chapter 18 (cf. 17:8, and as explicitly stated in 2 Sam 7:1); and it should be dated about 995 B.C. (cf. J.B. Payne, *An Outline of Hebrew History* [Grand Rapids: Baker, 1954], pp. 103, 108).

The chapter contains three major sections. The first is David's desire to erect a permanent temple for the ark, which was not granted (vv. 1–6). The second section is on God's promise that even though David could not build a house for him, the Lord would still build a house for the king (vv. 7–15). Just as God had prospered David up to this point, so he would continue to prosper his kingdom. The next member of the dynasty would construct the temple (vv. 11–12). Then, in what was eschatological time for David (NT times for us), his ultimate successor in this dynasty of men would also be acknowledged as the Son of God (v. 13); and in that eternity yet to come, the Son of David would establish God's kingdom on earth (v. 14). The third section records the king's praise to God for such incredible grace (vv. 16–27).

1 By quoting David's full statement, "the ark of the covenant of the LORD" (cf. 2 Sam 7:2, simply, "the ark of God"), the Chronicler calls initial attention to the significance of this chapter within the history of covenantal thought (cf. comment on v. 12). Nathan the prophet had already been God's agent to guide David in organizing the Levitical musicians (cf. comment on 16:4), and he is best known for how he would later rebuke David for his sin with Bathsheba (2 Sam 12). Nathan aided Solomon in the latter's rise (1 King 1:10–11) and recorded some of the historical sources on which Ezra was able to draw for his own work (1 Chron 29:29; 2 Chron 9:29).

2–3 In reply to David's inquiry about building a temple, Nathan did tell him to "do it." But this was his immediate, human reaction: unofficial, noninspired (God's word did not come to him till that night, v. 3), and, as it turned out, wrong.

4 While 2 Samuel 7:5 had been content to record God's question, "Are you the one to build me a house?" Chronicles includes his strong prohibition: "You are not the one to build me a house." The reason, given only later (in 22:8; 28:3), lay in David's ruthless warfare (cf. 2 Sam 8:2). Yet Chronicles preserves another addition over 2 Samuel: the Hebrew text says literally, "build me *the* house." The idea of there being such a house *was* legitimate, just that David was not the one to build it.

5–6 Historical precedent shows that since the days of the Exodus, God had not "dwelt in a house," except briefly in Eli's building at Shiloh (1 Sam 3:3); and this had been destroyed by the Philistines after the first battle at Ebenezer (Jer 7:12).

9 For this verse context (cf. 2 Sam 7:1) suggests, and the Hebrew permits, a past rather than a future rendering: "I have provided . . . and have planted them so that they have a home . . . and are no longer disturbed" (so Keil, in loc.).

God's words that the wicked do not oppress Israel "as they did at the beginning" serve as a reminder of the sufferings of the Hebrews in Egypt (Exod 1:13–14).

10–11 God's promise to "build a house" for David is a play on words: the king could not build God a house, i.e., a structure "of cedar" (v.6); but God would build him one, a dynasty of descendants ("offspring," v.11).

12 While God did not here employ the term covenant, what he revealed was one; and it is so designated subsequently (2 Sam 23:5; Pss 89:3, 34; 132:11–12). This Davidic covenant was the sixth, and last, to be established in OT times (ZPEB, 1:1007–10). God's plan had moved onward from the Edenic (Gen 3:15), Noachian (9:9), Abrahamic (15:18), and Sinaitic covenants (Exod 19:5–6), through the Levitical (Num 25:12–13; cf. comment on 1 Chron 9:19), down to this revelation; and it involves three stages.

First, God promised David a successor, the "one who will build" the temple, viz., Solomon, an identification confirmed by God's words that Ezra included in v.11 (though they are not preserved in 2 Sam 7:10): "one of your own sons." Second, God promised to "establish his throne," as a continuing dynasty. Third, it would be established "forever," a feature made possible by Jesus Christ, who, as God's Son (next verse), is the only one to possess a rule that is endless (Luke 1:32–33); and in this lay David's own salvation (2 Sam 23:5). As Messiah he would set up his kingdom, in men's hearts, at his first coming (Dan 2:44a; Luke 17:21), though its external realization, over the world, awaits his second coming (Dan 2:44b; Luke 17:24).

13 This verse along with Psalm 2:7, 12, is one of the major OT revelations on the deity of the Messiah. It foretells Jesus' being uniquely God's son (Heb 1:5; cf. Acts 13:33; Heb 5:5), for it is not really applicable to Solomon (cf. comment on 22:10) or to any other of David's more immediate successors (by some sort of "double fulfillment"; cf. Payne, *Theology*, pp. 22–23, 261–62; id., *Prophecy*, p. 226). Jesus, however, combined in his own Person a perfect humanity and full deity (Matt 22:42–45; Phil 2:9), so that he might, by the one, become an accredited substitute for sinful men in his death (Heb 2:17–18; 1 Peter 2:24) and yet, by the other, be able to compensate infinitely for their sins and restore them to heaven and to God the Father by his resurrection (John 1:18; 14:6).

14–15 Unlike David's predecessor, Saul, whom God removed (v.13), Jesus would possess a permanent status over God's kingdom. Here again the Chronicler brings out more of the personal messianic character of God's words to Nathan (2 Sam 7:16 had included only his speaking in the more impersonal terms of David's "kingdom" and "throne").

16 The king's sitting "before the LORD" suggests that he went to the tent that was enshrining the ark (16:1).

17 In the phrase "as . . . the most exalted of men" (*ketôr hā'ādām*), the first word in the Hebrew is a rare noun meaning a "turn"; and although the rendering is not certain, McCarter (*II Samuel*, AB, p. 233) may be correct in translating the phrase "the turn of mankind to come," i.e., "the generation to come." Second Samuel 7:19 reads: "Is this your [tôraṯ hāʾāḏām, lit., 'law of the man'] usual way of dealing with man?" though Ezra may here not so much have been interpreting as following a differing (Palestinian-Qumran?) type of text (see Introduction: Text). David was, however, expressing his awe at God's favor, compared to his own lowly origin (v. 7).

22 That Israel is the Lord's "people" and that he is "their God" restates the central promise of the Lord's reconciling testament (cf. comments to 16:15 and 37), found from Genesis (17:7) to Revelation (21:3).

27 David's conclusion is one of faith in God's words: claiming the immediate blessing and affirming its eternal outcome.

Notes

13 First Chronicles 17 omits the latter half of the parallel passage (2 Sam 7:14), about the Davidic line's more immediately having to be corrected when they committed iniquity. By the time of the Chronicler, that lesson had been adequately demonstrated by the tragedy of the Exile; note an amplified messianism in the next verse (see comment on v. 14), made more explicit than in 2 Sam.

17 For a somewhat different understanding of this difficult verse and its relation to 2 Sam 7:19, see W.C. Kaiser, Jr., "The Blessing of David: A Charter for Humanity," *The Law and the Prophets*, ed. John Skilton (Philadelphia: Presbyterian and Reformed, 1974), pp. 298–318.

19 Alternatively the latter term in the phrase "for the sake of your servant and according to your will"—וּכְלִבְּךָ (ûḵᵉlibbᵉḵā, lit., "according to your heart")—could be pointed וְכַלְבְּךָ (wᵉḵalbᵉḵā, "[your servant] and your dog"), an address of humility, which has been documented in Lachish letter 2, 586 B.C. (ANET, p. 322).

---

6. Conquests and administration

18:1–17

¹In the course of time, David defeated the Philistines and subdued them, and he took Gath and its surrounding villages from the control of the Philistines.

²David also defeated the Moabites, and they became subject to him and brought tribute.

³Moreover, David fought Hadadezer king of Zobah, as far as Hamath, when he went to establish his control along the Euphrates River. ⁴David captured a thousand of his chariots, seven thousand charioteers and twenty thousand foot soldiers. He hamstrung all but a hundred of the chariot horses.

⁵When the Arameans of Damascus came to help Hadadezer king of Zobah, David struck down twenty-two thousand of them. ⁶He put garrisons in the Aramean kingdom of Damascus, and the Arameans became subject to him and brought tribute. The Lord gave David victory everywhere he went.

⁷David took the gold shields carried by the officers of Hadadezer and brought them to Jerusalem. ⁸From Tebah and Cun, towns that belonged to Hadadezer, David took a great quantity of bronze, which Solomon used to make the bronze Sea, the pillars and various bronze articles.

⁹When Tou king of Hamath heard that David had defeated the entire army of

Hadadezer king of Zobah, [10]he sent his son Hadoram to King David to greet him and congratulate him on his victory in battle over Hadadezer, who had been at war with Tou. Hadoram brought all kinds of articles of gold and silver and bronze.

[11]King David dedicated these articles to the Lord, as he had done with the silver and gold he had taken from all these nations: Edom and Moab, the Ammonites and the Philistines, and Amalek.

[12]Abishai son of Zeruiah struck down eighteen thousand Edomites in the Valley of Salt. [13]He put garrisons in Edom, and all the Edomites became subject to David. The Lord gave David victory everywhere he went.

[14]David reigned over all Israel, doing what was just and right for all his people. [15]Joab son of Zeruiah was over the army; Jehoshaphat son of Ahilud was recorder; [16]Zadok son of Ahitub and Ahimelech son of Abiathar were priests; Shavsha was secretary; [17]Benaiah son of Jehoiada was over the Kerethites and Pelethites; and David's sons were chief officials at the king's side.

The order of chapters in this part of Chronicles (cf. comments on 18:1; 19:1) is based on the sequence found in 2 Samuel, which is topical rather than chronological. Second Samuel 8 is the source that underlies 1 Chronicles 18. The subject of the chapter is twofold: David's wars of conquest—to the west, against Philistia (v.1); to the east, against Moab (v.2); to the north, against the Arameans of Syria (vv.3–11); and to the south, against Edom (vv.12–13)—followed by a descriptive survey of his administration (vv.14–17). The theme, twice repeated (vv.6, 13), is one of encouragement to all believers: that the Lord gave victory to David wherever he went.

1 The NIV's "In the course of time" is an effective rendering of *'aḥᵃrê-ḵēn*, (lit., "after such"), but actually indicates no more than a succession of topics. By strict chronology chapter 18 precedes 17 (cf. 17:8 and the introductory discussion to ch. 17), and chapter 19 (introduced by the same phrase) likewise precedes 18 (cf. comment on v.3).

David was now able to take the offensive and capture Gath, the most inland of the five Philistine "mother cities" (2 Sam 8:1 ASV), which made it the one most threatening to Judah (20:6, 8; cf. 1 Sam 5:8; 17:52).

2 Though the Chronicler does not seek to cover up David's acts of vengeance (cf. 20:3), he does omit the details about his harsh treatment of Moab (2 Sam 8:2).

3 Zobah was an Aramean state of Syria lying northeast of Damascus and south of Hamath. The attempt of its king Hadadezer to "establish his control along the Euphrates" could refer to some early, eastward campaign but seems rather to be based on the situation in 19:16, his gathering of forces along this river, with the aim of recouping the losses that he suffered because of his first defeat by Israel (detailed in 19:6–15).

4 Seven thousand is the correct number for the "charioteers" (cf. 19:18) that David took captive; the seventeen hundred in 2 Samuel 8:4 (cf. NIV mg.) is a scribal slip. To preserve the peace David took the strong measure of hamstringing most of the enemy's chariot horses.

8 The towns of Tebah (cf. NIV mg.) and Cun (called Berothai, 2 Sam 8:8) lay in the Coele Syria valley between the Lebanons. The tribute that David gained (cf. v.11) contributed to the vast resources (outlined in 22:2–5, 14–15) that he furnished to

Solomon for making "the bronze Sea," etc. (cf. 2 Chron 4:2–5 and, on the incalculable quantity of bronze employed, v.18).

12 Instead of Abishai (cf. comment on 11:20) overcoming the eighteen thousand Edomites, 2 Samuel 8:13 speaks of David's supreme leadership; and the title to Psalm 60 names Joab (the senior commander, v.15; cf. on 11:6) as a conqueror of twelve thousand. "The victory evidently involved a number of contingents acting to some extent individually" (NBCrev., p. 379).

15 Within David's "cabinet" some of the civil officers seem to have followed the pattern of Egyptian administration. The post of Jehoshaphat the "recorder" (*mazkîr*, lit., "one who reminds") corresponds to the Egyptian "chief of protocol," whose responsibilities included audiences and communications (Myers, *Chronicles*, 1:138).

16 Shavsha (Seraiah, 2 Sam 8:17), with no father listed, seems himself to have been foreign, though his office of *sōp̱ēr* implies more than just the literal "scribe," but in reality "secretary (of state)."

17 Benaiah (cf. comment on 11:23), in contrast to Joab (v.15), who led the general Israelite militia, commanded David's standing force of professional, foreign troops: the Kerethites, a people connected with the Philistines (1 Sam 30:14; Ezek 25:16), probably Cretans—notice the Egyptian name, up until the 1300s, of "Keftiu" (Heb., Caphtor; see comment on 1:12)—and the Pelethites, seemingly a shortened name for the Philistines themselves.

Notes

17 The position of David's sons as "chief officials" appears in 2 Sam 8:18 as כֹּהֲנִים (*kōhᵃnîm*), a term that by Ezra's time was restricted to "priests" but that in Samuel preserves an older, broader meaning of "official ministers" (cf. NBCrev., p. 379). Liberal interpreters prefer to see v.17 as an attempt on the part of the Chronicler to deny an earlier heterodoxy that permitted non-Levitical priests (cf. comment on 16:1).

7. Victories over Ammon

19:1–20:3

¹In the course of time, Nahash king of the Ammonites died, and his son succeeded him as king. ²David thought, "I will show kindness to Hanun son of Nahash, because his father showed kindness to me." So David sent a delegation to express his sympathy to Hanun concerning his father.

When David's men came to Hanun in the land of the Ammonites to express sympathy to him, ³the Ammonite nobles said to Hanun, "Do you think David is honoring your father by sending men to you to express sympathy? Haven't his men come to you to explore and spy out the country and overthrow it?" ⁴So Hanun seized David's men, shaved them, cut off their garments in the middle at the buttocks, and sent them away.

⁵When someone came and told David about the men, he sent messengers to

meet them, for they were greatly humiliated. The king said, "Stay at Jericho till your beards have grown, and then come back."

⁶When the Ammonites realized that they had become a stench in David's nostrils, Hanun and the Ammonites sent a thousand talents of silver to hire chariots and charioteers from Aram Naharaim, Aram Maacah and Zobah. ⁷They hired thirty-two thousand chariots and charioteers, as well as the king of Maacah with his troops, who came and camped near Medeba, while the Ammonites were mustered from their towns and moved out for battle.

⁸On hearing this, David sent Joab out with the entire army of fighting men. ⁹The Ammonites came out and drew up in battle formation at the entrance to their city, while the kings who had come were by themselves in the open country.

¹⁰Joab saw that there were battle lines in front of him and behind him; so he selected some of the best troops in Israel and deployed them against the Arameans. ¹¹He put the rest of the men under the command of Abishai his brother, and they were deployed against the Ammonites. ¹²Joab said, "If the Arameans are too strong for me, then you are to rescue me; but if the Ammonites are too strong for you, then I will rescue you. ¹³Be strong and let us fight bravely for our people and the cities of our God. The Lord will do what is good in his sight."

¹⁴Then Joab and the troops with him advanced to fight the Arameans, and they fled before him. ¹⁵When the Ammonites saw that the Arameans were fleeing, they too fled before his brother Abishai and went inside the city. So Joab went back to Jerusalem.

¹⁶After the Arameans saw that they had been routed by Israel, they sent messengers and had Arameans brought from beyond the River, with Shophach the commander of Hadadezer's army leading them.

¹⁷When David was told of this, he gathered all Israel and crossed the Jordan; he advanced against them and formed his battle lines opposite them. David formed his lines to meet the Arameans in battle, and they fought against him. ¹⁸But they fled before Israel, and David killed seven thousand of their charioteers and forty thousand of their foot soldiers. He also killed Shophach the commander of their army.

¹⁹When the vassals of Hadadezer saw that they had been defeated by Israel, they made peace with David and became subject to him.

So the Arameans were not willing to help the Ammonites anymore.

²⁰:¹In the spring, at the time when kings go off to war, Joab led out the armed forces. He laid waste the land of the Ammonites and went to Rabbah and besieged it, but David remained in Jerusalem. Joab attacked Rabbah and left it in ruins. ²David took the crown from the head of their king—its weight was found to be a talent of gold, and it was set with precious stones—and it was placed on David's head. He took a great quantity of plunder from the city ³and brought out the people who were there, consigning them to labor with saws and with iron picks and axes. David did this to all the Ammonite towns. Then David and his entire army returned to Jerusalem.

The climax of David's international struggles came in 995 B.C. (before the birth of Solomon, 2 Sam 12:24) and arose out of two campaigns against the Ammonites. These people were related to the Hebrews (cf. v.1) and lived directly east of them in the portion of Transjordan that lies east of the Jabbok River (Deut 3:16), as it flows northward before bending west to enter the Jordan. A major teaching value to be found in this section of 1 Chronicles (19:1–20:3) is summarized by Joab's words of trust and encouragement in v.13: "The Lord will do what is good in his sight." The topical units of the section include the causes of the Ammonite struggle (19:1–5); the first campaign, embracing the crisis that Joab surmounted against the combined forces of Ammon and their Aramean allies (vv.6–15); David's crushing of the attempted return by the Arameans (vv.16–19); and the second campaign, which resulted in Joab's overrunning the Ammonite state (20:1–3). These units closely parallel the corresponding paragraphs in their canonical source (2 Samuel 10–12), though Chronicles omits direct reference to David's sin with Bathsheba, which forms a large part of the Samuel narrative (11:2–12:25).

1 On the chapter's introductory phrase, see the comment on 18:1. "The Ammonites" were descendants, by incest, from Abraham's nephew Lot (Gen 19:36–38). During the chaotic days of the Hebrew judges, they had been guilty of repeated incursions against the Israelite tribes to their west (Judg 3:13; 10:7–9, 17–11:33; 1 Sam 11:1); but they had been first repelled and then subdued by Saul (1 Sam 11:11; 14:47).

2 Their late king "Nahash" would hardly have been the same oppressor who had precipitated Saul's elevation half a century earlier (1 Sam 11:1) but may have been his son. The latter's relationship to David had been one of *ḥesed,* meaning not so much "kindness" as "loyalty" to covenanted treaties and their obligations (cf. comment on 16:41). These may have had their origin in the common threat that both men faced in Saul, perhaps when David had been fleeing from him some twenty years earlier. One might compare the help that David received from the neighboring king of Moab (1 Sam 22:3). Some interpreters have suggested that it would inevitably discredit the sincerity of David's concern for the Hebrews in Gilead (2 Sam 2:5; cf. North, "The Chronicler," 1:411). But if this is a different Nahash from the tyrant who threatened Jabesh Gilead, then David could well have been loyal to both.

4 Hanun's shaving of David's emissaries is explained in 2 Samuel 10:4 as involving half their beards. For an Oriental this was an insult of the worst sort (v.5), and particularly after David's expression of faithful concern (v.2; cf. the vengeance in which it resulted, 20:3).

6 The quantity of silver paid out by Hanun for mercenary support (not specified in 2 Sam) amounts to over thirty-seven tons (NIV mg.). The value, however, represents a unique, once and for all payment. Since it was sent in desperation, it was not impossible.

"Aram Naharaim" (Mesopotamia, NASB) occupied land between the Tigris and Euphrates rivers; and it was this area that provided reinforcements for the second Syrian advance (v.16). The Chronicler uses its more general name to include the states of Beth Rehob and Tob, mentioned in 2 Samuel 10:6, 8 (cf. Gen 36:37; KD, *Samuel,* p. 377).

7 In the light of 2 Samuel 10:6, the total of 32,000 mercenaries seems to include foot soldiers and horsemen (cf. v.18) as well as charioteers. The same verse has 1,000 in the contingent from Maacah. Their gathering point was near "Medeba" (a fact not stated in 2 Sam) in north Reuben in Transjordan (Josh 13:16), though why they selected this location southwest of the Ammonite border is not known.

9 Joab's battle with Ammon was finally engaged before the gates of "their [capital] city," i.e., Rabbah (v.15; 20:1), modern Amman.

13 After appealing to his men to do their utmost for their people and their God (cf.

1 Cor 16:13), Joab in faith committed the outcome to the will of the Lord (cf. the same sort of balance that is stressed in one's spiritual salvation, Phil 2:12–13).

15 Joab did not at this time follow up the victory by laying siege to Rabbah; it may have been too late in the year (cf. 20:1).

16 This regathering of Aramean forces beyond the Euphrates seems to provide the setting for 18:3 (q.v.).

28 In the light of 18:4, the Chronicles figure of 7,000 charioteers, or horsemen, is to be seen as the original that lies behind the numeral 700 in the present MT of 2 Samuel 10:18 (its LXX = Chron). Likewise Chronicles' identification of 40,000 as "foot soldiers" is the correct reading, as opposed to Samuel's "horsemen" (NIV mg.), because the figure approximates the total of 20,000 plus 22,000 foot soldiers given in chapter 18 (vv.4–5; cf. the listing in Appendix A). As Wenham ("Large Numbers," p. 45) summarizes it, "1 Chronicles 18:4–5 is the fullest and most coherent text, and it is fairly easy to see how the other texts could have derived from it."

19 The "vassals" of Hadadezer included his client kings (2 Sam 10:19).

20:1 Springtime marked the end of the rainy season and permitted the resumption of warfare. The Chronicler's statement that "David remained in Jerusalem" suggests to his readers, without having to retrace all the sordid details, what 2 Samuel here records (11:2–27) on David's shameful adultery with Bathsheba and the murder of her incorruptible husband, the king's hero Uriah (1 Chron 11:41).

2 Joab did, however, summon David to Rabbah in time for its capitulation (2 Sam 12:27–29), so that his ruler was present to take the crown from the head of Ammon's national idol, Milcom (NIV mg.; cf. 1 Kings 11:5, 33; Zeph 1:5)—its very weight in gold ("about 75 pounds" NIV mg.) precluded any regular wearing of it by a man.

3 Second Samuel 12:31 adds to the labor with saws, picks, and axes, work in the brickkiln.

Notes

---

17 The defectively written phrase, he advanced "against them" (אֲלֵהֶם, ['ªlēhem]) may be traceable to 2 Sam 10:17's he advanced חֵלָאמָה (ḥēlā'māh, "Helam-ward"; cf. v.16). Helam lay in the Coele Syria Valley near Hamath (cf. comments on 18:3 and 8), which formed the northern border of Zobah.

20:2 The rendering that Milcom's crown was set with "precious stones" (אֶבֶן יְקָרָה, ['eben yᵉqārāh]) might more naturally be taken, with NASB, RSV, as singular, "a (particular) precious stone," rather than as collective.

3 The translation "consigning them to labor with saws" might at first suggest the Hebrew of 2 Sam 12:31: וַיָּשֶׂם (wayyāśem, "and he put [them to work] with saws"), from the root שִׂים (śîm). Yet it could also represent the verb form in the present text, וַיָּשַׂר (wayyāśar), if from the root שָׂרַר (śārar, "lead, conduct"; 15:22 MSS), "and he conducted (them to work) with saws." It need not be derived from נָשַׂר (nāśar, "to saw"), and be pointed וַיִּשַׂר (wayyiśśar, "and he sawed [them] with saws"). David could be ruthless (cf. comment to 18:2), but he was not cruel.

---

8. Philistine wars

20:4–8

⁴In the course of time, war broke out with the Philistines, at Gezer. At that time Sibbecai the Hushathite killed Sippai, one of the descendants of the Rephaites, and the Philistines were subjugated.

⁵In another battle with the Philistines, Elhanan son of Jair killed Lahmi the brother of Goliath the Gittite, who had a spear with a shaft like a weaver's rod.

⁶In still another battle, which took place at Gath, there was a huge man with six fingers on each hand and six toes on each foot—twenty-four in all. He also was descended from Rapha. ⁷When he taunted Israel, Jonathan son of Shimea, David's brother, killed him.

⁸These were descendants of Rapha in Gath, and they fell at the hands of David and his men.

Ezra's treatment of David's ascendancy (1 Chron 11–20) concludes with the record of three incidents that occurred during battles with the Philistines (20:4–8). Even as the preceding section (19:1–20:3) had elaborated on one aspect of the survey of David's conquest (ch. 18)—namely, the Ammonite struggle, as the basis for the Aramean wars that were introduced in 18:3—so the present, brief section elaborates on David's Philistine wars and capture of Gath, which had been mentioned in 18:1 (cf. the references to Gath in 20:6, 8). The first two incidents are not pinpointed historically (cf. comment on v.4 below) but also seem to belong to the period between the two initial Philistine offenses against David in 1003 B.C. (14:8–17) and the rest that God granted him from his enemies in about 995 (17:8; 2 Sam 7:1). Their canonical source is found in one of the appendices to 2 Samuel (21:15–22, which catalogs four such encounters; cf. comment on v.8)—though Chronicles omits the first, in which David's own life was imperiled (2 Sam 21:15–17).

4 On this section's introductory phrase, see the comments on 18:1; 19:1. "Gezer" may indicate the general location of the otherwise obscure place-name Gob (2 Sam 21:18); the former identifies the border city the Philistines had retreated to after David's victories in his war for independence (cf. comment on 14:16).

The champion "Sibbecai," from the Judean town of Hushah (4:4), was one of David's "Thirty" heroes (11:29) and the commander of his eighth corps (27:11). The Philistine "Sippai" ("Saph," 2 Sam 21:18), whom he overcame, is traced back to the "Rephaites" (BV, "Rephaim"), an ancient people (Gen 14:5) noted for their large size (Deut 2:21; hence RSV, "giants"). Except for those remaining in the kingdom of Og in Bashan, the Rephaim had generally died out by the time of Moses (Deut 3:11), which may account for their name rᵉpāʾîm ("ghosts"; Isa 26:14).

5 This second battle too took place in Gob (2 Sam 21:19). "Lahmi" was brother to Goliath, the well-known victim of David's heroism (1 Sam 17). But perhaps because of his unfamiliar and indeed unique name, a later copyist of the parallel passage in 2 Samuel (21:19) introduced a small but far-reaching corruption (see Notes), as if

Elhanan, now given the title "the Bethlehemite" (2 Sam 21:19), had killed Goliath himself. Liberal interpreters usually disregard the above explanation and first accuse 1 Samuel 17 of glorifying David by (falsely) attributing to him the exploit of Elhanan and then accuse Chronicles of twisting the text of 2 Samuel 21 so as to falsely promote harmony within Scripture (Curtis, p. 243). Still another suggestion has been proposed that Elhanan son of Jair (at Gob) might be another name of David son of Jesse (at Elah, 1 Sam 17:2)!

On the "weaver's rod," see the comment on 11:23.

6 The use of the article with "Rapha" (also in v.8; lit., "the ghost"; see comment on v.4) suggests that this is not a personal, individual name, except perhaps in the sense of an eponymous ancestor of "the Rephaim" (cf. how the plural in v.4 has in its parallel verse, 2 Sam 21:18, the singular with the article, $h\bar{a}$-$r\bar{a}p\bar{a}h$).

8 Instead of the demonstrative pronoun "These" (were descendants of . . .), 2 Samuel 21:22 has "these four," because of the additional incident that Chronicles has omitted (cf. the introductory discussion to this section).

Notes

4 The identity of the Rephaim is still obscure. Important studies include A. Caquot, "Les rephaim ougaritiques," *Syria* 37 (1960): 75–93, and Johannes C. DeMoor, "Rapi'ūma–Rephaim," *ZAW* 88 (1976): 323–47.

5 It is helpful to see the texts in parallel columns.

2 Sam 21:19	1 Chron 20:5
וַיַּךְ אֶלְחָנָן בֶּן־יַעֲרֵי אֹרְגִים	וַיַּךְ אֶלְחָנָן בֶּן־יָעוּר
בֵּית הַלַּחְמִי אֵת גָּלְיָת	אֶת־לַחְמִי אֲחִי גָלְיָת
(*wayyak 'elḥānān ben-yaᵉrê 'ōrᵉgîm*	(*wayyak 'elḥānān ben-yāᵓiwr*
bêt hallaḥmî 'ēt gālᵉyāt,	*'et-laḥmî 'ᵃḥî gālᵉyāt,*
"[and] Elhanan son of Jaare-Oregim	"[and] Elhanan son of Jair killed
the Bethlehemite killed Goliath")	Lahmi the brother of Goliath")

Several errors are apparent in 2 Sam 21:19.

1. The copyist of Samuel has confused the Elhanan mentioned on this occasion with David's officer by that name (cf. 2 Sam 23:24; 1 Chron 11:26).

2. The above made it necessary to alter the definite article before Lahmi to give his proper identity—hence, the Bethlehemite.

3. The above alteration (or miscopying), involving a single letter in the consonantal text (ח [*ḥ*] to ת [*t*]), followed easily, especially since Lahmi's spear rivaled that of his brother (cf. 1 Sam 17:7; 2 Sam 21:19 with 1 Chron 20:5).

4. The אֹרְגִים (*'ōrᵉgîm*, "weavers"), probably a dittography from the succeeding line ("weaver's rod"), yielded the compound name "son of Jaare-Oregim."

Thus the text of Chronicles appears to preserve the correct reading, a reading that underwent corruption in a later edition of Samuel.

C. David's Latter Days (21:1–29:30)

1. The census

21:1–30

¹Satan rose up against Israel and incited David to take a census of Israel. ²So David said to Joab and the commanders of the troops, "Go and count the Israelites from Beersheba to Dan. Then report back to me so that I may know how many there are."

³But Joab replied, "May the LORD multiply his troops a hundred times over. My lord the king, are they not all my lord's subjects? Why does my lord want to do this? Why should he bring guilt on Israel?"

⁴The king's word, however, overruled Joab; so Joab left and went throughout Israel and then came back to Jerusalem. ⁵Joab reported the number of the fighting men to David: In all Israel there were one million one hundred thousand men who could handle a sword, including four hundred and seventy thousand in Judah.

⁶But Joab did not include Levi and Benjamin in the numbering, because the king's command was repulsive to him. ⁷This command was also evil in the sight of God; so he punished Israel.

⁸Then David said to God, "I have sinned greatly by doing this. Now, I beg you, take away the guilt of your servant. I have done a very foolish thing."

⁹The LORD said to Gad, David's seer, ¹⁰"Go and tell David, 'This is what the LORD says: I am giving you three options. Choose one of them for me to carry out against you.' "

¹¹So Gad went to David and said to him, "This is what the LORD says: 'Take your choice: ¹²three years of famine, three months of being swept away before your enemies, with their swords overtaking you, or three days of the sword of the LORD—days of plague in the land, with the angel of the LORD ravaging every part of Israel.' Now then, decide how I should answer the one who sent me."

¹³David said to Gad, "I am in deep distress. Let me fall into the hands of the LORD, for his mercy is very great; but do not let me fall into the hands of men."

¹⁴So the LORD sent a plague on Israel, and seventy thousand men of Israel fell dead. ¹⁵And God sent an angel to destroy Jerusalem. But as the angel was doing so, the LORD saw it and was grieved because of the calamity and said to the angel who was destroying the people, "Enough! Withdraw your hand." The angel of the LORD was then standing at the threshing floor of Araunah the Jebusite.

¹⁶David looked up and saw the angel of the LORD standing between heaven and earth, with a drawn sword in his hand extended over Jerusalem. Then David and the elders, clothed in sackcloth, fell facedown.

¹⁷David said to God, "Was it not I who ordered the fighting men to be counted? I am the one who has sinned and done wrong. These are but sheep. What have they done? O LORD my God, let your hand fall upon me and my family, but do not let this plague remain on your people."

¹⁸Then the angel of the LORD ordered Gad to tell David to go up and build an altar to the LORD on the threshing floor of Araunah the Jebusite. ¹⁹So David went up in obedience to the word that Gad had spoken in the name of the LORD.

²⁰While Araunah was threshing wheat, he turned and saw the angel; his four sons who were with him hid themselves. ²¹Then David approached, and when Araunah looked and saw him, he left the threshing floor and bowed down before David with his face to the ground.

²²David said to him, "Let me have the site of your threshing floor so I can build an altar to the LORD, that the plague on the people may be stopped. Sell it to me at the full price."

²³Araunah said to David, "Take it! Let my lord the king do whatever pleases him. Look, I will give the oxen for the burnt offerings, the threshing sledges for the wood, and the wheat for the grain offering. I will give all this."

²⁴But King David replied to Araunah, "No, I insist on paying the full price. I will

not take for the LORD what is yours, or sacrifice a burnt offering that costs me nothing."

²⁵So David paid Araunah six hundred shekels of gold for the site. ²⁶David built an altar to the LORD there and sacrificed burnt offerings and fellowship offerings. He called on the LORD, and the LORD answered him with fire from heaven on the altar of burnt offering.

²⁷Then the LORD spoke to the angel, and he put his sword back into its sheath. ²⁸At that time, when David saw that the LORD had answered him on the threshing floor of Araunah the Jebusite, he offered sacrifices there. ²⁹The tabernacle of the LORD, which Moses had made in the desert, and the altar of burnt offering were at that time on the high place at Gibeon. ³⁰But David could not go before it to inquire of God, because he was afraid of the sword of the angel of the LORD.

After 995 B.C., about twenty years elapsed between the concluding events in David's rise to power (chs. 11–20) and the resumed narrative of deeds performed in the latter part of his reign, which occupies the balance of the book (chs. 21–29). The intervening period was one of crisis and personal failure on David's part, triggered by his sin of adultery with Bathsheba (2 Sam 11). This in turn set off a chain reaction of crime: the king's murder of Uriah (ch. 11) and a series of similarly wanton acts on the part of Amnon (cf. 13:4: "you the king's son"), Absalom (chs. 14–19), and even such less obviously motivated rebels as Sheba (ch. 20).

Since Absalom's revolt occupied a total of eleven years (2 Sam 13:23, 38; 14:28; 15:7 variant reading), or about 990–979, 1 Chronicles brings us down to about 975. Here our Chronicler takes up his account with David's census, which is recorded also in 2 Samuel 24. His reasons for a gap of this length are not difficult to surmise: little of what transpired during those two decades would encourage a postexilic Judah, before whom Ezra was seeking to portray a piety that characterized David at his best (see Introduction: Occasion and Purpose).

With the census (1 Chron 21), however, a chain reaction of a different caliber was inaugurated. Despite its sinful inception, it provided the immediate setting for God's revelation of the site of his temple and for the preparation that ensued (ch. 22). This in turn leads into David's administrative arrangements, whether in matters of religious (chs. 23–26) or civil organization (ch. 27). First Chronicles concludes with a final charge from David that both Solomon and all Israel would continue faithful to their God (chs. 28–29). Events like these definitely *were* germane to the purpose of the Chronicler. Beyond the opening chapter, however, there is no direct parallel elsewhere in the OT.

For the events of chapter 21, Scripture presents us with no less than four explanations (see vv.1, 3). Yet however complex the motivation for Israel's census and for the disaster that followed, Ezra's record now serves a double function. On the one hand, the various aspects of David's repentance remain exemplary for readers up to this moment (cf. vv.8, 13, 17, and 24). On the other hand, the decision of God to establish his altar and temple at Moriah in Jerusalem have affected all history (cf. Rev 11:1); for this mountain became the focus of the Holy City (v.2), where his Son was crucified (v.8). And it will continue to affect history; for from this "city he loves" (20:9), he will some day rule the nations of earth (v.4; cf. Isa 2:2–4) and then eternally heal the dwellers of his new earth (Isa 65:17–19; Rev 21:1–2; 22:2).

1 For the first time in Scripture, the word "Satan" appears without the definite article as a proper noun. He is still *haś-śāṭān*, "the adversary" (as in Job 1–2; Zech

3:1–2), with his changeless malice toward God and men (vs. liberalism's theories of an originally neutral, angelic "prosecuting attorney" (cf. Payne, *Theology*, pp. 291–95); but Satan has now become his name (cf. the similar development of *hammāšîaḥ*, "the anointed one," which is used for the first time without the article as a proper noun, *Messiah*, in Dan 9:25–26). David's numbering of his people was thus brought about, in the first instance, by the Devil's hatred of God's people and of God himself (cf. Job 1:11; 2:5).

Yet the parallel verse in 2 Samuel (24:1) goes deeper and shows that Satan, the instrument (cf. 1 Kings 22:22–23; Job 1:12; 2:6), was actually being used to accomplish, in the second instance, "the anger of the LORD . . . against Israel." That is, the disaster that was brought on because of the census served to punish the nation (1 Chron 21:7) for her sins, including repeated revolts against God's anointed king, David. The last revolt under Sheba had terminated only shortly before (cf. the introductory discussion to ch. 21). In the third instance there were, of course, God's ultimate and positive goals, insuring that the results of it all would mean the establishment of his altar and temple (cf. above).

3 Finally there was the immediate, human factor—meaning David's own motivation —that was evil (vv. 7–8, 17) and, as Joab dared point out to the king, contributed to "bring guilt on Israel." A census was not in itself wrong (cf. the God-directed census in Num 1 and 26). But on this occasion David seems to have ordered this because he was placing his trust in "multiplied troops" rather than in the promises of God (contrast 27:23 with Ps 30:6, the title of which indicates its composition at this time; cf. comment on 22:1).

4 The route of Joab and his officers "throughout Israel" is outlined in 2 Samuel 24:4 –6; and v.8 adds that it took almost ten months.

5 The total figures that they gathered require clarification in two directions. First, in comparison with those given in 2 Samuel 24:9, Ezra's sum of 1,100,000 for *all* Israel is larger than Samuel's 800,000, which probably did not include the regularly organized army (note the lack of an "all" before "Israel") of 288,000 (1 Chron 27:1–15; NBCrev., p. 292); but his sum of 470,000 for Judah is a bit smaller than Samuel's 500,000, which may here simply be a round number. Second, on the basis of the noun *'alāpîm*, denoting either "thousands" or "chiefs," "specially trained warriors" (cf. comments to 7:3–4; 12:24), we should probably think in terms of a muster of 1,570 outstanding military figures and not necessarily of over a million and a half "men . . . who could handle a sword."

6 Joab's exemption of Levi from this census (the tribe *was* numbered in 23:3) had precedent, because of that tribe's special religious status (Num 1:49–50). This fact may also explain his deliberate exclusion of Benjamin, since both Jerusalem (with God's ark) and Gibeon (with the tabernacle, v.29) lay within its borders (Josh 18:25, 28). We do know that his work was interrupted by God's "wrath [that] came on Israel" (1 Chron 27:24), in this very Benjamite area (21:15).

8 David's confession resulted from his troubled heart, or conscience (2 Sam 24:10), perhaps pricked by Joab's rebuke.

9 "Gad" the "seer" had already counseled David, both before he became king (1 Sam 22:5) and after (2 Chron 29:25), and was later to compose one of the source documents for his reign that was used by Ezra (1 Chron 29:29).

12 The alternate punishments set before David were of approximately equal severity. The pattern of "threes" in the time-units involved favors the "three years of famine" recorded in Chronicles and the LXX text of 2 Samuel 24:13, rather than the "seven years" found in the present MT of Samuel (NIV mg.).

God's instrument for executing the plague would be "the angel of the LORD." Compare the similar situations both before (1 Sam 6:3–6) and after (2 Kings 19:35). But while those cases may have involved the divine Angel of the Testament (cf. Exod 23:20–21; Mal 3:1), presumably preincarnate appearances of Christ (Payne, *Theology*, pp. 167–70), this one apparently did not; it was simply *an* ordinary "angel" (v.15; compare 1 Kings 19:5, 7). All angels, however, excel in might (Ps 103:20).

13 The king's submission to the word of the Lord through his prophet is both commendable, personally, and sets apart Hebrew religion from the lack of such ethical restraint within paganism generally (cf. comments on 11:3). David wisely chose the punishment from God (a plague) rather than that from men (invasion).

14 Punishment as such, however, remained inescapable; and "seventy thousand men of Israel fell"—a tragically appropriate sentence on a king whose sin had been that of trusting in the numbers of his troops (see comment on v.3).

16 David and his civic officials, "the elders," were already in penitence ("sackcloth"), perhaps on their way to the tabernacle (v.30), at Gibeon (v.29), when they saw the destroying angel with his drawn sword facing Jerusalem. But his hand was withdrawn (2 Sam 24:16).

17 The second confession of David (cf. v.8) is recorded more fully here than in the 2 Samuel parallel (24:17). It illustrates David's willingness to accept full responsibility and to sacrifice himself for his people's sake. The latter he calls "sheep," and Scripture frequently compares leader and people with a shepherd and his flock (11:2; cf. Ps 23; Jer 23:1–4). But while the king was indeed to blame for having "sinned and done wrong," the plague in question was not entirely a case of an innocent nation suffering for the crimes of its leader (see comment on v. 1).

18–22 The Chronicler omits Araunah's opening question (2 Sam 24:21) and moves directly to David's words (v.22), which show his compliance with Gad's instructions to build an altar there on his threshing floor (v.18).

23 The "oxen" would have been present to pull the wooden "threshing sledges" over the wheat. The grain offering always had to accompany the sacrifices of flesh (Exod 29:40–41; Lev 23:18; Num 15:4)—its name in the KJV, "meat offering" (in which "meat," by archaic usage, means "food"), is today peculiarly inappropriate, because this was the one major OT offering that did *not* involve flesh.

24 By refusing to present an "offering that costs me nothing," David confirmed the truth that God takes no pleasure in the man who yields only what involves no sacrifice. He requires of his followers a totally surrendered life (Rom 12:1; cf. Luke 21:1–3).

25 So David bought "the site"—*hammāqôm,* which may have included the whole area of Mount Moriah—for 240 ounces of gold (cf. NIV mg.). This was worth about one hundred thousand dollars, on a standard of about 1 ounce to four hundred dollars (cf. comment on 19:6). Second Samuel 24:24 notes a much smaller amount, 20 ounces of silver, for the threshing floor itself (NBCrev. p. 380).

26 God's answer of "fire from heaven on the altar" publicly attested his acceptance, both of the king's repentance and of the altar site (note similar miracles: in the past, in reference to the tabernacle, Lev 9:24; and yet to be revealed, in Solomon's temple, 2 Chron 7:1).

27 Furthermore the angel's sword was sheathed and the plague ceased (2 Sam 24:25).

29 On the tabernacle's contemporaneous location at Gibeon, see the comment on 16:39.

Notes

15 In light of the explicit supernaturalism of the plague—via the angel of God's punishment —modern theories of "epidemics inadvertently spread by the census takers themselves as they went from town to town" (Myers, *Chronicles,* 1:146) appear incongruously banal.

Instead of "Ornan" (אָרְנָן, *'ornān*), the LXX reads more properly "Ornah" (ορνα, *orna;* cf. NIV mg.). The Samuel MT Kethiv, הָ(אוֹרְנָה) ([*hā*]*'ôre'nāh*) agrees with this; cf. the Qere, הָ(אֲרַוְנָה) [*hā*]*'arawnāh*), whence the English "Araunah" (cf. W.C. Kaiser, Jr. "Araunah," ZPEB, 1:257–58). The name seems to be Hurrian in origin (North, "The Chronicler," 1:412), though doubtfully to be identified with an ancient semilegendary king or with a Jebusite king of similar name. (For details see P.K. Carter, Jr., *Samuel,* AB, 2:508, 512; H.A. Hoffner, "The Hittites and Hurrians," in *Peoples of Old Testament Times,* ed. D.J. Wiseman [Oxford: Clarendon, 1973], p. 225.)

2. Temple preparations

22:1–19

¹Then David said, "The house of the Lord God is to be here, and also the altar of burnt offering for Israel."
²So David gave orders to assemble the aliens living in Israel, and from among them he appointed stonecutters to prepare dressed stone for building the house of God. ³He provided a large amount of iron to make nails for the doors of the gateways and for the fittings, and more bronze than could be weighed. ⁴He also provided more cedar logs than could be counted, for the Sidonians and Tyrians had brought large numbers of them to David.
⁵David said, "My son Solomon is young and inexperienced, and the house to be built for the Lord should be of great magnificence and fame and splendor in

the sight of all the nations. Therefore I will make preparations for it." So David made extensive preparations before his death.

⁶Then he called for his son Solomon and charged him to build a house for the Lord, the God of Israel. ⁷David said to Solomon: "My son, I had it in my heart to build a house for the Name of the Lord my God. ⁸But this word of the Lord came to me: 'You have shed much blood and have fought many wars. You are not to build a house for my Name, because you have shed much blood on the earth in my sight. ⁹But you will have a son who will be a man of peace and rest, and I will give him rest from all his enemies on every side. His name will be Solomon, and I will grant Israel peace and quiet during his reign. ¹⁰He is the one who will build a house for my Name. He will be my son, and I will be his father. And I will establish the throne of his kingdom over Israel forever.'

¹¹"Now, my son, the Lord be with you, and may you have success and build the house of the Lord your God, as he said you would. ¹²May the Lord give you discretion and understanding when he puts you in command over Israel, so that you may keep the law of the Lord your God. ¹³Then you will have success if you are careful to observe the decrees and laws that the Lord gave Moses for Israel. Be strong and courageous. Do not be afraid or discouraged.

¹⁴"I have taken great pains to provide for the temple of the Lord a hundred thousand talents of gold, a million talents of silver, quantities of bronze and iron too great to be weighed, and wood and stone. And you may add to them. ¹⁵You have many workmen: stonecutters, masons and carpenters, as well as men skilled in every kind of work ¹⁶in gold and silver, bronze and iron—craftsmen beyond number. Now begin the work, and the Lord be with you."

¹⁷Then David ordered all the leaders of Israel to help his son Solomon. ¹⁸He said to them, "Is not the Lord your God with you? And has he not granted you rest on every side? For he has handed the inhabitants of the land over to me, and the land is subject to the Lord and to his people. ¹⁹Now devote your heart and soul to seeking the Lord your God. Begin to build the sanctuary of the Lord God, so that you may bring the ark of the covenant of the Lord and the sacred articles belonging to God into the temple that will be built for the Name of the Lord."

The Chronicler was vitally concerned to insure support for the Jerusalem temple in his day (Ezra 7:15–17; 8:25–30, 33–34). No more fitting stimulus for dedication in this regard could then be found than in the example set by David when he made preparations for the construction of that temple in his day; and this is the subject of 1 Chronicles 22 (cf. also chs. 28–29). Ezra first summarized David's own efforts (vv. 2–5) and then recounted the words of exhortation by which he privately encouraged Solomon to carry through in its building (vv. 6–16) and publicly charged the leaders of Israel to assist his son in this task (vv. 17–19). Though no parallels to the chapter now appear in Scripture, Ezra must have been able to use sources that are no longer available for us today.

1 In view of the revelations of God's presence that occurred in the preceding chapter (cf. esp. 21:15 and 26), David announced that his new altar on Araunah's threshing floor had become the designated place for Israel's burnt offerings, and that this site on Mount Moriah (2 Chron 3:1) was in fact "the house of the Lord God," even though the building had yet to be erected. Such words therefore explain how the title to Psalm 30 can simultaneously claim authorship by David and yet also be an occasion for its composition at "the dedication of the temple." For the psalm does fit historically at this point; notice how vv. 5–6 so precisely correspond to David's attitudes and experiences in 1 Chronicles 21.

2 The king began by drafting the *gērîm*, or resident "aliens," of the land for work as stone cutters. The situation is attested by the existence of a cabinet post on corvée labor, held by Adoram (2 Sam 20:24; cf. NIV mg.), and is confirmed by Solomon's similar arrangements later on (2 Chron 2:17–18 and 8:7–9, q.v.). An earlier parallel may be found in the way the Hebrews assigned certain of the conquered Canaanites to be "nethinim," or temple servants (cf. comment on 1 Chron 9:2).

3 The king's provision of "a large amount of iron" reflects how conditions had changed during his time—known archaeologically as Iron I—due, no doubt, to the incorporation of iron-producing Philistines within the sphere of Hebrew control (contrast the situation described in 1 Sam 13:19–22).

4 To handle the "cedar logs," Solomon was later forced to draft a considerable number of Israelites (1 Kings 5:13–14), though foreigners were used for the stone-work (cf. comments on v.2).

5 Nowhere does Scripture connect Solomon's age with some historically datable point (as it does with most of the kings at their accession; cf. 2 Sam 5:4). As a result we do not know exactly how *young* Solomon then was, in about 975 B.C. Josephus suggested fourteen (Antiq. VIII, 211 [vii.8]); and while some of his other figures for Solomon are unreliable (e.g., assigning him a reign of eighty years), he may be correct in this matter. For Solomon, after reigning forty years (2 Chron 9:30), was succeeded by his son Rehoboam, then aged forty-one (12:13); and Solomon could well have had a one-year-old son at his accession in 970, if Solomon himself had been born about 990. This would make him twenty at the time. Furthermore, though David's relationship with Bathsheba dates from about 995 (cf. the introductory discussions to chs. 17 and 19), Solomon was apparently not the first son that she bore to David but the fourth (1 Chron 3:5), which brings us once again to about 990 for his birth.

7 That the temple was to be built "for the Name of the LORD" means more than his reputation or honor but ultimately for his Person. In the OT most names were more than mere identifications. They might connote attributes or, for God, in OT theology, his general revelation (cf. Ps 8:1, 9: "How majestic is your name in all the earth!"), but usually his special revelation in theophanies (cf. Isa 30:27, on his "Name" coming to punish Assyria). Specifically God's "Name" stood for the glory-cloud of his presence in the tabernacle or the temple (Deut 12:11; 2 Chron 6:20); and so it seems to be here.

8 The "word of the LORD" David referred to had been brought to him by the prophet Nathan, before Solomon's birth (17:4). But the king here first revealed why God had refused him permission to build the temple: he had "fought many wars" (stated again in 28:3). The point was not simply that warfare had preempted his energies (cf. 1 Kings 5:3), but that it had polluted his hands with undue bloodshed. War may on occasion be necessary, right, and divinely ordained (1 Chron 14:10; 19:13); but David had become guilty of excessive violence (e.g., in 2 Sam 8:2). His explanation carries serious ethical implications for us today (Matt 5:9).

9 Though Solomon's succession was later disputed by his older brother Adonijah (1 Kings 1:5–13, 24–25), he had been divinely favored, even before birth (2 Sam

12:24–25); and he is here designated to "reign" over Israel, as David himself proceeded to acknowledge to Bathsheba on oath (1 Kings 1:13, 30). (On his status as king by divine choice, cf. Braun, "Apologetic," and "Temple Builder.")

God moreover promised Solomon a reign "of peace" (*šālôm*, cf. NIV mg. on the wordplay in Heb. with his name "Solomon," *šelōmōh*). Fulfillment came by his having to engage in only one known battle (vs. Hamath, 2 Chron 8:3).

10 In this verse David directly quotes from Nathan's prophecy in 17:12–14 (which he does also in 28:6). As predicted in the first clause, Solomon did "build a house" for God's name (cf. comment on v.7); and, as in the last, "the throne of his kingdom" did come to be established "over Israel forever." The middle clause, however, where God prophesies, "He will be my son," must be read in the light of a condition that was attached and that demanded a faithfulness (cf. comment on 28:7), which Solomon failed to achieve but was rather accomplished in Jesus Christ (cf. comment on 17:13). David seems to have quoted the entire passage, including its middle part so as to identify the more immediately relevant promises that both preceded and followed it in context. Compare Peter's citation of the whole of Joel 2:28–32 in Acts 2:17–21, concerning Pentecost, even though the middle portion (vv.19–20), concerning Christ's second coming, applied to a later situation and was included in what some have called a "sandwich structure," because of his quoting the entire passage.

11–13 David's blessing on his son, in its various aspects, set a pattern for subsequent benedictions. In v.11 he particularly invoked success for Solomon as he should "build the house"; compare this same stress in 28:10. In vv.12–13 David (harking back to Josh 1:7–8) emphasized how he should keep "the law . . . that the LORD gave Moses" (cf. the reappearance of this stress in 1 Kings 2:3).

14 The tremendous quantities of gold and silver (cf. NIV mg.) that David provided add up to over forty thousand tons, which represents a fabulous amount, with a far greater ancient purchasing value. This, together with smaller but related amounts given in 29:4 and 7 (q.v.), constitutes the one place in the Book of Chronicles where its figures are large enough to justify invoking God's special providence to account for them (cf. Appendix B). Keil (pp. 247–48), it is true, observes that "in the capitals of the Asiatic kingdoms of antiquity, enormous quantities of the precious metals were accumulated"; and he quotes ancient documents on how Cyrus obtained 500,000 talents of silver in his Asiatic campaigns. He concludes (ibid.), in respect to David's offering of twice this much silver, that "we cannot therefore regard the sums mentioned as incredible." But it may be that the historical reliability of these two passages in 1 Chronicles is better explained by "the special providence of God, in bestowing on His servant David a weight of riches commensurate with their intended employment for the house of His glory" (Payne, "Validity," p. 220).

19 David's goal, expressed here to the leaders of Israel, of bringing "the ark of the covenant . . . into the temple" was in fact to be accomplished in 2 Chronicles 5:7, and this act would mark the achievement of all his various efforts on its behalf, and on God's behalf, as so far described throughout chapters 13, 15, 16, 17, and now 22.

Notes

2 Because of the absence of parallels in 2 Samuel for the material found in this portion of 1 Chronicles, the historicity of David's orders, and indeed of his preparations as a whole (v.3), has been denied by proponents of the historical-critical method. Dentan (p. 137), for example, says, "The story is the product of the author's devotion to the Temple . . . he knew what he would have done if he had been king, and he could not imagine that David did otherwise."

3. Levitical organization

23:1–26:32

¹When David was old and full of years, he made his son Solomon king over Israel.

²He also gathered together all the leaders of Israel, as well as the priests and Levites. ³The Levites thirty years old or more were counted, and the total number of men was thirty-eight thousand. ⁴David said, "Of these, twenty-four thousand are to supervise the work of the temple of the LORD and six thousand are to be officials and judges. ⁵Four thousand are to be gatekeepers and four thousand are to praise the LORD with the musical instruments I have provided for that purpose."

⁶David divided the Levites into groups corresponding to the sons of Levi: Gershon, Kohath and Merari.

⁷Belonging to the Gershonites:
Ladan and Shimei.
⁸The sons of Ladan:
Jehiel the first, Zetham and Joel—three in all.
⁹The sons of Shimei:
Shelomoth, Haziel and Haran—three in all.
These were the heads of the families of Ladan.
¹⁰And the sons of Shimei:
Jahath, Ziza, Jeush and Beriah.
These were the sons of Shimei—four in all.
¹¹Jahath was the first and Ziza the second, but Jeush and Beriah did not have many sons; so they were counted as one family with one assignment.

¹²The sons of Kohath:
Amram, Izhar, Hebron and Uzziel—four in all.
¹³The sons of Amram:
Aaron and Moses.
Aaron was set apart, he and his descendants forever, to consecrate the most holy things, to offer sacrifices before the LORD, to minister before him and to pronounce blessings in his name forever. ¹⁴The sons of Moses the man of God were counted as part of the tribe of Levi.
¹⁵The sons of Moses:
Gershom and Eliezer.
¹⁶The descendants of Gershom:
Shubael was the first.
¹⁷The descendants of Eliezer:
Rehabiah was the first.
Eliezer had no other sons, but the sons of Rehabiah were very numerous.
¹⁸The sons of Izhar:
Shelomith was the first.

19 The sons of Hebron:

Jeriah the first, Amariah the second, Jahaziel the third and Jekameam the fourth.

20 The sons of Uzziel:

Micah the first and Isshiah the second.

21 The sons of Merari:

Mahli and Mushi.

The sons of Mahli:

Eleazar and Kish.

22 Eleazar died without having sons: he had only daughters. Their cousins, the sons of Kish, married them.

23 The sons of Mushi:

Mahli, Eder and Jerimoth—three in all.

24 These were the descendants of Levi by their families—the heads of families as they were registered under their names and counted individually, that is, the workers twenty years old or more who served in the temple of the Lord. 25 For David had said, "Since the Lord, the God of Israel, has granted rest to his people and has come to dwell in Jerusalem forever, 26 the Levites no longer need to carry the tabernacle or any of the articles used in its service." 27 According to the last instructions of David, the Levites were counted from those twenty years old or more.

28 The duty of the Levites was to help Aaron's descendants in the service of the temple of the Lord: to be in charge of the courtyards, the side rooms, the purification of all sacred things and the performance of other duties at the house of God. 29 They were in charge of the bread set out on the table, the flour for the grain offerings, the unleavened wafers, the baking and the mixing, and all measurements of quantity and size. 30 They were also to stand every morning to thank and praise the Lord. They were to do the same in the evening 31 and whenever burnt offerings were presented to the Lord on Sabbaths and at New Moon festivals and at appointed feasts. They were to serve before the Lord regularly in the proper number and in the way prescribed for them.

32 And so the Levites carried out their responsibilities for the Tent of Meeting, for the Holy Place and, under their brothers the descendants of Aaron, for the service of the temple of the Lord.

24:1 These were the divisions of the sons of Aaron:

The sons of Aaron were Nadab, Abihu, Eleazar and Ithamar. 2 But Nadab and Abihu died before their father did, and they had no sons; so Eleazar and Ithamar served as the priests. 3 With the help of Zadok a descendant of Eleazar and Ahimelech a descendant of Ithamar, David separated them into divisions for their appointed order of ministering. 4 A larger number of leaders were found among Eleazar's descendants than among Ithamar's, and they were divided accordingly: sixteen heads of families from Eleazar's descendants and eight heads of families from Ithamar's descendants. 5 They divided them impartially by drawing lots, for there were officials of the sanctuary and officials of God among the descendants of both Eleazar and Ithamar.

6 The scribe Shemaiah son of Nethanel, a Levite, recorded their names in the presence of the king and of the officials: Zadok the priest, Ahimelech son of Abiathar and the heads of families of the priests and of the Levites—one family being taken from Eleazar and then one from Ithamar.

7 The first lot fell to Jehoiarib,

the second to Jedaiah,

8 the third to Harim,

the fourth to Seorim,

9 the fifth to Malkijah,

the sixth to Mijamin,

10 the seventh to Hakkoz,

the eighth to Abijah,

¹¹ the ninth to Jeshua,
  the tenth to Shecaniah,
¹² the eleventh to Eliashib,
  the twelfth to Jakim,
¹³ the thirteenth to Huppah,
  the fourteenth to Jeshebeab,
¹⁴ the fifteenth to Bilgah,
  the sixteenth to Immer,
¹⁵ the seventeenth to Hezir,
  the eighteenth to Happizzez,
¹⁶ the nineteenth to Pethahiah,
  the twentieth to Jehezkel,
¹⁷ the twenty-first to Jakin,
  the twenty-second to Gamul,
¹⁸ the twenty-third to Delaiah
  and the twenty-fourth to Maaziah.

¹⁹This was their appointed order of ministering when they entered the temple of the LORD, according to the regulations prescribed for them by their forefather Aaron, as the LORD, the God of Israel, had commanded him.

²⁰As for the rest of the descendants of Levi:
  from the sons of Amram: Shubael;
    from the sons of Shubael: Jehdeiah.
  ²¹ As for Rehabiah, from his sons:
  Isshiah was the first.
²² From the Izharites: Shelomoth;
  from the sons of Shelomoth: Jahath.
²³ The sons of Hebron: Jeriah the first, Amariah the second, Jahaziel the third
  and Jekameam the fourth.
²⁴ The son of Uzziel: Micah;
  from the sons of Micah: Shamir.
  ²⁵ The brother of Micah: Isshiah;
  from the sons of Isshiah: Zechariah.
²⁶ The sons of Merari: Mahli and Mushi.
  The son of Jaaziah: Beno.
²⁷ The sons of Merari:
  from Jaaziah: Beno, Shoham, Zaccur and Ibri.
²⁸ From Mahli: Eleazar, who had no sons.
²⁹ From Kish: the son of Kish:
  Jerahmeel.
³⁰ And the sons of Mushi: Mahli, Eder and Jerimoth.

These were the Levites, according to their families. ³¹They also cast lots, just as their brothers the descendants of Aaron did, in the presence of King David and of Zadok, Ahimelech, and the heads of families of the priests and of the Levites. The families of the oldest brother were treated the same as those of the youngest.

^{25:1}David, together with the commanders of the army, set apart some of the sons of Asaph, Heman and Jeduthun for the ministry of prophesying, accompanied by harps, lyres and cymbals. Here is the list of the men who performed this service:

²From the sons of Asaph:
  Zaccur, Joseph, Nethaniah and Asarelah. The sons of Asaph were under the supervision of Asaph, who prophesied under the king's supervision.
³As for Jeduthun, from his sons:
  Gedaliah, Zeri, Jeshaiah, Shimei, Hashabiah and Mattithiah, six in all, under the supervision of their father Jeduthun, who prophesied, using the harp in thanking and praising the LORD.
⁴As for Heman, from his sons:

Bukkiah, Mattaniah, Uzziel, Shubael and Jerimoth; Hananiah, Hinani, Elia-thah, Giddalti and Romamti-Ezer; Joshbekashah, Mallothi, Hothir and Mahazi-oth. ⁵All these were sons of Heman the king's seer. They were given him through the promises of God to exalt him. God gave Heman fourteen sons and three daughters.

⁶All these men were under the supervision of their fathers for the music of the temple of the LORD, with cymbals, lyres and harps, for the ministry at the house of God. Asaph, Jeduthun and Heman were under the supervision of the king. ⁷Along with their relatives—all of them trained and skilled in music for the LORD—they numbered 288. ⁸Young and old alike, teacher as well as student, cast lots for their duties.

⁹The first lot, which was for Asaph, fell to Joseph,	
his sons and relatives,	12
the second to Gedaliah,	
he and his relatives and sons,	12
¹⁰the third to Zaccur,	
his sons and relatives,	12
¹¹the fourth to Izri,	
his sons and relatives,	12
¹²the fifth to Nethaniah,	
his sons and relatives,	12
¹³the sixth to Bukkiah,	
his sons and relatives,	12
¹⁴the seventh to Jesarelah,	
his sons and relatives,	12
¹⁵the eighth to Jeshaiah,	
his sons and relatives,	12
¹⁶the ninth to Mattaniah,	
his sons and relatives,	12
¹⁷the tenth to Shimei,	
his sons and relatives,	12
¹⁸the eleventh to Azarel,	
his sons and relatives,	12
¹⁹the twelfth to Hashabiah,	
his sons and relatives,	12
²⁰the thirteenth to Shubael,	
his sons and relatives,	12
²¹the fourteenth to Mattithiah,	
his sons and relatives,	12
²²the fifteenth to Jerimoth,	
his sons and relatives,	12
²³the sixteenth to Hananiah,	
his sons and relatives,	12
²⁴the seventeenth to Joshbekashah,	
his sons and relatives,	12
²⁵the eighteenth to Hanani,	
his sons and relatives,	12
²⁶the nineteenth to Mallothi,	
his sons and relatives,	12
²⁷the twentieth to Eliathah,	
his sons and relatives,	12
²⁸the twenty-first to Hothir,	
his sons and relatives,	12
²⁹the twenty-second to Giddalti,	
his sons and relatives,	12
³⁰the twenty-third to Mahazioth,	
his sons and relatives,	12
³¹the twenty-fourth to Romamti-Ezer,	
his sons and relatives,	12

^{26:1}The divisions of the gatekeepers:

From the Korahites: Meshelemiah son of Kore, one of the sons of Asaph.
²Meshelemiah had sons:
 Zechariah the firstborn,
 Jediael the second,
 Zebadiah the third,
 Jathniel the fourth,
 ³Elam the fifth,
 Jehohanan the sixth
 and Eliehoenai the seventh.
⁴Obed-Edom also had sons:
 Shemaiah the firstborn,
 Jehozabad the second,
 Joah the third,
 Sacar the fourth,
 Nethanel the fifth,
 ⁵Ammiel the sixth,
 Issachar the seventh
 and Peullethai the eighth.
 (For God had blessed Obed-Edom.)

⁶His son Shemaiah also had sons, who were leaders in their father's family because they were very capable men. ⁷The sons of Shemaiah: Othni, Rephael, Obed and Elzabad; his relatives Elihu and Semakiah were also able men. ⁸All these were descendants of Obed-Edom; they and their sons and their relatives were capable men with the strength to do the work—descendants of Obed-Edom, 62 in all.
⁹Meshelemiah had sons and relatives, who were able men—18 in all.

¹⁰Hosah the Merarite had sons: Shimri the first (although he was not the first-born, his father had appointed him the first), ¹¹Hilkiah the second, Tabaliah the third and Zechariah the fourth. The sons and relatives of Hosah were 13 in all.

¹²These divisions of the gatekeepers, through their chief men, had duties for ministering in the temple of the Lord, just as their relatives had. ¹³Lots were cast for each gate, according to their families, young and old alike.

¹⁴The lot for the East Gate fell to Shelemiah. Then lots were cast for his son Zechariah, a wise counselor, and the lot for the North Gate fell to him. ¹⁵The lot for the South Gate fell to Obed-Edom, and the lot for the storehouse fell to his sons. ¹⁶The lots for the West Gate and the Shalleketh Gate on the upper road fell to Shuppim and Hosah.

Guard was alongside of guard: ¹⁷There were six Levites a day on the east, four a day on the north, four a day on the south and two at a time at the storehouse. ¹⁸As for the court to the west, there were four at the road and two at the court itself.

¹⁹These were the divisions of the gatekeepers who were descendants of Korah and Merari.

²⁰Their fellow Levites were in charge of the treasuries of the house of God and the treasuries for the dedicated things.

²¹The descendants of Ladan, who were Gershonites through Ladan and who were heads of families belonging to Ladan the Gershonite, were Jehieli, ²²the sons of Jehieli, Zetham and his brother Joel. They were in charge of the treasuries of the temple of the Lord.

²³From the Amramites, the Izharites, the Hebronites and the Uzzielites:

²⁴Shubael, a descendant of Gershom son of Moses, was the officer in charge of the treasuries. ²⁵His relatives through Eliezer: Rehabiah his son, Jeshaiah his son, Joram his son, Zicri his son and Shelomith his son. ²⁶Shelomith and his relatives were in charge of all the treasuries for the things dedicated by King David, by the heads of families who were the

commanders of thousands and commanders of hundreds, and by the other army commanders. [27]Some of the plunder taken in battle they dedicated for the repair of the temple of the LORD. [28]And everything dedicated by Samuel the seer and by Saul son of Kish, Abner son of Ner and Joab son of Zeruiah, and all the other dedicated things were in the care of Shelomith and his relatives.

[29]From the Izharites: Kenaniah and his sons were assigned duties away from the temple, as officials and judges over Israel.

[30]From the Hebronites: Hashabiah and his relatives—seventeen hundred able men—were responsible in Israel west of the Jordan for all the work of the LORD and for the king's service. [31]As for the Hebronites, Jeriah was their chief according to the genealogical records of their families. In the fortieth year of David's reign a search was made in the records, and capable men among the Hebronites were found at Jazer in Gilead. [32]Jeriah had twenty-seven hundred relatives, who were able men and heads of families, and King David put them in charge of the Reubenites, the Gadites and the half-tribe of Manasseh for every matter pertaining to God and for the affairs of the king.

David's concern for the worship of God in the temple went beyond the material preparations that he made for the construction of its building, just described (ch. 22). Of even more lasting significance were the arrangements that he made for the organization of its ministering personnel, the Levites (chs. 23–26). Guided by the Lord through his prophets (2 Chron 29:25), the king exercised his administrative genius to establish a system of procedures that helped maintain legitimate worship under his successors, that provided the operational framework for promoting the revival of Mosaic theocracy in the days of Ezra the Chronicler (see the introductory discussion to ch. 6), and that continued to meet the needs of God's worshiping people on into NT times (cf. 24:10 as reflected in Luke 1:5, 8).

In 970 B.C. (26:31, cf. comment on v. 1), David took a census of the male Levites aged thirty and above; and he found that they numbered 38,000 at that time. His fundamental idea was to divide the men of the tribe into four operational units (23:1–5). The remainder of chapter 23 pauses to review the Levitical genealogies (cf. ch. 6) by outlining the main clans and family groups (vv.6–23), and this is followed by a brief survey of their duties (vv.24–32). The four units are then enumerated: a main body of 24,000 were assigned "to supervise the work of the temple of the LORD" (ch. 24; cf. 23:4), and this chapter proceeds to describe how the priestly descendants of Aaron were organized into "groups" (23:6; "courses," KJV; cf. 24:1–19), as were also the nonpriestly Levites who assisted them (vv.20–31); 4,000 others were appointed as musicians (ch. 25); 4,000 worked as doorkeepers, under whom were incorporated a variety of positions such as the temple treasurers (26:1–28); and the remaining 6,000 "were assigned duties away from the temple, as officials and judges over Israel" (26:29–32). The priests, the musicians, and presumably the temple Levites as well were specifically assigned to twenty-four different courses. These subdivisions provided a means for rotating them in service on a monthly basis.

1 David's full life is witnessed to by the fact that these events are dated in the fortieth, i.e., the last, year of his reign (26:31; 29:27); they are identified, indeed, as being his "last instructions" (23:27).

The process by which Solomon was then "made . . . king" is passed over in Chronicles. The unhappy details of his disputed succession (see comment on 22:9;

cf. 1 Kings 1) and of the ruthless consolidation that followed on his recognition as ruler (1 Kings 2) were common knowledge and contributed little to the purposes Ezra was seeking to achieve.

2–3 The Levites "thirty years old or more" (v.3) were numbered, as in Moses' day (Num 4:3, 23), but also those down to twenty years of age (cf. on v.24). The total of 38,000 has, like so many of the figures in Chronicles, been roundly criticized, but unnecessarily so. Under Moses in the wilderness, a more limited enumeration of the Levites—only those who were between the age of thirty and fifty, and who were able to do the work of transporting the tabernacle—had produced a sum of 8,580 (Num 4:47–48); and the Hebrew tribes as a whole had averaged over 50,000 warriors each (1:46; 26:51). Under David the main Levitical body of 24,000 was divided into twenty-four monthly courses; and, as has been observed, "1,000 on duty at any one time, considering the scale of the work, is not unreasonable" (NBCrev., p. 381). The critics too have conceded, "There might have been more Levites than the work merited" (Wenham, "Large Numbers," p. 47).

5 The instruments the king "provided" exhibit another aspect to David's musical prowess, which was long remembered in Israel (Amos 6:5).

6 The review of the genealogy of Levi, which extends from this point down through v.23, is paralleled by the listings in 6:16–30 (cf. the introductory discussion to ch. 6 and particularly the comments to vv.1–3 for references to earlier biblical sources) and by those in 24:20–30. Minor variations exist in the spellings of some of the names and in other details.

7 The fact that the Gershonite "Ladan" is listed in first place connects him with Libni, which was the senior subclan of Gershon (see the charted genealogy of Levi, pp. 352–53). No allusion is made to Libni's son Jahath (as in 6:20), since the purpose of chapter 23 is not that of providing a complete genealogy but rather of marking out those divisions within the clans of Levi on which the Davidic organization was based.

8 Jehiel, Zetham, and Joel were ancient Levitical patriarchs. They should not be confused with the individual, division chiefs of David's day, as listed in 24:20–30 (cf. Jehdeiah, descended from the patriarch Shubael, v.20), though at certain points in chapter 24 only the patriarchal family-founders are listed, without the current chiefs (as in v.23).

9 Since the "Shimei" of this verse belongs to "the families of Ladan," he should probably be distinguished from the Shimei of vv.7 and 10, his great-uncle (after whom he seems to have been named), the brother of Libni (6:17).

11 By combining the senior Shimei's latter two families into "one assignment," or course, David secured nine Levitical courses organized out of the clan of Gershon: six from Ladan and three from Shimei.

14 As in Deuteronomy 33:1 and in the title to Psalm 90, Moses is set apart as "the man of God." He ranks as perhaps the greatest purely human figure in the OT (Deut 34:10–12; cf. the similarly crucial character of Paul, in establishing the people of God in the NT).

16–20 From the four sons of Kohath (not including the priestly descendants of Aaron, v.13), nine more courses are derived, though "the [Davidic division] chiefs" (NIV, "the first") are specified for only the first three (vv.16–18).

22 The sons of Mahli's son Kish "married their cousins," the daughters of Eleazar. The property of the subclan of Mahli was thus preserved intact, according to Moses' regulation (Num 36:6–9; cf. v.11); but this left it with only one course, of Kish.

23 The sons of Mahli's brother, Mushi, account for three more. So to bring Merari's courses up to six, and thus to gain a total for all Levi of twenty-four (nine, nine, and six), two more were probably derived from the four sons of the Merarite Jaaziah (24:27; cf. the chart of Levi on pp. 352–53, and Keil, pp. 258–60, 269).

24 David's Levitical census actually extended to those "twenty years old or more" (cf. Moses' lower limit of thirty, v.3). Yet even Moses had later included in the tribe's assigned work force Levites down to the age of twenty-five (Num 8:24); and David lowered it five years further. His reasoning may have been that with the permanent establishment of the tabernacle and the ark in Jerusalem, physical requirements for the service were no longer so demanding (v.26); or it may have been that he simply anticipated increasing needs in manpower for the construction and operation of the new temple.

29 "The bread set out on the table" was "the showbread" (cf. comment on 9:32). On "the grain offering," see the comment on 21:23.

30 The daily services of praise by the Levites accompanied the regular sacrifices that were prescribed for every morning and evening and were offered up by the priests (Exod 29:38–39; Num 28:3–8).

31 More elaborate sacrifices were required for the weekly sabbaths, for the beginnings of months, and for the annual feasts (Num 28:9–29:39). The last named involved Israel's five set celebrations, the "appointed feasts" of Passover, Pentecost, and Tabernacles, which was preceded in turn by Trumpets and the Day of Atonement (Lev 23). The first three were also designated pilgrimage feasts, for which the presence of every adult Israelite male was expected at the central sanctuary (Exod 23:14–17; Deut 16:16).

32 Ezra made it clear that the main body of the Levites were "under their brothers the [priestly] descendants of Aaron" (see Introduction: Purpose, 2). They were to be the priests' helpers (v.28) in such matters as preparing the sacrifices and other matters of service and in maintaining the sanctuary, just as Moses had prescribed (Num 3:6–9; 4:23–33).

24:1 Ezra now takes up the priests. This followed logically on his presentation concerning the Levites as a whole (ch. 23), of which they formed but a part (v.13). For observations on "the sons of Aaron" and the development of their priestly families, together with references to the biblical sources on which they are based, see the comments to 6:3–8.

The primary subject of the first nineteen verses of chapter 24 is how David organized the priests of his time into "divisions," or courses (see comment on 23:6). Ezra does, however, grant this a priority in treatment, before he describes the corresponding set of courses for the rest of the Levites in vv.20–31.

2 The death of Aaron's two older sons, together with the reasons involved, are recorded in Leviticus 10:1–2.

3 The men who advised David in establishing the courses were official representatives of the branches of Aaron's two surviving sons: for Eleazar it was the high priest Zadok; for Ithamar, however, it was no longer Abiathar (as in 15:11), "who was too old by this time to be troubled with administrative details" (NBCrev., p. 381), but (as in 18:16) his son Ahimelech II (24:6), grandson of that Ahimelech I (see comment on 6:3), who had served as high priest prior to David's own kingship (1 Sam 22:9–20; 23:6).

4 By dividing the priests into "sixteen" courses taken from the descendants of Eleazar and "eight" from those of Ithamar, David secured a total of twenty-four. This made possible either a system of monthly shifts, as had been the case for certain rotating groups of priests in Egypt's mortuary temples, ever since the Old Kingdom in the third millennium B.C. (Myers, *Chronicles*, 1:167), or a system of fortnightly shifts once each year, as developed in NT times (NBCrev., p. 381).

5 The king's impartiality is significant. Even though Eleazar, as senior surviving son, had been designated leader of the Levites and of those who worked in the sanctuary (Num 3:32), and even though he had eventually succeeded his father Aaron as high priest (20:28), it was only the physical fact of the "larger number" (v.4) of priests who traced their ancestry to him that gave Eleazar numerical superiority in courses; those of Ithamar received an equal standing (cf. the even-handedness of Exod 28:1, 40–43).

6 Assignment was objective, by lot (v.7); it was witnessed by the king, Zadok, and Ahimelech—all three; and it was recorded by an unbiased (and otherwise unknown) nonpriestly Levite, Shemaiah. Indeed, while the Hebrew of this verse is not completely clear, it would appear that the lots alternated between Eleazar and Ithamar for the first sixteen courses, with half of Eleazar's descendants having to accept the remaining eight (Keil, pp. 265–66).

7 Listings of the actual divisions appear not simply here but also at three later points in the OT, in postexilic times (Neh 10:2–8; 12:1–7; 12:12–21); and there are several incomplete references as well (1 Chron 9:10–12 [cf. comment on v.10]; Ezra 2:36–39; Neh 11:10–12). The eighth course is specifically cited in the NT (cf. v.10); the names of the first, second, fourth, ninth, and twenty-fourth have been found in a MS in the fourth cave at Qumran; and a fragmentary inscription from Caesarea may refer to the fifteenth, sixteenth, and seventeenth (Myers, *Chronicles*, 1:167–68).

With the passage of time, some of the Davidic courses died out or had to be consolidated with others, and new ones were formed to take their places. At the first return from exile in 537 B.C., only four courses were registered: David's second, third (Ezra 2:36–39; Neh 7:39–42), fifth (if Pashhur had come to represent the older Malkijah; cf. 9:12 and Neh 11:12), and sixteenth. By 520 twenty-two were again operative (Neh 12:1–7), but only half of them were the courses as originally organized by David; see the chart that follows.

THE PRIESTLY COURSES

1000 B.C.	537 B.C.	530(?)B.C.	500 B.C.	444 B.C.
1 Chron 24:7-18	Ezra 2:36-39	Neh 12:1-7	Neh 12:12-21	Neh 10:2-8
1. Jehoiarib		Seraiah	Seraiah	Seraiah
2. Jedaiah	Jedaiah	Jeremiah	Jeremiah	Azariah
3. Harim	Harim	Ezra	Ezra	Jeremiah
4. Seorim	Pashhur	Amariah	Amariah	Pashhur
5. Malkijah		Malluch	Malluch	Amariah
6. Mijamin		Hattush	------	Malkijah
7. Hakkoz	Hakkoz	Shecaniah	Shecaniah	Hattush
8. Abijah		Rehum	Harim	Shebaniah
9. Jeshua		Meremoth	Meremoth	Malluch
10. Shecaniah		Iddo	Iddo	Harim
11. Eliashib		Ginnethon	Ginnethon	Meremoth
12. Jakim		Abijah	Abijah	Obadiah
13. Huppah		Mijamin	Miniamin	------
14. Jeshebeab		Moadiah	Moadiah	Daniel
15. Bilgah		Bilgah	Bilgah	Ginnethon
16. Immer	Immer	Shemaiah	Shemaiah	Baruch
17. Hezir		Joiarib	Joiarib	Meshullam
18. Happizzez		Jedaiah	Jedaiah	Abijah
19. Pethahiah		Sallu	Sallu	Mijamin
20. Jehezkel		Amok	Amok	Maaziah
21. Jakin		Hilkiah	Hilkiah	Bilgai
22. Gamul		Jedaiah	Jedaiah**	Shemaiah
23. Delaiah				
24. Maaziah*				

*Curtis, p. 271.
**KD, *Ezra*, et al., p. 267.

Jehoiarib, who received the first assignment, headed the course that later produced the Maccabees (1 Macc 2:1; 14:29). Some negative critics have appealed to this phenomenon to cast doubt on the Davidic authenticity of the entire section (cf. Curtis, p. 269), dating its arrangement to Maccabean times, long after the postexilic lists of Nehemiah, in which Jehoiarib does not have the preeminence (though cf. the immediately *pre*exilic sequence of 1 Chron 9:10, in which Jedaiah, David's second, had already replaced Jehoiarib in its primary position).

10 The seventh course, of Hakkoz, is documented down into the days of the Maccabees (1 Macc 8:17). The eighth, Abijah, was the one under which Zechariah the father of John the Baptist performed his priestly ministry (Luke 1:5).

15 The family of the seventeenth course, Hezir, was prominent in intertestamental times; and the name appears on one of the major tombs in the valley to the east of Jerusalem (N. Avigad, *Ancient Monuments in the Kidron Valley* [Jerusalem: Bialik, 1954], pp. 37–78).

20 The phrase "the rest of the descendants of Levi" identifies the bulk of the Levites, who were not descended from Aaron and who served as temple assistants (cf. comment on 23:32). Verses 20–31 proceed to describe their allocation into divisions that corresponded to the priestly courses, just listed. For some reason the nine divisions of the clan of Gershon (23:7–11; cf. comment on v.11) are not discussed. The next nine (24:20–25) correspond to the family groups that arose from Levi's second son Kohath through his four sons, Amram, Izhar, Hebron, and Uzziel (23:12–20). For each of their courses, Ezra also listed the name of the man who served as division chief during the time of David—e.g., for "Shubael" (cf. note to 23:16) the chief was Jehdeiah (cf. comment on 23:8)—except for the four courses of Hebron, the names of whose Davidic chiefs may simply not have been available to Ezra when he was writing.

21 So for the clause "Isshiah was the first" (NIV) read rather, "Isshiah was the chief" (ASV, RSV) or "leader" (BV).

22 "Shelomoth" is a variant of the name "Shelomith" (23:18).

29–30 The last four courses listed for the clan of Merari correspond to the four Merarite family divisions described in 23:21–23, though the only chief's name to appear is that of Jerahmeel, representing in David's day the Mahlite group of Eleazar and Kish, which had been consolidated into one (see comment on 23:22). Two other courses, however, should probably be assigned to the groups descending from Jaaziah (cf. comment on 23:23). Jaaziah is stated to have been a Merarite (24:27) and yet is distinguished from Mahli and Mushai, the actual sons of Merari (v.26). He may have been a later member of the clan, the numerical growth of whose offspring had reached such proportions that by the time of David they achieved separate recognition among the Levitical courses.

31 The subject of the clause "they also cast lots" must be the chiefs of the divisions of the nonpriestly Levites, as sketched in vv.20–30. The stated correspondence of their method of organization with that of "their brothers the descendants of Aaron" favors a similar division of their followers into twenty-four rotating courses, even though not spelled out, as it was for the latter. Josephus claimed it for them (*Antiq.* VII, 365 [xiv.7]); and the contextual evidences—cf. the same sort of casting lots (vv.5, 7) and of emphasizing equality between "families of the oldest" and "the youngest" (cf. comments on vv.5–6)—suggest that he was right.

25:1 Chapter 25 concerns David's organization of the four thousand Levitical musicians (23:5) into courses of service that correspond to those of the priests and temple Levites (ch. 24). On the authenticity of this kind of activity by the king, see the comments to 6:31 and 16:4 (also the note to 15:16). The statement that they were set apart by David "with the commanders of the army" (*weśārê haṣṣābāʾ*) is rendered by

Myers (*Chronicles*, 1:170) as "(by David) and the cult officials." But while *śārê* may indeed describe "the officials of" (twice in 24:5) and *ṣābāʾ* their "service" (Num 8:25), the combination does mean "the commanders of the army" (KB, pp. 790–91). Keil would prefer to broaden this idea to include "the chiefs of Israel, as the host of Yahweh, Exod 12:17, 41, etc." (p. 269); and he refers to "the leaders of Israel," whom David is known to have assembled to assist him in organizing the Levites (23:2). Yet David did give high regard to the counsel of his military commanders (11:10; 12:32; 28:1), even in liturgical affairs (cf. 13:1; 15:25).

Division heads for the musicians consisted of "the sons of Asaph, Heman and Jeduthun," the chief musicians who belonged, respectively, to the Levitical clans of Gershon, Kohath, and Merari. David had commissioned them some thirty years earlier to minister before the ark in Jerusalem (16:4–7, 37, 41–42). Their service, moreover, is identified as a form of "prophesying" (cf. Heman's description as "the king's seer," v.5). The association is legitimate.

On the one hand, much Hebrew prophecy is set in a poetic form. In the following century God's Spirit used the Asaphite singer Jahaziel to predict victory for Jehoshaphat (cf. comment to 2 Chron 20:14, on the possible identification of his words with Ps 83); and we note also how earlier groups of prophets could go about their prophesying while in ceremonial procession and accompanied by instruments (1 Sam 10:5–6).

On the other hand, much of Hebrew poetry was religious (cf. comments on v.4) and could be called "prophecy"—not necessarily in the sense of special revelations from God's Spirit, but in the sense of general ascriptions of praise or of repetition in worship of prophecies or psalms that had already been revealed and recorded as Holy Scripture. This would apply particularly to group prophecy and "supervised prophecy," as in v.2 (cf. Aubrey R. Johnson, *The Cultic Prophet in Ancient Israel* [Cardiff: University of Wales, 1948]).

On the particular musical instruments, such as zithers (*kinnōrōt*, here rendered "harps"), or cymbals, see the comment on 15:16. It was with specific reference to the Levites who performed on these instruments that God, through Nathan and Gad, gave David his instructions for their designated stations (2 Chron 29:25); and the importance of music in worship should never be underestimated or disregarded by the people of God.

2 Asaph, however, "prophesied" to a degree beyond that of simply recreating the hymns of others, as directed "under the king's supervision." For Asaph and his descendants were directly inspired to compose at least twelve of the canonical psalms (50, 73–83; cf. comment on 16:5).

3 Jeduthun (as in 9:16; 16:41–42), also called Ethan (see comment on 6:44), was twice singled out in titles to the psalms as the chief musician responsible for the public presentation of King David's compositions (Pss 39, 62).

4 The name of the Kohathite musician Heman's fourth son, Shubael, of the subclan of Izhar, is not to be confused with the Kohathite course (No. "x" among those of the temple Levites, pp. 352–53) of the same name but drawn from the senior subclan of Amram (23:16; 24:20). Just as in chapter 23, nevertheless, the NIV reads "Shubael," with the LXX and 25:20, in place of the MT's Shebuel (cf. note to 23:16).

Commencing with Heman's sixth son, Hananiah, the names of his remaining nine sons could be translated consecutively from the Hebrew to constitute the following prayer, which fitly describes the work of Heman as "the king's seer" and poet:

(6th—Hananiah) Be gracious, Yahweh,
(7th—Hanani) be gracious to me!
(8th—Eliathah) My God, Thou,
(9th—Giddalti) I've praised
(10th—Romamti-Ezer) and exalted for helping.
(11th—Joshbekashah) Though sitting forlorn,
(12th—Mallothi) I've proclaimed
(13th—Hothir) highest (14th—Mahazioth) visions.

5 Heman's status as "seer" received further witness, if he was perhaps the inspired composer of some of twelve other psalms (cf. comment on v.2), which were written by "the sons of Korah" (Pss 42–49, 84–85, 87–88), of whom he was one (6:33, 37).

In Hebrew linguistic psychology, Heman's "horn" (NIV mg.) represents power—as with a ram or bull—and abundance. God's blessing him with "fourteen sons" would be, to the Oriental mind, nothing short of a doubly perfect heritage of power, though the mention of his "three daughters" reminds us of the lack of discrimination in OT worship, where women shared fully in the musical services (cf. Ps 68:25).

8 The singers "cast lots" to determine without prejudice the arrangement of the twenty-four courses, serving under the sons of Asaph, Heman, and Jeduthun. Yet all took part, whether "teacher," probably referring to the 288 skilled musicians of v.7 (twelve per course), or "student," which suggests that all 4,000 of the Levitical musicians were involved in the allocation.

9–12 As it worked out, the third, second, and fifth courses did go, respectively, to Asaph's three oldest sons.

26:1 The first twenty-eight verses of chapter 26 describe King David's third unit of Levites (cf. the introductory discussion to ch. 23), i.e., the 4,000 gatekeepers (23:5; cf. the comments to 9:19; 15:21). These were the temple guards (vv.1–19); and with them were included certain other officials, such as treasurers, who were responsible for the physical operation of the sanctuary (vv.20–28). The temple itself had not yet been built; but the king seems to have made these arrangements in anticipation, while the actual casting of lots "for each gate" (v.13) may have come later, after the structures were completed. God's assignment of this section of his Word to "businessmen" suggests something of the importance he attaches to each person's part in the kingdom, material and spiritual.

The Chronicler had already identified two groups of gatekeepers, appointed by David when the ark was first brought to Jerusalem (16:38); and a number of later listings occur as well, either shortly before the Exile (9:17–29) or after (Ezra 2:42; Neh 11:19; 12:25). A remarkable persistence is exhibited in the names of some of the Levitical gate-keeping families. An example appears in the first and leading group, of (Me)shelemiah (v.1 and comment on v.14), though also cited simply as Shallum (9:17, 19 [though cf. v.21]; Ezra 2:42) or Meshullam (Neh 12:25).

The name "Asaph," father of Kore, is an abbreviation for Ebiasaph, who was a son of the rebellious Kohathite, Korah (cf. comments to 6:22 and 9:19). It should therefore not be confused with that of David's contemporary Asaph, the more famous chief musician, who belonged to the clan of Gershon.

4 Obed-Edom was another Kohathite descendant of Korah (v.1), who is best known for the divine blessing that he received for having faithfully cared for the ark, following the death of Uzzah (13:13–14). Though he had gained appointment as a Levitical musician, he continued also to maintain his status as a doorkeeper (cf. comments to 15:21; 16:38).

8 In the thirty years since the ark first came to Jerusalem, the number of those associated with Obed-Edom exhibited a net decrease of six, down to sixty-two (cf. 16:38).

9 Yet with the 18 "sons and relatives" of Meshelemiah, plus 13 more of Hosah (v.11), the total number of hereditary leaders for the sanctuary guards totals 93. By the time of Jerusalem's fall in 586 B.C., the figure had risen to 212 (cf. comment to 9:22), though the number of Levites available to serve under them may have become much less than the 4,000 present in David's day (23:5).

10 The king had commissioned Hosah of Merari to be a gatekeeper along with Obed-Edom (16:38).

13 The purpose of the "lots" that "were cast" was to assign the gatekeepers to locations about the sanctuary, not, at this point, to determine periods for their rotation, as had been the case for the priests, temple Levites, and musicians (chs. 24 –25).

14 "Shelemiah" (cf. NIV mg.) represents an abbreviated form of the name Meshelemiah (vv.1–2, 9). Together with his son Zechariah, he and his associated leaders received responsibility for two of the gates, east and north, leaving one each for Obed-Edom and Hosah.

15 Because the palace complex lay to the south of the Mount Moriah sanctuary, some have questioned the possibility of a south gate, "though it probably cannot be ruled out altogether" (Myers, *Chronicles*, 1:77, citing Ezek 40:24, 28). Most of the palaces, however, were erected after David's time (1 Kings 7:1–12); and even then their presence would seem to suggest the need for such a gate, for both the rulers and the people (Ezek 46:9–10). Obed-Edom was honored with this assignment toward the south and its palaces (cf. comment to 15:21).

16 The "Shalleketh Gate" is known only to have faced west and to have been located on the "upper [or 'ascending' NASB] road," probably one coming northward up through the Tyropoeon Valley from the lower city to the higher elevation of Mount Moriah. The word "Shalleketh" itself is a proper noun (cf. J. Simons, *Jerusalem in the Old Testament* [Leiden: Brill, 1952], p. 426). In Isaiah 6:13 *šalleket* means a "cutting down," as of a tree; but this hardly justifies Stinespring's criticism that "here the Chronicler forgets entirely his historical pose and describes the temple as it was in his time" (*Oxford Annotated Bible*, in loc.).

"Shuppim" is not otherwise identified, but his association with Hosah suggests that he may have been another leading gatekeeper from the clan of Merari.

17 Because the east gate was the main one, six guards were assigned to it, as compared with four to the north (and to the other directions). This gave Meshelemiah ten guard posts.

Since the latest noun ($^{a}supp\hat{\imath}m$) is plural, it should perhaps be rendered, here and in v.15, as "storehouses" (Myers, *Chronicles*, 1:175), and the preceding phrase as "two and two" (KJV, ASV) or "two each" (BV). This would then give Obed-Edom four guard posts at the south gate and four more at the storehouses, making a total of eight.

18 With Hosah's four posts at the west gate and two at the "court" (Heb., *parbār*, a term of uncertain meaning, but probably denoting a colonnade or court), his group of six stations brings us up to a total of twenty-four guard posts that were assigned by lot (v.13; cf. this same number of lots for the other units of Levi, chs. 24–25).

20 The gatekeepers' "positions of trust" (see comments to 9:22) included two major treasurerships: the one over the treasuries of the temple (vv.20–22), with their offerings and valuable equipment (cf. 9:28–29), and the other over the treasuries of dedicated objects (vv.23–28).

21 The former were placed in the charge of "Jehieli," which is an adjectival form meaning "Jehielites" (the group of Jehiel). This name, in turn, identifies the Gershonite course no. i of temple Levites (cf. chart on pp. 352–53).

22 The treasurers chosen from "Zetham and . . . Joel," which are Gershonite courses nos. ii and iii (23:8), are then called "sons of Jehiel"; for the leadership was recognized as pertaining to the senior branch.

23–24 The latter treasuries were placed under the care of Levites chosen from the clan of Kohath and, particularly, from within its four listed subclans, from the "Amramite" sons of Moses. These belonged to the courses nos. x ("Shubael") and xi ("Rehabiah").

25 In David's day the individual treasurer for the dedicated objects was from Rahabiah, i.e., "Shelomoth" (ASV)—reading this spelling with the consonantal MT in vv.25–26 and the LXX[BL] in v.28, instead of Shelomith (NIV). His name is not to be confused with Shelomoth, Gershonite course no. iv of the temple Levites (23:9), or with Shelomith, Kohathite course no. xii, from the subclan of Izhar (23:18; cf. comment on 24:22).

26 Examples of "the things dedicated by King David" are cited in 18:11 and 2 Chronicles 5:1.

29 The latter four verses of chapter 26 describe David's fourth and last major operational unit of Levi, the six thousand external officials and judges (23:4). Moses himself had first directed that the Levites, who would be responsible to teach the Word of God (Deut 33:10), should perform the corresponding function of interpreting it in judgment (Deut 17:9; cf. 2 Chron 19:8–11). These officers were then drawn primarily from the second and third subclans of Kohath, namely Izhar and Hebron. On the Izharite Kenaniah, King David's "head Levite," see the comment on 15:22.

427

30–31 Among the Hebronites, Hashabiah is probably that son of Kemuel who served as David's "officer over the tribe of Levi" (27:16–17); and Jeriah identifies the senior course, no. xiii, belonging to the subclan of Hebron (23:19). These two, between them, accounted for 4,400 (1,700 plus 2,700, v.32) of the 6,000 Levitical judges.

32 The statistic that 2,700 Levites maintained the laws of "God and . . . the king" among the tribes west of the Jordan (v.30) "seems strange . . . but contains a hint of the importance of the district of Gilead" (Curtis, p. 288).

Notes

4 The words "David said" are not in the Hebrew text but are necessarily supplied on the basis of the first person in v.5.
16 The NIV form "Shubael" (שׁוּבָאֵל, šûḇāʾēl; corresponding to LXX^AB and 24:20) is here properly given preference over the MT's "Shebuel" (שְׁבוּאֵל, šᵉḇûʾēl), despite the latter's attestation in 26:24 (cf. note below) and archaelogically on an eighth-century jar-handle stamp (Myers, *Chronicles*, 1:158).
24:23 As indicated by the NIV mg., the word "Hebron" is necessarily supplied on the basis of 23:19; and the words "the first" (as in BV), from the following context (not "the chief," ASV, RSV: cf. comment on 24:21, since v.23 is dealing with ancient patriarchal families, not David's division chiefs).
25:4 For Heman's fifth son, read "Jeremoth" (יְרֵמוֹת, yᵉrēmôṯ), with the LXX and v.22, rather than MT's "Jerimoth" (יְרִימוֹת, yᵉrîmôṯ).
26:14–16 Added to each of the Hebrew words for the four directions, NIV has supplied the clarifying word "gate," based on the context of v.13.
24 NIV reads "Shubael," with the Vulgate and 24:20 (cf. note to 23:16), in place of MT's "Shebuel."

4. *The civil organization*

27:1–34

¹This is the list of the Israelites—heads of families, commanders of thousands and commanders of hundreds, and their officers, who served the king in all that concerned the army divisions that were on duty month by month throughout the year. Each division consisted of 24,000 men.

²In charge of the first division, for the first month, was Jashobeam son of Zabdi-el. There were 24,000 men in his division. ³He was a descendant of Perez and chief of all the army officers for the first month.

⁴In charge of the division for the second month was Dodai the Ahohite; Mikloth was the leader of his division. There were 24,000 men in his division.

⁵The third army commander, for the third month, was Benaiah son of Jehoiada the priest. He was chief and there were 24,000 men in his division. ⁶This was the Benaiah who was a mighty man among the Thirty and was over the Thirty. His son Ammizabad was in charge of his division.

⁷The fourth, for the fourth month, was Asahel the brother of Joab; his son Zebadiah was his successor. There were 24,000 men in his division.

8 The fifth, for the fifth month, was the commander Shamhuth the Izrahite. There were 24,000 men in his division.

9 The sixth, for the sixth month, was Ira the son of Ikkesh the Tekoite. There were 24,000 men in his division.

10 The seventh, for the seventh month, was Helez the Pelonite, an Ephraimite. There were 24,000 men in his division.

11 The eighth, for the eighth month, was Sibbecai the Hushathite, a Zerahite. There were 24,000 men in his division.

12 The ninth, for the ninth month, was Abiezer the Anathothite, a Benjamite. There were 24,000 men in his division.

13 The tenth, for the tenth month, was Maharai the Netophathite, a Zerahite. There were 24,000 men in his division.

14 The eleventh, for the eleventh month, was Benaiah the Pirathonite, an Ephraimite. There were 24,000 men in his division.

15 The twelfth, for the twelfth month, was Heldai the Netophathite, from the family of Othniel. There were 24,000 men in his division.

16 The officers over the tribes of Israel:

over the Reubenites: Eliezer son of Zicri;
over the Simeonites: Shephatiah son of Maacah;
17 over Levi: Hashabiah son of Kemuel;
over Aaron: Zadok;
18 over Judah: Elihu, a brother of David;
over Issachar: Omri son of Michael;
19 over Zebulun: Ishmaiah son of Obadiah;
over Naphtali: Jerimoth son of Azriel;
20 over the Ephraimites: Hoshea son of Azaziah;
over half the tribe of Manasseh: Joel son of Pedaiah;
21 over the half-tribe of Manasseh in Gilead: Iddo son of Zechariah;
over Benjamin: Jaasiel son of Abner;
22 over Dan: Azarel son of Jeroham.

These were the officers over the tribes of Israel.

23 David did not take the number of the men twenty years old or less, because the Lord had promised to make Israel as numerous as the stars in the sky. 24 Joab son of Zeruiah began to count the men but did not finish. Wrath came on Israel on account of this numbering, and the number was not entered in the book of the annals of King David.

25 Azmaveth son of Adiel was in charge of the royal storehouses.

Jonathan son of Uzziah was in charge of the storehouses in the outlying districts, in the towns, the villages and the watchtowers.

26 Ezri son of Kelub was in charge of the field workers who farmed the land.

27 Shimei the Ramathite was in charge of the vineyards.

Zabdi the Shiphmite was in charge of the produce of the vineyards for the wine vats.

28 Baal-Hanan the Gederite was in charge of the olive and sycamore-fig trees in the western foothills.

Joash was in charge of the supplies of olive oil.

29 Shitrai the Sharonite was in charge of the herds grazing in Sharon.

Shaphat son of Adlai was in charge of the herds in the valleys.

30 Obil the Ishmaelite was in charge of the camels.

Jehdeiah the Meronothite was in charge of the donkeys.

31 Jaziz the Hagrite was in charge of the flocks.

All these were the officials in charge of King David's property.

32 Jonathan, David's uncle, was a counselor, a man of insight and a scribe. Jehiel son of Hacmoni took care of the king's sons.

33 Ahithophel was the king's counselor.

Hushai the Arkite was the king's friend. 34 Ahithophel was succeeded by Jehoiada son of Benaiah and by Abiathar.

Joab was the commander of the royal army.

Having outlined David's religious organization (chs. 23–26), the Chronicler adds chapter 27 on his civil arrangements. The year 970 B.C. had constituted a high-water mark in Israel's political experience; and its splendor was a far cry from the impoverished condition of the Jewish subprovince that existed in Ezra's day (cf. Hag 2:16–17; Zech 14:10). But even though it could have had little organizational relevance for the returned exiles in 450—and even less for us today—this rehearsal of past glories must have thrilled Ezra's discouraged people (as it can us as well) with the truth that tangible political results are included in God's decree for his faithful servants (cf. Rev 2:26).

First Chronicles 27 surveys three aspects of the Davidic regime: its military system, of twelve army corps, each with its own commanding general and twenty-four skilled chiefs (cf. comment to v.1), who were committed to a term of active duty one month each year (vv.1–15); the ethnic organization, of twelve listed Hebrew tribes (cf. comment to v.17) in their various geographical regions, each with its responsible officer (vv.16–24); and the royal administration, including both the central "cabinet" executives and the overseers of the king's properties in the field (vv.25–34).

1 A significant key to our understanding of these first fifteen verses appears in the Chronicler's introductory emphasis on the "commanders of thousands" (*śārê hā-ʾᵃlāpîm*). When the verse therefore concludes by referring to each "division's 24,000 *ʾalep*" (there is no word for "men" in the original), this phrase may indicate "chiefs" (who could command a thousand troops) rather than numerical "thousands" (cf. comment to 7:3–4, and the stress in 27:3 on leaders of "all the army officers for the first month"). For while the idea of a national militia of 288,000 organized into twelve corps of "24,000 men" each is reasonable enough (cf. over 600,000 in Moses' day, Exod 12:37; Num 1:46; 2:32; 11:21; 26:51), the alternative rendering of "24 chief men" (throughout vv.1–15) has two advantages: negatively, it relieves the capital of the congestion of some 48,000 rotating troops, who, literally, "came in and went out month by month" (NASB); and positively, as Wenham proposes, "this would be a means whereby the king could keep in touch with his military leaders" ("Large Numbers," p. 48; cf. "Validity," p. 217).

2 Each "lieutenant general" who commanded one of the twelve army corps was a distinguished military figure in his own right and is cited in the roster of David's heros (11:11–47 and 2 Sam 23:8–39), though with occasional variations in spelling and with facts of family information added here. "Jashobeam" was the first of "the Three" great champions (11:11).

3 Jashobeam's ancestor "Perez" was the fourth son of Judah and founder of its major clan (cf. chart, pp. 332–33).

4 "Dodai" was the father of Eleazar, the second of "the Three" (see comment on 11:12). "Mikloth was the leader," or, as we might say, executive officer, for this second corps.

5-6 The exploits (see 11:22–25) of "Benaiah" (v.5) son of Jehoiada the priest (cf. comment on 12:27–28) elevated him to the leadership of David's Cretan guard (see comment on 18:17). This probably explains why "his son Ammizabad" exercised actual command over the third corps. On Benaiah's position in respect to "the Thirty," see 11:25 and the comments on 11:15 and 12:4.

7 Holding the title of commander of the fourth corps (but "merely *honoris causâ*," Keil, p. 286) was Asahel, the first man to be named in David's legion of honor, which made up "the Thirty." "His son Zebadiah was his successor," due to Asahel's untimely death at the hands of Abner (see comments on 11:26).

8 Over the fifth corps was "Shamhuth the Izrahite." This defining adjective really means "of Zerah," the other leading clan of Judah (cf. comments on v.3 and the equivalent term "Zerahite," vv.11, 13). His name appears third among the Thirty (11:27).

9–15 The remaining seven generals, for the sixth to the twelfth corps, were selected from among the next nine members of the Thirty (11:27–31). "Heldai," commander of the twelfth (27:15), was a descendant of Othniel, the first of the Hebrew judges (Judg 1:13; 3:9–11).

17 While most of the tribes of Israel had one outstanding individual chosen to be the ethnic "officer" (vv.16–25), two were appointed for Levi: the high priest "Zadok," to represent its Aaronic or priestly branch (cf. comments on 6:8; 12:27–28; 16:39), and "Hashabiah," for the remainder (see comment on 26:30–31). Manasseh also had two officers, corresponding to its two regional halves, west (v.20) and east (v.21) of the Jordan. The tribes of Gad and Asher remain unlisted, either because the names of their tribal officers were not available to Ezra, or because they were dropped from the text by later copyists' mistakes.

18 Judah's representative, Elihu, is called "a brother of David." This could possibly identify the unnamed brother born between Ozen and David; but it then becomes difficult to explain why his name was not mentioned in 2:15, if he did survive (cf. comment on 2:15). Elihu may actually have been a more distant "brother" (= relative); or the name might be a variant for Jesse's oldest son, Eliab (2:13).

21 The tribal officer for Benjamin was "Jaasiel," a "son of Abner" who had commanded the troops of his nephew King Saul and had been the power behind Saul's son Ish-bosheth (26:28; cf. chart, pp. 362–63, and the comments on 8:33 and 11:2).

23 The Lord's promise "to make Israel as numerous as the stars" dated back to Abraham (Gen 15:5; 22:17; cf. 12:2; 13:16), over a thousand years before David. The king, therefore, did not order a total numbering of Israel (including minors); for that might have seemed to cast doubt on the prophecy. He did, however, sinfully decree a census of the men of fighting age, apparently through a lack of faith in God's protection of his kingdom (cf. comment on 21:3).

24 The Hebrew of this verse says simply that Joab "began to count but did not finish." Some have proposed that he started to enroll Israel's minors too (North, "The Chronicler," 1:413), but this seems unlikely in light of his opposition to the whole project (cf. comment on 21:6) and Ezra's contextual stress on "fighting men" (v.5; cf. v.3). Joab put off "even this numbering . . . [of] the men capable of bearing arms" (Keil, p. 287).

25 In the remainder of the chapter, with its list of royal administrators (vv.25–32), Azmaveth must have had charge of the central stores in Jerusalem, which contrasts with Jonathan's similar post "in the outlying districts."

28 "The western foothills" (Heb., šᵉpēlāh, "Shephelah") constituted the piedmont area between the Philistine coastal plain and the Judean hill country. The king depended on his personal properties in all the areas such as these, rather (as far as we can tell) than on taxes, to support his growing administration.

32 A concluding list of major counselors supplements the earlier outlines of David's cabinet as presented in 18:15–17 (cf. 2 Sam 8:15–18; 20:23–26).

33 Hushai's post of "king's friend" (cf. 2 Sam 15:37) may have begun on an informal and personal basis; but it became an official advisory position (cf. 1 Kings 4:5), for which parallels exist in ancient Egypt (examples are listed in Myers, *Chronicles*, 1:186). Ahithophel was the ill-fated "counselor" who deserted David for his son, the rebel Absalom (2 Sam 15:12, 31; 16:20–23), but whose advice was subverted by Hushai (15:32–37; 17:1–16).

34 After his suicide (17:23), Ahithophel "was succeeded by Jehoiada," son of the commander Benaiah (cf. comment on 27:5), and grandson of his namesake, the militant priest (see comment on 12:27–28).

Notes

Some critical scholars exhibit an ambivalence toward this chapter, claiming on the one hand that "the source may be a compilation of Davidic accounts . . . which contained both historical and fictional material" (Myers, *Chronicles*, 1:182), and, yet on the other hand, that it "reflects the situation in the Chronicler's period" (ibid., p. LVI).

27 The "wine vats," over whose vineyards Zabdi was placed in charge, are אֹצְרוֹת הַיַּיִן (ʾōṣᵉrôṯ hayyayin), literally, "the supplies of wine," but may refer to "wine cellars" (M. Dahood, "Is ʾeben Yiśrāʾel a divine title [Gen 49:24]?" *Biblica* 40 [1959]:164).

5. *Final words*

28:1–29:30

¹David summoned all the officials of Israel to assemble at Jerusalem: the officers over the tribes, the commanders of the divisions in the service of the king, the commanders of thousands and commanders of hundreds, and the officials in charge of all the property and livestock belonging to the king and his sons, together with the palace officials, the mighty men and all the brave warriors. ²King David rose to his feet and said: "Listen to me, my brothers and my people. I had it in my heart to build a house as a place of rest for the ark of the covenant of the LORD, for the footstool of our God, and I made plans to build it. ³But God said to me, 'You are not to build a house for my Name, because you are a warrior and have shed blood.' ⁴"Yet the LORD, the God of Israel, chose me from my whole family to be king

over Israel forever. He chose Judah as leader, and from the house of Judah he chose my family, and from my father's sons he was pleased to make me king over all Israel. [5]Of all my sons—and the LORD has given me many—he has chosen my son Solomon to sit on the throne of the kingdom of the LORD over Israel. [6]He said to me: 'Solomon your son is the one who will build my house and my courts, for I have chosen him to be my son, and I will be his father. [7]I will establish his kingdom forever if he is unswerving in carrying out my commands and laws, as is being done at this time.'

[8]"So now I charge you in the sight of all Israel and of the assembly of the LORD, and in the hearing of our God: Be careful to follow all the commands of the LORD your God, that you may possess this good land and pass it on as an inheritance to your descendants forever.

[9]"And you, my son Solomon, acknowledge the God of your father, and serve him with wholehearted devotion and with a willing mind, for the LORD searches every heart and understands every motive behind the thoughts. If you seek him, he will be found by you; but if you forsake him, he will reject you forever. [10]Consider now, for the LORD has chosen you to build a temple as a sanctuary. Be strong and do the work."

[11]Then David gave his son Solomon the plans for the portico of the temple, its buildings, its storerooms, its upper parts, its inner rooms and the place of atonement. [12]He gave him the plans of all that the Spirit had put in his mind for the courts of the temple of the LORD and all the surrounding rooms, for the treasuries of the temple of God and for the treasuries for the dedicated things. [13]He gave him instructions for the divisions of the priests and Levites, and for all the work of serving in the temple of the LORD, as well as for all the articles to be used in its service. [14]He designated the weight of gold for all the gold articles to be used in various kinds of service, and the weight of silver for all the silver articles to be used in various kinds of service: [15]the weight of gold for the gold lampstands and their lamps, with the weight for each lampstand and its lamps; and the weight of silver for each silver lampstand and its lamps, according to the use of each lampstand; [16]the weight of gold for each table for consecrated bread; the weight of silver for the silver tables; [17]the weight of pure gold for the forks, sprinkling bowls and pitchers; the weight of gold for each gold dish; the weight of silver for each silver dish; [18]and the weight of the refined gold for the altar of incense. He also gave him the plan for the chariot, that is, the cherubim of gold that spread their wings and shelter the ark of the covenant of the LORD.

[19]"All this," David said, "I have in writing from the hand of the LORD upon me, and he gave me understanding in all the details of the plan."

[20]David also said to Solomon his son, "Be strong and courageous, and do the work. Do not be afraid or discouraged, for the LORD God, my God, is with you. He will not fail you or forsake you until all the work for the service of the temple of the LORD is finished. [21]The divisions of the priests and Levites are ready for all the work on the temple of God, and every willing man skilled in any craft will help you in all the work. The officials and all the people will obey your every command."

[29:1]Then King David said to the whole assembly: "My son Solomon, the one whom God has chosen, is young and inexperienced. The task is great, because this palatial structure is not for man but for the LORD God. [2]With all my resources I have provided for the temple of my God—gold for the gold work, silver for the silver, bronze for the bronze, iron for the iron and wood for the wood, as well as onyx for the settings, turquoise, stones of various colors, and all kinds of fine stone and marble—all of these in large quantities. [3]Besides, in my devotion to the temple of my God I now give my personal treasures of gold and silver for the temple of my God, over and above everything I have provided for this holy temple: [4]three thousand talents of gold (gold of Ophir) and seven thousand talents of refined silver, for the overlaying of the walls of the buildings, [5]for the gold work and the silver work, and for all the work to be done by the craftsmen. Now, who is willing to consecrate himself today to the LORD?"

[6]Then the leaders of families, the officers of the tribes of Israel, the commanders of thousands and commanders of hundreds, and the officials in charge of the

433

king's work gave willingly. ⁷They gave toward the work on the temple of God five thousand talents and ten thousand darics of gold, ten thousand talents of silver, eighteen thousand talents of bronze and a hundred thousand talents of iron. ⁸Any who had precious stones gave them to the treasury of the temple of the LORD in the custody of Jehiel the Gershonite. ⁹The people rejoiced at the willing response of their leaders, for they had given freely and wholeheartedly to the LORD. David the king also rejoiced greatly.

¹⁰David praised the LORD in the presence of the whole assembly, saying,

> "Praise be to you, O LORD,
>   God of our father Israel,
>   from everlasting to everlasting.
> ¹¹Yours, O LORD, is the greatness and the power
>   and the glory and the majesty and the splendor,
>   for everything in heaven and earth is yours.
> Yours, O LORD, is the kingdom;
>   you are exalted as head over all.
> ¹²Wealth and honor come from you;
>   you are the ruler of all things.
> In your hands are strength and power
>   to exalt and give strength to all.
> ¹³Now, our God, we give you thanks,
>   and praise your glorious name.

¹⁴"But who am I, and who are my people, that we should be able to give as generously as this? Everything comes from you, and we have given you only what comes from your hand. ¹⁵We are aliens and strangers in your sight, as were all our forefathers. Our days on earth are like a shadow, without hope. ¹⁶O LORD our God, as for all this abundance that we have provided for building you a temple for your Holy Name, it comes from your hand, and all of it belongs to you. ¹⁷I know, my God, that you test the heart and are pleased with integrity. All these things have I given willingly and with honest intent. And now I have seen with joy how willingly your people who are here have given to you. ¹⁸O LORD, God of our fathers Abraham, Isaac and Israel, keep this desire in the hearts of your people forever, and keep their hearts loyal to you. ¹⁹And give my son Solomon the wholehearted devotion to keep your commands, requirements and decrees and to do everything to build the palatial structure for which I have provided."

²⁰Then David said to the whole assembly, "Praise the LORD your God." So they all praised the LORD, the God of their fathers; they bowed low and fell prostrate before the LORD and the king.

²¹The next day they made sacrifices to the LORD and presented burnt offerings to him: a thousand bulls, a thousand rams and a thousand male lambs, together with their drink offerings, and other sacrifices in abundance for all Israel. ²²They ate and drank with great joy in the presence of the LORD that day.

Then they acknowledged Solomon son of David as king a second time, anointing him before the LORD to be ruler and Zadok to be priest. ²³So Solomon sat on the throne of the LORD as king in place of his father David. He prospered and all Israel obeyed him. ²⁴All the officers and mighty men, as well as all of King David's sons, pledged their submission to King Solomon.

²⁵The LORD highly exalted Solomon in the sight of all Israel and bestowed on him royal splendor such as no king over Israel ever had before.

²⁶David son of Jesse was king over all Israel. ²⁷He ruled over Israel forty years —seven in Hebron and thirty-three in Jerusalem. ²⁸He died at a good old age, having enjoyed long life, wealth and honor. His son Solomon succeeded him as king.

²⁹As for the events of King David's reign, from beginning to end, they are written in the records of Samuel the seer, the records of Nathan the prophet and the records of Gad the seer, ³⁰together with the details of his reign and power, and the circumstances that surrounded him and Israel and the kingdoms of all the other lands.

434

The occasion for the final chapters of 1 Chronicles is a continuation of what was introduced in chapter 23: the assembling by the king of the leaders of Israel (23:2 = 28:1 and 29:1). The date is still 970 B.C. (26:31), and the subject is a final portion of "the last instructions of David" (23:27). The king's purpose has been not simply to organize the Levites on a permanent basis (chs. 23–26), but also to arouse the whole nation to the momentous task of erecting God's temple in Jerusalem (cf. 22:6, 11, 19). Now David once again charged the people (28:2–8) and his son Solomon (vv.9 –10) to consecrate themselves to this holy effort. David then presented his son with the inspired, written plans for the temple (vv.11–19) and encouraged him for the work that lay ahead (vv.20–21). He turned also to the nation, represented by its assembled leaders, and urged on them an all-out campaign of giving for the building (29:1–5). They rose to the challenge (vv.6–9), and David praised the Lord for their devotion (vv.10–22). Solomon was then confirmed on the throne of Israel by a second ceremony of anointing (cf. comment on v.22), and David passed on to his eternal reward (vv.22–30).

In describing David's plans for building the temple, Chronicles has paid special attention to portray David as a second Moses and Solomon as a second Joshua. In "Accession of Solomon," Williamson shows in detail how that was done. So does Dillard in "Chronicler's Solomon." Their arguments go as follows. In spite of many achievements by both Moses and David, neither one finished the task. Moses did not lead the people into the Promised Land, nor did David build the temple. Furthermore in both cases it was God who prohibited them from completing the work. Since the task fell on their successors, Chronicles depicts Solomon as a second Joshua by noting several resemblances between the two: (1) both were chosen privately and declared the support of all the people; (2) both received the support of the people without resistance or opposition; (3) both were magnified by God; (4) both led God's people into "rest." Aside from these similiarities, the language used in describing these events is striking: (5) both were told, "Be strong and courageous" (Deut 31:6; 1 Chron 22:13); "The LORD your God goes with you" (Deut 31:6, 8, 23; Josh 1:5, 9; 1 Chron 22:11, 16); and "He will never leave you nor forsake you" (Deut 31:6, 8; Josh 1:5; 1 Chron 28:20). These similarities show Joshua and Solomon as the ones chosen by God to finish the great work of their predecessors. (SBM)

1–2 On the king's previous desire to build a temple, see 17:1–4. The structure is here identified as "a place of rest for the ark" (Ps 132:8, 14; i.e., a more permanent one than the tent in which it had been kept heretofore, 16:1) and as God's "footstool" (Ps 132:7; Lam 2:1). The latter term points specifically to "the place of atonement" or "mercy seat" (v.11, i.e., the golden cover of the ark, over which the glory-cloud of God's presence was enthroned; Exod 25:20–22; 2 Sam 6:2).

3 David's desire to build the temple, however, had been denied because of his excessive bloodshed (cf. comment on 22:8). The king's public explanation at this point corresponds to what he had already told Solomon privately (22:7–16).

4 David's statement that God "chose me from my whole family to be king over Israel forever" must refer, not to him personally, but to his "family," i.e., his dynasty (cf. vv.5, 7), which would culminate in Jesus Christ, who would reign forever (17:14). The divine choice had been revealed through a process of progressive elimination: from the whole of national "Israel," through the tribe of "Judah," down to the

435

Davidic "family" in particular (Gen 28:14; 35:10–11; 49:10; 1 Sam 16:1–3; 1 Chron 17:16–17, 23–27). Compare its earlier stages of clarification: from "the seed of woman," through Noah and Shem, to Abraham (Gen 3:15; 6:17–18; 9:26; 12:1–3; Payne, *Theology,* pp. 258–60, 283).

5 Yet in a deeper sense what David acknowledged was not his own kingship but "the kingdom of the LORD over Israel." He, and all of earth's rulers, are but vice-regents, deputies who act as representatives of God to uphold his standards (29:23; 1 Sam 12:14; Rom 13:1–6).

6-7 Solomon did build God's "house" (v.6; 2 Chron 5:1); but as far as being "established" (v.7), or being "chosen to be" God's "son" (v.6) are concerned, v.7 states an explicit condition: "*if* he is unswerving in carrying out my laws"—which Solomon was not (1 Kings 11:1–11). Moreover between God's words "Solomon . . . will build my house" and "I have chosen him to be my son," the full prophecy, through Nathan, had originally included an intervening statement that shifted the point of reference beyond Solomon to the more distant future, i.e., "and I will establish his throne forever" (17:12). That is, the fulfillment of true sonship to God the "Father" was not achieved by Solomon (cf. comment on 22:10); it was "an ideal that actualized only in Christ" (Payne, *Prophecy,* p. 226).

9 David's appeal to his son to serve God with his whole heart and a "willing mind" parallels his similar final admonition recorded in 1 Kings 2:2–4.

11 The Hebrew phrase underlying the words "the place of atonement" is *bêt hak-kappōreṯ* (lit., "the house of the atoning cover," or "mercy seat," KJV; cf. comment on v.2). It denotes the room that housed the ark of the covenant, designated in the tabernacle as "the most holy place" and in the temple as "the oracle" (KJV) or "inner sanctuary" (NIV, NASB; 2 Chron 5:7, 9).

12 "The plans of . . . the temple" were directly revealed to David by the inspiration of the Holy Spirit (cf. comment on v.19), even as those for the tabernacle that preceded it had been given to Moses (Exod 25:9, 40; 27:8). The major pieces of its furnishings were symbolic of the great truths of God's salvation; and some—e.g., the altar, sea (= laver), ark, and even certain of the priestly garments—typified the atoning sacrifice, moral purity, incarnate presence, and holiness of Jesus Christ (Heb 8:5; 9:8–12, 23–24; cf. Payne, *Prophecy,* pp. 182–87).

16 Ezra referred to "each table" (Heb. plu., viz., "tables") because, in contrast to the single "table of show bread" (KJV; cf. comment on 9:32) made for the Mosaic sanctuary (Exod 37:10), the Solomonic would have ten of them (2 Chron 4:8).

18 Since the Lord could poetically be said to ride on cherubim as on a chariot (Ps 18:10; Ezek 1), they are here designated simply "the chariot." The Chronicler's reference is probably not to the small golden cherubim that formed part of the ark's holy cover, which had been made long before, but rather to those larger wooden but gold-plated cherub-angels of the inner temple, which were to "shelter the ark" as a whole (2 Chron 3:10–13). They emphasized the real presence of God in the temple.

436

19 Because the words "he gave me understanding" have no "and" before them in the Hebrew but are connected with the first part of the verse rather than its latter part, we should preferably follow the other EV and read: "the LORD gave me understanding in writing." David was saying that not only were the temple plans revealed by God (v. 12), but that they were given to him in written form from God, to be handed to Solomon (v.11)—an ultimate testimony to their divine character. Such "blueprint or possible scale model" (North, "The Chronicler," 1:413) goes beyond the verbal instructions and vision shown Moses for the tabernacle (Exod 25:40; 40:2).

20–21 David's final charge to Solomon (cf. vv.9–10; 22:11–16; Pss 27:13–14; 31:23 –24), that he should "be strong and courageous" because the Lord would "not fail . . . or forsake" him, reflects the stirring charges of Moses to Joshua (Deut 31:7–8, 23), and of the Lord himself (Josh 1:5–9, 18). Paul gives a similar closing admonition in 1 Corinthians 16:13.

29:1 David had expressed concern before, about Solomon's youthful inexperience and about his own need to compensate for this by preparing materials for the temple (v.2; cf. comments on 22:5 and 14).

2 The "stones of various colors" were probably mosaic pebbles (KB, p. 910).

3 "Over and above" the great amounts he had already prepared (cf. comments on 22:14), David next contributed his personal treasures.

4 Israel's finest gold was imported from "Ophir" (cf. comment on 2 Chron 8:18). This amounted to about 110 tons of gold (cf. NIV mg.) and 260 tons of silver (NIV mg.; cf. on v.7).

5 The king's appeal for each giver to "consecrate himself" reads literally "to fill his hand." This was a technical phrase used to describe ordination to the priesthood; and Scripture, significantly, places the act of giving on this same level of devotion.

7 The "daric" was a Persian gold coin, first issued by Darius I in the century before Ezra, though in David's day this figure—equivalent to about two and one-half talents—would have represented the corresponding weight in small pieces of the precious metal. The weight of gold contributed by David's leaders comes to about 190 tons (NIV mg.), and there was about 375 tons of silver (NIV mg.). David's example (v.4) thus incited a gift on the part of his officers that was half again as large as his own. Since it was a rarer commodity then than it is today, 3,750 tons of iron (NIV mg.) is also mentioned. The total of just the silver and gold adds up to an enormous sum by contemporary values. While the sum is only one twenty-fifth of the quantity tabulated in chapter 22, it still amounts to so much, particularly in ancient purchasing power, that it too should be recognized, as the other large figures in Chronicles, that it is to be accounted for through an act of divine providence (cf. comment on 22:14).

8 On "Jehiel" and course no. i of "the Gershonite" temple-Levites, see the comments on 26:21.

9 A "willing response" to the needs of the Lord's worship produced great rejoicing on the part of both the king and the people; and, still today, God loves cheerful givers (2 Cor 9:7).

10 David's reaction to his people's devotion was to praise the Lord (vv. 10–20). The phrase "our father Israel" here signifies the patriarch Jacob (Gen 32:28); he too (cf. v. 15) had had occasion to praise God for his goodness (Gen 32:10; 33:11). It is true that the Hebrew word order could suggest divine fatherhood—"Yahweh, God of Israel, our Father"—rather than a patriarchal characteristic (Dentan, p. 129); but see v. 18.

11 This verse supplies the conclusion to the Lord's Prayer: "For thine is the kingdom" (Matt 6:13, KJV).

14 The truth that "everything" we have "comes from" God is the foundation for the doctrine of stewardship. Its basis is this: since our property is his (Ps 24:1), and since we hold it only temporarily and in trust (1 Chron 29:15–16), it should therefore be used for him (Luke 17:10; cf. Payne, *Theology*, pp. 434–35).

21 When Ezra spoke of the "sacrifices in abundance for all Israel," he probably intended peace offerings, the one major category of sacrifice in which all the worshipers participated, feasting as guests around the table of the Lord (cf. v. 22 and comment on 16:1).

22 The "great joy" of those at this gathering, particularly in respect to Solomon's being "acknowledged," is reflected also in 1 Kings 1:40. By stating that David's son was acknowledged for "a second time," the Chronicler makes no attempt to conceal but rather recalls to his readers the well-known facts, which he does not recount, about Solomon's first induction to the throne. This had been precipitated by the attempt of his older half-brother Adonijah to displace him (1 Kings 1:25, 39). Such confirmatory rites, even to the point of reanointing, had value, particularly in cases of disputed succession (cf. the illustrations afforded by Saul, 1 Sam 10:1, 24; 11:14 –15, or by David, 16:13; 2 Sam 2:4; 5:3).

The position Solomon acceded to is here defined as that of "ruler" or "leader" (*nāgîd*, lit., "a conspicuous one"). It was a characteristic title among the early sovereigns of Israel (1 Sam 9:16; 13:14; 25:30; 1 Chron 5:2; 11:2; 17:7). Zadok too (cf. comments on 6:8; 16:39) was reanointed, though for him it was to the position of sole high priest (cf. Notes), his previous colleague Abiathar having been disqualified in connection with Adonijah's plot (1 Kings 1:7; 2:26).

26–30 In his concluding summary of David's reign, the Chronicler itemizes those aspects of his success that had the greatest appeal to Oriental thought: "long life, wealth and honor" and a "son" who "succeeded him" (v. 28)—which form a not inappropriate incentive for seeking the blessing of God in Occidental thought as well. First Kings, unhappily, adds certain specific features to David's final characterization that are of a less complimentary nature (1:1–4, 15; 2:5–6, 8–9).

Ezra's closing reference (v. 30) to his written sources, and particularly to the way Samuel, Nathan, and Gad recorded the circumstances of "Israel and the kingdoms of all the other lands," probably relates to those kingdoms that immediately surrounded Israel, so many of whom David had been enabled to incorporate within his own realm (cf. ch. 18).

Notes

17 In the three clauses of this verse, the words "the weight of," "of gold," and "of silver," respectively, have no equivalent in the Hebrew but have been supplied in the NIV by context (cf. vv.16, 18).

29:22 Liberalism denies the historicity of the ceremony of Zadok's reacknowledgment and insists that high priests were first anointed only in postexilic times—when they replaced the kings as political leaders (so de Vaux, AIs, pp. 347, 400).

29 That the Chronicler used many sources (see Introduction: Sources) does not mean that these were "lost biblical books" but merely indicates the honest research he conducted in writing his inspired account. Nothing in the Chronicler's remarks need be construed as suggesting that the canon is incomplete or that the entirety of the sources named here was inspired.

III. The Reign of Solomon (2 Chron 1:1–9:31)

A. *Solomon's Inauguration*

1:1–17

¹Solomon son of David established himself firmly over his kingdom, for the LORD his God was with him and made him exceedingly great.

²Then Solomon spoke to all Israel—to the commanders of thousands and commanders of hundreds, to the judges and to all the leaders in Israel, the heads of families—³and Solomon and the whole assembly went to the high place at Gibeon, for God's Tent of Meeting was there, which Moses the LORD's servant had made in the desert. ⁴Now David had brought up the ark of God from Kiriath Jearim to the place he had prepared for it, because he had pitched a tent for it in Jerusalem. ⁵But the bronze altar that Bezalel son of Uri, the son of Hur, had made was in Gibeon in front of the tabernacle of the LORD; so Solomon and the assembly inquired of him there. ⁶Solomon went up to the bronze altar before the LORD in the Tent of Meeting and offered a thousand burnt offerings on it.

⁷That night God appeared to Solomon and said to him, "Ask for whatever you want me to give you."

⁸Solomon answered God, "You have shown great kindness to David my father and have made me king in his place. ⁹Now, LORD God, let your promise to my father David be confirmed, for you have made me king over a people who are as numerous as the dust of the earth. ¹⁰Give me wisdom and knowledge, that I may lead this people, for who is able to govern this great people of yours?"

¹¹God said to Solomon, "Since this is your heart's desire and you have not asked for wealth, riches or honor, nor for the death of your enemies, and since you have not asked for a long life but for wisdom and knowledge to govern my people over whom I have made you king, ¹²therefore wisdom and knowledge will be given you. And I will also give you wealth, riches and honor, such as no king who was before you ever had and none after you will have."

¹³Then Solomon went to Jerusalem from the high place at Gibeon, from before the Tent of Meeting. And he reigned over Israel.

¹⁴Solomon accumulated chariots and horses; he had fourteen hundred chariots and twelve thousand horses, which he kept in the chariot cities and also with him

in Jerusalem. [15]The king made silver and gold as common in Jerusalem as stones, and cedar as plentiful as sycamore-fig trees in the foothills. [16]Solomon's horses were imported from Egypt and from Kue—the royal merchants purchased them from Kue. [17]They imported a chariot from Egypt for six hundred shekels of silver, and a horse for a hundred and fifty. They also exported them to all the kings of the Hittites and of the Arameans.

Just as the Book of 1 Chronicles paralleled and drew on 1 and 2 Samuel (starting at 1 Sam 31), so the Book of 2 Chronicles parallels 1 and 2 Kings. Its first nine chapters constitute the third out of the four major divisions into which the Chronicler's history naturally falls (see Introduction: Outline). These chapters are devoted to the reign of Solomon (970–930 B.C.), the son of David, and correspond to 1 Kings 1–11. Even more so than in 1 Kings, the Solomonic record in 2 Chronicles shows a greater concern for Solomon's temple—six out of the opening nine chapters (chs. 2 –7)—than it shows for Solomon's kingship. In 1 Kings the temple occupies four and one-half chapters out of the opening eleven (5:1–9:9). Nevertheless this third division of Chronicles does commence and conclude (chs. 1 and 8–9) with basic facts about Solomon's reign.

Chapter 1 concerns the king's inauguration. Shortly before his death in 970 (1 Chron 29:26), King David had seen his son Solomon safely seated on the throne of a united Israel (cf. comment on 23:1); and, by means of a second anointing, he had insured the allegiance of the nation's leaders to him (see comment on 29:22). Solomon's personal career as monarch, however, was inaugurated when God appeared to him in a dream at Gibeon (2 Chron 1:1–13, paralleling 1 Kings 3:4–15). This event, perhaps more than any other in history, brings to mind the biblical principle that "if any of you lacks wisdom, he should ask God . . . and it will be given to him" (James 1:5). The Chronicler, however, omits the material that immediately follows in 1 Kings, namely, how the reality of his divinely bestowed wisdom was demonstrated by an insightful decision, regarding the children of the two harlots (3:16–28)—probably because this was of a limited and somewhat personal interest (see Introduction: Purpose, 2). Instead Ezra validated Solomon's talents by adducing the economic prosperity that marked his reign (vv.14–17, paralleling 1 Kings 10:26–29).

1 The opening verse of 2 Chronicles draws together two other references: (1) that Solomon was "established firmly" recalls the struggle at his accession as this was recorded in 1 Kings 1 (cf. comment on 1 Chron 29:22); and (2) that God made him "exceedingly great" picks up the thought of 1 Chronicles 29:25.

2–4 Ezra clarifies 1 Kings 3:4 by identifying the various elements that made up Solomon's "whole assembly" (v.3), those who represented "all . . . Israel" (v.2) and who accompanied him to Gibeon. At the time Moses' tabernacle, "God's Tent of Meeting," was located at this center, seven miles northwest of Jerusalem (see comment on 1 Chron 16:39). With the ark now at the Jerusalem capital (v.4; cf. 1 Chron 13, 15–16), these two cities became the only legitimate places for divine atonement. First Kings 3:2 does recognize the reality of deviation in popular practice; but the principle of centralized worship, of services of sacrifice only where God revealed himself, had been established by Moses almost five hundred years earlier (Exod 20:24; Lev 17:3–9; Deut 12:5). Other "high places," even if used in the name of Yahweh, God of Israel, were necessarily excluded. This was because of their contamination through association with Canaanitish Baal worship; they stood under God's ban (Num 33:52; Deut 12:2). Indeed Solomon's first drift toward sin became apparent by his recognition and use of such unauthorized high places (plural, 1 Kings 3:3).

5 The "bronze altar" made by Bezalel (see comment on 1 Chron 2:20) had a frame of acacia wood, but it was overlaid with bronze (Exod 38:1-2).

7 When that night God "appeared to Solomon," it was in the form of a dream (1 Kings 3:5, 15; cf. 1 Sam 28:6).

8 The "kindness" that God showed Solomon was in *ḥesed,* literally, faithfulness to what he had previously covenanted (see comment on 1 Chron 16:41): in this instance, that Solomon should succeed David as king (see comment on 22:9).

9 God's "promise to . . . David"—primarily as revealed in 1 Chronicles 17:11–14—that Solomon prayed might "be confirmed" included the permanent establishment of David's seed on the throne of Israel and the erection of the temple at Jerusalem. The Lord had already fulfilled to the letter his promise to Abraham, that he should have descendants "as numerous as the dust of the earth" (Gen 13:16; 22:17; cf. 1 Kings 4:20).

10 The central teaching of chapter 1 (cf. the introductory discussion) lies in Solomon's selfless prayer for wisdom, which was the precise characteristic that his father David had already invoked for him (1 Chron 22:12). The newly inaugurated king's desire to have it so that he might "lead this people" Israel reads, literally, that he might "go out and come in before this people" (NASB). Such words referred originally to military leadership (1 Chron 11:2; cf. 1 Sam 18:13) but are here broadened into representing good governmental administratorship in general.

12 God granted Solomon's request. His factual knowledge was to some extent limited by his cultural environment; but his "wisdom," in the sense of that divinely given abililty that can apply knowledge to life situations (as shown by his authorship of Prov, Eccl, and S of Songs; cf. 1 Kings 4:29, 32), has never been surpassed (1 Kings 3:12). God also granted him an unparalleled concentration of wealth (v. 15; cf. comment on 1 Chron 22:14) and honor (1 Chron 29:25; Matt 6:29), which illustrates Christ's teaching: "Seek first his kingdom and his righteousness, and all these things will be given to you" (Matt 6:33).

14 Chapter 1 concludes (vv. 14–17) by adducing historical evidences for the fulfillment of God's promises. King Solomon's "chariot cities" and other urban constructions have been validated archaeologically by excavations at cities of his period from Hazor in the north to Gezer in the southwest. Megiddo too contains Solomonic structures, including an intricate gateway complex, a palace area, and perhaps even its well-known subterranean water system. Two huge, stone stables holding about 450 horses were formerly attributed to the wise king—and may still be based on his planning—but, at least to the level to which they have been so far recovered, they seem now to be datable to King Ahab in the next century (Y. Yadin, "Megiddo," in *Archaeology and OT Study,* ed. D. Winton Thomas [Oxford: University Press,

1969]; cf. Howard F. Vos, *Archaeology in Bible Lands* [Chicago: Moody, 1977], p. 191). (Currently there is some doubt as to whether these were even stables, but perhaps were grain storage bins.)

15 Solomon's silver, "and [his] gold," too (which does not receive mention in the parallel passages: 9:27; 1 Kings 10:27), were as common as "stones"—whose abundance are plainly evident to any tourist to the Holy Land. Solomon also made cedar as plentiful as the sycamore-fig trees, which abound in "the foothills" (Heb., Shephelah; cf. comment on 1 Chron 27:28).

16 Cilicia (cf. NIV mg.), in what is now southern Turkey, at the east end of the Mediterranean, was a prime ancient supplier of horses.

17 The price for chariots and horses (cf. NIV mg.) ran about fifteen pounds and three and three-fourths pounds of silver each, respectively. The chariots cost four times as much each, because of the craftsmanship required and because the wood itself had to be imported into Egypt (cf. Myers, *Chronicles*, 2:5). The law of Moses, significantly, forbade excess in these very matters (Deut 17:16); they were, in fact, the sorts of sin that Solomon's prosperity eventually precipitated.

Notes

13 The NIV reads, with the ancient versions, that Solomon went to Jerusalem "from the high place" at Gibeon, מֵהַבָּמָה (*mēhabbāmāh*); cf. the present MT, לַבָּמָה (*labbāmāh*, "to the high place"), which is incorrect.

B. *Solomon's Temple (2:1–7:22)*

1. *Preparations*

2:1–18

¹Solomon gave orders to build a temple for the Name of the LORD and a royal palace for himself. ²He conscripted seventy thousand men as carriers and eighty thousand as stonecutters in the hills and thirty-six hundred as foremen over them. ³Solomon sent this message to Hiram king of Tyre:

"Send me cedar logs as you did for my father David when you sent him cedar to build a palace to live in. ⁴Now I am about to build a temple for the Name of the LORD my God and to dedicate it to him for burning fragrant incense before him, for setting out the consecrated bread regularly, and for making burnt offerings every morning and evening and on Sabbaths and New Moons and at the appointed feasts of the LORD our God. This is a lasting ordinance for Israel.

⁵"The temple I am going to build will be great, because our God is greater than all other gods. ⁶But who is able to build a temple for him, since the heavens, even the highest heavens, cannot contain him? Who then am I to build a temple for him, except as a place to burn sacrifices before him?

⁷"Send me, therefore, a man skilled to work in gold and silver, bronze and

iron, and in purple, crimson and blue yarn, and experienced in the art of engraving, to work in Judah and Jerusalem with my skilled craftsmen, whom my father David provided.

8"Send me also cedar, pine and algum logs from Lebanon, for I know that your men are skilled in cutting timber there. My men will work with yours 9to provide me with plenty of lumber, because the temple I build must be large and magnificent. 10I will give your servants, the woodsmen who cut the timber, twenty thousand cors of ground wheat, twenty thousand cors of barley, twenty thousand baths of wine and twenty thousand baths of olive oil."

11Hiram king of Tyre replied by letter to Solomon:

"Because the LORD loves his people, he has made you their king."

12And Hiram added:

"Praise be to the LORD, the God of Israel, who made heaven and earth! He has given King David a wise son, endowed with intelligence and discernment, who will build a temple for the LORD and a palace for himself.

13"I am sending you Huram-Abi, a man of great skill, 14whose mother was from Dan and whose father was from Tyre. He is trained to work in gold and silver, bronze and iron, stone and wood, and with purple and blue and crimson yarn and fine linen. He is experienced in all kinds of engraving and can execute any design given to him. He will work with your craftsmen and with those of my lord, David your father.

15"Now let my lord send his servants the wheat and barley and the olive oil and wine he promised, 16and we will cut all the logs from Lebanon that you need and will float them in rafts by sea down to Joppa. You can then take them up to Jerusalem."

17Solomon took a census of all the aliens who were in Israel, after the census his father David had taken; and they were found to be 153,600. 18He assigned 70,000 of them to be carriers and 80,000 to be stonecutters in the hills, with 3,600 foremen over them to keep the people working.

Despite the greatness of King Solomon's armies, wealth, and material possessions (1:14–17), it is not these things that are the most important for us today; nor were they for Ezra in his day. Modern men would be inclined to think of his inspired writings as his greatest contribution: Proverbs, Ecclesiastes, the Song of Songs. But for Ezra's postexilic community, it was Solomon's temple that captured their greatest concern. This building was, after all, the place where they worshiped God, until Jesus Christ came and replaced it (John 4:21; cf. Matt 27:51) with a new and better way to the Father, through his own Person (John 14:6).

To the Jews of 450 B.C., the temple overshadowed every other aspect to the career of Solomon. Through the rites of atonement that were performed at its altar, God brought Israel into reconciliation with himself (cf. 2 Cor 5:18); and continuously these rites symbolized the presence of the Lord in the midst of his redeemed people (2 Chron 7:1–2; Exod 29:45–46). Salvation was bound up in the temple, even if in a preliminary and anticipatory way. For even as its altar and priests were a figure that pointed forward to Christ's sacrifice on the cross (Heb 7:27; 8:4–5; 9:9–12), so the structure itself was a type, a material prophecy of that day when the Word of God would become flesh and "tabernacle" among us (John 1:14 ASV mg.). Still today it serves as a type of that future glorification that awaits men in the heavenly presence of God himself (Exod 24:18; Heb 9:24; cf. Payne, *Theology*, pp. 361–63).

As noted in the introductory discussion to chapter 1, the Chronicler devoted six of his nine chapters on Solomon to the Jerusalem temple: to the preparations for it (ch. 2), to its construction (chs. 3–4); and to its dedication (chs. 5–7). These sections parallel 1 Kings 5–6 and 7:13–8:66, and provide an amplification to this earlier history.

Solomon's preparations for the temple (2 Chron 2) possessed considerable antecedents. King David had already prepared in many ways: providing the design for the whole complex, gathering supplies, and enlisting personnel (1 Chron 22, 28–29). Solomon, however, still needed to organize the labor force (2 Chron 2:2, 17–18). A further aspect, and perhaps the most significant of his preparations, lay in the young king's search for technical assistance from Hiram king of Tyre (cf. v.12). This way Solomon could gain an experienced superintendent of construction and also a supply of timbers from the incomparable cedars of Lebanon (vv.3–10). A suitable contract was soon negotiated (vv.11–16).

Several recent publications have shown the striking similarities between the building of the tabernacle in Exodus and the temple in 2 Chronicles. The detailed discussion may be read in Braun's "Message of Chronicles" and "Solomon, the Chosen Temple Builder." Also very helpful is Dillard's "The Chronicler's Solomon."

The resemblances between building the tabernacle and building the temple are as follows: (1) both Bezalel and Solomon were specifically singled out by God to be in charge of the building project (Exod 35:30; 1 Chron 28:6); (2) both men were from the tribe of Judah; (3) both were empowered by God to do the task they were chosen for (Exod 35:31: 2 Chron 2:7–12); (4) both built the bronze altar for the Lord (2 Chron 1:5; 4:1); (5) both built the furnishings for the tabernacle/temple (Exod 31; 2 Chron 4). Additional similarities may be noted: (6) both the tabernacle and the temple had a specific design that came from God (Exod 25:9; 1 Chron 28:11–19); (7) the people gave gifts freely and generously for the building project (Exod 25:1–7; 1 Chron 29:1–9; (8) when both structures were finished, the glory of God filled the place in a magnificent way (Exod 40:34–35; 2 Chron 7:1–3). These remarkable similarities bear witness to the divine inspiriation under which the Chronicler wrote. (SBM)

1 In addition to the temple, Solomon is said to have constructed a palace for himself (cf. v.12). Though repeatedly mentioned, little is known about it except for the time involved in its building and for some of the costly wood used in its construction (8:1; 9:11; cf. comment on 7:11). It seems to have lain south of the temple on Mount Moriah, but north of the older city of Jerusalem on Mount Zion (cf. comment on 1 Chron 26:15), in the space that existed between them.

2 The distribution of the king's "conscripted" laborers between "carriers and . . . stone cutters" (repeated in v.18) is based on the total of 153,600 given in v.17. These workers were drafted from the alien population that was resident in Israel (cf. note to v.17), according to plans that had already been formulated by David (see comment on 1 Chron 22:2). The total figures are validated by 1 Kings 5:15–16 (cf. comments on 2 Chron 2:18). Solomon also conscripted some 30,000 men out of Israel, to labor in relays of 10,000 men each, one month out of every three (1 Kings 5:13–14). Precedent for such monthly rotation appears in Egypt, where the system grew out of the three-month period for the annual innundation of the Nile (*Herodotus* 2.124).

3 The king then sent a communication, the text of which appears in vv.3b–10, to "Hiram [a shortened form of Ahiram] king of Tyre." This city was a Phoenician port,

newer and lying to the south of its counterpart Sidon, and situated on an island off the Mediterranean coast. Tyre lies, indeed, just north of the white cliffs that marked the northern border of Israel and specifically the tribe of Asher. It possessed the finest harbor in the area, and its inhabitants were noted for their ship building and commerce.

The occasion for King Solomon's writing had been furnished by the arrival of a Phoenician delegation sent by Hiram to console Solomon over the death of his father, David, who had been Hiram's friend, and to congratulate him on his own accession (1 Kings 5:1). The new king's request that Hiram send him "cedar logs as you did for my father David" (cf. 1 Chron 14:1) must not be misunderstood as implying either that the logs were to be used for a palace, as had been the case with David (cf. v.4), or that they were the first timber to be provided for the temple (cf. David's previous accumulations in this regard, 1 Chron 22:4, 14).

4 Concerning the activities projected for accomplishment within the temple, the "burning [of] fragrant incense" before the Lord was an act that was performed twice daily on the altar of incense (Exod 30:6–8). In reference to the "consecrated bread," or "showbread," see the comment on 1 Chronicles 9:32; on the daily "burnt offerings," 23:30; and on the "appointed feasts," 23:31.

5 Solomon's affirmation that "our God is greater than all other gods" testifies to his religious commitment, even when dealing with a powerful pagan king. The latter's response then indicates a corresponding willingness on Hiram's part to recognize Yahweh (cf. comment on v.12).

6 Even though the temple was designed to house the glory cloud of God's presence (5:13–14; cf. the introductory discussion to ch.2), Solomon, from the very outset, acknowledged that it could not "contain him," in the sense of restricting or in any way confining his infinitude to this one location (cf. 6:18; Acts 7:48–49). God in his grace has seen fit, on various occasions, to manifest himself for purposes of revelation and redemption; the supreme demonstration of this fact lies in the incarnation of Jesus Christ (John 1:14). Yet in all such cases, significant qualifications are present that prevent any reduction in the Lord's glory or any manipulation of God on the part of men. Such localization is always voluntary on his part, undertaken on his initiative alone (6:5–6); it is paralleled by his continuing and simultaneous omnipresence (16:9); and it is revocable at his will, capable of termination whenever he may deem it to have become detrimental to his purposes (cf. comment on 1 Chron 13:3; cf. Payne, *Theology*, pp. 152–53).

In the light of the greatness of God, Solomon confessed his own inadequacy: "Who then am I?" His humility becomes all the more noteworthy in view of his own unsurpassed wealth, wisdom, and power (cf. comments on 2 Chron 1:12, 14–15).

7 Solomon requested from Hiram a skilled workman and in fact hired a number of experienced Phoenicians (vv.8, 14) to work with his own men. For despite a growing number of "skilled craftsmen" in Israel, their techniques remained inferior to those of their northern neighbors, as is demonstrated archaeologically by less finely cut building stones and by the lower level of Israelite culture in general.

8 The materials that the king requested consisted preeminently of "cedar logs." The

445

fragrant cedars of Lebanon were famed throughout the ancient world. They were resistant to decay and superior to any timber native to Palestine. This valuable resource was particularly squandered under Turkish rule, so that today only a few isolated groves of magnificent trees survive. The further product, rendered "pine" (Heb., *berôš*), probably refers to the *Phoenician juniper* (KB, p. 148), while the "algum" or almug (not mentioned in the parallels that occur in 1 Kings 5:6, 8, 10) was a foreign import. It has been traditionally translated as "sandalwood," because it was brought in from Ophir (9:10) and used for ornamental woodwork and for musical instruments (9:11). Sandalwood, however, does not grow in Lebanon; and the term seems here, as indicated by the NIV margin, to represent another variety of *juniper*.

10 Solomon's payment to the Phoenicians was based on the charges that he had asked them to quote (1 Kings 5:6). First Kings goes on to speak of his delivering an identical "twenty thousand cors of wheat" but of only twenty cors of "pressed" oil (5:11 NIV mg.; cf. the listing in 2 Chron of "twenty thousand baths of" ordinary "olive oil"). Ten baths are contained in one cor; but the Chronicles figure still represents 115,000 gallons (NIV mg.), as compared to 1,200 gallons in Kings. The latter makes no mention at all of the "barley" and "wine"; and the verdict of negative criticism is that "Chronicles exaggerates figures most absurdly" (Montgomery, *Kings*, p. 136). Before drawing a hasty conclusion, however, one should observe that the objects being counted do not claim to be the same. Kings puts a limitation both on the product—in respect to the oil, it is speaking of a special, luxury kind—and on its recipients; for Kings refers only to the royal household of Hiram and not, as in Chronicles, to the larger group of Phoenician "servants, the woodsmen who cut timber." Furthermore Kings concerns an annually repeated delivery, while in Chronicles it is a one-time payment. Seen in this light, the differing figures suggest no unreasonable proportions (Payne, "Validity," p. 121).

As to the actual amounts involved, the 125,000 bushels of the two different grains and the 120,000 gallons of the two liquids (cf. NIV mg.) represent, as Keil (KD, *Kings*, p. 61) points out, "considerable quantities"; but they are not beyond the magnitude either of Solomon's resources or of the temple project that he was financing. Furthermore, at least in respect to the wheat, 1 Kings 5:11 does not simply validate the Chronicler's figure but actually makes its own far greater, because of the repeated character within Kings, as indicated above (cf. Payne, "Validity"). Such payments constituted a heavy drain on the economy of Israel. When they were prolonged, because of Solomon's private building projects (cf. comment on v. 1 and 1 Kings 7:1–2), they exhausted the kingdom (1 Kings 9:10–11).

12 Hiram's answer to Solomon (vv. 11–16) includes words of praise to the Lord and of appreciation for his love to Israel (v. 11), which are not recorded in 1 Kings 5. Though dismissed by some scholars as a fictitious "touch by the Chronicler" (Curtis, p. 322), there is some parallel to Hiram's reply in 1 Kings, even though more briefly recorded, which commences, "Praise be to the LORD" (5:7). Moreover this speech is appropriate, not simply theologically, but also practically, coming from the lips of an accomplished businessman, who was dealing with a promising prospective customer—whatever may have been Hiram's individual doctrinal commitments, or lack of same (cf. the comment on 36:22 on the pious phraseology found in the decree of Cyrus).

13 The name of the master craftsman whom Hiram sent to Solomon is "Huram-Abi." This may be rendered "Huram, my father," not in the sense of a physical relationship (Hiram's father is known to have been Abibaal), but of social status, meaning, "my (trusted) administrator," or "adviser" (as in Gen 45:8; Judg 17:10).

14 Huram-Abi's mother was, by tribal descent, literally, "a woman from the daughters of Dan" (Chron), but by immediate situation, "a widow from the tribe of Naphtali" (1 Kings 7:14). Yet the fact that his father came "from Tyre" gave Huram-Abi a combined Phoenician-Hebrew endowment, which enabled him to deal both linguistically and culturally with the two nationalities of workmen who would be responsible to him.

This superintendent's diversified skills included the capacity to handle precious metals, wood, stone, and fabrics (1 Kings 7:14 mentions only his skill with bronze). He thus presents a parallel to the wide-ranging abilities of Bezalel, the master builder of the Mosaic tabernacle (Exod 31:2–5). The "purple" cloth that he could employ was produced from what was actually a deep red dye, obtained from the murex shellfish of the Phoenician coast. Such material was called "royal purple" because of its quality, scarcity, and cost. Concerning the "blue," see Notes.

16 Despite limited facilities, Joppa had a small projecting point of rocks that set it apart from the generally unprotected sands and beaches of southern Palestine. It is mentioned in Egyptian documents as early as the time of Thutmose III (ANET, pp. 22, 242), who was probably the Pharaoh of the Hebrew oppression, dying just before the Exodus in 1446 B.C. (Exod 4:19). Joppa served as the port (cf. Jonah 1:3) for inland Judah and for the city of Jerusalem. Before one reached Solomon's capital, however, there were some thiry-five miles of flat, then hilly, and finally rugged terrain.

17–18 Ezra here itemizes "3,600 foremen" (v.18) out of the total of 153,600 aliens (v.17). There were, in addition, 250 chief Israelite officers (8:10), making a total of 3,850. The parallel passages in 1 Kings list only 3,300 foremen (5:16) but then have a correspondingly larger number of chief officers, "550" (9:23), again making a total of 3,850. Since Kings does not distinguish the aliens from the Israelites (cf. Notes), the differences in figures would seem to be due to the ways the respective authors distinguished the "chief" officers. As Wenham ("Large Numbers," p. 49) puts it, "one group of 300 men has been reckoned with one category in Kings and with another in Chronicles" (cf. Appendix A, in which the disagreement of the Chronicler's number is accounted for in terms of a "different method of reckoning").

Notes

7 The word translated "blue yarn" (also in v.14), תְּכֵלֶת (tᵉ<u>k</u>ēle<u>t</u>) is more precisely rendered as "violet purple-wool" (KB, p. 1028); cf. comment on v.14, above, on the "purple" being properly a "deep red." The blue color represented by the NIV is not without merit, however; see TWOT, 2:969–70.

17 Solomon's census for drafting workers concerned specifically "the aliens in Israel." Since neither v.2 nor the parallel passage in 1 Kings (5:13) records this specification, liberal

commentators have been quick to criticize the restriction to aliens (and the exemption of Israelites) in v.17 as "quite contrary to the impression given in 1 Kings" (Dentan, p. 141). Yet it is a basic principle in hermeneutics to interpret the general passage by the more specific, particularly when 1 Kings itself later goes on to explain that Solomon did levy forced laborers from among the surviving Canaanites (9:21), as opposed to the sons of Israel (vv.20, 22).

---

2. Construction

3:1–4:22

¹Then Solomon began to build the temple of the LORD in Jerusalem on Mount Moriah, where the LORD had appeared to his father David. It was on the threshing floor of Araunah the Jebusite, the place provided by David. ²He began building on the second day of the second month in the fourth year of his reign.

³The foundation Solomon laid for building the temple of God was sixty cubits long and twenty cubits wide (using the cubit of the old standard). ⁴The portico at the front of the temple was twenty cubits long across the width of the building and twenty cubits high.

He overlaid the inside with pure gold. ⁵He paneled the main hall with pine and covered it with fine gold and decorated it with palm tree and chain designs. ⁶He adorned the temple with precious stones. And the gold he used was gold of Parvaim. ⁷He overlaid the ceiling beams, doorframes, walls and doors of the temple with gold, and he carved cherubim on the walls.

⁸He built the Most Holy Place, its length corresponding to the width of the temple—twenty cubits long and twenty cubits wide. He overlaid the inside with six hundred talents of fine gold. ⁹The gold nails weighed fifty shekels. He also overlaid the upper parts with gold.

¹⁰In the Most Holy Place he made a pair of sculptured cherubim and overlaid them with gold. ¹¹The total wingspan of the cherubim was twenty cubits. One wing of the first cherub was five cubits long and touched the temple wall, while its other wing, also five cubits long, touched the wing of the other cherub. ¹²Similarly one wing of the second cherub was five cubits long and touched the other temple wall, and its other wing, also five cubits long, touched the wing of the first cherub. ¹³The wings of these cherubim extended twenty cubits. They stood on their feet, facing the main hall.

¹⁴He made the curtain of blue, purple and crimson yarn and fine linen, with cherubim worked into it.

¹⁵In the front of the temple he made two pillars, which together, were thirty-five cubits long, each with a capital on top measuring five cubits. ¹⁶He made interwoven chains and put them on top of the pillars. He also made a hundred pomegranates and attached them to the chains. ¹⁷He erected the pillars in the front of the temple, one to the south and one to the north. The one to the south he named Jakin and the one to the north Boaz.

⁴:¹He made a bronze altar twenty cubits long, twenty cubits wide and ten cubits high. ²He made the Sea of cast metal, circular in shape, measuring ten cubits from rim to rim and five cubits high. It took a line of thirty cubits to measure around it. ³Below the rim, figures of bulls encircled it—ten to a cubit. The bulls were cast in two rows in one piece with the Sea.

⁴The Sea stood on twelve bulls, three facing north, three facing west, three facing south and three facing east. The Sea rested on top of them, and their hindquarters were toward the center. ⁵It was a handbreadth in thickness, and its rim was like the rim of a cup, like a lily blossom. It held three thousand baths.

⁶He then made ten basins for washing and placed five on the south side and five on the north. In them the things to be used for the burnt offerings were rinsed, but the Sea was to be used by the priests for washing.

⁷He made ten gold lampstands according to the specifications for them and placed them in the temple, five on the south side and five on the north.

⁸He made ten tables and placed them in the temple, five on the south side and five on the north. He also made a hundred gold sprinkling bowls.

⁹He made the courtyard of the priests, and the large court and the doors for the court, and overlaid the doors with bronze. ¹⁰He placed the Sea on the south side, at the southeast corner.

¹¹He also made the pots and shovels and sprinkling bowls.

So Huram finished the work he had undertaken for King Solomon in the temple of God:

¹²the two pillars;
 the two bowl-shaped capitals on top of the pillars;
 the two sets of network decorating the two bowl-shaped capitals on top of the pillars;
¹³the four hundred pomegranates for the two sets of network (two rows of pomegranates for each network, decorating the bowl-shaped capitals on top of the pillars);
¹⁴the stands with their basins;
¹⁵the Sea and the twelve bulls under it;
¹⁶the pots, shovels, meat forks and all related articles.

All the objects that Huram-Abi made for King Solomon for the temple of the LORD were of polished bronze. ¹⁷The king had them cast in clay molds in the plain of the Jordan between Succoth and Zarethan. ¹⁸All these things that Solomon made amounted to so much that the weight of the bronze was not determined.

¹⁹Solomon also made all the furnishings that were in God's temple:

 the golden altar;
 the tables on which was the bread of the Presence;
²⁰the lampstands of pure gold with their lamps, to burn in front of the inner sanctuary as prescribed;
²¹the gold floral work and lamps and tongs (they were solid gold);
²²the pure gold wick trimmers, sprinkling bowls, dishes and censers; and the gold doors of the temple: the inner doors to the Most Holy Place and the doors of the main hall.

Having explained something of Solomon's preparations for the temple (ch. 2), the Chronicler moves into a description of its actual construction (chs. 3–4). His material forms a parallel to and represents an abridgment of 1 Kings 6–7. The reason for his omitting certain details probably lies in their less relevance for his own fifth-century period, or because of the less luxurious structure that Zerubbabel and Joshua were actually able to reconstruct on the Solomonic site in 515 B.C. (Ezra 6:14–15, and note Hag 2:6–9 or Zech 4:9–10). Still the accomplishment of Solomon back in 959 had value for Ezra's contemporaries, both as a reminder of the glories of Israel in the past and as a pattern or portent of greater things that could yet be accomplished in their time and in the future (cf. Hag. 2:7). In any event, and for men of every age, the major feature of the Solomonic temple—like those of the Mosaic tabernacle that preceded it, and which came to be housed in it (1 Kings 8:4), and on which the temple was modeled—provided typical illustrations of the changeless truths of the gospel (cf. the introductory discussion to ch. 2).

Second Chronicles 3 parallels 1 Kings 6 and describes the temple building as a whole; chapter 4 parallels 1 Kings 7 and deals with its equipment. Concerning the latter, except for the altar of incense and the most holy ark, the furnishings of the Solomonic temple were considerably more elaborate than the corresponding pieces that were made for the tabernacle of Moses.

1 "Mount Moriah" was the summit, in the area of that same name, on which Abraham had shown his willingness to sacrifice his son Isaac (Gen 22:2), over one thousand years earlier. "The threshing floor" of Araunah (cf. the note to 1 Chron 21:15), which was located on Mount Moriah, was then sanctified even further by David's encounter with God at that place (1 Chron 21:18–22:1).

2 Construction on the site did not begin till "the fourth year" of Solomon's reign, probably because of the planning and preparation that had to precede it (2 Chron 2). This particular regnal year extended from the fall of 967 B.C. to the fall of 966; but since "the second month" begins in April/May, the exact date must have fallen in the spring of 966 (E.R. Thiele, *The Mysterious Numbers of the Hebrew Kings* [Chicago: University of Chicago Press, 1951], pp. 30–31).

3 Cubits "of the old standard" represented an earlier, sacred measure. These ran about three inches longer than the ordinary cubit, which was a trifle under eighteen inches (see Ezek 40:5; 43:13, concerning the sacred, or longer, standard). On this basis the temple building measured about 105 feet by 35 feet, rather than 90 by 30; and it had double the dimensions of the tabernacle.

4 Along the entire front of the temple stretched a porch, or portico, that was open on the front. First Kings 6:3 gives its depths, of 10 cubits (c. 15 feet); but it is the text of 2 Chronicles, despite its confessedly difficult Hebrew, that tells how high its side walls rose, namely 20 cubits (30 feet). The MT suggests 120 cubits, which would imply a greater tower, or pylon (as in Egypt). But such a height, of over 200 feet, seems unlikely as far as architecture at that time is concerned; and it is doubtful as far as the written text is concerned. Critical scholars observe that the MT reading of 120 cubits "is universally regarded as a textual corruption" (see Notes); and the NIV is to be commended for its restored rendering of "twenty cubits high" (cf. NIV mg.).

5 "The main hall" refers to the temple proper, and particularly to its outer room, which corresponded to the "Holy Place" in the tabernacle. Compare the reference in v.8 to the inner room as the "Most Holy Place," called elsewhere the "oracle" (v.16; 4:20 KJV; cf. comment on 5:7). As for the wood that the king used (i.e., pine), see the comment on 2:8; and cedar was employed as well (1 Kings 6:9).

The paragraphing in the NIV connects Solomon's provision of a layer of "pure gold" for "the inside" (v.4) with this same main hall. The expenditure was enormous (cf. the amounts indicated in v.8 for the inner room, which was only half as long and high). But it was with these very projects in mind that David had proceeded with his earlier, massive preparations (cf. comment on 1 Chron 22:14; 29:4, 7).

6 The reference to "precious stones" may suggest mosaics, inlaid in the floor (cf. comment on 1 Chron 29:2). The gold "of Parvaim" cannot be identified with certainty. It seems to denote a place name, either the Arabian *El Farwaim*, perhaps in southeastern Arabia; or it may be a variant name for Ophir (cf. comment on 8:18).

7 The term rendered "doorframes" (*sippîm;* sing., *sap*) usually is limited to the "threshold" or "sill," i.e., to "the horizontal lower stone of the doorframe" (KB, p. 663); but the present context, of beams overlaid with gold, favors a broader mean-

ing. The carved decorations included palm trees and flowers (1 Kings 6:29) but especially "cherubim." The appropriateness of depicting these angelic creatures lay in their association with the holy and majestic presence of God (Gen 3:24; cf. their major function in vv.10–14, concerning the inner room). They appear normally in human form but with wings (Ezek 1:5–6). (Some critics attempt to connect the cherub with some mythological sphinx, half man and half beast. See the comment on Ezekiel 1:4–14; EBC, 6:757–58.)

8 The "six hundred talents of fine gold" with which the interior of the oracle was overlaid are not mentioned in 1 Kings 6. They consumed only a fraction of what David had provided (1 Chron 22:14) but still constituted a huge amount (cf. NIV mg.), about twenty-three tons of gold.

9 The "nails," on the other hand, which fastened the gold sheets to the walls, involved a much smaller amount of gold, totaling only twenty ounces (one and one-fourth pounds, NIV mg.), a figure that is again not mentioned in 1 Kings. So for once some critics have charged Ezra, not with exaggeration, but of claiming too little for holding all the gold sheeting in place. As Curtis (p. 327) says, fifty shekels "is clearly impossible, and it is doubtful whether even the Chronicler would make such a careless statement"; and he proceeds to emend the text. Yet if we follow Keil's suggestion (p. 317) of "gilding," there should be an adequate amount for nails, or even spikes.

11 The two large cherubim, when placed side by side, had a total wingspread of thirty-five feet (v.11). They are thus not to be confused with the small cherubim on the ark but were great gold-plated figures of olive wood (1 Kings 6:23), which filled the Most Holy Place (v.10) and overshadowed the whole ark.

14 The temple's "curtain" corresponds to the "veil" that separated the two rooms in the Mosaic tabernacle (Exod 26:31), and it was supplementary to the wooden doors mentioned in 4:22 (q.v.) and 1 Kings (6:31–32). It emphasized the fact that even though the awesome presence of God, represented by the glory cloud in the Most Holy Place, was present with men, it was still at the same time separated from them. The curtain portrayed the spiritual truth that the way to God was not yet open (Heb 9:8) and that it would not be till Christ would perform the true atonement to reconcile God and man. This then would end the anticipatory forms of the older testament, including the veil (Matt 27:51).

15 The "two pillars" were freestanding, set up at the portico in front of the temple (1 Kings 7:21). Their size, as stated in the present MT, namely, "thirty-five cubits long," seems to be the result of a copyist's error. The whole building was only twenty cubits high (cf. comments on v.3); and the parallel passage in 1 Kings (7:15) specifies that they were eighteen cubits each (twenty-seven feet), a figure confirmed by 2 Kings 25:17 (NIV mg.) and Jeremiah 52:21. Some have suggested that the thirty-five cubits in Chronicles might approximate the sum of the length of both pillars. Keil (KD, *Kings*, p. 97) objects, "But this mode of reconciling the discrepancy is improbable and is hardly in harmony with the words of Chronicles." He suggests instead: "The number 35 evidently arose from confounding the numerical letters *yodh-heth* (= 18) with *lamedh-he* (= 35)." Such a confusion would have been even more likely in the early, cursive Phoenician script than in the later, Aramaic square character (Payne, "Validity," pp. 121–22).

Each pillar had an ornamented capital (cf. the NIV mg. to v.16), which added "five cubits" (c. nine feet) to its height. The existence of ornamental pillars has been repeatedly attested by archaeology; subbases for such pillars were found in front of the temple at Hazor, and obelisks constitute an Egyptian illustration of the same sort of thing. Their very names (NIV mg. to v.17) symbolized the sustaining power of God, concretely exhibited by the permanence of the temple (cf. the discussion by Albright, *Archaeology*, pp. 144–48).

4:1 Turning in chapter 4 to the furnishings of the temple, Ezra first describes its main "altar." This has particular value because the corresponding description in 1 Kings 7, which once stood between v.22 and v.23, seems to have been lost by scribal paraleipsis: the eye of a copyist must have jumped from the "He made," found in 2 Chronicles 4:1 (now lost in Kings), to the "He made" of v.2 (1 Kings 7:23), since Kings does subsequently allude to this altar (8:64; 9:25). It was large— about thirty feet square (NIV mg.)—made of "bronze," and apparently in stages, with connecting stairs, since it rose to a height of fifteen feet (for an illustration, cf. J.B. Pritchard, *The Ancient Near East in Pictures Relating to the Old Testament* [Princeton: University Press, 1954], fig. 627). Just as in the tabernacle, the altar was the first main object to be met as one entered the sanctuary court. It demonstrates that God may be approached only through sacrifices, i.e., through the substitutionary and testamentary death of Christ (Heb 8:2–3; 9:12).

2 The "Sea of cast metal" corresponded to the more modest bronze laver of the tabernacle (Exod 30:18). It was used by the priests for washing (v.6; cf. Exod 30:21) and taught the necessity for purity on the part of those approaching God. It pointed typically to the washing of regeneration and sanctification provided in Christ (Titus 3:5; Heb 9:10). The circumference of the Sea, given as forty-five feet, was only approximate; for its diameter was a full fifteen feet (ten cubits).

3 The "cast figures of bulls" (*beqārîm*) "in two rows," "below the rim," are called simply "gourds" (*peqāʿîm*) in 1 Kings 7:24. Unless this is a copyist's mistake due to the similarly sounding words, the explanation may lie in a more general description in Kings of these ornamental bands of round-shaped animal heads.

4 Distinct from these cattle were the "twelve bulls" that stood under the Sea and served as its base (cf. illustration in ZPEB, 5:318). They probably denoted the twelve tribes of Israel (cf. Exod 24:4), just as the tribes had once camped, three on each side of the tabernacle (Num 2).

5 That the Sea was "a handbreadth" thick refers to a person's four fingers held together (i.e., a little over three inches; cf. KB, p. 355). The capacity stated in the present Chronicles text of "three thousand baths" (cf. NIV mg.) should be read with 1 Kings 7:26 as "two thousand." The suggestion of C. Wylie (BA 12 [1949]: 89), that Chronicles speaks of the Sea as a cylinder and Kings as a hemisphere is unacceptable on two counts: (1) because it denies the historicity of at least one of the records, since the actual Sea could not have been both shapes at the same time; and (2) because even a perfect cylinder, fifteen feet wide and seven and one-half feet (five cubits, v.2) deep, would hold only fifteen hundred baths (ZPEB, 5:317). There must have been a considerable bulge to account even for the two-thousand-bath (= twelve hundred gallon) capacity; and some criticism concludes, "The Chronicler, as often, expands the figure" (Curtis, p. 173).

Yet before accusing the Bible of deliberate and unconcealable falsification, one should consider the likelihood of accidental corruption by a later scribe (see Appendix A). Chronicles' larger number could have arisen either through a mistaken reading of the dual *'alpayim* ("two thousand") in Kings as plural (*'alāpîm,* "thousands") and then through supplying a "three" (which occurs four times in the preceding verse), or through an unclear reading of the numerical symbols—the use of which is demonstrable archaeologically, from the eighth-century Samaritan ostraca down to the fourth-century Elephantine papyri—i.e., reading three short vertical strokes for an original two (cf. Payne, "Validity," p. 122).

6 The large reservoir that constituted the Sea then supplied the "ten" smaller "basins" (holding 40 baths, or 230 gallons each) on their wheeled carts or bases (described in detail in 1 Kings 7:27–39). Archaeological attestation for the latter dating to about 1150 B.C. has been found in Cyprus; this was almost two centuries before the time of Solomon (see illustration in NBD, p. 1244). Their function (contrast comment on v.2) was for rinsing the offerings, a point not brought out in the parallel passage in 1 Kings (7:38–39).

7 As compared with the one golden lampstand in the tabernacle, the temple had "ten" (cf. the plural as mentioned in 1 Chron 28:15; Jer 52:19); and they were no doubt made "according to the specifications" as in Exodus 25:31–40. Once again (cf. comment on v.1) vv.7–10 find no corresponding, parallel passages in 1 Kings 7, and probably for the same reason (i.e., scribal paraleipsis): compare how 2 Chronicles 4:7 (now lost in Kings) commences—"He made," just as 4:11 does (= 1 Kings 7:40); yet Kings does mention the contents of vv.7–10 in its concluding summary (vv.48–49 = 2 Chron 4:19–20 on the lampstands and tables; cf. 1 Kings 7:12 on the courts). The lampstands, each one with its seven branches, continue to symbolize the perfection with which God's church must unceasingly shine for him (Lev 24:3–4; Matt 5:14), as supplied by the oil of God's powerful Holy Spirit (Zech 4:2–6; cf. Payne, *Prophecy,* p. 184).

8 The "ten tables" present us with a similar augmentation, over the single one that was made for the tabernacle (cf. comment on 1 Chron 28:16). But it does seem that only one table at a time (13:11; 29:18) was used for displaying the bread, as it was set out fresh every Sabbath, to symbolize Israel's reestablished communion with God and their life in his Presence (v.19; Lev 24:5–8; cf. the comments on 1 Chron 9:32; 28:16, and the Notes below).

The "sprinkling bowls" were not particularly associated with the tables but seem rather to have been used for collecting the blood of sacrifices, which was then sprinkled about the altar in the temple services of atonement (cf. Exod 24:6; 29:16; Lev 1:5; 3:2).

9 Moses' tabernacle had only a single court. The more developed ritual of the temple led to a division between the inner courtyard of the priests (1 Kings 6:36; 7:12)—also called the upper court, because it was elevated, so that the priests would be more visible as they performed their sacred duties (Jer 36:10)—and the outer "larger court" for Israel's general worshipers. Yet this very division into two courts (2 Kings 23:12) gave concrete expression to the fact that under the older testament there had not yet been achieved that universal priesthood of believers that would come about through Jesus Christ. In him all the people of God have direct access to the Father (Jer 31:34; Gal 3:28; Heb 4:14-16). The further distinction, however, of a separate "court of the women" arose only under intertestamental Judaism and is not an OT teaching (ZPEB, 5:649-50).

12 In the summary of the work performed by Huram (cf. comment on 2:14) for the temple (vv.12-16), the first items to be mentioned are the two bronze pillars (cf. comment on 3:15) with their "bowl-shaped capitals," which are described in 1 Kings 7:17-20. Their bulbous lower capitals were covered by an ornamented network or grating, while the upper sections consisted of a flaring crown, like opened lilies.

16 The name "Huram-Abi" connotes "Huram my administrator" (see comment on 2:13).

17 The places at which Huram cast the bronze articles for the temple were located "in the plain east of the Jordan," about halfway between Galilee and the Dead Sea. "Succoth," modern Deir Allah, has been excavated by H. Franken; and "Zarethan" (cf. NIV mg. and 1 Kings 7:46), probably the modern Saʿidiyeh, by J. Pritchard. Here the deep clay provided suitable molds (*ʿbî*, literally, "thickness") for the great metal objects.

21 In the summary of the temple furnishings (vv.19-22), the "gold floral work" refers to the ornamentation on the lampstands (Exod 25:33).

22 The "gold doors" were made of carved olive wood, which was in turn overlaid with gold (3:7; 1 Kings 6:31-35). The "doors of the main hall" opened onto the portico and the courts and led from the "Holy Place," which was the outer room of the temple (cf. comment on 3:5). The inner doors, to the oracle, provided protection additional to the veil, or curtain, for sealing off this Most Holy Place (cf. comment on 3:14).

Notes

4 The present MT for the latter part of this verse is רֹחַב הַבַּיִת אַמּוֹת עֶשְׂרִים וְהַגֹּבַהּ מֵאָה (*rōḥab habbayit ʾammôṯ ʿeśrîm wehaggōḇah mēʾāh*, "the width of the house, cubits twenty; and the heighth, hundred and twenty"). But for the last two words, the BH mg. (p. 1380) reads אַמּוֹת עֶשְׂרִים (*ʾammôṯ ʿeśrîm*, "cubits twenty"), as supported by a number of Greek and Syrian MSS; cf. Ezek 42:16: אֵמוֹת (*ʾēmôṯ*); Kethiv: אַמּוֹת (*ʾammôṯ*, "cubits"); Qere: מֵאוֹת (*mēʾôṯ*, "hundreds").

10 The term describing the large cherubim as "sculptured" (צַעֲצֻעִים, *ṣaʿaṣuʿîm*) occurs only here and denotes "things fashioned by melting," and hence "images" (KB, p. 810) or "image work" (BDB, p. 847).

4:8 Some critics are skeptical of the Chronicler's multiple tables of show bread. They speak either of "an exaggeration here" or, self-contradictory, that "they may have been used for . . . the ten lampstands" (Myers, *Chronicles*, 2:24)—all this despite v.19's attestation, both to their plurality and to their use for holding "the bread of the [divine] Presence."

---

3. Dedication

5:1–7:22

¹When all the work Solomon had done for the temple of the LORD was finished, he brought in the things his father David had dedicated—the silver and gold and all the furnishings—and he placed them in the treasuries of God's temple.

²Then Solomon summoned to Jerusalem the elders of Israel, all the heads of the tribes and the chiefs of the Israelite families, to bring up the ark of the LORD's covenant from Zion, the City of David. ³And all the men of Israel came together to the king at the time of the festival in the seventh month.

⁴When all the elders of Israel had arrived, the Levites took up the ark, ⁵and they brought up the ark and the Tent of Meeting and all the sacred furnishings in it. The priests, who were Levites, carried them up; ⁶and King Solomon and the entire assembly of Israel that had gathered about him were before the ark, sacrificing so many sheep and cattle that they could not be recorded or counted.

⁷The priests then brought the ark of the LORD's covenant to its place in the inner sanctuary of the temple, the Most Holy Place, and put it beneath the wings of the cherubim. ⁸The cherubim spread their wings over the place of the ark and covered the ark and its carrying poles. ⁹These poles were so long that their ends, extending from the ark, could be seen from in front of the inner sanctuary, but not from outside the Holy Place; and they are still there today. ¹⁰There was nothing in the ark except the two tablets that Moses had placed in it at Horeb, where the LORD made a covenant with the Israelites after they came out of Egypt.

¹¹The priests then withdrew from the Holy Place. All the priests who were there had consecrated themselves, regardless of their divisions. ¹²All the Levites who were musicians—Asaph, Heman, Jeduthun and their sons and relatives—stood on the east side of the altar, dressed in fine linen and playing cymbals, harps and lyres. They were accompanied by 120 priests sounding trumpets. ¹³The trumpeters and singers joined in unison, as with one voice, to give praise and thanks to the LORD. Accompanied by trumpets, cymbals and other instruments, they raised their voices in praise to the LORD and sang:

> "He is good;
> his love endures forever."

Then the temple of the LORD was filled with a cloud, ¹⁴and the priests could not perform their service because of the cloud, for the glory of the LORD filled the temple of God.

^{6:1}Then Solomon said, "The LORD has said that he would dwell in a dark cloud; ²I have built a magnificent temple for you, a place for you to dwell forever."

³While the whole assembly of Israel was standing there, the king turned around and blessed them. ⁴Then he said:

> "Praise be to the LORD, the God of Israel, who with his hands has fulfilled what he promised with his mouth to my father David. For he said, ⁵'Since the day I brought my people out of Egypt, I have not chosen a city in any tribe of Israel to have a temple built for my Name to be there, nor have I chosen anyone to be the leader over my people Israel. ⁶But now I have chosen Jerusalem for my Name to be there, and I have chosen David to rule my people Israel.'
>
> ⁷"My father David had it in his heart to build a temple for the Name of the LORD, the God of Israel. ⁸But the LORD said to my father David, 'Because it was in your heart to build a temple for my Name, you did well to have this in

your heart. ⁹Nevertheless, you are not the one to build the temple, but your son, who is your own flesh and blood—he is the one who will build the temple for my Name.'

¹⁰"The Lord has kept the promise he made. I have succeeded David my father and now I sit on the throne of Israel, just as the Lord promised, and I have built the temple for the Name of the Lord, the God of Israel. ¹¹There I have placed the ark, in which is the covenant of the Lord that he made with the people of Israel."

¹²Then Solomon stood before the altar of the Lord in front of the whole assembly of Israel and spread out his hands. ¹³Now he had made a bronze platform, five cubits long, five cubits wide and three cubits high, and had placed it in the center of the outer court. He stood on the platform and then knelt down before the whole assembly of Israel and spread out his hands toward heaven. ¹⁴He said:

"O Lord, God of Israel, there is no God like you in heaven or on earth—you who keep your covenant of love with your servants who continue wholeheartedly in your way. ¹⁵You have kept your promise to your servant David my father; with your mouth you have promised and with your hand you have fulfilled it—as it is today.

¹⁶"Now Lord, God of Israel, keep for your servant David my father the promises you made to him when you said, 'You shall never fail to have a man to sit before me on the throne of Israel, if only your sons are careful in all they do to walk before me according to my law, as you have done.' ¹⁷And now, O Lord, God of Israel, let your word that you promised your servant David come true.

¹⁸"But will God really dwell on earth with men? The heavens, even the highest heavens, cannot contain you. How much less this temple I have built! ¹⁹Yet give attention to your servant's prayer and his plea for mercy, O Lord my God. Hear the cry and the prayer that your servant is praying in your presence. ²⁰May your eyes be open toward this temple day and night, this place of which you said you would put your Name there. May you hear the prayer your servant prays toward this place. ²¹Hear the supplications of your servant and of your people Israel when they pray toward this place. Hear from heaven, your dwelling place; and when you hear, forgive.

²²"When a man wrongs his neighbor and is required to take an oath and he comes and swears the oath before your altar in this temple, ²³then hear from heaven and act. Judge between your servants, repaying the guilty by bringing down on his own head what he has done. Declare the innocent not guilty and so establish his innocence.

²⁴"When your people Israel have been defeated by an enemy because they have sinned against you and when they turn back and confess your name, praying and making supplication before you in this temple, ²⁵then hear from heaven and forgive the sin of your people Israel and bring them back to the land you gave to them and their fathers.

²⁶"When the heavens are shut up and there is no rain because your people have sinned against you, and when they pray toward this place and confess your name and turn from their sin because you have afflicted them, ²⁷then hear from heaven and forgive the sin of your servants, your people Israel. Teach them the right way to live, and send rain on the land you gave your people for an inheritance.

²⁸"When famine or plague comes to the land, or blight or mildew, locusts or grasshoppers, or when enemies besiege them in any of their cities, whatever disaster or disease may come, ²⁹and when a prayer or plea is made by any of your people Israel—each one aware of his afflictions and pains, and spreading out his hands toward this temple— ³⁰then hear from heaven, your dwelling place. Forgive, and deal with each man according to all he does, since you know his heart (for you alone know the hearts of men), ³¹so that they will fear you and walk in your ways all the time they live in the land you gave our fathers.

32"As for the foreigner who does not belong to your people Israel but has come from a distant land because of your great name and your mighty hand and your outstretched arm—when he comes and prays toward this temple, 33then hear from heaven, your dwelling place, and do whatever the foreigner asks of you, so that all the peoples of the earth may know your name and fear you, as do your own people Israel, and may know that this house I have built bears your Name.

34"When your people go to war against their enemies, wherever you send them, and when they pray to you toward this city you have chosen and the temple I have built for your Name, 35then hear from heaven their prayer and their plea, and uphold their cause.

36"When they sin against you—for there is no one who does not sin—and you become angry with them and give them over to the enemy, who takes them captive to a land far away or near; 37and if they have a change of heart in the land where they are held captive, and repent and plead with you in the land of their captivity and say, 'We have sinned, we have done wrong and acted wickedly'; 38and if they turn back to you with all their heart and soul in the land of their captivity where they were taken, and pray toward the land you gave their fathers, toward the city you have chosen and toward the temple I have built for your Name; 39then from heaven, your dwelling place, hear their prayer and their pleas, and uphold their cause. And forgive your people, who have sinned against you.

40"Now, my God, may your eyes be open and your ears attentive to the prayers offered in this place.

41"Now arise, O LORD God, and come to your resting place,
    you and the ark of your might.
May your priests, O LORD God, be clothed with salvation,
    may your saints rejoice in your goodness.
42O LORD God, do not reject your anointed one.
    Remember the great love promised to David your servant."

7:1When Solomon finished praying, fire came down from heaven and consumed the burnt offering and the sacrifices, and the glory of the LORD filled the temple. 2The priests could not enter the temple of the LORD because the glory of the LORD filled it. 3When all the Israelites saw the fire coming down and the glory of the LORD above the temple, they knelt on the pavement with their faces to the ground, and they worshiped and gave thanks to the LORD, saying,

"He is good;
    his love endures forever."

4Then the king and all the people offered sacrifices before the LORD. 5And King Solomon offered a sacrifice of twenty-two thousand head of cattle and a hundred and twenty thousand sheep and goats. So the king and all the people dedicated the temple of God. 6The priests took their positions, as did the Levites with the LORD's musical instruments, which King David had made for praising the LORD and which were used when he gave thanks, saying, "His love endures forever." Opposite the Levites, the priests blew their trumpets, and all the Israelites were standing.

7Solomon consecrated the middle part of the courtyard in front of the temple of the LORD, and there he offered burnt offerings and the fat of the fellowship offerings, because the bronze altar he had made could not hold the burnt offerings, the grain offerings and the fat portions.

8So Solomon observed the festival at that time for seven days, and all Israel with him—a vast assembly, people from Lebo Hamath to the Wadi of Egypt. 9On the eighth day they held an assembly, for they had celebrated the dedication of the altar for seven days and the festival for seven days more. 10On the twenty-third day of the seventh month he sent the people to their homes, joyful and glad in heart for the good things the LORD had done for David and Solomon and for his people Israel.

¹¹When Solomon had finished the temple of the LORD and the royal palace, and had succeeded in carrying out all he had in mind to do in the temple of the LORD and in his own palace, ¹²the LORD appeared to him at night and said:

"I have heard your prayer and have chosen this place for myself as a temple for sacrifices.

¹³"When I shut up the heavens so that there is no rain, or command locusts to devour the land or send a plague among my people, ¹⁴if my people, who are called by my name, will humble themselves and pray and seek my face and turn from their wicked ways, then will I hear from heaven and will forgive their sin and will heal their land. ¹⁵Now my eyes will be open and my ears attentive to the prayers offered in this place. ¹⁶I have chosen and consecrated this temple so that my Name may be there forever. My eyes and my heart will always be there.

¹⁷"As for you, if you walk before me as David your father did, and do all I command, and observe my decrees and laws, ¹⁸I will establish your royal throne, as I covenanted with David your father when I said, 'You shall never fail to have a man to rule over Israel.'

¹⁹"But if you turn away and forsake the decrees and commands I have given you and go off to serve other gods and worship them, ²⁰then I will uproot Israel from my land, which I have given them, and will reject this temple I have consecrated for my Name. I will make it a byword and an object of ridicule among all peoples. ²¹And though this temple is now so imposing, all who pass by will be appalled and say, 'Why has the LORD done such a thing to this land and to this temple?' ²²People will answer, 'Because they have forsaken the LORD, the God of their fathers, who brought them out of Egypt, and have embraced other gods, worshiping and serving them—that is why he brought all this disaster on them.' "

After having described the construction of Solomon's temple in chapters 3 and 4, the Chronicler devotes his next three chapters to events that are connected with its dedication. The material makes up, in fact, a single unit that extends from the king's summons to the men of Israel in 5:2 down through their dismissal in 7:10, together with an introductory verse and an appended but related answer of God to the dedicatory prayer (7:11–22). These three chapters present a close parallel to their canonical source in 1 Kings 8:1–9:9. Much of their theological importance, moreover, lies in the light that Solomon's ceremonies of dedication throw on the significance of the temple concept as a whole.

When he had assembled the representative leaders of Israel, the king's first act was to conduct the ark of God's covenant into the temple and to enshrine it in the Most Holy Place (5:1–10). He thus constituted the structure on Mount Moriah as the successor to Israel's previous sanctuaries; and God confirmed the validity of Solomon's procedure by taking up his own, localized dwelling within the temple and filling it with the "shekinah," the cloud of his Presence (vv.11–14).

Chapter 6 consists primarily of two utterances by King Solomon: his blessing on the people, which is actually a testimony of praise to the Lord for his faithfulness in prospering the temple project up to this point (vv.3–11), and his long prayer to God, dedicating the building for his sanctuary and imploring his favorable response when Israel should submit their petitions toward his Presence within the structure (vv.12–42). This action too was visibly confirmed by Yahweh, as he sent down fire from heaven on the new altar (7:1–3). Two weeks of extensive dedicatory sacrifices and of feasting followed (vv.4–10).

A final section, dated some time later, after Solomon had completed his own palace, describes how the Lord appeared to the king by night and verbally confirmed his agreement to the request that he should dwell in the temple and answer the prayers that were addressed to him there. His blessing, however, was conditioned on Israel's continued faithfulness; and he threatened exile and the temple's destruction if the nation should become apostate (7:11–22).

1 A preliminary action of Solomon was to bring into the temple "the things his father David had dedicated," examples of which may be found itemized in 1 Chronicles 18:10–11; 22:14; 26:26–27; and 29:2–5. Some of David's treasures must have remained, even after the great outlays for erecting the temple. The "treasuries" themselves may have been located in the "upper parts" (3:9) of the building, in some of the rooms that surrounded the sanctuary proper (1 Kings 6:5–10).

2 The first step in the activities of dedication was for the king and the assembled national leaders to bring the ark up from the old citadel of Zion to the temple area situated on the more northerly ridge of Moriah (cf. comment on 3:1; Ps 48:2). For forty years the ark had remained in the tent that David had first pitched on its arrival in Jerusalem (cf. comments on 1 Chron 15:1; 16:1).

3 The assembly was delayed until "the festival in the seventh month," namely, until the climactic season in Israel's sacred calendar that centered about the harvest Feast of Tabernacles (cf. 7:8–10). The work on the structure as such had been finished (5:1) in the eighth month of Solomon's eleventh year (1 Kings 6:38), i.e., in September/October 960 B.C. (cf. comment on 3:2; ZPEB, 1:829–30). This therefore entails a lapse of eleven months, until the fall of 959, for the official dedication ceremonies; but there were doubtless other matters that had to be arranged after the completion of the building.

4 In transporting the ark Solomon took the added precaution of employing the priests, taken from among the total group of Levi, to perform this work (vv.5, 7; 1 Kings 8:3; cf. comments on 1 Chron 13:10; 15:4).

5 Also "brought up" was the "Tent of Meeting," or tabernacle (cf. comment on 1:3), from its previous location at Gibeon (cf. 1 Chron 16:39).

6 The large number of sheep and cattle sacrificed followed the more modest precedent set by David when he first brought the ark to Jerusalem (1 Chron 15:26; 16:1–3).

7 The holy object was placed in the temple's "inner sanctuary" (*deḇîr*). The KJV renders this noun as "oracle," as if from the root "to speak"; for God did speak forth his oracles, designed for the guidance of Israel, from the cloud of his Presence that rested over the ark (Exod 25:22; Lev 1:1). More likely, however, *deḇîr* derives from an Arabic word meaning "back," hence the shrine that was situated in the innermost, or back, portion of the temple, "the Most Holy Place" (cf. comment on 3:5). On "the cherubim," under whose wings it rested, see the comment on 3:11.

9 Though the curtain, or veil (cf. comment on 3:14), concealed the ark itself from view, the poles by which the ark was carried must have projected on one or both of

459

its sides, so as to be visible from the door. The statement that "they are still there today" must have been quoted by Ezra from his sources (9:29), particularly from 1 Kings (8:8), out of those portions that were written before the destruction of Jerusalem in 586 B.C. The ark had been gone for over a century by Ezra's day (cf. ZPEB, 1:310 on the fate of the ark).

10 The fact that by Solomon's time "there was nothing in the ark except the two tablets" of the Decalogue shows that the golden pot of manna (Exod 16:32–34) and Aaron's rod that budded (Num 17:10–11; Heb 9:4) must have been lost during the intervening vicissitudes through which the ark passed. The Chronicler's reference at this point to the Lord's Sinaitic covenant may be attributed to the fact that the Ten Commandments, as engraved on Moses' two tablets of stone, expressed the basic response that God expected from his covenant people, whom he had already redeemed (Exod 20:2; cf. 19:4–6). The tablets could in a sense be called "the testimony" (25:16, 21) to his covenant.

11 In the ceremony during which God granted his confirmation to this new home for the ark (vv. 11–14), Ezra's word that the priests were present "regardless of their divisions" refers to the way they had been organized by David into their twenty-four hereditary courses (1 Chron 24:3–19). But the normal rotations in service could be disregarded on an occasion as significant as this, in which all were present.

12 The Chronicler is the first OT writer to refer to the "fine linen" worn by the Levites (cf. comment on 1 Chron 15:27). The "120 priests sounding trumpets" (cf. 15:24 comment) may suggest a figure of five drawn from each of the twenty-four priestly courses (cf. on 1 Chron 24:4).

13 The idea expressed by the word *ḥeseḏ*, here rendered as God's "love," means more specifically his "faithfulness" (cf. on 1 Chron 16:41). The concluding words, about the presence of a "cloud," have provoked a series of skeptical explanations. Some have suggested that "the temple was filled with a blinding cloud, doubtless from the censers" (North, "The Chronicler," 1:416). Others have referred to smoke caused by the fire from heaven; but this event did not occur until the situation described in chapter 7, and even there (v. 1) it is distinguished from "the glory."

14 The cloud, which was in fact "the glory of the LORD," had first guided the people of Israel out of Egypt (Exod 13:21–22) and then through the wilderness (40:36–38); and it is associated with the angel of God (14:19; 23:20–23), presumably the preincarnate presence of Christ (Payne, *Theology*, pp. 46–47, 168). At the dedication of the Mosaic tabernacle, almost five hundred years before Solomon, the cloud of God's glory had filled that earlier sanctuary (40:34–35). In the days just before the Exile, Ezekiel had envisioned the sin of Israel as driving the glory cloud out of the sanctuary (Ezek 10:18–19; 11:23); and it had not returned to the second temple, of Ezra's day. Intertestamental Judaism still speculated about the "shekinah," as it came to be called, meaning God's "dwelling." It appeared during Christ's first coming (Matt 17:5; Acts 1:9), and it will accompany his glorious second advent (Acts 1:11; Rev 1:7; 14:14; cf. R.E. Hough, *The Ministry of the Glory Cloud* [New York: Philosophical Library, 1955]).

6:1 The first two verses of 2 Chronicles 6 are a reflection by Solomon on the immediately preceding event (5:11–14), when God had demonstrated his approval on the king's relocation of the ark in the new temple. The Lord's words that he mentions, about dwelling "in a dark cloud," refer to God's presence on the top of Mount Sinai, shrouded in a cloud (Exod 19:9; 20:21), and also in the Mosaic tabernacle, as veiled off in its most Holy Place (Lev 16:2).

2 Though the purpose of the temple was for the Lord "to dwell" there "forever," there was still the attached condition that Israel must continue faithful (7:19–20; Matt 23:37–38). They did not; and the temple was twice destroyed (586 B.C. and A.D. 70). But Christ has promised that he will yet reign on Mount Zion (Matt 23:39) and rule forever in the New Jerusalem (Rev 21:2).

3 While he was speaking with God (vv.1–2), Solomon had been facing the temple and the cloud of the divine Presence that filled it. Now, for his address (vv.3–11), with its blessing on the people, Solomon turned around and faced east, toward the crowd that stood beyond the altar.

4 Solomon's blessing on Israel consisted of a recalling of God's verbal promises to David—that the temple would be built and David's dynasty established (v.10; cf. 1 Chron 17)—and of God's material fulfillments of them "with his hands," i.e., in history.

6 These included God's choice of Jerusalem, as stated in 1 Chronicles 22:1, that his "Name" might be "there" (vv.8, 20; cf. comment on v.33), which meant his very Presence (cf. on 1 Chron 22:7).

7–9 Solomon's thoughts on David's relationship to the temple repeat the latter's own words from 1 Chronicles 28:2–3.

10–11 God's covenant could be said to be in the ark, insofar as the two tablets of the Decalogue that the ark contained did constitute "the testimony" to it (cf. on 5:10). This covenant is identified in 1 Kings 8:21 as the Sinaitic (cf. comments on 1 Chron 16:15 and 17:12), the one that God "made with our fathers when he brought them out of Egypt," though the Chronicler apparently felt that this was understood. Some critics have, however, associated his omission with certain antipathy against Sinai (see Introduction: Purpose, 2).

12 For making his major prayer to God in chapter 6 (vv.12–42), Solomon turned back from facing the people (cf. v.3) and, as he stood "before the altar," again faced west, toward the temple.

13 This verse forms an insertion made by Ezra and is not found in 1 Kings 8, between v.22 and v.23. It seems to clarify the fact that Solomon was not "before the altar" to perform a priestly function. He stood rather on an elevated "bronze platform" (cf. the NIV mg. on its dimensions) so that his prayer could be better seen and heard by the people. The term for "platform" (*kîyôr*) normally designates a "basin" but here denotes a "stage," especially if rounded (BDB, s.v., #4). (For a listing of archaeological parallels, as identified by Albright, Pritchard et al., cf.

Myers, *Chronicles*, 2:36.) The way that the king "then knelt down" (cf. 1 Kings 8:54) gave public acknowledgment to the fact that he too was only God's servant, administering a kingdom that was not his own (cf. comment on 1 Chron 28:5).

14 The prayer itself through v.39 closely approximated 1 Kings 8:23–50a. It consists of praise to the Lord for his faithfulness to his covenant (vv.14–15) and of petition for its preservation (vv.16–17). Then come more words of praise, for God's infinity in space (v.18), and yet of petition, for his attention to the king's and people's prayers when made toward the temple (vv.19–42). The Hebrew text speaks literally of God's keeping of "the covenant and the *ḥesed*." These synonymous expressions are rightly rendered "covenant of love" (NIV; cf. comments on 5:13; 1 Chron 16:41). In other words, God's covenantal love, made efficacious through the death of Christ, is the source of all blessings, both for believers today and for those who received "the promise of eternal inheritance . . . under the first testament" (Heb 9:15 KJV). He reserves these blessings, moreover, for those who are his "servants," because faith must always be manifested by obedience (v.16; James 2:17–26).

18 In reference to Solomon's constant recognition that "even the highest heavens" (KJV, "the heaven of heavens") cannot contain the infinite Person of Yahweh, see comment to 2:6.

19–21 It was because the king recognized God's infinity that he prayed concerning the requests men make toward "this place" (v.20), toward the earthly temple, that they may be answered by God "from heaven, your dwelling place" (v.21). He proceeded to identify seven concrete situations (vv.22, 24, et al.) for which he requested the Lord's intervention from heaven (vv.23, 25 et al.), as follows:

22–23 1. Swearing to an "oath . . . in this temple." Testimony in doubtful cases was confirmed by an oath at the sanctuary (Exod 22:10–11; Lev 6:3–5); so God is petitioned to intervene in order to "establish innocence" (v.23).

24–25 2. "Defeat" and exile "by an enemy." Prayer was needed in such calamities because both of them could be the result of God's punishing their sin (Lev 26:17, 23; Josh 7:11–12; cf. Deut 28:48).

26–27 3. Lack of "rain." The phenomena of nature sometimes have moral causes; specifically, Israel could suffer drought in times of apostasy (Lev 26:19; Deut 11:10 –15; 1 Kings 17:1).

28–31 4. "Disease" or other "disasters." "Plagues" of various sorts could likewise result from sin (Lev 26:16, 20, 25–26; cf. Deut 28 *passim*), because God "knows" what is in "the hearts of men" (v.30; 1 Sam 16:7).

32–33 5. "Foreigners" coming to pray "toward this temple." From its outset Israel's sanctuary was thus designed to be "a house of prayer for all nations" (Isa 56:6–8). The goal of the nation's election was a universal knowledge of God (v.33; Gen 12:3; Eph 2:11–13, 19); and even in OT times aliens who would come in faith to Yahweh were assured of reception as proselytes into Israel (Exod 12:38, 48; Ruth 1:16; 2:12).

They would be attracted by God's "great name," which involved his actual Presence in the temple (cf. comment on v.6). For when the structure is said to "bear" his Name (v.33), the Hebrew reads literally that his name "has been called on" it. This means that God has taken the temple to himself as possession and dominion (just as in election/adoption, Deut 28:10, or as in marriage, Isa 4:1).

34–35 6. In "war." God will fight for his own, who cry to him in the battle (14:11–12; Deut 28:7; 1 Chron 5:20).

36–39 7. In "captivity," caused by "sin." Solomon's confession that there is no one who does not sin emphasizes the consistent biblical teaching on man's total depravity (cf. Deut 28 *passim*; Jer 13:23; 17:9; Eph 2:3). The resulting exile to "a land far away," as well as Israel's subsequent restoration on repentance, had been predicted as early as Moses (Lev 26:33, 44–45); and it all came about (2 Chron 36:16, 22–23), even as Solomon had prayed.

40 At this point Chronicles omits most of the king's prayer that is recorded in the parallel passage of 1 Kings 8:50b–53, since it was less relevant for a Judah that was no longer in exile in Ezra's time.

41 Solomon drew his last two verses from Psalm 132:8–10 (not included in the parallel passage in 1 Kings 8, after v.53). This royal psalm, while anonymous, seems to have been written by David, or by one of his associates, for that similar occasion forty years before, when the ark was first installed in Jerusalem in its tent (cf. this verse and Ps 132:8 with Num 10:35, and Ps 132:13–14 with 1 Chron 16).

42 In his prayer "do not reject your anointed one," the king now meant himself, though in subsequent usage it would express Israel's hope in the coming Messiah, as the climax of Solomon's line (cf. Notes). In Psalm 132:10 it had referred to his father David. Furthermore, to the original wording of the psalm, and as the basis for his own blessing, Solomon added the request for God to "remember the great love" promised to David. Here again (cf. v.14) the word in Hebrew is *ḥesed*, meaning "acts" performed out "of" the Lord's "faithfulness" to his covenant promises. This same basis was later validated when it was taken up by God himself in words given through the prophet Isaiah (Isa 45:3).

7:1 Divine approval that rested on the temple services (cf. comments on vv.1–3) and Solomon's prayer of dedication in particular (ch. 6) was shown by "fire" that "came down from heaven" on the altar. It was in this same way that God had inaugurated the sacrificial services at the Mosaic tabernacle (Lev 9:24) and at the Davidic altar (on Moriah, but some forty years earlier, 1 Chron 21:26).

3 Now all the people also saw "the glory of the LORD above the temple," which constituted a greater manifestation of what had already been revealed to the priests inside (5:13–14). Thus they knelt on "the pavement," which was associated with the outer, lower court (Ezek 40:17; 42:3, though one probably existed in the upper, priestly area too, 40:18), and repeated the familiar refrain about the Lord's faithfulness to his covenant promises (v.6; comment on 5:13).

King Solomon then added a blessing of his own on the congregation (1 Kings 8:55 –61), which was omitted by the Chronicler, perhaps because by the time of Ezra the priests only were accustomed to do this.

5 In the festivities that followed (vv. 4–11), the large numbers of animals sacrificed— 22,000 cattle and 120,000 sheep (cf. 35:7 comment)—are confirmed by 1 Kings 8:63. It defines them as peace offerings to be eaten by the people (cf. comments on 1 Chron 16:1; 29:21). They provided the basis for fifteen full days of feasting (2 Chron 7:9–10).

6 Concerning the Levitical musicians, who stood east of the altar (5:12) away from the temple, see the comments on 1 Chronicles 6:31; 16:4; and chapter 25. The priestly trumpeters were stationed "opposite" them and were therefore west of the altar, between it and the temple.

7 "The fat" of the fellowship (= peace) offerings, along with certain other choice pieces, was presented as a token sacrifice to God, prior to the feasting on the part of the people (Lev 3). Concerning the "burnt offerings" (Lev 1) and "grain offerings" (Lev 2), see the comment on 1 Chronicles 21:23.

8 Solomon had delayed the temple's dedication for a number of months (cf. on 5:3) so that this might be celebrated along with the harvest Feast of Tabernacles, when at the latter season all Israel would be coming in pilgrimage to Jerusalem (Exod 23:16–17). They therefore gathered "from Lebo Hamath" in Lebanon, toward the Euphrates River in the northeast (cf. on 1 Chron 13:5), down "to the Wadi of Egypt," i.e., the Wadi el Arish, midway between Palestine and Egypt to the southwest (Josh 15:5, 47).

9 The "eighth day" marked the final convocation of the Feast of Tabernacles (Lev 23:36; Num 29:35), on the twenty-second day of the seventh month. The special dedication feast, in other words, had lasted "for seven days," from the eighth of the month to the fourteenth, including the great Day of Atonement on the tenth (Lev 16), which was followed by the regular Feast of Tabernacles "for seven days more," from the fifteenth to the twenty-second.

10 The Chronicler's statement that "on the twenty-third day" Solomon "sent the people to their homes" constitutes a summary of the more detailed information of 1 Kings 8:66, that on the eighth "day he sent the people away. They blessed the king and then went home, joyful." Keil's explanation (KD, *Kings*, p. 138) thus speaks of a royal dismissal on the twenty-second day and of the people's return "to their tents" on the twenty-third.

11 Chapter 7 concludes with the Chronicler's description of the Lord's appearance to the king, so as to assure him personally that his prayers on behalf of the temple would be answered (vv. 11–22). But this event occurred only after the king had also completed his "royal palace" (cf. on 1 Chron 14:1), some thirteen years later (1 Kings 7:1; 9:10). The interval brings us down to Solomon's twenty-fourth year, or to 947/946 B.C. (cf. on 2 Chron 3:2; 5:3).

12 This was the Lord's second appearance to Solomon (1 Kings 9:2), the first having occurred at Gibeon at the start of his reign (2 Chron 1:3–13).

13 God's speaking of times when he would "shut up the heavens," etc., specifically recalls the wording of the petitions in Solomon's dedicatory prayer (e.g., 6:26 et al.), which the Lord here promised to answer (vv. 15–16).

14–15 For a comment on the expression "my people, who are called by my name" (v.14), see the comments on 6:32. The sentence, as it continues, forms what is probably the best known and most loved verse in all Chronicles. It expresses, as does no other passage in the Bible, the stipulations that God lays down for a nation to experience his blessing, whether that nation be Solomon's, Ezra's, or our own. Those who have been chosen to be his people must cease from their sins, turn from living lives of proud self-centeredness, pray to the Lord, and yield their desires to his Word and his will. Then, and only then, will he grant heaven-sent revival (v.15).

16 Concerning the significance of God's "Name" being "there," see 6:6 and the comment on 1 Chronicles 22:7.

17–18 The Lord's promise that the Davidic dynasty would "never fail to have a man to rule over Israel" (v.18) emphasizes the messianic hope that characterizes the Chronicler's eschatology (see Introduction: Theology). This same wording reappears elsewhere (e.g., in Mic 5:2). God's covenant to "establish" the throne of David harks back to 1 Chronicles 17 (vv.12, 14); but in the remaining verses of the present revelation, the divinely imposed condition of faithful obedience, which was first revealed in 2 Samuel 7:14b, is made just as explicit as in the parallel passage of 1 Kings 9:6–9.

19–22 The possibility that Solomon and his successors (cf. NIV mg.) might "go off to serve other gods" was what actually happened (1 Kings 11:1–8; 2 Chron 36:16); and it led to the very results (vv.20–22; 36:20) that the king had himself anticipated (6:36).

Notes

5:9 The NIV reading, that "they [the ark's poles] are still there," follows some Hebrew MSS, the ancient version, and 1 Kings 8:8; the common MT reading is singular, that "it [the ark] is still there"—which carries the same implication; see the comment above.

6:28 The Hebrew that underlies the phrase "their cities" is literally "his gates," i.e., Israel's urban communities, fortified with walls and gates.

42 The Leningrad MS B 19ᴬ, together with others, reads plural: "your anointed ones." This would indicate prayer for the whole Davidic dynasty, climaxing in the Messiah (cf. on v.42 above), and perhaps Israel's anointed prophets and priests as well (Payne, *Theology*, pp. 257–58, 271).

C. Solomon's Kingdom (8:1–9:31)

1. Its achievements

8:1–18

[1]At the end of twenty years, during which Solomon built the temple of the LORD and his own palace, [2]Solomon rebuilt the villages that Hiram had given him, and settled Israelites in them. [3]Solomon then went to Hamath Zobah and captured it. [4]He also built up Tadmor in the desert and all the store cities he had built in Hamath. [5]He rebuilt Upper Beth Horon and Lower Beth Horon as fortified cities, with walls and with gates and bars, [6]as well as Baalath and all his store cities, and all the cities for his chariots and for his horses—whatever he desired to build in Jerusalem, in Lebanon and throughout all the territory he ruled.

[7]All the people left from the Hittites, Amorites, Perizzites, Hivites and Jebusites (these peoples were not Israelites), [8]that is, their descendants remaining in the land, whom the Israelites had not destroyed—these Solomon conscripted for his slave labor force, as it is to this day. [9]But Solomon did not make slaves of the Israelites for his work; they were his fighting men, commanders of his captains, and commanders of his chariots and charioteers. [10]They were also King Solomon's chief officials—two hundred and fifty officials supervising the men.

[11]Solomon brought Pharaoh's daughter up from the City of David to the palace he had built for her, for he said, "My wife must not live in the palace of David king of Israel, because the places the ark of the LORD has entered are holy."

[12]On the altar of the LORD that he had built in front of the portico, Solomon sacrificed burnt offerings to the LORD, [13]according to the daily requirement for offerings commanded by Moses for Sabbaths, New Moons and the three annual feasts—the Feast of Unleavened Bread, the Feast of Weeks and the Feast of Tabernacles. [14]In keeping with the ordinance of his father David, he appointed the divisions of the priests for their duties, and the Levites to lead the praise and to assist the priests according to each day's requirement. He also appointed the gatekeepers by divisions for the various gates, because this was what David the man of God had ordered. [15]They did not deviate from the king's commands to the priests or to the Levites in any matter, including that of the treasuries.

[16]All Solomon's work was carried out, from the day the foundation of the temple of the LORD was laid until its completion. So the temple of the LORD was finished.

[17]Then Solomon went to Ezion Geber and Elath on the coast of Edom. [18]And Hiram sent him ships commanded by his own officers, men who knew the sea. These, with Solomon's men, sailed to Ophir and brought back four hundred and fifty talents of gold, which they delivered to King Solomon.

The Spirit of God guided Ezra to encourage his people by rehearsing in 1 Chronicles the history of King David's God-given power (cf. the introductory discussion to 10:1–20:8). Second Chronicles now contains a corresponding presentation of the results of serving God as these are exhibited by Solomon with all his glory. The Chronicler thus concludes his record about David's son by outlining the achievements of his kingdom (ch. 8), to be followed, in turn, by illustrations of the splendor that surrounded his rule (ch. 9). Ezra's content corresponds to the material found in 1 Kings, except that he omits the following sections, probably because they would not have contributed to his goal of strengthening Judah's theocracy: the king's enlarged but bureaucratic organization (1 Kings 4), his extravagant palace complex (7:1 –12), the idolatry that resulted from his gross polygamy (11:1–8), and the political deterioration that resulted during his latter years (vv.9–40).

Second Chronicles 8 parallels 1 Kings 9, with its catalog of King Solomon's successful enterprises. These include his expansion, both civil and military (vv.1–6); his organization of manpower (vv. 7–10); his guidance of public worship (vv. 11–16); and his commercial achievements (vv. 17–18).

1 The date, after the "twenty years" indicated in the text, was 946 B.C. (cf. on 7:11).

2 The reference to "villages that Hiram had given" (KJV, "restored") to the king assumes without further comment the unhappy record preserved in 1 Kings 9:11–13, about how Solomon had previously had to surrender twenty non-Israelite towns in Galilee to the Tyrian, apparently because of unpaid building debts (cf. 2 Chron 2:10, 15). Hiram, moreover, found this collateral so poor that Solomon seems to have had to take back the territory. He did then alleviate the poverty of the towns by "settling Israelites in them" and thus succeeded in expanding his borders.

3 Solomon's only recorded military campaign resulted in his conquest of "Hamath" in Lebanon, perhaps for having abandoned its former friendship (1 Chron 18:9–10) and breaking the peace. Hamath bordered on "Zobah," which had already been occupied by the Hebrews (see on 18:3); and the two place names are combined, since by Ezra's day they had been joined into the one Persian province.

4 "Tadmor in the desert" was the oasis known in Roman times as Palmyra, home of the fabulous Queen Zenobia. It lay 150 miles northeast of Damascus, midway on the caravan route to Mari on the Euphrates River. It thus controlled the trade on this desert "cut-off" to Babylon. Some texts in the parallel passage of 1 Kings 9:18 read "Tamar" (so RSV), which was an insignificant village southwest of the Dead Sea (but cf. Bright, *Israel*, p. 192).

5 The two "Beth Horons" were located on the border between Ephraim and Benjamin and controlled a major pass, northwest of Jerusalem, that led down to the port of Joppa.

6 "Baalath" lay nearby in Dan (Josh 19:44; cf. comment on 1 Chron 13:6), and others of the cities that were rebuilt by Solomon are listed in 1 Kings 9:15–18 (cf. Myers, *Chronicles*, 2:49, for an itemized bibliography on their archaeological attestation). Concerning his chariot cities, see the comment on 1:14.

8 On Solomon's force of "conscripted" Canaanitish labor, see the comment on 1 Chronicles 22:2 and the note to 2 Chronicles 2:17.

10 Concerning the 1 Kings 9:23 figure of 550 supervisors, rather than the 250 cited here, see the comment on 2:18.

11 Early in his reign (1 Kings 3:1), Solomon had married a daughter of "Pharaoh" (cf. Alberto R. Green, "Solomon and Siamun: A Synchronism Between Early Dynastic Israel and the Twenty-First Dynasty of Egypt," JBL 97 [1978]: 353–67). But despite the attendant prestige and political advantages (e.g., as noted in 1 Kings 9:16), such marriages introduced foreign idolatries and, eventually, apostasy into Israel (11:1–4). At this point Solomon still retained enough spiritual sensitivity to keep her residence out of "places" made "holy."

12 Solomon "sacrificed," but only through priestly mediators (cf. on 1 Chron 16:1). He would not have assumed the right to do so directly, any more than he personally would have "built the altar" (cf. the wording of vv. 1–6).

13 The "requirement for offerings" on special days had been spelled out by Moses (Lev 23:37–38).

14 Solomon was careful to maintain the organization of the priests, Levites, musicians, and others, in their twenty-four respective "divisions," or courses, as these had been developed by David (1 Chron 23–25; cf. 26).

17 "Ezion Geber and Elath" were ports at the north end of the Gulf of Aqaba that provided a strategic commercial access southward into the Red Sea and beyond. While earlier archaeological judgments about the presence of copper smelters at the former site have had to be revised, some final refining may have indeed been performed here on metals that were mined farther north in the Arabah valley (cf. Y. Aharoni in *Archaeology and Old Testament Study*, ed. D.W. Thomas [Oxford: University Press, 1967], pp. 437, 439).

18 Solomon's refineries provided a product for export, to be exchanged for gold from "Ophir." Ophir was thus reached via the Gulf of Aqaba and the Red Sea. Because its precise location is uncertain, various sites have been suggested. While Gray (*I & II Kings* [Philadelphia: Westminster, 1970], pp. 256–57) places it in Arabia, it has been identified by Albright with the east African Somaliland, Egyptian *Punt* (*Archaeology*, pp. 133–35, 212), and by D.J. Wiseman with the Asian *(S)upara*, north of Bombay, India, which had a thriving sea trade from the second millennium B.C. onward (NBD, p. 911). Both places provided the various products noted in 9:21 (q.v.). An ostracon from Tell Qasile, near Tel Aviv, dating from the end of the kingdom, has been found marked *ZHB 'PR LBYT ḤRN* ("gold of Ophir for Beth Horon [30 shekels]"; see H. Lewy, "Nitokris-Naqî'a," JNES 10 [1951]: 265–67).

The statement that "Hiram sent him ships commanded by his own officers" (1 Kings 9:27 mentions only the officers) means that the Tyrians constructed ships from materials that had been sent overland to Ezion Geber. Some critics argue for a deficiency in Ezra's geographical knowledge, for an anachronism 2,400 years before the Suez Canal was built (Dentan, p. 143). They then guided the less experienced Hebrews so they could navigate the ships, making an expedition in three years (9:21).

The revenue from each trip, of "four hundred and fifty talents of gold," amounted to about seventeen tons of gold (NIV mg.). First Kings 9:28 presents a variant reading of "420 talents," probably due to a scribal confusion between the numerical letters for 20 (כ, kaph) and 50 (נ, nun) (KD, *Kings*, p. 149)—a shift that would have been even more likely in the old Phoenician script than in the present Aramaic square character. It is impossible to say which of the figures is the more original.

Notes

---

5 The term for "gates," דְּלָתַיִם (*delātayim*), dual of דֶּלֶת (*delet*, technically, "leaf of a door" [KB, p. 211]), signifies the double-leafed gate in a city wall.

6 The term for horses, פָּרָשִׁים (*pārāšîm*) is usually rendered "cavalry, horsemen"; but "chario-teers" (NIV mg.) is more to the point.

---

2 Its splendor

9:1–31

[1]When the queen of Sheba heard of Solomon's fame, she came to Jerusalem to test him with hard questions. Arriving with a very great caravan—with camels carrying spices, large quantities of gold, and precious stones—she came to Solomon and talked with him about all she had on her mind. [2]Solomon answered all her questions; nothing was too hard for him to explain to her. [3]When the queen of Sheba saw the wisdom of Solomon, as well as the palace he had built, [4]the food on his table, the seating of his officials, the attending servants in their robes, the cupbearers in their robes and the burnt offerings he made at the temple of the LORD, she was overwhelmed.

[5]She said to the king, "The report I heard in my own country about your achievements and your wisdom is true. [6]But I did not believe what they said until I came and saw with my own eyes. Indeed, not even half the greatness of your wisdom was told me; you have far exceeded the report I heard. [7]How happy your men must be! How happy your officials, who continually stand before you and hear your wisdom! [8]Praise be to the LORD your God, who has delighted in you and placed you on his throne as king to rule for the LORD your God. Because of the love of your God for Israel and his desire to uphold them forever, he has made you king over them, to maintain justice and righteousness."

[9]Then she gave the king 120 talents of gold, large quantities of spices, and precious stones. There had never been such spices as those the queen of Sheba gave to King Solomon.

[10](The men of Hiram and the men of Solomon brought gold from Ophir; they also brought algumwood and precious stones. [11]The king used the algumwood to make steps for the temple of the LORD and for the royal palace, and to make harps and lyres for the musicians. Nothing like them had ever been seen in Judah.)

[12]King Solomon gave the queen of Sheba all she desired and asked for; he gave her more than she had brought to him. Then she left and returned with her retinue to her own country.

[13]The weight of the gold that Solomon received yearly was 666 talents, [14]not including the revenues brought in by merchants and traders. Also all the kings of Arabia and the governors of the land brought gold and silver to Solomon.

[15]King Solomon made two hundred large shields of hammered gold; six hundred bekas of hammered gold went into each shield. [16]He also made three hundred small shields of hammered gold, with three hundred bekas of gold in each shield. The king put them in the Palace of the Forest of Lebanon.

[17]Then the king made a great throne inlaid with ivory and overlaid with pure gold. [18]The throne had six steps, and a footstool of gold was attached to it. On both sides of the seat were armrests, with a lion standing beside each of them. [19]Twelve lions stood on the six steps, one at either end of each step. Nothing like it had ever been made for any other kingdom. [20]All King Solomon's goblets were gold, and all the household articles in the Palace of the Forest of Lebanon were pure gold. Nothing was made of silver, because silver was considered of little value in Solomon's day. [21]The king had a fleet of trading ships manned by Hiram's men. Once every three years it returned, carrying gold, silver and ivory, and apes and baboons.

[22]King Solomon was greater in riches and wisdom than all the other kings of the earth. [23]All the kings of the earth sought audience with Solomon to hear the wisdom God had put in his heart. [24]Year after year, everyone who came brought a gift—articles of silver and gold, and robes, weapons and spices, and horses and mules.

²⁵Solomon had four thousand stalls for horses and chariots, and twelve thousand horses, which he kept in the chariot cities and also with him in Jerusalem. ²⁶He ruled over all the kings from the River to the land of the Philistines, as far as the border of Egypt. ²⁷The king made silver as common in Jerusalem as stones, and cedar as plentiful as sycamore-fig trees in the foothills. ²⁸Solomon's horses were imported from Egypt and from all other countries.

²⁹As for the other events of Solomon's reign, from beginning to end, are they not written in the records of Nathan the prophet, in the prophecy of Ahijah the Shilonite and in the visions of Iddo the seer concerning Jeroboam son of Nebat? ³⁰Solomon reigned in Jerusalem over all Israel forty years. ³¹Then he rested with his fathers and was buried in the city of David his father. And Rehoboam his son succeeded him as king.

Jesus spoke of "Solomon in all his splendor" (Matt 6:29), and 2 Chronicles 9 documents his glorious rule with a series of historical illustrations: the visit he enjoyed from the queen of Sheba (vv.1–12); the revenue he obtained, together with the shields, throne, and other luxury items that this produced (vv.13–21); and the extent of the fame and power that he achieved (vv.22–28). The chapter concludes with a summary of his reign as a whole. It closely parallels its canonical source in 1 Kings 10.

1 The partly Semite and partly Hamite kingdom of "Sheba" (1 Chron 1:9, 22) lay at the southwestern point of the Arabian peninsula and on across the Red Sea into eastern Ethiopia. Excavations at Marib, which was its capital at this time, and at other Sabean sites have confirmed its cultural developments (cf. R.L. Bowen and F.P. Albright, *Archaeological Discoveries in South Arabia* [Baltimore: Johns Hopkins, 1958]). Sheba was famed for its commerce in gold and spice, and it simply could not allow Israel's expanding trade from Ezion Geber (described in 8:18) to go unnoticed. Its queen, accordingly, visited Solomon, with commerce as an underlying issue, but also "to test" his God-given wisdom (1 Kings 10:1; cf. 4:29–34) "with hard questions" (*ḥîḏôt*, "riddles," as in Judg 14:12). Such verbal interchange remains a familiar Arabic custom up to the present.

4 The NIV reading—of the "burnt offerings" (*'ôlāṭô*) that Solomon made (cf. comment on 8:12)—is based on the ancient versions (LXX, Syr., Vul.) and 1 Kings 10:5 and is probably the preferred reading. The MT of Chronicles has *'ªlîyāṭô*, seemingly referring to "upper chambers" (as of the temple, 3:9; 5:1 comment), or perhaps being related to the noun for "ascent" (NIV mg.), which might suggest a procession by the royal party for temple worship.

5–6 On "the greatness" of the king's wisdom," see v.23, the note to v.5, and the comment to 1:12.

7–8 Even his pagan visitor was led to recognize that "the LORD," Yahweh, was the one by whom Solomon had been placed on Israel's throne and for whom he was ruling (cf. on 1 Chron 28:5). The king's desire "to maintain justice and righteousness" had, indeed, been the purpose of his request for wisdom in the first place (cf. on 1:10).

9 The queen's gift, also recorded in 1 Kings 10:10, amounted to over four and a half tons of gold (cf. NIV mg.).

10–11 On "Ophir" see the comment on 8:18. "Algumwood" is probably a variant for almugwood (cf. on 2:8).

12 The Hebrew that underlies the NIV wording "he gave her more than she had brought" (to the king) is compressed and difficult; but it should probably be rendered "every wish she desired, he gave her a return for," or, according to what "she had brought" (cf. 1 Kings 10:13, which literally reads, "he gave her according to the hand," i.e., "power" or "authority," of the king). The statement has usually been interpreted as describing the completion of a satisfactory commercial transaction or as an expression of Solomon's munificence. In Ethiopic and Jewish tradition, it is maintained that the queen of Sheba subsequently bore a son to Solomon (see E. Ullendorff, *Ethiopia and the Bible* [London: Oxford, 1968], p. 134).

13 Chronicles describes Solomon's annual revenue in gold as approximating twenty-five tons (cf. NIV mg.), as had been previously maintained in 1 Kings 10:14.

15–16 The unit of weight, by which the gold that was applied to the king's "large" and "small shields" was counted, does not appear in the Hebrew text. The NIV assumes the "beka," or half-shekel, so that the figure of 300 for the smaller shields (v.16) would approximate the amount recorded in 1 Kings 10:17, which is stated to be three minas; for if 1 mina equals 60 shekels, then the Kings figure would suggest 360 bekas but only 180 shekels. Yet unstated weights in Hebrew usually assume the unit of "shekels." Furthermore, since Kings and Chronicles are in exact agreement on the amount of gold in the large shields (v.15), it is probable that they agree on the amount (half as much) in the smaller as well—though in Kings this is expressed in a differing unit of measure, i.e., the heavy mina, equaling 1000 shekels. As elucidated in HDB (4:903–4): "The persistence, side by side, of the two standards, the heavy and the light, explains how the mina might by one writer be taken . . . as containing 100 light shekels" (cf. KD, p. 247). (For illustrations of both of the sizes of shields, cf. Pritchard, *Pictures*, pp. 184, 372.) Solomon's "Palace of the Forest of Lebanon," where the shields were placed, was located in Jerusalem but received its name from its rows of Lebanese cedar pillars (1 Kings 7:2–5).

17 For a comparison of Solomon's "great throne" and its ornamentation with various ancient Near Eastern archaeological parallels, see Myers, *Chronicles*, 2:58, and Montgomery, *Kings*, pp. 221–22.

21 Solomon's fleet of "trading ships" are designated in 1 Kings 10:22 as "ships of Tarshish" (NIV mg.). Since according to 8:17–18 they actually navigated in the Red Sea, it seems unlikely that they "went to Tarshish," in the western Mediterranean, perhaps referring to Sardinia (cf. F.V. Winnett, "A Monotheistic Himyant Inscription," BASOR 83 [1941]: 22). Perhaps they were "Tarshish-type" ships (cf. NIV mg. on the literal Hebrew, and see comment on 20:36). As is usual in Semitic time-reckoning, the "three years" occupied by the expedition need include only the last part of the first year and the first part of the last year, so that the minimum trip time need have consumed only a little over one year.

24 The term for "weapons" (*nēšeq*, technically, "equipment," KB, p. 640) describes "armor" as well.

471

25 Solomon's "four thousand stalls for horses" accords well with both the archaeological evidence (cf. comment on 1:14) and the reference in 1 Kings 10:26 to "fourteen hundred chariots" (cf. 1 Kings 9:19). The parallel passage in 1 Kings 4:26, however, which reads "forty thousand stalls," should be attributed to scribal corruption (Payne, "Validity," pp. 123–24).

26 The observation that Solomon's rule extended as far as the Euphrates "River" (cf. NIV mg. and 1 Kings 4:21, 24) corresponds to the limit that God had promised to Abraham over a millennium earlier (Gen 15:18).

27 Concerning the "foothills," or Shephelah, see the comment on 1 Chronicles 27:28.

28 On Solomon's imported horses, see the comment on 1:16.

29 The Chronicler's references to documents by Nathan, Ahijah, and Iddo are taken up in the Introduction (Sources, d). First Kings 11:41 refers to another source, "The book of the annals of Solomon."

Notes

5 The phrase translated "your achievements," דְּבָרֶיךָ (dᵉbārêkā), is literally "your words," the same noun rendered just before as the "report."

11 The Hebrew for "steps" is מְסִלּוֹת (mᵉsillôt), literally "highways," with raised pavement, dikes, etc., perhaps indicating "supports" (with 1 Kings 10:12: מִסְעָד, misʿād) or "terraces" for the temple. The NIV seems here to have emended the word (per KB, p. 542), with the LXX, into מַעֲלוֹת (maʿᵃlôt, "ascents"; cf. comment on v.4), "steps."

IV. The Kingdom of Judah (10:1–36:23)

A. *The Division of the Kingdom*

10:1–11:19

¹Rehoboam went to Shechem, for all the Israelites had gone there to make him king. ²When Jeroboam son of Nebat heard this (he was in Egypt, where he had fled from King Solomon), he returned from Egypt. ³So they sent for Jeroboam, and he and all Israel went to Rehoboam and said to him: ⁴"Your father put a heavy yoke on us, but now lighten the harsh labor and the heavy yoke he put on us, and we will serve you."

⁵Rehoboam answered, "Come back to me in three days." So the people went away.

⁶Then King Rehoboam consulted the elders who had served his father Solomon during his lifetime. "How would you advise me to answer these people?" he asked.

⁷They replied, "If you will be kind to these people and please them and give them a favorable answer, they will always be your servants."

⁸But Rehoboam rejected the advice the elders gave him and consulted the young men who had grown up with him and were serving him. ⁹He asked them,

"What is your advice? How should we answer these people who say to me, 'Lighten the yoke your father put on us'?"

¹⁰The young men who had grown up with him replied, "Tell the people who have said to you, 'Your father put a heavy yoke on us, but make our yoke lighter' —tell them, 'My little finger is thicker than my father's waist. ¹¹My father laid on you a heavy yoke; I will make it even heavier. My father scourged you with whips; I will scourge you with scorpions.' "

¹²Three days later Jeroboam and all the people returned to Rehoboam, as the king had said, "Come back to me in three days." ¹³The king answered them harshly. Rejecting the advice of the elders, ¹⁴he followed the advice of the young men and said, "My father made your yoke heavy; I will make it even heavier. My father scourged you with whips; I will scourge you with scorpions." ¹⁵So the king did not listen to the people, for this turn of events was from God, to fulfill the word the LORD had spoken to Jeroboam son of Nebat through Ahijah the Shilonite.

¹⁶When all Israel saw that the king refused to listen to them, they answered the king:

"What share do we have in David,
    what part in Jesse's son?
To your tents, O Israel!
    Look after your own house, O David!"

So all the Israelites went home. ¹⁷But as for the Israelites who were living in the towns of Judah, Rehoboam still ruled over them.

¹⁸King Rehoboam sent out Adoniram, who was in charge of forced labor, but the Israelites stoned him to death. King Rehoboam, however, managed to get into his chariot and escape to Jerusalem. ¹⁹So Israel has been in rebellion against the house of David to this day.

¹¹:¹When Rehoboam arrived in Jerusalem, he mustered the house of Judah and Benjamin—a hundred and eighty thousand fighting men—to make war against Israel and to regain the kingdom for Rehoboam.

²But this word of the LORD came to Shemaiah the man of God: ³"Say to Rehoboam son of Solomon king of Judah and to all the Israelites in Judah and Benjamin, ⁴'This is what the LORD says: Do not go up to fight against your brothers. Go home, every one of you, for this is my doing.' " So they obeyed the words of the LORD and turned back from marching against Jeroboam.

⁵Rehoboam lived in Jerusalem and built up towns for defense in Judah: ⁶Bethlehem, Etam, Tekoa, ⁷Beth Zur, Soco, Adullam, ⁸Gath, Mareshah, Ziph, ⁹Adoraim, Lachish, Azekah, ¹⁰Zorah, Aijalon and Hebron. These were fortified cities in Judah and Benjamin. ¹¹He strengthened their defenses and put commanders in them, with supplies of food, olive oil and wine. ¹²He put shields and spears in all the cities, and made them very strong. So Judah and Benjamin were his.

¹³The priests and Levites from all their districts throughout Israel sided with him. ¹⁴The Levites even abandoned their pasturelands and property, and came to Judah and Jerusalem because Jeroboam and his sons had rejected them as priests of the LORD. ¹⁵And he appointed his own priests for the high places and for the goat and calf idols he had made. ¹⁶Those from every tribe of Israel who set their hearts on seeking the LORD, the God of Israel, followed the Levites to Jerusalem to offer sacrifices to the LORD, the God of their fathers. ¹⁷They strengthened the kingdom of Judah and supported Rehoboam son of Solomon three years, walking in the ways of David and Solomon during this time.

¹⁸Rehoboam married Mahalath, who was the daughter of David's son Jerimoth and of Abihail, the daughter of Jesse's son Eliab. ¹⁹She bore him sons: Jeush, Shemariah and Zaham.

The work of the Chronicler falls into four major parts. The last of these, which makes up the latter portion of 2 Chronicles (chs. 10–36), concerns the kingdom of Judah. At the breakup of the united kingdom of David and Solomon, on the latter's death in 930 B.C., Judah came to represent a minority of the Hebrews, in the south of Israel. Its record in Chronicles may then be traced out in three unequal sections: (1) on the division (2 Chron 10–11); (2) on the rulers, good and bad, of the people of Judah (chs. 13:1–36:16); and (3) on its ultimate fate of exile into Babylon (36:17–23).

The final editor of the Book of Kings, writing midway in the Exile, recognized this tragedy as an outworking of the moral righteousness of Yahweh, as he rendered to his faithless people exactly what their deeds deserved (2 Kings 17:7–23; 24:1–4). But the Chronicler, writing after the restoration of 538–536, recognized how God had been at work throughout these four centuries of Judah's decline, sovereignly accomplishing his holy purposes, that were constructive as well as destructive. The Lord's faithfulness to David continued steadfast (1 Chron 17:13; cf. 2 Chron 7:18).

Even in chapters 10–11, on the initial division, Ezra could say of Rehoboam's refusal to grant reforms, and of the rebellion at Shechem that resulted (ch. 10), "This turn of events was from God" (v.15; cf. Gen 50:20; Acts 2:23); and on the young king's attempt to resubdue Israel (ch. 11), he could quote God's word through the prophet, by which he prevented any such reunion: "This is my doing" (v.4). The overriding divine purpose was to separate the godly in Judah from the apostate in Israel (11:6–22) and to concentrate in the south those who remained faithful out of the northern tribes: thus "they strengthened the kingdom of Judah" (v.17). The two chapters of this section draw largely on 1 Kings 12; but see the comments to 10:19, which calls attention to the omission from Chronicles of the history of the north. Furthermore 11:5–12 and 18–23 utilized some different, and later lost, source; for they now stand without parallel in the OT.

1 Solomon's son "Rehoboam went to Shechem" to be crowned ruler of Israel. He had already succeeded his father in Judah (9:31); but even though the Davidic dynasty had been constituted by the Lord's appointment (1 Chron 17:14), each king was still subject to popular confirmation (v.4; cf. comment on 1 Chron 11:3, on David himself). Rehoboam could reign only as a "constitutional" monarch and servant of the people (cf. on v.7), under God (cf. on 9:8 and on 1 Chron 28:5). Shechem lay thirty miles north of Jerusalem in Ephraim, on the border of Manasseh (Josh 17:7). It formed a center for the northern tribes and after this event became their first capital (1 Kings 12:25).

2 Some years before Jeroboam I ("son of Nebat") had been divinely anointed to be ruler over ten-twelfths of the nation of Israel (1 Kings 11:26–40). It was because of this very fact that he was "in Egypt," having "fled from Solomon."

4 The "heavy yoke" to which the northerners objected had resulted from Solomon's extravagances (1:17 comment) at the expense of his people (cf. Deut 17:17, 20).

5 Without acceding to their request, Rehoboam remained, so far, fair and prudent in his conduct.

7 The parallel passage in 1 Kings 12:7 quotes even stronger advice by the elders to the king: not simply that he "be kind" and "favorable" to the people, but that he "be a servant" and "serve" them.

8 The "young men" to whom Rehoboam preferred to turn were probably some of Solomon's many sons, rendered callous by upbringing in the luxurious harem and court at Jerusalem.

9 By his words "How should *we* answer these people," Rehoboam already identified himself with autocracy.

15 But the whole course of events "was from God" (cf. the introductory discussion to ch.10), who had, through his prophet "Ahijah the Shilonite," ordained the division of the kingdom of Israel as a punishment for Solomon's decline into idolatry (1 Kings 11:29–33).

16 The rebellious spirit of the Israelites, however, against the Davidic dynasty that God had established, was equally sinful (13:5–7). Their cry, literally, of "Every man to your tents," had been employed before, against David (2 Sam 20:1). For the situations of life in Palestine are naturally those of geographical isolation; its broken terrain encourages political disruption. Some interpreters not infrequently reject the Chronicler's commitment to the legitimacy of God's messianic revelations to the house of David and assume an opposite stance, that the "declaration of independence by the northern kingdom [was, instead,] restoring the more basic situation of the people of God" (North, "The Chronicler," 1:417).

18 In his position over the "forced labor," Adoniram hardly constituted a wise choice for quieting Israel. He was probably one of the most hated figures in the land, an embodiment of oppression.

19 After this verse that summarizes "Israel's rebellion" (paralleled by 1 Kings 12:19), 1 Kings 12:20 proceeds to describe how the northern tribes made Jeroboam their king. Chronicles, however, omits it. Ezra dismisses the history of Israel from this point onward and concentrates on the faithful remnant in Judah.

11:1 As had been prophesied by Ahijah (see on 10:15; cf. 1 Kings 11:31–32), only the two tribes of "Judah and Benjamin" remained loyal to the Davidic dynasty (vv.3, 12; cf. the introductory discussion on Simeon on 1 Chron 4:24–43). Their muster of 180,000 men seems to be the largest troop total found in Chronicles (granting the possibility that at some points the term rendered "thousands" may rather mean "chiefs"; cf. comments to 1 Chron 7:3–4; 12:27), and it corresponds to the sum given in 1 Kings 12:21. The figure is a plausible one, in light of the carefully enumerated listing of over 600,000 for the whole nation in Numbers 1 (v.46) and 26 (v.51). That, of course, was in the days of Moses; but the population would hardly have been less under Solomon than then (cf. the similar expressions of populousness given in Deut 1:10; 10:22; and 1 Kings 3:8; 4:20).

2 "Shemaiah the man of God" was the same prophet who later confronted Rehoboam, after his unfaithfulness and defeat by Egypt (12:5–7). He also composed one of the source records for his reign (12:15).

3 Ezra's phrase "all the Israelites in Judah and Benjamin" includes what 1 Kings 12:23 specifies as "the rest" of the other tribes, i.e., the godly survivors out of a larger, apostate group (Lev 26:39, 44; Isa 20–23).

4 On the Lord's word "This is my doing," see the comment on 10:15.

5 Having been prohibited from retaking Israel, Rehoboam proceeded to refortify "towns" in the territory that he still had "in Judah" (cf. Notes). In light of the unsettled times that lay ahead for Rehoboam (cf. 12:2, 15), he acted wisely.

6–10 The fifteen cities that Ezra lists lie toward Judah's southern and western borders. Their choice seems to have been dictated by threat from Egypt (12:2–4). Following a detailed study by G. Beyer in 1931, W.F. Albright has confirmed this list as historically trustworthy ("The Reform of Jehoshaphat," in *Alexander Marx Jubilee Volume* [New York: Jewish Theological Seminary of America, 1950], pp. 66 –67).

14 Jeroboam had rejected the Levites (cf. 1 Kings 12:31) as part of his total policy of separating Israel from her religious dependence on Judah (1 Kings 12:26–28). The expression "Jeroboam and his sons," i.e., his successors, indicates that migrations by the faithful to Judah was a process that continued down through the years.

15 In addition to his golden "calf idols" (1 Kings 12:28–29), this Ephraimite also set up images of "goats" (*śeʿîrîm*; cf. Lev 17:7). Because of the latter's characteristic of inhabiting ruins (Isa 13:21; 34:14), some critics claim that the superstitious OT Hebrews here reveal a primitive belief in mythological "satyrs."

17 Sinful as Jeroboam's idolatries undoubtedly were, with their further evil of seeking to supplant the true worship of God in Jerusalem, they still accomplished a providential function, by driving the godly southward, so that they "strengthened the kingdom of Judah." The reason their migrations that supported Rehoboam are limited to a period of "three years" may have been simply because the godly became depleted in the North, but it may also have been due to Rehoboam's own lapse in the South (12:1–2; cf. Keil, p. 346).

18–20 In a summary of the royal family, with which the chapter concludes (vv. 18– 23), Rehoboam's wife "Maacah" seems to have been a granddaughter of Absalom, through his immediate daughter Tamar, the wife of Uriel (13:2; cf. 2 Sam 14:27; 18:18). The relationships may be charted as follows:

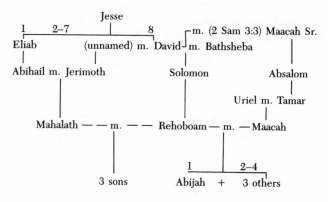

Mahalath was thus, simultaneously, Rehoboam's second cousin (via Eliab) and half-cousin (via her father Jerimoth's unnamed mother), while Maacah was the king's half-cousin once removed.

21 By taking "eighteen wives" Rehoboam willfully disregarded the law of God, both in respect to kingly abuse (Deut 17:17) and in respect to polygamous marriage (Lev 18:18; cf. John Murray, *Principles of Conduct* [Grand Rapids: Eerdmans, 1957], pp. 252–56), not to mention his disregard of the disastrous precedent set by his father, Solomon, from which he should have learned caution.

22 The king's appointment of Abijah (see on 12:16) "to be the chief prince" may imply some form of coregency; compare a similar elevation received by Abijah's grandfather Solomon, when threatened by a disputed succession (cf. the comments to 1 Chron 23:1; 29:22).

23 Rehoboam "acted wisely," not simply by delegating to some of his other sons a measure of the authority for national defenses that the divided kingdom of Solomon now required—and by providing them with property and wives—but particularly by "dispersing" them. It was a step that helped insure the smooth transfer of power to Abijah, the heir apparent (v.22).

Notes

---

12 The Hebrew that underlies the NIV rendering "Three days later" is literally "on the third day," which probably means "two days later" (cf. on 9:21).
14 Many witnesses to the MT, including the Leningrad MS B 19ᴬ, read "I will make" (your yoke heavy). But to maintain better parallelism between the two halves of the quotation, the NIV has followed the common Ben Hayyim (Bomberg) MT: "My father made" (your yoke heavy).
11:5 The Hebrew that underlies the NIV rendering "towns for defense" is literally "towns for siege," i.e., fortified cities (cf. vv.10, 23).

B. *The Rulers of Judah (12:1–36:16)*

1. *Rehoboam*

12:1–16

¹After Rehoboam's position as king was established and he had become strong, he and all Israel with him abandoned the law of the LORD. ²Because they had been unfaithful to the LORD, Shishak king of Egypt attacked Jerusalem in the fifth year of King Rehoboam. ³With twelve hundred chariots and sixty thousand horsemen and the innumerable troops of Libyans, Sukkites and Cushites that came with him from Egypt, ⁴he captured the fortified cities of Judah and came as far as Jerusalem.
⁵Then the prophet Shemaiah came to Rehoboam and to the leaders of Judah

who had assembled in Jerusalem for fear of Shishak, and he said to them, "This is what the LORD says, 'You have abandoned me; therefore, I now abandon you to Shishak.'"

[6]The leaders of Israel and the king humbled themselves and said, "The LORD is just."

[7]When the LORD saw that they humbled themselves, this word of the LORD came to Shemaiah: "Since they have humbled themselves, I will not destroy them but will soon give them deliverance. My wrath will not be poured out on Jerusalem through Shishak. [8]They will, however, become subject to him, so that they may learn the difference between serving me and serving the kings of other lands."

[9]When Shishak king of Egypt attacked Jerusalem, he carried off the treasures of the temple of the LORD and the treasures of the royal palace. He took everything, including the gold shields Solomon had made. [10]So King Rehoboam made bronze shields to replace them and assigned these to the commanders of the guard on duty at the entrance to the royal palace. [11]Whenever the king went to the LORD's temple, the guards went with him, bearing the shields, and afterward they returned them to the guardroom.

[12]Because Rehoboam humbled himself, the LORD's anger turned from him, and he was not totally destroyed. Indeed, there was some good in Judah.

[13]King Rehoboam established himself firmly in Jerusalem and continued as king. He was forty-one years old when he became king, and he reigned seventeen years in Jerusalem, the city the LORD had chosen out of all the tribes of Israel in which to put his Name. His mother's name was Naamah; she was an Ammonite. [14]He did evil because he had not set his heart on seeking the LORD.

[15]As for the events of Rehoboam's reign, from beginning to end, are they not written in the records of Shemaiah the prophet and of Iddo the seer that deal with genealogies? There was continual warfare between Rehoboam and Jeroboam. [16]Rehoboam rested with his fathers and was buried in the City of David. And Abijah his son succeeded him as king.

In the three and one-half centuries between the division of Solomon's kingdom in 930 B.C. and the Babylonian Exile in 586, Judah experienced twenty rulers. The nineteen men and one woman varied in their abilities, from the strongest and best to the weakest and worst. The destiny of any country depends to a great extent on the character of its leaders; and this was particularly the case among the Hebrews, into whose history God chose to intervene more directly than he has for other nations. The Chronicler could thus stimulate the men of his day to a greater devotion by pointing them back to his nation's more faithful monarchs and to those earlier miracles by which the Lord had delivered Judah; and still to the present, "faith is the victory" that overcomes the world (20:20; cf. 1 John 5:4).

Yet at the same time, and out of the same historical data, Ezra warns his people against compromise with the world, against disregard for the law of God, and against apostasy from the Lord himself. Judah's overall history was one of religious decline. Sin became so ingrained that even a ruler like Josiah could not reverse its downward courses: "The wrath of the LORD arose against his people, till there was no remedy" (36:16 KJV). In other words, in respect to any particular generation, God "can" cast away his people whom he foreknew (cf. Rom 11:1–2).

By and large 2 Chronicles 12:1–36:16 corresponds to 1 Kings 14:22–2 Kings 24:20; but significant differences remain. Much of the material found in Kings is omitted from Chronicles, specifically the detailed lives of some of the prophets and, most obviously, the entire history of Israel, the northern kingdom (cf. comment on 10:19, and Introduction: Purpose, 1). To the history, however, of Judah in the south, considerable material from other sources is added. Chronicles thus supplies us with inspiring (and inspired) examples of faith and deliverance that find no echo within the summaries provided by Kings.

The first ruler of the divided kingdom of Judah was Solomon's son Rehoboam, who reigned from 931 to 913 B.C. His kingship is the topic of 1 Kings 14:21–31, in parallel with which stands 2 Chronicles 12. The latter chapter commences with his establishment (v. 1a), after the division of Solomon's kingdom had once become permanent (chs. 10–11, which also include facts about Rehoboam). Chapter 12 then describes Rehoboam's punishment for abandoning the law of God (vv. 1b–6) and the restoration that followed on his resubmission to him (vv. 7–12). It concludes with a summary of the king's seventeen-year reign (vv. 13–16).

1 The term "all Israel" shifts, in this part of 2 Chronicles, from pointing to the entire nation (9:30) to either its northern half (in contrast to Judah, 11:1) or to "all the Israelites in Judah and Benjamin" (11:3), and, at this final juncture, to Judah alone, as constituting the true Israel (cf. NIV mg.; cf. Lemke).

Yet Rehoboam "abandoned" God's law by turning to the immoralities and polytheism of the surrounding Canaanites (1 Kings 14:23–24; 15:12). Herein lay the ultimate cause for Egypt's invasion of Judah (v. 2).

2 So in the king's "fifth year," 925 B.C., "Shishak attacked." Known in Egyptian history as Sheshonk I, he was the founder of the Twenty-Second Dynasty and its most energetic Pharaoh. This particular campaign is documented by a list of conquered Palestinian cities that stands to this day carved on the wall of his temple of Amon at Karnak, Thebes. It indicates that an immediate cause lay in his desire for plunder, which was directed even more against his former protege, Jeroboam, in the north (see on 10:2) than against Judah (cf. W.F. Albright, "New Light From Egypt on the Chronicles and History of Israel and Judah," BASOR 130 [1953]: 4–8).

3 The details preserved in vv. 3–8 have no parallel in 1 Kings 14. They would seem to derive from Ezra's special sources (cf. on v. 15), particularly from the records of Shemaiah.

Among Shishak's troops (cf. NIV mg.), the "Sukkites" are identified by Albright from an Egyptian document as being foreign mercenaries. He then adduces this fact in support of "the historical accuracy of the chronicler" (in H.H. Rowley, ed., *The Old Testament and Modern Study* [Oxford: University Press, 1951], p. 18).

4 Concerning Judah's "captured . . . fortified cities," the destruction of Lachish is particularly attested by archaeology.

5 On "Shemaiah" see the comment on 11:2.

7 "When . . . they humbled themselves," deliverance came soon (v. 12). This principle possesses permanent validity for Christian living (cf. 1 Peter 5:6), though Rehoboam seems not to have taken his own experience to heart (v. 14).

8 The point that God wanted them to grasp was "the difference" between what results from serving the Lord and from serving the world (Matt 11:28–30; cf. Notes).

10 Rehoboam's "bronze shields," with which he was forced to replace the gold (cf. comment on 9:15–16), dramatically illustrate how faithlessness reduced his condition to a mere imitation of the glory that had once been his.

13 Concerning God's putting his Name in Jerusalem, see the comments to 1 Chronicles 22:7 and 2 Chronicles 6:32.

15 Of the two literary sources that were cited by the Chronicler for this reign, it was the "records . . . of Iddo" that particularly dealt "with genealogies" (see Introduction: Sources, a, d).

16 The son who succeeded Rehoboam, "Abijah" (cf. the comment to 11:22–23), appears in 1 Kings 14:31; 15:1 et al., under the name "Abijam" (NIV mg.). The latter may have been his personal name, as contrasted with his throne name in Chronicles (cf. comments to 1 Chron 3:12, 15).

Notes

---

8 The MT lying behind the NIV phrase "the kings of" is מַמְלְכוֹת (*maml^{e}kôt*). On the basis of Phoenician, some would translate this as "kings" (Myers, *Chronicles,* 2:73); but the Hebrew means "kingdoms." The idea of the verse seems to be that God's people would experience the difference between his control and not simply that of particular foreign rulers, but that of the surrounding pagan imperial systems as a whole.

---

2. Abijah

13:1–14:1a

¹In the eighteenth year of the reign of Jeroboam, Abijah became king of Judah, ²and he reigned in Jerusalem three years. His mother's name was Maacah, a daughter of Uriel of Gibeah.

There was war between Abijah and Jeroboam. ³Abijah went into battle with a force of four hundred thousand able fighting men, and Jeroboam drew up a battle line against him with eight hundred thousand able troops.

⁴Abijah stood on Mount Zemaraim, in the hill country of Ephraim, and said, "Jeroboam and all Israel, listen to me! ⁵Don't you know that the LORD, the God of Israel, has given the kingship of Israel to David and his descendants forever by a covenant of salt? ⁶Yet Jeroboam son of Nebat, an official of Solomon son of David, rebelled against his master. ⁷Some worthless scoundrels gathered around him and opposed Rehoboam son of Solomon when he was young and indecisive and not strong enough to resist them.

⁸"And now you plan to resist the kingdom of the LORD, which is in the hands of David's descendants. You are indeed a vast army and have with you the golden calves that Jeroboam made to be your gods. ⁹But didn't you drive out the priests of the LORD, the sons of Aaron, and the Levites, and make priests of your own as the peoples of other lands do? Whoever comes to consecrate himself with a young bull and seven rams may become a priest of what are not gods.

¹⁰"As for us, the LORD is our God, and we have not forsaken him. The priests who serve the LORD are sons of Aaron, and the Levites assist them. ¹¹Every morning and evening they present burnt offerings and fragrant incense to the

LORD. They set out the bread on the ceremonially clean table and light the lamps on the gold lampstand every evening. We are observing the requirements of the LORD our God. But you have forsaken him. ¹²God is with us; he is our leader. His priests with their trumpets will sound the battle cry against you. Men of Israel, do not fight against the LORD, the God of your fathers, for you will not succeed."

¹³Now Jeroboam had sent troops around to the rear, so that while he was in front of Judah the ambush was behind them. ¹⁴Judah turned and saw that they were being attacked at both front and rear. Then they cried out to the LORD. The priests blew their trumpets ¹⁵and the men of Judah raised the battle cry. At the sound of their battle cry, God routed Jeroboam and all Israel before Abijah and Judah. ¹⁶The Israelites fled before Judah, and God delivered them into their hands. ¹⁷Abijah and his men inflicted heavy losses on them, so that there were five hundred thousand casualties among Israel's able men. ¹⁸The men of Israel were subdued on that occasion, and the men of Judah were victorious because they relied on the LORD, the God of their fathers.

¹⁹Abijah pursued Jeroboam and took from him the towns of Bethel, Jeshanah and Ephron, with their surrounding villages. ²⁰Jeroboam did not regain power during the time of Abijah. And the LORD struck him down and he died.

²¹But Abijah grew in strength. He married fourteen wives and had twenty-two sons and sixteen daughters.

²²The other events of Abijah's reign, what he did and what he said, are written in the annotations of the prophet Iddo.

¹⁴:¹And Abijah rested with his fathers and was buried in the City of David.

Second Chronicles 13 concerns the second man who ruled over post-Solomonic Judah, Rehoboam's son Abijah (cf. on 12:16). The one prominent event of his three-year reign (913 to 911 B.C.) was his war with Jeroboam (1 Kings 15:6–7). But while the parallel record about Abijah that appears in 1 Kings (15:1–8) contains only the briefest of summaries, Ezra's independent sources (cf. 2 Chron 13:22 on Iddo) furnished him with the details that are now unique to Chronicles. They describe the bravery against great odds of Judah's new king, which sprang from his trust in the God whose law he obeyed (vv.3–12), and the triumph over Israel that came as a result (vv.12–21): "The men of Judah were victorious because they relied on the LORD, the God of their fathers" (v.18). First Kings 15 does, however, include a negative evaluation of Abijah (vv.3–5), not reflected in Chronicles, "that his heart was not fully devoted to the LORD" (v.3).

2 It seems unnecessary to question that "Maacah" (cf. NIV mg.) was the literal "daughter of Uriel" (NIV mg.; cf on 11:20). The latter figure, incidentally, corresponds to the total given for the North in David's day, some sixty-five years earlier (cf. on 1 Chron 21:5; cf. 2 Sam 24:9); but this may be coincidental.

4 The exact location of "Mount Zemaraim" is uncertain. The town of Zemaraim lay with the territory of Benjamin (Josh 18:22); so the battle must have occurred on the border between the "country of Ephraim" (Israel) and Judah, perhaps near Bethel (v.19), on the northern boundary of Benjamin (cf. Notes).

5 The Lord had indeed "given the kingship of Israel to David and his descendants"; and this was to be "forever" (1 Chron 17:14), which seems to be the meaning of the phrase "a covenant of salt." Some commentators suggest that the term "salt" may have arisen simply because covenants could be ratified by a meal (Exod 24:11), at which salt was presumably used for seasoning (cf. Lev 2:13). More relevant is the observation that salt is well known as a preservative; hence the connotation of "everlastingness" (*'ôlām*, a word that occurs twice in Num 18:19, about things "given [to Aaron] . . . as a statute for ever: it is a covenant of salt for ever" [KJV]).

7 The term "scoundrels" represents the "sons of *b*e*liyaʿal* (KJV, "Belial"). But even though Belial, by NT times, had come to refer specifically to Satan (2 Cor 6:15) or to the Antichrist (2 Thess 2:3, q.v.), in the OT this word should be taken simply as a common noun, in its literal meaning of "worthlessness." Abijah recounts how such men "opposed Rehoboam . . . when he was young." In point of fact his chronological age was forty-one (12:13); but he still was "indecisive," literally, "weak of heart," i.e., immature in his understanding and experience (cf. 10:8–15), so that he was not "strong enough to resist them."

8 Scripture says that Jeroboam made the golden calves to be gods; they were "other gods, idols made of metal" (1 Kings 14:9). Some criticism, on the contrary, tends to minimize Jeroboam's apostasy by assuming that his calves were, like the ark, only "pedestals" for the invisible presence of Yahweh (Myers, *Chronicles*, 2:80); but see Jereboam's own words in 1 Kings 12:28: "Here are your gods, O Israel."

10 While at this point Abijah's affirmation "The LORD is our God" rings with sincerity, a longer view of his history requires some modification in evaluation; for "he committed all the sins his father had done before him" (1 Kings 15:3, witness his polygamy, described in v.21, and see Ezra's earlier evaluation of his father, Rehoboam, in 12:1). Also noteworthy is the fact that the prophets of the North and South had sanctioned the division. So Abijah used religious arguments for his own political ends. Yet since the North had acted in unbelief and apostasy, his words carried some conviction.

11 Concerning the king's loyalty to the ceremonial laws of Moses, see the comments at the following indicated places: on the daily "offerings," see 1 Chronicles 23:30; 2 Chronicles 4:1; on the "fragrant incense," 2 Chronicles 2:4; on the (show) "bread" and its "table," 1 Chronicles 9:32; 2 Chronicles 4:8; on the "gold lampstand," 2 Chronicles 4:7. Actually Solomon's temple contained ten such tables and lampstands (4:7–8); but one each of these may have been the original article dating back to Moses, hence the singular terminology.

12 The "priests with their trumpets" were to "sound the battle cry," specifically to call the Lord to their rescue (as in fact it came about, vv.14–15; cf. Num 10:9). The king's final appeal, "Men of Israel, do not fight against the LORD," was particularly appropriate for Ezra to include, in light of the opposition that the Jews of his day faced from the Samaritans, in this same area of northern Israel.

15 So "God routed Jeroboam," though whether this was through direct supernatural intervention, or through the courage of his embattled people as they saw themselves surrounded by the enemy, is not stated.

17 The slaughter inflicted on Ephraim of "five hundred chiefs," even if this term is not rendered as "thousands" (cf. on v.3), still represented the loss of over half "among Israel's" particularly "able men," a staggering blow for the limited northern kingdom.

19 Abijah "took . . . Bethel" (cf. on v.4), the actual center for Jeroboam's calf worship (1 Kings 12:29, 33), though the idol itself had probably been removed for safe keeping to some place farther north, before the city's capture. It is also to be noted that some eighteen years later Bethel was reoccupied by the Ephraimites (cf. 16:1). "Jeshanah and Ephron" were located four miles north and northeast of Bethel respectively.

20 Judah's victory may have encouraged the Arameans of Damascus to enter into a treaty with Abijah (cf. 1 Kings 15:19), which would further have impeded Jeroboam from "regaining power." The details on how "the LORD struck him down" are not elaborated elsewhere. His death occurred in 910 B.C., three years after Abijah's own.

22 This particular volume of "the prophet Iddo" (cf. 9:29; 12:15) is called his "annotations" (*midrash,* meaning a "commentary," perhaps on the king's official court record; cf. 24:27).

Notes

---

4 Some commentators consistently impugn the historicity of vv.3–21 as fanciful glosses on 1 Kings 15:6–7. North ("The Chronicler," 1:418) states that "the chronicler expands the note on war between Abijah and Jeroboam into a tissue of clichés drawn from famous biblical battles." Its author proceeds to cite the challenge to battle, in this verse, as if it were taken from Judg 9:7; v.13, on an ambush, as if it were taken from Judg 20:29; and v.14, on trumpets blown, from Num 10:9—apparently assuming that such happenings could be authentic only one time each!

---

3. Asa

14:1b–16:14

Asa his son succeeded him as king, and in his days the country was at peace for ten years.

²Asa did what was good and right in the eyes of the LORD his God. ³He removed the foreign altars and the high places, smashed the sacred stones and cut down the Asherah poles. ⁴He commanded Judah to seek the LORD, the God of their fathers, and to obey his laws and commands. ⁵He removed the high places and incense altars in every town in Judah, and the kingdom was at peace under him. ⁶He built up the fortified cities of Judah, since the land was at peace. No one was at war with him during those years, for the LORD gave him rest.

⁷"Let us build up these towns," he said to Judah, "and put walls around them, with towers, gates and bars. The land is still ours, because we have sought the LORD our God; we sought him and he has given us rest on every side." So they built and prospered.

⁸Asa had an army of three hundred thousand men from Judah, equipped with large shields and with spears, and two hundred and eighty thousand from Benjamin, armed with small shields and with bows. All these were brave fighting men.

⁹Zerah the Cushite marched out against them with a vast army and three hundred chariots, and came as far as Mareshah. ¹⁰Asa went out to meet him, and they took up battle positions in the Valley of Zephathah near Mareshah.

¹¹Then Asa called to the LORD his God and said, "LORD, there is no one like you to help the powerless against the mighty. Help us, O LORD our God, for we rely on you, and in your name we have come against this vast army. O LORD, you are our God; do not let man prevail against you."

¹²The LORD struck down the Cushites before Asa and Judah. The Cushites fled, ¹³and Asa and his army pursued them as far as Gerar. Such a great number of Cushites fell that they could not recover; they were crushed before the LORD and his forces. The men of Judah carried off a large amount of plunder. ¹⁴They destroyed all the villages around Gerar, for the terror of the LORD had fallen upon them. They plundered all these villages, since there was much booty there. ¹⁵They also attacked the camps of the herdsmen and carried off droves of sheep and goats and camels. Then they returned to Jerusalem.

¹⁵:¹The Spirit of God came upon Azariah son of Oded. ²He went out to meet Asa and said to him, "Listen to me, Asa and all Judah and Benjamin. The LORD is with you when you are with him. If you seek him, he will be found by you, but if you forsake him, he will forsake you. ³For a long time Israel was without the true God, without a priest to teach and without the law. ⁴But in their distress they turned to the LORD, the God of Israel, and sought him, and he was found by them. ⁵In those days it was not safe to travel about, for all the inhabitants of the lands were in great turmoil. ⁶One nation was being crushed by another and one city by another, because God was troubling them with every kind of distress. ⁷But as for you, be strong and do not give up, for your work will be rewarded."

⁸When Asa heard these words and the prophecy of Azariah son of Oded the prophet, he took courage. He removed the detestable idols from the whole land of Judah and Benjamin and from the towns he had captured in the hills of Ephraim. He repaired the altar of the LORD that was in front of the portico of the LORD's temple.

⁹Then he assembled all Judah and Benjamin and the people from Ephraim, Manasseh and Simeon who had settled among them, for large numbers had come over to him from Israel when they saw that the LORD his God was with him.

¹⁰They assembled at Jerusalem in the third month of the fifteenth year of Asa's reign. ¹¹At that time they sacrificed to the LORD seven hundred head of cattle and seven thousand sheep and goats from the plunder they had brought back. ¹²They entered into a covenant to seek the LORD, the God of their fathers, with all their heart and soul. ¹³All who would not seek the LORD, the God of Israel, were to be put to death, whether small or great, man or woman. ¹⁴They took an oath to the LORD with loud acclamation, with shouting and with trumpets and horns. ¹⁵All Judah rejoiced about the oath because they had sworn it wholeheartedly. They sought God eagerly, and he was found by them. So the LORD gave them rest on every side.

¹⁶King Asa also deposed his grandmother Maacah from her position as queen mother, because she had made a repulsive Asherah pole. Asa cut the pole down, broke it up and burned it in the Kidron Valley. ¹⁷Although he did not remove the high places from Israel, Asa's heart was fully committed to the LORD all his life. ¹⁸He brought into the temple of God the silver and gold and the articles that he and his father had dedicated.

¹⁹There was no more war until the thirty-fifth year of Asa's reign.

¹⁶:¹In the thirty-sixth year of Asa's reign Baasha king of Israel went up against Judah and fortified Ramah to prevent anyone from leaving or entering the territory of Asa king of Judah.

²Asa then took the silver and gold out of the treasuries of the LORD's temple and of his own palace and sent it to Ben-Hadad king of Aram, who was ruling in Damascus. ³"Let there be a treaty between me and you," he said, "as there was between my father and your father. See, I am sending you silver and gold. Now break your treaty with Baasha king of Israel so he will withdraw from me."

⁴Ben-Hadad agreed with King Asa and sent the commanders of his forces against the towns of Israel. They conquered Ijon, Dan, Abel Maim and all the store cities of Naphtali. ⁵When Baasha heard this, he stopped building Ramah and abandoned his work. ⁶Then King Asa brought all the men of Judah, and they

carried away from Ramah the stones and timber Baasha had been using. With them he built up Geba and Mizpah.

⁷At that time Hanani the seer came to Asa king of Judah and said to him: "Because you relied on the king of Aram and not on the Lᴏʀᴅ your God, the army of the king of Aram has escaped from your hand. ⁸Were not the Cushites and Libyans a mighty army with great numbers of chariots and horsemen? Yet when you relied on the Lᴏʀᴅ, he delivered them into your hand. ⁹For the eyes of the Lᴏʀᴅ range throughout the earth to strengthen those whose hearts are fully committed to him. You have done a foolish thing, and from now on you will be at war."

¹⁰Asa was angry with the seer because of this; he was so enraged that he put him in prison. At the same time Asa brutally oppressed some of the people.

¹¹The events of Asa's reign, from beginning to end, are written in the book of the kings of Judah and Israel. ¹²In the thirty-ninth year of his reign Asa was afflicted with a disease in his feet. Though his disease was severe, even in his illness he did not seek help from the Lᴏʀᴅ, but only from the physicians. ¹³Then in the forty-first year of his reign Asa died and rested with his fathers. ¹⁴They buried him in the tomb that he had cut out for himself in the City of David. They laid him on a bier covered with spices and various blended perfumes, and they made a huge fire in his honor.

The next three chapters in Chronicles concern Asa son of Abijah. The parallel section in 1 Kings that describes Asa is limited to sixteen verses (15:9–24); and these do not even touch on major sections in 2 Chronicles (14:3–15:15; 16:7–10), which are unique within Scripture to this latter writing. Out of the history of Asa's long reign, 911–870 B.C., Ezra selected four outstanding events for his record: (1) the king's first reform, dating to his initial ten years of peace (14:1b–8); (2) his victory over Zerah the Cushite in 897 (14:9–15); (3) Judah's second reform, that came as a result (ch. 15); and (4) the hostile moves made against him by Baasha of Israel in 895 and his series of religious deviations that followed (ch. 16). Asa, however, was still the most godly monarch to arise in Judah, from the division of Solomon's kingdom up to this point (1 Kings 15:11).

Asa's rule provides the Chronicler with an occasion to emphasize some of his theological concerns. His treatment of the reign of Asa may be seen in the series of contrasts he makes between the ruler's godly early years and his disappointing last years. The two periods may be contrasted by the following: (1) the king faced an overwhelming obstacle in Zerah and his forces but a less formidable foe in Baasha and his strategies; (2) the king turned to God for help against the first foe but sought the aid of Damascus against the second foe; (3) the Egyptians were routed in a crushing defeat, and Judah experienced victory and peace as the danger was eliminated. In the last years no such victory was experienced, and the problems did not go away; (4) Asa responded to God's word in two totally different ways. He received the exhortations of Azariah and heeded what was spoken to him by God; later on he rejected the warnings of the seer, became angry at him, and even put him in prison. Furthermore instead of repenting he continued in his disgraceful behavior by refusing to seek God's help when his foot became diseased, seeking only the help of physicians. By selecting specific historical events and presenting the material in terms of these contrasts, the Chronicler shows the blessings that come from seeking God as well as the folly of not turning to him in times of need. (SBM)

14:1b When Chronicles describes the country as being "at peace for ten years," this era would cover the first decade of Asa's rule, from 910 to 900 B.C., i.e., until the days before Zerah's invasion in 896 (cf. on 15:19). Nine years of this period over-lapped the reign of Baasha in Israel (909–886). First Kings 15:16 speaks of war between these two rulers " all their days" (KJV; cf. the present chapter's allusion in v.6 to Asa's building up "the fortified cities of Judah," so that North ["The Chroni-cler," 1:419] suggests "a kind of cold war with Baasha"). But since the same verse explains that he built the cities, "since the land was at peace," his actual conflict with Baasha must have broken out only subsequently. The peace, which may be traced back, in part, to Abijah's crushing defeat of Israel (13:17, 20), stemmed pri-marily from Asa's first reform (vv.3–5) because, as he said, "We have sought the LORD our God; . . . and he has given us rest" (v.7).

2–3 The king "removed . . . the high places" (v.3; cf. on 1:3), in obedience to Deuteronomy 12:2–3; but the people seem to have continued to resort to them, despite the royal purge (15:17). The "sacred stones" (ASV, "pillars"; Heb. *maṣṣēbôt*) were Canaanitish in origin and were thought quite literally to contain the local fertility gods, the Baalim. The "Asherah poles" (cf. NIV mg.) were wooden and were associated with Baal's goddess-consort who bore this name. Both, when carved, became idols (1 Kings 15:12). (For Asherah and her worship, see the com-ments in this volume on 1 Kings 14:15.)

7–8 As a conclusion to his description of Asa's initial reform and of the prosperity that resulted (v.7), the Chronicler enumerates Asa's army, with its "three hundred *specially trained* men from Judah" (v.8)—we are pointing the subject that is being counted as *'allûp*, i.e., "chief, officer, famous man, specially trained warrior" (Wen-ham, "Large Numbers," pp. 27, 30), rather than as *'elep*, "thousand"—with "two hundred and eighty" special warriors "from Benjamin"; for notice the contextual emphasis on their specialized weapons and their distinction as "brave fighting men."

9 Turning to the Cushite invasion (vv.9–15), Ezra enumerates the enemy as em-bracing, by contrast, "a thousand specialists" (NIV mg.; cf. on v.8) "and three hun-dred chariots" (Payne, "Validity," pp. 215–16). "Cushites," known also as Nubians (cf. on 1 Chron 1:8), served as Egyptian mercenaries and, by the close of the next century, had come to rule all Egypt, as the Twenty-Fifth Dynasty (cf. on 2 Chron 32:1). The name "Zerah" could suggest an attempt by Osorkon I, second Pharaoh of the Twenty-Second Dynasty, to duplicate the invasion and pillaging that had been accomplished by his predecessor Sheshonk (cf. on 12:2). His forces may have attract-ed a mixed following of bedouin Arabs as well (cf. the reference to "camels" in v.15). But the results this time, against godly Asa, were quite the opposite of what had permitted the easy plundering of Rehoboam (12:9).

10 The "Valley of Zephathah," where the battle was joined, remains unidentifiable; but it did lie "near Mareshah," which was a town that marks the entrance into the Judean hills and was situated between Gaza and Jerusalem, lying twenty-five miles farther along to the northeast. It was one of the points that Rehoboam had fortified in anticipation of just such an attack as this (11:10).

11 This climactic verse reads literally, "There is not with you, to help, between a mighty one and one without power; help us." Its words might express the idea, as in the NIV, that "there is not one" (person) who can help the powerless but also the mighty. Yet fully as meaningful is the idea (so KJV) that "it is nothing" (no harder) for you to help the powerless than the mighty (cf. 1 Sam 14:6). Still a third option is suggested in the JB (cf. Myers, *Chronicles*, 2:82–83): "Yahweh, numbers and strength make no difference to you when you give your help." The point seems to be that for God the humanly impossible is as nothing (Gen 18:14); and Asa had the faith to commit himself to Yahweh and to expect the impossible (cf. Mark 9:23).

12 Thus "the LORD struck down the Cushites," though again (cf. on 13:15) the detailed means that he employed are not stated (cf. v.13: "They were crushed before the LORD and his forces").

13 Asa's army "pursued them as far as Gerar," located southeast of Gaza, on their presumed flight back to Egypt. History attests to the fact that "they could not recover": Israel experienced no more interference from the decadent Twenty-Second and Twenty-Third dynasties. Only after 160 years, under its late eighth-century pharaohs, did Egypt reappear to trouble Israel (2 Kings 17:4).

15 Judah also attacked "the camps of the herdsmen" (lit., "tents of cattle," KJV) that belonged to the Philistinized seminomadic cattle tenders who were found in the area (cf. on v.9).

15:1 Asa's second great period of reform (cf. 14:2–8, on his earlier efforts) occupies 2 Chronicles 15. His actions came as a result of the victory in 896 B.C. over the Cushites (14:12–15), and particularly because of the preaching of "Azariah son of Oded," a prophet who remains unknown apart from this passage.

2 The clause "If you seek him" recalls David's admonition to Solomon (1 Chron 28:9); and Azariah went on (vv.3–6) to illustrate its truth from Israel's past history.

3 His words about the "long time" when "Israel was without the true God" probably refer to the lawless, and often faithless, days of the judges (Judg 21:25). Their being "without the law" was closely connected with their being "without a priest," since one of the latter's major functions was "to teach" the law that God had given through Moses (Lev 10:11).

4 On God's being "found by them" when "they sought him," see Judges 2:18.

5 On their situation being such that "it was not safe to travel about," literally, that "there was no peace for the one going out and the one coming in," see Judges 5:6.

7 This verse, which was the prophet's conclusion, appealed for resolute faith on their part, with the promise of reward from God.

8 Asa's renewed reformation (vv.8–15) involved the removal of Judah's "detestable idols," and also of the sexual immoralities that accompanied such originally Canaanitish worship (1 Kings 15:12). Much had already been accomplished earlier (14:3); but this second stage of reform took care of "all the still remaining idolatrous abominations" (Keil, pp. 356–57). It was also a more extensive removal, "from the whole land"; for it included areas Asa "had captured in the hills of Ephraim" during the five years of hostility that had immediately preceded (v.10; cf. 14:1). This in turn implies the accomplishment of certain Judean victories, not otherwise recorded, even as there must have been defeats too (cf. on 13:19; 16:1).

9 The statement that "large numbers had come over to him from Israel" illustrates how God's purpose in dividing Solomon's kingdom was in fact being achieved (cf. the introductory discussion to chs. 10–11 and the comments on 11:3, 14): a faithful "remnant" was being gathered and preserved. It may also help to explain, however, why Baasha of Israel proceeded to his acts of reprisal soon thereafter (16:1). On the coming of "people from . . . Simeon," see the introductory discussion to 1 Chronicles 4:24–43.

10 The "third month of" Asa's "fifteenth year" was May/June 895 B.C. The people may have "assembled at Jerusalem" then so as to observe the Feast of Weeks (Pentecost), one of Israel's three annual pilgrimage celebrations (cf. on 1 Chron 23:31; cf. Lev 23:15–21). This assembly probably took place in the year following Zerah's attack (cf. on v.19), since the pursuit, the gathering of plunder (v.11), and the occupying of the surrounding territories by Asa's forces (14:13–15) must have consumed several months.

12 The MT phrase about their "entering into a covenant" reads literally, "into the covenant," i.e., the one, great, everlasting testament of Yahweh (see on 1 Chron 16:15) that he decreed for the redemption of his people. The succeeding verses on Asa's "covenant renewal" bring out some of the testament's basic features. First, on the objective side God provided for the restoration of fallen man back into fellowship with himself. The reality of this restoration is indicated by the fact that he had become "the God of their fathers" (cf. v.15 that "he was found by them"). God thus entered into a saving relationship with his elect (Gen 17:7; Jer 31:34; John 17:6).

13 Second, on the subjective side men are to respond to him in faith and obedience. They therefore swore to "seek the LORD, the God of their fathers, with all their heart and soul" (v.12; cf. v.15; Gen 15:6; Exod 19:5; Luke 13:3; John 3:16). Conformity on this particular occasion was enforced on pain of "death" (cf. Deut 17:2–6). The principle is based on the fact that it is preferable for a man to be restrained in this life than for him, or for others who may be affected by him, to be lost for eternity (Deut 13:12–15; Mark 9:43–48).

15 Third, the result is an inheritance of peace: "the LORD gave them rest on every side." The immediate rest that he granted to Judah was one of relief from her enemies, but it was indicative of a more fundamental rest that comes to men because they have been accepted by God. Covenant rest embraces all the joys of redeemed life in the present (Ps 103), of heavenly life beyond the grave (Ps 73:23–26; Heb 4:9–11), and of ultimate life in the kingdom of God on earth (Ps 96:12–13; Rev 20:6; 22:5).

16 For the remaining verses of chapter 15, the parallel in 1 Kings (15:13–16) resumes, Scripture thereby attesting to the reality of Asa's reform. Rehoboam's second wife, "Maacah" (cf. on 11:20), was not only still living but must have been an influential figure at the Jerusalem court. Asa, however, has left a significant example to use through the way he placed religious loyalty above family loyalties, when he "deposed her from her position." The Kidron Valley, in which he burned her Asherah pole, is the gorge that lies between the east wall of Jerusalem and the Mount of Olives.

17 That Asa "did not remove the high places from Israel" is a commentary, not on the commendable programs of reform as instituted by the king himself (cf. on 14:3), but on the sad facts of the spiritual condition of his people.

18 The treasures Asa "brought into the temple" (cf. on 5:1) included "articles that he and his father had dedicated," namely, Abijah's spoils from Jeroboam (13:19) and his own from Zerah and his allies (14:13–15).

19 The often-heard rendering of this verse, suggesting that there was "no more war until the thirty-fifth year of" the king's reign, is subject to criticism on two counts. First, the Hebrew text lacks the word "more" and probably says simply, "There had not been war." Second, it is known that the king "was" involved in a serious conflict with Baasha (ch. 16), who died in the twenty-sixth year of Asa's reign (1 Kings 15:16, 33). Baasha had thus been dead for almost a decade before Asa's thirty-fifth year. Some commentators recognize this fact but still insist that the Chronicler asserts that there was peace till then, to prove (!) that virtue like Asa's brings peace and prosperity, and that the writer dismissed as "an inaccuracy" the record found in 1 Kings 15:16 of a long war with Baasha (North, "The Chronicler," 1:419).

Preferable, however, is Thiele's proposal (*Numbers,* pp. 57–60) that Ezra's reference is to the thirty-fifth year after the division of the Solomonic kingdom in 930 B.C. (cf. on 16:1) and that this verse relates then to Zerah's invasion in 896. It could thus be rendered, "There had not been war until the thirty-fifth year," which had reference to Asa's reign. It should be noticed, however, that the expression "the thirty-fifth year of Asa's reign" is exactly the same as that in 16:1. So it seems somewhat unlikely that the first dates from the beginning of the kingdom and the second from the beginning of his own reign. Another suggestion views the figures here and in 16:1 as twenty-fifth and twenty-sixth, respectively (NIV Study Bible; cf. 1 Kings 16:8).

16:1 Despite the king's two reforms and remarkable victory that are recorded in the two preceding chapters, chapter 16 proceeds to describe a series of religious deviations of which he became guilty in his later life: in relation to Israel (vv.1–9), to the prophet Hanani and others of his own people (v.10), and to his final illness (vv.11–14).

The "thirty-sixth year," which had reference to "Asa's reign" (cf. on 15:19), was 895 B.C.; and the event in question probably occurred after the assembly in May/June of that year (cf. on 15:10). At this point Judah was confronted by "Baasha king of Israel." The latter had overthrown the dynasty of Jeroboam I, had usurped the crown, and then reigned in Ephraim from 909 to 886 (1 Kings 15:27–29, 33). He had been consistently hostile toward Asa (1 Kings 15:16) and now became particularly aroused against him, probably because of the defection of many of his people to the Judean king (2 Chron 15:9). He advanced southward, apparently capturing Bethel at this time (cf. on 13:19). Baasha then "fortified Ramah," which lay on the main north-south highway along the Palestinian central ridge, only five miles north of Jerusalem. He thus effectively blockaded all movement into Judah.

2 Asa's response was to take "silver and gold"—all that he had (1 Kings 15:18)—from the Jerusalem temple and palace to purchase help from the Aramean king, Ben-Hadad I in Damascus. At one stroke Asa thereby sacrificed the results of his own piety (cf. on 2 Chron 15:18) and of God's blessing (14:13–14); he induced a pagan ruler to an act of perfidy (v.3); precipitated a pattern of Syrian intervention into the affairs of Israel that would have disastrous results throughout the succeeding century (cf. 2 Kings 10:32–33; 12:17–18); and, in the most serious deviation of all, he departed from the Lord by placing his primary trust in "the arm of flesh" (Jer 17:5).

3 The earlier Syro-Judean treaty Asa referred to must have existed between Ben-Hadad's father Tabrimmon, the son of Hezion (1 Kings 15:18), and Asa's father Abijah (cf. on 2 Chron 13:20). This earlier ruler Hezion may perhaps be equated with Rezon, the adversary of Solomon and the founder of the current kingdom in Damascus (1 Kings 11:23–25); so the Arameans themselves had a history of switching allies at their convenience.

4 Ben-Hadad therefore conquered "Ijon," located east of the Leontes River, as it flows southward out of the Syrian Beka Valley between the Lebanon ranges, shortly before its course turns west into the Mediterranean; Ijon thus lay on a natural route south into Israel. Eight miles farther south, on the headwaters of the Jordan, was "Abel Maim" (Abel Beth Maacah, 1 Kings 15:20, NIV mg.); and four miles east of it lay "Dan." The Arameans, indeed, took "all the store cities of Naphtali"—specified in 1 Kings as "all Kinnereth," meaning the plains on the northwest side of Galilee.

5 Faced with such losses in Israel's far north, "Baasha abandoned" his operation against Judah in the south, so that for the moment Asa's strategem appeared to have succeeded.

6 The men of Judah reused the materials from Ramah to "build up Geba and Mizpah." Though it was later associated with Asa's work (Jer 41:9), the site of Mizpah remains uncertain. Geba, however, usually identifies a town a little to the west and north of Ramah; so if Mizpah equals Tell en-Nasbeh to its northeast, Asa must then have been counterattacking by pushing Judah's borders northward again. Yet if Geba here refers to Gibeah of Saul, to the south of Ramah, and Mizpah equals Nebi Samwil, to its southwest, then Asa would have been defensively drawing in his lines, southward (cf. Myers, *Chronicles*, 2:94).

7 Verses 7–10 are unique to Chronicles. "Hanani the seer" was father to Jehu the seer, who would later serve Asa's son Jehoshaphat (19:2; 20:34). He not only condemned Asa's loss of faith (cf. on v.2) but went on to speak of the success the king would have enjoyed had he not deviated from trusting God: the Aramean army would have been his. The point is that "Aram" (unless one reads "Israel," with the LXX[L]), as Baasha's ally (v.3), would presumably have joined with Israel in attacking Judah; and God would then have delivered over the entire enemy force to Asa.

8 Hanani also reminded the king of the fate of the "Cushites" (cf. NIV mg.) and of their accompanying "Libyans" (cf. comments to 12:3; 14:9, 11). Hanani's reference to the "eyes of the LORD," as ranging "throughout the earth," was later repeated by God himself, speaking through a postexilic prophet (Zech 4:10). The emphasis is that no problem can arise for God's people of which the Lord is not aware, and from which he cannot deliver them (cf. Rom 8:32), provided their hearts are "fully committed" (*šālēm*, "whole, integrated") in respect to him. But King Asa, from then on, would "be at war," immediately with Baasha (1 Kings 15:32), and, after the latter's death in 886, with his successors; for the state of belligerency between Israel and Judah seems to have terminated only in the reign of Asa's son Jehoshaphat (18:1), shortly before 865 (cf. on 18:2; 22:2).

10 Asa's reaction was to compound his sin by putting Hanani "in prison," literally, "the house of stocks." This is the OT's first recorded royal persecution of a prophet, but many such instances were to follow (18:26; 24:21; Mark 6:17–18). One sin, moreover, leads to another; and he also "brutally oppressed some of the people."

11 Ezra here makes the initial reference in 2 Chronicles (cf. 1 Chron 9:1) to his primary literary source, "the book of the kings of Judah and Israel." This work cannot be our present 1–2 Kings, which, instead of providing a fuller description of "the events of Asa's reign, from beginning to end," contain only a fraction of what appears in Chronicles (cf. the introductory discussion to chs. 14–16). It seems to have consisted of some extensive court chronicle that is now lost (see Introduction: Sources, e).

12 In his thirty-ninth year, or 871 B.C., Asa deviated in still another direction, by seeking help for his foot disease "only from the physicians." While these may have been pagans, Scripture usually speaks positively of those who heal (Exod 21:19; Jer 8:22); medicine is God's gift (cf. 2 Kings 20:7). The king's sin lay in having recourse to them "only" and not seeking "help from the LORD," who is the ultimate healer of men's diseases (2 Kings 20:5; Ps 103:3).

14 Chronicles clarifies the general statement of 1 Kings 15:24 that Asa "was buried with [his fathers] in the city of . . . David" by speaking of "the tomb" (plu., *qibrō-ṭāyw*, "his burial chambers") that he had cut out for himself. The "huge fire," with "spices" and "perfumes," was not for cremation but "in his honor."

Notes

15:8 To preserve the absolute state of הַגְּבוּאָה (*hannᵉḇûʾāh*, "the prophecy," not const., "the prophecy of"), and to follow the ancient versions more closely, one should insert between the words "the prophecy" and "Oded" the full, relative clause אֲשֶׁר דִּבֶּר עֲזַרְיָהוּ בֶן (*ᵃšer dibber ᶜᵃzaryāh ḇen*, "which spoke Azariah the son of [Oded]").

16:8 The translation of the NIV text, "horsemen," is indeed a more normal rendering than that of the NIV mg., "charioteers" (cf. Notes on 8:6).

4. *Jehoshaphat*

17:1–20:37

¹Jehoshaphat his son succeeded him as king and strengthened himself against Israel. ²He stationed troops in all the fortified cities of Judah and put garrisons in Judah and in the towns of Ephraim that his father Asa had captured.

³The Lord was with Jehoshaphat because in his early years he walked in the ways his father David had followed. He did not consult the Baals ⁴but sought the God of his father and followed his commands rather than the practices of Israel. ⁵The Lord established the kingdom under his control; and all Judah brought gifts to Jehoshaphat, so that he had great wealth and honor. ⁶His heart was devoted to the ways of the Lord; furthermore, he removed the high places and the Asherah poles from Judah.

⁷In the third year of his reign he sent his officials Ben-Hail, Obadiah, Zechariah, Nethanel and Micaiah to teach in the towns of Judah. ⁸With them were certain Levites—Shemaiah, Nethaniah, Zebadiah, Asahel, Shemiramoth, Jehonathan, Adonijah, Tobijah and Tob-Adonijah—and the priests Elishama and Jehoram. ⁹They taught throughout Judah, taking with them the Book of the Law of the Lord; they went around to all the towns of Judah and taught the people.

¹⁰The fear of the Lord fell on all the kingdoms of the lands surrounding Judah, so that they did not make war with Jehoshaphat. ¹¹Some Philistines brought Jehoshaphat gifts and silver as tribute, and the Arabs brought him flocks: seven thousand seven hundred rams and seven thousand seven hundred goats.

¹²Jehoshaphat became more and more powerful; he built forts and store cities in Judah ¹³and had large supplies in the towns of Judah. He also kept experienced fighting men in Jerusalem. ¹⁴Their enrollment by families was as follows:

From Judah, commanders of units of 1,000:
Adnah the commander, with 300,000 fighting men;
¹⁵next, Jehohanan the commander, with 280,000;
¹⁶next, Amasiah son of Zicri, who volunteered himself for the service of the Lord, with 200,000.
¹⁷From Benjamin:
Eliada, a valiant soldier, with 200,000 men armed with bows and shields;
¹⁸next, Jehozabad, with 180,000 men armed for battle.

¹⁹These were the men who served the king, besides those he stationed in the fortified cities throughout Judah.

18:1Now Jehoshaphat had great wealth and honor, and he allied himself with Ahab by marriage. ²Some years later he went down to visit Ahab in Samaria. Ahab slaughtered many sheep and cattle for him and the people with him and urged him to attack Ramoth Gilead. ³Ahab king of Israel asked Jehoshaphat king of Judah, "Will you go with me against Ramoth Gilead?"

Jehoshaphat replied, "I am as you are, and my people as your people; we will join you in the war." ⁴But Jehoshaphat also said to the king of Israel, "First seek the counsel of the Lord."

⁵So the king of Israel brought together the prophets—four hundred men—and asked them, "Shall we go to war against Ramoth Gilead, or shall I refrain?"

"Go," they answered, "for God will give it into the king's hand."

⁶But Jehoshaphat asked, "Is there not a prophet of the Lord here whom we can inquire of?"

⁷The king of Israel answered Jehoshaphat, "There is still one man through whom we can inquire of the Lord, but I hate him because he never prophesies anything good about me, but always bad. He is Micaiah son of Imlah."

"The king should not say that," Jehoshaphat replied.

⁸So the king of Israel called one of his officials and said, "Bring Micaiah son of Imlah at once."

⁹Dressed in their royal robes, the king of Israel and Jehoshaphat king of Judah were sitting on their thrones at the threshing floor by the entrance to the gate of Samaria, with all the prophets prophesying before them. ¹⁰Now Zedekiah son of

Kenaanah had made iron horns, and he declared, "This is what the LORD says: 'With these you will gore the Arameans until they are destroyed.' "

¹¹All the other prophets were prophesying the same thing. "Attack Ramoth Gilead and be victorious," they said, "for the LORD will give it into the king's hand."

¹²The messenger who had gone to summon Micaiah said to him, "Look, as one man the other prophets are predicting success for the king. Let your word agree with theirs, and speak favorably."

¹³But Micaiah said, "As surely as the LORD lives, I can tell him only what my God says."

¹⁴When he arrived, the king asked him, "Micaiah, shall we go to war against Ramoth Gilead, or shall I refrain?"

"Attack and be victorious," he answered, "for they will be given into your hand."

¹⁵The king said to him, "How many times must I make you swear to tell me nothing but the truth in the name of the LORD?"

¹⁶Then Micaiah answered, "I saw all Israel scattered on the hills like sheep without a shepherd, and the LORD said, 'These people have no master. Let each one go home in peace.' "

¹⁷The king of Israel said to Jehoshaphat, "Didn't I tell you that he never prophesies anything good about me, but only bad?"

¹⁸Micaiah continued, "Therefore hear the word of the LORD: I saw the LORD sitting on his throne with all the host of heaven standing on his right and on his left. ¹⁹And the LORD said, 'Who will lure Ahab king of Israel into attacking Ramoth Gilead and going to his death there?'

"One suggested this, and another that. ²⁰Finally, a spirit came forward, stood before the LORD and said, 'I will lure him.'

" 'By what means?' the LORD asked.

²¹" 'I will go and be a lying spirit in the mouths of all his prophets,' he said.

" 'You will succeed in luring him,' said the LORD. 'Go and do it.'

²²"So now the LORD has put a lying spirit in the mouths of these prophets of yours. The LORD has decreed disaster for you."

²³Then Zedekiah son of Kenaanah went up and slapped Micaiah in the face. "Which way did the spirit from the LORD go when he went from me to speak to you?" he asked.

²⁴Micaiah replied, "You will find out on the day you go to hide in an inner room."

²⁵The king of Israel then ordered, "Take Micaiah and send him back to Amon the ruler of the city and to Joash the king's son, ²⁶and say, 'This is what the king says: Put this fellow in prison and give him nothing but bread and water until I return safely.' "

²⁷Micaiah declared, "If you ever return safely, the LORD has not spoken through me." Then he added, "Mark my words, all you people!"

²⁸So the king of Israel and Jehoshaphat king of Judah went up to Ramoth Gilead. ²⁹The king of Israel said to Jehoshaphat, "I will enter the battle in disguise, but you wear your royal robes." So the king of Israel disguised himself and went into battle.

³⁰Now the king of Aram had ordered his chariot commanders, "Do not fight with anyone, small or great, except the king of Israel." ³¹When the chariot commanders saw Jehoshaphat, they thought, "This is the king of Israel." So they turned to attack him, but Jehoshaphat cried out, and the LORD helped him. God drew them away from him, ³²for when the chariot commanders saw that he was not the king of Israel, they stopped pursuing him.

³³But someone drew his bow at random and hit the king of Israel between the sections of his armor. The king told the chariot driver, "Wheel around and get me out of the fighting. I've been wounded." ³⁴All day long the battle raged, and the king of Israel propped himself up in his chariot facing the Arameans until evening. Then at sunset he died.

^{19:1}When Jehoshaphat king of Judah returned safely to his palace in Jerusalem, ²Jehu the seer, the son of Hanani, went out to meet him and said to the king, "Should you help the wicked and love those who hate the LORD? Because of this, the wrath of the LORD is upon you. ³There is, however, some good in you, for you

have rid the land of the Asherah poles and have set your heart on seeking God."

⁴Jehoshaphat lived in Jerusalem, and he went out again among the people from Beersheba to the hill country of Ephraim and turned them back to the LORD, the God of their fathers. ⁵He appointed judges in the land, in each of the fortified cities of Judah. ⁶He told them, "Consider carefully what you do, because you are not judging for man but for the LORD, who is with you whenever you give a verdict. ⁷Now let the fear of the LORD be upon you. Judge carefully, for with the LORD our God there is no injustice or partiality or bribery."

⁸In Jerusalem also, Jehoshaphat appointed some of the Levites, priests and heads of Israelite families to administer the law of the LORD and to settle disputes. And they lived in Jerusalem. ⁹He gave them these orders: "You must serve faithfully and wholeheartedly in the fear of the LORD. ¹⁰In every case that comes before you from your fellow countrymen who live in the cities—whether bloodshed or other concerns of the law, commands, decrees or ordinances—you are to warn them not to sin against the LORD; otherwise his wrath will come on you and your brothers. Do this, and you will not sin.

¹¹"Amariah the chief priest will be over you in any matter concerning the LORD, and Zebadiah son of Ishmael, the leader of the tribe of Judah, will be over you in any matter concerning the king, and the Levites will serve as officials before you. Act with courage, and may the LORD be with those who do well."

²⁰:¹After this, the Moabites and Ammonites with some of the Meunites came to make war on Jehoshaphat.

²Some men came and told Jehoshaphat, "A vast army is coming against you from Edom, from the other side of the Sea. It is already in Hazazon Tamar" (that is, En Gedi). ³Alarmed, Jehoshaphat resolved to inquire of the LORD, and he proclaimed a fast for all Judah. ⁴The people of Judah came together to seek help from the LORD; indeed, they came from every town in Judah to seek him.

⁵Then Jehoshaphat stood up in the assembly of Judah and Jerusalem at the temple of the LORD in the front of the new courtyard ⁶and said:

"O LORD, God of our fathers, are you not the God who is in heaven? You rule over all the kingdoms of the nations. Power and might are in your hand, and no one can withstand you. ⁷O our God, did you not drive out the inhabitants of this land before your people Israel and give it forever to the descendants of Abraham your friend? ⁸They have lived in it and have built in it a sanctuary for your Name, saying, ⁹'If calamity comes upon us, whether the sword of judgment, or plague or famine, we will stand in your presence before this temple that bears your Name and will cry out to you in our distress, and you will hear us and save us.'

¹⁰"But now here are men from Ammon, Moab and Mount Seir, whose territory you would not allow Israel to invade when they came from Egypt; so they turned away from them and did not destroy them. ¹¹See how they are repaying us by coming to drive us out of the possession you gave us as an inheritance. ¹²O our God, will you not judge them? For we have no power to face this vast army that is attacking us. We do not know what to do, but our eyes are upon you."

¹³All the men of Judah, with their wives and children and little ones, stood there before the LORD.

¹⁴Then the Spirit of the LORD came upon Jahaziel son of Zechariah, the son of Benaiah, the son of Jeiel, the son of Mattaniah, a Levite and descendant of Asaph, as he stood in the assembly.

¹⁵He said: "Listen, King Jehoshaphat and all who live in Judah and Jerusalem! This is what the LORD says to you: 'Do not be afraid or discouraged because of this vast army. For the battle is not yours, but God's. ¹⁶Tomorrow march down against them. They will be climbing up by the Pass of Ziz, and you will find them at the end of the gorge in the Desert of Jeruel. ¹⁷You will not have to fight this battle. Take up your positions; stand firm and see the deliverance the LORD will give you, O Judah and Jerusalem. Do not be afraid; do not be discouraged. Go out to face them tomorrow, and the LORD will be with you.' "

¹⁸Jehoshaphat bowed with his face to the ground, and all the people of Judah and Jerusalem fell down in worship before the LORD. ¹⁹Then some Levites from the Kohathites and Korahites stood up and praised the LORD, the God of Israel, with very loud voice.

²⁰Early in the morning they left for the Desert of Tekoa. As they set out, Jehoshaphat stood and said, "Listen to me, Judah and people of Jerusalem! Have faith in the LORD your God and you will be upheld; have faith in his prophets and you will be successful." ²¹After consulting the people, Jehoshaphat appointed men to sing to the LORD and to praise him for the splendor of his holiness as they went out at the head of the army, saying:

> "Give thanks to the LORD,
> for his love endures forever."

²²As they began to sing and praise, the LORD set ambushes against the men of Ammon and Moab and Mount Seir who were invading Judah, and they were defeated. ²³The men of Ammon and Moab rose up against the men from Mount Seir to destroy and annihilate them. After they finished slaughtering the men from Seir, they helped to destroy one another.

²⁴When the men of Judah came to the place that overlooks the desert and looked toward the vast army, they saw only dead bodies lying on the ground; no one had escaped. ²⁵So Jehoshaphat and his men went to carry off their plunder, and they found among them a great amount of equipment and clothing and also articles of value—more than they could take away. There was so much plunder that it took three days to collect it. ²⁶On the fourth day they assembled in the Valley of Beracah, where they praised the LORD. This is why it is called the Valley of Beracah to this day.

²⁷Then, led by Jehoshaphat, all the men of Judah and Jerusalem returned joyfully to Jerusalem, for the LORD had given them cause to rejoice over their enemies. ²⁸They entered Jerusalem and went to the temple of the LORD with harps and lutes and trumpets.

²⁹The fear of God came upon all the kingdoms of the countries when they heard how the LORD had fought against the enemies of Israel. ³⁰And the kingdom of Jehoshaphat was at peace, for his God had given him rest on every side.

³¹So Jehoshaphat reigned over Judah. He was thirty-five years old when he became king of Judah, and he reigned in Jerusalem twenty-five years. His mother's name was Azubah daughter of Shilhi. ³²He walked in the ways of his father Asa and did not stray from them; he did what was right in the eyes of the LORD. ³³The high places, however, were not removed, and the people still had not set their hearts on the God of their fathers.

³⁴The other events of Jehoshaphat's reign, from beginning to end, are written in the annals of Jehu son of Hanani, which are recorded in the book of the kings of Israel.

³⁵Later, Jehoshaphat king of Judah made an alliance with Ahaziah king of Israel, who was guilty of wickedness. ³⁶He agreed with him to construct a fleet of trading ships. After these were built at Ezion Geber, ³⁷Eliezer son of Dodavahu of Mareshah prophesied against Jehoshaphat, saying, "Because you have made an alliance with Ahaziah, the LORD will destroy what you have made." The ships were wrecked and were not able to set sail to trade.

The regnal years of Asa's son Jehoshaphat reached from 873 to 848 B.C. (cf. on 17:7). Many of the features, moreover, that the Chronicler records of Asa's reign reappear in his description of the reign of his son. These parallels extend even to its organization under four major headings (cf. the introductory discussion to 2 Chron 14–16), which, for the career of Jehoshaphat, correspond to the textual divisions found in today's Book of 2 Chronicles (chs. 17–20). The first of these (ch. 17) reminds one of the account of Asa's first reform, as it describes how his son in 866 B.C. removed idolatry from Judah, taught God's law, and strengthened the kingdom. But even as Asa had entered into an unholy alliance with an Aramean king, Ben-Hadad I, so Jehoshaphat allied himself with the Ephraimite ruler, Ahab, and was thereby drawn into a nearly fatal campaign against Ramoth Gilead in 853 (ch. 18).

Furthermore, even as the prophet Azariah son of Oded had preached to Asa and inaugurated the earlier king's second reformation, so Jehu son of Hanani directed Jehoshaphat into a further reform in religion and into reorganization in the administration of justice (ch. 19). Finally, just as Asa had had to face the invading Cushites from the southwest, so Jehoshaphat met and overcame a vast army from the east (20:1–30), by trusting in the Lord. A concluding section then summarizes Jehoshaphat's reign and speaks to the failure of his commercial alliance with Israel (20:31–37). Out of these portions only chapter 18, together with the concluding remarks in 20:13–37, finds a parallel in 1 Kings (22:2–49).

By selecting carefully some of the many similarities in the reign of Asa and Jehoshaphat, the Chronicler can present the material so as to make the same theological message in chapters 17–20 that he had advocated in chapters 14–16. This message, with its emphasis on loyalty to God and the danger of disobedience, may be communicated in terms of a series of contrasting actions in the life of Jehoshaphat. Three contrasts should be noticed: (1) Jehoshaphat ignored the words of the prophet Micaiah but heeded the words of Jahaziel; (2) in the first military campaign he made a military alliance with Ahab, but in facing Moab and Ammon he relied completely on God for victory, in spite of the odds against him; (3) the results at Ramoth Gilead were catastrophic. Ahab was killed in battle and Jehoshaphat almost lost his life; however, when Judah faced its enemies Moab and Ammon, God destroyed the foreign armies. Furthermore it should be noted that at Ramoth Gilead, Jehoshaphat barely escaped with his own life when he called on the Lord for help. Similarly the nation escaped from the foreign danger by turning to the Lord for aid and deliverance. These series of contrasts emphasize the utter importance of depending on God and being loyal to him by obeying his Word and seeking his help. In other words, these series of contrasts make the same point in chapters 17–20 as in chapters 14–16. (SBM)

1 Jehoshaphat's strengthening of "himself against Israel" was directed specifically against Ahab (874–853), second king of the dynasty founded by the military leader Omri, and infamous for the Baal worship advocated by his wife Jezebel. Asa's hostility with the North thus continued, at least initially, under his son (cf. on 16:9; 18:1).

2 The Ephraimitic "towns . . . captured" by Asa included not simply the bastion of Ramah (cf. on 16:1), but other communities as well (cf. on 15:8).

3 There seems to be no compelling reason why the adjective *rî'šōnîm* ("first, former") need be taken adverbially, as in the NIV—"in his early years" (though the NIV also supplies "years")—rather than in the normal syntax of an attributive adjective, modifying its preceding noun, "ways" (cf. EV). The verse thus says that "Jehoshaphat walked in the former ways" of his ancestor David, the Chronicler's implication being that David's latter ways were less exemplary (cf. 2 Sam 11–21; see Introduction: Purpose, 3). Concretely Jehoshaphat disdained "the Baals" (plu.); for these were almost numberless, each individual field being treated as if it had its own guiding *ba'al* ("master, owner"), i.e., fertility spirit.

4 The practice of Israel, which Jehoshaphat also avoided, included Jeroboam's deviations in respect to the priesthood and the calendar, as well as his calf worship (cf. on 13:8; cf. 1 Kings 12:28–33).

6 Concerning "the high places and the Asherah poles" that Jehoshaphat removed, see the comment on 14:3. The introductory adverb *weʿod* (NIV, "furthermore") is more normally rendered "and again" (he removed the high places) (cf. EV). Jehoshaphat renewed his father Asa's earlier opposition to local shrines (14:3; cf. 1 Kings 22:46). Yet just as with Asa (cf. on 2 Chron 15:17), the king's official act was not sustained by his subjects: "The people continued to offer sacrifices and burn incense there," on the high places (1 Kings 22:43). Some commentators not infrequently accuse the Chronicler of deliberate alteration of the facts at this point, "to save the reputation of Jehoshaphat" (Dentan, p. 145). The point urged is that, to Ezra, "in view of Jehoshaphat's well-known zeal, the statement in Kings must be erroneous" (ibid., pp. 145–46)—it apparently being overlooked that 2 Chronicles itself (20:33) explicitly confirms the word of Kings, that "the high places were not removed," because "the people still had not set their hearts on the God of their fathers."

7–9 Though Jehoshaphat's "reign" (v.7) is said to have covered twenty-five years (20:31), 872–848 B.C., it can also be said to have terminated in only twenty-two years (eighteen, in 2 Kings 3:1, plus four more, in 8:16), i.e., from the death of his father Asa in 869. Jehoshaphat must therefore have enjoyed an additional three-year coregency, commencing in 872, a procedure that was probably necessary because of Asa's illness, which became increasingly serious in the following year (cf. on 16:12). Yet his dispatch of a religious teaching mission (17:7–9; cf. Notes) seems sufficiently independent to suggest that what v.7 calls his "third year" must have been that "of his" sole "reign," or 867.

The mission consisted of five government officials, nine Levites, and two priests, as named (v.8). For Jehoshaphat seems to have recognized how important it was for all the leaders of God's people (cf. Matt 28:20) "to teach" them "the Book of the Law of the LORD" (v.9; the Pentateuch, or at least Deuteronomy, though it could by this time have included the historical books through 2 Samuel and much of the Davidic and Solomonic poetry as well). Teaching was not limited to the professional Levites (Deut 33:10) and priests (Lev 10:11). They "went around to all the towns . . . and taught" (cf. the traveling evangelists mentioned in NT times, 3 John 7–8).

12 For a summarization of the evidence on Jehoshaphat's "store cities in Judah," see Y. Yadin, "The Fourfold Division of Judah," BASOR 163 (1961): 6–12.

13–18 The king's "experienced fighting men" that he "kept in Jerusalem" (v.13) involved five groups, that consisted respectively of 300, 280, 200, 200, and 180 specially trained leaders (reading in each verse, *ʾallûp*, "leader," rather than *ʾelep*, "thousand"; cf. the comments to 1 Chron 7:3–4 and 12:27). The total was thus 1,160 (not 1,160,000).

19 Yet even here, "these . . . who served the king" in the city of Jerusalem were specifically the five commanders, as listed. Portions of their followers would then have been stationed "in the fortified cities throughout Judah."

497

18:1 Second Chronicles 18 is taken from 1 Kings 22:2–35 and is the only extract from the records of Israel that was used by Ezra. His reason seems to have been because it involved the southern king, Jehoshaphat, almost as much as the northern ruler, Ahab, and also because the message of the prophet Micaiah, about which the chapter centers, had spiritual applications that extended far beyond the career of Ahab (cf. esp. the comments on vv.7, 13, 19–20, 27).

Jehoshaphat "allied himself with Ahab." This act is not simply condemned (19:2; cf. on 15:2); it is seen as the root of far-reaching consequences, made all too clear by a series of disasters that followed (18:31; 20:37; 21:6; 22:7, 10). Initially it entailed the "marriage" of Jehoshaphat's son Jehoram to Athaliah, the daughter of Ahab. Their marriage, in turn, furnishes an approximate date for the alliance, of about 865 B.C., because a child of this union (Ahaziah) was twenty-two at his own accession in 841 (22:2). A major cause that led to the alliance may be found in the growing threat of Assyria in the north. Its ruthless monarch Ashurnasirpal II (884–859) was already pressing into Lebanon; and his successor, Shalmaneser III, is known to have fought a drawn battle against a coalition of western states, including Damascus and Israel, at Qarqar on the Orontes River in 853.

2 Ahab urged Jehoshaphat to join him in a campaign to recover Ramoth Gilead. This was a key city on the eastern edge of Transjordanian Israel, south of the Yarmuk River, astride the Gilead trade route that went north to Damascus and beyond. It had been seized by the Aramean king of Damascus (16:4, or perhaps subsequently; cf. 1 Kings 20:34); but Ahab may have felt that the Arameans had been sufficiently weakened by their losses at Qarqar to permit its recapture at this time, later in 853.

4 Though Jehoshaphat had already committed himself to the enterprise (v.3), and though he went on to disregard the divine guidance that was given him (v.28), he still retained the religion of Yahweh to the extent that he insisted on seeking "the counsel of the LORD."

5 Jehoshaphat put little confidence in Ahab's four hundred court prophets (cf. v.6). These were men who confessedly spoke in the name of Yahweh and not of Baal (vv.5, 10). But it was a Yahweh in the corrupted form of a golden calf (cf. on 13:8); and their words were false (v.22), couched in terms that were calculated simply to please the hearers (v.12; cf. Mic 3:5, 11).

7 "Micaiah" remains unknown, apart from this incident. He never prophesied anything good about Ahab—because of the character of Ahab. The true prophets of Israel were, indeed, distinguished by the fact that they consistently warned their nation of the results of its sin (Jer 23:22; Mic 3:8).

9 The two kings set their thrones at "the gate of Samaria," the traditional place for rendering judgment (Gen 23:10; Ruth 4:1).

10–11 The "iron horns" (v.10) made by the false prophet Zedekiah were designed to symbolize victory for Ahab (Deut 33:17), but perhaps also to accomplish it, insofar as they were superstitiously believed to contain magical potency.

12–13 The true prophet Micaiah, by contrast, could tell the king "only what . . .

God says" (v.13). The revelations that he transmitted were objectively received and were distinguishable from the subjective thoughts and desires of his own heart (Jer 14:14; cf. 42:4, 7).

14–15 Micaiah's words "Attack and be victorious" (v.14) were spoken in irony, as the tone of his voice must have immediately indicated to Ahab (cf. v.15).

16 Micaiah's serious but figurative words "These people have no masters" (cf. Notes) continue the analogy of flocks and shepherds (cf. Num 27:16–17); they were a prediction of Ahab's death in battle (2 Chron 18:34). But the Hebrew troops would be free to "go home in peace," as brought about by the very orders of the Aramean king Ben-Hadad II, that his men were to fight only against Ahab (v.30).

18 As "Micaiah continued," with his vision of heaven itself, he spoke of "the host," or army, that was standing on either side of the Lord, which consisted of angelic spirits (cf. the "sons of God" in Job 1:6).

19 The Lord's question, "Who will lure Ahab . . . to his death?" testifies to the truth that God can work through spirits to incite evil men like Ahab to manifest their sin and thus be led, either to punishment or to repentance (cf. 1 Sam 16:14–15; 18:10 –11; Payne, *Theology,* pp. 197–200).

20 The Hebrew that underlies the phrase rendered "a spirit" (came forward) reads literally, "the (well-known) spirit," i.e., Satan the tempter (as in Job 1:6–12). Or perhaps this is an instance where the definite article is an "article of class." Apparently Micaiah seems to have assumed among his hearers a working knowledge of the Book of Job, as already recorded in the days of Solomon.

22 The seer's emphatic phrase "these prophets of yours" underlines their differentiation from God's (true) prophets.

23 The way Zedekiah "slapped Micaiah on the face" indicates in itself that the Holy Spirit was not present with him (James 3:17; but cf. 2 Kings 1:10–12). Yet his brazen claim to possess "the Spirit of the LORD" (NIV mg.) need not be watered down— though he may not have been personally aware that his optimistic message had in fact been supernaturally implanted in his mind, by Satan. Zedekiah's next words are difficult. He seems to be acknowledging Micaiah's claim that the Lord's Spirit had come "to speak to" him; but he asks, "Which way did the Spirit" actually "go when he went from me?" Not, presumably, to Micaiah!

24 Micaiah's rejoinder was to predict that Zedekiah would "go to hide in an inner room." Its fulfillment is unknown; but the prophecy seems to suggest an attempt on his part to escape pursuit, perhaps as Ahab's family would take vengeance on the false prophets, after the king's death.

25–26 Ahab's orders to send Micaiah back to the magistrate "Amon" (v.25) imply that the prophet had already been put in custody at the time. Note the precedent that had been set for persecution under Asa (cf. on 16:10).

27 The prophet's final statement, "Mark my words, all you people," was addressed to a plurality (*'ammîm,* "peoples, nations"). He was calling all the world to serve as his witness (cf. the identical words with which his namesake in the next century, Micah of Moresheth, would commence his prophecy, Mic 1:2).

28–29 Ahab's plan to "enter the battle in disguise" (v.29) was a futile attempt to escape the decree of God (v.16), and it failed (v.33).

30 Ben-Hadad's plan, in turn, to concentrate on no one "except the king of Israel" assumed that if Ahab could once be taken, the war would be won (cf. 2 Sam 21:17)—and it was also the means for fulfilling Micaiah's prophetic vision of v.16.

31–32 The words about Jehoshaphat with which v.31 concludes—"and the LORD helped him. God drew them away from him"—are an addition by Ezra, not found in the parallel passage of 1 Kings 22:32. They are significant, moreover, in at least three ways: (1) showing the seriousness of Jehoshaphat's deviation, how he would forthwith have reaped a fatal fruit from his sinful alliance with Ahab, had not God intervened; (2) suggesting the reality of his faith, that when "Jehoshaphat cried out," this was not just an expression of fear on his part but was apparently a prayer for divine help; and (3) demonstrating the greatness of the grace of God, rescuing men without a need for manmade alliances, or even, as in this case, in spite of them.

33 The arrow then struck the king in a vulnerable spot, literally, between the "scaly mail" armor and its "appendages," i.e., penetrating the abdomen.

34 With the death of Ahab, 2 Chronicles 18 closes. First Kings 22 has an additional five verses (36–40) with further details, which Ezra omitted as less relevant for his particular audience.

19:1 Jehoshaphat's safe return from Ramoth Gilead fulfilled a final detail in Micaiah's prophecy (cf. on 18:16).

2 Hanani the seer had confronted King Asa half a century earlier (cf. on 16:7); and his son Jehu the seer had already condemned the dynasty of Baasha in Israel, some thirty-five years before this occasion in 853 B.C. (1 Kings 16:1, 7). Jehu's message was once again a negative one, opposing Jehoshaphat's alliance with Israel (cf. on 18:1). But he went beyond the specific matter of this alliance (emphasized by the NIV mg.) and raised a more general ethical question, "Should you . . . love those who hate the LORD? " Certainly the Christian is to have a compassionate love for the hateful and the lost (Matt 5:44); but he must never compromise his stand for God (Ps 139:21–22) or "help the wicked" (cf. Rom 16:17; 2 John 10–11).

Jehu therefore announced to the king, "The wrath of the LORD is upon you." In fact it already had been (18:31); and it still would be (20:1, 37; 22:10). Unlike his father Asa, however, who had refused to humble himself before God when confronted by Jehu's father Hanani (see comment on 16:10), Jehoshaphat did submit to the judgment of God as conveyed by the seer Jehu. This encounter, indeed, seems to have precipitated the king's second great reform, both in its religious aspect (v.4) and in its judicial implications (vv.5–11).

3 Jehu himself seems to have anticipated the king's positive response by his balanced acknowledgment, both of "some good" in him (cf. the approval soon to be granted Jehoshaphat by Elisha, 2 Kings 3:14) and of some of the values that had emerged from his first reform, particularly the elimination of the "Asherah poles" (17:6; cf. on 14:3).

4 For a detailed discussion of the king's reforms, see Albright, "Reform of Jehoshaphat," pp. 61–82.

5–6 Jehoshaphat's admonition to the newly appointed judges (v.5), that they were "not judging for man but for the LORD" (v.6), is a standing reminder that good government springs from commitment to God (cf. v.7 and comment on 1 Chron 11:3).

8 "In Jerusalem" Jehoshaphat "appointed . . . Levites" (cf. on 1 Chron 26:29 on their judicial function) to serve on the central court of appeals and "to settle disputes." The NIV rendering, "And they lived in Jerusalem," represents a necessary repointing of the consonantal Hebrew verb so that it may be read *wayyēšᵉbû*. The MT pointing is *wayyāšûbû* ("And they returned"). But if the chronological order here is correct, this can hardly be correct, because Jehoshaphat's new judges had not been appointed at the time the king had gone out (v.4) among the provinces (so as to be able to "return" with him); they were, instead, already "in Jerusalem."

9–10 Israel's faithful judge was not simply to decide cases and render verdicts but was also to "warn" his "brothers" against sin in the sight of God. For he too was responsible to the Lord, and his ultimate motivation was that he might so live that divine "wrath" would not "come on" either him or his Hebrew brothers.

11 In the Pentateuch religious and civil law, or ceremonial and moral law, are juxtaposed, often without differentiation. Among the earlier prophets Samuel had begun to insist on certain priorities: that to obey was better than to sacrifice (1 Sam 15:22; though Moses too put love of God [Deut 6] and faith [Deut 7] before detailed legislation [Deut 12–26]). Now, at this point in the mid-ninth century, a distinction is explicitly made (though perhaps based on Deut 17:9, 12) between matters "concerning the LORD" and "matters concerning the king." Among the later prophets the difference between moral law and ceremonial law was sharply drawn (Isa 1:11–17; Amos 5:21–24; Payne, *Theology*, pp. 315–16; 321–22).

Under Jehoshaphat's judges, Levites were to "serve as officials" (*šōṭᵉrîm*). De Vaux (*Ancient Israel*, p. 155) proposes, "They seem to have been clerks attached to the court and, more generally, clerks attached to the judges."

20:1 Soon after 853 B.C. (cf. on 18:3; on 20:35), Jehoshaphat faced an unexpected invasion by the combined forces of Moab, Ammon, and "the Meunites" (NIV mg.; cf. 1 Chron 4:41; 2 Chron 26:7). These last were a people of Mount Seir in Edom (cf. vv.10, 22–23), perhaps from Maon, near Petra.

2 The enemy forces attacked by means of a little-used route, advancing around the south, or the Edomite (cf. Notes) end of the Dead Sea (per NIV mg.); for they took "En Gedi," about midway on its western shore.

3–4 Jehoshaphat "proclaimed a fast" (v.3) to emphasize in the presence of the "Lord" (v.4) Judah's distress (just as in Judg 20:26). Fasting did not exist as an official part of preexilic Hebrew religion, unless it be implied in Leviticus 16:29–31; but from the time of Samuel onward, it had been employed to stress the sincerity of the prayers of God's people when they were facing special needs (1 Sam 7:6; cf. Acts 13:2–3).

5 The "new courtyard" the king stood before was the temple's "large court" (cf. comment on 4:9); and it was probably called this because it was one of the innovations in Solomon's structure. Under him it had for the first time been separated from the "court of the priests." It is also possible that Jehoshaphat had recently restored it (cf. 17:12).

6–9 The king's plea, "If calamity comes upon us," was a quotation from Solomon's prayer that had been offered at the temple's dedication (6:28–30; cf. 7:13–15).

10–11 By referring also to Deuteronomy 2:5, which had recorded how God would not "allow Israel to invade" the lands of Seir, Jehoshaphat was in effect calling on the Lord to honor Israel's obedience in this regard. He spoke also of God's specific bestowal on Israel of the very land that these enemies were in the process of invading (v.11).

12 Jehoshaphat's conclusion—"We have no power . . . but our eyes are upon you"—embodies a faith similar to that demonstrated by his father Asa (14:11).

13–15 On the status of "Jahaziel" (v.14), descendant of the chief Levitical musician Asaph (cf. comment on 1 Chron 16:5), see Aubrey R. Johnson, *The Cultic Prophet in Ancient Israel* (Cardiff: University of Wales, 1944), pp. 61–62. Jahaziel's words, "the battle is not yours, but God's" (v.15), reflect the spirit of David against Goliath (1 Sam 17:47).

16 From a point seven miles north of En Gedi, "the Pass [*ma'ᵃlēh*, 'ascent'] of Ziz" wound inland, up to the Valley of Beracah (v.26), west of Tekoa, which was located south of Bethlehem toward Hebron. "Jeruel" lay on this same route, southeast of Tekoa.

17 Jahaziel's further words, "Stand firm and see the deliverance the Lord will give you," reflect the speech of Moses at the Red Sea (Exod 14:13). The situation has, however, provoked scorn from some, who refer to it as "legend . . . an ecclesiastical affair in which the army is expressly told before hand it will not need to fight . . . a kind of parable on man's need to trust in God" (Dentan, p. 146).

20 The "Desert of Tekoa" occupies a sharp drop-off, immediately to the east of the town. Jehoshaphat's words "have faith in the Lord your God and you will be upheld" were quoted a century later by Isaiah to King Ahaz (Isa 7:9; cf. 28:16; Mark 9:23).

21 At this point singers "went out at the head of the army," just as the ark of God and the priestly trumpeters had at Jericho (Josh 6:9). They praised the Lord "in (their) holy array" (cf. NIV mg., comment on 1 Chron 16:29, and Keil, p. 389), a rendering that seems preferable to that found in the NIV text: "for the splendor of his holiness."

22–30 The "ambushes" (v.22) that the Lord then set against the invaders are not identified; but they may have consisted of some of the more rapacious Seirites (Edomites), since the men of Ammon and Moab proceeded to turn on the men of Mount Seir (v.23). The result was that "they helped to destroy one another," just as had occurred at the triumph of Gideon (Judg 7:22).

On the location of the Valley of "Beracah" (v.26, meaning, "blessing" or "praise," NIV mg.), see the comment on v.16.

31–33 Here alone, for the concluding portion of chapter 20 (vv.31–37), information parallel to 1 Kings 22 appears (vv.41–49).

On the acknowledged failure to eliminate Judah's "high places," see the comment on 17:6.

34 On "the annals of Jehu" being "recorded in the book of the kings," see the comment on 32:32.

35 Jehoshaphat's "alliance with" Ahab's son "Ahaziah" belongs to the brief period of the latter's reign over Israel, 853–852 B.C.

36 On ships being "built at Ezion Geber," see 8:17. Archaeology indicates that after the demise of the original Solomonic settlement there, the site's second occupational level dates to the days of Jehoshaphat in the ninth century (T.J. Meek, "Bronze Swords From Luristan," BASOR 79 [1940]:8–9), though it seems soon to have fallen into Edomite hands (cf. 21:8). The phrase "trading ships" interprets a more literal rendering of the Hebrew, i.e., "ships that could go to Tarshish" (NIV mg.). The thought is that these vessels belonged to the class of ships that went to Tarshish (cf. comment on 9:21); their actual destination was Ophir (cf. on 8:18; 1 Kings 22:48).

37 The prophet "Eliezer . . . of Mareshah" is unknown apart from this passage. But because of Jehoshaphat's sin in allying himself with the wicked Ahaziah (v.35), which Eliezer condemned, the ships were wrecked; for God will not honor a compromising alliance (cf. comment on 19:2). The NIV text says that they were therefore "not able to set sail to trade," which represents the general idea of the Hebrew; but it may be rendered more closely that they were "never fit to sail to Tarshish" (JB; cf. NIV mg. and comment on 9:21), or to anywhere else, including their particular goal of Ophir (cf. on v.36).

First Kings 22:49 adds that Jehoshaphat then refused Ahaziah's offer for a joint-sailing endeavor. Some commentators proceed to censure Chronicles for seeking to explain Jehoshaphat's calamity as God's punishment for an alliance (v.35) that Kings says he refused to enter! As Keil (KD, *Kings*, p. 283), however, more plausibly points out, this was a "fresh proposal . . . to make another attempt."

Notes:

7 Some have cast doubt on the reality of Jehoshaphat's teaching mission, claiming it to be a reflection of conditions in the Chronicler's own day (Dentan, p. 146). North ("The Chronicler," 1:420) says that v.8 is "inserted, names and all," from Zech 6:10—actually, of the missionaries listed by Ezra, exactly one name (Tobijah's) out of the thirteen matches those that are found in Zechariah. Myers (*Chronicles*, 2:99) refers to the view that 17:7–9 is simply "another version of the judicial reform reported in 19:4–11." Finally Ackroyd ("Theology," p. 105) dismissed the whole idea of "Jehoshaphat, the reformer of justice" as "a theme . . . perhaps suggested by the exposition of his name, 'Yahweh judges.'" Yet Myers (*Chronicles*, 2:99), on his own part, concludes: "The fact that laymen are mentioned first . . . points to a tradition older than the Chronicler . . . perhaps quite old [prior to Hos 4:6]. . . . There is a strong probability that such a teaching mission was established to inform the people of the torah of the Lord" (cf. Albright's emphasis on the historical character of the king's judicial reform, "Reform of Jehoshaphat," pp. 74–82).

18:9 On the basis of Ugaritic, the noun for threshing floor, גֹּרֶן (*gōren*), has been rendered "plaza" (cf. "The *Goren* at the City Gate: Justice and the Royal Office in the Ugaritic Text 'Aqht'," PEQ [1953]: 118–20).

16 The noun for "master," אֲדֹנִים (*ᵃdōnîm*), is a Hebrew plural; the defeated Israelites will thus have no "masters" (unless this be a case of an enclitic mem [so Myers, *Chronicles*, 2:104]).

19:8 The phrase rendered "to administer the law of (the Lord)" reads in Hebrew simply לְמִשְׁפַּט (*lᵉmišpaṭ*, "for the judgment of [the Lord]," NASB; cf. v.11).

20:2 BH³ and NIV (mg.) read מֵאֱדֹם (*mēᵃdōm*, "from Edom"), though Y. Aharoni (*The Land of the Bible* [Philadelphia: Westminster, 1967], p. 393) feels that the MT's מֵאֲרָם (*mēᵃrām*, "from Aram") is "apparently correct. . . . It is not impossible that Aram-Damascus was in control of this region."

---

5. *Jehoram*

21:1–20

¹Then Jehoshaphat rested with his fathers and was buried with them in the City of David. And Jehoram his son succeeded him as king. ²Jehoram's brothers, the sons of Jehoshaphat, were Azariah, Jehiel, Zechariah, Azariahu, Michael and Shephatiah. All these were sons of Jehoshaphat king of Israel. ³Their father had given them many gifts of silver and gold and articles of value, as well as fortified cities in Judah, but he had given the kingdom to Jehoram because he was his firstborn son.

⁴When Jehoram established himself firmly over his father's kingdom, he put all his brothers to the sword along with some of the princes of Israel. ⁵Jehoram was thirty-two years old when he became king, and he reigned in Jerusalem eight years. ⁶He walked in the ways of the kings of Israel, as the house of Ahab had done, for he married a daughter of Ahab. He did evil in the eyes of the Lord. ⁷Nevertheless, because of the covenant the Lord had made with David, the Lord was not willing to destroy the house of David. He had promised to maintain a lamp for him and his descendants forever.

⁸In the time of Jehoram, Edom rebelled against Judah and set up its own king. ⁹So Jehoram went there with his officers and all his chariots. The Edomites surrounded him and his chariot commanders, but he rose up and broke through by night. ¹⁰To this day Edom has been in rebellion against Judah.

Libnah revolted at the same time, because Jehoram had forsaken the Lord, the God of his fathers. ¹¹He had also built high places on the hills of Judah and had caused the people of Jerusalem to prostitute themselves and had led Judah astray.

¹²Jehoram received a letter from Elijah the prophet, which said:

"This is what the LORD, the God of your father David says: 'You have not walked in the ways of your father Jehoshaphat or of Asa king of Judah. ¹³But you have walked in the ways of the kings of Israel, and you have led Judah and the people of Jerusalem to prostitute themselves, just as the house of Ahab did. You have also murdered your own brothers, members of your father's house, men who were better than you. ¹⁴So now the LORD is about to strike your people, your sons, your wives and everything that is yours, with a heavy blow. ¹⁵You yourself will be very ill with a lingering disease of the bowels, until the disease causes your bowels to come out.' "

¹⁶The LORD aroused against Jehoram the hostility of the Philistines and of the Arabs who lived near the Cushites. ¹⁷They attacked Judah, invaded it and carried off all the goods found in the king's palace, together with his sons and wives. Not a son was left to him except Ahaziah, the youngest.

¹⁸After all this, the LORD afflicted Jehoram with an incurable disease of the bowels. ¹⁹In the course of time, at the end of the second year, his bowels came out because of the disease, and he died in great pain. His people made no fire in his honor, as they had for his fathers.

²⁰Jehoram was thirty-two years old when he became king, and he reigned in Jerusalem eight years. He passed away, to no one's regret, and was buried in the City of David, but not in the tombs of the kings.

The sole reign of Jehoshaphat's son Jehoram extended from 848 to 841 B.C. and forms the subject of 2 Chronicles 21 (cf. v.1 comment). Dominating the chapter is the sad fact that Jehoram was married to Ahab's daughter and that he "walked in [their] ways" (v.6). It therefore describes, on the one hand, his viciousness and apostasy (vv.1–11) and, on the other, his condemnation, delivered through the prophet Elijah, and his overwhelming failures, both national and personal, that came as a result (vv.12–20). Much of the first half of the chapter corresponds to the same information (though cf. v.2 comment) found in 1 Kings 22:50 and 2 Kings 8:17 –22, with some elaboration by the Chronicler; but the second half (except for a few words in the king's death notice; cf. 2 Kings 8:24) is without biblical parallel.

1 "Jehoshaphat . . . was buried . . . and his son succeeded him," as sole monarch, in 848 B.C. But since Jehoshaphat's eighteenth year (2 Kings 3:1), four years before his death (17:7 comment), can simultaneously be designated as his son Jehoram's second year (2 Kings 1:17), it appears that the latter must have been associated with his father on Judah's throne since sometime in 853 (cf. Thiele, *Numbers*, pp. 64–65).

2 Because vv.3–4 have no parallel in Kings, their context would seem to have been drawn from the lost court chronicle mentioned elsewhere by Ezra (20:34; 25:26; cf. 16:11 comment) or from other, similar literary sources.

3 Jehoshaphat's giving his six younger sons "many gifts," but also dispersing them throughout the "cities in Judah," shows that he was following the wise policy established by his great-grandfather Rehoboam (cf. 11:23 comment).

4 When Jehoram, however, proceeded to massacre his brothers (cf. parallel atrocities recorded in 22:10 or Judg 9:5), along with certain "princes" (*śārîm*, or "prominent officials"), he was already demonstrating the unholy influence of his ruthless

505

wife, Athaliah. The latter herself became the instigator of the crime of 22:10 (cf. the similar record of her step-mother, Jezebel, in 1 Kings 18:4; 19:2; 21:7–15). The king's personality had thus become twisted to the point that he apparently suspected others of acting as he would have, if they were given the opportunity. Yet his brothers' principles were, in point of fact, much higher than his own (v. 13).

7 God's unwillingness "to destroy" the dynasty of David was what had preserved Judah previously as a kingdom, despite Solomon's sin (1 Kings 11:12–13). God had made a "covenant" with David. The actual term $b^e r\hat{\imath}t$ has not been preserved in the historical record of the Lord's promise (cf. 1 Chron 17:12 comment); but this was one of the successive revelations of God's redemptive testament, as confirmed by other passages (cf., e.g., 2 Sam 23:5; Isa 55:3).

8 At this time, and "because Jehoram had forsaken the LORD" (v. 10), "Edom rebelled" against its Hebrew governors (1 Kings 22:47); indeed Moab, to Edom's north, had already become independent (2 Kings 1:1).

9 When the king attempted to use force to reimpose his authority, "the Edomites surrounded his chariot commanders," almost overwhelming the Judean army. Jehoram then not simply "broke through" (cf. NIV); more positively he "struck them down" ($wayyak$) at Zair (2 Kings 8:21), possibly Zior, a few miles south of the site of his father's victory at Beracah (2 Chron 20:26).

10 Jehoram failed, however, to quell Edom's "rebellion." His campaign thus parallels Israel's failure shortly before, when it had attempted to resubdue Moab (2 Kings 3:6–27). Also in revolt at this time was "Libnah," a semi-Philistine city that may perhaps be identified with Tell Bornat in the vicinity of Gath (NBD, p. 734).

11 Jehoram built up the "high places," the very shrines that his father and grandfather had tried to eradicate (cf. the comments to 14:3 and 17:6). Here the people "prostituted themselves" ($z\bar{a}n\bar{a}h$, "committed fornication"). But though the Canaanitish worship thus reintroduced did involve sexual immorality (cf. 1 Kings 22:46), the emphasis at this point is how the king "led Judah astray," into faithlessness in respect to Yahweh, her divine husband. To Moses and the prophets, idolatry was adulterous prostitution (v. 13; Lev 20:5; cf. Num 25:1–2).

12–15 That Jehoram "received a letter from Elijah" (v. 12) has been labeled "a pure product of the imagination, since Elijah had nothing to do with the S. kingdom, and clearly was not living at this time (2 Kings 3:11 [i.e., before Jehoshaphat's death and Jehoram's installation in 848 B.C.])" (Curtis, pp. 415–16). Both criticisms, however, are answerable. Elijah's career did involve the south, specifically "Beersheba in Judah" (1 Kings 19:3); his flight took him, indeed, as far south as Sinai (v. 8). Also, though Elijah's last dated act occurred in 852 (2 Kings 1:3, 17), his translation to heaven (2:11) still need not have occurred till after Jehoram's accession as sole monarch over Judah and his crimes of slaughtering his brothers and his officials, in the year 848 (8:16). The words in 2 Kings 3:11 about Elisha "tell us only that the latter was Elijah's assistant . . . not that Elijah was no longer upon earth" (Keil, p. 397). Elijah may, however, have been gone by the time of the delivery of his letter, so that its sentence of doom could have had the force of a voice coming from the dead.

16–17 The land's fortunes suffered a complete reversal; for "the Philistines" (v. 16), who had rendered tribute to Jehoram's father (2 Chron 17:11), now "invaded Judah" (v. 17). They were joined, in fact, by "the Arabs who lived near the Cushites" (v. 16; cf. 14:9 comment), i.e., by nomads from the borderlands between Philistia and Egypt.

In the outworkings of God's justice, the man who began by massacring his own brothers (v. 4) ended by suffering the loss of his sons and wives (v. 17; 22:1).

18–20 The king's "incurable disease of the bowels" (v. 18) seems to have been some extreme form of dysentery. In further contrast to his father (cf. 16:14 comment), he died without "fire in his honor" (v. 19). Jehoram's death was unmourned, without even normal burial "in the tombs of the kings" (cf. 24:25 comment).

6. Ahaziah

22:1–9

> ¹The people of Jerusalem made Ahaziah, Jehoram's youngest son, king in his place, since the raiders, who came with the Arabs into the camp, had killed all the older sons. So Ahaziah son of Jehoram king of Judah began to reign.
> ²Ahaziah was twenty-two years old when he became king, and he reigned in Jerusalem one year. His mother's name was Athaliah, a granddaughter of Omri.
> ³He too walked in the ways of the house of Ahab, for his mother encouraged him in doing wrong. ⁴He did evil in the eyes of the LORD, as the house of Ahab had done, for after his father's death they became his advisers, to his undoing. ⁵He also followed their counsel when he went with Joram son of Ahab king of Israel to war against Hazael king of Aram at Ramoth Gilead. The Arameans wounded Joram; ⁶so he returned to Jezreel to recover from the wounds they had inflicted on him at Ramoth in his battle with Hazael king of Aram.
> Then Ahaziah son of Jehoram king of Judah went down to Jezreel to see Joram son of Ahab because he had been wounded.
> ⁷Through Ahaziah's visit to Joram, God brought about Ahaziah's downfall. When Ahaziah arrived, he went out with Joram to meet Jehu son of Nimshi, whom the LORD had anointed to destroy the house of Ahab. ⁸While Jehu was executing judgment on the house of Ahab, he found the princes of Judah and the sons of Ahaziah's relatives, who had been attending Ahaziah, and he killed them. ⁹He then went in search of Ahaziah, and his men captured him while he was hiding in Samaria. He was brought to Jehu and put to death. They buried him, for they said, "He was a son of Jehoshaphat, who sought the LORD with all his heart." So there was no one in the house of Ahaziah powerful enough to retain the kingdom.

The reign of Jehoram's son Ahaziah ran its course during the one year of 841 B.C. (cf. v.2 comment). Its theme is once again that of retribution (cf. 21:17 comment); and, in Ahaziah's case, it was his sinful alliance with the wicked house of Ahab in Israel that brought about its own punishment (22:4) in the form of premature death for the young monarch (v.9). The sequence of events is explained in more detail in the parallel passage of 2 Kings 8:25–10:14, though 2 Chronicles 22 adds unique details from its own special sources (vv.1, 9b), as well as certain observations by Ezra (vv.4b, 7a) that are not found in Kings.

1 The Chronicler's supplementary notice that Ahaziah was made king by "the people of Jerusalem" suggests that there was some uncertainty about the succession (cf. 23:13 comment and the instance in 2 Kings 23:30), perhaps because of the threat of Ahaziah's own mother, the ruthless Athaliah (cf. v.10). Concerning "the raiders who . . . had killed all" Jehoram's "older sons," see 21:17.

2 The reading found in the LXX and 2 Kings 8:26 for Ahaziah's age (NIV mg.) of "twenty-two years" is to be adopted, rather than the MT's "forty-two," which would make him older than his father (cf. 21:20). His reign of "one year" fell entirely within the twelfth year of Joram of Israel (2 Kings 8:25; cf. 3:1), whose death occurred at the same time as his own (9:24, 27), so that his rule must actually have been only a few months.

3–4 The way that Ahaziah's mother "encouraged him in doing wrong" is explained by this queen's patronizing of the Phoenician Baal worship of her step-mother Jezebel (23:17), and is a further testimony to the dominating influence of both these evil women (21:6; cf. 21:4 comment and Deut 7:3).

Ahaziah was not only encouraged to do evil by his mother, but he also followed the bad advice of "the members of the house related to him through his mother" (Keil, p. 404). This was "to his undoing" (v.4).

5 The Transjordanian Israelitish city of "Ramoth Gilead" had been seized by the Arameans (18:2 comment), and Ahab's attempt at its recovery in 853 had led instead to his own death (18:34). Yet with the murder of the Aramean king Ben Hadad II by Hazael some ten years later (2 Kings 8:7–15), Ahab's second son, "Joram" (cf. NIV mg.), recaptured the city, but only to be attacked in 841 by Hazael (2 Kings 9:14), who wounded Joram there.

6 So Joram returned from Ramoth (NIV mg.) to Jezreel, at the head of the Esdraelon Valley, where his father Ahab's palace was located (1 Kings 21:1), and where his nephew Ahaziah (cf. NIV mg.) "went down to see him."

7 The full record of how "the LORD had anointed Jehu to destroy the house of Ahab" is contained in 2 Kings 9.

8 It was only after Ahaziah's own death (v.9) that Jehu killed the forty-two relatives of Ahaziah (2 Kings 10:12–14; cf. Notes).

9 This verse should probably begin, as in the NASB, "he also [rather than 'he then,' NIV, which too is correct grammatically, with a waw consecutive, 'then'] went in search of Ahaziah." The final movements of Ahaziah are difficult to trace but may perhaps be reconstructed as follows: he fled south from Jezreel so as to hide "in Samaria. He was brought to Jehu," who fatally wounded him near Ibleam (between Jezreel and Samaria); he fled by chariot northwest to Megiddo, where he died (2 Kings 9:27); and his body was carried by Ahaziah's servants to Jerusalem (9:28), where they buried him (cf. KD, *Kings*, pp. 343–44).

Notes

8 The Hebrew underlying the phrase rendered "Ahaziah's relatives" is אֲחֵי (*ʾaḥê*). Keil (p. 405) et al. render it "the brothers of," which is a too restricted use of *ʾaḥê*. The literal sons, however, of Ahaziah's deceased (v.1) brothers, i.e., his nephews, would hardly have been old enough at this time (their grandfather Jehoram had been born only forty years previously, 21:5) to be "attending Ahaziah"; hence the more accurate rendering of the NIV.

8. *Athaliah*

22:10–23:21

¹⁰When Athaliah the mother of Ahaziah saw that her son was dead, she proceeded to destroy the whole royal family of the house of Judah. ¹¹But Jehosheba, the daughter of King Jehoram, took Joash son of Ahaziah and stole him away from among the royal princes who were about to be murdered and put him and his nurse in a bedroom. Because Jehosheba, the daughter of King Jehoram and wife of the priest Jehoiada, was Ahaziah's sister, she hid the child from Athaliah so she could not kill him. ¹²He remained hidden with them at the temple of God for six years while Athaliah ruled the land.

²³:¹In the seventh year Jehoiada showed his strength. He made a covenant with the commanders of units of a hundred: Azariah son of Jeroham, Ishmael son of Jehohanan, Azariah son of Obed, Maaseiah son of Adaiah, and Elishaphat son of Zicri. ²They went throughout Judah and gathered the Levites and the heads of Israelite families from all the towns. When they came to Jerusalem, ³the whole assembly made a covenant with the king at the temple of God.

Jehoiada said to them, "The king's son shall reign, as the LORD promised concerning the descendants of David. ⁴Now this is what you are to do: A third of you priests and Levites who are going on duty on the Sabbath are to keep watch at the doors, ⁵a third of you at the royal palace and a third at the Foundation Gate, and all the other men are to be in the courtyards of the temple of the LORD. ⁶No one is to enter the temple of the LORD except the priests and Levites on duty; they may enter because they are consecrated, but all the other men are to guard what the LORD has assigned to them. ⁷The Levites are to station themselves around the king, each man with his weapons in his hand. Anyone who enters the temple must be put to death. Stay close to the king wherever he goes."

⁸The Levites and all the men of Judah did just as Jehoiada the priest ordered. Each one took his men—those who were going on duty on the Sabbath and those who were going off duty—for Jehoiada the priest had not released any of the divisions. ⁹Then he gave the commanders of units of a hundred the spears and the large and small shields that had belonged to King David and that were in the temple of God. ¹⁰He stationed all the men, each with his weapon in his hand, around the king—near the altar and the temple, from the south side to the north side of the temple.

¹¹Jehoiada and his sons brought out the king's son and put the crown on him; they presented him with a copy of the covenant and proclaimed him king. They anointed him and shouted, "Long live the king!"

¹²When Athaliah heard the noise of the people running and cheering the king, she went to them at the temple of the LORD. ¹³She looked, and there was the king, standing by his pillar at the entrance. The officers and the trumpeters were beside the king, and all the people of the land were rejoicing and blowing trumpets, and singers with musical instruments were leading the praises. Then Athaliah tore her robes and shouted, "Treason! Treason!"

¹⁴Jehoiada the priest sent out the commanders of units of a hundred, who were in charge of the troops, and said to them: "Bring her out between the ranks and

put to the sword anyone who follows her." For the priest had said, "Do not put her to death at the temple of the Lord." ¹⁵So they seized her as she reached the entrance of the Horse Gate on the palace grounds, and there they put her to death.

¹⁶Jehoiada then made a covenant that he and the people and the king would be the Lord's people. ¹⁷All the people went to the temple of Baal and tore it down. They smashed the altars and idols and killed Mattan the priest of Baal in front of the altars.

¹⁸Then Jehoiada placed the oversight of the temple of the Lord in the hands of the priests, who were Levites, to whom David had made assignments in the temple, to present the burnt offerings of the Lord as written in the Law of Moses, with rejoicing and singing, as David had ordered. ¹⁹He also stationed doorkeepers at the gates of the Lord's temple so that no one who was in any way unclean might enter.

²⁰He took with him the commanders of hundreds, the nobles, the rulers of the people and all the people of the land and brought the king down from the temple of the Lord. They went into the palace through the Upper Gate and seated the king on the royal throne, ²¹and all the people of the land rejoiced. And the city was quiet, because Athaliah had been slain with the sword.

10 The reign of Israel's only queen, Athaliah the mother of Ahaziah, extended for six full years, from 841 to 835 B.C. (cf. 22:12; 23:1). It is described in the last three verses of 2 Chronicles 22 and in chapter 23. This section draws on its canonical source in 2 Kings 11 and follows it rather closely. It shows how Jehoshaphat's marriage alliance with the house of Ahab (18:1 comment) eventually resulted in an attempt to exterminate the dynasty of David and in the official paganizing of Judah. For after the death of her last remaining son (22:1, 9), Athaliah proceeded to slaughter her own royal grandchildren—so as to insure the throne for herself—and to establish the sort of Baal worship her mother Jezebel had been devoted to as the state religion of the southern kingdom. Under the protection, however, of the high priest Jehoiada, a single, one-year-old son of Ahaziah named Joash survived (22:10–12). Finally, when the lad had become seven, Jehoiada carried through a revolt that brought about the coronation of Joash (23:1–11), the execution of Athaliah (vv.12–15), and the extirpation of her false worship (vv.16–21).

11–12 "Jehosheba" (cf. NIV mg.; 2 Kings 11:2), a sister of the late king Ahaziah, rescued her infant nephew Joash by hiding him "in a bedroom" (v.11), i.e., in one of the palace rooms where mattresses and bedding were stored. Chronicles reveals the fact, otherwise unrecorded, that she was also the "wife of the [high] priest Jehoiada," who must have been many years her senior (cf. 24:15 comment). The two of them later removed Joash to "the temple of God" for safety (v.12).

23:1 As explained in 2 Kings 11:4, the five "commanders of units of a hundred" were the officers of the Carites (cf. the Cherethites, 1 Chron 18:17 comment) and of other elements of the royal guard.

2 The gathering of "the Levites and [clan] heads" is not mentioned in the parallel passage in 2 Kings 11, but such an action is not thereby rendered suspect (cf. the references in 11:5 and 9 to "Sabbath duty," which do assume the presence of Levites). It must have been accomplished with considerable secrecy, since the uprising caught Queen Athaliah wholly by surprise (v.13).

3 "The covenant with the king" was made specifically with Jehoiada as his protector (v.1; 2 Kings 11:4). Once again we see the requirement of popular confirmation, which played so prominent a part in the history of the succession of Israel's "constitutional monarchs" (cf. the comments to 1 Chron 11:3; 2 Chron 10:1).

4 The situation of the "priests and Levites" as "going on duty on the Sabbath" was that which concerned the changing of the Levitical courses in their temple service (cf. 1 Chron 24:4, 20 comments). The sentence reads literally, "the third (of you priests . . .)"—with the definite article in the Hebrew—since, as 2 Kings 11:5–7 makes clear, this group contrasts with the other two-thirds, who were going off duty. The former were "to keep watch at the doors," both of the palace (2 Kings 11:5) and of the temple, to prevent any unauthorized, non-Levitical personnel from entering the sanctuary (2 Chron 23:6).

5 This verse, as shown by its parallel in 2 Kings 11 (vv.5b–6), then constitutes a parenthesis that identifies the three parts of the third who were coming on duty: (1) those "at the royal palace" (which might mean simply "the house of the king," i.e., his chamber in the temple, 22:12, for Athaliah's palace remained open, 23:12); (2) those "at the Foundation Gate" (called the Sur Gate in 2 Kings 11:6, a temple gate of uncertain location); and (3) those "in the courtyards of the temple" (specified in Kings as stationed at the gate behind the guard).

8–9 Ezra here introduces the two companies of Levites "who were going off duty" (v.8): they had not been released but instead were assigned to guard the temple for the king (2 Kings 11:7) with the weapons that were being kept there (v.9).

10 When Jehoiada is said to have "stationed all the men," this company must have included the non-Levitical clan heads (v.2) and such of the royal guard as may have been considered faithful by the five commanders who had entered into the covenant with him (v.1).

11 The "copy of the covenant" that Joash was given (lit., *hā'ēḏûṯ*, "the testimony") may have been simply the terms of the contract under which he was to rule (Myers, *Chronicles,* 2:130) but was more likely the required scroll of the law of Moses, which testified both to his royal position under God and to his responsibilities for godly conduct while in office (Deut 17:18–19). Chronicles adds to 2 Kings 11:12 that it was the high priest "Jehoiada and his son" who "anointed" Joash.

13 In support of Joash there came "all the people of the land"—an expression identifying "the body of free men, enjoying civic rights" (de Vaux, *Ancient Israel,* p. 70), who are here distinguished from the military officers. They did not form "a party or a social class" (ibid., p. 71), though in postexilic times the expression did come to designate "the non-Jewish inhabitants of Palestine, who hindered the work of restoration" (p. 72).

16 Along with Jehoiada's political revolution came a corresponding religious revival —that king, priest, and citizenry would together "be the LORD's people." This included their reaffirmation of the southern kingdom's limited monarchy, in which all its social elements pledged allegiance to God as their ultimate Sovereign (cf. the comments to vv.3, 11).

17 The execution of "Mattan the priest of Baal" carried out the requirement of God's Word directed against those who should lead others into false religion (Deut 13: 5–10).

18 The priests then reestablished the true worship, according to the prescriptions of Moses and of David for the Levitical priests (1 Chron 23) and for the singers (ch. 25).

Notes

23:14 The meaning of Jehoiada's command to bring Queen Athaliah out between הַשְּׂדֵרוֹת (haśśᵉḏērōṯ), the "ranks," is no longer clear. The noun may connote, not so much surrounding lines of troops, as an architectural term (KB, p. 916; cf. NIV mg.), "the precincts," which is based on 1 Kings 6:9, where the NIV renders the same word as (cedar) "planks."

8. Joash

24:1–27

¹Joash was seven years old when he became king, and he reigned in Jerusalem forty years. His mother's name was Zibiah; she was from Beersheba. ²Joash did what was right in the eyes of the LORD all the years of Jehoiada the priest. ³Jehoiada chose two wives for him, and he had sons and daughters.

⁴Some time later Joash decided to restore the temple of the LORD. ⁵He called together the priests and Levites and said to them, "Go to the towns of Judah and collect the money due annually from all Israel, to repair the temple of your God. Do it now." But the Levites did not act at once.

⁶Therefore the king summoned Jehoiada the chief priest and said to him, "Why haven't you required the Levites to bring in from Judah and Jerusalem the tax imposed by Moses the servant of the LORD and by the assembly of Israel for the Tent of the Testimony?"

⁷Now the sons of that wicked woman Athaliah had broken into the temple of God and had used even its sacred objects for the Baals.

⁸At the king's command, a chest was made and placed outside, at the gate of the temple of the LORD. ⁹A proclamation was then issued in Judah and Jerusalem that they should bring to the LORD the tax that Moses the servant of God had required of Israel in the desert. ¹⁰All the officials and all the people brought their contributions gladly, dropping them into the chest until it was full. ¹¹Whenever the chest was brought in by the Levites to the king's officials and they saw that there was a large amount of money, the royal secretary and the officer of the chief priest would come and empty the chest and carry it back to its place. They did this regularly and collected a great amount of money. ¹²The king and Jehoiada gave it to the men who carried out the work required for the temple of the LORD. They hired masons and carpenters to restore the LORD's temple, and also workers in iron and bronze to repair the temple.

¹³The men in charge of the work were diligent, and the repairs progressed under them. They rebuilt the temple of God according to its original design and

reinforced it. ¹⁴When they had finished, they brought the rest of the money to the king and Jehoiada, and with it were made articles for the LORD's temple: articles for the service and for the burnt offerings, and also dishes and other objects of gold and silver. As long as Jehoiada lived, burnt offerings were presented continually in the temple of the LORD.

¹⁵Now Jehoiada was old and full of years, and he died at the age of a hundred and thirty. ¹⁶He was buried with the kings in the City of David, because of the good he had done in Israel for God and his temple.

¹⁷After the death of Jehoiada, the officials of Judah came and paid homage to the king, and he listened to them. ¹⁸They abandoned the temple of the LORD, the God of their fathers, and worshiped Asherah poles and idols. Because of their guilt, God's anger came upon Judah and Jerusalem. ¹⁹Although the LORD sent prophets to the people to bring them back to him, and though they testified against them, they would not listen.

²⁰Then the Spirit of God came upon Zechariah son of Jehoiada the priest. He stood before the people and said, "This is what God says: 'Why do you disobey the LORD's commands? You will not prosper. Because you have forsaken the LORD, he has forsaken you.'"

²¹But they plotted against him, and by order of the king they stoned him to death in the courtyard of the LORD's temple. ²²King Joash did not remember the kindness Zechariah's father Jehoiada had shown him but killed his son, who said as he lay dying, "May the LORD see this and call you to account."

²³At the turn of the year, the army of Aram marched against Joash; it invaded Judah and Jerusalem and killed all the leaders of the people. They sent all the plunder to their king in Damascus. ²⁴Although the Aramean army had come with only a few men, the LORD delivered into their hands a much larger army. Because Judah had forsaken the LORD, the God of their fathers, judgment was executed on Joash. ²⁵When the Arameans withdrew, they left Joash severely wounded. His officials conspired against him for murdering the son of Jehoiada the priest, and they killed him in his bed. So he died and was buried in the City of David, but not in the tombs of the kings.

²⁶Those who conspired against him were Zabad, son of Shimeath an Ammonite woman, and Jehozabad, son of Shimrith a Moabite woman. ²⁷The account of his sons, the many prophecies about him, and the record of the restoration of the temple of God are written in the annotations on the book of the kings. And Amaziah his son succeeded him as king.

Joash, the young son of Ahaziah and grandson of Athaliah, reigned over Judah for forty years, from 835 to 796 B.C. His rule, moreover, serves as a characterization in miniature for the historical course of his entire nation. During the earlier years of his reign, Joash lived uprightly, honoring the Lord and providing for the temple, whose structure and sacrificial services depicted God's eternal plan of salvation (vv. 1–14). But in later years he departed both from Yahweh and from his sanctuary (vv. 15–19; cf. Matt 21:13); he murdered the prophet who rebuked him, who was the son of the very priest who had preserved, enthroned, and guided him up to this point (vv. 20–22; cf. Matt 21:38); he suffered a humiliating subjugation to the forces of Damascus (vv. 23–24; cf. Luke 19:43–44); and he died incapacitated by battle wounds and slain by his own officials for his crimes (vv. 25–27; cf. Matt 21:41). Just as Asa's rejection of the prophetic word resulted in God's judgment, military troubles, downfall, and, ultimately, death (presumably from his diseased foot), so, similarly, was the fate of Joash. Second Chronicles 24 stands in general parallel to 2 Kings 12, but with supplements of varying length—ranging from the one verse summary of Joash's family (v.3) to the four paragraphs concerning his lapse at the death of Jehoiada (vv. 15–22)—which probably derived from Ezra's special source called the "annotations" (cf. v.27 comment).

1–2 Joash began his career by doing "what was right" (v.2), except that he had no success in removing Judah's high-place shrines (cf. 14:3 comment and 2 Kings 12:3); and he continued in his uprightness "all the years of Jehoiada" (cf. v.14), i.e., until some time after the twenty-third year of his reign, datable to 813 (2 Kings 12:6). Following the death of his protector, however, he fell into serious sin (vv.17–18).

3 The fact he had "two wives" was censurable (cf. Deut 17:17), though Jehoiada may have felt that this was an improvement over the state of some of his royal predecessors (cf. the comments to 1 Chron 14:3 or 2 Chron 11:21).

4 After the acts of vandalism and sacrilege committed under Athaliah (v.7), it had become necessary "to restore the temple."

5 The "money" to be collected is called *kesep*, literally, "silver"; for coinage entered the ancient world only during Israel's exilic period, and it reached Palestine even later (cf. 1 Chron 29:7 comment). "But the Levites did not act at once," both because of natural inertia (still true even of Christian workers), and because of the priestly demands that seem to have exhausted the normal revenues on current operations and on their own support (2 Kings 12:7; cf. Num 18:19). Yet the Chronicler, at least at this point, seems to view the priests in an overall better light than the Levites (v.6; see Introduction: Purpose, 2).

6 Concerning the "tax imposed by Moses," 2 Kings 12:4 specifies three sources of revenue: "money collected in the census," a half-shekel per head (Exod 30:14; 38:26; Matt 17:24; cf. Neh 10:32); "money received from personal vows," in substitutionary redemption payments, varying from three to fifty shekels (Lev 27:1–8; Num 18:15–16); and "money brought voluntarily to the temple."

7 On "the Baals," plural, see the comment on 17:3.

8 So Jehoiada (as stated in 2 Kings 12:9) "made a chest," with an opening in its lid (ibid.) to receive the donations. The priests agreed to surrender responsibility, both for taking collections and for making repairs for the temple (12:8); their needs were henceforth to be met by "the money from the guilt offerings and sin offerings" (12:16; cf. Lev 5:16). The high priest then had it "placed outside, at the [south] gate of the temple," that is, to the right of the altar (2 Kings 12:9).

9–12 A "proclamation was then issued" (v.9), to publicize the new procedures (v.5) and to insure the payment of the Mosaic tax (v.6).

13–14 Thus "they rebuilt the temple" (v.13); for none of the precious metal that was received was converted into sacred equipment (2 Kings 12:13), at least not till the repairs were finished (v.14). Second Kings does not discuss this matter of the subsequent surplus, but it does bring out the commendable honesty and faithfulness of the workmen (12:15).

15 The notice about the death of Jehoiada "at an age of a hundred and thirty" has led some to charge the Chronicler with a fictitious figure, i.e., "symbolical . . . older than Moses (120 years) or Aaron (123 years)" (Myers, *Chronicles*, 2:136). But the literal count corresponds to actual history. The precise placement of this priest within the gap that occurs in the Aaronic genealogy (cf. 1 Chron 6:10 comment) between Ahimaaz's grandson Johanan (born c. 960 B.C.) and Azariah II (in 751, 2 Chron 26:17) is unknown. If Jehoiada succeeded the high priest Amariah II (in 853, 2 Chron 19:11; 1 Chron 6:4 comment) at an age of 85, he would have expired in 808, some time before the death of his protege Joash in 796. Others have argued against a human life expectancy of more than 113½ years (EB, thirteenth ed., 13:1101); yet a more recent study includes photographs of a woman over 130 and of a man alleged to be 167 (*National Geographic*, 143 [Jan. 1973]: 99). Jehoiada's span of life was unique at this period, but not impossible, particularly for a man specially blessed of God ("Validity," pp. 109–28).

16 Jehoiada had become by marriage a brother-in-law to Joash's royal father Ahaziah (2 Chron 22:11); but burial "with the kings" was still a marked honor, which stands in distinct contrast to Joash's own eventual fate (24:25).

17–18 The "officials of Judah" (v.17), to whom Joash now listened, were of the class most attracted by the materialism of Baal worship (v.18; cf. Zeph 1:8). They were also the first to suffer God's penalty for it (cf. v.23 comment). Concerning "Asherah poles," see the comment on 14:3.

19 Among the "prophets sent to testify against" Israel, some of the earlier ones, as Shemaiah and Jehu, had been heeded (11:2; 12:5; 19:2); but the later ones—Hanani, Micaiah, and now Zechariah (16:7; 18:16; 24:20)— increasingly were not.

20 The expression that the Spirit "came upon" Zechariah means literally that he "clothed himself with" him (cf. 1 Chron 12:18 comment).

22 The expression that Joash did not remember Jehoiada's "kindness" (*hesed*) means the latter's "faithfulness" (1 Chron 16:41 comment). The king owed his power and position, and indeed his very life, to this priest's loyalty (2 Chron 23). Joash's murder of Jehoiada's son Zechariah has sometimes been interpreted as the event to which Jesus referred (Luke 11:51) as the last-recorded martyrdom in the OT canon; but this appears improbable (see Introduction: Canonicity). Our Lord's allusion most likely was to Zechariah the son of Berekiah (Matt 23:35; cf. Zech 1:1), coming at the close of the minor prophets.

Zechariah's dying prayer, "May the LORD see this and call you to account," is one of imprecation rather than of forgiveness (cf. Luke 23:34; Acts 7:60); but it is justified because of the official positions, both of the victim and of the oppressor: one involved the name and standards of God himself (v.20), and on the other was decreed the Lord's judgment of vengeance (vv.24–25).

23 The invading Arameans are first said to have killed Judah's "leaders" (*śārîm*, the identical noun that described the same social class previously rendered as "officials"; cf. v.17 comment). The raiders then sent to Damascus "all the plunder" of Jerusalem. Joash had stripped from the temple all the treasures that had been accumulated since the days of Asa (cf. 2 Kings 12:18), whose sin thus reaped its final reward (cf. the comments to 2 Chron 16:2 and 9).

24 "Only a few" Arameans overcame "a much larger" Judean army, just as Moses had threatened (Lev 26:17, as the reverse of his promise in 26:8).

25 The king's "officials" ('*bādîw*, "his [royal] servants") then assassinated him "in his bed" at the house of Millo (2 Kings 12:20), probably in Jerusalem (cf. 1 Chron 11:8 comment). Chronicles adds that the reason for the conspiracy (not recorded in 2 Kings 12:20–21) was to avenge Zechariah. But their act was still murder and is condemned (cf. 25:3). Second Kings 12:21 next describes his burial as being "with his fathers in the City of David"; but while Chronicles confirms this as to its general location, Ezra also specifies that it was "not in the tombs of the kings" (contrast v. 16 comment).

26 Variant forms for the names of the conspirators (NIV mg.) occur in 2 Kings 12:21 (q.v.).

27 The "many prophecies" about Joash probably refer to such prophetic threatenings as are noted in vv. 19–20. The title of the Chronicler's literary source for this reign, "the annotations [Heb. 'midrash' = commentary] on the book of the kings" suggests some interpretation of the more basic court chronicle (cf. 13:22) (see Introduction: Sources, e).

Notes

25 The NIV has followed the LXX and Vulgate in its reading "the son of (Jehoiada)." The MT is plural, "the sons of"; but this latter form seems less likely, since Joash is known to have murdered only the one son of Jehoiada, Zechariah (v. 21).

9. Amaziah

25:1–28

¹Amaziah was twenty-five years old when he became king, and he reigned in Jerusalem twenty-nine years. His mother's name was Jehoaddin; she was from Jerusalem. ²He did what was right in the eyes of the LORD, but not wholeheartedly. ³After the kingdom was firmly in his control, he executed the officials who had murdered his father the king. ⁴Yet he did not put their sons to death, but acted in accordance with what is written in the Law, in the Book of Moses, where the LORD commanded: "Fathers shall not be put to death for their children, nor children put to death for their fathers; each is to die for his own sins."

⁵Amaziah called the people of Judah together and assigned them according to their families to commanders of thousands and commanders of hundreds for all Judah and Benjamin. He then mustered those twenty years old or more and found that there were three hundred thousand men ready for military service, able to handle the spear and shield. ⁶He also hired a hundred thousand fighting men from Israel for a hundred talents of silver.

⁷But a man of God came to him and said, "O king, these troops from Israel must not march with you, for the LORD is not with Israel—not with any of the

people of Ephraim. [8]Even if you go and fight courageously in battle, God will overthrow you before the enemy, for God has the power to help or to overthrow."

[9]Amaziah asked the man of God, "But what about the hundred talents I paid for these Israelite troops?"

The man of God replied, "The LORD can give you much more than that."

[10]So Amaziah dismissed the troops who had come to him from Ephraim and sent them home. They were furious with Judah and left for home in a great rage.

[11]Amaziah then marshaled his strength and led his army to the Valley of Salt, where he killed ten thousand men of Seir. [12]The army of Judah also captured ten thousand men alive, took them to the top of a cliff and threw them down so that all were dashed to pieces.

[13]Meanwhile the troops that Amaziah had sent back and had not allowed to take part in the war raided Judean towns from Samaria to Beth Horon. They killed three thousand people and carried off great quantities of plunder.

[14]When Amaziah returned from slaughtering the Edomites, he brought back the gods of the people of Seir. He set them up as his own gods, bowed down to them and burned sacrifices to them. [15]The anger of the LORD burned against Amaziah, and he sent a prophet to him, who said, "Why do you consult this people's gods, which could not save their own people from your hand?"

[16]While he was still speaking, the king said to him, "Have we appointed you an adviser to the king? Stop! Why be struck down?"

So the prophet stopped but said, "I know that God has determined to destroy you, because you have done this and have not listened to my counsel."

[17]After Amaziah king of Judah consulted his advisers, he sent this challenge to Jehoash son of Jehoahaz, the son of Jehu, king of Israel: "Come, meet me face to face."

[18]But Jehoash king of Israel replied to Amaziah king of Judah: "A thistle in Lebanon sent a message to a cedar in Lebanon, 'Give your daughter to my son in marriage.' Then a wild beast in Lebanon came along and trampled the thistle underfoot. [19]You say to yourself that you have defeated Edom, and now you are arrogant and proud. But stay at home! Why ask for trouble and cause your own downfall and that of Judah also?"

[20]Amaziah, however, would not listen, for God so worked that he might hand them over to ˌJehoashˌ, because they sought the gods of Edom. [21]So Jehoash king of Israel attacked. He and Amaziah king of Judah faced each other at Beth Shemesh in Judah. [22]Judah was routed by Israel, and every man fled to his home. [23]Jehoash king of Israel captured Amaziah king of Judah, the son of Joash, the son of Ahaziah, at Beth Shemesh. Then Jehoash brought him to Jerusalem and broke down the wall of Jerusalem from the Ephraim Gate to the Corner Gate—a section about six hundred feet long. [24]He took all the gold and silver and all the articles found in the temple of God that had been in the care of Obed-Edom, together with the palace treasures and the hostages, and returned to Samaria.

[25]Amaziah son of Joash king of Judah lived for fifteen years after the death of Jehoash son of Jehoahaz king of Israel. [26]As for the other events of Amaziah's reign, from beginning to end, are they not written in the book of the kings of Judah and Israel? [27]From the time that Amaziah turned away from following the LORD, they conspired against him in Jerusalem and he fled to Lachish, but they sent men after him to Lachish and killed him there. [28]He was brought back by horse and was buried with his fathers in the City of Judah.

Second Chronicles 25 concerns the reign of Joash's son Amaziah (796–767 B.C.). Except for an introduction on Amaziah's succession (vv. 1–4) and a conclusion on his death (vv. 25–28), the chapter concentrates on two wars that he undertook and on the lessons that are to be learned from them: (1) his reconquest of Edom, through obedience to the Lord (vv. 5–16); and (2) his ensuing defeat by Israel, in punishment for engaging in a form of idolatry to which he succumbed after his earlier victory (vv. 17–24). His demise repeats a theme quite familiar by now: Rejecting God's prophetic word results in divine judgment, military defeat, downfall, and ultimately death. This data depends on, and closely follows, 2 Kings 14:1–20. It is considerably augmented, however, by fresh material concerning the king's Ephraimite mercenaries (vv.5–10, 13) and his Edomite idolatry (vv.14–16, 20), presumably as drawn from the Chronicler's larger source cited in v.26.

1–2 Amaziah "did what was right" (v.2; cf. vv.4, 10), "but not wholeheartedly" (see vv.14, 16, 20). Note also 2 Kings 14:4, on how he allowed the high places to remain standing (cf. 24:2 comment).

4 Though Amaziah executed his father's murderers (v.3; cf. 24:26), he spared "their sons," as had been prescribed by Moses (Deut 24:16 per NIV mg.; cf. Notes).

5 Because of such losses as had been suffered under his father, Joash (24:23), Amaziah's muster of able men with "spear and shield" fell considerably short of the enumerations made under Asa and Jehoshaphat (cf. the comments on 14:8; 17:14–18); but it still recorded the "three hundred" 'allūpîm (i.e., "specially trained warriors"; cf. the comments on 1 Chron 7:3–4; 12:37).

6 Amaziah then "hired a hundred" more "from Israel," at the cost of an equal number of silver "talents." At twelve hundred ounces each, this sum meant something over three and three-quarter tons. But no support that is purchased from the ungodly, such as these Ephraimites were, could enjoy the Lord's blessing (v.7; cf. 16:2 comment).

8 It is "God," after all, who "has the" controlling "power to help" (cf. v.9 and 14:11 comment).

10 So "Amaziah dismissed the [mercenary] troops," who, despite their payment, were furious over the loss of what they had anticipated as further plunder. But the king was placing his trust in God, just as his fathers had done (cf. 14:11; 20:12).

11–12 "Seir" (v.11), or Edom, had now continued independent from Judah for half a century (21:8); and it was ruthlessly subjugated (v.12). The decisive battle occurred at "the Valley of Salt," which had been the scene of David's victory two hundred years before (1 Chron 18:12). It probably lay at the southern end of the Dead Sea (or farther west, cf. Myers, *Chronicles*, 2:143). Ezra's figures for the slain Edomites have been criticized as an exaggeration; but, as Keil (p. 413) explains, "There were further battles; and in the numbers 10,000, manifestly the whole of the prisoners taken in the war are comprehended." Amaziah eventually occupied the Edomite capital of Sela (2 Kings 14:7), the later, famed city of Petra.

13 The Ephraimite mercenaries "that Amaziah had sent back" proceeded to vent their rage (v.10) by pillaging Judah's frontier towns in northwestern Benjamin (cf. 8:5 comment on Beth Horon). Wenham ("Large Numbers," p. 51) affirms the historicity of the tragedy that they "might well have killed 3,000 civilians in their lust for war and spoil." Thus Amaziah's initial reliance on "the arm of flesh" (vv.6–7) brought about its own punishment (cf. the introductory discussion to 22:1–9).

15 The futility of "gods, which could not save their own people" should have been obvious, but men still worship that which is demonstrably inadequate.

16 The king's silencing of the Lord's prophet at least involved no more than threats (contrast 16:10; 24:21).

17-19 Amaziah's pride over defeating Edom led him to challenge the far stronger kingdom of "Jehoash" (798-782) in "Israel" (v.17), the senselessness of which the latter proceeded to portray by his fable (vv.18-19).

20-21 The battle was joined at "Beth Shemesh" (v.21), fifteen miles west of Bethlehem, on Amaziah's own picked ground. For this town lay "in Judah" on its Danite border (Josh 15:10).

23 The disaster that resulted for the king included the destruction of the least defensible portion of Jerusalem's wall, namely the part facing north, "from the Ephraim Gate," on its west side, "to the Corner Gate," facing northeast.

24 It also included the loss of the temple treasures that were "in the care of Obed-Edom," i.e., of the old Levitical family of gatekeepers and musicians that bore his name (1 Chron 26:4 comment).

25-27 As a further divine punishment on Amaziah (cf. v.20), these losses led to a mounting conspiracy "against him in Jerusalem" (v.27). At a preliminary stage his sixteen-year-old son Uzziah was elevated to coregency—and to actual rule—in 790 (26:1). For while Amaziah died in the twenty-seventh year of the reign of Jeroboam II of Israel (2 Kings 15:1), in 767, the latter's death fourteen years later (14:23), in 753, is identified as the thirty-eighth year of Uzziah (15:8). A final stage was precipitated by Amaziah's flight to Lachish, twenty-five miles southwest of Jerusalem on the route to Egypt, in 767. If this represented an attempt by the ex-ruler to recover his throne, it failed; for his pursuers "killed him there" (cf. Thiele, *Numbers*, pp. 71-72).

28 Amaziah was buried in the "City of Judah" (= Jerusalem, as appears in D.J. Wiseman, *Chronicles of Chaldean Kings, 626-556 B.C., in the British Museum* [London: 1956], p. 73), a later term for "the City of David" (2 Kings 14:20).

Notes

4 Some critics tend to view the "Mosaic" law of Deut 24:16 as a "new norm of individual responsibility" that arose out of the insights of Jeremiah and Ezekiel (North, "The Chronicler," 1:422). Yet this same commentator appeals to the views of J. Scharbert ("Formgeschichte und Exegese von Ex 34:6f und seiner Parallelen," *Biblica* 38 [1957]: 130-50), who recognizes that individualism formed the implicit basis for the entire Mosaic legislation.

10. *Uzziah*

26:1–23

¹Then all the people of Judah took Uzziah, who was sixteen years old, and made him king in place of his father Amaziah. ²He was the one who rebuilt Elath and restored it to Judah after Amaziah rested with his fathers.

³Uzziah was sixteen years old when he became king, and he reigned in Jerusalem fifty-two years. His mother's name was Jecoliah; she was from Jerusalem. ⁴He did what was right in the eyes of the LORD, just as his father Amaziah had done. ⁵He sought God during the days of Zechariah, who instructed him in the fear of God. As long as he sought the LORD, God gave him success.

⁶He went to war against the Philistines and broke down the walls of Gath, Jabneh and Ashdod. He then rebuilt towns near Ashdod and elsewhere among the Philistines. ⁷God helped him against the Philistines and against the Arabs who lived in Gur Baal and against the Meunites. ⁸The Ammonites brought tribute to Uzziah, and his fame spread as far as the border of Egypt, because he had become very powerful.

⁹Uzziah built towers in Jerusalem at the Corner Gate, at the Valley Gate and at the angle of the wall, and he fortified them. ¹⁰He also built towers in the desert and dug many cisterns, because he had much livestock in the foothills and in the plain. He had people working his fields and vineyards in the hills and in the fertile lands, for he loved the soil.

¹¹Uzziah had a well-trained army, ready to go out by divisions according to their numbers as mustered by Jeiel the secretary and Maaseiah the officer under the direction of Hananiah, one of the royal officials. ¹²The total number of family leaders over the fighting men was 2,600. ¹³Under their command was an army of 307,500 men trained for war, a powerful force to support the king against his enemies. ¹⁴Uzziah provided shields, spears, helmets, coats of armor, bows and slingstones for the entire army. ¹⁵In Jerusalem he made machines designed by skillful men for use on the towers and on the corner defenses to shoot arrows and hurl large stones. His fame spread far and wide, for he was greatly helped until he became powerful.

¹⁶But after Uzziah became powerful, his pride led to his downfall. He was unfaithful to the LORD his God, and entered the temple of the LORD to burn incense on the altar of incense. ¹⁷Azariah the priest with eighty other courageous priests of the LORD followed him in. ¹⁸They confronted him and said, "It is not right for you, Uzziah, to burn incense to the LORD. That is for the priests, the descendants of Aaron, who have been consecrated to burn incense. Leave the sanctuary, for you have been unfaithful; and you will not be honored by the LORD God."

¹⁹Uzziah, who had a censer in his hand ready to burn incense, became angry. While he was raging at the priests in their presence before the incense altar in the LORD's temple, leprosy broke out on his forehead. ²⁰When Azariah the chief priest and all the other priests looked at him, they saw that he had leprosy on his forehead, so they hurried him out. Indeed, he himself was eager to leave, because the LORD had afflicted him.

²¹King Uzziah had leprosy until the day he died. He lived in a separate house —leprous, and excluded from the temple of the LORD. Jotham his son had charge of the palace and governed the people of the land.

²²The other events of Uzziah's reign, from beginning to end, are recorded by the prophet Isaiah son of Amoz. ²³Uzziah rested with his fathers and was buried near them in a field for burial that belonged to the kings, for people said, "He had leprosy." And Jotham his son succeeded him as king.

Chapter 26 concerns Amaziah's son Uzziah, whose total reign extended from 790 to 739 B.C. His career runs parallel to those of his father, Amaziah, and grandfather, Joash: for the earlier portion of all three of these long reigns was marked by piety and by a corresponding prosperity (in vv. 1–15). But the latter part of each introduced some more or less serious religious deviation, which in Uzziah's case resulted in his suffering a stroke of leprosy, a banishment from his own palace, and, eventually, death (vv. 16–23). Yet his failure was less far reaching than the outright idolatry practiced by his immediate predecessors, and his achievements mark him off as one of the half-dozen leading monarchs of Judah. The content of most of chapter 26 is unique to Chronicles, since the parallel sections in 2 Kings (14:21–22; 15:1–7) present little more than a summary of his reign.

1 The new king's designation, "Uzziah," was apparently his throne name (IDB, 4:742). His personal name, "Azariah" (NIV mg.), appears in eight of the twelve references that are made to him in Kings, and also in the genealogical recapitulation found in 1 Chronicles 3:12 (q.v.), perhaps because the use of his personal name may have been resumed after he became a leper. Since he was sixteen years old at his accession in 790, he must have been born when his father was fifteen (25:1; cf. 25:27 comment). Early marriages, however, were not uncommon in the ancient Near East.

2 The "Elath" that Uzziah "rebuilt" (cf. the comments to 8:17 and 20:36, and the note at the end of this chapter) has been identified with Period III of Tell el Kheleifeh by Nelson Glueck (BASOR 72 [1938]: 8; cf. Thomas, *Archaeology*, p. 444). The statement that this occurred only after Amaziah's death (in 767) confirms the reconstruction of Uzziah's accession, noted under 25:27, as occurring some time prior to the demise of his father.

4 "He did what was right," even though 2 Kings 15:4 cautions that the high places still remained (cf. the comments to 24:2; 25:2). Furthermore, below the surface prosperity that was enjoyed by both kingdoms at this time (v.5 comment), the contemporaneous preaching of Hosea and Amos indicates the presence of serious moral and spiritual decay.

5 Uzziah's mentor, Zechariah, though apparently familiar to Ezra, can no longer be identified today. His description as one "who instructed" the king "in the fear of God" has as its full, alternative reading (cf. NIV mg.): "one who had understanding in the visions of God" (so most of the Heb. textual representatives; cf. NASB). The God-given success that resulted for Uzziah is borne out historically. The four decades that marked his overlapping reign with Jeroboam II in the north, from 790 to 750 B.C., have been called Israel's "Indian summer" (cf. vv.8, 15): a time when the Assyrians, who had weakened Israel's Aramean enemies at Damascus on its northeastern border (cf. 2 Kings 12:17–19; 13:3–5), had not yet begun their own destruction of the Hebrew states (cf. 15:19, 29). Yet by the time of Uzziah's death, the prophets were expressing forebodings about what lay ahead (Isa 6:1, 11–12).

6 In his western offensive, the king overpowered three Philistine centers: "Gath," which was the most inland (and the most exposed to Hebrew attack), whose exact location—some twenty miles west of Hebron—is still in dispute, and whose destruction left the Philistines with only four main cities thereafter (cf. Amos 1:6–8; Zeph 2:4); and "Ashdod," near the Mediterranean, the one that lay almost directly west of Jerusalem. The smaller town of "Jabneh" stood about ten miles farther north, between Ekron and the Sea (Josh 15:11); it is better known as the Jamnia of NT times (and in 1 Macc 4:15).

7 "The Arabs" from the unknown site of "Gur Baal" and "the Meunites" (20:1 comment) seem to have been nomadic enemies of Judah, inhabiting its southeastern border.

9 "The Corner Gate" (25:23 comment), "the Valley Gate," and the "the angle of the wall" were located at northeastern, southwestern, and eastern points, respectively, of Jerusalem's fortifications (Neh 3:13, 19, 31).

10 The reality of Uzziah's "towers in the desert" (of arid southern Judah) has been validated by the discovery of an eighth-century tower at Qumran. Concerning "the foothills" (Heb. "Shephelah"), see the comment on 1 Chronicles 27:28. "The plain" then refers to the plateau of Transjordan; for though this area had formerly been under Ephraimitic control, Uzziah seems to have regained it from the Ammonites, who had occupied it (v.8).

11 To muster Judah's troops, "Maaseiah" held the post of "officer" (*šôṭēr*, here meaning "adjutant"), a scribal (cf. 19:11 comment) or mustering official (Exod 5:6).

13 While a figure of "2,600" for the "family leaders" placed "over the fighting men" (v.12) seems appropriate for a strong kingdom like Uzziah's, the enumeration of his more professional soldiers should probably be taken to read "300 alluphs," or "special warriors" (the same number as Amaziah's; cf. 25:5 comment), together with "7,500 men trained for war."

15 The description of his "machines . . . on the towers . . . to hurl stones" has been interpreted to mean "devices . . . [from which] to hurl stones"; i.e., they were shielding mantles, used to cover defending troops as they repelled enemies seeking to scale the walls; for question exists about the use of catapult machines at this time (Myers, *Chronicles*, 2:150).

16 In the chapter's latter section, on Uzziah's religious deviation (vv.16–23), his sin in entering the temple to burn incense consisted not simply in usurping what was an exclusively priestly prerogative (v.18; Exod 30:7–8; cf. Num 18:7), but perhaps also in arrogating to himself a Canaanitish type of office, of semidivine priest-king (see Gen 14:18; cf. Num 12:10).

17 "Azariah the priest," who withstood the king, is probably Azariah II, as listed in 1 Chronicles 6 (v.10 comment).

21 The "separate house" Uzziah as a leper had to stay in is literally *bêt hahopšît* (Qere; cf. 2 Kings 15:5) ("house of [the] freedom"; cf. NIV mg.). If Myers (*Chronicles*, 2:10–51) is correct in following John Gray's suggestion that its Ugaritic equivalent means "the house of pollution," this context may suggest a somewhat modified form of the OT's required quarantine (Lev 13:46) for the state of this severely disabled monarch. So his son "Jotham" assumed coregency in "the palace." The date of his transfer into power may be assigned to 751 B.C., since Jotham's twentieth year (2 Kings 15:30) was equivalent to his son Ahaz's twelfth (16:2), which is 732, as indicated by the correlations made in Kings with Hoshea in Israel (cf. 18:10 and J.B.

Payne, "The Relationship of the Reign of Ahaz to the Accession of Hezekiah," BS 126 [1969]: 40–52).

22 "The prophet Isaiah" recorded the other events of Uzziah's reign, though this work is now lost, even as Isaiah later did for those of Hezekiah's reign (32:32 comment).

23 Rather than suggesting that Uzziah was being "buried" only "near" his fathers because "he had leprosy" (NIV), one might more naturally render the Hebrew as that he was "buried with" (*'im*) them, and then conclude the thought either negatively—"in a field for burial . . . for" (as in the NIV) he was a leper—or more positively—"with them, although" (*kî*) he was a leper, viz., that he was honored in death despite his malady.

Notes

---

2 The NIV follows 2 Kings 14:22 and the versions in reading "Elath" (אֵילַת, *'êlat*), rather than the MT of Chronicles "Eloth" (אֵילוֹת, *'êlôt*; cf. the note at the end of ch. 8).
5 North ("The Chronicler," 1:422) would identify "Zechariah" with the slain son of Jehoiada, who had died half a century earlier, "by a dramatic license"(!).

---

11. *Jotham*

27:1–9

> [1]Jotham was twenty-five years old when he became king, and he reigned in Jerusalem sixteen years. His mother's name was Jerusha daughter of Zadok. [2]He did what was right in the eyes of the LORD, just as his father Uzziah had done, but unlike him he did not enter the temple of the LORD. The people, however, continued their corrupt practices. [3]Jotham rebuilt the Upper Gate of the temple of the LORD and did extensive work on the wall at the hill of Ophel. [4]He built towns in the Judean hills and forts and towers in the wooded areas.
> [5]Jotham made war on the king of the Ammonites and conquered them. That year the Ammonites paid him a hundred talents of silver, ten thousand cors of wheat and ten thousand cors of barley. The Ammonites brought him the same amount also in the second and third years.
> [6]Jotham grew powerful because he walked steadfastly before the LORD his God.
> [7]The other events in Jotham's reign, including all his wars and the other things he did, are written in the book of the kings of Israel and Judah. [8]He was twenty-five years old when he became king, and he reigned in Jerusalem sixteen years. [9]Jotham rested with his fathers and was buried in the City of David. And Ahaz his son succeeded him as king.

The official sixteen-year kingship of Uzziah's son Jotham extended from 751 to 736 B.C., but it overlapped the reigns of his predecessor (cf. 26:21 comment) and successor (v.8 comment) to such a degree that he himself is left with little independent notice in Scripture. The nine verses of chapter 27 furnish some elaboration on the even briefer notices that relate to this monarch in the parallel passage of 2 Kings 15:32–38; and they most notably concern his victory over the Ammonites, together with its evaluation (vv.5–6). Jotham was a good king, and God rewarded his righteousness (vv.2, 6).

1 Since Jotham's reign lasted for a total of "sixteen years," the reference to its "twentieth year" in 2 Kings 15:30 must be prophetic—for Jotham's successor had not yet been introduced in Kings at this point, or even Jotham himself for that matter.

2 The "corrupt practices" of his people are explained elsewhere in Scripture as consisting of sacrificial services carried out on Judah's high places, with accompanying immoralities, idolatries, and superstitions (2 Kings 15:35; cf. Isa 1–6, which pertains to this period).

3–4 The temple's "Upper Gate" (v.4; cf. 23:20), which "Jotham rebuilt," was situated on its north side (Jer 20:2; Ezek 9:2). The "hill of Ophel," on the other hand, lay to its south, in the upper part of the old city of David (cf. Kenyon's observations [1 Chron 11:8 comment] on "Millo" and the continuous repair that was entailed for the walls in this area).

5 Included in the tribute (NIV mg.) that the king gained from Ammon (cf. 26:10 comment) is a considerable sum of "silver." Though characteristically criticized by many writers as being exaggerated, the amount, for each of its three successive years, is identified by Curtis (p. 454), without adverse comment, as "United States value . . . some $187,500" [as per 1910, ed.]. A similar total amount was received at ancient Ebla from the city of Mari in just a single payment (Payne, "Validity," p. 207).

6 A testimony to Jotham's "power" has been the discovery of his official seal at Ezion Geber, Judah's outpost (26:2 comment) that continued under Hebrew control throughout his reign (but then cf. 28:5 comment).

7 The reference to "all" Jotham's wars suggests that prior to the Ammonite campaign (v.5), for which as king he had sole responsibility, he may have served as field commander for the alliance that was conceived by his quarantined father, Azariah-Uzziah (26:21), and which is mentioned in Assyrian annals (but not in the OT) as overcome by Tiglath-pileser III in about 743 B.C. (Thiele, *Numbers*, pp. 78–98).

8–9 Though "he reigned sixteen years" (v.8 repeats v.1), it was after only eight of these, in 743, that Jotham seems to have associated his son Ahaz with him on the throne (26:21 comment), perhaps because of this very defeat by Tiglath-pileser (v.7 comment; cf. 28:5 comment and 2 Kings 15:37).

12. Ahaz

28:1–27

> [1]Ahaz was twenty years old when he became king, and he reigned in Jerusalem sixteen years. Unlike David his father, he did not do what was right in the eyes of the LORD. [2]He walked in the ways of the kings of Israel and also made cast idols for worshiping the Baals. [3]He burned sacrifices in the Valley of Ben Hinnom and sacrificed his sons in the fire, following the detestable ways of the nations the

LORD had driven out before the Israelites. ⁴He offered sacrifices and burned incense at the high places, on the hilltops and under every spreading tree.

⁵Therefore the LORD his God handed him over to the king of Aram. The Arameans defeated him and took many of his people as prisoners and brought them to Damascus.

He was also given into the hands of the king of Israel, who inflicted heavy casualties on him. ⁶In one day Pekah son of Remaliah killed a hundred and twenty thousand soldiers in Judah—because Judah had forsaken the LORD, the God of their fathers. ⁷Zicri, an Ephraimite warrior, killed Maaseiah the king's son, Azrikam the officer in charge of the palace, and Elkanah, second to the king. ⁸The Israelites took captive from their kinsmen two hundred thousand wives, sons and daughters. They also took a great deal of plunder, which they carried back to Samaria.

⁹But a prophet of the LORD named Oded was there, and he went out to meet the army when it returned to Samaria. He said to them, "Because the LORD, the God of your fathers, was angry with Judah, he gave them into your hand. But you have slaughtered them in a rage that reaches to heaven. ¹⁰And now you intend to make the men and women of Judah and Jerusalem your slaves. But aren't you also guilty of sins against the LORD your God? ¹¹Now listen to me! Send back your fellow countrymen you have taken as prisoners, for the LORD's fierce anger rests on you."

¹²Then some of the leaders in Ephraim—Azariah son of Jehohanan, Berekiah son of Meshillemoth, Jehizkiah son of Shallum, and Amasa son of Hadlai—confronted those who were arriving from the war. ¹³"You must not bring those prisoners here," they said, "or we will be guilty before the LORD. Do you intend to add to our sin and guilt? For our guilt is already great, and his fierce anger rests on Israel."

¹⁴So the soldiers gave up the prisoners and plunder in the presence of the officials and all the assembly. ¹⁵The men designated by name took the prisoners, and from the plunder they clothed all who were naked. They provided them with clothes and sandals, food and drink, and healing balm. All those who were weak they put on donkeys. So they took them back to their fellow countrymen at Jericho, the City of Palms, and returned to Samaria.

¹⁶At that time King Ahaz sent to the king of Assyria for help. ¹⁷The Edomites had again come and attacked Judah and carried away prisoners, ¹⁸while the Philistines had raided towns in the foothills and in the Negev of Judah. They captured and occupied Beth Shemesh, Aijalon and Gederoth, as well as Soco, Timnah and Gimzo, with their surrounding villages. ¹⁹The LORD had humbled Judah because of Ahaz king of Israel, for he had promoted wickedness in Judah and had been most unfaithful to the LORD. ²⁰Tiglath-Pileser king of Assyria came to him, but he gave him trouble instead of help. ²¹Ahaz took some of the things from the temple of the LORD and from the royal palace and from the princes and presented them to the king of Assyria, but that did not help him.

²²In his time of trouble King Ahaz became even more unfaithful to the LORD. ²³He offered sacrifices to the gods of Damascus, who had defeated him; for he thought, "Since the gods of the kings of Aram have helped them, I will sacrifice to them so they will help me." But they were his downfall and the downfall of all Israel.

²⁴Ahaz gathered together the furnishings from the temple of God and took them away. He shut the doors of the LORD's temple and set up altars at every street corner in Jerusalem. ²⁵In every town in Judah he built high places to burn sacrifices to other gods and provoked the LORD, the God of his fathers, to anger.

²⁶The other events of his reign and all his ways, from beginning to end, are written in the book of the kings of Judah and Israel. ²⁷Ahaz rested with his fathers and was buried in the city of Jerusalem, but he was not placed in the tombs of the kings of Israel. And Hezekiah his son succeeded him as king.

The official reign of Jotham's apostate son Ahaz extended from 743 to 728 B.C.; he was, indeed, one of the weakest and most corrupt of all the twenty rulers of Judah.

His record in 2 Chronicles 28 is illumined by the prophecies of Isaiah that belong to this period (chs. 7–12), and it runs parallel to the history in 2 Kings 16. But apart from the opening four verses and the concluding formula in vv.26–27 (cf. 2 Kings 16:19–20), and a few words in v.16 (2 Kings 16:7), the composition of these two historical chapters remains distinct. Both report the reign of Ahaz through two stages: (1) his apostasy from the Lord and the defeat that he suffered as a result, at the hands of Syro-Ephraimitic attacks (2 Chron 28:1–7); and (2) his subsequent appeal and capitulation to Assyria, which led him into even further corruption and idolatry (vv.16–25). Between these sections, however, the Chronicler inserts a discussion of how the prophet Oded succeeded in rescuing a group of Judean captives out of Ephraim (vv.8–15), though none of this has been preserved in 2 Kings.

1 Since "Ahaz was twenty years old" when he acceded to coregency in 743 (cf. the comments to 26:21; 27:8), and since his father, Jotham, had been twenty-five at his own accession eight years previously (27:1), the time interval separating their births must have been only thirteen years. Jotham, and then Ahaz himself, have the lowest ages of paternity that are recorded for the Hebrew kings (cf. the comments on 26:1 and 29:1).

2 On the "Baals" see the comment on 17:3.

3 The "Valley of (the son of) Hinnom" (gê᾽ [ben] hinnōm) descended eastward below the southern edge of the city of Jerusalem; and it became noted as the scene of Judah's most revolting pagan practices (33:6). It was later defiled by King Josiah and converted into a place of refuse for the city (2 Kings 23:10); thus the perpetual fires of "Gehenna" became descriptive of hell itself (Mark 9:43). While 2 Kings 16:3 had recorded that Ahaz "sacrificed his son [sing.] in the fire," Ezra adds the fact that it was sons (pl.); that rendered his conduct even worse. The Canaanitish practice of child sacrifice had been forbidden to Abraham (Gen 22:12), and under Moses it was made a capital offense (Lev 20:1–5).

4 Concerning the "high places," see the comment on 14:3.

5 The kings of "Aram" and of "Israel" to whom God handed Ahaz over were, respectively, Rezin and Pekah (752–732 B.C.). These two may have turned against Judah because of the failure of the alliance that Uzziah had directed against Assyria (27:7 comment) and because of the sufferings that had resulted for them and their people (2 Kings 15:19; cf. v.37), but from which Judah had escaped unscathed. In what is called the Syro-Ephraimitic counteralliance, they besieged but could not capture Jerusalem (2 Kings 16:5; Isa 7:1). Rezin did, however, take Elath (2 Kings 16:6; cf. the comments on 2 Chron 26:2; 27:6); and it was not regained by Israel till A.D. 1948.

8 Even as v.6 should probably be understood as recording that "in one day Pekah killed 120 alluphs," or "specially trained warriors" (cf. the comments to 1 Chron 7:3 –4; 12:27), i.e., "all valiant men" (NASB), so too v.8 should best be treated as stating that "the Israelites took captive from their kinsmen" (lit., brothers) "200 alluphs, women, sons, and daughters"—a more plausible rendering than to think of 200,000 women, etc. (cf. Appendix B).

9–11 The northern prophet "Oded" is otherwise unknown, but he was God's spokesman for warning the Ephraimites that those who serve as the Lord's instruments for punishment must not exceed their appointed mission (cf. Isa 10:5–19). Their own standing, he observed, was hardly guiltless (2 Chron 28:10, 13).

14 The fact that Pekah's "soldiers gave up the prisoners and plunder" testifies to the feelings of brotherhood (v.8) that still existed between the two Hebrew kingdoms, to the authority of Israelite prophecy, and to the grace that God employed in his treatment of the nation of the worthless Ahaz.

15 Those who were "designated" to be responsible then "provided" for the prisoners, in accordance with the OT standard of showing love, even toward one's enemies (Exod 23:4; Prov 24:17; 25:21; cf. Matt 5:44).

16 In 734 B.C., in an act that amounted to a breach of faith with God (cf. the comments to 16:2, 9; 25:6, 10), Ahaz threw himself at the feet of Assyria's rulers (cf. Notes) for rescue and help. Isaiah had opposed this ill-advised act as being both useless and faithless (Isa 7:4–7). By his course what Ahaz really did was to place Judah under the iron heel of Tiglath-pileser (v.21 comment), to cause the deportation of three and one-half of the tribes of Israel to Assyria in 733 (2 Kings 15:29), followed by the remaining six and one-half tribes eleven years later (17:6), and eventually, in 701, to bring about Judah's own devastation by the armies of Sennacherib (18:13).

17 Again "the Edomites . . . attacked Judah," for they seemed ever on the alert to capitalize on Judah's calamities (cf. 2 Chron 20:10–11; 21:8). Their incursions of 735 and their seizure of prisoners may have been the occasion for the prophecies of Obadiah (v.11) and Joel (3:19).

18–20 "The Philistines" (v.18) did not simply rebel from Judean control (cf. 26:6 comment), but they also "raided towns in the foothills" (Heb., Shephelah; cf. 1 Chron 27:28 comment) of "Judah." The reality of their activity at this time (cf. Joel 3:4) is attested by a recently published Assyrian tablet that speaks of Tiglath-pileser's campaign against Philistia (D.J. Wiseman, *Iraq* 13 [1951]: 21–24).

21 But "that did not help" Ahaz; for, as Myers (*Chronicles*, 2:163) comments, "Though the rebellions were put down, the states involved were not returned to Judah but organized into Assyrian provinces."

22–23 The reverence Ahaz paid "to the gods of Damascus" (v.23) took a particular form; he sacrificed on an altar patterned after the one found there (2 Kings 16:10–13). Since "the kings of Aram" were by this time Assyrian (16:10a), interpreters until recently had assumed that the price of a nation's submission to the empire of Assyria included their compulsory worship of its deities (cf. Payne, "Chronicles," p. 412). Recent studies, however, have indicated that such was not necessarily the case (e.g., J. McKay, "Religion in Judea and the Assyrians," *Studies in Biblical Theology* [Naperville, Ill.: Allenson, 1973], 2:19, or M. Cogan, *Imperialism and Religion in Assyria, Judah, and Israel in the Eighth and Seventh Centuries B.C.E.*, SBL Monograph Ser. 19 [Missoula, Mont.: 1974]).

24–25 The paganism of Ahaz was designed not simply to supplement the worship of Yahweh, but to supplant it and close the Lord's temple.

27 The death of Ahaz occurred in the same year as that of "the rod that struck" the Philistines, i.e., of Tiglath-pileser III (Isa 14:28–29); and the official accession of "his son Hezekiah" is thus dated to 727/726 B.C. (cf. 31:1 comment). Yet since Ahaz's sixteen-year reign actually terminated in 728, it would appear that popular dissatisfaction must have forced his abdication and Hezekiah's assumption of defacto rule at least a year prior to the end of the king's life (cf. 2 Kings 18:9–10). Correspondingly, even though Ahaz "rested" (and was buried, 2 Kings 16:20) "with his fathers in . . . Jerusalem," his body "was not placed in the tombs of the kings" (compare similar harmonization that appears in 2 Chron 24:25, and cf. 21:20).

Notes

---

16 While the NIV (cf. mg.) adopts a variant reading, "king" (sing.), the plural form, "kings of Assyria," is not unprecedented; see v.27 or 32:4 (NIV mg.).

---

13. Hezekiah

29:1–32:33

¹Hezekiah was twenty-five years old when he became king, and he reigned in Jerusalem twenty-nine years. His mother's name was Abijah daughter of Zechariah. ²He did what was right in the eyes of the LORD, just as his father David had done.

³In the first month of the first year of his reign, he opened the doors of the temple of the LORD and repaired them. ⁴He brought in the priests and the Levites, assembled them in the square on the east side ⁵and said: "Listen to me, Levites! Consecrate yourselves now and consecrate the temple of the LORD, the God of your fathers. Remove all defilement from the sanctuary. ⁶Our fathers were unfaithful; they did evil in the eyes of the LORD our God and forsook him. They turned their faces away from the LORD's dwelling place and turned their backs on him. ⁷They also shut the doors of the portico and put out the lamps. They did not burn incense or present any burnt offerings at the sanctuary to the God of Israel. ⁸Therefore, the anger of the LORD has fallen on Judah and Jerusalem; he has made them an object of dread and horror and scorn, as you can see with your own eyes. ⁹This is why our fathers have fallen by the sword and why our sons and daughters and our wives are in captivity. ¹⁰Now I intend to make a covenant with the LORD, the God of Israel, so that his fierce anger will turn away from us. ¹¹My sons, do not be negligent now, for the LORD has chosen you to stand before him and serve him, to minister before him and to burn incense."

¹²Then these Levites set to work:
from the Kohathites,
    Mahath son of Amasai and Joel son of Azariah;
from the Merarites,
    Kish son of Abdi and Azariah son of Jehallelel;
from the Gershonites,
    Joah son of Zimmah and Eden son of Joah;
¹³from the descendants of Elizaphan,

Shimri and Jeiel;
from the descendants of Asaph,
Zechariah and Mattaniah;
¹⁴from the descendants of Heman,
Jehiel and Shimei;
from the descendants of Jeduthun,
Shemaiah and Uzziel.

¹⁵When they had assembled their brothers and consecrated themselves, they went in to purify the temple of the LORD, as the king had ordered, following the word of the LORD. ¹⁶The priests went into the sanctuary of the LORD to purify it. They brought out to the courtyard of the LORD's temple everything unclean that they found in the temple of the LORD. The Levites took it and carried it out to the Kidron Valley. ¹⁷They began the consecration on the first day of the first month, and by the eighth day of the month they reached the portico of the LORD. For eight more days they consecrated the temple of the LORD itself, finishing on the sixteenth day of the first month.

¹⁸Then they went in to King Hezekiah and reported: "We have purified the entire temple of the LORD, the altar of burnt offering with all its utensils, and the table for setting out the consecrated bread, with all its articles. ¹⁹We have prepared and consecrated all the articles that King Ahaz removed in his unfaithfulness while he was king. They are now in front of the LORD's altar."

²⁰Early the next morning King Hezekiah gathered the city officials together and went up to the temple of the LORD. ²¹They brought seven bulls, seven rams, seven male lambs and seven male goats as a sin offering for the kingdom, for the sanctuary and for Judah. The king commanded the priests, the descendants of Aaron, to offer these on the altar of the LORD. ²²So they slaughtered the bulls, and the priests took the blood and sprinkled it on the altar; next they slaughtered the rams and sprinkled their blood on the altar; then they slaughtered the lambs and sprinkled their blood on the altar. ²³The goats for the sin offering were brought before the king and the assembly, and they laid their hands on them. ²⁴The priests then slaughtered the goats and presented their blood on the altar for a sin offering to atone for all Israel, because the king had ordered the burnt offering and the sin offering for all Israel.

²⁵He stationed the Levites in the temple of the LORD with cymbals, harps and lyres in the way prescribed by David and Gad the king's seer and Nathan the prophet; this was commanded by the LORD through his prophets. ²⁶So the Levites stood ready with David's instruments, and the priests with their trumpets.

²⁷Hezekiah gave the order to sacrifice the burnt offering on the altar. As the offering began, singing to the LORD began also, accompanied by trumpets and the instruments of David king of Israel. ²⁸The whole assembly bowed in worship, while the singers sang and the trumpeters played. All this continued until the sacrifice of the burnt offering was completed.

²⁹When the offerings were finished, the king and everyone present with him knelt down and worshiped. ³⁰King Hezekiah and his officials ordered the Levites to praise the LORD with the words of David and of Asaph the seer. So they sang praises with gladness and bowed their heads and worshiped.

³¹Then Hezekiah said, "You have now dedicated yourselves to the LORD. Come and bring sacrifices and thank offerings to the temple of the LORD." So the assembly brought sacrifices and thank offerings, and all whose hearts were willing brought burnt offerings.

³²The number of burnt offerings the assembly brought was seventy bulls, a hundred rams and two hundred male lambs—all of them for burnt offerings to the LORD. ³³The animals consecrated as sacrifices amounted to six hundred bulls and three thousand sheep and goats. ³⁴The priests, however, were too few to skin all the burnt offerings; so their kinsmen the Levites helped them until the task was finished and until other priests had been consecrated, for the Levites had been more conscientious in consecrating themselves than the priests had been. ³⁵There were burnt offerings in abundance, together with the fat of the fellowship offerings and the drink offerings that accompanied the burnt offerings.

So the service of the temple of the LORD was reestablished. ³⁶Hezekiah and all the people rejoiced at what God had brought about for his people, because it was done so quickly.

30:1Hezekiah sent word to all Israel and Judah and also wrote letters to Ephraim and Manasseh, inviting them to come to the temple of the Lord in Jerusalem and celebrate the Passover to the Lord, the God of Israel. 2The king and his officials and the whole assembly in Jerusalem decided to celebrate the Passover in the second month. 3They had not been able to celebrate it at the regular time because not enough priests had consecrated themselves and the people had not assembled in Jerusalem. 4The plan seemed right both to the king and to the whole assembly. 5They decided to send a proclamation throughout Israel, from Beersheba to Dan, calling the people to come to Jerusalem and celebrate the Passover to the Lord, the God of Israel. It had not been celebrated in large numbers according to what was written.

6At the king's command, couriers went throughout Israel and Judah with letters from the king and from his officials, which read:

"People of Israel, return to the Lord, the God of Abraham, Isaac and Israel, that he may return to you who are left, who have escaped from the hand of the kings of Assyria. 7Do not be like your fathers and brothers, who were unfaithful to the Lord, the God of their fathers, so that he made them an object of horror, as you see. 8Do not be stiff-necked, as your fathers were; submit to the Lord. Come to the sanctuary, which he has consecrated forever. Serve the Lord your God, so that his fierce anger will turn away from you. 9If you return to the Lord, then your brothers and your children will be shown compassion by their captors and will come back to this land, for the Lord your God is gracious and compassionate. He will not turn his face from you if you return to him."

10The couriers went from town to town in Ephraim and Manasseh, as far as Zebulun, but the people scorned and ridiculed them. 11Nevertheless, some men of Asher, Manasseh and Zebulun humbled themselves and went to Jerusalem. 12Also in Judah the hand of God was on the people to give them unity of mind to carry out what the king and his officials had ordered, following the word of the Lord.

13A very large crowd of people assembled in Jerusalem to celebrate the Feast of Unleavened Bread in the second month. 14They removed the altars in Jerusalem and cleared away the incense altars and threw them into the Kidron Valley.

15They slaughtered the Passover lamb on the fourteenth day of the second month. The priests and the Levites were ashamed and consecrated themselves and brought burnt offerings to the temple of the Lord. 16Then they took up their regular positions as prescribed in the Law of Moses the man of God. The priests sprinkled the blood handed to them by the Levites. 17Since many in the crowd had not consecrated themselves, the Levites had to kill the Passover lambs for all those who were not ceremonially clean and could not consecrate their lambs to the Lord. 18Although most of the many people who came from Ephraim, Manasseh, Issachar and Zebulun had not purified themselves, yet they ate the Passover, contrary to what was written. But Hezekiah prayed for them, saying, "May the Lord, who is good, pardon everyone 19who sets his heart on seeking God— the Lord, the God of his fathers—even if he is not clean according to the rules of the sanctuary." 20And the Lord heard Hezekiah and healed the people.

21The Israelites who were present in Jerusalem celebrated the Feast of Unleavened Bread for seven days with great rejoicing, while the Levites and priests sang to the Lord every day, accompanied by the Lord's instruments of praise.

22Hezekiah spoke encouragingly to all the Levites, who showed good understanding of the service of the Lord. For the seven days they ate their assigned portion and offered fellowship offerings and praised the Lord, the God of their fathers.

23The whole assembly then agreed to celebrate the festival seven more days; so for another seven days they celebrated joyfully. 24Hezekiah king of Judah provided a thousand bulls and seven thousand sheep and goats for the assembly, and the officials provided them with a thousand bulls and ten thousand sheep and goats. A great number of priests consecrated themselves. ²⁵The entire assembly of Judah rejoiced, along with the priests and Levites and all who had assembled from Israel, including the aliens who had come from Israel and those who lived in Judah. ²⁶There was great joy in Jerusalem, for since the days of Solomon son of David king of Israel there had been nothing like this in Jerusalem. ²⁷The priests and the Levites stood to bless the people, and God heard them, for their prayer reached heaven, his holy dwelling place.

^{31:1}When all this had ended, the Israelites who were there went out to the towns of Judah, smashed the sacred stones and cut down the Asherah poles. They destroyed the high places and the altars throughout Judah and Benjamin and in Ephraim and Manasseh. After they had destroyed all of them, the Israelites returned to their own towns and to their own property.

²Hezekiah assigned the priests and Levites to divisions—each of them according to their duties as priests or Levites—to offer burnt offerings and fellowship offerings, to minister, to give thanks and to sing praises at the gates of the Lord's dwelling. ³The king contributed from his own possessions for the morning and evening burnt offerings and for the burnt offerings on the Sabbaths, New Moons and appointed feasts as written in the Law of the Lord. ⁴He ordered the people living in Jerusalem to give the portion due the priests and Levites so they could devote themselves to the Law of the Lord. ⁵As soon as the order went out, the Israelites generously gave the firstfruits of their grain, new wine, oil and honey and all that the fields produced. They brought a great amount, a tithe of everything. ⁶The men of Israel and Judah who lived in the towns of Judah also brought a tithe of their herds and flocks and a tithe of the holy things dedicated to the Lord their God, and they piled them in heaps. ⁷They began doing this in the third month and finished in the seventh month. ⁸When Hezekiah and his officials came and saw the heaps, they praised the Lord and blessed his people Israel.

⁹Hezekiah asked the priests and Levites about the heaps; ¹⁰and Azariah the chief priest, from the family of Zadok, answered, "Since the people began to bring their contributions to the temple of the Lord, we have had enough to eat and plenty to spare, because the Lord has blessed his people, and this great amount is left over."

¹¹Hezekiah gave orders to prepare storerooms in the temple of the Lord, and this was done. ¹²Then they faithfully brought in the contributions, tithes and dedicated gifts. Conaniah, a Levite, was in charge of these things, and his brother Shimei was next in rank. ¹³Jehiel, Azaziah, Nahath, Asahel, Jerimoth, Jozabad, Eliel, Ismakiah, Mahath and Benaiah were supervisors under Conaniah and Shimei his brother, by appointment of King Hezekiah and Azariah the official in charge of the temple of God.

¹⁴Kore son of Imnah the Levite, keeper of the East Gate, was in charge of the freewill offerings given to God, distributing the contributions made to the Lord and also the consecrated gifts. ¹⁵Eden, Miniamin, Jeshua, Shemaiah, Amariah and Shecaniah assisted him faithfully in the towns of the priests, distributing to their fellow priests according to their divisions, old and young alike.

¹⁶In addition, they distributed to the males three years old or more whose names were in the genealogical records—all who would enter the temple of the Lord to perform the daily duties of their various tasks, according to their responsibilities and their divisions. ¹⁷And they distributed to the priests enrolled by their families in the genealogical records and likewise to the Levites twenty years old or more, according to their responsibilities and their divisions. ¹⁸They included all the little ones, the wives, and the sons and daughters of the whole community listed in these genealogical records. For they were faithful in consecrating themselves.

¹⁹As for the priests, the descendants of Aaron, who lived on the farm lands around their towns or in any other towns, men were designated by name to distribute portions to every male among them and to all who were recorded in the genealogies of the Levites.

²⁰This is what Hezekiah did throughout Judah, doing what was good and right and faithful before the Lord his God. ²¹In everything that he undertook in the

service of God's temple and in obedience to the law and the commands, he sought his God and worked wholeheartedly. And so he prospered.

32:1After all that Hezekiah had so faithfully done, Sennacherib king of Assyria came and invaded Judah. He laid siege to the fortified cities, thinking to conquer them for himself. 2When Hezekiah saw that Sennacherib had come and that he intended to make war on Jerusalem, 3he consulted with his officials and military staff about blocking off the water from the springs outside the city, and they helped him. 4A large force of men assembled, and they blocked all the springs and the stream that flowed through the land. "Why should the kings of Assyria come and find plenty of water?" they said. 5Then he worked hard repairing all the broken sections of the wall and building towers on it. He built another wall outside that one and reinforced the supporting terraces of the City of David. He also made large numbers of weapons and shields.

6He appointed military officers over the people and assembled them before him in the square at the city gate and encouraged them with these words: 7"Be strong and courageous. Do not be afraid or discouraged because of the king of Assyria and the vast army with him, for there is a greater power with us than with him. 8With him is only the arm of flesh, but with us is the Lord our God to help us and to fight our battles." And the people gained confidence from what Hezekiah the king of Judah said.

9Later, when Sennacherib king of Assyria and all his forces were laying siege to Lachish, he sent his officers to Jerusalem with this message for Hezekiah king of Judah and for all the people of Judah who were there:

10"This is what Sennacherib king of Assyria says: On what are you basing your confidence, that you remain in Jerusalem under siege? 11When Hezekiah says, 'The Lord our God will save us from the hand of the king of Assyria,' he is misleading you, to let you die of hunger and thirst. 12Did not Hezekiah himself remove this god's high places and altars, saying to Judah and Jerusalem, 'You must worship before one altar and burn sacrifices on it'?

13"Do you not know what I and my fathers have done to all the peoples of the other lands? Were the gods of those nations ever able to deliver their land from my hand? 14Who of all the gods of these nations that my fathers destroyed has been able to save his people from me? How then can your god deliver you from my hand? 15Now do not let Hezekiah deceive you and mislead you like this. Do not believe him, for no god of any nation or kingdom has been able to deliver his people from my hand or the hand of my fathers. How much less will your god deliver you from my hand!"

16Sennacherib's officers spoke further against the Lord God and against his servant Hezekiah. 17The king also wrote letters insulting the Lord, the God of Israel, and saying this against him: "Just as the gods of the peoples of the other lands did not rescue their people from my hand, so the god of Hezekiah will not rescue his people from my hand." 18Then they called out in Hebrew to the people of Jerusalem who were on the wall, to terrify them and make them afraid in order to capture the city. 19They spoke about the God of Jerusalem as they did about the gods of the other peoples of the world—the work of men's hands.

20King Hezekiah and the prophet Isaiah son of Amoz cried out in prayer to heaven about this. 21And the Lord sent an angel, who annihilated all the fighting men and the leaders and officers in the camp of the Assyrian king. So he withdrew to his own land in disgrace. And when he went into the temple of his god, some of his sons cut him down with the sword.

22So the Lord saved Hezekiah and the people of Jerusalem from the hand of Sennacherib king of Assyria and from the hand of all others. He took care of them on every side. 23Many brought offerings to Jerusalem for the Lord and valuable gifts for Hezekiah king of Judah. From then on he was highly regarded by all the nations.

24In those days Hezekiah became ill and was at the point of death. He prayed to the Lord, who answered him and gave him a miraculous sign. 25But Hezekiah's heart was proud and he did not respond to the kindness shown him; therefore the

LORD's wrath was on him and on Judah and Jerusalem. ²⁶Then Hezekiah repent-ed of the pride of his heart, as did the people of Jerusalem; therefore the LORD's wrath did not come upon them during the days of Hezekiah.

²⁷Hezekiah had very great riches and honor, and he made treasuries for his silver and gold and for his precious stones, spices, shields and all kinds of valu-ables. ²⁸He also made buildings to store the harvest of grain, new wine and oil; and he made stalls for various kinds of cattle, and pens for the flocks. ²⁹He built villages and acquired great numbers of flocks and herds, for God had given him very great riches.

³⁰It was Hezekiah who blocked the upper outlet of the Gihon spring and chan-neled the water down to the west side of the City of David. He succeeded in everything he undertook. ³¹But when envoys were sent by the rulers of Babylon to ask him about the miraculous sign that had occurred in the land, God left him to test him and to know everything that was in his heart.

³²The other events of Hezekiah's reign and his acts of devotion are written in the vision of the prophet Isaiah son of Amoz in the book of the kings of Judah and Israel. ³³Hezekiah rested with his fathers and was buried on the hill where the tombs of David's descendants are. All Judah and the people of Jerusalem hon-ored him when he died. And Manasseh his son succeeded him as king.

The twenty-nine-year reign (2 Chron 29:1 comment) of Ahaz's son Hezekiah was counted officially from 726 to 697 B.C. (28:27 comment). Hezekiah's trust in the Lord (2 Kings 18:5) and strength of character, moreover, formed an exact antithesis to the apostasy and surrender to expediency that had stigmatized his father's rule. In the area of religion, where Ahaz had converted Jerusalem into a center for idola-try and its accompanying immoralities and atrocities, Hezekiah's first official act (29:3) was to cleanse the Lord's temple of its pollutions (ch. 29). He celebrated an epoch-making Passover (ch. 30); and he campaigned far and wide to stamp out the idolatrous and Canaanitishly oriented high places and to establish the pure religion of the OT (ch. 31). Then in the area of politics, where Ahaz had short sightedly surrendered himself and his kingdom to the empire of Assyria, Hezekiah planned and fought for Judah's ultimate welfare and freedom—not always wisely, but with eventual success (ch. 32).

The parallel passages in Kings touch only briefly on Hezekiah's religious reforms (2 Kings 18:1–6); indeed, once the two introductory verses in 2 Chronicles 29 (based on 2 Kings 18:1–3) are passed, no further parallels appear till the beginning of chapter 31. Yet the fact that such a body of data remains unique to the Chronicler need not thereby render his work suspect. As stated by Myers (*Chronicles*, 2:xxx), "There is nothing improbable in the outline of Hezekiah's reforming and missionary activity"; cf. W.F. Albright's conclusion (JBL 58 [1939]: 185) that the data in chapter 30, which is totally unparalleled, has been suspected unwarrantably. Second Kings does, however, provide a more detailed record of the contemporary political scene (18:7–20:21), which has been condensed into a single chapter in Ezra's history (2 Chron 32).

1 Hezekiah's "twenty-nine year" reign includes a divinely granted extension of fif-teen years (2 Kings 20:6), revealed to him in his fourteenth year (712 B.C., 18:13; 20:1), just before Merodach-Baladan's embassy, and embracing God's promise to deliver Jerusalem from Assyria (an event that occurred eleven years later, in 701). It is to be noted that the king's recorded accession is thus placed at 726; for even though this specification leaves a technical interregnum (actually, a regency by Hez-ekiah; cf. 2 Kings 18:1) that lasted over a year following the removal of Ahaz (2

Chron 28:27 comment), it also allows for Hezekiah, whose age was then twenty-five, to have been born when his father was about thirteen (cf. 28:1 comment; J. Barton Payne, "The Relationship of the Reign of Ahaz to the Accession of Hezekiah," BS 126 [1969]: 44–45).

2 Hezekiah not only did "what was right," but he so trusted in the Lord (cf. Isa 26:3 –4) that "there was no one like him among all the kings of Judah, either before him or after him" (2 Kings 18:5).

3 "The first year of his reign" must refer to the one that followed his official accession in 726 (cf. 30:1 comment) rather than to the one at the time of his rise to power two years before (see comments on v.1 and 28:27). "His first month" would then have been March/April 725. He then "opened the doors of the temple," which had been shut up by the apostate Ahaz (v.7; 28:24), "and repaired them," a project that included overlaying them with gold (2 Kings 18:16).

4 After this initial act the king's cleansing of the temple proceeded through four stages: (1) reconsecrating the Levitical personnel (vv.4–14); (2) directing them to purify the temple itself (vv.15–19); (3) rededicating the sanctuary and altar (vv.20–30); and (4) encouraging the populace to renew their presentation of sacrifices (vv.31 –36). To institute the first stage, he assembled the priests and Levites "in the square on the east side," presumably in the wide space in front of the temple (Ezra 10:9).

5 Concerning the Levites consecrating themselves (also in v.15), see the comment on 1 Chron 15:12.

9 The places Hezekiah could say that God had scattered the sons of Judah in captivity included Damascus, Samaria, Edom, and Philistia (28:5, 8, 17–18).

10 What the king desired is summed up as "a covenant" renewal (cf. 15:12 comment).

11 Hezekiah proceeded to address the Levites and priests (v.4), paternalistically, as "my sons." He reminded the former that God had chosen them to serve him (Num 3:7–8; Deut 10:8) and the latter that they possessed the special function of "burning incense" or, as the form *haqṭîr* is more properly rendered (e.g., in 1 Chron 23:13), of "offering sacrifices" (cf. v.21).

12 Kohath, Merari, and Gershon were the three clans that made up the tribe of Levi (1 Chron 6:1).

13–14 Separate mention, however, is given to "Elizaphan," a man who had been the leader of the Kohathites in the days of Moses (Num 3:30) and whose family had subsequently developed to almost assume the status of a subclan (1 Chron 15:8 comment). "Asaph," "Heman" (v.14), and "Jeduthun" were then the founders of the three families of the Levitical musicians (1 Chron 25).

15 Hezekiah's orders for cleansing the temple are said to have followed "the word of the LORD," for they were issued in conformity to the inspired Mosaic law (cf. Deut 12:2–4).

16 When the priests are said to have "brought out . . . everything unclean" that they found in the temple, this included not simply accumulated rubbish, but specifically the filthy idolatries and their accompanying equipment that King Ahaz had introduced (2 Kings 16:15). The Levites then "carried it out to the Kidron Valley," east of the temple. This was the same place where Asa had burned his queen-grandmother's repulsive Asherah object over a century and a half before (cf. 15:16 comment).

19 The faithless "Ahaz" had "removed," and even partially destroyed, "the articles" used in the Lord's worship (28:24; 2 Kings 16:17).

21 On the "sin offering" and its ritual that marked the temple's rededication, see Leviticus 4:1–5:13.

22 On the specific "sprinkling" of "the blood," see Leviticus 17:6; Numbers 18:17.

23 For the assembly to lay their hands on the goats of the sin offering was to designate these as substitutes for their own lives and to transfer their sins to the animal victims (Num 27:18–21; cf. 8:18–19). The goats thus served as types of Christ's death in the sinner's stead (2 Cor 5:21).

24 The blood of the slaughtered offerings was effective "to atone for all Israel" (as in Lev 4:13; 16:30). The verb *kappēr*, which Ezra used, means basically to "appease" or "pacify" (Gen 32:20; Prov 16:14), and hence to avert punishment by paying a ransom (Keil, p. 452; see also Leon Morris, *The Apostolic Preaching of the Cross* [Grand Rapids: Eerdmans, 1955, s.v.]). Ultimately what saved the Israelites was their anticipation of Christ's death on the cross, who bore the wrath of God that had been incurred by all men as sinners (Mark 10:45; Rom 3:25).

26 On the "instruments" of David, see the comments on 1 Chronicles 23:5.

27–30 On the "burnt offering" (v.27), see Leviticus 1. The Hebrew that lies behind the phrase "singing to the LORD" is literally "the song of the LORD" (NASB), which suggests a specific writing, i.e., perhaps including the canonical Psalms that were then available for use in worship. By Hezekiah's day this would have included the Psalter's Davidic Books I and IV and its Solomonic Book II (Pss 42–72; cf. 1 Chron 16:7 comments). Also mentioned are some of the compositions "of Asaph the seer" (v.30, whose name appears with Ps 50 and, in Book III, Pss 73–83).

31 Concerning the final resumption of sacrifice (cf. v.4 comment), the Chronicler observes that those who were particularly "willing brought burnt offerings"; for these were wholly consumed on the altar. In contrast were the more numerous "sacrifices" (the "consecrated" offerings of v.33, or "peace offerings," v.35 comment), which were largely eaten by the sacrificers in feasts that followed the services of presentation (cf. 1 Chron 29:21 comment). The "thank offerings" were a subcategory within the peace offerings (Lev 7:12–15).

535

34 The lower-ranked Levites, somewhat surprisingly (cf. 24:5 comment; Ezek 48:11), now showed themselves "more conscientious . . . than the priests" (but cf. 30:3 and the lack of principle evinced by the high priest Uriah only nine years before this, 2 Kings 16:10–11). For the truest faith is often found among the humble; and throughout history "professional" religious leaders have too often been among those least willing to submit to Christ and to the Word (cf. John 7:48).

35 The choice, and burnable, "fat of the fellowship offerings" ("peace offerings," NIV mg.) was presented to God on the altar prior to the time of the people's feasting (v.31 comment; Lev 3). On the "drink offerings" ("libations," NASB), see Numbers 15:5, 7, 10.

36 Thus Hezekiah and the people rejoiced at what the Lord had brought about, for in the last analysis all spiritual achievements find their origin in God's grace (30:12; 1 Kings 18:37; Acts 11:18).

30:1 Second Chronicles 30 concerns Hezekiah's epoch-making Passover Feast: first the preparations for it (vv.1–12) and then its observance (vv.13–27). The king "sent word" throughout Judah, but also sent letters inviting Ephraim and Manasseh, i.e., Israel, to come to Jerusalem for its celebration. Any such compliance had been prohibited during the two centuries that had followed Jeroboam's division of the Solomonic empire (vv.5, 26; 1 Kings 12:27–28). But now King Hoshea's capital in Samaria was subject to Assyrian siege (v.6; 2 Kings 17:5), and the northern ruler was powerless to interfere. The Assyrians, furthermore, would probably have encouraged anything that suggested defection from their rebelling vassal (contrast the note on 32:10). The sincerity of Hezekiah's concern for Israel is suggested by his subsequent naming of his son and crown prince Manasseh.

2 A Passover celebrated in the second month, in April/May 725, would be a month late. But this same amount of delay had been authorized by Moses himself, when circumstances made it necessary (Num 9:10–11), as was indeed the case here (cf. 2 Chron 29:17).

3 For the statement "They had not been able to celebrate it at the regular time," the Hebrew reads "at that time," i.e., during the first month (29:3), and particularly on its prescribed fourteenth day (cf. 29:17). Concerning the priests' not consecrating themselves, see the comments to 29:34 and 1 Chronicles 15:12.

5 That the feast "had not been celebrated in large numbers" meant, among other things, celebrated as a united kingdom (v.1 comment).

8 The ruler said, "Come to the sanctuary"; for Passover was one of the three annual pilgrimage feasts that required the presence of every male at the temple (1 Chron 23:31 comment).

9 His word of assurance that their exiled brothers would "be shown compassion . . . and will come back" was based on this same prediction, as made by Moses (Lev 26:40–42).

10 But the northerners—particularly those of Ephraim (cf. v.11 but also v.18)—still "scorned and ridiculed" the king's appeal: human depravity is so total that men will resist a gospel call even when on the brink of disaster (cf. Amos 4:10; Rev 9:20).

13 The "Feast of Unleavened Bread" continued on for a full seven days beyond the actual date of the Passover (Lev 23:5–6). It served to remind the Israelites of their hasty departure from Egypt and of their perpetual need to maintain lives separated from sin (Exod 12:11, 34; 1 Cor 5:7).

14 Jerusalem's idolatrous "altars" (28:24) were thrown "into the Kidron Valley" (cf. the comments on 15:16; 29:16).

15 The ceremony of the "slaughtered . . . Passover lamb" functioned as (1) a memorial to God's past deliverance of Israel from the tenth plague in Egypt (Exod 12:27); (2) a symbol of his present and continuing claim over sinners, which was met by a rite of redemption (Exod 13:15); and (3) a type of his future, ultimate justification for his people procured through the substitutionary death of Christ, the Lamb of God (1 Cor 5:7; cf. Payne, *Theology*, pp. 402–5). The religious leaders apparently were put to shame by the zeal of some of the people and responded accordingly.

16 "The priests sprinkled the blood" as it was "handed to them by the Levites," though normally it would have been presented to them directly by the head of each household (cf. Lev 1:11).

17 But here "the Levites had to kill the Passover lambs," because "many in the crowd had not consecrated themselves," so that they could stand before God in ritual purity (cf. Num 9:6). For the value of the sacrificial service, as a propitiation of God, depended on its typifying the perfect ransom of Christ (Heb 9:14).

18 "Yet they [did eat] the Passover": because of Hezekiah's prayer of intercession, the people were to this extent enabled to share in the feast. If they really sought God in their hearts (v.19), their failures in regard to outward conformity—at least on this first occasion—could be "healed" (v.20), i.e., pardoned. The whole situation reflects the biblical principle that faith takes precedence over ritual (John 7:22–23; 9:14–16).

23 The extension of "the festival" for "seven more days" parallels the way in which Solomon joined a special seven-day celebration for dedicating the temple with the regular week for the fall Feast of Tabernacles (cf. 7:9 comment).

24 The generous quantity of animals provided by the king and by his officials for the peace offerings (cf. 29:31 comment) may even have contributed to the decision to extend the feast. The Chronicler's combined totals, of two thousand bulls and seventeen thousand sheep, have been criticized as "quite possibly too big" (Wenham, "Large Numbers," p. 49). Yet on a similar (but less hurried) occasion, King Josiah and his officials were able to provide twice this number (cf. comment on 35:7–9; cf. even larger quantities that are elsewhere reported in Kings as well as in Chronicles; 7:5 comment).

27 The phrase "the priests and the Levites" may here be rendered as "the Levitical priests," since it was the priests whom Moses had authorized "to bless the people" (Num 6:23–27; cf. Lev 9:22). The grammatical principle is that of hendiadys (cf. the NIV translation of Gen. 3:16, lit., "pains and childbearing," but expressed as "pains in childbearing").

31:1 This next chapter moves on to describe Hezekiah's campaign to eradicate Canaanite idolatry from Israel and to reestablish true OT religion. The majority of its contents (vv.4–19) concern the king's efforts to ensure material support for the Levites, who constituted the nation's religious personnel. Only the opening sentence (v.1a) finds a parallel in 2 Kings (18:4); but just as in the Chronicler's two previous chapters (cf. the introductory discussion to ch. 29), this lack furnishes no warrant for questioning its authenticity. In his reforms the king had the support of his contemporary Judean prophets, Micah and Isaiah (Isa 13–27 applies particularly to Hezekiah's reign between the years 728 and 712). They were respected by the kings (32:20; cf. 2 Kings 19:2; Jer 26:18–19), and their writings illumine the entire period (cf. Isa 22:1–14; 24:1–13).

Concerning "the Asherah poles," see the comment on 14:3; concerning "the high places," see on 1:3. The monarch's crusade in Judah against both of these is attested by the summary in 2 Kings (18:4a). He was also compelled to destroy Nehushtan, the brazen serpent of Moses, which the people had perverted into an object of idolatry (18:4b). His campaign extended northward as well (cf. Notes); for some of the Ephraimites had repented, after two centuries of apostasy (30:11, 18), and the presence of Assyrian troops rendered those who remained obdurate incapable of opposing him (30:1 comment).

2 The Hebrew for Hezekiah's assigning the priests to divisions is definite: he "appointed THE divisions of the priests" (NASB, emphasis mine). He reestablished the twenty-four rotating courses (cf. the comments on 8:14; 23:4) that had been set up by David (1 Chron 25) to insure orderly worship. The word used for the Lord's "dwelling" is literally "camp," reflecting the wilderness situation under Moses (1 Chron 9:18 comment).

3 Just as Solomon had done (2 Chron 2:4 comment), "the king contributed" the regular "burnt offerings" for the temple. Specifications in this regard had, indeed, been set forth by Moses (Num 28–29). Concerning "the morning and evening burnt offerings," and those for the "appointed feasts," see the comments on 1 Chronicles 23:29–31.

4 Remunerations for "the priests" were derived primarily from certain designated parts of the sacrifices (cf. Lev 6–7) and from "the best of the firstfruits of your soil" (Exod 23:19; cf. Num 18:12), while that for the "Levites" came from tithes that were contributed by the other tribes (Lev 27:30–33; Num 18:21–24; cf. v.5). They "could devote themselves" to God's work, unhindered by secular pursuits, only if they received these portions regularly (cf. Neh 13:10).

5 Though the other commodities listed among the dedicated "firstfruits" could be used in Israel's offerings, the "honey" could not, even in the grain offerings that accompanied the other (animal) sacrifices (Lev 2:11). But it was still an acceptable gift for supporting the priests.

6 The "tithe of the holy things" may be a general term for these token portions of the offerings that became the property of the priests who presented them (cf. comment on v.5; cf. Num 8:8–11).

7 The Israelites began bringing their contributions "in the third month" (May/June), the time of the Feast of Pentecost and of the Palestinian grain harvest (Exod 23:16a); and they finished in the seventh month (Sept./Oct.), the time of the Feast of Tabernacles and of the ingathering of the fruit and vine harvests at the end of the agricultural year (23:16b).

10 The high priest Azariah III (also mentioned at the end of v.13; cf. 1 Chron 6:4 comment) is probably not the Azariah (II) who resisted Uzziah (2 Chron 26:17) almost thirty years before.

12 The office of the Levite "Conaniah" dated back to David, who had first organized some of the temple gatekeepers so as to have charge of the dedicated gifts (see comments on 1 Chron 26:20, 26).

14 The gatekeeper "Kore" (cf. 1 Chron 9:19 comment) was then responsible for "distributing the contributions"—whether of the "consecrated gifts" (cf. v.4) or of the additional "freewill offerings"— to their legitimate priestly recipients (Lev 7:14; cf. 6:29).

15 Deputy administrators carried out a final distribution locally, "in the towns of the priests," as these had been determined by Joshua, throughout the tribes of Israel (Josh 21:9–19). An alternative and perhaps more precise rendering to the statement that they "assisted him faithfully" might be that they "assisted him in their positions of trust" (as in 1 Chron 9:22, q.v.).

16 Portions were granted to "males three years old or more . . . who would enter the temple to perform the . . . various tasks." Assignments for work within the operational units of the Levites had originally been based on a minimum age of thirty (1 Chron 23:3); but if there is not a copyist's error here (cf. NIV Study Bible note), the priests' children who were as young as three must have accompanied their fathers in the service, and so received their portions, directly, in the temple.

17 Such reestablished distributions obviously gave a renewed, practical significance to "the genealogical records." On the reasons for service by "Levites twenty years old or more," see the comment on 1 Chronicles 23:24.

18 Thus Kore and his associates consecrated themselves, and the Hebrew adds "in holiness" (NASB). For it was no light responsibility, particularly in view of the numbers of women and children involved (cf. Acts 6:1), as they fulfilled "their positions of trust" (cf. v.15 comment, but rendered in the NIV as "were faithful").

21 "In everything" the king "worked wholeheartedly," in obedience to the law of Moses; "and so he prospered" (cf. 2 Kings 18:6–7).

32:1 After recounting all of Hezekiah's religious reforms (described in chs. 29–31), the Chronicler summarizes his political activity, generally on the assumption of the reader's knowledge of the more detailed accounts that are found in 2 Kings 18:7–20:21 and Isaiah 36–39. He records how in 701 B.C. "Sennacherib king of Assyria . . . invaded Judah"; but behind this deed lay a whole sequence of events.

Assyrian domination had come about in 734, through the specific invitation of Hezekiah's father, Ahaz (28:20–21). In 715 Ashdod and certain other Palestinian states had rebelled, urged on by Egypt (cf. 14:13 comment and 2 Kings 17:4) and by Marduk-apal-iddina of Babylon; for Ezra also records the latter's embassy to Hezekiah (cf. the comments to vv.25 and 31). Its arrival is dated to 712, which was the king's fourteenth year (2 Kings 18:13; 20:1, 12). But in 711 the Assyrians resubdued Ashdod (Isa 14:28–31; 20:1); and Hezekiah yielded to the will of God (20:2–6) by submitting to Sargon II, who called himself the "subjugator of Judah, whose situation is far away" (IB, 4:907).

On Sargon's death in 705, Hezekiah disregarded the Lord's word through Isaiah and became involved in plots with Egypt (Isa 30:1–5; 31:1–3). He assumed leadership in a western revolt and even imprisoned the Philistine king of Ekron, who had refused cooperation (2 Kings 18:8). The result was the above-cited invasion by Sargon's son Sennacherib—though the attacks of both monarchs are subsumed in 2 Kings 18:13 under the dateline of Hezekiah's fourteenth year (for notice how 20:6 must actually precede 18:13, by a full decade, even as in 2 Chron 32, vv.24–26, on the king's illness, precede vv.1–23, on his warfare).

Sennacherib's "thinking to conquer" Judah's "fortified cities" did in fact succeed (2 Kings 18:13; Isa 36:1), except in the case of Jerusalem.

4–5 To aid in their capital's defense, the Hebrews blocked all the springs, especially the Gihon (v.30 comment), directly east of city, "and the stream that flowed" (v.4) from it, i.e., its surface conduit into Jerusalem (Isa 7:3; cf. M. Burrows, "The Conduit of the Upper Pool," ZAW 70 [1958]: 221–27). Concerning the king's "reinforced supporting terraces" (v.5), see the NIV margin and 1 Chronicles 11:8 comment; then, for archaeological attestation to his building "another wall outside" the original one, see Myers, *Chronicles,* 2:187.

6 The Hebrew words for "he . . . encouraged them" are more literally "he spoke to their heart."

7 The king's statement that "there is greater power with us than with" Sennacherib recalls an earlier assurance made by Elisha (2 Kings 6:16); and it reflects the basic meaning of the name of the covenant God of Israel, Yahweh ("He is present [with us]," Exod 3:12, 14; cf. Isa 7:14; Matt 1:23).

8 Hezekiah's disparagement of the Assyrian, that "with him is only the arm of flesh," seems traceable to Isaiah (31:3), and was later quoted by Jeremiah (17:5). But Hezekiah's own "hard work" (v.5) had been criticized by Isaiah (Isa 22:9–10) because of the king's reliance on men rather than on the Lord (22:11; 30:15–16; cf. the comments on 2 Chron 16:2, 9; 25:6). In his annals for 701, Sennacherib was thus able to boast that he "shut up (the king) like a caged bird inside Jerusalem"; that Hezekiah was deserted by his Arabian mercenaries and compelled to release Sennacherib's pro-Assyrian Philistine vassal so as to be restored to his throne in Ekron; and finally that Hezekiah himself had to capitulate, paying a huge indemnity and surrendering over two hundred thousand captives to Assyria. These facts are assumed without comment in Chronicles, though the last two elements are elaborated by other Scriptures.

9–11 Later, i.e., after Hezekiah's payment of the stipulated tribute (2 Kings 18:14), the treacherous Assyrian proceeded to scrap the just negotiated peace treaty (cf. Isa 33:7–8), to lay "siege to Lachish" (v.9), twenty-five miles southwest of Jerusalem, and to make further demands on the beleaguered Hezekiah. To enforce them Sennacherib "sent his officers," including his supreme commander (2 Kings 18:17 NIV; the "tartan," KJV), with a large army "to Jerusalem." In view of the final results (v.21), it is not surprising that Sennacherib's annals say nothing further about this later aspect to his campaign. Indeed the very insolence of his message that follows (cf. vv.10–15 with 2 Kings 18:19–25, 28–35; Isa 36:4–10, 13–20) begins to provide justification for the stirring hopes expressed earlier by Hezekiah (vv.7–8; cf. v.11).

12 By his question, "Did not Hezekiah himself remove this god's high places?" Sennacherib must have been hoping to take advantage of any popular dissatisfaction that was felt against Hezekiah's reforms.

14 More straightforward was Sennacherib's blasphemy against Yahweh—as if God were no more "able to save his people" (v.14) from Assyria than had been the false deities of those nations the aggressor's ancestors had already destroyed (cf. v.19; Isa 10:15).

16–19 "Sennacherib's officers spoke further against the LORD" (v.16), excerpts of which appear in vv.18–19 (cf. the fuller record in 2 Kings 18:27–35). Sennacherib "also wrote letters" (v.17), since he had had to withdraw his troops attacking Jerusalem (v.9 comment) to meet an advance by an Egyptian force under Tirhakah, younger brother of the current Twenty-Fifth Dynasty ruler and himself later to become Pharaoh, from 690 to 664 B.C. (2 Kings 19:8–9). Because of this ruler's presence, and also to account for Sennacherib's initial success and yet subsequent defeat, some commentators have posited a second, separate, and otherwise undocumented campaign by Assyria against Hezekiah, in about 688. Such theories are now, however, acknowledged to be unnecessary historically and to be contrary to the thrust of Scripture, both in its chronology and in the logic of its narrative, particularly in Chronicles as it depicts a single chain of events (cf. NBD, pp. 1159–60, 1283; and Bright's excursus in *History of Israel,* pp. 282–87).

20 For details on the anguished pleas, and yet ringing affirmations of faith, with which Hezekiah and Isaiah "cried out in prayer," see 2 Kings 19:1–7, 14–34. This verse, it should be noted, is the only reference in Chronicles to the deeds of the prophet Isaiah (26:22 and 32:32 refer to his writings, about Uzziah and Hezekiah).

21 Then "an angel . . . annihilated all the fighting men . . . of the Assyrian king," specifically, 185,000 in one night (2 Kings 19:35). The proposal has been advanced that a plague carried by rodents was what struck down the invaders. This is based on an Egyptian legend—which does confirm the general fact of a miraculous deliverance—that Tirhakah (and Hezekiah) owed his victory to field mice that ate up the Assyrians' weapons (Herodotus, *Histories,* 2:141).

But while God can indeed make use of natural means for delivering his elect (and sometimes did [cf. Exod 14:21], even by plagues associated with mice, [1 Sam 6:4]), the rapidity and intensity of this disaster renders the plague proposal inadequate as a particular explanation for the happenings of 701 B.C., if viewed apart from a supernatural (angelic) agency. The event ranks, in fact, with Israel's crossing of the Red Sea as one of the two greatest examples of the Lord's intervention to save his people. So Sennacherib "withdrew to his own" land and was slain (2 Kings 19:36–37; Isa 37–38).

24 "In those days," fifteen years before his actual death (2 Kings 20:6), or in 712 (v.1 comment), Hezekiah, while seriously ill, prayed (contrast 16:12 comment and see 2 Kings 20:2–3); "and the prayer of faith shall save the sick" (James 5:15 KJV; cf. 2 Chron 16:12). "The LORD . . . answered him," promising him recovery (2 Kings 20:4 –6), "and gave him a miraculous sign," of the shadow that moved backward (2 Kings 20:8–11).

25 "But Hezekiah's heart was proud" (see on v.31); and the result was "the LORD's wrath," as declared through Isaiah's threat of impending exile to Babylon (2 Kings 20:16–18; Isa 39:6–7).

26 But because "Hezekiah repented, . . . the LORD's wrath did not come upon them" in his days (cf. 2 Kings 20:19; Isa 39:8; Jer 26:19; cf. Payne, *Prophecy,* p. 427, #8).

30 To insure a permanent water supply within his capital's walls, "Hezekiah . . . channeled" the flow of "the Gihon spring" through a 1,700 foot tunnel cut into the rock beneath Jerusalem. Archaeological confirmation of this engineering feat came in 1880, with the discovery, at its lower portal, of the Siloam Inscription, written in old Hebrew by the very workers who accomplished it.

31 The envoys of Babylon, to which Ezra here refers, were those sent by Marduk-apal-iddina, the Merodach-Baladan of 2 Kings 20:12–13. Their mission appears to have been not simply to inquire about the king's illness (v.24 comment) and about its accompanying "miraculous sign"—of understandable interest to astrologers such as the Babylonians—but also to arrange practical measures against Sargon's aggression, which did overpower Ashdod and the West in the following year, 711 (v.1 comment), and drove Marduk-apal-iddina from his throne in the East two years after that. The experience served "to test" Hezekiah, whether he would place his trust in human treaties or in God (again see v.1 comment); and it was his eagerness for the treaties that incurred the Lord's wrath (v.25).

32 Ezra's description of his main literary source as being "the vision of the prophet Isaiah" (= Isa 1:1) "in the book of the kings" (cf. 20:34 comment) indicates that at least chapters 36–39 of Isaiah (which are reproduced within 2 Kings 18–20) must have been incorporated into that larger court chronicle from which both he and the writer of Kings, prior to him, were accustomed to draw (see Introduction: Sources, e).

33 Underlying the NIV translation, that Hezekiah was buried "on the hill where the tombs . . . are," is the Hebrew phrase *bema'ᵃlēh qibrê*, which means literally, "in the going up [or 'ascent'] of the tombs of." But this expression could as well be rendered "in the upper section of the tombs," on the hypothesis of some additional excavation at a higher level, when the lower tombs had become occupied.

Notes

36 The temple's cleansing occurred פִּתְאֹם (*pit'ōm*, "suddenly"; NIV, "so quickly"). As an alternate rendering, KB (p. 786) lists the adverb "surprisingly," i.e., with remarkable effectiveness.

30:10 Myers (*Chronicles*, 1:xx) has proposed that behind the Ephraimites' scorning of Hezekiah's message lay an Assyrian policy that favored a continuing Bethel cult and opposed a reunification of Hebrew religion at Jerusalem; hence their appointment of a priest to maintain the North's form of worship (2 Kings 17:28). Yet Scripture suggests no such policy, the stated reason for the sending of the priest being the people's trouble with lions (v.25).

21 The NIV marginal rendering represents a more strict translation than the one presented in the text. For the verb הַלֵּל (*hallēl*) means to "praise" (and only by extension, "sing"); and the phrase בִּכְלֵי־עֹז (*biklê-'ōz*, lit., "with instruments of strength") is more closely represented by the margin's "resounding instruments" than by the text's "instruments of praise."

31:1 On the authenticity of Hezekiah's campaign of purification within the northern territory at the time of Samaria's fall, see W.F. Albright, "The Biblical Period" (in L. Finkelstine, ed., *The Jews: Their History, Culture, and Religion* [New York: Harper, 1948], 1:42). Confirmation of this ruler's expansion northward appears also from the identification of the mothers of the subsequent kings Amon and Jehoiakim as coming from Jotbah, to the northwest of Cana of Galilee (2 Kings 21:19), and from Rumah, south of Cana (2 Kings 23:36), respectively.

32:32 Hezekiah's "acts of devotion" (חֲסָדָיו, *hᵃsādāyw*) are more precisely "his acts of faithfulness" (cf. 1 Chron 16:41 comment).

14. Manasseh

33:1–20

¹Manasseh was twelve years old when he became king, and he reigned in Jerusalem fifty-five years. ²He did evil in the eyes of the LORD, following the detestable practices of the nations the LORD had driven out before the Israelites. ³He rebuilt the high places his father Hezekiah had demolished; he also erected altars to the Baals and made Asherah poles. He bowed down to all the starry hosts and worshiped them. ⁴He built altars in the temple of the LORD, of which the LORD had said, "My Name will remain in Jerusalem forever." ⁵In both courts of the temple of the LORD, he built altars to all the starry hosts. ⁶He sacrificed his sons in the fire in the Valley of Ben Hinnom, practiced sorcery, divination and witchcraft, and consulted mediums and spiritists. He did much evil in the eyes of the LORD, provoking him to anger.

⁷He took the carved image he had made and put it in God's temple, of which God had said to David and to his son Solomon, "In this temple and in Jerusalem,

which I have chosen out of all the tribes of Israel, I will put my Name forever. ⁸I will not again make the feet of the Israelites leave the land I assigned to your forefathers, if only they will be careful to do everything I commanded them concerning all the laws, decrees and ordinances given through Moses." ⁹But Manasseh led Judah and the people of Jerusalem astray, so that they did more evil than the nations the LORD had destroyed before the Israelites.

¹⁰The LORD spoke to Manasseh and his people, but they paid no attention. ¹¹So the LORD brought against them the army commanders of the king of Assyria, who took Manasseh prisoner, put a hook in his nose, bound him with bronze shackles and took him to Babylon. ¹²In his distress he sought the favor of the LORD his God and humbled himself greatly before the God of his fathers. ¹³And when he prayed to him, the LORD was moved by his entreaty and listened to his plea; so he brought him back to Jerusalem and to his kingdom. Then Manasseh knew that the LORD is God.

¹⁴Afterward he rebuilt the outer wall of the City of David, west of the Gihon spring in the valley, as far as the entrance of the Fish Gate and encircling the hill of Ophel; he also made it much higher. He stationed military commanders in all the fortified cities in Judah.

¹⁵He got rid of the foreign gods and removed the image from the temple of the LORD, as well as all the altars he had built on the temple hill and in Jerusalem; and he threw them out of the city. ¹⁶Then he restored the altar of the LORD and sacrificed fellowship offerings and thank offerings on it, and told Judah to serve the LORD, the God of Israel. ¹⁷The people, however, continued to sacrifice at the high places, but only to the LORD their God.

¹⁸The other events of Manasseh's reign, including his prayer to his God and the words the seers spoke to him in the name of the LORD, the God of Israel, are written in the annals of the kings of Israel. ¹⁹His prayer and how God was moved by his entreaty, as well as all his sins and unfaithfulness, and the sites where he built high places and set up Asherah poles and idols before he humbled himself— all are written in the records of the seers. ²⁰Manasseh rested with his fathers and was buried in his palace. And Amon his son succeeded him as king.

Manasseh, evil son of the godly Hezekiah, had the longest reign of all the Hebrew monarchs, from 697 to 642 B.C.; and he more than any other single person was responsible for the final destruction of the kingdom of Judah (2 Kings 23:26; 24:3; Jer 15:4). Most of his fifty-five-year reign was devoted to thoroughgoing paganism, religiously, and to a renewed subjection to Assyria, politically. This part of his record in 2 Chronicles (33:1–10) closely parallels its literary source in 2 Kings (21:1–10). During his closing years, a personal crisis did bring back Manasseh to repentance; but it was too late to produce a significant national effect (33:11–20). Most of this material, moreover, is unique to the Chronicler; for only two of its verses (18 and 20—which contain the normal formulas of concluding summarization) find correspondence in the material of 2 Kings (21:17–18; see Notes).

3 Concerning the "high places, . . . Baals, and . . . Asherah" poles, see the comments on 14:3 and 17:3. The king's apostate worship of "the starry host" had evil precedents going as far back as the time of Moses (Deut 4:19; Acts 7:42), but such practices were a particular sin of Assyro-Babylonians, with their addiction to astrology. Whether the Assyrians made it a policy to enforce their religion on the nations that became subject to their empire is subject to question (see 28:23 comment); but it is a fact that when Sennacherib's son Esarhaddon advanced westward against Egypt, Manasseh did weakly submit himself to him, in 676, which must have provided some stimulus for the astral worship in Judah.

4 About the Lord's "Name" remaining in Jerusalem forever, see the comments on 1 Chronicles 22:7; 2 Chronicles 6:2, 6.

5 On the two temple "courts," see on 2 Chronicles 4:9.

6 Manasseh "sacrificed his sons in the fire in the Valley of Ben Hinnom" (cf. NIV mg.), just as his grandfather Ahaz had (28:3 comment); and he "practiced sorcery," etc., attempting to communicate with the dead through the use of "mediums"— which Scripture uniformly condemns as contrary to faith in God (Exod 22:18; Deut 18:10–12). The Hebrew word for "spiritists" is *yiddeʿônî*, by etymology, "a knowing one." It referred originally to ghosts, who were supposed to possess superhuman knowledge; but it came to be applied to those who claimed power to summon them forth, i.e., to witches. Second Kings 21:16 adds that the king also engaged in tyranny, shedding "much innocent blood."

8 Yahweh had promised not to remove the Israelites but stipulated: "if only they will . . . do everything I commanded them . . . through Moses" (see comments on 7:14, 19).

10 "The LORD spoke" to Judah by "his servants the prophets," threatening their destruction (2 Kings 21:10–15); "but they paid no attention."

11 The occasion on which "the king of Assyria . . . took Manasseh prisoner . . . to Babylon" may have arisen in the year 648, when Ashurbanipal finally overcame a revolt that had been led in that city for four years by his own brother. Egypt, under a new dynasty (the twenty-sixth), had taken this opportunity to escape the Assyrian yoke; and Manasseh may have been tempted to try the same thing. But because Judah lay closer to Assyria, or because it lacked Egypt's greater resources, this attempt failed.

12 In any event, "in his distress he . . . humbled himself greatly before God"; for it sometimes takes a crisis to drive a man to God and to become converted (cf. Acts 9:3 –5).

14 On "Gihon" and "Ophel," see on 32:30 and on 27:3. The king's rebuilt fortifications extended as far as "the Fish Gate," in Jerusalem's north wall (Neh 3:3; cf. K.M. Kenyon, *Jerusalem: Excavating 3000 Years of History* [New York: McGraw-Hill, 1967], pp. 66–68).

17 Ezra explains that "the people, however, continued to sacrifice at the high places," because half a century of paganism could not be counteracted by half-a-dozen years of reform. It is true that Judah presented the offerings only to the Lord their God, but this was still contrary to Moses' law for a central sanctuary (cf. on 1:3). In practice, moreover, it meant little more than applying a new name to the old Baal worship, with all its debased rites.

18–19 The king's "prayer to his God" (v.18; cf. vv.12–13) is no longer preserved. These passages did, however, provide a basis on which someone shortly before the time of Christ composed the fifteen verses that make up the apocryphal Prayer of

Manasses. It appears in some LXX MSS as one of the fourteen books that make up their Apocrypha. It has the status of an official appendix to the Latin Vulgate but is not included in the eleven-book canon that was added to the OT by the Roman Catholic Council of Trent.

The Chronicler's special literary source for Manasseh was, according to the MT (cf. NIV mg.), the "history of Hozai" (ASV), an otherwise unknown prophet (see Introduction: Sources, d).

Notes

12 According to some, Manasseh's change of heart is only "supposed"—perhaps to furnish some theological justification for the outstandingly long reign that he enjoyed. But while his repentance is not permitted to be considered historical, it is conceded that his captivity may have been (Dentan, p. 152).

15. *Amon*

33:21–25

21Amon was twenty-two years old when he became king, and he reigned in Jerusalem two years. 22He did evil in the eyes of the LORD, as his father Manasseh had done. Amon worshiped and offered sacrifices to all the idols Manasseh had made. 23But unlike his father Manasseh, he did not humble himself before the LORD; Amon increased his guilt.

24Amon's officials conspired against him and assassinated him in his palace. 25Then the people of the land killed all who had plotted against King Amon, and they made Josiah his son king in his place.

The remainder of 2 Chronicles 33 (vv.21–25) deals with the brief reign of Manasseh's son Amon (642–640 B.C.). This man was the reflection of his father's essentially pagan life, and not of his repentant last years and death; for under the new king, Judah quickly relapsed into the superstitious practices of Manasseh before his conversion. After only two years Amon died at the hands of his own courtiers. His record follows and somewhat abbreviates its earlier source in 2 Kings 21:19–26.

22 When the Chronicler says that "Amon worshiped . . . all the idols Manasseh had made," this seems to suggest either that their removal (v.15a) had not involved their destruction, or that Manasseh's concentration on bringing about reform in Jerusalem (v.15b) had left intact those relics of his former paganism that characterized the local high places (v.17).

25 Concerning "the people of the land," who took vengeance on Amon's assassins and restored order to Judah, see the comment on 23:13.

16. *Josiah*

34:1–35:27

¹Josiah was eight years old when he became king, and he reigned in Jerusalem thirty-one years. ²He did what was right in the eyes of the LORD and walked in the ways of his father David, not turning aside to the right or to the left.

³In the eighth year of his reign, while he was still young, he began to seek the God of his father David. In his twelfth year he began to purge Judah and Jerusalem of high places, Asherah poles, carved idols and cast images. ⁴Under his direction the altars of the Baals were torn down; he cut to pieces the incense altars that were above them, and smashed the Asherah poles, the idols and the images. These he broke to pieces and scattered over the graves of those who had sacrificed to them. ⁵He burned the bones of the priests on their altars, and so he purged Judah and Jerusalem. ⁶In the towns of Manasseh, Ephraim and Simeon, as far as Naphtali, and in the ruins around them, ⁷he tore down the altars and the Asherah poles and crushed the idols to powder and cut to pieces all the incense altars throughout Israel. Then he went back to Jerusalem.

⁸In the eighteenth year of Josiah's reign, to purify the land and the temple, he sent Shaphan son of Azaliah and Maaseiah the ruler of the city, with Joah son of Joahaz, the recorder, to repair the temple of the LORD his God.

⁹They went to Hilkiah the high priest and gave him the money that had been brought into the temple of God, which the Levites who were the doorkeepers had collected from the people of Manasseh, Ephraim and the entire remnant of Israel and from all the people of Judah and Benjamin and the inhabitants of Jerusalem. ¹⁰Then they entrusted it to the men appointed to supervise the work on the LORD's temple. These men paid the workers who repaired and restored the temple. ¹¹They also gave money to the carpenters and builders to purchase dressed stone, and timber for joists and beams for the buildings that the kings of Judah had allowed to fall into ruin.

¹²The men did the work faithfully. Over them to direct them were Jahath and Obadiah, Levites descended from Merari, and Zechariah and Meshullam, descended from Kohath. The Levites—all who were skilled in playing musical instruments— ¹³had charge of the laborers and supervised all the workers from job to job. Some of the Levites were secretaries, scribes and doorkeepers.

¹⁴While they were bringing out the money that had been taken into the temple of the LORD, Hilkiah the priest found the Book of the Law of the LORD that had been given through Moses. ¹⁵Hilkiah said to Shaphan the secretary, "I have found the Book of the Law in the temple of the LORD." He gave it to Shaphan.

¹⁶Then Shaphan took the book to the king and reported to him: "Your officials are doing everything that has been committed to them. ¹⁷They have paid out the money that was in the temple of the LORD and have entrusted it to the supervisors and workers." ¹⁸Then Shaphan the secretary informed the king, "Hilkiah the priest has given me a book." And Shaphan read from it in the presence of the king.

¹⁹When the king heard the words of the Law, he tore his robes. ²⁰He gave these orders to Hilkiah, Ahikam son of Shaphan, Abdon son of Micah, Shaphan the secretary and Asaiah the king's attendant: ²¹"Go and inquire of the LORD for me and for the remnant in Israel and Judah about what is written in this book that has been found. Great is the LORD's anger that is poured out on us because our fathers have not kept the word of the LORD; they have not acted in accordance with all that is written in this book."

²²Hilkiah and those the king had sent with him went to speak to the prophetess Huldah, who was the wife of Shallum son of Tokhath, the son of Hasrah, keeper of the wardrobe. She lived in Jerusalem, in the Second District.

²³She said to them, "This is what the LORD, the God of Israel, says: Tell the man who sent you to me, ²⁴'This is what the LORD says: I am going to bring disaster on this place and its people—all the curses written in the book that has been read in the presence of the king of Judah. ²⁵Because they have forsaken me and burned

incense to other gods and provoked me to anger by all that their hands have made, my anger will be poured out on this place and will not be quenched.' ²⁶Tell the king of Judah, who sent you to inquire of the LORD, 'This is what the LORD, the God of Israel, says concerning the words you heard: ²⁷Because your heart was responsive and you humbled yourself before God when you heard what he spoke against this place and its people, and because you humbled yourself before me and tore your robes and wept in my presence, I have heard you, declares the LORD. ²⁸Now I will gather you to your fathers, and you will be buried in peace. Your eyes will not see all the disaster I am going to bring on this place and on those who live here.' "

So they took her answer back to the king.

²⁹Then the king called together all the elders of Judah and Jerusalem. ³⁰He went up to the temple of the LORD with the men of Judah, the people of Jerusalem, the priests and the Levites—all the people from the least to the greatest. He read in their hearing all the words of the Book of the Covenant, which had been found in the temple of the LORD. ³¹The king stood by his pillar and renewed the covenant in the presence of the LORD—to follow the LORD and keep his commands, regulations and decrees with all his heart and all his soul, and to obey the words of the covenant written in this book.

³²Then he had everyone in Jerusalem and Benjamin pledge themselves to it; the people of Jerusalem did this in accordance with the covenant of God, the God of their fathers.

³³Josiah removed all the detestable idols from all the territory belonging to the Israelites, and he had all who were present in Israel serve the LORD their God. As long as he lived, they did not fail to follow the LORD, the God of their fathers.

^{35:1}Josiah celebrated the Passover to the LORD in Jerusalem, and the Passover lamb was slaughtered on the fourteenth day of the first month. ²He appointed the priests to their duties and encouraged them in the service of the LORD's temple. ³He said to the Levites, who instructed all Israel and who had been consecrated to the LORD: "Put the sacred ark in the temple that Solomon son of David king of Israel built. It is not to be carried about on your shoulders. Now serve the LORD your God and his people Israel. ⁴Prepare yourselves by families in your divisions, according to the directions written by David king of Israel and by his son Solomon.

⁵"Stand in the holy place with a group of Levites for each subdivision of the families of your fellow countrymen, the lay people. ⁶Slaughter the Passover lambs, consecrate yourselves and prepare the lambs, for your fellow countrymen, doing what the LORD commanded through Moses."

⁷Josiah provided for all the lay people who were there a total of thirty thousand sheep and goats for the Passover offerings, and also three thousand cattle—all from the king's own possessions.

⁸His officials also contributed voluntarily to the people and the priests and Levites. Hilkiah, Zechariah and Jehiel, the administrators of God's temple, gave the priests twenty-six hundred Passover offerings and three hundred cattle. ⁹Also Conaniah along with Shemaiah and Nethanel, his brothers, and Hashabiah, Jeiel and Jozabad, the leaders of the Levites, provided five thousand Passover offerings and five hundred head of cattle for the Levites.

¹⁰The service was arranged and the priests stood in their places with the Levites in their divisions as the king had ordered. ¹¹The Passover lambs were slaughtered, and the priests sprinkled the blood handed to them, while the Levites skinned the animals. ¹²They set aside the burnt offerings to give them to the subdivisions of the families of the people to offer to the LORD, as is written in the Book of Moses. They did the same with the cattle. ¹³They roasted the Passover animals over the fire as prescribed, and boiled the holy offerings in pots, caldrons and pans and served them quickly to all the people. ¹⁴After this, they made preparations for themselves and for the priests, because the priests, the descendants of Aaron, were sacrificing the burnt offerings and the fat portions until nightfall. So the Levites made preparations for themselves and for the Aaronic priests.

¹⁵The musicians, the descendants of Asaph, were in the places prescribed by David, Asaph, Heman and Jeduthun the king's seer. The gatekeepers at each

gate did not need to leave their posts, because their fellow Levites made the preparations for them.

[16]So at that time the entire service of the LORD was carried out for the celebration of the Passover and the offering of burnt offerings on the altar of the LORD, as King Josiah had ordered. [17]The Israelites who were present celebrated the Passover at that time and observed the Feast of Unleavened Bread for seven days. [18]The Passover had not been observed like this in Israel since the days of the prophet Samuel; and none of the kings of Israel had ever celebrated such a Passover as did Josiah, with the priests, the Levites and all Judah and Israel who were there with the people of Jerusalem. [19]This Passover was celebrated in the eighteenth year of Josiah's reign.

[20]After all this, when Josiah had set the temple in order, Neco king of Egypt went up to fight at Carchemish on the Euphrates, and Josiah marched out to meet him in battle. [21]But Neco sent messengers to him, saying, "What quarrel is there between you and me, O king of Judah? It is not you I am attacking at this time, but the house with which I am at war. God has told me to hurry; so stop opposing God, who is with me, or he will destroy you."

[22]Josiah, however, would not turn away from him, but disguised himself to engage him in battle. He would not listen to what Neco had said at God's command but went to fight him on the plain of Megiddo.

[23]Archers shot King Josiah, and he told his officers, "Take me away; I am badly wounded." [24]So they took him out of his chariot, put him in the other chariot he had and brought him to Jerusalem, where he died. He was buried in the tombs of his fathers, and all Judah and Jerusalem mourned for him.

[25]Jeremiah composed laments for Josiah, and to this day all the men and women singers commemorate Josiah in the laments. These became a tradition in Israel and are written in the Laments.

[26]The other events of Josiah's reign and his acts of devotion, according to what is written in the Law of the LORD— [27]all the events, from beginning to end, are written in the book of the kings of Israel and Judah.

In contrast to his father, Amon, Josiah proved to be a good king over the people of Judah (640–609 B.C.). He was the last such, it is sad to say; but he was also in some respects their greatest (v.2). Josiah instituted the most thorough of all the OT reforms, dating to 622, and one that restored Israel's commitment to God's Book. It was this faith in holy Scripture that was then able to keep the nation's hope alive during their exile through most of the succeeding century (cf. Dan 9:2), during the difficult century of restoration that followed (Ezra 7:10; Mal 4:4), and during the next four hundred, silent years until the appearance of John the Baptist (Mal 3:1; 4:5 –6) and the kingdom of Jesus the Messiah, God's personal Word, who fulfilled the written Word (Matt 5:17–18).

Within 2 Chronicles Josiah's record occupies the two chapters (34–35) that immediately precede the closing chapter of the book; and they deal with four primary topics: (1) the earlier stages of the king's reforms (34:1–7); (2) the great reformation that occurred in the eighteenth year of his reign, beginning with the repair of the Jerusalem temple and climaxing with the discovery of the Mosaic Book of the Law and with Judah's responses to it (34:8–33); (3) Josiah's unsurpassed Passover observance (35:1–19); and (4) his tragic death (35:20–27). Parallel source material appears in a corresponding portion of 2 Kings (22:1–23:30). But the first of the four topics is less fully treated in Kings, and the third is barely touched on at all. For the others Chronicles does add certain explanatory verses (34:12–14, 33; 35:21–23, 25), but a number of their elements are more fully treated in Kings (as indicated below, cf. on 34:33).

1–2 Josiah "did what was right" (v.2), particularly in his devotion to "all the Law of Moses" (2 Kings 23:25), so that in this respect (cf. on 29:2, on the "trust" that was Hezekiah's area of strength) "neither before nor after Josiah was there a king like him" (2 Kings 23:25).

3 In the "eighth year" of his rule, in 632 B.C., when "he was still young," just sixteen, he began to seek the Lord personally; and in his "twelfth year," in 628, he began to purify Judah nationally of its high places and related paganisms (cf. on 33:3). The latter date identifies a particular time of chaos that occurred throughout the ancient Near East and that was precipitated by an invasion from the north of barbaric, nomadic horsemen known as the Scythians (628–626 B.C.) (cf. Richard Vaggione, "Over all Asia? The Extent of all the Scythian Domination in Herodotus," JBL 92 [1973]: 523–30). Their incursions wrought terror among complacent Jews (Jer 6:22-24; Zeph 1:12); and, though they never actually raided much beyond the open plains of coastal Palestine—where they were eventually stopped by the Egyptians—they did produce two major effects that concerned Judah.

In the area of religion, the Scythian presence seems to have conditioned the calls of the contemporary prophets Jeremiah (Jer 1:2, 14) and Zephaniah (Zeph 1:2, which refers to local Judean threats, vv.3–4; cf. Payne, "Prophecy," pp. 18, 440). It further correlates with the above noted second (628) stage of Josiah's revival; but this latter went far beyond the momentary fear usually associated with superficial "fox-hole" type religion (cf. 2 Chron 34:3–7). (For a contrasting view as to the effect of the Scythian invasion, see C.L. Feinberg's comments in EBC, 6:361–62.)

Then in the area of politics, the Scythian hordes succeeded in sweeping away the Assyrian imperial domination that had been Judah's nemesis throughout the preceding half century (cf. on v.6; 33:3). Indeed, after Ashurbanipal's death in about 631 (NBD, p. 98), and as a result of the barbarian tidal wave in 628, the way was cleared for Josiah to reestablish a united kingdom of Israel to the extent that it had occupied when it had first chosen David almost three centuries before (cf. F.M. Cross and D.N. Freedman, "Josiah's Revolt against Assyria," JNES 12 [1953]: 56–58).

Whether the king's achievement of political freedom involved a corresponding religious repudiation of Assyrian idolatry is, as previously noted (see on 28:23), open to question; only Canaanite forms appear as the objects of Josiah's purge. But the Chronicler's unique and yet inherently plausible outline of events is now being increasingly acknowledged as possessing historicity: "The chronological data is so reasonable in itself that it is difficult to see how the episode can be seriously questioned" (Myers, *Chronicles*, 2:205).

4 The term for "idols" (*pᵉsilîm*, also in v.7) means ones "cut out, carved," while the "images" (*massēḵôt*) were "cast" (as in v.3).

5–6 Josiah's campaign against idolatry included not simply Judah and Jerusalem (v.5), but extended also into "Manasseh" and "Ephraim" (v.6), just as Hezekiah's reform had a century earlier (cf. note on 31:1). On "Simeon" see the introductory discussion to 1 Chronicles 4:24–43. That Josiah's endeavor "reached as far as Naphtali" in Galilee shows that he recovered most of the formerly Assyrian province of Israel (cf. v.9), a fact that is archaeologically attested by seventh-century inscriptions from the land itself.

8 On Joah's position as "recorder," see the comment on 1 Chronicles 18:15. "Shaphan" is identified in 2 Kings 22:8 as "secretary" (see on 1 Chron 18:16).

9–10 The officials gave Hilkiah the high priest the money the Levitical doorkeepers had collected from the people of Ephraim, etc. Second Kings 22:4 suggests that it was the people who brought the silver far as the temple gate—perhaps to deposit it in a chest similar to the one once provided by King Joash (cf. on 2 Chron 24:8)—and that the Levites collected it from there.

11–12 The builders did the work so faithfully that no audit was required (2 Kings 22:7), just as had been true under Joash (2 Kings 12:15).

14 At this point in the year 622, Hilkiah found "the Book of the Law." It is later called the "Book of the Covenant" (v.30), which suggests Exodus 19–24 (cf. 24:7). Yet the curses that the book contained (v.24) suggests Leviticus 26 and Deuteronomy 28; and the ensuing stress on the central sanctuary (2 Kings 23:8–9) implies Deuteronomy 12, etc. "The Book" thus was at the least the Book of Deuteronomy. It is called "the covenant" in Deut 29:1, for example. It contains the curses (Deut 28) and it alone calls for a central sanctuary and was stored at the temple usually by the side of the ark (Deut 31:25–26). There is no internal evidence from this historical account that necessitates appeal to another book. "The Book," however, seems to have become misplaced during the apostate administrations of the previous kings, Manasseh and Amon, under whom the ark had been moved about (2 Chron 35:3).

The book is described as "the Law of the LORD that had been given through Moses," literally, *bᵉyad* ("by the hand of") Moses. For though all the passages in the Pentateuch do not claim to have been written down (cf. Exod 17:14; 24:4; 34:27; Lev 18:5 [Rom 10:5]; Num 33:2; Deut 31:9, 22) or even spoken by Moses (compare Deut 33 with 34), Scripture is nevertheless clear that all its contents do belong to a historical period no later than his (Deut 4:2; 12:32), and that they were composed *bᵉyad* ("under the guidance of") Moses (KB, p. 363, 5.b; cf. Christ's own belief in this fact, Luke 24:44; John 7:19). Indeed, and as if in anticipation of the current widespread denial of the Mosaic authorship of the Pentateuch, our Lord declared that those who refuse to believe Moses' words cannot consistently accept his own either (John 5:47).

19 In response the king "tore his robes," personally convicted by the immediate and terrifying relevance of threats such as those inscribed in Deuteronomy 28:36 (cf. Lev 26:32–33; 2 Chron 34:21, 24, 27), prophecies that were "written there concerning us" (2 Kings 22:13).

20 The variant forms of the names for "Abdon" and for the ancestors of Huldah's husband, "Shallum" (v.22; cf. NIV mg.), are derived from 2 Kings 22:12, 14.

22 Ezra's almost casual reference to the "Huldah" prophetess indicates how foreign the idea of discrimination based on sex was to the spirit of the OT (cf. Judg 4:4; 2 Sam 20:16). Restrictions on women, such as relegating them to a separate court in the temple (see on 4:9), arose only with the perversions of intertestamental Judaism.

Huldah's location in the second district can no longer be identified; but the name suggests one of the extensions to Jerusalem, either to the north or to the west.

24 The Lord confirmed that he would "bring disaster on . . . Judah," that he would "not turn away from the heat of his fierce anger, . . . because of all that Manasseh had done to provoke him" (2 Kings 23:26).

28 Josiah, however, was promised that his eyes would "not see all the disaster." Postponements of divine wrath had been granted previously to King Hezekiah (cf. on 32:26) and even to King Ahab of Israel (1 Kings 21:29) when they too displayed humility and repentance. Josiah would "be buried in peace," i.e., before the disastrous Fall of Judah that constitutes the point at issue here; for though the king was buried in honor, he did, in fact, die from battle wounds (35:23–24).

31 "The covenant" that Josiah "renewed" was the one contained in the Book of the Covenant (v.30), specifically the revelation of God's older testament—the pre-Christian revelation that was the Lord's eternal instrument for the redemption of his elect people (cf. the comments to 1 Chron 16:15; 2 Chron 15:12–13, 15). During this rite in the temple, the king stood ʿal-ʿomdô ("in his place," KJV), which was, more specifically, ʿal-ʿammûdô ("by his pillar," NIV), as in 23:13 (cf. LXX and 2 Kings 23:3), though the NIV is here technically reading with the Targum.

33 The Chronicler reports briefly that "Josiah removed all detestable idols." For more details on his thorough purging of the land of its high places—with their accompanying immoralities—of its astral worship, of its spiritism, and of its other paganisms, see 2 Kings 23:4–14, 24. His field of action included "all the territory belonging to the Israelites" (cf. its enumeration by tribes in v.6). In particular the king destroyed the altar of Jeroboam I at Bethel, along with the other high places of Samaria, and slew such of the priests as remained (2 Kings 23:15–20, exactly as had been predicted in 1 Kings 13:2, over three hundred years before).

In summary Ezra says of the Israelites under Josiah that "as long as he lived, they did not fail to follow the LORD." Yet the testimony of Jeremiah, who actively supported the king's reform (Jer 11:1–5), shows that for many this "following" may have consisted more in external compliance than in commitment from the heart (11:9–13).

35:1 The Chronicler's third major topic concerning the reign of Josiah (cf. the introductory discussion to the opening of ch. 34) describes how the king celebrated a great Passover (35:1–19). Its observance served to provide a public confirmation to his reform as a whole; it resulted, indeed, from Judah's obedience to that same rediscovered divine Law, "as it is written in the Book of the Covenant" (2 Kings 23:21). "The first month," to which the celebration is dated, is thus March/April within Josiah's climactic eighteenth year (2 Chron 35:18), namely 622 B.C.; contrast the way in which Hezekiah had had to postpone the keeping of his Passover to the second month (cf. on 30:2).

2–3 On the teaching office of Judah's "Levites" (v.3), see the comment on 17:7. Josiah told them to "put the sacred ark in the temple," because during the dark days of Manasseh and Amon (33:7; cf. 28:24) it seems to have been removed by these faithful ministers and carried elsewhere for its protection (cf. on 34:14).

4 Concerning their "divisions," or courses, "according to the directions written by David . . . and by . . . Solomon," see the comments, respectively, to 1 Chronicles 24:4, 20, and 2 Chronicles 8:14.

5–6 By directing the Levites to "slaughter the passover lambs" (v.6), the king continued the practice that had been worked out by Hezekiah (cf. on 30:17). But Josiah's goal was to prevent the sort of confusion that had arisen during the more precipitous reform and Passover of his godly great-grandfather, some 103 years earlier (cf. 30:16–18).

7 The historicity of the quantities of animals provided by Josiah (with supplements in the next verse) has been even more criticized than for those recorded in reference to Hezekiah's celebration (about half as many, 30:24 comment). Myers (*Chronicles*, 2:212), for example, calls it an "enormous number, highly exaggerated." Yet when one considers Josiah's more careful advanced planning, and the fact that the animals were prepared for "all Judah and Israel who were there [*hannimṣā'*, lit., 'all that could be found,' 35:18]," and that it was an unprecedented affair, that "none of the kings of Israel had ever celebrated such a Passover as did Josiah" (v.18; cf. comment), then his "thirty-thousand sheep and goats . . . and also three thousand cattle" appear to fall well within the category of the explainable (see Appendix B). Furthermore, when compared with the numbers of sacrificial animals that the Chronicler quotes from other Scriptures (cf. 2 Chron 7:5's citation of 1 Kings 8:63, about Solomon's dedication of the temple as requiring 120,000 sheep and 22,000 cattle), his own unique listing here for Josiah pales into relative insignificance.

While the flocks of sheep and goats provided for the paschal lambs, the cattle must have served for peace offerings, for feasting throughout the days of Unleavened Bread that followed the Passover (cf. on v.17, on 30:24, and on 1 Chron 29:21).

12–14 Ezra's statement that "they set aside the burnt offerings" (v.12) suggests that the Levites saved certain choice parts of the Passover lambs "to offer to the LORD" (cf. v.14), somewhat after the pattern of the peace offerings (Lev 3). Then the people roasted and ate the Passover itself (v.13, as in Deut 16:7).

16–19 Concerning "the Feast of Unleavened Bread" (v.17), see the comment to 30:13. To the time span of v.18, that "the Passover had not been observed like this . . . since the days of . . . Samuel," 2 Kings 23:22 adds what could be an even longer interval, "since the days of the judges." The point is that Josiah's feast came up to the Bible's ceremonial standards as no others had since those in the era of Moses and Joshua.

20 The phrase "After all this" introduces Ezra's final Josianic topic: the king's death. It is to be dated to the year 609 B.C. (W.F. Albright, BASOR 153 [1956]: 31–32). The cause lay in a military advance by "Neco King of Egypt," a leading Pharaoh of the Twenty-Sixth Dynasty, as he made an active bid to succeed to the rule of the Assyrian Empire in the west. Nineveh had fallen three years before, in 612; and the Egyptians opposed the rival claims of Babylon by going up the Euphrates River "on behalf of" (*ʿal*; cf. NIV), not "against" (KJV), the king of Assyria (2 Kings 23:29). Neco's immediate objective was to cross the river and retake the city of Haran (Wiseman, *Chaldean Kings*, p. 19). This town lay east of Carchemish, which constituted in its turn a key center on the westernmost bend of the Euphrates.

21 The Pharaoh addressed Josiah: "It is not you I am attacking"; for Neco desired, without further delay, to march along the Palestinian coast and so meet "the house with which I am at war," namely the Babylonian army under the capable crown-prince Nebuchadrezzar. His words for persuading Josiah, that "God has told me to hurry," would have had a special appeal for a godly king concerned about keeping God's word.

22 Josiah, like King Ahab at Ramoth Gilead, then "disguised himself" for protection against his fate (cf. on 18:29). For though this next truth might have come as a surprise to the king, "what Neco had said" actually had come "at God's command." The Lord's consistent message to his people had been that they must rely on him and, correspondingly, keep themselves from involvement in the international power politics of their day (cf. the comments on 16:2, 9; 28:16; 32:1, 5).

The reality of the contest at "Megiddo" has received archaeological confirmation from the ruins of the site's Stratum II. This level belonged to an unwalled town during the time of Josiah, and it evidences a measure of contemporaneous destruction (H.F. Vos, *Archaeology in Bible Lands* [Chicago: Moody, 1977], p. 192). Megiddo lies on the strategic pass through the ridge that separates Palestine's coastal plain from the Esdraelon Valley to its northeast. It has been the scene of key battles from the fifteenth century B.C. down to World War I. The conflict of the ages, against Christ at his second coming, will be joined at Armageddon (Rev 16:16), "the mountain of Megiddo."

25 "Jeremiah composed laments for Josiah," whom he highly esteemed (Jer 22:15–16). These dirges are then said to be "written in the Laments"—a book that is no longer extant and which is not to be confused with the prophet's later laments over Josiah's sons (22:10, 20–30) or over Jerusalem's fall (Lam).

Notes

25 As indicated by the NIV margin, the rendering that says that Judah had provoked God "by all that their hands have made," i.e., by idols, need not carry this exact connotation in the Hebrew, which reads literally, "by all the doings of their hands." It could mean simply, with the margin, "by everything they have done."

35:20 On the correctness of the Chronicler's portrayal of the death of Josiah, see M.B. Rowton, "Jeremiah and the Death of Josiah," JNES 10 (1951): 128–30, and Wiseman, "Chaldean Kings," pp. 18–20.

26 On Josiah's "works of devotion," see the note to 32:32.

17. *Jehoahaz*

36:1–4

¹And the people of the land took Jehoahaz son of Josiah and made him king in Jerusalem in place of his father.
²Jehoahaz was twenty-three years old when he became king, and he reigned in Jerusalem three months. ³The king of Egypt dethroned him in Jerusalem and

imposed on Judah a levy of a hundred talents of silver and a talent of gold. ⁴The king of Egypt made Eliakim, a brother of Jehoahaz, king over Judah and Jerusalem and changed Eliakim's name to Jehoiakim. But Neco took Eliakim's brother Jehoahaz and carried him off to Egypt.

The reign of the godly king Josiah's son Jehoahaz lasted only three months in the year 609 (v.2), following the death of his father in battle (35:24). But while the Chronicler includes no direct moral evaluation of Jehoahaz, the fuller account in 2 Kings (23:30–35), which served as Ezra's source, makes it clear that the young sovereign "did evil in the eyes of the LORD" (v.32). He, in fact, established a pattern of wrong doing that characterizes all the rest of the monarchs who make up the subject of the three concluding sections (vv.18–20; 2 Chron 36:5–16) in this major portion of 2 Chronicles (12:1–36:16), which concerns itself with the reigns of the twenty rulers of the southern kingdom of Judah. As a mark of divine justice, it was then the removal of Jehoahaz that marked the end of independent government in Israel.

1–2 At his accession in 609, Judah's new leader, Jehoahaz, "was twenty-three years old" (v.2), which made him two years younger than King Jehoiakim who succeeded him (v.5). The "people of the land" (v.1)—its free citizens (cf. on 23:13)—apparently saw more hope in Jehoahaz than in his older brother (1 Chron 3:15 comment). His "three month" reign continued only till Pharaoh Neco (II) of Egypt could find opportunity to replace him (cf. on 2 Chron 35:20–21).

3 Neco also "imposed on Judah" an indemnity of silver and gold (cf. similar amounts listed in 25:6 comment, 27:5 comment), amounting to about three and three-fourths tons and seventy-five pounds respectively (NIV mg.).

4 The Egyptian changed the name of Jehoahaz's brother from "Eliakim," meaning "God raises up," to "Jehoiakim," which means "Jehovah (Yahweh) raises up." This seems to indicate his willingness to continue the status of the Yahwistic religion of the Jews. More tangibly the Pharaoh's control over the king's name demonstrated Neco's lordship over his person (cf. on 6:6); indeed it would be four and a half centuries before the Jews should again be able to exercise political freedom, under the Maccabees. Neco then carried Jehoahaz off to Egypt, where he died (2 Kings 23:34; cf. Jer 22:10).

18. Jehoiakim

36:5–8

⁵Jehoiakim was twenty-five years old when he became king, and he reigned in Jerusalem eleven years. He did evil in the eyes of the LORD his God. ⁶Nebuchadnezzar king of Babylon attacked him and bound him with bronze shackles to take him to Babylon. ⁷Nebuchadnezzar also took to Babylon articles from the temple of the LORD and put them in his temple there.

⁸The other events of Jehoiakim's reign, the detestable things he did and all that was found against him, are written in the book of the kings of Israel and Judah. And Jehoiachin his son succeeded him as king.

The Chronicler's record about the kingship of Jehoahaz's older brother Jehoiakim (vv.5–8) again represents an abridgment of the previously written biblical history (in

2 Kings 23:36–24:7). On this occasion Ezra does include a moral judgment against Judah's new ruler (cf. on v.5); and in the political sphere his reign (609–598 B.C.) marked the transference of the Hebrew kingdom from Egyptian control to its ultimately fatal Babylonian domination.

5 During his "eleven years" Jehoiakim "did evil." As explained in Ezra's more detailed sources, this monarch first taxed his land to provide tribute to the Pharaoh (2 Kings 23:35)—though he himself lived in luxury (Jer 22:14–15). He perverted justice and oppressed the poor (Jer 22:13, 17); and he persecuted the prophets that God sent to reprove his sin (cf. 2 Chron 36:8, 16; Jer 26:21–24; 32:36).

6 After four years the Babylonian leader "Nebuchadnezzar" (whose name is more frequently and more accurately rendered as Nebuchadrezzar, Jer 21:2 mg.) "attacked" westward. In the spring of 605, he and his forces won a decisive victory over Neco at Carchemish (cf. on 35:20; Jer 46:2). As a consequence the Egyptians were driven back to their own borders; and the whole western Fertile Crescent, including Palestine, was given into the hands of Nebuchadnezzar (2 Kings 24:7). The victor proceeded to bind Jehoiakim "with bronze shackles" to carry him into captivity; such a threat may, however, have been sufficiently effective to render unnecessary his actual removal to Babylon.

7 The fact that "Nebuchadnezzar took to Babylon articles from the temple," together with an initial captivity of selected Jewish hostages, including the prophet Daniel (cf. Dan 1:1–3), marks the beginning of Israel's seventy-year Babylonian exile, 605–536 B.C. (Jer 29:10).

The historicity of Nebuchadnezzar's advance against Palestine in 605 and of this first stage of the Hebrew deportations was once widely questioned by scholars who were committed to the historical-critical method—it was recorded, after all, only in the highly suspected books of Chronicles and Daniel! Yet their authenticity was strikingly confirmed by D.J. Wiseman's publication in 1956 of two new tablets out of the Babylonian chronicles. In these Nebuchadnezzar states that in the summer of 605 he conquered "the whole land of Hatti," meaning the western Fertile Crescent, including Palestine, and "took heavy tribute of Hatti to Babylon" (cf. J.B. Payne, "The Uneasy Conscience of Modern Liberal Exegesis," BETS 1.1 [1958]: 14–18).

8 While Ezra refers only to his primary source, to Israel's major court record, for "the other events of Jehoiakim's reign," it is known that these events included three years of serving Nebuchadnezzar (until 602), which were followed by a rebellion (2 Kings 24:1–2). This presumably occurred in connection with a renewed rivalry between Egypt and Babylon, who fought a battle in the following year that resulted in a draw. Jehoiakim died on 9 December 598 (Thiele, *Numbers*, p. 168), just before his punishment could be meted out.

19. *Jehoiachin*

36:9–10

9Jehoiachin was eighteen years old when he became king, and he reigned in Jerusalem three months and ten days. He did evil in the eyes of the LORD. 10In the spring, King Nebuchadnezzar sent for him and brought him to Babylon, together with articles of value from the temple of the LORD, and he made Jehoiachin's uncle, Zedekiah, king over Judah and Jerusalem.

In these two verses the Chronicler summarizes the more extensive data about the reign of Jehoiakim's young son, Jehoiachin, which was found in his canonical source-document of 2 Kings (24:8–17). Like his uncle Jehoahaz of eleven years before (see 2 Chron 36:1–4), the current world power permitted Jehoiachin a kingship of but three months, at the close of 598 and at the beginning of 597 B.C. He thus reaped the bitter fruit of his father's rebellion (v.8 comment).

9 Since Jehoiachin had at least five children by the year 592 (cf. on 1 Chron 3:17), the variant reading (cf. NIV mg.) must be adopted, which says he "was eighteen years old when he became king"—and not "eight" (see Appendix A). His reign of "three months and ten days," by Hebrew counting, terminated on 16 March 597 (cf. on v.8), as indicated by the evidence of the new Nebuchadnezzar texts (see on v.7).

10 On 22 April 597, King Nebuchadnezzar had Jehoiachin deported from Jerusalem; and he was "brought . . . to Babylon" along with a second and more extensive deportation (see on v.7). This included the prophet Ezekiel and ten thousand of the leaders and skilled workers that made up the backbone of Jewish society (cf. 2 Kings 24:10–16).

20. Zedekiah

36:11–16

> **11**Zedekiah was twenty-one years old when he became king, and he reigned in Jerusalem eleven years. **12**He did evil in the eyes of the LORD his God and did not humble himself before Jeremiah the prophet, who spoke the word of the LORD. **13**He also rebelled against King Nebuchadnezzar, who had made him take an oath in God's name. He became stiff-necked and hardened his heart and would not turn to the LORD, the God of Israel. **14**Furthermore, all the leaders of the priests and the people became more and more unfaithful, following all the detestable practices of the nations and defiling the temple of the LORD, which he had consecrated in Jerusalem.
>
> **15**The LORD, the God of their fathers, sent word to them through his messengers again and again, because he had pity on his people and on his dwelling place. **16**But they mocked God's messengers, despised his words and scoffed at his prophets until the wrath of the LORD was aroused against his people and there was no remedy.

"Jehoiachin's uncle, Zedekiah" (v.10) was appointed to rule over the remnant of Judah by King Nebuchadnezzar of Babylon. As the last of the twenty monarchs of the southern kingdom, his eleven-year reign extended from 597 to 586 B.C. Through acts of infidelity toward his imperial master, he unwisely touched off the final revolt that brought down the vengeance of the Babylonians on Judah and Jerusalem; and thus both the state and the city were destroyed (vv.11–16). Yet ultimately Nebuchadnezzar served only as an instrument for accomplishing the sentence of God against his guilty nation: "The wrath of the LORD was aroused against his people and there was no remedy" (v.16).

As in the case of the three preceding reigns, the opening portion of this section represents a condensation of the parallel source materials that were available to Ezra from earlier Scriptures (2 Kings 24:18–19, with Jer 52:1–2). Yet v.13 and onwards presents a theological expansion of the explanation for Judah's fall that appears in 2 Kings 24:20; Jeremiah 52:3.

11 Being only "twenty-one" at the time of his appointment, Zedekiah was by far the youngest of Josiah's sons to occupy the throne (cf. on 1 Chron 3:15). Furthermore, though "he reigned in Jerusalem," the fact that seals have been discovered with the inscription "Eliakim steward of Yaukin" indicates that, at the least, his nephew Jehoiachin continued to wield influence as a recognized possessor, even if an absentee one, of royal property and, at the most, that Zedekiah may have ruled to some extent as a regent for his exiled predecessor.

12 The statement that Zedekiah "did not humble himself before Jeremiah" sums up a complex relationship that existed between the king and the prophet, as this developed historically. Zedekiah first disregarded Jeremiah's messages (Jer 34:1–10); he came in time to direct his inquiries to this same prophet (Jer 21); and he finally pled with him for help (Jer 37). But at no point did he sincerely submit to the requirements of the Lord that Jeremiah transmitted to him. Zedekiah was a weak man, largely controlled by a few vicious nobles that had been left to him, along with the inferior remnant of Judah (Jer 38:1–5; cf. the introductory discussion to v.11 above).

13 At the instigation of Hophra, a new Pharaoh (589–570 B.C.) of the Twenty-Sixth Dynasty in Egypt (cf. Jer 37:5; Ezek 17:15), "he rebelled against King Nebuchadnezzar, who had made him take an oath in God's name." Zedekiah, that is, had been bound as a vassal to the Babylonian monarch; and it was his faithlessness that became his own undoing (Ezek 17:13–19).

C. *The exile*

36:17–23

> [17]He brought up against them the king of the Babylonians, who killed their young men with the sword in the sanctuary, and spared neither young man nor young woman, old man or aged. God handed all of them over to Nebuchadnezzar. [18]He carried to Babylon all the articles from the temple of God, both large and small, and the treasures of the LORD's temple and the treasures of the king and his officials. [19]They set fire to God's temple and broke down the wall of Jerusalem; they burned all the palaces and destroyed everything of value there.
> [20]He carried into exile to Babylon the remnant, who escaped from the sword, and they became servants to him and his sons until the kingdom of Persia came to power. [21]The land enjoyed its sabbath rests; all the time of its desolation it rested, until the seventy years were completed in fulfillment of the word of the LORD spoken by Jeremiah.
> [22]In the first year of Cyrus king of Persia, in order to fulfill the word of the LORD spoken by Jeremiah, the LORD moved the heart of Cyrus king of Persia to make a proclamation throughout his realm and to put it in writing:
> [23]"This is what Cyrus king of Persia says:
> " 'The LORD, the God of heaven, has given me all the kingdoms of the earth and he has appointed me to build a temple for him at Jerusalem in Judah. Anyone of his people among you—may the LORD his God be with him, and let him go up.' "

Unlike the Book of Kings, with its central message of stern moral judgments (cf. the introductory discussion to ch. 12), Chronicles exists essentially as a book of hope, grounded on the grace of our sovereign Lord. The chapters on Judah's rulers (12:1–36:16) describe some great military victories and reforms, which sprang out of men's faith in God, even in the midst of the nation's overall spiritual deterioration. Then after having demonstrated that the Lord could, and did, reject his people for their disobedience (36:17–21), the Chronicler moves on to identify the groundwork by which Judah's postexilic restoration was effectuated, through the Persian king Cyrus's decree of 538 B.C. (vv.22–23). Thus in a repopulated land with a rebuilt temple—that still depicted God's changeless way of salvation—a nation refined by its trials could more adequately celebrate the Lord's continuing providence together with his anticipated triumph in the messianic kingdom that yet must come into being. History is a process, not of disintegration, but of sifting, of selection, and of development. When decades of exile have removed the dross, a remnant of purer gold (cf. the introductory discussion to ch. 10) will respond to the appeal for return to the Holy Land: "The LORD his God be with him . . . let him go up" (2 Chron 36:23).

17 On 15 January 588, the Lord "brought up" against Judah "the king of the Babylonians"; and on 28 July 586, the Hebrew capital at Jerusalem fell (Thiele *Numbers,* p. 169). For greater detail on the city's capture and pillage, see 2 Kings 25:1–21 and Jeremiah 39:1–10; 52:4–27. The 586 destruction of Judah is also the subject of the biblical prediction that involves more verses than any other direct prophecy that is to be found within Scripture—608, distributed among seventeen different books of the Bible (Payne, *Prophecy,* pp. 641–82).

18 "The articles from the temple" were "carried to Babylon," and on 14 August the sanctuary itself was burned (v. 19).

20 In describing "the remnant, who escaped from the sword," Ezra omitted, as less relevant to the restored, postexilic community, discussion about the regathering of refugees under Gedaliah and the flight of their remnant to Egypt (2 Kings 25:22–26; Jer 40–44), about the small fourth deportation of 582 B.C. (Jer 52:30), and about "the poorest people of the land" that were left scattered in Palestine (2 Kings 25:12). He speaks rather of those "carried into exile" in the third and great deportation, of 586 (cf. the comments on vv.7, 10). Correspondingly archaeology has demonstrated the thorough depopulation of Judah at this time.

Thus the exiles came "to Babylon" where "they became servants"; and yet, after an initial period of discouragement (Ps 137) and oppressive service (cf. Isa 14:2–3), at least some Jews gained favor and status (2 Kings 25:27–30; Dan 1:19; 2:49; 6:3). Those who were among the more worldly grew indifferent and drifted away from their faith (Ezek 33:31–32), but the more godly increased in their spiritual maturity (cf. Neh 1:4; Esth 4:14–16; Dan 1:8).

21 The statement that for "seventy years . . . in fulfillment of the word of the LORD spoken by Jeremiah" (cf. on v.7) "the land enjoyed its sabbath rests" seems to correlate the full span of the Exile with an equivalent number of sabbatical years (Lev 25:1–7; 26:34). This produces a total figure of 70 times 7 or 490 years; and the idea is that of making up for half a millennium of neglected sabbatical rests (G.F. Oehler, *Theology of the Older Testament* [Grand Rapids: Zondervan, n.d.], p. 34).

22 In October 539 Babylon fell to "Cyrus king of Persia," as he overthrew Nabonidus and his son Belshazzar, who were its last native rulers (Dan 5). Cyrus's policy of cooperating with local religions and of encouraging the return of exiles has received explicit archaeological confirmation from the inscriptions of the king himself (cf. esp. the famous "Cyrus Cylinder," ANET, p. 315).

On the correspondence of vv.22-23 with Ezra 1:1-3a, see the Introduction: Date and Authorship, last section.

23 Words such as the following, which were authorized by Cyrus: "The LORD [Yahweh], the God of heaven, has given me all kingdoms," should be recognized, from the viewpoint of Scripture, as constituting inspired truth, though from the viewpoint of contemporary Persian government they would probably have been understood more as diplomatic language (cf. on 35:21). Cyrus could thus address a Babylonian audience, saying, "Marduk, king of the gods [confessedly, the leading deity of the pantheon of Babylon, but not of Persia!] . . . designated me to rule over all the lands" (Cyrus Cylinder; cf. comment on v.22). But this monarch was still God's instrument for the providential restoration of Israel (Isa 44:28-45:5).

Appendix A

Numbers in Chronicles That Disagree
With Their Old Testament Parallels

	Higher	Lower		Parallel Passage	Evaluation of Chronicles
a)		1 Chron 11:11	300 slain by Jashobeam, not 800	2 Sam 23:8	Scribal error
b)	18:4		Hadadezer's 1,000 chariots and 7,000 horsemen, not 1,000 and 700 horsemen	8:4	Correct
c)	19:18a		7,000 Syrian charioteers slain, not 700	10:18a	Correct
d)		19:18b	and 40,000 foot soldiers, not horsemen	10:18b	Correct
e)	21:5a		Israel's 1,100,000 troops, not 800,000	24:9a	Different objects
f)		21:5b	Judah's 470,000 troops, not 500,000	24:9b	More precise
g)		21:12	Three years of famine, not seven	24:13	Correct
h)	21:25		Ornan paid 600 gold shekels, not 50 silver	24:24	Different objects
i)	2 Chron 2:		3,600 to supervise the temple contruction, not 3,300	1 Kings 5:16	Different method of reckoning
j)	2, 18				
k)	2:10		20,000 baths of oil to Hiram's woodmen, not 20 kors (= 200 baths)	1 Kings 5:11	Different objects
l)	3:15		Temple pillars 35 cubits, not 18	7:15	Scribal error
m)	4:5		Sea holding 3,000 baths, not 2,000	7:26	Scribal error
n)		8:10	250 chief officers for building the temple, not 550	9:23	Different method of reckoning
o)	8:18		450 gold talents from Ophir, not 420	9:28	Correct or Scribal error
p)	9:16 (Chron is same)		300 gold bekas per shield, not 3 minas	10:17	Different method of reckoning
q)		9:25	4,000 stalls for horses, not 40,000	4:26	Correct
r)	22:2		Ahaziah king at 42 years, not 22	2 Kings 8:26	Scribal error
s)		36:9	Jehoiachin king at 8, not 18	2 Kings 24:8	Scribal error

10	1	7	times Chronicles is
higher	same	lower	than its parallels.

Total disagreements: 19
(j repeats i) out of 213 paralleled numbers

Numbers Over 1,000 Unique to Chronicles

Unnoteworthy	Interpretable	Explainable	Providential		The Total of the Numbers over 1,000
a)		I Chron 5:18		44,760 Transjordanian troops	1
b)		5:21		Plunder and slain of the Hagarites	4
c)	7:2–11,40			Tribal masters, 17,200 to 87,000	7
d) 9:13				1,760 priests in Jerusalem	1
e)	12:24–37			Troops making David king, 3,000–120,000	12
f)			22:14	David's gold and silver talents for the temple	2
g)		23:3–5		Distribution of 38,000 Levites	5
h) 26:30, 32				1,700 and 2,700 Levitical officials	2
i)	27:1–15			24,000 for each militia group	13
j)			29:4,7	Metal offered for the temple	7
k)		2 Chron 2:10		Barley and wine to Hiram's woodsmen.	2
l)		12:3		Shishak's chariots and 60,000 horsemen	2
m)	13:3, 17			Abijah (400,000) vs. Jeroboam (800,000)	3
n)	14:8–9			Asa (580,000) vs. Zerah (1,000,000)	3
o)		15:11		7,000 of Zerah's sheep sacrificed	1
p) 17:11				7,700 Arab sheep and goats to Jehoshaphat	2
q)	17:14–18			Jehoshaphat's troops, 200,000 to 300,000 each division	5
r)	25:5–6			Amaziah's troops, 300,000 + 100,000	2
s)		25:11–12		Edomites slain and executed 10,000 each	2
t) 25:13				3,000 of Judah slain by mercenaries	1
u)	26:12–13			Uzziah's troops, 307,500 + 2,600 leaders	2
v)		27:5		Ammonite grain tribute, 10,000 kors	2
w)	28:6, 8			120,000 slain, 200,000 captive of Judah	2
x) 29:33				3,000 sheep for Hezekiah's celebration	1
y)		30:24		His Passover: 1,000 bulls + 10,000 sheep	2
z)		35:7–9		Josiah's Passover animals 30,000 +	4
5	9	10	2		90

EZRA-NEHEMIAH

Edwin M. Yamauchi

EZRA-NEHEMIAH

Introduction

1. Background*

The Babylonian exile in the sixth century B.C. was preceded by earlier deportations beginning in the eighth century by the Assyrians from both Israel and Judah. Deportation began with Tiglath-pileser III, who attacked Damascus and Galilee in 732 (2 Kings 15:29), carrying off at least 13,520 people to Assyria (ANET, pp. 283–84). Then Shalmaneser V and Sargon II besieged Samaria in 722 (2 Kings 17:6; 18:10). Sargon boasted that he carried off 27,290 (or 27,280) persons from Israel, replacing them with various other peoples from Mesopotamia and Syria (ANET, pp. 284–87).

Individual Israelite names have been recorded in Assyrian texts, particularly from Nimrud.[1] A Hananu, the governor of Til-Barsip and the eponym holder in 701, may have been an Israelite.[2]

Whereas Israel's population in the late eighth century B.C. has been estimated at 500,000 to 700,000, Judah's population in the eighth-to-sixth centuries has been estimated at between 220,000 and 300,000.[3] Population estimates for cities are made

---

*See E.M. Yamauchi, "The Archaeological Background of Ezra," BS (July-Sept. 1980): 195–211; id., "The Archaeological Background of Nehemiah," BS (Oct.-Nov. 1980): 291–309.

[1]W.F. Albright, "An Ostracon from Calah and the North-Israelite Diaspora," BASOR 149 (1958): 33–36; M. Heltzer, "Eight Century B.C. Inscriptions From Kalakh (Nimrud)," PEQ 110 (1978): 3–9.

[2]H. Tadmor, "Assyria and the West," *Unity and Diversity,* edd. H. Goedicke and J. Roberts (Baltimore: Johns Hopkins University Press, 1975), p. 41.

[3]J.P. Weinberg, "Demographische Notizen zur Geschichte der nachexilischen Gemeinde in Juda," *Klio* 54 (1972): 45ff.

on the basis of 40 to 50 persons per dunam (1,000 square meters or 1,200 square yards). As there are 4 dunams per acre, this would be an estimate of 160 to 200 persons per acre. Broshi suggests that Jerusalem was swelled by refugees from the north when Samaria fell in 722 and expanded to 500 dunams or 25,000 persons. At the time of Nehemiah, the city had contracted to 120 dunams or 6,000 persons.[4]

Judah had escaped the attacks of Tiglath-pileser III when Azariah (Uzziah) paid tribute to the king (ANET, p. 282), though Gezer was captured. But when Sennacherib attacked Judah in 701 B.C., he deported numerous Jews, especially from Lachish. His annals claim that he deported 200,150 from Judah (ANET, p. 22), but this may be an error for 2,150.[5]

The biblical references to the numbers deported by the Babylonians under Nebuchadnezzar are incomplete and somewhat confusing, giving rise to conflicting interpretations as to the actual number of Judeans deported. Until 1956 we had no extrabiblical evidence to confirm the attack on Judah in Nebuchadnezzar's first year.[6] Either in that year or soon after, Daniel and his companions were carried off to Babylon.[7]

In 597 Nebuchadnezzar carried off "all the officers and fighting men, and all the craftsmen and artisans—a total of ten thousand" (2 Kings 24:14). According to v.16, "the king of Babylon also deported to Babylon the entire force of seven thousand fighting men, . . . and a thousand craftsmen and artisans." If these figures represent only the heads of households, the total may have been closer to thirty thousand.[8]

On the other hand, Jeremiah enumerates for 597 but 3,023 captives (Jer 52:28) and for 586 only 832 captives from Jerusalem (v.29). In 582, after the murder of Gedaliah, 745 were deported, for a grand total of 4,600 (v.30). The smaller figures of Jeremiah probably represent only men of the most important families.

Albright accepted only the figures of Jeremiah and explained the discrepancy with the larger figures as due to losses suffered in the course of the trek.[9] He furthermore estimated the total population of Judah when the exiles returned at only 20,000 to 50,000. Such a radically minimalist view makes it impossible to accept the large number of returnees listed in Ezra 2–Nehemiah 7.

Other scholars assume that the numbers mentioned in 2 Kings and in Jeremiah are to be added, giving a total of about 15,000 deportees.[10] Kreissig estimates a total of 15,600 deportees.[11] Weinberg estimates that 10 percent of the population, or about 20,000, may have been deported.[12]

Impressed by the descriptions of widespread devastation found in 2 Kings 25:11;

---

[4]M. Broshi, "The Expansion of Jerusalem in the Reigns of Hezekiah and Manasseh," IEJ 24 (1974): 21 –26.

[5]A. Ungnad, "Die Zahl der von Sanherib deportierten Judäer," ZAW 59 (1942–43): 199–202.

[6]See D.J. Wiseman, Chronicles of Chaldaean Kings (London: British Museum, 1956).

[7]D.J. Wiseman et al., Notes on Some Problems in the Book of Daniel (London: Tyndale, 1956), pp. 16 –18.

[8]A. Malamat, "The Last Wars of the Kingdom of Judah," JNES 9 (1950): 223.

[9]W.F. Albright, The Biblical Period From Abraham to Ezra (New York: Harper & Row, 1963), p. 85.

[10]C.F. Whitley, The Exilic Age (Philadelphia: Westminster, 1957), p. 66.

[11]H. Kreissig, Die sozialökonomische Situation in Juda zur Achämenidenzeit (Berlin: Akademie Verlag, 1973), p. 22.

[12]Weinberg, "Demographische Notizen," p. 47; cf. Galling, Studien zur Geschichte Israels, pp. 51–52.

2 Chronicles 36:20; and Jeremiah 39:9–10, earlier scholars had proposed very high figures by multiplying the numbers in Jeremiah and 2 Kings by a factor as high as five to account for family members. Such scholars as R. Kittel, E. Meyer, E. Sellin, and G.A. Smith calculated as many as 40,000 to 70,000 deportees, or up to one-third of the population of Judah. A factor overlooked by most scholars is that no explicit figures are given for the deportation(s) before 597.

Depending on one's estimate of the numbers deported and the number of returning exiles, we have widely varying estimates for the population of postexilic Judah: 20,000 to 50,000 by W.F. Albright, 60,000 by H. Kreissig, 50,000 to 80,000 by J. de Fraine, 85,000 by R. Kittel, 100,000 by S. Mowinckel, 150,000 by J. Weinberg, and 235,000 by A. Schultz. An estimate of 150,000 is more probably correct than Albright's estimate.

An important difference between the deportations by the Babylonians and by the Assyrians is that the Babylonians did not replace the deportees with pagan newcomers. Thus Judah, though devastated, was not contaminated with polytheism to the same degree as was Israel (cf. McKay).

According to the biblical record, the Babylonian armies smashed Jerusalem's defenses (2 Kings 25:10), destroyed the temple and palaces (2 Kings 25:9, 13–17; Jer 52:13, 17–23), and devastated the countryside (Jer 32:43), killing many of the leaders and priests (2 Kings 25:18–21).

Though these biblical statements have been denied by skeptics such as C.C. Torrey, the severity of the Babylonian devastation has been amply confirmed by archaeology. Saul Weinberg concludes:

> A rapid review of the archaeological evidence from Judah of the sixth century B.C.E. thus gives a picture wholly in keeping with the literary evidence: thorough destruction of all fortified towns and cities by Nebuchadnezzar's forces in 586, a great decrease in population due to slaughter, deportation, collapse of the economy, which continued, but at a very low ebb, through the efforts of those who remained behind and those who slowly drifted back, so rudimentary must this existence have been that it has proved extremely difficult to pick up its traces in material remains.[13]

Evidences of the Babylonian attacks have been uncovered at Arad, Beth-Shemesh, Beth-Zur, Eglon, En Gedi, Gibeah, Jerusalem, Ramat Rahel, and Tell Beit-Mirsim. Thousands must have died in battle or of starvation (Lam 2:11–22; 4:9–10). After the deportations only the poor of the land—the vine-growers and farmers—were left (2 Kings 25:12; Jer 39:10; 40:7; 52:16). They occupied the vacant lands (Jer 6:12; see comment on Ezra 4:4). A few refugees who fled to different areas drifted back (Jer 40:11–12). For the next fifty years those left behind eked out a precarious existence under the Babylonian yoke (Lam 5:2–5), subjected to ill treatment and forced labor (vv.11–13).

The archaeological picture of this period has yet to be clarified by excavations, but the Israeli surveys of Judah of 1967–68 noted hundreds of new sites that date from this era. According to S. Weinberg:

---

[13]*Post-Exilic Palestine: An Archaeological Report* (Jerusalem: Israel Academy of Sciences and Humanities, 1969), pp. 6–7.

Most of these are villages or small towns, largely nameless and therefore not the kind of site that has hitherto attracted the archaeologists interested in biblical places. Yet a number of these have yielded material from the sixth century, and it now seems clear that it was in such places that most of the remaining inhabitants of Judah lived after the most important centers were destroyed by the Babylonians.[14]

During this time some limited forms of worship were continued in the ruined area of the temple (Jer 41:5). The Scriptures themselves pass over developments in Palestine and stress the contribution of the returning exiles from Babylonia. Some scholars question this emphasis. M. Noth, for example, comments that though "very important developments in life and thought took place among those deported to Babylon, . . . nevertheless even the Babylonian group represented a mere outpost, whereas Palestine was and remained the central arena of Israel's history."[15]

In light of the fact that the intellectual and spiritual leaders were the ones who were deported, the Scriptures must reflect the historical situation. As Gowan comments, "There does not exist sufficient evidence or probability of an active, creative group in the land during the exile, although the continuance of some form of Yahwism is not to be doubted."[16]

Most of those deported were from the upper classes and from cities. Judging from earlier Assyrian reliefs and texts, the men were probably marched in chains, with women and children bearing sacks of their bare possessions on wagons as they made their way to Mesopotamia. The exiled Judean king, Jehoiachin, was maintained at the Babylonian court and provided with rations (2 Kings 25:29–30), as a text from Babylonia explicitly confirms (ANET, p. 308).

After some years of initial hardship, the exiles made adjustments and even prospered (Jer 29:4–5). They were settled in various communities, for example, on the river Kebar near Nippur, sixty miles southeast of Babylon (Ezek 1:1–3; cf. Ezra 2:59 –Neh 7:61). When the exiles returned they brought with them numerous servants and animals and were able to make contributions for the sacred services (Ezra 2:65 –69; 8:26; Neh 7:67–72).

A fascinating light on the Jews in Mesopotamia is shed by the Murashu tablets. In 1893, 730 inscribed clay tablets were found at Nippur. W.R. Hilprecht and A.T. Clay published 480 of these texts in 1898. Additional texts were made available in 1974 by Stolper.[17] The archive dates from the reigns of Artaxerxes I (464–424) and Darius II (423–404).

Murashu and sons were wealthy bankers and brokers who loaned out almost anything for a price. Among their customers are listed about sixty Jewish names from the time of Artaxerxes I and forty from the time of Darius II. These appear as contracting parties, agents, witnesses, collectors of taxes, and royal officials. There seems to have been no social or commercial barriers between the Jews and the Babylonians. Their prosperous situation may explain why some chose to remain in Mesopotamia.[18]

---

[14]Ibid., p. 7.

[15]*The History of Israel*, rev. ed. (New York: Harper & Row, 1960), p. 296.

[16]D.E. Gowan, *Bridge Between the Testaments* (Pittsburgh: Pickwick, 1967), p. 37.

[17]M.W. Stolper, "Achaemenid Babylonia," Ph.D. diss., University of Michigan, 1974.

[18]M.D. Coogan, "Life in the Diaspora: Jews at Nippur in the Fifth Century B.C.," BA 37 (1974): 6–12.

With the birth of a second and a third generation, many Jews established roots in Mesopotamia. Josephus (Antiq. XI, 8 [i.3]) declared that "many remained in Babylon, being unwilling to leave their possessions." In like manner, during World War II Japanese immigrants and their American-born children were deported from the West Coast and placed in relocation camps. Given the opportunity to return to Japan after the war, few of the older Japanese did because of the superior conditions of their new home.

The spiritual life of the Jewish community in Mesopotamia is documented by Ezekiel, who was in exile either after 597 or 586. Ezekiel 8:1 refers to the prophet "sitting in my house and the elders of Judah were sitting before me" (cf. Ezek 3:15; 14:1; 20:1; 24:18; 33:30–33). Deprived of the temple, the exiles laid great stress on the observation of the Sabbath, on the laws of purity, and on prayer and fasting. It has often been suggested that the development of synagogues began in Mesopotamia during the Exile (but see comments on Neh 8:18).

The trials of the Exile purified and strengthened the faith of the Jews and cured them of idolatry. As Baron comments (p. 105): "The external grandeur of the 55 temples (of Babylon) devoted to the worship of the great gods . . . doubtless infused many a Judean onlooker with a sense of inferiority and shame. None the less, Jewish survival owes itself, paradoxically enough, not to those who remained at home but to the nationalistic vitality of those living so precariously in Exile."

The exiles who chose to return to Judah found their territory much diminished. According to Avi-Yonah (*Holy Land*, p. 19): "Its extent from north to south was about 25 miles, from east to west about 32 miles. The total area was about 800 square miles, of which about one third was an uncultivable desert."

The tiny enclave of Judah was surrounded by antagonistic neighbors. North of Bethel was the province of Samaria. South of Beth-Zur, Judean territory had been overrun by Idumaeans (cf. comments on Ezra 2:22–35). The eastern boundary followed the Jordan River, and the western boundary the Shephelah (low hills). The Philistine coast had been apportioned to Phoenician settlers.

The Persians did make Judah an autonomous province with the right to mint its own coins (see note on Neh 5:15). The archaeological evidence of coins and jar handles with YHD (for Yehud—Judah) comes from Jerusalem, Jericho, Gezer, Tell en-Nasbeh—all sites within the area demarcated as Jewish territory by Ezra-Nehemiah.

2. Reign of Artaxerxes I

Nehemiah served as the royal cupbearer of Artaxerxes I (Neh 1:1; 2:1), the Achaemenid king who ruled from 464 to 424, as an Elephantine papyrus (Cowley 30), dated to 407 B.C., mentions the sons of Sanballat, the governor of Samaria and adversary of Nehemiah (see ANET, p. 492). Though whether Ezra came in the seventh year (Ezra 7:7) of Artaxerxes I or of Artaxerxes II (403–359) is controversial, the traditional view places Ezra before Nehemiah in the reign of Artaxerxes I (cf. below, The Order).

Artaxerxes I was nicknamed Longimanus. According to Plutarch (*Artaxerxes* 1.1): "The first Artaxerxes, among all the kings of Persia the most remarkable for a gentle and noble spirit, was surnamed the Long-handed, his right hand being longer than his left, and was the son of Xerxes."

Longimanus was the third son of Xerxes and Amestris. His older brothers were named Darius and Hystaspes. Their father was assassinated in his bedchamber, between August and December 465, by Artabanus, a powerful courtier. In the ensuing months Artaxerxes, who was but eighteen years old, managed to kill Artabanus and his brother Darius. Then Artaxerxes defeated his brother Hystaspes in Bactria. His first regnal year is reckoned from 13 April 464 B.C.[19]

From 461 Artaxerxes lived at Susa (Yamauchi, "Achaemenid Capitals," pp. 5ff.). He used the palace of Darius I till it burned down near the end of his reign. He then moved to Persepolis, where he lived in the former palace of Darius I. He completed the Great Throne Hall begun by Xerxes, as a text in Old Persian and Akkadian indicates (Kent, no. A¹ Pa, pp. 113, 115). The only other extant Old Persian inscription of this king is an identical one-line text found on four silver dishes.

When Artaxerxes I came to the throne, he was faced with a major revolt in Egypt that was to last a decade. This rebellion was led by Inarus, a Libyan, and Amyrtaeus of Sais. They defeated the Persian satrap Achaemenes, the brother of Xerxes, and gained control of much of the Delta region by 462.

The Athenians, who had been at war with the Persians since the latter had invaded Greece in 490, sent two hundred triremes to aid the rebels (*Thucydides* 1.104). In 459 they helped capture Memphis, the capital of Lower Egypt. This was the situation that may have led the Persians to support Ezra's return in 458 to secure a loyal buffer state in Palestine.

In 456 Megabyzus, the satrap of Syria, advanced against Egypt with a huge fleet and army (*Diodorus Siculus* 11.77.1–5). During eighteen months he was able to suppress the revolt, capturing Inarus in 456. A fleet of forty Athenian ships with six thousand men sailed into a Persian trap. In spite of promises made by Megabyzus, Inarus was impaled in 454 at the instigation of Amestris, the mother of Artaxerxes I. Angered at this betrayal, Megabyzus revolted against the king from 449 to 446. If the events of Ezra 4:7–23 took place in this period, Artaxerxes I would have been suspicious of the building activities in Jerusalem. How then could the same king have commissioned Nehemiah to rebuild the walls of the city in 445? By then both the Egyptian revolt and the rebellion of Megabyzus had been resolved.

Artaxerxes I ended his long forty-year reign by dying from natural causes in the winter of 424 B.C.—a rarity in view of the frequent assassinations of Persian kings. He was buried in one of the four tombs, probably the second from the left, at Naqsh-i-Rustam, north of Persepolis.[20]

3. Chronology

Ezra 1:1 says that Cyrus issued a proclamation to the Jews in his first year. As Cyrus entered Babylon on 29 October 539 B.C., this was counted as his accession year. Babylonian and Persian scribes hold that his first regnal year over the Babylonians began on New Year's Day, 1 Nisan (24 Mar.) 538.

---

[19]J. Neuffer, "The Accession of Artaxerxes I," *Andrews University Seminary Studies* 6 (1968): 81.

[20]For the reign of Artaxerxes I, see Bengston, pp. 94ff., 340ff.; Myers, *Restoration*, pp. 103ff.; A.T. Olmstead, *History of Palestine and Syria to the Macedonian Conquest* (New York: Charles Scribners Sons, 1931), pp. 587ff.; id., *Persian Empire*, pp. 237ff.

The Jews used both a religious and a civil calendar. The former began the year with Nisan (Mar./Apr.). Many scholars assume that the calendar of Judah was identical with the Babylonian calendar, which also began in the spring.

Nehemiah 1:1 declares that Nehemiah was in Susa in the month of Kislev in the twentieth year of Artaxerxes I. According to a Nisan calendar, this regnal year ran from 13 April 445 to 2 April 444; Kislev would be the ninth month from 5 December 445 to 3 January 444. But Nehemiah 2:1 mentions a mission to Jerusalem in the month of Nisan in the twentieth year. Scholars who assume a Nisan-to-Nisan calendar assume a scribal error here because in such a spring-to-spring year Nisan precedes rather than follows Kislev. As Nehemiah 5:14 sets Nehemiah's tenure as governor from the king's twentieth to his thirty-second year, many scholars propose that Nehemiah 1:1 must have originally read the nineteenth year—*t⁼ša⁾ ⁼eśrēh* ("nineteen") instead of *⁼eśrîm* ("twenty").[21] Brockington (p. 127), however, believes that Nehemiah 2:1 should read the "twenty-first" year.

The Israelite civil year began with the seventh month, Tishri, in the fall. Some scholars conclude from Nehemiah 1 and 2 that the Israelites in the postexilic period reverted to a fall-to-fall calendar,[22] wherein the twentieth year of Artaxerxes I would have run from 7 October 445 to 25 September 444.[23] No emendation would then be needed.

4. Canon

The books now called Ezra and Nehemiah were known under the single title of Ezra in the earliest Hebrew MSS from the tenth century till the fifteenth century. The Masoretic scribes treated the works as one. The separation into two books appeared in a Hebrew MS dated 1448 and then in the printed Bomberg edition of 1525. Josephus (*Contra Apion* I, 40 [8]) and the Talmud (*Baba Bathra* 15a) also refer to the Book of Ezra, but not to a separate Book of Nehemiah.

The oldest MSS of the LXX (Vaticanus, Sinaiticus, Alexandrinus) treat Ezra-Nehemiah as one book, called Esdras B (see below, Esdras). Later MSS of the LXX, perhaps under Christian influence, treat Ezra and Nehemiah as two works. Melito of Sardis and Eusebius regarded Ezra-Nehemiah as one book. Origen (A.D. c.185–253) was the first Christian to distinguish between two books, which he called I Ezra and II Ezra, but he noted that they were one book in the Hebrew. Jerome in translating the Vulgate called the Book of Nehemiah *liber secundus Esdrae*.

Wycliffe's Bible (1382) refers to "The First and Second Book of Esdras." Myles Coverdale's translation (1535) has "The First Boke of Esdras" and "The Second Boke of Esdras, otherwyse called the Boke of Nehemias." Luther adopted the title "Nehemiah." Although Ezra and Nehemiah were regarded as one book from at least the

---

[21]D.J.A. Clines, "The Evidence for an Autumnal New Year in Pre-exilic Israel Reconsidered," JBL 93 (1974): 35–36.

[22]E.R. Thiele, *The Mysterious Numbers of the Hebrew Kings*, rev. ed. (Grand Rapids: Eerdmans, 1965), pp. 30, 161; S.H. Horn and L.H. Wood, *The Chronology of Ezra 7* (Washington, D.C.: Review & Herald, 1953), pp. 69–72; S.H. Horn, "The Babylonian Chronicle and the Ancient Calendar of the Kingdom of Judah," *Andrews University Seminary Studies* 5 (1967): 24.

[23]In this commentary Nisan dates will be given, with Tishri dates in parentheses. For the correlation of ancient with modern dates, see R.A. Parker and W.H. Dubberstein, *Babylonian Chronology 626 B.C.–A.D. 75* (Providence: Brown University Press, 1956).

third century B.C., the internal evidence indicates two separate compositions later combined (see Literary Form and Authorship). R.K. Harrison (IOT, p. 1136) points to another indication of originally separate compositions: "The fact that the second chapter of Ezra is repeated in Nehemiah 7:6–70."

Although some Palestinian MSS begin the historical section of the *Ketubim* (Writings) section with Chronicles and end it with Ezra-Nehemiah, the standard list as recognized by the Babylonian Talmud places Ezra-Nehemiah and Chronicles after Esther. Probably Ezra-Nehemiah was accepted into the Hebrew canon before Chronicles. Ezra-Nehemiah is omitted only from the canon of Theodore of Mopsuestia, of the Nestorians, and of certain Monophysite groups.

5. Literary Form and Authorship

a. *Lists and documents*

As in the closely related books of Chronicles, one notes the prominence of various lists in Ezra-Nehemiah. Evidently obtained from official sources, these comprise (1) the vessels of the temple (Ezra 1:9–11); (2) the returned exiles (Ezra 2:1–70; Neh 7:6–73); (3) the genealogy of Ezra (Ezra 7:1–5); (4) the heads of the clans (Ezra 8:1 –14); (5) those involved in mixed marriages (Ezra 10:18–43); (6) those who helped rebuild the wall (Neh 3); (7) those who sealed the covenant (Neh 10:1–27); (8) residents of Jerusalem and other cities (Neh 11:3–36); and (9) priests and Levites (Neh 12:1–26).

Genealogical lists of ancestors were especially important "during a period when people renewed their claims upon ancestral homes and needed evidence to substantiate their status in the community of the returnees."[24]

Also included in Ezra are seven official documents or letters (all, except the first, in Aramaic; the first is in Hebrew): (1) the decree of Cyrus (Ezra 1:2–4); (2) the accusation of Rehum et al. against the Jews (Ezra 4:11–16); (3) the reply of Artaxerxes I (Ezra 4:17–22); (4) the report from Tattenai (Ezra 5:7–17); (5) the memorandum of Cyrus's decree (Ezra 6:2b–5); (6) Darius's reply to Tattenai (Ezra 6:6–22); (7) the king's authorization to Ezra (Ezra 7:12–26).

In a study directed under A. Millard, C. Hensley examined these "Ezra Documents" in the light of thirty-two contemporary Persian documents and letters. Hensley (p. 233) concluded:

> The result has been that all of the questions raised concerning the authenticity of the ED (Ezra Documents) are answered in the positive in the light of our present state of knowledge of Achaemenid Persia. The study of the historical context of the ED in matters both general and specific has demonstrated that the ED can be considered authentic Persian documents, as far as history is concerned.
>
> The final conclusion drawn by the writer is that linguistically, stylistically, and historically the ED correspond perfectly to the non-Biblical documents of the Achaemenid period.

---

[24]H. Tadmor, "The Babylonian Exile and the Restoration," *A History of the Jewish People*, ed. H. Ben-Sasson (Cambridge: Harvard University Press, 1976), p. 159; cf. M. Johnson, *The Purpose of the Biblical Genealogies* (Cambridge: Cambridge University Press, 1969), p. 77.

b. *The Nehemiah memoirs*

Bowman ("Ezra-Nehemiah," p. 552) makes the following comment: "Although the extent of Nehemiah's narrative is debated, no one challenges the authenticity of the memoir concerning him that the Chronicler has incorporated in his work. . . . Nehemiah's memoirs, written not very long after 432 B.C. (cf. Neh 5:14) and preserved by the Chronicler literally, with relatively little interpolation or reworking, are one of the most accurate historical sources in the Old Testament."

Most scholars would include Nehemiah 1–6; 7:1–5; 11:1–2; 12:27–43; 13:4–31 in the Nehemiah memoirs, which vividly reflect the forcefulness of Nehemiah's personality. As Brockington comments (pp. 32–33), "Nehemiah's style is very much his own, simple, straightforward and business-like, yet reflecting at the same time a genuine religious zeal." Nehemiah's memoirs have been considered by Kellermann (*Nehemiah Quellen*, pp. 84–87) as an example of the "Prayer of the Accused," which was deposited at the temple. Smith (p. 126) draws comparisons with the Athenian reformer Solon and his poems and the Behistun Inscription of Darius I. Gerhard von Rad suggests comparisons with late Egyptian votive inscriptions that were deposited in temples or cemeteries, in which officials recorded their good deeds in providing for the poor and for the temples.[25] R.W. Klein comments: "Perhaps the most striking parallel is the biographical similarity between Nehemiah and Udjahorresnet (an Egyptian official under Cambyses and Darius I), but in style and form, and even in the idea of merit, . . . they are much different."[26] Like the Nehemiah memoirs the Udjahorresnet document is interspersed with prayers.

c. *The Ezra memoirs*

Part of the materials on Ezra are personal reminiscences: Ezra 7:27–28; 8:1–34; 9:1–15. According to Ryle (p. xviii), "The authorship of these extracts has never been disputed." There are, however, other sections about Ezra given in the third person—Ezra 7:1–26; 10; Neh 8—where, some conclude, a compiler has abridged the Ezra memoirs. But linguistic analysis has shown that both the first-person and the third-person extracts resemble each other. Kapelrud (p. 95) concludes: "The final result is that it has not been possible to prove any difference between those sections written in the first person, and the other sections of the Ezra-narrative." As P.R. Ackroyd notes, "This interchange of forms is not necessarily to be regarded as indicating separate sources; it is more probably to be seen as a difference of style even within the same narrative material. Examples are to be found in Isa. 6–7; Hos. 1 and 3."[27]

Bickerman (pp. 28–29) and S. Mowinckel[28] see numerous examples of such an interchange between the first person and the third person in extrabiblical texts, for example, from Egypt: the story of Sinuhe, the inscriptions of Kamose, Ramses II, Udjahorresnet; from Syria-Mesopotamia: the inscriptions of Idrimi, letters to Aššur, annals of Sargon II, texts of Nabonidus, and the story of Ahiqar.

Torrey (p. 243) suggested that "there is not a garment in all Ezra's wardrobe that

---

[25]"Die Nehemia-Denkschrift," ZAW 76 (1964): 176–87.

[26]"Ezra and Nehemiah in Recent Studies," in Cross, *Mighty Acts*, p. 366.

[27]"The Chronicler as Exegete," *Journal for the Study of the Old Testament* 1 (1977): 15.

[28]" 'Ich' und 'Er' in der Ezrageschichte," *Verbannung und Heimkehr*, ed. A. Kuschke (Tübingen: J.C.B. Mohr, 1961), pp. 211–33; id., *Ezra-Nehemiah III*, pp. 75–94.

does not fit the Chronicler exactly." Torrey and Kapelrud radically concluded that both the first-person and the third-person passages stemmed from the hand of the so-called Chronicler, who made up the Ezra memoirs from whole cloth. The same linguistic evidence, however, can be used to defend the authorship of the third-person passages by Ezra.[29]

d. The work of the Chronicler

Since the time of L. Zunz (1832) and F.C. Movers (1834), the view has grown, sponsored notably by Torrey and Kapelrud, that the author of Chronicles was also the author/compiler of Ezra-Nehemiah. This is based on certain characteristics common to both Chronicles and Ezra-Nehemiah.

1) Common verses

The verses at the end of Chronicles and at the beginning of Ezra are identical (cf. on Ezra 1:1). However, this may have been a device by the author of Chronicles (or less probably of Ezra) to dovetail the narratives chronologically (Williamson, *Israel*, p. 9).

2) Common words and themes

Both Chronicles and Ezra-Nehemiah exhibit a fondness for lists; for the description of religious festivals; for such phrases as "father's houses [NIV, 'families']" (Ezra 2:59; 10:16; Neh 7:61; 10:34, and more than twenty times in Chron),[30] "heads of fathers' houses" (frequently in Ezra-Neh and more than twenty times in Chron), and "the house of God" (frequently in Ezra-Neh and more than thirty times in Chron). Especially striking in these books is the prominence of the Levites and of temple personnel. Ryle (p. xxvii) comments: "Thus the Levites, who are only twice mentioned in the Books of Samuel (1 Sam. vi.15, 2 Sam. xv.24) and but once in the Books of Kings (1 Kings viii.4) are referred to by name more than 60 times in Ezra and Nehemiah, and about 100 times in the Books of Chronicles."

The words for "singer," "gatekeeper," and "temple servants" (*n*e*ṭînîm*) are used almost exclusively in Ezra-Nehemiah and Chronicles (cf. on Ezra 2:41–43). Because of his interest in the temple and the cult, it is assumed that the "Chronicler" was a Levite, or even a singer.

3) Common theology

Bowman ("Ezra-Nehemiah," p. 552) expresses the critical consensus as follows:

> The conclusion that Ezra-Nehemiah was originally part of Chronicles is further supported by the fact that the same late Hebrew language, the same distinctive literary peculiarities that mark the style of the Chronicler, are found throughout Ezra-Nehemiah. The same presuppositions, interests, points of view, and theological and ecclesiastical conceptions so dominate all these writings that it is apparent that Chronicles-Ezra-Nehemiah was originally a literary unit, the prod-

---

[29]W. F. Albright, "The Date and Personality of the Chronicler," JBL 40 (1921): 119–20; Rudolph, pp. 163–65.

[30]J.P. Weinberg, "Das BEĪT im 6.–4. Jh. v.u.z.," VetTest 23 (1973): 400-414.

uct of one school of thought, if not of a single mind, that can be called "the Chronicler."[31]

So widely established is the view that the Chronicler was responsible for Ezra-Nehemiah that so conservative a scholar as Wright (*Ezra's Coming*, p. 11) simply states, "It does not seem necessary, then, to spend longer in justifying the commonly held view that the Chronicler wrote Ezra-Nehemiah in addition to the Books known as Chronicles."

e. Estimates of the Chronicler's accuracy

The widespread agreement that Ezra-Nehemiah and Chronicles came from the same pen contrasts with the great disagreement over the value of the Chronicler's own contributions. Conservatives regard the Chronicler's work in Ezra-Nehemiah as that of an editor who has compiled authentic sources. Radical critics, however, view the Chronicler as an imaginative author who wrote fiction.

The outstanding proponent of the latter view was C.C. Torrey, who expressed his views initially in *The Composition and Historical Value of Ezra-Nehemiah*, published in 1896, and continued to maintain them in *The Chronicler's History of Israel*, published in 1954, just two years before his death.[32] According to Torrey the Chronicler was a highly imaginative writer but a poor historian who forged documents for apologetic purposes. Arguing from the failure of Ben Sirah (c. 180 B.C.) to mention Ezra, Torrey held that Ezra was a fictitious character. The entire episode of the return was created as a religious polemic against Samaritans. Torrey maintained, "We have no trustworthy evidence that any numerous company returned from Babylonia, nor is it intrinsically likely that such a return took place."[33] Torrey considered the Aramaic of Ezra to be late; and because of the presence of Greek words for coins, he dated the work of the Chronicler to 250 B.C.[34] His radical conclusions influenced A. Loisy, G. Hölscher, S.A. Cook, W.A. Irwin, and R.H. Pfeiffer.

Following in the wake of Torrey, there has been no lack of scholars who question the accuracy of the Chronicler. Noth viewed the Ezra narratives as largely the creation of the Chronicler.[35] Kapelrud (p. 96) conceded only that the Chronicler's circles were acquainted "perhaps with a very scanty tradition about Ezra." Although he does not believe that the Chronicler invented Ezra, Mowinckel dates the Chronicler's work even later than Torrey, with consequent confusions introduced by an even later redactor in the Maccabean period.

More recently H. Kellermann has offered a complex and radical analysis dividing the Ezra-Nehemiah materials into very precise categories: (1) an Ezra source, (2) a Nehemiah source, (3) the editorial work of the Chronicler, and (4) the work of a post-Chronicler redactor.[36]

---

[31]Cf. R. North, "Theology of the Chronicler," JBL 82 (1963): 369–81; J. Goldingay, "The Chronicler as a Theologian," BTh Bulletin 5 (1975): 99–126.

[32]W.F. Stinespring, "Prolegomenon," in Torrey, *Ezra Studies*, pp. XI–XXVIII; cf. Leesberg, pp. 79ff.

[33]Torrey, *Ezra Studies*, p. 288.

[34]E.M. Yamauchi, *Greece and Babylon*, p. 83; id., "The Greek Words in Daniel in the Light of Greek Influence," *New Perspectives on the Old Testament*, ed. J.B. Payne (Waco: Word, 1970), pp. 191–92.

[35]Martin Noth, *The History of Israel* (New York: Harper & Brothers, 1960), pp. 318–19.

[36]*Nehemiah Quellen*, pp. 4ff., 56ff., 76ff., 89ff., 94f., 148ff.; id., "Erwägungen zum Problem der Esradatierung," ZAW 80 (1968): 55–87.

In Kellermann's view the Chronicler had but a few scraps of information about Ezra. All other aspects of the Ezra story are fictional midrashim composed by the Chronicler with the aim of making Ezra overshadow Nehemiah. The Chronicler used the Nehemiah source because he approved of its anti-Samaritan bias but disapproved of Nehemiah's Zionist sympathies. The later redactor was a Zionist, a supporter of the Hasmoneans, who sought to counteract the Chronicler's attempt to minimize Nehemiah's role. Though ingenious and imaginative, Kellermann's reconstruction requires more faith than the narrative as it stands.[37]

As opposed to these radical views that are based on literary analyses of the texts, extrabiblical texts and archaeological evidence have supported an early date for the Chronicler and his accuracy (cf. Date). According to W.F. Albright, "Our respect for the accuracy of both the written and the oral tradition recorded by the Chronicler has been notably enhanced in recent years."[38] In his major commentary on Chronicles, J.M. Meyers concludes: "Furthermore, within the limits of its purpose, the Chronicler's story is accurate wherever it can be checked, though the method of presentation is homiletical."[39]

f. Ezra as the Chronicler?

Because the last verses of Chronicles are identical with the first verses of Ezra, some scholars argue that Ezra was written by the Chronicler. Other scholars, using the same data, argue that the Chronicler was Ezra himself. The Talmud (*Baba Bathra* 15a) states that Ezra wrote Chronicles—a view upheld by the church fathers and many of the older commentaries. This thesis, which was revived by A. von Hoonacker, received the influential endorsement of Albright in his 1921 (cf. n. 29) article, and is upheld by Albright's disciples, John Bright ("Ezra's Mission," p. 81) and J.M. Myers (*Ezra-Nehemiah*, p. XLVIII).

The view that Ezra was or may have been the Chronicler is widely held by evangelical scholars: e.g., E.J. Young,[40] G.L. Archer, Jr. (SOTIrev., p. 405), R.L. Harris (ZPEB, 2:470), and J.S. Wright (ZPEB, 2:472). This view, however, poses problems. First, late Jewish tradition is not very reliable. The genealogical data brings the work of the Chronicler down to about 400 B.C. (cf. Date). This was not a problem for Albright who dated Ezra's coming to 428 B.C. (cf. The Order). If Ezra was at least forty years old when he led the return, he would have been near seventy about 400 B.C. But on the traditional dating of his return in 458 (457), Ezra would have been about one hundred—not impossible, but improbable.

Despite numerous parallels between Chronicles and Ezra-Nehemiah, there are also many striking differences. Thus we conclude that Chronicles was composed by a close disciple of Ezra rather than by Ezra himself (Harrison, IOT, pp. 149ff.).

g. Differences between Chronicles and Ezra-Nehemiah

Though earlier scholars—e.g., W. de Wette, E. König, W. Rudolph, and M.H. Segal—had pointed out differences between Chronicles and Ezra-Nehemiah, it was

---

[37]See J.A. Emerton, "Review of U. Kellermann, *Nehemiah: Quellen, Überlieferung und Geschichte*," JTS, N.S., 23 (1972): 171–85.

[38]*Yahweh and the Gods of Canaan* (Garden City, N.Y.: Doubleday & Co., 1968), p. 182.

[39]*I Chronicles* (Garden City, N.Y.: Doubleday & Co., 1965), p. LXIII.

[40]*An Introduction to the Old Testament* (Grand Rapids: Eerdmans, 1958), p. 413.

especially the important analysis of Sara Japhet that pointed out many of the differences not noted before. Japhet listed words used in Ezra-Nehemiah that are not found in Chronicles and pointed to different uses of common terms. In the matter of theophoric names, the short form is used in Ezra-Nehemiah; but both short and long forms are used in Chronicles. She concluded ("Authorship," p. 371), "Our investigation of the differences between the two books, which was restricted to one field, has proven that the books could not have been written or compiled by the same author."

Recently J.D. Newsome suggests that while Ezra-Nehemiah is "unyieldingly separatist," there is a tentative kind of internationalism in Chronicles. Prophecy plays a central role in Chronicles but is a peripheral element in Ezra-Nehemiah. He writes, "In sum, our investigation leads to the conclusion that they are correct who see a different literary and theological hand in Ezra-Nehemiah from that in Chronicles."[41] Similarly R.L. Braun has noted that there is a marked difference between the openness shown to the north in Chronicles and the separatism manifested in Ezra 4:1–4 and Nehemiah 10:28–31.[42]

In his monograph Williamson (*Israel*, p. 64) noted other differences. The Chronicles emphasize the role of Jacob, an emphasis lacking in Ezra-Nehemiah. Conversely the Sabbath is important in Nehemiah. "In contrast, the Sabbath plays no significant role in Chr., and is most noticeably absent at 2 Chr. 36:11–16, where we should have expected a reference to it on the basis of Nehemiah's words" (p. 69). Williamson (ibid., p. 61) observes:

> When we turn with this in mind to the Chronicler's account of Solomon's reign, however, far from using such a golden opportunity of driving home this important lesson to his readers, we find that he actually omits from I Ki. 11:1ff. the very account to which Nehemiah refers. It is usually argued that this passage was omitted by the Chronicler because he wanted to make of Solomon an ideal figure. However, if Ezr. Neh. is an integral part of his work, that argument completely breaks down in view of Neh. 13:26. It seems far more sensible to see here the divergent emphases of separate authors.

h. *The Freedman-Cross reconstruction*

In 1961 D.N. Freedman proposed that most of Chronicles was written about 515 by a monarchist wishing to establish the claims of the house of David at the time of the completion of the second temple. First Chronicles 1–9 and Ezra-Nehemiah were then later attached by a clericalist. It was his conclusion "that the memoirs of Ezra and Nehemiah, who were roughly contemporaneous, and who together reconstituted the Jewish community in the latter half of the fifth century B.C., were attached, in a somewhat haphazard fashion, shortly after their time."[43]

More recently Cross ("A Reconstruction," pp. 4–18) has proposed a similar but three-staged reconstruction in the composition and editing of Chronicles and Ezra-Nehemiah:

1. In stage one (which he calls Chr_1) most of Chronicles (1 Chron 10–2 Chron 34) and the first part of Ezra (Ezra 1:1–3:13) were composed about 520 at the time of

---

[41]"Toward a New Understanding of the Chronicler and His Purposes," JBL 94 (1975): 201–17.
[42]"A Reconsideration of the Chronicler's Attitude Toward the North," JBL 96 (1977): 59–62.
[43]"The Chronicler's Purpose," CBQ 23 (1961): 436–42.

the foundation of the second temple, in support of the messianic movement centered about Zerubbabel and Jeshua.

2. In stage two (Chr₂), written about 450 B.C., shortly after Ezra's mission, an editor added the Aramaic source (Ezra 5:1–6:19) as a preface to the Ezra narratives (Ezra 7–10).

3. In stage three (Chr₃) a third editor added the Nehemiah memoirs and the genealogies of 1 Chronicles 1–9.

Cross's reconstruction is based on the assumption that papponymy (see below) was current among the high priests. He has to assume two haplographies in his reconstruction and the equation of Joiada and Jaddua. G. Widengren ("The Persian Period," J.H. Hayes and J.M. Miller, edd., *Israelite and Judean History* [Philadelphia: Westminster, 1977], pp. 507–9) notes that Cross mistakenly assumes that Eliashib was the brother of Joiakim, whereas Nehemiah 12:10 indicates that Eliashib was the son of Joiakim.

i. Conclusions

Though there are many complex relationships between Ezra-Nehemiah and Chronicles, we regard Nehemiah as the author of the Nehemiah memoirs and Ezra as the author of both the Ezra memoirs and the Ezra narrative, with a later follower of Ezra's circle as the Chronicler.

6. Date

a. Advocates of late dates

Though not from the same pen, Ezra-Nehemiah and Chronicles form a series and are assigned closely related dates. The *terminus ad quem* for dating the work of the Chronicler is about 200 B.C. as Ben Sirach (c. 180 B.C.) in Ecclesiasticus 47:8–10 draws on 1 Chronicles 23–29. Only Mowinckel has advocated a date as late as 200 B.C. Torrey, who believed that the words for coins in Ezra 2:69; 8:27 and Nehemiah 7:70–72 (cf. commentary) were references to the Greek drachma, dated the work of the Chronicler to 250 B.C.

Most critical scholars of the nineteenth and early twentieth centuries preferred a date about 300 B.C. because they believed that the Jaddua, in Nehemiah 12:10–11, 22, was the same Jaddua whom Josephus associated with Alexander the Great (cf. The High Priests). These scholars believed that the genealogy of 1 Chronicles 3:15 –24 lists six generations beyond Zerubbabel (c. 520 B.C.), which at thirty years per generation would date the passage at about 340 B.C.

Among those holding such a late date for the composition of Chronicles and Ezra-Nehemiah are L.W. Batten, R.A. Bowman, L.H. Brockington, J. de Fraine, K. Galling, F. Michaeli, M. Noth, W.O.E. Oesterley, H.W. Robinson, H.H. Rowley, H.E. Ryle, H. Schneider, and A. Weiser. Most of these critics have also advocated reversing the traditional order by placing Ezra after Nehemiah (cf. The Order). An exception is the conservative J.S. Wright, who, while advocating the traditional order of Ezra and Nehemiah, maintains this late date: "Unless strong evidence were forthcoming on other grounds, it would be reasonable to adopt 300 B.C. as the approximate date with a margin of up to about 30 years on either side of that date" ("Ezra's Coming," p. 12).

In a recent study H.G.M. Williamson concludes: "The date of Chronicles remains a controversial issue, but one in the later part of the Persian period, around 350 B.C., still seems to satisfy the evidence best."[44]

b. Advocates of an early date

Other scholars have argued that the genealogies of 1 Chronicles 3:15–24 originally listed four generations instead of six after Zerubbabel, i.e., about 400 B.C. Alternatively other scholars have calculated six generations of the passage at twenty years per generation, which would yield the same date. Those who advocate such an early date for the Chronicler argue that the Jaddua of Nehemiah 12:10–11, 22 was either a young man who lived to a ripe old age till Alexander's era, or that he is not to be identified with the Jaddua of Josephus.

A date of about 400 B.C. for the Chronicler and Ezra-Nehemiah has been advocated by Rudolph (p. xxv) and most notably by W.F. Albright, who declared: "The trend of recent study has been strongly in favor of raising the date of the compilation of the Chronicler's work from the third century (as supposed by nearly all competent scholars of the past generation) to the early fourth. With this goes a correspondingly higher respect for its historical value."[45] This position has also been defended by Myers[46] and Bright ("Ezra's Mission," p. 80). Cross ("A Reconstruction," p. 12) adds the following consideration: "Other arguments can be put for dating Chr_3 to circa 400. No hint of the conquest of Alexander is to be found, and perhaps more important, no reference to the suffering and chaos of the mid-fourth century B.C. when Judah joined in the Phoenician rebellion, harshly put down by Artaxerxes III and his general, Bagoas."

In conclusion, we would date the composition of the Ezra materials about 440, the Nehemiah memoirs about 430, and the Chronicles about 400.

7. The High Priests

The date and the order of Ezra-Nehemiah are connected with the list and the identification of the high priests mentioned in Ezra-Nehemiah. Advocates of a late date and of a reverse order assume that the list of high priests is relatively complete and that one can identify certain of these with those mentioned by Josephus.

a. Jeshua

Jeshua (Joshua) was the high priest who was the contemporary of Zerubbabel during the reign of Cyrus (Ezra 2:2; Hag 1:1, 12, 14; 2:2, 4; Zech 3:1, 3, 6, 9; 6:11).

b. Joiakim

Joiakim was evidently the high priest during the reign of Darius I (late sixth century B.C.). Those who assume that the list of priests is complete assume that the

---

[44]"The Origins of the Twenty-four Priestly Courses," VetTest Supplement 30 (1979): 265; cf. id., *Israel*, pp. 83–86.
[45]*Recent Discoveries in Bible Lands* (New York: Funk & Wagnalls, 1955), p. 105.
[46]*Ezra-Nehemiah*, p. LXX; id., *I Chronicles*, p. LXXXIX.

same Joiakim had an unusually long period in office, down to the mid-fifth century (Neh 12:12–21, 25–26).

c. Eliashib

Eliashib was the high priest at the time of Nehemiah, assisting in the rebuilding of the wall (Neh 3:1, 20–21; 13:28).

A priest named Eliashib was guilty of defiling the temple by assigning rooms to Tobiah the Ammonite (Neh 13:4, 7). Scholars disagree as to whether this Eliashib was the same as the high priest.

d. Joiada

Joiada was the son of Eliashib (Neh 12:10). It is uncertain from Nehemiah 13:28 whether Joiada or his father was high priest at the time of Nehemiah's second return.

e. Johanan

Johanan was the son of Joiada and grandson of Eliashib.

1. Ezra 10:6 mentions that Ezra went to the chamber of "Jehohanan the son of Eliashib."
2. Nehemiah 12:11 mentions the son of Joiada, named Jonathan, who was the father of Joiada.
3. Nehemiah 12:22 mentions a Johanan after Joiada and before Jaddua, and v.23 identifies Johanan as the son of Eliashib.
4. Elephantine papyri (Cowley 30:18; 31:17; dated 411–410 B.C.) refer to Johanan as high priest (ANET, p. 492).
5. Josephus (Antiq. XI, 297–301 [vii.1]) refers to a Johanan who killed his brother Jesus.

Are all five the same individual? Scholars who say so reason that in Nehemiah 12:11 Jonathan is an error for Johanan and that Nehemiah 12:23 indicates that Johanan was the descendant (i.e., grandson) of Eliashib. They would argue that since the Elephantine papyri indicate that Johanan was high priest in 410 B.C., it is more likely that Ezra came seven years later in the seventh year of Artaxerxes II (398 B.C.) rather than forty-eight years earlier under Artaxerxes I (458 B.C.) (Ackroyd, *Israel*, pp. 193, 285–86).

If these identifications are correct, this reasoning provides one of the strongest arguments for reversing the order of Ezra and Nehemiah. There are, however, a number of serious objections to such a reconstruction. For example, would Ezra have consorted with a known murderer, as he would have if he had arrived in 398 (cf. Ackroyd, *Chronicles*, p. 258)? This would have been the case if we were to identify Ezra's Jehohanan with the Jehohanan of Josephus. Such an identification would be undermined if Jehohanan was the son of Eliashib and the brother of Joiada rather than the grandson of Eliashib.[47] Jehohanan (Johanan), after all, was a most common name; it was used by fourteen different individuals in the OT, five in Maccabees, and seventeen in Josephus.[48] In Ezra 10:6, moreover, Jehohanan is not identified as a high priest.

---

[47]J.R. Porter, "Son or grandson, Ezr. X.6," JTS 17 (1966): 54–67.
[48]W.M.F. Scott, "Nehemiah-Ezra?" ExpT 58 (1946–47): 265.

C.G. Tuland concludes his analysis as follows: "Thus far three basic differences exclude the identification of the high-priestly Jehohanan-Eliashib 'set' (of Neh 3:1, 20, 21; 12:10, 11, 22, 23) found in the Aramaic papyri, Cowley 30 and 31, with the ordinary priest of Ezr 10:6: 1. the difference in rank and title; 2. the difference in office; 3. the difference in family relationship."[49]

f. Jaddua

A Jaddua, the son of Johanan, is mentioned in Nehemiah 10:21 (MT 22); 12:11, 22. Josephus (Antiq. XI, 302–7 [vii.2–viii.2]) identifies this Jaddua with the high priest at the time of Alexander's invasion of Palestine. Some conservative scholars try to maintain the traditional order of Ezra-Nehemiah by arguing that the biblical Jaddua may have been a young man about 400 B.C., who lived to an unusually advanced age in 333–332 B.C. (KD, p. 147). As this seems most unlikely, Josephus was probably mistaken and wrongly identified the Hellenistic Jaddua with his grandfather. H.G.M. Williamson notes that there are "strong grounds for believing that Josephus 'reduced' the Persian period by at least as much as two generations."[50] He may have been misled because there was an Artaxerxes and a Darius both in the fifth century and in the fourth century.

Inspired by the evidence of papponymy in the Samaria papyri, Cross ("A Reconstruction") has proposed a new reconstruction that offers a plausible harmonization of the biblical and extrabiblical data. Papponymy (the repetition of the same name in alternating generations so that grandsons are named after their grandfathers) was a common practice among leading Jewish families. Mazar (Mountain) argues that the name Tobiah alternates over nine generations. In a recently published Ammonite inscription, the royal name Amminadab recurs over six generations. The Samaria papyri indicate that the name Sanballat alternated over six generations.

Cross's reconstruction assumes that a pair of similar names has fallen out of our extant sources.[51] His reconstruction list would be as follows:

Name	Birth	Contemporary of
Jeshua	570	Zerubbabel
Joiakim	545	
Eliashib I	540	
Johanan I	520	Ezra
Eliashib II	495	Nehemiah
Joiada	470	
Johanan II	445	
Jaddua I[52]	420	
Johanan III	395	
Jaddua II	370	Alexander

---

[49]"Ezra-Nehemiah or Nehemiah-Ezra?" *Andrews University Seminary Studies* 12 (1974): 58–59.

[50]"The Historical Value of Josephus' Antiquities XI.297–301," JTS 28 (1977): 49–66.

[51]In Cross's reconstruction every high priest is the son of the preceding, except for Eliashib I, who is listed as the brother of Joiakim. But Neh 12:10 lists Eliashib as Joiakim's son.

[52]As Jaddua is a caritative or endearing form of Joiada, Cross uses the names Jaddua I, Jaddua II and Jaddua II, Jaddua III; but this may confuse readers.

By this reconstruction Cross resolves two key issues. Ezra's contemporary is Johanan I, son of Eliashib I, and not Johanan II, who is mentioned in the Elephantine papyri, as advocates of a reverse order have maintained. The Jaddua mentioned by Nehemiah would have been the grandfather of Jaddua II, high priest at the time of Alexander.[53]

8. The Order of Ezra and Nehemiah

A most important controversy concerns the order of Ezra and Nehemiah. Traditionally Ezra arrived in the seventh year of Artaxerxes I (Ezra 7:7) in 458 (457) B.C., and Nehemiah arrived in the king's twentieth year (Neh 2:1) in 445 B.C.

Critics have proposed a reverse order in which after Nehemiah's arrival in 445, Ezra arrived in the seventh year of Artaxerxes II in 398. Artaxerxes II, or Memnon (404–359 B.C.), is well-known from Xenophon's *Anabasis* as the king whose younger brother Cyrus led an unsuccessful revolt supported by Greek mercenaries.

Other scholars have favored an intermediate position that maintains the contemporaneity of the men but places Ezra later than the traditional order in the twenty-seventh or thirty-seventh year of Artaxerxes I, that is, in 438 or 428 B.C.[54]

There are numerous lines of argument that have been adduced in favor of the reverse order. We shall consider these and, at the same time, the counterarguments of those who favor either the traditional or intermediate position.

a. The list of high priests

As this is one of the weightiest arguments, it has been considered separately in the preceding section.

b. The contemporaneity of Ezra and Nehemiah

1. As the text stands Nehemiah and Ezra are noted together in Nehemiah 8:9, at the reading of the Law, and in Nehemiah 12:26, 36, at the dedication of the wall. Since Nehemiah's name is lacking in the 1 Esdras 9:49 parallel to Nehemiah 8:9, it has been argued that Nehemiah's name was inserted as a gloss. It has also been claimed that Nehemiah 12:26, 36 were added to the original text. J.A. Emerton has asserted, "No meeting between them is recorded and they never both play active parts in the same action, one is active, and at most, the other's name is mentioned in passing."[55]

2. But it is not true that one can delete Ezra or Nehemiah's name from Nehemiah 12:36, as some have argued, for to do so would leave one of the processions without a leader.

That references to the contemporaneity of Ezra and Nehemiah are few is readily explicable. Bright ("Ezra's Mission," p. 86) points out that "the Chronicler's interests were predominantly ecclesiastical, and to these Nehemiah was peripheral. Nehemiah, on the other hand, intended his memoirs as a personal *apologia*, not as a history of the contemporary Jewish community; he was concerned exclusively with

---

[53]Cross's reconstruction has been accepted by Talmon, "Ezra and Nehemiah."

[54]For a detailed consideration of the arguments, see Yamauchi, "Reverse Order," pp. 7–13.

[55]"Did Ezra Go to Jerusalem in 428 B.C.?" JTS 17 (1966): 16.

what he himself had done." We also have other examples of contemporary OT figures who do not refer to each other, e.g., Jeremiah and Ezekiel, Haggai and Zechariah.[56]

c. Meremoth the son of Uriah of the clan of Hakkoz

1. Ezra 2:61–62/Nehemiah 7:63–64 lists the family of Hakkoz as one of those not able to prove its priestly status. In Ezra 8:33 a Meremoth son of Uriah from this family is designated as one of the priests in charge of the temple treasury. In Nehemiah 3:4, 21 a Meremoth son of Uriah builds a double portion of the wall. Without a priestly title he is evidently considered a layman. Supporters of the reverse order argue that Meremoth in his youth aided in the building of the wall and in his old age (forty-seven years later in 398) served as a treasurer. They suggest that Meremoth's family must have regained its priestly status after Nehemiah's time at Ezra's coming.

2. On the other hand, it can also be argued that the situation can be explained on the basis of the traditional order. Koch (p. 190) suggests, "It seems as if Ezra acknowledged Meremoth at the time of his arrival in Jerusalem, but deposed him shortly afterward while carrying out his investigation."

Simpler is Kellermann's suggestion (*Nehemiah Quellen*, p. 69) that despite similar names and patronymics, we have to do with two individuals, one from a priestly and one from a lay family. Though Meremoth is not a very common name (three or four occurrences), Uriah is more common (six or seven occurrences).

d. The thirteen-year gap

1. As the present text is arranged, after Ezra's arrival in 458 and his activities in that first year, we hear nothing further about his ministry until the public reading of the Law some thirteen years later (Neh 8:1–8). A number of scholars would sever Ezra's association with Nehemiah and place the reading of the Law by Ezra in his first year.

2. Archer (SOTIrev., p. 412) responds: "Yet Nehemiah 8 only records a solemn reading of the law in a public meeting on the occasion of the Feast of Tabernacles. It by no means implies that Ezra had not been diligently teaching the law to smaller groups of disciples and Levites during the preceding twelve years." Less satisfactory are suggestions that Ezra may have returned to Mesopotamia, or that he may have fallen out of favor with the Persians by being associated with the attempt to rebuild the wall (Ezra 4:7–23).

e. The problem of mixed marriages

1. Both Ezra (9–10) and Nehemiah (13:23–28) deal with the problem of mixed marriages. Ezra adopted a more rigorous approach, demanding the dissolution of all such marriages. Apart from the expulsion of Joiada, Nehemiah simply forbade future mixed marriages. Brockington (pp. 19–20) holds that Ezra's handling most naturally follows Nehemiah's attempt and regards this as "the strongest argument" for the reverse order. Furthermore, others argue that the situation faced by Nehemiah

---

[56]Josephus (*Antiq*. XI, 158 [v.5]) has Ezra passing away before the arrival of Nehemiah, a state of affairs that is not taken seriously by scholars. But see Tuland (n. 49).

must have been one of long standing, since he found the children speaking in foreign dialects (Neh 13:23–24).

2. As to the latter argument, if Ezra's reforms took place in 457—some twenty-five years before Nehemiah's actions on his second return after 432—this would certainly be time enough for children of some age to have been born to renewed mixed marriages. The idea that a more rigorous handling of the problem should come later is purely subjective.

f. The alleged failure of Ezra

1. Closely allied to the preceding argument is the often-expressed idea that if he preceded Nehemiah, Ezra must have "failed," as Nehemiah had to correct the same abuse. Rowley (*Men of God*, p. 242), for example, avers, "It is curious that some of those who are zealous to defend the chronological order of Ezra and Nehemiah as it appears in the Bible are willing to do so at the cost of jettisoning the Biblical representation of the character of Ezra, and the reduction of him to the stature of an incompetent who had to be rescued by Nehemiah after his failure." The converse argument could of course be made, that if Nehemiah preceded Ezra, the former must have failed.

2. It should be noted that God's spokesmen do not "fail" when they faithfully deliver God's messages. The people who disobey are the ones who "fail." In the short period of time during Nehemiah's absence after his first term, numerous abuses appeared that he had to correct during his second term (Neh 13:4–31).[57]

g. Supporters of the reverse order

In 1889 M. Vernes first suggested the reverse order; A. van Hoonacker gave the view currency in publications from 1890 to 1924. The ablest exposition of this position was by H. H. Rowley in 1948, at a time when only a minority of scholars favored it.[58] Thereafter, however, this view came to predominate; and in 1970 Stinespring affirmed:

> Indeed, the placing of Ezra after Nehemiah may now be spoken of as part of "critical orthodoxy," having been incorporated into such works as *The International Critical Commentary, The Interpreter's Bible, The Interpreter's Dictionary of the Bible, The Oxford Annotated Bible,* and into much of the church-school literature of the leading Protestant churches in North America. The great German introductions of Eissfeldt and Sellin-Fohrer, now translated into English (1965 and 1968 respectively), have also joined the chorus of assent.[59]

h. Supporters of the intermediate date

Some scholars have attempted to retain the contemporaneity of Ezra and Nehemiah and yet date Ezra later by emending the number "7" of Ezra 7:7 to read either

---

[57]Many more arguments have been adduced, which cannot be discussed here (cf. Yamauchi, "Reverse Order").

[58]"The Chronological Order of Ezra and Nehemiah," *Ignace Goldziher Memorial Volume,* edd. S. Löwinger and J. Somogyi (Budapest, 1948), pp. 117-49; reprinted in *The Servant of the Lord,* rev. ed. (Naperville, Ill.: Allenson, 1965), pp. 135–68.

[59]"Prolegomenon," p. xiv.

"27" or "37." The former would date Ezra's arrival in 438, the latter in 428. The former was proposed by J. Wellhausen in 1895, the latter by J. Markwart in 1896. The first alternative has had relatively few supporters.

More attractive is the reading "37." Since both the Hebrew word for "30" and the word for "7" begin with the letter š, it has been argued that the former word may have dropped out. The most influential advocate here was Albright (*Biblical Period*, pp. 45–55, 62–65, 113). Bright ("Ezra's Mission," pp. 70–87) offered a persuasive exposition of this view. Though this position avoids the objections raised against the reverse position, there is no textual support for the proposed emendation.

i. Supporters of the traditional order

The traditional order has never lacked defenders.[60] In 1948 Rowley wrote: "Despite this impressive support [for the reverse order], this view has never been unchallenged, and there have always been scholars of eminence—even more numerous than its supporters—who have refused to adopt it, but have adhered to the traditional view."[61] U. Kellermann's article, published in 1968, refuted point by point the arguments for the reverse order.[62]

Other important scholars have since disagreed with the arguments for the reverse order and have supported the traditional view. Morton Smith, for example, comments: "The minor reasons commonly given for dating Ezra after Nehemiah are all of them trivial and have been disposed of by Kellermann."[63] Cross ("A Reconstruction," p. 14, n. 60) also rejected most of the arguments that claim that Ezra followed Nehemiah to Jerusalem. Talmon ("Ezra-Nehemiah," p. 320) concludes: "Such tenuous argumentation does not warrant a reordering of the biblical presentation. . . . Today a more optimistic appreciation of the biblical presentation seems to be gaining ground."

We believe that the traditional order of Ezra's arrival prior to Nehemiah in the seventh year of Artaxerxes I is the correct order.

9. Text

The Hebrew text of Ezra-Nehemiah has been well preserved; there are no major textual difficulties. Only one fragmentary MS—4QEzra, with a portion of Ezra 4–5—has been recovered from Qumran. Presumably the full MS would have also contained Nehemiah (see above: Canon).

The Hebrew of Ezra 1:1–4:7; 6:19–22; 7:1–11, 27–28; 8–10—that is, the non-Aramaic sections—and the Hebrew of Nehemiah 7:6–12:26—that is, the non-memoir sections—belong to the same late Hebrew as the Hebrew of the Chronicles. But the Hebrew of the Nehemiah memoirs (see Literary Form and Authorship)—Nehemiah 1:1–7:5; 12:27–13:31—is written in a more archaic Hebrew according to Robert Polzin.[64]

The Aramaic sections that are found in Ezra 4:8–6:18 and 7:12–26 consist largely

---

[60]For a defense of the traditional order, see Wright, *Ezra's Coming*, p.11.
[61]"Chronological Order," p. 122.
[62]"Esradatierung," pp. 55–87.
[63]"Ezra," *Ex Orbe Religionum*, edd. C.J. Bleeker et al. (Leiden: Brill, 1972), 1:143.
[64]*Late Biblical Hebrew* (Missoula: Scholars, 1976), pp. 70–74, 80.

of official documents. Out of these sixty-seven verses, fifty-two are records or letters and only fifteen are narrative. The author evidently found these documents in Aramaic and copied them with the insertion of connecting verses in Aramaic. The community he was writing for understood both Hebrew and Aramaic (cf. comment on Neh 8:8). J. Naveh asserts, "Aramaic, being the official language of the province *Yehud,* was perhaps most common in Judah, but the Hebrew language and script were still spoken and written at least by the people who were not exiled."[65]

Aramaic, a northwest Semitic language originally of the Arameans of Syria, became widespread as an international language first among the Assyrians and especially during the Persian Empire. The dialect of Aramaic used between 700 B.C. and 200 B.C. is known as Imperial Aramaic. This phase includes inscriptions from Anatolia to Afghanistan,[66] the passages in Ezra and in Daniel 2:4–7:28. Isolated Aramaic phrases appear in Genesis 31:47 and Jeremiah 10:11.

Torrey (*Ezra Studies,* pp. 140–61) had branded the Aramaic of Ezra and of Daniel as late Aramaic from the third to second century B.C., but extrabiblical sources clearly show that he was mistaken. Of greatest importance are the contemporary fifth-century B.C. Aramaic papryi recovered from the Jewish garrison at Elephantine in Upper Egypt.[67] Myers notes, "The Aramaic of Ezra . . . is that prevailing in the official documents of the Persian empire as may be seen from the Elephantine correspondence and other documents."[68]

The Aramaic of both Ezra and Daniel reveal the strong influence of Akkadian and Persian in numerous loan words and syntactic features, indicating its origin in the Persian rather than the Hellenistic period.[69]

10. Esdras

a. Nomenclature

Esdras is the Greek transliteration of Ezra. The arrangement and naming of the apocryphal works called Esdras are complicated as the canonical books of Ezra-Nehemiah were also called Esdras in the LXX and Vulgate. A chart can best clarify the relationship of the various titles.

EV:	Ezra	Nehemiah	1 Esdras	2 Esdras
LXX:	Esdras Beta	Esdras Gamma	Esdras Alpha	
Vul:	1 Esdras	2 Esdras	3 Esdras	4 Esdras

b. The Contents of 1 Esdras

First Esdras, the first book of the Apocrypha, differs from the other apocryphal books in that it is largely a divergent account of the canonical books of Ezra-

---

[65]"Hebrew Texts in Aramaic Script in the Persian Period?" BASOR 203 (1971): 32.

[66]See E.M. Yamauchi, "Documents from Old Testament Times," WTJ 41 (1978): 26–29.

[67]B. Porten with J.C. Greenfield, *Jews of Elephantine and Arameans of Syene* (Jerusalem: Hebrew University Press, 1976).

[68]*Ezra-Nehemiah,* p. LXIII. See J.A. Fitzmyer, *A Wandering Aramean* (Missoula: Scholars, 1979), p. 61.

[69]See Rosenthal, *Jerusalmi,* and also S. Kaufman, *The Akkadian Influence on Aramaic* (Chicago: University of Chicago Press, 1975).

Nehemiah. First Esdras parallels the last two chapters of 2 Chronicles, all of Ezra, and thirteen verses of Nehemiah from the section on Ezra (Neh 7:73–8:12).

In striking contrast to Ezra-Nehemiah, the writer of 1 Esdras concentrates exclusively on the ministry of Ezra. In the parallel to Nehemiah 8:9, the name of Nehemiah is omitted. As the Ezra narrative now found in Nehemiah 7:72–8:12 is placed in 1 Esdras 8:88–9:36 immediately after the events of Ezra 10, some claim that the 1 Esdras account is superior in that it avoids the gap of thirteen years found in the MT between Ezra's arrival and the reading of the Law.

c. 1 Esdras and the LXX

The Greek text of 1 Esdras is written in elegant Greek in contrast to the painfully literal LXX text of Ezra-Nehemiah.[70] The latter had been considered by Torrey (*Ezra Studies*, pp. 11–36, 66–82) as the work of Theodotion (second cent. A.D.) but is more probably a Palestinian translation by a forerunner of Theodotion.

In the LXX 1 Esdras precedes the LXX translation of Ezra-Nehemiah; the former is therefore designated Esdras Alpha, the latter Esdras Beta. First Esdras should be dated about 150 B.C.

d. 1 Esdras and Josephus

Josephus in Antiquities XI followed 1 Esdras rather than the MT-LXX perhaps because of its superior Greek. Josephus compounded the errors of 1 Esdras in his narrative. Both Ezra and Nehemiah are placed in the reign of Xerxes instead of in the reign of Artaxerxes.[71]

11. Postbiblical Traditions

Neither Philo nor the NT refers to Ezra or to Nehemiah. Myers (*Ezra-Nehemiah*, p. LXXV) detects a possible allusion to Nehemiah 9:6 in Acts 4:24.

a. Traditions about Ezra

Ben Sirach (Ecclus 49:11–13) in his catalog of famous men lists Nehemiah but not Ezra. Ben Sirach, however, was primarily concerned about men who were builders. According to some scholars Ben Sirach betrays a Sadducean bias and according to others an anti-Levitical one, either of which would explain Ezra's omission.[72]

Second Esdras 14:1–48 describes how God commanded Ezra to dictate the Scriptures in forty days to five rapidly writing scribes who produced twenty-four canonical books and seventy secret books.

The Talmud (*Megilla* 16b) tells us that Ezra was a disciple of the aged Baruch, who had been Jeremiah's scribe. The rabbis held that "if Moses had not anticipated him, Ezra would have received the Torah" (*Sanhedrin* 21b). *Baba Bathra* 14b–16a credits Ezra with the authorship of the books of Ezra and Chronicles.

---

[70]R. Hanhart, ed., *Esdrae Liber I* (Göttingen: Vandenhoeck & Ruprecht, 1974).

[71]C.G. Tuland, "Josephus, *Antiquities*, Book XI, Correction or Confirmation of Biblical Post-Exilic Records?" *Andrews University Seminary Studies* 4 (1966): 176–92. For a comparison of Josephus and the OT, see E. Yamauchi, "Josephus and the Scriptures," *Fides et Historia* 13 (1980): 42–63.

[72]P. Höffken, "Warum schwieg Jesus Sirach über Esra," ZAW 87 (1975): 184–201.

Baba Kamma 82a ascribes to Ezra ten *takkanot* (or regulations) covering miscellaneous practices as (1) holding the court on Mondays and Thursdays, (2) washing clothes on Thursdays and not Fridays, (3) eating garlic on Friday, (4) the combing of a woman's hair before taking a ritual bath, etc.[73]

The OT tells us nothing of Ezra's end. Josephus (*Antiq.* XI, 158 [v.5]) relates concerning Ezra that "it was his fate, after being honored by the people, to die an old man and be buried with great magnificence in Jerusalem." Later traditions spoke of his burial at Abu Ghosh or south of Nablus.[74]

From the eleventh century A.D., Jews in Mesopotamia held that Ezra was buried near the Persian Gulf at al-'Uzair ('Uzair is the Arabic for Ezra), on the right bank of the Tigris in southern Iraq.[75]

Samaritan tradition preserved in the medieval *Liber Josuae* blames "the cursed Ezra" for the excommunication of the Samaritans from the Jewish community.[76] This tradition may stem from the OT period but more probably reflects later hostility between the two communities.

The high regard with which the Jews of Arabia held Ezra may be reflected in the strange accusation found in the Quran 9:30: "And the Jews say: Ezra is the son of Allah, and the Christians say: The Messiah is the son of Allah." A late tradition holds that Ezra tried to persuade the Jews of Yemen in southwestern Arabia to return to Palestine, but they refused to go because they knew that the second temple would be destroyed.[77]

b. Traditions about Nehemiah

Nehemiah is extolled in Ecclesiasticus 49:13 (dated c. 180 B.C.): "The memory of Nehemiah also is lasting; he raised for us the walls that had fallen, and set up the gates and bars and rebuilt our ruined houses." Second Maccabees (first century B.C.) has some curious traditions about Nehemiah. Second Maccabees 1:18 refers to "the feast of the fire given when Nehemiah, who built the temple and the altar, offered sacrifices." Second Maccabees 2:13 reports: "The same things are reported in the records and in the memoirs of Nehemiah, and also that he founded a library and collected the books about kings and prophets, and the writings of David, and letters of kings about votive offerings."

Josephus (*Antiq.* XI, 183 [v.8]) speaks of Nehemiah's life and death as follows: "Then, after performing many other splendid and praiseworthy public services, Nehemiah died at an advanced age. He was a man of kind and just nature and most anxious to serve his countrymen; and he left the walls of Jerusalem as his eternal monument."

---

[73]S. Zeitlin, "Takkanot Ezra," *JQR* 8 (1917–18): 62–74.

[74]M. Munk, "Esra Hasofer nach Talmud und Midrasch," *Jahrbuch der jüdisch-literarischen Gesellschaft* 22 (1931): 228-29.

[75]D.S. Sassoon, "The History of the Jews in Basra," *JQR* 17 (1926–27): 407–69.

[76]J.D. Purvis, *The Samaritan Pentateuch and the Origin of the Samaritan Sect* (Cambridge, Mass.: Harvard University Press, 1968), p. 98.

[77]L. Ginzberg, *The Legends of the Jews* (Philadelphia: JPS, 1928), 6:432; E. Yamauchi, "Postbiblical Traditions About Ezra and Nehemiah," in *A Tribute to Gleason Archer*, ed. W. Kaiser and R. Youngblood (Chicago: Moody, 1986), pp. 167–76.

12. Purpose and Values

Ezra and Nehemiah record the return of the Jewish exiles from Babylonia and the rebuilding of the temple and the walls around Jerusalem. These accounts highlight the importance of the temple and its personnel. Of vital importance were the attempts to keep the community pure from the syncretistic influence of the neighbors who surrounded it.

The temptation to succumb to pagan syncretism was ever strong. In some cases Jewish communities compromised and were assimilated out of existence as at Elephantine in Egypt. Bright (*Israel*, p. 347) summarizes the situation:

> When one considers the magnitude of the calamity that overtook her, one marvels that Israel was not sucked down into the vortex of history along with the other little nations of western Asia, to lose forever her identity as a people. And if one asks why she was not, the answer surely lies in her faith: the faith that called her into being in the first place proved sufficient even for this. Yet this answer is not to be given to the utmost. That it won through was not something that transpired automatically, but only with much heart-searching and after profound readjustment.

The measures taken by Ezra and Nehemiah to safeguard the Jews from commingling with non-Jews may appear harsh to modern society, but in the light of history they were necessary. G. Widengren observes: "The exclusiveness of the Jews in Judah with the hard measures brought about by Nehemiah and Ezra caused a sharpening of the hostile attitude. Meyer has rightly emphasized the fact that these measures created Judaism. . . . As Nehemiah and Ezra saw the situation, they thought the way of exclusiveness the only possibility for the Jews to survive as a nation with a national religion."[78]

a. *The Book of Ezra*

The Book of Ezra reveals the providential intervention of the God of heaven on behalf of his people. In Ezra 1 the Lord is sovereign over all kingdoms (v.2) and moves even the heart of a pagan ruler to fulfill his will (v.1). He accomplishes the refining of his people through calamities like the conquest and the Exile. He stirs the heart of his people to respond and raises men of God to lead his people (v.11).

In Ezra 3 we see that the service of God requires a united effort (v.1), leadership (v.2a), obedience to God's Word (v.2b), courage in the face of opposition (v.3), offerings and funds (vv.4-7), and an organized division of labor (vv.8-9). Meeting these requirements would result in a sound foundation for later work (v.11), tears and joy (vv.11-12), and praise and thanksgiving to the Lord (v.11).

Ezra 4 teaches that doing the work of God brings opposition: in the guise of proffered cooperation from those who do not share our basic theological convictions (vv.1-2) to complete work we alone are responsible for (v.3); of opposition from those who would discourage and intimidate us (v.4), from professional counselors who offer misleading advice (v.5), from false accusers (vv.6, 13), and from secular authorities (vv.7, 21-24). Far from being discouraged, however, we need to be alert

---

[78]G. Widengren, "Persian Period," p. 512.

and vigorous, knowing that by God's grace we can triumph over all opposition and accomplish his will with rejoicing (6:14–16).

Ezra experienced the good hand of God. As a scribe he was more than a scholar—he was an expounder of the Scriptures (7:6, 12). He believed that God could guide and protect from misfortune (8:20–22). As an inspired leader he enlisted others and assigned trustworthy men to their tasks (7:27–28; 8:15, 24). He regarded what he did as a sacred trust (8:21–28).

Ezra was above all a man of fervent prayer (8:21; 10:1), deep piety, and humility (7:10, 27–28; 9:3; 10:6).

b. *The Book of Nehemiah*

The Book of Nehemiah perhaps more than any other book of the OT reflects the vibrant personality of its author. G. Campbell Morgan comments, "The book thrills and throbs and pulsates with the tremendous force of this man's will."[79] He is seen to have many admirable characteristics.

1. Nehemiah was a man of responsibility. That he served as the king's cupbearer (1:11–2:1) can only mean that he had proven himself trustworthy over a long period.

2. Nehemiah was a man of vision. The walls of Jerusalem had been in ruins for 141 years when Nehemiah learned of an abortive attempt to rebuild them (Ezra 4:23). He had a great vision of who God was and what he could do through his servants.

3. Nehemiah was a man of prayer. His first resort was to prayer (Neh 1:5–11). He prayed spontaneously even in the presence of the king (2:4–5).

4. Nehemiah was a man of action and of cooperation. He would explain what needed to be done (2:16–17) and inspire others to join him (2:18). He knew how to organize the rebuilding work (ch. 3). In spite of opposition the people responded so enthusiastically that they mended the wall in less than two months (6:15). He inspired the people with his own example (5:14–18). Nehemiah, a layman, was able to cooperate with his contemporary Ezra, the scribe and priest, in spite of the fact that these two leaders were of entirely different temperaments. In reaction to the problem of mixed marriages, Ezra plucked out his own hair (Ezra 9:3), whereas Nehemiah plucked out the hair of the offenders (Neh 13:25)!

5. Nehemiah was a man of compassion. He renounced his own privileges (Neh 5:18) and denounced the wealthy who had exploited their poorer brothers (5:8). He did this because of his reverence for God (5:9, 15).

6. Nehemiah was a man who triumphed over opposition. His opponents used every ruse to intimidate him. They started with ridicule (2:19; 4:2–3). They attempted slander (6:5–7). Hired prophets gave him misleading advice (6:10–14). Nehemiah responded with prayer (4:4), with redoubled efforts (v.6), with vigilance (v.9), and with trust in God (v.14).

7. Nehemiah was a man with right motivation. Although he justified his ministry, his primary motive was not to be judged aright by others or to be remembered by posterity. The last words of Nehemiah—"Remember me with favor, O my God" (13:31)—recapitulate a frequently repeated theme (5:19; 13:14, 22, 29). His motive throughout his ministry was to please and serve his divine Sovereign. His only reward would be God's approbation.

---

[79]*Living Messages of the Books of the Bible: Old Testament* (New York: Revell, 1912), p. 262.

13. Bibliography

Commentaries
Ackroyd, P.R. *Chronicles, Ezra, Nehemiah*. London: SCM, 1973.
Adeney, W.F. "Ezra, Nehemiah, and Esther." In *The Expositor's Bible*, ExB, vol. 13. Edited by W.R. Nicoll. London: Hodder & Stoughton, n.d.
Batten, L.W. *A Critical and Exegetical Commentary on the Books of Ezra and Nehemiah*. New York: Charles Scribner's Sons, 1913.
Bowman, R.A. "The Book of Ezra and the Book of Nehemiah." In *The Interpreter's Bible*, IB, vol. 3. Edited by G.A. Buttrick. Nashville: Abingdon, 1954, pp. 549–819.
Brockington, L.H. *Ezra, Nehemiah and Esther*. London: Nelson, 1969.
Clines, D.J.A. *Ezra, Nehemiah, Esther*. Grand Rapids: Eerdmans, 1984.
Coggins, R.J. *The Books of Ezra and Nehemiah*. New York: Cambridge University Press, 1976.
Fensham, F. Charles. *The Books of Ezra and Nehemiah*. Grand Rapids: Eerdmans, 1982.
Keil, C.F. *The Books of Ezra, Nehemiah and Esther*. Biblical Commentary on the Old Testament. KD. Grand Rapids: Eerdmans, n.d.
Kelly, B.H. *Ezra, Nehemiah, Esther, Job*. Richmond, Va.: John Knox, 1962.
Kidner, D. *Ezra-Nehemiah*. Leicester and Downers Grove: Inter-Varsity, 1979.
Michaeli, F. *Les livres des Chroniques, d'Esdras et de Néhémie*. Neuchâtel: Delachaux et Niestlé, 1967.
Myers, J.M. *Ezra-Nehemiah*. Garden City, N.Y.: Doubleday & Co., 1965.
Rudolph, W. *Esra und Nehemia*. Tübingen: J.C.B. Mohr, 1949.
Ryle, H.E. *The Books of Ezra and Nehemiah*. Cambridge: Cambridge University Press, 1901.
Slotki, J. *Daniel, Ezra and Nehemiah*. London: Soncino, 1951.
Turnbull, R.G. *The Book of Nehemiah*. Grand Rapids: Baker, 1968.
Williamson, H.G.M. *Ezra, Nehemiah*. Waco: Word, 1985.

Books
Ackroyd, P.R. *Exile and Restoration*. Philadelphia: Westminster, 1968.
———. *Israel under Babylon and Persia*. London: Oxford University Press, 1970.
Albright, W.F. *The Biblical Period from Abraham to Ezra*. New York: Harper & Row, 1963.
Avigad, N. *Bullae and Seals from a Post-Exilic Judean Archive*. Jerusalem: Hebrew University Press, 1976.
Avi-Yonah, M., ed. *The Holy Land*. Grand Rapids: Baker, 1966.
———. *The Herodian Period*. New Brunswick, N.J.: Rutgers University Press, 1975.
Barber, C.J. *Nehemiah and the Dynamics of Effective Leadership*. Neptune, N.J.: Loizeaux Bros., 1976.
Baron, S. *A Social and Religious History of the Jews I: Ancient Times*. Revised. New York: Columbia University Press, 1952.
Bengston, H. et al. *The Greeks and the Persians*. London: Weidenfeld and Nicolson, 1970.
Ben-Sasson, H., ed. *A History of the Jewish People*. Cambridge: Harvard University Press, 1976.
Bickerman, E. *From Ezra to the Last of the Maccabees*. Revised. New York: Schocken, 1962.
Bright, J. "The Date of Ezra's Mission to Jerusalem." In *Yehezkel Kaufmann Jubilee Volume*, edited by M. Haran. Jerusalem: Magnes, 1960, pp. 70–87.
———. *A History of Israel*. Revised. Philadelphia: Westminster, 1972.
Cameron, G. *Persepolis Treasury Tablets*. Chicago: University of Chicago Press, 1948, 1958, 1965.
Coogan, M.D. *West Semitic Personal Names in the Murašû Documents*. Missoula: Scholars, 1975.
Cowley, A.E. *Aramaic Papyri of the Fifth Century B.C.*. Oxford: Clarendon, 1923.

Cross, F.M., et al. edd. *The Mighty Acts of God*. Garden City, N.Y.: Doubleday & Co., 1976.

Driver, G.R. *Aramaic Documents of the Fifth Century B.C*. Oxford: Clarendon, 1954.

Freedman, D.N., and Greenfield, J.C., edd. *New Directions in Biblical Archaeology*. Garden City, N.Y.: Doubleday & Co., 1969.

Galling, K. *Studien zur Geschichte Israels im persische Zeitalter*. Tübingen: J.C.B. Mohr, 1964.

Gibson, J.C.L., ed. *Textbook of Syrian Semitic Inscriptions II: Aramaic Inscriptions*. Oxford: Clarendon, 1975.

Hallock, R.T. *Persepolis Fortification Tablets*. Chicago: University of Chicago Press, 1969.

Hayes, J.H., and Miller, J.M., edd. *Israelite and Judaean History*. Philadelphia: Westminster, 1977.

Horn, S.H., and Wood, L.H. *The Chronology of Ezra 7*. Washington, D.C.: Review and Herald, 1953.

Inscriptions Reveal. Revised. Jersualem: Israel Museum, 1973.

Janssen, E. *Juda in der Exilzeit*. Göttingen: Vandenhoeck & Ruprecht, 1956.

Jerusalmi, Isaac. *The Aramaic Sections of Ezra and Daniel*. Revised. Cincinnati: Hebrew Union College, 1970.

Kapelrud, A.S. *The Question of Authorship in the Ezra-Narratives*. Oslo: Dybwad, 1944.

Kellermann, U. *Nehemia: Quellen Überlieferung und Geschichte*. Berlin: A. Töpelmann, 1967.

Kent, R.G. *Old Persian*. Revised. New Haven: American Oriental Society, 1953.

Kenyon, K.M. *Jerusalem*. London: Thames & Hudson, 1967.

———. *Digging Up Jerusalem*. London: Benn, 1974.

Kraeling, E. *The Brooklyn Aramaic Papyri*. New Haven: Yale University Press, 1953.

Mazar, B. *The Mountain of the Lord*. Garden City, N.Y.: Doubleday & Co., 1975.

McKay, J.W. *Religion in Judah under the Assyrians*. London: SCM, 1973.

Moore, G.F. *Judaism in the First Centuries of the Christian Era I–III*. Cambridge: Harvard University Press, 1927–30.

Mowinckel, S. *Studien zu dem Buche Ezra-Nehemiah I–III*. Olso: Universitetsforlaget, 1964–65.

Myers, J.M. *The World of the Restoration*. Englewood Cliffs, N.J.: Prentice-Hall, 1968.

———. *I & II Esdras*. Garden City, N.Y.: Doubleday & Co., 1974.

North, R. "Civil Authority in Ezra." *Studi in onore di Edoardo Volterra*. Milan: Dott. A. Guiffrè, 1971, 6:377–404.

Obed, B. *Mass Deportations and Deportees in the Neo-Assyrian Empire*. Wiesbaden: L. Reichert, 1979.

Olmstead, A.T. *History of the Persian Empire*. Chicago: University of Chicago Press, 1948.

Porten, B. *Archives from Elephantine*. Berkeley: University of California Press, 1968.

Rainey, A.F. *The Scribe at Ugarit*. Jerusalem: Israel Academy of Sciences and Humanities, 1968.

Rosenthal, F. *A Grammar of Biblical Aramaic*. Wiesbaden: Harrassowitz, 1961.

Rowley, H.H. *Men of God*. London: Thomas Nelson, 1963.

———. *The Servant of the Lord*. Revised. Naperville, Ill.: Allenson, 1965.

Smith, M. *Palestinian Parties and Politics That Shaped the Old Testament*. New York: Columbia University Press, 1971.

Stern, Ephraim. *Material Culture of the Land of the Bible in the Persian Period 538–332 B.C*. Warminster: Aris & Phillips, 1982.

Talmon, S. "Ezra and Nehemiah." In *The Interpreter's Dictionary of the Bible, Supplementary Volume*. Edited by K. Crim et al. Nashville: Abingdon, 1976, pp. 317–28.

Torrey, C.C. *Ezra Studies*. Edited by W.F. Stinespring. 1910. Reprint. New York: KTAV, 1970.

Vogt, H.C. *Studien zur nachexilischen Gemeinde in Esra-Nehemiah*. Werl: Dietrich-Coelde, 1966.

Walser, G., ed. *Beiträge zur Achämenidengeschichte*. Wiesbaden: Franz Steiner, 1972.
Williamson, H.G.M. *Israel in the Book of Chronicles*. Cambridge: Cambridge University Press, 1977.
Wiseman, D.J., ed. *Peoples of Old Testament Times*. Oxford: Clarendon, 1973.
Wright, J.S. *The Building of the Second Temple*. London: Tyndale, 1958.
_____. *The Date of Ezra's Coming to Jerusalem*. Revised. London: Tyndale, 1958.
Yamauchi, E. *Greece and Babylon*. Grand Rapids: Baker, 1967.
_____. "Two Reformers Compared: Solon of Athens and Nehemiah of Jerusalem." *The Bible World: Essays in Honor of Cyrus H. Gordon*. Edited by G. Rendsburg et al. New York: KTAV, 1980, pp. 269–92.
_____. "Nehemiah, A Model Leader." *A Spectrum of Thought: Essays in Honor of Dennis F. Kinlaw*. Edited by Michael Peterson. Wilmore: Francis Asbury, 1982, pp. 171–80.
Zadok, Ran. *The Jews in Babylonia During the Chaldean and Achaemenian Periods*. Haifa: University of Haifa, 1979.

Dissertations
Ararat, N. "Ezra and His Deeds in the Sources." Ph.D. dissertation. Yeshiva University, 1971.
Breitkreuz, B. "The Person and Role of Ezra within the Framework of the Chronicler's History of Israel." Ph.D. dissertation. Hebrew Union College, 1969.
Hensley, C. "The Official Persian Documents in the Book of Ezra." Ph.D. dissertation. University of Liverpool, 1977.

Periodicals
Allrik, H.L. "The Lists of Zerubbabel (Nehemiah 7 and Ezra 2) and the Hebrew Numerical Notation." *Bulletin of the American Schools of Oriental Research* 136 (1954): 21–27.
Avi-Yonah, M. "The Walls of Nehemiah—A Minimalist View." *Israel Exploration Journal* 4 (1954): 239–48.
Bickerman, E.J. "The Edict of Cyrus in Ezra 1." *Journal of Biblical Literature* 65 (1946): 249 –75.
Cross, F.M. "The Discovery of the Samaria Papyri." *Biblical Archaeologist* 26 (1963): 110– 20.
_____. "A Reconstruction of the Judean Restoration." *Journal of Biblical Literature* 94 (1975): 4–18.
Japhet, S. "The Supposed Common Authorship of Chronicles and Ezra-Nehemiah." *Vetus Testamentum* 18 (1968): 330–71.
Klein, R. "Old Reading in I Esdras: The List of Returnees from Babylon (Ezra 2/Nehemiah 7)." *Harvard Theological Review* 62 (1969): 99–107.
Koch, K. "Ezra and the Origins of Judaism." *Journal of Semitic Studies* 19 (1974): 173–97.
Leesberg, M.W. "Ezra and Nehemiah." *Concordia Theological Monthly* 33 (1962): 79–90.
Rainey, A.F. "The Satrapy 'Beyond the River.'" *Australian Journal of Biblical Archaeology* 1 (1969): 51–78.
Talmon, S. "The Samaritans." *Scientific American* 236 (January 1977): 100–108.
Wallis, Gerard. "Jüdische Bürger in Babylonien während der Achämeniden-Zeit." *Persica* 9 (1980): 129–88.
Yamauchi, E. "The Achaemenid Capitals." *Near East Archaeological Society Bulletin* 8 (1976): 5–81.
_____. "The Archaeological Background of Ezra." *Bibliotheca Sacra* 137 (1980): 195–211.
_____. "The Archaeological Background of Nehemiah." *Bibliotheca Sacra* 137 (1980): 291– 309.
_____. "The Reverse Order of Ezra/Nehemiah Reconsidered." *Themelios* 5 (1980): 13–21.
_____. "Was Nehemiah the Cupbearer a Eunuch?" *Zeitschrift für die alttestamentliche Wissenschaft* 92 (1980): 132–42.

14. Chart and Maps

Dates are given according to a Nisan-to-Nisan Jewish calendar. The Jewish dates are indicated with Roman numerals representing months, Arabic numerals representing days.

NISAN YEAR			MODERN		EVENT	REFERENCE
Year	Month	Day	Month	Day		
539	VII	16	Oct	12	Babylon falls	
	VIII	3	Oct	29	Cyrus enters Babylon	Dan 5:30–31
538	III	24	Mar	24	Cyrus's first regnal year	Ezra 1:1–4
to			to			
537	III	11	Mar	11		
537?			spring		Return under Sheshbazzar	Ezra 1:11
	VII		Oct	5	Building the altar	Ezra 3:1–3
			to			
			Nov	2		
536	II		Apr	29	Work on the temple resumed	Ezra 3:8
to			to			
530			May	28	Opposition during Cyrus's reign	Ezra 4:1—5
520	VI	1	Aug	29	Haggai speaks to Zerubbabel	Hag 1:1
	VI	1	Aug/Dec (?)		Work resumed on temple under Darius	Ezra 5:1—2; Hag1:1,14–15
515	XII	3	Mar	12	Temple completed	Ezra 6:15
458	I	1	Apr	8	Ezra departs	Ezra 7:7
	V	1	Aug	4	Ezra arrives	Ezra 7:8–9
	IX	20	Dec	19	People assemble	Ezra 10:9
	X	1	Dec	29	Committee begins investigation	Ezra 10:16
457	I	1				
446			Mar	26	Nineteenth year of Artaxerxes I	
to			to			
445			Apr	12		
445			Apr	13	Twentieth year	Neh 1:1
to			to			
444			Apr	2		
445	I		Apr/May		Nehemiah approaches the king	Neh 2:1
			Aug?		Nehemiah arrives	Neh 2:11
	VI	25	Oct	2	Completion of the wall	Neh 6:15
	VII		Oct	8	Public assembly	Neh 7:73
			to			
			Nov	5		
	VII	15	Oct	22	Feast of Booths	Neh 8:14
		to		to		
		22		28		
	VII	24	Oct	30	Fast	Neh 9:1
433			Apr	1	Thirty-second year of Artaxerxes	Neh 5:14
to			to			
432			Apr	19	Nehemiah's recall and return	Neh 13:6

Number of Month	Name	Equivalent
I	Nisan	Mar./Apr.
II	Iyyar	Apr./May
III	Sivan	May/June
IV	Tammuz	June/July
V	Ab	July/Aug.
VI	Elul	Aug./Sept.
VII	Tishri	Sept./Oct.
VIII	Marcheshvan	Oct./Nov.
IX	Kislev	Nov./Dec.
X	Tebeth	Dec./Jan.
XI	Shebat	Jan./Feb.
XII	Adar	Feb./Mar.

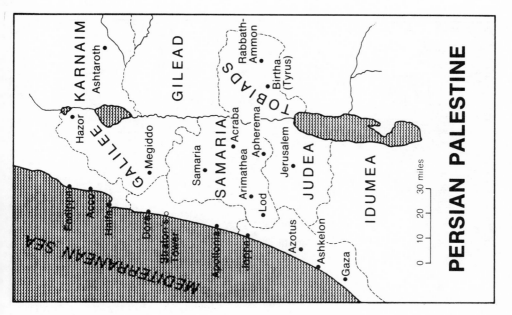

PERSIAN PALESTINE

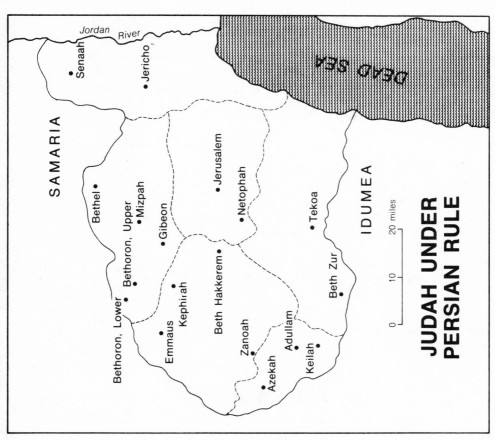

JUDAH UNDER
PERSIAN RULE

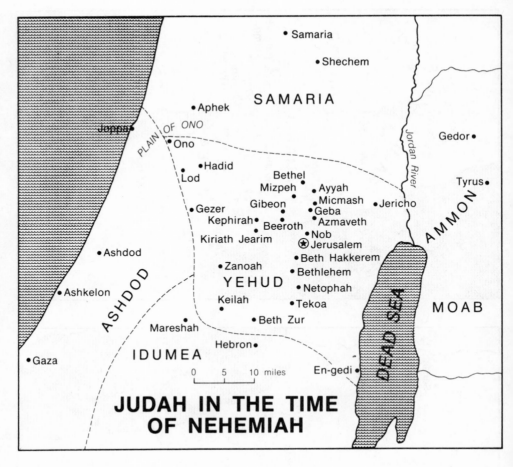

Samaria

Shechem

SAMARIA

Aphek

Joppa

PLAIN OF ONO

Ono

Hadid

Lod

Gezer

Bethel

Mizpeh

Gibeon

Kephirah

Beeroth

Kiriath Jearim

Ayyah

Micmash

Geba

Azmaveth

Nob

Jerusalem

Jordan River

Gedor

Tyrus

Jericho

AMMON

Ashdod

Ashkelon

Zanoah

YEHUD

Keilah

Beth Hakkerem

Bethlehem

Netophah

Tekoa

Beth Zur

DEAD SEA

MOAB

Gaza

IDUMEA

Mareshah

Hebron

En-gedi

0   5   10 miles

JUDAH IN THE TIME OF NEHEMIAH

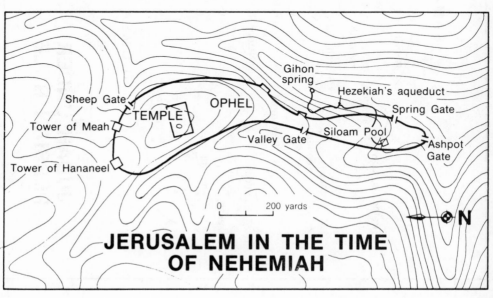

Sheep Gate

Tower of Meah

TEMPLE

OPHEL

Gihon spring

Hezekiah's aqueduct

Spring Gate

Tower of Hananeel

Valley Gate

Siloam Pool

Ashpot Gate

0   200 yards

N

JERUSALEM IN THE TIME OF NEHEMIAH

EZRA

Outline

Text and Exposition

I. The First Return From Exile and the Rebuilding of the Temple (1:1–6:22).

A. *The First Return of the Exiles (1:1–11)*

1. *The edict of Cyrus*

1:1–4

> ¹In the first year of Cyrus king of Persia, in order to fulfill the word of the LORD spoken by Jeremiah, the LORD moved the heart of Cyrus king of Persia to make a proclamation throughout his realm and to put it in writing:
>
> ²"This is what Cyrus king of Persia says:
> " 'The LORD, the God of heaven, has given me all the kingdoms of the earth and he has appointed me to build a temple for him at Jerusalem in Judah. ³Anyone of his people among you—may his God be with him, and let him go up to Jerusalem in Judah and build the temple of the LORD, the God of Israel, the God who is in Jerusalem. ⁴And the people of any place where survivors may now be living are to provide him with silver and gold, with goods and livestock, and with freewill offerings for the temple of God in Jerusalem.' "

It had been nearly seventy years since the first deportation of the Jews by the Babylonians to Mesopotamia. Though the initial years must have been difficult, the second and third generation of Jews born in the Exile had adjusted to their surroundings. Though some had become so comfortable that they refused to return to Judah when given the opportunity, still others, sustained by the examples and teachings of leaders like Daniel and Ezekiel, retained their faith in the Lord's promises and their allegiance to their homeland.

1 Ezra 1:1–3a is virtually identical with the last verses of Chronicles (2 Chronicles 36:22–23). (For the implications of this correspondence, see Introduction: Literary Form and Authorship.)

"In the first year" means the first regnal year of Cyrus, beginning in Nisan 538, after his capture of Babylon in October 539 (cf. Introduction: Chronology). Cuneiform texts record the Persian king's benefactions to Mesopotamian sanctuaries in the months following the capture of Babylon.

Cyrus, the founder of the Persian Empire and the greatest Achaemenid king, reigned over the Persians from 559 till 530 B.C. He established Persian dominance over the Medes in 550, conquered Lydia and Anatolia in 547–46, and captured Babylon in 539.

Isaiah 44:28 and 45:1 speak of Cyrus as the Lord's "shepherd" and his "anointed." Daniel (Dan 1:21; 6:28; 10:1) was in Babylon when Cyrus captured it.

"The word of the LORD spoken by Jeremiah" was the prophet's prediction (Jer 25:1–12; 29:10) of a seventy-year Babylonian captivity. The first deportations began in 605, in the third year of Jehoiakim, according to Daniel 1:1 (see Wiseman, *Notes on Daniel*, pp. 16–18). The seventieth year would be 536. We know that the Persian kings paid close heed to prophecies: Cambyses to Egyptian oracles, Darius and Xerxes to Greek oracles (*Herodotus* 8.133; 9.42, 151).

"Proclamation" (*qôl*) was an oral proclamation in the native language in contrast to the copy of the decree in 6:3–5, which was an Aramaic memorandum for the archives. In the case of the famous Behistun Inscription, Darius had copies sent throughout the empire in other languages, as we have copies in Akkadian from Babylon and on a papyrus in Aramaic from Egypt.

2 "The God of heaven" (*ᵉlōhê haššāmāyim*; cf. Aram. *ᵉlāh šᵉmayyāʾ*) is a phrase that occurs primarily in the postexilic books. Seventeen of the twenty-two occurrences are in Ezra, Nehemiah, and Daniel. It appears also in apocryphal works (Tobit 10:11 –12; Jud 5:8; 6:19; 11:17) (cf. D.K. Andrews, "Yahweh the God of Heavens," *The Seed of Wisdom*, ed. W.S. McCullough [Toronto: University of Toronto Press, 1964], pp. 45ff.).

The Holy City and the house of God are both prominent subjects in Ezra-Nehemiah. Jerusalem occurs eighty-six times, and the phrases "temple," "house of the LORD," and "house of God" appear fifty-three times. The phrase "a temple for him at Jerusalem in Judah" is literally "a house for him in Jerusalem that is in Judah." The formulation "Jerusalem that is in Judah" is characteristic of Persian bureaucratic style. The Elephantine papyri (Cowley 30:6) have "The temple of Yaw [i.e., Yahweh], the god, which is in the fortress of Yeb."

Cyrus instituted the enlightened policy of placating the gods of his subject peoples rather than carrying off their cult statues as the Assyrians, Elamites, Hittites, and Babylonians had done before. His generosity to the Jews was also paralleled by his benevolence to the Babylonians. Ultimately, however, it was the Lord who had "moved" his heart.

3 The religious orientation of the Achaemenid kings—Cyrus and his successors—is a controversial issue. We do not know whether they were influenced by Zoroaster (cf. V.V. Strouve, "The Religion of the Achaemenids and Zoroastrianism," *Cahiers d'histoire mondiale* 5 [1959–60]: 529–45; M. Boyce, *A History of Zoroastrianism* [Leiden: E.J. Brill, 1982], vol. 2).

4 "Where survivors may now be living" (*kol-hanniš'ār*, "everyone who remains over") refers to survivors of the capture and deportation (cf. Neh 1:2). The Hebrew word for "living" (*gār*) is cognate to the word for "resident alien" (*gēr*). The deportees continued to be regarded as aliens, as were the Susians and Elamites who were "resident" in Samaria years after their deportation (4:10, 17).

"The people of any place" could mean non-Israelite neighbors as in the case of the Exodus (Exod 12:35–36). More probably it designated the many Jews, especially of the second and the third generation, who did not wish to leave the land of their birth.

"Freewill offerings" (*nᵉḏāḇāh*, lit., "freewill offering") were voluntary giving (vv.4, 6; 2:68–69; 3:5; 7:13–16; 8:28) and voluntary service (v.5; 7:13), the keys to the restoration of God's temple and its service. A cognate form of *nᵉḏāḇāh* was used of those who volunteered to join the community at Qumran (1QS V.1, 6 et al.).

Notes

1 The name of Cyrus in Hebrew is כּוֹרֶשׁ (*kôreš*, cf. Old Pers. *kūruš*, Akkad. *kurašu*, Gr. *kyros*). The title "King of Persia" in extant Old Persian texts appears first in the Behistun

Inscription, but it is found in the Nabonidus Chronicle. The TEV translates the phrase "emperor of Persia."

The Assyrian king Esarhaddon declared in an inscription that the god Marduk reduced an original seventy-year period of depopulation for the city of Babylon and ordered its rebuilding in the eleventh year (cf. R. Borger, *Die Inschriften Asarhaddons Königs von Assyrien* [Graz: Archiv für Orientforschung, 1956], p. 15). For further discussions of the seventy-year period, see C.F. Whitley, "The Term Seventy Years Captivity," VetTest 4 [1954]: 60–72; G. Larsson, "When Did the Babylonian Captivity Begin?" JTS 18 [1967]: 417–23). There may also have been a return of exiles from the Syrian town of Neirab about 520 B.C., according to the interpretation of I. Eph'al, "The Western Minorities in Babylonia in the 6th–5th Centuries B.C.," *Orientalia* 47 (1978): 84–86.

---

2. The return under Sheshbazzar

1:5–11

⁵Then the family heads of Judah and Benjamin, and the priests and Levites—everyone whose heart God had moved—prepared to go up and build the house of the LORD in Jerusalem. ⁶All their neighbors assisted them with articles of silver and gold, with goods and livestock, and with valuable gifts, in addition to all the freewill offerings. ⁷Moreover, King Cyrus brought out the articles belonging to the temple of the LORD, which Nebuchadnezzar had carried away from Jerusalem and had placed in the temple of his god. ⁸Cyrus king of Persia had them brought by Mithredath the treasurer, who counted them out to Sheshbazzar the prince of Judah.

⁹This was the inventory:

gold dishes	30
silver dishes	1,000
silver pans	29
¹⁰gold bowls	30
matching silver bowls	410
other articles	1,000

¹¹In all, there were 5,400 articles of gold and of silver. Sheshbazzar brought all these along when the exiles came up from Babylon to Jerusalem.

5–6 The Lord stirred not only the heart of the Persian king but also the hearts of many of the exiles who had maintained their faith in the Lord in spite of the devastation of their homeland. A vivid attestation to this faith is an inscription carved at Khirbet Beit Lei, five miles east of Lachish, first published in 1963 by J. Naveh. F.M. Cross ("The Cave Inscriptions from Khirbet Beit Lei," *Near Eastern Archaeology in the Twentieth Century*, ed. J.A. Sanders [Garden City, N.Y.: Doubleday & Co., 1970], pp. 299–306) has translated the text as follows: "I am Yahweh thy God: I will accept the cities of Judah and will redeem Jerusalem." He has suggested that this may have been incised by a refugee to express his trust in God's faithfulness despite the desolation of the Holy City (cf. Lam 3:22–24).

Commenting on the tenacious faith that inspired the Jews to return to Palestine under the Persians and again in the twentieth century, W.F. Albright (*History, Archaeology and Christian Humanism* [New York: McGraw Hill, 1964], pp. 58–59) perceptively notes:

But how could the Jews have been so filled with the conviction that Israel would indeed be restored, even after complete destruction, unless there were prophecies of Restoration to believe? The rationalistic attempt to do away with prophecy raises new problems which are much more difficult to solve than acceptance of the uniform early tradition presented by our Biblical sources. So far as we know, no people except Israel has ever been restored to its native land after such a clean break. If there were any remaining doubt, surely it would be removed by the close analogy which we now have in the second restoration of Israel, after twenty-five more centuries! No one can dispute the fact that it was the firmly held rabbinic belief in their ultimate return as a nation to Palestine that brought the Jews back to their ancient home in recent generations.

7 Conquerers customarily carried off the statues of the gods of conquered cities. The Hittites took the statue of Marduk when they conquered the city of Babylon. The Philistines took the ark of the Jews and placed it in the temple of Dagon (1 Sam 5:2). As the Jews did not have a statue of the Lord, Nebuchadnezzar carried off the temple goods instead. The Hebrew of 2 Kings 24:13 indicates that he cut up the vessels of gold, no doubt the larger ones, to facilitate their transportation (cf. 2 Kings 25:13; Jer 52:17).

Jeremiah spoke of false prophets who prematurely predicted the return of these vessels (Jer 27:16–22; 28:6); he prophesied their ultimate return (27:22). Belshazzar had the audacity to drink from some of the temple vessels (Dan 5:23).

The Persian name "Mithredath" means "given by Mithra." Mithra(s) was the Persian god whose mystery religion became popular among Roman soldiers in the second century A.D. Another official with the same name appears in 4:7. Mithradates was the name of the king of Pontus in northern Turkey who warred against the Romans (cf. R.A. Bowman, *Aramaic Ritual Texts from Persepolis* [Chicago: University of Chicago Press, 1968], pp. 32, 73, 78, for the name "Dat-Mithra").

8 The word for "treasurer" is *gizbār*, from the Old Persian *ganzabara*. The word may be reflected in Gaspar (Caspar), the name of one of the magi according to the apocryphal Gospel of the Hebrews.

Sheshbazzar, who had a Babylonian name (cf. Notes), was probably a Jewish official who served as a deputy governor of Judah under the satrap in Samaria (cf. Ezra 5:14; 1 Esd 2:12).

9–11 When the Assyrian and Babylonian conquerors carried off booty, their scribes made a careful inventory of it. The actual figures in the Hebrew text add up to 2,499 rather than 5,400, perhaps because only the larger and more valuable vessels were specified. The RSV follows 1 Esdras and gives figures of 1,000, 1,000, 29, 30, 2,410, and 1,000—a total of 5,469. The exact meanings of the Hebrew words for the objects are uncertain (cf. Notes).

We know nothing about the details of Sheshbazzar's journey, which probably took place in the spring of 537. Judging from Ezra's later journey (7:8–9), the trip probably took about four months. The caravan would have proceeded from Babylonia up the Euphrates River and then south through the Orontes Valley of Syria to Palestine.

Notes

8 שֵׁשְׁבַּצַּר (*šēšbaṣṣar*, "Sheshbazzar") is a Babylonian name perhaps derived from one of the following Akkadian names:

    a. *Sin-ab-uṣur* ("Sin protect the father"; cf. LXX Sabanassaro, Sanabassaro; 1 Esd 2:12, 15). Sin was the moon god. This etymology is favored by Albright, Meyer, and Rosenthal.

    b. *Šamaš-ab-uṣur* ("Shamash protect the father") or *Šamaš-apla-uṣur* ("Shamash protect the son," favored by Brockington and Noth). Shamash was the sun god.

    c. *Šaššu-ab-uṣur* ("Shashu protect the father"). *Šaššu* is a variant for *Šamaš*. So says R. Berger, "Zu den Namen ששבצר und שנאצר," ZAW 83 (1971): 98–100.

Following a proposal by Imbert in 1888, supported by Albright in 1921, many scholars agree that Sheshbazzar is identical with Shenazzar (Akkad. *Sin-uṣur*) of 1 Chron 3:18. Sheshbazzar would then be of Davidic descent as the fourth son of King Jehoiachin; he would also be the uncle of Zerubbabel (cf. comment on 2:2).

9–10 אֲגַרְטְלִים (*ʾagarṭelîm*, "dishes") is rendered by the LXX as κάρταλλος (*kartallos*), a "basket with [a] pointed bottom" (cf. 2 Kings 10:7) or "a basket-shaped libation cup."

    מַחֲלָפִים (*maḥalāpîm*, "pans") occurs only here in the OT. In late Hebrew a related word is a technical term for the knives used in ritual slaughter of animals (so KJV; but cf. RSV, "censers").

    כְּפוֹרִים (*kepôrîm*, "bowls") occurs only here, in 8:27, and in 1 Chron 28:17. It is perhaps a late Hebrew word for מִזְרָק (*mizrāq*, "basin"; cf. Num 4:14; 1 Kings 7:40) or for קְעָרָה (*qeʿārāh*, "dish"; cf. Num 4:7).

Earlier scholars (Wellhausen, Kosters, Vernes, Torrey, Hölscher, Pfeiffer, Oesterley, Galling) questioned the authenticity of Cyrus's decree because of its Jewish phraseology. But documents from the Persian period and archaeological evidence have provided convincing evidences of its authenticity. Especially impressive are the "Verse Account of Nabonidus" (ANET, pp. 312–15) and the "Cyrus Cylinder" (ANET, pp. 315–16), which indicate that one of Cyrus's first acts was to return gods removed from their sanctuaries by Nabonidus. The latter document relates, "I (also) gathered all their (former) inhabitants and returned (to them) their habitations." A fragment of the Cyrus Cylinder, identified in 1970, recounts that Cyrus restored Babylon's inner wall and moats (cf. C.B.F. Walker, "A Recently Identified Fragment of the Cyrus Cylinder," *Iran* 10 [1972]: 158–59; P.-R. Berger, "Der Kyros-Zylinder mit dem Zusatzfragment BIN II Nr. 32," *Zeitschrift für Assyriologie* 64 [1975]: 192–234).

Excavations at Uruk and Ur reveal that Cyrus made restorations in temples there (cf. C.L. Woolley, *Ur of the Chaldees* [New York: Norton, 1965], p. 205; C.L. Woolley and M.E.L. Mallowan, *Ur Excavations IX: The Neo-Babylonian and Persian Periods* [London: The British Museum, 1962]).

The best expositions for the authenticity of the decree are E.J. Bickerman, "The Edict of Cyrus in Ezra 1," JBL 65 (1946): 249–75; R. de Vaux, "The Decrees of Cyrus and Darius on the Rebuilding of the Temple," *The Bible and the Ancient New East* (Garden City, N.Y.: Doubleday, 1971), pp. 63–96.

B. The List of Returning Exiles (2:1–70)

1. Leaders of the return

2:1–2a

> ¹Now these are the people of the province who came up from the captivity of the exiles, whom Nebuchadnezzar king of Babylon had taken captive to Babylon

(they returned to Jerusalem and Judah, each to his own town, ²in company with Zerubbabel, Jeshua, Nehemiah, Seraiah, Reelaiah, Mordecai, Bilshan, Mispar, Bigvai, Rehum and Baanah):

1 The list of returning exiles in vv. 1–70 almost exactly parallels the list in Nehemiah 7:6–73 (cf. 1 Esd 5:4–46). The list of localities indicates that people retained their memories of their homes and that exiles from a very wide background of tribes, villages, and towns returned.

The KJV's colon after Zerubbabel (v.2) implies that all those who followed were among those returning with Zerubbabel in 537. The NIV, RSV et al. place a comma after Zerubbabel, leaving open the possibility, according to some scholars, that the list may include those who returned to Judah at a later date.

A comparison of Ezra 2 with Nehemiah 7 reveals a number of differences in both the names and the numbers that are listed. Though the lists of temple personnel show few variations, there are differences in about half the cases of the lists of the laity. Of the 153 numbers, 29 are not the same in Ezra and Nehemiah. Many differences may be explained by assuming that a cipher notation was used with vertical strokes for units, horizontal strokes for tens, and stylized mems (the initial letter of the Hebrew word *mē'āh*) for hundreds. Single strokes could be overlooked or miscopied. Allrik (p. 27) states: "As for the lists in Nehemiah 7 and Ezra 2, while at first glance these textual-numerical differences may seem detrimental, actually they greatly enhance the value of the lists, as they bring out much of their real nature and age." For a fuller treatment of the discrepancies in names and numbers, see Gleason L. Archer, *Encyclopedia of Bible Difficulties* (Grand Rapids: Zondervan, 1982), pp. 229–30.

2a The list of eleven leaders in Ezra 2 is increased by the addition of "Nahamani" inserted before the name of Mordecai in Nehemiah 7:7 (cf. 1 Esd 5:8).

On "Zerubbabel" see the comments on 5:2.

"Jeshua" is a name similar to "Joshua" (Neh 8:17) and to the Greek "Jesus." It means "Yahweh is salvation." If he is the same as the Joshua of Haggai 1:1, he was the son of Jehozadak, the high priest carried into exile (1 Chron 6:15) and the grandson of Seraiah, the high priest put to death by Nebuchadnezzar (2 Kings 25:18 –21; cf. Ezra 5:2; Neh 12:1, 10, 26; Zech 3:1).

"Nehemiah" was not the same person as the king's cupbearer. On the name see the comment on Nehemiah 1:1.

"Seraiah" means "Yahweh is Prince." Nehemiah 7:7 has Azariah.

"Reelaiah" is paralleled in Nehemiah 7:7 by "Raamiah."

"Mordecai" is based on the name of the god of Babylon, Marduk (Jer 50:2). It is the name borne by Esther's uncle.

"Bilshan" is probably the Akkadian *Bel-šunu* ("their Lord").

"Mispar" is paralleled in Nehemiah 7:7 by "Mispereth."

"Bigvai," a Persian name meaning "happy," was borne by the Persian governor of Judea addressed by the Jews of Elephantine in 407 B.C.: B-g-w-h-y (*Bagohi*). Josephus (*Antiq.* XI, 297 [vii.1]) transliterated the name in Greek as *Bagoses*.

"Rehum" is a hypocoristicon (shortened form) for "(God) has been compassionate." Nehemiah 7:7 has "Nehum," which is probably a scribal error. The Murashu texts have a comparable name: *Raḥim*.

The practice of giving Babylonian or Persian names to Jews in captivity (Esth 2:7; Dan 1:7) is richly illustrated by the archives of Murashu. According to M.D. Coogan ("Life in the Diaspora: Jews at Nippur in the Fifth Century B.C.," BA 37 [1974]: 11): "It was not considered a serious compromise of one's Jewish identity to give a child a name which was not Yahwistic, nor even of Hebrew or Aramaic linguistic stock."

Notes

1 The simple, straightforward view of the lists in Ezra 2 and Nehemiah 7 as a list of the returnees under Zerubbabel is accepted by A. Alt, E. Meyer, F. Micheli, M. Noth, W. Rudolph, H. Schaeder, and G. Widengren. Other scholars (e.g., L.H. Brockington, R.J. Coggins, J.M. Myers, and R. North) doubt that so many people would have responded at first. Various alternative dates and explanations for the lists have therefore been proposed.

K. Galling ("The 'Gōlā list' according to Ezra 2//Nehemiah 7," JBL 70 [1951]: 149–58) has argued that the lists represent an official census drawn up in 519 B.C. for the governor Tattenai (Ezra 5) to show that the Jews could achieve the reconstruction of the temple. Others have held that the lists include the returnees down to the time of Ezra (458 B.C.) (cf. Batten, in loc.; Harrison, IOT, p. 1143).

Some scholars date the lists to Nehemiah's time, arguing that the ending in Neh 7:72b (73 EV)–8:1 provides a more satisfactory setting than Ezra 2:70–3:1. Others hold that the list was composed by the Chronicler about 400 B.C.

In the case of discrepant numbers, R. Klein ("Old Readings in I Esdras," HTR 62 [1969]: 99–107) notes that 1 Esdras supports Ezra thirteen times and Nehemiah but twice. He concludes that 1 Esdras preserves an older text than MT Ezra or the LXX. In some cases the 1 Esdras text can be used to correct some of the names and figures in the list.

In Ezra and Nehemiah there are about 80 different theophorous names bearing the divine element -iah for Yahweh, which are mentioned almost 270 times. We can compare these with similar names of Jews from the contemporary communities in Egypt and in Mesopotamia. At Elephantine in Egypt, of more than 160 Jewish names, only a few were nontheophorous.

In an early study of the Murashu names, S. Daiches (The Jews in Babylonia in the Time of Ezra and Nehemiah according to Babylonian Inscriptions [London: Jews' College, 1910], p. 31) remarked: "Some of these names do not even occur in the O.T. They are, therefore, not mere conventional names, which conveyed little or no meaning to those who gave them and those who bore them. They were coined with full consciousness, and the ideas expressed in them were the ideas that animate the fathers and the children in those times."

A striking example of such faith implicit in a name is found in a seal dated paleographically to the sixth century B.C. A father with the Babylonian name Šawaš-šar-uṣur ("Shamash protect the king") gave his daughter the Hebrew name Yehoyishma ("Yahweh will hear") (N. Avigad, "Seals of the Exile," IEJ 15 [1965]: 223–30).

מְדִינָה (mᵉdînāh, "province") is used of an administrative area, either a satrapy or its subdivision. The "province" here is Babylonia (cf. 7:16). The word also appears in the Aramaic papyri, e.g., Cowley 24:18, 35; 37:6 et al. (F. Charles Fensham, "Medina in Ezra and Nehemiah," VetTest 25 [1975]: 795–97).

2. Families

2:2b–20

The list of the men of the people of Israel:

[3]the descendants of Parosh	2,172
[4]of Shephatiah	372
[5]of Arah	775
[6]of Pahath-Moab (through the line of Jeshua and Joab)	2,812
[7]of Elam	1,254
[8]of Zattu	945
[9]of Zaccai	760
[10]of Bani	642
[11]of Bebai	623
[12]of Azgad	1,222
[13]of Adonikam	666
[14]of Bigvai	2,056
[15]of Adin	454
[16]of Ater (through Hezekiah)	98
[17]of Bezai	323
[18]of Jorah	112
[19]of Hashum	223
[20]of Gibbar	95

2b "The list of the men of the people of Israel" may have been of males only over the age of twelve; 1 Esdras 5:41 makes this explicit: "twelve or more years of age."

3 "The descendants of Parosh" represented the largest family of priests returning from Babylon. Members of this family returned with Ezra (8:3); some of them assisted in rebuilding the wall (Neh 3:25). "Parosh" means "flea" and may connote insignificance (cf. 1 Sam 24:14). On the other hand, S.D. Goitein ("Nicknames as Family Names," JAOS 90 [1970]: 517) suggests: "Fleas are tormenting bloodsuckers, and the idea expressed in this name, or by-name, is that its bearer should be a constant plague to his enemies. A distinguished Arab family in Jerusalem is called Barghūtī, which means the same thing; Arabic *barghūth* and Hebrew *par'ōsh* are identical phonetically and semantically."

Insect and animal names were common among the Hebrews (cf. comments on vv.5, 46; Neh 11:16; cf. Caleb ["dog"], Deborah ["bee"], Jonah ["dove"], Leah ["wild cow"], Rachel ["ewe"] et al.). An ostracon from the seventh century B.C. has the following names: Qore ("partridge"), Sorek ("bay horse"), and Qeres ("biting insect[?]") (*Inscriptions Reveal*, #138).

4 "Shephatiah" means "Yahweh has judged." Other members of the family returned with Ezra (8:8).

5 "Arah" means "wild ox." As the name appears elsewhere only in 1 Chronicles 7:39 and has been found in documents from Mesopotamia, it may have been adopted during the Exile.

6 "Pahath-Moab" means "governor of Moab" (cf. 8:4; 10:30; Neh 7:11; 10:14). These may be the descendants of the tribe of Reuben who were deported from the province of Moab by Tiglath-pileser III (cf. 1 Chron 5:3–8).

7 "Elam" was the name of the country in southwestern Iran in the area of Susa (cf. v.31; 8:7; 10:2, 26; Neh 7:12; 10:14).

9 "Zaccai" may mean "pure" or may be a shortened form of Zechariah ("Yahweh has remembered").

10 "Bani" is a shortened form of Benaiah ("Yahweh has built"). Nehemiah 7:15 has Binnui.

11 "Bebai" is "pupil of the eye"; cf. *Bi-bi-ya* in the Murashu texts (Coogan, *Personal Names*, p. 120).

12 "Azgad" ("Gad is strong") is either a reference to Gad, the god of fortune, or to the Transjordanian tribe of Gad. This name occurs only here and in Nehemiah 7:17. The greatest numerical discrepancy occurs here: Ezra lists 1,222 whereas Nehemiah lists 2,322.

13 "Adonikam" means "my Lord has arisen."

14 On "Bigvai" see comment on v.2.

15 "Adin" means "voluptuous."

16 "Ater" means "Lefty" (cf. Judg 3:15; 20:16). "Hezekiah" means "Yahweh is my strength."

17 "Bezai," a shorted form of Bezaleel, means "in the shadow of God."

18 "Jorah" is "autumn rain." Nehemiah 7:24 has Hariph.

19 "Hashum" means "broad nose."

20 "Gibbar" is "strong man." Nehemiah 7:25 has Gibeon.

3. *Villagers*

2:21-35

21the men of Bethlehem	123
22of Netophah	56
23of Anathoth	128
24of Azmaveth	42
25of Kiriath Jearim, Kephirah and Beeroth	743
26of Ramah and Geba	621
27of Micmash	122
28of Bethel and Ai	223
29of Nebo	52
30of Magbish	156
31of the other Elam	1,254
32of Harim	320
33of Lod, Hadid and Ono	725
34of Jericho	345
35of Senaah	3,630

Verses 21-35 list a series of villages and towns, most of them in Benjaminite territory north of Jerusalem. Significantly no references are to towns in the Negev south of Judah. When Nebuchadnezzar overran Judah (Jer 13:19), the Edomites (cf. Obad) opportunistically occupied the area. By the fifth century B.C., Nabataean Arabs (Mal 1:2-5) were pressing on the Edomites, who moved west and occupied the area south of Hebron, later known as Idumaea.

21 "Bethlehem"—among the returnees may have been the ancestors of Jesus (Mic 5:2).

22 "Netophah," a city south of Jerusalem, was settled by Levites (1 Chron 9:16).

23 "Anathoth," a village named after the Canaanite goddess Anath, was located three miles north of Jerusalem and was the home of the prophet Jeremiah (Jer 1:1).

24 "Azmaveth" was two miles farther north. Nehemiah 7:28 has Beth-Azmaveth ("the house of Azmaveth").

25 "Kiriath Jearim"—the Hebrew reads Kiriath Arim (cf. NIV mg.), probably an error for Kiriath Jearim ("village of the woods"), which is found in Nehemiah 7:29. The latter was the site eight miles northwest of Jerusalem where the ark rested (1 Sam 6:21; 7:1). "Beeroth" means "wells," modern Bireh, a site located twelve miles north of Jerusalem.

26 "Ramah" ("the height") was five miles north of Jerusalem. "Geba" was located east of Ramah.

27 "Micmash," eight miles northeast of Jerusalem, was the scene of Jonathan's exploit (1 Sam 13:23).

28 "Bethel" ("the house of God") was located at modern Beitin, twelve miles north of Jerusalem (cf. A.F. Rainey, "Bethel Is Still *Beitîn*," WTJ 33 [1971]: 175-88, who effectively refutes David Livingstone, "Location of Biblical Bethel and Ai Reconsidered," WTJ 33 [1970]: 283-300). Bethel, a border town, probably became a part of Judah in Josiah's reign. Cities such as Bethel, Mizpah, Gibeon, and Gibeah seemed to have escaped the Babylonian assault. Bethel, however, was destroyed in the transition between the Babylonian and Persian periods. Excavations reveal a small town on the site in Ezra's day.

29 "Nebo" was perhaps the same as Nob, which has been located on Mount Scopus, just to the east of Jerusalem (cf. Mordechai Cogan, "The Men of Nebo-Repatriated Reubenites," IEJ 29 [1979]: 37-39).

30 "Magbish" was perhaps southwest of Adullam.

31 On "Elam" see the comment on v.7.

32 "Harim" means "dedicated to God."

33 "Lod," modern Lydda, ten miles southeast of Jaffa, is today the site of the Israeli international airport.

34 "Jericho" is the famous oasis city just north of the Dead Sea.

35 "Senaah" means "the hated one." The largest number of returnees—3,630 (3,930 in Neh 7:38)—is associated with Senaah. Some have therefore suggested that this group did not come from a specific locality or family but represented low-caste people, as inferred from the meaning of the name.

4. Priests

2:36–39

36The priests:

the descendants of Jedaiah (through the family of Jeshua)	973
37of Immer	1,052
38of Pashhur	1,247
39of Harim	1,017

Four clans of priests are named with a total of 4,289, or about one-tenth the total. They may have been inspired by the hope of serving in a rebuilt temple.

36 "Jedaiah" ("Yahweh has known") was a family of priests noted during the time of David (1 Chron 24:7). The name appears as *Yadaʿyaw* in the Murashu texts (Coogan, *Personal Names*, p. 26).

37 "Immer" means "lamb" (cf. 1 Chron 24:14).

38 "Pashhur" is derived from the Egyptian *Psh Ḥr* ("the portion of Horus"; cf. T. Meek, "Moses and the Levites," AJSL 56 [1939]: 113–20). The name is found on a number of inscriptions and seals (cf. *Inscriptions Reveal*, #61).

39 On "Harim" see the comment on v.32

4. Levites and temple personnel

2:40–42

40The Levites:

the descendants of Jeshua and Kadmiel (through the line of Hodaviah)	74
41The singers:	
the descendants of Asaph	128
42The gatekeepers of the temple:	
the descendants of Shallum, Ater, Talmon, Akkub, Hatita and Shobai	139

40 The Levites, descendants of Levi (Gen 29:34), may have originally been regarded as priests (Deut 18:6–8); but they became subordinate to the priestly descendants of

Aaron, brother of Moses (Num 3:9–10; 1 Chron 16:4–42; 23:26–32). The Levites were then prohibited from offering sacrifices on the altar (Num 16:40; 18:7). As the Levites had no inheritance in land, they lived in forty-eight Levitical cities and were supported by tithes (Deut 12:12, 18; 14:29; Tobit 1:7). They were butchers, door-keepers, singers (1 Chron 15:22; 16:4–7), scribes and teachers (2 Chron 35:3; Neh 8:7, 9), and even temple beggars (2 Chron 24:5–11) (cf. D. Hubbard, "Levites," NBD, pp. 1028–31; E. Nielsen, "The Levites in Ancient Israel," *Annual of the Swedish Theological Institute* 1 [1964]: 16–27).

41 "The singers" (KJV, "temple singers"; JB, "cantors") are called "holy singers" by 1 Esdras 5:27 (cf. Neh 11:22–23; 12:29; 13:10). "Asaph" (lit., "he removed") was one of the three Levites appointed by David over the temple singers.

42 "Gatekeepers" are mentioned thirteen times in Ezra-Nehemiah, nineteen times in Chronicles. They are usually regarded as Levites (1 Chron 9:26; 2 Chron 8:14; 23:4; Neh 12:25; 13:22) but are sometimes differentiated from them (2 Chron 35:15) (cf. Jacob Liver, *Chapters in the History of the Priests and Levites* [Jerusalem: Magnes, 1968]).

At times as many as four thousand gatekeepers were mentioned (1 Chron 23:5). Their primary function was to tend the doors and gates of the temple (1 Sam 3:15; 1 Chron 9:17–32) and perform other menial tasks (2 Chron 31:14). The psalmist said he would rather be a doorkeeper in the house of his God than to dwell in the tents of the wicked (Ps 84:10; cf. the English word "janitor," which comes from the Lat. *janua*, ["door"]).

The 139 gatekeepers listed here belonged to six small clans. "Shallum" means "complete" and "Talmon" means "brightness." The name "Akkub" ("protected") appears eight times in the Murashu texts as *ʿaqqûb* (Coogan, *Personal Names*, pp. 32–33).

Notes

---

41 מְשֹׁרְרִים (*mᵉšōrᵉrîm*, "singers") is a Polel participle of the verb שִׁיר (*šîr*, "to sing"). At Ugarit there was a guild of musicians called *šrm*.

42 שֹׁעֲרִים (*šōᵃrîm*) are "singers." At Ugarit watchmen of the temple gates were called *tgrm*.

---

6. Temple servants

2:43–58

43The temple servants:

the descendants of
Ziha, Hasupha, Tabbaoth,
44 Keros, Siaha, Padon,
45 Lebanah, Hagabah, Akkub,
46 Hagab, Shalmai, Hanan,
47 Giddel, Gahar, Reaiah,

48 Rezin, Nekoda, Gazzam,
49 Uzza, Paseah, Besai,
50 Asnah, Meunim, Nephussim,
51 Bakbuk, Hakupha, Harhur,
52 Bazluth, Mehida, Harsha,
53 Barkos, Sisera, Temah,
54 Neziah and Hatipha

55The descendants of the servants of Solomon:

the descendants of
    Sotai, Hassophereth, Peruda,
56 Jaala, Darkon, Giddel,
57 Shephatiah, Hattil,
    Pokereth-Hazzebaim and Ami

58The temple servants and the
    descendants of the servants of Solomon   392

43 A long list of names (thirty-five in Ezra, thirty-two in Nehemiah) follows the heading "temple servants"; but the clans must have been very small, averaging about nine members. The temple servants and the sons of Solomon's servants together numbered 392 (v.58)—more than the total of the Levites, gatekeepers, and singers (vv.40–42). Though of a very menial status, they must have served God with true devotion.

The Hebrew word for "temple servants" (*nĕtînîm*, "Nethinim") occurs only in 1 Chronicles 9:2 and in Ezra-Nehemiah (cf. Notes). The Nethinim occupied a special quarter in Jerusalem (Neh 3:26, 31; 11:21) and enjoyed exemption from taxes (Ezra 7:24). They participated in the rebuilding of the wall (Neh 3:26) and signed Nehemiah's covenant (Neh 10:29).

"Hasupha" ("quick") appears only here and in Nehemiah 7:46; likewise "Tabbaoth" ("signet ring").

45 "Labanah" means "white" (cf. the name Lebanon).

"Hagabah" ("locust") may be derived from a root that in Arabic means "to cover," i.e., alluding to the covering of the ground by locust swarms (cf. Agabus in Acts 11:28).

46 "Shamlai" (Kethiv) is probably an error for "Shalmai" (Qere, NIV), which means "well being" (cf. Neh 7:48).

"Hanan" ("[God] is gracious") is derived from the verb *ḥānan* ("to be gracious"), and its derivatives are the components of numerous names borne by fifty-one persons in the OT. These include Baalhanan, Elhanan, Hananel, Hanani, Hananiah, Hannah, Hanun, Henadad, Jehohanan, Johanan, and Tehinnah (cf. the Punic names Hanno and Hannibal of Carthage). "Johanan" ("Yahweh is gracious") has given us the name John. The woman's name Hannah gives us Anna, Ann, Nan, and Nancy.

47 "Giddel," a shortened form of Geddeliah, means "Yahweh has made great."

48 "Rezin" is an Aramaic name that means "prince" (cf. Prov 14:28). It was borne by the kings of Damascus (Isa 7:8).

49 "Besai" is from Besodiah ("in the counsel of Yahweh").

50 "Asnah," an Egyptian name, means "he who belongs to Nah." "Meunim" seems to be related to the Maonites (Judg 10:12), an Arab tribe south of the Dead Sea subdued by Uzziah (2 Chron 26:7). A city near Petra is named Ma'an. "Nephussim" refers to a Bedouin tribe descended from Ishmael (Gen 25:15; 1 Chron 1:31; 5:18–22).

51 On "Bakbuk" ("bottle") Goitein ("Nicknames," p. 518) comments:

> This, no doubt, was originally a nickname. Baqbūq is a bottle, an earthenware container of bulging, protuberant form. . . . one might assume that the nickname characterized a fat man with a protuding belly, and this is indeed what Martin Noth . . . tentatively suggests. But instead of the shape of the vessel, the sound of the word might have been intended. In Arabic, *baqbaq* designates the gurgling, bubbling sound of water poured out from a bottle, and figuratively, the prattle of a chatterbox. Thus the original Mr. Baqbūq might have received his by-name because of his ceaseless *baq, baq, baq, baq, baq*.

"Hakupha" means "humpbacked."

52 "Bazluth" is "onion." "Mehida" is possibly an error for Mehira ("bought"). "Harsha" means "deaf" or "dumb."

53 For "Barkos" see Notes. "Sisera" is a name borne by the Canaanite general who fought Deborah (Judg 4–5).

54 "Neziah" is "faithful" and "Hatipha" means "snatched," as a captive in childhood?

55 The phrase "the descendants of the servants of Solomon" occurs only in this passage and in Nehemiah 7:60; 11:3. Note that the phrase does not appear in Chronicles. These may be the descendants of the Canaanites whom Solomon enslaved (1 Kings 9:20–21). But B.A. Levine ("The Netînîm," JBL 82 [1963]: 209) argues that they were instead the descendants of the royal officers who were merchants in the service of Solomon (1 Kings 9:22, 27).

"Hassophereth" is a feminine form that means "the scribe." Women scribes were rare. See the note on 7:6. Goitein ("Nicknames," pp. 517–18) remarks:

> Serving as a copyist or as a clerk was not a common occupation for a woman, but it was not entirely unknown even to Jewish or Islamic society in the Middle Ages. Cf. . . . an Iraqi Jew of noble descent whose family name was *Ibn an-Nāsikha*, son of the female copyist. The colophon of an exactly and beautifully written codex of the Pentateuch from Yemen, written by Miriam, the daughter of the renowned scribe Benayah, contained this remark: "Please be indulgent of the shortcomings of this volume; I copied it while nursing a baby."

57 For "Shephatiah" see v.4. "Hattil" means "babbler." "Pokereth-Hazzebaim" is "huntress of the gazelles." For "Ami" Nehemiah 7:59 has "Amon" ("faithful").

58 An analysis of the figures in these lists yields the following percentages of the total (v. 64):

Families	53.2
Villagers	29.6
Priests	14.7
Levites	0.2
Singers	0.4
Gatekeepers	0.5
Temple servants & descendants of the servants of Solomon	1.4
	100.0

Notes

43 נְתִינִים (*neṯînîm*, "temple servants"), only in the plural, is derived from the verb נָתַן (*nāṯan*, "to give," "to devote," "to dedicate"; cf. 8:20). Some scholars compare them with the *ytnm*, a special group with the priests at Ugarit.

E.A. Speiser ("Unrecognized Dedication," IEJ 13 [1963]: 69–73) has compared the Nethinim with the Babylonian *širkūtu* (derived from the verb *šarāku[m]*, "to present, grant"), who were dedicated by their masters or fathers to the gods and lived in special quarters. Though without biblical support, many scholars follow the rabbinic tradition (*Yebamoth* 79a) in viewing the Nethinim as the descendants of the Gibeonites whom Joshua made "woodcutters and water carriers for the house of my God" (Josh 9:21–23, 27). According to Ezra 8:20 it was David who dedicated the Nethinim as temple servants to the Levites (cf. Num 31:28–30).

An analysis of the thirty-five names of the Nethinim in Ezra 2:43–54 indicates that fifteen, or 45 percent, are not attested elsewhere in the OT or in epigraphic onomastica. Moreover 68 percent of the names are of foreign origin, as are 33–40 percent of the names of the sons of Solomon's servants. Whereas in postexilic times 90 percent of the priests and 82 percent of the Levites bore theophorous names, only 20 percent of the Nethinim had such names (cf. J.P. Weinberg, "N*eṯînîm* und 'Söhne der Sklaven Salomos' im 6.–4. Jh. v.u.Z.," ZAW 87 [1975]: 361ff.).

The majority of commentators (J. Wellhausen, E. Meyer, R. Kittel, R. de Vaux, J. Montgomery, S. Mowinckel et al.) view the Nethinim as the descendants of foreign slaves dedicated to the temple service. An example of such a practice from Mesopotamia was the dedication by Nabonidus of 2,850 captives from Que as servants of the temples of Nabu and Nergal (cf. I. Mendelsohn, "State Slavery in Ancient Palestine," BASOR 85 [1942]: 14–17; M. Haran, "The Gibeonites, the Nethinim, and the Sons of Solomon's Servants," VetTest 11 [1961]: 159–69). B.A. Levine ("The Nethînîm," JBL 82 [1963]: 207–12), however, has argued that the Nethinim were originally the "dedicated" members of a cultic guild rather than slaves.

53 בַּרְקוֹס (*barqôs*, "Barkos") is compounded with the name of the Edomite deity Qos (Qaus, Koze) (T.C. Vriezen, "The Edomite Deity Quas," *Oudtestamentische Studien* 14 [1965]: 330–53). In 1960 Crystal Bennet found a seal at Umm el-Biyara near Petra with the name of Qos Gabar, an Edomite king ("Fouilles d'Umm el-Biyara," RB 73 [1966]: 398ff.). M. Rose ("Yahweh in Israel–Qaus in Edom?" *Journal for the Study of the Old Testament* 1 [1977]: 28–34) has argued that Qaus was originally an Arab god adopted by the Edomites.

7. Individuals lacking evidence of their genealogies

2:59-63

59The following came up from the towns of Tel Melah, Tel Harsha, Kerub, Addon and Immer, but they could not show that their families were descended from Israel:

60 The descendants of	
Delaiah, Tobiah and Nekoda	652

61And from among the priests:

The descendants of
Hobaiah, Hakkoz and Barzillai (a man who had married a
daughter of Barzillai
the Gileadite and was called by that name).
62These searched for their family records, but they could not find them and so were excluded from the priesthood as unclean. 63The governor ordered them not to eat any of the most sacred food until there was a priest ministering with the Urim and Thummim.

59 "Tel Melah" ("mound of salt") is possibly a mound strewed with salt (cf. Judg 9:45). "Tel Harsha" is "mound of potsherds." "Kerub" is "meadow" (cf. Akkad. *kirûbû*). The Hebrew of "Addon" is "Addan" ("strong [place]").

The Hebrew word *tel* corresponds with the Akkadian *tillu* and the Arabian *tell* and designates hilllike mounds that cover the remains of ruined cities. Tel-Abib (Ezek 3:15) means the "mound of a flood," i.e., a place destroyed by a flood (Akkad. *abūbu*).

The Jewish exiles were settled along the Kebar River (Ezek 1:1) near the city of Nippur, a city in southern Mesopotamia that was the stronghold of rebels. The Jews were probably settled on the mounds of ruined cities depopulated by the Babylonians.

Of the exiles who returned, members of three lay families and three priestly families were unable at this time to prove their descent. Some may have derived from proselytes; others may have temporarily lost access to their genealogical records.

60 "Delaiah" is "Yahweh has drawn." "Tobiah" ("Yahweh is good") was the name also of one of Nehemiah's chief adversaries (Neh 2:10, 19). The name appears in the Murashu texts as *Ṭōbyaw* (Coogan, *Personal Names*, p. 26).

The total of 652 who could not prove their genealogies represents but 1½ percent of the total number given in v.64.

61 "Hobaiah" means "Yahweh has hidden." "Barzillai" ("man of iron") of Gilead in Transjordan helped David during his flight from his son Absalom (2 Sam 17:27-29; 19:31-39; 1 Kings 2:7). That the bridegroom took the name of his wife's father recalls the Mesopotamian *errēbu* ("to enter") marriage arranged by a father who had no sons but only daughters. The children belonged to the wife's family (cf. Gen 29 -31; 1 Chron 2:34-36).

62 Genealogies figure prominently in Chronicles, Ezra, and Nehemiah. The knowledge of relationships was highly regarded in ancient times, and it is important in many societies today. A.S. Kirkbride related "that on one occasion, while he was in an Arab encampment, an Arab got up and related the history of his forebears back to forty generations, and that there were others in the assembly who obviously could have done the same" (cited in *The Biblical Archaeologist Reader*, edd. G.E. Wright and D.N. Freedman [Garden City, N.Y.: Doubleday, 1961], p. 63, n. 18).

63 "The governor" probably refers here to either Sheshbazzar or Zerubbabel. The Hebrew word (cf. Notes) is used in Nehemiah 7:65 of Zerubbabel and in Nehemiah 8:9; 10:1 (2 MT) of Nehemiah. "The most sacred food" (*qōdeš haqqᵒdāšîm*), as in Leviticus 2:3, refers to the most holy part of the offering—the portion of the priests.

"The Urim [*'ûrîm*] and Thummim [*tummîm*]," objects kept in the breastplate of the high priest, were used for divining God's will. In the Pentateuch they are associated with Levi (Deut 33:8), Aaron (Exod 28:30; Lev 8:8; cf. Ecclus 45:10), and Eleazar (Num 27:21). The Urim and Thummim were probably two small objects made of wood, bone, or stone, perhaps of different colors or with different inscriptions, that would give a yes or no answer. The high priest would reach into his breastplate and extract one of the objects. The LXX translated the terms with abstractions: "Lights" and "Perfections"; elsewhere it translates the terms as "Manifestation" and "Truth."

According to rabbinical tradition, Urim and Thummim were used "only for the King, for the Court, or for one of whom the congregation had need" (*Yoma* 7.5). The rabbis held that "since the destruction of the first temple the Urim and the Thummim ceased" (*Tosefta Sota* 13.1). They held that Ezra 2:63 expressed, not a historical possibility, but an eschatological hope (b. *Sotah* 48a–b). Elsewhere in the Talmud (b. *Shebuoth* 16a), we read that Ezra had to reconsecrate the temple without benefit of the Urim and Thummim.

Notes

62 An ostracon from Arad, dated to the late seventh century B.C., has an eleven-line list of names such as "Shemaiahu son of Micaiahu . . . Tanhum son of Jedaiahu, Gealiahu son of Jedaiahu" (cf. *Inscriptions Reveal*, #137).

63 "Governor" is the Hebrew word תִּרְשָׁתָא (*tiršātā'*), which the KJV merely transliterates as "Tirshatah." W.T. In der Smitten ("Der Tirschātā' in Esra-Nehemiah," VetTest 21 [1971]: 618–20) has proposed that the word means "the circumcised one," identifying Nehemiah and Zerubbabel as Jews. But the word does not imply a contemptuous nickname. Earlier E. Meyer had proposed the meaning "palace eunuch" from the New Persian word *tārash*. Perhaps the best explanation is "the one to be feared or respected," i.e., "Excellency," assumed from the Old Persian *tarsa*, a view favored by I. Scheftelowitz, W. Rudolph, and K. Galling.

On the "Urim and Thummim," E. Lipinski ("Urīm and Tummīm," VetTest 20 [1970]: 495–96) cites an Assyrian text in which the god's answer was divined through two dice called *aban erēši* ("the desirable die") and *aban la erēši* ("the undesirable die"). The text reads: "conjuration to foretell the future by means of a white stone (alabaster) and a black stone (Haematite)."

8. Totals

2:64-67

[64]The whole company numbered 42,360, [65]besides their 7,337 menservants and maidservants; and they also had 200 men and women singers. [66]They had 736 horses, 245 mules, [67]435 camels and 6,720 donkeys.

64 The given total of 42,360 is considerably more than the sum of the actual figures given, as may be seen from a chart of the figures in Ezra 2, Nehemiah 7, and 1 Esdras 5.

Categories	Ezra	Nehemiah	1 Esdras
Men of Israel	24,144	25,406	26,390
Priests	4,289	4,289	2,388
Levites, singers, etc.	341	360	341
Temple servants	392	392	372
Men of unproven origin	652	642	652
Totals	29,818	31,089	30,143

To account for the difference of about twelve thousand between the given total and the actual total presents problems. Were these unspecified twelve thousand women and/or children? (First Esdras 5:41 explicitly states that its given total included "all those of Israel, twelve or more years of age.") If there were relatively few women among the returnees, the pressures for intermarriage would have been considerable.

Other scholars suggest that the numbers explicitly enumerated represent returnees from Judah and Benjamin, while the remainder were from other tribes. This seems preferable to the view of S. Mowinckel (*Studien zu dem Buche Ezra-Nehemiah I: Die Listen* [Olso: Universitetsforlaget, 1964], p. 69) that the given total represented only the heads of families, which would mean that the total number of returnees would have been an improbable 100,000 to 130,000.

Many have questioned whether such a large group of about 50,000 (42,360 + 7,337 slaves = 49,697) would have joined the initial return under Sheshbazzar. Some scholars have therefore suggested that the totals include others who came later. But surely the initial response would have been indeed the greatest for the many who had harbored memories of their homeland and who had nurtured hope in the fulfillment of prophecy.

J.S. Wright (*The Building of the Second Temple* [London: Tyndale, 1958], p. 14) adduces the modern parallel of the return of the Jews to Palestine after World War II: "One can estimate the likelihood by happenings in our own day. From the moment that a return to Palestine became possible, large numbers of Jews pressed back into what they regarded as their own land. They spurned the system of rationing that tried to stem the torrent of the return, and when that system was lifted, they poured in like a flood."

The former prime minister of Israel, David Ben-Gurion, described the modern emigration of Jews from Iraq to Israel: "Almost the whole community of Babylonian exiles who stayed when Babylon was destroyed came to this country ten years ago—and their number was nearly thrice the number of those who returned to Zion in the days of Ezra and Nehemiah" ("Cyrus, King of Persia," *Commémoration Cyrus* [Leiden: Brill, 1974], 1:133).

65 The ratio of slaves—one to six—is relatively high; that so many would return with their masters speaks highly of the relatively benevolent treatment of slaves by the Jews. Unlike the Hammurabi Code that permitted a master to kill his own slave with impunity, the Mosaic code denounced such a killing as murder (cf. H.L. Ellison, "The Hebrew Slave," EQ 45 [1973]: 30–35; N.P. Lemche, "The 'Hebrew Slave,'" VetTest 25 [1975]: 129–44).

The male and female singers listed here may have been secular singers who sang at weddings, funerals, etc. (2 Chron 35:25) as distinct from the male temple singers of v.41.

66 "Horses" in the OT are usually associated with royalty and the military. They were usually a royal monopoly. The horses listed here may have been a donation from Cyrus for the nobility.

"Mules" are hybrid offspring of donkey stallions and mares. They combine the strength and size of the horse with the patience and sure-footedness of the ass. They were not originally bred in Palestine; Solomon had to import them (1 Kings 10:25; 2 Chron 9:24). As precious animals they were used by the royalty and wealthy (1 Kings 1:33; Isa 66:20).

67 The "camels" mentioned in the OT were the one-humped Arabian camels as distinct from the two-humped Bactrian camels. The camel can carry its rider and about four hundred pounds and can travel three or four days without drinking.

"Donkeys" were sure-footed and able to live on poor forage. They were used to carry loads, women, or children. Sheep, goats, and cattle are not mentioned. They would have slowed the caravan (cf. G.S. Cansdale, *All the Animals of the Bible Lands* [Grand Rapids: Zondervan, 1970]).

9. Offerings

2:68–69

> [68]When they arrived at the house of the LORD in Jerusalem, some of the heads of the families gave freewill offerings toward the rebuilding of the house of God on its site. [69]According to their ability they gave to the treasury for this work 61,000 drachmas of gold, 5,000 minas of silver and 100 priestly garments.

68 The caravan probably followed the Euphrates River up to a point east of Aleppo, crossed west to the Orontes River Valley, then traveled south to Hamath, Homs, and Riblah. They would then have either passed through the Beqa'a Valley in Lebanon or have proceeded east of the Anti-Lebanon Mountains to Damascus and then to Palestine. The former route was followed by the Assyrian and Babylonian armies (Jer 39:5–7; 52:9–10, 26–27).

As the people were expending most of their savings, their giving demonstrated a true spirit of dedication to God's service (cf. Exod 36:5–7; 2 Cor 9:6–7).

69 The parallel passage in Nehemiah 7:70–72 gives a fuller and more systematic description than the account in Ezra. In Ezra the gifts come from the heads of the clans but in Nehemiah from three sources: the governor, the chiefs of the clans, and the rest of the people. The differences in the parallel accounts are as follows:

Ezra		Nehemiah	
Drachmas (or Darics) of gold		Governor	1,000
		Chiefs	20,000
		People	20,000
	61,000		41,000
Minas of silver		Chiefs	2,200
		People	2,000
	5,000		4,200

"Drachmas" translates the Hebrew *dark^emônîm* (cf. Neh 7:70–72). Another Hebrew word—*'ªdarkōnîm*—is used for coins in Ezra 8:27 and 1 Chronicles 29:7. The "drachma" was the Greek silver coin worth a day's wage in the late fifth century B.C. More probably the coin intended here was the Persian daric, which was a gold coin, named either after Darius I, who began minting it, or after the Old Persian word for gold, *dari*. The coin was famed for its purity, which was guaranteed by the king. It was 98 percent gold with a 2 percent alloy for hardness. It was ¾ of an inch in diameter and weighed 8.42 grams, or a little less than ⅓ of an ounce. Its value equalled the price of an ox or a month's wages for a soldier.

Since the coin was not in use until the time of Darius I (522–486 B.C.), its occurrence here in 537 B.C. has been labeled anachronistic. Its use is better viewed as a modernization by terms current at the time of the book's composition of earlier values, perhaps the Median shekel. The total of 61,000 darics equals some 1,133 pounds of gold (about the same if the term represented the Greek drachma).

A "mina" equaled 1.26 pounds of silver; five thousand minas would be 6,300 pounds of silver. In the sexagesimal system that originated in Mesopotamia, sixty shekels made a mina and sixty minas a talent. A shekel, about ⅓ ounce of silver, was the average monthly wage. Hence a mina would equal five years' wages and a talent three-hundred-years' wages (cf. R. Loewe, "The Earliest Biblical Allusion to Coined Money?" PEQ 87 [1955]: 141–50; J. Weingreen, "Coins," *Documents from Old Testament Times* [New York: Harper, 1961], p. 232; P. Naster, "Were the Labourers of Persepolis Paid by Means of Coined Money?" *Ancient Society* 1 [1970]: 129–34; H.G.M. Williamson, "Eschatology in Chronicles," *Tyndale Bulletin* 28 [1977]: 123–26).

Notes

68 Temples in the Near East had to be rebuilt on the same site. Galling (*Geschichte Israels*, p. 130) cites an inscription of Esarhaddon that refers to rebuilding "on the old foundation." The Aramaic papyrus Cowley 32:8 (c. 408 B.C.) refers to the rebuilding of the Jewish temple at Elephantine "in its place as it was before."

69 Torrey's belief that the Greek drachma was intended by the Chronicler led him to date his work to 250 B.C. The discovery of Greek coins in Palestine already in the Persian period undermines Torrey's argument. Albright (*Recent Discoveries,* p. 105) noted: "Most interestingly of all has been the finding (mostly outside of excavations) of many Atticizing coins following the drachma standard, belonging to the fifth and fourth centuries B.C. This is one of the many recent discoveries which prove that Torrey and his followers are wrong in holding that the references to 'dracmas' in the work of the Chronicler (including Ezra) belong to the Greek period."

E. Stern ("Israel at the Close of the Period of the Monarchy," BA 38 [1975]: 53) comments: "Indeed, the earliest coins discovered in Israel were minted in the mid-6th century, only some thirty years after the destruction of the Temple in 586." Later in the Persian period, Judean authorities were permitted to mint their own small silver coins with the name of the province Yehud in archaic Hebrew script (cf. Y. Meshorer, *Jewish Coins of the Second Temple* [Tel-Aviv: Am-Hassefer, 1967], pp. 36–37).

---

10. *Settlement of the exiles*

2:70

70The priests, the Levites, the singers, the gatekeepers and the temple servants settled in their own towns, along with some of the other people, and the rest of the Israelites settled in their towns.

70 Later Nehemiah would be compelled to move people by lot to reinforce the population of Jerusalem, as the capital city had suffered the severest loss of life at the time of the Babylonian attacks. The survivors, who came for the most part from towns in the countryside, naturally preferred to resettle in their hometowns.

C. The Revival of Temple Worship (3:1–13)

1. The rebuilding of the altar

3:1–3

1When the seventh month came and the Israelites had settled in their towns, the people assembled as one man in Jerusalem. 2Then Jeshua son of Jozadak and his fellow priests and Zerubbabel son of Shealtiel and his associates began to build the altar of the God of Israel to sacrifice burnt offerings on it, in accordance with what is written in the Law of Moses the man of God. 3Despite their fear of the peoples around them, they built the altar on its foundation and sacrificed burnt offerings on it to the LORD, both the morning and evening sacrifices.

1 "The seventh month" would be Tishri (Sept.–Oct.), about three months after the arrival of the exiles in Palestine. Tishri is one of the most sacred months of the Jewish year. The first day of Tishri is the New Year's Day (Rosh Hashanah) of the civil calendar, proclaimed with the blowing of trumpets and a holy convocation (Lev

23:24). Ten days later the Day of Atonement (Yom Kippur) is observed (Lev 23:27). From the fifteenth to the twenty-second day, the Feast of Tabernacles (Succoth) is celebrated (Lev 23:34–36).

"Assembled as one man" and similar expressions of the unity of Israel are found in Numbers 14:15; Judges 6:16; 20:1, 8, 11; 1 Samuel 11:7; 2 Samuel 19:14.

2 Jeshua, the priest, took precedence over Zerubbabel, the civil leader, in view of the nature of the occasions (cf. v.8; 5:2; Hag 1:1).

During their long stay in Babylon, the Jews were not able to offer any sacrifices, as this could only be done in Jerusalem. Instead they were surrounded by a myriad of pagan temples. About fifty temples are mentioned in Babylonian texts together with 180 open-air shrines for Ishtar, three hundred daises for the Igigi gods, and twelve hundred daises for the Anunnaki gods (cf. E. Yamauchi, "Babylon," *Major Cities of Bible Times*, ed. R.K. Harrison [Nashville: Nelson, 1985], pp. 32–48). Thus their first task in the midst of hostile neighbors was to erect once more an altar to sacrifice to the Lord.

The "enemies" did not have anything to fear from the rebuilding of the temple, as they did from the rebuilding of the wall (as we shall see in Nehemiah). Sincerely or not, they had at first offered their help to rebuild the temple (v.2). The rejection of this aid naturally aroused their hostility.

David first built an altar on the threshing floor of Araunah in Jerusalem (2 Sam 24:21). When it was later desecrated by Antiochus IV (1 Macc 1:54) with "a desolating sacrilege" in 167 B.C., the Jews dismantled it and rebuilt a new altar with great blocks of stones. Josephus (*Contra Apion* I, 198 [22]) quotes Hecataeus, who wrote: "Within this enclosure is a square altar, built of heaped up stones, unhewn and unwrought; each side is twenty cubits long and the height ten cubits" (cf. Notes).

The phrase "the man of God" occurs seventy-five times in the OT. It is used of Moses in Deuteronomy 33:1; Joshua 14:6; 1 Chronicles 23:14; 2 Chronicles 30:16; Psalm 90:1 et al. David is so described in Nehemiah 12:36.

3 "Despite their fear" is literally "for with fear" or "for in fear." The Hebrew word *'êmāh* means a terror inspired by men (Prov 20:2) or by animals (Job 39:20). The LXX reads *en kataplēxei* ("in consternation").

"The peoples around them" (*'ammê hā'ărāṣôt*) is literally "peoples of the lands" (cf. comment on 4:4).

Notes

1 Because of the similarity of the phrases in this verse and in Neh 8:1, some scholars have concluded that both passages describe the same assembly. But the assemblies described in Ezra 3 and Nehemiah 8 pursue entirely different matters.
2 Archaeologists have found Israelite altars at Arad, Dan, and Beersheba (cf. Y. Aharoni, "The Israelite Sanctuary at Arad," in Freedman and Greenfield, pp. 25–40; A. Biran, "Tel Dan," IEJ 22 [1972]: 164–65; Y. Aharoni, "Excavations at Tel Beer-Sheba," BA 35 [1972]: 111–27).

2. The Festival of Booths

3:4–6

> ⁴Then in accordance with what is written, they celebrated the Feast of Tabernacles with the required number of burnt offerings prescribed for each day. ⁵After that, they presented the regular burnt offerings, the New Moon sacrifices and the sacrifices for all the appointed feasts of the LORD, as well as those brought as freewill offerings to the LORD. ⁶On the first day of the seventh month they began to offer burnt offerings to the LORD, though the foundation of the LORD's temple had not yet been laid.

4 The English word "tabernacle" is derived from the Latin Vulgate's *tabernaculum* ("tent"). The original Hebrew word *sukkôt* refers to the "huts" constructed for the feast, which is sometimes simply called "the feast" or "the feast of the Lord." Originally a joyous harvest celebration (Exod 23:14–16; 34:22–23; Lev 23:33–43; Num 29:12–40; Deut 16:13–16), it is the only feast possibly referred to in the historical books (1 Sam 1:1–3; 1 Kings 12:32; cf. NIV Study Bible).

Jews celebrate the feast by building a hut covered with an open roof of branches, decorated with fruits and vegetables. Following Leviticus 23:40, Jews also use the palm, the willow, and the myrtle as the "lulav" ("a shoot or young branch," a Mishnaic term applied to all trees, but esp. the palm branch used at *sukkôt*) and the "ethrog" (a yellow citron known in Israel only from Hellenistic times; its name is of uncertain origin). During each of the nine days of the feast, the lulav and the ethrog are held in the hands and waved in all directions.

The "burnt offerings" were the holocausts prescribed for morning (Lev 1:13) and evening (Num 28:3–4).

5–6 The new moon marked the first day of the month and was a holy day (Num 28:11–15; cf. Col 2:16; cf. B.Z. Wacholder and D.B. Weisberg, "Visibility of the New Moon in Cuneiform and Rabbinic Sources," HUCA 42 [1971]: 227–41). "The appointed sacred feasts" include such festivals as the Passover, Weeks (Pentecost), and the Day of Atonement (Lev 23).

The renewal of the "freewill offerings" (cf. 1:4) fulfilled the promise of Jeremiah 33:10–11. Note that the revival of the services preceded the erection of the temple itself.

3. The beginning of temple reconstruction

3:7–13

> ⁷Then they gave money to the masons and carpenters, and gave food and drink and oil to the people of Sidon and Tyre, so that they would bring cedar logs by sea from Lebanon to Joppa, as authorized by Cyrus king of Persia.
>
> ⁸In the second month of the second year after their arrival at the house of God in Jerusalem, Zerubbabel son of Shealtiel, Jeshua son of Jozadak and the rest of their brothers (the priests and the Levites and all who had returned from the captivity to Jerusalem) began the work, appointing Levites twenty years of age and older to supervise the building of the house of the LORD. ⁹Jeshua and his sons and brothers and Kadmiel and his sons (descendants of Hodaviah) and the sons of Henadad and their sons and brothers—all Levites—joined together in supervising those working on the house of God.
>
> ¹⁰When the builders laid the foundation of the temple of the LORD, the priests in their vestments and with trumpets, and the Levites (the sons of Asaph) with cymbals, took their places to praise the LORD, as prescribed by David king of Israel.

¹¹With praise and thanksgiving they sang to the Lord:

"He is good;
his love to Israel endures forever."

And all the people gave a great shout of praise to the Lord, because the foundation of the house of the Lord was laid. ¹²But many of the older priests and Levites and family heads, who had seen the former temple, wept aloud when they saw the foundation of this temple being laid, while many others shouted for joy. ¹³No one could distinguish the sound of the shouts of joy from the sound of weeping, because the people made so much noise. And the sound was heard far away.

7 As with the first temple, the Phoenicians cooperated by sending timbers and workmen (1 Kings 5:7–12). The latter were paid in "money" (lit., "silver") that would have been weighed out in shekels (see comment on 2:69).

Ancient Phoenicia, modern Lebanon, was renowned for its cedars and other coniferous trees. Both the Mesopotamians and the Egyptians sought to obtain its timbers either by trade or by conquest. Cedars, mentioned seventy-one times in the OT, can grow to a height of 120 feet with a girth of 30 to 40 feet. Their fragrant wood resists rot and insects.

The wood was floated on rafts down the coast and unloaded at Joppa (cf. 1 Kings 5:9; 2 Chron 2:15–16). B. Maisler (Mazar) ("The Excavations at Tell Qasîle, Preliminary Report," IEJ 1 [1950–51]: 63) suggests the destination was Tell Qasîle on the Yarkon estuary just north of Joppa.

Sidon, modern Ṣaidā, twenty-eight miles south of Beirut, was one of the greatest of all the Phoenician cities (Gen 10:19; 1 Kings 5:6; 16:31; 1 Chron 22:4). After the conquest of Tyre by Nebuchadnezzar following a thirteen-year siege, Sidon became prominent (*Herodotus* 6.96–98; 8.67).

Tyre, modern Ṣûr, is located only a dozen miles north of the Israeli border. Renowned for its maritime trade (Ezek 26:4–14), the island of Tyre was later transformed into a peninsula by Alexander the Great's conquest.

8–9 The second month, Iyyar (Apr./May), was the same month when Solomon began his temple (1 Kings 6:1). As the Jews probably returned to Palestine in the spring of 537, the second year would be the spring of 536.

Previously the age limit for the Levites was thirty (Num 4:3) or twenty-five years (Num 8:24). It was reduced to twenty (1 Chron 23:24, 27; 2 Chron 31:17), no doubt because of the scarcity of Levites. Verses 8–10 indicate that Zerubbabel and Jeshua were involved in laying the foundation of the second temple, but 5:16 describes Sheshbazzar as also laying the foundation. On the apparent conflict, see the comment on 5:16.

10 "Trumpets" (*ḥᵃṣōṣrôt*) appears twenty-nine times, always in the plural, except in Hosea 5:8. Of these occurrences sixteen are in 1 and 2 Chronicles. The trumpets were made of beaten silver (Num 10:2). According to Josephus (*Antiq*. III, 291 [xii.6]), the trumpet was "in length a little short of a cubit; it is a narrow tube, slightly thicker than a flute." Except perhaps for their use at the coronation of Joash (2 Kings 11:14; 2 Chron 23:13), the trumpets were always blown by priests (Num 10:8; 1 Chron 15:24; 16:6; Ecclus 50:16). Trumpets were most often used on joyous occasions such as here and at the dedication of the rebuilt walls of Jerusalem (Neh 12:35; cf. 2 Chron 5:13; Ps 98:6).

"Cymbals" (*meṣiltayim*) appears thirteen times, all in 1 and 2 Chronicles except here and in Nehemiah 12:27. The cymbals were also played by priests and Levites.

11 "They sang" (from Heb. *'ānāh,* "to answer") is taken by the RSV in the sense of antiphonal singing by a choir divided into two groups, i.e., singing responsively.

"He is good," a constant refrain in Scriptures (1 Chron 16:34; 2 Chron 7:3; Pss 106:1; 136:1; Jer 33:10–11), implies the goodness of a covenant-keeping God (cf. A.R. Millard, "'For He Is Good,'" *Tyndale Bulletin* 17 [1966]: 115–17).

"Love" translates *ḥesed,* which more precisely means "steadfast love" (N. Glueck's monograph *Hesed in the Bible* [Cincinnati: Hebrew Union College Press, 1967] has been superseded by K.D. Sakenfeld's *The Meaning of Hesed in the Hebrew Bible* [Missoula: Scholars, 1978]).

12–13 Loud shouting—"a great shout"—expresses great jubilation or intense purpose (cf. 10:12; cf. Josh 6:5, 20; 1 Sam 4:5; Ps 95:1–2). The NEB has "shouted at the top of their voices"; the TEV adds: "so loud that it could be heard for miles."

The tears and outcries expressed the deep emotion of the occasion. The Israelis reacted similarly when they reached the Wailing Wall in their war against the Arabs in 1967. Traditionally Hebrews showed their emotions by weeping out loud (cf. 10:1; Neh 1:4; 8:9). V. Hamp ("*bākhāh,*" TDOT, 2:117) observes: "Like the Gk. *klaiō* and *daryō,* and the Lat. *fleo* and *lacrimo,* Heb. *bkh,* 'weeping,' comes from the mouth and voice. . . . Orientals do not weep quietly, but are quite inclined to loud weeping and lamenting, thus explaining the frequent connection of *bkh,* 'weeping,' with *qol,* 'the voice,' in the OT" (cf. T. Collins, "The Physiology of Tears in the Old Testament," CBQ 33 [1971]: 18–38, 185–97).

Whereas the elders were overcome with the memories of the splendors of Solomon's temple, the younger returnees shouted with great excitement at the prospect of a new temple. The God who had permitted judgment was also the God who had brought them back and would enable them to complete this project.

A Babylonian cornerstone reads, "I started the work weeping, I finished it rejoicing" (cf. Ps 126:5: "Those who sow in tears will reap with songs of joy").

D. The Opposition to the Rebuilding (4:1–24)

1. Opposition during the reign of Cyrus

4:1–5

> [1]When the enemies of Judah and Benjamin heard that the exiles were building a temple for the Lord, the God of Israel, [2]they came to Zerubbabel and to the heads of the families and said, "Let us help you build because, like you, we seek your God and have been sacrificing to him since the time of Esarhaddon king of Assyria, who brought us here."
>
> [3]But Zerubbabel, Jeshua and the rest of the heads of the families of Israel answered, "You have no part with us in building a temple to our God. We alone will build it for the Lord, the God of Israel, as King Cyrus, the king of Persia, commanded us."
>
> [4]Then the peoples around them set out to discourage the people of Judah and make them afraid to go on building. [5]They hired counselors to work against them and frustrate their plans during the entire reign of Cyrus king of Persia and down to the reign of Darius king of Persia.

This chapter summarizes various attempts to thwart the efforts of the Jews. In vv.1–5 the author describes events under Cyrus (539–530), in v.6 under Xerxes (485–465), in vv.7–23 under Artaxerxes I (464–424). He then reverts in v.24 to the time of Darius I (522–486), when the temple was completed (cf. Hag 1–2). The author drew on Aramaic documents from v.8 to 6:18, with a further Aramaic section in 7:12–26. See also the Introduction: Purpose and Values.

1–2 As most of the exiles were from Judah, their descendants became known as Jews (from Lat. *Iudaeus* = Old French *Ieu* = Middle English *Iewe*). Judith, the name of an apocryphal book, means "Jewess."

Benjamin, the small tribe occupying the area immediately north of Judah, was the only tribe beside Judah that remained loyal to Rehoboam when the ten northern tribes rebelled. Saul, the first king of Israel, came from this tribe, as did Saul of Tarsus (Phil 3:5).

The people who proffered their help were evidently from the area of Samaria, though they are not explicitly described as such. After the Fall of Samaria in 722, the Assyrian kings kept importing inhabitants from Mesopotamia and Syria "who feared the Lord and served their own gods" (2 Kings 17:24–33). The newcomers' influence doubtless diluted further the faith of the northerners who had already apostasized from the sole worship of the Lord in the tenth century. (In contrast, when the Babylonians deported the Jews in the sixth century, they did not take pagan settlers from elsewhere into Judah.)

Even after the destruction of the temple, worshipers from Shiloh and Shechem in the north came to offer cereals and incense at the site of the ruined temple (Jer 41:5). Moreover the northerners did not abandon faith in Yahweh, as we see from the Yahwistic names given to Sanballat's sons, Delaiah and Shelemaiah (Cowley 30:29). But they retained Yahweh, not as the sole God, but as one god among many gods; Sanballat's name honors the moon god Sin. Though Ezra-Nehemiah does not explicitly mention the syncretistic character of the northerners, evidence suggests that the inhabitants of Samaria were syncretists. (We should, however, distinguish the syncretistic inhabitants of Samaria from the strictly monotheistic Samaritans by calling the former Samarians.)

In 1962 the Ta'amireh Bedouins who had found the DSS discovered a cave in Wadi Daliyeh with fourth-century B.C. papyri. Paul Lapp in 1963 found there a great mass of skeletons, numbering between two hundred to three hundred men, women, and children: the remains of the leading families of Samaria who had fled in 331 from Alexander. A good proportion of their personal names included the names of such deities as Qos (Edomite), SHR (Aramaic), Chemosh (Moabite), Ba'al (Canaanite), and Nebo (Babylonian) (cf. Cross, "Samaria Papyri," pp. 110–20).

3 "You have no part with us" is literally "it is not for you and for us," a Hebrew idiom (cf. Judg 11:12; 2 Kings 3:13; Mark 1:24; John 2:4). The Jews tried tactfully to reject the aid proffered by the northerners by referring to the provisions of the king's decree. Nonetheless their response understandably aroused hostility and determined opposition.

4 "The peoples around them" is *'am hā'āreṣ*, literally, "the people of the land" (cf. Notes). Josephus (*Antiq.* XI, 19 [ii.1], 84–87 [iv.3]) describes these opponents explicitly as Cuthaeans or Samaritans. In the latter passage the Jews declined their cooperation "since none but themselves had been commanded to build the temple. . . . They would, however, allow them to worship there."

"To discourage" is literally "to weaken the hands," a Hebrew idiom (cf. Jer 38:4). As a participle, the verb *rāpāh* indicates a continuing process. The opposite idiom is "to strengthen the hands" (Ezra 6:22; Neh 6:9; Isa 35:3; Jer 23:14).

"Make them afraid"—the verb *bālah* means "to terrify" and often describes the fear aroused in a battle situation (Judg 20:41; 2 Sam 4:1; 2 Chron 32:18; Dan 11:44; Zech 8:10).

5 On the hiring of counselors, compare the hiring of Balaam (Deut 23:4–5) and the hiring of the prophets to intimidate Nehemiah (Neh 13:2). "Down to the reign of Darius king of Persia" passes over the intervening reign of Cambyses (529–522), who conquered Egypt in 525, and that of the usurper, the Pseudo-Smerdis, who seized power in 522 for seven months.

Notes

2 אֵסַר חַדֹּ֖ון (ʾēsar ḥaddōn, "Esarhaddon," for the Akkad. *Aššur-aḥ-iddin*, "Assur has given a brother") was the Assyrian king (680–669 B.C.) who succeeded Sennacherib (2 Kings 19:37; Isa 37:38). (A.R. Millard, "Assyrian Royal Names in Biblical Hebrew," JSS 21 [1976]: 1–14, demonstrates that Assyrian royal names have been preserved with remarkable accuracy in the Hebrew.) The deportations under Esarhaddon were probably connected with his conquest of Egypt in 671 (cf. ANET, p. 290).

4 The phrase עַם־הָאָרֶץ (ʿam-hāʾāreṣ, "people of the land"; NIV, "peoples around") and its plural variants עַמֵּי הָאָרֶץ (ʿammê hāʾāreṣ, "peoples of the land"; 10:2, 11; Neh 9:24; 10:31–32) and עַמֵּי הָאֲרָצֹות (ʿammê hāʾᵃrāṣôt, "peoples of the lands"; 3:3; 9:1, 2, 11; Neh 9:30; 10:30) occur between sixty and seventy times in the OT. Scholars have speculated that the phrase designates "foreign-born landowners" (Alt), "the landed nobility" (Daiches), "the rural population" (Gordis), "people of Judah who were collaborators of Samaria" (Rothstein), etc. E.W. Nicholson ("The Meaning of the Expression עַם הָאָרֶץ in the Old Testament," JSS 10 [1965]: 59–66) points out that the phrase seems to mean different groups at different times and situations. In 2 Kings 23:30 it designates landowning citizens. But during the exilic period, it often connoted the דַּלַּת הָאָרֶץ (dallat hāʾāreṣ, "the poor of the land"; 2 Kings 25:12; Jer 39:10; 40:7; 52:16), whom Gedaliah allowed to take possession of abandoned lands. These people felt that God had given them such lands (cf. Ezek 11:15; 33:24). The exiles' return would understandably bring tensions between those who had stayed and occupied the lands and the former landowners (cf. Jansen, pp. 49, 121). In Ezra-Nehemiah, except possibly for Neh 9:30, the phrase seems to refer to non-Jewish inhabitants of the land, principally the people of Samaria (cf. Vogt, p. 152; Weinberg, "Das BEĪT," p. 403; Williamson, *Israel*, p. 55).

In the NT period the rabbis used the phrase *ʿam hāʾāreṣ* of the common people who were ignorant of the ritual rules and who neglected tithing (cf. John 7:49; Luke 18:9–14). S. Zeitlin ("The am haarez," JQR 23 [1932–33]: 45–61) ascribes the hostility between the *ʿam hāʾāreṣ* and the rabbis to the fact that the farmers had to support the priests and Levites with their tithes whereas the developing urban population in the Maccabean period was free from such obligations.

2. Opposition during the reign of Xerxes

4:6

> ⁶At the beginning of the reign of Xerxes, they lodged an accusation against the people of Judah and Jerusalem.

6 "Xerxes" ('"*ḥašwērôš;* the "Ahasuerus" of Esther) is the Hebrew transliteration of the Old Persian *Xšayāršā,* the son of Darius. When Darius died at the end of 486, Egypt rebelled; and Xerxes had to march west to suppress the revolt. The Persians finally regained control by the end of 483. Rainey ("Satrapy," p. 57) comments: "Nothing is known about this incident beyond the brief biblical reference, but its timing to coincide with the Egyptian rebellion cannot be accidental."

"Accusation" (*śiṭnāh,* lit., "hostility") occurs only here and in Genesis 26:21, where it is the name of a well the herdsmen of Isaac and Gerar quarreled over.

Notes

6 Josephus (*Antiq.* XI, 121 [v.1]) incorrectly made Ezra a friend of Xerxes and (ibid., 159 [v.6]) called Nehemiah a cupbearer of Xerxes.

J. Morgenstern ("Jerusalem—485 B.C.," HUCA 27 [1956]: 101–79; 28 [1957]: 15–47; 31 [1960]: 15–47) postulated a destruction of Jerusalem in 485 B.C., in the reign of Xerxes, as the immediate background of Ezra-Nehemiah. Most scholars would agree with the judgment of Leesberg (p. 82), that "the arguments for [Morgenstern's] position rest upon an exegesis of many passages of the Old Testament which is highly subjective and in some cases is simply piling of one assumption upon a previous one" (cf. also Widengren, "Persian Period," p. 526).

3. Opposition during the reign of Artaxerxes I (4:7–23)

a. The letter to the king

4:7–16

> ⁷And in the days of Artaxerxes king of Persia, Bishlam, Mithredath, Tabeel and the rest of his associates wrote a letter to Artaxerxes. The letter was written in Aramaic script and in the Aramaic language.
>
> ⁸Rehum the commanding officer and Shimshai the secretary wrote a letter against Jerusalem to Artaxerxes the king as follows:
>
> ⁹Rehum the commanding officer and Shimshai the secretary, together with the rest of their associates—the judges and officials over the men from Tripolis, Persia, Erech and Babylon, the Elamites of Susa, ¹⁰and the other people whom the great and honorable Ashurbanipal deported and settled in the city of Samaria and elsewhere in Trans-Euphrates.
>
> ¹¹(This is a copy of the letter they sent him.)
>
> To King Artaxerxes,
>
> From your servants, the men of Trans-Euphrates:

¹²The king should know that the Jews who came up to us from you have gone to Jerusalem and are rebuilding that rebellious and wicked city. They are restoring the walls and repairing the foundations.

¹³Furthermore, the king should know that if this city is built and its walls are restored, no more taxes, tribute or duty will be paid, and the royal revenues will suffer. ¹⁴Now since we are under obligation to the palace and it is not proper for us to see the king dishonored, we are sending this message to inform the king, ¹⁵so that a search may be made in the archives of your predecessors. In these records you will find that this city is a rebellious city, troublesome to kings and provinces, a place of rebellion from ancient times. That is why this city was destroyed. ¹⁶We inform the king that if this city is built and its walls are restored, you will be left with nothing in Trans-Euphrates.

7 There were three Persian kings named "Artaxerxes": Artaxerxes I (464–424), Artaxerxes II (403–359), and Artaxerxes III (358–337). The king in this passage is Artaxerxes I.

Some scholars claim that the parallel account in Josephus (*Antiq.* XI, 21–25 [ii.1]), which substitutes Cambyses for Artaxerxes I, gives the correct order. Williamson (*Israel*, p. 50) points out that "at Ezra iv, however, it seems likely that the author has grouped by theme rather than by chronology. Josephus' corrections, therefore, which rest from one point of view on accurate historical knowledge, result in the end in unhistorical confusion" (cf. also Tuland, "Josephus," pp. 176–92).

"Bishlam" (*bišlām*) is rendered by the LXX as *en eirēnē* (i.e., revocalizing the Hebrew as *bišelôm*, "with the approval of"). The author of the letter would then be Tabeel writing with the approval of Mithredath (so NIV). On "Mithredath" see the comment on 1:8. "Tabeel" means "God is good" (cf. Isa 7:6).

Near Eastern kings used an elaborate system of informers and spies. Egyptian sources speak of the "ears and eyes" of the Pharaoh. Sargon II of Assyria had agents in Urartu whom he ordered, "Write me whatever you see and hear." The efficient Persian intelligence system is described by Xenophon (*Cyropaedia* 8.2.10–12). The King's Eye and the King's Ear were two distinct officials who reported to the monarch (cf. J. Balcer, "The Athenian Episkopos and the Achaemenid 'King's Eye,'" *American Journal of Philology* 98 [1977]: 252–63; A.L. Oppenheim, "The Eyes of the Lord," JAOS 88 [1968]: 173–79). But God's people could take assurance in their conviction that God's intelligence system is not only more efficient than any king's espionage network but is omniscient (cf. 2 Chron 16:9; Zech 4:10).

The letter was probably dictated in Persian to a scribe, who translated it into Aramaic and wrote it down in Aramaic script (see Introduction: Text). Aramaic was written in an alphabet borrowed from the Phoenicians. In the eighth century B.C., this became a distinct script that remained quite uniform till after Alexander's conquests, when a variety of scripts were developed for such Aramaic dialects as Nabataean, Palmyrenean, Syriac, and Mandaic (cf. J. Naveh, *The Development of the Aramaic Script* [Jerusalem: Israel Academy of Sciences and Humanities, 1970]. On the style and form of letters in Aramaic, see J.A. Fitzmyer, "Some Notes on Aramaic Epistolography," JBL 93 [1974]: 201–25; P. Dion, "Les types epistolaires hebreo-arameens . . . ," RB 86 [1979]: 544–79).

8 "Rehum" ("merciful"), "the commanding officer" (Aram. *beʿēl ṭeʿēm*, lit., "master of a decree"; cf. Akkad. *ṭêmu*, "order"), was an official with the role of a "chancellor" or a "commissioner" (cf. Driver, #3:7–8). "Shimshai" means "my sun" (cf. Samson [Heb. šimšôn]). The Akkadian name *Šam-ša-a* occurs in the Murashu texts (Coogan, *Personal Names*, p. 125).

Rehum dictated and Shimshai wrote the letter in Aramaic. It would then have been read in a Persian translation before the king (v.18). According to Herodotus (3.128), royal scribes were attached to each governor to report directly to the Persian king. A.L. Oppenheim ("A Note on the Scribes in Mesopotamia," *Studies in Honor of Benno Landsberger*, edd. H.C. Güterbock and T. Jacobsen [Chicago: University of Chicago Press, 1965], p. 253) comments, "Equally crucial is the scribe's position as the king's secretary, because in this capacity he exercised control over the communication of written information to the ruler" (cf. Rainey's *Scribe at Ugarit*).

A letter from the reign of Ashurbanipal (ABL, no.1250) warns: "Whoever you are, scribe, who is going to read [the preceding letter], do not conceal anything from the king, my lord. Speak kindly (of me) before the king, my lord, so that Bēl and Nabu should speak kindly of you to the king."

9 "Associates" is the plural of the Aramaic *keṇāt* and is found in vv.17, 23; 5:3, 6; 6:6, 13 (cf. Driver, #3:7). The Neo-Babylonian *kinatātu* or *kinattātu* were persons supported by the same fief, often children of the same parents. Persian bureaucracy reflected prominently the principle of collegiality; each responsibility was shared among colleagues.

"Judges" (Aram. *dînāyēʾ*) is transliterated by the KJV as "Dinaites." There was a tribe in western Armenia known as the *Dai-ia-e-ni*. But the word should be revocalized as *dayyānayyāʾ* ("judges") as in the Elephantine papyri.

"Persia" (Aram. *ᵃpārsāyēʾ*) was transliterated by the KJV as "Apharsites." The Assyrians first encountered the Medes and the Persians in the reign of Shalmaneser III (858–824 B.C.).

"Erech" (Aram. *ʾarkewāyēʾ*; KJV, "Archevites") was a great city (Gen 10:10) of the Sumerians, called Uruk, famed as the home of the legendary Gilgamesh. Excavations at the site, now called Warka, have produced the earliest examples of writing.

In the reign of the Assyrian king Ashurbanipal, a major revolt took place from 652 to 648 B.C., involving Shamash-shum-ukin, brother of the king and the ruler over Babylonia. After a long siege Shamash-shum-ukin hurled himself into the flames. Doubtless these men of Babylonia and the other cities were descendants of the rebels the Assyrians deported to the west (cf. H.W.F. Saggs, *The Greatness That Was Babylon* [New York: Hawthorn, 1962], p. 132).

"Elamites of Susa" (Aram. *šûšankāyēʾ dehāwēʾ ʿēlmāyēʾ*) was mistakenly transliterated by KJV as three nationalities: "Susanchites, the Dehavites, and the Elamites." The second, however, is not the name of a people but is to be revocalized *dehûʾ*, "that is" (cf. Rosenthal, p. 21, par. 35). "The people of Susa" is in apposition to "the Elamites"; Susa was the major city of Elam in southwest Iran. Because of Susa's part in the revolt, Ashurbanipal brutally destroyed Susa in 640. So thorough was the Assyrian destruction of Susa's ziggurat that only recently have excavators recognized its location (cf. M.-J. Steve and H. Gasche, *L'Acropole de Suse* [Leiden: Brill, 1971]).

10–11 Ashurbanipal, the last great Assyrian king (669–633 B.C.), was famed for his large library at Nineveh. He is not named elsewhere in the Bible but was probably the king who freed Manasseh from exile (2 Chron 33:11–13). He may be the unnamed Assyrian king who deported people to Samaria according to 2 Kings 17:24.

The descendants of such deportees, removed from their homelands nearly two centuries before, still commonly stressed their origins. Probably the murder of the Israelite king Amon (640–642 B.C.) was the result of an anti-Assyrian movement inspired by the revolt in Elam and Babylonia (cf. W.W. Hallo, "From Qarqar to Carchemish," BA 23 [1960]: 60–61). The Assyrians may then have deported the rebellious Samarians and replaced them with the rebellious Elamites and Babylonians.

11 "Trans-Euphrates" (Aram. *ʿabar-naharāh*, lit., "across the river" [i.e., the Euphrates River], corresponding to Akkad. *eber nāri*) is a phrase that first appeared in the reign of Esarhaddon. Palestinians defined the "land across the River" as Mesopotamia (Josh 24:2–3, 14–15; 2 Sam 10:16). Mesopotamians saw it as including Syria, Phoenicia, and Palestine (1 Kings 4:24). The Persians also called this area *Athura* ("Assyria"), hence the name "Syria."

When Cyrus conquered Babylon in 539, he appointed Gubaru governor of Babylon and the "land beyond the River." This became the official title of the fifth satrapy (5:3; 6:6; Neh 2:7 et al.). It is uncertain when the area was officially constituted a separate satrapy. Galling (p. 96) dated this to 524, in the reign of Cambyses; others to 520, in the reign of Darius I (*Herodotus* 3.89).

12 The Aramaic word for "repairing" (*yaḥîṭû*) is from either the root *ḥwṭ* ("to repair") or the root *yḥṭ* ("to lay"). S. Smith ("Foundations: Ezra iv.12; v.16; vi.3," *Essays in Honour of J.H. Hertz*, edd. I. Epstein, E. Levine, and C. Roth [London: Edward Goldstone, 1942], pp. 394–95) suggests a relation with the Akkadian *ḫāṭu*, which describes the process of searching for old foundations. He compares the Aramaic ʾ *uššayyāʾ* ("foundations") with the Akkadian *uššu*, derived from the Sumerian *uš*, a word used to designate the lower foundations as usually understood. Smith believes this resolves the alleged contradiction between the laying of the foundation by Sheshbazzar (5:16) and by Zerubbabel (Hag 2:15–18), which he holds was a ceremonial foundation (cf. ibid., pp. 387–96, and comments on 5:3).

13 "Taxes" (Aram. *mindāh*; cf. 7:24; elsewhere *middah* [4:20; 6:8]) is derived from the Akkadian *mandattu, maddattu*, a fixed annual tax paid by the provinces into the imperial treasuries. The word appears in the Elephantine texts as the rent due from the royal domains in Egypt to the Persians (cf. Cowley 10:3–4; Driver, pp. 33–34, 76; J.N. Postgate, *Taxation and Conscription in the Assyrian Empire* [Rome: Pontifical Biblical Institute, 1974], p. 119).

"Tribute" (Aram. *belô*; cf. Akkad. *biltu*) was the rent tax in Babylonia (Driver, 8:5, p. 70). Some scholars interpret this word as an impost or duty charged on merchandise (RSV, "custom") or as a poll tax (cf. Brockington, in loc.).

"Duty" (Aram. *halāk*; cf. Akkad. *ilku*, "feudal service") derives from the Akkadian verb *alāku* (lit., "to go"), as used in the Akkadian phrase *ana ḫarrān šarrim alākum* ("to go in the king's way"; cf. Hammurabi Code 26, 68–69; Postgate, *Taxation*, p. 86).

Estimates suggest that between twenty to thirty-five million dollars worth of taxes were collected annually by the Persian king. The Fifth Satrapy, which included Palestine, had to pay the smallest amount of the western satrapies. According to Baron (p. 162):

> The figures given by Herodotus (Herod. III.89–97 . . .) show that Palestine (Jewish, Samaritan, Gentile), together with Cyprus and the rich Phoenician cities, was assessed 350 silver talents, or about $680,000 (present gold value [as of 1952]) annually—an amount representing only some 2 per cent of the Treasury's total revenue in specie. Moreover, Palestine seems to have been free from contributions in kind which, in many other satrapies, equaled or exceeded the monetary payments.

The Persians took much of the gold and silver coins and melted them down to be stored as bullion. Very little of the taxes returned to benefit the provinces.

14 "We are under obligation to the palace" is literally "we eat the salt of the palace." Salt was made a royal monopoly by the Ptolemies in Egypt, and perhaps also by the Persians (Porten, *Archives*, p. 86, n. 121). Salt was used in the ratification of covenants (Lev 2:13; Num 18:19; 2 Chron 13:5; cf. S.H.C. Trumbull, *The Covenant of Salt* [New York: C. Scribner's Sons, 1899], pp. 17ff.). The English word "salary" is derived from the Latin *salarium*, the ration of salt given to soldiers (cf. the expression "a man who is not worth his salt").

15–16 "The archives" (Aram. *sᵉpar dokrānayyā'*, v.15) is literally "book of the records" (cf. 6:1–2; Esth 2:23; 6:1). There were evidently several repositories of such documents at the major capitals. The Greek physician Ctesias, who served at the court of Artaxerxes II, used the royal archives that preserved documents for centuries. Berossus in the third century B.C. used the Babylonian Chronicles that covered events from the Assyrian to the Hellenistic eras (cf. R. Drews, "The Babylonian Chronicles and Berossus," *Iraq* 37 [1975]: 39–55).

Notes

7 The Aramaic spelling of אַרְתַּחְשַׁשְׁתָּא (*'artaḥšaśtā'*, "Artaxerxes") in the Elephantine texts is ארתחששש (*'rtḥšś*). The original Old Persian name was *Artaxšathra*, which means "great" (*arta*) "kingdom" (*xšathra*).

D.B. Weisberg (*Guild Structure and Political Allegiance in Early Achaemenid Mesopotamia* [New Haven: Yale University Press, 1967], p. 15) has published a text (YBC 3499) from Uruk, from the fourth year of the reign of Cyrus, that confirms that local craftsmen in Mesopotamia were addressed in Aramaic: *ina lišānišunu iqbū* ("spoke in their language as follows").

8 The word for "secretary" is סָפְרָא (Aram. *sāprā'*, "scribe"; cf. vv.9, 17, 23; 7:12, 21). The Elephantine papyri have the phrases *spry 'wṣr'* ("scribes of the treasury") and *spry mdynt'* ("scribes of the province") (Cowley 2:12; 17:1, 6; Porten, *Archives*, pp. 51, 55). סֹפֵר (*sōpēr*) is the corresponding Hebrew word (cf. 7:6, 11; Neh 8:1, 4, 9, 13; 12:26, 36; 13:13). The Neo-Babylonian official (Akkad. *sipiru*) was a royal scribe capable of reading and interpreting a language other than Akkadian.

9 Torrey (p. 171) considered טַרְפְּלָיֵא (*ṭarpᵉlāyē'*, "Tripolis") as a derivation from Tetrapolis (the four cities of Antioch, Seleucia, Apamea, and Laodicea) and thus evidence for a

Hellenistic date for Ezra-Nehemiah. The most probable identification is with Tripoli (triple city) on the coast of Phoenicia, about fifty miles north of Beirut, and today the second largest city in Lebanon. Though the name Tripolis seems Greek, this does not necessarily require a Hellenistic date for the books. K. Galling ("Zur Deutung des Ortsnamens טרפל-Tripolis in Syrien," VetTest 4 [1954]: 418–22) has suggested that the name is a Hellenization of the Phoenician root *trpl*, designating a fruitful new land.

10 אָסְנַפַּר (*ʾosnappar*, "Ashurbanipal") is the Aramaized form of the Akkadian *Aššur-bān-apal* ("Ashur has made a son"). The shift of the final *l* to an *r* may be a sign of Persian influence as in the Old Persian *Babiruš* for Babylon; the loss of medial *rb* may be the result of scribal or oral ellipsis (cf. Millard, "Royal Names," p. 11).

---

b. *The letter from the king*

4:17–23

¹⁷The king sent this reply:

To Rehum the commanding officer, Shimshai the secretary and the rest of their associates living in Samaria and elsewhere in Trans-Euphrates:

Greetings.

¹⁸The letter you sent us has been read and translated in my presence. ¹⁹I issued an order and a search was made, and it was found that this city has a long history of revolt against kings and has been a place of rebellion and sedition. ²⁰Jerusalem has had powerful kings ruling over the whole of Trans-Euphrates, and taxes, tribute and duty were paid to them. ²¹Now issue an order to these men to stop work, so that this city will not be rebuilt until I so order. ²²Be careful not to neglect this matter. Why let this threat grow, to the detriment of the royal interests?

²³As soon as the copy of the letter of King Artaxerxes was read to Rehum and Shimshai the secretary and their associates, they went immediately to the Jews in Jerusalem and compelled them by force to stop.

17 "Greetings" is the Aramaic *šelām* (cf. Heb. *šālôm*, Arab. *salam*).

18 As the king was probably illiterate, documents would be read to him. Darius I related, "And it was inscribed and was read off before me" (cf. Esth 6:1).

"Translated" is literally "read separately," i.e., distinctively, but probably meaning here that the letter was translated from Aramaic into Persian (cf. comments on 4:8 and Neh 8:8).

19 There was some truth in the accusation. Jerusalem had rebelled against the Assyrians and the Babylonians in 701, 597, and 587 B.C. (2 Kings 18:7, 13; 24:1 et al.).

20 According to the Qere reading of the Hebrew text of 1 Kings 9:18, Solomon rebuilt Tadmor, the important oasis in the Syrian desert that controlled much of the Trans-Euphrates area. His international prestige is reflected in that he was given a pharaoh's daughter in marriage (1 Kings 3:1; 7:8).

21–23 After provincial authorities had intervened, the Persian king ordered a halt to the Jewish attempt to rebuild the walls of Jerusalem (see comment on Neh 1:3). Most scholars would date the episode of vv.7–23 before 445 B.C. The forcible destruction of these recently rebuilt walls rather than the destruction by Nebuchadnezzar would then be the basis of the report made to Nehemiah. Bowman, Olmstead, and Rudolph place this incident in the context of the revolt of the satrap Megabyzos against Artaxerxes I. Megabyzos was the king's brother-in-law and his greatest general.

To "compelled them by force to stop," the LXX adds "with horses and an (armed) force."

4. Resumption of work under Darius

4:24

> ²⁴Thus the work on the house of God in Jerusalem came to a standstill until the second year of the reign of Darius king of Persia.

24 The writer, after a long digression detailing opposition to Jewish efforts, returns to his original subject—rebuilding the temple (vv.1–3).

According to Persian reckoning the second regnal year of Darius I began on 1 Nisan (3 Apr.) 520 B.C., and lasted till 21 February 519. In that year the prophet Haggai (Hag 1:1–5) exhorted Zerubbabel to begin rebuilding the temple on the first day of the sixth month (29 Aug.). Work began on the temple on the twenty-fourth day of the month—21 September (Hag 1:15) (cf. J. Finegan, *Handbook of Biblical Chronology* [Princeton: Princeton University Press, 1964], pp. 212–13).

The date is significant. During his first two years, Darius fought numerous battles against nine rebels, as recounted in his famous Behistun Inscription (cf. Kent, pp. 107–8, 116–34; G. Cameron, "The Monument of King Darius at Bisitun," *Archaeology* 13 [1960]: 162–71). Only after the stabilization of the Persian Empire could efforts to rebuild the temple be permitted.

E. The Completion of the Temple (5:1–6:22)

1. A new beginning inspired by Haggai and Zechariah

5:1–2

> ¹Now Haggai the prophet and Zechariah the prophet, a descendant of Iddo, prophesied to the Jews in Judah and Jerusalem in the name of the God of Israel, who was over them. ²Then Zerubbabel son of Shealtiel and Jeshua son of Jozadak set to work to rebuild the house of God in Jerusalem. And the prophets of God were with them, helping them.

1 Beginning on 29 August 520 B.C. (Hag 1:1) and continuing till 18 December (Hag 2:1–9, 20–23), the prophet Haggai delivered a series of messages to stir the people to commence work on the temple. Two months after Haggai's first speech, Zechariah joined him (Zech 1:1).

Haggai 1:6 describes the deplorable situation: housing shortages, disappointing harvests, lack of clothing and jobs, and inadequate funds—perhaps as a result of inflation (see comments on Neh 5). Money went into bags full of holes.

Haggai rebuked the people with a paronomasia (play on words). He proclaimed that because the Lord's house had remained "a ruin" (ḥārēḇ, Hag 1:4, 9), the Lord would bring "a drought" (ḥōreḇ, Hag 1:11) on the land. Though this may be a hyperbole, it implies that very little progress was made in the sixteen years since the first foundation was laid.

Some scholars have held that there is an "irreconcilable difference" between Ezra 3:10 and the references in Haggai 2:18; Zechariah 4:9; 8:9, as the former speaks of the foundation of the temple in 536, the latter in 520. It is possible, however, to have more than one foundation ceremony for a particular building. Wright (Second Temple, p. 17) notes a Hittite ritual that speaks of the refoundation of a building (ANET, p. 356) and Akkadian rituals that tell of "founding anew the temple in question" (cf. also F.I. Andersen, "Who Built the Second Temple?" Australian Biblical Review 6 [1958]: 1–35; A. Gelston, "The Foundation of the Second Temple," VetTest 16 [1966]: 232–35; J. Baldwin, Haggai, Zechariah, Malachi [London: Inter-Varsity, 1972], pp. 52–53).

2 "Zerubbabel" is a Babylonian name after the Akkadian zēr-bābili ("seed of Babylon," referring to his birth in exile, probably before 570 B.C.). Here and in Ezra 3:2, Nehemiah 12:1, and Haggai 1:1, he is described as the son of Shealtiel—son of Jehoiachin, second last king of Judah (1 Chron 3:17). Though he was replaced by Zedekiah, Jehoiachin was regarded as the last legitimate king of Judah. Zerubbabel was the last of the Davidic line to be entrusted with political authority by the occupying powers.

In 1 Chronicles 3:19, however, Zerubbabel is listed as a son of Pedaiah, another son of Jehoiachin and brother of Shealtiel. Pedaiah may have married the widow of his dead brother, Shealtiel, in a levirate marriage (Deut 25:5–6). Note that the genealogy of Zerubbabel (as the son of Shealtiel) parallels the genealogy of Jesus (Matt 1:12; Luke 3:27).

Jeshua's father, Jozadak, had been carried off to Babylon by Nebuchadnezzar (1 Chron 6:15; cf. Ezra 3:2, 8–9; 4:3; Hag 1:1, 12, 14).

Notes

1 חַגַּי (ḥaggay, "Haggai," means "Festal," i.e., born on a feast) was a popular name. It was borne by eleven individuals at Elephantine and by four in the Murashu texts (Coogan, Personal Names, p. 23).

זְכַרְיָה (zᵉkaryāh, "Zechariah," i.e., "Yahweh has remembered") is described here as the "son" of Iddo, whereas according to Zech 1:1 he was the grandson of Iddo. The word "son" can designate a descendant. Iddo may have been the priest mentioned in Neh 12:4 as one of those who returned with Zerubbabel. The Zechariah of Neh 12:16 may have been a descendant of the prophet. On the other hand, it is possible that this Zechariah was the same as the prophet. In this case the prophet Zechariah was also the head of a priestly family (see W.C. Kaiser, ZPEB, 3:241).

2. The intervention of the governor Tattenai

5:3–5

> ³At that time Tattenai, governor of Trans-Euphrates, and Shethar-Bozenai and their associates went to them and asked, "Who authorized you to rebuild this temple and restore this structure?" ⁴They also asked, "What are the names of the men constructing this building?" ⁵But the eye of their God was watching over the elders of the Jews, and they were not stopped until a report could go to Darius and his written reply be received.

3–5 Batten (in loc.) in 1913 erroneously identified "Tattenai" with *Ushtannu*, the satrap over Babylon and Trans-Euphrates. A.T. Olmstead ("Tattenai, Governor of 'Across the River,'" JNES 3 [1944]: 46) pointed out the correct identification by referring to a document that can be dated to 5 June 502 B.C., which cites *Ta-at-tan-ni* as the *paḥaṭ* ("governor") who was subordinate to the satrap over *Ebir-nari*.

Shethar-Bozenai may have functioned as a Persian official known as the *patifrasa* ("inquisitor") or *frasaka* ("investigator"). A complaint was lodged before the "investigators" of the Egyptian satrap Arsames, according to Cowley (37:5; cf. Porten, *Archives*, p. 54).

"Structure" (Aram. *'uššarnā'*) is rendered "wall" by the KJV and ASV and "structure" in the RSV and NIV. The former rendering suggests an advanced stage in the rebuilding of the temple, the latter that Zerubbabel was fortifying the city. C.G. Tuland ("*Uššayyā'* and *'Uššarnā*," JNES 17 [1958]: 269–75), however, notes that the word—derived from the Old Persian **āċărna*—appears in the Aramaic papyri (Cowley 26:5, 9, 21; 27:1, 18; 30:1, 11), where it means "material" or "equipment." He therefore suggests that the clause here means "Who gave you a decree to build this house and to complete this (building) material?" Tuland concludes that Tattenai's investigations were thus made at a very early stage when the Jews were still gathering building materials (but see v.8). (Note: The asterisk before Persian words indicates a reconstructed form. See F. Rosenthal, *A Grammar of Biblical Aramaic* [Wiesbaden: Harrassowitz, 1961], pp. 58–59.)

The Persian governor gave the Jews the benefit of the doubt by not stopping the work while the inquiry (vv.3–5) was proceeding. Some scholars have suggested that Zechariah was promoting Zerubbabel as a messianic figure to lead a revolt against the Persians; evidently, however, from Tattenai's tolerant stance no such revolt took place. On the "elders" see v.9; 6:7–8, 14; Jeremiah 29:1; Ezekiel 8:1; 14:1. There was also an assembly of elders among the Egyptian exiles in Babylonia (cf. Eph'al, "Western Minorities," p. 76).

3. The report to Darius

5:6–17

> ⁶This is a copy of the letter that Tattenai, governor of Trans-Euphrates, and Shethar-Bozenai and their associates, the officials of Trans-Euphrates, sent to King Darius. ⁷The report they sent him read as follows:
>
> To King Darius:
>
> Cordial greetings.
>
> ⁸The king should know that we went to the district of Judah, to the temple of the great God. The people are building it with large stones and placing the

timbers in the walls. The work is being carried on with diligence and is making rapid progress under their direction.

[9] We questioned the elders and asked them, "Who authorized you to rebuild this temple and restore this structure?" [10] We also asked them their names, so that we could write down the names of their leaders for your information.

[11] This is the answer they gave us:

"We are the servants of the God of heaven and earth, and we are rebuilding the temple that was built many years ago, one that a great king of Israel built and finished. [12] But because our fathers angered the God of heaven, he handed them over to Nebuchadnezzar the Chaldean, king of Babylon, who destroyed this temple and deported the people to Babylon.

[13] "However, in the first year of Cyrus king of Babylon, King Cyrus issued a decree to rebuild this house of God. [14] He even removed from the temple of Babylon the gold and silver articles of the house of God, which Nebuchadnezzar had taken from the temple in Jerusalem and brought to the temple in Babylon.

"Then King Cyrus gave them to a man named Sheshbazzar, whom he had appointed governor, [15] and he told him, 'Take these articles and go and deposit them in the temple in Jerusalem. And rebuild the house of God on its site.' [16] So this Sheshbazzar came and laid the foundations of the house of God in Jerusalem. From that day to the present it has been under construction but is not yet finished."

[17] Now if it pleases the king, let a search be made in the royal archives of Babylon to see if King Cyrus did in fact issue a decree to rebuild this house of God in Jerusalem. Then let the king send us his decision in this matter.

6–7 That such inquiries were sent directly to the king has been vividly confirmed by the Elamite texts from Persepolis, where in 1933–34 several thousand tablets and fragments were found in the fortification wall. Some two thousand fortification tablets were published in 1969 by Halock. Dating from the thirteenth to the twenty-eighth year of Darius (509–494 B.C.), they deal with the transfer and payment of food products.

In 1936–38 additional Elamite texts were discovered in the treasury area of Persepolis. Over a hundred of these texts were published by Cameron in 1948, 1958, and 1965. They date from the thirtieth year of Darius to the seventh year of Artaxerxes I (492–458 B.C.). In addition to payment in kind, they include supplementary payment in silver coins, an innovation introduced around 493 B.C.

8 The interpretation of the phrase "large stones" (Aram. *'eben gᵉlāl;* cf. Akkad. *aban galâla*) is controverted. The LXX has "choice" or "splendid" stones (cf. 1 Kings 7:9 –11); 1 Esdras 6:9 (KJV) has "polished and costly" stones. The translation "large" is suggested because *gᵉlāl* means "rolling," i.e., such large stones that they were placed on rollers. Others believe *gᵉlāl* refers to the circular motion involved in polishing the stone. But Bowman concludes that by the Neo-Babylonian era the phrase *'eben gᵉlāl* simply means "stone(s)." See R. Bowman "*Aban galâlu* (Ezra 5:8; 6:4)," *Dōrōn,* edd. I. Naamani and D. Rudavsky (New York: National Association of Professors of Hebrew, 1965), pp. 64–74; Bowman, *Aramaic Ritual Texts,* p. 44.

"Placing the timbers in the walls" may refer to interior wainscoting (1 Kings 6:15 –18) or to logs alternating with the brick or stone layers in the walls (1 Kings 6:36).

9–12 According to 1 Kings 6:1, Solomon began building the temple in the fourth year of his reign, in 966 B.C. (see Gleason L. Archer, Jr., "The Chronology of the

Old Testament," EBC, 1:368). The project lasted seven years (1 Kings 6:38). Since Solomon employed Phoenician craftsmen (1 Kings 7:13–45), the temple evidently incorporated elements of foreign inspiration.

In 1936 a ninth-century temple was discovered at Tell Tainat (Tayinat) east of Antioch, which, though two-thirds the size of Solomon's temple, had a similar tripartite plan. Other parallels include a Late Bronze Canaanite temple at Hazor and a ninth or tenth-century royal chapel at Hamath. After a thorough examination of all possible prototypes of Solomon's temple, T. Busink (*Der Tempel von Salomo vis Herodes* [Leiden: Brill, 1970]), while acknowledging the Phoenician inspiration of certain elements, stresses the basic originality of his temple design (cf. also Paul Garber, "Reconstructing Solomon's Temple," BA 14 [1951]: 2–24; D. Ussishkin, "Building IV in Hamath and the Temples of Solomon and Tell Tayanat," IEJ 16 [1966]: 104–10).

In response to the challenge of the Persian authorities, the Jewish elders declared that they were the servants of the God of heaven and earth and recounted the building of the first temple by Solomon, which must have been an object of national pride. They then confessed that because of their fathers' sins, God had been provoked into using the pagan Babylonians in chastising them, just as Jeremiah had warned. We may be instructed that it is God who builds our institutions. If we take undue pride in them and thus provoke him, he can as readily destroy them for our chastening.

The Chaldeans inhabited the southern regions of Mesopotamia and established the Neo-Babylonian Empire (626–539 B.C.). Their origins are obscure. There may have been some original kinship with the Arameans, who came to occupy adjacent territories to the north of the Chaldeans. Nonetheless the Chaldeans were consistently distinguished from the Arameans in the Assyrian documents (cf. 2 Kings 24:2; Jer 35:11).

In the late seventh century B.C., the Chaldeans with the Medes, led by Nabopolassar, the father of Nebuchadnezzar, overthrew the Assyrians. In 1956 Wiseman published his *Chronicles of Chaldean Kings*, which gives us vital information for the first ten years of Nebuchadnezzar's reign (ibid., p. 73). Of the Fall of Jerusalem on 16 March 597, the chronicles laconically report: "He then captured its king (Jehoiachin) and appointed a king of his own choice (Zedekiah)" (cf. 2 Kings 24:17). Unfortunately, the extant Chaldean chronicles do not cover Nebuchadnezzar's final attack on Jerusalem.

Scholars are divided as to the year of Jerusalem's final capture. Second Chronicles 36:11 informs us that Zedekiah reigned eleven years (from 597 B.C.). Scholars (e.g., Albright, Freedman, Tadmor, Wiseman) who believe the Jews used a calendar beginning in Nisan (Apr.) date the Fall of Jerusalem to the summer of 587 B.C. Others (e.g., Horn, Malamat, Redford, Saggs, Thiele), who believe that the Jews used a calendar beginning in Tishri (Sept.), place the Fall in the summer of 586 B.C. The latter date might accord better with Ezekiel 33:21, which says that the Judean exiles in Babylonia heard of the disaster from a fugitive in December 586. (See K. Freedy and D. Redford, "The Dates in Ezekiel in Relation to Biblical, Babylonian and Egyptian Sources," JAOS 90 [1970]: 462–85; S. Horn, "The Babylonian Chronicle," pp. 12–27; A. Malamat, "A New Record of Nebuchadrezzar's Palestinian Campaigns," IEJ 6 [1956]: 246–56; H. Tadmor, "Chronology of the Last Kings of Judah," JNES 15 [1956]: 226–30.)

13 For the title "king of Babylon," see the comments on Nehemiah 13:6. In cuneiform contracts in Mesopotamia and in Syria, Darius is also designated "king of Babylon."

14 Cyrus appointed Sheshbazzar "governor" (*pehāh*, derived from Akkad. *pīhatu*). The LXX has "the treasurer who was over the treasury." Both Sheshbazzar and Zerubbabel were "governors" (v.14; Hag 1:1; 2:2). Both are said to have laid the foundation of the temple (v.16; 1:3; 3:2–8; Hag 1:1, 14–15; 2:2–4, 18). Josephus (*Antiq*. XI, 11–13 [i.3]) seems to identify Sheshbazzar with Zerubbabel, an identification accepted by a few scholars on the analogy of Daniel, who had both a Hebrew and a Babylonian name (see Keil, p. 27; J.O. Boyd, "The Historicity of Ezra," *Presbyterian and Reformed Review* 11 [1900]: 596). But both Sheshbazzar and Zerubbabel are Babylonian names.

Some scholars conclude that the Chronicler has telescoped the work of the two men and placed in retrospect the work done later by Zerubbabel in the time of Darius and credited it to Sheshbazzar in the age of Cyrus. That such an erroneous ascription was made lacks support. First, Sheshbazzar was probably an elderly man about fifty-five to sixty at the time of the return, whereas Zerubbabel was probably a younger contemporary about forty (cf. Myers, *Ezra-Nehemiah*, p. 28).

Secondly, Sheshbazzar may have been viewed as the official Persian "governor" whereas Zerubbabel served as the popular leader (3:8–11; see Sara Japhet, "Sheshbazzar and Zerubbabel—Against the Background of the Historical and Religious Tendencies of Ezra-Nehemiah," ZAW 94 [1982]: 66–98). This may be why the Jews mentioned Sheshbazzar here when speaking to the Persian authorities. Whereas the high priest Joshua is associated with Zerubbabel, no priest is likewise associated with Sheshbazzar.

With God all things are possible. Consider the fate of the temple and its vessels. How desperate and hopeless the situation of the Jews must have seemed from the destruction of Jerusalem by Nebuchadnezzar to the desecration of the temple vessels by Belshazzar in a feast the night Babylon fell to Cyrus (Dan 5)! Prior to that night there was utter destruction, deportation, and desecration; after that night reconsecration, return, and rebuilding. For those who could lift their hearts above the dismal prospects of earth to the God of heaven, a promise of an anointed one by the name of Cyrus had been made (Isa 44:28–45:1) long before the capture of Babylon by the Persians. What mere human prognosticator could have guessed such a turn of events?

15–17 It was important that the temple be built on its original "site" (v.15). Though Sheshbazzar presided over the laying of its foundation (v.16) in 536, so little actually was accomplished that Zerubbabel evidently had to preside over a second foundation some sixteen years later (see note on v.16; cf. Brockington, pp. 16–17, on the chronology of Zerubbabel's activity).

The fate of Sheshbazzar is uncertain. Though some have suggested that he returned to Mesopotamia, more probably, in view of his advanced age, he died soon after his return to Jerusalem.

Though there are references to Zerubbabel in Nehemiah 7:7; 12:1, 47, these are retrospective and yield no further information about his activities after the dedication of the temple. Some have therefore speculated that Zerubbabel might have been suspected of planning a revolt against the Persians. According to this scenario "the two sons of oil" of Zechariah 4:10–14 are references to Zerubbabel and Joshua as messianic figures (see L. Waterman, "The Camouflaged Purge of Three Messianic Conspirators," JNES 13 [1954]: 73–78; Ackroyd, *Exile and Restoration*, pp. 192 –94; K.M. Beyse, *Serubbabel und die Königserwartungen der Propheten Haggai und Sacharja* [Stuttgart: Calwer Verlag, 1972], pp. 40–41).

Bright (*History of Israel*, p. 373) concludes that "it is entirely possible that the Persians ultimately got wind of the sentiment in Judah and removed him. But we do not know. There is no evidence whatever for the assertion that he was executed. Yet, since we hear no more of him, and since none of his family succeeded him, it is likely that the Persians did strip the Davidic house of its political prerogatives." Tadmor (in Ben-Sasson, p. 172) suggests that Zerubbabel was probably summoned back to Persia since one of his descendants, Hattush, returned with Ezra (8:2; 1 Chron 3:19–22).

Notes

6 אֲפַרְסְכָיֵא (Aram. *ᵃparsᵉkāyēʾ*, "officials"; cf. 6:6) is transliterated "Apharsachites," as the name of people. This is probably a variant of אֲפַרְסַתְכָיֵא (*ᵃparsatkāyēʾ*) in 4:9 and describes a kind of official. Rosenthal (p. 58) suggests a derivation from the Persian **frasaka* ("investigator").

7 שְׁלָמָא כֹּלָּא (*šᵉlāmāʾ kōllāʾ*, "cordial greetings") is literally "well-being completely."

8 אָסְפַּרְנָא (*āsparnāʾ*, "with diligence") is a loan word from the Persian *asprṇa*, which means "exactly," "perfectly," "eagerly." The adverb is also found in 6:8, 12; 7:17, 21, 26.

12 נְבוּכַדְנֶצַּר (*Nᵉbûkadneṣṣar*, "Nebuchadnezzar"; Akkad. *Nabū-kudurri-uṣur*) means "Nabu protect my boundary stone" or "Nabu has protected the succession rights." The Hebrew form נְבוּכַדְרֶאצַּר (*Nᵉbûkadreʾṣṣar*, "Nebuchadrezzar"), used in Jeremiah and Ezekiel, is closer to the Akkadian. The variant used here in Ezra may be derived from an Aramaic form. Nebuchadnezzar, who reigned from 605 B.C. to 562 B.C., is mentioned almost a hundred times in the OT.

16 Hensley (p. 219) resolves the problem concerning the laying of the foundation thus: "It is sufficient to point out here that יהב (Y-H-B) is better understood in the sense of 'administer.' Thus Sheshbazzar is involved in the work as the official representative of the king, while Zerubbabel is the local authority in charge of the actual work."

17 בֵּית גִּנְזַיָּא (Aram. *bêṯ ginzayyāʾ*, "the royal archives," "house of treasures") comes from the Persian *ganza* ("treasure"; cf. the pl. of גִּזְבָּר [*gizbār*, "treasurer"] in 7:21 from the Pers. *bara* ["bearer"]). The *Genizah* was the storeroom where the Jews deposited worn-out Scriptures. The most important document of the Mandeans is called the *Ginza*.

4. The search for the decree of Cyrus

6:1–5

¹King Darius then issued an order, and they searched in the archives stored in the treasury at Babylon. ²A scroll was found in the citadel of Ecbatana in the province of Media, and this was written on it:

Memorandum:

³In the first year of King Cyrus, the king issued a decree concerning the temple of God in Jerusalem:

Let the temple be rebuilt as a place to present sacrifices, and let its foundations be laid. It is to be ninety feet high and ninety feet wide, ⁴with three courses of large stones and one of timbers. The costs are to be paid by the royal treasury. ⁵Also, the gold and silver articles of the house of God, which Nebuchadnezzar took from the temple in Jerusalem and brought to Babylon, are to be returned to their places in the temple in Jerusalem; they are to be deposited in the house of God.

1 "The archives" (Aram. *bêt siprayyā'*) is literally "house of books." The phrase then reads "in the house of the books where the treasures were laid up." Many Elamite documents were found in the so-called treasury area of Persepolis, along with precious stone objects, etc.

2 Diodorus (2.32.4) declared that the Persians had "royal parchments" recording their history. Persian officials wrote on scrolls of papyrus and leather, as discoveries made in Egypt show. The five books of Song of Solomon, Ruth, Lamentations, Ecclesiastes, and Esther are known to the Jews as the *Megilloth* or "Scrolls."

"Citadel" (Aram. *bîrtā'*) is probably from the Akkadian *bîrtu* ("fortress"). Widengren ("Persian Period," p. 499) comments on this verse: "Important documents were thus preserved in a fortress. This was a tradition which continued for many centuries, for in the Sassanian period, documents were still kept in the so-called *diz i nipišt*, 'the fortress of the archives.' Such a detail adds to the reliability of the story as to how the document was found."

Media was the homeland of the Medes in northwestern Iran. An Indo-European tribe related to the Persians, the Medes, after the rise of Cyrus in 550 B.C., became subordinate to the Persians. The name was retained down to the NT era (Acts 2:9).

"Ecbatana" (Aram. *'aḥmetā'*; KJV "Achmetha"; Old Pers. *Hagmatana* ["gathering place"]; Akkad. *Agmatanu*; Gr. *Agbátana*) was the capital of Media. Its ancient name is still preserved in the name of the modern Hamadan. This is the sole OT reference to the site. There are numerous references in the apocryphal books: Tobit 3:7; 7:1; 14:12–13; Judith 1:1–4; 2 Maccabees 9:1–3 (see Yamauchi, "Achaemenid Capitals," pp. 15–20).

In "The Decrees of Cyrus" (p. 89), de Vaux observes that "now we know that it was the custom of the Persian sovereigns to winter in Babylon and depart in the summer to Susa or Ecbatana, . . . and we also know that Cyrus left Babylon in the spring of 538 B.C. . . . A forger operating in Palestine without the information which we possess could hardly have been so accurate."

A similar "memorandum" (Aram. *dikrônāh*; cf. Egyp. Aram. *zkrn*) in the Aramaic papyri deals with permission to rebuild the Jewish temple at Elephantine (Cowley 32). The Aramaic memorandum of the decree of Cyrus in vv.3–5 is comparable with the Hebrew version of the king's proclamation (*qôl*) in 1:2–4. In contrast with the latter, the Aramaic is written in a more sober, administrative style without reference to Yahweh (see Hensley, pp. 86–88).

3 "Ninety feet high and ninety feet wide" is literally "60 cubits its height and 60 cubits its width." The cubit was the distance from the elbow to the finger tip, or slightly less than eighteen inches. No length is given here. These dimensions contrast with those of Solomon's temple, which was but 20 cubits wide by 30 cubits high by 60 cubits long (1 Kings 6:2). Keil (in loc.) accepts these figures and cites Herod's refurbished temple that was 100 or 120 cubits high. Bowman ("Ezra-Nehemiah," in loc.) suggests that the dimensions should be corrected to make the building 30 cubits high and 20 cubits wide (according to the Pesh.) like Solomon's. The dimensions are probably not descriptions of the temple as built, however, but specifications of the outer limits of a building the Persians would support. The second temple was manifestly not as grandiose as the first (3:12; Hag 2:3).

Kenyon has identified as the only visible remains of Zerubbabel's building a straight joint of stones with heavy bosses about 108 feet north of the southeast corner of the temple platform, which Dunand confirmed as similar to Persian masonry found in Phoenicia (cf. M. Dunand, "Byblos, Sidon, Jerusalem," VetTest Supplement 17 [1969]: 64–70; K. Kenyon, *Royal Cities of the Old Testament* [New York: Schocken Books, 1971], pp. 38–41; id., *Digging Up*, pp. 111–12, 177–78).

4 S. Smith ("Timber and Brick or Masonry Construction," PEQ 73 [1941]: 8) understands "large stones" (Aram. *'eben gelāl*, only here and 5:8) as "stones of rolling": "The stones meant are, then, large pebbles, rubbed smooth and flattened by the action of water, and therefore suitable for use in rubble courses."

The same kind of construction is mentioned in 1 Kings 6:36 and 7:12. Such use of timber beams with masonry is attested at Ras Shamra, Tell Tainat, Troy, Mycenae, Tiryns, Knossos et al. H.C. Thomas ("A Row of Cedar Beams," PEQ 92 [1960]: 61) remarks, "The most probable explanation is that protection against shock, and particularly earthquake shock, lies at the heart of this problem."

In 1973 French archaeologists discovered at Xanthos in Lycia in southwestern Turkey a cult foundation charter—written in Greek, Lycian, and Aramaic—dated to 358 B.C., a period when the area was controlled by a Persian satrap, that provided some striking parallels with the decree of Cyrus.

1. The Xanthos charter, though issued in response to a local request, would nonetheless have received ratification from the Persian court.

2. As in Ezra, amounts of sacrifices, names of priests, and responsibility for the upkeep of the cult are specified.

3. As in Ezra, gods were invoked to curse those who disregarded the decree of local gods.

A.R. Millard ("A Decree of a Persian Governor," *Buried History* [June 1974]: 88)

> Most obvious is the similarity of wording between Greek and Lycian requests and the satrap's Aramaic answer. Such resemblances in the Ezra passages, thought to show a forger's hand, are signs of normal practice. This practice explains how the Persian king or officer appears to know in detail about the cult in question; his information stems from its adherents. . . . The further objection that the Persians would have paid no attention to such details falls away.

5. Darius's order for the rebuilding of the temple

6:6–12

6Now then, Tattenai, governor of Trans-Euphrates, and Shethar-Bozenai and you, their fellow officials of that province, stay away from there. **7**Do not interfere with the work on this temple of God. Let the governor of the Jews and the Jewish elders rebuild this house of God on its site.

⁸Moreover, I hereby decree what you are to do for these elders of the Jews in the construction of this house of God:

The expenses of these men are to be fully paid out of the royal treasury, from the revenues of Trans-Euphrates, so that the work will not stop. ⁹Whatever is needed—young bulls, rams, male lambs for burnt offerings to the God of heaven, and wheat, salt, wine and oil, as requested by the priests in Jerusalem—must be given them daily without fail, ¹⁰so that they may offer sacrifices pleasing to the God of heaven and pray for the well-being of the king and his sons.

¹¹Furthermore, I decree that if anyone changes this edict, a beam is to be pulled from his house and he is to be lifted up and impaled on it. And for this crime his house is to be made a pile of rubble. ¹²May God, who has caused his Name to dwell there, overthrow any king or people who lifts a hand to change this decree or to destroy this temple in Jerusalem.

I Darius have decreed it. Let it be carried out with diligence.

6 "Stay away from there" (Aram. *raḥîq min tammāh*) is literally "be distant from there," an idiom found also in the Egyptian Aramaic papyri (Cowley 13:16; 25:4; 67:5; Kraeling 1:7).

7 On "on its site" see the comment on 5:15. When Babylonian kings like Nebuchadnezzar and Nabonidus rebuilt temples, they searched carefully to discover the exact outlines of the former buildings. An inscription of Nabonidus (cited by R. Ellis, *Foundation Deposits in Ancient Mesopotamia* [New Haven: Yale University Press, 1968], p. 181) reads: "I discovered its (i.e., the Ebabbara in Sippar) ancient foundation, which Sargon, a former king, had made. I laid its brick foundations solidly on the foundation that Sargon had made, neither protruding nor receding an inch."

8 "Treasury" (Aram. *niksîn*, Akkad. *nik[k]assū*; 7:26), literally "possessions," "properties," occurs frequently in extrabiblical Aramaic with a wide variety of meanings. Here it seems to mean royal "funds."

As the accounts in Haggai and Zechariah do not speak of support from the Persian treasury, some have questioned the promises made here. Extrabiblical evidence, however, makes it clear that Persian kings consistently helped restore sanctuaries in their empire. The memorandum concerning the rebuilding of the Jewish temple at Elephantine written by Bagoas, governor of Judah, and Delaiah, governor of Samaria, relates that they were "to rebuild it on its site as it was before, and the meal-offering and incense to be made on that altar as it used to be" (Cowley 32; ANET, p. 492). Kraeling (p. 107) sees this as "a directive presumably suggesting that the rebuilding be done at government expense," with a hint of government subsidies for the offerings.

Cyrus repaired the Eanna temple at Uruk and the Enunmah at Ur. Cambyses gave funds for the temple at Sais in Egypt. The temple of Amon at Hibis in the Khargah Oasis, excavated in 1941 by H. Winlock, was rebuilt from top to bottom by order of Darius. According to Jewish tradition Darius also restored the temple of Ptah in Egypt.

9 A lamb was offered every morning and evening; also two were offered on the Sabbath, seven each at great feasts and at the beginning of each month, and fourteen every day during the Feast of Tabernacles (Lev 1:3, 10; Num 28).

The "burnt offering" (lit., "holocaust") differed from the "welfare" or "fellowship" sacrifice (v.3) in that the sacrifice was wholly consumed on the altar. In the welfare sacrifice only the suet or fat was burned (Lev 3), with the meat divided between priest and sacrificer (Lev 7:11–36) (see R. de Vaux, *Ancient Israel* [New York: McGraw-Hill, 1961], pp. 417ff., 426ff.).

"Wheat" was offered as fine flour, either alone (Lev 5:11–13) or mixed as dough (Lev 2:1–3) or as cakes (Lev 2:4). "Salt" was offered with all oblations (Lev 2:13; Mark 9:49). "Wine" was poured out as a libation (Exod 29:40–41; Lev 23:13, 18, 37). "Oil" was used in the meal offerings.

Antiochus the Great gave the Jews money to complete the temple and large gifts of wine, oil, incense, wheat, and salt for sacrifices (Jos. *Antiq.* XII, 140 [iii.3]). Concerning "without fail," A.T. Olmstead ("A Persian Letter in Thucydides," AJSL 49 [1933]: 161) cites the parallel of a letter from Xerxes to the Spartan Pausanias (*Thucydides* 1.129.3): "And let neither night nor day hinder you from taking care to accomplish anything of what you have promised me, neither for expense of gold and silver let them be hindered."

That the Persian monarchs were interested in foreign cults is shown clearly by the ordinances of Cambyses and Darius I, regulating the temples and priests in Egypt. On the authority of Darius II (423–404 B.C.), a letter was written in 419 to the Jews at Elephantine (Cowley 21) concerning the keeping of the Feast of Unleavened Bread (ANET, p. 491; Cameron, *Persepolis Tablets,* pp. 12–13).

10 "Sacrifices pleasing" (Aram. *nîḥôḥîn*) is literally "sacrifices of sweet smell" (cf. Gen 8:21; Dan 2:46). In pagan religions the sacrifices were viewed literally as nourishment for the gods, but not in the worship of Yahweh (Ezek 44:7; see E. Yamauchi, "Anthropomorphism in Ancient Religions," BS 125 [1968]: 29–44; id., BS 127 [1970]: 212–22).

Darius commanded that the Jews be allowed to "pray for the well-being of the king and his sons." In the Cyrus Cylinder the king asks, "May all the gods whom I have resettled in their sacred cities ask daily Bel and Nebo for a long life for me" (ANET, p. 316). The Jews of Elephantine wrote to the Persian governor of Judah, Bagoas, that if he helped them get their temple rebuilt, "the meal-offering, incense, and burnt offering will be offered in your name, and we shall pray for you at all times, we, and our wives, and our children" (Cowley 30:26; ANET, p. 492). Herodotus (1.132) reported that among the Persians anyone who offered a sacrifice had to pray for the king.

11 Decrees and treaties customarily had appended a long list of curses against anyone who might disregard them (cf. some 250 lines of imprecations at the end of the Code of Hammurabi and the curses of the Vassal Treaties of Esarhaddon).

Anyone who would change Darius's decree would be "impaled" on a beam from his own house. The OT cites the hanging or fastening of criminals (Gen 40:22; 41:13; Num 25:4 et al.). According to Deuteronomy 21:22–23, a criminal was stoned and his corpse hung on a "tree" (cf. 2 Sam 21:6, 9). Esther 2:23; 5:14, and 9:14 speak of the seventy-five-foot-high gallows that Haman planned for Mordecai but on which Haman's ten sons were hung after they were slain. According to Herodotus (3.159), Darius I impaled three thousand Babylonians when he took Babylon, an act that Darius himself recorded in the Behistun Inscription (Kent, pp. 127–28).

"A pile of rubble" (Aram. *nᵉwālû;* "dunghill," KJV, RSV) is a word of uncertain etymology. Hensley (pp. 56–57), following Nöldeke, suggests it may mean the house was to be "confiscated" (cf. 1 Kings 14:10; 2 Kings 10:27; Job 20:7; Dan 2:5; 3:29; Zeph 1:17).

12 At the end of his famous Behistun Inscription, Darius warned: "If thou shalt behold this inscription or these sculptures, (and) shalt destroy them and shalt not protect them as long as unto thee there is strength, may Ahuramazda be a smiter unto thee, and may family not be unto thee, and what thou shalt do, that for thee may Ahuramazda utterly destroy!"

While Darius was expressing concern over the Jewish temple in Jerusalem, he was also giving orders for the reopening of the Egyptian temple at Sais in the Delta. Tuland ("Uššayyā'," p. 273) remarks:

> In Darius' reign, the work on the Temple recommenced in the autumn of 520 B.C.; it was well under way when the satrap made his inspection. . . . The king's reply then could not have been earlier than 519 B.C.; it was in this year that Darius wrote to his civil servants in Egypt, ordering them to prepare a codification of the sacred laws of that country, and it was probably about the same time that he granted Uzahor permission to reopen the temple at Sais.

6. *The completion of the temple*

6:13–15

> [13]Then, because of the decree King Darius had sent, Tattenai, governor of Trans-Euphrates, and Shethar-Bozenai and their associates carried it out with diligence. [14]So the elders of the Jews continued to build and prosper under the preaching of Haggai the prophet and Zechariah, a descendant of Iddo. They finished building the temple according to the command of the God of Israel and the decrees of Cyrus, Darius and Artaxerxes, kings of Persia. [15]The temple was completed on the third day of the month Adar, in the sixth year of the reign of King Darius.

13–14 Work on the temple made little progress because of opposition and the preoccupation of the returnees with their own homes (Hag 1:2–3). Because they had placed their own interests first, God sent them famine as a judgment (Hag 1:5–6, 10 –11). Spurred by the preaching of Haggai and Zechariah, and under the leadership of Zerubbabel and Joshua, a new effort was begun (Hag 1:12–15).

The reference to "Artaxerxes" seems out of place because this king did not contribute to the rebuilding of the temple. His name may have been inserted here because he contributed to the work of the temple at a later date under Ezra (7:21–26).

15 "Adar," the last Babylonian month, was February-March. The temple was finished on 12 March 515 B.C., a little over seventy years after its destruction. As the renewed work on the temple had begun 21 September 520 (Hag 1:4–15), sustained effort had continued for over four years.

According to Haggai 2:3, the older members who could remember the splendor of Solomon's temple were disappointed when they saw the smaller size of Zerubbabel's temple (cf. 3:12). Nonetheless the second temple, though not as grand as the first, lasted much longer. H.T. Frank (*Bible, Archaeology, and Faith* [Nashville:

Abingdon, 1971], p. 220) observes that "it was large and so well built as to serve as a fairly successful fortress on several occasions over the next five hundred years. The longevity of this Temple and the fact that the Maccabees undertook only strengthening of its defenses and no thoroughgoing rebuilding bespeak of adequacy and also of accumulated splendor."

The general plan of the second temple resembled the first. But the *dᵉbîr* ("the Most Holy Place") was left empty as the ark of the covenant had been lost through the Babylonian conquest. According to the Mishnah (*Yoma* 5.2), "after the Ark was taken away a stone remained there from the time of the early Prophets, and it was called 'Shetiyah'. It was higher than the ground by three fingerbreadths. On this he used to put [the fire-pan]" (cf. 1 Macc 1:21; 4:49–51). The *hêkāl* ("Holy Place") was furnished with a table for the showbread, the incense altar, and one menorah instead of Solomon's ten (see Mazar, *Mountain*, pp. 104ff.).

7. The dedication of the temple

6:16–18

> 16Then the people of Israel—the priests, the Levites and the rest of the exiles— celebrated the dedication of the house of God with joy. 17For the dedication of this house of God they offered a hundred bulls, two hundred rams, four hundred male lambs and, as a sin offering for all Israel, twelve male goats, one for each of the tribes of Israel. 18And they installed the priests in their divisions and the Levites in their groups for the service of God at Jerusalem, according to what is written in the Book of Moses.

16 For the dedication of Solomon's temple, see 1 Kings 8. This verse and v.19 emphasize that the leadership of the returned exiles was responsible for the completion of the temple.

"With joy" (Aram. *hedwāh*) occurs here; it is identical with the Hebrew form, found only in 1 Chronicles 16:27 and Nehemiah 8:10. In the former passage we read that "joy" together with "strength" are found in God's "place," that is, his sanctuary.

"Dedication" (Aram. *hᵃnukkāh*) occurs here, in v.17, and in Daniel 3:2–3; for the corresponding Hebrew word, see Numbers 7:10–11, 84, 88; 2 Chronicles 7:9; Nehemiah 12:27. The Jewish holiday in December that celebrates the discovery of pure oil, its prolongation, and the rededication of the temple captured by the Jews from the Seleucids is known today as Hanukkah.

17 The number of victims sacrificed was small compared to the thousands in similar services under Solomon (1 Kings 8:5, 63), Hezekiah (2 Chron 30:24), and Josiah (2 Chron 35:7). Nonetheless they represented a real sacrifice under the prevailing conditions.

18 This ends the Aramaic section that began in 4:8; another Aramaic section begins at 7:12.

The priests were divided into twenty-four courses, each of which served at the temple for a week at a time (cf. Luke 1:5, 8). In 1962 fragments of a synagogue inscription listing the twenty-four courses were found at Caesarea (cf. M. Avi-Yonah, "The Caesarea Inscription of the Twenty-four Priestly Courses," *The Teacher's Yoke*, ed. E.J. Vardaman [Waco: Baylor University Press, 1964], pp. 46–57).

8. The celebration of the Passover

6:19–22

[19]On the fourteenth day of the first month, the exiles celebrated the Passover. [20]The priests and Levites had purified themselves and were all ceremonially clean. The Levites slaughtered the Passover lamb for all the exiles, for their brothers the priests and for themselves. [21]So the Israelites who had returned from the exile ate it, together with all who had separated themselves from the unclean practices of their Gentile neighbors in order to seek the LORD, the God of Israel. [22]For seven days they celebrated with joy the Feast of Unleavened Bread, because the LORD had filled them with joy by changing the attitude of the king of Assyria, so that he assisted them in the work on the house of God, the God of Israel.

19 The date would have been about 21 April 515 B.C. Since the destruction of the temple by Titus in A.D. 70, Jews have not been able to sacrifice Passover lambs but have substituted eggs and roasted meat (see J.B. Segal, *The Hebrew Passover from Earliest Times to AD 70* [New York: Oxford University Press, 1963]). Only the Samaritans continue to slaughter lambs, for their place of worship is on Mount Gerizim (cf. John 4:20), though their temple has also been destroyed (see Talmon, "The Samaritans," pp. 100–108).

20 "Ceremonially clean" (Heb. Hithpael of *tāhēr*) is used almost exclusively of ritual or moral purity, occurring with its derivatives 204 times in the OT. Mostly these words appear in the priestly literature: about 44 percent in Leviticus and Numbers, about 16 percent in Exodus, and about 14 percent in Chronicles and Ezekiel. Priests and Levites had to be cleansed to fulfill their ritual functions. Second Chronicles 29:34 describes the Levites in the time of Hezekiah as more upright in heart in sanctifying themselves than the priests (2 Chron 30:17–19; cf. B. Porten, "Aramaic Papyri and Parchments," BA 42 [1979]: 92).

21 The returning exiles were not uncompromising separatists; they were willing to accept those who would separate themselves from the syncretism of the foreigners introduced into the area by the Assyrians.

"The unclean practices" (*tum'āh*) are literally "uncleanness," "filthiness." The antonym of *tāhēr* is *tāmē'* ("to be unclean"). It and its derivatives occur 279 times in the OT, about 64 percent in Leviticus and Numbers and 15 percent in Ezekiel. Idolatry defiled the land (Ezek 36:18; cf. Gen 35:2). The Lord asked Judah, "How can you say, 'I am not defiled, I have not run after the Baals'?" (Jer 2:23). Israel had been rendered unclean by the idols she had made (Ezek 22:4; 36:25).

22 Kelly (in loc.) remarks, "Over all there is sounded the constant note of 'joy.'" It was more than a political celebration or a displaced person's gladness at his return home. This was a deeply religious joy "because the Lord had filled them with joy" (see on v.16).

"King of Assyria" (*melek-'aššûr*) is a surprising title for Darius, the Persian king. Assyria was originally in the area in northeastern Mesopotamia along the banks of the upper Tigris River. In the eighth-seventh centuries B.C., the Assyrians expanded their empire to include Babylonia, Syria, Palestine, and even Egypt. They were finally overthrown by a coalition of Medes and Chaldeans.

Even after the Fall of Nineveh in 612, the term Assyrian was used for formerly occupied territories. Syria is an abbreviation for Assyria. Herodotus (1.178) refers to Babylon as the capital of Assyria, and Xenophon (*Cyropaedia* 2.1.5) speaks of "the Assyrians, both those from Babylon and those from the rest of Assyria." Persian kings adopted a variety of titles including "king of Babylon" (cf. 5:13; Neh 13:6). In Nehemiah 9:32 "kings of Assyria" could signify, not only Assyrian, but also Babylonian and Persian kings. The latter meaning may be intended here.

Notes

19–22 In 419 B.C. Darius II transmitted through the satrap Arsames to the Jewish colony at Elephantine an order to observe the Feast of Unleavened Bread: "Be ritually clean and take heed. . . . and anything whatever [in] which the[re is] leaven [do not eat . . .]" (Cowley 21; ANET, pp. 491).

II. Ezra's Return and Reforms (7:1–10:44)

A. *Ezra's Return to Palestine (7:1–8:36)*

1. Preparations

7:1–10

> [1]After these things, during the reign of Artaxerxes king of Persia, Ezra son of Seraiah, the son of Azariah, the son of Hilkiah, [2]the son of Shallum, the son of Zadok, the son of Ahitub, [3]the son of Amariah, the son of Azariah, the son of Meraioth, [4]the son of Zerahiah, the son of Uzzi, the son of Bukki, [5]the son of Abishua, the son of Phinehas, the son of Eleazar, the son of Aaron the chief priest— [6]this Ezra came up from Babylon. He was a teacher well versed in the Law of Moses, which the LORD, the God of Israel, had given. The king had granted him everything he asked, for the hand of the LORD his God was on him. [7]Some of the Israelites, including priests, Levites, singers, gatekeepers and temple servants, also came up to Jerusalem in the seventh year of King Artaxerxes.
> [8]Ezra arrived in Jerusalem in the fifth month of the seventh year of the king. [9]He had begun his journey from Babylon on the first day of the first month, and he arrived in Jerusalem on the first day of the fifth month, for the gracious hand of his God was on him. [10]For Ezra had devoted himself to the study and observance of the Law of the LORD, and to teaching its decrees and laws in Israel.

1 "After these things" refers to the completion and dedication of the temple in 515 B.C. (cf. ch. 6). The identity of the Artaxerxes mentioned here has been disputed. If this was Artaxerxes I as the traditional view maintains, which we believe is correct, Ezra arrived in Palestine in 458 (457). If this was Artaxerxes II, Ezra arrived in 398 (see Introduction: Chronology and The Order). The traditional view assumes a gap of almost sixty years between the events of chapter 6 and chapter 7. The only recorded event during this interval concerns opposition in Xerxes's reign (485–465 B.C.) (cf. 4:6).

The genealogy of Ezra given in vv. 1–5 is an extraordinary one that lists his ancestors back to Aaron, brother of Moses. Koch (p. 190) comments: "The long genealogy of Ezra consisting of sixteen ancestors is unique (for an individual) with the Old Testament, and has a parallel only among late Egyptian priests."

"Ezra" (*ʿezrāʾ*) is a shortened form of Azariah, a name that occurs twice in the list of his ancestors. The Greek form is Esdras.

"Seraiah" (*śᵉrāyāh*, "Yahweh is Prince") was the high priest under Zedekiah who was killed in 587 B.C. by Nebuchadnezzar (2 Kings 25:18–21; Jer 52:24) some 129 years before Ezra's arrival.

"Azariah" (*ʿazaryāh*, "Yahweh has helped") is the name of about twenty-five OT individuals, including one of Daniel's companions (Dan 1:6–7).

"Hilkiah" (*ḥilqîyāh*, "my portion is Yahweh") was the high priest under Josiah (2 Kings 22:4).

2 On "Shallum" see the comment on 2:42.

"Zadok" (*ṣāḏôq*, "righteous") was a priest under David whom Solomon appointed chief priest in place of Abiathar, who supported the rebel Adonijah (1 Kings 1:7–8; 2:35). Ezekiel regarded the Zadokites as free from idolatry (Ezek 44:15–16). The Zadokites held the office of high priest till 171 B.C. The Sadducees were named after Zadok, and the Qumran community looked for the restoration of the Zadokite priesthood (see J.R. Bartlett, "Zadok and His Successors at Jerusalem," JTS 19 [1968]: 1–18).

"Ahitub" (*ʾaḥîṭûḇ*, "my brother is good") was the grandfather of Zadok (Neh 11:11).

3 "Amariah" (*ʾamaryāh*) means "Yahweh has spoken."

4 "Zerahiah" (*zᵉraḥyāh*) is "Yahweh has shone forth"; "Uzzi" (*ʿuzzî*), "[Yahweh is] strength"; and "Bukki" (*buqqî*), "vessel [of Yahweh]."

5 "Abishua" (*ʾaḇîšûaʿ*, "my father is salvation") was the great grandson of Aaron (1 Chron 6:4–5 [5:30–31 MT]).

"Phinehas" (*pînᵉḥās*), from the Egyptian *p'-nḥsy* ("the Nubian") was the grandson of Aaron. Moses married a Negro woman from the Sudan, called "Ethiopian" in the KJV and "Cushite" in the NIV and RSV (Num 12:1) (see T. Meek, "Moses and the Levites," AJSL 56 [1939]: 113–20).

"Eleazar" (*elʿāzār*) is "God has helped." The Greek transliteration is Lazarus (John 11). The latter's town of Bethany is known today by the Arabic name Al-Azariyeh.

6 "A teacher" (*sōpēr*) is literally "a scribe" (cf. Aram. *sāpar* [4:8, 17, 23; 7:12, 21]; Akkad. *šāpirum;* see on 4:8, and Rainey, *Scribe at Ugarit*). Scribes served kings as secretaries, such as Shaphan under Josiah (2 Kings 22:3). Others took dictation, as Baruch, who wrote down what Jeremiah spoke (Jer 36:32; cf. N. Avigad, "Baruch the Scribe and Jerahmeel the King's Son," BA 42 [1979]: 114–18). From the exilic period the scribes were scholars who studied and taught the Scriptures. In the NT period they were addressed as "rabbis."

"Well versed" (*māhîr*) is a word that literally means "quick" or "swift." It occurs in only three other passages: Psalm 45:1, "a skillful writer"; Proverbs 22:29, "skilled in his work"; and Isaiah 16:5, "speeds the cause of righteousness." The phrase also occurs in the Aramaic Story of Ahiqar found at Elephantine (*Ahiqar* 1:1): *spr ḥkym w-mhry* ("a scribe wise and skilled"). A reflection of the root meaning of *māhîr* may be the apocryphal tradition in 2 Esdras 14:24: "In the meantime equip yourself with a good supply of writing tablets and engage . . . these five because they can write rapidly."

"The hand of the LORD his God was on him" is a striking expression of God's favor (cf. also vv.9, 28; 8:18, 22, 31; Neh 2:8, 18).

7–9 Most scholars assume that the seventh year of Artaxerxes I should be reckoned according to the Persian custom of dating regnal years from spring to spring (Nisan to Nisan, which was also the Jewish religious calendar). Thus Ezra would have begun his journey on the first day of Nisan (8 Apr. 458) and arrived on the first day of Ab (4 Aug. 458; see Introduction: Chronology, The Order; cf. also Finegan, *Handbook of Biblical Chronology*, # 336).

During the monarchy the Israelites had adopted a civil fall-to-fall calendar (Tishri to Tishri) as well. S.H. Horn and L.H. Wood ("The Fifth-Century Jewish Calendar at Elephantine," JNES 13 [1954]: 1–20) have argued that the Jews resumed such a calendar after the Exile partly on the basis of an Elephantine papyrus. The seventh year of Artaxerxes I would have run from Tishri 458 to Tishri 457. Ezra would have left on 27 March 457 and arrived on 23 July 457 (see Horn and Wood, *Ezra* 7, p. 115, and figs. 5–8). (For criticisms of this position, see R.A. Parker, "Some Considerations on the Nature of the Fifth-Century Jewish Calendar at Elephantine," JNES 14 [1955]: 271–74; Clines, "Autumnal New Year," p. 35.)

In either case the journey took 119 days (including an eleven-day delay indicated by 8:31), or four months. Spring was the most auspicious time for such journeys; most ancient armies went on campaigns at this season. Though the direct distance between Babylon and Jerusalem is about five hundred miles, the travelers would have had to traverse nine hundred miles, going northwest along the Euphrates River and then south (see comment on 1:11). The relatively slow rate is explicable by the presence of children and the elderly.

The full phrase "the gracious hand of his God was on him" occurs here, in 8:18, 22, and in Nehemiah 2:8, 18. Ezra 7:28 and 8:31 omit "gracious." The phrase denotes God's permanent help and grace that rest on a person or a congregation.

10 "Ezra set his heart" (Heb.). He is described as a scribe who was learned in the law of Moses (v.6), as a "teacher of the Law of God of heaven" (v.12). He not only studied the Scriptures but taught and interpreted them (Neh 8). Bible study was not merely an intellectual discipline but a personal study for his own life and for the instruction of his congregation.

2. *The authorization by Artaxerxes*

7:11–26

¹¹This is a copy of the letter King Artaxerxes had given to Ezra the priest and teacher, a man learned in matters concerning the commands and decrees of the LORD for Israel:

¹²Artaxerxes, king of kings,

To Ezra the priest, a teacher of the Law of the God of heaven:

Greetings.

¹³Now I decree that any of the Israelites in my kingdom, including priests and Levites, who wish to go to Jerusalem with you, may go. ¹⁴You are sent

by the king and his seven advisers to inquire about Judah and Jerusalem with regard to the Law of your God, which is in your hand. [15]Moreover, you are to take with you the silver and gold that the king and his advisers have freely given to the God of Israel, whose dwelling is in Jerusalem, [16]together with all the silver and gold you may obtain from the province of Babylon, as well as the freewill offerings of the people and priests for the temple of their God in Jerusalem. [17]With this money be sure to buy bulls, rams and male lambs, together with their grain offerings and drink offerings, and sacrifice them on the altar of the temple of your God in Jerusalem.

[18]You and your brother Jews may then do whatever seems best with the rest of the silver and gold, in accordance with the will of your God. [19]Deliver to the God of Jerusalem all the articles entrusted to you for worship in the temple of your God. [20]And anything else needed for the temple of your God that you may have occasion to supply, you may provide from the royal treasury.

[21]Now I, King Artaxerxes, order all the treasurers of Trans-Euphrates to provide with diligence whatever Ezra the priest, a teacher of the Law of the God of heaven, may ask of you— [22]up to a hundred talents of silver, a hundred cors of wheat, a hundred baths of wine, a hundred baths of olive oil, and salt without limit. [23]Whatever the God of heaven has prescribed, let it be done with diligence for the temple of the God of heaven. Why should there be wrath against the realm of the king and of his sons? [24]You are also to know that you have no authority to impose taxes, tribute or duty on any of the priests, Levites, singers, gatekeepers, temple servants or other workers at this house of God.

[25]And you, Ezra, in accordance with the wisdom of your God, which you possess, appoint magistrates and judges to administer justice to all the people of Trans-Euphrates—all who know the laws of your God. And you are to teach any who do not know them. [26]Whoever does not obey the law of your God and the law of the king must surely be punished by death, banishment, confiscation of property, or imprisonment.

11 Many scholars regard the Letter of Artaxerxes I permitting Ezra's return in 458 (or 457) as the *terminus a quo*, the beginning point, of Daniel's first 69 weeks (Dan 9:24–27). If each week represented a solar year, then 69 times 7 years equals 483 years, added to 457 B.C. equals A.D. 26, i.e., the traditional date for the beginning of Christ's ministry. Others, however, regard the commission of the same king to Nehemiah in 445 B.C. as the starting point (Neh 1:1, 11; 2:1–8). From this date by computing according to a lunar year of 360 days, the same date of A.D. 26 is reached. H.W. Hoehner ("Chronological Aspects in the Life of Christ VI: Daniel's Seventy Weeks and New Testament Chronology," BS 132 [1975]; 47–65), however, believes that the prophecy can be calculated to arrive at A.D. 29, when he believes Jesus' ministry began.

12 The text of the decree in vv. 12–26 is in Aramaic (see Introduction: Text). The phrase "king of kings" (Aram. *melek malkayyā'*) originally occurred in Akkadian as *šar šarrāni* (cf. *bēl šarrāni*), used by Assyrian kings from the time of Tukulti-Ninurta I as their empires incorporated many kingdoms. It was then adopted by Neo-Babylonian kings like Nebuchadnezzar (Ezek 26:7; Dan 2:37, 47). The Achaemenid kings from Darius I on used the Old Persian phrase *xšāyathiya xšāyathiyānām;* the deposed king of Iran was known in Modern Persian as *Shahinshah* ("king of kings"). The rabbis applied to God the title "King of the king of kings."

"The Law" (Aram. *dātā'*) is derived from the Persian *dāta*. R.N. Frye ("The Institutions," *Beiträge zur Achämenidengeschichte,* ed. G. Walser [Wiesbaden: Franz Steiner, 1972], p. 92) places the decree in its broader historical context as follows:

> Darius was actively concerned not only with his own "imperial" laws, to be promulgated throughout the empire, but also with the local laws and traditional practices in various provinces. . . . Darius wrote to his satrap in Egypt Aryandes to collect the wise men of the realm to make a new code of laws. Although the work was not finished before his death, the successors of Darius continued to be interested in the codification of the laws of their subject peoples. It is in this light that one must understand the efforts of Ezra (7, 11) and Nehemiah (8, 1) to codify the Mosaic law, which was not accomplished till the reign of Artaxerxes I.

"Greetings" (Aram. *gᵉmîr*) means "perfect" as an adjective and "completely" as an adverb. According to Slotki (in loc.), this would correspond to the rabbinic term *wegomer* ("etc."), referring to the other titles of respect attached to Ezra's name. Others see it as an adjective ("perfect") with an omitted word ("scribe") understood, or with the word *šᵉlām* ("greetings," i.e., "hearty [greetings]"; cf. NIV).

13 Note the use of the term "Israelites" rather than "Judeans." Ezra's aim was to make a united Israel of those who returned. W.J. Dumbrell ("Malachi and the Ezra-Nehemiah Reforms," *Reformed Theological Review* 35 [1976]: 45) observes:

> The Ezra narratives in both books [i.e., Ezra and Neh] use the term Israel some twenty-four times. It is the key term of the edict of Artaxerxes with which Ezra is armed (cf. Ezra 7:13). Likewise emphasized is the term "God of Israel" throughout the Ezra material. On the other hand Judah as a term occurs only four times in the Ezra material, and then only as a geographical term (Ezra 7:14, 9:9, 10:7, 9). Though necessarily in the more administratively geared book of Nehemiah the term Judah appears frequently, where a theological point has to be made it is the term Israel which is used (cf. in Nehemiah's prayer in 1:6 and again in 13:3).

Concerning "priests and Levites" Batten (in loc.) remarked, "Of all the official documents in our books this one arouses the greatest suspicion," because of its markedly Jewish tone. E. Meyer (*Die Entstehung des Judentums* [Tübingen: Niemeyer, 1896]) and others think this is the result of the king's using Jewish officials—possibly Ezra himself—to help him draw up the decree (see comment on 6:4).

14 "Seven advisers" corresponds with the Persian tradition (*Herodotus* 1.31; 3.84; 7.8; 8.67; Xenophon *Anabasis* 1.6.4f.; cf. Esth 1:14 on the seven princes "who had special access to the king").

Many scholars believe that "the Law" Ezra brought with him was the complete Pentateuch in its present form. D.N. Freeman (" 'Son of Man, Can These Bones Live?' " Int 29 [1975]: 183) asserts: "It was this altered situation that prompted Ezra to make the last and greatest change in the first part of the canon, the creation of the Pentateuch as a distinct unit, to be used as the legal instrument of a small quasi-autonomous enclave in the Persian Empire. Ezra brought with him to Palestine the Primary History in the text from which every subsequent manuscript was derived."

15-16 Critics ask whether the Persian king would be so generous. The Persian treasury had ample funds, and such benevolence was a well-attested policy. First

Esdras 8:13 adds: "all the gold and silver belonging to the Lord of Jerusalem which can be found in the province of Babylon." Though this phrase would hardly be in the king's letter, it expresses the truth found in Haggai 2:8: "'The silver is mine and the gold is mine,' declares the LORD Almighty."

There are close parallels to the directive of vv.15–16 in the Elephantine letters, i.e., in the so-called Passover Papyrus, in which Darius II ordered the Jews to keep the Feast of Unleavened Bread (Cowley 21; ANET, p. 491), and also in the temple reconstruction authorization: "Let meal-offering, incense and burnt-offering be offered upon the altar of the God Yahu in your name" (Cowley 31; ANET, p. 492).

The custom of sending gifts to Jerusalem from the Jews in the Diaspora was to continue down through the Roman Empire (Jos. Antiq. XVIII, 312–13 [ix.1]) till the Jewish-Roman War, when the Romans diverted these contributions to the temple of Jupiter instead.

18–19 See the comments on 5:17 and 6:1.

20–21 There are over three-hundred travel texts from Persepolis. According to Hallock (p. 6): "The travel-ration texts report the daily operations of a highly developed system of travel, transport, and communication. . . . The travel-ration texts also, by their very existence, imply an elaborate system for the transference of credits." Other Elamite texts from the treasury at Persepolis give examples of the royal disbursement of supplies and funds.

Some critics question how literally the Persian king's promise should be taken as Haggai 1:8–11 indicates that work on the temple was delayed because of a lack of contributions from the Jewish community. Perhaps the provincial officials did not cooperate in carrying out the royal commands. Commenting on Cyrus's earlier decree, North (p. 388) suggests: "Cyrus merely said the Jews could draw on tax-funds paid in by the Syrian population; . . . ultimately their disbursement would depend much on the good will of local Samaritan treasurers."

22 A "talent" (kikkār, "circle") in the Babylonian sexagesimal system was 60 minas, with a mina being 60 shekels. A talent weighed about 75 pounds. A hundred talents was an enormous sum, about 3¾ tons of silver. This amount, together with a talent of gold, was the tribute that Pharaoh Neco imposed on Judah (2 Kings 23:33).

A "cor" was a donkey load, about 6½ bushels. The total amount of wheat, 650 bushels, was relatively small. The grain would be used in meal offerings. A "bath" was a liquid measure of about 6 gallons; therefore the amount of oil was 600 gallons. "Salt without limit" is literally "salt without prescribing (how much)" (see comments on 4:14; 6:9).

A close parallel is the benefaction of Antiochus III as recorded by Josephus (Antiq. XII, 140 [iii.3]): "In the first place we have decided, on account of their piety, to furnish them for their sacrifices an allowance of sacrificial animals, wine, oil and frankincense to the value of twenty-thousand pieces of silver, and sacred artabae of fine flour in accordance with their native law, and one thousand-four hundred and sixty medimni of wheat and three hundred and seventy-five medimni of salt."

23 The urgency of the Persian king's command—"with diligence"—is reflected in a letter from Xerxes to Pausanias, the Spartan commander (Thucydides 1.129.3): "And let neither night nor day hinder you from taking care to accomplish anything of what you have promised me, neither for expense of gold and silver let them be hindered . . . *boldly* execute both my affairs and yours, whatever is finest and best for both" (emphasis mine).

"Wrath against the realm of the king" speaks of Egypt's revolt against the Persians in 460 B.C. and Egypt's expulsion of the Persians in 459 with the aid of the Persians. In 458 (457) when Ezra returned to Palestine, the Persians were involved in suppressing the revolt (see Introduction: Reign of Artaxerxes I). We do not know how many "sons" the king had at this time, but he ultimately had eighteen, according to Ctesias (*Persika* 44).

24 Priests and other temple personnel were often given exemptions from enforced labor or taxes. A Fifth-Dynasty pharaoh (twenty-sixth century B.C.) exempted personnel of the temple of Abydos from forced labor (ANET, p. 212). Antiochus III granted exemptions to the Jews: "the priests, the scribes of the temple and the temple-singers shall be relieved from the poll-tax and the crown-tax and the salt-tax which they pay" (Jos. *Antiq*. XII, 142–43 [iii.3]).

Some seven centuries after Ezra, Jewish rabbis cited this verse to claim exemption from Parthian taxes (third cent. A.D.): "You have transgressed against the writings, as it is written, *It shall not be lawful to impose upon them (priests and Levites) minda, belo, and halakh,* and Rav Judah explained '*Minda* means the portion of the king, *belo* is the poll-tax, and *halakh* is the *annona* (corvée [forced labor])" (J. Neusner, *There We Sat Down* [Nashville: Abingdon, 1972], p. 64).

25 "Magistrates" (Aram. *šāpt̲in*, a loan from the Heb. *šōpᵉṭîm*) is the literal name of the Book of Judges. Royal judges under the Persians had life tenure but were subject to capital punishment for misconduct in office (*Herodotus* 3.31; 5.25; 7.194). On the administering of justice, 1QapGen 20:13 reads: "For you are Lord and Master over all, and have power to mete out justice to all the kings of the earth."

Rudolph (*Ezra und Nehemiah*, in loc.) suggests that "to teach any who do not know them" does not mean converting Gentiles but bringing Jewish backsliders into conformity with the law.

26 "The law of the king" may be compared with the Akkadian phrase *data ša šarri*. G. Cameron ("Ancient Persia," in Robert C. Dentan, *The Idea of History in the Ancient Near East* [New Haven: Yale University Press, 1955], pp. 77–97) observes: "As early as his second regnal year, Darius' collection of existing laws was in use among the Babylonians, where, for the unusual guarantee by the seller, there is substituted the phrase: 'According to the king's law they shall make good.' "

The extensive powers given to Ezra—"must surely be punished by death"—are striking and extend to secular realms. Hensley (p. 225) cites a parallel from early Buddhist history: "Asoka's Rock Edict V grants basically the same authority to officials throughout his kingdom, also to regulate religious affairs." Some suggest that the implementation of these provisions may have involved Ezra in much traveling, which would explain the silence about Ezra's activities between 458 and 445. Though some have questioned the wide authority given to Ezra, extrabiblical parallels show that it was Persian policy to encourage both moral and religious authority that would enhance public order.

An outstanding parallel to the king's commissioning of Ezra is found in a similar commission of Darius I, who sent Udjahorresenet, a priest and scholar, back to

Egypt. He ordered the codification of the Egyptian laws in demotic and Aramaic by the chief men of Egypt—a task that took from 518 to 503. On the reverse side of the Demotic Chronicle, we are told that Darius ordered "that the wise men be assembled . . . from among the warriors, the priests and the scribes of Egypt so that they may set down in writing the ancient laws of Egypt" (Alan Gardiner, *Egypt of the Pharaohs* [Oxford: Clarendon, 1961], pp. 366ff.).

Notes

14 שְׁלִיחַ (*šelîaḥ*, "sent") is a passive participle that designates an ambassador or emissary; cf. the Greek ἀπόστολος (*apostolos*, "apostle"), which is derived similarly from the word "to send."

23 אַדְרַזְדָּא (ʾ*adrazdā*ʾ, "with diligence"), a hapax legomenon (i.e., occurs only here), derives from the Persian *drazdā ("diligently").

24 זַמָּרַיָּא (*zammārayyā*ʾ, "singers") is a hapax legomenon, the corresponding Hebrew word being *mešōrerîm*.

נְתִינַיָּא (*netînayyā*ʾ, "temple servants") is from the Hebrew *netînîm* (see comment on 2:43). Concerning their responsibilities, M. Avi-Yonah (*Herodian Period*, p. 266) suggests: "We may solve this problem if we assume that the Nethinim worked the Temple lands for the benefit of the High Priest, just as the ἱερόδουλοι [*hierodouloi*] did in [the] Temple-States. Indeed, Josephus translates Nethinim (Ezra 7:24) as ἱερόδουλοι, 'temple servants'; and similarly I Esdras."

26 שְׁרֹשִׁו *šrš* (Aram. Kethib *šerōšû*, Qere *šerōšî*, "banishment") is usually derived from the root *šrš* (cf. Heb. שָׁרֵשׁ [*šareš*, "to uproot"]). The LXX translates it *paideia* ("chastisement"). F. Rundgren, "Zur Bedeutung von *šršw*," VetTest 7 (1957): 400–404, calls attention to the Aramaic word סְרֹשִׁתָא (*serōšitā*), which appears in Driver # 3:5–7, which he associates with the Avestan word *sraošyā* ("punishment"; see also Z.W. Falk, "Ezra VII 26," VetTest 9 [1959]: 88–89).

3. *Ezra's doxology*

7:27–28

[27]Praise be to the LORD, the God of our fathers, who has put it into the king's heart to bring honor to the house of the LORD in Jerusalem in this way [28]and who has extended his good favor to me before the king and his advisers and all the king's powerful officials. Because the hand of the LORD my God was on me, I took courage and gathered leading men from Israel to go up with me.

27–28 Here is the first occurrence of the first person for Ezra, a trait that characterizes the "Ezra Memoirs" that continue to the end of chapter 9 (see Introduction: Literary Form and Authorship).

The Hebrew resumes in v.27. "Praise" (*bārûk*, lit., "blessed"; cf. the name Baruch) opens the prayers the Jews recite today: "Blessed are Thou O Lord, our God." Paul expressed his belief in Christ's deity by applying the corresponding Greek word (*eulogētos*) to him in 2 Corinthians 11:31 (cf. H.J. Schoeps, *Paul* [Philadelphia:

Westminster, 1961], p. 152). Ezra recognized fully that the ultimate source of the favor granted by the king was the sovereign grace of God (cf. 6:22).

"To bring honor" (*pā'ēr*, the Piel infinitive of a relatively rare root, used fourteen times in the OT) can mean "to glorify." Man can beautify, but only God can endow with true glory (cf. Isa 60:7b [RSV]: "I will glorify my glorious house").

Later passages show that Ezra was primarily a priest and scholar rather than an administrator. Yet the assurance that God had called him and had opened the doors gave Ezra the courage and strength to undertake this great task.

4. Returnees with Ezra

8:1-14

¹These are the family heads and those registered with them who came up with me from Babylon during the reign of King Artaxerxes:

²of the descendants of Phinehas, Gershom;
of the descendants of Ithamar, Daniel;
of the descendants of David, Hattush ³of the descendants of Shecaniah;

of the descendants of Parosh, Zechariah, and with him were registered 150 men;
⁴of the descendants of Pahath-Moab, Eliehoenai son of Zerahiah, and with him 200 men;
⁵of the descendants of Zattu, Shecaniah son of Jahaziel, and with him 300 men;
⁶of the descendants of Adin, Ebed son of Jonathan, and with him 50 men;
⁷of the descendants of Elam, Jeshaiah son of Athaliah, and with him 70 men;
⁸of the descendants of Shephatiah, Zebadiah son of Michael, and with him 80 men;
⁹of the descendants of Joab, Obadiah son of Jehiel, and with him 218 men;
¹⁰of the descendants of Bani, Shelomith son of Josiphiah, and with him 160 men;
¹¹of the descendants of Bebai, Zechariah son of Bebai, and with him 28 men;
¹²of the descendants of Azgad, Johanan son of Hakkatan, and with him 110 men;
¹³of the descendants of Adonikam, the last ones, whose names were Eliphelet, Jeuel and Shemaiah, and with them 60 men;
¹⁴of the descendants of Bigvai, Uthai and Zaccur, and with them 70 men.

1 Verses 1-14 list those who accompanied Ezra from Mesopotamia, including the descendants of 15 individuals. The figures of the men listed total 1,496, in addition to the individuals named. There were also a considerable number of women and children (v.21). An additional group of about 40 Levites (vv.18-19) and of 220 "temple servants" (v.20) are also listed.

2 On "Phinehas" see the comment on 7:5. "Gershom" ("sojourner") was also the name of the elder son of Moses and Zipporah (Exod 2:22). "Ithamar" ("isle of palms") was also the name of the fourth son of Aaron (Exod 6:23). For "Hattush" compare the Akkadian *ḫa-an-ṭu-šu* in the Murashu texts (Coogan, *Personal Names*, p. 125).

3 "Shecaniah" means "Yahweh has taken up his abode." On "Parosh" see the comment on 2:3.

"Zechariah" ("Yahweh has remembered") was the name of about thirty individuals in the Bible, including the prophet and the father of John the Baptist (Luke 1:5–67).

4 On "Pahath-Moab" see the comment on 2:6. "Eliehoenai" ("to Yahweh are my eyes") is found only here and in 1 Chronicles 26:3 (cf. Ps 25:15).

5 The Hebrew lacks "Zattu" (cf. 2:8), but the name is preserved by the LXX and 1 Esdras. "Jahaziel" means "May God see!"

6 On "Adin" see the comment on 2:15. "Ebed" (lit., "slave") is probably a shortened form of "Obadiah" ("slave of Yahweh"). It is found only here and in Judges 9:26 (see E. Yamauchi, "The Slaves of God," BETS 9 [1966]: 31–49). "Jonathan" ("Yahweh has given") is the name of sixteen individuals in the OT.

7 On "Elam" see 2:7. "Jeshaiah" means "Yahweh has saved." "Athaliah" ("Yahweh is exalted") was also the name of a famous queen, daughter of Ahab and Jezebel (2 Kings 11).

8 On "Shephatiah" see 2:4. "Zebadiah" means "Yahweh has given." "Michael" ("Who is like God?") is the name of ten OT individuals, including the archangel.

9 "Joab" means "Yahweh is father." "Jehiel" means "May God live!"

10 The Hebrew omits Bani (see 2:10), but the name is retained by the LXX and 1 Esdras. "Josiphiah" ("May Yahweh add!") appears only here, but it is a name closely related to Joseph. "Shelomith" means "complete" or "reward." A feminine form, it is usually a man's name as here. The Greek form is Salome.

11 On "Bebai" see 2:11; on "Zechariah" see v.3.

12 On "Azgad" see 2:12. "Johanan" ("Yahweh has been gracious") is the name of thirteen OT individuals. "Hakkatan" ("the little one") appears only here.

13 "The last ones" probably implies that these followed earlier members of the family who came with Zerubbabel. "Eliphelet" means "my God is escape." "Jeuel" is "Yahweh has stored up." "Shemaiah" ("Yahweh has heard") is the name of twenty-eight individuals in the Bible.

14 On "Bigvai" see 2:2. "Uthai" is perhaps hypocoristic for "(Yahu) has shown himself supreme." "Zaccur" ("remembered") is based on an emendation of the Hebrew Zabbud.

5. *The search for Levites*

8:15–20

> ¹⁵I assembled them at the canal that flows toward Ahava, and we camped there three days. When I checked among the people and the priests, I found no Levites there. ¹⁶So I summoned Eliezer, Ariel, Shemaiah, Elnathan, Jarib, Elnathan, Nathan, Zechariah and Meshullam, who were leaders, and Joiarib and Elnathan,

who were men of learning, [17]and I sent them to Iddo, the leader in Casiphia. I told them what to say to Iddo and his kinsmen, the temple servants in Casiphia, so that they might bring attendants to us for the house of our God. [18]Because the gracious hand of our God was on us, they brought us Sherebiah, a capable man, from the descendants of Mahli son of Levi, the son of Israel, and Sherebiah's sons and brothers, 18 men; [19]and Hashabiah, together with Jeshaiah from the descendants of Merari, and his brothers and nephews, 20 men. [20]They also brought 220 of the temple servants—a body that David and the officials had established to assist the Levites. All were registered by name.

15 "The canal that flows toward Ahava" probably flowed into either the Euphrates or the Tigris (cf. the "River" Kebar in Ezek 1:1, which was also a canal). Bowman ("Ezra-Nehemiah," in loc.) suggests the modern Mecîn, classical Maschana or Scenae, on the right bank of the Tigris River, which was near the beginning of two caravan routes.

"Three days" would be from the ninth to the twelfth of Nisan as the actual journey began on the twelfth (cf. v.31).

The "Levites" who were entrusted with many menial tasks may have found a more comfortable way of life in exile. A rabbinic midrash on Psalm 137 relates the legend that there were Levites in the caravan but that they were not qualified to officiate because when Nebuchadnezzar had ordered them to sing for him the songs of Zion, "they refused and bit off the ends of their fingers, so that they could not play on the harps."

Avi-Yonah (*Herodian Period*, p. 293) observes that in the Hellenistic era the role of the Levites declined sharply:

> From the sources it can be concluded with certainty that from the Hellenistic era onwards the Levites lost much of their status in the Temple. Whereas the Levites are continually mentioned in descriptions of the dedication of the altar in Ezra and Nehemiah, and still more frequently in the Books of Chronicles, they are ignored completely in the Books of Maccabees, when the dedication of the altar by Judah the Maccabee is described, as well as in Ben Sira's account of the service performed by Simeon the son of Onias.

16 "Eliezer" means "my God is help." "Ariel" ("Lion of God") appears only here as a personal name (cf. 2 Sam 23:20; 1 Chron 11:22). Elsewhere it is a cryptic name for Jerusalem (Isa 29:1, 2, 7).

The Hebrew lists two chiefs and a third man of learning with the name "Elnathan." First Esdras 8:44 lists only two men by this name. The name appears on the Lachish Ostracon III, in the Murashu texts as *'ēlnatan* (Coogan, *Personal Names*, p. 13), and on a postexilic bulla as *'lntn* (Avigad, *Bullae and Seals*, p. 6, fig. 5).

"Jarib" is a shortened form of "Joiarib" ("May Yahweh contend!"). "Nathan" is shortened from "Elnathan." "Meshullam" ("rewarded") is the name of nineteen OT individuals. He may be the same person who opposed the marriage reforms (10:15).

"Men of learning" is literally "those who cause to understand" (cf. 1 Chron 25:8; 2 Chron 35:3; Neh 8:7–9).

17 "Iddo" ("strength") is a shortened form of *'Aḏôn.* "In Casiphia" is literally "at the place Casiphia." Ackroyd (*Chronicles, Ezra, Nehemiah*, in loc.) speculates, "Since the word for 'place' is often used in the sense of 'holy place' it is natural to see here a reference to a sanctuary at this particular town." "Casiphia" means "silver town." Olmstead (*Persian Empire*, p. 306) locates the site at the place that later became the Parthian capital of Ctesiphon, on the Tigris River north of Babylon.

18 "Sherebiah" possibly means "Yahweh has sent scorching heat" (cf. *Yišribyaw* [Coogan, *Personal Names*, pp. 28, 85]). "A capable man" is literally "a man of insight." "Mahli" means "shrewd."

19 "Hashabiah" ("Yahweh has taken account") is the name of eleven OT individuals, primarily Levites. On "Jeshaiah" see v.7. "Merari" means "bitterness."

Only about forty Levites from two families were willing to join Ezra's caravan. The service of God requires dedication and sometimes moving from a comfortable situation.

20 On "temple servants" see 2:43. Humanly speaking, the dedication of this group is remarkable. Socially they were a caste of mixed origins and were inferior to the Levites in status. But God's Spirit had motivated them to respond in larger numbers than the Levites.

6. Prayer and fasting

8:21–23

> ²¹There, by the Ahava Canal, I proclaimed a fast, so that we might humble ourselves before our God and ask him for a safe journey for us and our children, with all our possessions. ²²I was ashamed to ask the king for soldiers and horsemen to protect us from enemies on the road, because we had told the king, "The gracious hand of our God is on everyone who looks to him, but his great anger is against all who forsake him." ²³So we fasted and petitioned our God about this, and he answered our prayer.

21 For the association of fasting and humbling oneself, see Psalm 35:13.

"A safe journey" (*derek yᵉšārāh*) is literally "a straight way" unimpeded by obstacles and dangers (cf. v.31). First Esdras 8:50 has *euodian* ("favorable journey"). The Jews before travel offer a prayer called *tephillath hadderech* ("prayer of the road"). Bowman ("Ezra-Nehemiah," p. 632) reports that this verse was the text of John Robinson's last sermon at Leiden before the Pilgrims sailed in 1620.

"Children" (*ṭap* as in Deut 1:39) designates those younger than twenty, with a stress on the younger ages. Such "little ones" are most vulnerable in times of war (cf. Deut 20:14; Judg 21:10; Ezek 9:6). The vast treasures they were carrying—"our possessions"—offered a tempting bait for robbers.

22 Scripture speaks often of unholy shame (Jer 48:13; Mic 3:7) and sometimes of a sense of holy shame. Ezra was quick to blush with such a sense of holy shame (cf. 9:6). Ezra had gone out on a limb by proclaiming his faith in God's ability to protect the caravan. Having done so, he was embarrassed to ask for human protection.

Grave dangers faced travelers between Mesopotamia and Palestine. Some thirteen years later Nehemiah was accompanied by an armed escort. The difference, however, does not mean that Nehemiah was a man of lesser faith (cf. Neh 2:9).

For the phrase "everyone who looks to him," see 1 Chronicles 16:10–11; 2 Chronicles 11:16; Psalms 40:16; 69:6; 70:4; 105:3–4.

23 Fasting implies an earnestness that makes one oblivious to food. For the association of fasting and prayer, see Nehemiah 1:4; Daniel 9:3; Matthew 17:21 (NIV mg.); Acts 14:23.

7. The assignment of the precious objects

8:24–30

24Then I set apart twelve of the leading priests, together with Sherebiah, Hashabiah and ten of their brothers, 25and I weighed out to them the offering of silver and gold and the articles that the king, his advisers, his officials and all Israel present there had donated for the house of our God. 26I weighed out to them 650 talents of silver, silver articles weighing 100 talents, 100 talents of gold, 2720 bowls of gold valued at 1,000 darics, and two fine articles of polished bronze, as precious as gold.

28I said to them, "You as well as these articles are consecrated to the LORD. The silver and gold are a freewill offering to the LORD, the God of your fathers. 29Guard them carefully until you weigh them out in the chambers of the house of the LORD in Jerusalem before the leading priests and the Levites and the family heads of Israel." 30Then the priests and Levites received the silver and gold and sacred articles that had been weighed out to be taken to the house of our God in Jerusalem.

24 This rendering implies that Sherebiah, Hashabiah, and ten others were the twelve leading priests. But according to vv.18–19, they were the leaders of the Levites at Casiphia. The verse can be rendered "I set apart twelve of the leading priests *besides* Sherebiah, Hashabiah, and ten of their brothers" (emphasis mine). According to v.30, both priests and Levites were entrusted with the sacred objects.

25 "Offering" (*terûmāh*) literally means "what is lifted" (i.e., "dedicated," or "given for the cult"; cf. Exod 25:2; 35:5; Lev 7:14; Deut 12:6). Note that the offerings came not only from the Jews but also from the king and his court.

26 For comparison "650 talents" equals 49,000 pounds or close to 25 tons of silver (cf. comment on 7:22). "100 talents" equals 7,500 pounds. These are enormous sums, worth millions of dollars.

27 "Darics" (*ᵃdarkōnîm*) appears only here and in 1 Chronicles 29:7. On its significance see the comment on 2:69 (cf. Neh 7:70–72), where the word *darkᵉmônîm* is used. According to Myers (*Ezra-Nehemiah*, p. 67), if this is the Persian gold daric, then 1,000 darics would weigh about eighteen and a half pounds; if the silver daric, about twelve and a fifth pounds. "Polished bronze" (*muṣhāḇ*) is found only here in the OT, possibly from a by-form of the root of gold. This kind of bronze may have been orichalc, a bright yellow alloy of copper highly prized in ancient times.

28 Both people and objects were sacred and "consecrated" (*qōḏeš*) to God.

29–30 Ezra carefully weighed out the treasures and entrusted them to others. He instilled a sense of the holiness of the mission and the gravity of each individual's responsibility. Each was responsible to guard his deposit, his "talent." The data were carefully recorded and rechecked at the journey's end (v.34).

8. The journey and arrival in Jerusalem

8:31–36

³¹On the twelfth day of the first month we set out from the Ahava Canal to go to Jerusalem. The hand of our God was on us, and he protected us from enemies and bandits along the way. ³²So we arrived in Jerusalem, where we rested three days.

³³On the fourth day, in the house of our God, we weighed out the silver and gold and the sacred articles into the hands of Meremoth son of Uriah, the priest. Eleazar son of Phinehas was with him, and so were the Levites Jozabad son of Jeshua and Noadiah son of Binnui. ³⁴Everything was accounted for by number and weight, and the entire weight was recorded at that time.

³⁵Then the exiles who had returned from captivity sacrificed burnt offerings to the God of Israel: twelve bulls for all Israel, ninety-six rams, seventy-seven male lambs and, as a sin offering, twelve male goats. All this was a burnt offering to the LORD. ³⁶They also delivered the king's orders to the royal satraps and to the governors of Trans-Euphrates, who then gave assistance to the people and to the house of God.

31 "We set out" (*nāsaʿ*) means literally "to pull up stakes" (i.e., of tents). After an initial three-day encampment (v.15), another eight days elapsed while Levites for the caravan were gathered. The actual departure was on the twelfth day. The journey was to take four months (see comment on 7:9).

According to Olmstead (*History of Palestine*, p. 585), "The Mesopotamian plains were in their full spring beauty, and Ezra must often have recalled Second Isaiah's prophecy that the desert would blossom like the crocus." The route between Babylonia and Syria is described by Strabo (16.1.26–27).

32 Nehemiah also "rested three days" after his arrival in Palestine (Neh 2:11).

33 "Meremoth son of Uriah" has the same name and patronymic (father's name) as Meremoth the son of Uriah who repaired two sections of the wall (Neh 3:4, 21) and who signed the covenant (Neh 10:5). This identification has been used by proponents of the reverse order of Ezra and Nehemiah. Kellermann ("Esradatierung," p. 69), however, denies the identification (cf. Introduction: The Order).

"Eleazar" ("God has helped") is *ʾelʿadar* in the Murashu texts (Coogan, *Personal Names*, p. 14). On "Phinehas" see the comment on 7:5. "Jozabad" means "Yahweh has given." "Noadiah" means "Yahweh has kept his appointment." In Nehemiah 6:14 it is the name of a prophetess.

34 According to Babylonian tradition (e.g., in the Hammurabi law code), almost every transaction, including sales and marriages, had to be recorded in writing. Ezra may have had to send back a signed certification of the delivery of the treasures.

35 The animal sacrifices were made as a thanksgiving to God for his mercies and as a sin offering to acknowledge their unworthiness for such mercies. Compared with the offerings of the returnees under Zerubbabel (6:17), when many more exiles were involved, the offerings on this occasion, except for the identical number of male goats, were far less.

36 "Satraps" (*ʾaḥašdarpᵉnayyāʾ*) comes from the Persian *xšathrapāna* (cf. Gr. *satrapēs;* see Esth 3:12; 8:9; 9:3; Dan 3:2–3, 27; 6:1–4, 6–7).

B. *Ezra's Reforms (9:1–10:44)*

1. *The offense of mixed marriages*

9:1–6a

> [1]After these things had been done, the leaders came to me and said, "The people of Israel, including the priests and the Levites, have not kept themselves separate from the neighboring peoples with their detestable practices, like those of the Canaanites, Hittites, Perizzites, Jebusites, Ammonites, Moabites, Egyptians and Amorites. [2]They have taken some of their daughters as wives for themselves and their sons, and have mingled the holy race with the peoples around them. And the leaders and officials have led the way in this unfaithfulness."
>
> [3]When I heard this, I tore my tunic and cloak, pulled hair from my head and beard and sat down appalled. [4]Then everyone who trembled at the words of the God of Israel gathered around me because of this unfaithfulness of the exiles. And I sat there appalled until the evening sacrifice.
>
> [5]Then, at the evening sacrifice, I rose from my self-abasement, with my tunic and cloak torn, and fell on my knees with my hands spread out to the LORD my God [6]and prayed:

1–2 Ezra had reached Jerusalem on the first day of the fifth month (7:9). The measures dealing with intermarriage were announced on the seventeenth day of the ninth month (cf. 10:8 with 10:9), or four and a half months after his arrival.

Those who brought Ezra's attention to this problem were probably the ordinary members of the community rather than the leaders, who were themselves guilty (v.2). When those in positions of responsibility fall, they lead many others astray. Those guilty of intermarriage were among the returnees (v.4). Humanly speaking there may have been reasons for such intermarriages, such as a disparity between the number of returning men and available Jewish women. (See the excursus on intermarriage at the end of ch. 10.)

"The neighboring peoples" (*ʿammê hāʾªrāṣôt,* lit., "peoples of the lands") included the pagan newcomers brought into Samaria by the Assyrians and who had infiltrated south, and Edomites and others who had encroached on former Judean territories.

The eight groups listed designate the original inhabitants of Canaan before the Hebrew conquest (Exod 3:8, 17; 13:5; 23:23, 28; Deut 7:1; 20:17; Josh 3:10; 9:1; 12:8; Judg 3:5; 1 Kings 9:20). Only the Ammonites, Moabites, and Egyptians were still extant in the postexilic period (cf. 2 Chron 8:7; Neh 9:8; cf. J.C.L. Gibson, "Some Important Ethnic Terms in the Pentateuch," JNES 20 [1961]: 217–38; Wiseman, *Peoples*). On "Canaanites" see John Gray, *The Canaanites* (New York: Praeger, 1964).

Though most scholars have identified the "Hittites" (*ḥittî,* which occurs forty-eight times in the OT) and the sons of *ḥēt* (Gen 10:15; 1 Chron 1:13) with the Anatolian Hittites (cf. O.R. Gurney, *The Hittites* [Harmondsworth: Penguin Books,

1966]), this poses problems. H.A. Hoffner ("Some Contributions of Hittitology to Old Testament Study," *Tyndale Bulletin* 20 [1969]: 27–55) suggests that the biblical term has nothing to do with the Anatolian Hittites. (But see A. Kempinski, "Hittites in the Bible," *Biblical Archaeology Review* 5 [1979]: 20–45.)

"Perizzites" is perhaps a designation for villagers from *perāzāh* ("hamlet"). The "Jebusites" occupied the city of Jerusalem (Josh 15:8; 18:16, 28), which was known as the city of Jebus (Judg 19:10; 1 Chron 11:4–5) before its capture by David. As the name Araunah (2 Sam 24:16) can be interpreted as Hurrian, and as the Amarna Letters (fourteenth cent. B.C.) indicate that the chief of Jerusalem was Abdi-ḫepa, a man with a Hurrian name, E.A. Speiser ("Hurrians and Hittites," *The World History of the Jewish People*, ed. B. Netanyahu [New Brunswick: Rutgers University Press, 1964], 1:158–61) has argued that the peoples in the conquest lists known as Jebusites, Hivites, and Hittites should be considered as branches of the Horites or Hurrians. (For a critique see R. de Vaux, "Les Ḥurrians de l'histoire et les Horites de la Bible," RB 74 [1967]: 481–503.)

"Ammonites," the descendants of Lot by an incestuous union with his younger daughter (Gen 19:38), occupied the area around Rabbath Ammon, modern Amman in Transjordan (see G.M. Landes, "The Material Civilization of the Ammonites," BA 24 [1961]: 65–86).

"Moabites," the descendants of Lot by his elder daughter (Gen 19:37), occupied the area of Moab east of the Dead Sea. Ruth was a Moabitess (Ruth 1:4). (See J.R. Bartlett, "The Moabites and Edomites," in Wiseman, *Peoples*, pp. 228–58; A.H. van Zyl, *The Moabites* [Leiden: Brill, 1960].)

According to the Pentateuch intermarriage with Egyptians was legitimate (see P. Montet, *Egypt and the Bible* [Philadelphia: Fortress, 1968]; R.J. Williams, "The Egyptians," in Wiseman, pp. 79–99).

"Amorites" derives from the Akkadian *Amurru* ("Westland," or Syria). (See A. Haldar, *Who Were the Amorites?* [Leiden: Brill, 1971]; K. Kenyon, *Amorites and Canaanites* [New York: Oxford University Press, 1966]; M. Liverani, "The Amorites," in Wiseman, *Peoples*, pp. 100–133.)

First Esdras 8:69 reads "Edomites" instead of "Amorites," which would require only minor changes: *hā'ᵃdōmî* instead of *hā'ᵉmōrî*. Because of the stereotyped nature of the list, the emendation is probably incorrect.

Though the Edomites are not mentioned by name in Ezra-Nehemiah, the harsh condemnation of them in Scripture (2 Chron 25:11 [NIV, "men of Seir"]; Ps 137:7; Ezek 25:12–14; Obad; Mal 1:4) suggests that the Edomites took advantage of the Babylonian conquest of Judah.

On "mingled the holy race," compare Psalm 106:35. "The holy race" is literally "the holy seed." For the phrase in a different context, see Isaiah 6:13.

"Leaders" derives from *śar* ("official," "chief," "leader"; KJV, "princes"). The "officials" (*segānîm*, pl. of *sāgān*, from Akkad. *šaknu;* cf. Jer 51:23, 28, 57) probably served the Persian government as tax collectors (see Bowman, *Aramaic Ritual Texts*, p. 26). In later Hebrew the word designated the assistant chief priest.

"Have led the way" is literally "their hand had been first." The leaders led or were "first," but in the wrong direction (cf. 10:18; Neh 6:18).

"In this unfaithfulness" derives from *ma'al* ("an act of unfaithfulness" or "breach of faith"; cf. 10:6; Lev 5:15; Josh 22:16; Dan 9:7). In Chronicles "it nearly always refers to an offense against the Jerusalem temple and the purity of its service (e.g., 2 Chron 26:16)" (Williamson, *Israel*, p. 53). Marrying those who did not belong to

Yahweh was infidelity for the people of Israel, who were considered to be the bride of Yahweh.

3 Note the use of the first person: "When I heard this, I tore my tunic and cloak." Rending one's garments commonly expressed distress or grief (cf. Gen 37:29, 34; Esth 4:1; Job 1:20; Isa 36:22; Jer 41:5; Matt 26:65). It is still practiced by some Jews after a bereavement.

Ezra's act of pulling out his own hair is unique in the Bible. In the apocryphal Additions to Esther 14:2, we read that "all the places of her joy she filled with her torn hair." Elsewhere the head is shaved (Job 1:20; Ezek 7:18; Amos 8:10). Nehemiah demonstrates how different his personality was from Ezra's: when confronted with the same problem of intermarriage, instead of pulling out his own hair, Nehemiah pulled out the hair of the offenders (Neh 13:25)!

Ezra's influence was not due to his official position but to the moral outrage he demonstrated. According to N.H. Snaith ("The Date of Ezra's Arrival in Jerusalem," ZAW 63 [1952]: 58), "his part was not an executive part, but comparable to that of Mahatma Gandhi in modern times. He is scandalized; he prays and he fasts (Ezr 9:3 –5; 10:6)."

4 Those with a proper perception of God's holiness will tremble at his word (see Heb 12:18–29, esp. v.21).

The word "appalled" is *mešômēm* (a Polel participle from *šmm*), which means "to be appalled or stupefied," "to be reduced to shuddering" (cf. Dan 4:19; 8:27). Rare is the soul who is so shocked at disobedience that he is appalled. (The English word originally meant "to make pale.")

The "evening sacrifice" took place about three P.M. (cf. Exod 12:6; Acts 3:1). The informants had probably visited Ezra in the morning, so that he must have sat in this position for many hours. The time of the evening sacrifice was also the appointed time for prayer and confession.

5–6a "Self-abasement" (*ta'anît*) means "mortification," "humiliation." It is used only here in the OT. In later Hebrew it meant fasting, as in the *Megillat Ta'anit* ("The Scroll of Fasting"), a rare Aramaic document from the NT period. Thus the RSV translates "I rose from my fasting."

"With my hands spread out" means with palms upwards (cf. Exod 9:29; 1 Kings 8:22; Isa 1:15).

Notes

1 Some critics (e.g., Brockington, p. 106) suggest that one should insert between Ezra 8 and 9 the narrative in Neh 8 (i.e., the reading of the Law by Ezra and the Levites before the assembly). But the texts, as they stand, describe two different assemblies.

2. Ezra's confession and prayer

9:6b–15

"O my God, I am too ashamed and disgraced to lift up my face to you, my God, because our sins are higher than our heads and our guilt has reached to the heavens. [7]From the days of our forefathers until now, our guilt has been great. Because of our sins, we and our kings and our priests have been subjected to the sword and captivity, to pillage and humiliation at the hand of foreign kings, as it is today.

[8]"But now, for a brief moment, the LORD our God has been gracious in leaving us a remnant and giving us a firm place in his sanctuary, and so our God gives light to our eyes and a little relief in our bondage. [9]Though we are slaves, our God has not deserted us in our bondage. He has shown us kindness in the sight of the kings of Persia: He has granted us new life to rebuild the house of our God and repair its ruins, and he has given us a wall of protection in Judah and Jerusalem.

[10]"But now, O our God, what can we say after this? For we have disregarded the commands [11]you gave through your servants the prophets when you said: 'The land you are entering to possess is a land polluted by the corruption of its peoples. By their detestable practices they have filled it with their impurity from one end to the other. [12]Therefore, do not give your daughters in marriage to their sons or take their daughters for your sons. Do not seek a treaty of friendship with them at any time, that you may be strong and eat the good things of the land and leave it to your children as an everlasting inheritance.'

[13]"What has happened to us is a result of our evil deeds and our great guilt, and yet, our God, you have punished us less than our sins have deserved and have given us a remnant like this. [14]Shall we again break your commands and intermarry with the peoples who commit such detestable practices? Would you not be angry enough with us to destroy us, leaving us no remnant or survivor? [15]O LORD, God of Israel, you are righteous! We are left this day as a remnant. Here we are before you in our guilt, though because of it not one of us can stand in your presence."

Ezra's prayer may be compared with that of Nehemiah (Neh 9:5b–38) and Daniel (Dan 9:4–19). The following elements are included: a general confession (v.6), sins of former times (v.7), a recital of God's mercy and goodness (vv.8–9), a further confession of Israel's sins (vv.10–12), and a final confession of guilt and the appeal (vv.13–15).

6b For "I am too ashamed and disgraced" (cf. Luke 18:13), the Hebrew uses two closely related words. The first (*bôš*) means "I am ashamed" as in 8:22. The second (a Niphal of *kālam*) means "to be humiliated or confounded," connoting the pain that accompanies shame. The latter has a more active "ring" in that it means "to be dishonored, be put to shame"; the former has a more passive connotation. Ezra felt both an inner shame before God and an outward humiliation before men for the sins of his people. The two verbs often occur together (Ps 35:4; Isa 45:16; Jer 31:19). In Ezra 9:6 the KJV translates the second verb "blush," a rendering used by the NIV in Jeremiah 8:12: "No, they have no shame at all; they do not even know how to blush." Our guilt reaches to the heavens, but his mercy extends above the heavens (Ps 108:4).

7 D.W. Thomas ("The Sixth Century B.C.: A Creative Epoch in the History of Israel," JSS 6 [1961]: 36) comments: "The language of bombast and self-glorification which is characteristic, for example, of the Assyrian records, contrasts remarkably with the acknowledgement of national failure which runs through the writing of the Hebrew historians."

"From the days of our forefathers"—the Hebrews were conscious of their corporate solidarity, unlike the individual emphasis of modern Christianity.

Ezekiel 21:16 vividly describes "the sword" (*ḥereḇ;* cf. Neh 4:13b) of Yahweh at work as an instrument of his judgment; though the king of Babylon wielded the sword, it was actually Yahweh himself who exercised divine judgment.

"Humiliation" (*bōšeṯ pānîm*) means literally "shame" or "confusion of faces" (cf. 2 Chron 32:21; Dan 9:7-8).

After the conquest of Judah by the Babylonians in 605 B.C., the Jews fell successively under the Persians, Alexander the Great, the Ptolemies, the Seleucids, the Romans, the Byzantines, the Arabs, the Turks, and the British. Only for about a century from the Maccabean Revolt in 165 B.C. till Pompey's intervention in 63 B.C. did the Jews enjoy autonomy, that is, until the establishment of the independent state of Israel in 1948.

8 In the archaic English of the KJV, "space" usually refers to a period of time (NIV has "for a brief moment"; cf. Gen 29:14; Lev 25:8; Deut 2:14; Acts 5:7; 19:8; Rev 8:1).

"Has been gracious" (*teḥinnāh*) means a prayer for grace in all but two passages of its twenty-four occurrences in the OT (e.g., in Solomon's prayer [1 Kings 8:30, 38, 49]). Here in v.8 it signifies the Lord's grace or mercy for the remnant of his people. In both cases the LXX has *eleos* ("mercy").

"A remnant" (*pelêṭāh*) is literally "those who have escaped" (cf. Gen 45:7). "A firm place" (*yāṯēr*) is literally a "nail" or a "peg," as a nail driven into a wall (cf. Isa 22:23) or a tent peg into the ground (Isa 33:20; 54:2). The LXX renders the word *stērigma* ("establishment"). The RSV translates "a secure hold," the NEB "foothold."

An increase in light—"gives light to our eyes"—means vitality and joy (1 Sam 14:27, 29; Ps 13:3 [4 MT]; 19:8 [9 MT]; Prov 15:30; 29:13; Eccl 8:1).

"Relief" (*miḥyāh*) is a relatively rare word that occurs but eight times, once here and in v.9 ("new life") where it means "relief," "reviving." Elsewhere it means "to save lives" (Gen 45:5), "emergence of raw flesh" (Lev 13:10, 24), "subsistence" (Judg 6:4 [NIV, "living thing"]; 17:10 [NIV, "food"]), "living" (2 Chron 14:13 [12 MT] [NIV, "recover"]).

The Jewish commentator Slotki (p. 166) observes poignantly: "A little grace had been granted by God to his people; a small remnant had found its weary way back to its home and driven a single peg into its soil; a solitary ray of light was shining; a faint breath of freedom lightened their slavery. How graphically Ezra epitomizes Jewish experience in these few words!"

9 The Achaemenid Persian kings were favorably disposed to the Jews: Cyrus (539–530 B.C.) gave them permission to return (Ezra 1). His son Cambyses (529–522), not named in the Bible, also favored them as we learn from the Elephantine papyri. Darius I (522–486) renewed the decree of Ezra (Ezra 6). Darius's son, Xerxes (485–465), granted Jews privileges and protection (Esth 8–10). Artaxerxes I (464–424) gave authorizations to Ezra (Ezra 7) and Nehemiah (Neh 1–2).

"New life" is the same word translated "relief" (v.8). "To repair" is literally "to cause to stand."

"Ruins" (*ḥorbāh*, "waste," "desolate places") occurs forty-two times in the OT.

The verb form means "to dry up," "to be in ruins," "to lay waste," or "to make desolate." Isaiah had prophesied that the Lord would raise up the ruins of Jerusalem (Isa 44:26). The city's ruins would break forth into singing (Isa 52:9; cf. 58:12; 61:4).

"A wall of protection" (*gādēr;* LXX *phragmos,* "fence") is used of a low fence around a sheepfold (Num 32:16) or of a wall bordering a path (Num 22:24). The qualifying phrase "in Judah and Jerusalem" indicates a metaphorical reference in the sense of "protection" (RSV; cf. Zech 2:1–5). Some critics take this reference to a wall as an argument for the priority of Nehemiah over Ezra, assuming an allusion to the wall that Nehemiah had repaired in his day. But most scholars (e.g., Ackroyd, Brockington, Bright, Kellermann) agree that the reference here is not to be taken literally (see Introduction: The Order).

10–11 On these two verses compare Leviticus 18:24–26; Deuteronomy 7:1–6; 2 Kings 17; 23:8–16; Ezekiel 5:11; Romans 3:19.

"Polluted by the corruption" (*niddāh hî ᵇeniddat*) is literally "polluted (land), it is by the pollution." *Niddāh* can mean menstrual flow (so Lev 12:2) or perversion (so Lev 20:21). Here it refers to both the corruption of Canaanite idolatry and the immoral practices associated with it (cf. 2 Chron 29:5; Lam 1:17; Ezek 7:20; 36:17). The noun *ṭumʾāh* ("impurity") occurs thirty-six times in the OT, twice in Ezra (see on 6:21).

The texts of the related Ugaritic culture reveal the degrading practices and beliefs of the Canaanites. According to J. Gray (*Canaanites,* p. 136), "Their gods were like the Greek gods, glorified human beings, contentious, jealous, vindictive, lustful, and even, like El, lazy" (cf. also C.H. Gordon, *Ugaritic Literature* [Rome: Pontifical Bible Institute, 1949]; W.F. Albright, *Archaeology and the Religion of Israel* [Baltimore: Johns Hopkins University Press, 1956]).

12 Verses 10–12 are not drawn from a single quotation but from many passages (Deut 11:8–9; Prov 10:27; Isa 1:19; Ezek 37:25). On the issue of intermarriage, see the excursus at the end of the chapter. In the NT era the problems of interfaith marriage were recognized by Christians as they had been by Jews. Marriages with unbelievers were condemned (2 Cor 6:14); widows were explicitly advised to marry within the faith (1 Cor 7:39).

13 "You have punished us less than our sins" is literally "you have withheld beneath our iniquities" (cf. Job 11:6).

14 "Angry" is related to the word *'ap,* which means both "nose" and "anger." For the association see Ezekiel 38:18: "My anger will rise up in my nose" (NIV, "my hot anger will be aroused") and Psalm 18:7–8: "because he was angry./Smoke rose from his nostrils." When God's anger came on the Israelites, it was because they had failed to perform their covenant responsibilities (cf. Deut 7:4; 11:17; 29:25–28; Josh 23:16; Judg 2:20).

15 A proper sense of God's holiness sheds light on our unworthiness (cf. Isa 6:1–5; Luke 5:8).

For comparable passages of national lament, see Psalms 44, 60, 74, 79, 80, 83, 85, 90, 108, 126, 129, 137.

Notes

---

7 בְּזָּה (*bizzāh*, "pillage," "booty," "plunder"; cf. Neh 4:4 [3:36 MT]; Esth 9:10, 15–16) is a late Hebrew word (cf. Polzin, ch. 4, # 10).

8–9 עַבְדֻת (*ʿabḏut̲*, "bondage") is found only here and in Neh 9:17 in the OT.

---

3. *The people's response*

10:1–4

> ¹While Ezra was praying and confessing, weeping and throwing himself down before the house of God, a large crowd of Israelites—men, women and children—gathered around him. They too wept bitterly. ²Then Shecaniah son of Jehiel, one of the descendants of Elam, said to Ezra, "We have been unfaithful to our God by marrying foreign women from the peoples around us. But in spite of this, there is still hope for Israel. ³Now let us make a covenant before our God to send away all these women and their children, in accordance with the counsel of my lord and of those who fear the commands of our God. Let it be done according to the Law. ⁴Rise up; this matter is in your hands. We will support you, so take courage and do it."

As noted above in comments on 7:9 (see also Introduction: Chronology), most scholars have followed a Nisan-to-Nisan calendar, placing Ezra's arrival in 458 B.C. Scholars who follow a Tishri-to-Tishri calendar say 457 B.C. Dates according to this alternative system are indicated in parentheses. Assuming the former system, we have the following chronological indicators in this chapter. Verse 9 indicates that the people assembled on the twentieth day of the ninth month (Kislev) of the first year, which would have been 19 December 458 (7 Dec. 457), amid the cold, rainy season. According to v.16, the examining committee began its work on the first day of the tenth month (Tebet), ten days later. The committee completed its work in three months (v.17), on the first day of the first month (Nisan)—27 March 457 (15 Apr. 456).

1 Hereafter Ezra is spoken of in the third person. (On the interchange between the first-person memoirs and the third-person narrative, see Introduction: Literary Form and Authorship.)

"Weeping," not silently but aloud (cf. on 3:12; Neh 1:4; Joel 1:12–17), like laughing, is contagious. The people also "wept bitterly," literally, "wept with a great weeping" (a Heb. idiom; cf. Jer 8:18–22).

"Throwing himself down" (*mit̲nappēl*, a Hithpael participle) implies that Ezra kept on "throwing himself down" on the ground. The prophets and other leaders used object lessons, even bizarre actions, to attract people's attention (Isa 7:3; 8:1–4, 18; Jer 19; 27). Note that women and children are mentioned. Entire families were involved.

2 Ezra, the wise teacher, waited for his audience to draw their own conclusions about what should be done. The Shecaniah here is distinct from that of 8:3 (q.v.). Possibly his father is the same Jehiel mentioned in vv.21 and 26 as he also was of the family of Elam (see comment on 2:7). Perhaps Shecaniah was grieved that his father had married a non-Jewish mother. Six members of the clan of Elam were involved in intermarriages (v.26).

3 "Make a covenant" (*kārat-b^erît*, lit., "to cut a covenant") derives from the practice of cutting a sacrificial animal. Originally it may have involved passing between the pieces with the implied curse that whoever did not keep the covenant should be cut up like the animals (Gen 15:9–18; cf. W.F. Albright, "The Hebrew Expression for 'Making a Covenant' in Pre-Israelite Documents," BASOR 121 [1951]: 21–22).

"All these women and their children" reflects the fact that in ancient societies, as in ours, mothers were given custody of their children when marriages were dissolved. When Hagar was dismissed Ishmael was sent with her (Gen 21:14). In Babylonia divorced women were granted their children and had to wait for them to grow up before remarrying (Codex Hammurabi 137; ANET, p. 172). In Greek divorces, however, the children remained with their fathers.

In "the counsel of my lord," the NIV has chosen to read the word for "lord" as vocalized *'^adōnî* ("my lord," i.e., Ezra) rather than as *'^adōnāy* ("Lord"). This reading is also adopted by the KJV, RV, and NEB. The general context, however, favors the rendering that the "counsel" is not simply that of Ezra but of the Lord (cf. Ps 33:11; Prov 19:21; Isa 19:17; Jer 49:20; 50:45).

4 "Rise up." Shecaniah gave a clarion call to action. Weeping was not enough. Courageous and painful decisions had to be made. The people themselves had to respond. Compare David's exhortation: "Arise and be doing! The LORD be with you!" (1 Chron 22:16, lit. tr.).

4. *The calling of a public assembly*

10:5-15

⁵So Ezra rose up and put the leading priests and Levites and all Israel under oath to do what had been suggested. And they took the oath. ⁶Then Ezra withdrew from before the house of God and went to the room of Jehohanan son of Eliashib. While he was there, he ate no food and drank no water, because he continued to mourn over the unfaithfulness of the exiles.

⁷A proclamation was then issued throughout Judah and Jerusalem for all the exiles to assemble in Jerusalem. ⁸Anyone who failed to appear within three days would forfeit all his property, in accordance with the decision of the officials and elders, and would himself be expelled from the assembly of the exiles.

⁹Within the three days, all the men of Judah and Benjamin had gathered in Jerusalem. And on the twentieth day of the ninth month, all the people were sitting in the square before the house of God, greatly distressed by the occasion and because of the rain. ¹⁰Then Ezra the priest stood up and said to them, "You have been unfaithful; you have married foreign women, adding to Israel's guilt. ¹¹Now make confession to the LORD, the God of your fathers, and do his will. Separate yourselves from the peoples around you and from your foreign wives."

¹²The whole assembly responded with a loud voice: "You are right! We must do as you say. ¹³But there are many people here and it is the rainy season; so we cannot stand outside. Besides, this matter cannot be taken care of in a day or two, because we have sinned greatly in this thing. ¹⁴Let our officials act for the whole assembly. Then let everyone in our towns who has married a foreign woman come at a set time, along with the elders and judges of each town, until the fierce anger of our God in this matter is turned away from us." ¹⁵Only Jonathan son of Asahel and Jahzeiah son of Tikvah, supported by Meshullam and Shabbethai the Levite, opposed this.

5 The Hebrew word for "oath" (*šᵉḇûʿāh*) is related to the word for "seven" (cf. Neh 5:12–13; 10:29). Another Hebrew word sometimes translated "oath" in the KJV is *'ālāh* (e.g., Gen 24:41; 26:28; Deut 29:12), which more properly connotes the implicit "curse" (Zech 5:3).

Ezra first enlisted the aid of the leaders of the priests, Levites, and laity and had them swear an oath. The oath, a solemn declaration made under divine sanction, could be assertive, exculpatory, or promissory. An assertive oath called God to witness the truth of a statement (1 Kings 18:10; Rom 1:9; Phil 1:8). An exculpatory oath sought to clear a person from an accusation (e.g., Codex Hammurabi 20, 23, 103; ANET, pp. 167, 170). An oath could be promissory about future undertakings, as was the case here.

In biblical oaths the implied curse for nonfulfillment is often expressed in the vague statement, "May the LORD deal with me, be it ever so severely, if . . ." (Ruth 1:17; 2 Sam 3:35; 1 Kings 2:23). On rare occasions the full implications of the curse are spelled out (Num 5:19–31; Job 31; Pss 7:4–5; 137:5–6). Peter progressively denied Christ (Matt 26:70), denied with an oath (v.72), and finally cursed, i.e., called down curses on himself (v.74; cf. S. Blank, "The Curse, Blasphemy, the Spell, and the Oath," HUCA 23 [1950]: 73–95; A. Crown, "Aposiopesis in the OT and the Hebrew Conditional Oath," *Abr-Nahrain* 4 [1963–64]: 96–111; G. Buchanan, "Some Vow and Oath Formulas in the New Testament," HTR 58 [1965]: 319–26).

6 Such complete fasting—"he ate no food and drank no water" (cf. Neh 1:4)—was twice observed by Moses (cf. Exod 34:28; Deut 9:18). The people of Nineveh also had a total fast after Jonah's preaching (Jonah 3:7). But such fasts were rare. Ordinary fasts involved abstaining from eating only (1 Sam 1:7; 2 Sam 3:35). The Mishnah (*Taanith* 1.4ff.) prescribes fasting from eating and drinking during daylight to pray for rain. Muslims observe a complete fast from food and drink during the daylight hours for the month of Ramadhan.

"He continued to mourn" (Hithpael of *'āḇal*), though often referring to the mourning rites for the dead (Gen 37:34; 2 Sam 13:31–37), also describes the reaction of those who are aware of the threat of deserved judgment (Exod 33:4; Num 14:39; 1 Sam 15:35; 16:1).

"The room" typifies chambers in the temple area that were used as storerooms (8:29; Neh 13:4–13). Jeremiah's prophecy was read in such a room before an assembly (Jer 36:10).

The identification of the names "Jehohanan son of Eliashib" and their relationship to the same names found in other sources is a complex issue that has an important bearing on the question of the order of Ezra and Nehemiah (see Introduction: The High Priest).

7 While Ezra continued to fast and pray, the chiefs and elders ordered all the exiles to assemble in Jerusalem. Though Ezra had been vested with great authority (7:25 –26), he used it sparingly and influenced the people by his example.

8 As the territory of Judah had been much reduced, the most distant inhabitants would not be more than fifty miles from Jerusalem. The borders were Bethel in the north, Beersheba in the south, Jericho in the east, and Ono in the west (see maps *a* and *b*). All could travel to Jerusalem "within three days."

"Would forfeit" (from *ḥērem*) means to ban from profane use and to devote, either to destruction (e.g., Exod 22:20; Deut 13:13–17) or for use in the temple as here (cf. Lev 27:28–29; Josh 6:18–19; 7:1–26).

9 Usually Judah alone is mentioned, but a few passages also refer to the exiles who came from or who settled in the area of Benjamin north of Jerusalem (1:5; 4:1).

"In the square" (*birᵉḥôḇ*) means "in a wide space." The KJV's "street" is misleading, though this is the meaning in modern Hebrew. The plaza or square was either in the outer court of the temple or more probably in the open space before the Water Gate (Neh 3:26; 8:1).

"Greatly distressed" is the Hiphil participle of a relatively rare verb (*rāʿaḏ*) that occurs only here, in Daniel 10:11, and in Psalm 104:32. Related nouns appear in Exodus 15:15; Job 4:14; Psalms 2:11; 48:5; 55:5; and Isaiah 33:14. The trepidation of the people was caused by two separate reasons: their transgressions and the weather.

"The rain" (*gᵉšāmîm*, pl. of intensity) indicates heavy torrential rains. The ninth month, Kislev (Nov.-Dec.), is in the middle of the rainy season, which begins with light showers in October and lasts to mid-April (see E. Yamauchi, "Ancient Ecologies and the Biblical Perspective," *Journal of the American Scientific Affiliation* 32 [1980]: 193–203).

December and January are also cold months in Jerusalem, with temperatures in the fifties and even forties. Sometimes it gets so cold that it snows (2 Sam 23:20; Ps 147:16–17; Prov 31:21; 1 Macc 13:22).

The assembly shivered, not only because they were drenched, but also because they sensed a sign of divine displeasure in the abnormally heavy rains (cf. 1 Sam 12:17–18; Ezek 13:11, 13).

10 Ezra was not only a scribe (7:11–12, 21) but also a priest (*kōhēn*, a word reflected in many Jewish names today: Cohen, Cohn, Kahane, Kahn et al.).

The sins and failures of the exiles were great enough; they added insult to injury by marrying pagan women, thus "adding to Israel's guilt" (cf. 2 Chron 28:13). In Exodus 9:34; Judges 3:12; 4:1, the Hebrew idiom is "added" to sin or to do evil.

11 "Confession" (*tôḏāh*) almost always means "thanksgiving" except here and in Joshua 7:19. A better translation than "foreign wives" might be "pagan wives," implying not only a different nationality, but adherence to a different religion.

12 The Lord so convicted the hearers that what Ezra had said was right that they spontaneously and unitedly responded in an extraordinary manner, "with a loud voice" (cf. 3:12; 2 Chron 15:14; Neh 9:4), acknowledging their need to do something about the situation.

The NIV's "You are right! We must do as you say" is literally "As you have said, so it is for us to do." The Hebrew word *kēn* is an adverb that means "so." In modern Hebrew it means yes.

13 A spokesman for the people nonetheless pointed out the practical difficulties in view of the inclement weather. "Sinned" (*pāšaʿ*) connotes an act of revolt or rebellion (cf. 1 Kings 12:19).

14 The "elders" (*z*eqēnîm) were the older men of the community who had beards (*zāqān*). They formed a governing council in every village (1 Sam 30:26–31). At Succoth there were seventy-seven elders (Judg 8:14). The elders at the gate of the town served as magistrates (Deut 19:12; 21:3, 19; Ruth 4:1–12).

In addition there were also "judges" (*šōpeṭîm*) appointed in every town (Deut 16:18–20; cf. de Vaux, *Ancient Israel*, pp. 137–38, 152–53, 156, 161–62).

"The fierce anger" (*ḥ*arôn *'ap*, lit., "glow of the nose") is a phrase used only of God's wrath (cf. 9:14; cf. also Exod 32:12; Num 25:4; Deut 13:17; Josh 7:26; Neh 13:18 et al.).

15 The truth of the narrative is indicated by the candor with which the opposition to the reform measures is recorded. Why these four men opposed the measure is unclear. Perhaps they were protecting themselves or their relatives. Perhaps they viewed the measures of separation as too harsh. Less probably they were fanatics who wished no delay in implementing the measure.

"Asahel" means "God has made" or "God has acted." "Jahzeiah" ("May Yahweh see!") is found only here. "Tikvah" ("hope") is found otherwise only in 2 Kings 22:14 (cf. "Yah is my hope" in Cowley 68:1).

On Meshullam's name see the comment on 8:16. If this is Meshullam the son of Bani in v.29, he himself had married a pagan wife.

"Shabbethai" occurs only here and in Nehemiah 8:7 and 11:16. It may mean one born on the Sabbath. The name occurs nine times in the Murashu texts (Coogan, *Personal Names*, pp. 34–35) as *šabbatay*, three times in the Elephantine texts (Cowley 2:21; 58:3; Kraeling 8:10) and once in a Hermopolis text (see B. Porten, "The Religion of the Jews of Elephantine in Light of the Hermopolis Papyri," JNES 28 [1969]: 116–17, 121). The Akkadian *Sa-ba-ta-ai* meant "one born on the day of the full moon."

5. Investigation of the offenders

10:16–17

> [16]So the exiles did as was proposed. Ezra the priest selected men who were family heads, one from each family division, and all of them designated by name. On the first day of the tenth month they sat down to investigate the cases, [17]and by the first day of the first month they finished dealing with all the men who had married foreign women.

16 For "Ezra the priest selected," the Hebrew reads "Ezra the priest, with certain heads of fathers' houses . . . were separated" (cf. KJV). The NIV and RSV follow 1 Esdras 9:16 and the Syriac.

17 The committee began its work ten days after the assembly had met in the rain. According to the Nisan calendar, they completed their work three months later on 27 March 457. The investigating elders and judges did their work carefully and thoroughly. They discovered that about a hundred couples were involved.

6. *The list of offenders*

10:18–43

[18] Among the descendants of the priests, the following had married foreign women:

From the descendants of Jeshua son of Jozadak, and his brothers: Maaseiah, Eliezer, Jarib and Gedaliah. [19](They all gave their hands in pledge to put away their wives, and for their guilt they each presented a ram from the flock as a guilt offering.)
[20] From the descendants of Immer:
Hanani and Zebadiah.
[21] From the descendants of Harim:
Maaseiah, Elijah, Shemaiah, Jehiel and Uzziah.
[22] From the descendants of Pashhur:
Elioenai, Maaseiah, Ishmael, Nethanel, Jozabad and Elasah.

[23] Among the Levites:

Jozabad, Shimei, Kelaiah (that is, Kelita), Pethahiah, Judah and Eliezer.
[24] From the singers:
Eliashib.
From the gatekeepers:
Shallum, Telem and Uri.

[25] And among the other Israelites:

From the descendants of Parosh:
Ramiah, Izziah, Malkijah, Mijamin, Eleazar, Malkijah and Benaiah.
[26] From the descendants of Elam:
Mattaniah, Zechariah, Jehiel, Abdi, Jeremoth and Elijah.
[27] From the descendants of Zattu:
Elioenai, Eliashib, Mattaniah, Jeremoth, Zabad and Aziza.
[28] From the descendants of Bebai:
Jehohanan, Hananiah, Zabbai and Athlai.
[29] From the descendants of Bani:
Meshullam, Malluch, Adaiah, Jashub, Sheal and Jeremoth.
[30] From the descendants of Pahath-Moab:
Adna, Kelal, Benaiah, Maaseiah, Mattaniah, Bezalel, Binnui and Manasseh.
[31] From the descendants of Harim:
Eliezer, Ishijah, Malkijah, Shemaiah, Shimeon, [32]Benjamin, Malluch and Shemariah.
[33] From the descendants of Hashum:
Mattenai, Mattattah, Zabad, Eliphelet, Jeremai, Manasseh and Shimei.
[34] From the descendants of Bani:
Maadai, Amram, Uel, [35]Benaiah, Bedeiah, Keluhi, [36]Vaniah, Meremoth, Eliashib, [37]Mattaniah, Mattenai and Jaasu.
[38] From the descendants of Binnui:
Shimei, [39]Shelemiah, Nathan, Adaiah, [40]Macnadebai, Shashai, Sharai, [41]Azarel, Shelemiah, Shemariah, [42]Shallum, Amariah and Joseph.
[43] From the descendants of Nebo:
Jeiel, Mattithiah, Zabad, Zebina, Jaddai, Joeland Benaiah.

18 Among those involved were the descendants of Jeshua, the high priest (see 2:2). On "Jozadak" see the comment on 3:2. "Maaseiah" ("the work of Yahweh") is the name of twenty-one OT persons. The name "Gedaliah" ("Yahweh has shown himself to be great") occurs twice in the Murashu texts as *Gadalyaw* (Coogan, *Personal Names,* p. 19).

19 For the symbolic handshake—"they all gave their hands"—see 2 Kings 10:15; Lamentations 5:6 (NIV, "We submitted to"); and Ezekiel 17:18.

According to Leviticus 5:14–19, a "ram" was the guilt offering for a sin committed unwittingly. Though the offenders may not have fully realized the gravity of their offense, they had no excuse; the Scriptures plainly set forth God's standards on marriage.

20 "Hanani" is a shortened form of "Hananiah" ("Yahweh has been gracious"). Nehemiah's brother bore this name (Neh 1:2). It occurs twelve times in the Murashu texts as *Ḥananī* (Coogan, *Personal Names*, p. 25). On "Immer" see the comment on 2:37; on "Zebadiah" at 8:8.

21 On "Harim" see the comment on 2:32; on "Maaseiah" on v.18 above. "Elijah" means "Yahweh is my God." On "Shemaiah" see on 8:13; on "Jehiel" on 8:9. "Uzziah" means "Yahweh is (my) might."

22 On "Pashhur" see the comment on 2:38. "Elioenai" is "my eyes are toward my God." Coogan (*Personal Names*, p. 124) believes this is patterned after the Akkadian *itti-ᵈX-īnāya*. On "Maaseiah" see on v.18. "Ishmael" means "May God hear!"; "Nethanel," "God has given." "Elasah" ("God has made") occurs only here and in Jeremiah 29:3.

23 "Shimei" is the shortened form of "Shemaiah" ("Yahweh has heard"). It appears on a bulla as *š-m-ʿ-y* (Avigad, *Bullae and Seals*, # 7). "Kelita" means "crippled, dwarfed one"; "Pethahiah," "Yahweh has opened (the womb)."

24 "Telem" ("brightness") occurs only here. "Uri" is the shortened form of Uriah (8:33).

Only one singer and three gatekeepers were involved. There is no representative of the Nethinim (2:43–54) or of the descendants of Solomon's servants (2:55–57). The lowest classes were the least involved in intermarriage; the pagan women were probably not very attracted to them.

25 "Ramiah" ("Yahweh is exalted") occurs only here, as does "Izziah" ("Yahweh sprinkled"). "Malkijah" means "Yahweh is my king." "Mijamin" ("luck") is literally "from the right hand," a contraction of Miniamin (Neh 12:17).

In place of the second "Malkijah," the RSV inserts "Hashabiah" following 1 Esdras 9:26. "Benaiah" is "Yahweh has built" (cf. *Banāyaw* in the Murashu texts; Coogan, *Personal Names*, p. 15).

26 The name "Mattaniah" ("the gift of Yahweh") occurs seven times in the Murashu texts as *Mattanyaw* (Coogan, *Personal Names*, p. 29) and on a seventh-sixth century B.C. bulla *M-t-n-y-h-w* (K. O'Connell, "An Israelite Bulla from Tell el-Ḥesi," IEJ 27 [1977]: 197–99).

"Abdi," a shortened form of Obadiah ("servant of Yahweh"), occurs in the Murashu texts as *ʿabdiya* (Coogan, *Personal Names*, p. 31). "Jeremoth" means "swollen"; "Zabad," "he has given" (cf. Coogan, *Personal Names*, p. 20). "Aziza" ("strong one") occurs only here.

28 "Hananiah" ("Yahweh has been gracious") is the name of fourteen OT individuals. It occurs three times in the Murashu texts as *Hananyaw* (Coogan, *Personal Names*, p. 25). "Zabbai" is perhaps a shortened form of "Zebadiah" ("Yahweh has given"). "Athlai," a shortened form of "Athaliah" ("Yahweh is exalted"), occurs only here.

29 "Malluch" means "counselor" and "Adaiah," "Yahweh has adorned himself." "Jashub" ("he will return") occurs only here and in Numbers 26:24 and 1 Chronicles 7:1. It occurs in the Murashu texts as *yašūb* (Coogan, *Personal Names*, p. 84). "Sheal" ("ask" or "may [God] grant") occurs only here. The name Š-ʾ-l occurs on a seal (Avigad, *Bullae and Seals*, p. 9).

30 "Adna" means "pleasure" and "Kelal," "perfection." "Bezalel" ("in the shadow of God") occurs only here and in Exodus 31:2 of the skilled craftsman who helped build the tabernacle. On "Binnui" see the comment on 2:10. "Manasseh" ("Yahweh causes to forget") occurs also in v.33.

31 "Ishijah" ("May Yahweh forget") occurs only here. On "Malkijah" see on v.25; on "Shemaiah" on 8:13. "Shimeon," derived from "Shemaiah" ("Yahweh has heard"), in Greek became the name "Simon." In the Murashu texts it appears as *šamaʿōn* (Coogan, *Personal Names*, pp. 35, 85).

32 "Benjamin" means "son of the right hand," and "Shemariah" is "Yahweh has preserved."

33 Both "Mattenai" and "Mattattah" (only here) mean "gift of God." "Jeremai" is a hypocoriston (pet name) of Jeremiah. One of the seals published by Avigad (*Bullae and Seals*, p. 7) has *l-y-r-m-y h-š-p-r* ("[seal] of Jeremai the scribe").

34 "Maadai" occurs only here (cf. Maadiah ["Yahweh assembles or promises"] in Neh 12:5). "Amram" is "people are exalted." "Uel" ("will of God") occurs only here.

35 Both "Bedeiah" ("branch of Yahweh") and "Keluhi" ("Yahweh is perfect") occur only here.

36 "Vaniah" (possibly Pers. *Vānyah* ["worthy of love"]) occurs only here.

37 "Jaasu" ("May Yahweh make!") occurs only here.

38 The NIV and RSV emend the Hebrew from *ûbānî ûbinnûy* ("and Bani and Binnui"; cf. KJV) to *ûmibᵉnê binnûy* ("and from the sons of Binnui"), following the LXX and 1 Esdras 9:34.

39 "Shelemiah" means "Yahweh has restored."

40 "Machnadebai" is possibly a corruption of "possession of Nebo" (cf. Brockington, pp. 119-20). "Shashai" occurs only here (cf. Cowley 49:1). "Sharai," possibly a shortened form of Sherebiah (8:18), occurs only here.

41 "Azarel" means "God has helped."

42 "Joseph" is "May (God) add (prosperity)!"

43 "Nebo" possibly derives from the Babylonian god Nabu. It occurs only here as a personal name. "Jeiel" ("God has healed") is the name of ten OT individuals, almost all in Chronicles. "Mattithiah" means "gift of Yahweh." "Zebina" ("purchased [as a child]") occurs in the Murashu texts six times as *Zabin* and five times as *Zabīnā* (Coogan, *Personal Names,* pp. 22–23, 72). "Jaddai," a shortened form of Jedaiah ("Yahweh has cared for"), occurs only here.

"Joel" means "Yahweh is God." On "Benaiah" see the comment on v.25.

7. The dissolution of the mixed marriages

10:44

> ⁴⁴All these had married foreign women, and some of them had children by these wives.

44 The Hebrew text reads literally: "And there were of them (masc. pl.) wives, and they (masc. pl.) put forth children." Some of the marriages produced children, but this was not accepted as a reason for halting the proceedings. As it was just under eight months from the time of Ezra's arrival (4 Aug.) to the committee's findings (27 March), the offspring mentioned here must be (1) a few prematurely born babies, which is not too likely; (2) the offspring of mixed marriages contracted in Mesopotamia; or (3) the offspring of mixed marriages contracted by those who had returned earlier to Palestine.

The text of 1 Esdras 9:36 reads: "And they put them away along with their children," a rendering adopted by the NEB and placed in the NIV margin.

Comparing the number of offenders to the numbers of the categories that returned with Zerubbabel (cf. Neh 7), we have the following percentages:

Classes	Those Who Returned	Those Who Intermarried	Percentages
Priests	4,289	17	0.4
Levites	74	6	8.1
Singers	128	1	0.8
Gatekeepers	139	3	2.2
Laity	24,144	84	0.3
Totals	28,774	111	0.4

J. Myers ("Ezra and Nehemiah," *Encyclopaedia Judaica* [New York: Macmillan, 1972], VI.1120) has some cogent comments on the list of offenders:

> 111 names appear in the unemended text of the list of those guilty of marriage infraction, an exceptionally small number in a community of some 30,000 persons. It is probably a truncated list, including representative names and pointing to the involvement of all classes, as the schematic arrangement may indicate. For

the most part members of the upper classes are named, which also seems to reflect the genuineness of the list since they alone were in a position to contract such marriages and stood to benefit most from them.

Excursus

Malachi, who prophesied in the early fifth century prior to Ezra's mission, indicates that some Jews had broken off marriages to their wives to marry women who were "daughters of a foreign god" (Mal 2:10–16), "the daughters of perhaps influential Palestinian landholders" (Dumbrell, "Malachi and Ezra-Nehemiah," p. 47).

Jewish rabbis in attempting to explain Malachi's remarks suggested that the women who returned had lost their beauty and aged before their time. Rabbi Johanan said, "When the Jews drew near from the Exile, the faces of the Jewish women had become blackened by the sun. They therefore left them and married heathen wives."

The situation for the returning exiles was probably aggravated by demographic and economic factors. A.C. Welch (*Post-Exilic Judaism* [Edinburgh: William Blackwood & Sons, 1935], p. 251) suggests: "As has already been noted, the lists of the men of the Return and the natural probabilities of the case prove that the large proportion of the newcomers were males, who must have had difficulty in finding wives among their fellow-Jews." Myers (*World of Restoration*, pp. 88–89) proposes that economic factors motivated the members of the upper classes who were most prominent in contracting intermarriages.

Though the actions of Ezra and later of Nehemiah may strike some readers as harsh, they were more than racial or cultural measures and were necessary to preserve the spiritual heritage of Israel. Both from the principle and from exceptions to the rule, warnings against intermarriage were clearly concerned not so much about racial miscegenation as about spiritual adultery. David Bossman ("Ezra's Marriage Reform: Israel Redefined," BTh 9 [1979]: 32–38) argues that Ezra's purification of the people followed a "priestly ideal of separation from all that is unclean."

What happened to a Jewish community that was lax concerning intermarriage can be seen from the example of the Elephantine settlement contemporary with Ezra and Nehemiah. Intermarriages took place among both lay leaders and priests. According to Porten (*Archives*, p. 174), "Some of the pagans who married Jews may have, like the early Samaritans, continued to worship their ancestral god(s) at the same time that they adopted the worship of YHW. Conversely, some of these Jews occasionally expressed devotion to the god(s) of their spouses at the same time that they continued to revere YHW." The Jews at Elephantine worshiped not only Yahweh, but the goddess Anath-Yahweh (cf. Jer 7:16–18; B. Porten, "The Religion of the Jews of Elephantine in Light of the Hermopolis Papyri," JNES 28 [1969]: 116–21).

Myers (*The World of the Restoration*, p. 122) concludes: "It is not accidental that Jewish communities in exile gradually disintegrated—for example, the one at Elephantine. . . . A pure cult with a pure people conducted in their religious and domestic affairs in a pure language was essential."

NEHEMIAH

Outline

Text and Exposition

I. Nehemiah's First Administration (1:1–12:47)

A. *Nehemiah's Response to the Situation in Jerusalem (1:1–11)*

1. *News of the plight of Jerusalem*

1:1–4

¹The words of Nehemiah son of Hacaliah:

In the month of Kislev in the twentieth year, while I was in the citadel of Susa, ²Hanani, one of my brothers, came from Judah with some other men, and I questioned them about the Jewish remnant that survived the exile, and also about Jerusalem.

³They said to me, "Those who survived the exile and are back in the province are in great trouble and disgrace. The wall of Jerusalem is broken down, and its gates have been burned with fire."

⁴When I heard these things, I sat down and wept. For some days I mourned and fasted and prayed before the God of heaven.

The walls of Jerusalem that had been destroyed by Nebuchadnezzar, despite abortive attempts to rebuild them (Ezra 4:6–23), remained in ruins for almost a century and a half. Such a lamentable situation obviously made Jerusalem vulnerable to her numerous enemies. Yet from a mixture of apathy and fear the Jews failed to rectify this glaring deficiency. They needed the dynamic catalyst of an inspired leader, a man named Nehemiah.

1 Though the books of Ezra and Nehemiah were bound together from the earliest times, "The words of" indicate the title of a separate composition (cf. Jer 1:1; Amos 1:1; see Introduction: Canon).

The name "Nehemiah" means "the comfort of Yahweh" or "Yahweh has comforted"; it contains the same verbal root found in the names Nahum and Menahem. The name appears as *Neḥemyahu* on an ostracon from Arad dated to the seventh century B.C. (cf. Y. Aharoni, "The 'Nehemiah' Ostracon from Arad," *Eretz-Israel* 12 [1975]: 72–76).

"Hacaliah" is contracted from "wait for Yahweh" (cf. Zeph 3:8). Such an imperative form is highly unusual. The name occurs only here and in 10:1–2. The reference to his paternal sepulchers in Jerusalem (2:3, 5) may mean that Nehemiah came from a prominent family.

For "the month of Kislev," see the Introduction: Chronology.

"Susa" was the major city of Elam, the area of southwestern Iran. Susa was located in a fertile alluvial plain 150 miles north of the Persian Gulf. In the Achaemenid period it served as a winter palace for the kings (Kislev = Nov.-Dec.), but the area became intolerably hot during the summer months.

Daniel (Dan 8:2) saw himself in a vision at Susa. It was the site of the story of Esther. Ezra 4:9–10 refers to the men of Susa who were deported to Samaria. At Susa, Artaxerxes I received the embassy of Callias (449 B.C.) that ended Greek-Persian hostilities. In his reign the palace that Darius I had built at Susa burned to the ground. Though no inscription attests to the building activity of Artaxerxes I, he may have begun the small palace in the Donjon area of the Ville Royale completed by his successor, Darius II. From this small hypostyle hall have come all the fragments of stone bas reliefs now on display at the Louvre (cf. Yamauchi, "Achaemenid Capitals," pp. 5–14).

2 "Hanani" is the shortened form of "Hananiah" ("Yahweh is gracious"). Here and in 7:2 it designates the brother of Nehemiah. The Elephantine papyri mention a Hananiah who was the head of Jewish affairs in Jerusalem. Many scholars believe that this Hananiah can be identified with Nehemiah's brother and assume that he succeeded Nehemiah (c. 427) (see C.G. Tuland, "Hanani-Hananiah," JBL 77 [1958]: 157–61; Porten, *Archives*, p. 130). Rowley (*Men of God*, pp. 235ff.), however, cautions against this identification.

"The Jewish remnant" is literally "Jews who had escaped" (cf. Ezra 4:12). "Jews" (*yᵉhûdîm*, Gr. *Ioudaioi*) became the name of the people of Israel after the Exile.

3 The lack of a city wall meant that the people were defenseless against their enemies. Kenyon (*Digging Up*, p. 170) notes: "The effect on Jerusalem was much more disastrous and far-reaching than merely to render the city defenceless. . . . The whole system of terraces down the (eastern) slope, dependent on retaining walls buttressed in turn by the fill of the next lower terrace, was ultimately dependent on the town wall at the base, forming the lowest and most substantial of the retaining walls."

Most scholars, however, do not believe that Nehemiah's distress was caused by the condition of walls torn down 140 years before his time but rather by the episode of Ezra 4:7–23. According to this passage Jews had attempted to rebuild the walls earlier, in the reign of Artaxerxes I. But after the protest of Rehum and Shimshai, the king ordered the Jews to desist. There was considerable suspicion of such attempts because of the revolt of Megabyzus.

4 Nehemiah "sat down" (cf. Ezra 9:3). Slotki (p. 183) comments: "The custom of mourners being seated (cf. Ps. 137:1; Job 2:13) has survived among Jews, the bereaved sitting on low stools during the seven days of mourning."

Nehemiah "mourned" (cf. comment on Ezra 10:6). Daniel mourned three weeks for the sins of his people (Dan 10:2).

Nehemiah also "fasted." During the Exile fasting became a common practice, including solemn fasts to commemorate the taking of Jerusalem and the murder of Gedaliah (Esth 4:16; Dan 9:3; 10:3; Zech 7:3–7; 8:19).

On "God of heaven" see the comment on Ezra 1:2.

2. Nehemiah's prayer

1:5–11

⁵Then I said:

"O LORD, God of heaven, the great and awesome God, who keeps his covenant of love with those who love him and obey his commands, ⁶let your ear be attentive and your eyes open to hear the prayer your servant is praying before you day and night for your servants, the people of Israel. I confess the sins we Israelites, including myself and my father's house, have committed against you. ⁷We have acted very wickedly toward you. We have not obeyed the commands, decrees and laws you gave your servant Moses.

⁸"Remember the instruction you gave your servant Moses, saying, 'If you are

unfaithful, I will scatter you among the nations, ⁹but if you return to me and obey my commands, then even if your exiled people are at the farthest horizon, I will gather them from there and bring them to the place I have chosen as a dwelling for my Name.'

¹⁰"They are your servants and your people, whom you redeemed by your great strength and your mighty hand. ¹¹O Lord, let your ear be attentive to the prayer of this your servant and to the prayer of your servants who delight in revering your name. Give your servant success today by granting him favor in the presence of this man."

I was cupbearer to the king.

5 "Awesome" (*nôrā'*) is a Niphal participle from the verb *yārē'* ("to fear, revere"). He is the one to be feared (cf. Deut 7:21; Dan 9:4).

"Who keeps his covenant of love" is literally "who keeps covenant and steadfast love." The latter word, *ḥeseḏ*, means the quality that honors a covenant through thick and thin (cf. comment on Ezra 3:11).

6 Scriptures often use anthropomorphic figures of speech—e.g., "let your ear be attentive"—without sharing in the anthropomorphic concepts of pagan mythology (cf. comment on Ezra 6:9; cf. E. Cherbonnier, "The Logic of Biblical Anthropomorphism," HTR 55 [1962]: 187–210).

Nehemiah did not exclude himself or members of his own family in his confession of sins. A true sense of the awesomeness of God reveals the depths of our own sinfulness (Isa 6:1–5; Luke 5:8).

7 "Commands" (*miṣwōṯ*, used 180 times in the OT, including 43 in Deut) is the usual word for commandment, as in the Ten Commandments (Exod 24:12).

"Decrees" (*ḥuqqîm*) indicates something prescribed as the statute of Joshua (Josh 24:25) and the commandment to keep the Passover (Exod 12:24).

"Laws" (*mišpāṭîm*) indicates legal decisions or judgments (Zech 7:9; cf. D.J. Wiseman, "Law and Order in Old Testament Times," *Vox Evangelica* 8 [1973]: 5–21). On the prominence of Moses in Ezra-Nehemiah, see Ezra 3:2; 7:6; Nehemiah 1:8; 8:1, 14; 9:14; 10:29; 13:1.

8 "Remember," a key word, recurs frequently in the book (4:14; 5:19; 6:14; 13:14, 22, 29, 31).

On "if you are unfaithful," Slotki (p. 185) comments: "The original does not include *if* and is more forceful: 'you will deal treacherously, I will scatter you,' expressing an inescapable sequel." In the centuries following the Babylonian conquest, Jews were scattered farther and farther. In the NT period there were more Jews in the Diaspora than in Palestine (John 7:35; Acts 2:9–11; James 1:1; 1 Peter 1:1).

9 "I will gather them" is a frequently made promise (Deut 30:1–5; Isa 11:12; Jer 23:3; 29:14; 31:8–10; Ezek 11:17; 16:37; 20:34, 41; 36:24; Mic 2:12).

The phrase "a dwelling for my Name" recalls Deuteronomy 12:5: "the place the LORD your God will choose . . . to put his Name there for his dwelling." Parallels are found in extrabiblical sources, e.g., in the Amarna Letters: "Behold the king has set his name [Akkad. *šakan šumšu*] in the land of Jerusalem." Shamshi-Adad I of Assyria boasted: "Thus I placed my great name . . . in the land of Lebanon."

10 Though they had sinned and failed, they were still God's people and his "peculiar" possession, a people for his treasure by virtue of his redemption (cf. Deut 4:34; 9:29).

11 On "success" W.J. Martin (ZPEB, 4:406) perceptively remarks: "For Nehemiah worldly success did not spell spiritual failure, and royal society left his appetite for divine fellowship unimpaired. The place of the fear of God in his heart was so great as to banish wholly the fear of man."

"Cupbearer" (*mašqeh* is a Hiphil participle of the verb *šaqāh*) literally means "one who gives (someone) something to drink." It occurs twelve times in the OT in the sense of "cupbearer," e.g., in 1 Kings 10:5 and 2 Chronicles 9:4 of Solomon's attendants. In the Joseph story it occurs nine times (Gen 40:1–41:9), but its significance is obscured by the KJV and the RSV, which translate the word "butler." That the cupbearer could have other responsibilities as well is indicated by Tobit 1:22: "Now Ahikar was cupbearer, keeper of the signet, and in charge of administration of the accounts, for Esarhaddon had appointed him second to himself." For archaeological evidence of Persian wine services, see P.R.S. Moorey, "Metal Wine-Sets in the Ancient Near East," *Iranica Antiqua* 15 (1980): 181ff.

Varied sources suggest something about Nehemiah as a royal cupbearer:

1. He would have been well-trained in court etiquette (cf. Dan 1:4–5).

2. He was probably a handsome individual (cf. Dan 1:4, 13, 15; Jos. *Antiq.* XVI, 230 [viii.1]).

3. He would certainly know how to select the wines to set before the king. A proverb in the Babylonian Talmud (*Baba Qamma* 92b) states: "The wine belongs to the master but credit for it is due to his cupbearer."

4. He would have to be a convivial companion, willing to lend an ear at all times.

5. He would have great influence as one with the closest access to the king, able to determine who was able see his master.

6. Above all Nehemiah had to be one who enjoyed the unreserved confidence of the king. The great need for trustworthy court attendants is underscored by the intrigues endemic to the Achaemenid court. Xerxes, father of Artaxerxes I, was killed in his own bedchamber by Artabanus, a courtier.

B. *Nehemiah's Journey to Palestine (2:1–20)*

1. *The king's response*

2:1–8

> [1]In the month of Nisan in the twentieth year of King Artaxerxes, when wine was brought for him, I took the wine and gave it to the king. I had not been sad in his presence before; [2]so the king asked me, "Why does your face look so sad when you are not ill? This can be nothing but sadness of heart."
>
> I was very much afraid, [3]but I said to the king, "May the king live forever! Why should my face not look sad when the city where my fathers are buried lies in ruins, and its gates have been destroyed by fire?"
>
> [4]The king said to me, "What is it you want?"
>
> Then I prayed to the God of heaven, [5]and I answered the king, "If it pleases the

king and if your servant has found favor in his sight, let him send me to the city in Judah where my fathers are buried so that I can rebuild it."

6Then the king, with the queen sitting beside him, asked me, "How long will your journey take, and when will you get back?" It pleased the king to send me; so I set a time.

7I also said to him, "If it pleases the king, may I have letters to the governors of Trans-Euphrates, so that they will provide me safe-conduct until I arrive in Judah? 8And may I have a letter to Asaph, keeper of the king's forest, so he will give me timber to make beams for the gates of the citadel by the temple and for the city wall and for the residence I will occupy?" And because the gracious hand of my God was upon me, the king granted my requests.

1 On a Nisan calendar "the twentieth year" would have been 13 April 445 to 1 April 444 (on a Tishri calendar, 7 Oct. 445 to 25 Sept. 444). On the problems of correlating this with 1:1, see the Introduction: Chronology. On the calculation of Daniel's seventy weeks (Dan 9:25) from the decree of Artaxerxes I to Nehemiah, see the comment on Ezra 7:11.

There was a delay of about four months from Kislev (Nov.-Dec.), when Nehemiah first heard the news (1:1), to Nisan (Mar.-Apr.), when he felt prepared to broach the subject to the king. There are various explanations for this. The king may have been absent in his other winter palace at Babylon. Perhaps the king was not in the right mood. Even though Nehemiah was a favorite of the king, he would not have rashly blurted out his request. We know it was politic to make one's requests during auspicious occasions such as birthday parties or when rulers were in a generous mood (Gen 40:20; Esth 5:6; Mark 6:21–25; Jos. *Antiq*. XVIII, 289–93 [viii.7]). It is certain that Nehemiah did not ask in haste but carefully bided his time, constantly praying to God to grant the proper opening.

"When wine was brought for him, I took the wine"; i.e., it was Nehemiah's turn to pour the wine. He was not "the" only cupbearer but one of several (in 1:11 the definite article is lacking; see J.J. Modi, "Wine Among the Ancient Persians," *Asiatic Papers* [Bombay: Royal Asiatic Society, 1905–29]: 3:231–46).

2 Persian works of art such as the great treasury reliefs from Persepolis indicate that those who came into the king's presence did so with great deference, placing the right hand with palm facing the mouth so as not to defile the king with one's breath (cf. R. Ghirshman, *The Art of Ancient Iran* [New York: Golden, 1964], pp. 205–6; R.N. Frye, "Gestures of Deference to Royalty in Ancient Iran," *Iranica Antiqua* 9 [1972]: 102–7).

Regardless of one's personal problems, the king's servants were expected to keep their feelings hidden and to display a cheerful countenance before him. So far Nehemiah had managed to do this; now his burden for Jerusalem betrayed itself, no doubt in his eyes. Artaxerxes seemed to trust Nehemiah to such a degree, however, that no suspicious thought seemed to have crossed his mind. Rather he perceived that it was not a matter of illness and was thus concerned to discover what was distressing his cupbearer.

The NAB's "I was seized with great fear" expresses well the anxiety that must have gripped Nehemiah—not so much for the king's question, but in anticipation of the request that he was to make, well knowing that the king himself had stopped the Jewish efforts at rebuilding the wall (Ezra 4:17–23).

3 "May the king live forever!" was a common form of address to kings (1 Kings 1:31; Dan 2:4; 3:9). Note that Nehemiah did not mention Jerusalem by name—"the city"— as he wished to arouse the king's sympathy by stressing first the desecration of ancestral tombs.

4 "Then I prayed to the God of heaven" is the most beautiful example of spontaneous prayer in the Scriptures. Before turning to answer the king, Nehemiah uttered a brief prayer to God. Despite his trepidation Nehemiah knew that he stood not only in the presence of an earthly monarch but before the King of the heavens. One of the most striking characteristics of Nehemiah was his recourse to prayer (cf. 4:4, 9; 5:19; 6:9, 14; 13:14). Those who are the boldest for God have the greatest need to be in prayer.

5 Fortified by his appeal to God and confident in the quality of his past service, Nehemiah was encouraged to make his bold request to the king. Nehemiah still did not mention Jerusalem by name but referred to it as "the city in Judah."

6–7 The word for "queen" (*šēgal*) comes from the root *šgl* ("to lie with" or "to ravish" a woman). It is used only here in v.6 and in Psalm 45:9. Though the word may simply mean a concubine (LXX has *pallakē*, "concubine"), the definite article indicates that she was the queen or the chief woman of the harem. Ctesias (# 44) reports that the queen's name was Damaspia and that the king had at least three concubines (F.W. König, *Die Persika des Ktesias von Knidos* [Graz: Archiv für Orientforschung, 1972], pp. 80–81, 124). Some have taken the queen's presence to conclude that this was a private audience and have even argued that this is one reason for considering Nehemiah a eunuch (cf. Notes). According to Daniel 5:2, however, royal women could be present on a public occasion.

The LXX and the Vulgate can be interpreted to mean that both the queen and the king spoke sympathetically to Nehemiah. Perhaps like Esther (Esth 4–5), she may have influenced the king. Rainey (*The Scribe*, p. 18) cites a letter from Ashur to Ugarit: "Now then, read the tablets that I have sent to you before the queen, and make entreaty before the queen with my favourable words." Extrabiblical sources reveal that the Achaemenid court was notorious for the great influence exercised by the royal women. Especially domineering was Amestris, the cruel wife of Xerxes and mother of Artaxerxes I. Darius II was dominated by his sister and wife, Parysatis.

In addition to safe-conduct letters (v.7), Nehemiah probably asked for a brief leave of absence, which was later extended. Nehemiah 5:14 implies that he spent twelve years on his first term as governor of Judah. In the thirty-second year he returned to report to the king and then returned to Judah for a second term (13:6).

8 The chief forester's name, "Asaph," means "(Yahweh) has gathered." *Pardēs* ("forest") is a loan word from Persian (Old Pers. *paradayadām*, Avestan *pairidaēza*) that originally meant "beyond the wall," hence an enclosure, a pleasant retreat, or a park. Such a park surrounded the tomb of Cyrus at Pasargadae with canals watering the grass and trees of every species. The Hebrew word occurs in the OT only here, in the Song of Songs 4:13 ("orchard"), and in Ecclesiastes 2:5 ("parks"). The Greek transliteration *paradeisos* is used here in the LXX and also of the Garden of Eden (Gen 3:8–10, 23–24; cf. also Xenophon *Oeconomicus* 4.13–14).

The location of the king's forest, where Nehemiah was to obtain timber for the gates, is unclear. Some place it in Lebanon, famed for its forests of cedars and other coniferous trees. Solomon obtained such cedars for his temple (1 Kings 5:6, 9; 2 Chron 2:8–9, 16), as did Zerubbabel for the rebuilding of the temple (Ezra 3:7) and Darius for his palace at Susa (Roland G. Kent, *Old Persian*, rev. ed. [New Haven: Yale University Press, 1955], pp. 77–97).

Others believe the king's forest should be identified with Solomon's Garden at Etham, about six miles south of Jerusalem, and well-known for its fine gardens (Jos. *Antiq.* VIII, 186 [vii.3]; cf. 2 Kings 25:4; Eccl 2:5–9; Jer 39:4; 52:7). This seems more probable. In the construction of city gates, indigenous oak, poplar, or terebinth (Gen 12:6; Josh 19:33; Judg 4:11; Hos 4:13) would most likely be used, not costly imported cedars from Lebanon.

"The citadel" (*bîrāh*; cf. 1:1) probably refers to the fortress north of the temple, which Josephus (*Antiq.* XV, 403 [xi.4]) called "Baris," and which was the forerunner of the Fortress Antonia built by Herod the Great (Acts 21:37; 22:24).

Notes

1 Though most scholars have identified the king in this passage as Artaxerxes I, especially in light of the Elephantine papyri, R.J. Saley, "The Date of Nehemiah Reconsidered," *Biblical and Near Eastern Studies*, ed. G.A. Tuttle (Grand Rapids: Eerdmans, 1978), pp. 151–65, opts for Artaxerxes II.

6 The presence of the queen has been used as an argument that Nehemiah was a eunuch. In 1:11 in place of the οὐνοχόος (*oinochoos*, "cupbearer") of the LXX Codex A, both א B have εὐνοῦχος (*eunouchos*, "eunuch"). Though it is true that there were many eunuchs at the Achaemenid court and that some cupbearers were eunuchs, for example at Herod's court (Jos. *Antiq.* XVI, 229–31 [viii.1]), the arguments used to support the thesis that Nehemiah was a eunuch are not convincing (see E. Yamauchi, "Was Nehemiah the Cupbearer a Eunuch?" ZAW 92 [1980]: 132–42).

8 The Greek word παράδεισος (*paradeisos*) during the intertestamental period acquired the sense of the abode of the blessed dead in such OT pseudepigrapha as Test Levi 18:10. It appears three times in the NT: Luke 23:43; 2 Cor 12:4; Rev 2:7.

2. The journey to Palestine

2:9–10

> ⁹So I went to the governors of Trans-Euphrates and gave them the king's letters. The king had also sent army officers and cavalry with me.
> ¹⁰When Sanballat the Horonite and Tobiah the Ammonite official heard about this, they were very much disturbed that someone had come to promote the welfare of the Israelites.

9 The text implies that Nehemiah set out immediately whereas Josephus (*Antiq.* XI, 168 [v.7]) indicates that Nehemiah returned in the twenty-fifth year (of Xerxes!). Unlike Ezra (Ezra 8:22) Nehemiah was accompanied by an armed escort, not, however, because his faith was weaker than Ezra's. As Adeney (p. 196) correctly notes: "But Nehemiah came straight from the court, where he had been a favourite servant

of the king, and he was now made the official governor of Jerusalem. It was only in accordance with custom that he should have an escort assigned him."

10 The name "Sanballat" derives from the Akkadian *Sin-uballit,* which means "Sin (the moon god) has given life." His epithet "the Horonite" identifies him as coming from (1) Hauran east of the Sea of Galilee, (2) Horonaim in Moab (Jer 48:34), or (3) most probably from either upper or lower Beth-Horon, two key cities twelve miles northwest of Jerusalem, which guarded the main road to Jerusalem (Josh 10:10; 16:3, 5; 1 Macc 3:15–16; 7:39).

Sanballat was the chief political opponent of Nehemiah (v.19; 4:1, 7; 6:1–2, 5, 12, 14; 13:28). Although not called governor, he had that position over Samaria (cf. 4:2). An important Elephantine papyrus (Cowley 30; ANET, p. 492), a letter to Bagoas, the governor of Judah, refers to "Delaiah and Shelemiah, the sons of Sanballat the governor [*pehah*] of Samariah." The letter is dated to 407 B.C. It is interesting that Sanballat's sons both bear Yahwistic names. In Cowley 32 (ANET, p. 492) Bagoas and Delaiah authorized the Jews to petition the satrap Arsames about rebuilding their temple at Elephantine.

In 1962 the same Beduoins who discovered the DSS found a cave in Wadi ed-Daliyeh, northwest of Jericho, which contained fourth-century B.C. papyri. With them were the grim remains of about two hundred men, women, and children from Samaria who unsuccessfully tried to flee from the troops of Alexander the Great. The data from the Samaria papyri include a Sanballat, who was probably the grandson of Nehemiah's foe (cf. H.H. Rowley, "Sanballat and the Samaritan Temple," BJRL 38 [1955]: 166–98; reprinted in his *Men of God*, pp. 246–76; Cross, "Samaria Papyri," pp. 110–20; id., "A Reconstruction," pp. 4–18; R.W. Klein, "Sanballat," IDB Supplement, pp. 781–82).

"Tobiah" means "Yahweh is good"; the name appears in the Murashu documents as *Tûbiâma.* He may have been a Judaizing Ammonite, but more probably he was a Yahwist Jew as indicated by his name and that of his son, Jehohanan (6:18). Some scholars speculate that Tobiah descended from an aristocratic family that owned estates in Gilead and was influential in Transjordan and in Jerusalem even as early as the eighth century B.C. (B. Obed, "The Historical Background of the Syro-Ephraimite War Reconsidered," CBQ 34 [1972]: 161). B. Mazar ("The Tobiads," IEJ 7 [1957]: 137–45, 229–38; cf. id., *Mountain*, pp. 66–68) has correlated varying lines of evidence to reconstruct the history of the Tobiad family to cover nine generations.

"Official" (*'ebed*) is literally "slave" or "servant" (cf. v.19; 13:1–3). The RSV believes this term was meant derisively: "Tobias, the Ammonite, the slave." But *'ebed* is often used of high officials both in biblical and in extrabiblical texts (e.g., 2 Kings 22:12; 24:10–11; 25:23; Jer 36:24; Lam 5:8). It is used of a Tobiah in Lachish Letter 3.19–21: "And a letter of Tobiah, the servant of the king," who is also cited in Letter 5.7–10 as "Tobiah, the arm of the king." Mazar believes that this Tobiah was an ancestor of Nehemiah's contemporary.

Tobiah was married to the daughter of Shecaniah (cf. 3:29; 6:18); and his son Jehohanan married the daughter of Meshullam, son of Berekiah, leader of one of the groups repairing the wall (cf. 3:4, 30; 6:18). Tobiah also was closely related to the priest Eliashib (13:4–7). Josephus (*Antiq.* XII, 160 [iv.2]) said that a later Tobiah was a leader of Jewish Hellenizers under Ptolemy II. This is confirmed by the important Zenon Papyri.

687

The region of Ammon is located in Transjordan around the modern capital, 'Amman (Ezra 9:1). Tobiah was no doubt the governor of Ammon or Transjordan under the Persians. His grandson Tobiah is called "the governor of Ammon." The site of 'Arâq el-Emîr ("caverns of the prince"), about eleven miles west of 'Amman, was the center of the Tobiads. The visible remains of a large building on top of the hill (Qaṣr el-'Abd, "castle of the slave," 60 by 120 feet) have been interpreted as a Jewish temple built by a later Tobiad. On two halls are inscriptions with the name Tobiah in Aramaic characters. The date of the inscriptions is much disputed. Mazar favored the sixth-fifth century B.C.; Naveh (*The Development*, pp. 62–64), the fourth century; Cross, the fourth-third century; and P.W. Lapp ("Soundings at 'Arâq el-Emî [Jordan]," BA-SOR 165 [1962]: 16–34; id., "The Second and Third Campaigns at 'Arâq el-Emîr," BASOR 171 [1963]: 8–39), who reexcavated the site in 1961–62, the third-second century (cf. also C.C. McCown, "The 'Arâ el-Emîr and the Tobiads," BA 20 [1957]: 63–76; M. Hengel, *Judaism and Hellenism* [Philadelphia: Fortress, 1974], 1:49, 267 –77).

The reason Sanballat and Tobiah "were very much disturbed" was not basically religious but political. The authority of the Samaritan governor in particular was threatened by Nehemiah's arrival.

Notes

10 W.F. Albright has suggested emending the Hebrew text by reading עֶבֶד (*ʿeḇeḏ*), not as "official," but as the proper name 'Abd, the individual called governor of Dedan in the Lihyanite inscription that also mentions Geshem. (See comment on v.19.)

3. Nehemiah's nocturnal inspection of the walls

2:11–16

[11]I went to Jerusalem, and after staying there three days [12]I set out during the night with a few men. I had not told anyone what my God had put in my heart to do for Jerusalem. There were no mounts with me except the one I was riding on. [13]By night I went out through the Valley Gate toward the Jackal Well and the Dung Gate, examining the walls of Jerusalem, which had been broken down, and its gates, which had been destroyed by fire. [14]Then I moved on toward the Fountain Gate and the King's Pool, but there was not enough room for my mount to get through; [15]so I went up the valley by night, examining the wall. Finally, I turned back and reentered through the Valley Gate. [16]The officials did not know where I had gone or what I was doing, because as yet I had said nothing to the Jews or the priests or nobles or officials or any others who would be doing the work.

11–12 After the long journey a few days of rest ("three," v.11) were necessary (cf. Ezra 8:32). Such was Nehemiah's discretion that he took only a few men into his confidence at first (v.12). He acted with great care going out at night, no doubt by moonlight, to inspect the situation firsthand.

13 Nehemiah did not make a complete circuit of the walls but only of the southern

area to see how much was preserved. Jerusalem was always attacked where she was most vulnerable, from the north; thus there was probably little preserved in that direction.

According to 2 Chronicles 26:9, Uzziah fortified towers in the west wall, on the Tyropoeon Valley. In the excavations of 1927–28, M. Crowfoot discovered remains of a gate with towers from the Persian and Hellenistic periods, which A. Alt (*Kleine Schriften* [Munich: Beck, 1959], 3:326–47) identified with the Valley Gate (see Mazar, *Mountain,* pp. 167, 182, 193; see also the map on page 600 in the Introduction).

"Jackal Well" (*'ên hattannîn*) is literally "spring of the dragons," the mythical water monsters (Gen 1:20–21; Exod 7:9; Ps 74:13; Jer 51:34; Ezek 29:3). The NIV and RSV emend to read *tannîm* ("jackals"; cf. Lam 4:3; Mic 1:8). Many scholars suggest this was the *'ên rogel* (Arab. Bir 'Ayub), at the junction of the Hinnom and Kidron valleys 275 yards south of the tip of the southeast ridge of Jerusalem (Kenyon, *Digging Up,* p. 152). J. Braslavi ("En-Tannin," *Eretz Israel* 10 [1971]: 90–93) argues, however, that this must be the major spring of Jerusalem, the Gihon, and that the name "Tannin" is derived from the serpentine course of the waters of the spring to the Pool of Siloam. (It is most probable that Hezekiah's tunnel followed a natural channel of water through limestone. Such naturally serpentine courses may be observed at Mammoth Cave, Kentucky.) Braslavi believes that the En-Rogel had been buried beneath the debris of the earthquake of Uzziah's reign and would not have been visible to Nehemiah.

"The Dung Gate" (*šā'ar hā'ašpōṯ;* cf. 3:13–14; 12:31; 2 Kings 23:10) led to the rubbish dump in the Hinnom Valley. It was situated about five hundred yards from the Valley Gate (3:13). Mazar interprets the Hebrew as *š-p-w-t,* a by-form of "Tophet," the "place of burning," where infant sacrifices were conducted in the days of Manasseh (2 Kings 23:10): "We may therefore conclude that the gate in question led from the City of David to the 'burning place' of Tophet in the valley of Hinnom" (*Mountain,* pp. 194–95).

Some propose a gate in the southwest corner, but most scholars prefer the great gate in the southeast corner (cf. J. Simons, *Jerusalem in the Old Testament* [Leiden: Brill, 1952], pp. 123–24). According to Josephus (War V, 145 [iv.2]), the Herodian Jerusalem had a "Gate of the Essenes," which was used by the Essenes to reach the *Bethso,* or latrines. This gate cannot be identified with Nehemiah's "Dung Gate," however; it is to be located much farther north on the grounds of the Institute of Holy Land Studies. (See Y. Yadin, "The Gate of the Essenes and the Temple Scroll," in Y. Yadin, *Jerusalem Revealed,* [Jerusalem: Israel Exploration Society, 1975], pp. 90–96; B.-G. Pixner, "An Essene Quarter on Mount Zion?" *Studia Hierosolymitanna* 1 [1976]: 255–57; R.M. Mackowski, *Jerusalem City of Jesus* [Grand Rapids: Eerdmans, 1980], pp. 62–66.)

14 "The Fountain Gate" was possibly in the southeast wall facing toward En-Rogel. According to 2 Kings 20:20 (2 Chron 32:30), Hezekiah diverted the overflow from his Siloam Tunnel to irrigate the royal gardens (2 Kings 25:4) located at the junction of the Kidron and Tyropoeon valleys. Kenyon (*Jerusalem,* pp. 69–71, 77) therefore identifies this with the Pool of Siloam or the adjacent Birket el-Hamra.

"There was not enough room." Kenyon's excavations between 1961 and 1967 on the eastern slopes of Ophel, the original hill of Jerusalem just south of the temple area, revealed the collapse of the terraces, which she identifies as the enigmatic "Millo" that David and Solomon had to keep repairing. She writes (*Jerusalem,* pp.

107f.): "The tumble of stones uncovered by our Trench 1 is a vivid sample of the ruinous state of the eastern side of Jerusalem that balked Nehemiah's donkey. The event shows that the sight of this cascade of stones persuaded Nehemiah that he could not attempt to restore the quarter of Jerusalem on the eastern slope of the eastern ridge, or the wall that had enclosed it."

15 The NIV and RSV indicate that Nehemiah retraced his steps and reentered the city at the Valley Gate on the west slope of Ophel.

16 "Nobles" (*ḥōrîm*) comes from the root "to be free" (cf. 4:14, 19; 5:7; 6:17; 7:5; 13:17). These were the notable men of the clans who directed public affairs (cf. J. van der Ploeg, "Les nobles israelites," *Oudtestamentische Studien* 9 [1951]: 54).

Notes

---

13 The Hebrew translated "examining" is שֹׂבֵר (*šōḇēr*, "breaking"). Rashi, the medieval Jewish commentator, suggested that Nehemiah was breaking the walls to bring conditions to the attention of the people! The Hebrew should be emended to read *śōḇēr* ("examining"; cf. v.15).

---

4. Nehemiah's exhortation to rebuild the walls

2:17–18

> ¹⁷Then I said to them, "You see the trouble we are in: Jerusalem lies in ruins, and its gates have been burned with fire. Come, let us rebuild the wall of Jerusalem, and we will no longer be in disgrace." ¹⁸I also told them about the gracious hand of my God upon me and what the king had said to me.
> They replied, "Let us start rebuilding." So they began this good work.

17 The walls and gates of Jerusalem had lain in ruins since their destruction by Nebuchadnezzar some 130 years before, despite attempts to rebuild them. The leaders and people had evidently become reconciled to this sad state of affairs. It took an outsider to assess the situation and rally the people to renewed efforts. *Ḥerpāh* appears seventy times in the OT either as "abuse," "scorn," or, as in this case, "disgrace" (cf. 1:3; 4:4; 5:9).

18 Nehemiah could personally attest that God was alive and active on his behalf. He had come, moreover, with royal sanction and authority. What was required and what Nehemiah provided was a vision and decisive leadership. Nehemiah was clearly a shaker, a mover, and a doer.

5. The opposition of Sanballat, Tobiah, and Geshem

2:19–20

> ¹⁹But when Sanballat the Horonite, Tobiah the Ammonite official and Geshem

the Arab heard about it, they mocked and ridiculed us. "What is this you are doing?" they asked. "Are you rebelling against the king?"

20I answered them by saying, "The God of heaven will give us success. We his servants will start rebuilding, but as for you, you have no share in Jerusalem or any claim or historic right to it."

19 On Sanballat and Tobiah, see the comment on v.10. "Geshem" (*gešem*, so also in 6:1-2), meaning "bulky" or "stout," is a common North Arabian name, *Jasuma*, found in various Arabic inscriptions including Safaitic, Lihyanite, Thamudic, and Nabataean.

Biblical and extrabiblical documents indicate that Arabs became dominant in the Transjordanian area from the Assyrian to the Persian periods (cf. Gen 25:13; Isa 60:7; Jer 49:28-33). Sargon II resettled some Arabs in Samaria in 715 B.C. (ANET, p. 286). Classical sources reveal that the Arabs enjoyed a favored status under the Persians. See Israel Eph'al, *The Ancient Arabs* (Jerusalem: Magnes; Leiden: E.J. Brill, 1982).

A Lihyanite inscription from Dedan (modern Al-'Ulā) in northwest Arabia reads: "Jašm son of Šahr and 'Abd, governor of Dedan." This Jašm is identified by Winnett and Albright with the biblical Geshem (F.V. Winnett, *A Study of the Lihyanite and Thamudic Inscriptions* [Toronto: University of Toronto Press, 1937], pp. 50-51; W.F. Albright, "Dedan," *Geschichte und Altes Testament* [Tübingen: J.C.B. Mohr, 1943], pp. 1-12).

In 1947 several silver vessels, some with Aramaic inscriptions dating to the late fifth century B.C., were discovered at Tell el-Maskhūta near Ismaila by the Suez Canal. One inscription bore the name "Qaynu the son of Gashmu, the king of Qedar." The son of Geshem records an offering to the goddess "Han-Ilat." Geshem was thus in charge of a powerful north Arabian confederacy of tribes that controlled vast areas from northeast Egypt (the LXX of Gen 45:10 reads "the land of Gesem of Arabia" instead of "the land of Goshen") to northern Arabia to southern Palestine. G.E. Wright ("Judean Lachish," BA 18 [1955]: 9-17; id., *Biblical Archaeology*, rev. ed. [Philadelphia: Westminster, 1962], pp. 206-7, fig. 148) has suggested that Geshem may have used the palace of the Persian period excavated at Lachish. Geshem may have been opposed to Nehemiah's development of an independent kingdom because he feared it might interfere with his lucrative trade in myrrh and frankincense. (See F.M. Cross, "Geshem the Arabian, Enemy of Nehemiah," BA 18 [1955]: 46-47; I. Rabinowitz, "Aramaic Inscriptions of the Fifth Century BCE," JNES 15 [1956]: 1-9; W.J. Dumbrell, "The Tell el-Maskhuṭa Bowls and the 'Kingdom' of Qedar in the Persian Period," BASOR 203 [1971]: 33-44; A.K. Irvine, "The Arabs and Ethiopians," in Wiseman, *Peoples*, pp. 287-311; J.R. Bartlett, "From Edomites to Nabataeans," PEQ 111 [1979]: 53-66.)

"Ridiculed" (from *bāzāh*) means "to show contempt for," "to despise" (cf. 2 Sam 6:16; 2 Kings 19:21; Esth 3:6; Prov 1:7).

20 Nehemiah appealed to historical claims to reject the interference of the Samaritan, Ammonite, and Arabian leaders in the affairs of Jerusalem. By his great confidence and dependence on God for success, he inspired the leaders and the people to a task they had considered beyond their abilities.

C. List of the Builders of the Wall (3:1–32)

This chapter is one of the most important in the OT for determining the topography of Jerusalem. Though some locations are clear, others are not. Opinions differ widely about whether the wall enclosed the southwest hill today called "Mount Zion" (the Maximalist view; cf. R. Grafman, "Nehemiah's 'Broad Wall'," IEJ 24 [1974]: 50–51; H. Geva, "The Western Boundary of Jerusalem at the End of the Monarchy," IEJ 29 [1979]: 84–91) or only the original settlement—including the temple area—of the southeast hill of Ophel (the Minimalist view).

The excavations of Kenyon from 1961 to 1967 have demonstrated that the southwest hill was settled only in the Hellenistic period. According to Mazar (*Mountain*, p. 193; cf. map on p. 192): "A detailed examination of the record left by Nehemiah shows, however, that his work was restricted to the eastern hill alone, which included, beside the Temple area, the southeastern ridge. This evaluation of Nehemiah's work *fits well with the results of recent archaeological excavations*" (emphasis mine). H.G.M. Williamson ("Nehemiah's Walls Revisited," PEQ 116 [1984]: 81–88), comparing Nehemiah 3:8 with 12:38, concludes that though there was a preexilic wall that enclosed the Mishneh (the Maximalist view), Nehemiah rebuilt a much more constricted wall (the Minimalist view), following perhaps a wall but newly started (Ezra 4). (See Avi-Yonah, "Walls of Nehemiah," pp. 239–48; Y. Aharoni and M. Avi-Yonah, *The Macmillan Bible Atlas* [New York: Macmillan, 1968], map 170; Kenyon, *Jerusalem*, p. 107; id., *Digging Up*, pp. 146–47, map fig. 26.)

Earlier critics (Wellhausen, Torrey, Mowinckel) questioned the authenticity of the list of builders. Though there are some striking omissions, e.g., Ezra and the city of Bethlehem, there is no real reason to question the genuineness of the list. According to J. Myers (*Encyclopaedia Judaica*, 6:1120), "An official document, this list reflects that actual rebuilding of the city as well as the extent of the organization of Judah."

The list, which was probably preserved in the temple, proceeds in a counterclockwise direction about the wall. Some forty-one parties are named as participating in the reconstruction of forty-two sections. The towns listed as the homes of the builders seem to have represented the administrative centers of the Judean province.

All together, ten gates are listed as follows:
1. the Sheep Gate (v.1)
2. the Fish Gate (v.3)
3. the Old (Jeshanah) Gate (v.6)
4. the Valley Gate (v.13)
5. the Dung (Ashpot) Gate (v.14)
6. the Fountain Gate (v.15)
7. the Water Gate (v.26)
8. the Horse Gate (v.28)
9. the East Gate (v.29)
10. the Inspection Gate (v.31).

The account suggests that most of the rebuilding was concerned with the gates as the enemy's assaults were concentrated on these structures.

According to the Maximalist position, the circuit of walls would have been about 2½ miles, enclosing some 220 acres. According to the Minimalist position, the circuit would have been just under 2 miles, enclosing about 90 acres. Each of the forty-two sections would then average about 250 feet, though an exceptionally long section of 1,500 feet is mentioned (v.3). Some sections were very short (vv.21–23); double sections were worked by some groups (e.g., v.27).

Clearly not all the sections of the walls or buildings in Jerusalem were in the same state of disrepair. Kenyon (*Digging Up*, p. 179) deduces a selective policy of destruction from 2 Kings 25:9 and concludes: "One can therefore accept as probable that quite a lot of the domestic buildings of Jerusalem survived (except those on the eastern slope): the hovels and the least important possibly completely, the medium-scale houses probably capable of easy repairs, only the grand houses seriously destroyed."

1. *The northern section*

3:1–7

¹Eliashib the high priest and his fellow priests went to work and rebuilt the Sheep Gate. They dedicated it and set its doors in place, building as far as the Tower of the Hundred, which they dedicated, and as far as the Tower of Hananel. ²The men of Jericho built the adjoining section, and Zaccur son of Imri built next to them.

³The Fish Gate was rebuilt by the sons of Hassenaah. They laid its beams and put its doors and bolts and bars in place. ⁴Meremoth son of Uriah, the son of Hakkoz, repaired the next section. Next to him Meshullam son of Berekiah, the son of Meshezabel, made repairs, and next to him Zadok son of Baana also made repairs. ⁵The next section was repaired by the men of Tekoa, but their nobles would not put their shoulders to the work under their supervisors.

⁶The Jeshanah Gate was repaired by Joiada son of Paseah and Meshullam son of Besodeiah. They laid its beams and put its doors and bolts and bars in place. ⁷Next to them, repairs were made by men from Gibeon and Mizpah—Melatiah of Gibeon and Jadon of Meronoth—places under the authority of the governor of Trans-Euphrates.

1 "Eliashib the high priest" was the son of Joaikim (see Ezra 10:6; see also Introduction: The High Priests). His house is mentioned in vv.20–21. It was fitting that the high priest should set the example. Among the Sumerians the king himself would carry bricks for the building of the temple.

"The Sheep Gate" (cf. v.32; 12:39) was no doubt located in the northeast section of the wall near the Birah fortress. John 5:2 locates it near the Bethesda Pool. Even today a sheep market is installed periodically near this area. (For the gates of the present walled city of Jerusalem, see S. Steckoll, *The Gates of Jerusalem* [Tel Aviv: am Hassefer, 1968].) Avi-Yonah ("Walls of Nehemiah," pp. 239–48) suggests that this gate replaced the earlier Gate of Benjamin (Jer 37:13; 38:7) that led to Anathoth in Benjamin (Zech 14:10).

"The Tower of the Hundred" (*migdal hammē'āh*) occurs only here and in 12:39. What the "hundred" refers to is unclear: either its height, one hundred cubits, or one hundred steps or a military unit (cf. Deut 1:15).

"The Tower of Hananel" is also mentioned in Jeremiah 31:38 and Zechariah 14:10 as the most northern part of the city. Some scholars (Brockington, in loc.; Coggins, in loc.) believe that "the Tower of the Hundred" may be a popular name for "the Tower of Hananel." But the NIV and other renderings suggest two separate towers with the Tower of Hananel to the west of the Tower of the Hundred. The towers were associated with "the citadel by the temple" (2:8) in protecting the vulnerable northern approaches to the city.

2 "Zaccur," short for "Zechariah," was a Levite who later signed the covenant (10:12).

3 "The Fish Gate" (cf. 12:39) was known in the days of the first temple (Zeph 1:10) as one of Jerusalem's main entrances (2 Chron 33:14). It may be the same as the Gate of Ephraim, which led out to the main road north from Jerusalem that then descended to the coastal plain through Beth-Horon. The consensus locates it close to the site of the present-day Damascus Gate. It was called the Fish Gate because merchants brought fish from either Tyre or the Sea of Galilee through it to the fish market (13:16).

Members of the "sons of Hassenaah" family appear in Ezra 2:35 (Neh 7:38) in the list of those returning from captivity. This is the largest group enumerated (3,630 in Ezra; 3,930 in Neh).

4 "Meremoth son of Uriah, son of Hakkoz," repaired a second section (v.21) and later signed the covenant (10:5). A priest named Meremoth the son of Hakkoz had difficulty establishing his lineage (Ezra 2:59, 61) but was entrusted with the treasures by Ezra (Ezra 8:33). According to Brockington (p. 135), "Meremoth is probably the only man who can be shown to have shared in the work of both Ezra and Nehemiah." Proponents of a reverse order have used this identification to argue that Nehemiah must have preceded Ezra, assuming that Meremoth labored on the wall in his youth rather than in his old age. Other scholars have questioned the identification (see Introduction: The Order).

"Meshullam" also repaired a second section (v.30) and signed the covenant (10:20). Nehemiah complained that he had given his daughter to a son of Tobiah (6:18). He may have been one of the men who accompanied Ezra (Ezra 8:16).

5 "Tekoa" was a small town five miles south of Bethlehem, famed as the home of the prophet Amos (Amos 1:1). Tekoa does not appear in the list of those who returned with Zerubbabel (Ezra 2:21–35).

"Nobles" (*'addîrîm*) is literally "exalted ones," "majestic ones" (cf. 10:29; 2 Chron 23:20; Jer 14:3; 25:34–36; Nah 2:5). These aristocrats disdained manual labor; they "would not put their shoulders to the work." The Hebrew for "shoulders" (*ṣawwā' r,* "neck") specifically refers to the back of the neck. The expression is drawn from the imagery of oxen that refuse to yield to the yoke (Jer 27:12). The common phrase "to backslide" is derived from the KJV rendering of Hosea 4:16: "For Israel slideth back as a backsliding heifer."

"Their supervisors" (*'adōnêhem*) comes from *'ādôn* (with pronominal suffix), a word used in the OT of an earthly lord about 300 times and 30 times of the divine Lord. The related *'adōnāy* is used 449 times of the Lord (cf. TDOT, 1:59–72; TWOT, 1:12 –13). The ASV and RSV render the word as the divine Lord. But the RV translates "their lord"; NEB, "their governor"; and TEV (like the NIV), "the supervisors."

In a remarkable coincidence six centuries later, complaining about Tekoans who had disregarded his mobilization orders and were seeking refuge in En-gedi, Bar Kochba warned, "Concerning every man of Tekoa who will be found at your place— the houses in which they dwell will be burned and you (too) will be punished" (Y. Yadin, *Bar Kochba* [New York: Random House, 1971], p. 125).

6 "The Jeshanah [*yᵉšānāh*] Gate" was situated in the northwest corner and is identified with the Corner Gate of 2 Kings 14:13 and Jeremiah 31:38. Its name has been interpreted in three ways: (1) literally as "The Old Gate" (KJV); (2) as the gate to Jeshanah, lying on the border between Judea and Samaria (2 Chron 13:19); and (3) Avi-Yonah ("Walls of Nehemiah," pp. 242–43) suggests an emendation to *Mišneh* ("second or new quarter") because the names of the gates were derived from what was outside the walls. The gate would then have led to the area of expansion (Zeph 1:10; cf. "New City Gate," NASB; "Gate of the New Quarter," JB).

7 "Mizpah" (*miṣpāh*, "Lookout Point") is identified with Tell en-Naṣbeh, excavated by W.F. Badè (cf. vv.7, 15, 19). According to H. Tadmor (in Ben-Sasson, p. 161): "At the same time, several cities lying north of Jerusalem, e.g. Bethel, Mizpah and Gibeon were not destroyed at all (by Nebuchadnezzar), and it is now assumed that this region—the land of Benjamin—submitted to the Babylonians in 588, with the commencement of the war, and thus escaped destruction." Part of the archaeological evidence for this assessment is the name Mozah (a city associated with Mizpah, e.g., in Josh 18:26) found inscribed on some twenty jar handles from the Persian period, which indicates that the vineyards in this area prospered during this period (cf. *Inscriptions Reveal*, p. 54).

"Under the authority" (*lᵉkissēʾ*) is literally "to the chair" or "throne." Fragments of a lion's paw and a bronze cylinder that belonged to the foot of a Persian throne similar to those depicted at Persepolis were found in Samaria. M. Tadmor ("Fragments of an Achaemenid Throne from Samaria," IEJ 24 [1974]: 42) remarks: "A throne of the Achaemenid kings might have belonged to their representative, the governor of Samaria."

The phrase can be interpreted in different ways: (1) as the satrap's residence in Jerusalem (cf. Avi-Yonah, *Holy Land*, p. 16); (2) as the satrap's residence at Damascus or Aleppo; or (3) interpreting "chair" as a symbol for the jurisdiction of the governor over the places from which the builders came, such as Gibeon and Mizpah (so NIV, RV, RSV).

2. The western section

3:8–13

> ⁸Uzziel son of Harhaiah, one of the goldsmiths, repaired the next section; and Hananiah, one of the perfume-makers, made repairs next to that. They restored Jerusalem as far as the Broad Wall. ⁹Rephaiah son of Hur, ruler of a half-district of Jerusalem, repaired the next section. ¹⁰Adjoining this, Jedaiah son of Harumaph made repairs opposite his house, and Hattush son of Hashabneiah made repairs next to him. ¹¹Malkijah son of Harim and Hasshub son of Pahath-Moab repaired another section and the Tower of the Ovens. ¹²Shallum son of Hallohesh, ruler of a half-district of Jerusalem, repaired the next section with the help of his daughters.
>
> ¹³The Valley Gate was repaired by Hanun and the residents of Zanoah. They rebuilt it and put its doors and bolts and bars in place. They also repaired five hundred yards of the wall as far as the Dung Gate.

8 "One of the goldsmiths" reflects the Hebrew *ben* ("son of," i.e., a member of a guild; cf. I. Mendelsohn, "Guilds in Ancient Palestine," BASOR 80 [1940]: 17–21). The industrial district of the goldsmiths and perfumers may have been located outside the walls (cf. vv.31–32).

"Perfume-makers" translates *raqqāḥîm*, which occurs only here, with the feminine form in 1 Samuel 8:13. The KJV translates the word "apothecaries." Mazar (*Mountain*, p. 194) discovered at Tell Garsen by Ein Gedi evidence of perfume manufacture from the balsam ointment from stratum V (c. 630–582 B.C.).

"They restored" comes from ' *āzaḇ*, which means "to abandon" (cf. LXX *katelipon*, "they left"). Mazar (*Mountain*, p. 194) takes the term literally to mean that Nehemiah abandoned areas as far as the Broad Wall. Other scholars believe that the word here must be a homonym meaning "to restore" or "to fortify," citing words in cognate languages (cf. Akkad. *ušezib*, Ugar. *'db*, Sabean *'ḏb*, etc.; see R. Gordis, *The Word and the Book* [New York: KTAV, 1976], p. 205).

"The Broad Wall" (*haḥômāh hārᵉḥāḇāh*) is usually understood as a thick wall, but R. Grafman ("Nehemiah's 'Broad Wall,'" IEJ 24 [1974]: 50–51) interprets the phrase to mean a long, extensive wall. In 1970–71 N. Avigad ("Excavations in the Jewish Quarter of the Old City of Jerusalem, 1971 [Third Preliminary Report]," IEJ 22 [1972]: 193–200), excavating in the Jewish Quarter of the walled city of Jerusalem, discovered a wall 7½ yards thick, 300 yards west of the temple area, and cleared it for some 44 yards. The wall is dated to the early seventh century B.C. and was probably built by Hezekiah (2 Chron 32:5). M. Broshi ("The Expansion of Jerusalem in the Reigns of Hezekiah and Manasseh," IEJ 24 [1974]: 21–26) surmises that the great expansion to and beyond the Broad Wall that caused a three-to-fourfold expansion of the city was occasioned by the influx of refugees from the Fall of Samaria in 722. Avigad believes that the wall, which curves west, turned south to enclose the Pool of Siloam. But Kenyon (*Digging Up*, p. 148) holds that the wall must have turned east, as she found no evidence of an early settlement on the southwest hill. (On the wall, see N. Avigad, "Excavations in the Jewish Quarter of the Old City, Jerusalem, 1970," IEJ 20 [1970]: 129–40; id., "Excavations, 1971," pp. 193–200.)

9 "Rephaiah" ("Yahweh has healed") had charge of half the central district, one of the five districts of Judea. "Harumaph" ("split nose" or "flat nose") is found only here. It made sense to have him and others repair the sections of the wall nearest their homes.

11 If "Malkijah son of Harim" is the individual mentioned in Ezra 10:31, the reference could support the contemporaneity of Ezra and Nehemiah. "Hasshub," short for "Hashabiah" ("Yahweh has considered"), was one who sealed the covenant (10:23).

"Another section" clearly indicates that our list is only partial, as no first section is mentioned.

The NIV's "Tower of the Ovens" (*migdal hattanûrîm*) is preferable to the alternative translation, "tower of the furnaces" (KJV). This tower is mentioned only here and was located on the western wall, perhaps in the same location as the one Uzziah built at the Corner Gate (2 Chron 26:9). The ovens may have been those situated in the bakers' street (Jer 37:21).

12 "Hallohesh" (*hallôḥēš*) is not a proper name but a participle that means "whisperer," in the sense of a snake charmer or an enchanter (Ps 58:5; Eccl 10:11). Michaeli (p. 316) comments: "It indicates, perhaps a kind of guild, rather than a family. He is the only person whose daughters are said also to work on the wall. Were these his actual daughters, or were they women practicing divination?" "With the help of his daughters" is a unique reference to women working at the wall. When the Athenians attempted to rebuild their walls after the Persians had destroyed them, it was decreed that "the whole population of the city, men, women, and children, should take part in the wall-building" (*Thucydides* 1.90.3). Less likely is the attempt to translate the word "daughters" as "dependent" villages (cf. 11:25–31).

13 Avi-Yonah (*Holy Land,* p. 22) comments: "The fact that Hanun and the inhabitants of Zanoah repaired a gate—a task usually left to a community rather than an individual—suggests that part of a district is meant here, with Hanun as its 'ruler.'"

"Five hundred yards" (lit., "a thousand cubits"—about 1,720 feet) is an extraordinary length, but probably most of the section was less damaged.

On the "Dung Gate" see the comment on 2:13. Almost all scholars identify this with the gate found by Bliss in the central (Tyropoeon) valley west of the Siloam Pool at the southern extremity of Ophel.

4. The southern section

3:14

¹⁴The Dung Gate was repaired by Malkijah son of Recab, ruler of the district of Beth Hakkerem. He rebuilt it and put its doors and bolts and bars in place.

14 "Recab" ("rider") was also the name of the father of an ascetic clan, the Recabites (Jer 35).

"Beth Hakkerem" ("house of the vineyard") is mentioned in Jeremiah 6:1 as a fire-signal point. Y. Aharoni ("Beth-haccherem," *Archaeology and Old Testament Study,* ed. D.W. Thomas [London: Oxford University Press, 1967], pp. 171–84) has identified the site with Ramat Rahel, two miles south of Jerusalem, which he excavated from 1954 to 1962. The site seems to have been the residence of a district governor in the Persian period.

4. The eastern section

3:15–32

¹⁵The Fountain Gate was repaired by Shallun son of Col-Hozeh, ruler of the district of Mizpah. He rebuilt it, roofing it over and putting its doors and bolts and bars in place. He also repaired the wall of the Pool of Siloam, by the King's Garden, as far as the steps going down from the City of David. ¹⁶Beyond him, Nehemiah son of Azbuk, ruler of a half-district of Beth Zur, made repairs up to a point opposite the tombs of David, as far as the artificial pool and the House of the Heroes.

¹⁷Next to him, the repairs were made by the Levites under Rehum son of Bani. Beside him, Hashabiah, ruler of half the district of Keilah, carried out repairs for his district. ¹⁸Next to him, the repairs were made by their countrymen under Binnui son of Henadad, ruler of the other half-district of Keilah. ¹⁹Next to him, Ezer son of Jeshua, ruler of Mizpah, repaired another section, from a point facing the ascent to the armory as far as the angle. ²⁰Next to him, Baruch son of Zabbai zealously repaired another section, from the angle to the entrance of the house of Eliashib the high priest. ²¹Next to him, Meremoth son of Uriah, the son of Hakkoz, repaired another section, from the entrance of Eliashib's house to the end of it.

²²The repairs next to him were made by the priests from the surrounding region. ²³Beyond them, Benjamin and Hasshub made repairs in front of their house; and next to them, Azariah son of Maaseiah, the son of Ananiah, made repairs beside his house. ²⁴Next to him, Binnui son of Henadad repaired another section, from Azariah's house to the angle and the corner, ²⁵and Palal son of Uzai worked opposite the angle and the tower projecting from the upper palace near the court of the guard. Next to him, Pedaiah son of Parosh ²⁶and the temple servants living on the hill of Ophel made repairs up to a point opposite the Water Gate toward the east and the projecting tower. ²⁷Next to them, the men of Tekoa repaired another section, from the great projecting tower to the wall of Ophel.

²⁸Above the Horse Gate, the priests made repairs, each in front of his own house. ²⁹Next to them, Zadok son of Immer made repairs opposite his house. Next to him, Shemaiah son of Shecaniah, the guard at the East Gate, made repairs. ³⁰Next to him, Hananiah son of Shelemiah, and Hanun, the sixth son of Zalaph, repaired another section. Next to them, Meshullam son of Berekiah made repairs opposite his living quarters. ³¹Next to him, Malkijah, one of the goldsmiths, made repairs as far as the house of the temple servants and the merchants, opposite the Inspection Gate, and as far as the room above the corner; ³²and between the room above the corner and the Sheep Gate the goldsmiths and merchants made repairs.

15 "The Fountain Gate" (*ša'ar hā'ayin*) may also be translated "Spring Gate." This may have faced the En-Rogel spring (see on 2:13). R. Weill identified it with a gate he discovered in 1923–24 in the eastern wall between the southern end of the city and the double wall of the Siloam Pool.

Mazar (*Mountain*, p. 174), however, derives the name from its location at the point at which the Siloam tunnel emerged from the ground with water from the Gihon Spring, the fountain par excellence of Jerusalem.

"Col-Hozeh" (lit., "everyone a seer") may indicate that the family practiced divination (cf. M. Jastrow, "Rô'eh and Hôzeh in the Old Testament," JBL 28 [1909]: 42–56).

The "Pool of Siloam [*šelaḥ*, 'sent'; KJV, 'Siloah']," a canal or water channel, is probably to be associated with the water of *šilōaḥ* (Gr. *Silōam*, John 9:7). Many would identify this with the Lower Pool of Isaiah 22:9, located at the present day Birket el-Ḥamra.

The "King's Garden" would have been located outside the walls where the Kidron and Hinnom valleys converge (2 Kings 25:4).

16 "Azbuk" ("Buq is mighty") occurs only here. "Beth Zur" was a district capital, twenty miles south of Jerusalem. Excavations conducted in 1931 and 1957 reveal that occupation was resumed in the fifth century B.C. and was sparse during the Persian period.

First Kings 2:10; 2 Chronicles 21:20; 32:33 confirm that David was buried in the city area (2:5; cf. also Acts 2:29). The so-called Tomb of David on Mount Zion venerated today by Jewish pilgrims is in the Coenaculum building, constructed in the fourteenth century A.D. Such a site for David's tomb is mentioned no earlier than the ninth century A.D.

"The House of the Heroes" (*bêt haggibbôrîm*, lit., "house of the mighty men, champions" [1 Sam 17:51], "warriors" [Isa 21:17]) may have been the house of David's mighty men, which served later as the barracks or the armory.

17–18 "Keilah" (v.17) was a city southwest of Jerusalem and eight miles northwest of Hebron, situated near the border with the Philistines. It played an important role in David's early history (1 Sam 23:1). For "Binnui" (v.18; cf. v.24; Ezra 2:10; 8:33) most Hebrew MSS read "Bavvai."

19 The last part of the verse is difficult to translate. The NAB reads: "the corner, opposite the ascent to the arsenal"; the JB has "opposite the slope up to the Armoury towards the Angle"; the NEB renders "opposite the point at which the ascent meets the escarpment."

20 "Baruch" is literally "blessed." A feminine form *barūkā* occurs in the Murashu texts (Coogan, *Personal Names*, p. 16; cf. *barīk*, id., pp. 69–70).
"Zealously" (*heḥerāh*) is from the root "to glow," "to burn," usually used of anger but also of zeal as here.

21 The residences of the high priest and his colleagues were located along the eastern wall of the city, corresponding with the retaining wall of the temple area above the Kidron Valley.

22 The Hebrew word *kikkār* ("the surrounding region") signifies something round as (1) a loaf of bread (1 Sam 10:3); (2) a weight, namely a talent (1 Kings 10:10); or (3) the lower plain of the Jordan Valley (Gen 13:10). Here it means the environs or surrounding territory.

23–24 On Benjamin (v.23) see the comment on Ezra 10:32. The name "Hasshub" also occurs in v.11, which means that we have either two men with the same name or the same man with two sections. An ostracon with the name Hasshub was found in the Yarkon basin near Tel Aviv (J. Kaplan, "The Archaeology and History of Tel Aviv-Jaffa," BA 35 [1972]: 87). "Ananiah" ("Yahweh has manifested himself") occurs only here as a personal name; it occurs in 11:32 as a site.
On "Henadad" (v.24) see Ezra 3:9.

25 "Palal" (possibly "[God] has judged") is found only here. "Uzai," perhaps short for "Azaniah" ("Yahweh has heard"), is also found only here. "Pedaiah" ("Yahweh has ransomed") occurs in the Murashu texts as *padāyaw* (Coogan, *Personal Names*, p. 33).
"The upper place" was probably the old place of David. Like Solomon's palace it would have a guardhouse (Jer 32:2). The "Gate of the Guard" (12:39) was probably located nearby.

26 "Ophel" ("swelling" or "bulge," hence a hill) was specifically the northern part of the southeast hill of Jerusalem that formed the original city of David, just south of the temple area (2 Chron 27:3; 33:14). Parts of the "wall of Ophel" were discovered by Charles Warren in 1867–70.
"The Water Gate" was a gate, not of the city, but of the palace-temple complex. It was called this because it led to the main source of water, the Gihon Spring. It must have encompassed a large area, for the reading of the Law took place there (8:1, 3, 16; 12:37). Other gates of the palace-temple were (1) the East Gate (v.29), (2) the Inspection Gate (v.31), and (3) the Gate of the Guard (12:39) (cf. 1 Macc 4:57; 2 Macc 1:8).

699

"The projecting tower" was on the crest of the Ophel Hill. In 1923–25 R.A.S. Macalister discovered a complex including a wall, a ramp, and a great tower, which he mistakenly ascribed to David and Solomon. Kenyon (*Jerusalem*, p. 115), in her excavations of 1961–67, demonstrated that the complex rests on ruins of houses destroyed by Nebuchadnezzar in 586 B.C. and must therefore be more recent. Kenyon believed that the tower dates to the second century B.C. Mazar (*Mountain*, p. 198; photos on pp. 196–97), however, comments thus on the tower: "It is not possible to determine whether it is hellenistic, or whether it had already been erected in Persian times. In the latter case, it may possibly be identified with the 'great projecting tower' described by Nehemiah (3:26–27)." Excavations in 1978 at the base of the tower revealed "for the first time in Jerusalem a Persian-period ceramic layer within clear stratigraphical context—solid archaeological evidence for that resettlement of the Babylonian exiles in the City of David" (Y. Shiloh, "City of David: Excavation 1978," BA 42 [1979]: 168). Shiloh, after excavations in 1978–82, dates the tower to the second century B.C. but has reinterpreted the ramp as a stepped stone structure supporting the Davidic Opel or central citadel area (see H. Shanks, "The City of David After Five Years of Digging," BAR 11.6 [1985]: 27–29).

27 The common people of Tekoa did double duty whereas the nobles of Tekoa shirked their responsibility (see v.5).

28 Athaliah entered "the entrance of the horse gate of the king's house" (RSV, 2 Chron 23:15) and was slain there. Jeremiah 31:40 states that the "Horse Gate," in the easternmost part of the city, was a gate through which one could reach the Kidron Valley.

29 The "East Gate" may have been the predecessor of the present "Golden Gate" (see Bowman, p. 694; Steckoll, *Gates of Jerusalem*, pp. 29–33). A storm that opened up a crack permitted the clandestine viewing of the arch of an earlier gate below the Golden Gate (G. Giacumakis, "The Gate Below the Golden Gate," *Near East Archaeological Society Bulletin*, 4 [1974]: 23–26; J. Fleming, "The Undiscovered Gate Beneath Jerusalem's Golden Gate," BAR 9.1 [1983]: 24–37).

30 "The sixth son of Zalaph" is an unparalleled expression. Perhaps the text is a corruption for "inhabitants of Zanoah."

31 Some of the goldsmiths apparently inhabited an area to the east of the walls of the temple area; others, however, worked on sections in the west (see v.8 above). Myers (*Ezra-Nehemiah*, p. 111) suggests that the "house" was not a residence but a building where temple functions were performed.

"The Inspection Gate" was in the northern part of the eastern temple. The word for "inspection," *mipqād*, is found in only three other passages beside this verse: (1) in 2 Samuel 24:9 where it means "numbering," "mustering"; (2) similarly in 1 Chronicles 21:5; and (3) in Ezekiel 43:21, where it means the "appointed" place for the sin offering to be burnt.

32 This verse brings us to the northeast corner of Jerusalem or back to the point of departure near the Sheep Gate (v.1).

We know from chapter 5 that there were deep economic differences in Judean society. With the exception of the nobles of Tekoa (v.5), everyone pitched in, from the high priest (v.1) to goldsmiths and perfume makers (vv.8, 31) and even women (v.12), to accomplish a common task. Some, like the commoners of Tekoa, even did more than their share (v.27). What an inspiring example of what can be done when God's people work together under dynamic leadership!

Viggo Olsen, who helped rebuild ten thousand houses in war-ravaged Bangladesh in 1972, derived unexpected inspiration from reading a chapter ordinarily considered one of the least interesting in the Bible: "I was struck . . . that no expert builders were listed in the 'Holy Land brigade.' There were priests, priests' helpers, goldsmiths, perfume makers, and women, but no expert builders or carpenters were named" (with J. Lockerbie, *Daktar* [Chicago: Moody, 1973], p. 324).

D. *Opposition to the Rebuilding of the Walls (4:1–23)*

1. *The derision of Sanballat and Tobiah*

4:1–5

> ¹When Sanballat heard that we were rebuilding the wall, he became angry and was greatly incensed. He ridiculed the Jews, ²and in the presence of his associates and the army of Samaria, he said, "What are those feeble Jews doing? Will they restore their wall? Will they offer sacrifices? Will they finish in a day? Can they bring the stones back to life from those heaps of rubble—burned as they are?"
>
> ³Tobiah the Ammonite, who was at his side, said, "What they are building—if even a fox climbed up on it, he would break down their wall of stones!"
>
> ⁴Hear us, O our God, for we are despised. Turn their insults back on their own heads. Give them over as plunder in a land of captivity. ⁵Do not cover up their guilt or blot out their sins from your sight, for they have thrown insults in the face of the builders.

1 The enumeration of the MT does not correspond to the English; 4:1 = 3:33 MT (see Notes). On "Sanballat" see the comment on 2:10.

"Became angry" derives from *ḥārāh*, which means "to be hot," as in "his nose became hot," i.e., his anger broke out (Gen 30:2; cf. 3:20; Ezra 10:14).

"Was greatly incensed" (from *kāʿas*) means "to be irritated" (cf. the reaction of Sanballat and his colleagues when they first heard of Nehemiah's arrival [2:19]).

2 "The army" translates *ḥayil*, which often means "strength," "wealth," but at times "army" (Exod 14:4; 2 Kings 6:14; Esth 8:11; Ezek 17:17). The LXX interprets it as part of a taunt: "So this is Samaria's strength, that the Judeans build a city!" Disputes between rival Persian governors were quite frequent, as the rivalry between the satraps Tissaphernes and Pharnabazus in western Asia Minor.

Sanballat rapidly fired five derisive questions to taunt the Jews and discourage them from their efforts.

1. "What are those feeble Jews doing?" The word "feeble" (*ʾǎmēlal*) is used only here in the sense of "frail," "miserable," "withered," "powerless." The JB renders the phrase "pathetic Jews" (cf. the cognate words *ʾǎmulāh*, "hot," "feverish," "weak" [Ezek 16:30], and *ʾumlal*, "to be frail," "to be in anguish," "to languish" [Ps 6:3]).

2. "Will they restore their wall?" The word translated "restore" usually means "to abandon." See comment on 3:8.

3. "Will they offer sacrifices?" The Jews eventually succeeded in offering sacrifices (12:43).

4. "Will they finish in a day?" Despite the furious activity of the Jews, the work seemed so great that it could hardly be finished in a short time.

5. "Can they bring the stones back to life ... burned as they are?" Fire had damaged the stones, which were probably limestone, and had caused much of the stone to crack and disintegrate.

3 On Tobiah see the comment on 2:10. The word translated "fox" (*šûʿāl*) occurs six times in the OT (Judg 15:4; Ps 63:10; S of Songs 2:15; Lam 5:18; Ezek 13:4). In some contexts it may designate "jackal." The jackal usually hunts in packs, whereas the fox is normally a nocturnal and solitary animal. The context therefore suggests that a fox is intended: the point of the sneer is that any wall the Jews built would be so flimsy that even the light footsteps of a solitary fox would collapse it (cf. G. Cansdale, *All the Animals of the Bible Lands* [Grand Rapids: Zondervan, 1970], pp. 124–26; H. Hoehner, "The Meaning of 'Fox,'" in *Herod Antipas* [Grand Rapids: Zondervan, 1972], pp. 343–47).

4–5 Compare 6:9, 14; 13:29. As in the imprecatory psalms (Pss 69:22–28; 79:12; 94; 109:14; 137:8–9; cf. ZPEB, 4:938–39), Nehemiah did not personally take action against his opponents but called down the vengeance of God. Ackroyd (*Chronicles, Ezra, Nehemiah,* pp. 277–78) remarked, "To understand such violent language, we need to appreciate fully the sense of the divine purpose at work, so that opposition is not seen in human terms but as opposition to God himself." Nehemiah's prayer borrows from the language of Jeremiah (Jer 12:3; 17:18; 18:21–23).

Notes

1 The verses of the EV do not follow the versification of the MT. The correspondences are as follows:

MT	EV
3:33	4:1
3:38	4:6
4:1	4:7
4:17	4:23

3 J.B. Bauer ("Der 'Fuchs' Neh 3,35 ein Belagerungsturm?" *Biblische Zeitschrift* 19 [1975]: 97–98) has made the unlikely suggestion that the term "fox" refers to a kind of siege tower.

2. The threat of attack

4:6–15

⁶So we rebuilt the wall till all of it reached half its height, for the people worked with all their heart.

⁷But when Sanballat, Tobiah, the Arabs, the Ammonites and the men of Ashdod heard that the repairs to Jerusalem's walls had gone ahead and that the gaps were being closed, they were very angry. ⁸They all plotted together to come and fight against Jerusalem and stir up trouble against it. ⁹But we prayed to our God and posted a guard day and night to meet this threat.

¹⁰Meanwhile, the people in Judah said, "The strength of the laborers is giving out, and there is so much rubble that we cannot rebuild the wall."

¹¹Also our enemies said, "Before they know it or see us, we will be right there among them and will kill them and put an end to the work."

¹²Then the Jews who lived near them came and told us ten times over, "Wherever you turn, they will attack us."

¹³Therefore I stationed some of the people behind the lowest points of the wall at the exposed places, posting them by families, with their swords, spears and bows. ¹⁴After I looked things over, I stood up and said to the nobles, the officials and the rest of the people, "Don't be afraid of them. Remember the Lord, who is great and awesome, and fight for your brothers, your sons and your daughters, your wives and your homes."

¹⁵When our enemies heard that we were aware of their plot and that God had frustrated it, we all returned to the wall, each to his own work.

6 "The people worked with all their heart" is literally "the people had a heart to work."

7 On Sanballat and Tobiah, see the comment on 2:10. On the Arabs see the comment at 2:19; on the Ammonites, at Ezra 9:1. Josephus (*Antiq.* XI, 174 [v.8]) also mentions the Moabites.

Ashdod, along with Ashkelon, Gaza, Ekron, and Gath, was one of the five major Philistine cities in the Late Bronze Age (Josh 11:22; 13:3). Ashdod was overrun by the Assyrians in the eighth century B.C. (Isa 20:1). As the prophets foretold (Jer 25:20; Zeph 2:4; Zech 9:6), Ashdod was then captured by the Neo-Babylonians (ANET, p. 308). With the Persian conquest alternate patches of the Palestinian coast were parceled out to the Phoenician cities of Tyre and Sidon, which provided ships for the Persian navy. During this period Ashdod was the most important city on the Philistine coast.

The site of Tel Ashdod was excavated from 1962 to 1972 by M. Dothan ("Ashdod of the Philistines," in Freedman and Greenfield, pp. 15–24; id., "Ashdod," in *Encyclopedia of Archaeological Excavations in the Holy Land*, ed. M. Avi-Yonah et al. [Jerusalem: Israel Exploration Society, 1975], 1:103–19).

The numerous enemies of the Jews became even more angry (see on v.1) as they heard of the progress on the repair of Jerusalem's walls.

8–9 "Plotted together" (v.8) comes from *qāṣar*, which means "to tie up," hence "to conspire" (cf. 1 Kings 15:27; 16:20).

"Trouble" (*tôʿāh*, "confusion," "chaos," "perversion") occurs only here and in Isaiah 32:6. Notice the balance between prayer and posting a guard (v.9).

10 "Laborers," the plural of *sabāl* ("burden bearer," "porter"), occurs only here and in 1 Kings 5:15; 2 Chronicles 2:2, 18; 34:13.

"Is giving out" (from *kāšal*, "to stumble," "to totter"; cf. Isa 3:8) depicts a worker tottering under the weight of his load and ready to fall at any step. The complaint, couched in poetic form in two lines of five words each, may reflect a song sung by the builders. Myers (*Ezra-Nehemiah*, p. 122) renders the refrain as follows:

> The strength of the burden bearer is drooping.
> The rubbish heap so vast;
> And we are unable by ourselves
> To rebuild the wall.

11 "Enemies" (pl. of *ṣar*, "adversary") would cause harm. A different word is used in v.15 (q.v.). Nehemiah must have had good sources of information to learn of these plots. The text indicates that the vigilance of Nehemiah and his fellow Jews forestalled any attempt at violent attack.

12 "Ten times over" is an idiomatic expression for "again and again" (Gen 31:41). The RSV emends *tāšûbû* ("you turn") to *yēšᵉbû* ("they live") and translates "from all the places where *they live* they will come up against us" (emphasis mine). This corresponds with the LXX: "They are coming against us from all sides."

13 "The exposed places" (pl. of *ṣᵉḥîaḥ*) derives from the verb *ṣāḥaḥ*, which means "to be white," thus a bare or exposed place. The word occurs only here and in Ezekiel 24:7; 26:4, 14. The related word *ṣᵉḥîḥāh* ("bare, scorched land") occurs only in Psalm 68:6.

Nehemiah posted men conspicuously in those areas most vulnerable along the wall—"the lowest points." The "sword" (*ḥereb*) is the most frequently mentioned weapon in the OT, occurring 407 times. For its metaphorical use see the comment on Ezra 9:7.

14–15 The best way to dispel fear—"Don't be afraid of them" (v.14; cf. Deut 3:22; 20:3; 31:6)—is to remember the Lord who alone is to be feared. "Enemies" (v.15) is the plural of *'ôyēb* (cf. Ezra 8:22, 31; Neh 5:9; 6:1, 16; 9:27–28).

3. *The rebuilding of the walls*

4:16–23

> ¹⁶From that day on, half of my men did the work, while the other half were equipped with spears, shields, bows and armor. The officers posted themselves behind all the people of Judah ¹⁷who were building the wall. Those who carried materials did their work with one hand and held a weapon in the other, ¹⁸and each of the builders wore his sword at his side as he worked. But the man who sounded the trumpet stayed with me.
>
> ¹⁹Then I said to the nobles, the officials and the rest of the people, "The work is extensive and spread out, and we are widely separated from each other along the wall. ²⁰Wherever you hear the sound of the trumpet, join us there. Our God will fight for us!"
>
> ²¹So we continued the work with half the men holding spears, from the first light of dawn till the stars came out. ²²At that time I also said to the people, "Have every man and his helper stay inside Jerusalem at night, so they can serve us as guards by night and workmen by day." ²³Neither I nor my brothers nor my men nor the guards with me took off our clothes; each had his weapon, even when he went for water.

16 "My men" derives from *na'ar*, which means "boy," "youth" (Gen 19:4); "young men" (1 Sam 30:17), "servants" (Gen 22:3), "a young man bearing armor" (1 Sam

14:1), and the member of a personal military retinue (1 Sam 21:2, 4). The term is used of the bodyguard of Nehemiah in 5:10 and 13:19.

"Spears" (*rᵉmāḥîm*) designates lances or spears with long shafts used as thrusting weapons (Num 25:7–8; 1 Kings 18:28). "Shields" (*māginnîm*) were small and round and were made of wood and wickerwork, for they were combustible (Ezek 39:9). From 2 Chronicles 18:33 it seems that *širyôn* ("armor") primarily designated breast-plates of metal or more probably of mail, which were joined to a lower appendage. In some cases such cuirasses may have been made of leather (cf. 1 Sam 17:38; 1 Kings 22:34; 2 Chron 26:14).

17 "Weapon" translates *šelaḥ*, which is a "missile" or a "javelin." The literal meaning would be that the burden bearers were so loaded that they could carry their loads with one hand and their weapons with the other. Others construe this to mean that the weapons were kept close at hand.

18–19 "Swords" were worn in a sheath (1 Sam 17:51) hung on a girdle (1 Sam 17:39; 18:4; 25:13; Ps 45:3). The trumpet mentioned here is the *shofar,* or ram's horn (Josh 6:4, 6, 8, 13), used for signaling as in times of attack (Num 10:5–10). Near the southwest corner of the temple, Mazar (*Mountain,* p. 138) found a stone from the parapet inscribed *le beit hat-teqi'ah* ("to the place of trumpeting"), which denoted the place where the trumpet was blown to mark the beginning of the Sabbath.

The MT and the Vulgate suggest that a single trumpeter accompanied Nehemiah; but the LXX and Peshitta, reading "next to him" (i.e., the builder), suggest a system of alarms. Josephus (*Antiq.* XI, 177 [v.8]) claims that Nehemiah stationed trumpeters at intervals of five hundred feet.

20 For the concept of the "Holy War" in which God fights for his people, see de Vaux, *Ancient Israel,* pp. 258–67 (cf. Josh 10:14, 42; Judg 4:14; 20:35; 2 Sam 5:24).

21 Work usually stopped at sunset (Deut 24:15; Matt 20:1–12). To work "till the stars came out" (cf. Job 9:9) indicates the earnestness of the people's efforts.

22 "His helper" is literally "his young man" or "servant" (cf. v.16 above). Though the ratio of returning slaves to free men was relatively high (see Ezra 2:65), it is improbable that each builder had a servant. More plausibly each builder had a young man as an assistant. Even those from outside Jerusalem stayed in the city at night so that some of them could serve as sentries.

23 The last three words of this verse—'*îš šilḥô hammāyim*—are notoriously difficult to interpret; they are literally "each man his weapon the water." Several possible interpretations of this puzzling phrase follow:

1. The NIV rendering is similar to that of the RV: "every one (went with) his weapon (to) the water," and the JPS: "every one that went to the water had his weapon." This would parallel the way Gideon's selected men drank their water with weapons in hand as an indication of their vigilance.

2. Many scholars would emend the word *hammāyim* ("water") to *bîmînô* ("in his right hand"; cf. NEB, "each keeping his right hand on his weapon"; RSV, "each kept his weapon in his hand").

3. The Vulgate took the word *šilḥô,* not in the sense of "his weapon," but as a verb

meaning "stripped himself": *unusquisque tantum nudabatur ad baptismum* ("every one stripped himself when he was to be washed"). This sense was followed by the KJV: "every one put them off for washing."

4. The LXX omitted the phrase altogether. Though the precise meaning of the verse is not clear, the implication is that constant preparedness was the rule. According to Josephus (*Antiq.* XI, 177 [v.8]), Nehemiah "himself made the rounds of the city by night, never tiring either through work or lack of food and sleep, neither of which he took for pleasure but as a necessity."

E. Social and Economic Problems (5:1–19)

1. The complaints of the poor

5:1–5

> ¹Now the men and their wives raised a great outcry against their Jewish brothers. ²Some were saying, "We and our sons and daughters are numerous; in order for us to eat and stay alive, we must get grain."
> ³Others were saying, "We are mortgaging our fields, our vineyards and our homes to get grain during the famine."
> ⁴Still others were saying, "We have had to borrow money to pay the king's tax on our fields and vineyards. ⁵Although we are of the same flesh and blood as our countrymen and though our sons are as good as theirs, yet we have to subject our sons and daughters to slavery. Some of our daughters have already been enslaved, but we are powerless, because our fields and our vineyards belong to others."

The economic crisis faced by Nehemiah is described in chapter 5, in the middle of his major effort to rebuild the walls of Jerusalem. Since the building of the wall lasted only fifty-two days (6:15), many scholars have considered it unlikely that Nehemiah would have called a great assembly (v.7) in the midst of such a project. They suggest that the assembly was called only after the rebuilding of the wall, taking v.14 as retrospective.

On the other hand, the economic pressure created by the rebuilding program may have brought to light problems long simmering that had to be solved before work could proceed. This is the position of E. Neufeld ("The Rate of Interest and the Text of Nehemiah 5:11," JQR 44 [1953–54]: 203–4).

Among the classes affected by the economic crisis were (1) the landless who were short of food (v.2); (2) the landowners who were compelled to mortgage their properties (v.3); (3) those forced to borrow money at exorbitant rates because of oppressive taxation (v.4); and (4) those forced to sell their children into slavery (v.5).

1 The gravity of the situation is underscored in that the wives joined in the protest as the people ran short of funds and supplies to feed their families. Significantly, also, their complaints were not lodged against the foreign authorities but against their own fellow countrymen who were exploiting their poorer brethren at a time when both were needed to defend the country. The poignant cry of the oppressed people is a cry to God for justice (cf. Exod 3:7; 22:22–23; Ps 9:12; Isa 5:7).

2 Some would prefer to read *rabbîm* ("numerous") as *'ōrᵉḇîm* ("taken for pledge"), as in v.3 (cf. Exod 21:2; Lev 25:39–41; Deut 15:12). Thus the NEB renders "daughters as pledges."

3 Economic conditions forced even the considerable property owners to mortgage to the aggrandizement of the wealthy few (cf. Isa 5:8). The rich got richer, the poor poorer.

The economic situation was aggravated by the natural conditions that had produced a famine. Some seventy-five years earlier the prophet Haggai had referred to a time of drought, when food was insufficient (Hag 1:5–11). Such hardships were considered expressions of God's judgment (Isa 51:19; Jer 14:13–18; Amos 4:6). In times of dire need the wealthy usually have enough stored up to feed themselves. It is the poor who suffer because of the huge rise in prices caused by scarcities.

4 On taxes see the comments at Ezra 4:13, 20; 6:8; 7:24. It is estimated that the Persian king collected the equivalent of twenty million darics a year in taxes. As Olmstead (*Persian Empire*, p. 298) points out: "Little of this vast sum was ever returned to the satrapies. It was the custom to melt down the gold and silver and to pour it into jars which were then broken and the bullion stored." At Susa alone Alexander found nine thousand talents of coined gold (about 270 tons) and forty-thousand talents of silver (about 1,200 tons) stored up as bullion.

As coined money was increasingly taken out of circulation, inflation became rampant. As M. Dandamayev ("Achaemenid Babylonia," *Ancient Mesopotamia*, ed. I.M. Diakonoff [Moscow: Nauka, 1969], p. 308) observes:

> Documents from Babylonia show that many inhabitants of this satrapy too had to mortgage their fields and orchards to get silver for the payment of taxes to the king. In many cases they were unable to redeem their property, and became landless hired labourers; sometimes they were compelled to give away their children into slavery. According to some Egyptian data, the taxation was so heavy that the peasants fled to the cities, but were arrested by the nomarchs and brought back by force.

The acquisition of land by the Persians and its alienation from production helped produce a 50 percent rise in prices (W.H. Dubberstein, "Comparative Prices in Later Babylonia," AJSL 56 [1939]: 20–43).

5 "Our daughters have already been enslaved [from *kābaš*, 'to subjugate']." As *kābaš* can mean "to rape a woman" (cf. Esth 7:8), the JB renders "have even been raped." But the context favors the rendering "enslaved." In times of economic distress, families would borrow funds using members of the family as collateral. If a man could not repay the loan and its interest, his daughters, his sons, his wife, or even the man himself could be sold into bondage. A Hebrew who fell into debt would serve his creditor as "a hired servant" (Lev 25:39–40). He was to be released in the seventh year (Deut 15:12–18), unless he chose to stay voluntarily. The Code of Hammurabi (# 117, ANET, pp. 170–71) limited such bond service to three years.

The ironic tragedy of the situation for the exiles was that at least in Mesopotamia their families were together. Now because of dire economic necessities, their children were being sold into slavery.

Notes

---

4 The NIV, RSV, and other EV supply "on" before "our fields," implying that the tax was on the lands. The Lucianic version of the LXX reads, "We have borrowed money on our fields and vineyards to pay the king's tax," that is, "we have borrowed the value in money of our field and vineyards."

---

2. The cancellation of debts

5:6–13

⁶When I heard their outcry and these charges, I was very angry. ⁷I pondered them in my mind and then accused the nobles and officials. I told them, "You are exacting usury from your own countrymen!" So I called together a large meeting to deal with them ⁸and said: "As far as possible, we have bought back our Jewish brothers who were sold to the Gentiles. Now you are selling your brothers, only for them to be sold back to us!" They kept quiet, because they could find nothing to say.

⁹So I continued, "What you are doing is not right. Shouldn't you walk in the fear of our God to avoid the reproach of our Gentile enemies? ¹⁰I and my brothers and my men are also lending the people money and grain. But let the exacting of usury stop! ¹¹Give back to them immediately their fields, vineyards, olive groves and houses, and also the usury you are charging them—the hundredth part of the money, grain, new wine and oil."

¹²"We will give it back," they said. "And we will not demand anything more from them. We will do as you say."

Then I summoned the priests and made the nobles and officials take an oath to do what they had promised. ¹³I also shook out the folds of my robe and said, "In this way may God shake out of his house and possessions every man who does not keep this promise. So may such a man be shaken out and emptied!"

At this the whole assembly said, "Amen," and praised the LORD. And the people did as they had promised.

6 Nehemiah "was very angry." There are times when we must speak out against social injustices (cf. Matt 21:18–19; Mark 11:12–18; Luke 19:45–48; Eph 4:26).

7 "Pondered" renders the Niphal of *mālak* ("to take counsel with oneself"); the NEB renders "I mastered my feelings."

"Accused" derives from *rîb*, which means "to dispute, quarrel, conduct a lawsuit with." The NEB renders "reasoned with"; the RSV has "brought charges against."

"Usury" (*maššā'*) occurs only here, in v.10, and in 10:31 (32 MT). It means to impose a burden or claim for repayment of debt. Compare the related word *maš-šā'āh* ("secured loan based on security"; Deut 24:10; Prov 22:26).

The OT passages (Exod 22:25–27; Lev 25:35–37; Deut 23:19–20; 24:10–13) prohibiting the giving of loans at interest were not intended to prohibit commercial loans but rather the charging of interest to the impoverished so as to make a profit from the helplessness of one's neighbors (E. Neufeld, "The Prohibition Against Loans at Interest in Ancient Hebrew Laws," HUCA 26 [1955]: 355–412; cf. Jos. *Antiq.* IV, 266 [iv.3]).

8 Though it was possible to use a poor brother as a bond servant, he was not to be sold as a slave (Lev 25:39–42). The sale of fellow Hebrews as slaves to Gentiles was

a particularly callous offense and was always forbidden (Exod 21:8). Joseph's brothers nonetheless sold him to the Egyptians. We know from Joel 3:6 that Jews were being sold to Greeks (c. 520 B.C. ; cf. J.M. Myers, "Some Considerations Bearing on the Date of Joel," ZAW 74 [1962]: 177–95). The people's guilt was so obvious that "they kept quiet," having no rebuttal or excuse (cf. John 8:7–10).

9 Failure to treat others, especially fellow believers, with compassion is an insult to our Maker and a blot on our testimony (cf. Prov 14:31; 1 Peter 2:12–15).

10 The granting of loans is not condemned nor is the making of profit (cf. Ecclus 42:1–5a). But the OT condemns the greed and avarice that seeks a profit at the expense of people (Ps 119:36; Isa 56:9–12; 57:17; Jer 6:13; 8:10; 22:13–19; Ezek 22:12–14; 33:31). In view of the urgency of the situation, Nehemiah urged the creditors to relinquish their rights to repayment with interest. Solon, the great Athenian reformer (594 B.C.), adopted a similar policy (cf. E. Yamauchi, "Two Reformers Compared: Solon of Athens and Nehemiah of Jerusalem," *The Bible World*, ed. G. Rendsburg et al. [New York: KTAV, 1980], pp. 269–92).

11 "The hundredth part" (*mē'āh*) literally means the "hundred" pieces of silver. But in the context it must mean 1 percent, i.e., per month, or as the Vulgate translates it, *centesiman pecuniae*. Some scholars prefer to emend the word to *maššā'* ("burden") in the sense of usury as in v.7, but this does not seem warranted.

12–13 On "oath" (v.12) see the comment on Ezra 10:5. *Ḥōṣen* (v.13; cf. Akkad. *ḥuṣannu*) means "robe," "sash," "girdle." The KJV and RV translate the word "lap." Here it probably refers to the fold of the robe or the sash in which objects were kept.

On "Amen" compare Numbers 5:22 and Deuteronomy 27:15–26, where the people also assented to an oath and its curse formula by saying "Amen." "Amen" is derived from the verbal root *'mn*, which means in the Hiphil "to believe or trust" and in the Niphal "to be reliable."

"Amen" occurs in the OT only twenty-four times, twelve of these in Deuteronomy 27:15–26. It is used in passages that praise God (e.g., 1 Chron 16:36; Neh 8:6; cf. 1 Cor 14:16) and in doxologies (e.g., Pss 41, 72, 89, 106).

3. Nehemiah's unselfish example

5:14–19

> [14]Moreover, from the twentieth year of King Artaxerxes, when I was appointed to be their governor in the land of Judah, until his thirty-second year—twelve years—neither I nor my brothers ate the food allotted to the governor. [15]But the earlier governors—those preceding me—placed a heavy burden on the people and took forty shekels of silver from them in addition to food and wine. Their assistants also lorded it over the people. But out of reverence for God I did not act like that. [16]Instead, I devoted myself to the work on this wall. All my men were assembled there for the work; we did not acquire any land.
>
> [17]Furthermore, a hundred and fifty Jews and officials ate at my table, as well as those who came to us from the surrounding nations. [18]Each day one ox, six choice sheep and some poultry were prepared for me, and every ten days an abundant supply of wine of all kinds. In spite of all this, I never demanded the food allotted to the governor, because the demands were heavy on these people.
>
> [19]Remember me with favor, O my God, for all I have done for these people.

14 On a Nisan calendar the thirty-second year of Artaxerxes I ran from 1 April 433 B.C. to 19 April 432 B.C. (on a Tishri calendar, 25 Sept. 433 to 13 Oct. 432; cf. Introduction: Chronology).

Nehemiah served his first term as governor for twelve years before being recalled to court (13:6), after which he returned for a second term of indeterminate length.

Provincial governors normally assessed the people in their provinces for their support, e.g., "food allotted to the governor." But Nehemiah, like Paul, bent over backwards and sacrificed even what was normally his due to serve as an example to the people (1 Cor 9; 2 Thess 3:8).

15 "Governors" is the plural of *peḥāh* (also the same in Aram.), which is used of Sheshbazzar (Ezra 5:14), Zerubbabel (Hag 1:1, 14; 2:2), and various Persian officials (Ezra 5:3, 6; 6:6-7, 13; 8:36; Neh 2:7, 9; 3:7 et al.). Nehemiah was certainly not referring here to Ezra and Zerubbabel. K. Galling ("Serubbabel und der Wiederaufbau des Tempels," *Verbannung und Heimkehr,* ed. A. Kuschke [Tübingen: J.C.B. Mohr, 1961], p. 96) believes that Judah did not have governors before Nehemiah and suggests that this refers to governors of Samaria. New archaeological evidence, however, confirms that the reference is to previous governors of Judah (cf. Notes; on Persian satraps see *Herodotus* 3.88; Xenophon *Cyropaedia* 8.6.1-7).

"Placed a heavy burden" literally means "made heavy (the burden of taxation)." The KJV's "were chargeable" is an inadequate rendering. Persian practice usually exempted temple personnel, which made the burden on the laity much heavier.

"Forty shekels of silver from them in addition to food and wine" is literally "of them for bread and wine after [*aḥar*] forty shekels of silver." The NIV follows the KJV ("beside") in rendering the preposition "in addition." Other scholars and versions follow the Vulgate, which reads "daily," that is, the cost of feeding the entourage amounted to about forty shekels per day (cf. comment on v.2).

If the governors themselves were extortionate, their "assistants" often proved even more oppressive (cf. Matt 18:21-35; 20:25-28).

A letter on a Hebrew ostracon from Meṣad Ḥashavyahu on the coast (seventh cent. B.C.) bears the poignant plea of a poor farmer whose garment had been taken by the governor's officer and had not been returned in contravention of Exodus 22:26-27 (cf. J. Naveh, "A Hebrew Letter From the Time of Jeremiah," *Archaeology* 15.2 [1962]: 108-11).

16 Nehemiah's behavior as governor was guided by principles of service rather than by opportunism. In the Roman period honest governors like Cicero were exceptional. Roman governors who came to Palestine were rapacious (cf. Jos. *War* II, 272-73 [xiv.1]).

17 When Solomon became king he sacrificed 22,000 oxen and 120,000 sheep and held a great seven-day feast for the assembly (1 Kings 4:23; 8:62-65). A text found at Nimrud has Ashurnasirpal II feasting 69,574 people for ten days (M.E.L. Mallowan, "Nimrud," in D.W. Thomas, ed., *Archaeology and OT,* p. 62).

As part of his social responsibility, a governor or ruler was expected to entertain lavishly. R. North ("Civil Authority," p. 436) comments, "The generosity of Nehemiah as of wealthy Bedouin sheiks is felt to consist in the fact that they let any number of poor relations come to dinner."

18 Compare Nehemiah's daily provisions with Solomon's (1 Kings 4:22–23). The people of Judah were afraid to present a defective sheep to Nehemiah's predecessor, but they were not above offering such an animal to the Lord (Mal 1:8).

"Poultry" (*ṣipporîm*, "birds") was domesticated in the Indus River valley by 2000 B.C. and was brought to Egypt by the reign of Thutmose III (fifteenth cent. B.C.). Poultry was known in Mesopotamia and Greece by the eighth century. The earliest evidence in Palestine is the celebrated seal of Jaazaniah (dated c. 600 B.C.), which depicts a fighting cock.

The meat listed here would perhaps be sufficient to provide one meal for 600 to 800 persons, including the 150 Jews and officials mentioned in v. 17.

19 Some have suggested that Nehemiah's memoirs were inscribed as a memorial set up in the temple (cf. 13:14, 22, 31). According to Ecclesiasticus 17:22, "the alms of a man are as a signet with him, and he will keep the good deeds of man as the apple of the eye" (cf. Heb 6:10). A striking parallel to Nehemiah's prayer is found in Nebuchadnezzar II's prayer to his god: "O Marduk, my lord, do remember my deeds favorably as good [deeds], may (these) my good deeds be always before your mind" (ANET, p. 307).

Notes

15 In 1974 a collection of about seventy bullae (clay seal-impressions) and two seals from an unknown provenance were shown to N. Avigad. One seal is the first to bear the inscription YHD, the Persian designation of the province of Judah as seal impressions and coins had indicated. Avigad dates the seals to the late sixth and early fifth century B.C. The mixture of the Hebrew language written in the Aramaic script is similar to the mixed linguistic character of Ezra and Daniel according to Avigad (*Bullae and Seals*, p. 19): "We may assume that in the period of the Return from Exile—the early Persian period in Eretz-Israel—the two tongues, Hebrew and Aramaic, were used concurrently."

The new evidence helps settle a controversy as to the interpretation of a word found on seal impressions from Ramat Rahel, which F. M. Cross ("Judean Stamps," *Eretz Israel* 9 [1969]: 20–27) read as *pḥr'* ("potter") instead of *pḥw'* ("governor"). The new bullae list several persons designated by a title that must be read as *pḥw'*, which disproves the contention of Alt, Rudolph, and Galling that there were no true governors of Judah before Nehemiah. On the basis of this new evidence, together with data from other sources, Avigad (*Bullae and Seals*, p. 35; cf. Talmon, IDBSup, pp. 325, 327) reconstructs a list of the governors of Judah.

Name	Source	Date
Sheshbazzar	Ezra 1:8; 5:14	538
Zerubbabel	Hag 1:1, 14	515
Elnathan	bulla and seal	late 6th
Yeho'ezer	jar impression	early 5th
Ahzai	jar impression	early 5th
Nehemiah	Neh 5:14; 12:26	445—433
Bagohi	Cowley 30:1	408
(Bagoas)		
Yehezqiyah	coins	330

F. *The Completion of the Walls Despite Opposition (6:1–19)*

1. *Attempts to snare Nehemiah*

6:1–9

> ^{6:1}When word came to Sanballat, Tobiah, Geshem the Arab and the rest of our enemies that I had rebuilt the wall and not a gap was left in it—though up to that time I had not set the doors in the gates— ²Sanballat and Geshem sent me this message: "Come, let us meet together in one of the villages on the plain of Ono."
>
> But they were scheming to harm me; ³so I sent messengers to them with this reply: "I am carrying on a great project and cannot go down. Why should the work stop while I leave it and go down to you?" ⁴Four times they sent me the same message, and each time I gave them the same answer.
>
> ⁵Then, the fifth time, Sanballat sent his aide to me with the same message, and in his hand was an unsealed letter ⁶in which was written:
>
> > "It is reported among the nations—and Geshem says it is true—that you and the Jews are plotting to revolt, and therefore you are building the wall. Moreover, according to these reports you are about to become their king ⁷and have even appointed prophets to make this proclamation about you in Jerusalem: 'There is a king in Judah!' Now this report will get back to the king; so come, let us confer together."
>
> ⁸I sent him this reply: "Nothing like what you are saying is happening; you are just making it up out of your head."
>
> ⁹They were all trying to frighten us, thinking, "Their hands will get too weak for the work, and it will not be completed."
>
> But I prayed, "Now strengthen my hands."

A description of further attempts to frustrate the efforts of Nehemiah is recorded in chapter 6. Barber (p. 97) notes that Nehemiah's enemies resorted "first to *intrigue* (Nehemiah 6:1–4), then to *innuendo* (6:5–9), and finally to *intimidation* (6:10 –14) to achieve their end."

1–4 On Sanballat, Tobiah, and Geshem (v.1), see the comments on 2:10, 19. "Ono" (v.2) was located seven miles southeast of Joppa near Lod (Lydda). It was in the westernmost area settled by the returning Jews (Ezra 2:33; Neh 7:37; 11:35). It may have been proposed as a kind of neutral territory, but Nehemiah recognized the invitation as a trap (cf. Jer 41:1–3; 1 Macc 12:39–53; 16:11–24).

Nehemiah's sharp reply (v.3) may seem like a haughty rebuff to a reasonable invitation. But he correctly discerned the insincerity of his enemies and their evil designs. His own utter dedication to the great enterprise of the wall made that his top priority. He refused to be distracted with lesser matters that would divert and dissipate his energies. Nehemiah's foes were persistent (v.4), but he was equally persistent in steadfastly resisting their blandishments.

5–7 Letters during this period were ordinarily written on a papyrus or leather sheet, rolled up, tied with a string, and sealed with a clay bulla (seal impression). The latter was intended to seal the letter and to guarantee its authenticity. Sanballat obviously intended that the contents should be made known also to the public at large (v.5). The Persian kings did not tolerate the claims of pretenders to kingship (v.6; cf. the Behistun Inscription of Darius 16–18 [Kent, p. 120]).

On v.7 compare vv.12, 14. Usurpers such as Jeroboam (1 Kings 11:29–31) and Jehu (2 Kings 9:1–3) hired false prophets. Such mercenary prophets were condemned by Amos (7:10–17). Kellermann (*Nehemiah Quellen*, pp. 156–59), who has argued that Nehemiah was of Davidic descent, believes there may have been some basis for the accusation "there is a king" (cf. Zech 6:9–14). Others are sharply critical of such a thesis (e.g., Emerton, "Review of Kellermann," p. 179).

8–9 Nehemiah does not mince words in his reply. He calls the report a lie (v.8). He may well have sent his own messenger to the king to assure him of his loyalty. "Making it up" is from *bāḏā'*, which occurs only here and in 1 Kings 12:33. The JB renders "It is a figment of your own imagination."

"Their hands will get too weak" (v.9) uses the verb *rāpāh* ("to become slack"). The Hebrew idiom "to cause the hands to drop" means to demoralize as in Ezra 4:4. Jeremiah was accused of "weakening [*merappē'*] the hands of the soldiers" (Jer 38:4; NIV, "discouraging the soldiers"). The Lachish Ostracon VI speaks of people in Jerusalem "who weaken the hands of the land and make the city slack so that it fails."

The Hebrew has an imperative: "strengthen." The RSV inserts "O God" to indicate that this is a prayer. This is to be preferred to the LXX, Vulgate, and Syriac, which have "I strengthened my hands" (cf. NEB, "So I applied myself to it with greater energy"; cf. Pss 28:7–8; 29:11; 46:1; Isa 40:31).

Notes

6 The variant *Gashmu* (cf. NIV mg.) is closer to the original Arabian form of the name than "Geshem."

2. *The hiring of false prophets*

6:10–14

> [10] One day I went to the house of Shemaiah son of Delaiah, the son of Mehetabel, who was shut in at his home. He said, "Let us meet in the house of God, inside the temple, and let us close the temple doors, because men are coming to kill you—by night they are coming to kill you."
>
> [11] But I said, "Should a man like me run away? Or should one like me go into the temple to save his life? I will not go!" [12] I realized that God had not sent him, but that he had prophesied against me because Tobiah and Sanballat had hired him. [13] He had been hired to intimidate me so that I would commit a sin by doing this, and then they would give me a bad name to discredit me.
>
> [14] Remember Tobiah and Sanballat, O my God, because of what they have done; remember also the prophetess Noadiah and the rest of the prophets who have been trying to intimidate me.

10 Since Shemaiah had access to the temple, Bowman (in loc.) suggests that he was probably a priest, "possibly one of those who were particularly friendly with Tobiah (cf. vss. 12, 18–19; 13:7–9)."

"Was shut in" (*āṣûr*) means "shut up" or "imprisoned" (cf. Jer 36:5). The significance of the phrase here is obscure. Three proposals have been suggested: (1) that Shemaiah had an ecstatic seizure (cf. 1 Kings 22:10; Isa 8:11; Ezek 3:14), (2) that Shemaiah was shut up temporarily because of ritual impurity (cf. 1 Kings 14:10; Jer 33:1), and (3) that Shemaiah had shut himself up as a symbolic action to indicate that his own life was in danger and to suggest that both must flee to the temple.

The last suggestion makes the most sense. Most would interpret Shemaiah's words as a ruse in which he pretended to be in personal danger and tried as a friend of Nehemiah to get him to take refuge in the temple. Shemaiah could legitimately have proposed that Nehemiah should take refuge in the temple area at the altar of asylum (Exod 21:13; 1 Kings 1:50–53; 2:28–34; 8:64; 2 Kings 16:14), but not for him to take refuge in "the house of God," the temple building itself.

A.L. Ivry ("Nehemiah 6,10: Politics and the Temple," JSJ 3 [1972]: 38) suggests an even more complex plot: "It would appear that Shemaiah is indeed suggesting something much more plausible and more diabolical than refuge in the temple, viz., commandeering and possession of it. This is the 'sin' against which Nehemiah reacts so sharply."

11–12 Even if his life was genuinely threatened, Nehemiah was not a coward who would run into hiding (v.11). Nor would he transgress the law to save his life. As a layman he was, of course, not permitted to enter the sanctuary (Exod 29:33; 33:20; Num 18:7). When King Uzziah dared offer incense in the sanctuary, he was stricken with leprosy (2 Chron 26:16–20). That Shemaiah proposed a course of action contrary to God's word revealed him as a false prophet (Matt 24:3–10).

13 Had Nehemiah wavered in the face of the threat, his leadership would have been discredited and morale among the people would have plummeted.

14 In the OT only three other women are mentioned as being prophetesses: (1) Miriam (Exod 15:20), (2) Deborah (Judg 4:4), and (3) Huldah (2 Kings 22:14; 2 Chron 34:22). The rabbinic traditions add another four: Sarah, Hannah, Abigail, and Esther. The prophets and prophetesses may have favored a policy of accommodation and objected to Nehemiah's work as divisive (cf. Isa 9:15; 28:7; Jer 2:26; 27:9–10; 28:9, 15–17; 29:24–32; Ezek 13:2, 17; Amos 7:14; Mic 3:5–11).

3. The completion of the walls

6:15–19

> 15So the wall was completed on the twenty-fifth of Elul, in fifty-two days. 16When all our enemies heard about this, all the surrounding nations were afraid and lost their self-confidence, because they realized that this work had been done with the help of our God.
>
> 17Also, in those days the nobles of Judah were sending many letters to Tobiah, and replies from Tobiah kept coming to them. 18For many in Judah were under oath to him, since he was son-in-law to Shecaniah son of Arah, and his son

Jehohanan had married the daughter of Meshullam son of Berekiah. ¹⁹Moreover, they kept reporting to me his good deeds and then telling him what I said. And Tobiah sent letters to intimidate me.

15 Assuming a Nisan calendar (see Introduction: Chronology), 25 Elul (the sixth month) would have been 27 October 445 B.C. Josephus (*Antiq.* XI, 168 [v.7]) gives 440 B.C. as the date of Nehemiah's arrival and dates the completion of the wall in December 437, two years and four months later. Albright and Bright favor the longer period of time for the rebuilding.

The archaeological investigations of Kenyon, however, confirm the biblical text. Her discoveries indicate that the circuit of the wall in Nehemiah's day was much reduced. She found what she believes was part of Nehemiah's wall on the crest of the rock scarp on the summit of Ophel: "It was solidly built, *c.* 2.75 metres thick, but its finish was rough, as might be expected in work executed so rapidly" (Kenyon, *Jerusalem,* pp. 111; id., *Digging Up,* pp. 183–84).

Remarkably the walls neglected for nearly a century and a half were rebuilt in less than two months when the people were galvanized into action by the catalyst of Nehemiah's leadership. One might have expected a description of the celebration and the dedication of the wall immediately on its completion, but we do not encounter this until 12:27.

16 "Lost their self-confidence" is literally "were much cast down in their own eyes." Some would emend *wayyipp⁽e⁾lû* ("were much cast down") to *wayyipālēʾ* ("it was a wonderful thing"; cf. JB, "they were deeply impressed"). The context, however, favors the unemended text. The rapid completion of the wall despite such odds could only have been accomplished with God's aid, and knowledge of this fact thoroughly discomfited Nehemiah's enemies (cf. 1 Chron 14:17).

17–18 Tobiah was doubly related to influential families in Judah. He was married to the daughter of Shecaniah, and his son Jehohanan was married to the daughter of Meshullam, who had helped repair the wall of Jerusalem (3:4, 30).

19 Tobiah's friends and relatives acted as a Fifth Column. They attempted both to propagandize on behalf of Tobiah and to act as an intelligence system for him. Tobiah himself kept on trying to frighten Nehemiah.

G. *The List of Exiles (7:1–73a)*

1. Provisions for the protection of Jerusalem

7:1–3

¹After the wall had been rebuilt and I had set the doors in place, the gatekeepers and the singers and the Levites were appointed. ²I put in charge of Jerusalem my brother Hanani, along with Hananiah the commander of the citadel, because he was a man of integrity and feared God more than most men do. ³I said to them, "The gates of Jerusalem are not to be opened until the sun is hot. While the

gatekeepers are still on duty, have them shut the doors and bar them. Also appoint residents of Jerusalem as guards, some at their posts and some near their own houses."

1 On the gatekeepers see Ezra 2:42, on the singers Ezra 2:41, and on the Levites Ezra 2:40. The gatekeepers normally guarded the temple gates (1 Chron 9:17–19; 26:12–19); but because of the danger in the city, they were appointed to stand guard at the city gates along with the singers and the Levites.

2 Hanani (see comment on 1:2) is a shortened form of the name Hananiah. Hanani was placed in charge of Jerusalem, that is, over Rephaiah and Shallum who were over sections of the city (3:9, 12).

The Hebrew phrase translated "along with Hananiah" may be interpreted in two ways: to denote two different individuals or as explanatory, i.e., "my brother Hanani, viz., Hananiah." Most EV (KJV, RSV, NEB, JB, NAB, NIV) translate the phrase to designate two individuals.

On "the citadel" (*bîrāh*), see the comment on 1:1. The KJV consistently translates the word "palace," but it was actually a fortress located at the northwest corner of Jerusalem (cf. Avi-Yonah, *Herodian Period*, p. 213).

Theoretically garrisons were directly controlled by the king, and their commanders were "enrolled upon the king's list" (Xenophon *Cyropaedia* 8.6.9). In practice, however, governors like Nehemiah could appoint their own men.

"A man of integrity" (*'îš 'emet*, lit., "a man of truth") is used once elsewhere, in the plural in Exodus 18:21: "select . . . trustworthy men" (cf. Paul's praise of Timothy [Phil 2:19–21]).

3 Normally the gates were opened at dawn, but this was to be delayed until the sun was high in the heavens (Gen 18:1; Exod 16:21; 1 Sam 11:9). The OT distinguishes the sun from the stars, not by its great light, but by its heat (Exod 16:21; 1 Sam 11:9; Ps 121:6; Isa 49:10). Inhabitants of the Near East are conscious of the sun's heat, especially during the summer (Ps 32:4). The gates were to be shut and bolted before the guards went off duty.

Notes

2 "Hananiah" occurs five times in the OT (cf. comment on Ezra 10:28). It also appears as *Hanana* on a bulla (Avigad, *Bullae and Seals*, p. 5, # 3). Both the long form *Ḥananyaw* and the short form *Ḥananī* appear in the Murashu texts (Coogan, *Personal Names*, p. 111).

---

2. Nehemiah's discovery of the list

7:4–5

⁴Now the city was large and spacious, but there were few people in it, and the houses had not yet been rebuilt. ⁵So my God put it into my heart to assemble the

nobles, the officials and the common people for registration by families. I found the genealogical record of those who had been the first to return. This is what I found written there:

4 "Large and spacious" (*raḥᵃbat yādayim ûgᵉdōlāh*) is literally "wide of two hands and large." This expression means extending to the right and left. *Rāḥāb* designates something "extensive" or "widespread," as the "wide sea" (Job 11:9; Ps 104:25), the "broad land" (Exod 3:8; Neh 9:35), and the "extensive" city of Babylon (Jer 51:58). As the actual circuit of the walls of the city had been contracted, the expressions must be relative to the number of people who could still be housed once the damaged houses were rebuilt.

5 On "registration by families" compare v.64; see Ezra 2:62 and 8:1, 3.

3. The list of exiles (7:6–69)

a. Families

7:6–25

⁶These are the people of the province who came up from the captivity of the exiles whom Nebuchadnezzar king of Babylon had taken captive (they returned to Jerusalem and Judah, each to his own town, ⁷in company with Zerubbabel, Jeshua, Nehemiah, Azariah, Raamiah, Nahamani, Mordecai, Bilshan, Mispereth, Bigvai, Nehum and Baanah):

The list of the men of Israel:

⁸the descendants of Parosh	2,172
⁹of Shephatiah	372
¹⁰of Arah	652
¹¹of Pahath-Moab (through the line of Jeshua and Joab)	2,818
¹²of Elam	1,254
¹³of Zattu	845
¹⁴of Zaccai	760
¹⁵of Binnui	648
¹⁶of Bebai	628
¹⁷of Azgad	2,322
¹⁸of Adonikam	667
¹⁹of Bigvai	2,067
²⁰of Adin	655
²¹of Ater (through Hezekiah)	98
²²of Hashum	328
²³of Bezai	324
²⁴of Hariph	112
²⁵of Gibeon	95

6–7 The following list of names is essentially the same as that found in Ezra 2:1–70. See the commentary on that section for the nature of the list and the reasons for the numerous variations in names and discrepancies in numbers.

"Raamiah" (v.7) means "Yahweh has thundered" (Ezra 2:2 has "Reelaiah"). "Nahamani" is a variant form for Nehemiah. It does not occur in Ezra 2:2. The name is found in the Murashu texts as *na-aḥ-ma-nu* (Coogan, *Personal Names*, p. 78). "Nehum" is probably an error for Rehum, which appears in the Ezra list.

10 Ezra 2:5 lists 775.

11 Ezra 2:6 lists 2,812.

13 Ezra 2:8 lists 945.

15 Ezra 2:10 has Bani and lists 642.

16 Ezra 2:11 lists 623.

17 Ezra 2:12 lists 1,222.

18 Ezra 2:13 lists 666.

19 Ezra 2:14 lists 2,056.

20 Ezra 2:15 lists 454.

22 Ezra 2:19 lists 223.

23 Ezra 2:17 lists 323.

24 "Hariph" means "sharp" or "autumn." Ezra 2:18 has Jorah.

25 Ezra 2:20 has Gibbar, which may be a corruption of Gibeon.

b. Villagers

7:26–38

[26]the men of Bethlehem and Netophah	188
[27]of Anathoth	128
[28]of Beth Azmaveth	42
[29]of Kiriath Jearim, Kephirah and Beeroth	743
[30]of Ramah and Geba	621
[31]of Micmash	122
[32]of Bethel and Ai	123
[33]of the other Nebo	52
[34]of the other Elam	1,254
[35]of Harim	320
[36]of Jericho	345
[37]of Lod, Hadid and Ono	721
[38]of Senaah	3,930

26 Ezra 2:21–22 has "the men of Bethlehem 123, of Netophah 56," which would total 179.

28 Ezra 2:24 has simply Azmaveth.

32 Ezra 2:28 lists 223.

718

33 Ezra 2:29 has simply Nebo.

37 Ezra 2:33 lists 725.

38 Ezra 2:35 lists 3,630.

c. Priests

7:39–42

39The priests:

the descendants of Jedaiah (through the family of Jeshua)	973
40of Immer	1,052
41of Pashhur	1,247
42of Harim	1,017

39–42 The names and numbers are identical with the parallel passage in Ezra 2:36 –69. Perhaps the lists of priests were kept more accurately than those of the laity.

d. Levites

7:43

43The Levites:

the descendants of Jeshua (through Kadmiel through the line of Hodaviah)	74

43 The very small number of Levites who returned is striking. When Ezra was about to leave Mesopotamia, he found not one Levite in the company; so he delayed his departure until he could enlist some Levites (Ezra 8:15–20).

e. Temple staff

7:44–60

44The singers:

the descendants of Asaph	148

45The gatekeepers:

the descendants of Shallum, Ater, Talmon, Akkub, Hatita and Shobai	138

46The temple servants:

the descendants of
Ziha, Hasupha, Tabbaoth,
47Keros, Sia, Padon,
48Lebana, Hagaba, Shalmai,
49Hanan, Giddel, Gahar,
50Reaiah, Rezin, Nekoda,
51Gazzam, Uzza, Paseah,
52Besai, Meunim, Nephussim,
53Bakbuk, Hakupha, Harhur,
54Bazluth, Mehida, Harsha,

⁵⁵Barkos, Sisera, Temah,
⁵⁶Neziah and Hatipha

⁵⁷The descendants of the servants of Solomon:

the descendants of
    Sotai, Sophereth, Perida,
    ⁵⁸Jaala, Darkon, Giddel,
    ⁵⁹Shephatiah, Hattil,
    Pokereth-Hazzebaim and Amon

⁶⁰The temple servants and the
    descendants of the servants of Solomon   392

44 Ezra 2:41 lists 128.

45 Ezra 2:42 lists 139.

47 Ezra 2:44 has Siaha instead of Sia.

48 The Hebrew MSS of Ezra 2:46 that we have has Shamlai, which is probably an error for Shalmai.

52 Ezra 2:50 includes Asnah, which is lacking in Nehemiah.

57 Ezra 2:55 has Hassophereth and Peruda instead of Perida.

59 Ezra 2:57 has Ami instead of Amon.

f. *Individuals without evidence of genealogies*

    7:61–65

⁶¹The following came up from the towns of Tel Melah, Tel Harsha, Kerub, Addon and Immer, but they could not show that their families were descended from Israel:

    ⁶²the descendants of
        Delaiah, Tobiah and Nekoda   642

⁶³And from among the priests:

    the descendants of
        Hobaiah, Hakkoz and Barzillai (a man who had married a
        daughter of Barzillai the Gileadite and was called by that
        name).
⁶⁴These searched for their family records, but they could not find them and so were excluded from the priesthood as unclean. ⁶⁵The governor, therefore, ordered them not to eat any of the most sacred food until there should be a priest ministering with the Urim and Thummim.

61 On these towns see the comment on Ezra 2:59.

62 Ezra 2:60 lists 652.

63–65 See the comments on Ezra 2:61–63.

720

g. Totals

7:66–69

⁶⁶The whole company numbered 42,360, ⁶⁷besides their 7,337 menservants and maidservants; and they also had 245 men and women singers. ⁶⁸There were 736 horses, 245 mules, ⁶⁹435 camels and 6,720 donkeys.

67 Ezra 2:65 lists 200 men and women singers.

68 Most Hebrew MSS lack this verse. On vv.66–69 see the comments on Ezra 2:64 –67.

4. Offerings for the work

7:70–72

⁷⁰Some of the heads of the families contributed to the work. The governor gave to the treasury 1,000 drachmas of gold, 50 bowls and 530 garments for priests. ⁷¹Some of the heads of the families gave to the treasury for the work 20,000 drachmas of gold and 2,200 minas of silver. ⁷²The total given by the rest of the people was 20,000 drachmas of gold, 2,000 minas of silver and 67 garments for priests.

70 "Drachmas" (*dark^emônîm*) were Greek coins weighing about 3/10 of an ounce; "1,000 drachmas" would weigh about 19 pounds. As a drachma was ordinarily a silver coin, the Hebrew word may designate the Persian daric. See the comment on Ezra 2:69.

71–72 The weight of "20,000 drachmas" (v.71) would be about 375 pounds; "2,200 minas" about 2,550 pounds; and "2,000 minas" (v.72) about 2,500 pounds.

5. Settlement of the exiles

7:73a

⁷³The priests, the Levites, the gatekeepers, the singers and the temple servants, along with certain of the people and the rest of the Israelites, settled in their own towns.

73a Many returning exiles may not have been from Jerusalem, whose population no doubt suffered the greatest casualties in the Babylonian attacks. These naturally returned to their own hometowns, leaving Jerusalem underpopulated (cf. 11:1–24).

H. Ezra's Preaching and the Outbreak of Revival (7:73b–10:39)

1. The public proclamation of the Scriptures

7:73b–8:12

When the seventh month came and the Israelites had settled in their towns, ^{8:1}all the people assembled as one man in the square before the Water Gate. They told Ezra the scribe to bring out the Book of the Law of Moses, which the LORD had commanded for Israel.

²So on the first day of the seventh month Ezra the priest brought the Law before the assembly, which was made up of men and women and all who were able to understand. ³He read it aloud from daybreak till noon as he faced the square before the Water Gate in the presence of the men, women and others who could understand. And all the people listened attentively to the Book of the Law.

⁴Ezra the scribe stood on a high wooden platform built for the occasion. Beside him on his right stood Mattithiah, Shema, Anaiah, Uriah, Hilkiah and Maaseiah; and on his left were Pedaiah, Mishael, Malkijah, Hashum, Hashbaddanah, Zechariah and Meshullam.

⁵Ezra opened the book. All the people could see him because he was standing above them; and as he opened it, the people all stood up. ⁶Ezra praised the LORD, the great God; and all the people lifted their hands and responded, "Amen! Amen!" Then they bowed down and worshiped the LORD with their faces to the ground.

⁷The Levites—Jeshua, Bani, Sherebiah, Jamin, Akkub, Shabbethai, Hodiah, Maaseiah, Kelita, Azariah, Jozabad, Hanan and Pelaiah—instructed the people in the Law while the people were standing there. ⁸They read from the Book of the Law of God, making it clear and giving the meaning so that the people could understand what was being read.

⁹Then Nehemiah the governor, Ezra the priest and scribe, and the Levites who were instructing the people said to them all, "This day is sacred to the LORD your God. Do not mourn or weep." For all the people had been weeping as they listened to the words of the Law.

¹⁰Nehemiah said, "Go and enjoy choice food and sweet drinks, and send some to those who have nothing prepared. This day is sacred to our Lord. Do not grieve, for the joy of the LORD is your strength."

¹¹The Levites calmed all the people, saying, "Be still, for this is a sacred day. Do not grieve."

¹²Then all the people went away to eat and drink, to send portions of food and to celebrate with great joy, because they now understood the words that had been made known to them.

Chapters 8–11 seem to interrupt the narrative of Nehemiah's work on the wall, but Keil (p. 227) maintains that "the facts narrated in chap. viii.-xi. might without any difficulty occur in the interval between the completion of the wall and its dedication."

The traditional view sees the reading of the Law by Ezra as the first reference to him in about thirteen years since his arrival in 458 B.C. Since Ezra was commissioned to teach the Law (Ezra 7:14, 25–26), it seems strange that there was such a long delay in the proclamation of it. Adeney (p. 273) suggests that "he had not found a fitting opportunity for revealing his secret to this people before all his reforming efforts were arrested, and the city and its inhabitants trampled under foot by their envious neighbours. Then came Nehemiah's reconstruction. Still the consideration of the Law remained in abeyance."

Other scholars have argued that Nehemiah 8 is out of place inasmuch as 1 Esdras 9:37–55 (which parallels Neh 7:73–8:13a) and Josephus (who follows Esdras) place the reading of the Law after Ezra 10. These scholars believe that the reading of the Law took place soon after Ezra's arrival—if this had been in the year of the arrival, the seventh month would have been 2 to 30 October (see Bright, *History of Israel*, p. 388). A number of scholars believe that Nehemiah 8 once stood between Ezra 8 and 9 (so Ackroyd, *Exile and Restoration*, p. 139; Brockington, p. 164; Rudolph, pp. xxii–xxiii; M. Smith, "Ezra," pp. 141–43). Others following Esdras would place Nehemiah 8 after Ezra 10. Such rearrangements would require the elimination of

Nehemiah's name (8:9) as a gloss, as Nehemiah would have come to Palestine about a dozen years later (Coggins, p. 107).

1 The phrase "all the people assembled as one man" is identical with Ezra 3:1, which also refers to an assembly called in the seventh month of the year. The object of that meeting, however, was to restore the altar of burnt offerings and sacrificial worship. Possibly Ezra had instituted the practice of holding such assemblies on the seventh month, Tishri, the beginning of the civil year.

"In the square before the Water Gate," which gate led to the Gihon Spring, may be the same as the broad place before the house of the Lord (Ezra 10:9); but it is not to be confused with the Water Gate in Herod's temple (*Middoth* 1.4). First Esdras 9:38 places the plaza in front of the sacred gate or the first port that is toward the east.

Assemblies were held by the city gates (Judg 19:15; 2 Chron 32:6). A plaza 64 feet by 31 feet has been uncovered by the gate at Dan. Mazar has found a broad plaza in front of the Huldah Gates of the temple.

There have been at least four views about what "the Book of the Law of Moses" represented: (1) a collection of legal materials (so R. Kittel, M. Noth, G. von Rad), (2) the priestly code (W.H. Kosters, H.-J. Kraus, A. Kuenen, A. Lods, E. Meyer, W.O.E. Oesterley, B. Stade), (3) Deuteronomic laws (R. Bowman, B. Browne, U. Kellermann, W. Scott), (4) the Pentateuch (W.F. Albright, J. Bright, F. Cross, O. Eissfeldt, S. Mowinckel, W. Rudolph, J. Sanders, H. Schaeder, E. Sellin, J. Wellhausen). Ezra could certainly have brought back with him the Torah, that is the Pentateuch. Bruce Waltke ("The Samaritan Pentateuch and the Text of the Old Testament," *New Perspectives on the Old Testament*, ed. J.B. Payne [Waco: Word, 1970], p. 234) writes: "Finally, the Pentateuch itself must be older than the fifth century. If the scribal scholars of the second Jewish commonwealth found it necessary to modernize the Pentateuch to make it intelligible to the people (cf. Neh 8) in the fifth century, then obviously the original Pentateuch antedates this period by many years."

2 "The first day of the seventh month" was the New Year's Day of the civil calendar (Lev 23:23–25; Num 29:1–6), celebrated also as the Feast of Trumpets with a solemn assembly and cessation from labor. "Women" did not participate in ordinary meetings but were brought together with children on such solemn occasions (Deut 31:12; Josh 8:35; 2 Kings 23:2).

"All who were able to understand" is rendered "children old enough to understand" by the JB (cf. v.3; 10:29).

3 "Daybreak" (*hāʾôr*) is literally "the light" (cf. Gen 44:3; Judg 16:2; 19:26; Job 3:3 –8; 24:14; Ps 139:11–12; Isa 58:8). The KJV translates the word "morning." At 4:21 (15 MT) the KJV also translates as "morning" *šaḥar*, which actually is the dawn—the light that appears a good hour before sunrise (Ps 139:9; Prov 4:18; Joel 2:2).

The people evidently stood for about five hours attentively listening to the exposition of the Scriptures. Christians on the mission fields have been known to listen with rapt attention for such extended periods of time.

4 "Platform" (*migdal*) usually means a "tower." Here it indicates a platform capable of holding Ezra and thirteen others. The JB renders it "dais."

"Shema" is a shortened form of Shemaiah; see the comment on Ezra 8:13. "Anaiah" ("Yahweh has answered") was one of those who signed the covenant (10:22 [23 MT]). "Mishael" ("Who is what God is?") was also the name of one of Daniel's friends (Dan 1:6 et al.). "Hashbaddanah" is perhaps a corruption of "Yahweh has considered (men)," found only here.

5 The "book" was a scroll rather than a codex or book, which did not become popular till the early Christian centuries (cf. C.H. Roberts and T.C. Skeat, *The Birth of the Codex* [London: Oxford University Press, 1983]).

The rabbis deduced from "the people all stood up" that the congregation should stand at the reading of the Torah. In Eastern Orthodox churches the congregation stands throughout the service.

6 "Praised the LORD" is literally "blessed the LORD." In Jewish synagogues a benediction is pronounced before the reading of each scriptural section.

On "the great God," compare 9:32; Deuteronomy 10:17; Jeremiah 32:18; Daniel 9:4. The Jews customarily "lifted their hands" in worship (cf. comment on Ezra 9:5; cf. Pss 28:2; 134:2; 1 Tim 2:8).

The repetition "Amen! Amen!" connotes the intensity of feeling behind the affirmation (2 Kings 11:14; Luke 23:21). The Amen as a congregational response is known from the time of David according to 1 Chronicles 16:36. It was later used in the synagogue (b. *Berakoth* 5.4; 8.8) and in the church (1 Cor 14:16). According to G. Dalman (*The Words of Jesus* [Edinburgh: T. & T. Clark, 1902], p. 226): "'Amen is affirmation, Amen is curse, Amen is making something one's own.' When he utters the word 'Amen,' the hearer affirms the wish that God may act, places himself under divine judgment, and joins in praise to God."

"Bowed down" (from *qādad*) occurs fifteen times in the OT (e.g., Gen 24:26, 48; 43:28; Exod 4:31; 12:27 et al.), always followed by the verb "to worship." The KJV renders it "bowed their heads"; it may mean "kneel down."

"Worshiped" is thought by some to be from the verb *ḥāwāh*, exclusively in the Hishtaphael stem as *hištaḥᵃwāh*. However J.A. Emerton ("The Etymology of *hištaḥᵃwāh*," OTS 20 [1977]: 41–55) regards it as a Hithpa'lel from *šḥt* (see Notes). The verb occurs 170 times in the OT, mostly of the worship of God, gods, or idols. Originally it meant to prostrate oneself on the ground as the frequently accompanying phrase *'ārṣāh* ("to the ground"; e.g., in v.6) indicates. The verb is used relatively rarely of an individual's worship of God (Gen 22:5; 24:26, 48). Such private acts of worship often involved actual prostration "to the earth" as with Abraham's servant (Gen 24:52), Moses (Exod 34:8), Joshua (Josh 5:14), and Job (Job 1:20). There are also three cases of spontaneous communal worship in Exodus (4:31; 12:27; 33:10). In 2 Chronicles 20:18 Jehoshaphat and the people "fell down in worship before the LORD" when they heard his promise of victory (see H.H. Rowley, *Worship in Ancient Israel* [London: SPCK, 1967]).

7 On "the Levites" see 2 Chronicles 35:3 and the comment on Ezra 2:40. "Jamin" means "right hand" or "good luck." "Hodiah" means "Yahweh is splendor." "Pelaiah" is "Yahweh has acted wonderfully." "Instructed" literally means "causing to understand" (cf. v.8; Ezra 8:16; Ps 119:34, 73, 130; Isa 40:14).

8 "They read" is from *qārā'*, which means "to call, proclaim," here "to read aloud" (Exod 24:7; Deut 17:19; 2 Kings 5:7; cf. Arab. *Qur'an*, "recitation," the name of the

Islamic scriptures). Reading in the ancient world was done aloud (Acts 8:28; cf. G. Hendricksson, "Ancient Reading," *Classical Journal* 25 [1929–30]: 182–96; W.P. Clark, "Ancient Reading," *Classical Journal* 26 [1930–31]: 698–700).

"Making it clear" (*mᵉpōrāš*) translates the Pual participle of the verb *pāraš*, a form that occurs only here (cf. the Aramaic Pael passive participle *mᵉpāraš* in Ezra 4:18). Many would derive its meaning from the sense "to separate," "to determine," hence "to make clear" (cf. RSV, "clearly").

Rabbinic tradition, however, from the epoch of Rab (A.D. 175–247) has understood this word as referring to translation from Hebrew into an Aramaic Targum. Thus the Babylonian Talmud (*Megillah* 3a) comments: "What is meant by the text: 'And they read in the book, in the law of God, *mephôrash*, and gave the sense and caused them to understand the meaning'? 'And they read in the book, in the Law of God': this indicates the Hebrew text; *mephôrash*: this indicates the targum" (see R. le Déaut, *Introduction à la Littérature Targuminque* [Rome: Institute Biblique Pontifical, 1966], p. 23; M. McNamara, *Targum and Testament* [Grand Rapids: Eerdmans, 1972], pp. 79–80).

This latter view has been adopted by the JB's "translating" and the NAB's "interpreting"; it is also listed in the margins of the RSV and NIV. But the Talmudic comment is clearly anachronistic as we have no evidence of targums from such an early date. The earliest extant targums are from Qumran and include a targum on Leviticus 16 and a targum on Job 3–5, both from Cave 4. An extensive targum on Job comes from Cave 11. This targum, dated to 150-100 B.C., may possibly be the Job Targum that Gamaliel ordered hidden (b *Sabbath* 115a).

9 Those who would place Ezra after Nehemiah deny their contemporaneity and excise the reference to Nehemiah as an interpolation. But the fact that Nehemiah is omitted in the parallel in 1 Esdras 9:49 is hardly significant, as he is completely ignored throughout the work.

On mourning (cf. Ezra 10:6; Esth 9:22; Isa 57:18–19; 60:20; 61:2–3; 66:10; Jer 31:13; 1 Macc 3:47–51; 4:38–40) and weeping (cf. Ezra 3:12; 10:1; Neh 1:4), see E. Feldman, *Biblical and Post-Biblical Defilement and Mourning* (New York: Yeshiva University Press, 1977).

The powerful exposition of the Word of God can bring deep conviction of sin. But repentance must not degenerate into a self-centered remorse but must issue into joy in God's forgiving goodness (cf. 2 Cor 2:5–11).

10 "Choice food" (*mašmannîm* from *šāman*, "to be fat") means delicious, festive food prepared with much fat (LXX has *lipasmata*, "fat"). Another Hebrew word for "fat" (*ḥēleb*) is used metaphorically for the "best" in Numbers 18:12, 29–30, 32, and the "finest" in Psalm 81:16 (17 MT) and 147:14. The fat of sacrificial animals was offered to God as the tastiest element of the burnt offering (Lev 1:8, 12), the peace offering (Lev 4:8–10), and the trespass offering (Lev 7:3–4). The fat was not to be consumed in these cases (cf. J. Heller, "Die Symbolik des Fettes im AT," VetTest 20 [1970]: 106–8).

"Sweet drinks" (*mamtāqqîm*) occurs only here and as "sweetness" in Song of Songs 5:16.

"Send some to those who have nothing prepared" reflects the Jews' tradition of remembering the less fortunate on joyous occasions (2 Sam 6:19; Esth 9:22; cf. 1 Cor 11:20–22). This was one example of the social conscience and concern of the Jews (Exod 23:11; Lev 19:10; 23:22; Deut 14:28–29; 26:12–13; Job 29:12, 16; 31:16–19;

Ps 112:9; Prov 1:6–8; 2:2; Ecclus 4:1, 3–8; 7:32; 29:20; see C. van Leeuwen, La de Leeuwen, *Le développement du sens social en Israel avant l'ère chrétienne* [Assen: Van Gorcum, 1955]).

"The joy" (*ḥedwāh*, only here and in 1 Chron 16:27; cf. the Aram. in Ezra 6:16), that is, our joy in the Lord as we eat and labor before him, will sustain us (Deut 12:7, 12, 18; 14:26; 16:11, 14).

"Strength" (*māʿōz*) means "stronghold," "fortress" (cf. Pss 27:1; 37:39; Jer 16:19).

11 "Be still" (*ḥassû* from *ḥas*) means "hush," "be quiet," as in Judges 3:19.

12 The day after Sukkoth (Tabernacles), the Jews celebrate a festival called *Simhat Torah* ("rejoicing over the Torah"), in which they parade in a circle inside the synagogue seven or more rounds with a different person holding the scrolls of the Torah each time. Children carry flags with inscriptions extolling the Word of God.

Notes

6 The verb for worship הִשְׁתַּחֲוָה (*hištaḥ°wāh*), formerly analyzed as a Hithpael of שָׁחָה (*šā-ḥāh*), is thought by some to be cognate with the Ugaritic *ḥwy* ("to bow down"; see G.R. Driver, "Studies in the Vocabulary of the Old Testament, "JTS 31 [1929–30]: 279–80; D. Ap. Thomas, "Notes on Some Terms Relating to Prayer," VetTest 6 [1956]: 229–30). But Emerton ("Etymology") rejects חוי (*ḥwy*) in favor of שחת (*šḥt*) (see commentary).

Prostration was a common act of self-abasement performed before relatives, strangers, superiors, and especially royalty (Gen 23:7, 12; 33:3, 6–7; Exod 18:7; Ruth 2:10; 1 Sam 20:41; 2 Sam 9:6, 8). Vassals in the Amarna Letters wrote to the Pharaoh: "Beneath the feet [of the king, . . .] seven times, and seven times [I fall]" (cf. ANET, p. 483).

The Greek word προσκυνέω (*proskyneō*, which is used to translate *hishtaḥ°wāh* 148 times in the LXX) had a semantic development similar to the Hebrew word. Like it *proskyneō* can mean either "I prostrate" or "I worship." In Mark 5:6 KJV translates "worshipped" when "prostrated" would have been more appropriate (cf. Mark 5:22, 33).

---

2. *The Festival of Booths*

8:13–18

13On the second day of the month, the heads of all the families, along with the priests and the Levites, gathered around Ezra the scribe to give attention to the words of the Law. 14They found written in the Law, which the Lᴏʀᴅ had commanded through Moses, that the Israelites were to live in booths during the feast of the seventh month 15and that they should proclaim this word and spread it throughout their towns and in Jerusalem: "Go out into the hill country and bring back branches from olive and wild olive trees, and from myrtles, palms and shade trees, to make booths"—as it is written.

16So the people went out and brought back branches and built themselves booths on their own roofs, in their courtyards, in the courts of the house of God and in the square by the Water Gate and the one by the Gate of Ephraim. 17The whole company that had returned from exile built booths and lived in them. From the days of Joshua son of Nun until that day, the Israelites had not celebrated it like this. And their joy was very great.

18Day after day, from the first day to the last, Ezra read from the Book of the Law of God. They celebrated the feast for seven days, and on the eighth day, in accordance with the regulation, there was an assembly.

13 Notice that the people in this revival had an insatiable appetite to learn more about the Scriptures.

14 "Booths" (*sukkôt*) were not "tabernacles," i.e., tents as the KJV translates in Leviticus 23:34, following the Vulgate, but booths made out of branches. This feast, celebrated from the fifteenth of Tishri (Sept.-Oct.) for seven days (Lev 23:39–43), was one of the three great feasts (along with Passover and Pentecost) during which all Jewish men were to assemble in Jerusalem. It was a joyous agricultural festival that celebrated the completion of the harvest. The rabbis said, "He who has not seen Jerusalem during the Feast of Tabernacles does not know what rejoicing means." (See Exod 23:16; Deut 16:13; Ezra 3:4; the feast of John 7 was probably the Feast of Booths.)

15 With the exception of palm trees and other leafy trees, the trees mentioned here are not the same as those prescribed in Leviticus 23:40. The latter included the willow, which is omitted here.

The olive tree (*Olea europaea, Eleagnus augustifolia*) is widespread in Mediterranean countries. According to Deuteronomy 8:8 it was growing in Canaan before the Conquest. It takes an olive tree thirty years to mature; so its cultivation requires peaceful conditions.

"Tree of oil" (*ēṣ šemen*) is commonly regarded as the "wild olive tree" (*Olea europaea oleaster*). But this is questionable since according to 1 Kings 6:23, 31–32, its wood was used as timber, whereas the wood of the wild olive tree would have been of little value for use in the temple's furniture. Also, the oleaster contains very little "oil." The phrase may have meant a resinous tree like the fir. The KJV renders the phrase as "pine."

"Myrtles" (*hᵃdās, Myrtus communis*) are evergreen bushes with a pleasing odor (Isa 41:19; 55:13; Zech 1:8, 10–11). "Palms" (from *tāmār, Phoenix dactylifera*) are date palms (cf. Exod 15:27; Lev 23:40; Num 33:9; Ps 92:12; S of Songs 7:8; Joel 1:12). Such trees were common around Jericho (Deut 34:3; 2 Chron 28:15). "Shade trees" (*ēṣ ᶜᵃbōt*) means literally "leafy trees" (Ezek 6:13; 20:28; see H.N. Moldenke and A.L. Moldenke, *Plants of the Bible* [Waltham, Mass.: Chronica Botanica, 1952]; *Fauna and Flora of the Bible* [London: United Bible Societies, 1972]).

Later Jewish celebrations of the Feast of Booths include the waving with the right hand of the *lulav*, made of branches of palms, myrtles, and willows, and the holding in the left hand of the ethrog, a citrus native to Palestine.

16 "Roofs" (pl. of *gāg*) in Palestine were flat so that one could walk on them (Josh 2:6; 1 Sam 9:25–26; 2 Sam 11:2; Mark 2:4; Acts 10:9). "Courtyards, in the courts" renders the plural of *ḥāṣēr*, which occurs in the singular 120 times and in the plural 25 times in the OT. Near Eastern houses were built around a court (see H.K. Beebe, "Ancient Palestinian Dwellings," BA 31 [1968]: 38–58; H. Orlinsky, "*Ḥāṣēr* in the Old Testament," JAOS 59 [1939]: 22–37).

The important Temple Scroll from Qumran has God describing an ideal temple in great detail. Columns 40–46 describe the outer court as follows: "On the roof of the third story are columns for the constructing of booths for the Festival of Booths to be occupied by the elders, tribal chieftains, and the commanders of thousands and hundreds (cf. Neh 8:16–17)" (J. Milgrom, "The Temple Scroll," BA 41 [1978]: 111). On "the square by the Water Gate," see 3:26; 8:1, 3; 12:37.

"The Gate of Ephraim" was a gate of the oldest rampart of Jerusalem, four hundred cubits east of the Corner Gate (2 Kings 14:13; 2 Chron 25:23). It was restored by Nehemiah (12:39).

17 The statement "from the days of Joshua son of Nun" hardly means that no celebration of the Feast of Booths had taken place since then, as such celebrations are mentioned after the dedication of Solomon's temple (1 Kings 8:65; 2 Chron 7:9) and after the return of the exiles (Ezra 3:4). It must mean that the feast had not been celebrated before with such exceptional joyousness (Slotki, in loc.) or strictness of observance (Ryle, in loc.).

The great joy compares to that experienced at the renewal of the Passover under Hezekiah (2 Chron 30:26) and at the revival under Josiah (2 Kings 23:22; 2 Chron 35:18).

18 "Assembly" (*⁽ᵃ⁾ṣereṭ*) is "a solemn or festal assembly" (cf. Lev 23:36; Num 29:35; Deut 16:8; 2 Kings 10:20; Joel 1:14).

Excursus

Problematic is the relationship between what is described in Nehemiah 8 and 9 (see comment on 9:37) and the origins of the synagogue. According to M. Avi-Yonah (*Herodian Period*, p. 333), "The basic elements of the synagogue—the public reading of the Law and congregational prayer—were first instituted by Ezra and Nehemiah." Many scholars (e.g., Moore, Oesterley [W.O.E. Oesterley and T.H. Robinson, *Hebrew Religion* (New York: Macmillan, 1930), p. 294]) have suggested plausibly that synagogues developed in the Exile after the destruction of the temple. Ackryod (*Israel Under Babylon and Persia*, p. 28) cautions: "But this is purely a supposition," then adds, "Neh. 8 perhaps provides us with a picture of a stage in the evolution of the institution, with reading and exposition specially stressed."

Actual epigraphic evidence for a synagogue, however, is first attested, not in Babylon or in Palestine, but rather in Egypt under Ptolemy III (247–221 B.C.), where two Greek inscriptions mention προσευχήν (*proseuchēn*, "[the house] of prayer"; cf. Acts 16:13, which M. Hengel ["Proseuche und Synagoge," *Tradition und Glaube*, ed. G. Jeremias et al. (Göttingen: Vandenhoeck & Ruprecht, 1971), pp. 157–84] interprets as a reference to a synagogue; J. Koenig, "L'origine exilique de la synagogue," *Mélanges d'Histoire des Religions* [Paris: Presses Universitaires de France, 1974], pp. 33–55). The word *synagōgē*, which originally meant the congregation itself rather than the building, first appears in first-century A.D. Palestine.

S. Zeitlin ("The Origin of the Synagogue," *Proceedings of the American Academy for Jewish Research* 3 [1932]: 69–81) has argued that the synagogue arose as a purely secular institution in the postexilic period with the rise of the Pharisees. E. Rivkin (*Ben Sira and the Non-Existence of the Synagogue* [Cincinnati: Hebrew Union College, 1969], pp. 29–31) associates its rise with the Hasmonean revolt (cf. J. Gutmann, "The Origin of the Synagogue: The Current State of Research," *Archäologischer Anzeiger* 87 [1972]: 36–40).

3. A day of fasting, confession, and prayer

9:1–5a

> [1]On the twenty-fourth day of the same month, the Israelites gathered together, fasting and wearing sackcloth and having dust on their heads. [2]Those of Israelite descent had separated themselves from all foreigners. They stood in their places and confessed their sins and the wickedness of their fathers. [3]They stood where they were and read from the Book of the Law of the LORD their God for a quarter of the day, and spent another quarter in confession and in worshiping the LORD their God. [4]Standing on the stairs were the Levites—Jeshua, Bani, Kadmiel, Shebaniah, Bunni, Sherebiah, Bani and Kenani—who called with loud voices to the LORD their God. [5]And the Levites—Jeshua, Kadmiel, Bani, Hashabneiah, Sherebiah, Hodiah, Shebaniah and Pethahiah—said: "Stand up and praise the LORD your God, who is from everlasting to everlasting!"

Interestingly, the ninth chapter of Ezra, of Nehemiah, and of Daniel are each devoted to confessions of national sin and prayers for God's grace.

1 Many scholars find it strange to have a day of penance following a festival of joy and consider the events of this chapter to have originally followed Ezra 10 (e.g., Rudolph, in loc.). There would thus have been a three-week interval between Ezra 10:17 and Nehemiah 9:1.

The text as it stands, however, refers to events that occurred two days after the end of the Feast of Booths, which took place from 15 to 22 Tishri. According to Leviticus 16:29, 10 Tishri was the great Yom Kippur, or Day of Atonement, on which every man searched his own heart. Though not held on the tenth day, this day of penance resembles the spirit of the Day of Atonement.

The month of Tishri was particularly a month of "fasting" (Zech 7:5; on fasting see Ezra 8:21; 10:6).

"Sackcloth" (*śaq*) was a goat-hair garment that covered the bare loins during times of mourning and penance (Gen 37:34; 2 Sam 3:31; 21:10; 1 Kings 21:27; Esth 4:1–4; Isa 58:5; Dan 9:3).

"Dust" (*'ᵃdāmāh*) occurs 221 times in the OT. It originally indicated reddish-brown earth.

Joshua 7:6, Lamentations 2:10, and Ezekiel 27:30 also mention the placing of *'āpār* ("ashes," often rendered "dust") on one's head (cf. also 2 Sam 13:19 [*'ēper*, "dust"]; Job 2:12). At the excavations at Beersheba in 1970–71, A. Rainey ("Dust and Ashes," *Tel-Aviv* 1 [1974]: 77–83, summarized as "The Archaeology of Dust and Ashes," *Biblical Archaeology Review* 1 [1975]: 14, 16) noticed that the streets were composed of gray ash made from the broom tree. The mourner could simply sit on the ground and pick up ashes and dust to place on his head, which was a sign of mourning (1 Sam 4:12; 2 Sam 1:2; 15:32).

2 "Those of Israelite descent" is literally "the seed of Israel" (cf. Ezra 9:2). On "had separated themselves" see Ezra 9:1; 10:8, 11, 16. On "confessed" see 1:6 (cf. Ezra 10:1; Dan 9:20).

3 The congregation spent about three hours in the study of Scriptures and three hours in the worship of the Lord (see comment on 8:6).

The Qumran Manual of Discipline (6:6–7) prescribes: "And in the place where the ten are, let there not lack a man who studies the Law night and day, continually, concerning the duties of each towards the other. And let the Many watch in common for a third of all the nights of the year, to read the Book and study the law" (A. Dupont-Sommer, *The Essene Writings from Qumran* [Cleveland: World, 1962], p. 85). This may mean that the brethren were divided into groups that studied the Scriptures in relays throughout the night. Members of the sect studied the Scriptures at least a third of every night, i.e., four hours (A. Leaney, *The Rule of Qumran and Its Meaning* [London: SCM, 1966], p. 185).

4 "Shebaniah" possibly means "turn, pray, O Yahweh." "Bunni" is short for "Benaiah" ("Yahweh has built"). On "Sherebiah" see the comment on Ezra 8:18. "Kenani," short for "Kenaniah" ("Yahweh strengthens"), occurs only here.

The "stairs" (*maʿªlēh*, "ascent") perhaps led to the platform mentioned in 8:4. On "loud voices" see the comment on Ezra 10:12.

5a Five of the eight names are the same as five names in the previous verse.

"Stand up and praise the LORD." Jews begin their prayers with *Baruch* ("Blessed") and stand for the benediction (cf. v.3).

4. A recital of God's dealings with Israel

9:5b–31

"Blessed be your glorious name, and may it be exalted above all blessing and praise. ⁶You alone are the LORD. You made the heavens, even the highest heavens, and all their starry host, the earth and all that is on it, the seas and all that is in them. You give life to everything, and the multitudes of heaven worship you.

⁷"You are the LORD God, who chose Abram and brought him out of Ur of the Chaldeans and named him Abraham. ⁸You found his heart faithful to you, and you made a covenant with him to give to his descendants the land of the Canaanites, Hittites, Amorites, Perizzites, Jebusites and Girgashites. You have kept your promise because you are righteous.

⁹"You saw the suffering of our forefathers in Egypt; you heard their cry at the Red Sea. ¹⁰You sent miraculous signs and wonders against Pharaoh, against all his officials and all the people of his land, for you knew how arrogantly the Egyptians treated them. You made a name for yourself, which remains to this day. ¹¹You divided the sea before them, so that they passed through it on dry ground, but you hurled their pursuers into the depths, like a stone into mighty waters. ¹²By day you led them with a pillar of cloud, and by night with a pillar of fire to give them light on the way they were to take.

¹³"You came down on Mount Sinai; you spoke to them from heaven. You gave them regulations and laws that are just and right, and decrees and commands that are good. ¹⁴You made known to them your holy Sabbath and gave them commands, decrees and laws through your servant Moses. ¹⁵In their hunger you gave them bread from heaven and in their thirst you brought them water from the rock; you told them to go in and take possession of the land you had sworn with uplifted hand to give them.

¹⁶"But they, our forefathers, became arrogant and stiff-necked, and did not obey your commands. ¹⁷They refused to listen and failed to remember the miracles you performed among them. They became stiff-necked and in their rebellion appointed a leader in order to return to their slavery. But you are a forgiving God, gracious and compassionate, slow to anger and abounding in love. Therefore you

did not desert them, [18]even when they cast for themselves an image of a calf and said, 'This is your god, who brought you up out of Egypt,' or when they committed awful blasphemies.

[19]"Because of your great compassion you did not abandon them in the desert. By day the pillar of cloud did not cease to guide them on their path, nor the pillar of fire by night to shine on the way they were to take. [20]You gave your good Spirit to instruct them. You did not withhold your manna from their mouths, and you gave them water for their thirst. [21]For forty years you sustained them in the desert; they lacked nothing, their clothes did not wear out nor did their feet become swollen.

[22]"You gave them kingdoms and nations, allotting to them even the remotest frontiers. They took over the country of Sihon king of Heshbon and the country of Og king of Bashan. [23]You made their sons as numerous as the stars in the sky, and you brought them into the land that you told their fathers to enter and possess. [24]Their sons went in and took possession of the land. You subdued before them the Canaanites, who lived in the land; you handed the Canaanites over to them, along with their kings and the peoples of the land, to deal with them as they pleased. [25]They captured fortified cities and fertile land; they took possession of houses filled with all kinds of good things, wells already dug, vineyards, olive groves and fruit trees in abundance. They ate to the full and were well-nourished; they reveled in your great goodness.

[26]"But they were disobedient and rebelled against you; they put your law behind their backs. They killed your prophets, who had admonished them in order to turn them back to you; they committed awful blasphemies. [27]So you handed them over to their enemies, who oppressed them. But when they were oppressed they cried out to you. From heaven you heard them, and in your great compassion you gave them deliverers, who rescued them from the hand of their enemies.

[28]"But as soon as they were at rest, they again did what was evil in your sight. Then you abandoned them to the hand of their enemies so that they ruled over them. And when they cried out to you again, you heard from heaven, and in your compassion you delivered them time after time.

[29]"You warned them to return to your law, but they became arrogant and disobeyed your commands. They sinned against your ordinances, by which a man will live if he obeys them. Stubbornly they turned their backs on you, became stiff-necked and refused to listen. [30]For many years you were patient with them. By your Spirit you admonished them through your prophets. Yet they paid no attention, so you handed them over to the neighboring peoples. [31]But in your great mercy you did not put an end to them or abandon them, for you are a gracious and merciful God.

5b "Your glorious name" is literally "the name of your glory." The Hebrew word for glory (*kābôd*) comes from a root that means "weighty," and then by extension "honored."

The RSV connects v.5b with what the Levites said in v.5a and inserts at the beginning of v.6: "And Ezra said," following the LXX (cf. the other prayers of Ezra [Ezra 7:27–28a; 9:6–15]). Michaeli (in loc.) notes that what follows is one of the most beautiful and most complete liturgical prayers outside the Psalms (cf. Pss 78, 105, 106). Myers (*Ezra-Nehemiah*, p. 167) comments: "This prayer psalm is a marvelous expression of God's continued faithfulness to his covenant despite the nation's equally continued apostasy."

The prayer reviews God's grace and power (1) in creation (v.6), (2) in Egypt and at the Red Sea (vv.9–11), (3) in the desert and at Sinai (vv.12–21), (4) at the conquest of Canaan (vv.22–25), (5) through the judges (vv.26–28), (6) through the prophets (vv.29–31), and (7) in the present situation (vv.32–37). Ezra's prayer is a marvelous mosaic of Scriptures (see Myers, *Ezra-Nehemiah*, pp. 167ff.; A. Welch, "The Source of Nehemiah IX," ZAW 47 [1927]: 130–37).

6 Ezra's prayer begins notably with the affirmation "You are alone the LORD," which, though not in the same words as the famous Shema of Deuteronomy 6:4, expresses the central monotheistic conviction of Israel's faith (cf. 2 Kings 19:15; Ps 86:10; Isa 37:16).

"The highest heavens" is literally "the heaven of heavens" (cf. Deut 10:14; 1 Kings 8:27; 2 Chron 2:6; 6:18; Ps 148:4; Jer 32:17). Ṣābā' (pl. ṣ*bā'ōt) literally means "army," "host," "warriors." The NIV interprets the host here as stars (cf. Gen 2:1), but the last clause indicates that angels are meant (cf. 1 Kings 22:19; Pss 103:20–21; 148:2). Elsewhere the KJV transliterates the word in the phrase "the Lord of Sabaoth" (Rom 9:29; James 5:4), which means "the Lord of hosts." The expression, which occurs three hundred times in the OT, is especially prominent in the prophetic books of this period, occurring fourteen times in Haggai, fifty-three in Zechariah, and twenty-four in Malachi.

Not only men, but also "the multitudes of heaven" worship before the Lord. These "multitudes" include the b*nê 'elîm (lit., "sons of gods"; Ps 29:1–2), rendered by the RV "sons of the mighty" and which probably means angels (cf. Ps 89:6 [7 MT]). According to Psalm 97:7 even "all gods" bow down before him.

7 On "chose" (from bāḥar), T. Vriezen (cited in H. Seebass, TWOT, 2:87) comments:

> "In the OT the choice is always the action of God, of his grace, and always contains a mission for man; and only out of this mission can man comprehend the choice of God." . . . Thus when Neh. 9:7 says that Yahweh has already chosen Abraham, this fits the situation of the prayer in this context, the purpose of which was to make known in the syncretism of the time of Ezra and Nehemiah that Judah has the mission of maintaining her identity and of resisting the temptation to be assimilated by the nations, as long as election is to mean a mission to the nations.

"Ur of the Chaldeans" ('ûr kaśdîm) is found only here and in Genesis 11:28, 31; 15:7. Ur is usually identified with the famous Sumerian city in southern Mesopotamia, occupied in the first millennium B.C. by the Chaldeans. The term "Chaldeans" was therefore a later gloss. C.H. Gordon, however, has advocated a site for Abraham's Ur in the north close to Harran ("Abraham and the Merchants of Ura," JNES 17 [1958]: 28–31; id., "Where Is Abraham's Ur?" Biblical Archaeology Review 3 [1977]: 20–21, 52; cf. H.W.F. Saggs, "Ur of the Chaldees," Iraq 22 [1960]: 200–209).

"Abram" ("the father is exalted") was changed to "Abraham" ("the father of a multitude") according to Genesis 17:4–5.

8 "Faithful" (ne'*mān) is used only a few times of individuals, for example, of Moses (Num 12:7) and Samuel (1 Sam 3:20, untr. in NIV). Whether the reference alludes to Abraham's faith in believing that God would grant him a son (Gen 15:6) or in being willing to sacrifice Isaac (Gen 22) is unclear. Ecclesiasticus 44:20 and 1 Maccabees 2:52 favor the latter (cf. James 2:21–23 with Rom 4:16–22).

On the different people, see v.24 and the comments on Ezra 9:1; the latter lists surrounding populations and so includes also Ammonites, Moabites, and Egyptians.

"Girgashites" is a Canaanite tribe listed seven times in the OT. It is of uncertain identity (cf. the Qaraqisha in Hittite records; the Ugaritic personal name grgš). On "because you are righteous," see Ezra 9:15; Psalm 119:137; Lamentations 1:18.

9 The "Red Sea" (*yam-sûp*, "Sea of Reeds") was probably one of the Bitter Lakes the Suez Canal now passes through.

10 "Signs" (pl. of *'ôt*, used eighty times) indicates "miracles," "signs of confirmation or warning." It is often used with the plural of *môpet* ("wonder"), especially of events connected with the plagues of Exodus (Exod 7:3; Deut 4:34; 6:22; 7:19; Pss 78:43; 105:27; 135:9; Isa 8:18; Jer 32:20–21).

"How arrogantly" renders the Hiphil of *zîd* (cf. Exod 18:11; Deut 1:43; 17:13; 18:20; Jer 50:29). On "you made a name," compare v.5, also 1:9, 11; Isaiah 63: 12, 14.

11 On "you divided the sea . . . and they passed through it," see Exodus 14:21–29; Psalm 78:13; 1 Corinthians 10:1–2; Hebrews 11:29; and on "you hurled their pursuers," see Exodus 15:4; Isaiah 43:16–17.

12 On "with a pillar of cloud you led them," see v.19; Exodus 13:21–22; Numbers 14:14; Deuteronomy 1:33; Psalms 78:14; 105:39; Isaiah 42:16; 58:8.

13 On regulations, etc., see the comment on 1:7. "Laws" (*tôrôt*) is the plural of *tôrāh*, which means "instruction," "law," and later, as the Torah, the Scriptures par excellence—the Pentateuch. Moore (1:263) explains the Jewish conception of Torah as follows:

> The comprehensive name for the divine revelation, written and oral, in which the Jews possessed the sole standard and norm of their religion is *Torah*. It is a source of manifold misconceptions that the word is customarily translated "Law," though it is not easy to suggest any one English word by which it would be better rendered. "Law" must, however, not be understood in the restricted sense of legislation, but must be taken to include the whole of revelation—all that God has made known of his nature, character, and purpose, and of what he would have man be and do.

14 On "your holy Sabbath," compare Exodus 20:8–11; 31:13–17; Deuteronomy 5:15; Ezekiel 20:12. According to the rabbis, "The Sabbath outweighs all the commandments of the Torah" (j. *Nedarim* 38b) (cf. 10:31; 13:15–22). Other references to "Moses" are Ezra 3:2; 7:6; Nehemiah 1:7–8; 8:1, 14; 10:29 (30 MT); 13:1.

15 "Bread from heaven" (Exod 16:4, 10–35; Pss 78:24; 105:40; John 6:32, 51, 58; see P. Borgen, *Bread from Heaven* [Leiden: Brill, 1965]), "water from the rock" (Exod 17:6; Num 20:8; Ps 105:41), and "take possession" (see v.23; Deut 11:31; Josh 1:11) recall significant events from Israel's past.

"You had sworn with uplifted hand" is literally "lifted up your hand" (i.e., as in an oath; cf. 5:13; Exod 6:8; Ezek 20:6; 47:14).

16 "Became arrogant" (from *zîd*, used in v.10) "and stiff-necked" (see vv.17, 29; cf. a similar phrase in 3:5) is a figure borrowed from the driving of stubborn oxen who resist guidance (Exod 32:9; Deut 10:16; 2 Kings 17:14; 2 Chron 36:13; Jer 7:26).

17 The forefathers "refused to listen" (cf. 1 Sam 8:19; Jer 11:10) and "failed to remember the miracles" (cf. Mark 6:52).

Seven Hebrew MSS and the LXX read *bᵉmiṣrāyim* ("in Egypt") instead of *bᵉmir-yām* ("in their rebellion"). Numbers 14:4 reports the proposal of "appointed a leader."

"A forgiving God" (lit., a God of "pardons") renders the plural of *sᵉlîḥāh*, a rare word that occurs only here, in Psalm 130:4, and in Daniel 9:9. In Modern Hebrew it is used in the expression "Excuse me." God is "gracious" (cf. v.31; Exod 34:6; 2 Chron 30:9; Pss 86:15; 103:8; 145:8; Joel 2:13; Jonah 4:2).

18 The "image of a calf" recalls Exodus 32:4–8 and Deuteronomy 9:16. "Blasphemies" translates *ne'āṣôt* (only here, in v.26, and Ezek 35:12), which means "abuses," "aspersions" (KJV, "provocations").

19 "Compassion" renders *raḥᵃmîm*, which is cognate with *reḥem* ("womb"). Girdlestone (SOT, p. 108) says this "expresses a deep and tender feeling of compassion, such as is aroused by the sight of weakness or suffering in those that are dear to us or need our help" (cf. also vv.27–28, 31, and 1:11).

20 The "good Spirit" and the "manna" recall Numbers 11. On "their thirst" see v.15; Isaiah 21:14; 44:3.

21 In the desert wanderings the people "lacked nothing" (cf. Deut 2:7; 8:4), and their "clothes" (pl. of *śalmāh*, specifically a "mantle"; cf. 1 Kings 10:25) "did not wear out" (cf. Deut 29:5 [4 MT]; contrast Josh 9:13). The absence of natural deterioration evidenced God's special guidance. "Become swollen" can mean "blistered"; *bāṣaq* occurs only here and in Deuteronomy 8:4.

22 Some would interpret *lᵉpē'āh* (lit., "to a corner"; NIV, "even the remotest frontiers") in the sense of "quarter by quarter," others as "adjoining land," viz., Transjordan.

Sihon refused the Israelites passage through his land, which was in Transjordan between the Jabbok and the Arnon (Num 21:21–33; Deut 2–3; Judg 11:19–21; Pss 135:11; 136:19–20). Excavations between 1968 and 1971 at Tel Ḥesban have not revealed any settlements earlier than the seventh century B.C.; so the location of Sihon's Heshbon remains uncertain.

"Og" was the Amorite king of Bashan with sixty cities (Deut 3:3–5; Josh 13:12). His defeat was one of the great victories of the Israelites (Josh 9:10; Pss 135:11; 136:20). The Babylonian Talmud (*Niddah* 61a) claims Og was the brother of Sihon. "Bashan" was the fertile area north of Gilead in Transjordan, called Batanea in the NT period.

23 On God's promise to Abraham, see Genesis 22:17; 26:4; Exodus 32:13; Deuteronomy 1:10; 10:22; 28:62; Judges 2:1; 1 Chronicles 27:23; Acts 7:5 (see A.A. MacRae, "Abraham and the Stars," JETS 8 [1965]: 97–100).

24 "Their sons went in and took possession" recalls Genesis 22:17; 26:4; Exodus 32:13; Deuteronomy 1:8; 10:22; 28:62; 1 Chronicles 27:23. On "you subdued before them the Canaanites," see v.8; Deuteronomy 9:3; Judges 1:4. On "along with their kings," see Deuteronomy 7:24; Joshua 11:12, 17.

25 The list of land, cities, etc., corresponds to the lists in the Sinai covenant and its renewal (Deut 6:10–11; Josh 24:13). "Fortified cities" (pl. of *bāṣûr*) designates such sites as Jericho (Josh 6), Lachish (Josh 10:32), and Hazor (Josh 11:11) (cf. also Deut 3:5; 9:1; Josh 14:12). "Fertile land" is literally "fat [*šᵉmēnāh*] land" (cf. v.35). A related phrase "the good land" appears in Numbers 14:7; Deuteronomy 8:7; Joshua 23:13; 1 Kings 14:15.

The lack of rainfall during much of the year made it necessary for almost every house to have its own well or cistern to store water from the rainy seasons (2 Kings 18:31; Prov 5:15). By 1200 B.C. the technique of waterproofing cisterns was developed, permitting the greater occupation of the central Judean hills. The chief cultivated trees of Palestine were the olive, fig, apple, almond, walnut, mulberry, sycamore, and pomegranate (cf. Deut 8:8; 2 Kings 18:32). Date palms grew in the Jordan Valley, especially at Jericho (see on 8:15). When they entered the land of Canaan, the Israelites were warned not to cut down any fruit trees (Deut 20:20). The Egyptian story of Sinuhe (early second millennium B.C.) says of Canaan: "Figs were in it, and grapes. It had more wine than water. Plentiful was its honey, abundant its olives. Every (kind of) fruit was on its trees" (ANET, p. 19).

Šāman ("grew fat"; NIV, "well-nourished") is used but four other times in the OT (Deut 32:15 [*bis*]; Isa 6:10; Jer 5:28). It always implies physical satiety and spiritual insensitivity. There is a similar connotation with the use of *ḥēleḇ* ("fat"). In Job 15:27 the godless man has hidden his face in "fat"; the eyes of the wicked "gleam through folds of fat" (NEB, Ps 73:7). The heart of the godless is "gross like fat" (RSV, Ps 119:70).

"They reveled" (Hithpaʿel of *ʿāḏan*, used only here) means "to luxuriate," "to enjoy the good life."

26 Putting the law "behind their backs" (cf. 1 Kings 14:9; Ezek 23:35), the forefathers "killed [the] prophets" (see 1 Kings 18:4; 19:10, 14; 2 Chron 24:20–22; Jer 26:20–23; Matt 23:37; Luke 11:47), thus committing "awful blasphemies" (see on v.18 above).

27 When God "handed them over" (cf. Ezek 39:23), "they cried out" to him (cf. Judg 4:3; Ps 107:6, 28); and "from heaven [he] heard" (see 2 Chron 6:21, 23, 25, 30, 33). He gave them "deliverers" (*môšîʿîm*, "saviors"), i.e., "judges" like Samson, Gideon et al. (Judg 2:16–18; 3:9, 15 et al.; 2 Kings 13:5). The English "judges," the Latin *judices*, and the Greek *kritai* are all misleading translations of the Hebrew *šōp ᵉṭîm*, who were military leaders rather than judicial magistrates.

28 The history of the "judges" is a cyclical story of deliverance, apostasy, and then deliverance (Judg 3:7, 12; 4:1; 6:1; 8:33–34 et al.).

29 The ordinances of God are such that "a man will live if he obeys them" (cf. Lev 18:5; Ps 119:25; Ezek 20:11). The people "stubbornly . . . turned their backs" (lit., "they presented a stubborn shoulder"; cf. the similar expressions in 3:5 and 9:16; also Hos 4:16; Zech 7:11).

30 By his "Spirit" (cf. Zech 7:12) and through his "prophets" (see 2 Kings 17:13; 2 Chron 24:19), God appealed to the people, but they "paid no attention" (cf. 1 Sam 8:19). So he "handed them over" (see Judg 6:1; 13:1; 2 Kings 13:3; Ps 106:41; Jer 20:4–5; Ezek 7:21).

31 God "did not put an end" to the erring people (see Jer 4:27; 30:11; 46:28).

Nehemiah's long recital of Israelite history significantly excludes any reference to the reigns of Saul, David, and Solomon.

5. Confession of sins

9:32–37

> 32"Now therefore, O our God, the great, mighty and awesome God, who keeps his covenant of love, do not let all this hardship seem trifling in your eyes—the hardship that has come upon us, upon our kings and leaders, upon our priests and prophets, upon our fathers and all your people, from the days of the kings of Assyria until today. 33In all that has happened to us, you have been just; you have acted faithfully, while we did wrong. 34Our kings, our leaders, our priests and our fathers did not follow your law; they did not pay attention to your commands or the warnings you gave them. 35Even while they were in their kingdom, enjoying your great goodness to them in the spacious and fertile land you gave them, they did not serve you or turn from their evil ways.
>
> 36"But see, we are slaves today, slaves in the land you gave our forefathers so they could eat its fruit and the other good things it produces. 37Because of our sins, its abundant harvest goes to the kings you have placed over us. They rule over our bodies and our cattle as they please. We are in great distress.

32 "Now" marks the transition from a survey of the past to a supplication for the present situation. God is "mighty" (cf. 1:5; Deut 10:17; Dan 9:4), and he "keeps his covenant" (see 1:5; Deut 7:9; 1 Kings 8:23; 2 Chron 6:14; Ps 89:28).

K. Baltzer (*The Covenant Formulary*, rev. ed. [Philadelphia: Fortress, 1971], pp. 43–47) compares Nehemiah 9–10 with the covenant formula found in the Pentateuch and in Hittite sovereignty treaties.

Treaty Form	*Nehemiah 9–10*
Title/Preamble	missing
Antecedent history	9:7–37
Stipulations: basic	10:29b
specific	10:30–39
Witnesses	9:38–10:29a
Curses and Blessings	10:29 (the curse is implied and future blessings are not specified)

The nation suffered "hardship" (*tᵉlāʾāh;* cf. Exod 18:8; Num 20:14; Lam 3:5).

One of the "kings of Assyria" was Shalmaneser III (858–824), who is not mentioned in the OT. He reported that he defeated Ahab at the important battle of Qarqar in 853 (D. Winton Thomas, ed., *Documents From Old Testament Times* [New York: Harper & Brothers, 1961], pp. 46–47). The first Assyrian king to expand his empire to the Mediterranean was the great Tiglath-pileser III, also know as Pul.

He attacked Phoenicia in 736, Philistia in 734, and Damascus in 732 (ibid., pp. 53ff.). Early in his reign (752–742) Menahem of Israel paid tribute to him (2 Kings 15:19–20; ANET, pp. 283–84). During his campaigns against Damascus, Pul also ravaged Gilead and Galilee and destroyed Hazor and Megiddo (2 Kings 15:29; ANET, p. 284).

Shalmaneser V (727–722) laid siege to Samaria—a task completed by Sargon II (721–705). Sargon's commander carried on operations against Ashdod (Isa 20:1). Sennacherib (704–681) failed to take Jerusalem in 701 (2 Kings 18:13–17) but captured Lachish (Thomas, *Documents,* pp. 64–73). Esarhaddon (681–669) conquered Egypt and extracted tribute from Manasseh of Judah (2 Kings 19:37; Isa 37:38; Ezra 4:2; Thomas, *Documents,* pp. 73–75). Ashurbanipal (669–633) was probably the king who freed Manasseh from exile and restored him as a puppet king (2 Chron 33:13; Ezra 4:9). (See W.W. Hallo, "From Qarqar to Carchemish: Assyria and Israel in the Light of New Discoveries," BA 23 [1960]: 34–61.)

33–34 In all that happened God had "been just" (v.33; cf. 2 Chron 12:6; Ezra 9:15; Ps 119:137; Jer 12:1; Dan 9:14), but the people still "did not pay attention" (v.34).

35 A.R. Millard (" 'For He is Good,' " *Tyndale Bulletin* 17 [1966]: 115–17) notes that "goodness" is used in extrabiblical covenants with the connotation of friendship. It is an attribute of God's covenant faithfulness, in a "spacious" (see comment on 7:4; cf. Exod 3:8; Judg 18:10; 1 Chron 4:40; Isa 22:18) and "fertile" (*šemēnāh,* "fat"; see v.25) land. Yet the people did not turn from their "evil ways" (cf. Deut 28:20; Judg 2:19; Ps 106:39; Isa 1:16; Jer 4:4; 21:12; 23:2, 22; Hos 9:15; Zech 1:4).

36 The people were "slaves" (see comments on Ezra 9:9; Neh 5:5) in the fruitful land God had given their forefathers (see 10:35 [36 MT], 37 [38 MT]; Isa 1:19; Jer 2:7).

37 On taxes see the comment on 5:4.

The term *gewiyyāh* ("bodies"), used thirteen times in the OT, characterizes man in weakness, oppression, or trouble (e.g., Gen 47:18–19). It is also used of a "corpse" (1 Sam 31: 10, 12; Ps 110:6; Nah 3:3) or of a "carcass" (Judg 14:8–9). The Persian rulers drafted their subjects into military service. Possibly some Jews accompanied Xerxes on his invasion of Greece.

The prayer of Ezra in Nehemiah 9:5–37 has had a profound impact on the Jewish synagogue service (so J. Liebreich, "The Impact of Neh 9.5–37 on the Liturgy of the Synagogue," HUCA 32 [1961]: 227–37).

6. A binding agreement

9:38

> 38"In view of all this, we are making a binding agreement, putting it in writing, and our leaders, our Levites and our priests are affixing their seals to it."

38 "Making" is literally "cutting"; see the comment on Ezra 10:3. "A binding agreement" translates *'amānāh,* which occurs only here and in 11:23, where it means a "royal prescription." The word is related to "Amen," and its root has the connotation of constancy. The KJV and RV translate it "sure covenant." The usual word for covenant (*bᵉrît*) appears in 1:5; 9:8, 32; 13:29; and Ezra 10:3. The Qumran community evidently practiced an annual renewal of their covenant with God. See Helmer Ringgren, *The Faith of Qumran* (Philadelphia: Fortress, 1963), pp. 225–27.

On seals and bullae (seal impressions), see Avigad, *Bullae and Seals*.

The Old Aramaic inscription of Panammu I, dated to the eighth century B.C., has a similar expression: *'mn krt* (*'mōn krît*) ("a sure covenant struck"; cf. J. Fitzmyer, *The Aramaic Inscriptions of Sefire* [Rome: Pontifical Biblical Institute, 1967], pp. 32 –33).

a. *A list of those who sealed it*

10:1–29

¹Those who sealed it were:

Nehemiah the governor, the son of Hacaliah.

Zedekiah, ²Seraiah, Azariah, Jeremiah,
³Pashhur, Amariah, Malkijah,
⁴Hattush, Shebaniah, Malluch,
⁵Harim, Meremoth, Obadiah,
⁶Daniel, Ginnethon, Baruch,
⁷Meshullam, Abijah, Mijamin,
⁸Maaziah, Bilgai and Shemaiah.
These were the priests.

⁹The Levites:

Jeshua son of Azaniah, Binnui of the sons of Henadad, Kadmiel,
¹⁰and their associates: Shebaniah,
Hodiah, Kelita, Pelaiah, Hanan,
¹¹Mica, Rehob, Hashabiah,
¹²Zaccur, Sherebiah, Shebaniah,
¹³Hodiah, Bani and Beninu.

¹⁴The leaders of the people:

Parosh, Pahath-Moab, Elam, Zattu, Bani,
¹⁵Bunni, Azgad, Bebai,
¹⁶Adonijah, Bigvai, Adin,
¹⁷Ater, Hezekiah, Azzur,
¹⁸Hodiah, Hashum, Bezai,
¹⁹Hariph, Anathoth, Nebai,
²⁰Magpiash, Meshullam, Hezir,
²¹Meshezabel, Zadok, Jaddua,
²²Pelatiah, Hanan, Anaiah,
²³Hoshea, Hananiah, Hasshub,
²⁴Hallohesh, Pilha, Shobek,
²⁵Rehum, Hashabnah, Maaseiah,
²⁶Ahiah, Hanan, Anan,
²⁷Malluch, Harim and Baanah.

²⁸"The rest of the people—priests, Levites, gatekeepers, singers, temple servants and all who separated themselves from the neighboring peoples for the sake of the Law of God, together with their wives and all their sons and daughters who are able to understand— ²⁹all these now join their brothers the nobles, and bind themselves with a curse and an oath to follow the Law of God given through Moses the servant of God and to obey carefully all the commands, regulations and decrees of the LORD our Lord.

1 This is a legal list, bearing the official seal and containing a roster of eighty-four names arranged according to the following categories: leaders, priests, Levites, and laymen.

2 Verses 2–8 contain twenty-one names, most of which reoccur in 12:1–7. "Jeremiah" ("May Yahweh raise up!") is the name of five persons including the prophet.

6 "Baruch" ("blessed") was also the name of Jeremiah's scribe. A seal with the latter's name and patronymic has been published (cf. N. Avigad, "Baruch the Scribe and Jerahmeel the King's Son," BA 42 [1979]: 114–18). On the subject of seals, see L. Gorelick and E. Williams, *Ancient Seals and the Bible* (Malibu: Undena, 1983); and O. Keel, "Ancient Seals and the Bible," JAOS 106 (1986): 307–11.

7 "Abijah" ("Yahweh is my father") is the name of nine individuals in the OT. It occurs in the Murashu texts as *'abī-ya-a-ma*, i.e., *'abîyaw* (Coogan, *Personal Names*, p. 12).

8 "Maaziah" ("Yahweh is a refuge") occurs only here and in 1 Chronicles 24:18. "Bilgai" ("cheerfulness") occurs only here.

In Ezra 2:36–39 four priestly families are listed; in the later list of 1 Chronicles 24:7–18, we have the arrangement of twenty-four courses that served as the basis of the rotation for priestly service (Luke 1:8). J. Liver (*Chapters in the History of the Priests and Levites* [Jerusalem: Magnes, 1968], p. ix) suggests that it may have been Nehemiah himself who established the twenty-four-course arrangement.

9 Of the Levites seventeen are mentioned by name. "Azaniah" ("Yahweh has heard") occurs only here.

10 "Associates" is literally "brothers."

11 "Mica" is a shortened form of Michael ("Who is like God?"). "Rehob" ("spacious") occurs only here and in 2 Samuel 8:3, 12 as a personal name.

13 "Beninu" ("our son") occurs only here.

14 Of the leaders of the people listed here (vv. 14–27), twenty are also found in the lists of Ezra 2 and Nehemiah 7. For the etymology of these names, see the comments on Ezra 2.

19 "Anathoth," a name derived from the Canaanite goddess Anath, is also the name of the city of Jeremiah (Jer 1:1). As a personal name it occurs only here and in 1 Chronicles 7:8. "Nebai," a name of unknown meaning, occurs only here.

20 "Magpiash," a name of unknown significance, occurs only here. "Hezir" means "swine" (cf. 1 Chron 24:15). On animal names as nicknames, see the comment on Ezra 2:3. The word *ḥᵃzîr* occurs only seven times in the OT. Leviticus 11:7 and Deuteronomy 14:8 forbid the eating of swine's flesh. Isaiah 65:4; 66:3, 17 describe apostate Jews who ate swine's flesh in heathen sacrifices. In Psalm 80:13 (14 MT) an enemy is described like a wild boar, and in Proverbs 11:22 a beautiful woman without discretion is likened to a golden ring in a pig's snout. Antiochus IV sought to compel Jews to eat pork (1 Macc 1:47; 2 Macc 6:18; cf. Matt 7:6; 2 Peter 2:22). (See Alfred von Rohr, "The Cultic Role of the Pig in Ancient Times," *In Memoriam Paul Kahle*, ed. M. Black and G. Fohrer [Berlin: A. Töpelmann, 1968], pp. 201–7.)

22 "Pelatiah" means "Yahweh delivers."

23 "Hoshea" means "May Yahweh save!" (cf. the name of the prophet Hosea).

24 On the name "Hallohesh" see the comment on 3:12. "Pilha" ("millstone") occurs only here, as does "Shobek" ("victor").

26 "Ahiah" ("my brother is Yahweh") occurs in the Murashu texts as *'aḥīyaw* (Coogan, *Personal Names,* p. 12). "Anan" (short for Ananiah ["Yahweh has manifested himself"]) occurs only here.

28 On Levites see the comment on Ezra 2:40; on gatekeepers and singers see on 2:41; on temple servants see on 2:43; and on wives and children see Nehemiah 8: 2–3.

29 This verse recalls Deuteronomy 27–29; see comments on Ezra 10:5 and Nehemiah 5:13. "A curse" (*'ālāh*) means an adjuration with an imprecation of grievous punishments in case of a failure to keep the oath (see J. Pedersen, *Der Eid bei den Semiten* (Strasbourg: Trübner, 1914); A.D. Crown, "Aposiopesis in the Old Testament and the Hebrew Conditional Oath," *Abr-Nahrain* 4 [1963–64]: 96–111; M.G. Kline, "Oath and Ordeal Signs," WTJ 27 [1965]: 115–39).

b. Provisions of the agreement (10:30–39)

1) Mixed marriages

10:30

> 30"We promise not to give our daughters in marriage to the peoples around us or take their daughters for our sons.

30 On mixed marriages see the excursus at the end of the commentary on Ezra 10.

2) Commerce on the Sabbath

10:31a

> 31"When the neighboring peoples bring merchandise or grain to sell on the Sabbath, we will not buy from them on the Sabbath or on any holy day.

31a "Merchandise," from *maqqāḥôṯ,* is only found here. "Grain" translates *šeḇer* (KJV, "victuals"). The provisions of vv.31–34 may have been a code drawn up by Nehemiah to correct the abuses listed in chapter 13 (e.g., vv.15–22).

Though the Sabbath passages in the Torah (Exod 20:8–11; Deut 5:12–15) do not explicitly prohibit trading on the Sabbath, this is clearly understood in Jeremiah 17:19–27 and Amos 8:5.

3) The sabbatical year

10:31b

Every seventh year we will forgo working the land and will cancel all debts.

31b According to the Mosaic legislation (Exod 23:10–11; Lev 25:2–7), in the seventh year the land was to lie fallow; and the collection of debts was not to take place (Deut 15:1–3).

F. Mezzacasas ("Esdras, Nehemias y el año Sabatico," *Revista Biblica* 23 [1961]: 1–9, 82–96) argues from parallels with Deuteronomy 31:10–11 that Nehemiah 8–10 is set in the context of a sabbatical year. He concludes that this is the year 430/429 B.C. Extrabiblical references include 1 Maccabees 6:49, 54; Philo (*Sp. Lege* 2.104); and Josephus (*Antiq*. III, 280–81 [xii.3]; XII, 378 [ix.5]; XIII, 234 [viii.2]; XIV, 202 [x.6], 206 [x.6], 475 [xvi.1]; XV, 7 [i.1]; *War* I, 60 [ii.4]). The Romans misrepresented the Sabbath and the sabbatical year as the result of laziness. According to Tacitus (*Histories* 5.4): "They were led by the charms of indolence to give over the seventh year as well to inactivity."

4) Offerings for the temple and its staff

10:32–39

32"We assume the responsibility for carrying out the commands to give a third of a shekel each year for the service of the house of our God: 33for the bread set out on the table; for the regular grain offerings and burnt offerings; for the offerings on the Sabbaths, New Moon festivals and appointed feasts; for the holy offerings; for sin offerings to make atonement for Israel; and for all the duties of the house of our God.

34"We—the priests, the Levites and the people—have cast lots to determine when each of our families is to bring to the house of our God at set times each year a contribution of wood to burn on the altar of the LORD our God, as it is written in the Law.

35"We also assume responsibility for bringing to the house of the LORD each year the firstfruits of our crops and of every fruit tree.

36"As it is also written in the Law, we will bring the firstborn of our sons and of our cattle, of our herds and of our flocks to the house of our God, to the priests ministering there.

37"Moreover, we will bring to the storerooms of the house of our God, to the priests, the first of our ground meal, of our grain, offerings, of the fruit of all our trees and of our new wine and oil. And we will bring a tithe of our crops to the Levites, for it is the Levites who collect the tithes in all the towns where we work.

38A priest descended from Aaron is to accompany the Levites when they receive the tithes, and the Levites are to bring a tenth of the tithes up to the house of our God, to the storerooms of the treasury. 39The people of Israel, including the Levites, are to bring their contributions of grain, new wine and oil to the storerooms where the articles for the sanctuary are kept and where the ministering priests, the gatekeepers and the singers stay.

"We will not neglect the house of our God."

32 Exodus 30:13–14 states that a "half shekel is an offering to the LORD" from each man twenty years old and older as a symbolical ransom. Later Joash used the annual

741

contributions to repair the temple (2 Chron 24:4–14). In the NT period Jewish men everywhere sent an offering of a half-shekel (actually its equivalent) for the temple in Jerusalem (Matt 17:24).

Several explanations have been suggested why the offering should be a third rather than a half shekel.

1. Some maintain that the half-shekel of Exodus (30:16; 38:25–28) was meant as a onetime offering for the construction of the tabernacle and therefore has no bearing on the offering in Nehemiah 10:32.

2. Others argue that the offering was reduced from one-half to one-third because of economic impoverishment.

3. Some argue that the later shekel was based on a heavier standard, thus one-third of the later shekel was equal to one-half of the earlier shekel. That is, the later Babylonian-Persian shekel was twenty-one grams, whereas the former Phoenician shekel was fourteen grams, hence one-third the former was equal to one-half the latter.

The weights of the Babylonian shekel varied from 8.3 grams to 16:7 grams, with an average of 11:42 grams. According to Kenyon (*Digging Up,* p. 103): "The surprising point to emerge is that the weight of 4 shekels in absolutely mint condition gave a shekel value of 11:34 grammes, and this can be taken as the standard in use in Jerusalem in the reign of Zedekiah, immediately before the Babylonian destruction of the city." A third of a shekel would normally weigh about 4 grams or about one-eighth of an ounce.

33 "The bread set out on the table" (*leḥem hamma'areḵeṯ*) is literally "bread of arrangement" (KJV, "shewbread"). These were twelve cakes of fine flour arranged in two rows of six set out each Sabbath (Lev 24:6–7). Elsewhere they are also called *leḥem happānîm* ("bread of the face"), that is, bread set before the presence of God (Exod 25:30; 1 Sam 21:6 [7 MT]; 1 Kings 7:48) (cf. P.A.H. de Boer, "An Aspect of Sacrifice I: Divine Bread," VetTest Suppl. 23 [1972]: 27–36).

On "regular grain offerings" see Exodus 29:38–41; Numbers 28:3–8. On "burnt offerings" compare Ezra 8:35.

"The Sabbaths, New Moon festivals and appointed feasts" recall Numbers 28:9–16. "To make atonement" translates *kipper* (Piel of *kāpar*), which means "to cover" or "to wipe away" one's sin, hence to expiate. It describes the effect of the sin and trespass offerings (Lev 4:20; Num 5:8).

34 "Lots" (pl. of *gôrāl*) were used frequently to determine the will of the Lord (1) to apportion the land among the tribes (Num 26:55; Josh 14:2; 18:10); (2) to detect a guilty person (Josh 7:14; 1 Sam 14:42; Jonah 1:7); (3) to choose the first king, Saul (1 Sam 10:19–21); (4) to settle disputes (Prov 18:18); (5) to determine the courses of the priests, singers, gatekeepers (1 Chron 24:5; 25:8; 26:13; Luke 1:9); (6) to determine who should dwell in Jerusalem (Neh 11:1); and (7) to choose the replacement of Judas Iscariot (Acts 1:26).

In a secular connection Haman cast lots to determine the time to act against the Jews (Esth 3:7; 9:24); and the soldiers cast lots to gain the garment of Jesus (Matt 27:35; Mark 15:24; Luke 23:34; John 19:24).

Though there is no specific reference to a wood offering in the Pentateuch, the perpetual burning of fires would have required a continual "contribution of wood" (cf. 13:31; Lev 6:12–13). Josephus mentions "the festival of wood-offering" on the fourteenth day of the fifth month (Ab), when all the people were accustomed to bring wood for the altar (*War* II, 425 [xvii.6]). The Mishnah (*Taanith* 4.5) lists nine times when certain families brought wood. See further J. Epstein, "Die Zeiten des Holzopfers," *Monatsschrift für Geschichte und Wissenschaft des Judentums* 78 (1934): 97–103; M. Avi-Yonah, "The Temple and the Divine Service," in *The Herodian Period*, ed. M. Avi-Yonah, pp. 64–69; L.I. Rabinowitz, *Torah and Flora* (New York: Sanhedrin, 1977), pp. 64–69.

Jubilees 21:13 specifies: "And of these kinds of wood lay upon the altar under the sacrifice, and do not lay (thereon) any split or dark wood, (but) hard and clean, without fault, a sound and new growth; and do not lay (thereon) old wood, for there is no longer fragrance in it as before."

Columns 23–25 of the newly published Temple Scroll from Qumran describe the celebration of the wood-offering festival. The provision of wood for the six days is assigned as follows: (1) first day, Levi and Judah; (2) second day, Benjamin and Joseph's son, Ephraim and Manasseh; (3) third day, Reuben and Simeon; (4) fourth day, Issachar and Zebulon; (5) fifth day, Gad and Asher; and (6) sixth day, Dan and Naphtali. See J. Milgrom, "The Temple Scroll," BA 41 (1978): 108; Y. Yadin, *The Temple Scroll* (London: Weidenfeld and Nicholson, 1985), pp. 101–11.

35 The offerings of the "firstfruits" were brought to the temple for the support of the priests and Levites (Exod 23:19; 34:26; Lev 19:23–24; Num 18:13; Deut 26:1–11; Ezek 44:30). Actually the Torah stipulated only seven kinds of plants for the firstfruits. The promise to bring the firstfruits of "every tree" was an act of exceptional piety.

36 The firstborn of men and beasts and the firstfruits of field and garden (Lev 19:23 –25) were to be given to God. They could be set free for secular use only by redemption (Exod 13:13, 15; 34:20; Lev 27:26–33; Num 3:44–51; 18:15–17; Deut 14:23–26). M. Tsevat (TDOT, 2:126) says, "It is not only the best that belongs to God, but also the first. It would be presumptuous for man to enjoy something without first giving God his portion."

37 On "storerooms" see Ezra 8:29; 10:6. "Ground meal" (*ʿărîsāh*) is mixed dough at the first stage (Num 15:20–21). On "offerings" (*tᵉrûmāh*), see Ezra 8:25; Nehemiah 10:39; 12:44; 13:5. Literally it means "what is lifted" (KJV, "heave offering"). These contributions were for the maintenance of the priests.

"New wine" is *tîrôš*, which the LXX always translates *oinos* ("wine") and not *gleukos* ("new wine"), the term used in Acts 2:13. Though *tîrôš* can refer to freshly pressed grape juice (Isa 65:8; Mic 6:15), it can still be intoxicating (Hos 4:11). The word is an archaic term often used in summaries of agricultural products (Gen 27:28; Deut 7:13; 11:14; 18:4; 2 Kings 18:32; Jer 31:12) and is used exclusively in the Qumran texts. *Yiṣhār* is an archaic term for olive oil used in the same lists of agricultural products as *tîrôš*.

"A tithe of our crops" is literally "tithe of our land." The practice of giving a tenth was an ancient one (Gen 14:20; 28:22). The law decreed that a tenth of the plant crops was holy to the Lord (Lev 27:30; Num 18:23–32). There is no reference here to a tithe of cattle (as in Lev 27:32–33). Earlier in the fifth century B.C., the prophet Malachi accused the Israelites of robbing God by withholding tithes and offerings (Mal 3:8). Tithes were meant for the support of the Levites (13:10–12; Num 18: 21–32).

"Towns where we work" (lit., "towns of our work") were perhaps agricultural towns.

38 The Levites were to give in their turn "a tenth of the tithes" they received (Num 18:25–32). Chambers in the outer courts of the temple were used as "storerooms" for silver, gold, and other objects (cf. vv.39–40; 12:44; 13:4–5, 9; Ezra 8:29; 1 Macc 4:38).

39 *Dāgān* means "grain" and cereal crops. Formerly people referred to a "corn" of salt. But "corn" in America means maize or Indian corn. In the KJV "corn" occurs 101 times; it is uniformly replaced by "grain" in the RSV.

The people pledged themselves to "not neglect" God's house. The prophet Haggai (1:4–9) had accused the people of neglecting the temple.

I. The New Residents of Judah and Jerusalem (11:1–36)

1. Selection of the new residents

11:1–2

> ¹Now the leaders of the people settled in Jerusalem, and the rest of the people cast lots to bring one out of every ten to live in Jerusalem, the holy city, while the remaining nine were to stay in their own towns. ²The people commended all the men who volunteered to live in Jerusalem.

1 On "lots" see the comments on 10:34. Lots were made out of small stones or small pieces of wood. The pre-Islamic Arabs used wooden arrows without points (cf. Ezek 21:21; Hos 4:12). They were shaken (Prov 16:33) and cast (Obad 11; Nah 3:10) on the ground (1 Chron 24:31; Ezek 24:6; Jonah 1:7). Lots are also described as "coming out" (Num 33:54; Josh 19:1, 17; 1 Chron 24:7; 25:9; 26:14).

"The holy city" (cf. v.18) is a rare use of the phrase in a historical narrative that is usually found in prophetic texts (e.g., Isa 48:2; 52:1; Dan 9:24; Joel 3:17). The designation is also used in the NT (Matt 4:5; 27:53; Rev 11:2). The Arabic name for Jerusalem is *al-Quds* ("The Holy [City]").

"The remaining nine" is literally "the nine of the hand (or parts)." According to Ecclesiasticus 49:14: "The memory of Nehemiah also is lasting; he raised for us the walls that had fallen, and set up the gates and bars and rebuilt our ruined houses." Josephus (*Antiq.* XI, 181 [v.8]) asserts: "But Nehemiah, seeing that the city had a small population, urged the priests and Levites to leave the countryside and move to the city and remain there, for he had prepared houses for them at his own expense."

The practice of redistributing populations was also used to establish Greek and Hellenistic cities. Known as *synoikismos*, the practice involved the forcible transfer from rural settlements to urban centers. The city of Tiberias on the western shore of the Sea of Galilee was populated by such a process by Herod Antipas in A.D. 18 (Jos. *Antiq.* XVIII, 36–38 [ii.3]).

Estimates of the population of Jerusalem in Nehemiah's day vary. D.E. Gowan (*Bridge Between the Testaments* [Pittsburgh: Pickwick, 1976], p. 20) suggests 8,000. Probably more accurate is the estimate of M. Broshi ("La population de l'ancienne

Jérusalem," RB 92 [1975]: 9–10, 13), who multiplies an area of 120 dunams (a dunam is 1,000 square meters or 1,200 square yards) by 40 persons to arrive at 4,800. This is quite a drop from an area of 500 dunams (125 acres) and 20,000 during the time of Josiah (c. 609 B.C.). Jerusalem suffered the greatest loss of life during the Babylonian attacks.

2 In addition to those chosen by lot, some men volunteered, from a sense of duty, to live in Jerusalem (v.2). Evidently most would have preferred to stay in their native towns and villages (cf. Ezra 2:1). "Commended" (lit., "blessed") is a word usually used of God but at times, as here, of men (cf. 1 Chron 16:2; 2 Chron 6:3; 30:27).

2. The provincial leaders (11:3–24)

a. A topical statement (11:3–4a)

11:3–4a

> ³These are the provincial leaders who settled in Jerusalem (now some Israel-ites, priests, Levites, temple servants and descendants of Solomon's servants lived in the towns of Judah, each on his own property in the various towns, ⁴while other people from both Judah and Benjamin lived in Jerusalem):

3–4a These verses succinctly preview the specifics of vv.4b–36. Verses 3–19 are a census roster that can be compared with the list in 1 Chronicles 9:2–21 of the first residents in Jerusalem after the return from Babylonia. About half the names in the two lists are identical.

b. From Judah

11:4b–6

> From the descendants of Judah:
>
> Athaiah son of Uzziah, the son of Zechariah, the son of Amariah, the son of Shephatiah, the son of Mahalalel, a descendant of Perez; ⁵and Maaseiah son of Baruch, the son of Col-Hozeh, the son of Hazaiah, the son of Adaiah, the son of Joiarib, the son of Zechariah, a descendant of Shelah. ⁶The de-scendants of Perez who lived in Jerusalem totaled 468 able men.

4b "Athaiah" ("Yahweh has shown himself preeminent") occurs only here. "Mahala-lel" means "God is one who illuminates." "Perez" ("Breach") was also the name of one of the twin sons born to Judah (Gen 38:29).

5 "Hazaiah" ("Yahweh has seen") occurs only here. For "Shelah" the MT has Shilo-nite, i.e., an inhabitant of Shiloh, which belonged to the northern kingdom rather than to Judah. The word therefore should be revocalized to indicate a descendant of Shelah, Judah's third son (Num 26:20).

6 "Able men" (*'anšê-ḥāyil*) literally means "men of valor." These were originally valiant, free men whose later descendants became wealthy and served in the armed forces (cf. v.14; 2:9; 4:2 [3:34 MT]; 2 Kings 15:20; Ezra 8:22).

c. From Benjamin

11:7–9

⁷From the descendants of Benjamin:

Sallu son of Meshullam, the son of Joed, the son of Pedaiah, the son of Kolaiah, the son of Maaseiah, the son of Ithiel, the son of Jeshaiah, ⁸and his followers, Gabbai and Sallai—928 men. ⁹Joel son of Zicri was their chief officer, and Judah son of Hassenuah was over the Second District of the city.

7 For "Benjamin" see the comment on Ezra 4:1. "Joed" ("Yahweh is witness") occurs only here. "Kolaiah" ("voice of Yahweh") occurs only here and in Jeremiah 29:21. "Ithiel" ("God is with me") occurs only here and in Proverbs 30:1.

8 "Gabbai" derives from the verb "to be high" (cf. Ugar. *gby; Gabābēl*, "Bel is exalted" [Coogan, *Personal Names*, p. 70]).

Notice that Benjamin provided twice as many men (928) as Judah (468) to protect the city of Jerusalem.

9 "Zicri" is short for Zechariah. "The Second District" translates *mišneh*, which some EV transliterate as "Mishneh." Like the "market district" (*maḵtēš*) in Zephaniah 1:11 (probably the Tyropoeon Valley area), the Mishneh was a new suburb to the west of the temple area. Excavations by B. Mazar and N. Avigad indicate that the city had spread outside the walls in this direction by the late eighth century B.C. before the "broad wall" was built about 700 B.C. by Hezekiah (see comment on 3:8; cf. Yadin, *Jerusalem Revealed*, pp. 8, 41–44. See also Zeph 1:10–11).

d. From the priests

11:10–14

¹⁰From the priests:

Jedaiah; the son of Joiarib; Jakin; ¹¹Seraiah son of Hilkiah, the son of Meshullam, the son of Zadok, the son of Meraioth, the son of Ahitub, supervisor in the house of God, ¹²and their associates, who carried on work for the temple—822 men; Adaiah son of Jeroham, the son of Pelaliah, the son of Amzi, the son of Zechariah, the son of Pashhur, the son of Malkijah, ¹³and his associates, who were heads of families—242 men; Amashsai son of Azarel, the son of Ahzai, the son of Meshillemoth, the son of Immer, ¹⁴and his associates, who were able men—128. Their chief officer was Zabdiel son of Haggedolim.

10 "Jakin" means "he establishes" (cf. the parallel in 1 Chron 9:10).

11 "Seraiah" was the descendant of the high priest, who was taken prisoner by Nebuchadnezzar (2 Kings 25:18–21). See also 10:2; 12:1, 12; Ezra 2:2.

"Supervisor" translates *nāgîd* ("chief," "leader," "prince"). Pashhur, who had Jeremiah put in stocks (Jer 20:1–2), was such a "chief officer."

12 "Pelaliah" ("Yahweh has interposed") occurs only here. "Amzi" ("my strong one") is an abbreviated form of Amaziah. It occurs here and in 1 Chronicles 6:46.

13 "Ahzai" is a shortened form of Ahaziah ("Yahweh has grasped"), which occurs only here.

14 "Able men" (*gibbōrê ḥayil*) is literally "mighty men of valor" (cf. 2:9; 4:2 [3:34 MT]; 11:6; 1 Chron 9:13; Ezra 8:22). "Zabdiel" ("God has given") occurs only here and in 1 Chronicles 27:2. "Haggedolim" means "the great ones."

e. From the Levites

11:15–18

15From the Levites:

Shemaiah son of Hasshub, the son of Hashabiah, the son of Bunni; 16Shabbethai and Jozabad, two of the heads of the Levites, who had charge of the outside work of the house of God; 17Mattaniah son of Mica, the son of Zabdi, the son of Asaph, the director who led in thanksgiving and prayer; Bakbukiah, second among his associates; and Abda son of Shammua, the son of Galal, the son of Jeduthun. 18The Levites in the holy city totaled 284.

15 For "Hasshub" see the comment on 3:11. In 1957 J. Kaplan found an ostracon with this name at Tell Abu Zeitun along with fifth century B.C. Attic sherds. "Azrikam" means "my help has arisen."

16 "The outside work" (*ḥîṣōnāh*) is literally "lying outside," "outer" (cf. 1 Chron 26:29). Slotki (p. 251) explains that it refers to "duties outside the Temple but connected with it; e.g. providing materials for repairing the fabric of the building."

17 "Mica" is short for Michael (cf. on 10:11) or possibly for Michaiah ("Who is like Yahweh?"). The latter name appears in the Murashu texts as *Mīkayaw* (Coogan, *Personal Names*, p. 28). "Asaph" was one of the three leaders of the temple choirs (cf. 1 Chron 25:1–2; Pss 50, 73–83). "Bakbukiah" possibly means "the bottle of Yahweh." See the comment on Ezra 2:51. The name "Abda" ("slave" or "servant," i.e., of Yahweh, as in the name Obadiah [1 Chron 9:16]) occurs here and in 1 Kings 4:6. It occurs nine times in the Murashu texts as *ʿabdā* (Coogan, *Personal Names*, p. 31). "Galal" means "tortoise." On animal names see the comment on Ezra 2:3. "Jeduthun" was the chief of one of the three choirs (1 Chron 16:42; 25:1; 2 Chron 5:12; Pss 39, 62, 77).

18 The relatively small number of Levites (284) compared to the priests (1,192—the total of 822, 242, and 128 in vv.12–13) is striking, as in Ezra 2:40.

f. From the temple staff

11:19–24

19The gatekeepers:

Akkub, Talmon and their associates, who kept watch at the gates—172 men.

20The rest of the Israelites, with the priests and Levites, were in all the towns of Judah, each on his ancestral property.
21The temple servants lived on the hill of Ophel, and Ziha and Gishpa were in charge of them.

> 22The chief officer of the Levites in Jerusalem was Uzzi son of Bani, the son of Hashabiah, the son of Mattaniah, the son of Mica. Uzzi was one of Asaph's descendants, who were the singers responsible for the service of the house of God. 23The singers were under the king's orders, which regulated their daily activity.
> 24Pethahiah son of Meshezabel, one of the descendants of Zerah son of Judah, was the king's agent in all affairs relating to the people.

19 On "the gatekeepers" see the comment on Ezra 2:42.

20 "Ancestral property" (*naḥᵃlāh*) designates the inalienable hereditary possession including land, buildings, and movable goods acquired either by conquest or inheritance (Gen 31:14; Num 18:21; 27:7; 34:2; 1 Kings 21:3–4). The word is used at Ugarit in connection with individuals concerned with the administration of landed property. But in the OT it describes the land of Canaan as the possession of both Yahweh and Israel, including the individual holdings of tribes and families. It also designated Israel as Yahweh's special possession (Deut 4:20; 9:26, 29; 1 Kings 8:51 –53). H.O. Forshey ("The Construct Chain *naḥᵃlat YHWH/ᵉlōhîm*," BASOR 220 [1975]: 51) comments: "There is no parallel elsewhere in the ancient Near East to this use of *naḥᵃlāh* as an appellative of the covenant community."

21 On "the temple servants" see the comment on Ezra 2:43; on "Ophel" see on Nehemiah 3:26. "Gishpa," perhaps a corruption of Hasupha (Ezra 2:43), occurs only here.

22 On "the singers" see the comment on Ezra 2:41.

23 David regulated the services of the Levites, including the singers (1 Chron 25). The Persian king Artaxerxes I may have given a royal stipend so that the Levite choir might sing and pray for "the well-being of the king" (Ezra 6:10).

24 "Zerah," short for Zerahiah (Ezra 7:4), means "Yahweh has shone forth" (cf. Akkad. *Zaraḥ-šameš*, "The sun (god) has shone forth" [Coogan, *Personal Names*, pp. 23, 72–73]). "The king's agent" is literally "was at the king's hand."

2. *Places settled by those from Judah*

11:25–30

> 25As for the villages with their fields, some of the people of Judah lived in Kiriath Arba and its surrounding settlements, in Dibon and its settlements, in Jekabzeel and its villages, 26in Jeshua, in Moladah, in Beth Pelet, 27in Hazar Shual, in Beersheba and its settlements, 28in Ziklag, in Meconah and its settlements, 29in En Rimmon, in Zorah, in Jarmuth, 30Zanoah, Adullam and their villages, in Lachish and its fields, and in Azekah and its settlements. So they were living all the way from Beersheba to the Valley of Hinnom.

This is an important list, which corresponds to earlier lists of Judean cities. All these names also appear in Joshua 15 except Dibon, Jeshua, and Meconah. The list, however, is not comprehensive as a number of cities listed in Ezra 2:20–34 and Nehemiah 3 are lacking. The limits of the Judean settlement after the return from

Babylon have been confirmed by archaeological evidence; none of the YHD-YHWD (the official designation of the Persian province of Judea) coins have been found outside the area demarcated by these verses.

25 "Kiriath Arba" ("city of four [giants]") was the archaic name of the city of Hebron (Gen 23:2; Judg 1:20), the important city twenty miles south of Jerusalem. In the Hellenistic era it fell to the Idumaeans. As Hebron is the traditional site of the burial of Abraham, Sarah, and other patriarchs, Jewish zealots of the Gush Emunim party have established a settlement on the outskirts of Arab Hebron known as Kiryat Arba.

"Its settlements" is literally "its daughters" (cf. Num 21:25, 32; 32:42: Josh 15:45, 47; 1 Chron 2:23; 2 Chron 13:19).

26 "Jeshua" is Tell es-Saʿweh (?), northeast of Beersheba. "Moladah" was not far from Beersheba (Josh 15:26); it was occupied by the Idumaeans and perhaps was the same as Malatha (Jos. *Antiq*. XVIII, 147 [vi.2]). "Beth Pelet," a site near Beersheba (Josh 15:27), means "house of refuge."

27 "Hazar Shual" means "enclosure of a fox [or jackal]" (see comment on 4:3; cf. Josh 15:28; 1 Chron 4:28).

According to Genesis 21:25–31, "Beersheba" means "well of the seven" or "well of the oath." About thirty miles south of Hebron, Beersheba represented the southernmost limit of population as in the expression "from Dan to Beersheba" (Judg 20:1; cf. 1 Chron 21:2). Tel Beersheba east of the modern city was excavated by Y. Aharoni from 1969 to 1976. He discovered a well sixty-five feet deep, but no material remains earlier than the early Iron Age. The settlement was destroyed by Sennacherib in 701 B.C. and only resettled in the Persian period. Some forty Aramaic ostraca have been recovered from the mid-fourth century B.C., though no buildings of this period have been discovered (cf. Y. Aharoni, "Beersheba, Tel," *Encyclopedia of Archaeological Excavations in the Holy Land*, ed. M. Avi-Yonah [London: Oxford University Press, 1975], 1:160–68).

28 "Ziklag" is celebrated as the town given to David by Achish, king of Gath (1 Sam 27:6), and taken by the Amalekites (1 Sam 30:1). "Meconah," a town near Ziklag, is of uncertain location, possibly Tell esh-Shārîʿah.

29 "En Rimmon" ("spring of the pomegranate") was probably Tell Halif nine and a half miles north northeast of Beersheba (cf. Josh 15:32; 19:7; 1 Chron 4:32). See J.D. Seger and O. Borowski, "The First Two Seasons at Tell Halif." BA 40 (1977): 156–66. "Zorah" is Sarʿah on the north side of the Wadi es-Sarar ("valley of Sorek"), the home of Manoah, Samson's father (Judg 13:2). "Jarmuth," eight miles northeast of Eleutheropolis (Beit-Jibrin), was one of five Canaanite cities in the south that attempted to halt Joshua's invasion (Josh 10:3–5).

30 "Zanoah" was a village in the Shephelah district of low hills between Judah and the area of Philistia (Josh 15:34). The men of Zanoah repaired the Valley Gate (Neh 3:13). The site has been identified with Khirbet Zānûʿ, three miles southeast of Beth-Shemesh. "Adullam" was the city between Jerusalem and Lachish where David hid in a cave from Saul (1 Sam 22:1).

"Lachish" is Tell ed-Duweir, a great Judean city midway between Jerusalem and Gaza. The site was excavated between 1932 and 1938 by James Starkey. Renewed excavations began in 1973 under David Ussishkin. The Assyrian king Sennacherib failed to take Jerusalem in 701 B.C. but did capture Lachish, a feat depicted on famous reliefs now in the British Museum. The city was later captured by Nebuchadnezzar (Jer 34:7) and was then resettled during Nehemiah's time for a Persian governor, identified as Geshem by G.E. Wright ("Judean Lachish," BA 18 [1955]: 9 –17). An inscribed Arabic incense altar from Nehemiah's time has been found at Lachish. See F.M. Cross, "Two Notes on Palestinian Inscriptions of the Persian Age," BASOR 193 (1969): 19–24. See also Y. Aharoni, "Trial Excavation in the 'Solar Shrine' at Lachish," IEJ 18 (1968): 157–69; D. Ussishkin, "Excavating at Tel Lachish 1973–77," Tel Aviv 5 (1978): 1–97; id., "Answers at Lachish," Biblical Archaeology Review 5.6 (1979): 16–39.

"Azekah" is Tell Zakarîyeh. Lachish and Azekah are mentioned together and in this order also in Jeremiah 34:7. One of the Lachish ostraca presents this dramatic message as Nebuchadnezzar's forces were approaching: "And let (my lord) know that we are watching for the signals of Lachish, according to all the indications which my lord hath given, for we cannot see Azekah" (ANET, p. 322).

"Hinnom" is the valley southwest of Jerusalem (NT Gehenna; cf. L.R. Bailey, "Gehenna: The Topography of Hell," BA 49 [1986]: 187–91). The direct distance from Jerusalem to Beersheba is only forty miles.

3. Places settled by those from Benjamin

11:31–35

> [31]The descendants of the Benjamites from Geba lived in Micmash, Aija, Bethel and its settlements, [32]in Anathoth, Nob and Ananiah, [33]in Hazor, Ramah and Gittaim, [34]in Hadid, Zeboim and Neballat, [35]in Lod and Ono, and in the Valley of the Craftsmen.

31 "Geba" ("height") is Jeba, six miles northeast of Jerusalem (cf. Josh 18:24; Ezra 2:26; Neh 7:30). Geba, the traditional northern limit of Judah (2 Kings 23:8; Zech 14:10), was fortified by Asa (1 Kings 15:22).

"Micmash" is Mukhmas, seven miles northeast of Jerusalem (cf. Ezra 2:27; Neh 7:31). Micmash was the location of the strategic pass to the Jordan Valley, where Saul and Jonathan fought the Philistines (1 Sam 13–14).

"Aija," an alternative name for "Ai" ("ruins"), has been identified with et-Tell, just three miles southeast of Bethel. This was a city taken by Joshua (Josh 7–8), though the excavations by J. Callaway at et-Tell between 1964 and 1970 did not uncover any Late Bronze remains. Nor is there anything later than 1050 B.C. at et-Tell.

"Bethel" ("house of God") is Beitîn, a site partially excavated by W.F. Albright and J.L. Kelso between 1934 and 1960. J.L. Kelso (The Excavation of Bethel [Cambridge: American Schools of Oriental Research, 1968], p. 52) observes: "The data in Ezra and Nehemiah parallel the archaeological finds. . . . Bethel was the northernmost town listed with the Benjaminites in Neh 11:31ff. but it was not listed at all among the people rebuilding the walls of Jerusalem. The tiny post-exilic village was doubtless close to the springs beneath the built-up area of modern Beitin."

32 "Anathoth" is Anata, three miles north of Jerusalem, the birthplace of Jeremiah

(Jer 1:1; cf. Ezra 2:23; Neh 7:27). "Nob," probably Mount Scopus, is just north of the Mount of Olives, where the sanctuary was established after the destruction of Shiloh (Jer 7:14; see 1 Sam 21:1–9; Isa 10:27–32). "Ananiah" was probably Bethany (i.e., "house of Ananiah"), which was two miles east of Jerusalem. Today the Arabs call the village el-Aziríyeh, after Lazarus.

33 "Hazor" is Khirbet Hazzur, west of Beit Hanina, which is north of Jerusalem. "Gittaim" ("two wine presses"; cf. 2 Sam 4:3) is probably at Râs Abū Ḥamîd near Ramleh. This site was mistakenly assumed to be the famous Philistine Gath in Eusebius's *Onomasticon* (cf. A.F. Rainey, "Gath of the Philistines," *Christian News from Israel* 17.2–3 [1966]: 30–31).

34 "Hadid" ("sharp") is el-Haditheh, three to four miles northeast of Lydda near the mouth of the Aijalon Valley (cf. Ezra 2:33; Neh 7:37). It was called Adida in the Hellenistic era (1 Macc 12:38). "Zeboim" ("hyenas") was possibly north of Lydda, perhaps Khirbet Sabieh. "Neballat" is Beit Nebala, four miles east of Lydda. The name may have preserved that of an Assyrian governor of Samaria (seventh cent. B.C.), Nabu-uballit.

35 "Lod" (Gr. Lydda, Arab. Ludd) is today the site of Israel's international airport, ten miles from the coast (cf. Ezra 2:33; Neh 7:37; 1 Macc 10:30, 38). Peter healed Aeneas at Lydda (Acts 9:32–38). It became a rabbinical center in the Talmudic period.

"Ono" is Kafr 'Anā, five and a half miles northwest of Lydda. The enemies of Nehemiah tried to lure him to a conference there (Neh 6:2; cf. Ezra 2:33; Neh 7:37).

"The Valley of the Craftsmen" (*gê haharāšîm;* cf. 1 Chron 4:14) may be the Wadi esh-Shellal, the broad valley between Lod and Ono. The name may preserve the memory of the Philistine iron monopoly (1 Sam 13:19–20). In any case the oak trees of the nearby Sharon plain would have been useful to artisans working in either wood or iron. See M. Har-El, "The Valley of the Craftsmen," *PEQ* 109 (1977): 75–86.

4. Transfer of Levites from Judah to Benjamin

11:36

³⁶Some of the divisions of the Levites of Judah settled in Benjamin.

36 Certain divisions of Levites, who had been located in Judah, were now transferred to Benjamin to rectify the disproportion presumably discovered in Nehemiah's census.

J. Lists of Priests and the Dedication of the Wall (12:1–47)

1. Priests and Levites from the first return

12:1–9

¹These were the priests and Levites who returned with Zerubbabel son of Shealtiel and with Jeshua:
Seraiah, Jeremiah, Ezra,

2 Amariah, Malluch, Hattush,
3 Shecaniah, Rehum, Meremoth,
4 Iddo, Ginnethon, Abijah,
5 Mijamin, Moadiah, Bilgah,
6 Shemaiah, Joiarib, Jedaiah,
7 Sallu, Amok, Hilkiah and Jedaiah.
These were the leaders of the priests and their associates in the days of Jeshua.

8 The Levites were Jeshua, Binnui, Kadmiel, Sherebiah, Judah, and also Mattaniah, who, together with his associates, was in charge of the songs of thanksgiving. 9 Bakbukiah and Unni, their associates, stood opposite them in the services.

1 "Shealtiel" was the father of Zerubbabel according to this verse and Ezra 3:2, 8; Haggai 1:1; but 1 Chronicles 3:17-19 lists him as the uncle of Zerubbabel. On this see the comment on Ezra 5:2.

"Jeshua" was the high priest about 560-490 B.C. (cf. Ezra 2:2; Neh 7:7; 12:10, 26). "Seraiah" (cf. 11:11; 12:12) is called Azariah in 1 Chronicles 9:11 (cf. on Ezra 2:2). On "Jeremiah" see the comment on 10:2.

This "Ezra" is, of course, not the same Ezra who returned eighty years later. On the name see on Ezra 7:1.

2 On "Amariah" see Ezra 7:3; "Malluch," Ezra 10:29; and "Hattush," Ezra 8:2.

3 On "Shecaniah" see on Ezra 8:3. On "Rehum" see on Ezra 2:2; in this verse it may be a corruption of Harim (cf. Ezra 2:39; Neh 7:42). On "Meremoth" see on Ezra 8:33.

4 "Iddo" (from ʿ$a\bar{d}\bar{a}y\bar{a}$ʾ, "timely") is the same name as that of the prophet Zechariah's grandfather (Zech 1:1). On "Abijah" see on 10:7.

5 On "Mijamin" see comment on Ezra 10:25 (cf. Miniamin, v.17; see Coogan, *Personal Names,* p. 77). "Moadiah" means "Yahweh assembles" (cf. v.17). "Bilgah" ("brightness") occurs only here, in v.18, and in 1 Chronicles 24:14.

6 On "Shemaiah" see the comment on Ezra 8:13; on "Jedaiah," on Ezra 2:36.

7 "Amok" means "deep," "unsearchable." On "Hilkiah" see on Ezra 7:1.

The rotation of twenty-four priestly houses may have been established at the time of David (cf. Jos. *Antiq.* VII, 365 [xiv.7]). There are twenty-two heads of priestly houses mentioned here in vv.1-7. Inscriptions listing the twenty-four courses of the priests probably hung in hundreds of synagogues in Palestine. Thus far only fragments of two such inscriptions have been recovered—one found at Ascalon in the 1920s and fragments from Caesarea in the 1960s (dated to the third and fourth century A.D.) (see M.A. Avi-Yonah, "The Caesarea Inscription of the Twenty-four Priestly Courses," in *The Teacher's Yoke,* ed. E.J. Vardaman et al. [Waco: Baylor University Press, 1964], pp. 46ff.).

8 On "Jeshua" see the comment on Ezra 2:2; on "Kadmiel," on Ezra 2:40; on "Sherebiah," on Ezra 8:18; on "Judah," on Ezra 3:9; and on "Mattaniah," on Ezra 10:26.

9 On "Bakbukiah" ("bottle of Yahweh"?) see on Ezra 2:51. "Unni," short for Anaiah (cf. 8:4), occurs only here and in 1 Chronicles 15:18, 20. The singing was in antiphonal fashion with two sections of the choir standing opposite each other (cf. v.24; 2 Chron 7:6; Ezra 3:11).

"Services" (*mišmārôt*, "wards" or "divisions") is the title of a work from Qumran that discusses in detail the rotation of the priestly families' service in the temple according to the sect's solar calendar, which was synchronized with the lunar calendar.

Notes

8 הַיְּדוֹת (*huyyᵉdôt*, "thanksgiving") is an unusual form for הוֹדָיוֹת (*hôḏāyôt*). The *Hodayoth* at Qumran were "Thanksgiving Hymns."

2. High priests and Levites since Joiakim

12:10–26

10Jeshua was the father of Joiakim, Joiakim the father of Eliashib, Eliashib the father of Joiada, 11Joiada the father of Jonathan, and Jonathan the father of Jaddua.

12In the days of Joiakim, these were the heads of the priestly families:
of Seraiah's family, Meraiah;
of Jeremiah's, Hananiah;
13of Ezra's, Meshullam;
of Amariah's, Jehohanan;
14of Malluch's, Jonathan;
of Shecaniah's, Joseph;
15of Harim's, Adna;
of Meremoth's, Helkai;
16of Iddo's, Zechariah;
of Ginnethon's, Meshullam;
17of Abijah's, Zicri;
of Miniamin's and of Moadiah's, Piltai;
18of Bilgah's, Shammua;
of Shemaiah's, Jehonathan;
19of Joiarib's, Mattenai;
of Jedaiah's, Uzzi;
20of Sallu's, Kallai;
of Amok's, Eber;
21of Hilkiah's, Hashabiah;
of Jedaiah's, Nethanel.

22The family heads of the Levites in the days of Eliashib, Joiada, Johanan and Jaddua, as well as those of the priests, were recorded in the reign of Darius the Persian. 23The family heads among the descendants of Levi up to the time of Johanan son of Eliashib were recorded in the book of the annals. 24And the leaders of the Levites were Hashabiah, Sherebiah, Jeshua son of Kadmiel, and their associates, who stood opposite them to give praise and thanksgiving, one section responding to the other, as prescribed by David the man of God.

25Mattaniah, Bakbukiah, Obadiah, Meshullam, Talmon and Akkub were gate-keepers who guarded the storerooms at the gates. 26They served in the days of Joiakim son of Jeshua, the son of Jozadak, and in the days of Nehemiah the governor and of Ezra the priest and scribe.

10–11 On the complex problem of the identification of these high priests, see the Introduction: The High Priests.

12 All but one of the twenty-two priestly families listed in vv. 1–7 are repeated in this later list that dates to the time of Joiakim, the high priest in the late sixth and early fifth century B.C. "Meraiah," probably from Amariah, occurs only here.

13 On "Meshullam" see on Ezra 8:16; on "Amariah," on Ezra 7:3; and on "Jehoha-nan," on Ezra 10:6.

14 On "Jonathan" see on Ezra 8:6. For "Shecaniah" the Hebrew MSS read "Sheba-niah," but this is probably an error (see v.3).

15 On "Harim" see on Ezra 2:32; on "Adna," on Ezra 10:30. For "Meremoth" (LXX, Syr.) the Hebrew MSS read "Meraioth," but this is probably an error (cf. 10:5). "Helkai," contracted from "Hilkiah" ("my portion is Yahweh"), occurs only here.

17 "Zicri" is short for Zechariah. "Miniamin" ("luck") is literally "from the right hand" (cf. Coogan, *Personal Names*, p. 28). On "Moadiah" see on v.5. "Piltai" ("[God is] deliverance") occurs only here.

20 For "Sallu" the MT has Sallai, but this is probably an error (cf. v.7). "Eber" was also the eponym of the Hebrews (Gen 10:21).

21 On "Hashabiah" see on Ezra 8:19.

22 On the identification of "Eliashib, Joiada, Johanan, and Jaddua" with those men-tioned in the extrabiblical sources, see the Introduction: The High Priests.
   "Darius the Persian" was either Nothus, Darius II (423–404 B.C.), or Codoman-nus, Darius III (335–331 B.C.), the king whose empire Alexander the Great con-quered. The fact that a Jaddua is mentioned as the high priest by Josephus (*Antiq*. XI, 302 [vii.2]) has caused some scholars to favor the later king. A Johanan appears, however, as the high priest in an Elephantine papyrus dated to 407 B.C. (ANET, p. 492); and this favors an identification with Darius II. The recently discovered Sa-maria papyri has persuaded some scholars that the Jaddua in Nehemiah was not the Jaddua in Josephus but the grandfather of the latter (see F.M. Cross, "The Discov-ery of the Samaria Papyri," BA 26 [1963]: 121; id., "Aspects of Samaritan and Jewish History in Late Persian and Hellenistic Times," HTR 59 [1966]: 203ff.).

23 The "book of the annals" (*sēper diḇrê hayyāmîm*, lit., "book of the words (deeds) of the days," or "chronicles"; cf. Neh 7:5) may have been the official temple chronicle containing various lists and records. Compare the annals of the Persian kings (Ezra 4:15; Esth 2:23; 6:1; 10:2); "the book of the annals of the kings of Israel," mentioned eighteen times in 1 and 2 Kings; and "the book of the annals of the kings of Judah," mentioned fifteen times in 1 and 2 Kings.

24 On "who stood opposite" see on v.9. On "David's directions" see 1 Chronicles 16:4; 23:27–31; 2 Chronicles 8:14.

25 From 11:17 we would have expected Mattaniah and Bakbukiah to be associated with the leaders of the choirs mentioned in v.24, rather than with the gatekeepers of v.25. On "gatekeepers" see the comment on Ezra 2:42 (cf. Neh 3:1).

26 This is one of the explicit references of the contemporaneity of Ezra and Nehemiah (see Introduction: The Order).

3. *Dedication of the walls of Jerusalem*

12:27–43

> [27]At the dedication of the wall of Jerusalem, the Levites were sought out from where they lived and were brought to Jerusalem to celebrate joyfully the dedication with songs of thanksgiving and with the music of cymbals, harps and lyres. [28]The singers also were brought together from the region around Jerusalem—from the villages of the Netophathites, [29]from Beth Gilgal, and from the area of Geba and Azmaveth, for the singers had built villages for themselves around Jerusalem. [30]When the priests and Levites had purified themselves ceremonially, they purified the people, the gates and the wall.
>
> [31]I had the leaders of Judah go up on top of the wall. I also assigned two large choirs to give thanks. One was to proceed on top of the wall to the right, toward the Dung Gate. [32]Hoshaiah and half the leaders of Judah followed them, [33]along with Azariah, Ezra, Meshullam, [34]Judah, Benjamin, Shemaiah, Jeremiah, [35]as well as some priests with trumpets, and also Zechariah son of Jonathan, the son of Shemaiah, the son of Mattaniah, the son of Micaiah, the son of Zaccur, the son of Asaph, [36]and his associates—Shemaiah, Azarel, Milalai, Gilalai, Maai, Nethanel, Judah and Hanani—with musical instruments ⌊prescribed by⌋ David the man of God. Ezra the scribe led the procession. [37]At the Fountain Gate they continued directly up the steps of the City of David on the ascent to the wall and passed above the house of David to the Water Gate on the east.
>
> [38]The second choir proceeded in the opposite direction. I followed them on top of the wall, together with half the people—past the Tower of the Ovens to the Broad Wall, [39]over the Gate of Ephraim, the Jeshanah Gate, the Fish Gate, the Tower of Hananel and the Tower of the Hundred, as far as the Sheep Gate. At the Gate of the Guard they stopped.
>
> [40]The two choirs that gave thanks then took their places in the house of God; so did I, together with half the officials, [41]as well as the priests—Eliakim, Maaseiah, Miniamin, Micaiah, Elioenai, Zechariah and Hananiah with their trumpets—[42]and also Maaseiah, Shemaiah, Eleazar, Uzzi, Jehohanan, Malkijah, Elam and Ezer. The choirs sang under the direction of Jezrahiah. [43]And on that day they offered great sacrifices, rejoicing because God had given them great joy. The women and children also rejoiced. The sound of rejoicing in Jerusalem could be heard far away.

27 On "dedication" (*ḥᵃnukkāh*) compare the dedication of the temple by Solomon (1 Kings 8) and the dedication of Zerubbabel's temple (Ezra 6:16). The dedication of the wall culminates the efforts of the people under Nehemiah's inspired leadership. Great enthusiasm must have characterized their march to the joyful music.

After the recapture of the temple by Judas Maccabeus from the Seleucids on 25 Kislev 165 B.C., the temple was again rededicated (2 Macc 1:18), an act that was the basis for the Jewish holiday of Hanukkah.

"Cymbals" (mᵉṣiltayim) were used for religious ceremonies (2 Sam 6:5; 1 Chron 16:42; 25:1; 2 Chron 5:12; 29:25; Ezra 3:10). Cymbals have been recovered from Beth-shemesh and from Tell Abu Hawam.

"Harps" (nᵉbel) occurs twenty-seven times. The KJV translated the word twenty-three times as "psaltry" (cf. Vul. psalterium) and four times as "viol." It was used mainly in religious ceremonies (e.g., 1 Sam 10:5; 2 Sam 6:5; 1 Chron 15:16, 20, 28; Ps 150:3) with a few exceptions (Isa 5:12; 14:11; Amos 5:23). The harp was an instrument with strings of varying lengths.

"Lyres" (kinnôr) occurs forty-two times. The LXX renders it twenty times as kithara and seventeen times as kinura. The KJV renders the term as "harp," the RSV as "lyre." The lyre was an instrument with strings of the same length but of different diameters and tensions (see Gen 4:21; 1 Sam 16:16, 23; 1 Chron 15:16, 21, 28; Pss 137:2; 149:3; 150:3; Isa 23:16; Dan 3:5, 7, 10, 15). See T.C. Mitchell and R. Joyce, "The Musical Instruments in Nebuchadnezzar's Orchestra," in Notes on Some Problems in the Book of Daniel, ed. D.J. Wiseman et al. (London: Tyndale, 1965), pp. 19–22.

28 "Netophathites" were from Netophah, a town near Bethlehem (1 Chron 2:54; 9:16; Ezra 2:22; Neh 7:26). The site is perhaps Khirbet Bedd Fālûḥ near the spring ʿAin en-Natuf.

29 "Beth-Gilgal" was perhaps the Gilgal near Jericho (Josh 4:19–20) or the Gilgal of Elijah (2 Kings 2:1), some seven miles north of Bethel.

30 On "purified" compare Ezra 6:20; see also comments on Nehemiah 13:9, 22, 30. The verb ṭᵃhēr occurs ninety-four times. It is used almost exclusively of ritual or moral purity, most frequently of the purification necessary to restore someone who had contracted impurity to a state of purity so that he might participate in ritual activities (Lev 22:4–7). The Levites are said to have cleansed all that was holy in the temple (1 Chron 23:28) and the temple itself (2 Chron 29:15) during the times of revival. Ritual purification was intended to teach God's holiness and moral purity (Lev 16:30).

31 There were two great processions, starting probably from the area of the Valley Gate (2:13, 15; 3:13) in the center of the western section of the wall. The first procession led by Ezra (v.36) and Hoshaiah (v.32) moved in a counterclockwise direction on the wall; the second with Nehemiah moved in a clockwise direction. They met between the Prison Gate and the Water Gate and then entered the temple area (cf. Ps 48:12–13).

"To the right" translates yāmîn. The literal rendering is misleading, as this procession went left to the south. The Semite oriented himself facing east; so the right hand represented the south (cf. the name of Yemen in southern Arabia; see Josh 17:7; 1 Sam 23:24; Job 23:9).

32 "Hoshaiah" ("Yahweh has saved") occurs only here and in Jeremiah 42:1.

33 "Ezra" here is not Ezra the scribe (v.36).

34 "Judah" is lacking in the LXX (cf. Hodaviah in Ezra 3:9).

35 On "trumpets" see on Ezra 3:10. Each choir was composed of seven priests blowing trumpets and the Levites playing on other musical instruments. "Asaph" was the founder of one of the three guilds of Levite musicians (1 Chron 25:1–2).

36 "Milalai," lacking in the LXX, is perhaps an error for "Gilalai," which occurs only here, as does "Maai." "Judah" is lacking in the LXX. On "Ezra the scribe" see on Ezra 7:1–6.

37 On the "Fountain Gate" see on 3:15; on the Water Gate," on 3:26.
The procession went around the southern end of the walls, then north up the eastern wall to the Water Gate near the Gihon Spring.

38 "The second choir" is literally "the second thanks," i.e., the thanksgiving choir. "In the opposite direction" (*lᵉmô'l*, to be emended to *liśᵉm ōl*) is literally "to the left" but means northwards (so Josh 19:27; Isa 54:3; Ezek 16:46; cf. the note on v.31).
The procession led by Nehemiah went north in a clockwise direction around the northwestern sections of the wall. On the "Tower of the Ovens," see the comment on 3:11; on "Broad Wall," on 3:8.

39 On the "Ephraim Gate" see the comment on 8:16. This gate is not mentioned as in need of repair in chapter 3. It stood between the Broad Wall and the Jeshanah Gate. On the "Jeshanah Gate" see the comment on 3:6; on the "Fish Gate," on 3:3; the "Tower of Hananel," on 3:1; and the "Tower of the Hundred," on 3:1.
Some scholars suggest that *maṭṭārāh* ("Gate of the Guard"; cf. "the courtyard of the guard," Jer 32:2) be emended to *mipqāḏ*, to make it the "Inspection Gate." On the latter see the comment on 3:31.

40 Other nations had such solemn processions, too. The famous fifth-century B.C. reliefs from the staircase of Darius's Apadana depict representatives from many nations bearing gifts for the royal treasury (cf. Yamauchi, "Achaemenid Capitals," pp. 32–33; R. Ghirshman, *The Art of Ancient Iran* [New York: Golden, 1964]; E.F. Schmidt, *Persepolis III* [Chicago: University of Chicago Press, 1970]). In Athens every fourth year the Panathenaic festival featured a procession from the Agora to the Acropolis for the presentation of a new garment for the stature of Athena (see N. Yalouris, *Classical Greece: The Elgin Marbles of the Parthenon* [Greenwich, Conn.: New York Graphic Society, 1960]). The famous Altar of Peace of Augustus depicts a solemn procession of the imperial family, senators, and priests. See D. Earl, *The Age of Augustus* (New York: Crown, 1968), pp. 120ff., figs. 51, 53, pp. 113–16.

42 "The choirs sang" is literally "the singers made (themselves) heard." "Jezrahiah" means "Yahweh shines forth" (cf. Izrahiah, 1 Chron 7:3).

43 "Great sacrifices" (cf. Judg 16:23) were offered because "God made them rejoice with great joy" (cf. 1 Chron 29:9; Jonah 4:6). "The women" (see 8:2; 10:28; Exod 15:20) "could be heard far away" (see on Ezra 3:13; cf. 1 Kings 1:40; 2 Kings 11:13).

Notes

27 Some scholars (e.g., Michaeli, Gelin) believe that vv.27–34 on the dedication of the wall should be placed after the passage (Neh 6:15–16) describing the completion of the wall. Myers (*Ezra–Nehemiah*, in loc) suggests that this passage "logically joins clearly with Neh. 11,36 of which it is a continuation." For the view that the נֶבֶל (*nēbel*) was not a harp but "a reed instrument with a windbag made of an animal hide," see Miriam Aharoni, "The Askos: Is It the Biblical *Nēbel*?," *Tel Aviv* 6 (1979): 95–97.

31 The MT reads וְתַהֲלֻכֹת (*wetahªlukōt*, "festal procession"). The NIV's "one was to proceed" reflects an emendation to וְהָאַחַת הֹלֶכֶת (*wehāʾaḥat hōleket*, "and the one went in procession").

---

4. Regulations of the temple offerings and services

12:44–47

44At that time men were appointed to be in charge of the storerooms for the contributions, firstfruits and tithes. From the fields around the towns they were to bring into the storerooms the portions required by the Law for the priests and the Levites, for Judah was pleased with the ministering priests and Levites. 45They performed the service of their God and the service of purification, as did also the singers and gatekeepers, according to the commands of David and his son Solomon. 46For long ago, in the days of David and Asaph, there had been directors for the singers and for the songs of praise and thanksgiving to God. 47So in the days of Zerubbabel and of Nehemiah, all Israel contributed the daily portions for the singers and gatekeepers. They also set aside the portion for the other Levites, and the Levites set aside the portion for the descendants of Aaron.

44–45 "Storerooms" (v.44) translates *niškāh*, which occurs only here, in 3:30, and in 13:7. On "contributions" see on 10:37, 39.

The people of Judah were "pleased" (i.e., it gave them great joy) to contribute their offerings to support the priests and Levites (cf. 2 Cor 9:7). "Ministering" is literally "standing" (cf. Deut 10:8, "to stand before the LORD to minister" to him).

46 Asaph, a founder of one of the three musical guilds, was a Gershonite Levite to whom David entrusted the "service of song" in the tabernacle (cf. 1 Chron 6:39; 2 Chron 29:30; 35:15; Pss 50, 73–83).

47 On "Zerubbabel" see on Ezra 2:2; 3:2, 8; 4:2–3; Neh 7:7; 12:1. "Contributed" translates a participle implying continued giving. "The daily portions" is literally "the matter of the day in its day" (cf. E. Yamauchi, "The Daily Bread Motif in Antiquity," *WTJ* 28 [1966]: 145–56). On "the Levites set aside," see the comment on 10:37–38.

II. Nehemiah's Second Administration (13:1–31)

A. *Abuses During His Absence (13:1–5)*

1. *Mixed marriages*

13:1–3

> [1]On that day the Book of Moses was read aloud in the hearing of the people and there it was found written that no Ammonite or Moabite should ever be admitted into the assembly of God, [2]because they had not met the Israelites with food and water but had hired Balaam to call a curse down on them. (Our God, however, turned the curse into a blessing.) [3]When the people heard this law, they excluded from Israel all who were of foreign descent.

1 The reference "the Book of Moses" is to Deuteronomy 23:3–6 (cf. Num 22–24). On marriages to Ammonites and Moabites, see the comment on Ezra 9:1. On the general subject of intermarriage, see the excursus after Ezra 10.

2 "Balaam" (*bil'ām*) was the seer summoned by Balak, the king of Moab, to curse Israel (Num 22–24). He came from Pethor, probably Pitru in northwestern Mesopotamia (Num 22:5). Though hired to curse the Israelites, through the inspiration of Yahweh he blessed them instead. Later, however, he was used to lead Israel into the worship of the Moabite god at Peor (Num 25:1–3; 31:16; cf. Rev 2:14). In the NT his name is symbolic of avarice (2 Peter 2:15; Jude 11). (See W.F. Albright, "The Oracles of Balaam," JBL 63 [1944]: 208–33.) A remarkable Aramaic inscription referring to Balaam, dated to the sixth century B.C., was found inscribed on wall plaster at Deir 'Alla in Transjordan (cf. J. Hoftijzer, "The Prophet Balaam in a 6th-Century Aramaic Inscription," BA 39 [1976]: 11–17; Jo Ann Hackett, *The Balaam Text from Deir 'Alla* [Chico: Scholars, 1984]).

Curses had a dynamic power of their own once uttered and could not simply be recalled. They could, however, be canceled by blessings (cf. Judg 17:1–2; see C.H. Gordon, *Adventures in the Nearest East* [London: Phoenix House, 1957], pp. 165–69; E.M. Yamauchi, *Mandaic Incantation Texts* [New Haven: American Oriental Society, 1967], pp. 1–67).

3 The same term for "foreign descent" (*'ēreb*; KJV "mixed multitude") is used in Exodus 12:38. There, however, the mixed multitude was welcomed as they had agreed to the worship of Yahweh, whereas it is implied that this was not the case here.

Notes

1 Schaeder would place Neh 10 (the covenant) after Neh 13 for what he believes would make a more satisfactory conclusion to Nehemiah's ministry.

2. Tobiah's occupation of the temple quarters

13:4–5

⁴Before this, Eliashib the priest had been put in charge of the storerooms of the house of our God. He was closely associated with Tobiah, ⁵and he had provided him with a large room formerly used to store the grain offerings and incense and temple articles, and also the tithes of grain, new wine and oil prescribed for the Levites, singers and gatekeepers, as well as the contributions for the priests.

4 Some scholars (e.g., Batten, Berman) identify "Eliashib" with the high priest of that name (cf. 3:1, 20; 13:28; see Introduction: The High Priests). Others argue that it is unlikely for a high priest to have been placed in charge of storerooms.

The word rendered "closely associated" (*qārôḇ*) is used in Ruth 2:20 to indicate that Boaz was related to Naomi and Ruth. We do not know exactly how Tobiah (cf. on 2:10) was related or associated with Eliashib.

5 During Nehemiah's absence from the city to return to the Persian king's court, Tobiah had used his influence with Eliashib to gain entrance into a chamber ordinarily set aside for the storage of tithes and other offerings (Num 18:21–32; Deut 14:28–29; 26:12–15). The storerooms mentioned in vv.4–5, 13 were evidently in the inner court of the temple. Those mentioned in 10:38–39 and Zechariah 3:7 were parts of the outer court. Elsewhere we read of the chamber of Jehohanan (Ezra 10:6) and of Meshullam (Neh 3:30).

One of the Aramaic letters from the governors of Judah and Samaria to the Jews of Elephantine (Cowley 32; ANET, p. 492) instructs that "the meal-offering and incense" was "to be made on that altar as it used to be" (cf. B. Porten, ed., *Jews of Elephantine and Arameans of Syene* [Jerusalem: Academon, 1976], pp. 98–99). Frankincense (*lᵉḇônāh*, NIV, "incense") like myrrh is a resin derived from trees that grow only in Somalia and in southern Arabia (cf. Gus W. van Beek, "Frankincense and Myrrh," BA 23 [1960]: 70–95; N. Green, *Frankincense and Myrrh* [London: Longman, 1981]).

B. Nehemiah's Return

13:6–7

⁶But while all this was going on, I was not in Jerusalem, for in the thirty-second year of Artaxerxes king of Babylon I had returned to the king. Some time later I asked his permission ⁷and came back to Jerusalem. Here I learned about the evil thing Eliashib had done in providing Tobiah a room in the courts of the house of God.

6 On the chronology see the comments on 1:1 and 2:1. The thirty-second year of Artaxerxes I (on a Nisan calendar) ran from 1 April 433 to 19 April 432 B.C. This verse and 5:14 indicate that Nehemiah's first term ran for about twelve years till 433/432. We do not know the exact length of his second term, but it must have ended before 407 B.C., when Bagohi (Bigvai) was governor of Judah according to the Elephantine papyri. Bright (*History of Israel*, p. 408) suggests that after Nehemiah's first term, he may have been succeeded by his brother Hanani (see on 1:2; 7:2), whom Bright would identify with the Hananiah mentioned in the Passover Papyrus of 419 B.C. (ANET, p. 491).

The Elephantine papyri provide us with an interesting parallel to Nehemiah's absence ("some time later"). Arsames, the satrap of Egypt, left his post in the fourteenth year of Darius I (414/413 B.C.) and was still absent at the Persian court in the seventeenth year (407/406). As in Nehemiah's case internal conflict and a breakdown of order took place during the governor's absence (see Cowley 27, 30).

7 Zerubbabel's temple had two courtyards (Zech 3:7; cf. Isa 62:9; 1 Macc 4:38, 48). Hecataeus of Abdera, a Greek historian of the fourth century B.C., described the inner court as being five hundred cubits long and one hundred cubits wide (see Jos. *Contra Apion* I, 198 [22]). However, he may have known of these dimensions only by hearsay.

C. Nehemiah's Expulsion of Tobiah

13:8–9

> [8]I was greatly displeased and threw all Tobiah's household goods out of the room. [9]I gave orders to purify the rooms, and then I put back into them the equipment of the house of God, with the grain offerings and the incense.

8 Nehemiah was a man of a volcanic temperament who quickly expressed his indignation by taking action (vv.25–28; cf. 5:6–13). Contrast the reaction of Ezra who "sat appalled" (Ezra 9:3). Kidner (p. 129) comments: "If on his first visit he had been a whirlwind, on his second he was all fire and earthquake to a city that had settled down in his absence to a comfortable compromise with the gentile world." Nehemiah's action reminds us of Christ's furious expulsion of the moneychangers from the temple area (Matt 21:12–13; Mark 11:15–16; Luke 19:45–46; John 2:13–22).

"Household goods" (*keli*) include "vessels," "equipment," "implements," etc. (cf. Gen 45:20; KJV "stuff" means movable property).

9 On "to cleanse" see the comment on 12:30 (cf. Lev 12; 14:4–32; 17:15–16). Though only a single chamber used by Tobiah has been mentioned before (vv.5, 7–8), the plural "rooms" here shows that other chambers were involved.

D. *Reorganization and Reforms (13:10–31)*

1. *Offerings for the temple staff*

13:10–14

> [10]I also learned that the portions assigned to the Levites had not been given to them, and that all the Levites and singers responsible for the service had gone back to their own fields. [11]So I rebuked the officials and asked them, "Why is the house of God neglected?" Then I called them together and stationed them at their posts.
>
> [12]All Judah brought the tithes of grain, new wine and oil into the storerooms. [13]I put Shelemiah the priest, Zadok the scribe, and a Levite named Pedaiah in charge of the storerooms and made Hanan son of Zaccur, the son of Mattaniah, their assistant, because these men were considered trustworthy. They were made responsible for distributing the supplies to their brothers.

¹⁴Remember me for this, O my God, and do not blot out what I have so faithful-
ly done for the house of my God and its services.

10 It appears that Nehemiah was correcting an abuse of long standing. Strictly
speaking the Levites had no holdings (Num 18:20, 23–24; Deut 14:29; 18:1); but
some may have had private income (Deut 18:8). The Levites were thus dependent
on the faithful support of the people. This may explain the reluctance of many
Levites to return from Exile. See the comment on Ezra 8:15. For the complaints of
those who found little material advantage in serving the Lord, see Malachi 2:17;
3:13–15.

11 Nehemiah's rebuke of the officials here recalls his earlier rebuke of the selfish
wealthy who exploited the less fortunate in granting them usurious loans. Less than
a century before, the prophet Haggai had rebuked the people for attending to their
own houses and neglecting the rebuilding of the house of God (Hag 1:1–9).

12 On tithes see the comment on 12:44. Temples in Mesopotamia also levied tithes
for the support of their personnel.

13 On the nature of the profession "scribe," see on Ezra 7:6.

"In charge of the storerooms" is literally "I made treasurers over the treasuries"
(cf. Ezra 8:33–34). Of the four treasurers one was a priest, one a Levite, one a
scribe, and one a layman of rank. They all needed to be "trustworthy" (ne'emān; cf.
9:8, "faithful"; see also 1 Sam 22:14; Prov 25:13; Isa 8:2; Jer 42:5) "for distributing
the supplies." This would ensure that supplies were distributed equitably just as the
church appointed deacons for this purpose (Acts 6:1–5).

14 Nehemiah was concerned that God would remember him (v.31; cf. 5:19) and "not
blot out" (see Exod 17:14; 32:32) what he had done "faithfully" (the pl. of ḥeseḏ),
viz., his good deeds inspired by steadfast love (see comment on 1:5).

2. The abuse of the Sabbath

13:15–22

¹⁵In those days I saw men in Judah treading winepresses on the Sabbath and
bringing in grain and loading it on donkeys, together with wine, grapes, figs and
all other kinds of loads. And they were bringing all this into Jerusalem on the
Sabbath. Therefore I warned them against selling food on that day. ¹⁶Men from
Tyre who lived in Jerusalem were bringing in fish and all kinds of merchandise
and selling them in Jerusalem on the Sabbath to the people of Judah. ¹⁷I rebuked
the nobles of Judah and said to them, "What is this wicked thing you are doing—
desecrating the Sabbath day? ¹⁸Didn't your forefathers do the same things, so
that our God brought all this calamity upon us and upon this city? Now you are
stirring up more wrath against Israel by desecrating the Sabbath."

¹⁹When evening shadows fell on the gates of Jerusalem before the Sabbath, I
ordered the doors to be shut and not opened until the Sabbath was over. I stationed some of my own men at the gates so that no load could be brought in on
the Sabbath day. ²⁰Once or twice the merchants and sellers of all kinds of goods
spent the night outside Jerusalem. ²¹But I warned them and said, "Why do you
spend the night by the wall? If you do this again, I will lay hands on you." From
that time on they no longer came on the Sabbath. ²²Then I commanded the

Levites to purify themselves and go and guard the gates in order to keep the Sabbath day holy.

Remember me for this also, O my God, and show mercy to me according to your great love.

15 Grapes were, of course, trodden by foot (Isa 16:10; 63:2), but not normally on the "Sabbath." There was always the temptation on the part of merchants to violate the Sabbath rest; this was especially true of non-Jewish merchants (see comment on 10:31; cf. Isa 56:1-8; 58:13; Jer 17:21; Amos 8:5). The high regard for the ideal of the Sabbath was, however, expressed by many parents who called their children Shabbethai (see comment on Ezra 10:15; cf. Neh 8:7; 11:16).

The word translated "food" (*ṣayid*, "provisions") occurs only here, in Joshua 9:5, 14, and in Job 38:41.

16 Tyre, modern Ṣûr, is located only a dozen miles north of the border between Israel and Lebanon. The Tyrians supplied some of their famous cedars for the rebuilding of the temple (Ezra 3:7). Tyre was renowned for its far-flung maritime trade (Ezek 26:5, 14). Originally an island, Tyre was transformed into a peninsula by Alexander's siege causeway (cf. H.J. Katzenstein, *The History of Tyre* [Jerusalem: Schocken Institute, 1973]; id., "Tyre in the Early Persian Period [539-486 B.C.E.]," BA 42 [1979]: 23-36).

The Tyrians also exported fish (Ezek 26:4-14). Most of the fish, which included sardines, were either dried, smoked, or salted. Fish were an important part of the diet (Lev 11:9; Num 11:5; Deut 14:9; Isa 19:8; Matt 15:34; Luke 24:42). They were sold at the market by the Fish Gate (2 Chron 33:14; Neh 3:3; 12:39; Zeph 1:10).

17 Nehemiah rebuked especially the nobles who were the leaders (cf. vv.11, 25; cf. 5:7).

"Desecrating" (*ḥālal*) means to turn what is sacred into common use, to profane (cf. Mal 2:10-11).

18 On the "Sabbath" see the comment on v.15 (cf. also Isa 58:13; Ezek 20:13, 16; 22:8, 26; 23:38).

19 The gates began to cast long "evening shadows" even before sunset when the Sabbath began. The Israelites, like the Babylonians, counted their days from sunset to sunset (the Egyptians reckoned their days from dawn to dawn). The precise moment the Sabbath began was heralded by the blowing of a trumpet by a priest. According to the Mishnah (*Sukkah* 5.5): "On the even of Sabbath they used to blow six more blasts, three to cause the people to cease from work and three to mark the break between the sacred and the profane." Josephus (*War* IV, 582 [ix.12]) describes the point on the parapet of the temple where the priests stood "in the afternoon of the approach, and on the following evening of the close, of every seventh day, announcing to the people the respective hours for ceasing work and for resuming their labors." Mazar's excavations by the temple mount recovered a stone from the parapet, which had fallen to the ground in Titus's siege, with the inscription *le beit hat-teqi'ah*, "for the place of the blowing (of the trumpet)" (*Mountain*, pp. 138-39).

20 When the gates were shut on the Sabbath eve, the persistent merchants carried on their activities outside the gates for two weeks until Nehemiah noticed them (v.21).

21 Nehemiah was not a man of idle words. He meant what he said and was not averse to backing up his words by force (v.25).

22 The Sabbath was sanctified, not just by a negative cessation of ordinary labor, but by a consecration of that day to joyous gatherings. Fasting and mourning were not to be observed on the Sabbath (Jub 50:12; Jud 8:6; CD 8.13; M *Taanith* 3.7). According to Moore (*Judaism*, 1:37–38): "As the Scribes learned from Isa 58,13 that God meant the sabbath to be set apart from other days not only by the things that were not done on it, but by what was done, that it was a day for men to enjoy themselves on, and in accordance with the notions of feast days in the Scriptures, gave a front place in this enjoyment to more sumptuous eating and drinking than on other days."

Notes

19 "When evening shadows fell on the gates" is literally "When the gates began to grow dark." צָלַל (*ṣālal*, "become dark, shady") appears in the Qal only here. In the Hiphil ("to give shade") it occurs in Ezek 31:3 and possibly in Jonah 4:6.

On the exact significance of "when the Sabbath was over," see J.H. Tigay, "*LIFNÊ HAŠŠABĀṬ* and *ʾAḤAR HAŠŠABĀṬ* 'On the Day Before the Sabbath' and 'On the Day After the Sabbath,'" VetTest 28 (1978): 362–65.

3. *Mixed marriages*

13:23–29

23Moreover, in those days I saw men of Judah who had married women from Ashdod, Ammon and Moab. 24Half of their children spoke the language of Ashdod or the language of one of the other peoples, and did not know how to speak the language of Judah. 25I rebuked them and called curses down on them. I beat some of the men and pulled out their hair. I made them take an oath in God's name and said: "You are not to give your daughters in marriage to their sons, nor are you to take their daughters in marriage for your sons or for yourselves. 26Was it not because of marriages like these that Solomon king of Israel sinned? Among the many nations there was no king like him. He was loved by his God, and God made him king over all Israel, but even he was led into sin by foreign women. 27Must we hear now that you too are doing all this terrible wickedness and are being unfaithful to our God by marrying foreign women?"

28One of the sons of Joiada son of Eliashib the high priest was son-in-law to Sanballat the Horonite. And I drove him away from me.

29Remember them, O my God, because they defiled the priestly office and the covenant of the priesthood and of the Levites.

23 Ezra had dealt with the same problem of intermarriage some thirty years before, according to the traditional dating (see Introduction: The Order, and the excursus after Ezra 10).

On "Ashdod" see the comments on v.24 and on 4:7.

Ammon was the area in Transjordan around the city of Amman (cf. on Ezra 9:1). Tobiah, Nehemiah's enemy, was influential in that area (cf. on Neh 2:10). The Ammonites worshiped the god Molech (Milcom) by sacrificing children in the fire (Lev 18:21; 2 Kings 23:10, 13). Extensive archaeological evidence of the burning of thousands of young children has come to light in the Phoenician colony of Carthage.

Excavations have uncovered some Ammonite inscriptions from the ninth to seventh century B.C. that feature the god Milcom (Jer 32:35; NIV, "Molech") to whom the children were offered (see S.H. Horn, "The Ammonite Citadel Inscription," BASOR 193 [1969]: 2–13). One seal was owned by an exile who returned from Assyria in the seventh century B.C. (cf. N. Avigad, "Seals of the Exile," IEJ 15 [1965]: 223–30). An ostracon from about 500 B.C. from Heshbon, southwest of Amman, indicates the mixed nature of the population, as a fragmentary name list has two West Semitic names, one Babylonian name, and one Egyptian name (cf. J. Naveh, "Hebrew Texts in Aramaic Script in the Persian Period?" BASOR 203 [1971]: 27–32).

The Moabites worshiped Chemosh, to whom they sacrificed their children (Num 21:29; 2 Kings 3:27). On the worship of Chemosh and of Milcom, see McKay, *Religion in Judah under the Assyrians,* pp. 39–41, 106–7.

24 Zechariah 9:6 declares: "Foreigners [*mamzēr*] will occupy Ashdod." The word means "bastard" (cf. Deut 23:3); the RSV renders "a mongrel people."

Myers (*Ezra-Nehemiah,* p. 216) comments: "Nehemiah observed it first in the speech of children—an interesting point, since the mothers naturally taught their children to speak the only language they knew." The Hebrews recognized other people as foreigners by their languages (cf. Exod 21:8; Deut 3:9; Judg 12:6; Ps 114:1; Isa 33:4–19; Ezek 3:5–6).

The excavations at Ashdod have uncovered an ostracon from Nehemiah's age in Aramaic script that reads *krm zbdyh* ("[from the] vineyard of Zebadiah"). The name means "Yahweh has given" (cf. Ezra 8:8; 10:20) (see *Inscriptions Reveal,* p. 71; M. Dothan in Freedman and Greenfield, p. 22). Unfortunately the inscription is too brief to shed any light on the Ashdodite language.

1. Was the Ashdodite language a survival of Philistine, which may have been an Aegean or Anatolian language? In 1966 W.H. Brownlee purchased eight crude parchment scrolls found in the Hebron area inscribed in a hitherto unknown script. He and G. Mendenhall have suggested that these may be in a "Philistine" language. Orthographic characteristics indicate a date about the ninth to eighth century B.C. But doubts have been expressed by others concerning the authenticity of these scrolls (cf. W.H. Brownlee, G.E. Mendenhall, and Y. Oweis, "Philistine Manuscripts from Palestine?" *Kadmos* 10 [1971]: 102–4, 173).

2. Possibly the dialect was Phoenician. In the Persian period the Philistine-Palestinian coastal area was divided into several jurisdictions. Ashkelon was under the Tyrians; Ashdod was the center of the Persian province. In 1964 Cross published an ostracon from Nebi Yunis in modern Ashdod with the Phoenician name *B'lṣd,* dating from about 350–300 B.C. This name *Ba'lṣīd* ("my lord is Ṣīd") may, however, be

a Persian loan word in Aramaic (cf. F.M. Cross, "An Ostracon from Nebī Yūnis," IEJ 14 [1964]: 185; Gibson, *Textbook*, p. 152).

3. A third possibility is that Ashdodite was a local dialect of Aramaic, the language that had become the lingua franca of the Near East (see Introduction: Text).

"One of the other peoples" (*'am wā'ām*, "people and people") is a late Hebrew idiom (cf. Ezra 10:14; Esth 1:22; 3:12; 8:9).

25 On Nehemiah's rebuke of the others, see vv.11, 17. Contrast Ezra's action (Ezra 9:3), who pulled out his own hair, with Nehemiah's here. Plucking the hair from another's beard was an action designed to show anger, to express an insult, and to mark someone to scorn (2 Sam 10:4; Isa 50:6; cf. Hammurabi Code 127; *Herodotus* 2.121). The *semirasus* ("half-shaven") marked the lowest type of slave or prisoner at Rome. On "oath" see the comment on Ezra 10:5.

Nehemiah's action was designed to prevent future intermarriages ("you are not to give"), whereas Ezra dissolved the existing unions. On the bearing of these different approaches on the chronological order of Ezra and Nehemiah, see the Introduction: The Order.

26 Solomon was Israel's outstanding king in wealth and political achievements (1 Kings 3:12–13; 2 Chron 1:12). Solomon reigned for forty years (1 Kings 11:42), either between 971–931 B.C. (according to Thiele) or 961–922 B.C. (according to Albright). He built the magnificent temple (1 Kings 6:1–38) and an even more splendid palace for himself (1 Kings 7:1). His fame spread beyond his borders so that the queen of Sheba in southwestern Arabia traveled fourteen hundred miles to test his fabled wisdom (1 Kings 10:1–3) (cf. J.B. Pritchard, ed., *Solomon and Sheba* [London: Phaidon, 1974]). His international prestige is demonstrated in that he was given the daughter of a pharaoh (probably Siamun) in marriage (1 Kings 3:1; 7:8; 9:16, 24; 11:1; 2 Chron 8:11). This is the only firmly attested instance in which a king of Egypt gave his daughter in marriage to an alien. (See K.A. Kitchen, *The Third Intermediate Period in Egypt* [Warminster: Aris & Phillips, 1973], pp. 281–83; A.R. Green, "Solomon and Siamun," JBL 97 [1978]: 353–67.)

According to 1 Kings 11:3, Solomon had seven hundred wives and three hundred concubines, among whom were Moabite, Ammonite, Edomite, Sidonian, and Hittite women (1 Kings 11:1). The mother of Rehoboam, Solomon's successor, was an Ammonite princess. Hellenistic sources suggest that Solomon also married the daughter of Hiram of Tyre.

Solomon began his reign humbly by asking for wisdom from the Lord (1 Kings 3:3–15). In later years, however, his foreign wives led him to worship other gods, so that he built a high place for Chemosh, the god of the Moabites on the Mount of Olives (1 Kings 11:7). McKay (*Religion in Judah*, pp. 95–96) notes later examples of foreign queens who led Israel astray: "Rehoboam's wife, Maacah, daughter of Abishalom, whose name is certainly not Yahwistic, erected an image to Asherah in the city (I Kings 15.10–13); Ahab's marriage to Jezebel brought the Sidonian Baal and Asherah to Samaria (I Kings 16.32–3); and in consequence of Jehoram's marriage to Ahab's daughter, Athaliah, a temple for the Sidonian Baal was erected in Jerusalem (II Kings 8.18; 11:1ff.)."

27 On "terrible wickedness" compare 2 Samuel 13:16; Jeremiah 26:19.

28 We do not know the name of "one of the sons of Joiada son of Eliashib the high priest." The Hebrew is ambiguous as the phrase high priest could refer to either Joiada or Eliashib. In the latter case Eliashib was still alive (see Introduction: The High Priests). More probably the epithet "high priest" designates Joiada (cf. 12:10). The offending son would then have been a brother of the man who succeeded Joiada as high priest, Johanan "II" (12:22–23). He was married to a daughter of Sanballat.

According to Leviticus 21:14, the high priest was not to marry a foreigner. The expulsion of Joiada's son may have followed this special ban or the general interdict against intermarriage. Such a union was especially rankling to Nehemiah in the light of Sanballat's enmity (see comment on 2:10).

29 On "remember them" compare 6:14.

Notes

29 "Defiled," the plural of גֹּאַל (gōʾal, "cultic pollutions") occurs only here.

4. Provisions of wood and firstfruits

13:30–31

> 30So I purified the priests and the Levites of everything foreign, and assigned them duties, each to his own task. 31I also made provision for contributions of wood at designated times, and for the firstfruits.
>
> **Remember me with favor, O my God.**

30 "Duties" (mišmārôt, "divisions") refers to the assignment of particular duties to groups of priests and Levites, possibly on a rotating basis.

31 On the wood offering, see the comment on 10:34; on firstfruits on 10:35.

The last words of Nehemiah—"Remember me with favor"—recapitulate an often-repeated theme running through the final chapter (vv. 14, 22). His motive throughout his ministry was to please and to serve his divine Sovereign.

Nehemiah provides us with one of the most vivid patterns of leadership in Scriptures.

1. *He was a man of responsibility,* as shown by his position as the royal cupbearer.

2. *He was a man of vision,* confident of who God was and what he could do through his servants. He was not, however, a visionary but a man who planned and then acted.

3. *He was a man of prayer,* who prayed spontaneously and constantly even in the presence of the king (2:4–5).

4. *He was a man of action and cooperation,* who realized what had to be done, explained it to others, and enlisted their aid. Nehemiah, a layman, was able to cooperate with his contemporary, Ezra the scribe and priest, in spite of the fact that these two leaders were of entirely different temperaments.

5. *He was a man of compassion,* who was moved by the plight of the poorer

members of society so that he renounced even the rights he was entitled to (5:18) and denounced the greed of the wealthy (5:8).

6. *He was a man who triumphed over opposition*. His opponents tried ridicule (4:3), attempted slander (6:4–7), and spread misleading messages (6:10–14). But through God's favor Nehemiah triumphed over all difficulties.

See C.J. Barber, *Nehemiah and the Dynamics of Effective Leadership* (Neptune, N.J.: Loizeaux Brothers, 1976); D.K. Campbell, *Nehemiah: Man in Charge* (Wheaton: Victor Books, 1979); Alan Redpath, *Victorious Christian Service* (Old Tappan, N.J.: Revell, 1958); R.H. Seume, *Nehemiah: God's Builder* (Chicago: Moody, 1978); E. Yamauchi, "Nehemiah: A Model Leader," in *A Spectrum of Thought*, edited by M.L. Peterson (Wilmore, Ky.: Francis Asbury, 1982), pp. 171–80.

Excursus

Josephus (*Antiq.* XI, 302–11 [vii.2–viii.2]) describes how Joannes was succeeded as high priest by his son Jaddus. Manasses, the latter's brother, married Nikaso, the daughter of Sanballetes, the satrap of Samaria. Many other Israelites including priests were involved in intermarriage. This took place in the time of Alexander.

The striking similarity between this account and that recounted in Nehemiah 13 has led many scholars (e.g., Cheyne, Kennett, Ryle, Wellhausen) to conclude that both accounts deal with the same Sanballat (cf. James A. Montgomery, *The Samaritans* [Philadelphia: John Winston, 1907], pp. 66–67). Josephus must simply have dated the episode a century too late.

On the other hand, C.C. Torrey proposed the radical solution of redating Nehemiah to the fourth century, i.e., the period of Alexander (see H.H. Rowley, "Sanballat and the Samaritan Temple," in *Men of God*, pp. 246–58).

The idea that there could have been two Sanballats was considered highly improbable by A.E. Cowley (*Aramaic Papyri of the Fifth Century B.C.* [Oxford: Clarendon University Press, 1923], p. 110): "The view that there were two Sanballats, each governor of Samaria and each with a daughter who married a brother of a High Priest at Jerusalem, is a solution too desperate to be entertained."

Though Rowley ("Sanballat," pp. 251ff.) conceded that there could have been two Sanballats, he also was skeptical: "For so exact a repetition of history at an interval of a century, at a distance of two generations on the wife's side and a single generation on the husband's, we should need stronger evidence than Josephus's account can supply."

Although we still do not have explicit evidence to confirm the details of the stories, we now have some dramatic evidence that indicates that there was a series of governors of Samaria named Sanballat.

In 1962 Bedouins discovered in caves at Wâdi ed-Dâliyeh, north of Jericho, rare fourth-century B.C. papyri and bullae belonging to Samaritans who had fled from Alexander the Great. A Sanballat who was called *pḥt šmrn* ("governor of Samaria") is listed. From this new evidence we can reconstruct the following list of governors over Samaria:

Name	Born	Floruit	Source
Sanballat I	c.485	445	Nehemiah
Delaiah	c.460	410	Elephantine Papyri
Sanballat II	c.435	380	Samaria Papyri
Hananiah	c.410	355	Samaria Papyri
Sanballat III	c.385	330	Josephus

(See F.M. Cross, "A Reconstruction of the Judean Restoration," JBL 94 [1975]: 4–18; S. Talmon, "Ezra and Nehemiah," IDB Suppl., pp. 327–28.)

This reconstruction is based on the principle of papponymy (i.e., the practice of naming a child after his grandfather). We know the Tobiads practiced this for nine generations, and high priests named Onias and Simon reappear over five generations.

In the light of the new evidence, we can see that the episodes in Nehemiah 13 and Josephus are distinct. The expelled priest of Josephus's account would have been the nephew of the expelled priest of Neh 13:28. Accordingly F.M. Cross ("Papyri of the Fourth Century B.C. from Dâli-yeh," in Freedman and Greenfield, p. 57) concludes: "Certainly we can no longer look at the episode [in Josephus] with the same historical skepticism. After all, the names and relationships are by no means identical. It appears that the noble houses of Samaria and Jerusalem were willing to intermarry despite the ire of certain strict Jews, presumably the progeny of the reforms of Nehemiah and Ezra" (cf. also J.D. Purvis, *The Samaritan Pentateuch and the Origins of the Samaritan Sect* [Cambridge: Harvard University Press, 1968], pp. 102–5).

The acceptance of the historicity of Josephus's account (*Antiq*. XI, 310–11 [viii.2]) of how Sanballat built a temple at Gerizim in Samaria for the deposed Manasses c.330 B.C. raises the larger question of the development of the Samaritan schism. Certainly by NT times the Samaritans and the Jews hardly spoke to each other (cf. John 4). Jewish pilgrims from Galilee took the long detour down to the Jordan Valley rather than the direct route, as Samaritians were known to waylay pilgrims. In A.D. 6 and 9 Samaritans scattered bones in the Jewish temple as an act of deliberate desecration.

How and when did the breach between the Jews and the Samaritans occur?

It has been customary to trace the origins of the Samaritans to the conquest of Samaria by the Assyrians in 722 B.C. According to Assyrian records over twenty-seven thousand were deported. In their place "the king of Assyria brought people from Babylon, Cuthah, Avva, Hamath and Sepharvaim and settled them in the towns of Samaria to replace the Israelites" (2 Kings 17:24). The later Assyrian kings, Esarhaddon and Ashurbanipal, brought in still others (Ezra 4:2, 10). We must bear in mind, however, that there was not a complete interchange of populations. A certain percentage was deported and their place taken by newcomers (see Introduction: Background).

It is noteworthy that the only place where the Samaritans (šōmᵉrōnîm) are explicitly mentioned is in 2 Kings 17:29. J. MacDonald ("The Discovery of Samaritan Religion," *Religion* 2 [1972]: 143) warns us to distinguish between the polytheistic "Samarians" of Nehemiah's day and the monotheistic "Samaritans":

> The word translated "the Samaritans" occurs (in 2 Kings 17:29) for the first and only time in the Old Testament. The Hebrew word *shomrōnîm* is everywhere [i.e., in all translations] rendered thus without question. It is only as the result of close study of the new materials to hand that it becomes plain that the word has always been wrongly translated and that for "the Samaritans" we must read "the Samarians". On linguistic grounds, it is abundantly clear that the word *shomrōn* . . . in the plural here means "the inhabitants/people of Samaria". . . . There is no connection here between the inhabitants of Samaria, as such, and the religious group called the Samaritans, who themselves derive their name from the Hebrew verb "to keep".

Some scholars believe they can detect anti-Samaritan allusions in some of the prophetic passages from the preexilic period (see M. Delcor, "Hinweise auf das

Samaritanische Schisma im Alten Testament," ZAW 74 [1962]: 281–91; R. Tournay, "Quelques reflectures bibliques antisamaritaines," RB 71 [1964]: 503–36).

According to their own accounts, such as the Samaritan Chronicles, the Samaritans originated when descendants of Joseph refused to follow Eli when he moved the ark from Shechem to Shiloh. This pro-Samaritan version has been defended by some scholars involved in Samaritan studies (see Moses Gaster, *The Samaritans* [London: Oxford University Press, 1925]; MacDonald, "The Discovery," p. 141).

Oppositions to the Jews who returned from exile came from the *'am hā'āreṣ* ("people of the land") who are described as descendants of the Assyrian colonists in Samaria (Ezra 4:1–5, 8–23). Nehemiah's efforts were opposed at every turn by Sanballat, the governor of Samaria (Neh 2:10).

Those who believe that Josephus's account of the building of the Samaritan temple should really be dated back to the fifth century B.C. have traditionally dated the Samaritan schism to this period. The Samaritan tradition itself connects the building of their temple with Sanballat, who is anachronistically considered a contemporary of Zerubbabel.

According to the conventional view, the expulsion of Tobiah's son-in-law (Neh 13) may have been the beginning of the rival worship established in Samaria. For example, D.M. Beegle ("Samaritans," WBE, p. 1509) writes: "It is preferable to follow the biblical data and date the beginning of the Samaritan schism *c.* 445 B.C." It has further been assumed from the rabbinical tradition that speaks of Ezra's introduction of the "Assyrian or Aramaic script" that the Samaritan Pentateuch, which was copied in Paleo-Hebrew, dates back to the fifth century B.C.

The recent trend in Samaritan studies, however, is to lower the date of the Samaritan schism from the time of Nehemiah to the fourth century B.C. or even later.

It can be argued that Sanballat's opposition was based, not on religious, but political motives. The Elephantine papyri indicate that his sons had Yahwistic names. See H.H. Rowley, "The Samaritan Schism in Legend and History," in *Israel's Prophetic Heritage*, edd. B. Anderson and W. Harrelson (New York: Harper & Bros., 1962), pp. 208–22. The fact that Sanballat's daughter married the son of the Jewish high priest (Neh 13:28) is evidence, according to Rowley, that there was no religious hostility between the Samaritans and the Jews at that date.

Rowley ("Sanballat and the Samaritan Temple," p. 270) argues that the feud reached an advanced stage by the fourth century B.C. and "at some time before the middle of the third century B.C., and perhaps before the beginning of that century the breach with the Samaritans had become complete."

Scholars who accept Josephus's account of the building of the Samaritan temple on Gerizim at the time of Alexander's conquest correlate this with the establishment of Macedonians at Samaria and a resettlement of the expelled Samaritans at Shechem (G.E. Wright, "The Samaritans at Shechem," HTR 55 [1962]: 357–66; F.M. Cross, "Aspects of Samaritan and Jewish History in Late Persian and Hellenistic Times," HTR 59 [1966]: 206).

Under the foundations of the Roman temple of Zeus built on Tell er-Ras on Mount Gerizim, archaeologists believe they have found a podium that may go back to this Samaritan temple (R.J. Bull and G.E. Wright, "Newly Discovered Temples on Mt. Gerizim in Jordan," HTR 58 [1965]: 234–37; R.J. Bull, "The Excavation of Tell er-Ras on Mount Gerizim," BA 31 [1968]: 58–72).

Cross ("Samaritan and Jewish History," p. 206) has argued that the building of the Samaritan temple need not have led to a final separation, though it certainly aggravated relations. He cites the building of rival temples by Onias IV at Leontopolis in Egypt in the second century B.C. and the shrine of Hyrcanus the Tobiad at Arâq el-'Emîr about 200 B.C.

Along with other scholars, Coggins has argued for a revision to a later and a more gradual rupture between the Samaritans and the Jews through a slow process of deterioration in relations from the third century B.C. to the beginning of the Christian Era (see R.J. Coggins, "The Old Testament and Samaritan Origins," *Annual of the Swedish Theological Institute* 6 [1967–68]: 35–48; id., *Samaritans and Jews* [Atlanta: John Knox, 1975]).

Frank Cross and his students have advocated a still later date in the second century B.C. for the Samaritan schism from an analysis of the Samaritan Pentateuch. Their study of the scripts convinces them that the Samaritan version branches off from the Paleo-Hebrew script no earlier than the first century B.C. (see Purvis, *Samaritan Pentateuch*, p. 85). The exemplar of the Samaritan Pentateuch must, however, be an older Palestinian edition of the Pentateuch that dates back to the fifth century B.C. (see Waltke, "Samaritan Pentateuch," pp. 212–39).

Cross and Purvis would interpret the development of the distinctive Samaritan script as a consequence of certain historical events. In 128 B.C. John Hyrcanus destroyed the Samaritan temple on Gerizim and a few years later probably destroyed Shechem as well. After Pompey freed Samaria from the Jews in 64 B.C., the Samaritans severed all ties with Judaism. Such a late date for the schism had been advocated earlier by Hölscher and Albright.

Questions may be raised about the adoption of such a late date, particularly since the Samaritans adopted as their Scriptures only the Pentateuch and not the Prophets or the Writings. Z. Ben-Hayyim, the noted Israeli scholar of Samaritans, comments: "Can one really come to an important historical and social conclusion such as the time of the formation of the Samaritan sect according to the orthographic form and the script of its Holy Writ?" ("Review of J. Purvis, *The Samaritan Pentateuch*," *Biblica* 52 [1971]: 255).

See also Wayne A. Brindle, "The Origin and History of the Samaritans," *Grace Theological Journal* 5 (1984): 47–75; H.G. Kippenberg, *Garizim und Synagoge* (Berlin: W. de Gruyter, 1971); J. MacDonald, *Theology of the Samaritans* (Philadelphia: Westminster, 1964); R. Pummer, "The Present State of Samaritan Studies," *JSS* 21 (1976): 39–61; id., "The *Book of Jubilees* and the Samaritans," *Église et Théologie* 10 (1979): 147–78; and S. Talmon, "The Samaritans," *Scientific American* 236 (Jan. 1977): 100–108.

ESTHER

F.B. Huey, Jr.

ESTHER

Introduction

1. Background

Five books that are found together in the third division of the Hebrew Bible are Song of Songs, Ruth, Lamentations, Ecclesiastes, and Esther. Collectively they are called the five Megilloth ("Scrolls"). The arrangement of the books differs in the various codices and printed editions of the Hebrew Bible.[1] However, the Book of Esther is generally the last of the five, probably because it is read during Purim, the last festival of the Jewish year. A few early MSS placed it after the Pentateuch. In our English Bibles it is found after Ezra and Nehemiah, probably because of the role of Persia in the three books.

The Book of Esther is called *the* Megillah (*the* "Scroll") by Jewish readers because of its immense popularity. However, since it was first written, it has continued to be controversial. Reactions to it are not neutral; they range from ecstatic delight for the victory of the Jews over their enemies to violent dislike and rejection because of what appears to be indefensible moral conduct and the absence of any reference to God.

Esther is one of two OT books named for a woman, the other being Ruth, and one of several not quoted in the NT. It is one of two OT books that does not mention God, the other being Song of Songs, and one of two that deals specifically with persecution of the Hebrew people, the other being Exodus. Esther contains the account of the origin of the Feast of Purim, one of two festivals adopted by the postexilic Jewish community that are not found in the Moasic law, the other being Hanukkah. The events of the book are set in Susa during the reign of Xerxes, king of Persia (486–465 B.C.), whose empire reached from India to Ethiopia. Esther is the only OT book in which the entire narrative takes place in Persia.

Against a background of centuries of persecution, it is understandable why the Feast of Purim became such a favorite of the Jews. It recalls a time when they were able to turn the tables on those who wanted to destroy them. Purim is celebrated today amid a carnivallike atmosphere, with masquerade parties, noisemaking, and revelry. The story is reenacted in synagogues with the audience hissing Haman and cheering Mordecai. The Book of Esther is a profound statement about the heroic resistance necessary for survival in the face of violent anti-Semitism that continues to the present day.

2. Authorship

The text of Esther nowhere names the author nor gives the date of its writing. Authorship of the book has been attributed to Mordecai by Ibn Ezra, Clement of Alexandria (Streane, p. xix), and, more recently, Wright (p. 46). However, it is unlikely that Mordecai would have penned the paean of praise about himself in 10:3 (Young, *Introduction*, p. 345). Augustine suggested that Ezra was the author of Esther, and *Baba Bathra* 15a proposed that the men of the Great Synagogue wrote the book. No one has seriously argued that Esther herself was the author. Therefore all that can be said is that the identity of the author remains unknown. If the book was written in the fifth or fourth century B.C. (see discussion under Date), the author was probably a Persian Jew (so Harrison, Keil, Paton, Streane). His intimate knowledge of Persian life and customs argues for his Persian domicile; the nationalism that permeates the story makes it almost certain that he was Jewish. If the book

---

[1]See Paton, *Esther*, pp. 1–5, for some examples.

was written in the second century B.C., the author was probably a Palestinian Jew (so Bloch, Knight).[2]

For some time questions have been raised whether Esther was the work of one or several authors. The unity of the book was first challenged by J.D. Michaelis in 1783, with his insistence that 9:20–10:3 came from a separate source. A number of scholars have agreed with Michaelis's analysis (e.g., Eissfeldt, Paton). However, Baldwin (p. 412) concluded that the arguments for these verses as an addition to the original literary unit are not persuasive (cf. Streane, p. xx). Alleged changes in vocabulary and style can be explained as a change from narrative style to directions for the observance of Purim. Baldwin points out that it is not quite accurate to say that Purim is only mentioned in this section, as it is anticipated in 3:7.

Cazelles argued that Esther is a conflation of two originally independent texts, based on what he identified as duplicate accounts (e.g., two banquets in ch. 1, two lists of the king's servants [1:10, 14]; Esther's two banquets [5:5; 7:1]).[3]

Bardtke (pp. 248–52) believed that the writer had three different sources available: (1) a story about Vashti's downfall, (2) an account of Esther's rise to royalty and her great deed, and (3) a narrative about the struggle between Mordecai and Haman.[4] Fuerst (p. 34) emphatically denies that there was ever any combining of three written sources to form the present Book of Esther.

Dommershausen made an extensive study of the various stylistic elements in the book to identify its various literary units. He determined that Esther was written by one author who used a large number of sources, but his conclusions have been refuted by Berg (pp. 8–9).

Harrison (p. 1087) does not go so far as to identify the book as a composite but says that the author had sources, such as some of the writings of Mordecai (9:20), books of the annals of the Median and Persian kings (2:23; 6:1; 10:2), and certain familiar oral traditions. However Harrison concluded (p. 1101) that the book is a fundamental unity.

It is apparent that attempts to find separate narrative elements in Esther have not been universally accepted. Rather the unity of the book is still vigorously defended. Striedl demonstrated persuasively that the characteristic style of the writer recurs throughout the book.[5] Others who join in support of the unity of the book include Anderson ("The structure . . . reveals its unity," p. 824), Berg ("appears to be a unified whole," p. 168), and Gordis ("a literary unity," "Studies in Esther," p. 44). Arguments based on stylistic difference fail to offer convincing objective evidence for fragmenting the Book of Esther into different sources. If it was "woven" together from different sources, the seams do not show. Therefore it is best to accept the book as a literary unit.

---

[2]Cf. Walter Harrelson, *Interpreting the Old Testament* (New York: Holt, Rinehart and Winston, Inc., 1964), p. 449, who follows a late fourth-century date but says the author lived in Judah.

[3]Henri Cazelles, "Note sur la composition du rouleau d'Esther," *Lex tua Veritas: Festschrift Hubert Junker*, edd. Heinrich Gross and Franz Mussner (Trier: Paulinus-Verlag, 1961), pp. 17–30.

[4]This view is accepted by Fohrer, p. 254; W.L. Humphreys, "Book of Esther," *IDB Supplementary Volume*, p. 280; Moore, *Esther*, p. li; but rejected by Berg, p. 5, and Gordis, "Book of Esther," p. 387.

[5]Hans Striedl, "Untersuchung zur Syntax und Stilistik des hebräischen Buches Esther," ZAW 55 (1937): 73–108.

3. Date

Since the author of the Book of Esther cannot be identified, there can be no absolute certainty about the date of its composition. The *terminus a quo* must be no earlier than the death of Xerxes (465 B.C.), as 10:2 suggests that his reign had ended. However the *terminus ad quem* is not so easy to determine. Based on an examination of the opinions of a number of scholars, two principal periods are usually proposed as the most likely date. They are an early date (450–300 B.C.) and a late date (175–100 B.C.). There is also a mediating position that Esther reached its final form in the second century B.C. but originated during the fourth century (Moore, *Esther*, pp. lvii–lviii). In addition some scholars insist that the evidence is not yet sufficient to settle the date (Anderson, p. 828; Berg, p. 173; Young, *Introduction*, p. 346).

Among those who support an early date are Childs ("towards the end of the Persian period," p. 602); Gordis ("late Persian or early Hellenistic," "Studies in Esther," p. 44); Harrison ("not later than 350 B.C.," p. 1090); Keil (400 B.C., p. 312); Moore ("the first edition probably goes back to the fourth century," *Esther*, p. lviii); Streane ("scarcely later than B.C. 300," p. xix); Young (tentatively, the "latter half of the fifth century B.C.," *Introduction*, p. 346).

Arguments for the earlier date include the numerous Persian names and loan words (cf. Paton, *Esther*, p. 65, for a list of Persian words found in Esther). It is unlikely that so many words of this type would have occurred in a composition written in the late Greek period without modification. Attempts to discover Greek influence on the book have been unsuccessful. Archer (p. 417) says there are no traces of Greek influence in language or thought in Esther (cf. Moore, *Esther*, lvii).

Moore (ibid.) also observes that the Hebrew of Esther is most like that of Chronicles, which is now dated no later than about 400 B.C.

Another argument for the early date is the author's intimate knowledge of Persian customs and the topography of Susa and the Persian royal palaces. Such familiarity with Persian life argues for a date in the Persian period and perhaps not long after Xerxes' reign, for this kind of knowledge would not likely have survived till the Maccabean period.

Late date proponents include Brockington (160–100 B.C., p. 218); Browne (between 150 and 100 B.C., p. 381); Fohrer (first half of second century B.C., p. 255); Kaiser (between 300 and 100 B.C., p. 203); Stiehl (165–140 B.C.).[6] Morris argued for a date in the early years of Antiochus IV Epiphanes.[7] Rowley proposed a date of not more than a few decades after 180 B.C.[8] Pfeiffer (p. 742) placed the date at 125 B.C.

One of the major arguments for the late date is that Ben Sira (180 B.C.) makes no mention of Esther, and therefore the book must have been written later (Pfeiffer, p. 741). However he does not mention Job or Ezra either, which unquestionably were in existence; so this argument from silence is not valid (Fohrer concurs, p. 255).

Another argument is that Purim is first referred to, though not by name, in 2 Maccabees 15:36 (a first-century-B.C. apocryphal book), where it is called the Day of Mordecai. It was observed the day after the Day of Nicanor, mentioned in the same verse, an event that celebrated the defeat of an enemy commander in 161 B.C. First

---

[6]Ruth Stiehl, "Das Buch Esther," *Wiener Zeitschrift für die Kunde des Morgenlandes* 53 (1956): 4–22.

[7]A.E. Morris, "The Purpose of the Book of Esther," ExpT 42 (December 1930): 126.

[8]H.H. Rowley, *The Growth of the Old Testament*, Harper Torchbacks reprint (New York: Harper and Row, 1963), p. 155.

Maccabees 7:49 (usually dated around 100 B.C.) mentions the Day of Nicanor without referring to Purim. On that basis Pfeiffer (p. 740) argued that Purim was unknown to Judas Maccabeus.

If the Feast of Purim really had been established during the reign of Xerxes, late-date proponents argue that it would surely have been mentioned in Jewish literature earlier than the Maccabean books. However they do not suggest the extant literature in which it should be found. Ezra and Nehemiah do not mention all the Jewish festivals by name that are found in the Mosaic law, but no one would argue that they did not then exist. A new festival like Purim would have been slow to gain a foothold among the other already established feasts (Wright, p. 39); therefore it would not be mentioned at an earlier date. Purim is not mentioned in the NT and only rarely in Jewish writings of the first few centuries of the Christian Era. Baldwin (p. 414) is correct in asserting that the absence of evidence does not prove that the book did not exist prior to the second century B.C. Streane (p. xviii) calls the argument from silence a "precarious" one; Schultz (p. 21) calls it "hazardous."

Many late-date proponents, following Spinoza, argue that the Book of Esther was appropriate only after the persecutions of Antiochus IV Epiphanes (175–164 B.C.), when enmity between Jews and Gentiles had been inflamed and when the Jews had triumphed over their heathen enemies through the heroic deeds of Judas Maccabeus (Brockington, p. 218; Paton, *Esther*, p. 61). They suggest that Haman was none other than Antiochus IV in disguise (so Morris, "Purpose of Esther," p. 126; Pfeiffer, pp. 741–42). This view has been widely repudiated (Eissfeldt calls it "hardly credible," p. 510; cf. Fohrer, p. 255; Harrison, p. 1089). Moore (*Esther*, p. lx) cites other so-called veiled figures in Esther of Jewish enemies in Maccabean times whom scholars have claimed to identify. Harrison (p. 1089) says the argument that the Jews would not have exhibited such bitter hatred toward Gentiles before about 165 B.C. as revealed in Esther does not hold up before the evidence discovered in the Elephantine papyri of anti-Semitism that resulted in the destruction of the Jewish temple at Yeb by their Egyptian enemies in 410 B.C. Harrison (ibid.) also points out that in Esther the Jews were not fighting for their religion, as in the Maccabean period, but for their right to exist.

The absence of copies of Esther at Qumran has also been cited as further evidence of its lateness. Fohrer (p. 255) is correct in asserting that the absence of any known copies of Esther at Qumran is irrelevant for dating the book (Moore, *Esther*, pp. xxi–xxii, lviii, concurs).

Arguments for the early date of the Book of Esther—the author's knowledge of Persian life and customs, the use of Persian loan words, and the style of Hebrew—outweigh the arguments for the late date of Esther.

4. Purpose

Many exegetes take the position that the major purpose of the Book of Esther was to explain the historical origin of Purim, to justify its celebration (since it is not mentioned in the Torah), and to regulate its manner of observance. Paton's attitude is typical: "The book has one purpose from beginning to end, that is, the institution of the feast of Purim" (*Esther*, p. 56; for the same view, cf. Anderson, p. 824; Keil, p. 304; Schultz, p. 3). Harrison prefers to say that "one important purpose" (rather than the major purpose) was to "furnish the historical background of the institution of a feast that was not prescribed in the Torah" (p. 1099; cf. Streane, p. xvii). Berg (p. 3) raises a serious objection to Purim as the central purpose of Esther by observing that "if the story was intended to explain and legitimate Purim, the narrator devotes a surprisingly small effort to his task." She notes that the festival is mentioned specifically only in 9:28–32 and is alluded to only in 3:7 and 9:24.

The purpose of Esther has been sought in political motives by some scholars. They believe that its purpose was to record the remarkable deliverance of the Jewish people at a critical time in their history and to keep the memory of that deliverance alive through the annual observance of Purim, in order to kindle their nationalistic fervor. Pfeiffer (p. 744) shares this view. An immediate purpose served by the book was to assure the Jews who did not return to their homeland after the Exile that God still loved them and would protect them from unjust oppression (Young, *Introduction*, p. 349).

Some Christian scholars have proposed that the real purpose of the book was to serve as a prophecy, i.e., a foreshadowing of the events and the revelation in the NT. By this interpretation Esther becomes a pattern of the Virgin Mary, and the gallows built by Haman foreshadows the cross (so Carthusiani, 1534; Ferns, 1567; Serarii, 1610; Bonartii, 1647; Celadaeis, 1648; cited by Schultz, p. 27; cf. Paton, *Esther*, p. 56; Fuerst, p. 38). The allegorical method of interpretation has been repudiated by modern Christian exegetes, but it still recurs now and then.[9]

Most commentaries overlook what may well be the actual intent of the Book of Esther—to teach God's providential care of his people (see Theological Values). This oversight is understandable because the doctrine of providence is presented so subtly in Esther; God's name is not even mentioned. Young (*Introduction*, p. 349) calls attention to the centrality of providence: "The book of Esther, then, serves the purpose of showing how Divine Providence overrules all things; even in a distant, far country, God's people are yet in His hands" (cf. Harrison, p. 1099). An acknowledgement of the frequently implied activity of God's providence in the book nullifies the recurrent observation that the book is totally secular in nature and also gives proper recognition to its significant theological content.

The possibility of another purpose is suggested under Special Problems—i.e., to show that God's displeasure may be manifested by his silence.

5. Literary Form

Esther has often been described as a "masterpiece of literature" (Striedl, "Buches Esther," pp. 107–8) and "a literary treasure" (Kaiser, p. 198), even by secular literary standards. Such high praise of the book is given even by those who do not highly regard its historicity. (The question of the historicity of Esther will be discussed under Special Problems.) It has been described as a historical romance (Gunkel), an etiological legend,[10] and a historical novel (Berg, p. 14; Moore, *Esther*, p. lii). It has been submitted to careful literary analysis by technical experts (e.g., Berg, Dommershausen), but its literary merits and readability are apparent even to the

[9]E.g., J. Vernon McGee, *Esther: The Romance of Providence* (Wheaton, Ill.: Van Kampen, 1951), p. 68.

[10]J. Alberto Soggin, *Introduction to the Old Testament*, Old Testament Library (Philadelphia: Westminster, 1976), p. 403.

untrained. The action is vigorous and quick with a dramatic turn of events, reminiscent of O. Henry or Guy de Maupassant. The plot is skillfully narrated with a paucity of words and swiftly carries the reader along to its climactic denouement.

In some respects the Book of Esther resembles the Joseph narrative, which also tells of the rise to power and influence of a Hebrew outsider within the royal court (Berg, pp. 123–65; also cf. Daniel). Its principal characters are skillfully portrayed with a minimum of words. Their clear delineation can be compared to Shakespearean characters: Haman, the consummate villain; Esther, the beautiful and courageous heroine; Mordecai, the shrewd advisor; and Xerxes, the sensual and indifferent king. Moore's statement (*Esther*, p. liii) that the characters are superficially drawn must be rejected; one evidence of the inspiration and genius of the author is his ability to communicate so much about the personalities of the leading figures with so few words.

Various literary techniques are apparent: contrast, irony, and humor. Poetic devices such as assonance, alliteration, hendiadys, parallelism, hyperbole, and chiasmus can also be identified (cf. Dommershausen, pp. 138–52). Form-critical analysis has been applied to the book with the result that form-critical categories such as "novella" (a long prose narrative written for a particular purpose), "report" (a narrative that tells what happened without overtly trying to arouse interest by creating tension that looks to a resolution), and "wisdom narrative" (an account in which judgments are made that result in the best kind of life) have been identified in Esther. Gordis ("Book of Esther," pp. 375–78) says it uses the form of a chronicle of the Persian court written by a Gentile scribe.[11]

The fact that literary forms and techniques can be discovered in Esther (as well as in the other books of the OT) and that literary evaluations of the book are made should not raise questions in the reader's mind as to the inspiration of the Scriptures. God's revelation has always come in understandable forms that communicate rather than obfuscate. His ultimate and greatest revelation, that of his Son, was communicated in human form (John 1:14; Heb 1:1–2).

6. Text

The Hebrew text of Esther is well preserved; there are few difficult passages (e.g., 1:22; 2:19; 7:4; these, as well as Qere and Kethiv readings, will be discussed as they are encountered). Numerous variants in vocalization and accents have been found, but none of these is significant so far as its effect on the meaning of a passage (cf. Paton, *Esther*, p. 9). The language is not in the style of classical Hebrew; Esther contains words that are characteristic of later Hebrew and also contains Persian words. Although more MSS copies of Esther exist than any other book of the OT (ibid., p. 5), thereby revealing Jewish esteem for it (see Moore, *Esther*, pp. 114–15, for a brief study of medieval illuminated MSS), no portions have yet been found at Qumran. Some scholars believe that its absence there can be explained by the practice that books containing the name of God were stored in genizahs rather than destroyed. Since Esther does not contain the name of God, old and worn copies of

---

[11]For a fuller form-critical analysis of Esther, see Dommershausen, pp. 138–43; Roland E. Murphy, *Wisdom Literature: Job . . . Esther, The Forms of the Old Testament Literature XIII* (Grand Rapids: Eerdmans, 1981), pp. 1–12, 153–70.

it could have been destroyed.[12] However it is unlikely that all the copies would have worn out at the same time and hence that all would have been destroyed together. Therefore the final explanation for the absence of Esther MSS at Qumran must await further information.

No other OT book has been amplified so greatly in its translations as Esther. Two Aramaic Targums contain large amounts of additional material (see Paton, *Esther*, pp. 18–24, for a convenient summary description of their contents). A comparison of the Greek and Hebrew texts reveals a number of additions in the LXX that are included in the Apocrypha, many omissions, some differences with the Hebrew text, and intentional references to God. One of the recensions, the Lucianic, is much briefer and often differs from other Greek witnesses to the text.

The major additions to Esther that are found in the Apocrypha are called collectively "The Additions to the Book of Esther" and appear to have been written to minimize or to correct the book's seemingly religious inadequacies and the absence of God's name. The Greek version totals 270 verses, whereas the MT has 163; these additional verses were almost certainly never part of the original Hebrew (Harrison, p. 1101; Paton, *Esther*, p. 43). The major additions according to the Vulgate verse order are (1) The Dream of Mordecai (11:2–12:6; before 1:1 in the LXX); (2) The First Edict of Artaxerxes (13:1–7; after 3:13 in the LXX); (3) The Prayer of Mordecai (13:8–14:19; after 4:17 in the LXX); (4) The Prayer of Esther (15:4–19; after [3] in the LXX); (5) The Second Edict of Artaxerxes (16:1–24; after 8:12 in the LXX); (6) The Interpretation of Mordecai's Dream (10:4–13; at the end of the book in the LXX); (7) The Colophon to the Greek Esther (11:1; after [6] in the LXX).

Significant omissions and additions will be noted as they are encountered in the exposition.[13] The MT, in spite of the many accretions made to Esther, unquestionably represents the purest form of the text that has come down to the present time; and it serves as the basis for the exposition that follows.

7. Place in the Canon

The question of the process by which biblical books came to be recognized as canonical goes beyond the scope of this study.[14] However, because the canonical worth of Esther has been questioned both in ancient times and in modern times, some comments are required concerning differing views regarding the process of canonization. At one extreme is the "dropped from heaven" mentality, which would eliminate all divine-human interaction in the writing of the Scriptures. Then there is the belief that "the books received immediate recognition and acceptance by the faithful as soon as they were made aware of the writings" (Archer, p. 79).[15] At the

---

[12]D. Winton Thomas, "The Dead Sea Scrolls: What May We Believe?" *Annual of Leeds University Oriental Society* 6 (1969): 15.

[13]For a collection of the variant readings of Esther, see Moore, *Esther*, pp. lxi–lxiv; id., *Daniel, Esther and Jeremiah: The Additions* (Garden City, N.Y.: Doubleday and Co., 1977); and Paton, *Esther*, pp. 5–47; id., "A Text-Critical Apparatus to the Book of Esther, *Old Testament and Semitic Studies*, vol. 2, eds. R.F. Harper et al. (Chicago: University of Chicago Press, 1908), pp. 3–51.

[14]For further reading, see Harrison, pp. 260–88; Moore, *Esther*, pp. xxi–xxxi; Milton C. Fisher, "The Canon of the Old Testament," EBC, 1:385–92, esp. for his distinction between "canonicity" and "canonization," p. 386).

[15]Cf. E.J. Young, "The Canon of the Old Testament," *Revelation and the Bible*, ed. C.F.H. Henry (Grand Rapids: Baker, 1958), p. 168.

other extreme is the belief that canonicity was determined wholly by human criteria, human judgment, church councils, etc. This stance seems to imply that if men had not accepted the books, they would not have been God's Word or could have been eliminated from the Scriptures.

God's Word is inspired, and canonicity is "an innate authenticity by virtue of divine inspiration" (Fisher, EBC, 1:386). That fact, however, does not require agreement with the belief that there was *immediate* acceptance by all "the faithful"; even the apostle Peter had some difficulty before accepting the Word of the Lord (Acts 10:13–16). The process by which the OT books reached canonical status cannot, of course, be recovered; but if it could, the divine-human interaction would be apparent. This suggests that the Scriptures are the inspired words that God intended to be preserved and that subsequently were acknowledged by believers as his revelation. Harrison (p. 262) calls the process by which the OT canon became acknowledged as authoritative "human activity and cogitation under divine guidance." The time framework involved in this process cannot be recovered.

On the human side the Book of Esther must have received immediate and widespread acceptance by the Jewish people because it preserved the account of one of their rare triumphs over their enemies. At the same time, though its canonicity was never in doubt, there was sporadic opposition to the book because of its vindictive spirit and lack of religious and moral teachings. Its absence at Qumran, where every other OT book has been found or represented in part, has been explained as the Essene community's rejection of the book for theological reasons;[16] but this is only a hypothesis without evidence, which ultimately may be remedied by additional discoveries.

Since it was about a great Jewish victory, the Book of Esther quickly became popular among the Jewish people. The *baraitha* (or unauthorized gloss in the *Baba Bathra*), which is usually believed to be of second-century B.C. origin, mentions Esther as part of the *Ketubim* (see Harrison, p. 271). Josephus (*Against Apion* I, 38 –40 [8]) made the earliest explicit reference to Esther as already being a part of the Jewish Scriptures. There is no doubt that the Jewish canon was complete, including Esther, by the beginning of the Christian Era and that all the books were accepted by early Christians, even though Esther is not specifically quoted in the NT. It is equally certain that discussion about Esther and certain other books continued. As late as the second century A.D., Rabbi Samuel declared that the Book of Esther was apocryphal. Athanasius (d. 373) and Gregory of Nazianzus (d. 389) did not include Esther in their canonical lists. Amphilochius (d. 394), bishop of Iconium, stated that Esther was "accepted only by some." However, whatever questions about it lingered during the early centuries of the church, Esther was recognized as part of the Christian canon at the Council of Hippo in A.D. 393 and at the Council of Carthage in 397 (cf. Moore, *Esther,* p. xxviii).

Though its canonicity was accepted, discussion about Esther continued. Maimonides (d. 1204) said that when the rest of the Scriptures passed away, the Law and Esther would still remain. By contrast Martin Luther said, "I am so hostile to this book [2 Macc] and to Esther that I wish they did not exist at all; for they Judaize too

---

[16]Cf. H.L.Ginsberg, "The Dead Sea Manuscript Finds," in *Israel: Its Role in Civilization,* ed. Moshe David (New York: Harper, 1956), p. 52; Bardtke, p. 257, n. 12.

greatly and have much heathen impropriety" (cited in Schultz, p. 12). Schultz (ibid.) believes that Luther's remark was not made in reference to the MT but rather to the Greek (i.e., apocryphal) portions. Bickerman also believes that the famous remark has been misunderstood. He said that Luther was lamenting the absence of material in the book that could be interpreted as foreshadowing the life of Jesus and thus contribute to Christian faith. Bickerman observed that in the preface of Luther's German translation of Esther, he acknowledged that "it contains much that is good."[17]

Today the Jewish people hold the Book of Esther in highest esteem. They say that it is equal or superior to the Torah because it includes the origin of one of their festivals. The Jerusalem Talmud says that though the Prophets and the Writings may come to nought, the Pentateuch and Esther will never perish.

Knight (p. 15) says that the test of canonicity is "whether it adds to our knowledge of the mighty acts of God for the salvation of the world in and through his chosen instrument and people" and concludes that Esther meets that test. Esther shows how the sovereign God (though not mentioned by name) overrules the efforts of those who would destroy his people. The doctrine of God's providence on behalf of his people so thoroughly permeates the book that it cannot be said to be lacking in theological content (see further discussion under Theological Values). For all the questions that have been raised about it, Esther is worthy of its canonical status.

8. Special Problems

Three problems are especially associated with the Book of Esther: (1) lack of a single mention of God's name in the book; (2) moral and ethical practices by Mordecai and Esther that are difficult to justify; and (3) a number of what appear to be historical inaccuracies. These are problems that cannot be ignored.

a. *Absence of God's name*

The Book of Esther's failure to mention God, the Law, the covenant, the temple, and other characteristic institutions of Israel's faith is noticeable even to the casual reader. Scholars have proposed many solutions to explain these puzzling omissions. Paton (*Esther*, p. 95) believes that since the book was meant to be read during a time of uninhibited merrymaking and drinking (*Megillah* 7b says: "A man is obligated to drink on Purim until he is unable to distinguish between 'Blessed be Mordecai' and 'Cursed be Haman' "), God's name might be profaned if read aloud. To avoid this possibility the name was omitted altogether.[18] However this reasoning seems to presuppose that the book was written after such boisterous practices had already become a traditional part of the celebration or that it was written to be read as part of the earliest Purim celebrations; therefore Paton's explanation should be rejected.

Some scribes claimed to find the divine name YHWH ("The LORD") in acrostics

---

[17]E.J. Bickerman, *Four Strange Books of the Bible: Jonah, Daniel, Koheleth, Esther* (New York: Schocken Books, 1967), pp. 212–13.

[18]Cf. Hayyim Schauss, *The Jewish Festivals* (New York: Schocken Books, 1962), pp. 250–71, for different ways the Jewish people have celebrated Purim.

based on the initial and final letters of successive words in 1:20; 5:4, 13; and 7:7. The four letters YHWH are written larger than others in some MSS to reveal the "hidden" name (cf. Browne, p. 381; Moore, *Esther,* p. 56; Paton, *Esther,* p. 8). However no one today takes these rabbinic devices seriously.

Other scholars have explained the absence of reference to God by linking Esther to wisdom literature, which characteristically does not stress God or the Hebrew religion (cf. Ecclesiastes, which says very little about the institutions of the Hebrew faith; and Proverbs, which mentions "Elohim" only five times and "Yahweh" only eighty-seven times, a relatively small occurrence when compared to the usage of Yahweh in other books). Talmon (p. 427) calls Esther "applied wisdom," as opposed to a collection of wisdom sayings, such as Proverbs (cf. Gordis, "Book of Esther," p. 365, who calls it wisdom "in action"; in fact, he says all the books of the Hagiographa belong to the genre of wisdom literature). Opposed to Gordis and Talmon, who are chief proponents of Esther as wisdom literature, Crenshaw denies the affinities between Esther and wisdom.[19] Though definitions of "wisdom" in OT studies are varied (e.g., "practical religion in daily life," Fohrer [p. 310]; "skill in the art of living," Dentan;[20] "the knowledge of good and evil," Pedersen;[21] "ability to make a proper judgment and use of the factual content of knowledge," Mallott[22]), they all suggest that wisdom seeks to find the best way to live. Esther cannot be classified as wisdom in order to explain the absence of God's name in the book because it does not exhibit the characteristics that are identified with wisdom literature.

The explanation for the absence of God's name in Esther can be more profitably sought in the providence of God and his hiddenness (see Theological Values). Many scholars (e.g., Keil) believe that there is an indirect reference to Esther's faith when she spoke of fasting (4:16; cf. 4:3; 9:31). The statement "relief and deliverance . . . will arise from another place" (4:14) comes very close to being an acknowledgement of God and probably should be understood that way.

b. *Moral and ethical practices*

The nationalistic and vengeful spirit of the Book of Esther caused many problems among early Jewish and Christian readers (see discussion at Place in the Canon) and continues to do so. Some scholars have a low opinion of the leading characters because they do not consistently exhibit noble qualities. Paton (*Esther,* p. 96) said, "There is not one noble character in this book." Xerxes was a cruel, sensual, and capricious despot. Esther was willing to hide her identity in order to become queen and did not appear to be reluctant to marry a Gentile. She showed no mercy when Haman pled for his life and even demanded that his sons be hanged. Not content with deliverance of her people, she and Mordecai with the king's permission wrote a decree authorizing their people to slaughter and plunder their enemies. Mordecai advised Esther to conceal her identity in order to become queen. He insolently refused to bow to Haman and joined Esther in bringing vengeance on their enemies. The author never explicitly condemns any of the moral shortcomings of Esther

---

[19]J. L. Crenshaw, "Method in Determining Wisdom Influence Upon 'Historical' Literature," JBL 88 (June 1969): 129–42.

[20]Robert C. Dentan, *The Knowledge of God in Ancient Israel* (New York: Seabury, 1968), p. 122.

[21]Quoted from Eduard Nielsen, "Johannes Pedersen and the Old Testament," *Annual of the Swedish Theological Institute* 8 (1972): 18.

[22]Floyd E. Mallott, *Is Life Worth Living?* (Elgin, Ill.: Brethren, 1972), p. 22.

or Mordecai but seems to describe their triumph with approval. Perhaps only someone who has experienced severe persecution can understand, without approving, the unrestrained exultation evoked by victory over one's persecutors that is reflected in this book.

Exegetes approach the moral problems of Esther in several ways: (1) defense of the actions of Esther and Mordecai (e.g., Keil), implying that because they are in the Bible, they cannot be wrong; (2) an extremely critical and condemning attitude toward the book because of its morality (e.g., Paton); (3) neither blind defense nor blanket condemnation. The third attitude has the greatest merit.

Not all conservative scholars find it necessary to defend the actions of Esther and Mordecai. Speaking of the Jews in Persia, Young (*Introduction*, p. 349) said, "Their theocratic spirit . . . was weak." Baldwin (p. 414) commented, "Mordecai and Esther . . . were positively blameworthy." Wright (p. 45) is more specific: "The Christian judgment of the Book of Esther has been unnecessarily cramped through our feeling that because Mordecai is a Bible character, he must be a good man. Yet, like Samson and Jehu, he may have been little more than a time-server. The Bible makes no moral judgment on him, but it expects us to use our Christian sense. He was raised up by God, but he was not necessarily a godly man." If immoral practices among the Israelites are found in the preexilic period (idolatry, adultery, lying, etc.), why should anyone be surprised to find other expressions of ungodly conduct in the postexilic period (e.g., in Malachi)? Criticism of the morality of Esther and Mordecai is no more an attack on the inspiration of the Scriptures than a condemnation of the idolatry of the Israelites during the monarchy is an attack on the Scriptures.

There is an explanation that addresses both the omission of God's name and the moral problems of the book (and at the same time reveals a link between the two) that most exegetes have not considered. It is that the entire book should perhaps be seen as a subtle but powerful reminder that God's people sometimes fail to consult him prior to acting, do things that are contrary to his will, and consequently experience his displeasure by his silence.

Liberal commentators tend to emphasize the immoral acts in Esther as some kind of implied condemnation of the Scriptures (e.g., Paton, Pfeiffer; see Keil's rebuttal, pp. 315–16). On the other hand, many conservative commentators ignore or feel bound to justify the unscriptural conduct of Mordecai and Esther (e.g., hiding her identity, marriage with a Gentile, ordering the slaughter of their enemies after the tables were turned), as though the integrity of the Scriptures is at stake; but this defensive posture assumes that God ordered them to do these things. "All Scripture is God-breathed and is useful for teaching, rebuking, correcting and training in righteousness" (2 Tim 3:16), but everything found in the Bible is not to be emulated. Sometimes the biblical narratives show us how we should *not* act. "In all things God works for the good of those who love him" (Rom 8:28), but that does not mean that all things that happen are in themselves good (e.g., a small child killed by a drunken driver). The disturbing ethical practices of Esther and Mordecai resulted in the deliverance of the Jewish people from a terrible pogrom, but their success does not prove that the means used were good or pleasing to God. Keil (p. 316) observes: "The book . . . neither praises nor recommends their actions or behaviour, but simply relates what took place without blame or approval."

There are numerous examples in the Bible of great men and women of God committing immoral acts (e.g., Abraham passed his wife off as his sister [Gen 12:10

–20];[23] Lot lived among the wicked people of Sodom [Gen 19]; David committed adultery with Bathsheba [2 Sam 11]; Rahab was commended for her faith but not for her harlotry [Heb 11:31]). In the examples cited there is no explicit rebuke by God, only his silence. However the silence of God—the feeling that he is very distant— can express his disapproval just as powerfully as his rebuke.

The people of Israel failed God numerous times throughout their history. Sometimes he rebuked and threatened them openly (e.g., Amos 6:1; Mic 3:12); sometimes he withdrew his presence.[24] He was frequently brokenhearted by their sins (Jer 8:21; Ezek 6:9). The postexilic Book of Malachi shows clearly that the Israelites still had not brought their practices into conformity with the moral and spiritual standards established by God through his law. Could not Esther also be interpreted as another example of the postexilic failure of the Jewish people to become the exemplary people of God that he meant them to be?

What is usually interpreted as the providence of God working silently but effectively on behalf of his people in Esther should be reexamined to see whether God's silence should be interpreted as evidence that the people were working out their own affairs without consulting him. There is no historical evidence that the Jewish people entered into a period of blessing after the events of Esther, a blessing that might have been expected if God were guiding their actions. In fact his clear promise was that if they would obey him, they would be blessed (Deut 28). Mordecai's elevation (10:3) may not have been God's "stamp of approval" on his actions. It may teach that if we use human means to achieve our purposes, we will receive human rewards (cf. Matt 6:5).

Is it possible that Mordecai's pride is the key for understanding the events of Esther? The entire confrontation with Haman could have been avoided if Mordecai had shown respect by bowing before him. To do so would not have been an admission that Haman was a god, as some commentators have argued (e.g., Keil). In fact many biblical examples can be found of Israelites bowing before another person (e.g., Gen 23:7; 33:6; 42:6; 49:8; 1 Sam 24:8; 1 Kings 1:16, 23; Jer 27:8–11). Should Esther have refused to marry a pagan Gentile? If she had, could not God have found another way to deliver his people? If Esther and Mordecai had forgiven their enemies instead of demanding vengeance, would God have been pleased and protected his people? Was there any other way to nullify the first decree than by revenge? Does the fact that the origin of Purim is found in the Bible and that the Jewish people observe Purim today prove that God ordained this festival as an addition to the festivals found in the Mosaic Law (Lev 23; 25; cf. Zech 7:5–6, where Jews were observing fast days but not by commandment of God; Amos 4:4–5, where they modified the observances to suit themselves)?

These and similar questions need to be asked about the Book of Esther. To do so may result in a fresh, insightful understanding of this controversial book. Its real

---

[23]See G.Ch. Aalders, *Genesis,* tr. by William Heynen, Bible Student's Commentary (Grand Rapids: Zondervan, 1981), 1:276.

[24]There are numerous verses that suggest the hiddenness or silence of God when he was angry with his people. A nonexhaustive list includes Gen 4:14; Exod 33:1–3; Deut 1:45; 3:26; 31:17–18; 1 Sam 8:18; 28:6; Job 13:23–24; 34:29; Pss 13:1; 22:1–2, 24; 27:9; 30:7; 51:11; 66:18; 88:14; 89:46; 104:29; Prov 1:28 –29; 15:29; Isa 1:15; 8:17; 54:8; 57:17; 59:2; 64:7; Jer 11:11, 14; 14:12 (though they fast); 33:5; Ezek 11:23; 39:23–24; Mic 3:4; John 9:31. See also Samuel E. Balentine, "A Description of the Semantic Field of Hebrew Words for 'Hide,'" VetTest 30 (April 1980): 137–53; idem, *The Hidden God: The Hiding of the Face of God in the Old Testament* (Oxford: University Press, 1983).

message may prove to be that God's people are prone to use the same means as ungodly people for achieving their goals rather than taking a bold step of faith that God will work out his purposes without human initiative (Exod 14:13–14), least of all resorting to immoral acts in a crisis situation (cf. 1 Sam 24:10; 26:9–11).

c. Alleged historical inaccuracies

Scholars have long debated and to the present day remain divided about the historicity of the events described in Esther. Some say it is historical in the fullest sense (e.g., Hoschander, Keil, Raven, Watson, Young). Others say that it is essentially historical or that it has a historical basis or that there is little in the book that could not have happened (e.g., S.R. Driver, Fohrer, Rowley, Streane). Harrison (p. 1098) says it has a "substantial historical nucleus." Others think it is neither pure fact nor pure fiction but a combination and call it a "historical novel" (Eissfeldt, Moore; Gordis ["Book of Esther," p. 387] calls it a "reworking of history" but elsewhere [p. 43] a "historical novel"). Some scholars call it an etiological legend that was composed in terms acceptable to the Jews of what was originally a pagan holiday.[25] Other scholars brand the entire story as fictitious and without a shred of historical evidence (cf. Bickerman, Browne, Gaster, Paton, Pfeiffer).

In order to settle the question of historicity, an examination of each of the major historical problems associated with the book is in order.

1) The neatness of the structure

Some say the story is too neatly balanced in its structure between the antagonists on either side and the monarch in the middle to be believable (e.g., Pfeiffer [p. 739] calls it "artificial symmetry"). They argue that the number of fortuitous happenings and the anticipated triumph of the Jews is artificial. (Of course there are no difficulties with the "coincidences" if one acknowledges the providence of God at work behind the scenes.) Gerleman argued that Esther was structured after the story of the Exodus.[26] Similarities with the literary structure of *A Thousand and One Nights* have also been alleged (Moore, *Esther*, p. 25). Gordis ("Studies in Esther," p. 45) makes a perceptive observation concerning the structure of Esther that explains what might appear to be an overly neat, almost artificial unfolding of events: "The outstanding literary characteristic of the author of Esther is his interest in the swift flow of the action. He, therefore, strips the plot of all non-essentials, concentrating on events rather than on motivations, on incidents rather than on descriptions of character." That truth is stranger than fiction could also be applied to the story of Esther. The tightly structured, fast-moving narrative in no way proves that any of the events in the book could not have taken place.

2) Accuracy of the descriptions of the Persian court and Persian customs

In spite of attempts to discredit the historical accuracy of the Persian background depicted in the book, the accuracy of the descriptions of the Persian court and the

---

[25]Soggin, *Introduction*, p. 403; cf. W. L. Humphreys, "A Life-Style for Diaspora: A Study of the Tales of Esther and Daniel," JBL 92 (June 1973): 211–13, who calls it a "festal legend" (p. 213); also Anderson, p. 824.

[26]Gillis Gerleman, *Studien zu Esther* (Neukirchen-Vluyn: Neukirchener Verlag, 1966); id., *Esther* (Neukirchen-Vluyn: Neukirchener Verlag, 1973).

customs of the times, as well as a profusion of precise dates and Persian names, continues to withstand attacks and provides impressive evidence for the historical nature of the book.[27] The character of Xerxes (Ahasuerus) is consistent with what is known about him through secular historians such as Herodotus, Aeschylus, and Juvenal (e.g., his sumptuous drinking parties, extravagant gifts, irrational temper). His Greek campaign fits perfectly within the events of his marital problems and explains the lapse of time between the third (1:3) and seventh years (2:16). The author also shows an accurate knowledge of certain features of Persian government. The antiquity of the festival of Purim itself and the acceptance of the book by the Jewish people in spite of its failure to mention God or any institutions of the Jewish religion also argue for its historicity.

3) The number of provinces

Esther 1:1 says there were 127 provinces, whereas the evidence is said to point to a number that varied between 20 and 29. It is true that Darius divided the kingdom into 20 satrapies, but the word used in 1:1 is *meḏînāh* ("province"), which should be understood as an administrative subdivision of a satrapy (cf. Ezra 2:1, where Judah is referred to as a province, a subdivision of what Herodotus called the fifth satrapy, Syria). Also Shea (p. 245) observes that there is a Hebrew-Aramaic word for satrapy that could have been used here if that is what the author meant. There could have been varying numbers of provinces at different times; thus the number preserved in Esther is not without historical credibility.

4) The length of the feast

A feast that lasted 180 days (1:4) has been questioned as an exaggeration. However an early ninth-century B.C. Assyrian record tells of 69,574 guests who were present for a ten-day palace dedication (Fuerst, p. 45). Also, as will be suggested in the comments, the guests may have come in rotation, as it would have been difficult for all administrative officials to be away from their posts for six months at the same time.

5) The identification of Xerxes' queen

One of the most serious objections raised against the historicity of Esther is that the only known wife of Xerxes was called Amestris, the daughter of a Persian general Otanes. Persian records do not mention a queen by the name of Vashti who was deposed, nor do they mention the name of Esther as Xerxes' wife. Amestris was known for her cruelty; Herodotus says she had the mother of her husband's paramour brutally mutilated and had fourteen noble Persian young men buried alive in an act of religious devotion.

The problem appears insoluble, but a number of answers have been proposed: (1) in a polygamous society a king may have had more than one wife (Baldwin, p. 413); (2) Esther may have been a subordinate wife or chief concubine (Schultz, p. 5; Dommershausen, p. 140, observed that the author regularly wrote "King Xerxes" but "Esther the Queen" to emphasize that Xerxes was king while Esther was only

[27]Cf. M. Dieulafoy, *L'Acropole de la Suse,* 1890; Gordis, "Studies in Esther," p. 44; Paton, *Esther,* pp. 65–71; Yamauchi, pp. 109–10.

one of his wives); (3) the most persuasive explanation is one mentioned by Streane (p. 5) and developed by Wright (pp. 40–42), which shows the similarity of the names "Vashti" and "Amestris" and concludes that they were one and the same person (cf. Shea, pp. 235–37).

6) *The fate of Vashti*

The fact that Persian records do not mention Vashti or the fate of Amestris is not proof that the king had only one wife and queen or that the events narrated in Esther should be repudiated.

7) *Esther's selection as queen*

The events of Xerxes' reign fit well with the choosing of a new queen between the third year (1:3) and the seventh year (2:16; see Shea for an excellent harmony of the chronology, pp. 227–46; cf. Wright, pp. 42–43). From 483 (Xerxes' third year) to 480 B.C., Xerxes was involved in his ill-fated campaign against Greece. Amestris and two of Xerxes' sons accompanied him; so he must have been married for some years to Amestris. Herodotus says that after Xerxes' disastrous defeat in Greece, he returned to Persia and consoled himself with his harem. His return was in 479 B.C., the seventh year of his reign and the year that Esther became queen, or another wife (2:16). Objections that the Persian king was required to choose his wife from one of seven noble families of the land (so Herodotus) can easily be overcome. Wright (p. 38) calls attention to the fact that Amestris was not from one of the seven noble families and that Darius had wives who also were not of the seven families. The marriages with daughters of the seven families may have been only a custom, not a binding law; and even if it were a law, the king could have ignored it. There is no valid evidence for the claim that a Persian king could not have had a Jewish girl or a foreigner in his harem.

8) *The age of Mordecai*

Esther 2:5–6 has frequently been cited as one of the principal historical inaccuracies of the book. It introduces Mordecai as the "son of Jair, the son of Shimei, the son of Kish, who had been carried into exile from Jerusalem by Nebuchadnezzar." If the antecedent of "who" is Mordecai, as many scholars claim (e.g., Pfeiffer), then he would have been at least 120 years old (cf. Paton, *Esther,* p. 168) and hardly the age to have a young, beautiful cousin. And, of course, if she had been near his age, she could never have won Xerxes' beauty contest! Grammatically it is just as likely that the antecedent of "who" is Kish, Mordecai's great-grandfather, thus removing the problem of Mordecai's age. Some commentators say the genealogy contains gaps and that Shimei is the one who cursed David (2 Sam 16:5–8) and that Kish is the father of Saul (1 Sam 9:1–2). There is absolutely no evidence for this interpretation of Mordecai's genealogy.

9) *Mordecai's rise to power*

Another argument against the historicity of Esther is Mordecai's rise to power. Critics say it would have been impossible for a foreigner and a Jew to have become prime minister under a Persian king. The evidence against this objection is overwhelming, as examples of foreigners rising to high political office in the ancient Near

East are numerous. Joseph became second in the land to Pharaoh (Gen 41:41–43). Daniel rose to great prominence in Babylon (Dan 2:48), and Nehemiah became the king's cupbearer (Neh 1:11). More than one hundred Jewish names have been found in a collection of tablets from the reigns of Artaxerxes I and Darius II of men who had important offices in the kingdom (Baldwin, p. 413).

The most impressive evidence for Mordecai's rise to power was the discovery of the name Marduka (= Mordecai) on a cuneiform tablet from Borsippa. He is identified as a high official in the royal court at Susa during the early years of Xerxes' reign. Some scholars interpret this discovery to mean only that it was possible for a foreigner like Mordecai to rise to power under Xerxes (e.g., Brockington, p. 220). Others insist that the two are to be equated. Gordis ("Book of Esther," p. 384) says, "Two officials with the same name is scarcely likely" (cf. Wright, p. 44; Yamauchi, p. 107). This inscriptional evidence offers remarkable archaeological confirmation of the biblical narrative.

10) *The orders to exterminate the Jews*

Critics say Haman would not have promulgated a vindictive decree for the extermination of the Jews and then waited eleven months to carry it out, as it would have given them time to escape or to prepare for defense. Keil (p. 307) says Haman resorted to casting the lot to determine a propitious day for carrying out his slaughter and had such confidence in the power of magical decisions that premature publication would not change the Jews' fate. Schultz (p. 9) says that the Jews' flight would not have been unwelcome to Haman as he would still accomplish his purpose of confiscating their property. As parallel support for the historicity of the delay in carrying out the decree, in 193 B.C. Antiochus III of Syria issued a decree that was forwarded by his viceroy in Persia four months later (cited by Gordis, "Book of Esther," p. 383).

11) *The king's willingness to destroy his own subjects*

Another objection to the historicity of Esther is that the king would never have signed a decree that would result in the destruction of thousands of his Persian subjects; and, in fact, Persian records do not mention such a slaughter or even a Jewish persecution during Xerxes' reign. However it is not inconceivable that a capricious, cruel tyrant like Xerxes would have agreed to the slaughter of his own people as a whim to please his wife. Unfortunately history is all too replete with mass slaughters of a ruler's own subjects or of other innocent people (see below).

12) *The number of people killed by the Jews*

The great number of people killed by the Jews has been cited as further evidence of the book's historical inaccuracy ("incredible," Fohrer, p. 253). The LXX reduces the number to fifteen thousand. Harrison (p. 1092) believes the figure of seventy-five thousand is symbolic of a great victory. Granted that a few hundred may have been killed in some skirmishes between Jews and Persians, critics say such a large number is the author's own invention. However, as noted above, mass slaughters have been all too common throughout history. In 90 B.C. Mithridates, king of Pontus, ordered the assassination of all Romans in his realm on a certain date; at least eighty thousand were killed. Hulagu sacked Baghdad in A.D. 1258 and killed between eight hundred thousand and a million people. King Ferdinand drove three hundred thousand Jews from Spain during his reign. Fifty thousand were killed in the Saint Bartholomew's massacre that began in Paris on 24 August 1572 and spread throughout France. In more recent memory Adolph Hitler was responsible for the liquidation of six million Jewish people. From what is known of the cruel, capricious nature of Xerxes, there is no reason to doubt that he was capable of agreeing to the slaughter of his own subjects.

13) The decrees in different languages

Decrees sent out in different languages (1:22; 3:12; 8:9) have also been called another historical inaccuracy of the book. This argument is without merit. The Persians had absorbed many people of different languages; Herodotus says sixty nations were under Persian rule. From what is known of their tolerant policies toward conquered people, it would have been quite normal for them to communicate official decrees to the subjects in their native tongues.

14) The non-Jewish origin of Purim

Many scholars have seen Babylonian, Persian, or Greek parallels with the Festival of Purim and therefore argue that the festival did not originate historically as described in the Book of Esther but was borrowed from pagan festivals (cf. Harrison, pp. 1093–94). They argue that the very name Purim (from the Akkad. word *puru*, "lot") proves its non-Jewish origin, and that its secular character (riotous celebration) also shows its pagan roots. However Moore (*Esther*, p. xlvii) is correct in observing that even though Purim is a Hebraized form of a non-Hebrew word, this does not prove that it was borrowed from a foreign festival. Gaster (p. 14) argued for a Persian origin of Purim in the Persian New Year festivals (also Hitzig [cited in Harrison, p. 1093], Kaiser [p. 202], Meier). Zunz (in Harrison, p. 1093) said it was adapted from a Persian spring festival. Gunkel (in Eissfeldt, p. 509) believed it was based on a Persian festival that was occasioned by the murder of the Magi (a story related by Herodotus).

Scholars have suggested many origins for Purim but have not been able to prove any of them. Even if the manner of celebration reveals some pagan links, this would in no wise deny the historicity of the event that Purim celebrates, any more than certain pagan accretions to the Christmas and Easter observances disprove the historicity of the events these two days celebrate. No non-Israelite festival can be shown to be the model for Purim in origin or manner of observance; therefore the historian must look to the Book of Esther as the only authentic explanation for the origin of Purim.

15) Parallels with ancient myths

Attempts have been made to explain Esther as a mythological narrative (esp. by P. Jensen and H. Zimmern [in Harrison, p. 1093]). The appeal of this theory is the similarity of the names of Mordecai and Esther to the Babylonian deities Marduk and Ishtar, and the names of Haman and Vashti to Elamite deities Human and Mashti. The story thus becomes the account of the triumph of the Babylonian deities over the Elamite gods. This interpretation of Esther has met with little acceptance even among liberal scholars (e.g., Eissfeldt and Fohrer reject it), since theophoric elements were commonly used in names.

An unbiased examination of all the arguments against the historicity of Esther leads one to the conclusion that there is no valid evidence for denying the historicity of any of the people or events found in the book, though, admittedly, the lack of confirmation of Vashti or Esther is a difficult problem. An observation by Keil (p. 305) should also be considered in making one's evaluation: "The objections that have been raised to its credibility have arisen, first from the habit of making subjective probability the standard of historical truth." There is nothing in Esther that could not have happened. After careful study of the historicity of Esther, Wright (p. 46) persuasively concluded: "There is obviously a need to take the book of Esther seriously as a first-hand historical document."[28]

9. Theological Values

Since the Book of Esther does not mention the name of God (though Xerxes is mentioned by name twenty-nine times) or any of the institutions of the Jewish faith, it has been assumed that its theological value is minimal ("The book has little to commend it to civilized persons," Pfeiffer, p. 747). Schauss said that Esther "has no religious content and can arouse no pious thoughts,"[29] but such conclusions are erroneous and reveal insensitivity to the theological ideas contained in the book. The omission of God's name does not detract from the theological worth of Esther (see further discussion of this omission under Special Problems). It could be interpreted as the hiddenness of God as he works out his purposes (cf. Berg, pp. 178, 183 –84). The hiddenness of God can also sometimes be explained as evidence of his displeasure; this fact may be the key to the ethical problems of Esther that disturb many sincere Christian exegetes. In the OT God sometimes spoke out to show his displeasure toward his people's sins (e.g., Isa 1:15; Jer 17:1; Amos 6:8). Sometimes he expressed his displeasure by withdrawal and silence (e.g., Ezek 11:23, God's withdrawal from Jerusalem; Amos 8:11, a famine of the Word).

It should be remembered that the conduct of the Israelites was frequently contrary to what God expected of them; but he continued to preserve them, if only as a remnant. The Jews in Esther's time did not deserve God's favor (no one ever does). Mordecai and Esther were not blameless. Baldwin's observation (p. 414) that Mordecai and Esther "in seeking to run all their enemies to the death . . . were positively blameworthy" should be carefully pondered by those who feel obligated to justify their attitude toward their enemies.

Esther implicitly teaches God's providential care of his people. Vashti's deposition, Esther's selection as her successor, and Mordecai's discovery of the plot against the king and his subsequent reward are only a few of the many "chance" happenings that are better explained by God's way of effecting the deliverance of his people from their persecutors.

---

[28]For further reading in support of the historicity of the Book of Esther, cf. Archer, pp. 419–21; Gordis, "Book of Esther," pp. 382–88; Harrison, pp. 1090–98; Hoschander, p. 20 *passim*; Shea, pp. 227 –46; Wright, pp. 37–47; Yamauchi, pp. 99–117; Young, *Introduction*, pp. 346–48.

[29]*Jewish Festivals*, p. 264.

Childs (p. 606) believes that Gordis has clearly formulated the basic theological issue at stake: 'It is fundamental to the Jewish world-outlook that the preservation of the Jewish people is itself a religious obligation of the first magnitude."[30] The book implies that even when God's people are far from him and disobedient, they are still the object of his concern and love, and that he is working out his purposes through them (4:14). There is also a reminder in 4:14 that if one fails to carry out God's tasks, he will work out his purposes through another.

The sovereignty of God is implicit in the events of the story. The fast-moving events that seem to be under the control of men such as Xerxes and Haman prove in the end to have been directed by God for the benefit of his people. Even the law of the Medes and Persians, which should have brought about the slaughter of the Jews, was overruled.

The Book of Esther teaches (1) the law of retribution for sin by the hanging of Haman on his own gallows, (2) that faithfulness is rewarded, and (3) the value of standing for one's convictions even in the midst of a dangerous situation. It reveals that the natural reaction to unjust oppression frequently is to fight back rather than to claim " 'It is mine to avenge; . . . ,' says the Lord" (Rom 12:19).

10. Bibliography

Books

Anderson, Bernhard W. "The Book of Esther: Introduction and Exegesis." In *The Interpreter's Bible*, vol. 3. IB. Edited by George Arthur Buttrick et al. New York and Nashville: Abingdon, 1954, pp. 823–74.

Archer, Gleason L., Jr. *A Survey of Old Testament Introduction*. Rev. ed. SOTIrev. Chicago: Moody, 1974.

Baldwin, Joyce G. "Esther." In *The New Bible Commentary Revised*. NBCrev. Edited by D. Guthrie et al. Grand Rapids: Eerdmans, 1970.

Bardtke, Hans. *Das Buch Esther*. Kommentar zum Alten Testament. Band XVII. Gütersloher Verlagshaus Gerd Mohn, 1963.

Berg, Sandra Beth. *The Book of Esther: Motifs, Themes and Structure*. Society of Biblical Literature Dissertation Series 44. Missoula, Mont.: Scholars, 1979.

Brockington, L.H. *Ezra, Nehemiah and Esther*. The Century Bible New Series. London: Thomas Nelson and Sons, 1969.

Browne, L.E. "Esther." In *Peake's Commentary on the Bible*. Edited by Matthew Black and H.H. Rowley. London: Thomas Nelson and Sons, 1962, pp. 381–85.

Childs, Brevard S. *Introduction to the Old Testament as Scripture*. Philadelphia: Fortress, 1979.

Davies, T.W. *Ezra, Nehemiah and Esther*. New Century Bible. New York: Oxford University Press, 1909.

Dommershausen, Werner. *Die Esterrolle: Stil und Ziel einer alttestamentlichen Schrift*. Stuttgarten Biblische Monographien VI. Edited by J. Hospecker and W. Pesch. Stuttgart: Katholisches Bibelwerk, 1968.

Eissfeldt, Otto. *The Old Testament: An Introduction*. New York: Harper and Row, 1965.

Fohrer, Georg. *Introduction to the Old Testament*. Nashville and New York: Abingdon, 1968.

---

[30]Robert Gordis, *Megillat Esther: The Masoretic Hebrew Text With Introduction, New Translation and Commentary* (New York: Rabbinical Assembly, 1972), p. 13.

Fuerst, Wesley J. *The Books of Ruth, Esther, Ecclesiastes, the Song of Songs, Lamentations*. The Cambridge Bible Commentary on the New English Bible. Cambridge: Cambridge University Press, 1975.

Gaster, Theodor H. *Purim and Hanukkah in Custom and Tradition*. New York: Abelard-Schuman, 1950.

Gerleman, Gillis. *Esther*. Biblischer Kommentar: Altes Testament. Neukirchen-Vluyn: Neukirchener Verlag, 1960.

Goldman, S. "Esther: Introduction and Commentary." In *The Soncino Books of the Bible: The Five Megilloth*. Edited by A. Cohen. London: Soncino, 1946, pp. 192–242.

Haller, Max. "Esther." *Die fünf Megilloth*. Handbuch zum Alten Testament. Tübingen: J.C.B. Mohr, 1940.

Harrison, R.K. *Introduction to the Old Testament*. Grand Rapids: Eerdmans, 1969.

Hoschander, J. *The Book of Esther in the Light of History*. Philadelphia: Dropsie College Press, 1923.

Kaiser, Otto. *Introduction to the Old Testament*. Minneapolis: Augsburg, 1975.

Keil, C.F. *The Books of Ezra, Nehemiah and Esther*. Biblical Commentary on the Old Testament. KD. 1888 Reprint. Grand Rapids: Eerdmans, 1956.

Kelly, Balmer H. *The Book of Ezra, The Book of Nehemiah, The Book of Esther, The Book of Job*. The Layman's Bible Commentary. Vol. 8. Richmond: John Knox, 1962.

Knight, George A.F. *Esther, Song of Songs, Lamentations: Introduction and Commentary*. London: SCM, 1955.

Moore, Carey A. *Esther: Translated with an Introduction and Notes*. The Anchor Bible. AB. Vol. 7b. Garden City, N.Y.: Doubleday & Co., 1971.

Orlinsky, Harry M., ed. *Studies in the Book of Esther*. In The Library of Biblical Studies. New York: KTAV, 1982.

Paton, Lewis Bayles. *A Critical and Exegetical Commentary on the Book of Esther*. The International Critical Commentary. ICC. Edinburgh: T. & T. Clark, 1908.

Pfeiffer, Robert H. *Introduction to the Old Testament*. New York: Harper and Row, 1948.

Schultz, Fr.W. "The Book of Esther." In *Commentary on the Holy Scriptures*. CHS. Vol. 7. Edited by John Peter Lange. New York: Charles Scribner's Sons, 1877.

Streane, A.W. *Esther*. The Cambridge Bible. Cambridge: Cambridge University Press, 1907.

Wright, J. Stafford. "The Historicity of the Book of Esther." In *New Perspectives on the Old Testament*. Edited by J. Barton Payne. Waco: Word, 1970.

Würthwein, Ernst. "Esther." *Die fünf Megilloth*. Handbuch zum alten Testament. 2d ed. Tübingen: J.C.B. Mohr, 1969.

Young, Edward J. *An Introduction to the Old Testament*. Grand Rapids: Eerdmans, 1953.

Periodicals

Gordis, Robert. "Studies in the Esther Narrative." *Journal of Biblical Literature* 95 (March 1976): 43–58.

———. "Religion, Wisdom and History in the Book of Esther." *Journal of Biblical Literature* 100 (September 1981): 359–88.

Littman, Robert J. "The Religious Policy of Xerxes and the Book of Esther." *Jewish Quarterly Review* 65 (January 1975): 145–55.

Millard, A.R. "The Persian Names in Esther and the Reliability of the Hebrew Text." *Journal of Biblical Literature* 96 (December 1977): 481–88.

Shea, W.H. "Esther and History." *Andrews University Seminary Studies* 14 (Spring 1976): 227–46.

Talmon, Shemaryahu. "'Wisdom' in the Book of Esther." *Vetus Testamentum* 13 (October 1963): 419–55.

Vischer, William. "The Book of Esther." *Evangelical Quarterly* 11 (January 1939): 3–21.

Yamauchi, Edwin. "The Archaeological Background of Esther." *Bibliotheca Sacra* 137 (April-June 1980): 99–117.

11. Outline

Text and Exposition

I. Esther Elevated to Queen of Persia (1:1–2:23)

A. *The Great Banquets of Xerxes*

1:1–9

> [1]This is what happened during the time of Xerxes, the Xerxes who ruled over 127 provinces stretching from India to Cush: [2]At that time King Xerxes reigned from his royal throne in the citadel of Susa, [3]and in the third year of his reign he gave a banquet for all his nobles and officials. The military leaders of Persia and Media, the princes, and the nobles of the provinces were present.
>
> [4]For a full 180 days he displayed the vast wealth of his kingdom and the splendor and glory of his majesty. [5]When these days were over, the king gave a banquet, lasting seven days, in the enclosed garden of the king's palace, for all the people from the least to the greatest, who were in the citadel of Susa. [6]The garden had hangings of white and blue linen, fastened with cords of white linen and purple material to silver rings on marble pillars. There were couches of gold and silver on a mosaic pavement of porphyry, marble, mother-of-pearl and other costly stones. [7]Wine was served in goblets of gold, each one different from the other, and the royal wine was abundant, in keeping with the king's liberality. [8]By the king's command each guest was allowed to drink in his own way, for the king instructed all the wine stewards to serve each man what he wished.
>
> [9]Queen Vashti also gave a banquet for the women in the royal palace of King Xerxes.

1 The story of Esther begins with *way^{e}hî* (lit., "And it was"; NIV, "This is what happened"). This phrase is traditionally translated "Now it came to pass" (KJV) but is omitted altogether in some translations (e.g., NAB, RSV). *Way^{e}hî* frequently begins a book (cf. Josh; Judg; Ruth; 1 and 2 Sam; Ezek; Jonah) or a sentence without any apparent syntactical relationship to what preceded.

The story is said to have taken place during the reign of the Persian monarch Xerxes. The Hebrew word used throughout the book is *'^{a}hašwērôš* ("Ahasuerus"), which is considered a variant of Xerxes' name. Xerxes is the Greek form of the Persian *Khshayârsha*. The LXX, however, mentions a later Persian ruler, Artaxerxes (understood as Artaxerxes I by Wright, p. 37, and as Artaxerxes II by Hoschander, p. 20 *passim*, and A.T. Olmstead, *History of Palestine and Syria* [New York: Charles Scribner's Sons, 1931], pp. 612–14). Xerxes ruled Persia 486–465 B.C. As grandson of Cyrus the Great (550–530 B.C.) by Atossa, Cyrus' daughter, Xerxes inherited an empire from his father, Darius I (520–486 B.C.), that stretched east to west from India (probably a reference to the northwestern part of the Indus River region that had been conquered by Darius) to Cush ("Ethiopia," KJV, RSV; that is, the Upper Nile region that had been conquered by Cambyses). Inscriptions have been found in which Xerxes referred to himself as "the great King, the King of Kings, the King of the lands occupied by many races, the King of this great world." Xerxes was the Persian monarch who made an ambitious but disastrous attempt to conquer Greece in 480–479 B.C. He divided much of his energy during the remaining years of his reign to an ambitious building project at Susa and Persepolis. He was murdered by his vizier Artabanus, who then placed Artaxerxes I on the throne.

For purposes of governing, Xerxes' empire was divided into 127 provinces (*m^{e}dînâh*). Provinces are not to be confused with satrapies, which is a different word (see

Introduction: Special Problems, c.3). There were twenty satrapies according to Herodotus and as many as thirty-one according to other sources. The Behistun Rock inscription says there were twenty-one satrapies, but later in the same inscription it says twenty-three, and still later, twenty-nine. Some scholars regard the number 127 as an exaggeration and another of the historical inaccuracies of the book, but the problem is solved when "provinces" are understood as political subdivisions of the "satrapies" (cf. 3:12).

2 "At the time King Xerxes reigned" suggests the beginning of his reign, but v.3 says it was in the third year. Many scholars (e.g., Bardtke) understand *kešeḇeṯ* (lit., "when sitting"; NIV, "reigned") to mean "when he sat securely," i.e., when Xerxes was established on his throne after quelling uprisings in Egypt and Babylon during the early years of his reign. It may only mean that Xerxes took up his residence in Susa ("Shushan," KJV), the royal winter residence and capital of ancient Elam. Royal residences were also located in Babylon, Ecbatana, and Persepolis. In the summer Susa was unbearably hot. Strabo, the Greek geographer (63 B.C.–A.D. 24?) said Susa was so hot that lizards and snakes burned to death if they crossed the street at noon and that cold water placed in the sun could be used for a bath immediately! Susa was both the name of the the city and the name of the royal fortress or citadel that occupied a separate part of the city. Fire destroyed the royal buildings during the reign of Artaxerxes I (465–424 B.C.), but they were rebuilt by Artaxerxes II (404–358). Susa's location made it a center of traffic on the roads to Persepolis, Sardis, and Ecbatana. In 324 Susa was the scene of the mass marriages between ten thousand of Alexander the Great's soldiers and Persian girls.

3 In the third year of his reign, Xerxes gave a great banquet to display his wealth and glory. Its purpose may have been to make plans for his Greek campaign (Baldwin, Keil, Schultz). His nobles and the military and political leaders of Persia and Media were all present. Ctesias, the court physician to Artaxerxes Mnemon, said that as many as 15,000 guests were entertained at once at Persian banquets. King Assurnasirpal of Assyria was reported to have entertained 69,574 guests for ten days.

4 For 180 days (half a year) Xerxes displayed his vast wealth and royal regalia to his guests. A question has been raised as to whether the guests could have exercised their administrative duties and also all have been present during the entire 180 days or whether they might have come by rotation till all had experienced the king's hospitality (cf. Introduction: Special Problems, c.4). Keil argued (p. 324) that vv.5–8 are a further description of the feast of v.3 and not a second feast. He believed the king displayed his wealth for 180 days and then gave a feast that lasted 7 days. The LXX preserves a distinction by calling the first a *dochē* ("banquet") and the second a *potos* ("drinking party").

5 Contrary to Keil, the context indicates that a seven-day banquet was given for all the men (*ʿām*, "people," but cf. v.9) who were in the citadel of Susa, from the greatest to the least (i.e., both nobles and commoners were included). The banquet was held in the king's enclosed garden. Persian palaces usually stood in the midst of a park (Gr. *paradeisos*, from which the word "paradise" comes) surrounded by a fortified wall.

6 With eyewitness accuracy the author described the white-and-blue linen hangings in the garden that were fastened with cords to silver rings on marble pillars. He described couches of gold and silver placed on a mosaic pavement of porphyry, marble, mother-of-pearl, and other costly stones. Herodotus (9.82) described couches of gold and silver that the Greeks captured from the Persians. The meaning of many of the materials described in v.6 remains uncertain. Archaeologists have found the remains of Xerxes' palace and have verified the accuracy of the opulence described in this verse (cf. Dieulafoy, *L'Acropole de Suse*; A.T. Olmstead, *History of the Persian Empire* [Chicago: University of Chicago Press, 1948], pp. 170–71; J:P. Free, *Archaeology and Bible History* [Wheaton, Ill.: Van Kampen, 1950], pp. 244–45).

7 Wine was served in golden goblets, no two alike. The Targum says they were the vessels taken from the temple in Jerusalem by Nebuchadnezzar in 587 B.C. (cited in Paton, *Esther*, p. 140; but cf. Ezra 1:7). The king's "liberality" (Heb., "according to the king's hand") assured an abundant supply of wine for all the guests.

8 The guests were served according to Persian law; the word for "command" (*dāt*, "law") here may mean the special rule made for this feast. The exact meaning of this verse remains uncertain. It probably means that no one was compelled to drink; at the same time no restrictions were placed on what a guest could consume. The king's wine stewards had been instructed to serve each man whatever he wanted, however much or little.

9 At the same time the men were being entertained by the king, Queen Vashti gave a banquet for the women in the royal palace, though such separation of the sexes at banquets was not required by Persian custom. The queen's name has raised a question about the historicity of the Book of Esther, as the only known name of Xerxes' queen was Amestris, who was a cruel and imperious woman. Answers to the problem have been varied. Some scholars say the king had more than one wife; others say this is one of the historical inaccuracies of the book; still others say Vashti was another name for Amestris (cf. Introduction: Special Problems, c.5).

Notes

1 The LXX and OL add seventeen verses between the title and 1:1 that describe a dream of Mordecai and his discovery of the plot against the king's life (cf. Introduction: Text).

The consonants of the Persian name *Khshayârsha* appear in the Elephantine papyri as *Kshy'rsh*, which is quite similar to Xerxes.

Haller (cited in Moore, *Esther*, p. 4) deletes "7" to make the number of provinces agree with Dan 6:1.

2 The infinitive כְּשֶׁבֶת (*keshebet*), a hapax legomenon, has the force of a preterite—"when sitting" (NIV, "reigned").

3 "Military leaders of Persia and Media" (NIV) is a translation of חֵיל פָּרַס וּמָדַי (*hêl pāram ûmāday*, "the power of Persia and Media," i.e., the army). It is unlikely that the entire army is meant; perhaps the king's elite bodyguard was intended.

Except in 10:2, which preserves the chronological order of the two kingdoms, the order "Persia and Media" is always maintained in Esther because of Persia's ascendancy over Media since the time of Cyrus the Great (550–530 B.C.). In Daniel the order is reversed, as Media was dominant at that time.

5 The LXX has "when the days of the marriage feast were completed" and "six days" instead of "seven days."

6 The first letter ח (ḥ) of the first word, חוּר (ḥûr, "white linen"), of this verse in the MT is somewhat larger than normal. It has been explained as an indication of a suspected omission before it or as the emphasis at the beginning of an impressive description, but its actual significance remains unknown.

For בַּהַט (bahaṭ, "porphyry"), the LXX has σμαραγαδίτης (smaragaditēs, "emerald"); the true identity of the material composing the mosaic pavement is uncertain. Except for "marble" the names of the other materials in the pavement are found only here in the OT, and their meaning is disputed.

8 The LXX says "drinking was not according to the law."

9 וַשְׁתִּי (waštî, "Vashti") may be related to the Old Persian word Vahista ("the best"; cf. BDB, s.v.; or possibly, "one who is desired," IDB, s.v.).

B. Vashti's Dethronement (1:10–22)

1. Vashti's refusal to obey the king

1:10–12

> 10On the seventh day, when King Xerxes was in high spirits from wine, he commanded the seven eunuchs who served him—Mehuman, Biztha, Harbona, Bigtha, Abagtha, Zethar and Carcas— 11to bring before him Queen Vashti, wearing her royal crown, in order to display her beauty to the people and nobles, for she was lovely to look at. 12But when the attendants delivered the king's command, Queen Vashti refused to come. Then the king became furious and burned with anger.

10–11 On the seventh day of the feast (the last day of the feast, not the Sabbath day), when the king was in high spirits (Heb., "the heart of the king was good with wine," v.10; cf. 2 Sam 13:28; Eccl 9:7), he sent his seven eunuchs (seven was a sacred number to the Persians as well as to the Hebrews; so Paton, *Esther*, p. 148) to bring the queen before him, wearing the crown (Heb., "turban"), so that he might display her beauty to the assembled guests (v.11). Some Jewish sources interpreted the order to mean that she was to appear nude, except for her crown. The name of the eunuchs are all Persian in origin. Eunuchs are usually associated with the king's harem, but they also played important roles in political and administrative affairs (cf. Jer 29:2 [NIV, "court officials"]; Dan 1:7 [NIV, "chief official"]; Acts 8:27).

12 The queen refused to answer the king's summons, and he became enraged. His male ego had suffered a public affront. Though the motive for her refusal is not stated, she probably did not choose to degrade herself before the king's drunken guests. Later writers, such as Plutarch, mistakenly asserted that wives were not customarily present at Persian feasts.

Notes

10 There are considerable variations in the names of the seven eunuchs in the LXX. Attempts to explain the differences from the MT names have not been very helpful (cf. Moore, *Esther*, pp. xli–xliv; Paton, *Esther*, pp. 66–68; Millard, p. 485, who concludes that the Hebrew text of Esther "can be trusted to give non-Hebrew names accurately, unless we have clear proof to the contrary").

12 The Hebrew verb מָאֵן (*mā'ēn*, "refuse") appears only in the Piel stem in the OT.

---

2. *The wise men's advice*

1:13–22

13Since it was customary for the king to consult experts in matters of law and justice, he spoke with the wise men who understood the times 14and were closest to the king—Carshena, Shethar, Admatha, Tarshish, Meres, Marsena and Memucan, the seven nobles of Persia and Media who had special access to the king and were highest in the kingdom.

15"According to law, what must be done to Queen Vashti?" he asked. "She has not obeyed the command of King Xerxes that the eunuchs have taken to her."

16Then Memucan replied in the presence of the king and the nobles, "Queen Vashti has done wrong, not only against the king but also against all the nobles and the peoples of all the provinces of King Xerxes. 17For the queen's conduct will become known to all the women, and so they will despise their husbands and say, 'King Xerxes commanded Queen Vashti to be brought before him, but she would not come.' 18This very day the Persian and Median women of the nobility who have heard about the queen's conduct will respond to all the king's nobles in the same way. There will be no end of disrespect and discord.

19"Therefore, if it pleases the king, let him issue a royal decree and let it be written in the laws of Persia and Media, which cannot be repealed, that Vashti is never again to enter the presence of King Xerxes. Also let the king give her royal position to someone else who is better than she. 20Then when the king's edict is proclaimed throughout all his vast realm, all the women will respect their husbands, from the least to the greatest."

21The king and his nobles were pleased with this advice, so the king did as Memucan proposed. 22He sent dispatches to all parts of the kingdom, to each province in its own script and to each people in its own language, proclaiming in each people's tongue that every man should be ruler over his own household.

13–14 Angered by Vashti's disobedience, the king consulted his wise men, "who understood the times," to determine what should be done to her. Like their Babylonian counterparts, these wise men were astrologers and magicians who gave counsel according to their reading of celestial phenomena (cf. 1 Chron 12:32; Isa 44:25; 47:13; Jer 50:35–36; Dan 2:27; 5:15). It was the king's custom to consult experts in matters of law and justice and to hear their opinions before he acted on any matter. There were seven of these wise men, all with Persian names, called "the seven nobles" ("the seven princes," KJV, RSV) of Persia and Media (cf. Millard, pp. 485 –87, on accuracy of foreign names). They were probably the Council of Seven mentioned in Ezra 7:14 and Herodotus 3.31. Their high rank (Heb., "who sat first in the kingdom") allowed them "special access" (Heb., "those seeing the king's face") into the king's presence (cf. 2 Sam 14:24, 32).

15 The king wanted to know what could be done legally to the queen for disobeying his command. It seems strange that he would have to consult others before dealing with a rebellious wife, but apparently the law protected her from his caprice.

16 Memucan, one of the seven nobles and perhaps their spokesman after they had discussed the matter, advised the king that Vashti had not only done "wrong" (Heb., "to be crooked") to the king but also to all the nobles and all the people throughout all the provinces of the kingdom. Verses 17–18 explain why her offense affected all the people.

Apparently there was no existing law to deal with the situation, hence the consultation between the king and his nobles.

17–18 More was involved than the queen's affront to the king. With keen perception Memucan saw that if left unpunished, Vashti's rebellious attitude toward her husband would influence other women in the kingdom to rebel against their husband's authority (v.17). If the defiant queen could successfully ignore the king's commands, the nobles anticipated there would be no end of disrespect and discord in their own homes (v.18). If the queen did not obey her husband, the wives of lesser nobles would be encouraged to disobey their husbands.

19 Memucan advised immediate and drastic action to deal with the situation. He spoke deferentially to the king ("if it pleases the king"; cf. 3:9; 5:4, 8; 7:3; 8:5; 9:13). Memucan advised Xerxes to issue a "royal decree" (Heb., "a word of the kingdom") to be included among the laws of the Persians and Medes that could not be repealed (Heb., "cannot pass away"; cf. 8:8; 9:27; Dan 6:8, 12, 15). The decree would forbid Vashti from ever again entering the presence of the king and would give her position to someone better than she. The Hebrew here could mean a more beautiful or more virtuous person. The advisors wanted to be sure that Vashti could never again be restored to the king's favor, lest she take vengeance on them.

20 Memucan further advised the king to proclaim the decree (Heb., "let the decree be heard") throughout the empire so that all women from the least to the greatest (Heb., "from great and to small," a phrase that can be used of age, physical size, or social status) would respect their husbands.

21–22 Memucan's advice pleased the king (Heb., "the word was good in the eyes of the king") and the other nobles; so the king did as Memucan had suggested (v.21). Xerxes ordered dispatches sent to every part of the kingdom, to each province in its own script and to each people in their own language, as many languages were spoken in the Persian empire (v.22). He wanted to be sure that all his subjects who spoke different languages and used different written scripts understood the decree, even though Aramaic was commonly understood and used for state business in all parts of the empire from Egypt to India. The decree proclaimed that every man should be ruler over his own household. Persia was noted for its excellent postal system; so it was not long before the contents of the king's decree were known throughout the kingdom.

Notes

13 A slight textual emendation from הָעִתִּים (*hā'ittîm*) to הַדָּתִים (*haddātîm*) is required to translate "who knew the times" (KJV, RSV) as ". . . the laws" (JB, NAB, NIV). The emendation is not supported by the ancient versions but by the parallel "that knew law and judgment" (KJV) of the same verse.

14 The LXX lists only three names.

15 כְּדָת (*kᵉdāt*, "according to law") has been read with the preceding verse—"highest in the kingdom according to law." It has been omitted as an instance of dittography with the consonants *bmlkwt* in בַּמַּלְכוּת ("in the kingdom") of v.14, or understood as emphatic or (most likely) resumptive (after the parenthetical expression of vv.13b–14).

16 The Kethiv of Memucan is מוֹמְכָן (*mᵉwmukān* [pointing uncertain]); the Qere is מְמוּכָן (*mᵉmûkān*), to agree with the spelling in v.14.

17 The Hebrew word for "husband" used here is בַּעַל (*baʿal*), which means "lord" or "owner." It is also the name of the Canaanite deity Baal.

The LXX omits "King Xerxes commanded . . . she would not come."

19 Outside the OT no evidence has been found that Persian laws were irrevocable. When Cambyses (530–522 B.C.) expressed a desire to marry his sister, his advisors told him that there was no law that allowed it but that there was a law that allowed a king to do whatever he pleased.

Up to this point in the narrative, Vashti has always been referred to as "the queen." Her title, however, is omitted in the remaining occurrences of her name (1:19; 2:1, 4, 17); the omission is probably an intentional literary device to suggest Vashti's demotion.

20 פִּתְגָם (*pitgām*, "edict") is from the Old Persian *patigāma* ("to come," "to arrive").

"All the women will respect" uses the third masculine plural verbal form instead of the expected feminine form. Disagreement in gender is not unusual in Hebrew.

A Targum says Memucan was having trouble with his own wife and wished to discipline her indirectly through the decree that he suggested to the king.

22 "Ruler" is the Qal active participle of the verb שָׂרַר (*śārar*, "to rule") that appears elsewhere only in Num 16:13; Judg 9:22; 1 Chron 15:22; Prov 8:16; Isa 32:1; Hos 8:4. The name Sarah comes from this word.

The last phrase of this verse is difficult and has caused considerable discussion among scholars. Literally it says, "and speaking according to the tongue of his people," which has been interpreted in two ways: (1) he should only speak his native tongue in his home (RSV, NASB), particularly if he had a foreign wife; (2) the decree should be proclaimed in every people's native tongue (NIV, KJV). It has been compared to the English idioms: "talk plain English to her," "say whatever suited him," and "have the last word." The LXX says, "in order that men might be feared in their own houses."

C. Choosing a New Queen (2:1–23)

1. The search

2:1–4

¹Later when the anger of King Xerxes had subsided, he remembered Vashti and what she had done and what he had decreed about her. ²Then the king's personal attendants proposed, "Let a search be made for beautiful young virgins for the king. ³Let the king appoint commissioners in every province of his realm to

bring all these beautiful girls into the harem at the citadel of Susa. Let them be placed under the care of Hegai, the king's eunuch, who is in charge of the women; and let beauty treatments be given to them. ⁴Then let the girl who pleases the king be queen instead of Vashti." This advice appealed to the king, and he followed it.

1 After Xerxes' wrath "had subsided" (the same verb [*šāḵaḵ*] is used in Gen 8:1 of the Flood receding; cf. 7:10), he remembered the deeds of Vashti and his decree that deposed her. It is uncertain whether he now regretted his rash action and wished to reinstate her but was prevented because his decree was irrevocable (cf. Dan 6:14–15) or whether it means only that his thoughts now turned to a replacement for the queen. The fate of Vashti is not revealed by the author, but according to rabbinic tradition she was executed.

The king divorced Vashti in the third year of his reign (1:3) and did not marry Esther till the seventh year (2:16). Verse 1 begins "Later" (NIV; Heb., "after these things") and then describes the events leading up to the king's marriage to Esther. Between the events of 1:3 and 2:16, Xerxes made his disastrous expedition to Greece. Returning from his naval defeat at Salamis in 480 and his humiliating rout at Plataea in 479, he turned his thoughts to remarriage, through which he hoped to find solace.

2 The king's personal attendants proposed that the king choose another wife from among the beautiful young virgins (Heb., "a young woman, a virgin, good of appearance"). Perhaps they feared retaliation from Vashti if she were reinstated to the king's favor, or they may have seen and felt more than others the king's unhappiness that the putting away of Vashti had caused him.

3–4 Verses 3–4 explain in detail how plans for assembling the virgins were to be carried out. In all the provinces officials were to be appointed to locate all the beautiful young virgins and bring them to the harem (Heb., "house of the women") in Susa. There they would be placed under the care of Hegai, the king's eunuch. Beauty treatments (from a word meaning "to scour, polish") of all kinds of ointments and cosmetics would be applied to each of the virgins for twelve months (cf. v. 12) in preparation for her presentation to the king. The one who pleased the king (Heb., "who is good in the king's eyes") would be made queen in the place of Vashti.

The courtiers' suggestion pleased the king (Heb., "the word was good in the eyes of the king"); so he ordered that the search begin. Fathers apparently did not voluntarily present their daughters as evidenced by the king's appointment of officials to search for the candidates.

Notes

1 The LXX says, "He no longer remembered Vashti."
3 The eunuch's name is spelled הֵגֶא (*Hēge'*) in v.3 but הֵגַי (*Hēgay*) in vv.8, 15. Herodotus (9.33) mentioned a eunuch of Xerxes with a similar name.

2. *Esther as a candidate*

2:5–11

> ⁵Now there was in the citadel of Susa a Jew of the tribe of Benjamin, named Mordecai son of Jair, the son of Shimei, the son of Kish, ⁶who had been carried into exile from Jerusalem by Nebuchadnezzar king of Babylon, among those taken captive with Jehoiachin king of Judah. ⁷Mordecai had a cousin named Hadassah, whom he had brought up because she had neither father nor mother. This girl, who was also known as Esther, was lovely in form and features, and Mordecai had taken her as his own daughter when her father and mother died.
> ⁸When the king's order and edict had been proclaimed, many girls were brought to the citadel of Susa and put under the care of Hegai. Esther also was taken to the king's palace and entrusted to Hegai, who had charge of the harem. ⁹The girl pleased him and won his favor. Immediately he provided her with her beauty treatments and special food. He assigned to her seven maids selected from the king's palace and moved her and her maids into the best place in the harem.
> ¹⁰Esther had not revealed her nationality and family background, because Mordecai had forbidden her to do so. ¹¹Every day he walked back and forth near the courtyard of the harem to find out how Esther was and what was happening to her.

5–6 At this juncture in the narrative, Mordecai is introduced for the first time. His name appears fifty-eight times in this book but nowhere else in the Bible. Another Mordecai is mentioned in Ezra 2:2 and Nehemiah 7:7; some have proposed that they are one and the same (Anderson; Wright [p. 46] says, "This is possible"). "Mordecai" is the Hebraized form of the Babylonian deity Marduk. Idolatrous names for devout Jews grew out of a practice during the Diaspora of giving both a Babylonian and a Hebrew name to the same person (cf. Dan 1:6–7). He is called a "Jew," a word derived from "Judah" that was used from the time of the Exile to refer to an Israelite. Wright (p. 45) says Mordecai was a eunuch because no wife or family is mentioned (v.7) and because he had access to the women's quarters (v.11). His ancestry is traced through his father, Jair, and his grandfather, Shimei, to his great-grandfather, Kish, of the tribe of Benjamin. The reader is not told why he was in Susa.

Verse 6 contains one of the critical problems of the book. It begins: "who had been carried into exile from Jerusalem . . . with Jehoiachin." If the antecedent of "who" is Mordecai, he would now be approximately 120 years of age if he had been exiled as a child (reckoning from 597 B.C., the year of exile, to 486, the beginning of the reign of Xerxes). Esther would have probably been at least 70. This unlikelihood has been used as evidence that the story is fictitious. However the antecedent of "who" may also be explained as the nearer name "Kish." If so, it was Kish, Mordecai's great-grandfather, who was carried away into captivity with King Jehoiachin (known also as Coniah and Jeconiah) in 597 B.C. (cf. further discussion at Introduction: Special Problems, c.8).

The genealogy has also been understood by Jewish tradition, as well as by some modern commentators, to contain gaps (Goldman, p. 202; Moore, *Esther*, p. 26). Thus Shimei becomes the Shimei known to David (cf. 2 Sam 16:5; 1 Kings 2:8, 36), and Kish becomes the father of Saul (cf. 1 Sam 9:1; 1 Chron 8:33). There is, however, no evidence to support these supposed gaps (cf. discussion under Special Problems).

7 Mordecai "brought up" ('*ōmēn*, the participial form of a Hebrew word that means "confirm," "support," the same word from which "Amen" is derived) his cousin (rabbinic tradition and Josephus say that he was her uncle), whose Hebrew name was Hadassah ("myrtle"). She is better known by her Persian name Esther, which is derived from the Persian word for "star," or from the name of the Babylonian deity Ishtar (known in Hebrew as Ashtoreth). Some scholars think the two names reflect different literary traditions (Bardtke) or that she was given the name Esther at the time of her coronation (Anderson). Her age at the time of the death of her parents is not given, but Mordecai took her as his own daughter; he probably adopted her (cf. v.15; the Hebrew word used here means literally "to take"). Her father's name is given in v.15, but nothing is known about him. The author describes her as "lovely in form and features."

8 After the king's edict had been proclaimed, girls from all over the empire were brought to Susa, including Esther. Josephus (*Antiq.* XI, 200 [vi.2]) says there were four hundred girls. They were placed in the care of Hegai, who was in charge of the harem. The Hebrew says Esther "was taken" to the king's palace. The verb *lāqaḥ* can mean "taken by force" and has so been interpreted by some scholars, though most feel there is no indication that she was taken by coercion. It is difficult to understand why Mordecai would have wanted his cousin to marry a heathen (cf. the attitudes of Ezra and Nehemiah toward mixed marriages; Ezra 9:1–4, 14; 10:3, 11, 18–44; Neh 10:30; 13:23–27).

9 Hegai must have discerned that Esther had the qualities that would please the king, for she "won his favor" (Heb., "she lifted up grace before his face"). Immediately (Heb., "he hastened") he began to provide her with beauty treatments and special food ("with such things as belonged to her," KJV) so that the required twelve months of preparation could be completed without delay. Esther apparently did not object to breaking the Jewish dietary laws (cf. Dan 1:8). Hegai assigned seven maids from the king's palace to take care of her and transferred Esther and her maids to the best quarters of the harem.

10 Mordecai forbade Esther to reveal her Jewish nationality, and she dutifully obeyed him. Why he swore her to silence remains an unanswered enigma. Obviously she would have stood little chance to be selected queen if she were not Persian, but why would Mordecai want her to marry a Gentile? Such a marriage was a violation of Jewish laws. Also there was no threat by Haman or known antipathy to the Jews at the time to warrant his secrecy. Mordecai has been accused of ambition for political advancement that could be realized if his cousin were queen. The author expresses no disapproval of the subterfuge. Gordis ("Book of Esther," pp. 377, 385) says she did not reveal her origin so there would be no known legal impediment to her marriage. But 4:14 suggests that the providence of God was at work in the events.

11 Mordecai was careful to keep close check on Esther. Every day he walked near the courtyard of the harem to try to gain information about his cousin. The reader may want to know how he was able to communicate with her, since she was in the royal harem; but it was not important to the writer's purpose to give an explanation.

Notes

5 Attempts to relate the name Mordecai with the Persian *mordkai* ("little man"; cf. Schultz, p. 41) have not met with success. His name is usually associated with the Babylonian deity Marduk. He was not the only Jew whose name contained a foreign deity's name (cf. Dan 1:7).

Those who believe there are gaps in Mordecai's genealogy cite a Jewish Targum that says David discerned prophetically that Mordecai would descend from Shimei and therefore ordered Solomon to put him to death only after he had ceased from having sons (cf. 1 Kings 2:8–9).

Mordecai is called "the Jew" seven times in the fifty-eight occurrences of his name in Esther (cf. 2:5; 5:13; 6:10; 8:7; 9:29, 31; 10:3).

6 The crux of the critical question hinges on the identification of the antecedent of אֲשֶׁר (*ʾªšer*, "who"). Keil (p. 336) and most modern commentators (e.g., Kaiser, Pfeiffer) say it is more in accordance with normal Hebrew narrative style for *ʾªšer* to refer to the chief person in the clause preceding it, which in this case would be Mordecai. However it can be argued just as legitimately that the phrase introduced by *ʾªšer* modifies the word that immediately precedes it, which would be Kish (e.g., Archer, Wright).

7 The name "Hadassah" is missing from all the ancient versions except the Vulgate.

See TDOT, 1:292–323, for further study of the etymology of אֹמֵן (*ʾōmēn*, "brought up").

The OL and Vulgate have "niece" instead of "his uncle's daughter" (i.e., cousin). The LXX adds "daughter of Aminadab."

Instead of "had taken her as his daughter," the LXX has "took her for a wife for himself." But since she was taken to the king's harem, she was obviously a virgin (cf. vv.2–3).

9 חֶסֶד (*ḥesed*, "favor") is a word that is often translated as "steadfast love." See Katharine Doob Sakenfeld, *The Meaning of Hesed in the Hebrew Bible*, Harvard Semitic Monographs 17 (Missoula, Mont.: Scholars, 1978), for a study of this word.

10 The Lucianic recension of Esther omits vv.10–13; the Hebrew is difficult.

C.H. Gordon (*Introduction to Old Testament Times* [Ventnor, N.J.: Ventnor, 1953], pp. 278f.) has called attention to an Iranian doctrine called *kitman* or *taqiyya* that has survived to the present, which allows a person to deny his faith and pretend to be part of another religion when faced with personal danger. He believes this was the practice Esther followed, and later the Persians who out of fear pretended to be Jews for the same reason (8:17).

---

3. *The traditional procedure*

2:12–14

> 12Before a girl's turn came to go in to King Xerxes, she had to complete twelve months of beauty treatments prescribed for the women, six months with oil of myrrh and six with perfumes and cosmetics. 13And this is how she would go to the king: Anything she wanted was given her to take with her from the harem to the king's palace. 14In the evening she would go there and in the morning return to another part of the harem to the care of Shaashgaz, the king's eunuch who was in charge of the concubines. She would not return to the king unless he was pleased with her and summoned her by name.

12 Further information is given about each candidate's beauty treatment. The treatment required twelve months (Jos. *Antiq*. XI, 201 [vi. 2] has six months) before a

candidate was allowed into the king's presence. For six months oil of myrrh was applied to her and for six months, perfumes and cosmetics.

13 When each candidate was ready to be presented to the king, whatever she desired to take with her (Heb., "with all that she said") from the harem to his palace was given to her (i.e., jewels, clothing, and other ornaments).

14 The maiden chosen would go into the king's presence in the evening to spend the night with him. The next morning she would return to another part (Heb., "the second house") of the harem and be placed under the care of Shaashgaz, the king's eunuch who was in charge of the concubines. She never returned to the king again unless he was pleased with her and summoned her by name. Those rejected lived the rest of their lives like widows (cf. 2 Sam 20:3). Parallels with a story in *The Arabian Nights* have been noted by many commentators. In that story King Shehri-yar had a new bride each evening but had her executed the next day. Finally Scheherazade won his heart and became queen.

Notes

14 שֵׁנִי (šēnî, "second") has caused many problems for exegetes. Moore (*Esther*, pp. 23–24) understands it to modify בֵּית הַנָּשִׁים (bêt hannāšîm, "the harem"; lit., "the house of the women") and thereby interprets it as a second harem. NIV understands it as "another part" of the harem. Gordis ("Studies in Esther," pp. 53–54, following Ryssel) translates it "a second time" or "again," which gives a satisfactory meaning in the context.

Shaashgaz is called Gai in the LXX. He is not mentioned again in Esther.

---

4. Esther chosen as queen

2:15–18

> 15When the turn came for Esther (the girl Mordecai had adopted, the daughter of his uncle Abihail) to go to the king, she asked for nothing other than what Hegai, the king's eunuch who was in charge of the harem, suggested. And Esther won the favor of everyone who saw her. 16She was taken to King Xerxes in the royal residence in the tenth month, the month of Tebeth, in the seventh year of his reign.
> 17Now the king was attracted to Esther more than to any of the other women, and she won his favor and approval more than any of the other virgins. So he set a royal crown on her head and made her queen instead of Vashti. 18And the king gave a great banquet, Esther's banquet, for all his nobles and officials. He proclaimed a holiday throughout the provinces and distributed gifts with royal liberality.

15 When Esther's turn came to be taken to the king, she did not request any of the usual ornaments or cosmetics to enhance her beauty. She only took the things that Hegai, the king's eunuch, had suggested. She trusted him to know what would please the king. Her modesty and humility impressed everyone who saw her (Heb.,

"Esther was lifting up grace in the eyes of all who saw her"). Her father's name is given in this verse as Abihail. This name occurs in the OT twice as a woman's name (1 Chron 2:29; 2 Chron 11:18).

16 It was the tenth month, called Tebeth (i.e., December-January), and the seventh year of Xerxes' reign when Esther was taken to the king. It was four years after Vashti had been deposed (cf. 1:3). Various explanations have been given for the long lapse of time before Esther's turn came. It is best explained as the time when Xerxes was occupied with military campaigns in Greece. His return from his disastrous defeat at the hands of the Greeks in 479 B.C. would correspond to the seventh year.

17 None of the previous candidates had attracted the king sufficiently for him to make her his wife; but he immediately loved Esther and placed the royal crown on her head, thereby making her queen in place of Vashti. Vashti is not mentioned again in the book. After seeing Esther the king had no desire to continue the search for a queen.

18 A great wedding feast was given by the king for all his nobles and officials. As a generous gesture to mark the occasion, he proclaimed a holiday, i.e., a release from work (Heb., "a causing to rest"; "granted a remission of taxes," RSV; "amnesty," NEB mg.), throughout the provinces. He distributed "gifts" (*maś'ēt*, from *nāśā'*, "to lift up") liberally as befitted such a monarch.

Notes

15 The LXX omits "who had adopted her as his own daughter" (RSV).

For "Abihail" the LXX has "Aminadab" both here and in 9:29.

16 The LXX gives a different date. It has "in the twelfth month, which is Adar."

The Syriac has "fourth" year instead of "seventh."

Tebeth is one of the names of the Babylonian months adopted by the Jews after the Exile to replace the Canaanite names they had formerly used. BDB (p. 372) derives Tebeth from the root טבת (*ṭbt*, "to sink in," i.e., the muddy month). The word occurs only here in the OT.

5. *An attempt on the king's life thwarted*

2:19–23

[19]When the virgins were assembled a second time, Mordecai was sitting at the king's gate. [20]But Esther had kept secret her family background and nationality just as Mordecai had told her to do, for she continued to follow Mordecai's instructions as she had done when he was bringing her up.

[21]During the time Mordecai was sitting at the king's gate, Bigthana and Teresh, two of the king's officers who guarded the doorway, became angry and conspired to assassinate King Xerxes. [22]But Mordecai found out about the plot and told Queen Esther, who in turn reported it to the king, giving credit to Mordecai. [23]And

when the report was investigated and found to be true, the two officials were hanged on a gallows. All this was recorded in the book of the annals in the presence of the king.

19–20 The meaning of v.19 is difficult to ascertain. All the virgins were assembled again. At that time Mordecai was sitting at the king's gate. No reason is given for the assembly. Some commentators believe these were virgins who arrived after Esther's selection. Others think that certain officials brought them, hoping that one would appeal to the king and supplant Esther in his affections. Keil thinks it took place at the time the two courtiers conspired against Xerxes (cf. vv.21–22). Gordis ("Studies in Esther," p. 47) believes the verse refers to a second procession of the unsuccessful maidens at the conclusion of the ceremonies that elevated Esther to the throne, after which they were sent home (see Paton, *Esther*, pp. 186–88, for further study).

Esther had been careful to keep her nationality secret, as Mordecai had instructed her. From the time she first came under his care, she had been obedient to his commands and continued to listen to him, even after being elevated to the position of queen. Her continued obedience to Mordecai becomes important to the plot. Mordecai's position at the gate was not that of an "idler" but represented some kind of duty or official position he occupied. He may have been appointed to this position by Esther to give him easier access to the royal quarters (Gordis, "Studies in Esther," p. 48). Men who "sat at the gate" were frequently elders and leading, respected citizens who settled disputes that were brought to them.

21–22 Verse 21 resumes the narrative of v.19 that had been interrupted by the parenthetical observation of v.20. During the time he was sitting at the king's gate, Mordecai either overheard or was informed about a plot to kill Xerxes (Heb., "to send a hand against the king") by two of the king's officers, Bigthana and Teresh (cf. 6:2). They were eunuchs, guards of the door—i.e., men who protected the king's private apartment—who had become angry with Xerxes. The cause of their anger with the king is not stated. Mordecai got word to Esther about the plot; and she relayed the information to the king, giving credit to Mordecai, without mentioning their relationship. Plots against Persian monarchs were not uncommon. Xerxes was in fact assassinated in his bedroom in a similar situation in 465 B.C. in a conspiracy led by his chiliarch Artabanus.

23 When Mordecai's report was investigated and found to be true, the two men were hanged on a "gallows" (Heb., "tree"). The entire event was recorded in the "book of the annals" (Heb., "the book of the matters of the day," i.e., official court records of memorable events) in the presence of the king. It is hard to understand why Xerxes forgot to reward Mordecai at that time.

Notes

19 The Lucianic recension of Esther omits vv.19–23 altogether.

Instead of "at the king's gate," the LXX has "in the king's courtyard/palace" (αὐλή; also in 3:2; 5:9; 6:10, 12).

20 The LXX adds that Mordecai instructed Esther "to fear God and to perform his commandments."

21 One of the guards here is בִּגְתָן (*bigtān*, "Bigthan"). In 6:2 his name is בִּגְתָנָא (*bigtānā'*, "Bigthana").

The LXX adds that the two men hated the king "because Mordecai had been promoted."

II. The Feud Between Haman and Mordecai (3:1–8:17)

A. *Haman's Plot to Kill Mordecai (3:1–15)*

1. *Haman's anger with Mordecai*

3:1–6

> [1]After these events, King Xerxes honored Haman son of Hammedatha, the Agagite, elevating him and giving him a seat of honor higher than that of all the other nobles. [2]All the royal officials at the king's gate knelt down and paid honor to Haman, for the king had commanded this concerning him. But Mordecai would not kneel down or pay him honor.
> [3]Then the royal officials at the king's gate asked Mordecai, "Why do you disobey the king's command?" [4]Day after day they spoke to him but he refused to comply. Therefore they told Haman about it to see whether Mordecai's behavior would be tolerated, for he had told them he was a Jew.
> [5]When Haman saw that Mordecai would not kneel down or pay him honor, he was enraged. [6]Yet having learned who Mordecai's people were, he scorned the idea of killing only Mordecai. Instead Haman looked for a way to destroy all Mordecai's people, the Jews, throughout the whole kingdom of Xerxes.

1 Some time later (Heb., "after these things," a vague reference to a later date that might have been any time between the seventh and twelfth years of Xerxes' reign; cf. 2:16; 3:7), the king elevated Haman by giving him a place of honor above all the other nobles of the empire. It was probably the same office that was later given to Mordecai (cf. 10:2). This is the first mention of Haman. The text identifies him as the son of Hammedatha the Agagite (otherwise unknown). Scholars have linked the names "Haman" and "Hammedatha" to Persian words or to the Elamite god Human or Humban, but these associations cannot be verified. Jewish tradition considers him to have been a descendant of the Amalekite king, Agag, an enemy of Israel during Saul's reign (cf. 1 Sam 15:7–33; cf. Notes for other explanations of the name Agag). The Amalekites were ancient enemies of the Jews (cf. Exod 17:8–14; Num 24:7; Deut 25:17–19). Saul failed to destroy the Amalekites completely as God had ordered him to do, and consequently the kingdom was taken from him (cf. 1 Sam 15:23). The author may be informing the reader subtly that the ancient feud between the Amalekites and the Israelites has been inherited by Haman, a descendant of Agag, and Mordecai, a descendant of Saul.

2–4 By command of the king, all the royal officials at the king's gate knelt down and paid honor to Haman. Mordecai, however, refused to kneel before Haman or to honor him (v.2). In spite of repeated appeals by the royal officials, Mordecai refused to obey the king's command (vv.3–4). Apparently he had told them that as a Jew he could not bow before any man. Streane (p. 20) suggests two reasons for Mordecai's refusal: (1) it would have been an act of idolatry; (2) he refused to bow before the hereditary enemy of Israel. The officials informed Haman of Mordecai's insolence to see whether it would be "tolerated" (Heb., "to see whether the words of Mordecai would stand"). It is unlikely that Mordecai's refusal to bow to Haman was caused by a claim to divine honor by Haman (a view followed by Josephus, Keil et al.). There are many examples of God's people prostrating themselves before a king or other superiors (cf. Gen 23:7; 27:29; 1 Sam 24:8; 2 Sam 14:4; 1 Kings 1:16). It also is unlikely that Mordecai could have been elevated next to the king if he had refused to kneel before Xerxes. The most probable reason was, as a Targum suggests, Mordecai's pride; no self-respecting Benjaminite would bow before a descendant of the ancient Amalekite enemy of the Jews.

5–6 On learning that Mordecai refused to kneel before him or to pay him honor, Haman was enraged (Heb., "filled with anger"). So great was his wrath and his injured pride that he determined to destroy all the Jews in Xerxes' kingdom. Haman was not satisfied with killing only Mordecai but was determined to succeed where Saul had failed (cf. 1 Sam 15:9); Haman would destroy all his enemies.

Notes

1 Streane (p. 19) cites three explanations of "Agagite": (1) a descendant of Agag the Amalekite (Exod 17:8–16; 1 Sam 15; see Jos. *Antiq*. XI, 209 [vi. 5]); (2) a nickname, indicating that in spirit he was like the earlier Amalekite king; (3) a place or family otherwise unknown. Keil argues that the connection with the Amalekite king of 1 Samuel 15:33 cannot be proved. An inscription of Sargon mentions Agag as a district in Persia; Haman may have been a native of that place. The LXX has *Bougaion* for "Agagite."

In 9:24 "Macedonian" appears in the LXX instead of *Bougaion*.

6 Josephus (*Antiq*. XI, 211 [vi. 5]) said Haman's hatred of the Jews grew out of the destruction of his own race, the Amalekites, by the Jews.

2. *A day of revenge chosen by lot*

3:7–15

> [7]In the twelfth year of King Xerxes, in the first month, the month of Nisan, they cast the *pur* (that is, the lot) in the presence of Haman to select a day and month. And the lot fell on the twelfth month, the month of Adar.
>
> [8]Then Haman said to King Xerxes, "There is a certain people dispersed and scattered among the peoples in all the provinces of your kingdom whose customs are different from those of all other people and who do not obey the king's laws; it is not in the king's best interest to tolerate them. [9]If it pleases the king, let a decree be issued to destroy them, and I will put ten thousand talents of silver into the royal treasury for the men who carry out this business."
>
> [10]So the king took his signet ring from his finger and gave it to Haman son of Hammedatha, the Agagite, the enemy of the Jews. [11]"Keep the money," the king said to Haman, "and do with the people as you please."
>
> [12]Then on the thirteenth day of the first month the royal secretaries were summoned. They wrote out in the script of each province and in the language of each people all Haman's orders to the king's satraps, the governors of the various

provinces and the nobles of the various peoples. These were written in the name of King Xerxes himself and sealed with his own ring. ¹³Dispatches were sent by couriers to all the king's provinces with the order to destroy, kill and annihilate all the Jews—young and old, women and little children—on a single day, the thirteenth day of the twelfth month, the month of Adar, and to plunder their goods. ¹⁴A copy of the text of the edict was to be issued as law in every province and made known to the people of every nationality so they would be ready for that day.

¹⁵Spurred on by the king's command, the couriers went out, and the edict was issued in the citadel of Susa. The king and Haman sat down to drink, but the city of Susa was bewildered.

7 In the twelfth year of Xerxes' reign (474 B.C.), in the first month of the year (called Nisan, i.e., March-April), five years after Esther had become queen (2:16), the *pûr* (i.e., the lot) was cast in Haman's presence to determine the day for the slaughter of the Jews. The exact way lots were cast is unknown. The purpose of the lot may have been only to determine an auspicious day for Haman to go before the king to make his request to kill the Jews. The lot fell on the twelfth month (called Adar, i.e., February-March). The names of the months are those that were adopted from the Babylonian calendar by the Jews after the Exile. The non-Hebraic word *pûr* (probably the Akkad. word *puru* ["die" or "lot"], which is explained by the Hebrew *gôrāl* ["lot"]) anticipates the institution of Purim (i.e., "lots") in chapter 9. The casting of lots to determine God's will was a well-known practice in Israel (cf. Lev 16:8; Num 26:55–56; Josh 14:2; 1 Sam 14:41–42; 1 Chron 26:14; Neh 10:34; Ps 22:18; Prov 16:33; 18:18; Joel 3:3; cf. Acts 1:26). (For an explanation of the delay of eleven months before carrying out the plan, see Introduction: Special Problems, c.10.)

8 To gain the king's support for his plan, Haman described the Jews who were scattered in all the provinces of Persia as a people who kept themselves aloof, who had different customs (Heb., "statutes"), and who would not obey the king's laws. Haman reasoned that it was not in the king's best interest to "tolerate them" (Heb., "to cause them to rest," i.e., "to leave them alone"). Haman did not mention Mordecai as the special object of his wrath.

9 In order to obtain the king's permission to destroy the Jews, Haman appealed to the monarch's greed, offering to put ten thousand talents of silver of his own private fortune into the royal treasury to pay the men who would carry out the pogrom (Heb., "I will weigh out on the hands of the doers of the business"). It is impossible to determine the value of the silver in current monetary equivalents. It was a fabulous sum that is estimated to weigh approximately 375 tons. It has also been estimated to represent the equivalent of two-thirds of the annual income of the Persian Empire (Paton). Perhaps Haman planned to acquire such a large sum by confiscating the Jews' property.

10–11 The proposal apparently was immediately acceptable to the king. He removed the signet ring from his finger and gave it to Haman with instructions to keep the money and to do whatever he pleased with the Jews. The signet ring was a symbol of royal authority and in ancient times was used instead of a written signature to seal official documents. Thus Haman was given unlimited authority to carry out his plan. The king was unaware that by giving blanket authority to Haman to execute the Jews, he had also placed his own wife under a death sentence. The king's rejection of Haman's silver may have been only an example of Oriental politeness that did not actually mean he rejected the payment (cf. 4:7, where it seems that the bribe was paid; cf. Gen 23:3–18). The fact that Haman did not actually mention the Jews by name in his conversation with the king has been interpreted by some scholars (e.g, Anderson, p. 850) as an intentional effort to withhold the identity of the intended victims from Xerxes.

12 On the thirteenth day of the first month (Nisan), the royal secretaries were summoned to write out in the script of each province and in the language of each people Haman's orders to the satraps, governors, and nobles. The orders were written in the king's name and sealed with his ring. Three echelons of officials are named—satraps, who ruled over the twenty major divisions of the empire; the governors, who ruled smaller subdivisions of the satrapies; and nobles, who served under the governors and were perhaps chiefs of the conquered peoples.

13 Dispatches were sent by "couriers" (Heb., "runners") to all the provinces with orders to annihilate all the Jews, young and old, and to plunder their goods on the thirteenth day of the twelfth month (Adar). No reason is given for the lapse of almost a year from the time of the decree till its implementation. With so much advance notice, some scholars (e.g., Paton) point out that the Jews would have had time to escape. The piling up of verbs—"destroy, kill and annihilate"—is a literary device that expresses the idea of thoroughness.

14 The decree was to be made law in every province, and all were to know about it so they would be ready for the day.

15 The couriers departed in haste for the provinces at the king's command. The edict was also circulated in the citadel of Susa. Then the king and Haman sat down to drink, unconcerned about the tragedy soon to be inflicted on the Jews. The people of Susa were bewildered by what was happening. Apparently they did not share Haman's passionate anti-Semitism.

Notes

7 See Paton, *Esther*, pp. 77–94, for a comprehensive discussion of various theories of the origin of Purim. Purim is celebrated by Jews with a carnivallike festive spirit.

William F. Albright, "Some Recent Archaeological Publications," BASOR 67 (1937): 37, called attention to the word *pūru* in Assyrian texts with the meaning "lot."

The Lucianic recension of Esther says "thirteenth" day instead of "fourteenth." The LXX adds "and the lot fell on the fourteenth of. . . ." The phrase was probably omitted in the MT by haplography.

9 Goldman (p. 212) cites a Midrash that asks, "With what can the wicked Haman be compared?" The answer: "With a bird which made its nest on the seashore and the sea swept away its nest, whereupon it said, 'I will not move from here until I turn the dry land into

sea and the sea into dry land.' What did it do? It took water from the sea in its mouth and poured it on the dry land, and it took dust from the dry land and cast it into the sea. Its companions came and stood by it and said, 'Luckless unfortunate, with all your labour what will you effect?' "

11 הַכֶּסֶף נָתוּן לָךְ (*hakkesep nātûn lāk*, "the silver is given to you") is interpreted by most scholars, following the LXX, to mean "Keep the money" (NIV, JB); but Moore (*Esther*, p. 40) translates, "Well, it's your money," i.e., "If you want to spend it that way, it's all right with me."

13 Between v.13 and v.14 the LXX inserts a copy of a supposed anti-Jewish decree of Artaxerxes, composed of seven verses.

15 נָבוֹכָה (*nābôkāh*, "bewildered") is from a word that means "confused," "agitated"; cf. Exod 14:3; Joel 1:18.

B. *Mordecai's Plan to Save His People (4:1–17)*

1. *Reaction to the edict*

4:1–3

> [1]When Mordecai learned of all that had been done, he tore his clothes, put on sackcloth and ashes, and went out into the city, wailing loudly and bitterly. [2]But he went only as far as the king's gate, because no one clothed in sackcloth was allowed to enter it. [3]In every province to which the edict and order of the king came, there was great mourning among the Jews, with fasting, weeping and wailing. Many lay in sackcloth and ashes.

1 On learning what Haman was plotting, Mordecai expressed his grief and humiliation in typical Oriental fashion. He tore his clothing, put on sackcloth, and sprinkled ashes on himself. Then he walked about the city wailing loudly (cf. Gen 37:29; 1 Sam 4:12; 2 Sam 1:2; 3:31; 13:19; 1 Kings 20:31; 2 Kings 6:30; Job 1:20).

2 Mordecai went no farther than the king's gate, as no one was permitted within the gate who was wearing sackcloth. Apparently a person in mourning was considered ceremonially unclean. Perhaps Mordecai hoped to attract Esther's attention (cf. 4:4).

3 Not only was Mordecai in mourning, but in every province where the edict was announced, it was greeted by the Jews with fasting, weeping, and wailing. Many of them lay down on sackcloth and ashes.

Notes

---

1 The LXX adds that Mordecai was wailing, "An innocent people is condemned to death."

---

2. Mordecai's appeal to Esther

4:4–17

⁴When Esther's maids and eunuchs came and told her about Mordecai, she was in great distress. She sent clothes for him to put on instead of his sackcloth, but he would not accept them. ⁵Then Esther summoned Hathach, one of the king's eunuchs assigned to attend her, and ordered him to find out what was troubling Mordecai and why.

⁶So Hathach went out to Mordecai in the open square of the city in front of the king's gate. ⁷Mordecai told him everything that had happened to him, including the exact amount of money Haman had promised to pay into the royal treasury for the destruction of the Jews. ⁸He also gave him a copy of the text of the edict for their annihilation, which had been published in Susa, to show to Esther and explain it to her, and he told him to urge her to go into the king's presence to beg for mercy and plead with him for her people.

⁹Hathach went back and reported to Esther what Mordecai had said. ¹⁰Then she instructed him to say to Mordecai, ¹¹"All the king's officials and the people of the royal provinces know that for any man or woman who approaches the king in the inner court without being summoned the king has but one law: that he be put to death. The only exception to this is for the king to extend the gold scepter to him and spare his life. But thirty days have passed since I was called to go to the king."

¹²When Esther's words were reported to Mordecai, ¹³he sent back this answer: "Do not think that because you are in the king's house you alone of all the Jews will escape. ¹⁴For if you remain silent at this time, relief and deliverance for the Jews will arise from another place, but you and your father's family will perish. And who knows but that you have come to royal position for such a time as this?"

¹⁵Then Esther sent this reply to Mordecai: ¹⁶"Go, gather together all the Jews who are in Susa, and fast for me. Do not eat or drink for three days, night or day. I and my maids will fast as you do. When this is done, I will go to the king, even though it is against the law. And if I perish, I perish."

¹⁷So Mordecai went away and carried out all of Esther's instructions.

4 Some of Esther's maids and eunuchs must have seen Mordecai at the king's gate; so they reported his behavior to Esther. No reason is given why they felt one Jew's grief should be reported to their queen since they apparently did not know about her relationship to Mordecai, though they did know the two were acquainted (cf. 2:11, 22). Esther was distressed (*tithalhal*, lit., "writhed in pain") to learn of Mordecai's sorrow. She sent clothes for him to wear in place of the sackcloth, probably so that he could enter the palace; but he refused to accept them. No reason is given for Mordecai's refusal to take the clothing. It may have indicated to Esther that his actions were not caused by personal sorrow but by a public calamity.

5 Since Mordecai would not come to her, Esther sent Hathach, one of the king's eunuchs who had been assigned to attend her, to find out what was troubling Mordecai.

6–7 Hathach looked for Mordecai in the open square of the city in front of the king's gate, an area probably used as a marketplace. There Mordecai told the eunuch what had happened that caused him to be in mourning. He told Hathach how much money Haman had agreed to pay into the royal treasury for the privilege of destroying the Jews (cf. comment on 3:11). The reader is not told how Mordecai learned about the transaction between the king and Haman.

8 Mordecai had a copy of the edict for the Jews' annihilation that was being circulated in Susa. He asked the eunuch to give it to Esther and to explain it to her. He told Hathach to urge Esther to go to the king to plead for mercy for the Jewish people. Mordecai's request would require that the queen reveal her Jewish identity.

9-11 After Hathach told the queen what Mordecai had said, she instructed him to return to her cousin to remind him that no one could approach the king in the inner court without a royal summons. The penalty for such a transgression was death. On occasion the king had been known to extend his golden scepter to an uninvited person as a gesture of mercy. Herodotus (3.118) mentions the Persian custom that anyone who approached the king uninvited would be put to death unless pardoned by the king. Herodotus also said, however, that a person could send a letter to the king asking for an audience. Why this procedure did not occur to Esther can only be surmised. Since she had not been summoned by the king for a month, Esther did not know whether he would forgive her if she approached him without a royal summons. She may have concluded that she had lost the king's favor. It appears that initially Esther was more concerned about her own welfare than about her people.

12-14 Mordecai responded to Esther's words by telling her that she would not escape Haman's edict against the Jews because she was in the king's house. He warned her that if she remained silent, deliverance of the Jews would come from another source; but because of her cowardice, she and her father's family would perish. Not even royal status could protect her from the king's edict. Then Mordecai asked the question that has become the *locus classicus* for support of the doctrine of providence as a key to the understanding of the Book of Esther: "Who knows but that you have come to royal position for such a time as this?" (v.14). Her exaltation as a queen may have been God's way of obtaining a savior for his people. Mordecai confronted her with the options. Going to the king would involve the risk of death for her, but refusing to go would mean certain death for Esther and her father's house.

The phrase "from another place" remains an enigma. Lucian's recension of Esther, Josephus (*Antiq.* XI, 227 [vi. 7]), and the Targums consider "place" (*māqôm*) as a veiled reference to God (cf. Berg, p. 76; Streane, p. 29). This seems to be the correct interpretation, though some scholars believe it refers to political help that would come from another source, perhaps a foreign power (e.g., Anderson, p. 854).

15-16 Esther sent a reply to Mordecai, affirming her willingness to risk her life in behalf of her people. She asked him to assemble all the Jews who were in Susa to fast for her for three days and nights. She and her maids would also participate in the fast. Afterward she would go to the king, even though to do so was contrary to the law. In a final expression of courage and willing submission, she said, "If I perish, I perish" (v.16). Her remark has also been interpreted as "a despairing expression of resignation to the inevitable" (Paton, *Esther*, p. 326; cf. Jacob's statement in Gen 43:14). Prayer and fasting before God were customary concurrent practices in times of sorrow, anxiety, or penitence (cf. 1 Sam 1:7-10; 2 Sam 12:16-17; Ezra 8:23; Isa 58:2-5; Jer 14:12; Dan 9:3; Zech 7:3-5). The author of Esther is careful, however, to avoid the mention of God or that prayer was made to him.

17 Mordecai departed from the open square in front of the king's gate and carried

out Esther's instructions. The Hebrew only says he "crossed over," which may mean he crossed the city square or crossed the river that separated Susa from the citadel.

Notes

---

4 The LXX adds that Esther was distressed "when she heard what had happened."

5 Various versions spell the name Hathach differently (the LXX, "Achrathaios"; Josephus, "Achratheon"; OL, "Aetac"; Vul., "Athac"). The name may mean "companion" or "courier." The Targums call him "Daniel."

The Hebrew of "to find out what was troubling Mordecai and why" is "to know what [is] this and upon what/why [is] this."

7 The LXX and OL add the amount that was to be paid: "ten thousand talents" (cf. 3:9).

8 The Greek versions add to this verse: "Remembering your humble background when you were supported by my hand because Haman who is second to the king has spoken against us for death. Call on the Lord and speak to the king concerning us, to deliver us from death."

9 After "reported," the LXX and Vulgate add "everything."

11 The Lucianic recension, OL, and Vulgate add "and how can I go without being summoned?"

12 For וַיַּגִּידוּ לְמָרְדֳּכָי (*wayyaggîdû lᵉmordᵉkāy*, "and they told to Mordecai"), the LXX and OL read "When Hathach had reported to Mordecai." It is difficult to explain how additional people had become involved in the communications between Esther and Mordecai, as the Hebrew for "they told" suggests. NIV's rendering skirts the issue.

13 "Do not think" is אַל־תְּדַמִּי בְנַפְשֵׁךְ (*'al-tᵉdammî bᵉnapšēk*, "Do not think in your soul"). נֶפֶשׁ (*nepeš*, "soul") is the life principle, the self.

14 The Hebrew word for "relief" is רוּחַ (*rûaḥ*), which in other contexts may be translated "breath," "wind," or "spirit." Knight (p. 36) says that here it has the meaning of "breathing freely."

17 After v.17 the LXX adds a prayer by Mordecai and a prayer by Esther.

C. *Esther's First Banquet*

5:1-8

¹On the third day Esther put on her royal robes and stood in the inner court of the palace, in front of the king's hall. The king was sitting on his royal throne in the hall, facing the entrance. ²When he saw Queen Esther standing in the court, he was pleased with her and held out to her the gold scepter that was in his hand. So Esther approached and touched the tip of the scepter.

³Then the king asked, "What is it, Queen Esther? What is your request? Even up to half the kingdom, it will be given you."

⁴"If it pleases the king," replied Esther, "let the king, together with Haman, come today to a banquet I have prepared for him."

⁵"Bring Haman at once," the king said, "so that we may do what Esther asks."

So the king and Haman went to the banquet Esther had prepared. ⁶As they were drinking wine, the king again asked Esther, "Now what is your petition? It will be given you. And what is your request? Even up to half the kingdom, it will be granted."

⁷Esther replied, "My petition and my request is this: ⁸If the king regards me with

favor and if it pleases the king to grant my petition and fulfill my request, let the king and Haman come tomorrow to the banquet I will prepare for them. Then I will answer the king's question."

1 "On the third day," i.e., when the fasting was completed (cf. 4:16), Esther dressed in her royal splendor (Heb., "put on royalty") and went to the inner court of the palace in front of the king's hall. Xerxes was sitting on his throne in the hall, facing the entrance. From this position he could see Esther standing in the court. She had waited to see what he would do, as she had already violated the law by entering the inner court (cf. 4:11).

2 Esther's beauty evidently pleased the king; so he did not rebuke her. The Hebrew says that "she lifted up favor in his eyes." Instead, he held out the golden scepter in his hand as a gesture of favor toward her. Esther approached the throne and touched the tip of the scepter.

3 The king sought to know why she had come to him. He assured her that any request she might make, even up to half the kingdom, would be granted. He realized that only a pressing need could have caused Esther to risk coming to him unsummoned. The offer of half the kingdom was probably an example of Oriental courtesy that was not intended to be taken too literally (cf. Mark 6:23).

4 Esther's response was not what the reader would expect. Instead of forthrightly pleading for her people, she invited the king and Haman to a banquet she had prepared that day. She undoubtedly realized that it was not a psychologically propitious moment to plead for her people. The commentaries have proposed numerous explanations for Haman's inclusion in the invitation—e.g., to make the king suspicious (or jealous) of Haman, to avoid being alone with Xerxes, or to lull Haman into a false sense of security. Perhaps she thought it best for Haman to be present when she made her accusations against him.

5–6 The king ordered that Haman be summoned at once (v.5). The two men then went to Esther's banquet. Again the king asked to know the nature of Esther's request while they were drinking wine (Heb., "at the banquet of wine"). The king's words are almost identical with those of v.3.

7–8 For a second time Esther postponed giving a direct answer to the king. Instead she invited the king and Haman to a second banquet the following day. She indicated that she would present her petition to the king at that time (see Berg, pp. 77–78, for some explanations of Esther's delay).

Notes

1 The LXX expands vv.1–2 considerably. It tells how Esther fainted when she saw the anger on the king's face. Her fear softened the king's attitude toward her. He sprang from his throne, embraced her, and assured her that she would not be put to death. The LXX attributed his change of attitude to God.

3 "What is it?" translates מַה־לָּךְ (*mah-llāk*, lit., "What to/for you?"). The same expression occurs in Jonah 1:6.
4 The Lucianic recension and OL describe Haman as "your friend."
6 The LXX omits "even up to half the kingdom."

D. *Haman's Plot Against Mordecai*

5:9–14

⁹Haman went out that day happy and in high spirits. But when he saw Mordecai at the king's gate and observed that he neither rose nor showed fear in his presence, he was filled with rage against Mordecai. ¹⁰Nevertheless, Haman restrained himself and went home.

Calling together his friends and Zeresh, his wife, ¹¹Haman boasted to them about his vast wealth, his many sons, and all the ways the king had honored him and how he had elevated him above the other nobles and officials. ¹²"And that's not all," Haman added. "I'm the only person Queen Esther invited to accompany the king to the banquet she gave. And she has invited me along with the king tomorrow. ¹³But all this gives me no satisfaction as long as I see that Jew Mordecai sitting at the king's gate."

¹⁴His wife Zeresh and all his friends said to him, "Have a gallows built, seventy-five feet high, and ask the king in the morning to have Mordecai hanged on it. Then go with the king to the dinner and be happy." This suggestion delighted Haman, and he had the gallows built.

9–10 Haman left the banquet happy and in "high spirits" (Heb., "good of heart") because of the honor that had been accorded him by the invitations to the queen's private banquets. When he encountered Mordecai at the king's gate, however, Haman was filled with rage against the Jew because Mordecai did not stand up nor show fear (Heb., "did not tremble") in his presence (cf. 3:2). But Haman controlled himself and went to his home and called his wife, Zeresh (a Persian name that perhaps means "golden" or "one with disheveled hair"), and his friends together to tell them about the great honor accorded him by the king and the queen. Mordecai had apparently heard that Esther had been favorably received by the king and was encouraged by this turn of events; he had removed his sackcloth (cf. 4:2).

11–12 In an expansive mood Haman boasted about his wealth, his many sons, and the honor shown him by the king. He also exulted about the invitation to Esther's private banquet to which only he and the king had been invited. Haman's boasting only accentuated his later humiliation and fall from favor (cf. Prov 16:18).

13 In spite of the things that should have brought him happiness, Haman had no satisfaction as long as he saw Mordecai sitting at the king's gate. Haman's wealth and honors could not satisfy him when he thought of one Jew who failed to show him the proper respect he felt he deserved!

14 Haman's wife and friends suggested a plan that would remove the source of his irritation. She told Haman to have a gallows (*ʿēṣ*, "a tree") erected seventy-five feet ("fifty cubits") in height and then to ask the king to have Mordecai hanged on it.

With that business out of the way, Haman could go with the king to Esther's banquet and be happy. His wife's suggestion delighted Haman, and he had the gallows built, confident that the king would approve his request. The height of the gallows was exorbitant and is not taken seriously by some commentators, but it is consistent with what we know of Haman's vanity and obsessive desire for revenge.

Notes

---

10 The Hebrew word for "friends," אֲהָבִים (*ʾ ohāḇîm*), is also the same word that is usually translated "lovers" (e.g., Ezek 23:5; Hos 2:5); but it does not have that meaning here or in several other passages in the OT (cf. 2 Chron 20:7; Prov 14:20; 18:24; Jer 20:4).

11 A Targum says Haman had 208 sons in addition to 10 who held government offices and one who was the king's scribe (9:10 says he had 10 sons). Herodotus (1.136) said that those Persians were held in highest esteem who had the greatest number of sons.

E. Haman's Humiliation (6:1–13)

1. Discovery of an unrewarded deed

6:1–5

> ¹That night the king could not sleep; so he ordered the book of the chronicles, the record of his reign, to be brought in and read to him. ²It was found recorded there that Mordecai had exposed Bigthana and Teresh, two of the king's officers who guarded the doorway, who had conspired to assassinate King Xerxes.
> ³"What honor and recognition has Mordecai received for this?" the king asked.
> "Nothing has been done for him," his attendants answered.
> ⁴The king said, "Who is in the court?" Now Haman had just entered the outer court of the palace to speak to the king about hanging Mordecai on the gallows he had erected for him.
> ⁵His attendants answered, "Haman is standing in the court."
> "Bring him in," the king ordered.

1 The same night of Esther's first banquet, the king was unable to sleep (Heb., "the sleep of the king fled"; cf. Dan 6:18); so he ordered the royal annals (cf. 2:23) to be brought in and read to him. The annals have been variously called "the book of the chronicles" (NIV); "the book of memorable deeds, the chronicles" (RSV); "the Record Book, the Chronicles" (JB); "the chronicle of notable events" (NAB); and "the chronicle of daily events" (NEB). The Hebrew translated literally means "the book of remembrances, the words/matters of the days." The annals contained written records of facts and events that were important to the kingdom (see 2:23; cf. Ezra 4:15; Mal 3:16). It would be futile to speculate on the cause of the king's sleeplessness, but we can be sure that God was behind it.

The entire chapter shows how a series of seemingly trivial circumstances fit together to overrule the evil intentions of Haman (e.g., the king happened to be unable to sleep; he happened to ask that the royal annals be read to him; Haman happened to be in the palace).

2–3 In the course of reading the annals, the record of Mordecai's exposure of the plot of Bigthana and Teresh against the king was found (cf. 2:21). On inquiring what "honor and recognition" (this may be a hendiadys for "great honor") had been bestowed on Mordecai, the king was told that nothing had been done to honor him. The oversight must have disturbed Xerxes, as it was a reflection on him for not rewarding one of his benefactors. Herodotus indicated that it was a point of honor with Persian kings to reward promptly and generously those who had benefitted them (cf. Moore, *Esther*, p. 64, n. 3).

4–5 Though the hour was late, the king inquired if anyone was in the court. He intended to set the matter right without further delay. By chance, obsessed with his hatred of Mordecai, Haman had just entered the outer court to speak to the king about having Mordecai hanged on the gallows he had erected. The attendants advised the king of Haman's presence; so the king ordered that he be brought to his bedchamber at once. It seems strange that Haman came in the middle of the night to make his petition, but perhaps he knew the sleeping habits of the monarch well. The Book of Esther is filled with fortuitous coincidences.

Notes

---

1 The LXX and the Targums say that God took away the king's sleep.

The MT has "read before the king." The NIV follows the LXX: "read to him."

2 The LXX omits the names of the two conspirators in this verse.

---

2. *Mordecai honored*

6:6–11

> ⁶When Haman entered, the king asked him, "What should be done for the man the king delights to honor?"
>
> Now Haman thought to himself, "Who is there that the king would rather honor than me?" ⁷So he answered the king, "For the man the king delights to honor, ⁸have them bring a royal robe the king has worn and a horse the king has ridden, one with a royal crest placed on its head. ⁹Then let the robe and horse be entrusted to one of the king's most noble princes. Let them robe the man the king delights to honor, and lead him on the horse through the city streets, proclaiming before him, 'This is what is done for the man the king delights to honor!' "
>
> ¹⁰"Go at once," the king commanded Haman. "Get the robe and the horse and do just as you have suggested for Mordecai the Jew, who sits at the king's gate. Do not neglect anything you have recommended."
>
> ¹¹So Haman got the robe and the horse. He robed Mordecai, and led him on horseback through the city streets, proclaiming before him, "This is what is done for the man the king delights to honor!"

6 The text suggests that abruptly and without an exchange of greetings the king asked Haman what should be done for a person whom the king delighted to honor.

Haman assumed the king meant to honor him. It is one of the great ironies of the story that Haman was to decide how the man he desired to hang would be honored.

7–9 The vain Haman, not needing additional wealth, suggested that the one to be honored be given a royal robe that had been worn by the king along with a horse the king had ridden and that had a royal crest placed on its head (vv.7–8). As verification of this practice, horses wearing crowns or head ornaments are depicted on both Assyrian and Persian reliefs (cf. Bardtke, p. 348). Haman further suggested (v.9) that one of the king's most noble princes lead the "honoree," garbed in the king's robe, on the horse through the city streets. As he led horse and rider through the streets, the prince was to proclaim, "This is what is done for the man the king delights to honor!" Haman must have been ecstatic in anticipation of the high honor he thought was about to be accorded him before all the people of Susa.

10 The suggestion delighted the king. He ordered Haman to carry out the plan at once. Then for the first time the king named the man who was to be honored—Mordecai, Haman's adversary. The king warned Haman not to "neglect" (Heb., "cause to fall") any of the honors he had proposed. It seems strange that the king would knowingly honor a Jew so soon after enacting an edict to destroy all the Jews in his kingdom.

11 Haman had no choice but to carry out the king's orders. No writer, however gifted, could adequately describe the chagrin and mortification Haman must have experienced as he robed Mordecai and led him through the streets. One wonders what brought the greatest enjoyment to Mordecai—remembrance by the king, the people's adulation, or Haman's humiliation!

Notes

6 The Hebrew of "Haman thought to himself" is literally "Haman said in his heart."

---

3. *Haman's wife affirms his downfall*

6:12–13

> [12]Afterward Mordecai returned to the king's gate. But Haman rushed home, with his head covered in grief, [13]and told Zeresh his wife and all his friends everything that had happened to him.
>
> His advisers and his wife Zeresh said to him, "Since Mordecai, before whom your downfall has started, is of Jewish origin, you cannot stand against him—you will surely come to ruin!"

12 Afterward Mordecai returned to the king's gate, where he had been sitting before Haman had been forced to lead his foe through the streets of Susa mounted on the king's horse. The honor had not changed Mordecai's position before the king as a Jew awaiting the execution of Haman's edict. Haman, however, rushed home with his head covered, an expression of his grief and wretchedness. Covering the head was a way of expressing mourning (cf. 2 Sam 15:30; Jer 14:3–4). Haman must have hoped to find solace from his wife and friends.

13 Haman told his wife and friends all the details of his humiliating experience. If he expected comfort from them, he did not receive it. Instead they, seeing the handwriting on the wall, warned Haman that the Jew had been responsible for the beginning of his downfall. They were convinced that he could not stand against Mordecai; Haman's ruin was already assured. They seem to have conveniently forgotten that his humiliation was largely the result of their suggestion (cf. 5:14). The men who were called Haman's "friends" in 5:10, 14 and in this verse are also now called "advisers" (Heb., "wise men"). Most commentators think the author was injecting into the mouths of Haman's friends the Jewish belief in the ultimate victory of the Jews over the Amalekites.

Notes

13 For "advisers" the LXX has "friends." The Hebrew is חֲכָמָיו (ḥ°kāmāyw, "wise men"). The LXX may reflect a harmonizing with 5:14.

All the versions except the Vulgate add "for God is with him" at the end of this verse.

F. Esther's Second Banquet (6:14–7:10)

1. Haman summoned to the banquet

6:14

> [14]While they were still talking with him, the king's eunuchs arrived and hurried Haman away to the banquet Esther had prepared.

14 The conversation between Haman and his friends was interrupted by the appearance of eunuchs sent by the king to escort Haman to Esther's banquet. The Hebrew says that "they hastened to bring" him. The statement has been interpreted by some scholars to mean that, as the result of his humiliating experience with Mordecai (cf. 6:11), Haman had either forgotten about the queen's banquet or did not want to attend it. Others think it emphasizes his importance, for it was a common custom to escort guests to a banquet (Moore, *Esther*, p. 69; cf. Luke 14:17). The statement probably is intended to convey the urgency with which a command issued by the king was carried out.

2. Haman exposed and executed

7:1–10

> [1]So the king and Haman went to dine with Queen Esther, [2]and as they were drinking wine on that second day, the king again asked, "Queen Esther, what is your petition? It will be given you. What is your request? Even up to half the kingdom, it will be granted."

³Then Queen Esther answered, "If I have found favor with you, O king, and if it pleases your majesty, grant me my life—this is my petition. And spare my people—this is my request. ⁴For I and my people have been sold for destruction and slaughter and annihilation. If we had merely been sold as male and female slaves, I would have kept quiet, because no such distress would justify disturbing the king."

⁵King Xerxes asked Queen Esther, "Who is he? Where is the man who has dared to do such a thing?"

⁶Esther said, "The adversary and enemy is this vile Haman."

Then Haman was terrified before the king and queen. ⁷The king got up in a rage, left his wine and went out into the palace garden. But Haman, realizing that the king had already decided his fate, stayed behind to beg Queen Esther for his life.

⁸Just as the king returned from the palace garden to the banquet hall, Haman was falling on the couch where Esther was reclining.

The king exclaimed, "Will he even molest the queen while she is with me in the house?"

As soon as the word left the king's mouth, they covered Haman's face. ⁹Then Harbona, one of the eunuchs attending the king, said, "A gallows seventy-five feet high stands by Haman's house. He had it made for Mordecai, who spoke up to help the king."

The king said, "Hang him on it!" ¹⁰So they hanged Haman on the gallows he had prepared for Mordecai. Then the king's fury subsided.

1–2 The king and Haman went "to dine" (Heb., "to drink") with Esther at her invitation (v.1). At her second banquet (Heb., "banquet of wine"), the king once again sought to discover the nature of Esther's petition (v.2). Again he assured her that it would be granted, "even up to half the kingdom" (cf. 5:3, 6). He made his inquiry while they were drinking wine, which was customarily served after the meal. The "second day" here does not refer to a banquet that lasted two days but to the second day's banquet.

3 The queen no longer withheld her request from the king. She began courteously by asking if she had "found favor with you, O king, and if it pleases your majesty." She dared not presume on the good will of Xerxes. She unmasked Haman, but by doing so she revealed her own identity without knowing what the king's reaction would be. The king must have looked at her in stunned silence when she asked for her life and also for the lives of her people. It probably took him some time to grasp the fact that she also was a Jew. The abruptness of her words (Heb., "my life as my request and my people as my request") may reflect the queen's desperation and her anxiety about the king's response to her petition.

4 Without waiting for the king to speak, Esther hastened to explain that she and her people had been sold for destruction, slaughter, and annihilation. She added that if it had been a matter of selling them as slaves rather than killing them, she would not have troubled the king with such a petty problem. If he had sold them, at least he would have benefited monetarily. The verb "sell" (*māḵar*) can be used in the general sense of "deliver up to enemies" (e.g., Judg 2:14; 3:8), but here it probably alludes to the monetary agreement between Haman and the king (cf. 3:11; 4:7). The Hebrew of the latter part of this verse—"no such distress would justify disturbing the king"—is quite obscure, resulting in a number of translations and interpretations of Esther's words. It is considered to be the most difficult clause in all the

Book of Esther to translate. It has been interpreted to mean that the death of Xerxes' Jewish subjects would be a more grievous loss to him than enslavement would be to the Jews (JB, NAB, RSV). It has also been understood to mean that selling the Jews as slaves was not sufficient grounds to trouble the king (NIV, NEB, Moore). Either interpretation could be justified from the Hebrew. The second, however, is preferable. It seems to imply the first, i.e., if selling the Jews as slaves was all that was involved, Esther would have kept silent; but more than that was involved—their destruction, which would be an economic loss to the king.

5 The king's reaction was immediate and wrathful. He demanded to know who had dared to do such a thing (Heb., "to fill his heart to do thus"). He must have felt that the plot to kill the Jews that also encompassed his wife was a personal affront. Either he ignored his complicity in the affair, or he felt that he had been duped into agreeing to the Jews' destruction. A careful reading of chapter 3 shows that Haman did not mention the Jews by name; so perhaps the king was unaware of the full contents of the decree he had signed.

6 Without hesitation Esther identified Haman as the adversary and enemy. Haman was struck with terror ("dumbfounded," Moore, *Esther*, p. 97) by the accusation, for he understood that his fate was automatically sealed by Esther's words.

7 The enraged king arose abruptly and went into the palace garden, probably to consider the appropriate punishment before speaking; or he may have been too angry to speak. Also the situation created a dilemma for the king because he could hardly condemn Haman for carrying out orders that bore his royal seal. Xerxes probably needed some time to collect his thoughts before acting. Haman, knowing that the king had already decided his fate (Heb., "he saw that the evil was completed/determined for him from the king"), remained to beg Esther for his life.

8 Haman's timing could not have been worse. Just as he fell on the couch where Esther was reclining to plead for his life, the king walked in. A Targum adds that the angel Gabriel pushed Haman as the king entered the room! Angrily he accused Haman of attempting to molest the queen even while she was with her husband. As soon as the words left the king's mouth, servants or court officials (we are not told whether they had been present all along or whether the commotion in the room brought them) covered Haman's face. The king's angry words were a sentence of death. Although there is no evidence that it was a Persian custom to cover the face of a condemned criminal before he was led away to execution, that was probably its meaning here. Esther looked on in silence as her enemy was led away. Bardtke (p. 359) says court etiquette prevented her from speaking to the king, as strict harem regulations had been violated.

9 One of the king's eunuchs, Harbona, remembered the gallows that Haman had erected for the execution of Mordecai and so informed the king. If the king had been considering mercy for Haman, Harbona's reminder that Haman had knowingly plotted the death of a man who had saved the king's life was sufficient to seal Haman's fate. The king's immediate response was "Hang him on it!"

10 No mention is made of the time that elapsed between the pronouncement of the sentence and its execution, but Haman was probably carried away and hanged immediately. The king's wrath "subsided" ("abated," NAB, NEB; the same Hebrew verb [šākak] is found in Gen 8:1 to describe the waters of the Flood receding; cf. 2:1). Goldman (p. 229) says Haman's fate is an example of "measure for measure" justice (cf. Exod 21:24). As an act of poetic justice, Haman lost his life on the very gallows that he had anticipated would bring him such joy at Mordecai's execution.

Notes

2 The Lucianic recension adds to this verse: "Esther was terrified about telling him because her enemy was before her, but God gave her the courage when she called on him."

4 The JPS translation reads: "For the adversary is not worth bothering the king about." The LXX says, "For the slander is not worthy of the king's palace." No satisfactory translation has yet been found for this verse. See Paton, *Esther*, pp. 261–62, for the variety of interpretations that have been proposed.

5 NIV's "Where is the man?" translates אֵי־זֶה הוּא (*'ê-zeh hû'*, "Where is he?"), which the LXX omits.

Adam Clarke (*One-Volume Commentary on the Holy Bible*, abridged ed. by Ralph Earle [Grand Rapids: Baker, 1967], p. 430) believed that the abruptness of the Hebrew reveals the agitated state of mind of the king: "Who—he—this one?—and—where?—this one—he—who—he to fill—his heart—to do—thus?"

The Lucianic recension adds after this verse: "And when the queen saw that it seemed terrible to the king and that he hated the evil, she said, 'Do not be angry, my lord. It is enough that I have gained your pity. Enjoy the feast! Tomorrow I will act in accordance with your command!' Then the king urged her to tell him who had dared to do thus, and with an oath he promised to do for her whatever she asked."

6 The Lucianic recension says, "Haman your friend."

Attempts have been made to read הָרָע (*hārā'*, "vile"; "wicked," RSV) as *hārēa'* ("the lover"), the argument being that Esther deliberately called Haman her lover to incite the king's wrath; but the reading has not gained wide support.

7 One Targum said the king went into the garden to work off his anger by cutting down trees! Another says he rushed angrily into the garden because he saw Haman's sons (actually angels impersonating them) cutting down his trees.

8 On the basis of the LXX, some would change the reading of "they covered Haman's face" to "his face became flushed," i.e., with shame and dismay. The verb חָפָה (*ḥāpāh*, "to cover, veil") has also been interpreted intransitively: "Haman's face was covered," i.e., he covered it himself in shame and confusion.

9 חַרְבוֹנָה (*ḥarbônāh*, "Harbona") is probably the same person mentioned in 1:10, though the name is spelled there with an א (', aleph) as the final letter; here the final letter is ה (h, he). The LXX calls him *Bougathan*.

10 The MT uses a construction that does not name the subject: "They hanged Haman." The LXX uses an impersonal passive: "Haman was hanged."

G. Mordecai's Elevation (8:1-17)

1. Exaltation over the house of Haman

8:1-2

> [1]That same day King Xerxes gave Queen Esther the estate of Haman, the enemy of the Jews. And Mordecai came into the presence of the king, for Esther had told how he was related to her. [2]The king took off his signet ring, which he had reclaimed from Haman, and presented it to Mordecai. And Esther appointed him over Haman's estate.

1-2 On the same day that Haman was executed, King Xerxes gave Haman's entire "estate" (*bêt*, "house") to Esther, probably as compensation for all she had suffered. Persian law gave the state the power to confiscate the property of those who had been condemned as criminals (cf. Herodotus 3.128-29; Jos. *Antiq*. XI, 17 [i.3]). The queen revealed her relationship to Mordecai, whereupon the king invited him into his presence. Xerxes removed from his finger the signet ring that he had "reclaimed" (*he'ĕbîr*, "caused to pass") from Haman and gave it to Mordecai, thereby making him prime minister with power to act in the king's name (cf. 3:10). Mordecai became one of the select group of courtiers who had the right of access into the king's presence (cf. 1:10, 14; 7:9). Esther placed her kinsman in charge of Haman's estate. Haman's wealth, title, and power now belonged to his enemy Mordecai.

Notes

1 The text of the Lucianic recension that corresponds to 8:1-12 is quite different from the MT and the LXX (q.v.).

For "had told how he was related to her" (Heb., "had made known what he was to her"), the LXX has "had shown that he was related to her"; and the Vulgate says, "He was her father."

2. Reversal of Haman's decree

8:3-14

> [3]Esther again pleaded with the king, falling at his feet and weeping. She begged him to put an end to the evil plan of Haman the Agagite, which he had devised against the Jews. [4]Then the king extended the gold scepter to Esther and she arose and stood before him.
>
> [5]"If it pleases the king," she said, "and if he regards me with favor and thinks it the right thing to do, and if he is pleased with me, let an order be written overruling the dispatches that Haman son of Hammedatha, the Agagite, devised and wrote to destroy the Jews in all the king's provinces. [6]For how can I bear to see disaster fall on my people? How can I bear to see the destruction of my family?"
>
> [7]King Xerxes replied to Queen Esther and to Mordecai the Jew, "Because Haman attacked the Jews, I have given his estate to Esther, and they have hanged him on the gallows. [8]Now write another decree in the king's name in behalf of the Jews as seems best to you, and seal it with the king's signet ring—

for no document written in the king's name and sealed with his ring can be re-voked."

⁹At once the royal secretaries were summoned—on the twenty-third day of the third month, the month of Sivan. They wrote out all Mordecai's orders to the Jews, and to the satraps, governors and nobles of the 127 provinces stretching from India to Cush. These orders were written in the script of each province and the language of each people and also to the Jews in their own script and language. ¹⁰Mordecai wrote in the name of King Xerxes, sealed the dispatches with the king's signet ring, and sent them by mounted couriers, who rode fast horses especially bred for the king.

¹¹The king's edict granted the Jews in every city the right to assemble and protect themselves; to destroy, kill and annihilate any armed force of any national-ity or province that might attack them and their women and children; and to plun-der the property of their enemies. ¹²The day appointed for the Jews to do this in all the provinces of King Xerxes was the thirteenth day of the twelfth month, the month of Adar. ¹³A copy of the text of the edict was to be issued as law in every province and made known to the people of every nationality so that the Jews would be ready on that day to avenge themselves on their enemies.

¹⁴The couriers, riding the royal horses, raced out, spurred on by the king's command. And the edict was also issued in the citadel of Susa.

3 With a great show of emotion, Esther fell at the feet of the king and begged him to "put an end" (*lᵉhaᶜᵃbîr*, "to cause to pass over") to the evil plan Haman had devised against the Jews. Haman's overthrow and Mordecai's elevation could not give Esther comfort so long as Haman's decree against the Jews remained un-revoked.

4 Some commentators (e.g., Paton) assume that Esther risked her life a second time to come uninvited into the king's presence, because the king again extended his scepter to her (cf. 4:11; 5:1-2). However, the scepter was extended only after her emotional plea and not at the moment of her entrance before the king. Therefore his gesture was intended to encourage her to rise from her prostrate position before continuing to speak.

5-6 With proper deference to the king and an expressed hope that she enjoyed the king's favor, Esther petitioned him to issue an order "overruling" (*lᵉhāšîb*, "to cause to return") Haman's dispatches (v.5). She reminded him that Haman's orders had been sent with the explicit purpose of destroying the Jews in all the king's prov-inces. Esther expressed her grief in face of the impending disaster about to fall on her people (Heb., "the evil that will find my people") and her kinsmen, thus reveal-ing her true character—that she was not merely self-serving, as might have been inferred from her previous statements. Esther was careful to place the blame on Haman for the wicked plot and not on the king.

7-8 The king responded by first reminding Esther and Mordecai that he had exe-cuted Haman and given his estate to her. The king then told them to write another decree in his name in behalf of the Jews. He gave them permission to word the decree as seemed best to them (Heb., "according to the good in your eyes"). He reminded them that he could not write the new decree himself, as no prior docu-ment written in his name and sealed with his ring could be "revoked" (*lᵉhāšîb*, "to cause to return"; cf. v.5), even by the king himself (cf. comment on 1:19; cf. Dan 6:8, 12, 15). It could only be neutralized by another decree.

9 The royal secretaries were summoned "at once" ("at that time," Heb., RSV). It was the twenty-third day of the third month, Sivan (May-June), two months and ten days after Haman had issued his order (cf. 3:12). They wrote out Mordecai's orders to the Jews and to the other government officials of the 127 provinces. The orders were written in the script and language of the Jews (cf. 1:1; 3:12). Therefore no one in the Persian Empire would be able to plead ignorance of Mordecai's orders.

10 Because of the authority granted him by Xerxes, Mordecai wrote the orders in the king's name and then sealed the dispatches with the king's signet ring. They were then sent throughout the empire by "mounted couriers" (Heb., "runners on the horses"). The horses the couriers rode had been especially bred for the king's use. Although the Hebrew of this verse contains some obscure technical terms, the meaning is clear that strong, fast horses were used to carry Mordecai's message throughout the empire without undue delay.

11–12 These verses contain the substance of Mordecai's edict that was sent in the king's name. It granted the Jews the right to "protect themselves" (Heb., "stand on their soul") against anyone who might attack them, to slaughter women and children (cf. Notes), and to plunder the property of their enemies (v.11). The day set apart for the Jews to take revenge on their enemies was the thirteenth day of the twelfth month, Adar (v.12). The decree was almost a paraphrase of Haman's edict (cf. 3:13). Some commentators interpret the edict only as giving the Jews the right to defend themselves. Anderson (p. 866) calls it "measure-for-measure" retaliation (cf. Exod 21:24). It is difficult to understand why the Persian ruler would allow a Jewish minority to massacre his subjects at will. Yet we have already observed Xerxes' indifference to the value of human life (cf. 3:11), and it was the only way to neutralize the preceding edict.

13 Mordecai's edict was to be issued as law in every province of the empire and made known to all the subjects, regardless of their nationality. Everyone would be on notice that the Jews would be ready on the designated day to take vengeance on their enemies. The verse is almost identical with 3:14.

14 Riding the royal horses, the couriers hastened to deliver the edict to all parts of the kingdom, knowing it was a royal decree. The decree was also circulated in the citadel of Susa. The verse is similar to 3:15.

Notes

5 The phrase "thinks it the right thing to do" contains the verb כָּשֵׁר (kāšēr), from which "kosher" comes, a word used to describe food that is ritually clean or "right" for eating. The LXX omits "son of Hammedatha, the Agagite."
Many Syriac MSS have "all the Jews" instead of simply "the Jews."

7 The LXX, OL, and Syriac omit "and to Mordecai the Jew." However the plural verbs of v.8 ("write . . . seal") support the MT. There is no reason to assume that Mordecai was not present with Esther when she pleaded with the king (cf. 8:1–2).

The LXX adds to this verse "What do you still seek?"

The OL reads "They hanged him with all his house."

8 One of the Targums has "Make haste to write" instead of "Write."

9 This is the longest verse in the Hagiographa; it contains forty-three words totaling 192 letters (cf. 3:12).

The LXX has "the first month which is Nisan" instead of "the twenty-third day . . . Sivan."

10 The KJV's "mules, camels, and young dromedaries" is markedly different from other translations and reflects a misunderstanding of the difficult words of the MT. The LXX omits the obscure, technical words of this verse and has only that "they sent the letters by the couriers."

11 Some EV suggest that "women and children" refers to enemy action against Jewish women and children (NIV; RSV and JB are ambiguous). According to the Hebrew grammatical construction, these words may be interpreted as objects of the infinitives "to destroy, kill and annihilate" and therefore would refer to Jewish action against their enemies (with KJV, NAB, NASB, NEB).

Because of the problems created by this verse, Hoschander (cited in Gordis, "Studies in Esther," p. 50) preferred to delete "their women and children" as a gloss without supporting evidence. Paul Haupt ("Critical Notes on Esther," AJSL 24 [January 1908]: 160) understood it as an order to kill only the women and children who attacked the Jews. Gordis ("Book of Esther," p. 378; cf. "Studies in Esther," pp. 49–53) says the presumed cruelty practiced by the Jews in exterminating their enemies together with their wives and children is based on "a failure to comprehend the form and context of the passage." The author is only quoting Haman's decree that would have resulted in the destruction of the Jewish women and children: "the order to destroy . . . all the Jews—young and old, women and little children" (3:13). The new decree allowed the Jews to defend themselves and "to destroy . . . any . . . that might attack their women and children" (8:11). This interpretation is also reflected in the NIV. Further support for this interpretation is found in 9:15–16, which indicates the Jews did not take booty from their enemies. If Mordecai's order had included the killing of women and children, surely booty would have been taken.

12 After v.12 the LXX adds twenty-four verses that purport to be a copy of a new decree of "Artaxerxes."

13 The LXX has "fight against" instead of "avenge themselves on."

14 "Spurred on" is NIV's translation of מְבֹהָלִים וּדְחוּפִים (mᵉḇōhālîm ûdᵉḥûpîm, "hastened and hurried"), both passive participles.

---

3. Popular reaction

8:15–17

> [15]Mordecai left the king's presence wearing royal garments of blue and white, a large crown of gold and a purple robe of fine linen. And the city of Susa held a joyous celebration. [16]For the Jews it was a time of happiness and joy, gladness and honor. [17]In every province and in every city, wherever the edict of the king went, there was joy and gladness among the Jews, with feasting and celebrating. And many people of other nationalities became Jews because fear of the Jews had seized them.

15 Mordecai left the king's presence wearing royal garments of blue and white that befitted his new position. He also wore a large crown of gold and a purple robe of fine linen. The verse closes with the statement that the city of Susa had a "joyous celebration" (Heb., "shouted and rejoiced"). As it is difficult to understand why the Persian residents of Susa would rejoice at a decree that could be used against them, the statement probably refers to the joy of the Jewish residents of Susa. Verses 16 –17, as well as Josephus (*Antiq*. XI, 284–85 [vi.13]), support this interpretation.

16–17 When the edict became known throughout the provinces, there was great joy among the Jewish people, accompanied by feasting and other celebrations. "People of other nationalities" (Heb., "peoples of the land") became Jews out of fear of what the Jews might do to them (Heb., "terror of the Jews fell on them"). The statement that they "became Jews" may mean that they pretended to be Jews or took the side of the Jews. The tables had turned so completely that it was now dangerous not to be a Jew.

Notes

---

16 "For the Jews it was a time of happiness" is literally "For the Jews there was light." Light was a symbol of well-being and prosperity (cf. Job 22:28; 30:26; Pss 27:1; 36:9; 97:11).
17 "Celebrating" is literally "a good day" ("a holiday," NASB, RSV).
  "People of other nationalities" (Heb., "peoples of the land/earth") is here a technical term for non-Jews. Elsewhere "people [sing.] of the land" refers to Jewish inhabitants. It could designate the general population of an area. It was sometimes used as a technical term for a specific social class or political body and sometimes referred to male, property-owning people (i.e., responsible citizens).
  The LXX adds that those who became Jews "were circumcised."
  "Fear of the Jews" is taken by some scholars (e.g., Dommershausen, p. 110; Hoschander, p. 247; K.V.H. Ringgren and A. Weiser, *Das Hohelied, Klagelieder, Das Buch Esther, Das Alte Testament Deutsch* XVI [Göttingen: Vandenhoeck und Ruprecht, 1958], p. 140) to be a veiled reference to God, but in the context the expression should be understood literally.

III. The Jews' Day of Vengeance (9:1–19)

A. *A Great Slaughter*

9:1–10

¹On the thirteenth day of the twelfth month, the month of Adar, the edict commanded by the king was to be carried out. On this day the enemies of the Jews had hoped to overpower them, but now the tables were turned and the Jews got the upper hand over those who hated them. ²The Jews assembled in their cities in all the provinces of King Xerxes to attack those seeking their destruction. No one could stand against them, because the people of all the other nationalities were afraid of them. ³And all the nobles of the provinces, the satraps, the governors and the king's administrators helped the Jews, because fear of Mordecai had seized them. ⁴Mordecai was prominent in the palace; his reputation spread throughout the provinces, and he became more and more powerful.
⁵The Jews struck down all their enemies with the sword, killing and destroying

them, and they did what they pleased to those who hated them. ⁶In the citadel of Susa, the Jews killed and destroyed five hundred men. ⁷They also killed Parshandatha, Dalphon, Aspatha, ⁸Poratha, Adalia, Aridatha, ⁹Parmashta, Arisai, Aridai and Vaizatha, ¹⁰the ten sons of Haman son of Hammedatha, the enemy of the Jews. But they did not lay their hands on the plunder.

1 The thirteenth day of the twelfth month, Adar, arrived for the carrying out of both edicts (cf. 3:7, 13; 8:12). The nine months that elapsed since the second decree was signed are passed over in silence (cf. 8:9). The day was originally set aside for the Jews' enemies to overpower them, but now "the tables were turned" (Heb., "it was turned over/changed"). Now the Jews had "the upper hand" (Heb., "gained power") over those who hated them. This chapter assumes a universal hatred of the Jews (cf. vv.2, 5, 16) that was not expressed previously. Earlier only Haman's hatred of the Jews was stated (3:8).

2 The Jews gathered in their cities throughout the provinces to "attack" (Heb., "stretch out a hand against") anyone who tried to destroy them. Fear seized the people of other nationalities; no one was able to stand against the Jews. All resistance to them was ineffective.

3–4 The nobles and other political leaders "helped" (Heb., "lifted up"; "supported," NAB, JB) the Jews because of their fear of Mordecai and the influence he had with the king (v.3). Mordecai was not only prominent in the palace, but "his reputation spread" (Heb., "his reputation was walking") throughout the empire (v.4). He had become increasingly powerful during his brief months as prime minister.

5 The Jews showed no mercy to their enemies. They massacred those who hated them; there were no restraints imposed on them by the king. The Jews did not limit themselves to self-defense. They hunted out and destroyed those who might harm them. Their fury can only be understood by those who have experienced a long history of unjustified persecution.

6–10 In the citadel of Susa, the Jews killed five hundred men and also killed the ten sons of Haman, whose names are carefully recorded in these verses. Their names are Persian and are not found elsewhere in the OT. The Jews did not, however, take any plunder in Susa, though the edict granted them this right (cf. 8:11); their restraint shows their motive was not personal enrichment. Although the reader has not been told that the sons participated in their father's plot, as Amalekites and hereditary enemies of the Jews, they shared in their father's guilt (cf. Korah [Num 16:27, 32–33] and Achan [Josh 7:24–25], whose entire families suffered the consequences of one person's sins).

Notes

3 "The king's administrators" (Heb., "the doers of the business that [belonged] to the king") is translated in the LXX as "the royal scribes."

5 The LXX omits this verse.

6–9 See Moore, *Esther*, p. 87, and Paton, *Esther*, p. 284, for explanations of the unusual vertical arrangement in the MT of the names of Haman's sons. The arrangement may suggest the way the sons were hanged. When these verses are read during Purim today, the names of the ten sons and the word "ten" are read in one breath because they all died together. For a discussion of the meaning of the son's names, see Paton, *Esther*, pp. 70 –71; his discussion reveals that the meaning of the names is far from certain.

10 The LXX says they took plunder and adds "the Bougaion" to "son of Hammedatha."

B. Vengeance in Susa

9:11–15

[11]The number of those slain in the citadel of Susa was reported to the king that same day. [12]The king said to Queen Esther, "The Jews have killed and destroyed five hundred men and the ten sons of Haman in the citadel of Susa. What have they done in the rest of the king's provinces? Now what is your petition? It will be given you. What is your request? It will also be granted."

[13]"If it pleases the king," Esther answered, "give the Jews in Susa permission to carry out this day's edict tomorrow also, and let Haman's ten sons be hanged on gallows."

[14]So the king commanded that this be done. An edict was issued in Susa, and they hanged the ten sons of Haman. [15]The Jews in Susa came together on the fourteenth day of the month of Adar, and they put to death in Susa three hundred men, but they did not lay their hands on the plunder.

11–12 The king was informed of the slaughter of the five hundred and of the ten sons of Haman in the citadel of Susa. He reported the figures to Esther and asked whether she knew what the Jews were doing elsewhere in the provinces. He also encouraged her to make any other request of him that she desired, and it would be granted. Xerxes' only desire was to please his queen; he showed no concern for his subjects who were being killed.

13 Esther asked for an extension of another day for the Jews in Susa to continue killing their enemies. She also asked that Haman's ten murdered sons be hanged on gallows as an additional act of degradation on Haman's house. She may have hoped the deed would serve as a deterrent against further Jewish persecution.

14–15 The king granted Esther's request without demurrer. He issued an order for the hanging of Haman's ten sons. On the next day, the fourteenth of Adar, the Jews killed an additional three hundred of their enemies in Susa but did not take any plunder.

Notes

---

11 The LXX omits "the citadel."

C. Celebration in the Provinces and in Susa

9:16–19

[16]Meanwhile, the remainder of the Jews who were in the king's provinces also assembled to protect themselves and get relief from their enemies. They killed seventy-five thousand of them but did not lay their hands on the plunder. [17]This happened on the thirteenth day of the month of Adar, and on the fourteenth they rested and made it a day of feasting and joy.

[18]The Jews in Susa, however, had assembled on the thirteenth and fourteenth, and then on the fifteenth they rested and made it a day of feasting and joy.

[19]That is why rural Jews—those living in villages—observe the fourteenth of the month of Adar as a day of joy and feasting, a day for giving presents to each other.

16–17 Elsewhere in the Persian provinces, the Jews killed seventy-five thousand of their enemies on the thirteenth day of Adar but took no plunder. On the fourteenth day they rested and celebrated their victory with feasting (Heb., "drinking") and rejoicing. (For confirmation of the historical likelihood of such a great slaughter, see Introduction: Special Problems, c.12.)

18–19 The author added these verses to explain why in his time Jews living in the city kept the Feast of Purim on the fifteenth of Adar whereas Jews living in the country observed it on the fourteenth of Adar. The Jews in Susa were permitted two days for killing their enemies (the thirteenth and fourteenth of Adar) and therefore celebrated their victory on the fifteenth. Jews elsewhere had only one day for slaughtering their enemies (the thirteenth day of Adar) and therefore celebrated their victory on the fourteenth. In addition to feasting, they gave presents to each other (Heb., "sending portions of a man to his friend").

Notes

16 The LXX says 15,000 were killed. The Lucianic recension says 10,107.

19 The Hebrew word for "rural" Jews is הַפְּרָזוֹים (*happerāwzîm*) and occurs here, in Deut 3:5, and in 1 Sam 6:18. The definition of what constituted a village and a city later gave rise to elaborate Talmudic discussions.

IV. Institution of the Feast of Purim (9:20–10:3)

A. Mordecai's Letter

9:20–28

[20]Mordecai recorded these events, and he sent letters to all the Jews throughout the provinces of King Xerxes, near and far, [21]to have them celebrate annually the fourteenth and fifteenth days of the month of Adar [22]as the time when the Jews got relief from their enemies, and as the month when their sorrow was turned into joy and their mourning into a day of celebration. He wrote them to

observe the days as days of feasting and joy and giving presents of food to one another and gifts to the poor.

²³So the Jews agreed to continue the celebration they had begun, doing what Mordecai had written to them. ²⁴For Haman son of Hammedatha, the Agagite, the enemy of all the Jews, had plotted against the Jews to destroy them and had cast the *pur* (that is, the lot) for their ruin and destruction. ²⁵But when the plot came to the king's attention, he issued written orders that the evil scheme Haman had devised against the Jews should come back onto his own head, and that he and his sons should be hanged on the gallows. ²⁶(Therefore these days were called Purim, from the word *pur*.) Because of everything written in this letter and because of what they had seen and what had happened to them, ²⁷the Jews took it upon themselves to establish the custom that they and their descendants and all who join them should without fail observe these two days every year, in the way prescribed and at the time appointed. ²⁸These days should be remembered and observed in every generation by every family, and in every province and in every city. And these days of Purim should never cease to be celebrated by the Jews, nor should the memory of them die out among their descendants.

20–21 When Mordecai learned that the Jews were celebrating their victory on two different days, he recorded what had happened and then sent letters to all the Jews in all the provinces of the kingdom. In the letter he authorized them to celebrate their victory over their enemies thereafter on both the fourteenth and fifteenth days of Adar. The statement that Mordecai "recorded these events" should not be interpreted to mean that Mordecai was the author of the Book of Esther. It probably refers to the recent events that had resulted in two different days on which the Jews celebrated their victory.

22 The two-day celebration would be observed as a memorial to the time when the Jews "got relief" ("rid themselves," JB; "obtained rest," NAB) from their enemies. Their sorrow and mourning had been transformed into joy and celebration by the turn of events. Mordecai instructed them to observe the days by feasting and by giving food to one another and gifts to the poor.

23 The Jews agreed to observe their celebration every year in the same way as they did that first time and in accordance with the instructions given them by Mordecai.

24 The narrator summarizes for the reader in the following verses the events that led to the establishment of the Jewish festival of Purim. Haman, the Jews' enemy, had cast the *pûr* to determine on which day he would destroy the Jews (cf. 3:7). Perhaps vv.24–25 contain the substance of Mordecai's letter to the Jews (cf. 9:20, 23).

25 When the plot was brought to the king's attention, "he issued written orders" (Heb., "he said with the scroll") that Haman's evil scheme should come back onto his own head. He also ordered the death of Haman and his sons on the gallows (though not at the same time; cf. 7:10; 9:14).

26–27 In the first explicit reference to the Jewish festival of Purim, the author explains that the name finds its origin in the word *pûr* (cf. 3:7; 9:24; *pûrîm* is the plural form). As a result of the instructions given them in Mordecai's letter, the Jews took it on themselves to observe the fourteenth and fifteenth days of Adar every year in the way prescribed and at the time appointed. The festival would be observed by their descendants and "all who join them" (Heb., "all the ones attaching themselves on them," i.e., proselytes to the Jewish faith). Thus Purim became the first Jewish festival for which there is no basis in the Torah, but it is considered just as binding as the other festivals. (See Lev 23:1–44; 25:1–17 for a complete list of the holy days and seasons prescribed under Mosaic law.)

28 The author makes a final exhortation for the Jews to remember the days of Purim in every generation by every family wherever they may live. The days of Purim should never cease to be celebrated by the Jews nor forgotten by their "descendants" (Heb., "seed").

Notes

20 The LXX has "wrote these things in a book."
22 Instead of "days of feasting," the LXX has "days of marriage."
  The OL adds that gifts were to be given to "widows and orphans" as well as to the poor. The Talmud says gifts should be given to at least two poor persons.
23 The verb קִבֵּל (qibbēl, "agreed," NIV; "undertook," KJV, RSV, NASB, NEB, JB) is singular in the MT but has a plural subject, "the Jews." Many Hebrew MSS do use the plural verb, however.
24 The Lucianic recension omits vv. 23–26. The OL omits vv. 24–27.
  The LXX has "the Macedonian" instead of "the Agagite."
25 The MT may read either "when she" or "when it came before the king," since Hebrew does not have a separate neuter form (cf. GKC, pars. 80a, 122q). Esther is understood as the subject by KJV, NAB, RSV. But NIV, NASB, NEB take the feminine form to be a neuter and therefore understand it as a reference to Haman's plot. The LXX has "and when he [i.e., Haman] went in to the king" (so JB). All these interpretations can be justified grammatically and contextually.
26 Attempts to link Purim to pagan festivals such as Babylonian (P. Jensen, "Elamitische Eigennamen. Ein Beitrag zur Erklärung der elamitischen Inschriften," *Wiener Zeitschrift für die Kunde des Morgenlandes* 6 [1892]: 47–70, 209–26; H. Winckler, "Esther," *Altorietalische Forschungen* 3 [1902]: 1–66, esp. p. 4; Heinrich Zimmern, "Zur Frage noch dem Ursprunge des Purimfestes," ZAW [1891]: 157–69) or Persian (Hermann Gunkel, *Esther* [Tübingen: Mohr, 1916], p. 115; Julius Lewy, "The Feast of the Fourteenth Day of Adar," HUCA [1939]: 127–51 [p. 149 gives a summary statement of his position]) have been unsuccessful. For further discussion see the Introduction: Special Problems, c. 14.
28 The Lucianic recension omits vv. 28–32; the OL omits vv. 30–32.

B. Esther's Confirmation
9:29–32

29So Queen Esther, daughter of Abihail, along with Mordecai the Jew, wrote with full authority to confirm this second letter concerning Purim. 30And Mordecai sent letters to all the Jews in the 127 provinces of the kingdom of Xerxes—words of goodwill and assurance— 31to establish these days of Purim at their designated times, as Mordecai the Jew and Queen Esther had decreed for them, and as they had established for themselves and their descendants in regard to their times of fasting and lamentation. [32]Esther's decree confirmed these regulations about Purim, and it was written down in the records.

29 Esther, together with Mordecai, wrote with the full authority of her position to confirm "this second letter concerning Purim." Scholars are divided as to the meaning of the "second letter." Most assume it refers to the letter described in vv.29–31 and was intended to add authority to Mordecai's previous letter (vv.20–22). However it would seem unusual for Esther and Mordecai to confirm their own joint letter.

30 Mordecai sent letters to all the Jews in the 127 Persian provinces that contained words of "good will and assurance" (Heb., "peace and truth," KJV, NASB, RSV; "peace and security," NAB, NEB; "kindness and friendship," JB).

31 The purpose of the letter was to establish the days of Purim at the times decreed by Mordecai and Esther, i.e., the fourteenth and fifteenth days of Adar. Purim was to be observed with fasting and lamentation. It is known that by the ninth century A.D. the Jews were observing the thirteenth day as a fasting day—"Esther's fast."

32 Esther's decree confirmed the regulations about Purim. It was written down "in the records" (Heb., "in the scroll"; cf. 9:25) in order to be available to future generations for verification. Some commentators understand this verse to be a reference to the Book of Esther itself. Others believe it refers to the scroll used by the compiler of Esther.

Notes

29 Many scholars believe vv.29–32 are an addition to the book (e.g., Moore).
  The word "second" is omitted by the LXX, OL, and Syriac.
31 The LXX has "concerning their health and their plan" instead of "their times of fasting and lamentation."

C. *The Greatness of Mordecai*

10:1–3

[1]King Xerxes imposed tribute throughout the empire, to its distant shores. [2]And all his acts of power and might, together with a full account of the greatness of Mordecai to which the king had raised him, are they not written in the book of the annals of the kings of Media and Persia? [3]Mordecai the Jew was second in rank to King Xerxes, preeminent among the Jews, and held in high esteem by his many fellow Jews, because he worked for the good of his people and spoke up for the welfare of all the Jews.

1 Even as it had begun, the book closes with a statement that reveals the imperial power and wealth of Xerxes. He was able to impose "tribute" (*mas*, used elsewhere of forced taxation or involuntary labor; cf. Exod 1:11; 1 Kings 5:13 [27 MT]; 9:21) to the most distant shores of his empire. It is unclear as to what the relevance of this verse is to the rest of the book. It may imply that Mordecai was a factor in augmenting the king's power over other nations under his control (cf. Joseph in Gen 41).

2 The reader is told that the mighty acts of Xerxes as well as a full account of the greatness of Mordecai were recorded in the book of the official annals of the kings of Media and Persia (cf. 6:1; 1 Kings 11:41; 2 Chron 25:26; cf. Introduction: Special Problems, c.9). Notice that Media is mentioned first here, whereas it follows the mention of Persia in 1:3, 14, 19.

3 The book closes with a paean of praise to Mordecai, who rose to be second in rank to King Xerxes and "preeminent" (Heb., "great") among the Jews. He was held in "high esteem" (Heb., "favored"; "popular," RSV) by his fellow Jews because he worked for their good "and spoke up for the welfare of all the Jews" (Heb., "speaking peace to all his seed"; cf. Ps 85:8; Zech 9:10).

Notes

1 For "imposed tribute" the LXX has "wrote" tribute.
3 The word translated "welfare" (NIV) is שָׁלוֹם (šālôm), one of the most theologically significant words in the OT, occurring 237 times. It can mean "absence of strife, war"; but "completeness," "wholeness," "harmony," "fulfillment" more accurately encompass the meaning of the word.

After v.3 the LXX has additional verses that give the interpretation of a dream attributed to Mordecai and a concluding witness to the date and authenticity of the LXX "letter of Purim" ("Phrourai").

JOB

Elmer B. Smick

JOB

Introduction

1. Background
2. Authorship and Unity
3. Date and Source
4. Canonicity
5. Text
6. Purpose
7. Major Characters

    a. Job
    b. The Three Counselors

8. Mythopoeic Language
9. Bibliography
10. Outline

1. Background

The uniqueness of the Book of Job derives from its depth and thoroughness in dealing with the relationship of human suffering to divine justice, commonly called theodicy (from Gk. *theos* ["god"] and *dikē* ["justice"]). Numerous documents, especially from ancient Mesopotamia and Egypt, demonstrate that this genre of wisdom writing was well established in the OT world; but none touch on these matters so eloquently and fully as this OT book. In a Sumerian document he calls "The First Job," Kramer relates the tale of a man who in his affliction complained to his "personal" god while wailing for mercy:

> My companion says not a true word to me,
> My friend gives the lie to my righteous word . . .
> My God . . . how long will you neglect me, leave me
> unprotected?[1]

Like the biblical Job, this "Job" was restored; "his god harkened to his bitter tears and weeping," which "soothed the heart of his god."[2]

Another poetic monologue also written in the second millennium B.C. is commonly called "I Will Praise the Lord of Wisdom" (ANET, pp. 434–37). This Babylonian "Job" is like the Sumerian one. As a righteous sufferer he also reckoned with the thought that Marduk, the cosmic god, allowed him to suffer. Yet he hoped that

---

[1]Samuel N. Kramer, *History Begins at Sumer* (Garden City, N.Y.: Doubleday, 1959), pp. 114–18.
[2]Ibid.

by means of ritual piety he would obtain mercy; but he had his doubts: "Oh that I only knew that these things are well pleasing to a god!" (II.33). He too was restored and ended with a thanksgiving hymn and offerings that "made happy their [i.e., the gods] mood" and "gladdened their heart" (IV.40).

These documents share literary structures and lament language in common with Job but deal with the meaning of suffering in a way that expresses their own social, ethical, and cultic standards—all polytheistic. The Book of Job is emphatically monotheistic, but the sufferer's predicament is the same; so similar issues and solutions are discussed. For example, in "A Dispute Over Suicide" (ANET, pp. 405–7), a man of Egypt debates with his KA (soul?) over suicide because times (between the Old and Middle kingdoms) are so bad that there is no more justice or love. He finally decides death is better because men then become like gods in the nether world. As Job longed for an advocate (9:33; 16:19, 21; 19:25–27), so this man pled for the advocacy of the gods and felt that he was presenting his case before a divine tribunal (ANET, p. 405, n. 2).

As for literary structure, this document has a striking likeness to the Book of Job in its A-B-A pattern that begins, as does Job, with a short prose prologue, followed by a long poetic section, and ends with an epilogue in prose. This pattern finds expression in other ancient Near Eastern documents.

Still another document, from as early as 1000 B.C., is called "A Dialogue About Human Misery" (ANET, p. 438). This is even more like Job. It is a dialogue involving a friend who accuses the sufferer of imbecility and evil thoughts and suggests he put aside such thoughts and seek the gracious favor of a god. The sufferer complains that animals do not have to make offerings, and that even men who get rich quickly do so without paying attention to the gods, while he who has done all the right things from his youth suffers. The friend warns him in these words:

> The mind of the god,
>   like the center of the heavens,
> is remote;
>   His knowledge is difficult,
> men cannot understand it.
>   [lines 256–57]

The friend's view seems to be that the gods have made men perverse, and there is nothing that can be done about it. "Falsehood and untruth they [the gods] conferred upon them [men] forever" (line 280). The sufferer finally appeals to the gods for mercy, and the dialogue ends there on a fatalistic note.

So while the literary genre and overall format of the Book of Job came from the world it was a part of, there is really nothing extant that compares with the biblical book in its philosophical and theological profundity. Moreover the Book of Job cannot be forced into any single literary classification. It is generally called Wisdom literature, but that describes more the subject matter than the form. John Milton classified the Book of Job as a subspecies of epic. C.S. Lewis, for one, considered this reasonable.[3] Although the book is not an epic, the Prologue has the stereotyped forms and expressions of an old epic tradition. The book also displays a dramatic intention that says something about its authorship and unity (see below). Job's antiwisdom in contrast to the wisdom of the counselors intensifies the dramatic aspect.

---

[3]*A Preface to Paradise Lost* (New York and London: Oxford University Press, 1961).

The book is largely poetry of various genres (lament, wisdom, proverbs, hymns, etc.), and in places it is more difficult to understand than any other part of the OT. This appears to be due more to the language than to textual corruption, though critics still claim the text has suffered greatly in transmission. Pope (pp. XX, L) considers chapters 24–27 thoroughly scrambled. Job abounds in *hapax legomena* (words occurring only once). The grammar, syntax, and orthography (spelling) often stand outside the regular forms of classical Hebrew. The more extensive literature of the cognate languages helps us interpret the difficult parts of the language of Job. Scholars have long used Arabic and Aramaic for help in vocabulary and elements of grammar. The Elihu speeches have an Aramaic flavor. Aramaic elements scattered throughout the book have led Tur-Sinai (*Job*) to view it as originally written in Aramaic and later translated into Hebrew (cf. also Guillaume, "Arabic Background"). On the other hand, Dahood (*Philology*) views the book as strongly influenced by earlier Canaanite patterns detectable through Ugaritic.

Although there is little scholarly consensus on their views, Dahood and his students have attempted to use the poetic texts from Ugarit (Ras Shamra) to shed light on the language of Job (cf. Blommerde, Ceresko, and the articles by Dahood). The book has often been looked on as some form of Edomite since Job is called a "man . . . of the East" (1:3). Edom was a reputed center of wisdom (cf. 1 Kings 4:30), but we have no Edomite literary documents to test this view. Arabic, Aramaic, Hebrew, Ugaritic, and Phoenician are all northwest Semitic; and all may be included in what Isaiah calls "the language of Canaan" (Isa 19:18). We have no written Arabic from OT times, nor any appreciable amount of Edomite or Ammonite; but one of the oldest and longest documents from preexilic Transjordan is the Moabite Stone (Mesha Inscription). Being prose, it throws little light on Job. It does, however, show how this nearby language could have been understood easily by any Hebrew. So the unique Hebrew of Job and his counselors may fall into a similar category as another dialect perhaps of Edomite origin.

Since Ugaritic has a sizeable extant corpus of west Semitic poetic literature, it lends itself to comparative usage. Arabic grammar is especially instructive since it has preserved archaic forms (case endings, etc.). Aramaic and Phoenician have little poetic material, but there are many documents from the OT period. Babylonian-Assyrian provides poetry for comparison, but it must be used cautiously since its morphology and syntax are east Semitic.

In this commentary we will use comparative linguistics to deal with difficult passages involving *hapax legomena*, rare meanings of homonyms, and rare syntax. Revocalizing will be resorted to only where a problem appears, that is, where the Hebrew as it stands is obviously strange or yields little sense.

2. Authorship and Unity

Is Job of single or composite authorship? One critical approach would make it a gradual aggregation of materials on an original base. The wisdom poem of chapter 28, the Elihu speeches in 32–37, and the Yahweh discourses in 38 and 41 are said to be additions. Much has been made of the supposed incongruities between the Prologue-Epilogue and the Dialogue. In the former Job is presented as a saint of God who will not curse God and die; in the latter his complaints are bitter to the point of being shocking, while his friends seem to be saying all the right things.

Then comes the unexpected rebuke of the friends and the commendation of Job in the Epilogue (42:7–8). Some scholars think this destroys the unity of the book. When they consider these things along with the different literary form (prose vs. poetry) and Job's ritual piety in the Prologue-Epilogue (features missing in the Dialogue), they have concluded that the Prologue-Epilogue came from a different source.

The Prologue-Epilogue, it is said, represents an old epic-tale used as a framework by the author of the Dialogue. This tale about a legendary figure named Job (Ezek 14:14, 20) was used to give more advanced concepts about theodicy an impressive hoary antiquity. But Ewald (p. 20) says that it is not fully legitimate to ask "whether the work of the poet as we possess it contains history or fiction, as if a third thing were not possible." His idea is that the book is an artistic masterpiece skillfully put together by a great poet who used materials available to him. While it is true that the book makes no claim of having been written by Job (the Prologue-Epilogue is about him but does not cite him as author), nevertheless the discourses claim to be from the lips of the same sufferer referred to in the Prologue. If this is not so, the integrity of the book is impaired.

To return to the problem of the apparent incongruities mentioned above, the Israeli scholar Y. Kaufmann explains the problem of God's rebuking the friends and not Job himself by suggesting that the friends were guilty of clichés and empty phrases while Job's challenge to God reflects a moral duty to speak only the truth before him.[4] This is more satisfactory than assuming, as some do, that the book has lost a large portion in which the friends, like his wife, told Job to curse God and die. Job himself accused his friends of currying favor with God by saying things they did not believe (13:7-8).

One cannot, of course, assume that there are no deletions or interpolations at all in Job. Yet a fair mind must recognize the singular organic unity of this extensive piece of OT literature. The brevity of Bildad's speech and the omission of Zophar in chapters 24–27, combined with Job's use of the argument of his detractors (27:13–23), may indicate such a deletion and/or interpolation. It is possible but by no means certain. Commentators cannot agree on how to handle the problem in chapters 24–27. Most shift sections around to suit themselves. Pope claims the material was deliberately scrambled by someone who tried to refute Job's arguments by confusing the picture. This is only a guess; so it is just as satisfactory to work with the text as it is, assuming a breakdown in the debate and a final attempt by Job to be as eloquent as they on the fate of the wicked. See comments on chapter 27.

Much is made of the fact that Elihu is ignored in the Epilogue as if this were proof that he was put in by an interpolater. But Satan is also ignored in the Epilogue; and even Pope, who takes a dim view of the authenticity of the Elihu speeches, admits they have been blended in with the rest of the book with great skill. Much depends on how one views the speeches themselves. On the role of Elihu, see comments introducing that section. The complaints against the first divine speech (ch. 38) on the basis that God is indifferent to man's predicament is a misunderstanding of the purpose of the divine speeches. (See Purpose and also the comments introducing the divine speeches.)

---

[4]*History of the Religion of Israel from the Babylonian Captivity to the End of Prophecy*, tr. by C.E. Froymsen (New York: KTAV, 1976), p. 335.

Some critics accept as even more spurious the second divine speech on Behemoth and Leviathan. But others regard it as the climax of the book and even more original than the first. Some writers have satirized the divine speeches making God appear cruel and indifferent to human suffering.[5] Such abysmal lack of sensitivity to what many see as a literary and theological triumph is all too typical.

The overall A-B-A literary structure this book shares with other ancient compositions (see "A Dispute Over Suicide" above and also "The Code of Hammurabi," ANET, pp. 164–80) is only the most obvious structural accomplishment of the author. There are other artful and balanced structures throughout the book, witnessing to a creative composition, not merely an arbitrary compilation. Job opens the Dialogues with a lengthy lamentation of his condition. This expected genre is used throughout by Job, but not in the specialized form of individual lament found in the Psalms.[6] The one exception is Psalm 88, which sounds much like Job (cf. Ps 88:8 and Job 19:13–19); but in keeping with the spirit of the Psalms, even 88 begins with a strain of hope (v. 1). Job's laments, like Psalm 88, tend to be mostly negative; but the attempt to make them totally negative is an unfortunate scholarly quibble. The lengthy lament of chapter 19 clearly ends in hope.

Much of the book takes the form of legal disputation. Although Job's friends come to console him, they soon fall into a bitter dispute over the reason for his suffering. The argument breaks down in the third cycle, and Job is left to deliver a peroration on a theme he has repeatedly brought up: his own vindication (chs. 29–31). The wisdom poem in chapter 28 is the work of the unknown author who views the failure of the dispute as evidence of a lack of wisdom. In praise of true wisdom, he centers this structural apex between the three cycles of dialogue-dispute and the three monologues: Job's (29–31), Elihu's (32–37), and God's (38–41). In chapters 29–31 Job turns directly to God for a legal decision—that he is innocent of the charges the counselors have leveled against him. Elihu's monologue is another human perspective on why Job has suffered. More needed to be said on the value of divine chastisement and the redemptive purpose of suffering.

God's monologue presents the divine perspective. Job is not condemned as one who is being punished for sin, but neither is he given a logical or legal reason for his suffering. It remains a mystery to Job, though the reader is ready for Job's restoration in the Epilogue, because he has had the heavenly vantage point of the Prologue. So the architectonics and the theological significance of the book are beautifully tied together. (See diagram on page 850.)

It is neither prudent nor necessary to assume a view of the composition of the book that rules out the possibility of the use of source materials and some kind of literary development involved in the composition of the Book of Job. But the fact is, any attempt to know exactly what that was is sheer guesswork. There is as much reason to believe that the book, substantially as we have it, was the work of a single literary and theological genius as to assume it is the product of numerous hands often with contrary purposes. We do not know who the writer was, but his work has witnessed to the spirits of the faithful through the ages that he was divinely inspired.

---

[5]Cf. A. MacLeish, *Job, A Play in Verse* (Boston: Houghton Mifflin, 1957).
[6]Cf. C. Westermann, *The Psalms, Structure, Content and Message* (Minneapolis: Augsburg, 1980).

Architectonics of the
Book of Job[7]

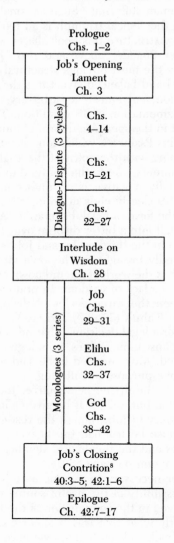

Prologue
Chs. 1–2

Job's Opening
Lament
Ch. 3

Dialogue-Dispute (3 cycles)

Chs.
4–14

Chs.
15–21

Chs.
22–27

Interlude on
Wisdom
Ch. 28

Monologues (3 series)

Job
Chs.
29–31

Elihu
Chs.
32–37

God
Chs.
38–42

Job's Closing
Contrition[8]
40:3–5; 42:1–6

Epilogue
Ch. 42:7–17

It is likely that the poet based the material on wisdom poetry passed down through the generations. The wisdom poetry of the speeches in Job includes poetic genres such as laments, hymns, proverbs, and oracles. But, as in all Semitic poetry,

---

[7]Cf. Sawyer, pp. 253–57; also Westermann, *Structure of Job*, p. 6.

[8]Job's words of contrition are divided to provide a response to each divine speech. The first is preparatory to the second.

parallelism is foremost. This comes from an artistic urge toward symmetry through balanced lines and other units of composition. The double line or bicolon tends to prefer a balance in form, that is, an equal weight of syllables (or accents) on either side of the line, except where unbalanced lines are used for other reasons. We call these unbalanced bicola "the lament form" (*qinah*), but it is not limited to lamentations. The balance of thoughts (meaning) on either side operates similarly. The latter may be partially or fully synonymous (the same) or antithetical (opposite) or may be entirely absent.

The poet, however, was a free spirit; so he created unique and intricate patterns of relationship between thought and form parallelism. Although the bicolon is usual, a rare monocolon and more frequent tricolon are also employed, as is the double bicolon (quatrain). The patterns the poet creates with these principles are limitless, and they have given rise to many terms to describe the parallelism: introverted, stairstep, climactic, complete, incomplete, void, etc. The symmetrical urge also applies to strophes, stanzas, and whole poems where the climax is as likely to be in the middle as at the end. Structure on a wide scale that includes whole speeches and books has only recently begun to be appreciated. The strophic patterns play a role in literary and textual criticism and consequently in interpretation. See the commentary for various structures and patterns that often illuminate meaning. Line parallelism can only be fully appreciated on the basis of the Hebrew word order; so translations can only approximate what is there. The few samples below are an attempt (somewhat in vain) to overcome that problem.

Job 13:12 illustrates complete synonymous parallelism in a balanced bicolon with chiasm (crossing of elements):

> Your-maxims (are) • proverbs-of-ashes;
> defenses-of-clay (are) • your-defenses.

Hebrew syllables (form) 8 / / 8
Pattern (thought) a • b / / b' • a' (chiasm).

Job 5:9 illustrates incomplete synonymous parallelism in a balanced bicolon:

> He-performs • wonders • that-cannot-be-fathomed,
> miracles • that-cannot-be-counted.

Hebrew syllables (form) 7 / / 7
Pattern (thought) a • b • c / / b' • c'.

Job 8:20 illustrates incomplete antithetical parallelism in a balanced bicolon:

> Surely-God • does-not-reject • a-blameless-man
> or-strengthen • the-hand-of-evildoers.

Hebrew syllables (form) 6 (8) / / 8
Pattern (thought) a • b • c / / B' • C'.[9]

---

[9]The capital letters B and C indicate heavier elements originally used to balance the weight in syllables, but here the first line lost some final original vowels that contributed a number of additional

Job 38:2 illustrates synthetic parallelism (no parallel thoughts) in a balanced bicolon:

> Who-is-this • that-darkens • my-counsel
> with-words • without-knowledge.

Hebrew syllables (form) 6 / / 6
Pattern (thought) a • b • c / / d • e.

Job 20:23 illustrates the balanced tricolon with synthetic and synonymous elements. Tricola are often formed by combining an opening line with a bicolon that completes the sense:

> When-he • has-filled • his-belly,
> (God)-will-vent • against-him • his-burning-anger
> and-rain-down • upon-him • his-blows.

Hebrew syllables (form) 8 / / 8 / / 8
Pattern (thought) a • b • c / / d • e • f / / d' • e' • f'.

Job 19:27 illustrates the tricolon with two synonymous lines completed with a synthetic line:

> Whom-I • will-see • for-myself
> my-eyes • will-see • and-not-another
> (How)-yearns • my-heart • within-me.

Hebrew syllables (form) 8 / / 8 / / 8
Pattern (thought) a • b • c / / a' • b' • c' / / d • e • f.

Job 15:2 [1 MT] illustrates a quatrain made of two synonymously parallel bicola that are tied together in thought and form:

> Would-a-wise-man • answer • with-empty-notions
> or-fill • with-(hot)-east-wind • his-belly?
> Would-he-argue • with-words • that-are-useless,
> with-speeches • that-have-no-value?

Hebrew syllables (form)   8 / / 7 / 8 / / 7
Pattern (thought)   a • b • c / / b' • c' • a'
                          a • b • c / / b' • C'.

3. Date and Source

As is true with much Wisdom literature, the actual composition of the Book of Job as we have it is very hard to date with precision. Suggestions range from the Mosaic era[10] (with Moses as author!), to the Solomonic era (Delitzsch, 1:21), on into the

---

syllables. This whole matter becomes somewhat theoretical; therefore one should avoid dogmatism about the balance of lines and certainly should not emend the text on that basis.

[10]So the Talmud (j *Sota* 5.8; b *Bathra* 15a), Origen, Jerome, and other church fathers.

seventh century B.C. and the unsettled and unfortunate times of Judah's king Manasseh (Ewald, p. 76) after Sennacherib had besieged Jerusalem. Davidson argues for a seventh-century date by observing that the questions of providence entered a new phase when God's laws were no longer calmly expounded but subjected to doubt and that a condition of great disorder and misery forms the background of the Book of Job.[11]

Buttenwieser asserts that the Book of Job was written by "at least 400 B.C."; and at the same time he insists that arguments purporting to show that the existence of a folk tale of Job was current in the sixth century B.C.,[12] during the time of Ezekiel's ministry,[13] are ultimately mistaken.

Doctrinal clues are mentioned by some authors as considerations one must take into account in trying to establish a probable date for the Book of Job. Delitzsch (1:22), in support of his view of a Solomonic date, claims that Job in 19:29 reflects only a personal belief regarding future judgment of mankind, whereas later Wisdom writings (e.g., Eccl 12:14) expressed it as a "settled element of general religious consciousness." Nor is Job 19:25–27 "an echo of an already existing revelation of the resurrection of the dead," but it is an "acknowledgment of revelation which we see breaking forth and expanding throughout Isa. xxvi.19, comp. xxv.8, and Ezek. xxxvii. comp. Hos. vi.2, until Dan. xii.2" (ibid.).[14] The representations of the future in the Book of Job are the same as those in Psalms, which come from the time of David and Solomon, and in the Proverbs of Solomon.[15]

A religious evolution from an early conception of the gods as arbitrary figures to be appeased on a changeable, sometimes whimsical basis to a later conception of rule by God according to his self-imposed laws of righteousness and justice is put forth by Jastrow in his argument for a postexilic date of approximately 400 B.C. He

---

[11]Davidson (p. lx) argues that the "new phase" is seen in that one scarcely finds a trace of the problems and questions that fill the Book of Job in Proverbs, even though the same general subjects are treated in both books. An interesting and rather extended contrast with Delitzsch's view is found in Davidson (pp. lx–lxii). The reader of these two views is left with the impression that either era is still open as a possibility, rather than that one sufficiently negates the other to the point of becoming a preferable view.

[12]"All that follows from this bare reference is that alongside Noah and Daniel, Job had enjoyed the renown of exemplar piety . . . the likelihood must be granted that the Job of the story current at the time of Ezekiel had little, if anything, in common with the suffering hero of the Book of Job. Ezekiel, who most consistently developed the view that there can be no punishment without sin and who made this the basis of his preaching, could not but have viewed Job's calamity in exactly the same light as the friends did" (pp. 8f.).

[13]Argued by K. Budde, *Das Buch Hiob*, Nowack Handkommentar, 2d ed. (Göttingen: Vandenhoeck & Ruprecht, 1913), pp. xiif., on the evidence of Ezek 14:14–20.

[14]A case may be made that the resurrection in Isaiah, Ezekiel, and Hosea are not personal but national. But cf. M.J. Dahood (*Psalms I*, AB, vol. 16 [New York: Doubleday, 1965], p. xxxvi) on the concept of resurrection and immortality in preexilic times.

[15]Delitzsch (1:23) lays stress on Heman being the author of Ps 88. "Besides, the greatest conceivable fulness of allusion to the book of Job . . . is found in Ps. lxxxviii. and lxxxix, whose authors, Heman and Ethan . . . [were] the contemporaries of Solomon mentioned in 1 Kings v.11 [4:31 EV]." The agreement in either thought or expression of these Psalms and Job have "no such similarity as suggests a borrowing, but an agreement which, since it cannot possibly be accidental, may be most easily explained by supposing that the book of Job proceeds from just the same Chokma-fellowship to which, according to 1 Kings v.11, the two Ezrathites . . . belong.

"One might go further, and conjecture that the same Heman who composed Ps lxxxviii, the gloomiest of all the Psalms, and written under circumstances of suffering similar to Job's, may be the author of the book of Job."

feels that Job contrasts what is with what ought to be. The problem of Job is thus "one which directly arises out of the basic doctrine of post-exilic Judaism, . . . and it was inevitable that the question would sometime be raised, whether what the prophets taught of the nature of God which the people accepted as guidance in their lives was compatible with the facts of experience" (Jastrow, p. 36).

Davidson (p. lxi) contrasts Wisdom as perceived in Job and Proverbs 1–9. In Proverbs 1–9 Wisdom earnestly presses herself on men: she loves them that love her. Even when she rises to the highest conception of herself as architect of the world, she still offers herself to men and may be embraced by them (Prov 8:32). But the speaker in Job 28 despairs of wisdom: it can nowhere be found, neither in the land of the living nor in the place of the dead, neither by man nor by any creature (ibid.).

Jastrow (p. 36) agrees and feels that Job and Proverbs 1–9, "being two such opposing representations, can hardly be contemporaneous." But in stating this view, Jastrow perhaps unwittingly lends additional support to Delitzsch's position. It does indeed seem improbable that two such opposing views would be contemporaneous, but Delitzsch (1:21) maintains that there are three Wisdom periods: (1) Proverbs and Song of Solomon—Solomonic era, (2) Proverbs 1–9—Jehoshaphat's time, and (3) Ecclesiastes—postexilic.

A postexilic date for Job is rejected by Pope on the grounds that Job's suffering would have been seen as a parable of the nation's fate, and there is no hint of this nor of any nationalistic concerns in the book. Moreover the choice of an Edomite hero would be extremely unlikely due to the strong feeling against Edom by the prophets as a result of their aiding and abetting the enemy at the Fall of Jerusalem (cf. the Book of Obadiah).

Modern views have been many and varied, but the most recent tendency supports an early date. Urbrock points out that

> evidence is mounting for the antiquity of both the poetic and prose portions of Job. Robertson has shown that "verbal patterns of early poetry occur extensively in . . . Job" and that a clustering in Job of other linguistic forms characteristic of archaic Hebrew verse points similarly to an early date . . . he suggests as a working hypothesis the dating of Job to the "eleventh-tenth centuries." Again, Dahood and Pinar, Pope's commentary, Blommerde's grammatical analysis, and Michel's studies of mythological expressions in Job . . . have all demonstrated the usefulness of interpreting Job in the light of linguistic principles and thematic motifs exhibited in the Ugaritic texts from the fourteenth century B.C. On the other hand, the prose prologue and epilogue have been shown to be "saturated with poeticisms in vocabulary and style" and to employ "some unique forms explicable by reference to Ugaritic," so that "the considerable amount of epic substratum indicates that our present narrative framework is directly derived from an ancient Epic of Job (Sarna JBL 76:25)."[16]

In his dissertation Urbrock suggests that the formulaic nature of the poetry, when considered along with the thematic structure of the dialogue, indicates that a traditional oral song-cycle of Job lies behind the Book of Job now preserved in the OT. This is quite convincing in itself as an argument for the possible antiquity of Job.

---

[16]"Oral Antecedents," p. 132 *passim*. See also his *Evidences of Composition*.

Such a traditional oral song-cycle may indeed have very early roots, perhaps even preceding the eleventh-tenth century B.C. date mentioned by Urbrock.[17]

It is possible then that the Book of Job, or perhaps parts of the book, existed outside Israel for a long time as oral tradition or even in written form until an unknown Israelite author under divine inspiration gave it its present literary form. This would account for the non-Israelite flavor of the book as well as for its unquestioned place in the Hebrew canon. It seems likely that Job himself lived in the second millennium B.C. (2000 to 1000 B.C.) and shared a tradition not far removed from that of the Hebrew patriarchs. Job's longevity of 140 years, his position as a man whose wealth was measured in cattle and who acted as priest for his family, and the picture of roving Sabean and Chaldean tribesmen fit the second millennium better than the first. The book, however, may not have reached its final form until the first millennium. Anywhere in the OT biblical period is a possible date, but attempts to place the authorship of Job as late as the second or first century B.C. have been dealt a decisive blow by the discovery of parts of a Targum of Job in the Qumran caves.[18]

The exact place of origin is as difficult to determine as the exact date. As mentioned already, the book shows considerable Aramaic flavor that may mean Job and his friends lived near centers of Aramaic influence. Aram-Naharaim was such a center in northern Mesopotamia. At the end of the millennium, some Aramean tribes moved south and settled on the borders of Babylonia and Palestine; but Arameans continued to control the caravan route through the Khabur River area. This was the time when Aleppo and Damascus became Aramean centers and when the Chaldean tribes invaded Babylonia (CAH, 3:4). If Job 1:17 means that Chaldean tribes were still roving, the event could reflect a time before they settled at about 1000 B.C. Job himself lived in the land of Uz (1:1). Genesis 10:23 ties Uz with the Arameans, as does Genesis 22:20–22. The latter passage (v.22) also ties in Kesed (the Chaldeans) with the Arameans and the Uzites but does not make them identical. These passages refer to nations or tribes that were related sometimes mainly by their proximity. The land of Uz was east of Palestine, but its precise location cannot be determined. Job had great influence in a unnamed town (29:7). According to Lamentations 4:21, Edom was in the land of Uz. It seems then that Uz might have been the name of a region east of Palestine including the Edomites and adjacent tribes.

4. Canonicity

Presently the Book of Job is found in printed Hebrew Bibles in the third place among the eleven books of the third division of the Hebrew Scriptures, the Writings, following Psalms and Proverbs; but it has not always been so. The Talmudic list (b • *Bathra* 14b) and certain Spanish MSS place Job before Proverbs, and Jerome's list places Job before Psalms and Proverbs; but generally in Jewish lists it is grouped with the Psalms and Proverbs after the Prophets at the head of the Writings. The Targum, however, and certain Greek and Latin texts (having abandoned

[17]"Oral Antecedents," p. 132.
[18]See footnote 28.

the tripartite Hebrew division of Scriptures) have given Job many assignments, sometimes with the poetical books, sometimes with the historical, and sometimes after the Prophets. Since the thirteenth century (as in Vaticanus), Job has come after the historical books, before Psalms. Sinaiticus, on the other hand, bowing to the theories that connect Job with Moses, places the book between Deuteronomy and Joshua.

Childs in his "canonical function" approach looks at Job as Israel and the church have traditionally done,[19] from the perspective of a community whose religious and theological confessions are being addressed by a divine word; the implication of this is to allow the book to perform a variety of different roles within the one community whose unity is not threatened by the presence of tension.

The tension in Job, resultant from the reader's awareness of the scene in heaven and Job's ignorance of it, serves to address the continuing community with basic issues of faith. The book poses two sets of questions, one for the reader who views the Dialogue from the framework of the Prologue, the other for the reader who chooses to share Job's stance of ignorance of the divine will in order to pursue his probing questions. One can agree with Childs's consideration that

> it is a serious misunderstanding of the diversity of the book's canonical role when someone, such as Rowley (*New Century Bible Commentary* 13) sets these two perspectives in irreconcilable conflict and eliminates one. Because the reader is told in the prologue why Job is suffering, the truth of another solution is not ruled out which arises from the perspective of an ignorance of God's purpose in which the Job of the dialogue has been placed.[20]

Childs still agrees, however, with those who question the book's literary unity but maintains that that has nothing to do with its canonical integrity. This leads him to the very pertinent statement that "the issue at stake is whether or not the reader who stands within the community of faith is given sufficient guidelines from the book to obtain a clear witness for a variety of different issues of faith."[21]

It is amazing that a book about a man outside the sphere of Israel's covenant bond whose experience illustrates both the highest and the lowest levels of faith became part of the Hebrew canon and was never seriously challenged. This proves that the Hebrews recognized the superior spiritual message of this book. The book did not become authoritative by an edict of an official body like the rabbinical synod at Jamnia in 90 A.D. It was accepted as a divine word by the community of God's people at a time well before the LXX was completed or else it would not have been included. Some books like Song of Solomon and Ecclesiastes were under discussion at Jamnia; but even the criticisms of Ecclesiastes were merely academic, and there were no such attacks on Job. Although, as Gordis notes (*God and Man*, p. 221), it would have been easy "to point to passages in Job's speeches that incline to skepticism and heresy." Gordis's view is that Job was readily accepted because "only the Job of the prose tale impinged on the consciousness of ancient readers. . . . The disturbing ideas were couched in difficult poetry" (ibid, p. 222). This may be true for the later community, but it begs the question of why the earlier community

---

[19]Brevard S. Childs, *Introduction to the OT as Scriptures* (Philadelphia: Fortress, 1979), p. 533.
[20]Ibid., p. 534. See pp. 534–43 for Childs's extended description of this diversity of canonical function.
[21]Ibid., p. 543.

accepted Job and for that matter the Song of Solomon and Ecclesiastes as well. The theological tensions within the book were purposeful and were included to lift the teaching of the book to a new level of theological profundity.

The authority of the Book of Job is tied to its place in the Hebrew canon that the Jewish community held in common with Jesus and the early church as Scripture. Despite its difficulties theologically and linguistically, its place in the canon was never seriously challenged. The book itself, however, remains one of the greatest exegetical challenges facing the biblical scholar.

5. Text

The great Greek MSS of the OT (Vaticanus, Sinaiticus, and Alexandrinus) have approximately the same number of verses for Job as the MT, but both Origen and Jerome make it clear that the oldest Greek text of the LXX of Job was shorter than the MT by about one-sixth.[22] Everyone agrees that the old Greek was free and interpretive, but some have held that the theologically offensive passages were toned down or omitted.[23] Others (e.g., Gerleman, pp. 25–26) stress the ignorance of the translators; for example, the Hellenistic Jews did not appreciate the earlier discursive Hebrew style; so they often chose to give a simplified summary. Orlinsky (35:58) disagrees with both positions and maintains that in numerous passages the Hebrew pattern of the LXX differed from the preserved Hebrew text, and that in many places the divergences are simply stylistic Greek.[24]

Some believe there were two versions of Job and that the shorter version was the original. But this too is seriously disputed.[25] Origen, who expressly tells us about the omissions and additions, filled in the missing lines largely from Theodotion's minor Greek version using diacritical marks to show the differences. But the MSS on which this knowledge is based yield conflicting evidence as to the exact extent of these additions.[26] The Coptic (Sahidic) version, based on the Greek, is thought to preserve the pre-Origen text. It was particularly in Job where Jerome felt the greatest need to make a translation directly from the Hebrew. Jerome was

---

[22]On this matter cf. Dhorme (pp. cxcix–cciii); Driver and Gray (pp. lxxi–lxxvi).

[23]See D.H. Gard, "The Exegetical Method of the Greek Translation of the Book of Job," JBL Monograph Series, vol. 8 (1952): 71–93. But Orlinsky (vols. 30, 32) corrects the notion that the Greek translator demonstrates a broad theological or philosophical bias.

[24]Orlinsky's "Studies in the Septuagint Book of Job" are the most definitive yet to appear. But in 1982 Heater (pp. 41–42) made an important contribution toward a better understanding of the Greek text in which he demonstrates an anaphoric translation technique used in the LXX of Job. The technique was to adopt words or phrases from other passages of Scripture into the translation where the underlying idea was the same or similar. For example, the LXX of Job 3:16—"Or as a stillbirth coming from the mother's womb"—is not a paraphrase of the Hebrew (Dhorme) but an anaphoric translation coming verbatim from Num 12:12a. The awaited Göttingen edition of the LXX of Job will be an important step forward for OT text-critical studies.

[25]The oral antecedents that underlie the written composition of Job, according to Urbrock ("Oral Antecedents," p. 113), have had a role in producing the two versions of Job, the longer of the MT and the shorter of the Old Greek. But cf. Pope, p. XLIV.

[26]F. Buhl (Canon and Text of the Old Testament [Edinburgh: T. & T. Clark, 1892], pp.129–30), citing Field's work on Origen's Hexapla, notes that Job had 1,600 lines (stichs) but with the additions marked by asterisks 2,200. He maintains, however, that filling up the gaps from Theodotion began before Origen. See Driver and Gray (p. lxxii).

influenced by the rabbis who taught him Hebrew but also by Origen's Hexaplaric version of the LXX that he translated into Latin.

Jerome's attitude can be appreciated only when a comparison of the MT and the LXX is made. In the LXX Job 5:4–5, 14–16, Eliphaz tells what ought to happen (optative) to the wicked instead of asserting what does happen. This makes Job's irony lose its point in 6:8, 14. In general the LXX tends to make Job less defiant and more patient. In 32:1 the MT says that the friends ceased to answer Job "because he was righteous in his own eyes." The LXX presents a better view of Job by translating "because they considered him righteous." The Testament of Job, a pseudepigraphal work based on the LXX, goes all the way in simplifying the theology. The LXX translators were not above making additions. Many of these are exegetical comments. A rather lengthy one is attached to 2:9, involving Job's wife's complaint of her own sorrows.

In other places the translator adapts the text to his audience—the Alexandrian Jews of Hellenistic times. For example, in 42:11 the Hebrew says each of Job's friends brought him "a gold ring" (nezem, always translated enōtion ["ring"] elsewhere in the LXX). But here it is a tetradrachma, a coin common in Ptolemaic times; but to avoid any idolatrous overtones, he says it was "unstamped."

Despite the poor quality of the LXX as a translation, it still has value for textual criticism when used along with other ancient versions. On occasion the LXX translation is completely wrong and yet is still a good witness to the consonants of the Hebrew text (cf. Notes on 18:15). Sometimes the LXX handles difficult lines in Job by translating ad sensum (according to the general sense of the context). In such a case it is a paraphrase and has no divergent Hebrew text behind it, though the latter is always a possibility.

A good paraphrastic example is in 8:14a. The NIV has rendered the word yāqôṭ as "fragile" with some but little linguistic support (see NIV mg.) and translates the line "What he trusts in is fragile." The LXX has "For his house shall be uninhabited." Did the LXX see the word "house" in the text in the first line? It is not likely. It is more likely that they did not know how to render this line and so made an ad sensum paraphrase based on the second line that speaks of "the spider's house" (web). The Syriac is much closer to the Hebrew: "Whose confidence [Heb., 'What he trusts in'] shall be cut off." Here the Syriac was based on the same Hebrew as our MT with a unique choice for the root of the dubious word. Gesenius-Buhl lists this as qṭṭ ("to cut off").[27] In this case the Syriac is a good witness to the original text and the LXX is unreliable.

A reversal of this situation appears in 15:23a. Here the RSV follows earlier versions, all of which were led astray by the MT vocalization ('ayyēh ["where"] for 'ayyāh ["vulture"]). They therefore had to paraphrase: "He wanders abroad for bread, saying, 'Where is it?' " Even though the LXX paraphrases some of this context, it alone caught the correct idiom in the Hebrew text with the words "food for vultures." Partly following the LXX the NIV reads: "He wanders about–food for vultures." The Syriac uses an ad sensum meaning that fits the context but omits the difficulties, reading: "He flees because of the threat of judgment." See the note on 6:7 for another good example of the LXX providing a reading that is superior.

---

[27]Wilhelm Gesenius' Hebräisches und Aramäisches Handwörterbuch über das Alte Testament, F. Buhl (Berlin: Gottingen, Heidelberg: Springer-Verlag, 1949).

No general rule can be formulated on how to use these ancient versions. Each line of each text must be independently evaluated, and even then room must be left for difference of opinion. More than is generally realized, the Syriac Peshitta version translated directly from the Hebrew, and shows an understanding of numerous rare Hebrew forms or words. Like the LXX, even where it gives an erroneous translation, the Syriac may confirm the consonants of the MT. Such is the case in Job 35:11, where the Syriac reads *mn qdm* ("from before"), as if the Hebrew read *millipnê* ("from before"). This confirms the consonants of the MT, where we have a contracted form of the root *'lp* ("teach"; cf. Notes on 35:11).

The MT is still overwhelmingly the best source for the text of Job. This conclusion receives additional support from the several pieces of a lost Targum (Aramaic paraphrase) of Job found in Cave 11 at Qumran and published in 1971. The Aramaic of this Qumran Targum appears to be from some time in the second century B.C., though the document may not have received its present form until the first century A.D.[28] The MT order of chapters 24–27, which scholars have disputed (see comments below), is confirmed by this Targum; and the document ends the book at 42:11 in contrast to the LXX, which adds a lengthy and highly interpretative paragraph beyond v.17 of the MT. The document proves some Targumic material was already written down in pre-Christian times. Since the Targums were the Jewish community's attempt to put the Scriptures in a language the people could understand, it may be that the Book of Job was chosen early-on because of its great difficulty.

Studies in comparative Semitic linguistics have shed light on rarer meanings and unusual grammar and often supported the MT. Evidence for this will be supplied in the Notes along with the commentary. An unknown nuance or little known homonym may be obscured by a very common meaning of a word. An interesting example is in the last line of Job 30:13. Following many scholars BHS suggests emending the word *'ōzēr* ("one helping") to *'ōṣēr* ("one hindering"). The RSV's "no one restrains them" did not need to follow this emendation, for G.R. Driver had already pointed out that in both Arabic and Akkadian *'zr* can mean "hinder."[29] So the presence of *'zr* as a homonym or as a verb with opposite meanings—"help" and "hinder"–is likely (Pope, p. 221). The Hebrew text needs no adjustment. The NIV rejected this option, but its footnote shows uneasiness about the choice.

In the Massora (notes of the Jewish scribes of the Middle Ages) we have information concerning several places in Job where the pre-Masoretic scribes emended the text for theological reasons. These *Tiqqune sopherim* (Guides for the Scribes) should be seriously considered for establishing the original text. One of these is in Job 7:20, where the simple omission of one Hebrew letter kaph (*k*) made Job say, "I have become a burden to myself" (cf. KJV), instead of "Have I become a burden to you" (cf. RSV, NIV, also LXX). The latter was felt by the scribes to verge on blasphemy; so the pronoun "you" was dropped, but a record was kept.

Another example in 32:3 is an even more substantive change. It lacks the support

---

[28]J.P. van der Ploeg and A.S. van der Woude, *Le Targum de Job de la Grotte XI de Qumrân* (Leiden: E.J. Brill, 1971). For a brief evaluation in English, see Pope, pp. XLV–XLVI; cf. also A. York, *A Philological and Textual Analysis (11Qtg Job)*, Univ. Microfilms International (Ann Arbor, Mich.: University of Michigan Press, n.d.); M. Sokoloff, *The Targum to Job from Qumran Cave XI* (Ramot-Gan, Israel: Bar Ilan University, 1974).

[29]"Problems in Job," AJSL 52 (1935-36): 163.

of the LXX; so the NIV has stayed with the MT, which says, "and yet had condemned Job." Again this was considered blasphemous (see Notes in loc.); so "Job" was substituted for "God."[30] That there are only eighteen such emendations in the entire Hebrew Bible, and that a record was kept of them is a tribute to the Masoretic diligence in preserving the text they had inherited.

Frequently the Masoretes put in their marginal notes variants that came about when they observed a difference between texts coming from the two Masoretic schools (the Eastern and Western) or even within a school. These are usually minor vocalization or accent variants. Rarely a Qere (what is read) will substantively change the meaning of the Kethiv (what is written). An example of such a substantive change may be found in the last word of 19:29 (see Notes). On even rarer occasions our increased lexical knowledge (from extrabiblical sources) enables us to revocalize (make a different choice of vowels) the correctly preserved consonants and thus make good sense of the text. See for example 28:11: *mibbᵉkî* does not mean "from overflowing (weeping)," as in the KJV, but refers to the "sources" of the rivers (see Notes).

6. Purpose

The purpose of the Book of Job cannot be reduced to a single simple statement. The author appears to have had a multifaceted purpose under the general theme of wisdom teaching about God and human suffering. The various parts of the book speak with somewhat different purposes in mind. The Prologue teaches the wisdom of man's total submission to the will of his Creator. The reader views the drama from the divine perspective where he learns of God's secret purpose to expose the falsehood of the Accuser and prove Job's faith. The Dialogue, on the other hand, gives the human perspective. Job knows nothing of what transpired in the heavenly council. The author's purpose is to teach the believing community some profound lessons positively and negatively about honesty and reality in our relationship with God and about man's limited knowledge of the divine purposes. Here we see a deeper probing into the problem of evil than current views of theodicy had gone.

The author of the Book of Job purposes to show how the theological position of Job's friends represents a shallow and only partial observation of life; that is, man's suffering is always in proportion to his sins. Overall there is no studied attempt to justify God with regard to the suffering of the innocent. But the author finally demonstrates that God does not abandon the sufferer but communicates with him at the proper time.

Another subsidiary purpose of the book is to show that though men are often sinful, weak, and ignorant, they can, like Job, be relatively pure and upright even when in the midst of physical distress, emotional turmoil, and spiritual testing. In the divine speeches the purpose is to prove to Job that God is Creator and Sustainer of all things and yet is willing to communicate with Job as his friend and not his enemy, as Job had imagined him to be. While this does not answer all Job's questions, it is really all Job needs to know.

---

[30]For more information see C.D. Ginsburg, *Introduction to the Masseretico-Critical Edition of the Hebrew Bible,* 1897 reprint (New York: KTAV, 1966), pp. 347–67.

Satan was permitted to afflict Job and then test him through the instrumentality of would-be helpers who used all the words of traditional piety. Job's major problem was this vexing question of theodicy. How can God be both good and sovereign in the light of the suffering of the innocent and the prospering of the wicked? The book pursues a middle course between the concepts of an evil deity on the one hand and a limited deity on the other. But there is no attempt to give a rational or philosophical solution. The picture is the same as that given in Genesis where the Serpent (Satan) as a creature of God subject to his will is also in rebellion. Here the Accuser bears the responsibility for Job's trouble, though he is permitted to do so by God. The problem of theodicy is left on the note that God in his omnipotence and omniscience can and does use secondary means to bring about his higher and perfect purposes. One such purpose in Job's suffering is to humiliate the Accuser, proving Job's devotion to God is pure.

Initially Job stands the test even when his wife says, "Curse God and die!" (2:9). But as his troubles multiply, Job has second thoughts; he wrestles with God, challenges God, and sinks into depths of despair, with moments of trust and confidence, only to fall again into despair. Throughout Job defends his own essential innocence (not sinlessness) against the view of his friends, who rarely move from the single theme that suffering is the immediate corollary of sin, and that because Job has grievously sinned God has become his enemy. But Job's own view of why he is suffering is in a state of flux. So he says many unfortunate things and yet in it all does not do what Satan said he would; he does not curse God to his face (2:5).

While the counselors make no progress in their arguments, Job grows somewhat less belligerent. He appears to us to be self-righteous in his peroration (chs. 29–31), but this must be understood in its cultural context. He persistently calls for an audience with God to argue his case. He also calls for a friend in heaven to plead his cause at the divine tribunal. He is confident he will be vindicated (13:18; 19:26). The counselors consistently stand on God's side, sometimes uttering beautiful hymns; but they could not seem to move from their fallacious notion that the righteous always prosper and sinners always suffer and, conversely, that suffering proves sinfulness and prosperity proves righteousness.

Eliphaz is not quite so crass; but he still insists that though the righteous suffer a little and the unrighteous prosper a little, the righteous never come to an untimely end (4:7; 5:16–19), and the wicked even when they prosper are in dread of calamity (15:20–26). Bildad is convinced that Job's children died for their sins and warns Job that he will receive the same fate unless he gets right with God (8:4–6). Zophar is bent on denouncing Job as a mocker of God. Job's suffering is ample proof of his sinfulness, and repentance is his only hope (11:13–15).

Much of what Job's counselors said is theologically sound and true in the abstract, but it did not necessarily apply to Job. It is not so much what they say but what they leave out that makes their counsel so shallow. They all finally reach the conclusion that Job is obstinate and that his refusal to humble himself and repent proves he has committed sins of great enormity. The OT accounts of the innocent sufferers Abel, Uriah, Naboth et al. question this simplistic approach. Jesus, of course, taught his disciples that the innocent do suffer to accomplish God's higher purpose. "Neither this man nor his parents sinned," said Jesus of a man born blind (John 9:3), "but this happened so that the work of God might be displayed in his life."

Some have suggested that normative OT theology also teaches the counselors' erroneous view. For example, Psalm 1:3 says of the righteous, "Whatever he does prospers"; and Psalm 37:25 says, "I was young and now I am old,/ yet I have never seen the righteous forsaken/ or their children begging bread." The tension is real; but the discrepancy is superficial since the Psalms are not making specific applications, as were the counselors of Job, but are expressing general truth. Job agonized over how to integrate this general truth with his own experience. He had no answer, for he did not have the heavenly perspective given in the Prologue. Therefore he blew hot and cold. Sometimes he blamed the Lord for tormenting him (13:21, 25) and wished God would leave him alone (7:17–21; 10:20; 19:22). At other times he yearned for God to communicate with him (14:15) that he might be vindicated (13:15). Job's emotional instability arose from his internal conflict over the fantasy that God was unjustly punishing him for sins he had not committed (9:21–24). So there are moments when he perceives God to be his enemy (7:20; 10:16–17; 16:9).

As noted, the book does not attempt to formulate a rational solution to the problem of evil, especially that aspect of the problem that tries to relate God's goodness and sovereignty to the suffering of the innocent. Although Job is exercised about God's justice, his ultimate concern is more practical than theoretical. His practical concern is not healing and restoration but his own vindication as an upright man. Job does not ask for rational answers; nor does God give such to him when he appears, though Job is finally vindicated (42:7–9). There were no heinous sins for which he was being punished. When God does rebuke Job, it is for his ignorance (38:2) and presumption while arguing his case (42:2), not for a profligate life. God is apparently telling Job in chapters 38–41 that man does not know enough about God's ways to make judgments concerning his justice.

In his appearance to Job, God ignores the problem of theodicy. He gives no rational explanation or excuse for Job's suffering, but Job is not crushed; he is only rebuked and then shown to be basically right while the friends are condemned for their presumptive and arrogant claim to a knowledge of God's ways (42:7). Job thus realizes that God does not need man's advice to control the world and that no extreme of suffering gives man the right to question God's wisdom or justice, and on this he repents (42:2–6).[31] On seeing the power and glory of God, Job's rebellious attitude dissolves and his resentment disappears. Job now gets what he sought for. His friends do not see him pronounced guilty; so their view of his suffering is refuted.

Job is not told why God tested him. He comes to accept God on God's own terms; and while we know the full story, Job had to walk by faith even after he was vindicated. That God never impugns Job's character proves that Satan has failed and that Job's testing has come to an end. Though he has not demanded restoration, God, having achieved his higher purpose through Job, now restores him. Job in his suffering, despite moments of weakness, surpassed in righteousness his detractors who had not suffered as he had. After all his doubts and bitterness, Job arrived at that point of spiritual maturity where he could pray for those who abused him (42:10; cf. Luke 6:28).

The issues raised in the book are among the most profound and difficult of human existence. The answer was already on Job's lips in the Prologue when he said, "The LORD gave and the LORD has taken away;/ may the name of the LORD be praised"

---

[31]On Job's repentance see the discussion in the commentary on 42:2–6.

(1:21b); and "Shall we accept good from God, and not trouble?" (2:10). The truth Job learned was that God must be God and that of all values and all existence only God and his glory must ultimately prevail.

7. Major Characters

a. Job

Apart from the Bible nothing is known of Job. He was not an Israelite and showed no knowledge of the covenant between Yahweh and his chosen people. Indeed there is not in the book the slightest hint of any acquaintance with the history of the Hebrew people. There is, however, no good reason to question Job's historicity as a well-to-do patriarch who lived east of the Jordan at a time before the emergence of the Hebrews as a nation.

The English name "Job" comes from the Greek *Iōb*, which derives from the Hebrew form '*iyôb*. Earlier attempts to determine an etymology of the name have given way to evidence from a well-attested west Semitic name in the second millennium found in the Amarna Letters, Egyptian Execration texts, Mari, Alalakh, and Ugaritic documents. The original form of the name was '*Ayyāb(um)*, which can mean "Where is [my] father?" or possibly "no father." Either form might suggest an orphan or illegitimacy. The word '*iy*, from an original '*ay* ("where" or "no"), was often connected with other substantives such as "brother" ('*ah*) instead of "father" ('*āb*). Compare the name Ichabod ('*î-kābôd*), which might be translated "no-glory" (1 Sam 4:21 mg.). In the Hebrew '*iyôb* a weak aleph (glottal stop) between vowels is dropped out.[32]

Job assumes two roles, but this does not imply there are two "Jobs" as critics have often maintained. The author of this masterly work was not that clumsy. He had purpose in the apparent discrepancy between Job's role as one who "did not sin in what he said" (2:10) and his role as the protester who shocked the somewhat discreet Eliphaz into saying, "Your own mouth condemns you. . . . you vent your rage against God" (15:6, 13). Job in either of these roles alone would have produced just another statement on suffering, of which there were many in the ancient world. What lifts the book to literary and theological greatness is the author's deft presentation of a truly righteous man whose commitment to God is total, yet who can still struggle with God to the point of rage over the mystery of God's ways. Job does not know what the reader knows—that God honors him by testing, thus expressing his total confidence in Job. But Job must remain ignorant of this for it to be genuine. For the intended message of the book, the raging Job is just as important as the patient Job. In his suffering Job served God supremely, not as a stoic, but as a feeling man who had to come to terms with the mystery of the divine will.

b. The Three Counselors

These men play a unique role. They have the same underlying theory of suffering, but each develops his case against Job in his own way.

---

[32]For extrabiblical sources see Pope, pp. 5–6. For the negative meaning of '*iy*, cf. Notes on 22:30.

1) *Eliphaz*

Based on a variety of passages, we have good reason to believe Eliphaz was an Edomite. According to Genesis 36:4, a man named Eliphaz was the firstborn of Esau, the progenitor of the Edomites, and Teman was his son (v.11). A number of prophets mention Teman as a place, an Edomite city or district (Jer 49:7, 20; Ezek 25:13; Amos 1:12; Obad 8–9). Jeremiah assumes Teman was known for its wisdom. The site may be the same as the Arabian town of Tema mentioned in Babylonian sources.[33] Apparently Eliphaz was the senior member since he spoke first. Throughout his speeches, at least till his final speech in chapter 22, he shows a broader spirit than the others, accepting Job as a pious man gone astray. Though failing in compassion, he alone of the three showed some consideration and respect.

2) *Bildad*

This non-Hebrew name is not mentioned in any other OT book. Bildad considers Job's struggle over the justice of God as blasphemy and uses his erudition, his knowledge of ancient wisdom tradition, to prove to Job that his family got what they deserved and warns him about a similar doom. Genesis 25:2, 6 provides some helpful information about his tribe, the Shuites. They were descendants of Abraham through Keturah and inhabitants of "the land of the east." There is a land of *Suhu* on the Middle Euphrates mentioned in Assyrian records (ANET, *passim*); but apart from a possible phonetic problem, Genesis 25:3 suggests this tribe lived near Dedan, which Jeremiah locates near Tema and Buz (Jer 25:23), far from the Euphrates. Bildad's name is probably a combination of Bil (*ba'al*, "Lord"; cf. LXX Baldad) and Adad (Hadad, Dadda), the well-known storm god. Compare Ben-hadad, the Aramean royal name, and the Edomite kings Hadad the son of Bedad (Gen 36:35) and Baal-Hanan (v.38).

3) *Zophar*

Zophar is from Naamah, but not the little Israelite town in the western foothills (Josh 15:41). The LXX took the liberty to identify him with a known kingdom, calling him Zophar the king of the Minaeans (2:11; 11:1; 20:1; 42:9), which has led to the conjecture that there was a transposition of the consonants n and m in the MT. This is not likely. The LXX also has Zophar for Zepho the son of Eliphaz ben Esau (Gen 36:11, 15). The fact is that scholars cannot agree on either the derivation of Zophar's name nor the location of the place. But it must have been somewhere in north Arabia or Edom. Dhorme (p. xxvii) gives several possible locations based on data from Eusebius's *Onomasticon* and from topographical surveys. Zophar was the most caustic of the counselors. His message to Job was repent or die the horrible death the wicked deserve.

4) *Elihu*

This character appears only in chapters 32–37, where his speeches are recorded. Some critics have banished him as nongenuine, a late addition, etc. He has the distinction of having his father's name recorded, which G.B. Gray (Driver and Gray,

---

[33]cf. W.F. Albright, "The Name of Bildad the Shuhite," AJSL 44 (1927–28): 36.

1:278) takes as evidence of different authorship. It is just as likely that the name "Barakel the Buzite" (32:2) is given to identify Elihu as one whose father was a leading figure in a clan more closely related to Job. Uz and Buz were brothers according to Genesis 22:21. Elihu's name means "He is my God" and is the only one of the five (including Job) used by Israelites (cf. 1 Sam 1:1; 1 Chron 12:20; 26:7; 27:18). The Aramaisms in Elihu's speeches fit the statement that Buz was the son of Abraham's brother Nahor whose son Laban speaks Aramaic (Gen 31:47). Elihu gives his youth as the reason he dared not speak while the older men held forth. The character of his speeches and the author's intended use of them will be discussed later.

8. Mythopoeic Language

The Book of Job, like a microcosm of the OT, bears witness to the will and purpose of the one God who created and rules over nature and all creatures, especially his crowning work of creation—man. In Genesis 3, as a result of the work of the Tempter, God put in effect the death penalty of Genesis 2:17. But only the Tempter, the Serpent, is cursed. Along with immediate punitive effects, man suffers alienation from God as a token of the death penalty.

The Book of Job brings us a step closer to the mystery of godliness by adding a new dimension to the concept of punitive suffering. The ancient Near Eastern documents from Babylonia and Egypt agree with this punitive aspect of suffering but, as mentioned above, are shallow in the way they deal with the problem. In those documents man must humble himself before the gods who are often perverse, or not interested, or they are incapacitated. Job's problem is the opposite. He thinks God is too interested and too powerful for him. Job is a strict monotheist (9:8; 23:13). He disavows any false worship (31:26–28) and yet was knowledgeable of many mythological concepts of the pagan religions current in the ancient Semitic world.

H.W. Wolff says:

> The more distinctly the old Oriental religions are reconstructed before our eyes, the more clearly we see that the O.T. actively resists the attempt to understand it in analogy to the cults of its environment. This is all the more surprising since the connection of Israel with its environment in matters of a general world view, of profane and sacral usage, of Cultic institutions, yes even of prophetic phenomena, is constantly becoming clearer.[34]

To this may be added the observation that the mythological elements in Job conform remarkably well with the religious expressions from contemporary sources. But careful attention to certain features in context will show that any special problem these allusions may appear to pose for the monotheistic outlook of the author of this book is superficial.

Our present purpose is to defend this last statement. Here we use the term *myth*

---

[34]"The Hermeneutics of the Old Testament," in C. Westermann, ed., *Essays on Old Testament Hermeneutics*, tr. J.L. Mays (Atlanta: John Knox, n.d.), p. 167.

in its traditional sense, not as another way of expressing the truth,[35] but as the way a polytheistic people understood deity. In this sense, to see wide mythological commitment, as some have been prone to do,[36] results in as much misinterpretation as does the attempt to ignore mythological expression to protect the Scriptures from such "contamination." Reading primitive meaning into a piece of monotheistic literature because the language is infused with the idiom of a primitive substratum is poor methodology. It is true that sometimes it is impossible to tell when the terms are mere figures and when they represent the view of the speaker.[37] We must be guided by the thrust of the context.

The language of mythology is inherent in every language from every age and is often used in religious contexts that are strongly monotheistic.[38] The Jews in Babylon borrowed pagan festival names for their religious calendar. Fanatically monotheistic Jews embellished their synagogues with zodiacal mosaics borrowed from Roman art depicting the sun god riding his chariot.[39] Matthew 12:24 uses the pagan deity name Beelzebub (2 Kings 1:3) for Satan simply as an idiom without a thought given to its origin. Isaiah and Ezekiel, both monotheists, were prone to using mythological allusion as a vehicle through which they communicated their messages.[40]

Nature is a theme that frequently evoked mythological language: the storm, fire, the sea, the heavens and the earth, and creatures in both spheres. Job 3:8 begins with a reference to an occult practice involving the celebrated Leviathan. Regarding the day of his birth, Job says, "May those who curse days curse that day,/ those who are ready to arouse Leviathan."

Dhorme (p. 29) says that "Those who curse days" may refer to other sufferers like Job who also cursed the day of their birth. But in light of the parallelism, the expression more likely refers to professional cursers like Balaam. Job appears to be making a play on the similar sound of the words yām ("sea") and yōm ("day") and the parallel between Leviathan, the sea monster, and the Yam as a deity in Canaanite mythology.

Job, in a cursing mood, employs the most vivid and forceful proverbial language available to call for the obliteration of that day.[41] There is no way of knowing how valid Job considered the work of such cursers, but in his negative confession Job presents himself as a monotheist who rejected current mythological conceptions of the sun (31:26–28). Job's error, for which he can scarcely be excused, was in damning the day of his birth, questioning the sovereign purpose of God. But we must not be like his friends who failed to understand his frustration. He felt

---

[35]John L. McKenzie ("Myth and the Old Testament," CBQ 21 [1959]: 265–82), following Cassirer, defines myth in this way; but it assumes a unique set of presuppositions.

[36]Pope seems to take this position. He takes issue with Gordis's statement that Job takes monotheism for granted (Pope, p. XXXIX).

[37]See quote from Gaster below.

[38]John Milton drew heavily on Greek mythology to enrich his poetic imagery even in his picture of Creation.

[39]Rachel Hachlili, "The Zodiac in Ancient Jewish Art: Representation and Significance," BASOR 228 (1977): 61ff.

[40]Isa 14 and 27; Ezek 28.

[41]Although the NEB renders 3:8b "those whose magic binds even the monster," the same stem of the verb 'ûr means "to rouse" the dead in Sheol in Isa 14:9.

constrained to speak out what he truly felt and so came perilously close to cursing God to his face as Satan had predicted.

Many of Job's words then are not normative, that is, they were not meant to teach a doctrine but are to show us the extent of Job's disturbance. Even where a passage may be considered normative, however, mythic language may be used.

These mythological expressions uniquely serve the purpose of the book. The way they are used sometimes reverses the effect of the polytheism and shows that Job's God is the Sovereign Lord over all creation. Notice what Job says in 9:13: "God does not restrain his anger;/ even the cohorts of Rahab cowered at his feet." Who are these cohorts of Rahab? Are they literal sea monsters? Why then is God angry with them? It is more likely a metaphor describing those great cosmic powers that oppose God's will.

Sometimes these terms are simple metaphors, and at other times the biblical author is consciously antimythologizing. Psalm 121 appears to be, for example, a polemic against the hill shrines and the notion of many patron deities. Since the pagan deities are no-gods (Ps 5:4), where can one turn for help? The psalmist says (121:1):

> I lift up my eyes to the hills—
> where does my help come from?
> My help comes from the LORD,
> the Maker of heaven and earth.

The psalmist goes on (vv.5, 7) to reinforce this with his concept of the Lord as the only true patron deity:

> He will not let your foot slip—
> he [Yahweh] who watches over you will not slumber;
> ....
> The LORD will keep you from all harm.

We think immediately of Eliphaz's taunt of Job in 5:1:

> Call if you will, but who will answer you?
> To which of the holy ones will you turn?

The "holy ones" are the *benê hā'elōhîm* ("the sons of God") of the Prologue.

The divine council concept may be considered an ideologic continuity with Canaanite religion,[42] but the author of Job and Psalms 82 and 89:5–8 have introduced a discontinuity in the way they handle the concept. The discontinuity can be appreciated in terms of the Hebrew hierarchy of *'elōhîm* (godlike beings). There is only one Creator—all the *qehal qedōšîm* ("council of holy ones") fear him and none can be compared with him (89:7–8). Men are *'elōhîm* to the animals, rulers and judges are *'elōhîm* to ordinary men, and the heavenly beings are *'elōhîm* to men.

In the Canaanite mythology there were lesser divine beings created by the cosmic gods to serve them. They were sometimes available as patron deities or personal intercessors and were generally lackeys in the divine assembly. In Job 33:23 Elihu speaks of such an intercessor, calling him a *mal'āk*[43] ("messenger"; NIV, "angel") and a *mēlîṣ* ("interpreter"; NIV, "mediator"). Both Job and his friends believe that

---

[42]See H.L. Ginsberg's translation of Ugaritic mythological texts in ANET, pp. 130–55.

[43]The same term is used in Ugaritic for the lackey gods; cf. A. Herdner, *Corpus des tablettes en cuneiformes alphabetiques decouvertes à Ras Shamra-Ugarit de 1929 à 1939* (Paris: Imprimere Nationale, 1963), 1.2.17–21; 3.4.76–80 et al.; also C. Gordon, UT, 137:40–41; cf. ANET, p. 130.

among such "holy ones" a man might find a defender. Three times Job mentions such a one: first as an arbiter (9:33), then as a witness to his integrity (16:19–21), and finally as his (redeemer) vindicator (19:25–27). This is certainly evocative and part of the ideological preparation for the mediatorial work of Christ who could stand between God and man, sharing the nature of each, as Job says in 9:33: "to lay his hand upon us both."

The Book of Job is replete with vivid imagery based on the colorful mythic literature deeply engrained in the language and passed on through generations. There are many themes, but we will only sample a few.

A widely used theme is the quelling of Chaos known in West Semitic literature as Yam ("Sea") and in Babylonia as Tiamat ("the Deep"). The sea monsters variously called Rahab ("the boisterous"), Tannin ("the dragon"), and Leviathan ("the serpent") also play a part.

In 7:12 Job speaks out in anguish over his imagined harassment by God and says: "Am I the sea [Yam] or the monster of the deep [Tannin],/ that you put me under guard?" The tales of the conquest of Yam, Tannin, and Lotan (Leviathan) by Baal and Anat are well-known (ANET, pp. 137–38). The Babylonian Tiamat is killed by hero gods who then proceed to create the land and sea from the pieces. The West Semitic literature provides no Creation account but stresses the control of the sea by the weather God, Baal (ANET, p. 131). Job and his friends knew well the West Semitic myths. But they were not committed to them as part of their view of deity. This we know from the total thrust of their words.

A look at the Chaos terminology in the first part of chapter 9 will help us capture the thrust of Job's concept of deity. According to Job, El (one of Job's epithets for God) is indeed the God of profound wisdom and cosmic force and as such is too much for mere man. In vv.5–13 he moves mountains and shakes the earth off its foundations—the earthquake. He speaks and the sun does not rise—the eclipse. He seals up the stars from sight—movement of the stars and planets. He stretches out the heavens and tramples on the back of Yam (bom°tê yām; NIV, "the waves of the sea")—creation and the overcoming of Chaos. He made the Bear, Orion, Pleiades, and the southern chambers; and when he is angry even the cohorts of Rahab (the boisterous sea-monster) cower at his feet. Job here described his Deity as one who is unique and all powerful when compared with the description of any single contemporary god.

The Ugaritic El (the head of the pantheon) is a character variously represented. Sometimes he is a forceful patriarch living in a tent, at other times a frightened deity who is forced to give up the young Baal to the messengers of Yam. Baal can take things in his own hands and destroy Yam with the weapons supplied by the craftsman god, Kothar wa-Hasis (ANET, p. 131). But then Baal is killed by Mot. The issue is always sovereignty. El and the divine assembly are faced with the question of ascribing kingship to Yam. Baal asserts kingship, not only by eliminating Yam, but by demonstrating his power in the storm. This West Semitic story was imported to the east where Marduk, chosen as king by the gods, asserts kingship by slaying Tiamat.[44]

---

[44]Yahweh's lordship over Chaos is the theme of Ps 29. There the benê 'ēlim are called to honor the one who controls and sits enthroned forever over the flood (29:10).

The point is that Job's God assumes all the functions of the gods, whether Baal, El, or Yam. Job's El is never subordinated to any of the *benê hā'elōhîm* ("sons of God"). In 9:8 he exercises his creative power all by himself (*lebaddô*). The line in Hebrew is the same as a line in Isaiah 44:24. He is not only a deity who does not share his power and authority, but he performs his numberless wonders while being invisible (v.11): "When he passes me, I cannot see him;/ When he goes by, I cannot perceive him."

The psalmist expresses a similar discontinuity in Psalm 89:5–8:

> The heavens praise your wonders, O LORD,
>   your faithfulness too, in the assembly of the holy ones.
> For who in the skies above can compare with the LORD?
>   Who is like the LORD among the heavenly beings?
> In the council of the holy ones God is greatly feared;
>   he is more awesome than all who surround him.
> O LORD God Almighty, who is like you?
>   You are mighty, O LORD, and your faithfulness
>   surrounds you.

As in Job and Isaiah, this theme is linked to God as Creator; for it is precisely at this point the psalmist describes the LORD (Yahweh) as Creator of the heavens and earth and the one who rules over the surging sea, crushing Rahab and all his enemies. In his creating and saving power he is unique and incomparable.

The psalmist's God also had that mysterious quality of invisibility. Was it not this quality that disturbed his idolatrous contemporaries when they chided, "Where is your God?" (42:3, 10; 79:10). Psalm 115:2 reads:

> Why do the nations say,
>   "Where is their God?"
> Our God is in heaven;
>   he does whatever pleases him.
> But their idols are silver and gold,
>   made by the hands of men.

Even though the Hebrew God is invisible, he exists in heaven and is supreme. Job likewise asserts that God is both invisible and all powerful.

Turning to another theme, in Job 5:7 most translations read: "Yet man is born to trouble/ as surely as sparks fly upward." A more literal translation is "Man is born to trouble/ as sure as Resheph's sons soar aloft."

Who are "Resheph's sons"? Is this a metaphor for flames, sparks, or lightning? Resheph is equated with Nergal, the Mesopotamian god of pestilence and the nether world. In Deuteronomy 32:24 the word is parallel with *qeteb* ("destruction") and in Habakkuk 3:5 with *deber* ("pestilence"), and the plural is used of lightning in Psalm 78:48. In Psalm 76:4, however, "the reshephs" ("arrows") of the bow are in apposition to the shield, the sword, and the battle. Resheph, like Baal, is a thunder god and a god of battle. In Ugaritic Resheph is called "Lord of the arrow," either referring to his skillful use of lightning or his attendance on arrows in flight. Just as death's firstborn (Job 18:13) devours the bodies of wicked men, so here the sons of Resheph are active troublemakers.

On Resheph, T.H. Gaster observes: "When *Resheph* is said (Hab 3:5) to attend upon Yahweh, or when the pangs of love are described as 'fiery *reshephs*' (Song of Songs 8:6), do the writers really have in mind the figure of the Canaanite plague-god of that name, or is this simply a case of metonymy? This is a problem which I will not even attempt to resolve, but it must at least be mentioned."[45]

From my point of view, Gaster is asking the wrong question. It makes little difference whether the figure of the plague god is in mind or not. Habakkuk is using a highly anthropomorphic figure of Yahweh. The real questions are Did Habakkuk believe Yahweh existed in the form of a warrior? and Did Job and Habakkuk believe Resheph or Resheph's sons really existed as gods? That must be answered in the light of other things these writers say.

Job 26 is replete with mythological allusions—the denizens of Sheol, Zaphon the cosmic mountain, Yam, and Rahab—all in a cosmography with some rather sophisticated observations. Verses 5–14 may be translated:

> The spirits of the dead write,
>   the Waters below and their denizens.
> Sheol is naked in God's presence,
>   Abaddon is uncovered.
> He spreads out Zaphon over emptiness;
>   he hangs the earth on nothing.
> He wraps up the waters in his clouds;
>   yet the clouds do not burst under the weight.
> He covers the face of the full moon
>   spreading his clouds over it.
> He marks out the horizon on the face of the waters
>   for a boundary between light and darkness.
> The pillars of the heavens quake
>   stunned at his rebuke.
> By his power he churned up the sea,
>   by his skill he pierced Rahab.
> By his breath the skies become fair;
>   his hand pierced the gliding serpent.
> And these are only the outer fringes of his power;
>   how faint the whisper we hear of him!
> Who then can understand the thunder of his might?

Buttenweiser commenting on v.7 (in loc.) said:

> Our author, though naturally ignorant of the law of gravitation, had outgrown the naive view of his age about the universe, and conceived of the earth as a heavenly body floating in space, like the sun, moon, and stars. It is not surprising to meet with such a view in the book of Job when one considers the advanced astronomy in Babylonia, Egypt, and Greece. As early as 540–510 B.C. Pythagoras of Samos, in his travels in Egypt and the East, acquired the knowledge of the obliquity of the ecliptic and of the earth's being a sphere freely poised in space. . . . Job 38:6 bears out rather than contradicts the conclusion that the writer of Job had attained a more advanced view of the universe, since the question, "Whereon were its foundations set?" shows that he no longer shared the primitive notion that the earth was resting on pillars erected in the sea.

Both Buttenweiser and Dhorme contend "the north" (ṣāpôn, 26:7) is the celestial pole formed by the seven stars of Ursa Minor from which the movement of the universe was believed to proceed. Two observations are needed. First, the cosmography is not in itself the purpose of the passage. Again God's power is in focus.

---

[45]*Myth, Legend and Custom in the Old Testament*, p. xxxvi, as quoted in Michel, p. 8.

Second, we cannot ignore what Ugaritic literature tells about Mount Zaphon as the Canaanite Olympus.[46]

The cosmic-mountain concept is related to Sinai as the place God reveals himself from and Zion as God's dwelling place.[47]

Psalm 48:1–2 says:

> Great is the LORD, and most worthy of praise,
>   in the city of our God, his holy mountain.
> It is beautiful in its loftiness,
>   the joy of the whole earth.
> Like the utmost heights of Zaphon is Mount Zion,
>   the city of the Great King.

Eschatological Zion in Isaiah 2:2–4 is the place where the Lord's house is established at the head of the mountains with all the nations flowing to it, where the Lord is enthroned and rules over a world of universal peace (cf. Isa 24:23).

The passage that most closely approximates Job 26:7 is Isaiah 14:13–14. Here the king of Babylon desires to place himself where the Most High dwells. We translate it:

> You said in your heart,
> "I will ascend to heaven;
>   above the stars of God;
> I will set my throne on high;
>   I will sit on the mount of assembly.
> On the slopes of Zaphon,
>   I will ascend above the heights of the clouds;
> I will make myself like the Most High."

There is a difference in the way the two passages (Job 26:7; Isa 14:13–14) use Zaphon. In the mouth of the pagan king, it is used quite literally to mean the mount of assembly that indeed reaches into the heavens and is the divine abode. But in Job the choice of words points to metonymy. This is the conclusion Clifford makes in a similar observation: "Zaphon's meaning seems to be practically 'heavens.' *Nōṭek* elsewhere is used of 'heavens' in the Old Testament and it forms a reasonable merism with *'ereṣ* in the passage from Job. It is easy to imagine the development of the meaning of Zaphon, under Israelite impulse, from 'mountain (dwelling of God)' to 'heavens (dwelling of God).'"[48] So the mountain of all mountains is the mountain that God stretched out like a canopy, which is his dwelling place—the heavens.

Even though mythopoeic language is used, there is a hint that the author is demythologizing. In 26:12 he carefully placed the definite article on the word *yam* ("sea"), which shows that he did not consider it a proper name but "the sea."[49]

In this highly figurative language, "the pillars of the heavens" (26:11), like the pillars of the earth (9:6), are the mountains. In both cases God makes them quake. The writer does not have a rigid cosmography. His language is phenomenological, and his purpose is not to tell us how much he knows of the cosmos but how powerful

---

[46]Now called *Mons Casius* due north of Israel. In Canaanite myth the god Baal-Hadad had his marvelous dwelling built there. This explains why the Hebrew word *ṣāpôn* means "north." Compare Negev (dry) for south, Yam (sea) for west.

[47]See Richard J. Clifford, "The Cosmic Mountain in Canaan and the Old Testament," *Harvard Semitic Monographs* 4 (1972).

[48]Ibid., p. 162, n. 85.

[49]In contrast to 7:12, where *yam* is used without the definite article as a name: "Am I Yam?"

God is. Job is saying El is the God of the heavens and the God of the earth—the God of all nature. Stretching out the heavens over emptiness and hanging up the earth on nothing are bold figures derived from actions common to man. The marvel is that he can do these things with nothing for support.

Other marvels of nature are also attributed to his vast power and dominion. He fills the clouds with water, and they do not burst. He uses the clouds as a drape over the face of the full moon.[50] He marks out the circle of the horizon as with cosmic calipers. By a mere word he makes the mountains shake, and by his power he controls the raging sea and its monstrous creatures. All this is only a whisper of his power, only the fringe of his dominion.[51]

As noted above, understanding the mythological background sometimes accomplishes just the opposite of what some assume. Rather than showing ideological commitment to the pagan way of handling the mysteries of nature, it throws the discontinuity into relief and helps us appreciate how monotheistic the writer was. For example, Sheol is the realm of the god Mot (Death) in Ugaritic where Baal enters and is powerless. In 26:6 Sheol is open (NIV, "naked") before God so that its denizens tremble—a uniquely biblical concept that fits only monotheism.

Generally the mythology allots to the gods their separate domains. There are the gods of the heavens and the gods of the earth. With Baal dead, Ashtar, the Rebel god, is permitted by El to attempt to sit on Baal's throne; but not having the stature, he does not succeed and must be content to reign on the earth.[52] Each god is powerful in his own domain. As personifications of nature, they are often in conflict with one another. The hero Baal faces a losing battle with Mot but has victory over Yam. Unlike the Ugaritic El who sires deities but cannot control them, Job's "El" is the sovereign Lord over all natural forces—especially the domains of Mot, Yam, and Baal.

This is what prompts Wolff to write:

> Following the signposts of the OT itself, we must seek to understand it on the basis of the peculiar nature of Yahweh, the God of Israel. In his essence, Yahweh is not a figure of mythology in the sense that one could speak of him in the manner of the myths of the neighboring lands, which chatter so much of the "private life" of their gods and of their life together in the pantheon. Yahweh is the one beside whom no other is god, and before whom all others are shown to be no gods.[53]

On this general subject W.F. Albright has made some cogent remarks, speaking of the OT as a "masterpiece of empirical logic not expressed in formal categories."[54] He claims the OT has demythologized the language on which some Hebrew

---

[50]In 26:9 scholars differ over reading *kissēh* ("throne") or *kēseh* ("full moon"). The latter is on the basis of Ps 81:3 [4 MT] and Prov 7:20. See Gordis, *Job* (in loc.).

[51]As early as 1957 Dahood suggested *derek* sometimes means "power" or "dominion" ("Some Northwest-Semitic Words in Job," *Biblica* 38 [1957]: 306–20). In this he since has been generally supported (Pope, p. 186).

[52]Herdner, *Corpus de tablettes*, 6.1.39–65. Clifford (*Cosmic Mountain*, p. 168) mentions another place where Ashtar does exercise kingship from Zaphon.

[53]"OT Hermeneutics," in Westermann, ed., *Essays*, p. 168.

[54]*History, Archaeology, and Christian Humanism* (New York: McGraw-Hill, 1964), p. 94.

literature is based. "Old words are kept but they have a new meaning, divested of all clear mythological connotations."[55]

There may be partial demythologizing in some cases. On 38:7 Andersen (*Job*, p. 274) says, "It is noteworthy that 11Qtg Job has completed the demythologizing, making the stars shine instead of sing, and calling the *sons* 'angels.'" Is use of the plural in *'elōhîm* ("God") and *'adōnāy* ("Lord") demythologizing? In Hebrew this appears to mean the totality of all the manifestations and attributes of deity that polytheism broke down into single elements. In some Canaanite documents a single high god is referred to with the plural ending, the so-called plural of majesty (Amarna and Ugaritic). The Hebrews had no problem distinguishing between the plural of majesty for the true God and the same plural word for "the gods." Sometimes they are used in the same sentence (cf. Ps 82:1). The Chronicler in postexilic times heard no polytheism in Solomon's words to Hiram king of Tyre when he said, "Our God is greater than all other gods" (2 Chron 2:5; cf. Pss 86:8; 95:3; 136:2). Despite this apparent attributing existence to the gods, Psalm 96:5 says, "For all the gods of the nations are idols."

Albright observes that

> much of the onslaught on early Israelite monotheism comes from scholars who represent certain theological points of view with reference to monotheism, i.e. who deny that orthodox trinitarian Christianity—or orthodox Judaism or orthodox Islam are monotheistic. I do not need to stress the fact that neither of the last two religions can be called monotheistic by a theologian who insists that this term applies only to Unitarian Christianity or liberal Judaism. But no dictionary definition of monotheism was ever intended to exclude orthodox Christianity.[56]

9. Bibliography

Books

Andersen, F.I. *Job, An Introduction and Commentary*. Downers Grove, Ill.: Inter-Varsity, 1976.

Blommerde, A.C.M. *Northwest Semitic Grammar and Job*. Biblica et Orientalia 22. Rome: Pontifical Biblical Institute, 1969.

Buttenwieser, M. *The Book of Job*. London: Hodder and Stoughton, 1922.

Calvin, J. *Sermons from Job*. Selected and translated by L. Nixon. Grand Rapids: Eerdmans, 1952.

Ceresko, A.R. *Job 29–31 in the Light of Northwest Semitic*. Biblica et Orientalia 36. Rome: Pontifical Biblical Institute, 1980.

Cowles, H. *The Book of Job*. New York: Appleton and Company, 1887.

Dahood, M. *Ugaritic-Hebrew Philology*. Rome: Pontifical Biblical Institute, 1965.

Davidson, A.B. *The Book of Job*. Cambridge Bible. Cambridge: Cambridge University Press, 1918.

Delitzsch, F. *Biblical Commentary on the Book of Job*. KD. Reprint. Grand Rapids: Eerdmans, 1971.

Dhorme, E. *A Commentary on the Book of Job*. Paris, 1926. Translated by H. Knight. London: Nelson and Sons, 1967.

Driver, S.R. *The Book of Job in the Revised Version*. Oxford: Clarendon, 1906.

---

[55]Ibid.

[56]*History*, p. 155.

Driver, S.R., and Gray, G.B. *A Critical and Exegetical Commentary on the Book of Job.* ICC. 2d ed. Edinburgh: T. & T. Clark, 1950.

Eerdmans, B.D. *Studies in Job.* Leiden: Burgersdijk and Niermans, 1939.

Ellison, H.L. *From Tragedy to Triumph: The Message of the Book of Job.* Grand Rapids: Eerdmans, 1958.

Ewald, G.H.A. *Commentary on The Book of Job.* Translated by J.F. Smith. 1836. Reprint. Edinburgh: Williams & Norgate, 1882.

Fohrer, G. *Das Buch Hiob.* Gutersloh: G. Mohn, 1963.

Gerleman, G. *The Book of Job.* Studies in the Septuagint. Volume 1. Lund: Gleerup, 1946.

Glatzer, N.N. *The Dimensions of Job.* New York: Schocken, 1969.

Good, E.M. *Irony in the Old Testament.* London: Allenson, 1965, pp. 146–240.

Gordis, R. *The Book of God and Man: A Study of Job.* Chicago: University of Chicago Press, 1966.

———. *The Book of Job: Commentary, New Translation and Special Studies.* New York: KTAV, 1978.

Grabbe, L.L. *Comparative Philology and the Text of Job, A Study of Methodology.* SBL Dissertation Series No. 134. Missoula, Mont.: Scholars, 1975.

Guilleaume, A. *Studies in the Book of Job.* Annual of the Leeds University Oriental Society. Supplement II. Leiden: E.J. Brill, 1968.

Habel, N.C. *The Book of Job.* The Cambridge Bible Commentary on the N.E.B. Cambridge: Cambridge University Press, 1975.

———. *The Book of Job.* The Old Testament Library. Philadelphia: Westminster, 1985.

Hanson, A., and Hanson, M. *The Book of Job.* London Torch Bible Commentary. 1953. Reprint. London: SCM, 1970.

Heater, Homer, Jr. *A Septuagint Translation Technique in the Book of Job.* Catholic Biblical Quarterly Monograph Series 11. Washington, D.C., 1982.

Irwin, W.A. *Job: Peake's Commentary on the Bible.* Edited by M. Black and H.H. Rowley. London: Thomas Nelson and Sons, 1962.

Janzen, J.G. *Job, Interpretation, A Bible Commentary for Teaching and Preaching.* Atlanta: John Knox, 1985.

Jastrow, M., Jr. *The Book of Job.* Philadelphia: J.B. Lippencott, 1920.

Kissane, E.J. *The Book of Job.* Dublin: Browne and Nolan, 1939.

McFadyen, J.E. *The Problem of Pain, A Study in the Book of Job.* London: James Clarke and Co., n.d.

Peake, A.S. *Job.* The Century Bible. Edinburgh: T.C. and E.C. Jack, 1905.

———. *The Problem of Suffering in the Old Testament.* Reprint. London: Epworth, 1947.

Polzin, R., and Robertson, D.A., edd. *Studies in the Book of Job, Semeia 7.* An Experimental Journal for Biblical Criticism. Missoula: Scholars, 1977.

Pope, M.H. *Job.* Anchor Bible. Vol. 15. 3d ed. New York: Doubleday, 1973.

Reichert, V.E. *Job: with Hebrew Text and English Translation.* Hindhead, Surrey: Soncino, 1946.

Robinson, T.H. *Job and His Friends.* London: SCM, 1954.

Rowley, H.H. *The New Century Bible Commentary: The Book of Job.* Grand Rapids: Eerdmans, 1980.

Sanders, P.S. *Twentieth Century Interpretations of the Book of Job.* Englewood, N.J.: Prentice-Hall, 1968.

Snaith, N.H. *The Book of Job, Its Origin and Purpose.* Studies in Biblical Theology. Second Series. London: SCM, 1968.

Stevenson, W.B. *Critical Notes on the Hebrew Text of the Poem of Job.* Aberdeen: University Press, 1951.

Terrien, S. *The Book of Job, Introduction and Exegesis.* The Interpreter's Bible. Vol. 3. New York and Nashville: Abingdon-Cokesbury, 1954.

Tur-Sinai, N.H. *The Book of Job: a New Commentary.* Jerusalem: Kiryath Sepher, 1957.

Vawter, B. *Job and Jonah, Questioning the Hidden God.* New York: Paulist, 1983.

Weiser, A. *Das Buch Hiob*. Göttingen: Vandenhoeck & Ruprecht, 1951.
Westermann, C. *The Structure of the Book of Job, A Form-Critical Analysis*. Philadelphia: Fortress, 1981.

Articles
Aharoni, R. "An Examination of the Literary Genre of the Book of Job." *Tarbiz* 49 (1979): 1–13.
Baker, J. "Commentaries on Job." *Theology* vol. 66, no. 515 (May 1963): 179–85.
Baker, J.A. "The Book of Job: Unity and Meaning." *Studia Biblica 1978 I*. Edited by E.A. Livingstone. Sheffield: JSOT, 1979, pp. 17–26.
Canney, M.A. "The Hebrew *mēlîs*." *American Journal of Semitic Languages and Literatures* 40 (1923–24): 135–37.
Clines, D.J.A. "Job 5:1–8: A New Exegesis." *Biblica* 62 (1981): 185–94.
_____. "The Arguments of Job's Three Friends." *Art and Rhetoric in Biblical Literature*. Edited by J.G. Davies et al. Sheffield: JSOT, 1982, pp. 199–214.
Couroyer, B. "Qui est Behemoth?" *Revue Biblique* 82 (1975): 418–43.
Curtis, J.B. "On Job's Witness in Heaven." *Journal of Biblical Literature* 102:4 (1983): 549–62.
Dahood, M.J. "Some Northwest Semitic Words in Job." *Biblica* 38 (1957): 306–20.
_____. "Northwest Semitic Philology and Job." *The Bible in Current Catholic Thought*. Edited by J.L. McKenzie. New York: Herdner & Herdner, 1962, pp. 55–74.
_____. "Hebrew-Ugaritic Lexicography I–XII." *Biblica* 44 (1963) to 55 (1974).
_____. "The Metaphor in Job 22:22." *Biblica* 47 (1966): 108–9.
_____. "Nest and Phoenix in Job 29:18." *Biblica* 48 (1967): 542–44.
_____. "S'RT 'Storm' in Job 4:15." *Biblica* 48 (1967): 544–45.
_____. "Is the Emendation of *Yādîn* to *Yāzîn* Necessary in Job 36:31?" *Biblica* 53 (1972): 539–41.
_____. "Ugaritic-Phoenician Forms in Job 34:36." *Biblica* 62 (1981): 548–50.
_____. "The Dative Suffix in Job 33:13." *Biblica* 63 (1982): 258–59.
Davidson, A.B., and Toy, C.H. "Job." *Encyclopaedia Britannica*. Eleventh edition. New York: Encyclopaedia Britannica, 1911, 15:422–27.
Dick, M.B. "The Legal Metaphor in Job 31." *Catholic Biblical Quarterly* 41 (1979): 37–50.
DiLella, A. "An Existential Interpretation of Job." *Biblical Theology Bulletin* 15 (1985): 49–55.
Driver, G.R. "Problems in the Hebrew Text of Job." *Supplements to Vetus Testamentum* 3 (1960): 72–93.
Freedman, D.N. "The Structure of Job 3." *Biblica* 49 (1968): 503–8.
_____. "The Elihu Speeches in the Book of Job." *Harvard Theological Revue* 61 (1968): 51–59.
Fullerton, K. "Double Entendre in the First Speech of Eliphaz." *Journal of Biblical Literature* 49 (1930): 320–74.
Gammie, J.G. "Behemoth and Leviathan: On the Didactic and Theological Significance of Job 40:15–41:26." *Israelite Wisdom*. Edited by G.G. Gammie et al. Missoula: Scholars, n.d., pp. 217–31.
Good, E.M. "Job and the Literary Task: A Response." *Soundings* 56 (1973): 470–84.
Gordon, C. "Leviathan: Symbol of Evil." *Biblical Motifs*. Edited by A. Altmann. Cambridge: Harvard University Press, 1966, pp. 1–10.
Gordis, R. "The Temptation of Job: Tradition Versus Experience." *Judaism* 4 (1955): 195–208.
_____. "Elihu, the Intruder." *Biblical and Other Studies*. Edited by A. Altmann (Cambridge: Harvard University Press, 1963), pp. 60–78.
Guilleaume, A. "The Arabic Background of the Book of Job." *Promise and Fulfillment*. Edited by F.F. Bruce. Edinburgh: T. & T. Clark, 1963, pp. 106–27.

———. "The Unity of the Book of Job." *Annual of Leeds University Oriental Society* 4 (1964): 26–46.

Habel, N.C. " 'Naked I Came . . .': Humanness in the Book of Job." *Die Botschaft und die Boten. Festschrift für Hans Wolter Wolff zum 70 Geburtstag.* Edited by E. Jeremias and L. Perlitt. Neukirchen Vluyn: Neukirchener Verlag, 1981, pp. 373–92.

———. "Of Things Beyond Me: Wisdom in the Book of Job." *Currents in Theology and Mission* 10 (1963): 142–54.

———. "The Narrative Art of Job. Applying the Principles of Robert Alter." *Journal for the Study of the Old Testament* 27 (1983): 101–11.

———. "The Role of Elihu in the Design of the Book of Job." *In the Shelter of Elyon: Essays on Palestinian Life and Literature in Honor of G.W. Ahlstrom.* JSOT Supplement 31. Edited by W.B. Barrick and J.S. Spencer. Sheffield: JSOT, 1984.

Harris, R.L. "The Book of Job and Its Doctrine of God." *Grace Journal* 13:3 (1972): 3–33.

Hoffman, Y. "The Use of Equivocal Words in the First Speech of Eliphaz (Job 4–5)." *Vetus Testamentum* 30 (1980): 114–18.

———. "The Relation Between the Prologue and the Speech Cycles in Job: A Reconsideration." *Vetus Testamentum* 31 (1981): 160–70.

———. "Irony in the Book of Job." *Immanuel* 17 (1983/84): 7–21.

Holbert, J.C. " 'The Skies Will Uncover His Iniquity': Satire in the Second Speech of Zophar (Job XX)." *Vetus Testamentum* 31 (1981): 171–79.

Kuyper, L.J. "The Repentance of Job." *Vetus Testamentum* 9 (1959): 91–94.

Laurin, R. "The Theological Structure of Job." *Zeitschrift für die alttestamentliche Wissenschaft* vol. 84, no. 1 (1972): 86–89.

MacKenzie, R.A.F. "The Purpose of the Yahweh Speeches in the Book of Job." *Biblica* 40 (1959): 435–45.

Meek, T.J. "Job 19:25ff." *Vetus Testamentum* 6 (1956): 99–103.

Melamed, E.Z. "Break-Up of Stereotyped Phrases as an Artistic Device in Biblical Poetry." *Scripta Hierosolymitana.* Volume 8. Studies in the Bible. Edited by C. Rabin. Jerusalem: Magnes, 1961.

Moore, R.D. "The Integrity of Job." *Catholic Biblical Quarterly* 45 (1983): 17–31.

Newell, L.B. "Job: Repentant or Rebellious." *Westminster Theological Journal* Fall (1984): 298–316.

O'Conner, D.J. "Job's Final Word—'I am Consoled . . .' (42:6b)." *Irish Theological Quarterly* 50 (1983/84): 181–97.

Orlinsky, H. "Studies in the Septuagint of Job." *Hebrew Union College Annual* 28 (1957): 53–74; 29 (1958): 229–71; 30 (1959): 153–57; 32 (1961): 268–93; 33 (1962): 119–51; 35 (1964): 57–78; 36 (1965): 37–47.

Oswalt, J.N. "The Myth of the Dragon and Old Testament Faith." *Evangelical Quarterly* vol. 49, no. 3 (1977): 163–72.

Patrick, D. "The Translation of Job 42:6." *Vetus Testamentum* 26 (1976): 369–71.

Payne, J.B. "Inspiration in the Words of Job." *The Law and the Prophets. Old Testament Studies in Honor of O.T. Allis.* Edited by J.H. Skilton. Nutley, N.J.: Presbyterian and Reformed, 1974, pp. 319–36.

Polzin, R. "The Framework of the Book of Job." *Interpretation* 28 (1974): 182–200.

Rad, G. von "Job 38 and Ancient Egyptian Wisdom." *The Problem of the Hexateuch and Other Essays.* Edinburgh: Oliver and Boyd, 1966, pp. 281–91.

Raurell, F. "Ètica de Job i llibertat de Déu." *Revista Catalana de Teologia* 4 (1979): 5–24.

Roberts, J.J.M. "Job and the Israelite Religious Tradition." *Zeitschrift für die alttestamentliche Wissenschaft* 89 (1977): 107–14.

Robertson, D. "The Book of Job: A Literary Study." *Soundings* 56 (1973): 446–69.

Rowley, H.H. "The Book of Job and Its Meaning." *Bulletin of the John Rylands Library* 41 (1958): 167–207.

Sanders, J.A. "Suffering as Divine Discipline in the Old Testament and Post-biblical Judaism." *Colgate Rochester Divinity School Bulletin* 38 (1955).

Sarna, N.M. "Epic Substratum in the Prose of Job." *Journal of Biblical Literature* 76 (March 1957): 13–25.

––––––. "The Mythological Background of Job 18." *Journal of Biblical Literature* 88 (1963): 315–18.

Sawyer, J.F.A. "The Authorship and Structure of the Book of Job." *Studia Biblica 1978 I*. Edited by E.A. Livingstone. Supplement Series 11. Sheffield: JSOT, 1979, pp. 253–57.

Scholnick, S.H. "The Meaning of *mišpaṭ* in the Book of Job." *Journal of Biblical Literature* 101 (1982): 521–29.

Shapiro, D.S. "The Problem of Evil and the Book of Job." *Judaism* 5 (1956): 46–52.

Skehan, P.W. "Job's Final Plea (Job 29–31) and the Lord's Reply (Job 38–41)." *Biblica* 45 (1964): 51–62.

––––––. "Strophic Patterns in the Book of Job." *Catholic Biblical Quarterly* (1961): 129–43.

Smick, E.B. "Another Look at the Mythological Elements in the Book of Job." *Westminster Theological Journal* vol. 40, no. 2 (1978): 213–28.

––––––. "Semeiological Interpretation of the Book of Job." *Westminster Theological Journal* 48 (1986): 235–49.

––––––. "Architectonics, Structured Poems, and Rhetorical Devices in the Book of Job." In *A Tribute to Gleason Archer. Essays on the Old Testament*. Edited by W.C. Kaiser, Jr., and R.F. Youngblood. Chicago: Moody, 1986, pp. 87–104.

Terrien, S. "The Yahweh Speeches and Job's Responses." *Review and Expositor* 68 (1971): 497–509.

Thompson, K.T. "Out of the Whirlwind: The Sense of Alienation in the Book of Job." *Interpretation* 14 (1960): 51–63.

Tsevat, M. "The Meaning of the Book of Job." *Hebrew Union College Annual* 37 (1966): 73–106.

Urbrock, W.J. "Oral Antecedents to Job, a Survey of Formulas and Formulaic Systems." *Semeia* 5 (1976): 111–37.

Webster, C.W. "Strophic Patterns in Job 3–28." *Journal for the Study of the Old Testament* 26 (1983): 33–60.

––––––. "Strophic Patterns in Job 29–42." *Journal for the Study of the Old Testament* 30 (1984): 95–109.

Whedbee, W. "The Comedy of Job." *Semeia* 7 (1970): 1–39.

Williams, J.G. " 'You have not spoken truth of me': Mystery and Irony in Job." *Zeitschrift für die alttestamentliche Wissenschaft* 83 (1971): 231–55.

Williams, R.J. "Theodicy in the Ancient Near East." *Catholic Journal of Theology* 2 (1956): 14–26.

Wilson, J.V.K. "A Return to the Problems of Behemoth and Leviathan." *Vetus Testamentum* vol. 25, no. 1 (1975): 1–14.

Zink, J.K. "Impatient Job: An Interpretation of Job 19:25–27." *Journal of Biblical Literature* 84 (1965): 147–52.

Zuckerman, B. "Two Examples of Editorial Modification in 11Qtg JOB." In *Biblical and Near Eastern Studies*. Edited by G.A. Tuttle. Grand Rapids: Eerdmans, 1978, pp. 269–75.

Unpublished Works

Kantz, J.R., III. "A Hermeneutical Study of Job 29–31." Th.D. Dissertation, Southern Baptist Theological Seminary, Louisville, 1970.

Michel, W.L. "The Ugaritic Texts and the Mythological Expressions in the Book of Job." Ph.D. Dissertation, University of Wisconsin, 1970.

Urbrock, W.J. "Evidences of Oral-Formulaic Composition in the Poetry of Job." Ph.D. Dissertation, Harvard University, 1975.

11. Outline

Text and Exposition

I. The Prologue (1:1–2:13)

The Prologue contains some epical features of a story passed on from generation to generation (cf. Sarna, "Prose of Job," pp. 13–25). This does not remove it from the realm of sober history any more than the poetic features of historical psalms, like Psalm 78 or Psalm 106, make them unhistorical. But it does help us appreciate the stylized and therefore identical phraseology of the two interviews with the Accuser (Satan) (1:6–8, 12; 2:1–3, 6–7) and the consummate skill of the storyteller who by repeating the simple phrase "while he was still speaking" (1:16, 17, 18) creates an effective tragic climax. Exegetical awareness of such features can be of value to the preacher and expositor.

The Prologue introduces us to Job as a man of faith and shows how his fortunes on earth were directed by heavenly forces beyond his control. But its full purpose lies even deeper. It is a deliberately planned foundation on which the spiritual message of the book is based. Without this prologue the Job of the dialogues and monologues might justly be considered a man with an insufferable self-righteousness, and the reader would be left without a heavenly perspective much as in the other theodicies of the ancient Near East. With this Prologue the purpose of the book is clarified—to show that in a world where evil is a reality, good people may appear to unjustly suffer, but that such injustice is precipitated by the Accuser and, though permitted by God, it is an expression of God's total confidence that the faith of his servant will triumph.

Job, then, is like the guiltless Sufferer in Psalm 22 and Isaiah 53. His attitude in the Prologue is an OT anticipation of the truth that God's servants are honored when they are "counted worthy of suffering disgrace for the Name" (Acts 5:41). Job started with the triumphant spirit of the postresurrection disciples (1:20–21; 2:10); but like the prophet Jeremiah (20:7–9) and that greatest of prophets John the Baptist (Luke 7:18–20), Job, as a man of like passions, was not above a struggle for faith. This is what creates the dramatic power of the book and provides courage for all faithful sufferers who also struggle to understand the mysteries of divine providence.

The Prologue consists of a series of vignettes. The opening scene introduces Job in his domestic felicity (1:1–5), and the closing scene introduces his three friends who are moved to an extravagant display of mourning over the extent of Job's suffering (2:11–13). In between the scenes shift back and forth from heaven to earth, unveiling the secret purpose for it all—a purpose unknown to Job.

A. Job's Felicity

1:1–5

> ¹In the land of Uz there lived a man whose name was Job. This man was blameless and upright; he feared God and shunned evil. ²He had seven sons and three daughters, ³and he owned seven thousand sheep, three thousand camels, five hundred yoke of oxen and five hundred donkeys, and had a large number of servants. He was the greatest man among all the people of the East.
>
> ⁴His sons used to take turns holding feasts in their homes, and they would invite their three sisters to eat and drink with them. ⁵When a period of feasting had run its course, Job would send and have them purified. Early in the morning

he would sacrifice a burnt offering for each of them, thinking, "Perhaps my children have sinned and cursed God in their hearts." This was Job's regular custom.

1–5 Job is presented as a man who worships (fears) God and shuns evil and whose life is crowned with prosperity. Fearing the Lord and shunning evil (v.1) are the controlling principles of wisdom (28:28). Although the author does not use the term wisdom (*ḥokmāh*) here, this repeated description of Job (1:1, 8; 2:3) labels him a truly wise man. The insertion of an excursus on wisdom in chapter 28 appears to be a deliberate structural feature of the book. Placed between the three cycles of dialogue and the three monologues, it tells the reader how a man so renowned for his wisdom cannot take it for granted. Wisdom is the essence of true religion in this OT literary genre.

That Job was "blameless" (*tām*) and "upright" (*yāšār*) should not be construed to imply he was sinless (cf. 13:26; 14:16–17). The former, from the root "be complete" (*tmm*), usually refers to a person's spiritual maturity and the integrity (purity) of his inner being. The latter, meaning "straight," "right" (*yšr*), is used in many contexts dealing with human behavior that is in line with God's ways. Together they provided an idiomatic way to describe Job's high moral character.

Job lived in Uz, a land somewhere east of Canaan on the edge of the desert (vv.1, 19). He lived in an area where farming could be carried on (v.14) but also near a town (29:7). In v.3 Job's wealth is described in terms similar to those used of the patriarchs, the stress being on animals and servants (Gen 12:16). Job was greater (richer) than any of the people of the East. This shows he was a well-known sage among the easterners. Such easterners may be contrasted with the Mediterranean people who came from the west, like the Philistines. Verse 5 reveals that Job, like the patriarchs, functioned as a priest for his family. He took his sacrificial obligation seriously, viewing it as expiation for sin. To Job this included even sins of the heart, for he made special offerings just in case his sons had secretly cursed God. The matter of cursing God or not cursing God is to be a key theme in the development of this drama.

Notes

1 The idiom אִישׁ הָיָה (*'iš hāyāh*, "there lived a man") indicates that the story has no connection with any earlier event. It is the Hebrew way to begin a totally independent narrative (Dhorme, in loc.).

The following passages tie עוּץ (*'ûṣ*, "Uz") to the Arameans: Gen 10:22–23; 22:21; 1 Chron 1:17. But Gen 36:28; Jer 25:19–21, and Lam 4:21 tie Uz to Edom. The conflict may only be apparent since Gen 10 (1 Chron 1) is a table of nations, and Gen 22:21 deals with Uz before the birth of Esau, the progenitor of the Edomites. Since, as Delitzsch notes, the Arabic name of Esau is *'iṣ*, Uz may be the place in what is now North Arabia where the two cultures (Aramean and Edomite) met or divided from a common origin. *Uṣṣa* in Shalmaneser III's annals is undoubtedly the same place.

5 וּבֵרֲכוּ (*ûbērᵃkû*, lit. "and blessed"; NIV, "and cursed") is an euphemism by the original writer, not a later scribe (so Pope, p. 8). For similar use of original euphemisms (cf. 2 Sam 12:14) in Egyptian documents, see K.A. Kitchen, *Ancient Orient and Old Testament* (Chicago: Inter-Varsity, 1966), p. 166 (cf. Job 1:11; 2:5, 9; 1 Kings 21:10, 13; Ps 10:3).

B. Job Tested (1:6–2:13)

1. Satan's accusations of Job

1:6–12

> ⁶One day the angels came to present themselves before the LORD, and Satan also came with them. ⁷The LORD said to Satan, "Where have you come from?"
>
> Satan answered the LORD, "From roaming through the earth and going back and forth in it."
>
> ⁸Then the LORD said to Satan, "Have you considered my servant Job? There is no one on earth like him; he is blameless and upright, a man who fears God and shuns evil."
>
> ⁹"Does Job fear God for nothing?" Satan replied. ¹⁰"Have you not put a hedge around him and his household and everything he has? You have blessed the work of his hands, so that his flocks and herds are spread throughout the land. ¹¹But stretch out your hand and strike everything he has, and he will surely curse you to your face."
>
> ¹²The LORD said to Satan, "Very well, then, everything he has is in your hands, but on the man himself do not lay a finger."
>
> Then Satan went out from the presence of the LORD.

6–12 There are two scenes in heaven, each depicting the divine council (1:6–12 and 2:1–6). Each is followed by a series of events that result from the encounter between the Lord and Satan. The divine council (v.6) is made up of the *bᵉnê hāʾᵉlōhîm* ("the sons of God" [NIV, "angels"], which here [but probably not in Gen 6:2] refers to these supernatural beings who are above men but created by God [Ps 8:5]). The heathen nations used the same terminology for their lackey gods who were considered created beings. The author of Job applies the term to the beings the Hebrews otherwise called the Lord's messengers (*malʾāḵîm*, Gen 19:1; 24:7; 48:16; Ps 104:4; Mal 3:1 et al.). The Accuser (*haśśāṭān*, "the Satan") is such a being, but one whose business is to roam the earth (v.7) as the Accuser of those committed to serving God (1 Peter 5:8; Rev 12:10). Here we find him questioning Job's motive for religious devotion. "Does Job fear God for nothing?" (v.9). It is not the Accuser but the Lord who initiates the testing of Job; for the Lord says: "Have you considered my servant Job? There is no one on earth like him" (v.8). God's statement that Job is his servant implies more than mere servitude; it means God and Job are in a covenant relationship based on solemn oaths.

As in Genesis 3, God sets the stage and allows man to be put to the test. Here the Lord sees fit to use secondary means to accomplish his purpose. That purpose is not just to test Job as an end in itself but to give Job the opportunity to honor his Lord to whom he has pledged his allegiance with a solemn oath. That allegiance becomes a significant part of the cosmic struggle between Job's adversary and the Lord. Will Job curse God or not?

Understanding this struggle is basic to understanding the Book of Job as well as the whole historical-religious drama of the Bible (Gen 3:15; Rom 16:20). The Accuser insinuates that Job's allegiance is hypocritical (v.9). If only God would remove the protective hedge he has placed about Job (v.10), this "devout" servant would certainly curse God to his face. The attack is on God through Job, and the only way the Accuser can be proven false is through Job. So Satan is given limited but gradually increased access to Job—first to his possessions, then to his family, and finally to his physical well-being. But through it all, in the words of M. Kline (WBC, p. 461), "the primary purpose of Job's suffering, unknown to him, was that he should stand before men and angels as a trophy of the saving might of God, an exhibit of that divine wisdom which is the archetype, source, and foundation of true human wisdom."

Notes

6 In וַיְהִי הַיּוֹם (*wayₑhî hayyôm*, "One day . . . came . . . and"), stress is on the particularity of this day; the same is true in v.13.

The terminology לְהִתְיַצֵּב עַל־יְהוָה (*lₑhityaṣṣēḇ ʿal-yhwh*, "to present themselves before the LORD") is used of servants or courtiers who present themselves before their king. Sarna ("Prose of Job," pp. 22–23) sees it as a Canaanite term used especially for the convocation of celestial beings.

In rendering הַשָּׂטָן (*haśśāṭān*, "Satan"), the NIV has taken the liberty to leave out the definite article that the Hebrew uses consistently here (1:6–12; 2:1–7). The article means the author wants the root meaning of this title to be emphasized. Whether this represents an earlier stage in the development of the doctrine of Satan is a debatable question. Both here and in Zechariah (3:1–2), a postexilic prophet, the definite article and the context emphasize the accusatory role of this superhuman adversary. The root is not used very often in the OT and is usually of human adversaries (1 Sam 29:4; 2 Sam 19:22; 1 Kings 5:4; 11:14, 23, 25; Ps 109:6). By the time of the Chronicler (cf. 1 Chron 21:1, where no article is used), the LXX, and the NT, this term had become a proper name for the arch-adversary; but there is no data on when the concept originated. Here it should be rendered "the Adversary" or "the Accuser."

2. Job's integrity in loss of family and property

1:13–22

[13]One day when Job's sons and daughters were feasting and drinking wine at the oldest brother's house, [14]a messenger came to Job and said, "The oxen were plowing and the donkeys were grazing nearby, [15]and the Sabeans attacked and carried them off. They put the servants to the sword, and I am the only one who has escaped to tell you!"

[16]While he was still speaking, another messenger came and said, "The fire of God fell from the sky and burned up the sheep and the servants, and I am the only one who has escaped to tell you!"

[17]While he was still speaking, another messenger came and said, "The Chaldeans formed three raiding parties and swept down on your camels and carried them off. They put the servants to the sword, and I am the only one who has escaped to tell you!"

[18]While he was still speaking, yet another messenger came and said, "Your sons and daughters were feasting and drinking wine at the oldest brother's house, [19]when suddenly a mighty wind swept in from the desert and struck the four corners of the house. It collapsed on them and they are dead, and I am the only one who has escaped to tell you!"

[20]At this, Job got up and tore his robe and shaved his head. Then he fell to the ground in worship [21]and said:

> "Naked I came from my mother's womb,
>   and naked I will depart.
> The LORD gave and the LORD has taken away;
>   may the name of the LORD be praised."

²²In all this, Job did not sin by charging God with wrongdoing.

13–19 Again the use of the article on the word "day" (v.13; cf. v.6) suggests the translation "Now it was the day his sons and daughters were eating." According to v.5 Job's custom was to make offerings for them at that time. So the very day he made these offerings, this devastation took place. The meaning of the suffering then is even a deeper mystery for Job. As noted the stylistic nature of the text indicates that the account is an old and frequently told story based on sober history. Indeed the coming of the messengers of misfortune each on the heel of the other (vv.14, 16, 17, 18), all on that one fateful day, has its dramatic effect heightened by the narrator's style; but such fact is often stranger than fiction. We are informed, however, that it is really the work of the Accuser, this master of evil, who can and does use both the elements of nature and men to accomplish his purpose. Why does God allow such a devastating series of blows? Is it not a part of his higher purpose and design to humiliate the Adversary all the more?

As Delitzsch notes (p.63), Satan is a great juggler and has manifested himself as such in Paradise and in the temptation of Jesus Christ: "There is in nature as among men an entanglement of contrary forces which he knows how to unloose, because it is the sphere of his special dominion."

20–22 Tearing one's outer garment and cropping his hair (v.20) were common gestures of violent grief in the biblical world (cf. Gen 37:34; Josh 7:6; Ezra 9:3, 5). Such response to grief including weeping and wailing (Ps 42:3; John 11:33–35) is more natural and beneficial to human needs than the suppression of grief prevalent in the modern western world.

The wisdom quatrain (v.21; cf. Eccl 5:15) introduces us to the poetic parallelism found in all the speeches beginning in chapter 3. Here the attitude of Job in contrast to that in the Dialogue is one of supreme faith and total resignation to the sovereign will of God. Job did not understand why but believed that his trouble came from God. "The LORD gave and the LORD has taken away" (v.21). Job was ignorant of what had taken place in the divine council—that God allowed the Accuser to strike thus far. But Job was right, it was the Lord who had taken away. The use of secondary means does not solve the problem of evil, nor is it the purpose of the Book of Job to solve this logical dilemma. In a very real sense, Job's statement of trust in God went as far as he or any human can go in solving this mystery.

When Job said, "May the name of the LORD be praised" (v.21), he was using, as noted, the same word that Satan used in v.11 as an euphemism with the opposite meaning. The play on the root *brk* ("bless") is forceful. It stresses how the Accuser is foiled at this point. Instead of cursing God to his face, Job praised him.

Here the author, being a Hebrew, uses that special covenant name (YHWH) for God (see Notes). Job and his friends were not Hebrews; so they use other Hebrew epithets for God—most often the general epithet *ʾelôah*. Here in the Prologue the composer of the book carefully identifies the Job of faith and wisdom as the same Job with questions and defiance in the Dialogue and Monologue. But more important is his identification of the God of the Dialogue with the true God whom the Hebrews worshiped.

Up to this point (v.22), though deprived of family and possessions, Job did not sin with his lips (cf. 2:10) by accusing God of "wrongdoing" (*tiplāh*, see Notes).

Notes

15 שְׁבָא (*šeḇāʾ*, "the Sabeans"), north Arabian nomads, are to be distinguished from the people of Sheba, who had a wealthy south Arabian kingdom, and whose queen visited Solomon in 1 Kings 10:1–13 (cf. Pope, p. 13).

16 אֵשׁ אֱלֹהִים (*ʾēš ʾelōhîm*, "the fire of God") may be either lightning (Pope, p. 14) or brimstone (Delitzsch, 1:61). The terminology "of God" as part of a cliché does not mean God is considered the immediate source in this context. It is simply phenomenological language because it came from heaven.

17 כַּשְׂדִּים (*kaśdîm*, "the Chaldeans") were roving marauders before they settled down in the south, west of the Tigris, in the ninth century B.C.

שְׁלֹשָׁה רָאשִׁים (*šelōšāh roʾšîm*, "three raiding parties") is an ancient military stratagem that is still used (Judg 7:16, 20; 9:34, 43–45; 1 Sam 11:11; 13:17).

לְפִי־חָרֶב (*lepî-ḥāreḇ*, "to the sword"; lit. "to the mouth of the sword") reflects the custom of making swords with a hilt in the shape of a lion's head, with the blade coming from the mouth (see Pope's note, pp. 13–14), just as Messiah is figured with the sword proceeding from his mouth (Isa 11:4; Rev 1:16; 2:16; 19:15). To this may be added the reverse OT figure of words as sharp instruments of destruction (Ps 52:2–4; Hos 6:5), on which is based the NT figure of the Word of God as a sharp two-edged sword (Heb 4:12).

18 עַד (*ad*, "while") is an example of defective spelling following plenary spellings. Compare Notes on 37:24.

21 The so-called Tetragrammaton יהוה (*yhwh*) is translated "the LORD" in the KJV and NIV. Because it was considered too sacred to pronounce in post-OT Judaism, it was vocalized with the vowels of ʾaḏōnāy ("Lord"; cf. LXX *Kyrios*). The original vowels were consequently lost though scholars, on the basis of early transliterations (Epiphanius and Theodoret use the Gr. ʾIabé), pronounce it "Yahweh." The exact meaning is debated but always tied to some form of the Hebrew verb meaning "to be, become" (Exod 3:13–15). It was Israel's unique name for God and as such had special significance for their relationship to him in the covenant renewal at Sinai (Exod 6:2–5). The sage Job probably did not know God by this name, but the author of the book identifies Job's God as the very same God whom Israel worshiped.

אָשׁוּב שָׁמָּה (*ʾāšûḇ šāmāh*, "will depart") is literally "return there." In OT terminology the body is formed in mother earth, the womb is considered a place of darkness like Sheol (Ps 139:13, 15). So returning to it means going to the place where the departed go. It did not mean nonexistence as some have maintained. The ancient Semitic world viewed man as having an existence in Sheol, however drab it may have been. But Job here probably speaks merely of burial (Gen 3:19).

22 Much has been written about תִּפְלָה (*tiplāh*, "wrongdoing"). Dhorme's explanation (in loc.) is the best. He links the word with the root *tpl* ("tasteless"; 6:6). As our words "insipid" and "insipient" are related, so the root *tpl* also means "worthless" in Lam 2:14. If Job did not charge God with doing anything worthless, he must have believed God had a high purpose.

3. Satan's further accusations

2:1–6

> [1]On another day the angels came to present themselves before the Lᴏʀᴅ, and Satan also came with them to present himself before him. [2]And the Lᴏʀᴅ said to Satan, "Where have you come from?"
>
> Satan answered the Lᴏʀᴅ, "From roaming through the earth and going back and forth in it."
>
> [3]Then the Lᴏʀᴅ said to Satan, "Have you considered my servant Job? There is no one on earth like him; he is blameless and upright, a man who fears God and shuns evil. And he still maintains his integrity, though you incited me against him to ruin him without any reason."
>
> [4]"Skin for skin!" Satan replied. "A man will give all he has for his own life. [5]But stretch out your hand and strike his flesh and bones, and he will surely curse you to your face."
>
> [6]The Lᴏʀᴅ said to Satan, "Very well, then, he is in your hands; but you must spare his life."

1–3 At a special time set aside for it, the Accuser again appeared with "the sons of God" and as a subordinate presented himself before the Lord (v.1). The terminology is formulaic, using the same words as 1:6–9. The Accuser has continued to roam the earth (v.2), obviously looking for those he would take "captive to do his will" (2 Tim 2:26). He lost the first round of this contest. For the third time the Lord triumphantly described Job as a unique servant (no one like him), a pure and devout man who has become even stronger as a result of the testing. "He still maintains his integrity" (v.3). The stem (Hiphil) of the verb "maintains" indicates a strengthening of the grip he already had.

As if to add a bit of irony, the Lord said to the Accuser, "You incited me against him to ruin him without any reason" (v.3). The words are typical OT empirical logic. They should not be used to imply that God can somehow be stirred up to do things that are against his will. On the contrary, God suggested Job to the Accuser (1:8; 2:3) in the first place. All Job's suffering was part of the divine purpose, as God says in 38:2: "Who is this that darkens my counsel with words without knowledge?" But when God uses a secondary cause to affect the life of a human, even Satan can be said to stir him up.

The word *ḥinnām*, sometimes translated "without cause" (KJV, RV, NEB), needs some clarification. Satan had a cause or reason for doing it—to discredit God, and certainly God was accomplishing his own cause or purpose. In 1:9 Satan used the same word to accuse Job of having an ulterior purpose for serving God. Now God taunts the Accuser with the counteraccusation that Satan himself is the one who wants to see injustice done. The translation of this key word (*ḥinnām*) as "without any reason" is good at this point. It means there was no immediate sinfulness in Job that called for punishment. Another possible translation for *ḥinnām* is "in vain" (cf. JB). This would suggest that Satan has wasted his energy on Job. But that meaning is rare in the OT (cf. Prov 1:17; Mal 1:10; NIV, "useless").

4–6 Satan did not consider his energy to have been wasted. His next move was to obtain permission to attack Job's body. With the adage "Skin for skin! A man will give all he has for his own life" (v.4), Satan suggested that even Job's triumphant faith expressed in his doxology (1:21) was only a ploy by which he was purchasing his personal well-being. He was even willing to sacrifice the skin of his loved ones to save his own. If God would send his hand against Job's body (i.e., permit Satan to do so), Job's verbal piety would prove to be a sham; and he would curse God to his face (v.5). The contest was about to take on a new intensity. God placed Job in the hands of their mutual adversary but limited his power—"you must spare his life" (v.6). The suffering of the innocent is a mystery that defies all human logic. The Book of Job deals with this subject profoundly but does not attempt to give a neat logical solution.

Notes

4 Scholars have pondered over the origin and precise meaning of the proverb עוֹר בְּעַד־עוֹר (*ʿôr beʿad̲-ʾôr,* "skin for skin"). The sentence that follows it clearly explains its application. Satan was implying that Job was willing to give the life of another to save his own. Dhorme (in loc.) sees the use of skin as indicative of a superficial wound (a scratch) on Job in contrast to the attack on his bone and flesh.

5 As a strong adversative אוּלָם (*ʾûlām,* "But") might be rendered "On the other hand." יְבָרֲכֶךָ (*yebār˙kekkā,* "He will . . . curse you") is the same euphemism as in 1:11.

6 The verb שְׁמֹר (*šemôr,* "spare") means "to safeguard." Because of the choice of word, it would appear Satan was being made responsible for the life of Job.

4. Job's integrity in personal suffering

2:7–10

> ⁷So Satan went out from the presence of the LORD and afflicted Job with painful sores from the soles of his feet to the top of his head. ⁸Then Job took a piece of broken pottery and scraped himself with it as he sat among the ashes.
>
> ⁹His wife said to him, "Are you still holding on to your integrity? Curse God and die!"
>
> ¹⁰He replied, "You are talking like a foolish woman. Shall we accept good from God, and not trouble?"
>
> In all this, Job did not sin in what he said.

7–8 It is not important for us to know about Job's disease. The symptoms were many. The "painful sores" all over his body (v.7), from the soles of his feet to the tip of his head, were perhaps only the initial stage of the malady. Job speaks of other complications in 30:17, 27, 30. The Semitic root *šḥn* ("sores") denotes fever and inflammation, but in the OT it describes diseases that have symptoms appearing on the skin (Exod 9:9; Lev 13; Deut 28:27, 35). The scratching Job did with the potsherd (v.8) was because of the nature of his disease. He used this only as a counterirritant and not for the ancient practice of laceration as a sign of mourning for the dead (Deut 14:1). If it was the latter, it would have been mentioned in conjunction with the loss of his family.

9–10 Not knowing the limitation God had put on the Accuser, Job's wife at this point diagnosed the disease as incurable and recommended that he curse God and die (v.9). Chrysostom's explanation of why Satan did not destroy Job's wife with the rest of the family was so that she could become his tool. Job's mental anguish was certainly intensified by his wife's advice. Had he followed it, the contest would have ended with the Accuser as the victor.

Job's reply is remarkable in the compassion he showed toward his wife and in his total acceptance of God's will for his life (v.10). He might have accused his wife of blasphemy but chose to accept it as a statement of desperation. Her "talking like a foolish woman" does not refer to intellectual foolishness but to religious apostasy as in Psalms 14:1 and 53:1, where "the fool [nābāl] says in his heart, 'There is no God.'" To curse God was essentially a way of denying he is God. Job was willing to believe that his wife was only talking like a blasphemer. Job's wisdom, on the other hand, was to receive with meekness whatever prosperity or disaster God might send. Such wisdom was not rooted in his intellectual capacity but in his fear of (worship of) God.

Now the author repeats practically the same testimony of Job's verbal innocence given in 1:21. Despite all that has happened to him, up to this point Job did not err with his lips. This section of the Prologue provides the basis of the NT description of Job as a man of perseverance (James 5:11).

Notes

8 Though somewhat messy, הָאֵפֶר (hā'ēper, "the ashes") were perhaps the most sterile place a man with sores could sit. That aspect may be only coincidental; but the ancients, by practice, may have found it physically advantageous.
9 בָּרֵךְ (bārēk, "curse") is the same as in 1:11 and 2:5.
10 The root of נְקַבֵּל (neqabbēl, "we accept") is not a late Aramaism (BDB), nor is it fully synonymous with lqḥ ("receive") (Dhorme). Canaanite evidence from the Amarna Letters shows it can mean "receive meekly, patiently" (Kline, WBC, p. 464).

5. The coming of the counselors

2:11–13

11When Job's three friends, Eliphaz the Temanite, Bildad the Shuhite and Zophar the Naamathite, heard about all the troubles that had come upon him, they set out from their homes and met together by agreement to go and sympathize with him and comfort him. 12When they saw him from a distance, they could hardly recognize him; they began to weep aloud, and they tore their robes and sprinkled dust on their heads. 13Then they sat on the ground with him for seven days and seven nights. No one said a word to him, because they saw how great his suffering was.

11–13 It took time, possibly months, for the news to pass by word of mouth and for the three sages, friends of Job, to come (cf. 7:3). Teman, an Edomite city, is the only place of the three that can be definitely located. The friends arranged a meeting (see Notes) so they could join together to console Job (v.11). Teman was a center of wisdom (Jer 49:7). Shuah was the name of an eastern tribe according to Genesis 25:2, 6. Pope (p. 24) (with Janssen and Savignac) puts Naaman at *Jebel el Naʿameh* in Arabia.

When the counselors join together near Job's home, they are stunned by what they see (v. 12). Like the Suffering Servant of Isaiah 53, Job is disfigured beyond recognition, at least from a distance. The friends had come to show grief (*nûd*) and console (*nāḥam*) Job. The same words are used in 42:11, where other members of his house perform this eastern ritual after Job is restored. The verb *nûd* ("to show grief") means literally "to shake the head." The three friends may have come largely to go through the proper motions. It does not appear that they were ready for what they encountered.

Instead of rituallike acts that seem to have been taking place in 42:11, the friends immediately went into a more drastic form of mourning usually reserved for death or total disaster. They tore their robes of nobility, wailed, and threw dust into the air. Then they sat in silence before Job for seven days and nights (v. 13). (For mourning seven days over the dead, see Gen 50:10; 1 Sam 31:13, and Ecclus 22:12; cf. also Josh 7:6; 1 Sam 4:12; 2 Sam 13:19; Lam 2:10; Ezek 27:30.) Some consider the seven days of silence a display of grief in its most intense form (Dhorme, p. 23). Like the elders of fallen Jerusalem in Lamentations 2:10, Job's friends sat on the ground with dust on their heads and kept silent. For one of them to speak prior to the sufferer would have been in bad taste.

Notes

11 אֱלִיפָז (*ᵉlîpaz*, "Eliphaz") probably does not mean "God is fine gold" (Pope, p. 24) but possibly "God is the Victor," from the Arabic *paʾza* ("win," "gain victory"). Bildad seems most likely to derive from *Bil-ʾada* ("Baal is lord"). See Pope (p. 24) for other suggestions on Bildad. On Zophar, Pope follows Dhorme who sees a diminutive here meaning "little bird" (see the Introduction: The Three Counselors).

The verb וַיִּוָּעֲדוּ (*wayyiwwāʿᵃdû*, "by agreement") means more than simply "to agree" but rather "to have an appointment," including a time and place. Amos 3:3 proves the point (contrary to Dhorme), for two people cannot walk together unless they agree on a time and place.

II. The Dialogue–Dispute (3:1–27:23)
Excursus

The Dialogue is not strictly dialogue but alternating speeches given with an audience in mind. Sometimes they are directed toward what one or the other has previously said, but in Job's case they are also directed to God or given as soliloquy. Often there is highly emotional language with no closely reasoned argumentation. Each man gives a distinctive character to his utterances, and certain issues are taken up and often repeated. For example, Job repeatedly struggles over God's justice and his own vindication. And the friends often defend God and warn and condemn Job. A significant difference between their speeches comes from a difference in relationship with God. Job is determined to be absolutely honest with God. Job tells God everything, every fear and every doubt. They tell God nothing. They only talk about God, never to him. This should be kept in mind as we become impatient with Job. We should also keep in mind that despite all the hair-raising things Job will say, he never asks for restoration. His main concern is about his relationship with God, and that is why he puts so much stress on vindication. Without vindication all that he is suffering is proof God is his enemy. So when Job calls God his enemy, the reader must remember these are words of poetic passion used analogically as the total context proves.

The use of the poetic format beginning in 3:3 will help the reader remember that as Job breaks the silence, his words are highly figurative, poetic rhetoric. The reader has already seen this prosodic power and beauty in the doxology in 1:21. But now the genre is not blessing or praise but malediction replete with a full-bodied hyperbole and other poetic tropes.

The counselors will prove just as adept as Job in this media. Some of their poems are masterly, and whole speeches show architectonic structure; each has a tone distinctively his own, and each has an overall coherence to his series of speeches. Discovering the tonality of a speech is aided by being sensitive to certain sentences that clearly express the speaker's mood. Clines ("Arguments," pp. 199–214) calls these important features "nodal sentences" and lists some that he considers crucial for perceiving the real message, e.g., 4:6 and 5:8; for Eliphaz, 15:4–5; 22:21, 30; for Bildad, 8:4–6; 18:4; 25:4; and for Zophar, 11:4–5. Clines also worries that failure to understand the practice of using stylized descriptions with certain rhetorical patterns as literary building blocks can lead the commentator astray. These rhetorical devices are subordinate and function in a way that is not always obvious. So the interpreter must not give a disproportionate emphasis to what is being used only as an aside, a rhetorical tool. For example, is Eliphaz insulting Job in 4:8–11, or is he merely giving an excursus on the fate of the wicked? At this point he really does not think Job is wicked and encourages him to be patient on that account (4:6; 5:19–26).

A further point made by D.J.A. Clines ("Verbal Modality and the Interpretation of Job 4:20–21," VetTest 30 [1980]: 354–57) is the importance of seeing the possible modal force of a verb in Hebrew (the language is not as precise as Greek in this respect), which may change one's understanding of what the speaker is saying. For example, in 4:20–21 Eliphaz is talking about how fragile man is, not about the brevity of life. He is saying that it is possible for a man to die without even gaining wisdom.

As we get into the speeches, these rhetorical issues and a host of other linguistic challenges of this essentially atypical Hebrew will constitute an interpretative challenge. The so-called Dialogue itself has a structure. Job opens with a sizzling malediction (ch. 3) that brings on three cycles of emotive prosody that fades out with Bildad's brief poem in chapter 25. Job then closes the verbal duel with a final statement employing both oath and imprecation (ch. 27) as big weapons to silence the arguments of his opponents.

A. *Job's Opening Lamentation*

3:1–26

¹After this, Job opened his mouth and cursed the day of his birth. ²He said:

> ³"May the day of my birth perish,
>   and the night it was said, 'A boy is born!'
> ⁴That day—may it turn to darkness;
>   may God above not care about it;
>   may no light shine upon it.

⁵May darkness and deep shadow claim it once more;
    may a cloud settle over it;
    may blackness overwhelm its light.
⁶That night—may thick darkness seize it;
    may it not be included among the days of the year
    nor be entered in any of the months.
⁷May that night be barren;
    may no shout of joy be heard in it.
⁸May those who curse days curse that day,
    those who are ready to rouse Leviathan.
⁹May its morning stars become dark;
    may it wait for daylight in vain
    and not see the first rays of dawn,
¹⁰for it did not shut the doors of the womb on me
    to hide trouble from my eyes.

¹¹"Why did I not perish at birth,
    and die as I came from the womb?
¹²Why were there knees to receive me
    and breasts that I might be nursed?
¹³For now I would be lying down in peace;
    I would be asleep and at rest
¹⁴with kings and counselors of the earth,
    who built for themselves places now lying in ruins,
¹⁵with rulers who had gold,
    who filled their houses with silver.
¹⁶Or why was I not hidden in the ground like a stillborn child,
    like an infant who never saw the light of day?
¹⁷There the wicked cease from turmoil,
    and there the weary are at rest.
¹⁸Captives also enjoy their ease;
    they no longer hear the slave driver's shout.
¹⁹The small and the great are there,
    and the slave is freed from his master.

²⁰"Why is light given to those in misery,
    and life to the bitter of soul,
²¹to those who long for death that does not come,
    who search for it more than for hidden treasure,
²²who are filled with gladness
    and rejoice when they reach the grave?
²³Why is life given to a man
    whose way is hidden,
    whom God has hedged in?
²⁴For sighing comes to me instead of food;
    my groans pour out like water.
²⁵What I feared has come upon me;
    what I dreaded has happened to me.
²⁶I have no peace, no quietness;
    I have no rest, but only turmoil."

The spiritual tone of Job's life changed dramatically here. The man of patience and faith sank into a state of despondency and spiritual depression, so frequently a major problem to those who endure severe physical illness or impairment. (See our comments about the Job of the Prologue and the Dialogue in the Introduction: Major Characters.) In chapter 3 Job established an attitude that largely colored all that he said in the succeeding chapters. In all his many words of despair, nowhere would he come closer to cursing God to his face (2:5) than here in chapter 3. By cursing the day of his birth, he was questioning the sovereign wisdom of his Creator. At this point the drama is intense, for the Accuser whom we shall never see again seems to have triumphed. Whether he has or not will be determined by what follows.

Freedman ("Structure") and Habel (*Job*, 1985, pp. 102–3) have contributed enormously to full appreciation of this chapter by analyzing its structure. Habel points to two poetic units: a curse (vv.3–10), followed by a complimentary lament (vv.11–26). Each unit has a framing device (inclusio). Each opens by announcing the subject and closes by giving the reason. So the following pattern emerges:

> The Curses
>   A. Subject: Day and Night (v.3)
>   Curses on that day (vv.4–5)
>   Curses on that night (vv.6–9)
>   A₁ Reason for His Curse: His Misery (v.10)
> The Lament
>   A. Subject: Why Did He Not Die at Birth (v.11)
>   Laments on why God permits suffering (vv.12–24)
>   A₁ Reason for His Lament (vv.25–26)

Worthy of note are the thematic similarities between Job 3 and Jeremiah 20:14–18 (see Habel, p. 103) and the cosmogonic connections suggested by M. Fishbane ("Jer. 4 and Job 3: A Recovered Use of the Creation Pattern," VetTest 21 [1971]: 151–67).

1–2 The words "After this" (v.1), which typically mark a literary transition (Gen 15:14 [NIV, "afterward"]; 23:19; 25:26), introduce the Dialogue, a major division of the book. In fact, the entire third chapter, though a part of the Dialogue, is transitional.

3–10 The way Job cursed the day of his birth has two interesting features in these verses. First, he expressed a desire for the annihilation of that day, a would-be negation of God's creative act in bringing such a day into being (v.3). As God had said in Genesis 1:3, "Let there be light," so Job, using the same terminology in v.4, said, "As for that day, let there be darkness" (lit. tr.). All this is a logical absurdity; but it is poetry, and Job meant to give full vent to his feelings. He wished that day could be so annihilated that even God would forget it (v.4b). Job wanted the day lost in total darkness, not even numbered anymore as a day in the calendar (vv.5–6).

The second feature is Job's use of personification. He personified both the night of his conception and the day he was born. In Hebrew v.3b reads: "the night that said." That night speaks about what it has witnessed, the birth of a boy. It is more vivid to imagine the day perishing as a person (v.3a) than as a span of time. Jeremiah (20:14) also cursed the day of his birth but feeling the need for concreteness shifted the curse to the man who brought the news of his birth to his father. The first half of v.7 uses personification, but the second half does not. We must not press any figure too far. A barren night (figurative) unable to conceive results in a literal night in which no shout of joy will be heard.

Dhorme (in loc.) says that "those who curse days" in v.8 refers to other sufferers like Job who also cursed the day of their birth. But the expression more likely refers to professional cursers like Balaam (Num 22–24). In v.8a Job appears to be making a play on the similar sound of the words *yām* ("sea") and *yôm* ("day") and the sound-alikes *'ōrēr* ("curser") and *'ōrēr* ("arouser"). Current mythology used the term Leviathan for a monster of chaos who lived in the sea, and the Sea itself was a boisterous deity who could be aroused professionally. But to Job, a strict monotheist (31:26–28), this was simply vivid imagery, the use of proverbial language tailored to his call for the obliteration of that day. The verb *'ûr* means "to awaken" or "to arouse" the dead in Sheol in Isaiah 14:9. The figure then may be of an awakened monster of chaos who could perhaps swallow that day or even usher in the end of days.

11–26 Job continued his pitiable complaint with a series of rhetorical questions. There is a progression in his thought. Since the day of his birth did happen (v.10), the next possibility was a stillbirth (vv.11–12, 16). But since he was alive, he longed for a premature death (vv.20, 23). In vv.13–19 Job conceived of death as falling into restful sleep (v.13). It is clear that he did not consider it annihilation. The dead are in a place where there is no activity, where everyone finds rest; even the wicked stop making trouble there (v.17).

In addition to the progression of thought, there is also a symmetry of ideas in these verses. Job wished he had been a stillbirth (vv.11–12) and then imagined himself joining the great (kings, counselors, rulers) who rested in Sheol (vv.13–15). Then in v.16 he repeated the issue and followed with a description of the small (the wicked, the weary, the captives) who also rested in Sheol. A concluding line wraps it up with the thought that the small and great were all alike (see Notes) in Sheol, where even the slave was freed from his master (v.19).

The last of Job's rhetorical questions comes in vv.20–23. To paraphrase: Why is light given to a man who is miserable (v.20a)? Why is life given to a man who has no future (v.23a)? His suffering was so intense both physically (v.24) and mentally (vv.20b, 23b) that death in comparison would be an exquisite pleasure, like finding hidden treasure (vv.21b–22). The very thing he dreaded the most happened. It thus appeared to him that the very God who had put a hedge of protection and blessing about him (1:10) subsequently hemmed him in with trouble and distress (vv.23c, 26).

What does this chapter teach us? What is its function as part of Scripture? Job's attitude is certainly not normative—just the opposite. We should hardly look to this chapter to tell us what to believe about the state of the dead. What we can see in the chapter is how even a man of great faith can fall into the slough of despond. That one as great as Job should have such a struggle of faith is a source of support to those similarly afflicted, especially when viewed in the light of the rest of the Book of Job. God prefers we speak with him honestly, even in our moments of deepest gloom, than that we mouth innocuous clichés far removed from reality.

Notes

3 The NIV takes אָמַר (*'āmar*) as a verb with an indefinite subject, viz., "one said."
4 The basic meaning of the root of יִדְרְשֵׁהוּ (*yiḏrᵉšēhû*, "care about it") is "to seek, search for." The point is that the day might be lost in darkness.

The epithet אֱלוֹהַּ (*'ᵉlôah*, "God") is used forty times exclusively by Job and the counselors. Except for one instance in 12:9 (and it is doubtful), the name YHWH ("LORD") is used only by the Hebrew author in the Prologue and Epilogue and in 38:1 and 40:1, 3, and 6.
5 Dhorme, following early Jewish interpretation, derives יִגְאָלֻהוּ (*yig'āluhû*, "claim it once

more") from a root that means "to pollute." "To claim" or "reclaim" is an extended meaning of *g'l* I ("to redeem").

The vowels of צַלְמָ֫וֶת (*ṣalmāwet*) make it read "shadow of death" (KJV); but these vowels, though ancient, probably do not reflect the original spelling. Other Semitic languages use the root *ṣlm*, meaning simply "darkness." The word is used ten times in Job; two of the contexts are about death (10:21–22; 38:17). We may conclude that from early on the word was used with "the shadow of death" etymology. Job 38:17 revolves around that meaning. That spelling in Ps 23:4 may also have been deliberate by the original poet; but that does not seem likely in Job 3:5; 12:22; 16:16; 24:17; 28:3; and 34:22.

Most agree that the root of כִּמְרִירֵי (*kimrîrê*, "darkens"; NIV, "blackness") is *kmr* ("be dark, black"; cf. KJV). But the MT vowels read "like the bitternesses of," which some link to an eclipse. See Pope (in loc.) for data (cf. NEB).

6 For אַל־יִחַדְּ (*'al-yiḥadde*, "may it not be included"), NIV reads *yēḥad* (*yḥd*), as in Gen 49:6, literally, "be joined" (cf. KJV). BDB (p. 292) takes it from *ḥdh* ("rejoice") (cf. Driver and Gray, in loc.). KB and W.L. Holladay (*A Concise Hebrew and Aramaic Lexicon of the Old Testament* [Grand Rapids: Eerdmans, 1971], p. 96) derive it from *ḥdh* II (cf. *ḥzh*), "be seen, appear," as does Blommerde following Dahood.

The use of יְרָחִים (*yerāḥîm*, "months") proves this is not standard OT Hebrew, which would use חֳדָשִׁים (*ḥodāšîm*, "months" or "new moons").

10 If we understand בִטְנִי (*biṭnî*) in its usual genitive, "my womb" seems to mean the womb out of which he came, i.e., his mother's. But Habel (*Job*, 1985, p. 109) thinks it is deliberately ambiguous since Job's parents are left out of the earlier curse. The NIV avoids the issue by rendering the pronoun suffix in a rare dative relationship to the noun (cf. N.C. Habel, "The Dative Suffix in Job 33:13," *Biblica* 63 [1982]: 258–59).

11 In this bicolon the principle of double duty usage of elements is applied on each side:

> Why did I not (come out) from the womb and die;
> (Why did I not) come out from the belly and expire?

14 The meaning of חֳרָבוֹת (*ḥorābôt*) has been troublesome to some. Its ordinary meaning "ruins" is perfectly acceptable here, for it was considered a great achievement for kings to excavate, uncover, and rebuild the ruins of their ancestors. The verb בָּנָה (*bānāh*) can mean rebuild as well as build. Nebuchadnezzar bragged in his building inscriptions: "Ebarra . . . abode of Šamaš which since distant days . . . was fallen to ruins. . . . Its ancient location I found and beheld . . . as of old I made and completed" (Stephen Langdon, *Building Inscriptions of the Neo-Babylonian Empire, Part I, Nabopolassar and Nebuchadnezzar* [Paris: Ernest Leroux, 1905], pp. 443, 445).

19 It is now recognized that הוּא (*hû'*, "he"), like ὁ αὐτός (*ho autos*), can mean "the same." In Ps 102:27 the heavens and earth change, but God is the same. Contrary to the NIV, the context would also favor the reading "There the small and great are alike (the same)."

B. *The First Cycle of Speeches (4:1–14:22)*

1. *Eliphaz*

4:1–5:27

> [1]Then Eliphaz the Temanite replied:
>
> > [2]"If someone ventures a word with you, will you be impatient?
> > But who can keep from speaking?
> > [3]Think how you have instructed many,
> > how you have strengthened feeble hands.

⁴Your words have supported those who stumbled;
    you have strengthened faltering knees.
⁵But now trouble comes to you, and you are discouraged;
    it strikes you, and you are dismayed.
⁶Should not your piety be your confidence
    and your blameless ways your hope?

⁷"Consider now: Who, being innocent, has ever perished?
    Where were the upright ever destroyed?
⁸As I have observed, those who plow evil
    and those who sow trouble reap it.
⁹At the breath of God they are destroyed;
    at the blast of his anger they perish.
¹⁰The lions may roar and growl,
    yet the teeth of the great lions are broken.
¹¹The lion perishes for lack of prey,
    and the cubs of the lioness are scattered.

¹²"A word was secretly brought to me,
    my ears caught a whisper of it.
¹³Amid disquieting dreams in the night,
    when deep sleep falls on men,
¹⁴fear and trembling seized me
    and made all my bones shake.
¹⁵A spirit glided past my face,
    and the hair on my body stood on end.
¹⁶It stopped,
    but I could not tell what it was.
 A form stood before my eyes,
    and I heard a hushed voice:
¹⁷'Can a mortal be more righteous than God?
    Can a man be more pure than his Maker?
¹⁸If God places no trust in his servants,
    if he charges his angels with error,
¹⁹how much more those who live in houses of clay,
    whose foundations are in the dust,
    who are crushed more readily than a moth!
²⁰Between dawn and dusk they are broken to pieces;
    unnoticed, they perish forever.
²¹Are not the cords of their tent pulled up,
    so that they die without wisdom?'

^{5:1}Call if you will, but who will answer you?
    To which of the holy ones will you turn?
²Resentment kills a fool,
    and envy slays the simple.
³I myself have seen a fool taking root,
    but suddenly his house was cursed.
⁴His children are far from safety,
    crushed in court without a defender.
⁵The hungry consume his harvest,
    taking it even from among thorns,
    and the thirsty pant after his wealth.
⁶For hardship does not spring from the soil,
    nor does trouble sprout from the ground.
⁷Yet man is born to trouble
    as surely as sparks fly upward.

⁸"But if it were I, I would appeal to God;
    I would lay my cause before him.
⁹He performs wonders that cannot be fathomed,
    miracles that cannot be counted.

893

¹⁰ He bestows rain on the earth;
    he sends water upon the countryside.
¹¹ The lowly he sets on high,
    and those who mourn are lifted to safety.
¹² He thwarts the plans of the crafty,
    so that their hands achieve no success.
¹³ He catches the wise in their craftiness,
    and the schemes of the wily are swept away.
¹⁴ Darkness comes upon them in the daytime;
    at noon they grope as in the night.
¹⁵ He saves the needy from the sword in their mouth;
    he saves them from the clutches of the powerful.
¹⁶ So the poor have hope,
    and injustice shuts its mouth.

¹⁷ "Blessed is the man whom God corrects;
    so do not despise the discipline of the Almighty.
¹⁸ For he wounds, but he also binds up;
    he injures, but his hands also heal.
¹⁹ From six calamities he will rescue you;
    in seven no harm will befall you.
²⁰ In famine he will ransom you from death,
    and in battle from the stroke of the sword.
²¹ You will be protected from the lash of the tongue,
    and need not fear when destruction comes.
²² You will laugh at destruction and famine,
    and need not fear the beasts of the earth.
²³ For you will have a covenant with the stones of the field,
    and the wild animals will be at peace with you.
²⁴ You will know that your tent is secure;
    you will take stock of your property and find nothing missing.
²⁵ You will know that your children will be many,
    and your descendants like the grass of the earth.
²⁶ You will come to the grave in full vigor,
    like sheaves gathered in season.

²⁷ "We have examined this, and it is true.
    So hear it and apply it to yourself."

With artistic flare (see Notes), Eliphaz sounded the keynote for all else that he and his companions would say. Job in chapter 3 was so obviously wrong that it was not hard for Eliphaz to appear to be right. His words are so good that the apostle Paul quotes 5:13 in 1 Corinthians 3:19. But we must keep in mind that the overall purpose of the book includes the concept that the counselors were basically wrong even though their words were often right (42:7–8). Fullerton (pp. 326–27) rightly warns that while on the surface the speech is orthodox and is given with "dignity and sobriety" in contrast to Job's "almost ungovernable outbursts," yet there is "a subtle overtone" of flaws that can be easily missed by a casual reading.

1–11 Eliphaz, a man from Teman, an Edomite city noted as a center of wisdom (Jer 49:7), on the surface spoke as if he thought Job was basically righteous and that his sufferings were temporary. But in reality Eliphaz was not so convinced of this. Later he openly agreed with a harder line against Job used by his other friends (22:1–11). His opening statement in v.2 can be taken as a conditional sentence (NIV) or as a question without the conditional sentence, viz., "Should one attempt to speak with you while you are (so) weary?" This opening line sounds like Eliphaz was truly concerned for Job's welfare but could not resist the temptation to give Job some "proper" instruction—"But who can keep from speaking?" Some compliments are offered. Job is called a "wisdom teacher"—like himself (vv.3–4). But the compliment is followed by a warning to Job (v.5) who had instructed and strengthened those in trouble that he must now be careful lest he fail to apply to himself the lessons he taught others.

In v.6 Eliphaz was willing to affirm that Job was basically an upright man who only needed the wisdom to see that all deserve some punishment for sin, for no one is completely pure (4:17). Compare 22:4 where he speaks of Job's piety. Is it with tongue-in-cheek?

According to Eliphaz, Job's faith in God and blameless conduct (1:8; 2:3) should have saved him; for "who, being innocent, has ever perished?" (v.7). Verses 8–11 may be an excursus about the fate of the wicked without reference to Job (cf. Clines, "Arguments," p. 201), or they may reveal that he really is not all that certain about Job. Moreover Job's experience does not support the idea that the innocent never perish. With the perspective of the Prologue, the reader has insight that proves Eliphaz's statement in vv.7–8 is shallow. Although he was shallow especially with reference to Job, Eliphaz would also say things that were not so shallow. For example, he would admonish Job to be patient and see the disciplinary aspect of suffering (5:17–18).

12–21 At this point Eliphaz bolstered the authority of his words by an appeal to the supernatural—an eerie and hair-raising experience in which he received a divine oracle (vv.12–15). Uncertain about what it was he saw (v.16), he claimed "a form" spoke in the silence of the night. The NIV runs the words of the oracle from v.17 through v.21. Others reduce the oracle to v.17 alone, with the balance of the verses being Eliphaz's comment on it. The NIV supports the traditional translation of v.17. But the thought that a man could be more righteous than God is hardly the issue. Many grammarians (e.g., Dhorme, Pope; cf. RSV) render it "Can a mortal be found righteous in the presence of God?" (see Notes).

Eliphaz went on to tell how far inferior the angels are to God (v.18). More so man, whose body like a house of clay (v.19; cf. Gen 2:7), is as fragile as a moth. It is clear that Eliphaz saw man as almost zero in God's sight—hardly more than an insect that may perish unnoticed (v.20). Like collapsing tents people "die without wisdom" (v.21). This appears to be far more than a simple statement about the death of the ignorant. Eliphaz was saying, "They die and it is not by (of) wisdom." That is, there is no special purpose in it. To a God so transcendent that he does not even trust the angels, the death of a sinful man is of little consequence.

It would hardly seem possible to stress too much that God is transcendent. Eliphaz, however, succeeded in taking this important truth and misapplying it. In fairness to Eliphaz, the verbs in vv.19–21 may have an optative force. Hence they may only express possible consequences of man's sinfulness (see Notes), not what happens to every sinner. Eliphaz's point then is that since all deserve this, we should be patient when temporary suffering comes.

5:1–7 Eliphaz next directed his words more explicitly toward Job. There was no mediator among the holy servants of God (the angels) who would dare answer a plea from Job (v.1). Why? Because he was behaving like a fool (v.2). The fool in wisdom language is a man who pays no proper heed to God (Ps 14:1). What happens to such fools? Their houses are cursed, their children crushed, and their wealth depleted (vv.3–5; cf. 1:13–19). Eliphaz was not quite explicit, but Job no doubt got the point; but see Cline's view ("Arguments") mentioned above. Similarly Habel (*Job*, 1985, p. 121) makes a distinction between Eliphaz's role here as a friend and the poet's playing with his speeches. In vv.6–7 Eliphaz was establishing a connection between moral and physical evil. Trouble does not sprout up like weeds in the field. He was implying that one must sow and cultivate trouble.

Dhorme (in loc.) suggests v.7a should read "man engenders trouble" instead of "man is born to trouble." The suggestion is attractive and within grammatical bounds if one will allow a Hebrew vowel (pointing) change from passive to active (see Notes). Thus "man engenders trouble" emphasizes the point Eliphaz has already made: man's active role as an evildoer rather than seeing man as a victim of circumstances.

The "sparks [that] fly upward" (v.7b) are literally Resheph's sons (see Introduction, p. 869; also W.J. Fulco, *The Canaanite God Rešep*, AO series 8 [New Haven: American Oriental Society, 1976]). The name is used seven times in the OT including this passage, mostly for flames or lightning (Deut 32:23–24; 1 Chron 7:25 [proper name]; Pss 76:4; 78:48; S of Songs 8:6; Hab 3:5). As we have noted above, this imagery from the current mythology is a literary trope and marks linguistic richness. Its use need not imply anything about the theology of the speaker or author. Eliphaz was probably saying that man like the sons of this colorful and pestering figure stirs up his own trouble or is the victim of uncontrollable natural forces such as disease, plague, and death.

8–16 Verses 9–16 are in the form a creedal hymn on the nature of God as the Lord of creation and salvation. So Job was admonished to appeal to God who does only what is right. He punishes the unjust and delivers the lowly. This is of course exactly what Job believed, but such advice did not help him understand why his suffering was so intense. On the contrary, since it implies he was getting just what he deserved, it only added to his confusion.

These lines are a fine example of hymn genre in OT poetry. A similar creedal hymn appears in Isaiah 44:24–28. That is why the apostle Paul could cite a line from v.13 in 1 Corinthians 3:19: "He catches the wise in their craftiness." But in Eliphaz's case what is absolutely true is misapplied—the sick room is not the place for theological strictures that may turn out to do more harm than good. Eliphaz as a counselor is a supreme negative example. Great truths misapplied only hurt more those who are already hurting.

17–27 Eliphaz continued his lofty words with another unit of fine poetry. So the purpose of the creedal poem in 5:9–16 was to show a sinner (fool) how transcendent and holy God is. Sinners get what they deserve, and only the righteous have hope. It is a terrifying statement that God, because he is a holy God, hates sinners. But as a man dedicated to wisdom, Eliphaz balanced this with another poem (vv.17–26) addressed to anyone who understands God's "discipline" (*mûsar*, v.17; cf. Prov 1:2, 7; 3:12; 23:12 [NIV, "instruction"], 23 et al.). The parallel expression in 5:17 and Proverbs 3:11 shows that in the Wisdom genre such language was common. Typical gnomic truth (vv.19–26) maintained that the correcting wounds of God were temporary—the truly good man will always be rescued. The very God who injured him will heal him, and he will be blessed and again enjoy the good things of life.

In the light, however, of Job's experiences—the loss of his family, his economic ruin, his sickness—there is a thoughtless cruelty inherent in applying the words of vv.19–26 to him. For example, if Job benefits from God's discipline (v.17), then "his children will be many" (v.25); but Job's children were dead. Is it possible that the author of the Book of Job included this speech for a very subtle reason? Perhaps it was meant to be a satire on all such mechanical use of theology with its heartless superiority. It is not what Eliphaz knew that is wrong; it is what he was ignorant of—God's hidden purpose—that made all his beautiful poetry and grand truth only a snare to Job. Moreover, while things he said are good even for a sufferer to contemplate—such as the disciplining aspect of suffering—even these words, we know from the Prologue, do not apply to the case in hand.

Eliphaz's patronizing attitude revealed in his closing sentence (v.27) must have been galling to Job his peer.

Notes

Andersen (*Job*, p. 111) sees in Eliphaz's speech throughout chs. 4–5 what he calls a symmetrical introverted structure. It is a keen observation and worth repeating. It is based on subject matter as follows:

    A. Opening Remark (4:2)
      B. Exhortation (4:3–6)
        C. God's Dealings With Men (4:7–11)
          D. The Revelation of Truth (4:12–21)
        C'. God's Dealings With Men (5:1–16)
      B'. Exhortation (5:17–26)
    A'. Closing Remark (5:27).

For more on this subject, see Smick, "Architectonics."

4:2 מִלִּין (*millîn*, "speaking") is a clear Aramaism used thirteen times in the Book of Job—the Hebrew spelling *millîm* is used ten times. Compare v.10 where נָתַע (*nāta'*, "to be broken") would appear normally in Hebrew as נָתַץ (*nātaṣ*). Such Aramaic influence has little to do with dating the book. It simply reveals the dialect of the speaker. Dhorme (p. cv) has shown conclusively that Elihu's speech had an Aramaic color.

17 מִין (*mîn*), a preposition used commonly for comparison, here has the meaning "before" or "in the presence of." This meaning serves the context better and is attested in Num 32:22 and Jer 51:56 (see Notes on 32:2).

20 Some render מִבְּלִי מֵשִׂים (*mibbᵉlî mēśîm*, "unnoticed") "nameless," reading שֵׁם מִבְּלִי(ם) (*mibbᵉlî[m] šēm*) (Pope, p. 38). The NIV also considers the second *m* as enclitic but takes the word *śim* ("put") as it stands. The idiom שָׂם לֵב (*śim lēb*, "put to mind," "pay attention"; cf. 1:8; 2:3; 34:14) appears with ellipsis of *lēb* as in 23:6; 24:12; 34:23; and Isa 41:20; so here NIV translates "without putting to mind," i.e., "unnoticed." Compare Notes on 17:3 and 12.

21 יִתְרָם בָּם (*yitrām bām*, "the cords of their tent") is literally "their tent-cord(s) is pulled away from them" (a rare use of *b* meaning "from" as is common in Ugaritic). The KJV's rendering, which is scarcely intelligible—"Doth not their excellency *which is* in them go away?"—is based on some ancient versions (Targ., Vulg., Syr.).

5:4 For בַּשַּׁעַר (*baššaʿar*, "in court," "in the gate"), Andersen (*Job*, in loc.) suggests reading *baśaʿar* ("in the storm") as a cruel reference to the way Job's children were lost (1:19); this spelling of the Hebrew word meaning "storm" is attested in Isa 28:2.

5 The translation of וְאֶל־מִצִּנִּים (*wᵉ'el-miṣṣinnîm*) as "even from among thorns" makes little sense and fails to do justice to all the Hebrew consonants. The line is difficult (Pope [in loc.] says "impossible"), but the Joseph story in Genesis may provide information to help us interpret the line. Genesis 37:7 uses the word אֲלֻמָּה (*ᵃlummāh*, "sheaf") and Gen 41:23 the word צְנֻמוֹת (*ṣᵉnumôt*, "thin," "emaciated"). The line would not require any change of consonants to read *w' lm-ṣnym* with the meaning "the emaciated [cf. 'the hungry' in v.5a] take away ['consume' in v.5a] his [double duty pronoun from v.5a] sheaves ['harvest' in v.5a]." (For this we are partially indebted to Michel, pp. 267–68.)

7 The Masoretes have vocalized יוּלָד (*yûllād*, "is born") as a Pual perfect, but the presence of the waw creates a problem. The versions seem to read *yiwwālēd* (Niphal). Dhorme's suggestion (see comment above) to read *yôlîd* accounts for the waw but then takes the preposition *l* on the preceding word as a sign of the accusative, a rarer Aramaism.

15 In addition to rendering מֵחֶרֶב (*mēhereb*) as "from the sword," the NIV has brought the word "needy" from 15b to 15a and inserted "them" in 15b. It also renders *min* ("from") as "in." The latter is perhaps possible; but neither expediency is necessary if we are willing to adopt Dhorme's pointing *moḥᵒrāb* (Hophal participle from *ḥrb* III), which means "the desolate." The verse reads: "He saves the desolate from their mouth;/ the needy from the clutches of the powerful."

19, 21 The preposition בְּ (*b*) meaning "from"—בְּשֵׁשׁ (*bᵉšēš*, "from six"), בְּשׁוֹט (*bᵉšôṭ*, "from the lash")—is attested (4:21 [NIV, "without"]; Deut 1:44); but the reverse, i.e., מִן (*min*) meaning "in" (as in NIV v.15a), is less likely. The Dead Sea Psalms scroll (11QPsᵃ) substituted *min* for *b* when they understood the meaning to be "from" (cf. Ps 119:87).

23 In light of the parallelism with "wild animals," the א (ʾ, aleph) here could be understood as prothetic, rendering אַבְנֵי (*ʾabnê*, "the stones of") as "the sons [offspring] of the field." Pope (in loc.) carries the meaning a step too far with his "sprites of the field." For similar use of *ʾabnê*, see Gen 49:24; Isa 14:19; Ezek 28:14 (cf. Andersen, *Job*, p. 122, n. 3). These are the same as v.23b—wild animals that kill domestic animals. The latter was the measure of one's wealth; so it was important to have a covenant with these beasts. It was important to take a count and find no sheep, goats, or cattle that had been killed.

---

2. Job's reply

6:1–7:21

¹Then Job replied:

²"If only my anguish could be weighed
  and all my misery be placed on the scales!
³It would surely outweigh the sand of the seas—
  no wonder my words have been impetuous.
⁴The arrows of the Almighty are in me,
  my spirit drinks in their poison;
  God's terrors are marshaled against me.
⁵Does a wild donkey bray when it has grass,
  or an ox bellow when it has fodder?
⁶Is tasteless food eaten without salt,
  or is there flavor in the white of an egg?
⁷I refuse to touch it;
  such food makes me ill.

⁸"Oh, that I might have my request,
  that God would grant what I hope for,
⁹that God would be willing to crush me,
  to let loose his hand and cut me off!
¹⁰Then I would still have this consolation—
  my joy in unrelenting pain—
  that I had not denied the words of the Holy One.

¹¹ "What strength do I have, that I should still hope?
    What prospects, that I should be patient?
¹² Do I have the strength of stone?
    Is my flesh bronze?
¹³ Do I have any power to help myself,
    now that success has been driven from me?

¹⁴ "A despairing man should have the devotion of his friends,
    even though he forsakes the fear of the Almighty.
¹⁵ But my brothers are as undependable as intermittent streams,
    as the streams that overflow
¹⁶ when darkened by thawing ice
    and swollen with melting snow,
¹⁷ but that cease to flow in the dry season,
    and in the heat vanish from their channels.
¹⁸ Caravans turn aside from their routes;
    they go up into the wasteland and perish.
¹⁹ The caravans of Tema look for water,
    the traveling merchants of Sheba look in hope.
²⁰ They are distressed, because they had been confident;
    they arrive there, only to be disappointed.
²¹ Now you too have proved to be of no help;
    you see something dreadful and are afraid.
²² Have I ever said, 'Give something on my behalf,
    pay a ransom for me from your wealth,
²³ deliver me from the hand of the enemy,
    ransom me from the clutches of the ruthless'?

²⁴ "Teach me, and I will be quiet;
    show me where I have been wrong.
²⁵ How painful are honest words!
    But what do your arguments prove?
²⁶ Do you mean to correct what I say,
    and treat the words of a despairing man as wind?
²⁷ You would even cast lots for the fatherless
    and barter away your friend.

²⁸ "But now be so kind as to look at me.
    Would I lie to your face?
²⁹ Relent, do not be unjust;
    reconsider, for my integrity is at stake.
³⁰ Is there any wickedness on my lips?
    Can my mouth not discern malice?

^{7:1} Does not man have hard service on earth?
    Are not his days like those of a hired man?
² Like a slave longing for the evening shadows,
    or a hired man waiting eagerly for his wages,
³ so I have been allotted months of futility,
    and nights of misery have been assigned to me.
⁴ When I lie down I think, 'How long before I get up?'
    The night drags on, and I toss till dawn.
⁵ My body is clothed with worms and scabs,
    my skin is broken and festering.

⁶ "My days are swifter than a weaver's shuttle,
    and they come to an end without hope.
⁷ Remember, O God, that my life is but a breath;
    my eyes will never see happiness again.
⁸ The eye that now sees me will see me no longer;
    you will look for me, but I will be no more.

⁹As a cloud vanishes and is gone,
   so he who goes down to the grave does not return.
¹⁰He will never come to his house again;
   his place will know him no more.

¹¹"Therefore I will not keep silent;
   I will speak out in the anguish of my spirit,
   I will complain in the bitterness of my soul.
¹²Am I the sea, or the monster of the deep,
   that you put me under guard?
¹³When I think my bed will comfort me
   and my couch will ease my complaint,
¹⁴even then you frighten me with dreams
   and terrify me with visions,
¹⁵so that I prefer strangling and death,
   rather than this body of mine.
¹⁶I despise my life; I would not live forever.
   Let me alone; my days have no meaning.

¹⁷"What is man that you make so much of him,
   that you give him so much attention,
¹⁸that you examine him every morning
   and test him every moment?
¹⁹Will you never look away from me,
   or let me alone even for an instant?
²⁰If I have sinned, what have I done to you,
   O watcher of men?
Why have you made me your target?
   Have I become a burden to you?
²¹Why do you not pardon my offenses
   and forgive my sins?
For I will soon lie down in the dust;
   you will search for me, but I will be no more."

Job attacked the counselors (ch. 6) and God (ch. 7), giving as his excuse for his rage the depth of his misery (6:3; 7:11). His words, disturbing as they are, arose from a limited knowledge (38:2) and his determination to speak only the truth as he saw it. "How painful are honest words!" (6:25). He viewed God as the author of his misery and opened (6:4) and closed (7:20) the speech with a figure of God shooting arrows in him. He found life an unbearable arena of torment. Once again Job's suffering was so intense that death would come as an exquisite release (6:8–10). Few suffer as intensely as Job; so it is difficult for us to identify with his rage. But for those who have a similar experience, the words of Job can bring immense comfort for the simple reason that many sufferers have felt rage but have been too ashamed to express it. That a man who had experienced such faith should speak from the depth of his being such words of anguish can only strengthen those in anguish.

Job argued persuasively his case against the counselors. They had been no help. Their words were bad medicine or, as Job put it, bad food (6:6–7). They were undependable (6:14–23), cruel (6:27–30), and viewed him as too great a risk to offer any help (6:21). Job challenged them to prove he was wrong (6:24) and pleaded with them for the milk of human kindness (6:14, 28).

1–7 The two themes of his speech are introduced here. In vv.1–4 Job complained against God and in vv.5–7 against the counselors. First he attempted to justify his own "impetuous" words (v.3) with an appeal to his overwhelming misery brought on by the arrows of God (v.4). Then he claimed the right to bray like a donkey or bellow like an ox deprived of fodder and left to starve (v.5). Job starved for the right words that, like food (Amos 8:11), could bring strength and nourishment. The food Eliphaz dished out was absolutely tasteless; worse, it turned Job's stomach (vv.6–7). Despite his bodily misery Job's major concern was for the needs of his spirit. If only he could hear words that would nourish his soul rather than sicken him more!

8–10 Again (cf. 3:21) Job earnestly asked God to bring an end to his suffering by bringing an end to his life—a mercy killing! He would then have some joy even in pain. He would have one consolation left before he died—that he had not denied the words of the Holy One, though he emphatically rejected the words of Eliphaz. Verses 1–10 form a unit based on a theme about the use of words: Job's words (v.3), Eliphaz's words (vv.6–7), and God's words (v.10).

11–13 Job complained that he had no reason to be patient, for he had nothing to look forward to (v.11). As a vulnerable creature made of flesh, he had no human resources left (v.12). Even his natural ability, the gifts that contributed to his success, had been driven from him (v.13). This is a reply to Eliphaz's words in 4:2–6.

14–21 Turning, in despair, to his friends, Job pled for kindness (*ḥesed*; NIV, "devotion"), even though they may have thought that he no longer feared God (v.14). Instead he found them like wadis that run dry (vv.15–20). Verse 21 is the climax of Job's reaction to his friends' counsel. They offered no help. The verse is like a sermon about the special strength needed to be willing to make oneself available when we see others in a truly dreadful condition. The risk involved makes us afraid.

22–23 Job never asked his friends for anything tangible (v.22). It was not as if they were being asked to pay a ransom to save him (v.23). The thought goes back to v.14, where he asked only for what would cost them nothing—their faithful love (*ḥesed*), despite what they thought he had done.

24–27 Job's words were a challenge and an indictment. His friends needed to be specific about his sins and be sure they were right (v.24). He insisted that they speak the truth just as he affirmed a compelling desire to speak only the truth before God. His words may have been painful, but they were honest, even though his friends treated them as wind (vv.25–26). In his mind it was their arguments that are specious (v.25b). He labeled them as men of such severe cruelty that they could have cast lots for an orphan or bartered away a friend (v.27).

28–30 Here Job softened his tone and appealed to his friends as men of compassion (v.28). He pled for justice, for a reconsideration of their indictment of him (v.29). His integrity was at stake, and that was more important to him than life itself. In v.30 Job again employed the figure of words as morsels of food. He reaffirmed the honesty of his own words and claimed for himself a discriminating taste for the truth.

7:1–2 These verses form a complaint to God: The life of man, so full of toil and suffering, is like hard military service—like a toiling slave longing for the shade. He is a hireling laboring for his pittance. Certainly this negative view of life, this language of dejection, represents a feeling shared at times by almost every human being.

3–10 These are the words of a chronic sufferer. There have been months of futility and nights of tossing in misery, nights that seem to drag on endlessly (vv.3–4). Yet almost in the same breath Job described his purposeless life as passing with incredible speed (v.6)—a complaint heard on the lips of the aging or any who feel their days are numbered (vv.7–10). In v.5 Job described one of the symptoms of his disease—scabs that crack and fester. Was it elephantiasis? We cannot be sure. But worse than the disease itself, Job lost all hope of being healed. He believed his only release from pain was death.

Beginning in v.7 Job addressed God directly, and this continues throughout the chapter. His words are an empirical view of the human lot on this earth. Man's life is only a breath. He goes down to the grave and never returns (v.9). Death is so final—a person disappears like a cloud, and his family sees him no more (v.10).

11–21 Again in v.11 Job asserted his determination to cry out in agony of spirit over the apparent injustice of God who, it seems, would not leave him alone. Even when sleep did come, he blamed God for his terrifying dreams (vv.13–14). This blaming of God brings up several theological issues. First, does the Book of Job teach a lesson about God's willingness to allow for Job's rage? Job's extreme language fits his cultural setting but was a source of great offense to postbiblical Jews who sometimes felt the need to theologically correct his words. That is exactly what was done in v.20 by scribes who preceded the Masoretes. Both an ancient scribal tradition and the LXX show the original reading of the final line to be "Have I become a burden to you?" (cf. NIV mg.). The present MT reads "I have become a burden to myself" —an early attempt to remove what was thought blasphemous. Fortunately a scribal note (*Tiqqune sopherim*) was kept. It is not only this verse but the whole passage that shares this raging attitude of Job's. If reprehensible in the eyes of later men, it was accepted by God (though not desired, cf. 38:2) as part of the struggle of a man who was determined to open himself wholly to God.

Secondly, was Job giving a parody of Psalm 8 (as Gordis, *God and Man,* in loc. maintains)? Like the psalmist, Job asked, "What is man that you make so much of him?" (v.17). The biblical answer is of course that man is the work of God's hands, created in his own image. God's purpose for the world centers around man, his crowning creation, to whom he gave the world. God makes much of man, for he was meant to be God's surrogate on earth. But Job, in his current condition, believed God's interest in him was only negative—as if God's only interest were to torment him for his sin, not letting him alone long enough to swallow his spittle (v.19). God even used him as a target for his arrows (v.20).

Contrary to all this, the reader knows from the Prologue that a loving God waited, with great concern, for that moment when Job's test would be over and the hand of the tormentor (the Accuser) would be removed. But at this moment it appears to Job that God is the tormentor. The reader knows God was using a secondary means and that Job's conception of God as tormentor was askew. The reader also knows that because God is sovereign, the problem remains logically unresolved. This age-old dilemma between divine sovereignty and divine goodness is a permanent back-drop throughout the Book of Job. The dilemma is there, but it is not the purpose of the Book of Job to attempt to resolve the problem. Job never received logical answers to the questions he asked. Satan and man may try to thwart the divine purpose. But that purpose can never be thwarted, for the one behind it is absolutely sovereign. It is precisely there that the Book of Job and the entire Bible leaves the question.

It would be a mistake to think, however, that Job was wrestling with a purely intellectual problem. No, his concern was more experiential than cognitive, though he was also seeking a way to make his experience (suffering) agree with his theology (the justice of God). Hebrew sages in the OT were not trying to solve logical syllogisms. Job's pathetic words at the end of this chapter show that he still entertained doubts about his own blameworthiness, but they also suggest that he felt God was being unjust. These are words he would eventually regret (40:4).

Notes

6:6 In rendering בְּרִיר חַלָּמוּת (berîr ḥallāmût) "in the white of an egg," the NIV follows the Targums as does Dhorme. Pope (in loc.) says this means "slimy cream cheese." But A.R. Millard ("What has no taste? [Job 6:6]," *Ugaritische Forschungen* 1 [1969]: 210) has pointed to the word *hilimitu* in the Alalakh Tablets, which means some kind of unknown vegetable, and this is close to the Syriac (slime of purslane). For *rîr* as "saliva" see 1 Sam 21:13.

7 Various translations of נַפְשִׁי (napšî) are "my soul," "my throat," "my appetite." All are possible, but NIV's "I" (lit. "myself") is a good choice.

The NIV's rendering of הֵמָּה כְּדְוֵי לַחְמִי (hēmmāh kidwê laḥmî) as "such food makes me ill" may be excused for being paraphrastic because the line as it stands in the MT is very difficult. But the witness of the LXX should be heeded, for it saw in the Hebrew text the letters *zhmh* (third fem. sing. perfect) as the first word of v.7b. Two factors favor the LXX: (1) the usage in 33:20 of the verb *zhm* ("be loathsome") with *lḥm* ("food") and (2) that the paleo-Hebrew letters ' (*y*, yod) (preceding) and ז (*z*, zayin) were written almost identically in certain periods. The line can then be literally rendered: "It is loathsome like bad food." Pope (in loc.) suggests another attractive solution. Taking *lḥm* to mean "flesh" as in 20:23 (RSV mg.; NIV, "upon him") and Zeph 1:17 (RSV; NIV, "entrails"), he renders the line "They (their words) are putrid as my flesh."

10 The NIV renders כִּי־לֹא כִחַדְתִּי (kî-lō' kiḥadtî) as "that I had not denied." The basic meaning of *kḥd* in Hebrew is "to hide" (15:18; 27:11); but in Ethiopic it means "to apostatize," which may be closer to its force in this context.

16 Since snow becomes dark as it melts, the NIV has captured the meaning of יִתְעַלֶּם־שָׁלֶג (yit 'allem-šāleg) as "with melting snow"; but the full force of *'lm* ("to be dark," "to conceal") as parallel with *qdr* ("to become dark") in v.16a cannot be appreciated in English. Pope (p. 53) has shown that the Arabic cognate to *'lm* is used of overflowing wadis.

21 The Greek and Syriac paraphrase 21a to read "and you have been against me," understanding לֹא (lō', NIV, "no help") as לִי (lî, "against me"). Another expedient in this difficult verse is to change כִּי (kî, "too") to כֵּן (kēn), reading "thus you have been to me." But there is no textual evidence for this. Others go with לֹו (lô), the Qere of a Western reading, and render "For now you have become His" (JPS). The NIV has done well to stay with the MT taking *lō'* to mean "nothing" (cf. KJV), that is, "no help."

7:6 Ibn Ezra noted long ago the play on the word תִּקְוָה (tiqwāh, "hope"), which can also mean "thread." Job's days move fast like a weaver's shuttle, and they come to an end through want of thread. Both meanings were equally intended. This is the kind of overtone in meaning that cannot be reflected in a translation without a footnote.

8 The precise meaning of this verse is problematic, not because the words are difficult, but because we are not sure who "the beholder" is in 8a nor how 8b relates to 8a. There is an emphasis on both the finality of death and God's constant attention to man. Is Job repeating himself, saying in both lines that God will not be able to find him after he dies? Andersen takes it this way, suggesting a rare assertative לֹא (*l*) in 8a (*Job*, p. 136, n. i; cf. also the note on 11:11). But it is possible that the "beholder" is his fellowman while v.8b gives the reason he will no longer be seen, for "God's eyes were against him and he will be gone."

12 This verse draws on mythological imagery. The Hebrew יָם (*yām*, "sea") is personalized and used like a proper name (Sea) without the article. It is also in apposition with תַּנִּין (*tannîn*, "monster of the deep"); so it may be taken as a reference to the Canaanite god of the sea (*Yam* in Ugar.). The NIV by translating it "the sea" has rejected this meaning, probably because some felt it would imply Job believed in Yam (but see Introduction, p. 868). According to the Canaanite myths, Yam was a boisterous opponent of Baal who was taken captive by him. Job denies that he is like this. M. Dahood ("MIŠMR 'MUZ-ZLE' in Job 7:12," JBL 80 [1961]: 270–71) has made a good case that מִשְׁמָר (*mišmār*) means "muzzle." In Ugaritic the goddess Anat boasts of muzzling the sea monster. But as Pope (p. 61) points out, the captive notion fits better with other OT texts (Ps 104:9; Jer 5:22) about the boisterous sea that is kept within bounds by God. Again we have overlapping semantic nuances that could be appreciated by those who felt the full range of meaning of a word like *mišmār*.

14 The parallel preposition בְּ (*b*) on בַחֲלֹמוֹת (*baḥălōmôt*, "with dreams") to the מ (*m*) in וּמֵחֶזְיֹנוֹת (*ûmēḥezyōnôt*, "with visions") proves the overlapping meaning of these two prepositions. See DSS 11QPsᵃ on Ps 119:87.

15 In rendering נַפְשִׁי (*napšî*) "I," the NIV takes *nepeš* to mean "I," "myself." But in this context the more concrete meaning "throat" fits better with the idea of strangulation and the parallel word "bones." Sarna (cited in Andersen, *Job*, p. 131; cf. also H.D. Hummel, "Enclitic MEM in Early Northwest Semitic," JBL 76 [1957]: 85–107) sees in the מ (*m*) prefixed to the word עַצְמוֹתָי (*ʿaṣmôtāy*, "bones") an enclitic *m* going with the preceding מָוֶת (*māwet*, "death"). He would read "so that my throat prefers strangling, my bones welcome death." Andersen (*Job*, pp. 137–38) follows this view but with mythological overtones. He sees Death (the god Mot) as the Strangler in Job's terrifying dream.

16 The NIV has added to מָאַסְתִּי (*māʾastî*, "I despise") the words "my life," but not without good reason. In 9:21 the same language is used including the object חַיָּי (*ḥayyāy*, "my life"), while in 42:6 the same word מָאַס (*māʾas*) in the imperfect tense is used as it is here, with the object suppressed.

19 Unfortunately the NIV in its attempt to give genteel English has paraphrased עַד־בִּלְעִי רֻקִּי (*ʿad-bilᵉʿî ruqqî*) as "even for an instant." This colorful figure is still used in Arabic, meaning a very brief moment, literally, "long enough to swallow my spit."

20 There is nothing in the Hebrew that demands the "If" that suggests Job thought God should be indifferent to sin in the NIV's rendering of חָטָאתִי (*ḥāṭāʾtî*, "If I have sinned"). No one in the OT world would entertain such an idea. The key to the text is to understand that there were many kinds of sin. Job says, "I have missed the mark of perfection, but what have I done against you?" That is, have I committed the high-handed sin? His point is that the extent of his suffering goes beyond his sin.

For עָלַי (*ʿālay*, NIV, "to you") the MT reads "to myself." This is one of the *Tiqqune sopherim* (see Introduction: Text) where the ancient Hebrew scribes recorded a change in the text. In this case it was made for theological reasons. Someone early in the transmission of the text felt it was sacrilegious for Job to say to God, "Have I become a burden to you?" The BHS text critical note shows that the LXX also supports the second person singular.

3. *Bildad*

8:1–22

¹Then Bildad the Shuhite replied:

²"How long will you say such things?
  Your words are a blustering wind.
³Does God pervert justice?
  Does the Almighty pervert what is right?
⁴When your children sinned against him,
  he gave them over to the penalty of their sin.
⁵But if you will look to God
  and plead with the Almighty,
⁶if you are pure and upright,
  even now he will rouse himself on your behalf
  and restore you to your rightful place.
⁷Your beginnings will seem humble,
  so prosperous will your future be.

⁸"Ask the former generations
  and find out what their fathers learned,
⁹for we were born only yesterday and know nothing,
  and our days on earth are but a shadow.
¹⁰Will they not instruct you and tell you?
  Will they not bring forth words from their understanding?
¹¹Can papyrus grow tall where there is no marsh?
  Can reeds thrive without water?
¹²While still growing and uncut,
  they wither more quickly than grass.
¹³Such is the destiny of all who forget God;
  so perishes the hope of the godless.
¹⁴What he trusts in is fragile;
  what he relies on is a spider's web.
¹⁵He leans on his web, but it gives way;
  he clings to it, but it does not hold.
¹⁶He is like a well-watered plant in the sunshine,
  spreading its shoots over the garden;
¹⁷it entwines its roots around a pile of rocks
  and looks for a place among the stones.
¹⁸But when it is torn from its spot,
  that place disowns it and says, 'I never saw you.'
¹⁹Surely its life withers away,
  and from the soil other plants grow.

²⁰"Surely God does not reject a blameless man
  or strengthen the hands of evildoers.
²¹He will yet fill your mouth with laughter
  and your lips with shouts of joy.
²²Your enemies will be clothed in shame,
  and the tents of the wicked will be no more."

Bildad's speech contains an important negative lesson about human nature in general and about the qualities of a good counselor. He heard Job's words with his ears, but his heart heard nothing. This truth should be viewed in the light of Job's plea for compassion in chapter 6. All people under the most ordinary circumstances need compassion; how much more Job in his extremity! Repeatedly in chapter 6 Job called himself a helpless (v. 13) and despairing man (vv. 14, 26) in need of the devotion of his friends. It seems almost incredible that Bildad would reply so callously.

There is not only steely indifference to Job's plight but an arrogant certainty that Job's children got just what they deserved and that Job was well on his way to the same fate. The lesson we must learn is that there are such people in the world and that they do their heartless disservice to mankind under the guise of being the special friend of God.

As he appears in the Dialogue, Job becomes a man whose frame of mind is not totally conducive to loving relationships with others. Anyone who curses the day of his birth and looks on death as preferable to life is in need of help. His three friends were there for that purpose, but Job came to view them as part of his problem rather than as those who offer therapy. Their view that people do suffer for their sins and need to be brought face to face with that reality was not wholly wrong. The assumption that Job was one of these is what led them astray as counselors.

The lessons we learn from Job's friends about counseling are negative, but the three are not alike. The book presents three counselors instead of one because each had his own approach and message for Job. Eliphaz began somewhat sensitive to Job's needs but eventually lost patience (ch. 22). The other two were aloof and superior. None of them was able to accept Job unconditionally. It is true that Job was a stubborn patient, but they were unable or unwilling—or both—to become involved with him. Their advice was well-meant and often accurately and artistically stated, but it succeeded in making Job even more stubborn and resistive to them. No doubt a large part of the problem was their academic commitment to a viewpoint they refused to alter, namely, that sin brings suffering and suffering is evidence of sin.

Job forced his counselors to accept or reject his contention that he was not suffering for his sins. In 6:24 he said, "Teach me, and I will be quiet;/ show me where I have been wrong." That they did not accept Job's contention made them unwilling to listen and hence miserable as counselors. Bildad could only reply, "God does not reject a blameless man" (v.20). However, had they accepted Job's contention, the book would have lost a major part of its message, a message that centers around the mystery of God's purposes in dealing with his creatures. An important lesson to be learned from the book is that counselors must not be sacrosanct. They must be willing to listen, become involved, and have respect for the integrity of the human personality they are trying to help. And they must always bear in mind that they may not fully understand the nature of the case.

1–10 Bildad was blunt. Eliphaz might only "venture a word" (4:2), but Bildad opened with a blast. "Your words are blustering wind" (v.2), said Bildad, as a preface to his one and only theological point: Job's suffering was the proof of his sinfulness. Since God cannot be unjust (v.3), there is only one conclusion—Job and his family (v.4) had received the punishment they deserved. Job should plead for mercy (v.5). Then, if he deserved it (v.6), God would restore him (v.7). Bildad failed to see that mercy implies the forgiveness one receives even though he does not deserve it. Eliphaz had appealed to revelation; Bildad appealed to tradition. To Bildad nothing less than the teachings of the ancients (vv.8–10) proved the orthodoxy of his viewpoint. If Job would only take the time to consider ancient tradition, he would find that God only does right. Sinners get just punishment, and good men are blessed with health and prosperity.

11–19 This poem on the destruction of the wicked has a literary quality similar to that demonstrated by Eliphaz in his masterly poem on the good man in 5:17–26. The man who ignores God, Bildad called a *ḥānēp* (NIV, "godless"; v.13). The word means something like our word "hypocrite." Such a man's hope is unreliable. Like a spider's web (v.14), it provides no support. The godless are like papyrus plants without water (vv.11–12) or a vine with shallow roots clinging to rocks, destined to be pulled up or left to wither and die (vv.16–19).

20–22 Bildad thought he heard Job say that God perverts justice (v.3). Job had problems about divine justice; but he had not yet blatantly accused God of being unjust, though he came close to it (6:20). Job found it difficult if not impossible to understand God's justice. Although Job did not claim perfection (v.21), he considered himself a blameless man (*tām*, v.20). This was also God's view of him in the Prologue (1:8; 2:3), but Bildad was sure that God had rejected Job. Since God does not reject blameless men (8:20), Job could not be one. So he must be a hypocrite (*ḥānēp*). The situation, however, could be remedied: if only he would turn to God, Job's lips might laugh again.

Notes

6 The NIV renders נְוַת צִדְקֶךָ (*nᵉwat ṣidqekā*) "your rightful place." "Estate" would be a better way to translate *nāweh*, which has pastoral overtones (also 5:3). The word *ṣedeq* has legal overtones yielding "your rightful (lawful) estate."

8 There is no need to emend כּוֹנֵן (*kônēn*, "find out") to בּֽנֵן (*bonēn*) (Ehrlich, Fohrer). Driver-Gray and Dhorme understood it correctly. A colloquial ellipsis of לֵב (*lēḇ*, "mind") yields the meaning "fix (your mind) to," which fits with a similar colloquial use of the verb שִׂים (*śîm*, "to put"; 4:20; 23:6; 24:12; 34:23). The verb כּוּן (*kûn*, "fix") appears with similar meaning in Isa 51:13 (NIV, "bent") and probably in Job 28:27 (NIV, "confirmed") and Judg 12:6 (NIV, "pronounce"). The two verbs in this verse—שָׁאַל (*šāʾal*, "ask," "inquire") and *kûn*—are used together with the same meanings in Ugaritic (Blommerde, p. 50).

11 The practical wisdom poem of vv.11–19 are the words of instruction that come from the fathers. The rhetorical question is a common wisdom form Job has already used effectively in 6:5–6.

13 There is no need to amend אָרְחוֹת (*ʾorḥôt*, "paths") to אַחֲרִית (*ʾaḥᵃrît*) to get the meaning "destiny," "fate." The Ugaritic evidence here is indirect (Blommerde, p. 52); but Dhorme (in loc.) has shown *ʾorḥôt* in Prov 1:19 (NIV, "end") has the same meaning, and to that may be added Prov 24:14b (NIV, "future hope") (cf. Blommerde, p. 52, and NIV).

14 The NIV margin says that the meaning of יָקוֹט (*yāqôṭ*, "fragile") is unknown, but see our discussion of this in the Introduction (p. 858). The various changes in the text suggested by commentaries accomplish nothing better than the *ad sensum* rendering of the NIV.

17 The NIV has added the words "a place" to יֶחֱזֶה (*yeḥᵉzeh*, "looks for") because the most common meaning of *ḥāzāh* is "to look." But nothing needs to be added if we understand the root to be אָחַז (*ʾāḥaz*, "to seize"), with a suppression of the א (ʾ, aleph) as in 2 Samuel 20:9 (*yōḥᵃzāh*, NIV, "took"; cf. BDB, p.28). The translation would read "It ['the plant' of v.16] takes hold among the stones." Pope (in loc.) makes the verb plural: "They [the roots] take hold." For the use of the word בֵּית (*bêṯ*, "among") as a preposition, see Holliday, *Concise Lexicon*, p. 39.

19 The NIV renders הֶן־הוּא מְשׂוֹשׂ דַּרְכּוֹ (*hēn-hûʾ mᵉśôś darkô*) as "Surely its life withers away." The MT is very difficult because the two major words can be taken in more than one way. The NIV goes along with the NEB. The word *mᵉśôś* is identified with the same form in Isa 8:6 meaning "to wither (melt) away" instead of the other meaning "joy" (so NIV, KJV,

RSV et al.), which does not fit the context at all. Dhorme (in loc.) may be right in giving *derek* a literal rather than a metaphorical meaning—"there by its path [*derek*] it rots."

4. Job's reply

9:1–10:22

¹Then Job replied:

²"Indeed, I know that this is true.
But how can a mortal be righteous before God?
³Though one wished to dispute with him,
he could not answer him one time out of a thousand.
⁴His wisdom is profound, his power is vast.
Who has resisted him and come out unscathed?
⁵He moves mountains without their knowing it
and overturns them in his anger.
⁶He shakes the earth from its place
and makes its pillars tremble.
⁷He speaks to the sun and it does not shine;
he seals off the light of the stars.
⁸He alone stretches out the heavens
and treads on the waves of the sea.
⁹He is the Maker of the Bear and Orion,
the Pleiades and the constellations of the south.
¹⁰He performs wonders that cannot be fathomed,
miracles that cannot be counted.
¹¹When he passes me, I cannot see him;
when he goes by, I cannot perceive him.
¹²If he snatches away, who can stop him?
Who can say to him, 'What are you doing?'
¹³God does not restrain his anger;
even the cohorts of Rahab cowered at his feet.

¹⁴"How then can I dispute with him?
How can I find words to argue with him?
¹⁵Though I were innocent, I could not answer him;
I could only plead with my Judge for mercy.
¹⁶Even if I summoned him and he responded,
I do not believe he would give me a hearing.
¹⁷He would crush me with a storm
and multiply my wounds for no reason.
¹⁸He would not let me regain my breath
but would overwhelm me with misery.
¹⁹If it is a matter of strength, he is mighty!
And if it is a matter of justice, who will summon him?
²⁰Even if I were innocent, my mouth would condemn me;
if I were blameless, it would pronounce me guilty.

²¹"Although I am blameless,
I have no concern for myself;
I despise my own life.
²²It is all the same; that is why I say,
'He destroys both the blameless and the wicked.'
²³When a scourge brings sudden death,
he mocks the despair of the innocent.
²⁴When a land falls into the hands of the wicked,
he blindfolds its judges.
If it is not he, then who is it?

25 "My days are swifter than a runner;
    they fly away without a glimpse of joy.
26 They skim past like boats of papyrus,
    like eagles swooping down on their prey.
27 If I say, 'I will forget my complaint,
    I will change my expression, and smile,'
28 I still dread all my sufferings,
    for I know you will not hold me innocent.
29 Since I am already found guilty,
    why should I struggle in vain?
30 Even if I washed myself with soap
    and my hands with washing soda,
31 you would plunge me into a slime pit
    so that even my clothes would detest me.

32 "He is not a man like me that I might answer him,
    that we might confront each other in court.
33 If only there were someone to arbitrate between us,
    to lay his hand upon us both,
34 someone to remove God's rod from me,
    so that his terror would frighten me no more.
35 Then I would speak up without fear of him,
    but as it now stands with me, I cannot.

10:1 I loathe my very life;
    therefore I will give free rein to my complaint
    and speak out in the bitterness of my soul.
2 I will say to God: Do not condemn me,
    but tell me what charges you have against me.
3 Does it please you to oppress me,
    to spurn the work of your hands,
    while you smile on the schemes of the wicked?
4 Do you have eyes of flesh?
    Do you see as a mortal sees?
5 Are your days like those of a mortal
    or your years like those of a man,
6 that you must search out my faults
    and probe after my sin—
7 though you know that I am not guilty
    and that no one can rescue me from your hand?

8 "Your hands shaped me and made me.
    Will you now turn and destroy me?
9 Remember that you molded me like clay.
    Will you now turn me to dust again?
10 Did you not pour me out like milk
    and curdle me like cheese,
11 clothe me with skin and flesh
    and knit me together with bones and sinews?
12 You gave me life and showed me kindness,
    and in your providence watched over my spirit.

13 "But this is what you concealed in your heart,
    and I know that this was in your mind:
14 If I sinned, you would be watching me
    and would not let my offense go unpunished.
15 If I am guilty—woe to me!
    Even if I am innocent, I cannot lift my head,
for I am full of shame
    and drowned in my affliction.

> ¹⁶If I hold my head high, you stalk me like a lion
>   and again display your awesome power against me.
> ¹⁷You bring new witnesses against me
>   and increase your anger toward me;
>   your forces come against me wave upon wave.
>
> ¹⁸"Why then did you bring me out of the womb?
>   I wish I had died before any eye saw me.
> ¹⁹If only I had never come into being,
>   or had been carried straight from the womb to the grave!
> ²⁰Are not my few days almost over?
>   Turn away from me so I can have a moment's joy
> ²¹before I go to the place of no return,
>   to the land of gloom and deep shadow,
> ²²to the land of deepest night,
>   of deep shadow and disorder,
>   where even the light is like darkness."

In these chapters Job's words move from extolling God (9:1–13)—perhaps as a display of theological acumen to impress the counselors—to blaming God. Would God ever treat him justly? He doubted it (vv.14–31). Does God mock the innocent? Job thought probably so (vv.21–24). "If it is not he, then who is it?" (v.24). These are hard words, but his question instead of a statement implies doubt. These words are followed in vv.32–35 with a yearning for someone strong enough to take up his cause with God. But in chapter 10 Job decided to plead his own cause and direct all his words to God. How could God who created him want to destroy him and that without any formal charges?

1–24 In vv.1–13 Job intended to show that his problems were not due to gross ignorance of God's ways. Those ways are past finding out, but he knew as much about them as they do. His opening remark—"Indeed I know that this is true" (v.1)—is a grudging admission that what Bildad had said contained the right theology. But he had more than Bildad's words in mind. Job immediately called to mind Eliphaz's rhetorical question in 4:17: "Can a mortal be more righteous than God?" Some think Eliphaz and Job were each using the root *ṣdq* ("righteous") in a slightly different sense. Eliphaz's righteousness was based on ontological superiority while Job was thinking of juridical vindication, that is, innocence (see David Robertson, *The Old Testament and the Literary Critic* [Philadelphia: Fortress, 1977], p. 41). The word covers both meanings.

Bildad's accusations in chapter 8 turned Job's mind to the subject of legal vindication. In 8:20 Bildad said, "Surely God does not reject a blameless man." To Bildad God's justice required punishing the guilty and blessing the innocent (see also 8:3–6). Job fervently believed that he was innocent of any sin that would warrant the kind of punishment he was enduring. But he was frustrated in his attempt to vindicate himself. God's wisdom was too profound and his power too great for Job to debate in court (vv.3–4).

Verses 4–13 constitute a hymn in which Job described God's awesome power. God shakes the earth from its place and makes its pillars tremble (v.6); he speaks to the sun, and it does not shine (v.7); he stretches out the heavens and treads on the waves of the sea—the creation and control of all natural forces (v.8). Job closed the hymn with the words of Eliphaz used in 5:9: "He performs wonders that cannot be fathomed, miracles that cannot be counted." But Job was applying these words in a way opposite to how Eliphaz used them.

In chapter 5 Eliphaz was showing how God, by his power, does what is good and right. He lifts to safety those who mourn and delivers the poor from the clutches of the powerful. But Job saw God's power as if it were amoral, a sovereign freedom, an uncontrollable power that works mysteriously (v.11) to do whatever he wills so that no one can stop him and ask, "What are you doing?" (v.12). Yes, God's anger makes even the armies of Rahab (the boisterous demonic power associated with the sea) cower at his feet (v.13). Job thought such a God would overwhelm him in any attempt to show his innocence. Job could only plead for mercy; even worse, Job doubted God would give him a hearing. For no reason at all, God would overwhelm him in any attempt to show his innocence. Job could only plead for mercy; even worse, Job doubted that God would even give him a hearing, but believed that for no reason at all God would crush him.

This awful indictment of God presents us with a very contemporary theological issue. There are those within the bounds of the modern church who think that in the OT God is sometimes a bully and therefore this view of God must be written off as only a phase in man's understanding. Due to Job's frustration and illness, these words (vv.14–31) must not be considered normative. But unfortunately even normative passages are sometimes written off as sub-Christian. All God's sovereign acts are rooted in his righteous character, even when they are outside the bounds of human ability to evaluate them. And that applies especially here as Job struggled to understand.

In vv.21–24 this God of Job's imagination was worse than morally indifferent (v.22); he even mocked the despair of the innocent (v.23) and blocked the administering of justice (v.24). Since everyone gets treated the same way—the blameless and the wicked—Job threw all caution to the wind: "I have no concern for myself; I despise my own life" (v.21). He added, "If God is not responsible for this, then who is?" (cf v.24).

These are words of a sick and desperate man. They are a forceful reminder to anyone who has to counsel the sick, that people who face deep trials often say irresponsible things in their struggle to understand their suffering in the light of God's compassion. Not all Job's words are wrong, but it is a mistake to try to make them all represent valid theology rather than the half-truths of a man struggling to understand. They deal with the mystery at the very heart of the Book of Job: the problem of evil for which no human being has a logical explanation. So Job reasoned, as many have, that if God is sovereign, truly sovereign, he is responsible for all evil.

Job did not mention the corollary: If there is evil beyond God's control, then he is not truly sovereign. Job stressed only God's irresistible might; and it appears to him that if God held him to be guilty, there was nothing that he could do to establish his innocence. Yet he believed he was innocent and was concerned with disproving the contention of his friends that God only destroys the wicked and always cares for the righteous. Job's experience told him that sometimes God crushes the innocent for no reason at all (v.17). We who are privileged to see the drama from the divine perspective know that Job was innocent and that God did have a cause, a cause beyond the purview of Job, a cause that could not be revealed to Job at that moment.

25–35 Verses 25–31 fall together as an expression of deep despair. Job was unable to suck sweetness from a single day; there was not a glimpse of joy, not a smile (v.27), only one unending blur of suffering (v.28). Since God arbitrarily chose to treat him as a criminal, what could he do to purge himself (v.29)? Even if he were able to purge himself (v.30), God would plunge him again into a slime pit so that even his clothes would detest him (v.31).

In vv. 32–35 Job went back to the theme of vv.14–20. He was so frustrated over the immenseness of God! No doubt Andersen (*Job*, p. 151) is correct in saying that the real issue in the Book of Job is not the problem of suffering but the obtaining of a right relationship between Job and God. What Job did not realize was that in wrestling with God, he was moving in the direction of a right relationship with his Maker. If he only understood what God was doing, that would have made his suffering bearable. But as it was then, he bore a burden that was even greater than his suffering—his apparent inability to stand in God's presence as an upright and blameless man (v.32).

In v.33 Job touched on the mystery through which God would eventually provide godliness for man. He yearned for a mediator between himself and God. A *môkîah* ("someone to arbitrate") does not have to be one who stands over God and Job in order to judge between them (Pope, in loc.). As "one who argues a case," he is a mediator or negotiator who is able to bring parties together. We should not infer from this that the Book of Job here is directly predictive of the NT doctrine of Christ as mediator. For one thing Job was not looking for a mediator to forgive him of his sins so that he might be received by God; Job was yearning for a mediator who could prove that he was innocent and could somehow be effective with God despite his infinite power and wisdom. But having said that, we have here a rudimentary idea that is certainly evocative of that NT concept. Even here in the Book of Job, the idea will move on to greater ramifications in 16:20–21 and 19:25–26.

10:1–22 In chapter 10 Job continued to bewail his sorrowful condition. Life had become an unbearable burden. In his bitter anquish he determined to speak out (v.1), once again directing his words to God. He called on God, not for healing and restoration, which incidentally he nowhere ever asked for; but he wanted to know again why he was suffering. "Tell me what charges you have against me" (v.2).

Job could not understand how God, the Creator, who looked on his original creation and considered it good, could turn his back on the work of his hands (v.3). Had not Job dedicated his life to God, in contrast to the wicked who received God's smile? Job knew that God was not limited like human beings who have mere eyes of flesh and a certain number of years (vv.4–5). Did God have to search out Job's faults when he knew that he was innocent (vv.6–7)? Job put God on the witness stand and plied him with questions. Job could not understand how the God who so marvelously made him in the womb, who gave him life and showed him such providential care, could be willing to destroy him (vv.8–12).

The NIV takes v.13 with what follows, but some do not agree (cf. Andersen, *Job*, pp. 153–54). If the NIV is correct (see Notes), then in v.13 Job was saying that God brought him into being so that he might hound him over his sin and let no offense go unpunished. It seemed that Job was saying that it did not make any difference whether he was innocent or guilty because he was full of shame and drowned in affliction anyhow (vv.14–15). No matter how much he tried to assert his integrity, it seems that God insisted on stalking Job like a lion, showing his awesome power in wave after wave of oppression (vv.16–17).

Poor Job, the God he imagined was so angry with him was not angry with him at all; but in his current state of mind, he reverted back to his original wish to have died at birth, to have been carried straight from the womb to the tomb (vv.18–19). In chapter 3 Job saw Sheol as a place where he might have found some rest from his troubles; here in chapter 10 he longed for a few days of release on earth before he had to go to that place of no return, which he envisioned as a land of gloom and deepest night (vv.20–23).

Job had reached about as far as a human being can go into the depths of depression and despair, but it would do us well to be reminded that even the apostle of hope said in 2 Corinthians 1:8–9: "We were under great pressure, far beyond our ability to endure, so that we despaired even of life. Indeed, in our hearts, we felt the sentence of death. But this happened that we might not rely on ourselves but on God, who raises the dead." In his despair Job still wrestled with God, but it was still to the living God that his cry was lifted up. An important question yet to be faced is, Did Job have any hope that transcended this life?

Notes

9:2 Gordis (*Job*, p. 103) claims עִם־אֵל (*'im-'ēl*, "before God") carries a double connotation: "in the estimation of God" and "in a contest with God." To passages using the latter meaning may be added Isa 7:14, where the rest of the chapter shows the prophet has a dual-cutting edge to that epithet Immanuel: God is with us—to bless—and God is in contest with us—to punish. Here in v.2 Job quoted Eliphaz in 4:17, but he substituted *'im* for *min*. This lends weight to our contention that *min* means "before" spatially rather than express comparison in 4:17.

4 Is this verse a description of God or the man who would dare dispute with him? While the latter is possible (Pope, in loc.), it requires turning the line into a conditional sentence. Dhorme thinks the idea is too subtle. The same problem exists in v.3a, where Pope also goes against most by taking God as the subject: "If he (God) deigned to litigate." The NIV considers the subject of v.3a to be indefinite, meaning "anyone." Verses 5–12 are clearly hymnic, extolling God's fearsome power. The NIV has chosen to include vv.4, 13 in the hymn.

5 The NIV's rendering of וְלֹא יָדָעוּ (*welō' yādā'û*, "without their knowing it") makes it sound as if the mountains do not know when they are moved. Again an indefinite subject leads to the translation "and no one knows it"—i.e., earthquakes in uninhabited places.

7 We have assumed the astronomical phenomena here are the eclipse of the sun and the periodic behavior of the planets and stars, but that may not be the primary reference. The Targum may have caught the intent of this context with its paraphrase: "The clouds seal up the stars" (Dhorme, p. 129). The NIV renders זָרַח (*zārah*) "shine," but its basic meaning is "rise." Is it a brief eclipse or sustained darkness? Verses 5–7 describe what God does in his anger—the quaking of the mountains often includes volcanic activity with clouds darkening the sky.

8 The word לְבַדּוֹ (*lebadô*, "alone") stresses the monotheism of Job. Isaiah 44:24 uses identical language. See the Introduction, p. 868.

As many have noted, the rhetoric is mythopoeic (Pope, p. 70). The myth told of the defeat of the sea god; but since Job's God alone is God (v.8a), the meaning must be limited to his control over his creation. יָם (*yām*, "Yam"; NIV, "sea") was a cosmic deity (a dragon). The back parts בָּמֳתֵי (*bomotê*) of Yam is a metaphor for "the waves of the sea" (NIV).

9 Compare 38:31–33. The LXX shows the familiarity of the translator with Greek pagan literature. These heavenly phenomena are called "Pleiades, Hesperus, and Arcturus." For views on the identification of these constellations, see G.R. Driver ("Two Astronomical Passages in the Old Testament," JTS, n.s., 4 [1953]: 208–12; id., "Two Astronomical Passages in the Old Testament," JTS, n.s., 7 [1956]: 1–11); Pope (pp. 70–71, 301); Dhorme (pp. 131–32). Although their roots are obscure, Pleiades (כִּימָה, kîmāh) and Orion (כְּסִיל, keꜱîl) are generally accepted. But עָשׁ (ʿāš; cf. ʿayiš in 38:32) as "Bear" is uncertain. It may be "Leo" (cf. NIV mg. at 38:32). On "the constellations [chambers] of the south," G. Schiaparelli (Astronomy in the Old Testament [Oxford: University Press, 1905], pp. 63 –67) notes that as a result of precession many stars that were visible on the southern horizon in Palestine (the 32d degree of north lattitude) are no longer visible there. This heavenly display begins at the star Argus (Canopus) and ends with Centaurus and is the brightest part of the whole sky. In this area are five stars of the first magnitude (there are only twenty in the whole stellar sphere) and five more of the second magnitude. It actually produces a faint twilight illumination.

11 Job was frustrated—וְלֹא אֶרְאֶה (welōʾ ʾerʾeh, "I cannot see him")—because he wanted to see God but could not. What is this invisibility of God? Is Job's God by his very nature invisible compared with visible idols? In the Introduction (p. 869) we suggest this, but Job did finally "see" God in 42:5. It is our contention that even if the "seeing" is a literal viewing of something, it is only God's majesty and splendor (37:21–22); for the Lord spoke to Job out of the storm (38:1). Here and in 42:5 "seeing God" probably means a personal encounter that goes beyond head knowledge, which in 42:5 Job called "hearing with the ears."

13 Pope (in loc.) translates "a god could not turn back his anger." But the word אֱלוֹהַ (ʾelôah, "God") is used forty-two times in Job of the true God; and Job 12:6 is the only additional passage where it could mean a god or an idol but that, like this, is subject to the other interpretation (cf. NIV mg. at 12:6).

15–16 Andersen (Job, p. 147, n. 2) sees v.15 as pivotal for understanding the chapter. Job's claim to innocence makes it unlikely that he would appeal for mercy as admonished. He suggests לֹא (lōʾ) in v.15a does double duty and reads v.15b: "I do not need to plead with my judge for mercy." Andersen points out that Elihu accused Job of "justifying himself" and accused the friends of failing to prove Job was wrong. In v.16a Andersen finds difficulty in Job's accusation of God as cruel and unfair (also v.17). Not fairness but exposure to the divine presence (v.34) is Job's concern according to Andersen; so he turns the negative of v.16b into an assertative אל (l). Of course, any negative can be made positive by turning it into a question. The text would read: "If I summoned him and he responded, would he not give me a hearing?" But this makes what follows seem unnatural.

19 On יוֹעִידֵנִי (yôʿîḏēnî, "summon him") and the third masculine singular pronoun, see the note on v.35.

20 The NIV understands the subject of וַיַעְקְשֵׁנִי (wayyaʿqešēnî, "it would pronounce me guilty") to refer back to "my mouth" rather than to "God." The Hebrew (masc.) will allow for either, but the NIV softens the overt injustice Job imputed to God who would pronounce him guilty even if he was innocent.

27 Although against normal usage, ʾim with the infinitive and pronoun—אִם־אָמְרִי (ʾim-ʾomrî, "If I say")—is preferable to following the one MS that changes the verb to אָמַרְתִּי (ʾāmartî; cf. BHS mg.).

29 This verse is pure irony. Since the tone of irony cannot be conveyed in writing, NIV has done next best—made it a hypothetical statement.

30 The Hithpael in אִם־הִתְרָחַצְתִּי בְמֵו־שָׁלֶג (ʾim-hiṭrāḥaṣtî bemēw-šāleg, "even if I washed myself with soap") may be iterative, not reflexive (cf. Andersen, Job, p. 150, n. 1), meaning "Even if I repeatedly washed." The Kethiv and the LXX are right in reading bemô, the poetic preposition "with." Pope (p. 75) gives linguistic proof that šeleg here means "soap," not "snow."

33 The NIV goes with the LXX and other versions reading לוּ (*lû*), which expresses "desire," rather than the negative לֹא (*lō'*). The MT pointing probably arose for theological reasons (cf. 16:4).

35 כִּי לֹא־כֵן אָנֹכִי עִמָּדִי (*kî lō'-kēn 'ānōkî 'immādî*, "but as it now stands with me, I cannot") is difficult. The NIV has rendered the line *ad sensum*. Blommerde (p. 8) suggests that *'immādî* has the yod as a rare third person singular pronoun suffix on the basis of Phoenician and Ugaritic evidence. But Z. Zevit ("The Linguistic and Contextual Arguments in Support of a Hebrew 3 m.s. suffix -y," *Ugarit Forschungen* 9 [1977]: 315–28) argues against any such use in the OT. Zevit claims the Ugaritic evidence is questionable; and while the Phoenician evidence is well attested, the yod appears only with nouns or verbs ending in a long vowel and with singular nouns in the genitive case (cf. F.M. Cross and D.N. Freedman, "The Pronominal Suffixes of the Third Person Singular in Phoenician," *JNES* 10 [1951]: 228–30). Zevit claims all but five of Dahood's Psalms examples of third singular yod are either not necessary or impossible; so he falls back on the confusion between waw and yod during several periods when the two graphemes looked very much alike in the square script. If the third masculine singular yod were attested in Hebrew inscriptional material as it is in Phoenician, he would have to revise this opinion. Since this is not so, we accept only those passages in Job that are supported by the LXX as third singular or can be easily considered a graphic confusion of two similarly written letters.

The form *'immādî* ("with me") here, however, creates a special problem since the form *'immādô* ("with him") is not attested in the OT. This makes it difficult to see how the Greek arrived at the third singular. But Greek that reads "I do not think myself unjust with him" is too far from the MT. If *'immādô* were possible, the line would render excellent sense: "but it is not so between us," reading the last two Hebrew words "I with him." Of the thirty-one examples of third singular yod in Job given by Blommerde, the following have a context clearly favoring the third person: 9:9; 14:3; 19:28; 21:16; 22:18; 31:18. In some of these cases the LXX has the third masculine singular.

10:2 The meaning of אַל־תַּרְשִׁיעֵנִי (*'al-taršî'ēnî*, "Do not condemn me") is literally "treat a person as wicked." That was Job's problem with God. It appeared to him that the Almighty was giving him what a wicked man deserved when he knew Job was not a wicked man ("guilty" in v.7 is the same verb).

3 הֲטוֹב (*h²ṭôb*, "Does it please [you]") is literally "Is it good?" The idiom has overtones of Genesis 1, where God looked on all his creation and "it was good." How can he now despise the work of his hands?

8–12 Is this poem on the creation of man or his gestation? Verses 8–9 use the "potter" figure while vv.10–12 are figures of procreation and gestation—Job was poured out like milk (semen) and knit together in the womb.

15 Job claimed it was his affliction that made it appear he was guilty. This verse hardly means he was willing to concede that point. The two verbs at the end of this verse are imperative in form. The meaning then of v.15b is "be satisfied with my shame, be aware of my affliction." See the NIV mg., which is closer to the MT. The NIV text has "drowned" from the root *rwh* ("be saturated") instead of *r'h* ("to see"). The difference in meaning is whether Job was calling on God for mercy or was stating his own sad condition.

16 The subject of the first verb is ambiguous. The Hebrew appears to be third masculine singular. The NIV goes with the Syriac (first person), but there are other ways to handle the problem. W.F. Beck (*The Holy Bible, An American Translation* [New Haven, Mo.: Leader, 1976]) takes *yig'eh* as an adverb—"Bold like a lion you hunt me down." Pope (in loc.) does the same but reading *gē'eh*.

20 יָשִׁית מִמֶּנִּי (*y²šît mimmennî*, "turn away from me") is literally "put from me," another example of ellipsis of either *lēb* ("heart") or *yād* ("hand") (cf. 38:11 for this verb and note on 4:20 for ellipsis).

5. *Zophar*

11:1–20

¹Then Zophar the Naamathite replied:

> ²"Are all these words to go unanswered?
>   Is this talker to be vindicated?
> ³Will your idle talk reduce men to silence?
>   Will no one rebuke you when you mock?
> ⁴You say to God, 'My beliefs are flawless
>   and I am pure in your sight.'
> ⁵Oh, how I wish that God would speak,
>   that he would open his lips against you
> ⁶and disclose to you the secrets of wisdom,
>   for true wisdom has two sides.
>   Know this: God has even forgotten some of your sin.
>
> ⁷"Can you fathom the mysteries of God?
>   Can you probe the limits of the Almighty?
> ⁸They are higher than the heavens—what can you do?
>   They are deeper than the depths of the grave—what can you
>   know?
> ⁹Their measure is longer than the earth
>   and wider than the sea.
>
> ¹⁰"If he comes along and confines you in prison
>   and convenes a court, who can oppose him?
> ¹¹Surely he recognizes deceitful men;
>   and when he sees evil, does he not take note?
> ¹²But a witless man can no more become wise
>   than a wild donkey's colt can be born a man.
>
> ¹³"Yet if you devote your heart to him
>   and stretch out your hands to him,
> ¹⁴if you put away the sin that is in your hand
>   and allow no evil to dwell in your tent,
> ¹⁵then you will lift up your face without shame;
>   you will stand firm and without fear.
> ¹⁶You will surely forget your trouble,
>   recalling it only as waters gone by.
> ¹⁷Life will be brighter than noonday,
>   and darkness will become like morning.
> ¹⁸You will be secure, because there is hope;
>   you will look about you and take your rest in safety.
> ¹⁹You will lie down, with no one to make you afraid,
>   and many will court your favor.
> ²⁰But the eyes of the wicked will fail,
>   and escape will elude them;
>   their hope will become a dying gasp."

Zophar was a severe man. Like Bildad he lacked compassion and was ruthlessly judgmental. He thought Job, who was suffering to the point of despair, was getting much less than he deserved.

1–12 Zophar considered Job's words pure mockery (vv.2–3), for he thought Job was claiming flawless doctrine and sinless perfection (v.4). Job has steadfastly maintained his innocence or blamelessness in contrast with wickedness (9:22), but he did not claim to be perfect (7:21). Though he complained bitterly of the treatment God appeared to be giving him, to this point he has not been particularly sarcastic nor has he mocked God or even ridiculed his friends. He has accused them of being shallow in their arguments and callous in the way they have dealt with him (6:24–27).

Zophar spoke with eloquence about God's infinitude (vv.7–8), justice, and omniscience (vv.10–11). Job needed a stiff rebuke from the lips of God because God had favored him by forgetting some of his sin, or at least had allowed Job to forget some of his sin (see note on v.6). Either way the words are designed to suggest the enormity of Job's sin. Zophar's only reason to believe Job had sinned to such an extent was derived from the extent of Job's suffering, which he took to be God's way of exposing secret sin. That Job would not admit it was taken to be additional evidence of his pride and hardness of heart. So Job needed to be humbled. The best way to humble him was to bring him face to face with God. In vv.7–9 he expounded on the immensity of God in spatial terms. If the limits of the created cosmos were beyond Job's understanding, how much more the mysteries of God!

In vv.10–11 Zophar touched on the omnipotence and omniscience of God who sees through the deceit of men like Job and keeps a permanent record of it. All this was designed to humble Job, but Zophar apparently doubted that it would. He then attempted heavy handed shock treatment to get through to Job. The sharpness of his sarcasm is demonstrated in v.12. Zophar labeled Job a witless, empty-headed man with as much chance to become wise as a wild donkey has to be born tame (see Notes).

13–20 Job's only hope was to stretch out his hands to God and repent (v.13). This is of course good advice for a person who has lived a life of sinful indulgence, but to Job's ears it was pious arrogance. And it was arrogant for Zophar to assume he knew why Job was suffering; he had reduced the solution of this very complex human problem to a simplistic formula—every pain has a sin behind it. Zophar erroneously suggested that if one repents and gets right with God, this guarantees that the struggles and troubles of life will dissolve (vv.14–16). This common error is made by many well-meaning Christians who fail to distinguish between forensic forgiveness that cancels the guilt of sin and the immediate consequences of a profligate life that often brings trouble and distress. But we know from the Prologue that Job's troubles were not the result of a profligate life; so Zophar was wrong on both counts. Job's troubles did not come as a penalty from God; and even if they did, Job's repentance would not guarantee that life from then on would be "brighter than noonday" (v.17) and that people would stop molesting him and instead "court his favor" (vv.18–19).

Notes

4 Used mainly in Proverbs, the word לִקְחִי (liqḥî, "my beliefs") means "teaching." But in Deut 32:2, where it is parallel with אִמְרָתִי ('imrāṭî, "my speech"; NIV, "my word"), it may mean "my testimony" (cf. Habel, Job, 1985, p. 207). But the subject here is Job's doctrine.

6 True, effective wisdom (תוּשִׁיָּה, tûšîyāh) includes understanding the dialectical tension— כִּפְלַיִם (kiplayim, "two sides")—often involved in the balance of truth. But is this the meaning here? Zophar may have meant the hidden (deeper) part of wisdom axioms. The precise meaning is not agreed on, but in wisdom literature the מָשָׁל (māšāl, "proverb,"

"riddle," "parable") had a hidden as well as an obvious meaning. Jesus frequently used this method of teaching. Zophar was chiding Job for being obvious and therefore shallow.

The NIV's translation of יַשֶּׁה לְךָ אֱלוֹהַ (yaššeh leḵā ʾelôah)—"God has forgotten"—leaves out the force of the leḵā. Literally it reads "God has forgotten for you some of your sin." The verb nāšāh usually takes a direct object. If the lamed is a mark of the accusative (Aramaism), then we could read "God has made (allowed) you to forget."

8 The NIV should not have used the word "grave" for שְׁאוֹל (šeʾôl) in this context. The stress is on a place that is opposite to heaven and very deep—the nether world.

11 The NIV has chosen to make the readings positive with a question. This may be another case of the assertive or emphatic לֹא (lʾ; cf. BHS mg. See also note on 7:8).

12 The NIV's margin seems preferable. See Pope (p. 86) who claims עַיִר (ʿayir) means a male domesticated donkey, not a colt of a wild donkey. Dahood ("Zacharia 9:1, ʾên ʾādām," CBQ 25 [1963]: 123–24) claims פֶּרֶא אָדָם (pereʾ ʾādām) means "a wild ass of the steppe," reading ʾādām as ʾadāmāh; but see Speiser (Genesis, AB, vol. 1 [New York: Doubleday, 1964], p. 118).

---

6. Job's reply

12:1–14:22

[1]Then Job replied:

> [2]"Doubtless you are the people,
>   and wisdom will die with you!
> [3]But I have a mind as well as you;
>   I am not inferior to you.
>   Who does not know all these things?

> [4]"I have become a laughingstock to my friends,
>   though I called upon God and he answered—
>   a mere laughingstock, though righteous and blameless!
> [5]Men at ease have contempt for misfortune
>   as the fate of those whose feet are slipping.
> [6]The tents of marauders are undisturbed,
>   and those who provoke God are secure—
>   those who carry their god in their hands.

> [7]"But ask the animals, and they will teach you,
>   or the birds of the air, and they will tell you;
> [8]or speak to the earth, and it will teach you,
>   or let the fish of the sea inform you.
> [9]Which of all these does not know
>   that the hand of the LORD has done this?
> [10]In his hand is the life of every creature
>   and the breath of all mankind.
> [11]Does not the ear test words
>   as the tongue tastes food?
> [12]Is not wisdom found among the aged?
>   Does not long life bring understanding?

> [13]"To God belong wisdom and power;
>   counsel and understanding are his.
> [14]What he tears down cannot be rebuilt;
>   the man he imprisons cannot be released.
> [15]If he holds back the waters, there is drought;
>   if he lets them loose, they devastate the land.

16 To him belong strength and victory;
  both deceived and deceiver are his.
17 He leads counselors away stripped
  and makes fools of judges.
18 He takes off the shackles put on by kings
  and ties a loincloth around their waist.
19 He leads priests away stripped
  and overthrows men long established.
20 He silences the lips of trusted advisers
  and takes away the discernment of elders.
21 He pours contempt on nobles
  and disarms the mighty.
22 He reveals the deep things of darkness
  and brings deep shadows into the light.
23 He makes nations great, and destroys them;
  he enlarges nations, and disperses them.
24 He deprives the leaders of the earth of their reason;
  he sends them wandering through a trackless waste.
25 They grope in darkness with no light;
  he makes them stagger like drunkards.

13:1 My eyes have seen all this,
  my ears have heard and understood it.
2 What you know, I also know;
  I am not inferior to you.
3 But I desire to speak to the Almighty
  and to argue my case with God.
4 You, however, smear me with lies;
  you are worthless physicians, all of you!
5 If only you would be altogether silent!
  For you, that would be wisdom.
6 Hear now my argument;
  listen to the plea of my lips.
7 Will you speak wickedly on God's behalf?
  Will you speak deceitfully for him?
8 Will you show him partiality?
  Will you argue the case for God?
9 Would it turn out well if he examined you?
  Could you deceive him as you might deceive men?
10 He would surely rebuke you
  if you secretly showed partiality.
11 Would not his splendor terrify you?
  Would not the dread of him fall on you?
12 Your maxims are proverbs of ashes;
  your defenses are defenses of clay.

13 "Keep silent and let me speak;
  then let come to me what may.
14 Why do I put myself in jeopardy
  and take my life in my hands?
15 Though he slay me, yet will I hope in him;
  I will surely defend my ways to his face.
16 Indeed, this will turn out for my deliverance,
  for no godless man would dare come before him!
17 Listen carefully to my words;
  let your ears take in what I say.
18 Now that I have prepared my case,
  I know I will be vindicated.
19 Can anyone bring charges against me?
  If so, I will be silent and die.

20 "Only grant me these two things, O God,
  and then I will not hide from you:
21 Withdraw your hand far from me,
  and stop frightening me with your terrors.
22 Then summon me and I will answer,
  or let me speak, and you reply.
23 How many wrongs and sins have I committed?
  Show me my offense and my sin.
24 Why do you hide your face
  and consider me your enemy?
25 Will you torment a windblown leaf?
  Will you chase after dry chaff?
26 For you write down bitter things against me
  and make me inherit the sins of my youth.
27 You fasten my feet in shackles;
  you keep close watch on all my paths
  by putting marks on the soles of my feet.

28 "So man wastes away like something rotten,
  like a garment eaten by moths.

14:1 Man born of woman
  is of few days and full of trouble.
2 He springs up like a flower and withers away;
  like a fleeting shadow, he does not endure.
3 Do you fix your eye on such a one?
  Will you bring him before you for judgment?
4 Who can bring what is pure from the impure?
  No one!
5 Man's days are determined;
  you have decreed the number of his months
  and have set limits he cannot exceed.
6 So look away from him and let him alone,
  till he has put in his time like a hired man.

7 "At least there is hope for a tree:
  If it is cut down, it will sprout again,
  and its new shoots will not fail.
8 Its roots may grow old in the ground
  and its stump die in the soil,
9 yet at the scent of water it will bud
  and put forth shoots like a plant.
10 But man dies and is laid low;
  he breathes his last and is no more.
11 As water disappears from the sea
  or a riverbed becomes parched and dry,
12 so man lies down and does not rise;
  till the heavens are no more, men will not awake
  or be roused from their sleep.

13 "If only you would hide me in the grave
  and conceal me till your anger has passed!
  If only you would set me a time
  and then remember me!
14 If a man dies, will he live again?
  All the days of my hard service
  I will wait for my renewal to come.
15 You will call and I will answer you;
  you will long for the creature your hands have made.
16 Surely then you will count my steps
  but not keep track of my sin.

¹⁷My offenses will be sealed up in a bag;
 you will cover over my sin.

¹⁸"But as a mountain erodes and crumbles
 and as a rock is moved from its place,
¹⁹as water wears away stones
 and torrents wash away the soil,
 so you destroy man's hope.
²⁰You overpower him once for all, and he is gone;
 you change his countenance and send him away.
²¹If his sons are honored, he does not know it;
 if they are brought low, he does not see it.
²²He feels but the pain of his own body
 and mourns only for himself."

There is good reason to question the chapter division in this long speech. The most natural break comes in 13:20. Job first answered his counselors (12:1–13:19), then addressed God (13:20–14:22). With his patience running out, he chose to match Zophar's harshness with sarcasm—"Doubtless you are the people,/ and wisdom will die with you" (12:1). Job was sure he knew as much as they did and begged to differ with their view of suffering. Being comfortable themselves they could afford to be contemptuous toward him. If only he were treated justly, Job would not be suffering the way he was. He repeated the unanswerable question: Why did God treat him so badly? Why should a man who is righteous and blameless be made a laughingstock (v.4) when sinners and idolaters go undisturbed (v.6). This is the kind of question that made them brand Job as a man whose feet were slipping (v.5).

1–25 This poem breaks neatly into three stanzas. The first (vv.4–6) states Job's problem: "Why me, God, and not those who really deserve misfortune?" In the second (vv.7–12) Job complained that the whole world was afflicted with the same apparent injustice. Why should this be when all things, including the very breath of man, are in God's hands (v.10)? Bildad had already accused Job of attributing evildoing to God (8:3) and had appealed to the authority of past generations to prove Job was wrong. Now Job appealed to the experience of mankind and all creation to support his view that it makes no difference whether people are good or bad. God does not use morality as the basis for granting freedom from affliction. The issue over the problem of theodicy is joined, an issue every believer must wrestle with eventually. Job's counselors were so superficial that they had not yet struggled with this difficult problem. Their thoughts on the subject were simplistic. Job considered their words bland and superficial, certainly not a worthy part of the wisdom of elders (vv.11–12). He had already accused them of serving tasteless food (thoughts) (6:6–7).

In the third stanza (vv.13–25), Job expounded on God's sovereign freedom—with his power and wisdom he does whatever he wishes (v.13). Job stressed the negative use God makes of his power. God tears down what man builds (v.14), sends drought and flood (v.15), makes fools out of judges (v.17), sends priests and nobles into captivity (vv.18–19), and deprives kings of their reason (v.24).

According to Robertson (*Old Testament*, p. 43; cf. id., "Job," pp. 446–69), Job began in v.13 to speak tongue-in-cheek. He was criticizing God for not being very wise. A wise man destroys in order to rebuild; but when God destroys, it is impossible to rebuild (v.14). A wise man would use the weather for good, but God "holds back the waters, there is drought; if he lets them loose, they devastate the land" (v.15). Robertson says Job was charging God with mismanaging the universe. Habel (*Job*, 1985, p. 216) also labels this a satirical hymn that deliberately reverses the wisdom tradition of Proverbs 8:14–16.

The correct interpretation of this section probably lies in a more restrained view of what Job was saying. This may be a mockery of the lopsidedness of Eliphaz's creedal hymn in 5:18–26, where everything good happens to the righteous. It is hardly a parody on God's wisdom since in the introduction to the poem (v.13) Job ascribed wisdom to God in conjunction with his purpose and understanding. In this context Job's problem is with the counselor's wisdom, not God's. He was attempting to answer Zophar's question: "Can you fathom the mysteries of God?. . . What can you know?" (11:7–8). He was saying that God's actions were indeed mysterious and strange. Job could not figure them out, but he knew as much about them as the others.

In other words Job believed the mystery was profound; and he was amazed that the "sages" would be so shallow (v.12). Job saw God so wise and powerful that he cannot be put in a box. He has sovereign freedom. Job illustrated this by drawing a word picture of the mystery of God's acts in the history of man. God humbles great men and nations, showing himself to be the only truly sovereign being (vv.16–25).

13:1–27 Job continued to show his irritation at Zophar's remark about his being an inane, witless person (11:12). His friends talked about God—Job maintained he could do that as skillfully as they (v.2). He was confident that given the opportunity he could prove his case before God, for he knew their accusations were false (v.3). Despite the unfortunate things he had said about God in chapter 9—"He would not give me a hearing" (cf. v.16) but "multiply my wounds for no reason" (v.17), and "he destroys both the blameless and the wicked" (v.22)—Job still believed all this could be reconciled if only he could argue his case directly with God. But his counselors smeared him with lies. They were quacks and fake healers who could show their wisdom only if they kept quiet (vv.4–5; cf. Prov 17:28).

Job's argument in vv.6–12 has the following interesting twist. How dare his friends argue God's case deceitfully and use lies to flatter God? Job warned them about lying even while they uttered beautiful words in defense of God. If they were going to plead God's case, they had better do it honestly. God would judge them for their deceit even if they used it in his behalf (vv.8–9). This proves what Job believed about God. We know from the Epilogue (42:7) that Job's assessment was right. Job's friends' words about God may have been true, but they were worthless because they were empty maxims—mere clichés (v.12). Moreover their assessment of Job was wrong. If God would have examined their lives, they would not have been able to deceive him the way they deceived men. For their hypocritical partiality toward God and their dishonest charges against Job, God would surely punish them (vv.10–11).

On the other hand, Job was so sure he would be vindicated that he repeated his desire for a hearing before God (vv.13–19). He viewed this boldness on his part as one of the evidences that what they said about him was not true. If Job were a hypocrite, would he be willing to put his life in jeopardy in this way (v.16)? Such a man would not dare come before God. The much disputed v.15 (see Notes) expresses neither the trusting commitment of 1:21 nor the hopelessness of the NIV margin.

The negative should be maintained in v.15a, but Job was more positive than negative in this context. Even if slain he would not wait (*yāḥal*, NIV, "hope") but would defend his ways before God and was sure God would vindicate him. Although certain that their charges were false, Job did not claim sinless perfection. He admitted the sins of his youth for which he hoped he had been forgiven (v.26). Why, then, did God keep frightening him with his terrors and treating him as an enemy, indeed, as an enslaved prisoner of war whose feet have been branded (v.27)? He saw himself as helpless, as swirling chaff or a wind-blown leaf. If God would only stop tormenting him and communicate, Job felt all would end well.

13:28–14:22 Job's mercurial mood changed again. At the end of chapter 13 he again lost grip on his confidence and regressed to a hopeless feeling. From 13:28 to 14:6 Job mused on the misery of man in his pathetically brief life, uttering a brief but structured poem (see Notes), a literary device designed to introduce the theme of the plight of the human race. People are impure; so they are worthy of punishment. Job, however, uttered a plea that the sovereign God, who gives to each a short span of numbered days, would let his poor creature alone until his hard labor on earth was over. Again we must be reminded that a key factor remained a mystery to Job—the presence and power, albeit limited, of the Accuser who understandably is not mentioned at all in the Dialogue.

In 14:7–22 Job turned again to death as the only way out of his impasse. A tree may be cut down and its stump appear to be dead (vv.7–8); yet at the scent of water, it springs to life and sends out new shoots (v.9). Such a phenomenological observation cannot be asserted for man. He is more like a lake run dry (vv.10–11). A man's lifetime runs out and cannot be renewed (v.12). But Job suggested that God could provide a remedy by simply taking his life till his anger was over and then, by resurrection, call him back from Sheol.

Was Job being only hypothetical here while really rejecting all possibility of resurrection? Note his pessimistic assertions in vv.18–22. Critical scholars have held that a doctrine of bodily resurrection did not come into Hebrew theology until Hellenistic times, and even then it was resisted in the wisdom schools. It is sometimes noted that the LXX turns the question in v.14 into an assertion: "If a man dies, he will live again!" This was done despite the clear sign of the question in the Hebrew text.

While it may be true that a fully developed doctrine of resurrection and the afterlife comes into Hebrew literature in Hellenistic times and later, Dahood (*Psalms*, AB [Garden City, N.Y.: Doubleday, 1966–70], 17A: XLI-LII) has correctly shown that these concepts were not foreign to preexilic Israel. This chapter proves Job believed in the possibility of resurrection, though he saw man differently than the tree that can be cut down and immediately renewed. Man lies down and does not rise till the heavens are no more (v.12). But the assumption is that man will be raised.

Job was not giving a general polemic against resurrection. On the contrary, he was saying that if God wanted to, he could hide Job in Sheol till his anger passed and then raise him (v.13). Job's pessimism arose, not from a skepticism about resurrection, but from God's apparent unwillingness to do anything immediately for him. Therefore his hopes were dashed, his life had become a nightmare of pain and mourning—with nothing to look for but death.

Job knew that eventually God would cover all his offenses and long for him as the beneficent Creator who delights in those he made. But despite his faith in God's power over death, Job was convinced that God would not even allow him the exquisite release of death (cf. note on 14:14). The waters of suffering continue to erode till his bright hope was a dim memory (v.19) and nothing mattered anymore but the pain of his body and the continual mourning of his soul (v.22).

Notes

12:2 Job started out clearly speaking to his friends. אַתֶּם (*attem*, "you") is second person plural in vv.2–3, but the second singular appears in v.7. On this basis some (e.g., Duhm) have suggested that vv.7–12 are a redactor's insertion, pointing also to the use of יהוה (*yhwh*, "Yahweh") in v.9. This is the only place it is used in the entire Dialogue. Dhorme notes that some MSS have אֱלוֹהַּ (*ᵉlôah*), which he thinks is original, "Yahweh" having come in at an early time because the line is identical to Isa 41:20c.

It is unlikely that vv.7–12 are an addition. Job's words at any point might be directed to what one of the counselors had said. In this case that one is Zophar, the last to speak, who had just called Job an evil and deceitful man (11:11). Job wanted Zophar to face the truth that instead of suffering the wicked often prosper. Appalled at Zophar's lack of wisdom, he uttered v.12, which might be translated "The aged ought to have wisdom and the old understanding."

Dahood's suggestion (*Psalms*, 16:113) that עָם (*ʿām*, "the people") comes from ʿ*mm* ("be strong") as an epithet of deity has not been generally accepted because the root has not been clearly attested with this meaning. The usual rendering requires a nuance of irony and suggests the elite, the strong, and the sagacious among the people (cf. 34:20).

4 What can וַיַּעֲנֵהוּ (*wayyaᵃnēhû*, "and he answered") mean when one of Job's major complaints has been that God would not even give him a hearing (9:16). Although this is the Qal stem, hence meaning "answer," the solution may lie in understanding a double entendre. The homonym עָנָה (*ʿānāh*) in the Piel stem means "to answer" or "to afflict." Job has become a laughingstock: the more he called on God, the more God answered by afflicting him.

5 For לַפִּיד בּוּז (*lappîd bûz*, "contempt for misfortune"), the MT reads literally "a contemptible torch belongs to the thought of one at ease." Though Rashi thought this torch (KJV "lamp") was hellfire, NIV correctly divides the first word into the preposition *l* ("for") and the word *pîd* ("misfortune"), which makes much better sense.

6 It is not the abrupt shift in number (common in Heb.) but the use of the relative pronoun *ᵃšer* that leads one to prefer the margin over the text in the NIV for לַאֲשֶׁר הֵבִיא אֱלוֹהַּ בְּיָדוֹ (*laᵃšer hēbîʾ ᵉlôah bᵉyadô*, "those who carry their god in their hands"). In the NIV text Job was saying that even idolaters who provoke God prosper. In the margin Job complained that God's hand provides security even for sinners who provoke him.

11–12 The NEB makes these two verses a parenthesis with some justification, but there is no justification in the dislocation of v.10. As noted above Job was chiding his counselors for their lack of wisdom. He was talking about theodicy—a subject difficult only for those who have a sovereign God. Job had spoken honestly about the depths of his dilemma; he was amazed at the shallowness of their thinking and uttered a hymn (not tongue-in-cheek, see above) in honor of God's sovereign control over all the affairs of men and nations. It is much as if Job were saying, "I cannot understand God's apparent injustice, but I know he is wise and in control."

12 The root שֹׁשׁ (*yšš*, "aged," "old") appears in the poetry of Job (15:10; 29:8; 32:6) and in 2 Chron 36:17. It does not show Job was written at the time of the Chronicles but is a good example of how a word spanning long centuries of usage may be attested only rarely in the extant literature. In the verse Job was chiding them for being elders and yet so lacking in true wisdom. His tone must be caught.

18 The idea of וַיֶּאְסֹר אֵזוֹר (wayye'sōr 'ēzôr, "ties a loincloth") is that God frees those shackled by kings and sends kings into captivity.

21 וּמְזִיחַ אֲפִיקִים רִפָּה (ûmᵉzîaḥ 'ᵃpîqîm rippāh, "disarms the mighty") is literally "loosens the belt of." The word for belt⁻ (mᵉzîaḥ) is a *hapax legomenon* as vocalized. Psalm 109:19 clearly limits it to something wrapped around a person. It may be an Egyptian loan word (cf. BDB, p. 561).

13:2 The second person pronouns in vv.1–12 are plural; e.g., כְּדַעְתְּכֶם (kᵉda'tᵉkem, "what you know"). Job was as theologically astute as they were, but he was not satisfied with easy solutions.

11 Andersen (*Job,* in loc.) cogently suggests that הֲלֹא (hᵃlō', "would not") might be rendered "should not." If they had true understanding of who God is, if they were truly wise men, their "fear of the Lord" would prevent them from indulging in such a perilous exercise as mouthing clichés in honor of the God they do not know. See Andersen's comments on Kierkegaard (ibid., p. 165, n. 2).

14 Since the LXX does not have the expression עַל־מָה ('al-māh, "why") and in the MT the same letters appear immediately before these, some consider this a scribal repetition or dittography and would translate the verse as a strong assertion: "I will!" But the question fits well with v.16—"Why? Because this could mean deliverance for me."

15 The interpretation of הֵן יִקְטְלֵנִי לֹא אֲיַחֵל (hēn yiqtᵉlēnî lō' 'ᵃyaḥēl, "Though he slay me, yet will I hope in him") has produced considerable disagreement. Much depends on how to understand lō'. Most of the Hebrew MS tradition takes it as a negative, which would change the meaning from hope to despair: "Behold he will slay me; I have no hope" (RSV). Many other Hebrew MSS, some ancient versions, and the Hebrew oral tradition have לוֹ (lô, "in him"), which is the basis for the NIV. There are a number of ways, however, that one could translate the line positively. For example, Dhorme, Rowley, and Pope translate the verb "tremble," "quaver," "I will not quaver." Andersen (*Job,* in loc.) chooses to render the written tradition as לָא (la'), a rare assertative particle common in Arabic—"Certainly" (see M. Dahood, "Two Pauline Quotations from the Old Testament," CBQ 17 [1955]: 24, n. 23). Other positive renderings are Calvin's making the negative positive as a question: "Shall I not have hope?" The LXX probably read אל (l) instead of לא (l) and therefore translated it "the Mighty One" (ho dynastes). Dahood (*Psalms,* 16:144) understands the LXX to be the translation of a rare epithet of deity spelled לֵא (lē ', common as a description of Baal in Ugar.), reading, "If the Victor should slay me, I will yet hope." Whatever the reading, the context appears to require a translation that expresses Job's faith, not his doubt. Though Job in other contexts (ch. 9) was troubled about it, here he expressed his conviction that God is just. Since Job was not a hypocrite ("godless man," v.16), if he could only argue his case in God's presence, he would be vindicated (v.18). We of course know from the Prologue that he was right.

17 אֲחֲוָתִי ('aḥᵃwātî, "what I say") is a noun with a "prothetic" aleph (cf. note on 37:13).

20 The NIV renders אַךְ־שְׁתַּיִם אַל־תַּעַשׂ עִמָּדִי ('ak-šᵉttayim 'al-ta'aś 'immādî) "Only grant me these two things, O God." Since the MT is clearly negative ("Do not do to me"; cf. KJV), the NIV had to have a reason to repoint 'al (negative) to 'ēl ("O God"). There is no textual evidence; so the context is the compelling reason. It helps the reader to understand that God is now addressed. But more important the things requested are positive acts, though the negative aspect of the first may have prompted the MT vocalization that produced the negative particle 'al. What are the two things? It is somewhat difficult to determine, but they seem to be, first, for God to withdraw his hand and stop terrifying him (note the negative aspect). Job asked for deliverance from suffering but nowhere requested restoration to riches. Second, he was more interested in communication with God: "Then summon me and I will answer, or let me speak, and you reply" (v.22).

In אָז מִפָּנֶיךָ לֹא אֶסָּתֵר ('āz mippāneykā lō' 'essātēr, "then I will not hide from you"), the Niphal 'essātēr can be passive or reflexive. Andersen (*Job,* in loc.) claims it is passive, an expression of Job's fear, and that it should be translated "then I will not be hidden from your presence" (cf. Gen 4:14). In this context Job was not hiding from God but was seeking God's presence. Compare v.24: "Why do you hide your face?"

25 תַּעֲרוֹץ (taʿarôṣ, "Will you torment") is open to two possibilities: (1) "Do you wish to torment?" or (2) "Will you keep on tormenting?" In Job's mind the rhetorical questions required a negative answer. There is no list of sinful omissions or transgressions that can be brought against him. God should not consider himself Job's enemy, nor should he want to torment Job.

26 The Deity's record book—כִּי־תִכְתֹּב עָלַי מְרֹרוֹת (kî-tiktōb ʿālay merōrôt, "For you write down bitter things against me")—is an ancient concept well-known in OT times (cf. Exod 32:32–33; Ps 69:28).

27 Job saw himself as a prisoner of war with his feet in stocks and branded as a slave, viz., ה עַל־שָׁרְשֵׁי רַגְלַי תִּתְחַקֶּה (ʿal-šoršê raglay titḥaqqeh, "putting marks on the soles of my feet"). For this practice see Hammurabi's Code (ANET, p. 176, n. 227). The middle of this tricolon ("you keep close watch . . .") applies equally to the colon that precedes and the one that follows. There is no dislocation (cf. Pope, in loc.).

28 It appears that the subject matter of chapter 14 begins here. The NIV assumes ʾādām ("man") in 14:1 is the referent of וְהוּא (wehûʾ, "So he"; NIV, "So man"). Dhorme, Pope et al. consider the verse misplaced and put it after 14:2.

14:3 The LXX, Vulgate, and Syriac all read וְאֹתִי תָבִיא (weʾōtî tābîʾ, "Will you bring him?"), the antecedent being "such a one." The MT uses the first person. Contextually it makes little difference since in either case it is Job.

4 Gray, Pope et al. think this verse is also out of place and unbalanced, but Andersen (Job, in loc.) sees the verse as pivotal in this poem (vv.1–6) and therefore very important. But we question Andersen's introverted structure (vv.3, 5 going together as do vv.2, 6). In subject matter we see vv.2, 5 and vv.3, 6 belonging together with v.4 as the apex. The introduction, which establishes the tone of the poem, is formed by 13:28 and 14:1. The poem would read as follows:

He wastes away like something rotten, like a garment eaten by moths— man born of woman.	Introduction

Few of days and full of trouble
  he springs up like a flower and withers away;
  like a fleeting shadow he does not endure.
	A

Do you fix your eye on such a one? Will you bring him before you for judgment?	B

Who can bring what is pure from the impure?
  No one! (Or: "The Mighty One alone"
  [see Blommerde, p. 69]).
	Apex

Man's days are determined;
  you have decreed the number of his months
  and have set limits he cannot exceed.
	A'

So look away from him and let him alone, till he has put in his time like a hired hand.	B'

6 Though one Hebrew MS reads as a regular imperative—וַחֲדָל (waḥadāl)—the consonants of 10:20 support the notion that וְיֶחְדָּל (weyeḥdāl) may have an imperative force (so NIV, "and let him alone").

10 The NIV has rejected the notion that וְאַיּוֹ (weʾayyô) means "and where is he?" (KJV) and has gone with the LXX ("and is no more"). אַי (ʾî) is an old negative as in the name Ichabod ("No-glory," 1 Sam 4:21; and Job 22:30, "one who is not innocent").

14 To capture the force of Job's meaning of חֲלִיפָתִי (ḥalîpātî, "my renewal"), we must note that the same root is used in v.7 concerning the tree. There the NIV translated it

"sprout." A basic meaning is "to have succession." In this verse Job is speaking of succession after death, not the healing of his body in this life.

It is important to see this verbal tie with v.7 because many commentators think Job has only relief in mind and any thought of life after death is considered impossible by Job. To make this idea clear, Pope (in loc.) uses the verbal auxiliary "would" instead of "will" in vv.14–17: "I would wait . . . you would call." The Hebrew text does not require such a rendering, nor is it necessary to assume that Job gives a totally negative answer to his question "If a man die, will he live again?" Scholars have assumed this because of their preconceptions about OT theology, which ruled out ideas of resurrection in preexilic and early postexilic Israel (cf. W. Kaiser, Jr., *Toward an Old Testament Theology* [Grand Rapids: Zondervan, 1978], pp. 99, 181, 249).

19 What is וְתִקְוַת אֱנוֹשׁ (wᵉtiqwat ᵉnôš, "man's hope")? It should be connected with the hope mentioned in v.7 and elaborated in vv.13–17. In vv.18–22 Job felt that the fulfillment of this resurrection hope is so far off ("till the heavens are no more," v.12) that for all practical purposes it offered no solution to his current dilemma. So he suggested that God might hide him in the grave temporarily and then resurrect him when his anger subsides (v.13). But he did not believe this would happen; so he fell back to all the empirical evidence that contradicted his hope and so ended his speech in the slough of despond.

C. The Second Cycle of Speeches (15:1–21:34)

1. Eliphaz

15:1–35

¹Then Eliphaz the Temanite replied:

> ²"Would a wise man answer with empty notions
> or fill his belly with the hot east wind?
> ³Would he argue with useless words,
> with speeches that have no value?
> ⁴But you even undermine piety
> and hinder devotion to God.
> ⁵Your sin prompts your mouth;
> you adopt the tongue of the crafty.
> ⁶Your own mouth condemns you, not mine;
> your own lips testify against you.
>
> ⁷"Are you the first man ever born?
> Were you brought forth before the hills?
> ⁸Do you listen in on God's council?
> Do you limit wisdom to yourself?
> ⁹What do you know that we do not know?
> What insights do you have that we do not have?
> ¹⁰The gray-haired and the aged are on our side,
> men even older than your father.
> ¹¹Are God's consolations not enough for you,
> words spoken gently to you?
> ¹²Why has your heart carried you away,
> and why do your eyes flash,
> ¹³so that you vent your rage against God
> and pour out such words from your mouth?
>
> ¹⁴"What is man, that he could be pure,
> or one born of woman, that he could be righteous?
> ¹⁵If God places no trust in his holy ones,
> if even the heavens are not pure in his eyes,

927

16 how much less man, who is vile and corrupt,
   who drinks up evil like water!

17 "Listen to me and I will explain to you;
   let me tell you what I have seen,
18 what wise men have declared,
   hiding nothing received from their fathers
19 (to whom alone the land was given
   when no alien passed among them):
20 All his days the wicked man suffers torment,
   the ruthless through all the years stored up for him.
21 Terrifying sounds fill his ears;
   when all seems well, marauders attack him.
22 He despairs of escaping the darkness;
   he is marked for the sword.
23 He wanders about—food for vultures;
   he knows the day of darkness is at hand.
24 Distress and anguish fill him with terror;
   they overwhelm him, like a king poised to attack,
25 because he shakes his fist at God
   and vaunts himself against the Almighty,
26 defiantly charging against him
   with a thick, strong shield.

27 "Though his face is covered with fat
   and his waist bulges with flesh,
28 he will inhabit ruined towns
   and houses where no one lives,
   houses crumbling to rubble.
29 He will no longer be rich and his wealth will not endure,
   nor will his possessions spread over the land.
30 He will not escape the darkness;
   a flame will wither his shoots,
   and the breath of God's mouth will carry him away.
31 Let him not deceive himself by trusting what is worthless,
   for he will get nothing in return.
32 Before his time he will be paid in full,
   and his branches will not flourish.
33 He will be like a vine stripped of its unripe grapes,
   like an olive tree shedding its blossoms.
34 For the company of the godless will be barren,
   and fire will consume the tents of those who love bribes.
35 They conceive trouble and give birth to evil;
   their womb fashions deceit."

For the first thirteen verses of this chapter, Eliphaz plied Job with questions designed to shame him into silence. Verses 14–16 reveal again some interesting architectonics. These verses form an apex about which Eliphaz's words hinge. They derive from his vision in 4:17–19 and here state his thesis: God's holiness versus man's corruption. The remaining half of the chapter is a dramatic description of the dreadful fate of the wicked.

1–6 Eliphaz was angry. He had run out of patience. The time to be polite (4:2) and indirect was over. He considered Job's words not only valueless but deceitful and irreverent. In his opening lines Eliphaz accused Job of belching out a hot wind of useless words (vv.2–3). Worse, his mouth spoke as it did because of the sin in his heart (v.5). Job had condemned himself by his ungodly talk. Such irreligion made him a dangerous person able to lead others astray (v.4).

7–13 Here Eliphaz chided Job for arrogance. Note the questioning format, a motif used most effectively in the divine speeches in chapters 38–41. Was Job wise enough to sit in the council of God's angels (vv.7–8)? In reality he was not even wise enough to be in harmony with the elders and wise men on earth (v.10). "God's consolations" (v.11) are the gentle words Eliphaz tried to use with Job (see 4:1–6) only to receive a raging response (vv.12–13).

14–16 Eliphaz repeated the thought that came to him by "revelation" (4:17–19)— that man is too vile to even stand before God. The oracle had made a deep impression on the counselor.

17–20 Here Eliphaz bolstered this "revelation" with wisdom that came from tradition—the wicked never escape the torment they deserve; and even if they do, for a moment, trouble is just around the corner.

21–35 Eliphaz next presented a poetic discourse on the fate of the wicked. To the counselors Job's idea that the wicked prosper was a great heresy. The poem refutes this notion (compare his poem in 4:17–26, in which he described the righteous man). He refused to believe that any wicked person prospers, except perhaps for the briefest moment. Eliphaz believed that wicked people always suffer distress and anguish (vv.21–22). They know disaster is stored up for them (v.23). He pictured the wicked man as a quixotic figure who uselessly attacks God with full armor and thick shield (vv.25–26). No doubt it is all a caricature of Job whose "eyes flash" as he "vents his rage against God" (vv.12–13).

In vv.27–35 the caricature continues with a variety of figures—the fat, rich, wicked man who finally gets what he deserves (vv.27–32). He is like a grapevine stripped before its fruit is ripe or an olive tree shedding its blossoms (v.33). As long as Eliphaz rejected the notion that the wicked prosper and its corollary that the innocent sometimes suffer, he would never have to wrestle over the disturbing mystery of how this fits with the justice of God. Eliphaz viewed man as either all good or all bad. He allowed no room for a good man to have doubts and struggles, and those who are bad Eliphaz wanted to reduce to zero.

In his query "What is man, that he could be pure?" (vv.14–16), Eliphaz's view of man comes through clearly. There is nothing in his words that would lead one to the conclusion that God has any love for sinful human beings. Indeed, the deity Eliphaz worshiped was mechanical; he behaved like the laws of nature; so sinners could expect no mercy. The sinner always gets paid in full—trouble and darkness, terror and distress, the flame and the sword. God will see to it.

In describing such a fate, Eliphaz made sure that all the things that had happened to Job were included—fire consumes (vv.30, 34; cf. 1:16), marauders attack (v.21; cf. 1:17), possessions are taken away (v.29; cf. 1:17), and houses crumble (v.28; cf. 1:19). Although the modern reader often misses the point that these barbs are all directed at Job, we can be sure that Job himself felt their sting.

Notes

2 The Piel וִיְמַלֵּא (*wîmallē'*, "or fill") can also mean "to empty" or "to overflow" (cf. TEV).

4 יִרְאָה (*yir'āh*, "piety"; lit., "fear" of God) is the OT term for true religion.

12 The root *rzm* is used only here in יְרְזְמוּן עֵינֶיךָ (*yirzᵉmûn 'êneykā*, "your eyes flash"). Tur-Sinai (*Job*, in loc.) cites an Arabic cognate "become weak, dim" with the meaning "What has blurred your eyes?" The NIV has chosen to follow Dhorme (in loc.) who sees by metathesis the root *rmz* ("wink" or "flash the eyes").

15 These created heavenly beings—viz., בִּקְדֹשָׁו (*biqḏōšāw*, "in his holy ones")—were referred to by Eliphaz in 5:1. If holy, why are they not trusted? The basic meaning of the word is "to set apart" (the root is even used of temple-prostitutes). Not all such beings were good (the Accuser; cf. 2 Peter 2:4).

19 Andersen (*Job*, in loc.) thinks וְלֹא־עָבַר זָר (*wᵉlō'-'āḇar zār*, "when no alien passed") may be "wisdom that is uncontaminated by foreign influence." That it refers to Israel's inheritance of the land is unlikely since it would be the only reference to Israelite history in Job.

21 קוֹל־פְּחָדִים (*qôl-pᵉḥāḏîm*, "terrifying sounds") are reports of terrorism such as Job received in chapter 1.

23 The MT vocalization of לַלֶּחֶם אַיֵּה (*lallehem 'ayyēh*) is followed in the RSV: "He wanders abroad for bread; saying, 'Where is it?'" The LXX failed to understand the first verb but correctly rendered this line: "He has been appointed food for vultures," seeing the object as *'ayyāh*, "a vulture" (cf. 28:7 and Introduction, p. 858).

27–28 Being fat in that world was not objectionable. It was the proof of prosperity. Here Eliphaz was admitting that the wicked do prosper; but as he said in v.29, "His wealth will not endure."

2. *Job's reply*

16:1–17:16

¹Then Job replied:

²"I have heard many things like these;
miserable comforters are you all!
³Will your long-winded speeches never end?
What ails you that you keep on arguing?
⁴I also could speak like you,
if you were in my place;
I could make fine speeches against you
and shake my head at you.
⁵But my mouth would encourage you;
comfort from my lips would bring you relief.

⁶"Yet if I speak, my pain is not relieved;
and if I refrain, it does not go away.
⁷Surely, O God, you have worn me out;
you have devastated my entire household.
⁸You have bound me—and it has become a witness;
my gauntness rises up and testifies against me.
⁹God assails me and tears me in his anger
and gnashes his teeth at me;
my opponent fastens on me his piercing eyes.
¹⁰Men open their mouths to jeer at me;
they strike my cheek in scorn
and unite together against me.

¹¹ God has turned me over to evil men
and thrown me into the clutches of the wicked.
¹² All was well with me, but he shattered me;
he seized me by the neck and crushed me.
He has made me his target;
¹³   his archers surround me.
Without pity, he pierces my kidneys
and spills my gall on the ground.
¹⁴ Again and again he bursts upon me;
he rushes at me like a warrior.

¹⁵ "I have sewed sackcloth over my skin
and buried my brow in the dust.
¹⁶ My face is red with weeping,
deep shadows ring my eyes;
¹⁷ yet my hands have been free of violence
and my prayer is pure.

¹⁸ "O earth, do not cover my blood;
may my cry never be laid to rest!
¹⁹ Even now my witness is in heaven;
my advocate is on high.
²⁰ My intercessor is my friend
as my eyes pour out tears to God;
²¹ on behalf of a man he pleads with God
as a man pleads for his friend.

²² "Only a few years will pass
before I go on the journey of no return.

^{17:1} My spirit is broken,
my days are cut short,
the grave awaits me.
² Surely mockers surround me;
my eyes must dwell on their hostility.

³ "Give me, O God, the pledge you demand.
Who else will put up security for me?
⁴ You have closed their minds to understanding;
therefore you will not let them triumph.
⁵ If a man denounces his friends for reward,
the eyes of his children will fail.

⁶ "God has made me a byword to everyone,
a man in whose face people spit.
⁷ My eyes have grown dim with grief;
my whole frame is but a shadow.
⁸ Upright men are appalled at this;
the innocent are aroused against the ungodly.
⁹ Nevertheless, the righteous will hold to their ways,
and those with clean hands will grow stronger.

¹⁰ "But come on, all of you, try again!
I will not find a wise man among you.
¹¹ My days have passed, my plans are shattered,
and so are the desires of my heart.
¹² These men turn night into day;
in the face of darkness they say, 'Light is near.'
¹³ If the only home I hope for is the grave,
if I spread out my bed in darkness,
¹⁴ if I say to corruption, 'You are my father,'
and to the worm, 'My mother' or 'My sister,'

> ¹⁵where then is my hope?
>   Who can see any hope for me?
> ¹⁶Will it go down to the gates of death?
>   Will we descend together into the dust?"

In these chapters we find a direct contradiction of what the counselors have said. Job's thoughts match, by means of contrast, those of Eliphaz in chapter 15; but his opening words are an answer to the opening words of all three (cf. 8:2; 11:2–3; 15:2 –6). In 15:12–13, 25–26, Eliphaz accused Job of attacking God, but Job claimed the reverse was true; God assailed him (16:8–9, 12–14). Eliphaz saw all men as vile and corrupt in God's eyes (15:14–16). Job believed he had been upright and would be vindicated (16:15–21). Eliphaz thought the words of the wise supported him (15:17 –18). Job was convinced that there was not a word of wisdom in what he had to say (17:10–12). Because God had closed their minds to understanding (17:4), they were incapable of doing anything but scold him (16:4–5; 17:2).

1–5 Job, with purpose, chose a word (*ʿāmāl*) Eliphaz used to suggest Job had conceived his own misery ("trouble," 15:35); and he threw it back at him in the epithet "miserable comforters" (v.2). He affirmed how he would have given real encouragement to them if the tables were turned, but all he got were arguments and scoldings (vv.3–5). The opening words of chapter 16 are full of meaning for all who aspire to counsel others. It is a powerful negative example. The counselors had become gadflies pestering Job who was certain that they had no understanding of his real problem.

6–14 In v.6 Job turned again to the enemy—the god his mind had created—the one who wore him out and tore him in his anger. He viewed himself as one whom God had seized by the scruff of the neck and thrown into the clutches of the wicked (v.11). God had made Job his target, an object of attack; like a warrior he pierced him without pity. The figure was no doubt suggested by Eliphaz's description of the wicked man (meaning Job) who shakes his fist at God, defiantly attacking the Almighty (15:25–26). Job saw it as just the reverse of that in vv.12–14. Job recognized that God could do whatever he wished. But Job was anguished by the thought that God acted like his enemy. So Job and Eliphaz were polarized in their respective views. Was God attacking Job or Job attacking God?

In v.7 because of a sudden shift in Hebrew to third person singular, the NIV has inserted the word "God" and changed the third person to the second person: "you have worn me out." It is possible that the Hebrew third singular refers back to the pain in v.6: "surely now it (my pain) has worn me out." But there was no question in Job's mind that God sent the pain—"you have devastated my entire household" (v.7). A similar problem exists in v.8, where the antecedent in the clause "and it has become a witness" is Job's condition. So in vv.6–8 Job said that it did not make any difference whether he spoke or did not speak, his pain was still there. It wore him out and had become the major witness against him, for on it his detractors had based their arguments. To them it was proof of his sinfulness. As if that were not bad enough, he thought God had assailed him, crushed him, and turned him over to his detractors (vv.9–14).

15–17 Here we see a pathetic figure in sackcloth, sitting with brow in the dust, eyes sunken and face bloated with tears, avowing innocence. From this sad figure arises a baneful cry, but one that has not totally lost hope as vv.18–21 show.

16:18–17:2 Verses 18, 22, and 17:1 indicate that Job thought he would die before he could be vindicated before his peers; so he was concerned that the injustice done to him should never be forgotten. That is what he meant when he called on the earth never to cover his blood or bury his cry (v.18). In Genesis 4:10–11 Abel's innocent blood was crying out to God as a witness against Cain. So Job was consoled to think his cry would continue after his death. And there is one in heaven who would listen to it (vv.19–21). He firmly believed that he had a friend, an advocate, an intercessor on high who would plead his cause. Those who say (e.g., Andersen, Dhorme) this is God himself must deal with v.21—"he pleads with God."

There are indications, however, that Job considered this advocate to be greater than man. He was in heaven (v.19). In 9:33 the Arbitrator was a mere wish but was described as one who could put his hand on both God and Job. In 19:25 the Vindicator who lived must also be a heavenly figure since Job made a special point of how he would eventually stand on the earth (dust). We must be careful how we apply all this as predictive. Certainly God gave Job this hope in the midst of his darkest hours to point to the one who would ultimately fulfill it. But Job probably understood only a limited part of its fullest meaning. Having a heavenly advocate was not a novel thought in that society as may be inferred from 5:1 and 33:23.

3–5 What pledge or guarantee was Job asking for? The translation of v.3 is difficult. The following paraphrase (cf. Notes) may help clarify the meaning: "Give attention (O God) to becoming my guarantor (that I am right) with you,/ for who else will shake my hand to prove it?" If God put up such a guarantee for Job, it would not only silence his mockers (the counselors, v.2) but would prove they were guilty of false accusation and deserve the sanctions and punishment they had implied Job deserved. Verse 5 is a proverb. Job was reminding his counselors of the dire consequences of slander.

6–9 Unfortunately such a guarantee from God was not evident. On the contrary, Job saw God as the one who made him suffer humiliation (v.6). There were few who believed he was innocent. Most people thought they did God a favor by spitting in Job's face. At least that is how Job felt. But in vv.8–9 he was saying that truly good men can pity him in his suffering without turning away from what is right. This is what his counselors could not understand. To them every pain had a sin behind it, and God could not be doing this to Job unless he deserved it. Another interpretation of vv.8–9 is that Job was being sarcastic. He was saying, "You upright men are appalled at this." He had already accused them of having contempt for sufferers like him (12:5).

10 Job was outraged at his friends' attitude, which he considered completely devoid of wisdom. The verse lends added weight to the interpretation of vv.8–9 as sarcasm.

11–16 The counselors had said that night would be turned to day for Job if only he would get right with God (cf. 11:17). In vv.12–16 Job made a parody of their advice. It is was like going to the grave with the notion that all you have to do is treat it like home where warmth and loved ones are and it will become so. No, Job's fondest desires were shattered (v.11); he had no hope but death. He closed this section as he opened it, with the despair of the grave (16:22–17:2). This despair was not quite as reprehensible as was their faulty advice.

Notes

6 מַה (*mah*) may be negative as in NIV ("not"; cf. Arabic and 1 Kings 12:16), or it may mean "how much" (Isa 21:11).

7 הֶלְאָנִי (*helʾānî;* NIV, "you have worn me out") is third masculine singular perfect—"he (it) has made me weak." The reason the NIV has made it conform to the second half of the verse, which is clearly second person, is because such a shift in Hebrew is not unusual. But the subject could very likely be his pain already mentioned in v.6.

כָּל־עֲדָתִי (*kol-ʿᵃdātî,* "my entire household") means literally "all my company," and the concept is difficult to fit into this context. The NEB and modern commentaries have emended the text (Pope [following Duhm] suggests רָעָתִי [*rāʿatî,* "my evil"] for *ʿᵃdātî*). Considering the Aramaic flavor of Job, it seems that the word עֲדִית (*ʿᵃdît,* "scurf," "scab") found in the Targum on Lev 13:2 would yield a good reading. Taking this word with what follows and the waw as emphatic, the reading would be "All my scurvy has surely seized me" (cf. 22:16 for the verb *qmṭ,* "to seize").

This would break vv.7–8 into three equal lines. It is very difficult to know what to do with הֲשִׁמּוֹתָ (*hᵃšimmôtā,* "you have devastated"). Dhorme (p. 232) comes closest to a solution. With the simple expedient of dropping the final *ā* and considering the ה (*h*) as the definite article, he reads *haššimmôt,* meaning "the one who rejoices in the misfortunes of others." Hence v.7a reads "The one rejoicing in misfortunes has wearied me." The reference is to God.

9–11 These verses are impassioned Semitic hyperbole. Job viewed God as a beast of prey. He "assails" or possibly "sniffs out" (cf. שָׂטַם [*śāṭam*] in Gen 27:41; 49:23; 50:15; Job 30:21). It does not mean "hate" (KJV) or "hold a grudge" (BDB, s.v.; see T.L. Fenton, "Ugaritica-Biblica," *Ugaritic Forschungen,* vol. 1 [1969]: 65–66). And he "tears" (טָרַף, *ṭārap*) his victim. In 10:16 Job said, "You stalk me like a lion."

9 צָרִי (*ṣārî,* "my opponent") is too mild for these blazing verses. Job looked on God as his enemy. In 13:24 and 19:11, Job thought God considered him an enemy. In 13:24 the synonym אוֹיֵב (*ʾôyēb,* "enemy") is used, but in 19:11 the word is the same as here. Job never pictured himself as fighting God (v.17a), but as a pitiful victim (vv.12–14), even an innocent one (v.17b).

17 The preposition עַל (*ʿal,* "yet") is a shortened form of עַל־אֲשֶׁר (*ʿal-ʾᵃšer,* "although"). The word is used the same way in 10:7: "though you know."

20 מְלִיצַי רֵעָי (*mᵉlîṣay rēʿāy,* "my intercessor is my friend"), as it is vocalized in the MT, may be read "the ones deriding me (are) my friends." This would be based on a Hiphil participle of the root *lîṣ* ("to deride, scorn"). But in 33:23 and Isa 43:27 the word *mēlîṣ* means "an intermediary between God and man," a meaning that fits this context well. In several other passages it simply means "an interpreter or ambassador" (Gen 42:23; 2 Chron 32:31). Other suggestions based on this meaning are "the interpreter of my thoughts" (compare רֵעִי [*rēʿî,* "my thoughts"], Ps 139:2; BDB, p. 946) or "my cries [from רוּעַ (*rûaʿ*, 'cry out')] intercede for me." The latter carries on the thought of v.18, but v.21 goes on to describe a very personal function of this one as an "intercessor" with God. So the NIV is justified in its choice of possible meanings. In the light of v.21, one can hardly agree with Dhorme (p. 239) that the witness is God himself. The concept here should be tied to the גֹּאֵל (*gōʾēl,* "redeemer") of 19:25 and then probably to the מוֹכִיחַ (*môkîaḥ,* "advocate") of 9:33. Here was Job's answer to Eliphaz's taunt in 5:1: "To which of the holy ones will you turn?" Job believed there was a holy one he could turn to as his Intercessor.

22 The NIV has left a space to show that this verse goes better with ch. 17, leaving v.21 as a climax.

17:1 נִזְעָכוּ (*nizʿāḵû*, "are cut short") is used only here, but some MSS use the Aramaic spelling that comes from the root דָּעַךְ (*dāʿak*, "to extinguish").

The Hebrew reads "graves [קְבָרִים (*qᵉḇārîm*)] (belong) to me." The grave is conceived of as a dwelling place here (cf. Ps 49:11). The word is plural with singular meaning because of a peculiar grammatical feature that used this plural form for dwellings (cf. Pope, p. 384).

2 וּבְהַמְּרוֹתָם (*ûḇᵉhammᵉrôṯām*, "on their hostility") may not be about mockers and hostility but a continuation of Job's preoccupation with his impending death. For slightly different approaches see Pope (p. 128) and Dahood (*Psalms*, 16:278–79).

3 The NIV's rendering of שִׂימָה־נָּא עָרְבֵנִי עִמָּךְ (*śîmāh-nnāʾ ʿārḇēnî ʿimmāḵ*, "Give me, O God, the pledge you demand") is somewhat paraphrastic and difficult to understand. Some vocalize ʿārḇēnî as ʿerḇōnî and read "Put my pledge beside you" (Dhorme, in loc.), in which case Job was offering a pledge to God and in the next line was asking God for a mutual pledge (Pope, in loc.). But as the MT stands, it can be translated: "Consider (this O God) [see note on this idiom on 4:20]; become my guarantee [go surety for me] with yourself. For who else is there that is prepared to strike [shake] my hand." For handshaking as a way to ratify a pledge, see Prov 6:1; 17:18; 22:26.

4 Unless one changes the vowels or adds a מ (*m*), לֹא תְרֹמֵם (*lōʾ ṯᵉrōmēm*, "you will not let them triumph") does not include the pronoun "them." The text can be understood by seeing the prefix *ṯ* as an indication of the third masculine plural as in Ps 106:38 (*watte hᵉnap*) and Ps 68:3 (*tindōp*). In Ugaritic the prefix *t* is so used (UT, 9.14). The JB has caught the sense by vocalizing it as passive: "and not a hand is lifted." Quite literally the text reads "that is why they do not do anything (rise up to help)." For this use of רוֹם (*rûm*), see Gen 41:44.

5 יַגִּיד (*yaggîḏ*, "denounces"), a very common word normally meaning "declare," clearly means "denounce" or "inform on" in Jer 20:10.

12 יָשִׂימוּ (*yāśîmû*, "These men turn") could be the same idiom noticed above in v.3 (cf. Notes on 4:20). The verb *śîm* means "put (to heart)" or "consider" (suppressing the word *lēḇ*, "heart"). The idiom applies to both sides of the parallelism—"they think light is near"; so there is no need to supply the words "they say."

14 The NIV has followed the way the LXX translates לַשַּׁחַת (*laššaḥaṯ*, "to corruption") in Ps 16:10. Here the LXX uses "death" but there "corruption." The NT interpretation of the psalm (cf. Acts 2:31–32) hangs on that meaning instead of the usual "pit." N.J. Tromp (*Primitive Conceptions of Death and the Nether World in the Old Testament* [Rome: Pontifical Biblical Institute, 1969], pp. 69ff.) has drawn on evidence from Ugarit and Qumran to support this meaning.

16 The NIV has seen fit to make the figure בַּדֵּי שְׁאֹל (*baddê šᵉʾōl*, "to the gates of death") more direct. The Hebrew has "the bars of Sheol." The figure (synecdoche) here uses the part (the bars) for the whole (the gates).

---

3. Bildad

18:1–21

¹Then Bildad the Shuhite replied:

²"When will you end these speeches?
Be sensible, and then we can talk.
³Why are we regarded as cattle
and considered stupid in your sight?

⁴You who tear yourself to pieces in your anger,
  is the earth to be abandoned for your sake?
  Or must the rocks be moved from their place?

⁵"The lamp of the wicked is snuffed out;
  the flame of his fire stops burning.
⁶The light in his tent becomes dark;
  the lamp beside him goes out.
⁷The vigor of his step is weakened;
  his own schemes throw him down.
⁸His feet thrust him into a net
  and he wanders into its mesh.
⁹A trap seizes him by the heel;
  a snare holds him fast.
¹⁰A noose is hidden for him on the ground;
  a trap lies in his path.
¹¹Terrors startle him on every side
  and dog his every step.
¹²Calamity is hungry for him;
  disaster is ready for him when he falls.
¹³It eats away parts of his skin;
  death's firstborn devours his limbs.
¹⁴He is torn from the security of his tent
  and marched off to the king of terrors.
¹⁵Fire resides in his tent;
  burning sulfur is scattered over his dwelling.
¹⁶His roots dry up below
  and his branches wither above.
¹⁷The memory of him perishes from the earth;
  he has no name in the land.
¹⁸He is driven from light into darkness
  and is banished from the world.
¹⁹He has no offspring or descendants among his people,
  no survivor where once he lived.
²⁰Men of the west are appalled at his fate;
  men of the east are seized with horror.
²¹Surely such is the dwelling of an evil man;
  such is the place of one who knows not God."

Following the pattern of Eliphaz and Zophar, only Bildad's opening lines were directly addressed to Job (cf. 15:2–3 and 20:2–5 with vv.2–4 here). In the rest of the speech, with typical redundant and discursive rhetoric, he launched into a poem on the fate of the wicked. In this chapter he made no attempt to admonish Job as he did in 8:5–7, 20–22. The same is true of the words of Eliphaz and Zophar in chapters 15 and 20. The dispute intensifies (cf. 22:2–5), giving additional evidence of the planned structure of the Dialogue. For further observations on this compositional make-up and disputational form of the friends' speeches, see Westermann (*Job*, pp. 17–30).

1–4 Bildad considered Job beside himself, a man no longer acting fully responsible (v.2). He resented Job's attitude toward them as belittling and accused Job of being irrationally self-centered. The world was going to remain the same no matter how much Job ranted against the order of things (v.4).

5–21 Bildad felt Job did not really understand the doctrine of retribution. He probably considered Job weak on this subject because Job kept harping on how the righteous suffer and the wicked prosper. In these speeches Job and his friends had nothing to say about future retribution at the day of final judgment or the balancing of the scales of justice after death. This is a truth that unveils gradually (progressive revelation) in the OT.

For example, in Psalm 73 the psalmist struggles like Job. He says, "For I envied the arrogant when I saw the prosperity of the wicked" (v.3). But through revelation the psalmist came to understand the "final destiny" (Ps 73:16–17). Some dispute whether he means this life or the next, but the psalmist's triumph of faith in vv.23 –28 sounds like a hope that transcends life itself.

Bildad's concern, however, was to establish in Job's mind the absolute certainty that every wicked man gets paid in full, in this life, for his wicked deeds. He said nothing of a final judgment but was sure the lamp of the wicked would be snuffed out (vv.5–6). As his step weakens (v.7), he is trapped and devoured (vv.8–10). "Terrors startle him on every side and dog his every step" (v.11). Death is part of the punishment, not a dividing line after which punishment comes. The only after-death retribution for Bildad was having one's memory (name) cut off, with no offspring or survivors. Death is personified in vv.13–14. This king of terrors reminds us of the Canaanite deity Mot (Death) whose gullet reaches from earth to sky—the devouring deity (cf. ANET, p. 138). Isaiah reverses the figure and sees the LORD (Yahweh) swallowing up death forever (Isa 25:8; cf. 1 Cor 15:54).

Notes

2–3 The NIV (KJV) follows the LXX and 11QtgJob reading קֵץ (*qēṣ*, "end") as in 16:3 and 28:3. As spelled in the MT, קִנְצֵי (*qinṣê*, "end") is used only here. BDB (p. 890) suggests it means "a hunter's snare." So Gordis (*Job,* in loc.) translates: "How long will you go hunting for words?" W. Gesenius may have been right in viewing it as an Aramaic spelling of the word meaning "end" (BDB, p. 890). The very next word מִלִּין (*millîn,* "speeches") is a clear Aramaism.

Notice the KJV's "ye (make an end)." Throughout vv.2–3 the Hebrew uses the second masculine plural. The text quickly shifts to the singular from v.4 on. Since the plural is repeated (both verb and pronoun), it is not a copyist's error. Dhorme (in loc.) thinks Bildad was addressing the audience that prevented him from speaking. But there is no evidence of this. Perhaps Bildad chose to categorize Job as one of the problem people ("you people") who make life difficult by being unreasonable.

12 The jussive form of the verb (*yᵉhî*) in יְהִי־רָעֵב אֹנוֹ (*yᵉhî-rāʿēb ʾōnô,* "calamity is hungry for him") must be translated indicative. As *tertia*-weak, this verb would have originally ended in a diphthong (*yihyāy*). This vestige of the original dialect represents a contraction of the diphthong without the element *eh* common to the later spelling in Judah. The MT regularly treats a dangling consonantal yod by vocalizing it as *î*. Compare 20:23 and 24:14 for similar spelling. Although *ʾōnô* is open to several possibilities (Dhorme, "wealth"; Gordis [*Job*], "child"), NIV takes it as parallel with אֵיד (*ʾêd,* "disaster"), though limited OT usage does not employ these words in parallel elsewhere. Dahood (*Psalms,* 16:237) sees here אָנָה (*ʾānāh;* "to meet"). This provides the meaning "Famine has become (and continues to be) his partner." This provides a good parallel with the other half: "disaster is stationed at his side [lit., 'at his rib']."

14 Justification for וְתַצְעִדֵהוּ (*wᵉtaṣʿidēhû*) to be translated "and marched off" depends on understanding the verb as a rare third person masculine plural imperfect with prefix *t* (cf. Blommerde, pp. 15–16, 84–85). Other examples are found in 19:15 and Pss 68:3; 106:38.

The indefinite plural subject ("they march him off") is logically equivalent to a third masculine singular passive ("he is marched off").

15 The NIV has chosen to vocalize מִבְּלִי־לֹו (*mibbᵉlî-lô*, "fire . . .") as *mabbēl* + *l*, in which case the last letter introduces the second colon as emphatic *l* (lamed). The MT has preserved the consonants of a rare word meaning "fire." The root appears in both Akkadian and Ugaritic but nowhere else in the OT. This identification is now widely accepted (cf. BHS mg.) but was seen first by M. Dahood ("Some Northwest Semitic Words in Job," *Biblica* 38 [1947]: 312–14). The parallelism with גָּפְרִית (*goprît*, "burning sulfur") is compelling. The passage is also an example of how the LXX (and Theodotian) can completely misunderstand the Hebrew but still be a good witness to the original consonants (*en nukti auto = bᵉlîlô*, "in his night").

---

4. Job's reply

19:1–29

¹Then Job replied:

²"How long will you torment me
   and crush me with words?
³Ten times now you have reproached me;
   shamelessly you attack me.
⁴If it is true that I have gone astray,
   my error remains my concern alone.
⁵If indeed you would exalt yourselves above me
   and use my humiliation against me,
⁶then know that God has wronged me
   and drawn his net around me.

⁷"Though I cry, 'I've been wronged!' I get no response;
   though I call for help, there is no justice.
⁸He has blocked my way so I cannot pass;
   he has shrouded my paths in darkness.
⁹He has stripped me of my honor
   and removed the crown from my head.
¹⁰He tears me down on every side till I am gone;
   he uproots my hope like a tree.
¹¹His anger burns against me;
   he counts me among his enemies.
¹²His troops advance in force;
   they build a siege ramp against me
   and encamp around my tent.

¹³"He has alienated my brothers from me;
   my acquaintances are completely estranged from me.
¹⁴My kinsmen have gone away;
   my friends have forgotten me.
¹⁵My guests and my maidservants count me a stranger;
   they look upon me as an alien.
¹⁶I summon my servant, but he does not answer,
   though I beg him with my own mouth.
¹⁷My breath is offensive to my wife;
   I am loathsome to my own brothers.
¹⁸Even the little boys scorn me;
   when I appear, they ridicule me.
¹⁹All my intimate friends detest me;
   those I love have turned against me.

²⁰ I am nothing but skin and bones;
   I have escaped with only the skin of my teeth.

²¹ "Have pity on me, my friends, have pity,
   for the hand of God has struck me.
²² Why do you pursue me as God does?
   Will you never get enough of my flesh?

²³ "Oh, that my words were recorded,
   that they were written on a scroll,
²⁴ that they were inscribed with an iron tool on lead,
   or engraved in rock forever!
²⁵ I know that my Redeemer lives,
   and that in the end he will stand upon the earth.
²⁶ And after my skin has been destroyed,
   yet in my flesh I will see God;
²⁷ I myself will see him
   with my own eyes—I, and not another.
   How my heart yearns within me!

²⁸ "If you say, 'How we will hound him,
   since the root of the trouble lies in him,'
²⁹ you should fear the sword yourselves;
   for wrath will bring punishment by the sword,
   and then you will know that there is judgment.'"

The chapter divides into four logical stanzas. In the first Job shows increasing irritation over his counselors' shameless attacks and his impatience with their superior claims (vv. 2–5). Then follows Job's feeling of abandonment by God and perception that God's attack on him is wrong (vv. 6–12). Then he blames God for alienating his kinsmen and household, even his wife (vv. 13–20). In vv. 21–27 he ends this lament, to our amazement, with a triumphant expression of faith in the one who will ultimately champion his cause and vindicate him (vv. 23–27). This stanza is bracketed by words to his friends whom Job does not believe will ever have pity (v. 21). So he warns them of the dire consequences of their false accusations (vv. 28–29).

1–5 Verse 4 literally reads "my error lives (remains) with me." Job implied his friends had no right to interfere, no right to behave as if they were God (cf. v. 22).

By an unusual handling of v. 6, Andersen (*Job*, p. 191) claims Job was not accusing God of injustice but of no-justice (v. 7b). This would be attractive if there were not so many other places where Job made the same charge. Notice the following:

He mocks the despair of the innocent . . .
   If it is not he, then who is it? (9:23–24)
You search out my faults . . . though you know that I am not guilty. (10:6–7)
God has turned me over to evil men . . . shattered me, . . . crushed me . . .
   without pity he pierces my kidneys. (16:11–13)

In the light of these lines, it is easy to render 19:6 "God has wronged me." These are the very thoughts that elicited Bildad's retort, "Does God pervert justice?" (8:3), and later Elihu's words, "It is unthinkable that God would do wrong, that the Almighty would pervert justice" (34:12). The only way to handle Job's words in 19:6 is along the lines already suggested, that it was Job's faulty perception or, better, his lack of full perception. The exasperated Job perceived things in this way. He did not know God's plan (42:2). But even without heavenly knowledge, Job's perception was better than Bildad's, who also lacked the heavenly knowledge that it was God who was permitting the Accuser to strike Job.

In a sense the Accuser was acting as the hand of God, for he had said to God, "But stretch out your hand and strike his flesh" (2:5). And God had replied, "Very well, then, he is in your hands" (2:6). So Job was not totally wrong when he said, "The hand of God has struck me" (19:21). Bildad with his truncated theological formula could not begin to appreciate Job's predicament. And because he had reduced God and his actions to an impersonal formula, Bildad was incapable of showing any mercy toward Job.

6–12 In Job's mind God was at war with him. God's troops laid siege as if Job were a fortified city; but, alas, he was only a tent. In a series of largely military images, the tension of Job's lament rises with each succeeding verse; but with poetic license the chronological sequence is in reverse of the way it really happened. In v.8 his paths are blocked or walled up, that is, he is in captivity (cf. 3:23; 13:27). In v.9 he suffers royal dethronement—stripped of his honor and crown as a defeated king (see his words in 29:14, where Job claimed righteousness and justice as his robe and turban). In v.10 he is torn down (like a wall) and uprooted (like a tree, more drastic than the figure in 14:7). And finally in vv.11–12 God's troops advance and build a siege ramp against him. Reverse this order and you have a step-by-step description of what happened in siege warfare.

13–19 Leaving this compelling figure, Job spoke quite literally of how his family and friends had turned against him (vv. 13–17). In any society nothing hurts more than rejection by one's family and friends, but what could be worse in a patriarchal society than to have children ridicule the patriarch (v.18)?

20 What does escaping with only the skin of one's teeth mean? The NIV takes this to mean that only Job's gums were left unaffected by his ailment. Since the word *only* must be inserted to get this meaning, many are not satisfied with it. The line is difficult. The KJV made a literal translation of it and thereby created an idiom in the English language for a narrow escape (by the skin of my teeth). But is Job talking about a narrow escape here? Commentators list many attempts to find a suitable meaning for the line (see Rowley, p. 170). Rowley himself offers no solution but suggests Job was saying his disease had reduced him to a shadow of his former self and that he had barely survived at all. G.R. Driver ("Problems in the Hebrew Text of Job," in *Wisdom in Israel and the Ancient Near East*, eds. M. Noth and D.W. Thomas [Leiden: Brill, 1960], p. 80) offers some cogent lexical and grammatical reasons for rendering the line "I gnaw myself on (the) skin (with) my teeth," like an unnerved person may gnaw at his lips.

Too often 19:21–29 has been isolated from what Job has said earlier. Job has stressed a number of themes that to a degree find their resolve here. Despite this resolve the dissonance of the dialogue continues after this; but Job's bitterness toward God, if not his puzzlement over what God was doing, was washed away as a result of the faith and hope expressed here.

Up to this point Job had come to the conclusion that he was soon to die (10:20; 16:22–17:1). His experience created in him a sense of amoral chaos in the world and in his life. His sense of being crushed caused him to look repeatedly toward death as a kind of hopeless release (14:18–22; 16:11–16). He knew he was innocent and sought above all else to be vindicated. His compassionless counselors had reiterated their impersonal theology that declared him guilty. He felt that God was angry with him and had become the enemy who attacked and crushed him. He perceived that he was alone in a cruel and amoral world. There was no one left who understood, no one to plead his cause or bear witness to his innocence. And this was what he wanted most of all, not release, not retribution, but only justice, someone to vindicate him.

In two earlier chapters (9; 16) where he expressed deep bitterness toward God, Job also touched on this same "Advocate" theme. In chapter 9 it was only a desire— "If only there were someone to arbitrate between us" (9:33). But in chapters 16 and 19 it becomes a firm conviction—"my witness is in heaven" (16:19) and "I know that my Redeemer lives" (19:25). As in 13:15, here in chapter 19 this hope extends to include Job himself as a participant in the process of vindication—"I myself will see him on my side" (v.27; see Notes).

21 Deserted by loved ones Job needed radical friendship, not theological banter. This was not the first time Job called for pity (cf. 6:14). It is necessary to feel with Job his sense of total desertion if we are to understand the passage. It is within this context that he turned to God in vv.25–26.

22 Job's appeal failed. He thought his counselors had joined forces with God as "the hound of heaven" to sniff him out and to be in on the kill (cf. 16:9). Although Job's perception of God may have been wrong (not understanding the role of the Accuser), his perception of them was correct. They had presumed to take on themselves the role of divine judicial authority, as is evident in Eliphaz's remark in 15:11a, where he assumed his words were God's words. As part of the "Chase" metaphor, in v.22b Job included a typical Semitic idiom for slander—they devour his flesh.

23–24 These words arise from Job's desire to defend his integrity. Believing that he was at the point of death, Job felt he had nothing to lose by speaking out (7:7–11; 10:1; 13:3, 13–28; 16:18). But they are also a direct response to Bildad's taunt in 18:17 suggesting Job would be permanently forgotten. Both men were fully aware of Wisdom teachings like Proverbs 10:7: "The memory of the righteous will be a blessing, but the name of the wicked will rot."

With no hope left of proving his righteousness, Job looked to the future, leaving his case with posterity (Ps 102:18). His wish to inscribe his words (v.24) was uttered with poetic expansiveness that contemplated several possible ways—in a scroll (copper? see Dhorme) or on a rock. Whether the lead was to be used on the rock or was another medium is not clear. Permanency is the issue—inscribed forever.

25–27 Are these the only words Job wanted inscribed or did he mean all his words where he had over and over proclaimed his innocence? The conjunction that begins v.25 (not reflected in the NIV) may be the adversative "But." This would mean Job was leaving the thought of inscribing his words permanently to the even more favorable situation of having a living Redeemer (Vindicator) who would champion his cause even after he was gone (v.26). Job's hope in the midst of despair reached a climax. Slandered by his friends and with death imminent, Job looked to the future where his Defender waited. This time it sounds like God himself, for there is no mention of his Defender pleading with God as in 16:21. But is it God? This is difficult to determine from the immediate context. The larger context, namely chapters 9 and 16, where the same third-party theme appears, lends weight to the notion that that theme finds its climax here. We have noted that the theme was already ancient in Job's day.

In pagan theology a personal patron-deity acted as a champion for an individual human, pleading his cause in the council of the gods. In the Book of Job the angels perform this role. In 33:23 Elihu clearly presented this theology of angels that took the place of the pagan servant-deities. He employed the very root (*mlṣ*) used in 16:20 to describe Job's "Intercessor." In each of these Advocate passages, the third party is greater than man; and in chapter 16 he lives in heaven. Yet he is fully capable of taking his stand to testify on earth (19:25). It is even possible, though not necessary, that Job used the word "lives" (*ḥāy*) in its extended meaning "lives forever" (cf. Dahood, *Psalms*, 16:91; R.B.Y. Scott, *Proverbs and Ecclesiastes*, AB, vol. 18 [Garden City, N.Y.: Doubleday, 1965], p. 91) just as he wished his words were inscribed forever (v.24).

The meaning of the word *gō'ēl* ("redeemer") is fundamental to understanding this passage. The word is important in OT jurisprudence. It had both a criminal and a civil aspect. As "blood avenger," a *gō'ēl* had a responsibility to avenge the blood of a slain kinsman (Num 35:12–28). He was not seeking revenge but justice. On the civil side he was a redeemer or vindicator. Here he had the responsibility to "buy back" and so redeem the lost inheritance of a deceased relative. This might come by purchasing from slavery or marrying the decedent's widow in order to provide an heir. As such he was the defender or champion of the oppressed as in the Book of Ruth. See Proverbs 23:10–11, where God is the Defender (*gō'ēl*) of oppressed individuals. In the Exodus and the Exile he is the *gō'ēl* of his oppressed nation (Exod 6:6; Isa 43:1). The Lord also as *gō'ēl* delivers individuals from death (Ps 103:4). Here Job had something more in mind than one who will testify to his integrity. In 16:18 he cried, "O earth, do not cover my blood." Job saw himself a murder victim. He depended on his *gō'ēl* to testify for him but also to set the books straight. God who had become his enemy would become his friend, and those who had joined in the kill would be punished (vv.28–29).

In Hebrew the emphatic position of the pronoun "I" in v.25a shows Job had a settled conviction: "I, yes I know." The words "my Redeemer [Vindicator]" indicate a personal relationship, and the word "lives" must mean more than merely "alive" but implies he would continue his work of vindicating Job's integrity and avenging Job's death, as Job implied in vv.28–29.

In v.25b the Hebrew word *'aḥᵃrôn* ("in the end") does not have a preposition, though the NIV translation is permissible, being understood as an adverb meaning "afterward." Another possibility is to take it as a substantive referring to the Redeemer as "the Last." According to A. Schoors ("Literary Phrases," in *Ras Shamra Parallels*, 2 vols., ed. L.R. Fisher [Rome: Pontifical Biblical Institute, 1972, 1975], 1:12), the term is juridicial and refers to the one who has the last word at a trial. Dhorme (in loc.) recalls such passages as Isaiah 44:6 and 48:12, where God is called "the first and the last"; but the term never stands alone as an epithet of deity. It may be best to see it as an adjective "as the one coming after (me)." Job thought his vindication would come after his death. The Hebrew alone in v.25b is not clear enough for us to determine whether Job was speaking of the end of his life or the end of the world. But since the latter concept is not mentioned elsewhere in the Book of Job, the former is a safer interpretation.

Similarly, at the end of v.25, does "upon the dust" mean "upon the earth" (NIV) or does it mean Job's grave (NIV mg.)? The term refers to the grave in 7:21; 17:16; 20:11; 21:26; and in Psalm 22:29 and Isaiah 26:19; but it can mean "the earth" as in Job 41:33. So Job could have meant merely that the human arena here on earth is where his Vindicator would testify; but since the context is about Job's decaying body, it may be a specific reference to his grave. Are, then, the two succeeding verses a reference to Job's resurrection? In 14:10–14 Job said nothing about general eschatological resurrection; but he believed in God's power to raise the dead and had a desire and hope that God would set a time and raise him. So here in chapter 19 we may see a similar resurrection in which Job would see God with his own eyes and as his friend. While he was anticipating the doctrine of resurrection, he was not spelling out the teaching of a final resurrection for all the righteous.

Verse 26a is a most difficult line. Literally it reads "after my skin they have struck off—this!" The general meaning alludes to the ravages of Job's disease, but the precise meaning is variously interpreted. Habel's understanding (*Job*, 1985, in loc.) of the line is appealing. He considers v.26a to be a continuation of the thought in v.25 and the word "after" (*'aḥar*) to be explanatory of the preceding "afterward" (*'aḥarôn*, "in the end" in NIV), reading: "After, that is, my skin is peeled off!" This, then, emphasizes Job's confidence that even after he died, his "redeemer" would arise to testify in his behalf. Dogmatism should be avoided and the precise meaning here perhaps held in abeyance (cf. Notes).

Verse 26b is clearer. What is very clear is that Job expected to see God. Two verbs meaning "see" are used here and in v.27. The debate centers around whether it is "in the flesh" or "apart from the flesh" that Job had this experience. The Hebrew could go either way (cf. Notes); but since Job spoke of using his own eyes, and in light of what has been said about Job's view of possible resurrection, the NIV text "in the flesh" is preferred. So Job was convinced that even if he died, he would live again to witness his own vindication.

At the end of chapter 16 Job was obsessed with the notion that someone in heaven would stand up for him and plead his case. But here in chapter 19 he expected to witness his own vindication on earth. Indeed his own eyes would gaze on his Vindicator. As it turned out Job did not need the intermediary (*mēlîṣ*) mentioned in chapter 16 because his idea that God was against him proved to be without foundation. The lesson that suffering does not show that God is alienated is one of the most enduring themes in the book. Job's feelings of alienation and the condemnation by his friends produced in him a consequent feeling of need for a Redeemer (Vindicator), which is strongly evocative of sinful man's basic need before a holy God (cf. 1 Tim 2:5–6). But in Job's case, as an innocent sufferer he finally realized that God himself would appear to him, whom he would see with his own eyes (cf. 19:27 with 42:5); and then Job would learn that his God was not alienated or unconcerned but was both his Vindicator (*gō'ēl*) and his friend.

Notes

2 The alternation between the Hebrew plural with mem (ten times) and the Aramaic plural with nun (thirteen times) does not follow a particular speaker (in 26:4 Job used *n* [nun]). מִלָּה (*millāh*, "word") is so common in Aramaic that its usage in Hebrew tends to be Aramaized.

11 For כְצָרָיו (keṣārāyw, "among his enemies"), the RSV has "as his adversary," based on the Vulgate. The plural in the MT shows this to be dative rather than accusative, literally, "as (one) of his enemies."

15 In three places the second or third feminine plural with pronoun is vocalized as second masculine (Jer 2:19; S of Songs 1:6; and here). The original vocalization of תַחְשְׁבֻנִי (taḥšebunî, "you count me") was probably taḥšebānnî ("[my maidservants] count me"). Moreover the poetic balance also favors taking "my guests" with the preceding line rather than following the Masoretic punctuation as does the NIV. The masculine plural pronoun at the end of the verse includes everyone from v.13 on.

17 לִבְנֵי בִטְנִי (libnê biṭnî, "to my own brothers") is literally "to the sons of my belly." What does it mean? The RSV and NIV take the belly to be his mother's. The fact that Job's sons were killed may simply mean these were the children of concubines, but not all agree. See Dhorme (pp. 277–78) for detailed discussion. He extends the meaning to include "relatives."

18 The idiom וַיְדַבְּרוּ־בִי (wayedabberû-bî, "they ridiculed me") in Ps 78:19 must mean "speak against." This weakens the case of those who see here an old meaning of a similar root evidenced in the Tell Amarna glosses. That meaning is "to flee" (G.R. Driver, "Hebrew Notes," ZAW 52 [1934]: 55f.). It was used widely in Old Babylonian and understood in the West. Since culturally it is more likely children would flee from rather than ridicule a sick patriarch, the case still has some merit.

22 In וּמִבְּשָׂרִי (ûmibbeśārî, "of my flesh"), the min clearly shows its overlapping quality with the preposition בּ (b, "with," "in," "from").

25 In Isa 44:6 the prophet speaks of God as the Redeemer or Vindicator (גֹּאֵל, gōʾēl), and in Isa 48:12 God calls himself "the first" (רִאשׁוֹן, riʾšôn) and "the last" (אַחֲרוֹן, ʾaḥarôn). Dhorme and Rowley see a similar meaning for וְאַחֲרוֹן (weʾaḥarôn) in v.25: "As the Last (One) upon the earth (dust) he shall stand (rise)." That the term does not stand alone as an epithet of deity should not rule against seeing God as the one who will have the last word in Job's trial. The NIV adds a preposition to capture an adverbial force since ʾaḥarôn can mean "afterward," but the eschatological tone "in the end" is questionable.

As mentioned above, it is best to see ʾaḥarôn as an adjective (BDB, p. 30, b), "as one coming after (me)." This fits the NIV margin where עַל־עָפָר (ʿal-ʿāpār) is rendered "upon my grave." The missing pronoun î ("my") may be due to haplography with the first letter י (y, yod) of the next word יָקוּם (yāqûm, "he will stand") or a case of single writing of a consonant where the morphology requires two (cf. Dahood, Psalms, 17A:371). Job has repeatedly lamented the fact that death is near (7:21b; 10:8–9; 14:10–12; 16:22–17:1).

26 וּמִבְּשָׂרִי (ûmibbeśārî, "yet in my flesh") is identical to the form in v.22, but here the meaning of the preposition is much more difficult. In its text and margin, the NIV has given the two major possibilities. They are opposite in meaning. The margin "apart from my flesh" (i.e., in the disembodied state) is at best a rare concept in the OT. In the next verse Job asserted he would see God with his own eyes (v.27). The preposition refers to the viewer's vantage point: "from (within) my flesh I shall see God."

27 In וְלֹא־זָר (welōʾ-zār, "and not another"), we may take zār ("stranger") as a genitive referring back to the "eyes," viz., "and not (the eyes) of a stranger." Or equally defensible is the meaning "and not (as) a stranger." The latter expresses Job's desire for a friendly relationship with God.

28 The LXX, Theodotian, the Vulgate, and many Hebrew MSS take בִי (bî, "in me") as third masculine—בּוֹ (bô, NIV, "in him"), which is another example of the confusion between the ו (w, waw) and י (y, yod) in the square script. In this case the context demands the third masculine meaning.

29 שַׁדִּין (šaddyyn, "judgment"), a hapax legomenon, may be simply a variant of the divine epithet Shaddai. (For full treatment of this view, see L.R. Fisher, "šdyn in Job 19:29," VetTest 2 [1961]: 342–43.) Most relate it to the noun דִּין (dîn, "judgment"), following the interpretation of Aquila, Symmachus, and Theodotian, and understand the שׁ (š) as the

relative *še* (BDB, p. 979). But this use of *še* does not appear in Job. The LXX and the Hebrew oral tradition indicate ancient uncertainty, but Shaddai does appear in 29:5. The NIV margin is to be preferred.

---

5. Zophar

20:1–29

¹Then Zophar the Naamathite replied:

> ²"My troubled thoughts prompt me to answer
> because I am greatly disturbed.
> ³I hear a rebuke that dishonors me,
> and my understanding inspires me to reply.

> ⁴"Surely you know how it has been from of old,
> ever since man was placed on the earth,
> ⁵that the mirth of the wicked is brief,
> the joy of the godless lasts but a moment.
> ⁶Though his pride reaches to the heavens
> and his head touches the clouds,
> ⁷he will perish forever, like his own dung;
> those who have seen him will say, 'Where is he?'
> ⁸Like a dream he flies away, no more to be found,
> banished like a vision of the night.
> ⁹The eye that saw him will not see him again;
> his place will look on him no more.
> ¹⁰His children must make amends to the poor;
> his own hands must give back his wealth.
> ¹¹The youthful vigor that fills his bones
> will lie with him in the dust.

> ¹²"Though evil is sweet in his mouth
> and he hides it under his tongue,
> ¹³though he cannot bear to let it go
> and keeps it in his mouth,
> ¹⁴yet his food will turn sour in his stomach;
> it will become the venom of serpents within him.
> ¹⁵He will spit out the riches he swallowed;
> God will make his stomach vomit them up.
> ¹⁶He will suck the poison of serpents;
> the fangs of an adder will kill him.
> ¹⁷He will not enjoy the streams,
> the rivers flowing with honey and cream.
> ¹⁸What he toiled for he must give back uneaten;
> he will not enjoy the profit from his trading.
> ¹⁹For he has oppressed the poor and left them destitute;
> he has seized houses he did not build.

> ²⁰"Surely he will have no respite from his craving;
> he cannot save himself by his treasure.
> ²¹Nothing is left for him to devour;
> his prosperity will not endure.
> ²²In the midst of his plenty, distress will overtake him;
> the full force of misery will come upon him.
> ²³When he has filled his belly,
> God will vent his burning anger against him
> and rain down his blows upon him.

24 Though he flees from an iron weapon,
    a bronze-tipped arrow pierces him.
25 He pulls it out of his back,
    the gleaming point out of his liver.
    Terrors will come over him;
26   total darkness lies in wait for his treasures.
    A fire unfanned will consume him
    and devour what is left in his tent.
27 The heavens will expose his guilt;
    the earth will rise up against him.
28 A flood will carry off his house,
    rushing waters on the day of God's wrath.
29 Such is the fate God allots the wicked,
    the heritage appointed for them by God."

The entire chapter is another poem on the ghastly fate of the wicked (see Bildad's words in 8:11–19 and in ch.18, and Eliphaz in 15:20–35). The poem must be read with full attention given to the use of figurative language, parallelism, and strophic structure, all basic elements of Hebrew poetry. Despite the error of Zophar's application, the poem itself ought to be appreciated as a masterly piece of literature.

We should also try to appreciate the elements of truth contained herein. As Gordis (*God and Man,* p. 90) notes, Zophar was "performing a vital task . . . defending man's faith in a moral universe, a world governed by the principle of justice, which was not merely a deep desire of the human soul but an indispensable instrument of social control." It is unfortunate that one able to make such an eloquent statement of this truth should fail so miserably in properly applying it.

1–3 Zophar took Job's words, especially his closing words in 19:28–29, as a personal affront. Job had dared to assert that on Zophar's theory of retribution Zophar himself was due for punishment. To Zophar such could only happen to the wicked.

Zophar was the most emotional of the three; and he was not about to let Job's rebuke go unanswered, though in chapter 19 Job had earnestly pled for a withdrawal of their charges. Here he had nothing new to say to Job but said it with passion. The speech is full of terrifying imagery.

4–11 Zophar could not abide the thought that the wicked prosper (cf. 9:22; 12:5–6). Underneath the words lie the comfortable fact that he was a healthy and prosperous man, which, in his view, was itself proof of his goodness and righteousness. To him the joy and vigor of the wicked would always be brief and like a fantasy (cf. Ps 73:19 –20). Oppressing the poor is the mark of the truly wicked (vv.10, 19). On this subject Job had no quarrel with Zophar (see 31:16–23). But, of course, he denied being that kind of person.

12–19 The evil man's wicked deeds, especially robbing the poor, are tasty food that pleases his palate but turns sour in his stomach. God will force him to vomit up such ill-gained riches. In his peroration (chs. 29–31) Job would stress his own social conscience and strongly deny Zophar's veiled accusation.

20–28 When a wicked man's belly is filled and there is nothing left for him to devour, God then vents his anger against him (vv.20–21). The man flees from an iron weapon only to be shot in the back by a glittering bronze arrow that must be pulled out of his liver (vv.24–25). Such attention to figurative detail is often overlooked as meaningless. On the contrary, the more eloquently it could be said, the more the ancient speaker was able to convey how deeply he felt and how sincerely he was trying to make his point. But Zophar, despite his eloquence and sincerity, had no compassion. He left no room for repentance and put all his stress on the importance of material possessions, while Job at this point was increasingly concerned over his relationship with God, no matter what happened to his body or possessions (19:23–27).

29 Like Bildad in 18:21, Zophar concluded his speech with a summary statement in which he claimed all he had said was in accord with God's judicial order for the wicked.

Notes

2 On חוּשִׁי (ḥûšî, "greatly disturbed"), see BDB (ḥûš II, pp. 301f.).

10 On יְרַצּוּ (yeraṣṣû, "must make amends"), compare 14:6. Contrary to its usual meaning, Dhorme (in loc.) has shown that the Piel form of this root means "to satisfy, pay off a debt."

17 The deletion of נַהֲרֵי (naharê, "the rivers") or the addition of the word for "oil" is suggested by those who feel the first line in Hebrew is too short (cf. Pope). There is no textual evidence to help; so any corruption of the text was very early. Such unbalanced poetic lines do not always call for emendation. If one counts syllables there are other unbalanced lines in the poem (1, 16, 29). But the grammar is also difficult—if not impossible—which prompts BHS to call for deletion of this word. A more satisfactory explanation comes from an understanding of paleography, that is, the early shape of the square letters נ (n, nun) and צ (ṣ, ṣadē). The error in our text could have come from the loss of a short diagonal stroke that changed the ṣadē (Y) to a nun (J) (the additional vowel ending being secondary). For the basic root šhr meaning "fresh oil," see the denominative verb in 24:11. We render the text "He will not enjoy the streams of oil, nor the rivers of honey and cream." This solves the problem of both balance and grammar.

19 There is a question whether בַּיִת (bayit, "houses") refers to "houses he did not build" or "houses he cannot rebuild" or "domains on which he cannot build a house." Andersen (Job, p. 196) suggests the meaning is the last.

20 From לֹא יְמַלֵּט (lōʾ yemalleṭ) the NIV gets "save himself" from comparing Amos 2:15. Here napšô ("himself") is suppressed.

23 On יְהִי (yehî, "When he has"), compare the Notes on 18:12 and 24:14. As in 18:12, here yehî (jussive) really represents the indicative yihy(eh).

With some revocalizing and a different division of the letters, some scholars read בִּלְחוּמוֹ (bilḥûmô, "with his blows") either as mabbûl ḥammô ("a flood of his wrath") or mabbēl ḥammô ("the fire of his wrath") (cf. BHS). The NIV derives this from the root lḥm, meaning "to fight" (cf. Pss 35:1; 56:2 [3 MT]) or as a noun in Judg 5:8). It might also mean "with his flame" (Deut 32:24; NIV, "consuming") or even "into his intestines" (cf. the first line and Zeph 1:17) or even with Arabic "into his flesh" (see Dhorme); but KJV's "while he is eating" and RSV's "as his food" should be ruled out.

24 קֶשֶׁת נְחוּשָׁה (qešet neḥûšāh, "a bronze-tipped arrow") literally reads "a bow of bronze." The NIV is not wrong, however, for no bows were made of bronze. It means either a bow that shoots arrows "tipped" with bronze or capable of piercing bronze targets (ANET, p. 244).

26 "A fire unfanned" does not sound very hot, but the point is a fire that needs no fanning by man to make it hot, which might be lightning.

6. *Job's reply*

21:1–34

[1] Then Job replied:

[2] "Listen carefully to my words;
  let this be the consolation you give me.
[3] Bear with me while I speak,
  and after I have spoken, mock on.

[4] "Is my complaint directed to man?
  Why should I not be impatient?
[5] Look at me and be astonished;
  clap your hand over your mouth.
[6] When I think about this, I am terrified;
  trembling seizes my body.
[7] Why do the wicked live on,
  growing old and increasing in power?
[8] They see their children established around them,
  their offspring before their eyes.
[9] Their homes are safe and free from fear;
  the rod of God is not upon them.
[10] Their bulls never fail to breed;
  their cows calve and do not miscarry.
[11] They send forth their children as a flock;
  their little ones dance about.
[12] They sing to the music of tambourine and harp;
  they make merry to the sound of the flute.
[13] They spend their years in prosperity
  and go down to the grave in peace.
[14] Yet they say to God, 'Leave us alone!
  We have no desire to know your ways.
[15] Who is the Almighty, that we should serve him?
  What would we gain by praying to him?'
[16] But their prosperity is not in their own hands,
  so I stand aloof from the counsel of the wicked.

[17] "Yet how often is the lamp of the wicked snuffed out?
  How often does calamity come upon them,
  the fate God allots in his anger?
[18] How often are they like straw before the wind,
  like chaff swept away by a gale?
[19] It is said, 'God stores up a man's punishment for his sons.'
  Let him repay the man himself, so that he will know it!
[20] Let his own eyes see his destruction;
  let him drink of the wrath of the Almighty.
[21] For what does he care about the family he leaves behind
  when his allotted months come to an end?

[22] "Can anyone teach knowledge to God,
  since he judges even the highest?
[23] One man dies in full vigor,
  completely secure and at ease,
[24] his body well nourished,
  his bones rich with marrow.
[25] Another man dies in bitterness of soul,
  never having enjoyed anything good.
[26] Side by side they lie in the dust,
  and worms cover them both.

27"I know full well what you are thinking,
  the schemes by which you would wrong me.
28You say, 'Where now is the great man's house,
  the tents where wicked men lived?'
29Have you never questioned those who travel?
  Have you paid no regard to their accounts—
30that the evil man is spared from the day of calamity,
  that he is delivered from the day of wrath?
31Who denounces his conduct to his face?
  Who repays him for what he has done?
32He is carried to the grave,
  and watch is kept over his tomb.
33The soil in the valley is sweet to him;
  all men follow after him,
  and a countless throng goes before him.

34"So how can you console me with your nonsense?
  Nothing is left of your answers but falsehood!"

In this closing speech of the second cycle, Job was determined to prove that he had listened to what his counselors had said. This he did by quoting or otherwise alluding to their words and then refuting them. Compare 20:11 with 21:7, 18:19 with 21:8, 18:5 with 21:17, 5:4 and 20:10 with 21:19, and 20:4 with 21:29.

1-3 If the counselors could give Job no other consolation, they should have at least paid close attention to his words. Evidently he sensed that the dialogue was about to break up since he implied the other parties were not even listening.

4-6 Job was appalled at the counselors' failure to have any compassion (v.5); but if his complaint were only against them (man), he thought his bitterness would not be justified. His rage was based on the idea that God may be responsible. Job was terrified because he knew how awesome a task it is to complain against God (v.6). Yet in all honesty, he could find no other way out of his predicament. The scriptural lesson in these hard words can be understood only when we place them in their canonical context. God would rather have us complain than be indifferent toward him or to handle his truths arrogantly and so reduce them to dead maxims. Job's anguish over not understanding what God was doing is proof that he was not indifferent or arrogant. It was the counselors who assumed they knew what was going on.

7-15 The counselors had elaborated on the horrible fate of the wicked (15:20-35; 18:5-21) against Job's claim that the wicked often prosper. Those who wish to know nothing of God's ways, who even consider prayer a useless exercise (vv.14-15), flourish in all aspects of their lives. Far from dying prematurely, as Zophar said in 20:11, they live long and increase in strength (v.7). Bildad's claim that the wicked have no offspring or descendants to remember them (18:19-21) was flatly denied by Job (v.8). Job painted a word picture in vv.7-13 illustrating the domestic pleasantness and prosperity often enjoyed by godless people who dare to defy the Almighty (v.15).

16 This verse as translated is difficult to understand. The NIV has not caught fully the correct interpretation. The way Eliphaz used these words in 22:17-18 helps interpret Job's words (see Notes). Job knew God controls the prosperity of the wicked, and that is what makes it an enigma when the "counsel of the wicked" is so far from God (cf. Ps 1:1). "Why *do* the wicked live on . . . and increase in power?" (v.7, emphasis mine).

17–21 Job alluded directly to Bildad's words in 18:5, with the retort "How often . . . ?" (v.17). And if children have to pay for their father's sins as Eliphaz (5:4) and Zophar (20:10) said, then the wicked being evil are encouraged to say, "What do we care?" (cf. v.21). Job was disturbed at the apparent injustice of it all. As noted the Book of Job does not deal with the matter of final future judgment that would set right the tables of justice. Such revelation will come later. Job, therefore, felt that immediate punishment for the wicked would be the only just procedure; but he found just the opposite in life. Again failure to understand fully God's ways had led both Job and the counselors astray; but Job did not pretend to understand, and they did. Moreover Job was suffering physically and emotionally, and they were not.

22–26 Job admitted that his knowledge of God's ways was defective (v.22), but it was precisely his high view of God that had created a problem. Those who do not believe in an absolutely sovereign God cannot possibly appreciate the depth of the problem Job presented in vv.23–26. The answer still alludes us. Even with all our additional revelation (Rom 8:28), we often stand in anguish over the apparent injustice and seeming cruelty of God's providence.

27–33 Job realized his counselors were going to repeat the same worn-out clichés that implied he was a wicked man. They have repeatedly suggested the destruction of his house was proof of it (cf. 8:15; 15:34; 18:15, 21). He called these clichés schemes by which they wronged him (v.27). He challenged them to investigate the total experience of people throughout the world to determine whether he was right (v.29). He was saying that it is impossible to derive a just law of retribution from what we observe in this present world. Their simplistic view was wrong, claimed Job, for all too often there was no one to denounce the wicked for what he had done, and there was no one to punish him (v.31, NEB; see Notes). Contrary to the description of the wicked in chapters 8 and 20, the ungodly man is often buried with the highest honors (vv.32–33).

34 Job opened this discourse with a plea for a kind of consolation based on his counselors' quiet listening. He closed by returning to that thought with a blast at what they had offered as consolation, their answers riddled with falsehood and nonsense.

Notes

---

3 תַּלְעִיג (*talʿig*, "mock on") in the Hiphil probably has an elative meaning here, that is, not a little but increased mocking. The shift between singular and plural in Hebrew is merely a stylistic matter.

8 For לִפְנֵיהֶם (*lipnêhem*, "they see"), BHS wrongly suggests a deletion. It is tempting to repoint עִמָּם (*ʿimmām*, "around them") to *ʿammān* ("their kinsmen and their offspring"), but neither the Masoretes nor the LXX understood it this way. The NIV is on the right track even if a little loose. The Hebrew is asyndetic—"established before them, [even] around them."

13 יְבַלּוּ (*yeballû*, "they spend") is a good example of where the written and oral traditions diverge, each preserving a word with a different basic meaning: בָּלָה (*bālāh*, "wear out," "use to full") versus כָּלָה (*kālāh*, "complete"). In this context the meanings converge; so either is possible.

The context witnesses against the common meaning for בְּרָגַע (*berāgaʿ*) as "in an instant" (NIV mg.). The NIV ("in peace") has followed the rarer meaning usually in the Hiphil, "to be at rest." See Ps 35:20 for the adjective with this meaning.

16 The words of this verse are easy to understand, and most translations have rendered them rather literally; but the problem lies with the strange result. Some attach it to what follows (RV). The latter inserts the words "ye say," as most translations do, for v. 19 to solve the problem of Job's apparent agreement with the counselors in the middle of a speech in which he was so heartily in disagreement. Rashi took v. 16a as a question, while Ibn Ezra felt the context was served better by a statement that implied God must be held responsible for allowing the wicked to prosper. There is no reason to question whether v. 16b should be taken as Job's repudiation of all the words of the wicked recorded in vv. 14–15.

It helps to compare 22:17–18 with 21:14–16. In chapter 22 Eliphaz was using Job's words to his own advantage. So Eliphaz's words are a commentary on these. Job was saying, "Look, the prosperity of the wicked is from God despite the fact that their counsel is far from him." While in 22:18a Eliphaz was using only the substance of Job's words, he clarified the meaning of 21:16a. The words of 22:18b are identical with 21:16b. The relationship between the "a" and "b" clauses in both passages is concessive and refers to the distance between God and the wicked, not Job and the wicked. This implies reading מֶנִּי (*mennî*, "from me") as מֶנּוּ (*mennû*, "from him") or accepting a third singular pronoun suffix written with yod (9:19, 35 [note]; 14:3; 19:28; 21:16; 22:18; 31:18). Compare Blommerde (pp. 92–93) who interprets בְּיָדָם (*beyādām*) as "from his hand." This may be possible but not necessary.

17 Whether כַּמָּה (*kammāh*, "yet how often") is an interrogative or exclamatory "how" cannot be determined from the Hebrew. See the NIV margin on vv. 17–20. If it is exclamatory, we must assume Job was being ironic as in 26:2–3 and had already begun to quote his friends (cf. the clarifying "It is said" in v. 19). It is easier to take v. 17 and v. 18 as questions, realizing he still had the words of Bildad in 18:5 in mind.

19 The brackets indicate "[It is said]" is not in the Hebrew. But it clarifies the meaning. See Gordis on "The Use of Quotations in Job" (*God and Man*, pp. 169–89).

24 עֲטִינָיו (*ʿatînāyw*, "his body") is used only here. The NIV has loosely followed the ancient versions that rendered this word "thigh." The word חָלָב (*ḥālāb*, "milk") is taken as *ḥeleb* ("fat")—hence the RSV's "his body is full of fat." In Rabbinic *ʿatîn* probably means "a pail" or "bucket." But "his pails are full of milk" (BDB, p. 742) is contextually a problem.

25 Scholarly opinion (Driver-Gray, Dhorme) now sees the preposition בְּ (*b*) on בְּטוֹבָה (*battôbāh*, "anything good") as partitive, hence "anything." This fits the overlapping of the prepositions *b* and *min* as we have noted earlier (e.g., "from").

30 The problem with לְיוֹם אֵיד (*leyômʾêd*, "from the day of calamity") stems from the meaning given to the preposition לְ (*l*) and the verb יוּבָלוּ (*yûbālû*, "he is delivered") in v. 30b. Because of the demands of the context, NIV has chosen rare meanings for each. The margin—"man is reserved for the day of calamity,/ that he is brought forth to"—is the more normal usage. Some feel the normal meaning fits Job's thesis in the sense that the wicked escape disaster during their lifetime even though they may have to face it after death. Gordis (*Job*, in loc.) solves the problem by considering the line a quotation of the friends' opinion. But if Pope (in loc.) and others are correct in giving the meaning "from" to the *l*, the problem dissolves.

D. *The Third Cycle of Speeches (22:1–26:14)*

1. *Eliphaz*

22:1–30

¹Then Eliphaz the Temanite replied:

²"Can a man be of benefit to God?
   Can even a wise man benefit him?
³What pleasure would it give the Almighty if you were righteous?
   What would he gain if your ways were blameless?

⁴"Is it for your piety that he rebukes you
   and brings charges against you?
⁵Is not your wickedness great?
   Are not your sins endless?
⁶You demanded security from your brothers for no reason;
   you stripped men of their clothing, leaving them naked.
⁷You gave no water to the weary
   and you withheld food from the hungry,
⁸though you were a powerful man, owning land—
   an honored man, living on it.
⁹And you sent widows away empty-handed
   and broke the strength of the fatherless.
¹⁰That is why snares are all around you,
   why sudden peril terrifies you,
¹¹why it is so dark you cannot see,
   and why a flood of water covers you.

¹²"Is not God in the heights of heaven?
   And see how lofty are the highest stars!
¹³Yet you say, 'What does God know?
   Does he judge through such darkness?
¹⁴Thick clouds veil him, so he does not see us
   as he goes about in the vaulted heavens.'
¹⁵Will you keep to the old path
   that evil men have trod?
¹⁶They were carried off before their time,
   their foundations washed away by a flood.
¹⁷They said to God, 'Leave us alone!
   What can the Almighty do to us?'
¹⁸Yet it was he who filled their houses with good things,
   so I stand aloof from the counsel of the wicked.

¹⁹"The righteous see their ruin and rejoice;
   the innocent mock them, saying,
²⁰'Surely our foes are destroyed,
   and fire devours their wealth.'

²¹"Submit to God and be at peace with him;
   in this way prosperity will come to you.
²²Accept instruction from his mouth
   and lay up his words in your heart.

> 23 If you return to the Almighty, you will be restored:
>   If you remove wickedness far from your tent
> 24 and assign your nuggets to the dust,
>   your gold of Ophir to the rocks in the ravines,
> 25 then the Almighty will be your gold,
>   the choicest silver for you.
> 26 Surely then you will find delight in the Almighty
>   and will lift up your face to God.
> 27 You will pray to him, and he will hear you,
>   and you will fulfill your vows.
> 28 What you decide on will be done,
>   and light will shine on your ways.
> 29 When men are brought low and you say, 'Lift them up!'
>   then he will save the downcast.
> 30 He will deliver even one who is not innocent,
>   who will be delivered through the cleanness of your hands."

Eliphaz, the least vindictive, was provoked to agree with his friends that Job had been a very wicked man (vv.4–5). He did not even attempt to answer Job's shocking statements in chapter 21 but moved on to accuse Job of various social sins (vv.6–11) and of failing to appreciate the wonderful attributes of God, especially God's omniscience (vv.13–14) and his justice, goodness, and mercy (vv.16–18). All Eliphaz felt he could do for Job was to make a final plea for repentance (vv.21–30).

1–3 What was Eliphaz's argument here (cf. Elihu in 35:7)? Was it that God could have no ulterior motive in dealing with Job, since there was nothing Job could do to benefit God (Pope)? That may be part of it. But Eliphaz was here reacting to Job's notion that God allowed human wickedness to go unpunished (ch. 21), and in his reactionary mood he went to the opposite extreme of suggesting there was nothing man could do to benefit God. It is the now familiar unbalanced stress on divine transcendence: the concept that man is nothing in God's eyes, even his virtue is useless. God does not need man; it is man who needs God. Since everything has its origin in God, man's giving it back—even in service—does not enhance God in any way.

Verse 3 carries the thought a step further. A translation that fits well into the context might be: "Would it please the Almighty if you were vindicated?/ Would he gain anything if you did live a blameless life?" Two observations are in order. First, Eliphaz did not know of God's contest with the Accuser over Job's former blameless life. The Almighty had especially chosen Job to be an instrument through whom he would gain glory and the Accuser be humiliated. Second, Eliphaz seemed so convinced of Job's wickedness—even to the point of exaggeration (v.5)—that he did not believe he could be vindicated. So in his mind Job's blamelessness was hypothetical nonsense. For Job to be vindicated would be a lie; so how could God take pleasure in that?

4–11 Verse 4 is pure irony. In 4:6 Eliphaz had been sincere about Job's piety, but here he spoke of it tongue-in-cheek. He no longer believed Job was basically a God-fearing man. Job's troubles were God's rebuke. That they were great testified to the extent of his sin. So Eliphaz felt free, perhaps obligated, to expound on the possible nature of those sins (vv.5–9). Job's sins are described in terms of social oppression and neglect. In other words, Eliphaz felt Job had deceived himself by trusting in his ritual piety (what he had done for God) while his real sin was what he failed to do for his fellow man. For this God sent snares and peril, darkness and floods (vv. 10–11). These were not literal but commonly used figures of trouble and distress in the OT (cf. Pss 42:7; 91:3–6; Isa 8:7, 22; 43:2).

12–20 As noted, Eliphaz's tone had been more positive and sympathetic than the others, but here he threw the weight of his argument with Bildad and Zophar, though not completely. Having become convinced Job was a man who followed the path of the ungodly (v. 15), Eliphaz used Job's own words to refute him. Had not Job complained that the blessing of the wicked was God's doing (21:13–16)? Eliphaz turned that around by saying that the wicked are destroyed before their time (v. 16), that is, before they can fully enjoy the good things God provides (vv. 18–20).

21–30 Eliphaz was, no doubt, sincere in this his last attempt to reach Job through a call to repentance. Some feel the author of the book through a subtle "double entendre" has used Eliphaz to show the incapacity of the standard wisdom ideas to handle the realities of human experience (Fullerton [pp. 320–41] developed this notion for Job 4 and 5). At any rate this call for Job to submit; to be at peace with God (v. 21); to hear God's word and hide it in his heart (v. 22); to return to the Almighty and forsake wickedness (v. 23); to find delight in God rather than in gold (vv. 24–26); and to pray, obey (v. 27), and become concerned about sinners (vv. 29–30) could not be improved on by prophet or evangelist.

There are some problems, however, that beset these powerful words. They assume Job was an ungodly man and that his major desire was a return to health and prosperity (v. 21). The fact is that Job was not ungodly and that he had already made clear his desire to see God and be his friend (19:25–27). But Job's words have not always sounded friendly toward God, and Eliphaz did not have the capacity to understand the nature of Job's wrestling with God where Job expressed to God his deepest feelings of fear and bafflement over what appeared to be an unjust and cruel providence. To Eliphaz's black-and-white mentality, those words (backed by Job's troubles) were sad proof of Job's need to repent and "get right" with God. His assumption that Job did not know how to pray aright would be controverted by God himself, and Eliphaz would have to depend on Job's prayers (42:8).

Notes

8 Again see Gordis's view on "The Use of Quotations in Job" (*God and Man*, pp. 169–89). Some think this verse is out of place since Job was being addressed directly. Gordis adds the words "For you believe." The Qumran Targum also felt this need and added "and you say." But Pope (p. 165) thinks it is "an oblique reference to Job as a land-grabber." This is essentially the way the NIV interprets it.

11 For אוֹר־חֹשֶׁךְ (ʾô-ḥōšek, "so dark"), the LXX reads "light" (ʾôr), which would make the Hebrew read "light becomes darkness so you cannot see." But also possible is the reading "the land becomes dark" (cf. Isa 24:15; 26:19; and possibly Job 33:30 for ʾur meaning "land").

12 In גֹבַהּ שָׁמָיִם (gōbah šāmāyim, "in the heights of heaven"), the Hebrew has no preposition "in" (cf. NEB, "at the zenith of the heavens"). Dahood (Psalms, 16:62) reads gabōah (adjective) instead of the MT noun and רְאֵה (rō'eh, "see") (participle) instead of the MT imperative re'ēh (LXX has third sing. indicative). The MT asks Job to see how high stars are. Dahood (ibid.) reads "Is not God the Lofty One of Heaven, and the One who sees the top of the stars though they are high?" Andersen's view (Job, in loc.) that v.12a is comparative—"Is not God higher than the heavens"—also seems to fit the context well. The point is that God is so lofty that he looks down on the top of the stars. Eliphaz used this thought to accuse Job of believing God is so far away and so separated by thick clouds that he cannot see what evil people are doing. Job has complained that God seems indifferent to wickedness, but he has also complained of the opposite problem—God's overbearing surveillance.

15 As noted by Pope (p. 166), the meaning of הָאֹרַח עוֹלָם (ha'ōrah 'ôlām, "the old path") may be "the dark path," based on a homonymous root common in Ugaritic (glm) but also attested in 42:3: מַעְלִים עֵצָה (ma'elîm 'ēṣāh, "makes dark [obscures] my counsel").

17 The LXX, Syriac, and Qumran Targum appear to go against the MT's לָמוֹ (lāmô, "to them") claims lmw can mean "for (to) us." The LXX et al. have "to us." Dahood ("Hebrew-Ugaritic Lexicography III," 46:324; 47:409). The NIV follows the ancient versions without a footnote.

18 For רָחֲקָה מֶנִּי (rāhaqāh mennî, "I stand aloof"), the LXX reads "the counsel of the wicked is far from him." The NEB and JB go in this direction. The NIV, Pope, Gordis et al. do not and so make this line a parenthesis. Andersen (Job, in loc.) thinks v.18 is a quote of Job's words (who claimed God blesses the wicked) in order to refute them (see above). That the MT uses the yod instead of the waw here and in 21:16 brings up again the question of a third singular pronoun suffix written with the yod (see Notes on 9:35; 14:3; 19:28; 21:16; 31:18).

20 Instead of קִימָנוּ (qîmānû, "our foes"), the ancient versions, following an otherwise unattested root (Arab. qiyām), render this "their substance" (cf. NEB, "riches"); but the root (qûm) often means "to rise up against," even without an accompanying preposition (cf. Exod 15:7: "those who opposed you").

23 Just how the LXX arrived at "and humble yourself" (perhaps from תֵּעָנֶה, tē'āneh) instead of "you will be restored" (from תִּבָּנֶה, tibbāneh) is a mystery; but the NEB, JB, and RSV all adopt the LXX's reading. The Niphal of bnh means literally "be rebuilt," but that it can mean "be made prosperous" is clear from Jer 12:16 and Mal 3:15.

25 תּוֹעָפֹת (tô'āpōt) is used four times in the OT, but its meaning is still dubious. For the NIV's "choicest," see KB, p. 1022. BDB (p. 419) gives "eminence" based on "the horns" in Num 23:22 and 24:8 and "the mountains" in Ps 95:4 (opposite "the depths of the earth"). Pope guesses "piled up" (silver) is the meaning.

29 This verse is notoriously difficult, and there are many solutions; but it seems the simplest is to take the וּ (û, sign of the plural) on הִשְׁפִּילוּ (hišpîlû) as dittography (with the following word) and translate "He (God) will bring (you) low if you speak in pride, but the humble he will save."

30 אִי־נָקִי ('î-nāqî, "one who is not innocent") is an excellent example of how modern linguistic studies have really clarified the meaning. The reader need only compare the KJV's "the island of the innocent." The use of 'î as a negative in both Hebrew and Phoenician can no longer be doubted. Both Pope (p. 169) and Gordis ("Corporate Personality in Job: A Note on Job 22:29–30," JNES 4 [1945]: 54–55) stress the fact that v.30b requires a negative meaning since the innocent have no need of the clean hands of the righteous man.

2. Job's reply

23:1–24:25

¹Then Job replied:

²"Even today my complaint is bitter;
   his hand is heavy in spite of my groaning.
³If only I knew where to find him;
   if only I could go to his dwelling!
⁴I would state my case before him
   and fill my mouth with arguments.
⁵I would find out what he would answer me,
   and consider what he would say.
⁶Would he oppose me with great power?
   No, he would not press charges against me.
⁷There an upright man could present his case before him,
   and I would be delivered forever from my judge.

⁸"But if I go to the east, he is not there;
   if I go to the west, I do not find him.
⁹When he is at work in the north, I do not see him;
   when he turns to the south, I catch no glimpse of him.
¹⁰But he knows the way that I take;
   when he has tested me, I will come forth as gold.
¹¹My feet have closely followed his steps;
   I have kept to his way without turning aside.
¹²I have not departed from the commands of his lips;
   I have treasured the words of his mouth more than my daily
   bread.

¹³"But he stands alone, and who can oppose him?
   He does whatever he pleases.
¹⁴He carries out his decree against me,
   and many such plans he still has in store.
¹⁵That is why I am terrified before him;
   when I think of all this, I fear him.
¹⁶God has made my heart faint;
   the Almighty has terrified me.
¹⁷Yet I am not silenced by the darkness,
   by the thick darkness that covers my face.

^{24:1}Why does the Almighty not set times for judgment?
   Why must those who know him look in vain for such days?
²Men move boundary stones;
   they pasture flocks they have stolen.
³They drive away the orphan's donkey
   and take the widow's ox in pledge.
⁴They thrust the needy from the path
   and force all the poor of the land into hiding.
⁵Like wild donkeys in the desert,
   the poor go about their labor of foraging food;
   the wasteland provides food for their children.
⁶They gather fodder in the fields
   and glean in the vineyards of the wicked.
⁷Lacking clothes, they spend the night naked;
   they have nothing to cover themselves in the cold.
⁸They are drenched by mountain rains
   and hug the rocks for lack of shelter.
⁹The fatherless child is snatched from the breast;
   the infant of the poor is seized for a debt.
¹⁰Lacking clothes, they go about naked;
   they carry the sheaves, but still go hungry.

¹¹ They crush olives among the terraces;
    they tread the winepresses, yet suffer thirst.
¹² The groans of the dying rise from the city,
    and the souls of the wounded cry out for help.
    But God charges no one with wrongdoing.

¹³ "There are those who rebel against the light,
    who do not know its ways
    or stay in its paths.
¹⁴ When daylight is gone, the murderer rises up
    and kills the poor and needy;
    in the night he steals forth like a thief.
¹⁵ The eye of the adulterer watches for dusk;
    he thinks, 'No eye will see me,'
    and he keeps his face concealed.
¹⁶ In the dark, men break into houses,
    but by day they shut themselves in;
    they want nothing to do with the light.
¹⁷ For all of them, deep darkness is their morning;
    they make friends with the terrors of darkness.

¹⁸ "Yet they are foam on the surface of the water;
    their portion of the land is cursed,
    so that no one goes to the vineyards.
¹⁹ As heat and drought snatch away the melted snow,
    so the grave snatches away those who have sinned.
²⁰ The womb forgets them,
    the worm feasts on them;
    evil men are no longer remembered
    but are broken like a tree.
²¹ They prey on the barren and childless woman,
    and to the widow show no kindness.
²² But God drags away the mighty by his power;
    though they become established, they have no assurance of
    life.
²³ He may let them rest in a feeling of security,
    but his eyes are on their ways.
²⁴ For a little while they are exalted, and then they are gone;
    they are brought low and gathered up like all others;
    they are cut off like heads of grain.

²⁵ "If this is not so, who can prove me false
    and reduce my words to nothing?"

While the meaning of chapter 23 is quite clear, scholars have seen serious problems in chapter 24. In addition to the difficulties in making sense of the text, there is the issue of determining whose words these are. There is no general agreement about what should be done. Some leave the verses as they are and consider the whole a disconnected series of short pieces that cannot be put together with any certainty (Snaith). Others try to create a complete third cycle by rearrangement. For example Pope puts vv.9, 21 between v.3 and v.4 and v.14c after v.15. He shifts vv.18–20 and vv.22–25 to follow 27:8–23 and labels them as Zophar's words, since Zophar does not reply for a third time. The NAB attributes vv.18–25 to Bildad, while Habel (*Job*, 1985, pp. 37–38) considers all of chapter 24 and 27:13–23 as the words of Zophar.

All the above is done on the basis of what appears to be the thoughts of the counselors, not of Job. Some even claim that there was early scribal doctoring of the text to make Job sound more orthodox. One must not overlook the practice of unannounced quotations. The RSV added *"You say"* before v.18 and looked on this as a quotation by Job of what the counselors have said (cf. Gordis, *God and Man*, pp. 169–80). Such an ancient rhetorical device is disturbing to us because we are not used to it, but it may be the correct approach to these verses. Since there is absolutely no agreement about handling chapter 24, it seems wiser to let the text stand and above all refuse to force modern categories of logic and rhetoric on it.

Job's statements about God in these chapters must be constantly evaluated in the light of the wider canonical context. Job has wrestled with the concept that God is free to do anything he pleases (23:13). For example, in 9:12 Job complained, "Who can say to him, 'What are you doing?' " What God does appeared unjust and led Job to fantasize about God as if God were his enemy (16:7–14). But these words are not normative, and a correct hermeneutic begins with the principle of the analogy of Scripture (comparing Scripture with Scripture) and continues with the principle of contextualization. We must allow Job the right to use the language of feeling rejected (23:14–17) just as the psalmist freely does (Ps 88:3–18).

In the final verses of chapter 23, Job made his apology for his emotional language, which had been so misunderstood by his friends. He had been terrified by what he came to accept as God's plan for his life (vv.14–16). The mystery, however, was still there. Job did not understand what God was doing. So in all honesty he still needed to speak out and call for the thick darkness to be removed (v.17).

1–2 Job was becoming less fractious. His play on words in v.2 leaves somewhat open the question of whether he was still rebellious or just bitter (see Notes).

3–7 Job's spiritual movement during this dispute is evident again when we compare his attitude about a hearing with God in chapter 9 with his thoughts on the same subject here. Job still wanted a fair trial, for he was certain he was blameless, that is, above the charges that had been made (vv.3–4). He doubted in 9:14–20 that God would even give him a hearing and that even while pleading for mercy he would be crushed. At this point he admitted he was not totally innocent (9:15–20), though he still considered himself blameless (*tām*) (9:21). After Zophar's abuse in chapter 11, where he was flatly labeled a wretched sinner (11:5, 14), Job reacted with a bolder assertion of his blamelessness (13:13–15). In chapter 22 we noticed how Eliphaz, the least accusatory of the three, had moved closer to the others with his quip, "Are not your sins endless?" (22:5). So here Job reasserted his claim to be an upright man with renewed confidence that God agreed with him. This is why having an audience with God was very important to Job (v.5). He continued to be positive (13:18) about the outcome of such an encounter (23:6–7).

Our knowledge of the doctrine of justification by faith with its premise of the depravity of man (Rom 1–3) makes it difficult for us to understand this part of the message of the Book of Job. It is helpful to look on Job as illustrative of Christ who also suffered unjustly to fulfill the purpose of God (cf. Joseph, Gen 37–50). We have seen how Job's upright life was so rooted in the fear of God that even God himself used Job as an example of godliness (1:8; 2:3). So Job was not wrong in calling for his own vindication. The psalmist did the same (Pss 17:2–3; 26:1–3 et al.).

8–12 Job was still frustrated, however, over the matter of finding God (cf. v.3). Job could not find him. God was absent. Later in 42:5 Job would say, "But now my eyes have seen you." At this point, though he wrestled with God verbally (as he had done in chs. 7, 10, 13, 14, 17), he had no immediate sense of God's presence nor of God's voice communicating with him. Yet in reply to Eliphaz (22:21), Job claimed to have heard God's words and treasured them in his heart (v.12). He rejected Eliphaz's call for him to return to God (22:23), for he felt he had never turned away from God. Job did not think God was testing him (v.10b) as a means to purge away his sinful dross. It was rather to prove he was pure gold. Job's words in vv.11–12 have to be the words either of a terrible hypocrite or of a deeply committed believer. They remind us of Psalm 119:11, 101, and 168.

The Hebrew of v.10 reads literally, "But/For he knows the/a way with men." The line is difficult to interpret. Does "the way" mean the way Job took (NIV) or God's way with Job? If it means the latter, Job was being submissive to God's will—an answer to the stricture "Submit to God" in 22:21. Eliphaz had in mind Job's earlier demand to know why God was afflicting him (7:20–21; 10:2). With this interpretation Job was accepting his testing but with assurance that he would come forth as gold (a veiled rebuke of Eliphaz's accusation in 22:24). The NIV has taken the verse in the other sense, that God knew Job was following God's way. This he expressed more fully in vv.11–12. In either case Job answered Eliphaz's strictures.

13–17 Verse 13 is a monotheistic affirmation. Job said, "He (God) is the unique (one)." The Hebrew expression is rare in the OT but idiomatic. A preposition is used between two words to express equivalence (see Notes). Job's God was the same as Israel's God—he was the only one; there was no other (Deut 6:4). As the all-powerful sovereign Deity, God did what he pleased (v.13b). Job's fear (vv.15–16) was the necessary corollary to the truth that God was sovereign and therefore could not be put in a box and told what he could and could not do by human beings. What might this God who does what he pleases have had in mind for Job (v.14)? A real part of the living faith Job expressed in vv.8–12 was his determination not to be silenced despite the darkness he felt over the intention of God, who had no one to answer to for his behavior. This has led to M. Tsevat's observation about God's being viewed as amoral ("The Meaning of the Book of Job," HUCA 37 [1966]: 73–106). There is a sense in which God is above human conceptions of what is moral or right; but we must be careful in a formulation like Tsevat's lest we sound like God is pictured as immoral, which Tsevat does not mean. See our comments below on this subject under the theophany.

24:1 Job began by expressing in one bicolon (v.1) the mood that dominates here—a complaint on why God did not set straight the balance of justice. Why did not his promised retribution come at set times against all ruthless oppressors? The chapter alternates in a rather discursive way between a description of the criminals and their victims. This theme is an exceedingly important part of the major message of the book. Job felt God should demonstrate his justice by openly punishing the wicked. In the divine speeches God would teach him a tremendous lesson about this, which he did not now understand. That lesson centers around the idea that the principle of retribution does not operate mechanically in this world but according to the divine will. Although God is free to do as he pleases, Job knew he did not deserve his suffering. But how then does the age-old principle of retribution fit in?

In this chapter Job presented a picture of a world that was still a deep enigma to him. His courageous honesty led him to expound on the mystery of how the wicked get by unpunished while they perform their evil deeds against the innocent. The touching pathos of these word-pictures should be felt by the reader, for they give us some insight into Job's contempt for wickedness and his ability to empathize with those in distress (cf. 31:13–22).

2–12 The wicked were so brazen they pastured stolen flocks on stolen land, or possibly as the LXX has it, they dared to seize the shepherd along with his flock (v.2). Since the orphan (v.3) is without inheritance, his donkey would represent all he owned. Job appreciated those ancient civil laws that protected widows and the fatherless (cf. Exod 22:22). In contrast to this passage, the psalmist stresses how God himself is "the father of the fatherless and the defender of widows" (Ps 68:5) and the dispenser of justice to the wicked (Ps 68:1–2).

This is a moving description of the ruthless exploitation of the poorest of the poor. Note the pitiful case of the destitute who must carry food while they go hungry (v.10) and tread the winepress while they suffer thirst (v.11). The climax is v.12c, which returns to the theme of v.1. The great enigma is that all this was going on and God did nothing (cf. Ps 73:2–3; Hab 1:13; Mal 3:15). Also see the Notes on an alternate reading: "God does not pay attention."

13–17 The tone-setting bicolon (v.1) is followed by a stanza stressing the deeds of the wicked (vv.2–4). Then vv.5–12 stress the suffering and misery of the poor, and vv.13–17 return to the deeds of the wicked. The murderer (v.14), the adulterer (v.15), and the thief (v.16) share a characteristic that is self-condemning: they all love darkness rather than the light (cf. 38:12–15; Ps 82:5; John 3:20; Eph 5:8; 1 Thess 5:5).

18–24 As stated many have insisted that these are not Job's words because they do not sound like his sentiments about the wicked. But there is nothing wrong with viewing them all as Job's words since he never claimed the wicked always prosper or never come to a bad end. His problem was that God treats the good and bad alike. But here again (cf. Gordis, *Job*) this may be an unannounced quotation of the conventional view of the friends. Gordis (ibid., in loc.) supports this by showing how Job cited their words in order to refute them in 21:19, where the quote is definitely unannounced, and in 21:28, where Job announced the quotation with the words "You say." Chapter 21:13–25 as such a quotation is less clear. The problem here in vv.18–24 is that the refutation is missing. Gordis (*Job*, in loc.) thinks that is because this third cycle of speeches has become disarranged. We think Job had a good reason for mouthing his friends' view here (see below).

25 It is curious that in v.25 Job spoke as if he had just made an argument against the views of his friends rather than partially agreeing with them. The verse is a clue to the rhetoric of the chapter. It is not a disconnected assemblage of pieces put together by scribes who wanted to make Job sound more orthodox. An argument based on this verse can be made for literary unity in this chapter. We must go back to the nodal statement in v.1 and examine it carefully. The verb ṣāp, there translated "set," means literally "store up." Job's query was "Why is there not a storing up of judgment by the Almighty so his friends could eventually see the day (v.2) of his wrath on the wicked." Job was anticipating "the day of the LORD," a theme stressed by some of the prophets (cf. Joel).

The query of v.1 fits in with Job's view that the wicked prosper. After developing a series of vignettes, with as much pathos as possible, about the deeds of the wicked and the sufferings of their victims (vv.1–17), Job finally mouthed the view of his friends about God's judgment on the wicked. Job may have been either quoting them with irony or complaining that this judgment comes piecemeal, a little here and a little there (see esp. vv.23–24).

Eventually the wicked die and are forgotten; they lack security and have their day only for a little while (22:16–18)—but where are the great days of stored-up judgment so the righteous can be sure that justice for such horrors is meted out? Job was not convinced that piecemeal judgment was truly just since the righteous often suffered the same. So v.25 is not a disconnected verse. Literally it forms an *inclusio* with the original query in v.1. Here the Book of Job again anticipates a step forward in theological understanding (cf. 14:14–15; 19:25–27). There is no direct teaching of final judgment to set right the balance of justice, but there is a concept here that anticipates the teaching that God must have his day.

Notes

23:2 In מְרִי שִׂחִי (meّrî śiḥî, "my complaint is bitter"), the consonants *mry* point, not to *mrr* ("bitter"), but to *mrh* ("to be contentious"); and the primary meaning of *śiḥî* is "to speak." So read "my speech is contentious (for) his hand, etc." But there may be a wordplay between his being defiant and resentful (cf. Andersen, *Job*, p. 108).

On יָדִי כָּבְדָה עַל (yāḏî kāḇeḏāh ʿal, "his hand is heavy in spite of"), the NIV agrees with the LXX and Syriac. The MT reads "my hand" or possibly "the hand on me" (dative suffix, see NIV mg.). If we follow the LXX, either the likeness between the two letters yod (my) and waw (his) in late script or the rare third singular yod are a viable explanation (cf. Blommerde, pp. 92–93, but see Notes on 9:35). For a similar use of *ʿal* meaning "notwithstanding, in spite of" in Job, see 10:7 and 24:6.

3 תְּכוּנָתוֹ (teّḵûnāṯô, "his dwelling") means a place prepared or arranged. A good translation would be "his tribunal, courtroom."

6 Commenting on הַבְּרָב־כֹּחַ (habbeّrāḇ-kōaḥ, "would he . . . with great power"), Tur-Sinai (*Job*, in loc.) cogently shows that *rāḇ-kōaḥ* means "an attorney." The meaning is "Will he argue against me through an attorney?"

On יָשִׂם בִּי (yāśim bî, "press charges against me"), the NIV is paraphrastic because of failure to appreciate the Hebrew idiom *śîm lēḇ* ("put to mind," "pay attention to"), with *lēḇ* suppressed as in 4:20; 24:12; 34:23; and Isa 41:20. Job answered his own question: God would not use an attorney but "surely he, himself [אַךְ־הוּא, *ʾaḵ-hûʾ*] will give me full attention."

7 Instead of מִשֹּׁפְטִי (miśśōp̄eّṭî, "from my judge"), some Hebrew MSS and the versions read *miśpāṭî* ("my case"). Combining this with the verb פָּלַט (pālaṭ, "to deliver"), Job was certain he would be vindicated. He said, "I will permanently bring my case to a successful conclusion" (delivery or birth, cf. *plṭ* in 21:10b).

9 The stress of בַּעֲשֹׂתוֹ (baّʿaśōṯô, "when he is at work") is not on God's working but on his being there, passing the time as in Eccl 6:12. Some say the root is *ʿśh*, which has a cognate that means "to turn" in Arabic and Ugaritic (cf. 1 Sam 14:32, Kethiv).

13 On וְהוּא בְאֶחָד (wᵉhûʾ bᵉʾeḥād, "But he stands alone"), Budde's emendation from bʾḥd to bḥr (dropping aleph and changing daleth to resh) is thought justified by the fact that bḥr ("choose") and ʾwh ("desire") (v.13b) appear in Ps 132:13 as parallel synonyms. Here the first line says, "When God chooses, who can oppose him." We prefer to let the text stand and view the preposition as beth essentiae (GKC, par. 119 i; cf. Job 37:10 and Ps 68:5), meaning "he is unique." Dahood (Psalms, 16:325; id., "NSPJ," p. 67) calls it beth emphaticum.

17 In כִּי־לֹא נִצְמַתִּי (kî-lōʾ niṣmattî, "Yet I am not silenced"), the verb in Hebrew consistently means "to be exterminated, put to an end" (cf. KJV). But in the Arabic and Syriac, it means "becoming speechless"; and the NIV has followed the NEB in choosing this meaning. The verse is very difficult.

24:1 יָמִיו (yāmāyw, "such days") is literally "his days," i.e., the Almighty's. This strengthens our view that Job anticipated the "day of the LORD" concept.

6 On בְּלִילֹו (bᵉlîlô, "fodder"), the MT says, "his fodder they cut (harvest)." The words mean "mixed fodder," not as it grows in the field. The LXX has a doublet witnessing to a dual reading of the MT consonants. Dhorme (in loc.) and Fohrer (in loc.) chose the first half of the LXX "(they reap) at night" (בְּלֵילֹו, (bᵉlêlô), while the Vulgate, Syriac, and Targum read the other half "(in a field) not his" (בְּלִי לֹו, bᵉlî lô). Pope and others emend to בְּלִיַּעַל (bᵉlîya ʿal, "[they reap in the field of] the villain"), which fits the parallelism but may be too drastic.

9 Instead of MT's עַל (ʿal, lit., "upon"), the LXX provides a better reading—ʾul ("in front of").

11 שׁוּרֹתָם (šûrōtām) may mean "walls" or "terraces" (cf. Gen 49:22; 2 Sam 22:30; Ps 18:29; Jer 5:10). It is probably a figure of speech (synecdoche) for "oil presses" (cf. NIV mg.).

12 וְנֶפֶשׁ (wᵉnepeš, "and the souls of") almost certainly means "and the throats of" (the wounded)—a generally accepted primitive meaning for nepeš.

For תִּפְלָה (tiplāh, "with wrongdoing"), the Syriac and two Hebrew MSS read tᵉpillāh ("the prayer"). This appears to be an attempt to make Job's theology more acceptable.

יָשִׂים (yāśîm, "charges") is another example of the ellipsis of lēb ("heart") in the idiom śîm lēb ("pay attention"; cf. 4:20; 23:6; 34:33). "God does not pay attention to wrongdoing."

14 The translation of לָאֹור (lāʾôr) as "when daylight is gone" depends on the l being negative or separative ("from the light") as in Ugaritic.

The NIV makes יְהִי (yᵉhî, "he steals forth") more colorful than it is. It literally says, "He becomes" (like a thief). But this jussive form of the verb "to be" appears several times in Job as an indicative (cf. Notes on 18:12 and 20:23).

17 The words כִּי יַחְדָּו (kî yaḥdāw, "For all") seem strangely out of place. The Hebrew reads "For together morning to them (is) deep darkness." Some (e.g., Rowley, NEB) suggest the first two words go with the preceding line. Pope omits them as a marginal comment. Following the plural in v.16, this may be a case where revocalization is in order. In 3:6 (see Notes) we saw the root חדה (ḥdh II) used and meaning "be seen," "perceive," "view" (cf. KB). It may be vocalized יֶחְדּוּ (yeḥᵉdû) meaning "the morning is seen by them as deep darkness" or "they view deep darkness as morning to them."

18 The third masculine singular pronoun is very awkward here—הוּא (hûʾ, "they are"). In 37:6 the verb הֱוֵא (hᵉwēʾ) means "fall." We may vocalize this as a participle from the same root and render it "Like scum falling on the surface of the water, may their portion . . . be cursed."

24 Combining the force of the parallelism in the following line—"they are cut off like heads of grain"—with the witness of the ancient versions leads to the conclusion that the meaning of כַּכֹּל (kakkōl) is not "like all others." The LXX transliterates μολόχη (molochē), which in Hebrew is מַלּוּחַ (mallûaḥ, "saltwort" or "mallow"). Compare the NEB—"they wilt like a mallow flower." The Qumran Targum reads in Aramaic kyblʾ ("like crab grass").

3. *Bildad*

25:1-6

¹Then Bildad the Shuhite replied:

²"Dominion and awe belong to God;
  he establishes order in the heights of heaven.
³Can his forces be numbered?
  Upon whom does his light not rise?
⁴How then can a man be righteous before God?
  How can one born of woman be pure?
⁵If even the moon is not bright
  and the stars are not pure in his eyes,
⁶how much less man, who is but a maggot—
  a son of man, who is only a worm!"

This is the last we hear from Job's three counselors. Some have thought they had exhausted their arguments (e.g., Ewald, p. 246). Others (e.g., K. Fullerton, "The Original Conclusion of the Book of Job," ZAW, N.F., 1 [1924]: 121) have considered this an unlikely solution. Most modern critical scholars have lengthened this short speech by including 26:5-14, but there is no obvious reason why this should be done. The theme is similar but not the same. Indeed Job in 9:4-13 looked in awe at nature (cf. 26:5-14), while Bildad looked at God's transcendence to show his purity and dominion over the moral order so he (Bildad) could prove the impurity of man. MacKenzie ("Yahweh Speeches," pp. 435-45) has noted that in celebrating God's power, Job stressed arbitrary power, the friends stressed justice, and God in his speeches stressed mystery and love.

1-3 Bildad in these few lines did not bother to answer Job's recent argument, nor did he present a new one. He only repeated what had already been said by Eliphaz (4:17-21; 15:14-16). In 9:4-13 Job demonstrated his penchant for answering Bildad's moral argument with a lengthy description of God's arbitrary power in the universe. As noted above, each had his own reason for dwelling on the power of God. Here Bildad wanted to show how God's power established order in the heavenly realm and that his dominion extends to all created beings.

4-6 God's majesty palls everything (moon and stars, v.4), and it reaches everywhere (v.3b). So how can any man be considered righteous or pure in God's eyes? We can recognize the truth here; but as we have seen earlier, it is the next statement that reveals what Bildad really had in mind. His point was that man is a maggot (v.6). Unlike the apostle Paul who developed the doctrine of total depravity in Romans 1 -3 to prepare the way for grace, we know from the rest of Bildad's remarks that he left no room for mercy or forgiveness.

Eliphaz was the first to question the possibility of anyone's purity before God (4:17). In chapter 8 Bildad's words left the door open only for those who were truly blameless (8:20). Job, repeating the issue in 9:2, wanted to know how he could prove his blamelessness since God was so inaccessible. In 15:14-16 Eliphaz came very close to a nihilistic view of man—he is hopelessly "vile and corrupt, who drinks up evil like water!" But in chapter 22 Eliphaz left the door open for Job to be restored, but not on the basis of mercy, for he must bear the penalty for whatever he has done. Then if there is repentance, Job could be restored (22:21-23). But

Bildad repeated the old question of 9:2 with an implied negative answer. If God is inaccessible, it is because he is too pure; and man, like Job, is a hopeless worm.

Notes

3 Instead of אוֹרֵהוּ (*ʾôrēhû*, "his light"), the LXX reads as if it saw אוֹרְבוֹ (*ʾōrēḇô*, "his ambush"). This parallels "his forces" and would read "against whom does not his ambush rise up?" NEB chose this reading, but most reject it.
5 It is unlikely that there is any such root as אהל (*ʾhl*) meaning "be bright." The MT's וְלֹא יַאֲהִיל (*wᵉlōʾ yaʾᵃhîl*, "is not bright") could be an example of aleph as an internal *matres lectionis*, reading יָהֵל (*yāhēl*) from the root הָלַל (*hālal*, "shine"; Job 31:26, cf. also 41:18).

4. Job's reply

26:1–14

¹Then Job replied:

²"How you have helped the powerless!
How you have saved the arm that is feeble!
³What advice you have offered to one without wisdom!
And what great insight you have displayed!
⁴Who has helped you utter these words?
And whose spirit spoke from your mouth?

⁵"The dead are in deep anguish,
those beneath the waters and all that live in them.
⁶Death is naked before God;
Destruction lies uncovered.
⁷He spreads out the northern skies over empty space;
he suspends the earth over nothing.
⁸He wraps up the waters in his clouds,
yet the clouds do not burst under their weight.
⁹He covers the face of the full moon,
spreading his clouds over it.
¹⁰He marks out the horizon on the face of the waters
for a boundary between light and darkness.
¹¹The pillars of the heavens quake,
aghast at his rebuke.
¹²By his power he churned up the sea;
by his wisdom he cut Rahab to pieces.
¹³By his breath the skies became fair;
his hand pierced the gliding serpent.
¹⁴And these are but the outer fringe of his works;
how faint the whisper we hear of him!
Who then can understand the thunder of his power?"

The chapter clearly breaks into two parts: Job's reaction to Bildad (vv. 1–4) and a poem celebrating God's omnipotence (vv. 5–14). The poem is frequently regarded as reflecting a line of argument inconsistent with Job's general position (but compare with 9:5–10 for many of the same arguments); and it is felt that, as such, it more properly should be assigned to one of the other speakers. Before giving the reason for leaving this poem where it is, a word might be said about the generally agreed on disruption of the text in chapters 24–27.

Kissane (p. xli), who does not hesitate to move passages, complains that "the text has suffered much more at the hands of some modern critics than it had suffered throughout the ages of its history." One cannot help but wonder about such whole-sale rearrangements as that of Tur-Sinai (*Job*, in loc.) or M.P. Reddy's reconstruction ("Reconstruction," ZAW 90 [1978]: 49–94). Reasons put forth to "explain" such a corruption of the text are speculative and range from scribal errors, such as "accidental displacement" of lines or "straying" of a passage because it became attached to the wrong column of the text (Kissane, p. xliif., and J. Strahan, *The Book of Job*, 2d ed. [Edinburgh: T. & T. Clark, 1914], p. 219), to the suggestion by Snaith (p. 61) that Job represents an unfinished work by an author who died before he proceeded very far. For summaries of the host of scholastic opinions, see Rowley (pp. 215f.) and Driver-Gray (p. xli). There is little to be gained by attempting to interact with such variety on an individual basis. We shall simply note some arguments in support of accepting the text as it stands and call for the reader to draw his own conclusion.

Pope (p. xlvi) calls attention to the fact that the Qumran Targum (11QtgJob), dating to the first half of the second century B.C., supports the Masoretic order of chapters 24–27.

Long ago Ewald (pp. 249f.) saw chapter 26 as befitting Job's lips because it demonstrates his superiority over his "friends" and seems to show that he was in fact striving after higher knowledge with resignation and diffidence. Certainly Job assumed an attitude of "out-doing" his friends' knowledge in 12:1–4 and 13:1–2. But in 26:14 he gives a modest confession that he is able to do no more than describe the barest and most distant outlines of divine power. Here Job's contention is that in God there remains so much that is incomprehensible. Seen as such it would be strange indeed to hear such an admission coming from the lips of one like Bildad, whose primary concern was to keep God neatly packaged and demystified so that nothing remains "problematic." In earlier speeches it was Job who dwelt on God's mysterious ways (9:4–13; 12:13–25). Zophar mentioned the subject only as a way to rebuke Job (11:7–9).

1–4 Bildad has struck a most sensitive nerve. In all Job's speeches nothing has been more important to him than his determination to be vindicated, shown blameless, in God's tribunal (10:1–7; 13:3, 13–19; 16:18–21; 19:23–27; 23:2–7). Bildad has just labeled that impossible. Job could not restrain himself. He leveled a sarcastic reply directly at the speaker (Hebrew second singular). He had nothing but contempt for Bildad's wisdom. In his colorful ironic exclamations, he considered himself powerless, feeble, and without wisdom, but not a maggot (vv. 2–4). If Bildad would only impute to him the dignity every human being deserves, he could have some compassion. The RSV had already caught this ironic tone departing from the question format in the KJV (LXX). Understanding vv. 2–3 as sarcasm makes Job's question about the source of such wisdom equally tongue-in-cheek.

Job wanted to know who "wrote" Bildad's material (v. 4). He certainly knew Bildad was mouthing Eliphaz's words (4:17). Job considered inane Bildad's argument that the majesty and power of God are the reasons why man cannot be righteous before him. It is proof of the poverty of his thought. It angered Job because he knew they all agreed that he was a reprobate sinner and so had given up the idea that he was an upright person temporarily suffering for sins. No, he was a worm whose case was hopeless. So Job dared to remind them that they too were hopeless as counselors.

The sharp transition to a poem about God and the cosmos has led to the conclusion that these verses belong with Bildad's short speech. But there are two additional reasons this is not so. First, this lofty poem does not appear to have the kind of material we are used to hearing from Bildad. Second, sharp transitions are common in these discourses. All the speechs tend to be very discursive. Some think this belongs to Bildad because its theme is like his, but that may be the very reason Job presented his view of the subject. The controlling theme is indeed similar to Bildad's—God's vast power. Job took up where Bildad left off. Bildad had used the theme to reduce sinful humans to the status of worms. Job wished to correct what he saw as an unwarranted connection. He did not see God's power related to the possibility or impossibility of human reconciliation with God. Both men dealt with the cosmos, but Job ended on a note that left man standing before the mystery of God's power with unanswered questions (v.14), but not as a maggot (25:6).

5–6 The term $hār^epā\hat{}îm$ ("the dead," v.5) in this and other OT passages means "shades or spirits of the dead." Isaiah 14:9 pictures the Rephaim in Sheol rising from their thrones to greet the king of Babylon on his descent. Here they tremble as God casts his eye on them in Sheol (v.6). But who are those that "live in the waters"? Some (e.g., Pope, p. 183) take it as the "watery abyss" that Sheol is thought to be. Rowley (p. 217) asserts that the mention of the waters is in reference to the nether world, "entrance to which is often depicted in terms of being overwhelmed by waters." He cites 2 Samuel 22:5: "the waves of death . . . torrents of destruction." Jonah was in Sheol in the belly of the great fish (Jonah 2:2). But this language is metaphorical for life-threatening situations (cf. 27:20). Job's earlier allusion to Sheol as "the land of gloom and deep shadow" (10:21) is more like this passage. It is possible that those "beneath the waters" (v.5) are those conceived of as buried in "the lowest pit, in the darkest depths" (Ps 88:6). Many commentators take those in the waters as the fishes, etc. Others feel this does not do justice to this context.

The thrust of these verses is that there is no place hidden from God. Job's remark was an emphatic rejoiner to Bildad's statement (25:3) that the light of God shines on everyone. Job heightened the observation dramatically by drawing attention to the searching eye of God from which even Sheol and Abaddon provide no hiding place. The proverbist whose purpose was different than Job's took it a step further: "Death and Destruction lie open before the LORD—how much more the hearts of men!" (Prov 15:11).

7–8 The word "skies" (v.7) is a justifiable insertion. Although $ṣāpôn$ means "north," the verb $nōṭeh$ ("spreads out") is never used of the earth and is often used in reference to the heavens. As in 9:8, where "(God) alone stretches out the heavens," $nōṭeh$ carries the idea of "stretching out" as a tent. This imagery is continued by the words "over empty space," or "over the void." It is difficult to postulate what "void" might be intended by Job if he were referring to a northern region of the earth where the majestic mountains rise. In the Introduction we drew attention to two points worthy of consideration again. First, that cosmography is not in itself the purpose of the passage. God's power is in focus. Second, we cannot ignore what Ugaritic literature tells about Mount Zaphon as the Canaanite Olympus. The Canaanite "cosmic mountain" concept is paralleled in the OT by both Sinai and Mount

Zion as the dwelling place of God and the place from which he chooses to reveal himself. But here it is that holy place where God dwells, that greatest of tents that he spreads out and where he dwells, the heavens.

Is there any substance to the suggestion that "the north" is the celestial pole formed by the Ursa Minor constellation? Such a view would imply the text refers to spreading out the stars, for only at night is the "void" (absence of stars) noticeable. Other passages that describe the heavens stretched out like a tent do not limit it to the stars (cf. Jer 10:12 et al.). Job pointed to God's power as incomprehensible. The heavens are visible; yet they do not fall to earth; there is no visible means of support. Even the earth itself can be said to hang on nothing.

While it is doubtful whether we should ascribe with Buttenweiser much significance to Job's scientific insights, Fohrer's interpretation (in loc.) is also highly questionable. The earth, he thinks, was thought of like a plate over empty space supported with pillars at the edges. He uses 9:6 as evidence, but there earth's pillars are clearly the mountains. Such an explanation destroys the mystery Job was seeking to present. The fact that God can spread out the heavens over empty space, hang the earth on nothing, and fill the clouds with water without their bursting is intended to make us stand in awe (v.8). Job was boldly expressing in poetic terms the marvelous, majestic power of God. Those clouds, though they contain an impressive quantity of water, do not split and dump all the water at once. Even with today's scientific explanation of cloud formation in terms of temperature, pressure, condensation, etc., one is still moved to wonder at the extreme complexity and yet ingenious simplicity of such a phenomenon.

9 Does God cover the face of "his throne" or "the full moon" (see Notes)? If the text is speaking of God's throne, then this line can be tied to God's appearance in the storm (38:1). God uses the clouds to enshroud him in his lofty abode (Ps 104:3–13; Amos 9:6). He appears in heaven (*ṣāpôn*, "the north") in golden splendor and awesome majesty. But people can no more look at him directly than they can the sun (37:21–22). So the clouds must cover the face of his throne—an apt word-picture of a theophany.

10 The NIV interprets the literal Hebrew "He draws a circle" as God's establishment of the horizon, which acts as the line of demarcation between light and darkness (day and night). Job was ascribing to God, and not to the incantations and rituals of the nature cults, the authority and dominion over night and day.

11 The Akkadian term for "the horizon" was *isid šamê* (lit., "the foundation of heaven," cf. *The Assyrian Dictionary*, 21 vols., ed. E. Reiner [Chicago: The Oriental Institute, 1956–], 7:240). Here the mountains are called the "pillars of the heavens" while in 9:6 they are the "pillars of the earth." They are pillars because their foundations go beneath the waters of the sea (Jonah 2:6) and reach to the clouds as if supporting the vault of the sky. The thought was common that the earth would shake at its foundations when God expressed his anger (Ps 18:7, 15; Isa 2:19, 21; 13:13; Ezek 38:19 et al.). Such phenomenological language was based on volcanoes and earthquakes. The force exerted by a thunderclap (Ps 77:18) is perceived as "the blast of the breath from your [God's] nostrils" (Ps 18:15).

12–13 Job continued his exaltation of God as Creator and Ruler of all nature. In the process he demythologized the language of the popular myths that described creation as the overcoming of chaos (see J.N. Oswalt, "The Myth of the Dragon and Old Testament Faith," EQ 49.3 [1977]: 163–72). The Akkadian creation epic (ANET, pp. 66–69) tells of the defeat of the chaotic goddess Tiamat (the Deep) by the hero god Marduk (Bel). In west Semitic literature, Tiamat's counterpart was boisterous Yam (the Sea) who fought Marduk's counterpart Baal. Job's intent to demythologize is quite evident. Here the sea that God subdues is not the deity Yam. Job depersonalized Yam by using the definite article (the sea), thus expressing his innate monotheistic theology. Marduk employed seven winds (ANET, p. 66) to overthrow Tiamat; here God's own breath clears the heavens. All the power of the wind is his breath. Further, by his own wisdom, skill, and power he "cut Rahab to pieces" and "pierced the gliding serpent," unlike Marduk who depended on the enablement of the father-gods.

A study of the OT names for the well-known Canaanite mythological sea monsters like Rahab shows how purposefully the OT authors used the language to enrich their own poetic conceptions of the supremacy of the one and only true God. This is especially true of poetry that deals with cosmological, historical, and eschatological themes. For example, Psalm 89:9–10 reads:

> You rule over the surging sea;
> when its waves mount up, you still them.
> You crushed Rahab like one of the slain;
> with your strong arm you scattered your enemies.

Compare also Psalm 74:13–14; Isaiah 27:1; 51:9–10.

Making the heavens beautifully bright by his breath could be a reference to the creation account of Genesis when God separated the light from the darkness of the initial chaos (Gen 1:2–4), but it more likely refers to the clearing of the skies after a storm. Job, then, demonstrated God's authority over the domain of Mot (the god of death) in vv.5–6 and over the domain of Baal (the cosmic storm god in vv.7–10). And in vv.12–13 Job drew attention to God's awe-inspiring power over the domain of Yam (the stormy sea-god). The same imagery was evoked and the same theology taught when Jesus stilled the waves (Matt 8:23–27), a powerful demonstration of the deity of the Son of Man.

14 For Job these manifestations and deeds are but mere shadows or whispers of the smallest part of God's might. We stand merely at the fringe of his majestic power. Who among us can even begin to fully comprehend this, let alone to fully realize the thunderous might of which he is capable? How beautifully and humbly Job asserted the majestic omnipotence of God! But he ended the poem convinced of the mystery that surrounds that omnipotence.

Notes

2 Andersen's translation ("How have you saved with your arm the strengthless?" *Job*, p. 217) of זְרוֹעַ (*zᵉrôaʿ*, NIV, "the arm") is good. In poetry prepositions are often not written. In OT literature "the arm" saves, it is not saved. So read "saved by (your) arm the feeble."

5 On the use of רְפָאִים (*rᵉpāʾîm*, "the dead") in Ugaritic and the Bible, the reader may consult J.C. de Moor ("Rapiūma-Rephaim," ZAW 88.3 [1976]: 323–45) and C. L'Heureux ("The Ugaritic and Biblical Rephaim," HTR 67 [1974]: 265–74).

Both the Hebrew and resultant translations of מִתַּחַת (*mittaḥat*, NIV, "those beneath") are difficult to understand. Blommerde's solution should be given serious consideration. He takes the mem as enclitic with the preceding word and vocalizes *tht* as Hiphil of *ḥtt* ("be dismayed"). Thus *tēḥat* is third feminine singular followed by a subject considered collective (cf. BDB, p. 565, for "waters" with singular subject), giving the meaning "the waters and those living in them are dismayed" (cf. Pope, p. 182).

6 אֲבַדּוֹן (*ᵃbaddôn*, "Destruction," "Abaddon," from the root *ʾābad*, the "place of destruction") is the nether world; and only rarely does this word mean general "destruction" (see Job 31:12 and perhaps also in 1QM fragment 9:3, TDOT, p. 23), though often so translated in modern versions. Gordis (*Job*, p. 279) suggests that the term Abaddon came into use later than Sheol and may carry the meaning of "the land of destruction of evildoers," as against the older idea of Sheol as the undifferentiated domicile of the dead. Among the plethora of suggestions for the etymology of Sheol, Gordis thinks the proposal that it derives from the Hebrew שָׁאַל (*š'l*, "ask," "inquire") has the most support. As "the place of inquiry," Sheol does not refer to necromancy (M. Jastrow, Jr., "The Babylonian Term *šu'alu*," AJSL 14: 170) but to "the place of God's inquiry" (ibid.).

7 Concerning צָפוֹן עַל־תֹּהוּ (*ṣāpôn ʿal-tōhû*, "the northern [skies] over empty space"), in the Introduction and comments above, we have preferred to render צָפוֹן (*ṣāpôn*) "the heavens" (the celestial mountain) as God's abode. Though תֹּהוּ (*tōhû*) can mean "wasteland" (cf. 6:18 and 12:24 and possibly Gen 1:2), here and in Isa 40:17, 23 it means "the void, nothing" as is proved by the parallelism.

9 Gordis (*Job*, in loc.) disagrees with many—including NIV—who render כֶּסֶה (*kissēh*) "full moon," which he claims should be read as in the MT: "throne" (not *keseh*, which he claims means "the day of the full moon" in Ps 81:3 and in Phoenician and Syriac). The NIV needs a margin note, for the KJV "throne" is still a viable translation (cf. comments above). Habel (*Job*, 1985, p. 372) points out that it is "his cloud" (*ᵃnānô*) that is "God's own cloud, not clouds in general" that covers his throne.

The quadriliteral פַּרְשֵׁז (*paršēz*, "spreading") is unique. There is no consensus on its origin, but all agree it is a variant of the word *pāraś* ("spread").

12 The RV margin adopted by the RSV is based on a homonym of רָגַע (*rāgaʿ*, "churned up"), which has the opposite meaning "to still" (see BDB, p. 921). But the NIV has been guided by the similar texts of Isa 51:15 and Jer 31:35.

13 In שָׁמַיִם שִׁפְרָה (*šāmayim šiprāh*, "the skies became fair"), the masculine plural going with the feminine singular raises a question about the translation of *šiprāh* ("brightness") as "became fair." Some see the preposition בְ (*b*) at the beginning of the line as dittography with the final consonant in v.12. Therefore "his breath (wind)" is the subject of a verb "*šiprāh* (Piel)" meaning (from Arabic) "sweeps clean" (Dhorme). Others feel the parallel line "pierced the gliding serpent" is mythopoeic language; so this line cannot be the clearing of the sky after a storm but something that goes with the parallel. Dhorme, Gordis, and Habel view the בְ (*b*) before רוּחוֹ (*rûḥô*) as a dittograph; and Habel follows Gordis, reading: "his breath spread out (cf. *šaprîr*, Jer. 43:10, BDB 1051) the heavens" (Gordis, *Job*). Tur-Sinai (*Job*, in loc.), followed by Pope, resorts to the Akkadian *sapāru* ("net" or "bag") and completely redivides and revocalizes *šāmayim* ("the skies") to read *śîm yām šiprāh* ("he put the sea in a bag").

14 דְּרָכָו (*dᵉrākāw*) is literally "his ways." Dahood et al. (cf. *Psalms*, 16:2, for bibliography) have extrapolated from the Ugaritic word *drkt* ("throne") the meaning "dominion," "power," which they think is sometimes applicable to OT texts (cf. Prov 8:22). Here and in 40:19, the NIV has translated the word "work," since it frequently refers to actions (cf. BDB, p. 203).

E. *Job's Closing Disclosure*

27:1–23

¹And Job continued his discourse:

> ²"As surely as God lives, who has denied me justice,
> the Almighty, who has made me taste bitterness of soul,
> ³as long as I have life within me,
> the breath of God in my nostrils,
> ⁴my lips will not speak wickedness,
> and my tongue will utter no deceit.
> ⁵I will never admit you are in the right;
> till I die, I will not deny my integrity.
> ⁶I will maintain my righteousness and never let go of it;
> my conscience will not reproach me as long as I live.

> ⁷"May my enemies be like the wicked,
> my adversaries like the unjust!
> ⁸For what hope has the godless when he is cut off,
> when God takes away his life?
> ⁹Does God listen to his cry
> when distress comes upon him?
> ¹⁰Will he find delight in the Almighty?
> Will he call upon God at all times?

> ¹¹"I will teach you about the power of God;
> the ways of the Almighty I will not conceal.
> ¹²You have all seen this yourselves.
> Why then this meaningless talk?

> ¹³"Here is the fate God allots to the wicked,
> the heritage a ruthless man receives from the Almighty:
> ¹⁴However many his children, their fate is the sword;
> his offspring will never have enough to eat.
> ¹⁵The plague will bury those who survive him,
> and their widows will not weep for them.
> ¹⁶Though he heaps up silver like dust
> and clothes like piles of clay,
> ¹⁷what he lays up the righteous will wear,
> and the innocent will divide his silver.
> ¹⁸The house he builds is like a moth's cocoon,
> like a hut made by a watchman.
> ¹⁹He lies down wealthy, but will do so no more;
> when he opens his eyes, all is gone.
> ²⁰Terrors overtake him like a flood;
> a tempest snatches him away in the night.
> ²¹The east wind carries him off, and he is gone;
> it sweeps him out of his place.
> ²²It hurls itself against him without mercy
> as he flees headlong from its power.
> ²³It claps its hands in derision
> and hisses him out of his place.

We are faced with the problem of how this speech fits in. Critics have given various reasons for the change from "Then Job replied" (6:1; 9:1; 12:1; 16:1; 19:1; 21:1; 23:1; 26:1) to "And Job continued his discourse" (27:1). Most feel the new formula was not original but was added because of a jumbled text. The same formula is used in 29:1 to mark off a clearly separate discourse. So here it also marks a separate discourse (ch. 27), probably as a concluding statement by Job to balance the introductory statement in chapter 3 (cf. Andersen, *Job*, p. 219).

The poem is mainly about God's just punishment of the wicked. Job opened by denying he was such, though his counselors had so labeled him. The chapter divides into two major parts: vv.1–12, where Job spoke directly to his friends with words a falsely accused victim would utter before an ancient Semitic tribunal—including oaths and an imprecation. Then in vv.13–23 he closed with a poem about the fate of the wicked, a favorite theme of the counselors. Many take these verses to be a fragment of Zophar's final speech (cf. Gordis, *Job*, p. 291; Dhorme, p. 386). But as Andersen says (*Job*, pp. 219–20), we do not need to take this as a sudden change in Job's point of view, nor as a later scribe's attempt to make him sound orthodox, nor as Zophar's words. Job has never categorically denied God's justice but simply differed with his counselors on how it was carried out in particular cases, especially his own.

1–6 An oath based on the existence of God was the most extreme measure available (the last resort) in Job's society for a condemned person to plead innocent. Either he was innocent, or he suffered the divine sanctions; for if Job was a liar, he blasphemed God. He was saying that his integrity (blamelessness, not sinlessness) was more important to him than life itself (v.5). But Job did not fear death because he spoke the truth. He knew he could swear before God without forfeiting his life. He felt God had denied him justice but inconsistently still knew that somehow God was just; so he could swear by his life. This same incongruity applies also to his earlier fantasies, when with highly emotional words he viewed God as his enemy (9:14–31; 16:7–14; 19:7–12). Refusal to accept the possibility of incongruous rhetoric baffles interpreters and makes them want to attribute Job's remarks to the counselors. It also baffled Elihu in 34:5–9.

We can all agree with Elihu that God never does wrong (34:10)—we can agree till tragedy comes into our lives. Then we may begin to ask ourselves what we have done wrong, or we may even question God's goodness. Deep down we know that neither question is right. So Job too emphatically denied either alternative. He was throwing the mystery into God's lap, as it were, and leaving it there. Andersen (*Job*, p. 220) calls it Job's paradoxical appeal to God against God. Here at the very heart of the problem of evil, the Book of Job lays the theological foundation for an answer that Job's faith anticipates but which Job did not fully know. God, the Sovereign and therefore responsible Creator, would himself in the person of his eternal Son solve this human dilemma by bearing the penalty of the sins of mankind, thus showing himself to be both just and the justifier (vindicator) of all who trust in him (Rom 3:26).

7–10 Job's oath is followed by this imprecation against his detractors (v.7). Imprecatory rhetoric is difficult for Westerners to understand. But in the Semitic world it is still an honorable rhetorical device. The imprecation had a juridical function and was frequently a hyperbolic (cf. Pss 109:6–15; 139:7–9) means of dealing with false accusation and oppression. Legally the false accusations and the very crimes committed are called down on the perpetrator's head. Since the counselors had falsely accused Job of being wicked, they deserved to be punished like the wicked. They knew nothing of mercy though Job pled for it (19:21). They spoke only of God's justice and power; yet they would become the objects of God's mercy despite Job's imprecation that was later changed to prayer on their behalf (42:7–9). The imprecation, however, still served a purpose. It was a dramatic means by which Job, as a blameless man, declared himself on God's side.

11–12 Here Job added a warning and made an application directly to his "friends." He was reminding them of an issue on which they all agreed—that the wicked deserve God's wrath. But they have put Job in that category falsely. He did not have to explain to them about God's ability to set things straight. Verse 11 can and should be understood as a question. Job was saying, "Must I teach you about God's power to punish? Indeed, I could never conceal from you a subject on which you have expounded at length."

13–23 Job is here to expound eloquently the subject the counselors know so much about. We might say he was giving this stanza on the fate of the wicked to dramatize in "living metaphor" the punishment they deserved for their false and arrogant accusation.

The stanza has an *inclusio* structure, that is, the opening and closing lines answer to each other. But his can only be seen when two items in v.23 are understood. First, the verbs and pronoun should be taken as third masculine singular. The reference is to God in v.13, not to the storm in the preceding verse. Second, "his place" at the end of v.23 means "heaven," God's place. Both prepositions in the Hebrew text will then make sense. The verse will read: "He claps his hands against them and hisses at them from his dwelling (heaven)" (see Notes).

Notes

1 מְשָׁלוֹ (*mᵉšālô*, "his discourse") means a poetic discourse, but no single English word can express fully its meaning. The etymology is "a similitude or comparison" that many of the *mašals* (proverbs) in the Book of Proverbs were. In usage the term includes parables, riddles, and other difficult sayings. Jesus frequently used *mašal* language (cf. John 4:13; 6:53–58; 10:6–10; 11:25). There were also the professional singers (*mōšᵉlîm*, Num 21:27) and oracular poems of Balaam (Num 23:7, 18; 24:3, 15, 21–23) where the same verb is employed (נָשָׂא, *nāśā'*) as here in Job—"he took (lifted) up his *mašal*" (cf. Isa 14:4; Hab 2:6). The verb expresses the public aspect of this communication, and the auxiliary verb יָסַף (*yāsap*, "to add") shows this is a continuation of what Job had been doing.

6 There is a problem translating לֹא־יֶחֱרַף (*lō'-yehᵉrap*) as "will not reproach me" since there is no "me" in the text and the verb in this root would have to be Piel for this transitive meaning. This is the only place it appears in the Qal imperfect. Guilleaume (*Studies in Job*, p. 109) relates it to the Arabic *ḥarafa* ("to change the mind"). This gives the reading "my mind will not change as long as I live." But using the Arabic dictionary in this way can be precarious (cf. Pope, Dhorme).

7 The jussive establishes יְהִי כְרָשָׁע (*yᵉhî kᵉrāšā'*, "may my enemies be like") as an imprecation. This terminology (*hāyāh + k*, "be like") here means "suffer the fate of."

11 Pope ignores אֶתְכֶם (*etkem*, "you"), the second masculine plural pronoun, when putting these words into Zophar's mouth. At least Dhorme does not begin Zophar until v.13. But we have given reasons for leaving these as Job's words.

In בְּיַד־אֵל (*bᵉyad-'ēl*, "about the power of God"), the term *yād* ("hand") should not be limited to "power." It could be rendered "his dealings, what he does" with his hand, which may be used for blessing or punishment. He seems to be warning them.

13 For עִם־אֵל ('*im-'ēl*), NIV's "God allots" gets the sense; but the Hebrew says, "the fate of the wicked man *from God*." There is no need to get rid of the ayin as a dittograph (BHS). Ugaritic supports '*im* (usually "with") to mean also "from" (cf. Dahood, *Ugaritic-Hebrew Philology*, p. 32, or Pope, p. 191, for details).

15 Those who escape war and famine (v.14) will die בַּמָּוֶת (*bammāwet*, "the death"), which can be any tragic death, not just "the plague" (NIV). Even worse than tragic death is the absence of mourning for them.

18 On כָּעָשׁ (*kā'āš*, "like a moth's cocoon"), Pope notes that it is not necessary to read "cocoon" into the text since though '*āš* means "moth," it also means "a night watchman" in Arabic, which yields better poetry: "He builds a house like a watchman, like a hut the guard makes" (Pope, pp. 188, 193).

19 In rendering וְלֹא יֵאָסֵף (*welō' yē'āsēp*) "but will do so no more," the NIV has followed the LXX (*yôsîp*) without a footnote. The MT says, "And he shall not be gathered." It is probably a rhetorical question and therefore refers to his death with his eyes still open.

20 Since both "tempest" and "night" are feminine, either could be the subject. "The night snatches them away like a tempest" creates a better parallel (Dahood, "Hebrew-Ugaritic Lexicography VII," p. 342).

23 The grammatical difficulties with which Pope wrestles are solved if the verse is understood as an *inclusio* with v.13 as mentioned above. For מָקֹם (*māqōm*) as God's "place, abode," see 1 Kings 8:30; 2 Chron 6:21; Isa 26:21; Hos 5:15; Mic 1:3.

III. Interlude on Wisdom

28:1-28

¹There is a mine for silver
    and a place where gold is refined.
²Iron is taken from the earth,
    and copper is smelted from ore.
³Man puts an end to the darkness;
    he searches the farthest recesses
    for ore in the blackest darkness.
⁴Far from where people dwell he cuts a shaft,
    in places forgotten by the foot of man;
    far from men he dangles and sways.
⁵The earth, from which food comes,
    is transformed below as by fire;
⁶sapphires come from its rocks,
    and its dust contains nuggets of gold.
⁷No bird of prey knows that hidden path,
    no falcon's eye has seen it.
⁸Proud beasts do not set foot on it,
    and no lion prowls there.
⁹Man's hand assaults the flinty rock
    and lays bare the roots of the mountains.
¹⁰He tunnels through the rock;
    his eyes see all its treasures.
¹¹He searches the sources of the rivers
    and brings hidden things to light.

¹²"But where can wisdom be found?
    Where does understanding dwell?

> ¹³ Man does not comprehend its worth;
>   it cannot be found in the land of the living.
> ¹⁴ The deep says, 'It is not in me';
>   the sea says, 'It is not with me.'
> ¹⁵ It cannot be bought with the finest gold,
>   nor can its price be weighed in silver.
> ¹⁶ It cannot be bought with the gold of Ophir,
>   with precious onyx or sapphires.
> ¹⁷ Neither gold nor crystal can compare with it,
>   nor can it be had for jewels of gold.
> ¹⁸ Coral and jasper are not worthy of mention;
>   the price of wisdom is beyond rubies.
> ¹⁹ The topaz of Cush cannot compare with it;
>   it cannot be bought with pure gold.
>
> ²⁰ "Where then does wisdom come from?
>   Where does understanding dwell?
> ²¹ It is hidden from the eyes of every living thing,
>   concealed even from the birds of the air.
> ²² Destruction and Death say,
>   'Only a rumor of it has reached our ears.'
> ²³ God understands the way to it
>   and he alone knows where it dwells,
> ²⁴ for he views the ends of the earth
>   and sees everything under the heavens.
> ²⁵ When he established the force of the wind
>   and measured out the waters,
> ²⁶ when he made a decree for the rain
>   and a path for the thunderstorm,
> ²⁷ then he looked at wisdom and appraised it;
>   he confirmed it and tested it.
> ²⁸ And he said to man,
>   'The fear of the Lord—that is wisdom,
>   and to shun evil is understanding.' "

The purpose and function of this poem has brought about considerable debate. Many view it as extraneous and make no effort to integrate it with the rest of the book. Although it stresses a typical theme (the inaccessibility of wisdom except through piety), it appears to be more than that. There is a deeper reason it is in the book. Dhorme (p. 1) suggests that it is to express a judgment on the previous chapters. Since the dialogue has reached an impasse, the author now makes his own comment on the powerlessness of man's efforts to penetrate secrets that belong only to God. No speaker is identified at the beginning of the poem, though one might assume the author meant it to be Job. But the change goes beyond the usual discursiveness to a complete change in literary genre. The tone is so irenic that one need not assume Job was speaking. When we hear Job again in chapter 29, he is still in the midst of his struggle. As both Dhorme and Andersen (*Job*, in loc.) observe, this is a calm meditation compared with Job's hot words. The unknown author who composed the book in its present ABA (prose-poetry-prose) pattern now uses another trifold symmetrical pattern within the poetry. He inserts between the dialogue in chapters 3–27 (three rounds corresponding to the three counselors) and the monologue format in chapters 29–41 (three speeches based on three characters) his own wisdom poem as an apex. Chapter 28 is not the climax that is reserved for the theophany at the end. The drive toward symmetry is an important aesthetic principle of OT poetry. Parallelism appears at every level. It is imbedded in lines, stanzas, poems, and books. The structure of this poem is as follows:

Introduction: The Source of All Treasure (vv.1–2)

I. First Stanza: The Discovery of Treasure (vv.3–11)

Refrain and Response: Wisdom Elusive (vv.12–14)

II. Second Stanza: Wisdom as Treasure (vv.15–19)

Refrain and Response: Wisdom Elusive (vv.20–22)

III. Third Stanza: God and Wisdom (vv.23–27)

Conclusion: The Source of Wisdom (v.28)

The content of the chapter about the elusiveness of wisdom is climaxed with the admonition that wisdom may be attained only through submission to God. The theme is stated twice in the refrain, which appears in vv.12, 20. Job was frustrated and unable to find a wisdom solution to the mystery behind his suffering. The counselors had been only a hindrance. So this theme—"Where can you find wisdom?"—is certainly not extraneous.

The poem develops the theme with skill by first concentrating on man's inquisitive nature and technological ability that enable him to find the riches of the earth no matter how difficult they are to obtain (vv.1–11). The second stanza dwells on the value of wisdom and its scarcity compared with even the greatest treasure on earth (vv.13–19). The third stanza (vv.21–28) finally addresses the question asked in the refrain. Wisdom has a source, but it is so elusive that only God knows the way to it. That is because he is omniscient (v.24) and is wisdom's Master (v.27). Man finds it only when he fears God and honors him as God (v.28).

The chapter as the literary apex of the book anticipates the theophany but does so without creating a climax. God alone has the answer or better *is* the answer to the mystery Job and his friends have sought to fathom.

1–2 Verses 1–2 state what appears to be a truism—earth's material riches have a source. But these two verses accomplish a rhetorical purpose. They set the tone without explicitly stating the theme. Dahood (*Semitic Philology,* p. 67) has missed the real parallelism by assuming *môṣā'* ("place of going forth") does not mean "mine" or "source" but "smelter," derived from an obscure root. The quatrain (vv.1–2) is clear. The first line of each bicolon refers to mining and the second to smelting.

3–11 These verses illustrate ancient man's technological ability in mining. Our scant knowledge of mining technique in the OT world has increased in recent years. B. Rothenberg's *Timna, Valley of the Biblical Copper Mines* (London: Thames & Hudson, 1972) presents the evidence for six thousand years of metallurgy in the Arabah. There smelting was done near the mines, but shaft mining is not evident till Roman times.

Searching in the blackest darkness required light (v.3). This could be accomplished by cutting a shaft and letting in sunlight or by torches. We know mining lamps were used in Nubia in the first century B.C. (Gordis, *Job,* p. 304). The ability to cut shafts through rock is seen in the elaborate "waterworks" in cities like Jerusalem and Megiddo. It began long before the tunnel of Hezekiah, whose Siloam Inscription tells of the rigors of boring through hard limestone. The mines at Serabit el Khadem demonstrate the same ability to cut through long distances of solid rock. Copper was mined in Edom and the Sinai Peninsula from Chalcolithic times on.

While there was no gold in Palestine, Egypt controlled rich mines in Nubia. Tushratta, king of Mitanni, wrote Amenhotep III that the gold in Egypt was like dust in the streets (CAH, 2.3, pt. 1, p. 486). As for iron, it was not used widely in Palestine till shortly before 1200 B.C., but there is evidence of working terrestrial iron (as opposed to meteorite iron) back to about 6000 B.C. (see W. Kaiser, Jr., "The Literary Form of Genesis 1–11," in *New Perspectives on the Old Testament*, ed. B.J. Payne [Waco: Word, 1970], p. 55). The OT reflects Israel's lack of technical knowledge in smelting and smithing iron before the time of David. The Philistine monopoly is mentioned in 1 Samuel 13:19–21. Iron mining was developed on the plateau east of the Jordan Valley, and clay in the floor of the valley was used in making large bronze castings for Solomon's temple (1 Kings 7:46). He also imported (1 Kings 10:11) large quantities of gold and precious stones from Ophir (v.16, Africa?).

Apart from the translation difficulties at the beginning of v.4 (see Notes), we now have knowledge of miners being lowered down deep shafts in cages or baskets. Verse 5 could be a reference to volcanic action, but there is very ancient evidence of shaft mining where fire was used to split rocks and to reach ore (see below).

Recent discoveries at Vincă near Belgrade and Rudna Glava in Yugoslavia reveal advanced knowledge of metallurgy dating back to 4500 B.C. (carbon-14 dating). Mining was a well-developed art in Europe long before the age of metals and on a small scale existed ten thousand years ago. This information fits the remembrance of early metallurgy reflected in Genesis 4:22. Shaft mining is evident showing the miners used ropes to haul out ore. Smelting was done with goatskin bellows. The often vertical shafts varied in diameter up to five feet and followed the veins of ore (see B. Jovanovic and B.S. Ottaway, "Copper Mining and Metallurgy in the Vinca Group," *Antiquity* 50 [1976]: 104–13).

In the Late Bronze Age, an interesting form of shaft mining was carried on in the Austrian Alps at Mitterberg, where ore was separated by setting fire to the shafts and letting them burn for days and weeks. They also used small fires in the shafts to facilitate quarrying by alternate heating and cooling with water to crack the rock. In the Early Bronze Age in Iran (Veshonveh) and in Central Turkey (Koslu), underground shafts over 150 feet long were worked. All this happened in places far removed from the biblical scene, but its early date makes the knowledge in Job 28 far from surprising (see B. Jovanovic, "The Origins of Copper Mining in Europe," *Scientific American*, vol. 242, no. 5 [1980]: 152–67).

Man, the dauntless technologist, in his search for treasure reaches paths that even a falcon's eye (one of the best eyes in nature) cannot see; yet man's eye sees them (v.7). Where beasts at the top of the food chain (v.8) cannot set foot, man's hand touches as he "lays bare the roots of the mountain" (v.9).

12–14 The refrain states the theme and is followed by a response. Compare the refrain followed by response in Psalm 107:8 and 9, 15 and 16, 21 and 22, 31 and 32. In v.13 the response is clearer when the Hebrew translated "comprehend its worth" is rendered "know its abode" (see Notes). It is important to observe how as a refrain vv.12–14 are parallel in form and meaning with vv.20–22. In v.14 "the deep" and "the sea" give the same negative response as do "Destruction" and "Death" in v.22.

The thrust is that even if one were able to probe these inaccessible places, wisdom could not be found.

15–19 Unlike Proverbs 8 and 9, here wisdom is not personified but is hypostatized, that is, given substance and objectivity so that the author could compare the search for it with man's search for treasures of gold, etc. The point is that man's intelligence and determination enable him to accomplish amazing feats of technical ingenuity, but left to himself he cannot find wisdom. Wisdom as a treasure is rarer than any other. Even with a wealth of technical knowledge, man cannot purchase wisdom. The author piles up words for precious metals and stones to lay stress on how exceedingly rare and costly wisdom is. He uses four different terms for gold of which the exact nuances elude us: the finest (red?) gold (*seḡôr*, v.15), gold of Ophir (*keṭem 'ôp̄îr*, v.16), fine gold (*pāz*, v.17), and pure gold (*keṭem ṭāhôr*, v.19). To emphasize his point he adds eight kinds of precious jewels in vv.16–19. Human beings may be clever, even ingenious and wealthy, but they are rarely wise.

20–22 Verses 12 and 20 are identical except for the verb. But there is no special significance to the change in verbs and no reason to change the text. They are clearly the same refrain. Verses 13 (Notes) and 21 give the same answer to the questions, though in different terms. Verse 13 stresses man's ignorance of wisdom and v.21 nature's blindness to wisdom. That Destruction and Death have a rumor about wisdom (v.22) probably means those who reach that place have a belated understanding they missed in life (cf. the rich man in Luke 16:19–31).

23–27 The poem reaches its climax. God alone knows where the wisdom is (v.23), for he is omniscient. Man must search for his treasure (vv.3–11), but God sees everything without searching (v.24). When he brought order out of the primeval chaos (vv.25–26), he used wisdom to do it. Wisdom is the summary of the genius God used to fashion the universe. In some sense it is objective to God (Prov 8:22), for he looked at it as if it were a blueprint of creation. He examined and approved it (v.27) and

> By wisdom the LORD laid the earth's foundations,
>> by understanding he set the heavens in place;
> by his knowledge the deeps were divided,
>> and the clouds let drop the dew.
>>>> Prov 3:19–20

28 Having shown God as the Source of wisdom, the author now makes his application to man. Man must look to God for wisdom. Man may share in it only through a knowledge of the revealed mind of God. To acknowledge him as God and live within the sphere of his life-giving precepts is wisdom for man (Deut 4:5–6; Ps 111:10; Prov 8:4–9; 9:10). In the process of studying God's revelation, man will learn that the price of wisdom—perfect obedience to God—is still beyond his reach. In the spirit of Job 28, the apostle in Romans 11:33 speaks of "the depth of the riches of the wisdom and knowledge of God" and of "how unsearchable his judgments." He assures us this mystery is hidden in Christ through whom is revealed "the full riches of complete understanding" and "all the treasures of wisdom and knowledge" (Col 2:2–3). And in Ephesians 3:8–10 he calls the gospel "the unsearchable riches of Christ" and "the manifold wisdom of God."

977

Notes

1 The particle כִּי (kî) is asseverative and does not so need to be translated (cf. Exod 15:1).

2 The passive participle יָצוּק (yāṣûq, "is smelted") has adjectival force. This is an example of a double duty preposition. The מִן (min, "from") is carried over (cf. Blommerde, in loc.).

3 In this verse the third line lacks a verb and prepositions. As in v.2 the verb is implied from line 2 and prepositions are supplied as the context requires. Gordis (Job, p. 305) takes this third line with what follows. He sees "the rock of darkness and gloom" as lava.

4 מֵעִם־גָּר (mē'im-gār, "Far from where people dwell") is difficult. Ancient and modern versions vary greatly. The KJV flooded the mines by taking naḥal (NIV, "shaft") as a flowing wadi. Gordis (Job, p. 305) takes gār as a "crater" and reads "The lava . . . cleaves a channel from the crater." Dhorme and Graetz (cf. NEB) vocalize 'im as 'am ("people") and use the initial mem to pluralize naḥal, rendering "a foreign people has pierced shafts."

9 For הָפַךְ מִשֹּׁרֶשׁ (hāpak miššōreš), the NIV reads hāpak-ma (enclitic mem) followed by the direct object—"he lays bare the roots of" (H.D. Hummel, "Enclitic mem in Early Northwest Semitic, Especially Hebrew," JBL 76 [1957]: 103).

11 On מִבְּכִי נְהָרוֹת (mibbekî nehārôt, "the sources of the rivers"), compare the KJV's "He bindeth the floods from overflowing." The Ugaritic mbk nhrm ("the source of the two rivers," i.e., the place of the god El's abode; cf. H.L. Ginsburg, "The Ugaritic Texts and Textual Criticism," JBL 62 [1943]: 111; Pope, p. 203) has provided clarity for this passage, which the NIV has followed. But the NIV margin, following the RSV, is unnecessary; the Hebrew text does not have to be translated "dams up" (from ḥbš, "binds") for פ (p) and ב (b) can interchange. As Hebrew npš can be nbš in Phoenician, so ḥpš ("searches") might be written ḥbš in this dialect.

12 There is no discrepancy in meaning between תִּמָּצֵא (timmāṣē', "be found") and תָּבוֹא (tābô', "come from") in v.20. Hosea 14:8 (9 MT) shows mṣ' can be used with min (as here) with the meaning "comes from."

13 On עֶרְכָּהּ ('erkāh), in our comments above we have not gone along with the NIV translation ("its worth"), for there no longer need be a choice between the LXX (presumably based on original Hebrew darkāh, "its way"; cf. RSV and BHS mg.) and the MT ("worth," "price"). Dahood ("Hebrew-Ugaritic Lexicography VII," p. 355) has shown that the root 'rk can mean "house," "abode" (cf. Pope, p. 203, for additional information). This fits beautifully our idea that vv.12–14 and vv.20–22 are refrain units that parallel each other.

16 The exact identification of most of these precious stones—e.g., בְּשֹׁהַם (bešōham, "with . . . onyx")—is guesswork.

17 On זְכוֹכִית (zekôkît, "crystal"), Pope's note is illuminating. This is glass (cf. Arab., Syr.), which at that time was considered precious enough for jewels.

21 Concerning וְנֶעֶלְמָה (wene'elemāh, "It is hidden"), Blommerde (in loc.) notes the presence of the emphatic waw (cf. 31:30), which ties this verse nicely to v.20, answering, "It is hidden, indeed."

23 Instead of הֵבִין (hēbîn, "understands"), six MSS and the LXX would have us read הֵכִין (hēkîn, "establishes"); but the pairing with יָדַע (yāda', "knows") rules it out (cf. Fisher, Ras Shamra Parallels, 1:198).

26 חֹק (ḥōq) can mean "a decree"; in Prov 8:29 and Jer 5:22, however, NIV renders it "boundary" in reference to God's limitation of the sea. But here "rain" is in view, as in Job 38:25, where different words are used; but the idea is the same: "Who cuts a channel for the torrents of rain?" The force of the parallelism in v.26b and of the root חקק (ḥqq, "to engrave, cut") allows one to render ḥōq "conduit," "channel."

27 The existence of a few MSS and editions reading הֵבִינָה (hēbînāh, "he understood") instead of הֱכִינָהּ (hekînāh, "he confirmed it") has led Dhorme and Pope to accept the former. But the Hiphil use of kûn is similar to this in Judg 12:6. That also could be a mistake for bîn

except that the Hiphil of *kûn* ("direct") + *lēb* ("the heart") means "give attention" (cf. Job 11:13; Ps 78:8 et al.). Just as *śîm lēb* ("pay attention") sometimes appears with ellipsis of *lēb* (see Notes on 4:20; 23:6; 24:12; 34:23), the idiom here and in Judg 12:6 might better be translated "he gave attention to it" (cf. BDB, p. 466).

28 Reasons presumed to be strong are listed for taking this verse as an editorial appendage, making the poem an agnostic statement about man and wisdom (Fohrer). The arguments, however, are not so strong as they appear to be (see Habel, *Job*, 1985, pp. 400–401).

1. The introductory formula "And he said to man" is said to be too short for a poetic line and hence was a splice (Pope). But Ps 50:16 is the same kind of formula followed by a series of synonymous bicola. Including the formula in the balance of lines creates a tricolon (cf. vv.3–4) with an acceptable syllable count of 6/9/6 (cf. Prov 4:4).

2. That form of the divine name *'adōnāy*, used here only in Job, is supposed to prove this verse was added. It merely supports our contention that this entire chapter must be the words of the author who is using this term for God in contrast to those used by the non-Israelite characters. Many MSS have YHWH (cf. BHS mg.).

3. It is also said that there is too sharp a cleavage between "metaphysical wisdom" and "practical wisdom." The latter (v.28) was supposedly added by the conservative school as an antidote to the agnostic tenor of the poem. But note how "wisdom" (*ḥokmāh*) is balanced by "understanding" (*bînāh*) in vv.12, 20, and 28. By asking about the source of wisdom, the refrains set the stage for the conclusion. Moreover the poem opened with a statement about the source of man's treasure and closes with a statement about the source of man's greatest treasure.

IV. The Monologues (29:1–42:6)

A. *Job's Peroration (29:1–31:40)*

1. *His past honor and blessing*

29:1–25

¹Job continued his discourse:

> ²"How I long for the months gone by,
>   for the days when God watched over me,
> ³when his lamp shone upon my head
>   and by his light I walked through darkness!
> ⁴Oh, for the days when I was in my prime,
>   when God's intimate friendship blessed my house,
> ⁵when the Almighty was still with me
>   and my children were around me,
> ⁶when my path was drenched with cream
>   and the rock poured out for me streams of olive oil.
>
> ⁷"When I went to the gate of the city
>   and took my seat in the public square,
> ⁸the young men saw me and stepped aside
>   and the old men rose to their feet;
> ⁹the chief men refrained from speaking
>   and covered their mouths with their hands;
> ¹⁰the voices of the nobles were hushed,
>   and their tongues stuck to the roof of their mouths.
> ¹¹Whoever heard me spoke well of me,
>   and those who saw me commended me,

¹²because I rescued the poor who cried for help,
and the fatherless who had none to assist him.
¹³The man who was dying blessed me;
I made the widow's heart sing.
¹⁴I put on righteousness as my clothing;
justice was my robe and my turban.
¹⁵I was eyes to the blind
and feet to the lame.
¹⁶I was a father to the needy;
I took up the case of the stranger.
¹⁷I broke the fangs of the wicked
and snatched the victims from their teeth.

¹⁸"I thought, 'I will die in my own house,
my days as numerous as the grains of sand.
¹⁹My roots will reach to the water,
and the dew will lie all night on my branches.
²⁰My glory will remain fresh in me,
the bow ever new in my hand.'

²¹"Men listened to me expectantly,
waiting in silence for my counsel.
²²After I had spoken, they spoke no more;
my words fell gently on their ears.
²³They waited for me as for showers
and drank in my words as the spring rain.
²⁴When I smiled at them, they scarcely believed it;
the light of my face was precious to them.
²⁵I chose the way for them and sat as their chief;
I dwelt as a king among his troops;
I was like one who comforts mourners.

Like a lawyer summing up his case, Job began the monologue with an emotional recall of his former happiness, wealth, and honor (ch. 29) and proceeded to lament, not the loss of wealth, but the loss of his dignity and God's friendship (ch. 30). He completed this trilogy with a final protestation of innocence (ch. 31). This chapter is sometimes called a negative confession. It is really an oath of innocence that effectively concludes with Job's signature in 31:35. There is no more Job could say; the case rested in God's hands. Job had to be shown to be a liar and suffer the punishment he calls upon himself or be vindicated.

Chapter 29 is a classic example of Semitic rhetoric with one of the elements of good style being a symmetrical structure. Unfortunately scholars have imposed their own notions of what the rhetoric should be and so have changed its order and obscured its beauty (cf. Dhorme, Pope, Skehan, NEB). These authors all move vv.21–25 up to follow v.10. In the writer's opinion the order of the verses in the Hebrew text present the author's original symmetrical intention. The pattern is as follows:

Blessing (vv.2–6)

Honor (vv.7–10[11])

Job's benevolence (vv.11[12]–17)

Blessing (vv.18–20)

Honor (vv.21–25)

The chapter deals with both active and passive aspects of Job's former life. He was blessed by God and honored by men. But he was also socially active, a benefactor and leader. His benevolence was an important part of the high position he held in his society where social righteousness was expected of every ruling elder. The Ugaritic literature and Hammurabi's Code both stress the responsibility of rulers to protect the poor and champion the cause of widows and orphans. So a description of Job's benevolence is in the climactic position in this oration, with the key line (v.14) in the exact middle of the poem. This verse sums up his benevolence in a striking metaphor about his being clothed with righteousness. Such benevolence established his right to the honor and blessing the surrounding verses describe. This chapter then is setting the stage for chapter 30.

1–6 These words are charged with emotion. Job longed for the precious days when he had enjoyed God's watchcare (v.2) and guidance (v.3). God had been his friend (vv.4–5a). Job had enjoyed the blessings of family and wealth (vv.5b–6). Like v.14, v.6 sums up the blessing in figurative language that reminds us of the words used to describe Israel's blessing in the land of promise—there it was "milk and honey," here "cream" and "olive oil." In Deuteronomy 32:13, Israel was blessed with oil and honey from the rock; in Psalm 81:16 the figure is honey flowing from the rock. The point Job made was not just that he had cream and olive oil but that he had it in such abundance that only hyperbole can describe it—drenched with cream and streams of olive oil.

7–11 The public square (v.7) was the business center, town hall, and courthouse combined. We have no idea what city this was, but any city that had a gate and public square was a major urban center. Job was a city father who occupied a prominent seat (v.8). The reaction to Job in the square seems exaggerated to the western mind, but it is fully in keeping with his culture and times. This deference to Job from young and old, princes and nobles (vv.8–10), shows he was a ruler. In the Prologue he was "the greatest man among all the people of the East" (1:3). Correct protocol demanded silence till the most honored person had spoken. The language excels in its descriptive power: Hushed, with their tongues sticking to the roof of their mouths, all waited in silence for Job to speak (v.10). Verse 11 implies that he had spoken and registers the effect. Seeing v.11 as transitional is another good reason for not disrupting the pattern by jumping to v.21. While it is true v.21 picks up again the story of Job's honor, so does v.18 continue the theme of v.6.

12–17 There may be good reason to make the stanza break after v.11 with the word "because" (*kî*) of v.12 toned down to "for." This is not certain, but it is clear that these verses are a unit (stanza) about Job's social benevolence. The stanza is both the apex (structurally) and the climax (conceptually) of this first unit of the trilogy. Verse 14 stands in the center of the stanza and the poem. It sums up in a metaphor what the surrounding verses present in action. The entire stanza is the climax because it presents Job's major point in the trilogy as well as the reason he was so honored and blessed. In these few verses Job covered a large area of the social responsibility of rulers who aspired to be godlike (Ps 68:5). The figure in v.14 is striking. Literally Job said, "I put on righteousness and it robed me," implying a veritable incarnation of righteousness.

The passage should be read as instruction, as a stimulus to our social conscience. Job responded to the poorest of the poor, gave comfort to the dying and joy to widows, assisted the blind and lame, and assumed the role of father and advocate for those who had no one else to look to. He was not just a protector but militantly opposed the wicked. It is important to see that Job did not concentrate on ritual righteousness (but compare 1:5) nor other ethical or religious responsibilities but on that area where humans most often fail—in their response to the sufferings of others. Compassion that knew no bounds is what characterized the life of the one who was truly the righteousness of God incarnate, who "took up our infirmities and carried our diseases" (Matt 8:17).

There is not even a hint that Job had any power to perform miracles. The dying blessed him (v.13), not because he could keep them from dying, but perhaps because he provided a way for them to die with dignity. He even found ways to make a widow's heart sing.

Although this stanza is idealistic—Job no doubt failed in some ways—it is to be accepted, not as self-righteousness, as some insist, but as an eloquent testimony to the tenor of Job's life as "a blameless and upright" man who "feared God and shunned evil" (1:1, 8; 2:3).

18-20 The man who had provided for others faced the prospect of a shortened life instead of the patriarchal ideal of 110 years with family gathered about (cf. Gen 50:22). He had hoped to flourish "like a tree planted by streams of water" (Ps 1:3) and to remain strong and virile. But was Job thinking of his family in v.18? Should the Hebrew word translated "nest" be taken figuratively (metonymy) and rendered "house" (NIV)? The problems in v.18 are formidable. The verse reads literally: "I thought, 'With (in) my nest I will expire (die).'" The LXX has "my age will grow old," which has led to the surmise that the Hebrew text behind the LXX had *zqny* ("my old age") instead of *qny* ("my nest"). But the Greek translators had a habit of simplifying what they did not understand. The Targum saw the same letters as the MT giving the Aramaic for "nest" (Pope, p. 214).

Some translators accept the old rabbinic opinion that the second half of the line speaks of the phoenix (cf. KD, 2:127; cf. NAB, NEB mg. et al.). The question seems to hinge on whether the word *ḥôl* (usually "sand") can mean "phoenix" at all. Pope (pp. 214-15) rejects Dahood's (originally Albright's) Ugaritic derivation. If this bird with its legendary long life and power to renew itself is in view, then "nest" fits the figure: "I shall die in my nest and multiply my days as the phoenix." If not, then the NIV's *ad sensum* translation may be acceptable; but see the Notes. In view of the figurative language already used in vv.14, 17, 19, and 20, rendering *qny* ("nest") as "house" certainly impairs the poetic effect.

In v.20 Job thought of his former "glory" as a warrior and hunter. His "glory remaining fresh" means his continued prowess, vehemence, and splendor with weapons. The parallel "the bow ever new" proves the point (cf. Isa 21:15, *kōbed* ["vehemence"; NIV, "heat"]; BDB, p. 458).

21-25 To bring to a balanced conclusion this first of the three connected poems, Job returned to the theme of vv.7-11. Again we emphasize the importance of seeing the stanza in its place, not only for the strophic parallelism mentioned above, but because it must stand immediately before the theme of chapter 30 to create the desired contrast between the high honor Job had enjoyed with the extreme dishonor he presently suffered. The language on both subjects is choice. Job's effect on others was charismatic. Men waited expectantly to drink in his words (v.23). Even his smile carried a blessing. The terminology of v.24 is not unlike the priestly blessing of Numbers 6:24–25 and the words of Psalm 4:6: "Let the light of your face shine upon us, O Lord." So in this way Job again was godlike, so much so that his counsel was valued (vv.21–23), his approval sought (v.24), and his leadership accepted with gratitude (v.25).

Notes

2 יַרְחֵי (*yarḥê*, "the months"; cf. 3:6; 7:3; 39:2) as used is typically archaic or Canaanite (Edomite?) since the Israelites regularly used חֹדֶשׁ (*ḥōdeš*, "new moon"), never used in Job. The chapter reveals in a number of places such language: e.g., the archaic (full) form of the preposition עֲלֵי (*ᵃlê*, vv.3–4, 7; used ten times in Job) and the word קָרֶת (*qāreṯ*) for "city" (v.7; cf. Prov 8:3; 9:3, 14; 11:11).

3 The NIV renders חֹשֶׁךְ (*ḥōšek*) "through darkness." The implied preposition is normal in poetry.

4 For בְּסוֹד (*besôḏ*, "when [God's] intimate friendship"), the ancient versions have a variety of *ad sensum* readings, but all based on the root *śwk* (*śkk*), from which some arrive at the meaning "When God *protected* my tent." This was the verb used when the Accuser said to God, "Have you not put a hedge around him?" (1:10). But the NIV has stayed with the MT as an infinitive or noun form *swd*, meaning "to counsel or hold council." The problem has been the preposition עֲלֵי (*ᵃlê*, "upon" [Pope]; NIV, "blessed"), but compare Rowley's simple rendering: "When the friendship of God was upon my tent."

7 If Gordis and Pope are right in their claim that public squares were outside the gate as implied in 1 Sam 31:12; 2 Sam 21:12; Neh 8:1, then *ᵃlê* may mean "from," as in Phoenician (cf. 30:2, 4, and, following Dahood, Cerensko, p. 15). Another rendering, however, could be "When I went out the gate [cf. 31:34, *lō'-'ēṣē' pāṯaḥ*, 'I . . . would not go outside'] to the city." קָרֶת (*qāreṯ*, "city") may be used metaphorically to mean the people of the city as in Prov 11:10–11.

11 The particle כִּי (*kî*) is asseverative and thus not represented in the translation of the NIV.

12 Here the כִּי (*kî*) may or may not be asseverative depending on whether the verse should be closely tied to v.11.

18 In עִם־קִנִּי (*'im-qinnî*, "in my own house"), the preposition is thought to be a problem. Driver-Gray, followed by Gordis, see no problem rendering *'im* "within" (cf. Exod 22:24; Lev 25:35–36, 39, 47). For fuller discussion, see Driver-Gray, pp. 201–4. There is no linguistic support for the translation "with my nestlings" (cf. Rowley, pp. 238–39).

24 For לֹא יַפִּילוּן (*lō' yappîlûn*), the NIV has given a paraphrase: "was precious to them." The Hebrew words say, "They did not allow to fall." Dhorme's paraphrase is better: "Nor was my smile lost on them!" Both amount to the same idea, that Job's approval encouraged them. But others (e.g., Rowley) take it to mean that Job's cheerfulness was not clouded by their despondency. Indeed, Rowley sees both sides of the colon in this sense, reading: "I smiled on (laughed at) them when they had no confidence;/ and the light of my countenance they did not cast down."

25 The last line of this verse is awkward as currently translated, but there is no need to drop the line as NEB does nor to emend the text. Not a single consonant or word needs to be changed. Only a change in the vowels of the last two words creates the line *kaᵃšer 'ôḇîlēm yonḥu(ma)*, which reads: "as I conducted them they were led." This concludes with the use of enclitic mem (cf. Hummel, "Enclitic *mem*," pp. 85–107) and builds on the Hiphil of יָבַל (*yāḇal*, "to conduct") and the Hophal of נָחָה (*nāḥāh*, "to lead") (cf. Pope, p. 212). The verse, then, is a chiasm: a • b // b' • a'.

2. *His present dishonor and suffering*

30:1–31

¹ But now they mock me,
  men younger than I,
 whose fathers I would have disdained
  to put with my sheep dogs.
² Of what use was the strength of their hands to me,
  since their vigor had gone from them?
³ Haggard from want and hunger,
  they roamed the parched land
  in desolate wastelands at night.
⁴ In the brush they gathered salt herbs,
  and their food was the root of the broom tree.
⁵ They were banished from their fellow men,
  shouted at as if they were thieves.
⁶ They were forced to live in the dry stream beds,
  among the rocks and in holes in the ground.
⁷ They brayed among the bushes
  and huddled in the undergrowth.
⁸ A base and nameless brood,
  they were driven out of the land.

⁹ "And now their sons mock me in song;
  I have become a byword among them.
¹⁰ They detest me and keep their distance;
  they do not hesitate to spit in my face.
¹¹ Now that God has unstrung my bow and afflicted me,
  they throw off restraint in my presence.
¹² On my right the tribe attacks;
  they lay snares for my feet,
  they build their siege ramps against me.
¹³ They break up my road;
  they succeed in destroying me—
  without anyone's helping them.
¹⁴ They advance as through a gaping breach;
  amid the ruins they come rolling in.
¹⁵ Terrors overwhelm me;
  my dignity is driven away as by the wind,
  my safety vanishes like a cloud.

¹⁶ "And now my life ebbs away;
  days of suffering grip me.
¹⁷ Night pierces my bones;
  my gnawing pains never rest.
¹⁸ In his great power ˎGodˌ becomes like clothing to me;
  he binds me like the neck of my garment.
¹⁹ He throws me into the mud,
  and I am reduced to dust and ashes.

²⁰ "I cry out to you, O God, but you do not answer;
  I stand up, but you merely look at me.
²¹ You turn on me ruthlessly;
  with the might of your hand you attack me.
²² You snatch me up and drive me before the wind;
  you toss me about in the storm.
²³ I know you will bring me down to death,
  to the place appointed for all the living.

²⁴ "Surely no one lays a hand on a broken man
  when he cries for help in his distress.

²⁵ Have I not wept for those in trouble?
  Has not my soul grieved for the poor?
²⁶ Yet when I hoped for good, evil came;
  when I looked for light, then came darkness.
²⁷ The churning inside me never stops;
  days of suffering confront me.
²⁸ I go about blackened, but not by the sun;
  I stand up in the assembly and cry for help.
²⁹ I have become a brother of jackals,
  a companion of owls.
³⁰ My skin grows black and peels;
  my body burns with fever.
³¹ My harp is tuned to mourning,
  and my flute to the sound of wailing.

The contrast between chapter 29 and chapter 30 is purposeful and forceful. The threefold use of "But now" in 30:1, 9, 16 ties the chapter together and reveals the author's contrastive intention. Moreover the very first verb seems to be used to heighten the contrastive effect. In 29:24 Job said, "I laughed [*šḥq*] at them" (at his people who were discouraged) and now a brood of ruffians "laugh [*šḥq*] at me." This is the second of the two possible interpretations of 29:24 mentioned above. Throughout vv.1–15 he expanded this theme: the loss of his dignity. If one feels Job exaggerated his honor in chapter 29, the hyperbole on his loss of honor in chapter 30 is even more extreme. Verses 3–8 are typical. Having your peers mock you is bad; but to prove how honorless he was, Job told how boys, whose fathers he could not trust to handle his sheep dogs, mocked him. This lengthy description of these good-for-nothing fathers is a special brand of rhetoric. The modern Western mind prefers understatement; so when Semitic literature indulges in overstatement, such hyperbole becomes a mystery to the average Western reader. To define every facet of their debauchery, to state it in six different ways, is not meant to glory in it but to heighten the pathetic nature of his dishonor.

To achieve a full measure of contrast, Job dwelt on the negative side of the three themes of chapter 29 in the following order: honor, blessing, and benevolence. The removal of God's blessing is far worse than affliction by men; so it is put in the climactic central position. The contrastive arrangement is as follows:

I. No honor from men (vv.1–15)
   A. Young mockers and their elders (vv.1–8; compare 29:7–11)
   B. Job assaulted (vv.9–15; compare 29:21–25)

II. No blessing from God (vv.16–23; compare 29:2–6, 18–20)
   A. Job suffers (vv.16–17)
   B. God afflicts (vv.18–19)
   C. Job pleads (v.20)
   D. God afflicts (vv.21–23)

III. No benevolence for Job (vv.24–31; compare 29:12–17)
   A. Plea for mercy and help (v.24)
   B. Reminder of his benevolence (v.25)
   C. No benevolence for Job (v.26)
   D. Result: His present condition (vv.27–31)

1–10 The conceptual correspondence with 29:7–11 is striking. Note the emphasis on the young and old (29:8) and on the chief men and nobles (29:9–10). The highest strata in society had stood hushed in respect (29:9–10) and then had spoken well (29:11) of Job. Here the lowest riffraff mocked him. Indeed they could not be kept quiet, for he had become a byword among them (v.9). There men had commended him (29:11); here they detested him (v.10). There they had covered their mouths with their hands (29:9); here they spit in his face (v.10).

11–15 These verses begin with a line that takes us right back to 29:20, where Job had mused on his former life as a hero with his bow ever new in his hand. But here God has unstrung his bow, resulting in the opposite situation as pictured in 29:21–25. Job's tribe had gathered about to hear every good word that fell from the lips of their benevolent leader. But here he was no longer leading the way like "a king among his troops" (29:25). Instead he saw himself like a city under siege (civil war?). Verses 12–14 use the terminology of siege warfare known from other biblical passages (Hab 1:10). Job had already used similar language of God's imagined attack on him (19:10–12). Here the language was even more precise. The "siege ramps" at the end of v.12 are called literally "roads of ruin." Verse 14 is very vivid. Job thought of himself as a city with a wide, gapping breach in its wall. The stones come crashing down, and amid the rubble the instruments of siege warfare roll through. The tranquility and dignity he had so enjoyed have vanished like a cloud.

16–23 Job shifted from this sorry relationship with his fellow man to an even sorrier subject, the removal of God's blessing from his life. He cried out to God but got no answer. When God was his friend, it was like having a light over him in the midst of darkness (29:3). But at this time his days were full of suffering and his nights of misery (v.16). These verses are important in that they show us that Job's basic complaint still remained. It was not only God's silence (v.20) but his violent treatment of Job that had become the sufferer's greatest problem. It would be no problem at all if only Job's concept of God was limited. That not being the case, in Job's mind, it must have been God who was responsible for all this.

The figure in v.18 is strange as it appears in the NIV. Most believe the agent in v.18 is God; but since the subject is hid in the verb, some take it as the pain of v.17 (cf. RSV). Some commentators suspect that this very difficult verse (v.18) has been disturbed by a well-meaning, pious scribe who could not abide what appeared to him blasphemous (Pope, p. 223). The problem with this is that the succeeding lines are just as bad if not worse, and they are not disturbed. The Qumran Targum now supports the LXX in reading "seizes my garment" (see Notes). This greatly simplifies the text (RSV).

The NIV translation of v.18 does not do justice to the key word (ḥpś), which it renders "becomes." The Hithpael of ḥpś can mean "to disguise oneself" ("let oneself be searched for"; cf. 1 Sam 28:8; BDB, p. 344). The point might be that since God is all powerful, he can do anything. He can even disguise himself as Job's clothing and bind Job's neck at the collar (NIV). But this is unlikely. The use here is more like the Niphal of ḥpś as in Obadiah 6, where Esau "is plundered" or "exposed." Here perhaps Job's clothing "is ripped off," and in the process he is choked by the collar of his tunic and hurled into the mud.

Job saw his problem with God as twofold. First, God would not answer him; and, second, God actively afflicted him. This was exactly the bifold nature of his complaint in chapter 13:20–27, even including the point of his being tossed about by the wind (13:25). As in that speech (chs. 13–14), Job's only prospect for the future was death (v.23). What was so devastating to Job was not the fear of death, for he had already asked for it as a relief (6:8–10; 14:3), but that he should have to face it with God as his enemy (13:24). God's constant attack, his ruthless might (v.21), was so completely the opposite of Job's "intimate friendship" with God in those bygone days when he had still perceived that God was on his side (29:4–5).

24–31 These verses complete the contrast with chapter 29. Here Job was in the position of those poor wretches to whom his heart and strength went out in 29:12–17. As a summation of his case, he packed his argument with emotion and righteous indignation. Justice was all on his side. The very benevolence he so freely had dispensed (v.25) he now looked for ·in vain (v.26). Verse 26 also reminds us of his expectations in 29:18–20. So here (vv.27–31) he presented himself to the court as he was, his body marred and burning with fever; he himself was exhibit A. As he often did, Job closed the stanza (v.31) with a strong figure of speech (cf. 29:6, 14, 17, 25; 30:15). His "path had been drenched with cream" (cf. 29:6), now his "harp is tuned to mourning and [his] flute to the sound of wailing."

Notes

2 That *kālaḥ* means "vigor" or "strength" in עָלֵימוֹ אָבַד כָּלַח (*ʿālēmô ʾābad kālaḥ*, "since their vigor had gone from them") seems clear from its only other use in 5:26. No doubt the KJV derived "old age" from the same connection, but "old age" makes no sense with the verb *ʾābad* ("perish"). There is a general consensus on the meaning but not on the derivation of *kālaḥ* (cf. Rowley, p. 191; Pope, p. 219). Even more vexing is how to fit these verses into Job's thought. Andersen (*Job*, in loc.) does not think Job was still talking about the fathers of v.1, which would imply Job refused to employ them simply because they were decrepit. Verses 2–8, then, are a commentary on these young scoundrels. NIV rejects this line of reasoning by inserting the words "their sons" (not in Heb.) into v.9.

3 Did the men "gnaw" or "roam" the parched land? הַעֹרְקִים (*haʿōreqîm*) in v.17 means "gnaw." Although the spelling is the same, we cannot be certain they are the same root; for the ayin in Hebrew can represent two different Semitic phonemes. On the basis of an Aramaic root, the verse is rendered "flee" in KJV. This is also the origin of the Targum "roaming" whence came the NIV ("they roamed"). Verse 17, however, unquestionably means "gnaw."

The RSV attaches אֶמֶשׁ (*ʾemeš*, "at night") to what precedes and omits the last two Hebrew words in the verse in an effort to create good poetry since the lines are said to be unbalanced. Pope (in loc.) observes that the alliteration here is too striking to be emended away (cf. 38:27). Moreover the final idiom שׁוֹאָה וּמְשֹׁאָה (*šôʾāh ûmešōʾāh*, "desolate waste-lands") also appears in 38:27 and Zeph 1:15 in contexts that demand a similar meaning.

The tricolon is not unbalanced as supposed (Pope) and therefore should not be changed. The Psalms present numerous lines like this where a short middle element of a tricolon applies equally to both the preceding and the following lines as here (cf. Pss 84:3; 98:2; 121:6).

4 Because לַחְמָם (*laḥmām*) is used in Isa 47:14 (as an infinitive of the root *ḥmm*, "to warm oneself"), and because it is claimed that "broom tree roots" are not edible and are used to make charcoal, Gesenius (BDB, p. 328) long ago rejected "their food" (NIV) as the meaning here (cf. RSV, NIV mg.). Andersen (*Job*, in loc.) appeals to the Qumran Targum, which supports the general idea of "eating." The 11QtgJob then is an excellent witness to

the ancient Masoretic oral tradition. In light of the Isaiah passage (which has the same vowels), the interpretation here must be left open.

8 נְכָּאוּ (*nikkᵉʾû*, "they were driven") is thought to come from *nkh* ("to strike") and therefore to mean "to whip or scourge," but this is not certain. It may mean they were driven from the arable land to the steppe.

11 Because the context of כִּי־יִתְרוֹ פִתַּח (*kî-yitriw pittaḥ*, "now that God has unstrung my bow") is about the deeds of these degenerate sons, and because the first two verbs in this verse are singular, Pope wants to emend them to plurals. Most translations assume God is the subject. What is not absolutely certain is what kind of "cord" (*yeter*) this is and whether it is God's or Job's. The oral tradition says "my cord," the written "his cord." But what does "God loosens his cord" mean? "My cord" could be Job's "tent cord" as in 4:21 (cf. KD, in loc., "the cord of life"). But since the word is clearly used for a "bowstring" in Ps 11:2, the NIV has the most satisfactory interpretation, especially in light of Job's statement in 29:20 and the relationship we have sought to establish between these two chapters.

12 The meaning of פִּרְחַח (*pirḥaḥ*, "the tribe") is conjectural. The KJV based its "youth" on a similar word in 39:30, Deut 22:6, and Ps 84:3, which means "young birds." Gordis (*Job*, p. 333) suggests it is used contemptuously here as is our word "bird." Perhaps "brood" would be better.

13 G.R. Driver ("Problems in Job") pointed out long ago that עֹזֵר (*ʿōzēr*, "helping") appears in Arabic as one of those verbs that carries opposite meanings. So RSV's "no one restrains them" is better without any emendation (see Introduction, p. 859).

14 In תַּחַת שֹׁאָה הִתְגַּלְגָּלוּ (*taḥat šōʾāh hitgalgālû*, "amid the ruins they come rolling in"), *šōʾāh* connotes the noise as well as the devastation that may have a variety of causes. Here it is not the storm but the battle. The verb has nothing to do with "billows" (Andersen, Rowley) but is a verbalizing of the word גַּלְגַּל (*galgal*, "wheel"; cf. the war chariot in Isa 5:28; Jer 47:3).

18 Concerning יִתְחַפֵּשׂ לְבוּשִׁי (*yitḥappēś lᵉbûšî*, "becomes like clothing to me"), the Qumran Targum agrees with the LXX: "grasps my clothing." This does not mean the MT should be emended, for there may be a meaning of the root *ḥpś* that we do not know. The usual meaning is "to disguise oneself," but see the comment above based on Obad 6 where it means "plundered." A clue to the meaning might lie in a west Semitic gloss found in a letter to the king of Tyre among the El Amarna tablets, where the word *ḥapši* means "arm," "force" (J.A. Knudtzon, *Die El-Amarna Tafeln*, 2d ed. [Aalen: O. Zeller, 1964], 147:12; so W.F. Albright, "Canaanite *hofši*, "free," in the Amarna Tablets," *Journal of the Palestine Oriental Society* 4 [1924]; 169f.). The verb תָּפַשׂ (*tāpaś*, "to seize, grasp") seems to be behind the LXX and the Qumran Targum. If *yittāpēś* (Niphal, "is seized") was the original form, then an auditory corruption (addition of ח) took place after 11QtgJob was written (c. 100 B.C.).

20 The problem with NIV's translation of וַתִּתְבֹּנֶן בִּי (*wattitbōnen bî*) as "but you merely look at me" is that the verb in this stem is "to give diligent attention," which hardly fits the notion "merely look at." Andersen (*Job*, in loc.) is on the right track. We have here a double duty use of the negative: "but you do not give diligent attention."

24 This is a very difficult verse. Many solutions have been suggested. The NIV is about as accurate as possible except that it seems to ignore לָהֶן (*lāhen*, "to them" [fem.]), which might mean "with regard to these things," i.e., his affliction (cf. RV). The words "on a broken man" is a paraphrase of "on (against) a ruin." See Rowley (p. 197) for a summary of the many interpretations of this verse.

3. *His negative confession and final oath*

31:1–40

¹I made a covenant with my eyes
    not to look lustfully at a girl.
²For what is man's lot from God above,
    his heritage from the Almighty on high?
³Is it not ruin for the wicked,
    disaster for those who do wrong?
⁴Does he not see my ways
    and count my every step?

⁵"If I have walked in falsehood
    or my foot has hurried after deceit—
⁶let God weigh me in honest scales
    and he will know that I am blameless—
⁷if my steps have turned from the path,
    if my heart has been led by my eyes,
    or if my hands have been defiled,
⁸then may others eat what I have sown,
    and may my crops be uprooted.

⁹"If my heart has been enticed by a woman,
    or if I have lurked at my neighbor's door,
¹⁰then may my wife grind another man's grain,
    and may other men sleep with her.
¹¹For that would have been shameful,
    a sin to be judged.
¹²It is a fire that burns to Destruction;
    it would have uprooted my harvest.

¹³"If I have denied justice to my menservants and maidservants
    when they had a grievance against me,
¹⁴what will I do when God confronts me?
    What will I answer when called to account?
¹⁵Did not he who made me in the womb make them?
    Did not the same one form us both within our mothers?

¹⁶"If I have denied the desires of the poor
    or let the eyes of the widow grow weary,
¹⁷if I have kept my bread to myself,
    not sharing it with the fatherless—
¹⁸but from my youth I reared him as would a father,
    and from my birth I guided the widow—
¹⁹if I have seen anyone perishing for lack of clothing,
    or a needy man without a garment,
²⁰and his heart did not bless me
    for warming him with the fleece from my sheep,
²¹if I have raised my hand against the fatherless,
    knowing that I had influence in court,
²²then let my arm fall from the shoulder,
    let it be broken off at the joint.
²³For I dreaded destruction from God,
    and for fear of his splendor I could not do such things.

²⁴"If I have put my trust in gold
    or said to pure gold, 'You are my security,'
²⁵if I have rejoiced over my great wealth,
    the fortune my hands had gained,
²⁶if I have regarded the sun in its radiance
    or the moon moving in splendor,

27 so that my heart was secretly enticed
  and my hand offered them a kiss of homage,
28 then these also would be sins to be judged,
  for I would have been unfaithful to God on high.

29 "If I have rejoiced at my enemy's misfortune
  or gloated over the trouble that came to him—
30 I have not allowed my mouth to sin
  by invoking a curse against his life—
31 if the men of my household have never said,
  'Who has not had his fill of Job's meat?'—
32 but no stranger had to spend the night in the street,
  for my door was always open to the traveler—
33 if I have concealed my sin as men do,
  by hiding my guilt in my heart
34 because I so feared the crowd
  and so dreaded the contempt of the clans
  that I kept silent and would not go outside

35 ("Oh, that I had someone to hear me!
  I sign now my defense—let the Almighty answer me;
  let my accuser put his indictment in writing.
36 Surely I would wear it on my shoulder,
  I would put it on like a crown.
37 I would give him an account of my every step;
  like a prince I would approach him.)—

38 "if my land cries out against me
  and all its furrows are wet with tears,
39 if I have devoured its yield without payment
  or broken the spirit of its tenants,
40 then let briers come up instead of wheat
  and weeds instead of barley."

The words of Job are ended.

We now arrive at the climax of the peroration. The material is similar in form, if not in content, to the negative confession given by the deceased who stands before Osiris in the Egyptian Book of the Dead (ANET, p. 34). Under oath the subject lists the evil things he has not done with the hope he will be vindicated and pass through the portals unscathed. Although the form is negative, the oration has a positive purpose as an attestation of loyalty to God as his sovereign Lord. To make this effective the subject calls down curses on his own head if his words are proved false. It is easy to interpret it as a prime example of self-righteousness, but to do so would fly in the face of Job's just call for vindication. Indeed, he has been doing this throughout the dialogue, and it reaches a climax in 27:5.

I will never admit you are in the right;
  till I die, I will not deny my integrity.
I will maintain my righteousness and never let go of it;
  my conscience will not reproach me as long as I live.

Job fleshed out that statement with a recital of the details of his virtuous life before God's hand struck him. This is the "shun evil" aspect of the description of Job that God repeated to Satan in the Prologue (1:8; 2:3). As stated before, because such was God's view of Job, he must not be labeled as self-righteous when he spoke the truth, even though it was about himself.

The chapter, then, as to its literary format, is a negative testament by which Job closes the matter of whether he was being punished for his sins. After such a state-ment, in the jurisprudence of the ancient Near East, the burden of proof fell on the court. That is why v.40 says that "the words of Job are ended." Each disavowal had to be accompanied by an oath that called for the same punishment the offense deserved on the basis of the principle of *lex talionis,* that is, "an eye for an eye and a tooth for a tooth" (vv.5–10). Since the charges against Job were wide and varied, he needed to give a similarly wide disavowal. He had already done this in a general way (cf. 23:10–12), but here he specified and called for condemnation and punish-ment from both God and man (vv.8, 11–12, 14, 22–23) if he was guilty of any of those sins.

Even though this is a poetic statement and should not be interpreted as if it were a legal brief, Job added his signature as a gesture to show his intentions to make it an official disclaimer of any indictment brought against him (v.35).

Critical scholars have rearranged the contents of the chapter by putting together any verses that touch on the same subject. We agree with Andersen (*Job,* in loc.) that by moving whatever annoys "their tidy minds" they do harm to the "living art of the whole poem." He points out, however, that this is poetry from a sufferer sitting on an ash heap. We have sympathy for such a sentiment but must keep in mind the goodly measure of orderly rhetoric we have seen even in Job's passionate and explosive utterances. Too much order should not be pressed; but even where the order is incomplete, it always seems to be present in these poems. In this poem a structure of themes is built around the repeated-oath formula. The formula does not always have to have an apodosis to follow the "if" clause. It can be implied (vv.29–34). Also several totally different "if" clauses may be given before a single apodosis completes the formula (vv.16–22; 24–28). In vv.5–8 the formula is used with two "if" clauses on basically the same theme followed by one apodosis. Verses 9–12 have a complete formula with protasis and apodosis followed by moral observa-tion tied to a divine sanction. In vv.13–15 the "if" clause has a moral observation also coupled to a word of divine sanction, which serves as an apodosis. The following is an attempt to show the thematic structure:

Job's Oaths of Allegiance to God

Introduction: No idolatry toward the fertility goddess—see below (vv.1—4)
    Covenant ban (v.1)
    Divine sanction (vv.2–4)   Lust of the eye//God's eye

A. First list of sevenths oaths (vv. 5–22)
    Oath (v.5)
    Self-imprecation (v.6)
    Oath (v.7)   Falsehood and deceit//God's scales
    Self-imprecation (v.8)

    Oath (v.9)
    Self-imprecation (v.10)   Adultery//God's fire
    Divine sanction (vv.11–12)

    Oath (v.13)
    Self-imprecation (v.14)   Mistreatment of slaves//God's court
    Moral observation (v.15)

Oath (vv. 16–18)
Oath (vv. 19–20) $\Big\rangle$ Neglect of needy

Oath (v. 21)
Self-imprecation (v. 22) $\Big\rangle$ Abuse of helpless//God's terror

B. Divine sanction (v. 23)   The fear of God

C. Second list of seven oaths (vv. 24–34)
   Oath (v. 24)
   Oath (v. 25) $\Big\rangle$ Idolatry (gold or gods)
   Oath (vv. 26–27)

   Divine sanction (v. 28)   Unfaithfulness to God

   Oath (v. 29)
   Oath (without *'im*) (v. 30) $\Big\rangle$ Hatred of enemy

   Oath (vv. 31–32)   Selfishness

   Oath (vv. 33–34)   Hypocrisy

D. The climax: Job presents his signed defense and challenges God to indict him
   on specific charges (vv. 35–37)

E. The anticlimax: a literary device (vv. 38–40)
   Oath (v. 38)
   Oath (v. 39) $\Big\rangle$ Avarice
   Self-imprecation (v. 40)

1–4 These verses need to be examined from the standpoint of subject and form. Why does the chapter begin like this? Why would a statement concerning sexual lust be at the head of the list, and why is not the oath formula used here? Some have emended the text; others have considered v. 1 misplaced, belonging with vv. 9–12 (NEB). Pope's observation (p. 228) that this would leave vv. 2–4 unconnected is worthy since these verses form a poetic unit. The covenant ban on Job's eyes (v. 1) parallels God's all-seeing eye (v. 4), and these verses enclose vv. 2–3, which speak of God's judgment on the wicked whose sins he sees.

The lines are, then, an introduction to Job's catalog of oaths protesting his loyalty to God. So Job, by declaring a covenant ban on his own eyes in conjunction with his Sovereign's ability to see all, appropriately brought to the fore the covenant theme that underlies and gives meaning to the oaths he was about to make.

There is, however, still more to it. Job's making a covenant with his eyes was not merely a promise not to lust after a girl. The sin he had in mind was more fundamental, or it would not have commanded this position in the poem. Job was emphatically denying an especially insidious and widespread form of idolatry: devotion to the *bᵉtûlāh* ("the maiden"), the goddess of fertility. As the Venus of the Semitic world, she was variously known as the Maiden Anat in Ugaritic (ANET, pp. 132–33), Ashtoreth in preexilic Israel (Judg 2:13; 10:6; 1 Sam 7:3–4; 1 Kings 11:5, 33), and Ishtar in Babylonian sources wherein she is described as "laden with vitality, charm, and voluptuousness" (ANET, p. 383). She is probably the Queen of Heaven mentioned in Jeremiah 7:18 and 44:16–19. G. Jeshurun had already suggested this interpretation in 1928 (cf. Pope, p. 228). Pope (p. 229) still chose to emend 31:1, even though he admits that with this interpretation the difficulties that led to the emendation vanish (cf. D. Freedman, JBL 102 [1983]: 143). Even token worship of the sun and moon is disavowed in the middle of the poem (vv.24–34); so a disavowal of the temptation to even look at the sex goddess is rendered very likely when we keep in mind that *btlt* ("the maiden") in Ugaritic is the very word used here. The Hebrews were constantly warned about this ubiquitous fertility cult (cf. Deut 16:21 –22; Hos 4:14). Clay plaques and figurines of the virgin's nude form may be seen in archaeology museums (cf. J.B. Pritchard, *The Ancient Near East in Pictures* [Princeton: N.J.: Princeton University Press, 1969], pp. 160–65).

See Hans Walther Wolff (*Hosea, A Commentary on the Book of the Prophet Hosea*, Hermenia, tr. G. Stansell, ed. P.D. Hanson [Philadelphia: Fortress, 1974], p. 14) for material on the sex cult. It would strengthen the case if a reference to the goddess using only *btlt* were available. However, in Proverbs 6:25 lusting (*ḥmd*) in the heart after a prostitute is not unlike Job's statement. Job used here the Hithpolel of *bîn* ("to give full attention to"). Earlier (9:11) he had used the Qal/Hiphil of *bîn* parallel with *rā'āh* ("to see") to complain about his inability to see God. On the other hand, the fertility goddess was everywhere to be seen.

The covenant-ban language (v.1) is a forceful way for Job to stress his allegiance to God, and the divine sanction in vv.2–3 is equivalent to the self-imprecation in the oath format (vv.6, 8, 10, 14, 22). Indeed that is the force of the imprecations as may be seen by the references to God's judgment in almost every case.

Not all accept the text here as a reference to the goddess. Driver-Gray understood vv.1–4 as a general claim to a virtuous life, giving God's judgment on evil as the grounds that led to a choice virtue. Such an understanding of v.1 is rather narrow to express such a general claim, but on this point Andersen (*Job*, in loc.) agrees with Driver-Gray.

5–8 In Job's world there were no atheists or even secularists. Everyone believed in the validity of divine sanction. This made the oath the ultimate test of integrity (cf. Num 5:20–22). Job opened the series of oaths by clearing himself of being false (Ps 26:4) and deceitful (Hos 12:8). In v.6, which may be either a parenthesis (NIV, RSV) or a "then" clause (Pope), Job mentioned commercial dishonesty and moved on in v.7 to clear himself of avarice ("my heart has been led by my eyes"). Clearly v.7 is talking about any evil deed his hands may do. But the verb *dābaq* translated "defiled" really means "cling to." If we follow the Oriental Kethiv (see Notes), then the text says, "if anything has stuck to my hands"—referring to thievery. With God's honest scales in mind, Job completed the oath with a self-imprecation that would balance the scales: May he not get any gain from what his hands may plant (v.8)!

9–12 From here to v.23 Job cleared himself of social sins. The sin of adultery heads the list (v.9). In the biblical world adultery was heinous, because it struck at the roots of the family and clan. It meant, as is clear here, relations with another man's wife. In Hammurabi's Code it does not have to be a capital offense, but in the Mosaic Law it was (Lev 20:10). Here Job's hypothetical sin calls for "eye for eye" justice—the same would happen to his wife. In the versions and the Talmud, v.10a was also thought to have sexual connotations since the parallel in v.10b is explicit (Pope, p. 231; Gordis, *Job*, p. 346). The moral observation that follows states that adultery is an offense punished both by the law of man (v.11) and the law of God (v.12).

In v.12 Job used a striking figure also found in Deuteronomy 32:22, in which fire kindled by God's wrath "burns to Sheol" and "devours the earth and its harvests." The figure was, no doubt, common poetic rhetoric. "It" refers to the sin but by metonymy means "God's wrath on the sinner." On the problem of the wife as victim when she was sinned against in v.10, see Gordis (*Job*, pp. 346–47), who explains it on the basis of the ancient Semitic concept of corporate responsibility.

13–15 We may truly stand amazed at Job's egalitarian spirit, for he took seriously the rights of his servants (slaves?). He did not just admit their right to have grievances but to openly express them and expect justice (v.13). Even more amazing in terms of what we know about slavery in the OT world, Job based this right on the principle that all human beings are equal in God's sight, because he who created them all is both their (his servants') Master and his, and that Master shows no favoritism (vv.14–15; cf. Eph 6:9). So Job considered any act of injustice to those under him as an affront to God (v.14).

16–23 Eliphaz had already accused Job of gross sins against the poor in 22:6–9, and in 29:12–17 Job had spoken positively about the depth of his social conscience. Here he closed the issue with a series of oaths of clearance enforced by a final fierce self-imprecation (v.22). There are several interesting touches to his phraseology that should be noted. In v.16 "the desires of the poor" parallel "the eyes of the widow" and present a touching picture suggesting sensitivity to their wants beyond merely meeting basic needs for survival. The word *ḥēpēṣ* ("desires") is never translated "needs" since the root means "take delight in." In v.20 "his heart" really means "his loins." The force of the parallelism is lost unless one can feel the pathos of a shivering body thankfully warmed by Job's fleece. In v.21 the verb "I have raised" comes from *nûp* ("to swing"). So it means literally "cuffing" the fatherless with impunity because of one's political power.

On the principle of *lex talionis*, the breaking off of the offending arm creates a dramatic imprecation (v.22). The hyperbolic language of Christ as he called for holiness (God-fearing life) has its roots in this self-imprecatory rhetoric (Matt 5:29–30). Verse 23 is pivotal. It is meant to be a statement that applies to all the oaths; for it contains an absolutely necessary ingredient for such clearance oaths to have meaning—the fear of God, that is, complete faith in his power to effect the curses. Thus his terror set Job to trembling.

24–28 Job began again with another firm denial of idolatry. But here the temptations are different. Instead of the appeal of the ever popular sex goddess, it is the appeal of gold (vv.24–25) and the apparent luster of two of the most commonly worshiped astral deities, the sun and moon (v.26). Job denied even secret homage to them (v.27).

29–34 Verses 31–32 as given in the NIV are somewhat difficult to understand because of the double negative. It can best be understood as Job's oath that his servants never complained about his lack of generosity (cf. Notes on v.31). He had freely shared food and home with all who came his way. Despite the inconvenience, Job's servants were of one mind with him. Pope following Tur-Sinai (*Job*, in loc.) sees in v.31 a denial of homosexual intentions in Job's household like those against strangers in Genesis 19:1-10. The interpretation has some merit but is difficult to prove.

Job denied hypocrisy in vv.33-34. Linguistically it is impossible to determine whether or not he was making a reference to Genesis 3 (cf. KJV, NIV mg.: "as Adam did") since the word *'āḏām* can be generic in meaning (NIV). M.G. Kline (WBC, p. 482) takes it as an allusion to the fall of Adam because then the imprecation in v.40 that "invokes the elementary primeval curse upon the ground" follows naturally. But Job was dealing with hypocrisy here—hiding one's sins. Adam hid himself in shame, but not his sins, as a hypocrite does. That Job admitted to sin is important to see since one might easily assume he was claiming perfection in this chapter. Reading behind the lines in v.34, one can appreciate how important an issue general knowledge of his sins might be and how great the temptation would be to maintain his public image (cf. v.21).

35-37 Job strategically brought his oration to its climax with a sudden change in tone. In 13:14-16 he was not so certain about his innocence and thought he might even put his life in jeopardy by calling for a hearing. But even then he affirmed that "no godless man would dare come before him [God]!" He was now sure of his innocence, so confident of the truthfulness of these oaths that he affixed his signature and presented them as his defense with a challenge to God for a corresponding written indictment.

How does this brash attitude (vv.36-37) toward "his accuser" fit the statements accompanying the oaths about Job's fear of God's terror? This strange paradox in Job's mind that God to whom he appealed for support was also his adversary is the main point of the chapter. Fearing the terror of God (v.23) is meant for those who break covenant with him. Job knew he had not done this. But he could not deny the existential reality that he stood outside the sphere of covenant blessing. Something was wrong.

There was only one way Job knew to make this absurd situation intelligible. That was to appeal to his just and sovereign Lord as a vassal prince who has been falsely accused. Even though he had repeated it often, he obstinately refused to accept as final that God was his enemy.

There is always a place in the lament rhetoric of the OT for the sufferer to remind God of his justice and covenant love. But Job was not just reminding God. He wanted God to reply to his defense with a list of the charges against him so whatever doubts were left may be publicly answered.

Verse 36 has been called a gesture of equality (Terrien, *Job*, p. 1124) where Job approached God as a prince to force God to accept his unblemished record and prove the counselors were wrong about his being punished for his sins. Commentators have never been able to agree on whether Job was doing right or wrong. Some are satisfied to leave it as the poet's (the author's) responsibility. He has chosen to present "the problem of the relationship between God and man in the sharpest possible delineation" since "nowhere in the ancient Near East does man approach the deity as a prince" (ibid.).

Others believe Job put himself in a false position. Neither his blamelessness nor his suffering gave him the right to tell God what he ought to do. Thus R.A.F. MacKenzie agrees with Weiser that "Job's precious integrity has become a barrier between him and God—a condition God must accept. Job overshot the mark"

("Job," in *Jerome Bible Commentary*, hereafter JBC, ed. R.E. Brown et al. [Englewood Cliffs, N.J.: Prentice-Hall, 1968], p. 527).

The opening words of the theophany (God's answer to Job in chs. 38–41) throw some light on the posture of Job in these verses. God rebuked Job's brashness (38:2 –3) as a darkening of his counsel. And as for the proud prince wearing the indictment like a badge of honor, God set aside his majesty and assumed a human stance calling on Job to brace himself and prepare to wrestle with the Almighty.

38–40 These verses are clearly anticlimactic, but that does not mean they belong in another place in this chapter. In several places before Job has shown his penchant for anticlimax (e.g., 3:23–26; 14:18–22). Job denied avarice in these verses. He had not eaten of the produce of his land without paying for the labor or by cheating the tenant farmers (NIV). The second line of v.39 might mean "causing the death of the owners" (cf. RSV, Dhorme, Pope). In that case it is something similar to Jezebel's illegal seizure of Naboth's vineyard in 1 Kings 21 (see Notes). That the land personified as a witness cries out and weeps over the horrible deeds done there (v.38) lends support that murder as well as avarice is in mind. And that in turn is why the primeval curse on the land is invoked. This is like Genesis 4:8–12, where Abel's blood cried out to God who then cursed the land so that it no longer yielded its crops to Cain.

Notes

---

1 On מָה (*māh*, "not"), compare KJV, RSV et al. The NIV has handled this in keeping with *māh* in 16:6 (cf. Arab., rare in Heb.).
7 מְאוּם (*mu'ûm*, not reflected in NIV) as spelled means "spot," "blemish." The Syriac, Targum, and Oriental Kethiv read *me'ûmāh* ("anything"). The MT would read "A spot has stuck to my hands."
9 Note the secret enticement to idolatry in v.27.
11 "Shameful" is hardly strong enough for זִמָּה (*zimmāh*). The term is used with some of the worst sexual aberrations in Lev 18:17 and 20:14. RSV's "heinous" is better. The second half of this verse is literally "a sin of the judges," stressing the human court, while v.12 is God's judgment.
18 גְּדֵלַנִי (*gedēlanî*) is literally "he grew up with me," which means essentially what the NIV has: "I reared him."
23 This statement of the certainty of God's sanctions against all who violate his law need not be limited to the preceding verse. Like vv.2–3 (cf. אֵיד [*'ēd*, "disaster," "destruction"] in vv.3, 23), the concept is foundational to the validity of the oaths in this chapter.
27 On the kissing of idols, compare 1 Kings 19:18 and Hos 13:2. The MT has "and my hand kissed my mouth." Since the heavenly bodies are remote, the kiss is not direct as with idols. So we read "my hand passed a kiss from my mouth." This assumes the rare meaning "from" for the preposition לְ (*l*).
31 This translation of אִם־לֹא (*'im-lō'*) as "if . . . have never" has obscured the meaning with the use of the word "never" to represent the *lō'* in the second colon. The *'im-lō'* of the first colon is an oath formula and as such is positive, not negative. So it would mean "If the men of my house have ever said."
   On לֹא . . . מִי־יִתֵּן (*mî-yittēn . . . lō'*, "who has not"), certainly the idiomatic meaning of *mî-yittēn* ("would that") should be preserved; and there is no problem if the *lō'* is vocal-

ized *la'*, indicating a rare assertative (cf. Andersen, *Job*, p. 136, n. 1): "Would that we might eat of his flesh until satisfied."

33 Concerning כְּאָדָם (*keʾādām*, "as men do"), as noted above, *'adām* can be "mankind" or "Adam." In this context Job denied hypocrisy—the hiding was not from God but from his fellow man.

בְּחֻבִּי (*beḥubbî*, "in my heart") is from *ḥbb* and is an Aramaism. It's Hebrew equivalent is *ḥēq* ("bosom").

35 תָּוִי (*tāwî*, "my signature") is literally "my mark"—that which authenticates a document. סֵפֶר (*sēper*, "indictment") simply means "a scroll." Some have suggested the translation "acquittal." "Let my prosecutor [אִישׁ *rîbî*] write out an acquittal." But why would a prosecutor, opponent, or accuser do what is not his duty? It is better to leave the brash Job intact.

39 The NIV has rendered וְנֶפֶשׁ בְּעָלֶיהָ הִפָּחְתִּי (*wenepeš beʿāleyhā hippāḥtî*) "broken the spirit of its tenants." In 11:20 נָפַח (*nāpaḥ*) with *nepeš* was translated "dying gasp." It would be better to render it in a similar way here. RSV has "caused the death of its owners." If *baʿal* means "owner," then it must mean the former owner, implying exploitation of the land (cf. 1 Kings 21). Dahood ("Ugaritic Studies and the Bible," *Gregorianum* 43 [1962]: 75; id., "Book Review on *Le Livre de Job* by Jean Steinmann," *Biblica* 41 [1960]: 303; id., "Qoheleth and Northwest Semitic Philology," *Biblica* 43 [1962]: 362) maintains "workers," not "owners," are in view. This is based on the shift between *b* and *p* as attested in Ugaritic and Phoenician—the usual Hebrew *p'l* ("to work") being spelled *b'l* here.

B. *Elihu Speeches (32:1–37:24)*

Some critics tend to be fierce in their opposition to Elihu. Peake (p. 29) held the author of this section dissented with the Prologue and attacked the original poet for permitting God to participate in the debate. According to Peake, this author thought he could solve the problem. To Rowley (p. 266) the original author made Elihu self-important and banal as a parody on such people. Pope (p. xxvii) considered the speeches diatribes that echo what has already been said but is offered by Elihu as novel and decisive. Generally the criticisms of those who find Elihu prolix, etc., are too severe. For example, Elihu's pride in his "superior knowledge" may not be a claim to superior knowledge but only to eloquence ("speech," see comment on 36:4). Eloquence was highly regarded in the OT world; but like any aesthetic judgment, it is personal. What makes Elihu sound insufferably prolix to us might have been considered the essence of good style. Scholars had to learn about the tautological style of the Ugaritic poems before they were willing to stop emending Hebrew poetry for this reason.

The list of those who see the section as a later addition is impressive and includes Delitzsch (KD, 2:309). The speeches according to Strahan (pp. 24–25) were the first commentary on the Book of Job. As such they have high doctrinal value but are really extraneous to the book. The view that the chapters were added by the author of the book has been stated in several ways. Gordis (*Job*, pp. 548–49; id., *God and Man*, ch. 9) believes the author may have learned through his life the lessons of the disciplinary aspect of suffering and woven this into the already completed book with which he was occupied throughout his life. Freedman ("Elihu Speeches") thinks these speeches were written by the author but never fully integrated into the book, that being done by another hand.

Other critics have gone so far as to say Elihu's words represent the climax of the book since only here we find an answer given to the problem of suffering—that it is disciplinary and redemptive (see C.H. Cornill *Introduction to the Canonical Books of the Old Testament,* tr. G.H. Box [London: Williams and Norgate, 1907], pp. 426 –27). Rowley finds this a problem because the reader is told in the Prologue why Job is suffering, and it is not to discipline him but "to vindicate God's trust in him." So Rowley considers all that Elihu says irrelevant to the purpose of the book. The point is quite legitimate and deserves real consideration.

We have suggested in the Introduction (Purpose) the answer to Rowley. The canonical Book of Job does not have a single purpose. It is true Elihu is not mentioned elsewhere in the book; so his speeches could be left out. But at the beginning (ch. 32) and at the end (ch. 37), they are skillfully woven into the fabric of the book and made to play a legitimate role. Whether put in immediately or later by the same author or added at an even later time by another, the speeches are part of the canonical book and serve as a transition leading to the theophany. They give another human perspective in which we find a more balanced theology than that of the counselors. This differs with the view that Elihu was the divine forerunner whose role was to prepare Job for the theophany. How could that be since Elihu saw no need for a confrontation between Job and God (34:23–24)? The idea should not be totally discarded but tempered with the thought that Elihu was merely human. So we need not assume everything he said is normative even though he claimed a special inspiration (32:8, 18). Elihu's attack on Job was limited to his statements during the dialogue. He did not accuse Job of a wicked life for which he was being punished. So Elihu was not guilty of false accusation, and that may be the reason he was not rebuked by God (42:7).

Elihu tried to be sensitive to Job but deserved some criticism for a weakness common to man—his overconfidence in his ability to do what the others could not. This makes him sound sanctimonious; but once Elihu got into his message, he seemed to improve as he went along. His poems in chapters 36–37, while at points difficult to understand, have a masterly quality similar to other great poems in the book.

Dhorme is correct in seeing a different mode of discussion here. The counselors and Job did not quote each other directly. Elihu had the debate before him and quoted Job frequently using his name (cf. 32:12; 33:1, 31; 34:5–7, 35–36; 35:16; 37:14). The Yahweh speeches call into question Job's words in totality but not in particular as Elihu did. So here the author's purpose is to deal with Job's extreme language.

Job was extreme at times (cf. 9:14–24), but it was due to his determination to be honest. He was also inconsistent. He questioned God's justice on the basis of his experience but was deeply committed to it since he laid all his hope for vindication on it. Elihu sensed this inconsistency and scored Job for wanting vindication while also accusing God of indifference to man's behavior (35:2–3). Elihu assured Job that God's wisdom coupled with his power to carry out his wise purposes guaranteed his discipline would ultimately prove redemptive (36:11–16). Despite his anger (32:2–3) and wordy lecturing style, Elihu never got bitter as did Bildad and Zophar. Nor did he stoop to false accusation about Job's earlier life (cf. Eliphaz, 22:4–11). He presented God as a merciful teacher (33:23–28; 36:22–26). Suffering is disciplinary (33:19–22), not just judgmental. The counselors glorified God with their hymns but remained cold and detached. Elihu had a warmer personal response to the greatness of God (37:1–2). He included himself as one who should be hushed in awe before

God. Elihu said God reveals both his justice and his covenant love in his sovereign control of the world (37:13, 23); and this is the reason the wise of heart should worship him. That is a fitting note of introduction for Yahweh's appearance.

1. Introduction

32:1–5

> ¹So these three men stopped answering Job, because he was righteous in his own eyes. ²But Elihu son of Barakel the Buzite, of the family of Ram, became very angry with Job for justifying himself rather than God. ³He was also angry with the three friends, because they had found no way to refute Job, and yet had condemned him. ⁴Now Elihu had waited before speaking to Job because they were older than he. ⁵But when he saw that the three men had nothing more to say, his anger was aroused.

1–5 Job had closed his peroration with a final flourish of bravado. He was so certain of his blameless life that he would be willing to march like a prince into the presence of God and give an account of his every step. The attempt of his friends to convince him of his sinfulness had failed. Job could have no more to say, having challenged God. The friends had no more to say because they considered him a hopeless hypocrite (v.1; 22:4–5).

The book at this point introduces Elihu, a young man who in deference to age has waited with increasing impatience for the opportunity to speak (vv.2–4). Four times in the Hebrew text we are told he was angry. First at Job (v.2 *bis*) for justifying himself rather than God and then at the friends because of their inability to refute Job (v.3; cf. v.5). We are not told explicitly why or under what circumstances he was there. The Prologue says nothing of bystanders, though it implies Job sat in an open public place where the friends could see him at a distance (2:12). These verses simply imply that Elihu was among bystanders who listened to Job and his counselors. One must assume a fictional quality to this narrative if the Elihu speeches were by a later author or even by the same author as an afterthought (Gordis). Authorship itself is not the crucial issue since we do not know who authored the book. What is important is that this is an authentic part of the canonical text and was accepted as such by successive communities of faith.

This introduction that stresses Elihu's anger has led to the conclusion that he is the original "angry young man" (MacKenzie, JBC). But his tone is not full of anger compared with some of the counselors' speeches. Andersen (*Job*, p. 51) sees him as an adjudicator who gives the human estimate of what has been said in chapters 3–31. There is no reason to believe the speeches were intended as an alternate answer that was inserted much later because someone felt the divine reply was inadequate (Pope, p. xxviii). However one may judge their quality, the speeches are only presented as a human reaction to Job's apparent "self-righteousness" and the counselors' ineptitude. Elihu's concern was not that they falsely condemned Job (v.3) but, that in failing to disprove Job's claims about his blameless life, they succeeded in condemning God. After all, they held that God never afflicts the innocent and always punishes the wicked. This interpretation follows the ancient scribal tradition mentioned in the NIV margin. See the Notes for other interpretations. Verses 4–5 reveal clearly that Elihu's major target was Job. He "waited before speaking to Job." Elihu's reply to the counselors was secondary as is evident in his speeches.

Notes

1 Instead of בְּעֵינָיו (be'ênāyw, "in his own eyes"), the LXX, Symmachus, and the Syriac have "in their eyes." Dhorme follows this, but nothing in the counselors' words even hints at such a change of mind showing that they were now convinced that Job was righteous.

2 Concerning מֵאֱלֹהִים (mē'elōhîm, "rather than God"), in 4:17 we suggested that the preposition מִן (min) can also mean "in the presence of" (cf. Dhorme). Both the LXX and the Vulgate so translate it here. Despite his statement that Job was not only prepared to vindicate himself before God but also to bring an indictment against God, Rowley (p. 207) does not back that up with a specific reference. Job certainly questioned God's justice but always relied on it for ultimate vindication.

3 Concerning וַיַּרְשִׁיעוּ אֶת־אִיּוֹב (wayyaršî'û 'et-'iyôb, "and yet had condemned him"), Jewish scribal tradition says that out of reverence the text was changed (cf. Introduction: Text). Originally it read "and so had condemned God" (NIV mg.). That is, because the counselors failed to prove their case against Job, they made God responsible for being unjust to him. Most modern commentators accept this reading. However Tur-Sinai (*Job,* in loc.) and Rowley accept the MT, but not as the NIV has it. They read, "They would not refute Job and so show him to be wrong" (a mere repetition). Andersen (*Job,* in loc.) wants to apply the negative to both verbs: "They didn't find an answer and (didn't) prove Job wrong."

---

2. *The first speech: part 1*

32:6–22

⁶So Elihu son of Barakel the Buzite said:

"I am young in years,
  and you are old;
that is why I was fearful,
  not daring to tell you what I know.
⁷I thought, 'Age should speak;
  advanced years should teach wisdom.'
⁸But it is the spirit in a man,
  the breath of the Almighty, that gives him understanding.
⁹It is not only the old who are wise,
  not only the aged who understand what is right.

¹⁰"Therefore I say: Listen to me;
  I too will tell you what I know.
¹¹I waited while you spoke,
  I listened to your reasoning;
while you were searching for words,
¹² I gave you my full attention.
But not one of you has proved Job wrong;
  none of you has answered his arguments.
¹³Do not say, 'We have found wisdom;
  let God refute him, not man.'
¹⁴But Job has not marshaled his words against me,
  and I will not answer him with your arguments.

¹⁵"They are dismayed and have no more to say;
  words have failed them.
¹⁶Must I wait, now that they are silent,
  now that they stand there with no reply?

> ¹⁷ I too will have my say;
>   I too will tell what I know.
> ¹⁸ For I am full of words,
>   and the spirit within me compels me;
> ¹⁹ inside I am like bottled-up wine,
>   like new wineskins ready to burst.
> ²⁰ I must speak and find relief;
>   I must open my lips and reply.
> ²¹ I will show partiality to no one,
>   nor will I flatter any man;
> ²² for if I were skilled in flattery,
>   my Maker would soon take me away.

Driver-Gray feel the major division here is not in 33:1 but in 33:8, where Elihu shifted from preliminary remarks to the substance of his speech. Up to v.8 he told why he had to speak and how he would go about it. His opening words (vv.6–14) are mainly an apology to the friends but also a rebuke for their failure with Job. Verses 15–22 take the form of a soliloquy about his urgency heard as part of his apology.

6–14 Elihu's reason for daring to intrude on ground usually reserved for sages was the fact that wisdom comes from God—the old may lack it, the young may have it—if the Spirit of God grants it (vv.6–9). Obviously Elihu believed he had been thus blessed. "Therefore," he said, "listen to me" (v.10). The counselors' reasoning had not impressed him. He caricatured them as groping for words and unable to handle bombastic Job. In v.13 Elihu seemed to be accusing them of using a falsely pious appeal to let God handle Job as a way out of their responsibility to refute him. But they had not made any such statement. Rowley (*Job,* p. 209), following Peake, thinks the verse is a polemic against the author for including the divine speeches. It is unlikely he would suggest there was no need for God because he (Elihu) could handle the situation. He had just said how dependent on the Spirit of God he was. The NEB goes the opposite direction, making v.13b Elihu's own claim that God, not man, will rebut Job.

In v.14 Elihu avowed that he would have used a different set of arguments had he been in the Dialogue with Job. Some critics have accused Elihu of saying absolutely nothing new, of using the counselors' old traditional arguments all over again as if they were novel (cf. Pope, p. xxvii). Others see the Elihu speeches as authentic and meaningful (Gordis, *Job,* pp. 358, 546–54). His speeches, though verbose and pompous from our standards, are not diatribes (Pope); and while they contain some of the thoughts already mentioned by the counselors, they are given in a different spirit (cf. 33:1–7). This is why the NIV's "your arguments" for *'imrêkem* ("your words") may not be a wise translation. He certainly did use some of their arguments as well as some of Job's, but one's words often convey more than an argument. In light of the increasingly biting tone and mood in the dialogue, it seems unfair to accuse Elihu, however overconfident he may have been, of continuing in the same vein as the counselors.

15–22 The shift to the third person in v.15 shows how Elihu used the same discursive style as in the Dialogue. Here he launched out on a soliloquy all about words—his words. Words have failed Job's counselors, but here he was standing by with so many words inside him that he was fairly bursting at the seams (v.18). There was no way that he could hold them back (v.19). He promised himself (and anyone listening) that he would be absolutely impartial (v.21). As is usual in Semitic rhetoric, he carried the matter of impartiality to a hyperbolic extreme (v.22; cf. Job in 13:8–9). He would not even use honorific titles (see Notes on v.21), something he had never learned to do skillfully for fear of God's punishment.

Almost all modern interpreters have found Elihu to be insufferably wordy. Mac-Kenzie (JBC, in loc.) says it takes him twenty-four verses to say, "Look out! I'm going to speak." He even suggests the Elihu speeches may be a parody on "some particular 'younger school' of wisdom teachers" (Ibid.). Whether successful or not from the modern viewpoint, Elihu meant to be eloquent; and wordiness was the essence. This loquacious style to some degree makes all the speeches in chapters 3 –41 difficult for the modern reader to appreciate. In Egypt even judges were impressed by the lengthy rhetoric of a defendant called "The Eloquent Peasant" (ANET, pp. 407–10). The peasant is brought in before the magistrates nine times just to keep him talking; and when the Herakleopolitan king of Egypt (twenty-first cent. B.C.) hears of it, the peasant's speeches are put into writing for his majesty to enjoy. No doubt Aaron possessed some of this gift that Moses feared he himself lacked.

Elihu then appeared on the scene to present eloquently a human viewpoint free of the acrimony that ultimately bound the thoughts of the three friends. Whether we see him as prolix or not, his intention was noble. See the comments on 36:1–4, which suggest Elihu is referring to his "speech," not his "knowledge" here in 32:6 and 10.

Notes

6 זָחַלְתִּי (zāḥaltî, "I was fearful") is another Aramaism found only here in the OT, attested as early as the ninth century Zakir inscription (see H. Donner and W. Röllig, *Kanaanäische und Aramäische Inschriften*, 3 vols. [Wiesbaden: Otto Harrassowitz, 1968], 3:32, text 202).

9 For רַבִּים (rabbîm, "the old"), the NIV mg. reads, "Or *many;* or *great*." The versions understood the word to mean "older men." Genesis 25:23, where *rab* means "older," supports this, as does 1QS, where *rabbîm* are the senior members (cf. v.7, where *rōb sānîm* ["great in years"] means "old"). The NIV's use of "only" avoids a categorical assertion that no old people are wise (cf. Andersen, *Job*, p. 247).

10 Two Hebrew MSS and the Versions make שִׁמְעָה (šimʿāh, "Listen") plural and thus harmonize the grammar with the second plural pronouns in v.6. The MT is an emphatic imperative and should not be changed.

On דֵּעִי (dēʿî, "what I know"), see Pope's comment based on the Qumran Targum (p. 243) and H.L. Ginsberg's studies ("The Legend of King Keret, A Canaanite Epic of the Bronze Age," BASOR Suppls. 2–3 [1946]: 42f.), which point to the root *dʿw* (Arab.) meaning "speech" also in vv.6, 17. In 36:3–4 this may also be the meaning (see below; cf. 37:16). Even if one insists this is from the familiar root *ydʿ* ("to know"), it is still a mark of Elihu's distinctive style since in the Dialogue the infinitive is always *daʿat*.

11 הוֹחַלְתִּי (hôḥaltî, "I waited")—here and in v.16 Elihu again revealed a difference between his speech and that of Job and the friends. They consistently used the Piel and not the Hiphil of this root (cf. 6:11; 14:14; 29:21, 23; 30:26). There is no difference in meaning, but the Piel is used widely in poetry of the Psalms and Isaiah. The Hiphil is another evidence of Elihu's style.

תְּבוּנֹתֵיכֶם (tᵉbûnōtêkem, "your reasoning") is still preferred, despite the Syriac and the Qumran Targum translation "(until) you finish" based on the root klh.

13 Concerning אֵל יִדְּפֶנּוּ ('ēl yiddᵉpennû, "let God refute him"), the verb is stronger than mere refutation; it means "drive" or "beat" (as the wind does). This is the only place it is used of words. The Arabic "strike" (as with a mallet) fits this context.

14 The Book of Job shifts back and forth with the plural spelling מִלִּין (millîn, "words"). Notice millîm in the next verse. Although the Hebrew reads smoothly in v.14a, Dhorme unnecessarily sees a difficulty in understanding why Elihu said Job did not marshall words against him when he was not even present. That is certainly no reason to see two haplographies, etc., in this verse. Elihu may have been pointing out the reactionary nature of their arguments, of which he intended not to be guilty. Or as Pope suggests, לֹא (lō', "not") might be read לֻא (lu', "would that").

17 The Hebrew of חֶלְקִי (ḥelqî, "my say") is literally "(speak) my piece."

18-19 In the second half of v.18, the Hebrew clearly reads "wind swells my belly," which should be kept as a figure in light of v.19. This figure was used by Eliphaz in 15:2 as derogatory of Job's "hot wind." It is only from the parallelism that we know אֹבוֹת ('ōbôt) means "wineskins" (cf. Matt 9:17).

21-22 The use of אַל-נָא ('al-nā') is hardly indicative mood. Elihu seems to have been saying, "Please do not expect me to show partiality." In the second half of this verse and in the first half of v.22, the verb כָּנָה (kānāh) means "to call someone by his honorific title," a practice Elihu felt God disapproved.

---

3. The first speech: part 2

33:1-33

¹But now, Job, listen to my words;
  pay attention to everything I say.
²I am about to open my mouth;
  my words are on the tip of my tongue.
³My words come from an upright heart;
  my lips sincerely speak what I know.
⁴The Spirit of God has made me;
  the breath of the Almighty gives me life.
⁵Answer me then, if you can;
  prepare yourself and confront me.
⁶I am just like you before God;
  I too have been taken from clay.
⁷No fear of me should alarm you,
  nor should my hand be heavy upon you.

⁸"But you have said in my hearing—
  I heard the very words—
⁹'I am pure and without sin;
  I am clean and free from guilt.
¹⁰Yet God has found fault with me;
  he considers me his enemy.
¹¹He fastens my feet in shackles;
  he keeps close watch on all my paths.'

¹²"But I tell you, in this you are not right,
  for God is greater than man.
¹³Why do you complain to him
  that he answers none of man's words?
¹⁴For God does speak—now one way, now another—
  though man may not perceive it.

15 In a dream, in a vision of the night,
   when deep sleep falls on men
   as they slumber in their beds,
16 he may speak in their ears
   and terrify them with warnings,
17 to turn man from wrongdoing
   and keep him from pride,
18 to preserve his soul from the pit,
   his life from perishing by the sword.
19 Or a man may be chastened on a bed of pain
   with constant distress in his bones,
20 so that his very being finds food repulsive
   and his soul loathes the choicest meal.
21 His flesh wastes away to nothing,
   and his bones, once hidden, now stick out.
22 His soul draws near to the pit,
   and his life to the messengers of death.

23 "Yet if there is an angel on his side
   as a mediator, one out of a thousand,
   to tell a man what is right for him,
24 to be gracious to him and say,
   'Spare him from going down to the pit;
   I have found a ransom for him'—
25 then his flesh is renewed like a child's;
   it is restored as in the days of his youth.
26 He prays to God and finds favor with him,
   he sees God's face and shouts for joy;
   he is restored by God to his righteous state.
27 Then he comes to men and says,
   'I sinned, and perverted what was right,
   but I did not get what I deserved.
28 He redeemed my soul from going down to the pit,
   and I will live to enjoy the light.'

29 "God does all these things to a man—
   twice, even three times—
30 to turn back his soul from the pit,
   that the light of life may shine on him.

31 "Pay attention, Job, and listen to me;
   be silent, and I will speak.
32 If you have anything to say, answer me;
   speak up, for I want you to be cleared.
33 But if not, then listen to me;
   be silent, and I will teach you wisdom."

Elihu spoke directly to Job, appealing to him by name (vv.1, 31). He ended the speech admonishing Job to reply (v.32). At the very end of his speeches (37:19), Elihu made another such appeal. And in 34:5, 7, 35–36, and 35:16 he referred again to Job by name. The counselors studiously avoided even mentioning Job's name, which indicates how formal their relationship was. From chapter 12 on Job had lost all confidence in the sincerity of his friends (cf. 12:2; 13:4–5; 16:2–5; 19:2–6, 28–29; 21:3, 34; 26:1–4). Elihu was aware of this; so he opened his speech stressing his own honest intent (cf. 1 Chron 29:17; Ps 119:7).

The refutation of Job beginning in v.8 immediately reveals Elihu's style—direct quotation of Job's words. In the Dialogue Job and his friends had replied in a more general way to one another's ideas. Elihu was not satisfied with this. Even though he said, "I heard the very words," some feel Elihu had the advantage of also seeing them. Whether that is so or not, he was concerned with the very words and quoted them fairly accurately three times (33:9–11; 34:5–6; 35:2–3) as the starting points for his rebuttal of Job's claim to innocence.

1–7 As vv.1–3 form a unit of thought, so do vv.4–7. There is no need to shift v.4 (Dhorme) since the verses form an a • b/a' • b' pattern. Verse 4 goes with v.6 and v.5 with v.7. Having in mind Job's earlier words to God in 13:21—"Withdraw your hand far from me, and stop frightening me with your terrors"—Elihu said that he, like Job, was only a creature of God nipped from clay; so Job needed to have no fear in marshaling arguments against him. But the words "if you can" in v.5 belie an attitude of superiority despite his attempt to allay Job's fears (see Notes on v.7 on the linquistic play on words between 13:21 and 33:7).

8–22 Finally Elihu began his argument. He had already shown an awareness of Job's precise wording. Now with some freedom he quoted the sufferer, picking out lines from various speeches. In 9:21 Job had claimed to be "blameless" (*tām*). In 10:6–7 he had complained, asking why God had to probe for sin in him when God knew he was not guilty. In 13:19 he had challenged anyone to bring charges against him and in 13:23 had requested God to show him his sin. We can be quite sure chapter 13 is referred to because 33:10b–11 are virtually identical to 13:24b and 27a. However quoting accurately does not necessarily mean verbatim. The NIV's "the very words" (v.8) unfortunately give that impression (see Notes on v.9).

Some of Job's words, especially out of context, sound like a claim to sinlessness. For example in 23:10–12 Job had said that he never had turned aside from God's steps or departed from his commands. Eliphaz certainly had that impression from Job's words (15:14–16). But the precise words of v.9 were not uttered by Job, and on occasions Job admitted to being a sinner (7:21; 13:26). His words in chapters 9, 10, 13, 19, and 23:7, 10–12 have in mind sins for which he was being punished; and he claimed nothing more for himself than what (unknown to him) God already had pronounced him to be (1:8; 2:3). Elihu then did not understand what was happening from the divine perspective, nor could we expect him to. His defense of God was like that of the counselors, especially in their earlier speeches, but without their rancor against Job's person.

In v.12 Elihu appealed to God's transcendence as the reason Job was wrong to dispute with him. His words sound banal, for hymns have already been uttered about God's greatness (4:8–16; 9:2–13; 11:7–9; 12:13–25; 25:2–6); but his purpose is commendable. God's thoughts and purposes are beyond man's ability to comprehend; so how can anyone know what God is doing? But for the moment, beginning in v.13, Elihu set aside the issue of Job's guilt or innocence and of God's transcendence (both of which he would return to) to answer Job's frequent complaint, that God would not give him a hearing (cf. 9:16, 35; 13:22; 19:7; 23:2–7).

God did communicate with man in various ways (v.14) and often (vv.29–30). Elihu expounded on two of these ways—through dreams (vv.15–18) and through illness (vv.19–22). The dream was considered an important channel for divine revelation. A repeated dream (vv.14–15) confirmed the revelation (Gen 41:32). Dreams and visions continued as a legitimate means to determine God's will in Israel (1 Sam 28:6) and in the early church (Acts 10:9–16).

Elihu tailored the possibility of this kind of revelation to Job's case. Job had already experienced dreams and visions from God, but they had only terrified him

(7:14). This was, however, just the kind of revelation Elihu thought Job needed. And Job should have interpreted this as God's instruction to keep him from ultimate destruction. Although v.16b is somewhat of a problem, it would be closer to the MT to translate it "and he sets the seal on (confirms) their discipline" (cf. Notes). Unfortunately Elihu overlooked the real question about which Job wanted an audience with God, namely: What are the sins I am accused of?

The second, but nonverbal, way Elihu found God revealing himself is even more tailored to Job's case. "Or a man may be chastened on a bed of pain" (v.19). As C.S. Lewis (*The Problem of Pain* [New York: Macmillan, 1943], p. 93) effectively observed, "God whispers to us in our pleasures, speaks in our conscience, but shouts in our pains: it is His megaphone to rouse a deaf world." God's purpose in suffering is to chasten man for his own good lest he find himself face to face with death (on v.22, "the messengers of death," see Notes). But Elihu did not make the crude claim so often on the lips of the counselors—that Job's sufferings were the proof of a wicked life.

Elihu's message is not exactly new, for Eliphaz had at least touched on the disciplinary aspect of suffering in 5:17–18. The subject, however, has not been broached again till now. Its emphasis by Elihu is commendable, but it is not exactly the kind of communication from God Job has had in mind.

In chapters 3, 6–7, 10, 14, 16–17, 29, and 30, Job spoke about death, either longing for it or complaining that it was his only hope. The emphasis was not lost on Elihu. After each of the two descriptions of how God communicates with man, Elihu ended on the theme that God does so to redeem man's life from the pit. In vv.18 and 22, after describing symptoms just like Job's (vv.19–21), Elihu pictured the sufferer at the edge of the pit—exactly where Job found himself—about to go on "the journey of no return" (16:18–22). There can be no question that Elihu had in mind chapter 16 as he picked up the subject of an interceding angel.

23–30 Eliphaz was convinced that there was no heavenly mediator who would listen to Job (5:1). In 16:18–21 Job had dared to suggest that he had such a witness, an advocate in heaven who would intercede for him, pleading as a man does for his friend. The word *mēliṣ* translated in 16:20 as "my intercessor" (but see Notes on the vocalization) is rendered here (v.23) as "mediator." It also means "interpreter," as one who stands between two others to make communication possible. The life of the "hypothetical" sufferer here hangs in the balance; no mere mortal can save him. Elihu considered such an event only a possibility, and even then this heavenly mediator would be "one out of a thousand"—a rare one indeed—who might do the job. His job was first "to tell a man what is right for him" (but see Notes). So in a sense this "angel" became a third means of revelation from God to man. He also provided for mercy in behalf of the sufferer and even provided a ransom to save his life (v.24). All this would happen only if man listened to the revelation and turned to God for grace (v.26a). Such a redeemed person would openly admit his sin and praise God for his grace (v.27).

So Elihu had both agreed and disagreed with Job and with the counselors. He had added the element of God's mercy, a subject avoided by the counselors who constantly appealed to God's justice. Man must reap what he sows even when he repents and is healed. Elihu felt there was a place for grace. A ransom may have to be paid, but the man is restored and only then comes to make his public confession.

Verses 26–28 present a person who has truly had a conversion experience. He has joyous communion with God; he is thankful and contrite. In vv.29–30 Elihu made a case for the patience of God who will favor a man even when he falls away two or even three times. This should encourage Job who had not yet even experienced it once.

31–33 Unfortunately like so many well-meaning messengers of grace, Elihu was so fully convinced of his good intentions toward Job that he became insufferably overbearing.

Notes

5 עֶרְכָה (ʿerkāh, "prepare yourself") means "set things in order," usually troops in battle array; here it is arguments. Elihu wanted to do battle with Job, but only as his equal. Yahweh in his challenge to Job (38:3; 40:7) used a significantly different figure and different word for "answer" (see Notes in loc.).

6 The idiom כְּפִיךָ (kᵉpîkā, "just like you") in Exod 15:11 et al. means "in proportion to" or "the same in measure."

קֹרַצְתִּי (qōraṣtî) means "I . . . have been taken from." In Assyrian the verb means "nipped off" (BDB, p. 902). It is what the potter does with clay.

7 In rendering אֶכְפִּי (ʾakpî) as "my hand," the NIV has followed the LXX (cf. KJV); but the verb of this rare root (ʾkp) is attested in Prov 16:26 and Ecclus 46:5, where it means "to press on." So the RSV's "my pressure" is better. The line is a play on 13:21 where Job called for God "to withdraw his hand" (kap). Elihu may have considered it elegant to substitute the rarer "like-sounding" word.

9 Elihu announced in v.8 that he was quoting Job and yet he used חַף (ḥap, "clean"), which is found nowhere else in the OT. This suggests the NIV of v.8—"the very words" for "the sound of the words"—may be overdone. It certainly reveals that modern verbatim quotation was not a feature of the ancient Semitic mentality. The NT quotations of OT share that viewpoint.

13 דְּבָרָיו (dᵉbārāyw, "man's words") is literally "his words." The problem here is what is the antecedent of the pronoun "his"? NIV has made it refer to "man's words," but it may refer to man's inability to answer God's words. That, however, contradicts the next verse.

The interpretation in the NIV mg., where it is God who does not answer for his actions, does not fit the context at all. Dahood ("Dative Suffix," pp. 258–59) sees here the participle with the dative suffix reading, "Why do you complain to Him that he answers none who speak to him." That fits both the wider and the immediate contexts well.

16 וּבְמֹסָרָם יַחְתֹּם (ûbᵉmōsārām yaḥtōm, "and terrify them with warnings") has been variously interpreted. As vocalized the MT reads "and seals their fetters." With the vowel change to mûsār, we get "and seals (confirms) their discipline" (cf. KJV). Most modern EV (NIV, RSV et al.) follow the vocalization of the LXX in the second word (yᵉhittēm), yielding "he terrifies them with mûsār [disciplinary warning]." The suffix ām is considered objective genitive (Gordis, Job, p. 375): "with warnings to them."

17 Understanding the use of מַעֲשֶׂה (maʿăśeh, "from wrongdoing") as implicitly evil (cf. Gen 44:15) in this context is supported by the use of the synonym poʿal ("deed"), parallel with pešaʿ ("transgression") in 36:9. We see here also the aforementioned tendency in this poetry to leave out prepositions.

18 Both the parallelism and the root ʿbr ("pass over, on, or by") support the identification here—מֵעֲבֹר בַּשָּׁלַח (mēʿăbōr baššālaḥ, "from perishing by the sword")—of the Akkadian cognate šalḫu ("a water channel") used in Mesopotamian mythology with reference to the river of death (see Rowley, Pope, Tsevat, "The Canaanite God šālaḥ," VetTest 4 [1954]:

43). If we read "sword," "javelin," or "missile" from 2 Sam 18:14, we must justify the use of the verb *ʿbr*. It is used consistently in this idiom by Elihu (cf. 34:20; 36:12; cf. also Ps 37:36) and in Nahum 1:12 where it clearly means "to die."

21 יָכֵל (*yikel*, "wastes away") is again in Job clearly the apocopated form of the weak verb, not the jussive. See Notes on 18:12.

22 לַמְמֻתִים (*lamᵉmitîm*, "to the messengers of death") is a reference to the angels of death as in 2 Sam 24:16; 2 Kings 19:35; 1 Chron 21:15; and Ps 78:49, whose work can be accomplished by plague. Pope revocalizes assuming the use of enclitic mem. But that involves questionable methodology. When a text is grammatically clear and fits culturally, one should not emend or revocalize to support a thesis over which there is some disagreement. The "waters of death" as the nether world is not that well attested in the OT. The line only appears unbalanced until one counts the syllables.

24 Concerning פְּדָעֵהוּ (*pᵉdāʿēhû*, "spare him"), there is no known word *pdʿ* meaning "to spare." Gordis (*Job*, in loc.) follows the two MSS that read *prʿ*, but his attempt to show that the meaning in Prov 4:15 ("avoid") fits here is not convincing. Dhorme, also unconvincing, says the ayin stands for hey in *pdh* ("to ransom"). Guilleaume (Pope) sees the conjunction *p* ("and"; Arab., Aram., Ugar. et al.) followed by the root *wdʿ* ("to release"), which, it is claimed, is used in 1 Sam 21:3 (cf. J. Barr, *Comparative Philology and the Text of the Old Testament* [London: Oxford University Press, 1968], pp. 20–21).

25 Gordis gives four explanations of רֻטֲפַשׁ (*ruṭᵃpaš*, "is renewed"). Guilleaume (*Studies in Job*, p. 119) relates it to the Hebrew *rṭb* ("be soft, tender"), with the final sibilant as used in Arabic. Others say it is from *ṭps* ("grow fat") with prefixed resh. It may be a combination of the two verbs like *paršez* ("spreading") in 26:9 (see Notes). All are guesses.

26 For וַיָּשֶׁב (*wayyāšeb*) the MT reads "And he restores man." The NIV assumes the subject is God: "he is restored by God." Because of the sudden shift in subject, some emend it to read *yᵉbaššēr* ("he [the man] announces [to men]"; cf. RSV). The NEB moves the line up to v.23. Gordis (*Job*, p. 379) attempts to show *šwb* ("return") can mean "proclaim." If this is so, the RSV is preferred.

27 Most revocalize יָשֹׁר (*yāšōr*, "then he comes") to *yāšîr* ("he sings," RSV), but the NIV takes it as is from *šûr* II (KB, p. 957).

30 בְּאוֹר הַחַיִּים (*bᵉʾôr haḥayyîm*, "that the light of life may shine on him") might possibly read "that he may be given light in the land of the living." See Notes on 22:11.

---

4. The second speech

34:1–37

¹Then Elihu said:

> ²"Hear my words, you wise men;
> listen to me, you men of learning.
> ³For the ear tests words
> as the tongue tastes food.
> ⁴Let us discern for ourselves what is right;
> let us learn together what is good.

> ⁵"Job says, 'I am innocent,
> but God denies me justice.
> ⁶Although I am right,
> I am considered a liar;
> although I am guiltless,
> his arrow inflicts an incurable wound.'
> ⁷What man is like Job,
> who drinks scorn like water?

⁸ He keeps company with evildoers;
    he associates with wicked men.
⁹ For he says, 'It profits a man nothing
    when he tries to please God.'

¹⁰ "So listen to me, you men of understanding.
    Far be it from God to do evil,
    from the Almighty to do wrong.
¹¹ He repays a man for what he has done;
    he brings upon him what his conduct deserves.
¹² It is unthinkable that God would do wrong,
    that the Almighty would pervert justice.
¹³ Who appointed him over the earth?
    Who put him in charge of the whole world?
¹⁴ If it were his intention
    and he withdrew his spirit and breath,
¹⁵ all mankind would perish together
    and man would return to the dust.

¹⁶ "If you have understanding, hear this;
    listen to what I say.
¹⁷ Can he who hates justice govern?
    Will you condemn the just and mighty One?
¹⁸ Is he not the One who says to kings, 'You are worthless,'
    and to nobles, 'You are wicked,'
¹⁹ who shows no partiality to princes
    and does not favor the rich over the poor,
    for they are all the work of his hands?
²⁰ They die in an instant, in the middle of the night;
    the people are shaken and they pass away;
    the mighty are removed without human hand.

²¹ "His eyes are on the ways of men;
    he sees their every step.
²² There is no dark place, no deep shadow,
    where evildoers can hide.
²³ God has no need to examine men further,
    that they should come before him for judgment.
²⁴ Without inquiry he shatters the mighty
    and sets up others in their place.
²⁵ Because he takes note of their deeds,
    he overthrows them in the night and they are crushed.
²⁶ He punishes them for their wickedness
    where everyone can see them,
²⁷ because they turned from following him
    and had no regard for any of his ways.
²⁸ They caused the cry of the poor to come before him,
    so that he heard the cry of the needy.
²⁹ But if he remains silent, who can condemn him?
    If he hides his face, who can see him?
    Yet he is over man and nation alike,
³⁰   to keep a godless man from ruling,
    from laying snares for the people.

³¹ "Suppose a man says to God,
    'I am guilty but will offend no more.
³² Teach me what I cannot see;
    if I have done wrong, I will not do so again.'
³³ Should God then reward you on your terms,
    when you refuse to repent?
    You must decide, not I;
    so tell me what you know.

34 "Men of understanding declare,
  wise men who hear me say to me,
35 'Job speaks without knowledge;
  his words lack insight.'
36 Oh, that Job might be tested to the utmost
  for answering like a wicked man!
37 To his sin he adds rebellion;
  scornfully he claps his hands among us
  and multiplies his words against God."

Elihu claimed he wanted Job to be cleared. It seems Elihu had repentance in mind as he called on Job "to speak up" (33:32) or else listen and learn wisdom. He saw himself as a teacher of wisdom (33:33). As he proceeded to do that in chapter 34, he believed even the wise could benefit from his chosen words (vv.2–4). Once again his method was to quote Job (vv.5–6), and his purpose was to show that Job's words were theologically unsound. He did not always claim to quote the very words of Job (33:8–11). Sometimes he gave only a summary of what the sufferer had said (vv.5–6, 8). As we examine this chapter, we should keep in mind that Elihu had picked out of Job's speeches those words and ideas that sounded particularly damaging. Job had had questions about the justice of God, and he had emphatically asserted his innocence. But none of this should be viewed independently of Job's total statement. His claim to innocence was always given in the context of his reason for suffering. And while he had questioned the mystery of theodicy, he had also made clear he believed in God's justice so much that he was willing to rest his entire case, all his hope, on that one issue (13:13–19; 23:2–7). Like the counselors, Elihu picked out only those words of Job that he needed in order to prove his point.

Elihu, however, was not in all respects like the counselors. For example, he did not express their view of suffering. As we have seen in chapter 33, he considered the disciplinary aspect of suffering to be one of the ways God communicates with man. Unlike the counselors, Elihu did not totally condemn Job. He thought Job, through association with the wicked, had picked up some of their views (vv.8–9). The counselors in defending God had stressed God's transcendence almost to the point of denying his concern over man. They viewed man in his sin as nothing. Elihu accused Job of talking like a wicked person (v.36) and of being rebellious rather than submissive (v.37). But in 33:23–28 he had shown some understanding of God's free grace in dealing with human waywardness.

Like the counselors, Elihu had a compelling desire to uphold the truth that God always does what is right (vv.10–12). They saw this only in terms of black and white. God punishes and rewards. Elihu presented the sovereign Creator as one who intentionally and momentarily exercised benevolence toward all mankind (vv.13–15). Elihu was zealous to counter Job's complaint that God treats the wicked and the righteous alike (9:22; 10:3; 21:7–8; 24:1–12). This would mean God does evil (vv.10–30). Elihu was convinced Job needed to repent over such a rebellious notion (vv.33–37). He, like Job and the counselors, revealed no knowledge of the events in the divine council. So it appears Elihu was not an angelic messenger from God, for he had a limited perspective and presented, therefore, only a human estimate of Job's spiritual condition.

Apart from the introductory statement (vv.2–4), the chapter divides into three main themes. The quotation of Job and the condemnation of his views (vv.5–9) is followed by a long defense of God (vv.10–30) and then a return to his polemic against Job (vv.31–37).

1–4 In 12:11–12 Job was sarcastic about the bad "food" the counselors had been dishing up to him under the guise of "the wisdom of the aged." Elihu here was determined to show where real wisdom lay, where food may be found that was really good. He called for all who were wise to join him in his banquet of words to find out how good they were.

5–9 The quote in v.5 is accurate. Job used the very words of himself. For v.5a compare 12:4; 13:18; 27:6; and for v.5b compare 27:2. Where he had not used the very words, he used the thoughts of v.5; but he never labeled himself as in v.6, a person "without transgression" (*beʾlî-pāšaʿ;* NIV, "guiltless"). Despite Elihu's claim in 33:32 that it would please him if Job were shown to be in the right, we were told by the narrator that Elihu had already made up his mind; he was angry at Job for justifying himself rather than God (32:2). Here his anger surfaces.

The first half of v.6 presents a special problem. The NIV's "I am considered a liar" (cf. RSV) does not say who considered Job a liar. If it means Job accused God of calling him a liar, there is no evidence for that. If it means the counselors accused Job of this, there is some evidence. Eliphaz said Job had a "crafty tongue" (15:5). Certainly Job accused them of lying about him (13:4). Here in v.6 some modern translations follow the LXX, which reads "He (God) lies about my case" (Pope, NEB). The claim is that a pious scribe changed the Hebrew text for theological reasons. But there is no scribal tradition to support this (as in 32:3). The LXX has its own propensity to change the text for theological reasons. It is interesting that it has a theologically difficult reading here. What makes it unlikely is the absence of any such remark by Job.

The MT is clearly first person. The RV margin (cf. Rowley) is perhaps a better way to handle v.6a: "Should I lie against my right (that is, when I am innocent)?" The latter is close to what Job said in 6:28–29 (cf. 6:14): "Would I lie to your face . . . my integrity is at stake." Their implication that Job was lying is what has drawn this comment; so Elihu may have both 6:28–29 and 15:5 in mind. God's "arrow [that] inflicts an incurable wound" (v.6) is surely based on 16:13 (see Notes on v.6).

In v.7 Elihu drew again from the words of Eliphaz. The latter had said Job "drinks up evil like water" (15:16) and had censured Job for venting his rage against God and shaking his fist at the Almighty and defiantly attacking him (15:25–26). Elihu did not go as far as Eliphaz in accusing Job of this, but it is enough that Job kept company with such people. Verse 9 is not a direct quote from Job. Job had imagined the wicked saying this in 21:15 and then had complained that calamity did not come very often on them (21:17). So it is only by implication that Elihu could accuse Job. His accusation was based on Job's sentiment that the righteous get the same treatment as the wicked.

10–15 Intrinsic to v.9 is the accusation that God is not just. From this point on throughout the next twenty-one verses, Elihu expounded on the theme "God only does right." Notice how he repeated himself to emphasize this theme in vv.10 and 12. Job had wailed "that those who provoke God are secure" (12:6) while one who is "righteous and blameless" is made "a laughingstock" (12:4; cf. 10:3; 21:7–8; 24:1 –12). To Elihu this could mean nothing else than an accusation that God does wrong, and it is unthinkable that God would do wrong. But that does not solve the mystery. Job was probing when he questioned, "Why do the innocent suffer?" Job saw that "the fatherless child is snatched from the breast, the infant of the poor is seized for a debt" (24:9), "the murderer . . . kills the poor and needy" (24:14), "but God charges no one with wrongdoing" (24:12). "No!" said Elihu, "God repays a man for what he has done" (v.11). Whether Job saw it or not, Elihu insisted on that most basic truth. "For truly ['It is unthinkable,' NIV] God cannot perpetrate evil" (v.12).

Up to this point Elihu has not attempted to use logic but has countered Job's problem with a strong affirmation of God's righteousness. Without this affirmation all his words would be meaningless. The righteousness of God is self-evident as truth because of the image of God in man. That is the reason man understands justice. Indeed, that Job had a problem on this issue is in itself a reflection of his Creator's justice, and God cannot be inferior to Job. Elihu's next words get us deeper into the mystery. They infer that God is the Creator and therefore not accountable to Job (v.13). Further, in vv.14–15 he asserts man's complete dependence on the continuing exercise of God's free grace to continue his existence.

16–20 From all this Elihu maintains that man is not in a position to stand as God's judge (v.17). Without God's impartial judgment, especially on those who hold power (vv.18–19), the world would dissolve into hopeless anarchy. Because of his omnipotence, no one can influence him as he actively governs.

21–30 Such impartial governance of the world is typified by God's punishment of the wicked rulers who disregard his ways. This justice lies behind all the order there is, and it is confirmed and guaranteed by God's omniscience as well as his omnipotence. Job had complained over the delay of justice (21:19; 24:1). Elihu maintained that God does not have to set times for inquiry and judgment. His omniscience enables him to judge all the time. God hears the cry of the poor and needy and punishes the wicked openly, but it is his prerogative to remain silent if and when it pleases him (v.29). Even then he keeps his control over individuals and nations for the common good (vv.29c–30). And even then he may use the wicked to punish the wicked and so keep the godless from ruling. But on vv.29–30, see Notes.

31–37 Having closed his defense of God, Elihu resumed admonishing Job. That much is clear, but vv.31–33 are among the most difficult to put together. The NIV has taken some small liberties with v.33 in order to make it a simple and direct call to repentance. The Hebrew of v.33 reads, "Should he pay back (reward) on your terms because you object." It appears Elihu was trying to show Job how untenable his position was by means of an illustration. If a man should repent after God has disciplined him, must God be subject to man's wishes as he governs the world? The implied answer is "Of course not!" But this is what Job expected by making himself equal with God, by accusing God of injustice and demanding God present to him an indictment. Elihu was certain that any wise man he might consult would agree that Job's behavior was like the wicked who multiply words against God. So Job deserved to be tested to the utmost.

Furthermore the illustration in vv.31–32 is probably given to shame Job for lack of contriteness (see Notes for some variations in the way the verses should read). The question in v.33 could be meant to startle Job. Must God recompense (šlm) him for unfair treatment? Obviously not. Again Job's sin was that he arrogantly made himself equal with God and played the part of a rebel (v.37).

Notes

6 For עַל־מִשְׁפָּטִי אֲכַזֵּב (ʿal-mišpāṭi ᵘkazzēḇ, "although I am right, I am considered a liar"), the LXX has "he lies," meaning God. Some maintain the MT was changed to avoid the offensive theology (Dhorme, Pope, NEB et al.). This fits nicely with ʿal-mišpāṭi ("concerning my case"). The NIV may be based on the intransitive Piel (cf. GKC, par. 52 k), but for this reading Gordis (*Job*, p. 386) has a better explanation: the indirect quote, reading, "In spite of my right, they say that I lie." Some want to change the vowels to Niphil (ʾekkāzēḇ, "I am proven a liar"), as in Prov 30:6 (Duhm); but Rowley's suggestion—following the RV margin—"should I lie" seems best. See comments above.

חִצִּי (ḥiṣṣî, "his arrow") is literally "my arrow [is incurable]." Gordis (*Job*, p. 386) calls this a transferred epithet, meaning "the arrow that is in me" (cf. 6:4).

11 On יַמְצִאֶנּוּ (yamṣiʾennû, "he brings upon him"), compare the use of mṣʾ in 31:25.

13 אָרְצָה (ʾarᵉṣāh, "the earth") is possibly an old accusative.

14 אִם־יָשִׂים אֵלָיו לִבּוֹ (ʾim-yāśîm ʾēlāyw libbô, "If it were his intention") is the idiom used in 1:8 and 2:3. See also v.23 below. The RSV follows the LXX and the Oriental Kethiv in reading yašiḇ ("take back") and dropping lēḇ ("heart," "mind").

18 For הַאֲמֹר (haʾᵃmōr, "Is he not the One who says"), the MT has the interrogative hey with the infinitive construct, which means "Is it right to say" (Pope [in loc.] has "Does one say . . ."). The NIV seems to be a combination of the interrogative and the active participle ʾōmēr. The ancient versions (LXX et al.) have the participle with the article: "The One who says" (RSV, NEB, Dhorme). The participle with the article is preferred since v.19 continues the idea with the relative pronoun אֲשֶׁר (ʾᵃšer).

21 Compare 14:16; 24:23; 31:4.

23 It is usually assumed יָשִׂים עוֹד (yāśîm ʿôḏ, "to examine men further") is a haplography and there were two mems; the second word being môʿēḏ ("appointed time"; cf. BHS mg.). "For he has not appointed a time for any man" (RSV). Modern versions and commentaries (Dhorme, Pope) have followed this since it was proposed by Reiske (*Conjecturae in Jobum et Proverbia*, 1779). Gordis (*Job*, in loc.) drops the yod and reads śîm (infinitive, "to set"): "It is not for man to set the time." The NIV keeps the MT with yāśîm as the idiom "pay attention" (cf. v.14) with the ellipsis of lēḇ as in 4:20; 23:6; 24:12; and Isa 41:20 (cf. Driver-Gray, p. 299).

26 In rendering תַּחַת־רְשָׁעִים (taḥaṭ-rᵉšāʿîm), the NIV (RSV) vocalizes the Hebrew as rišᵉʿām ("their wickedness") (cf. Syr.), taking taḥaṭ ("under") to mean "in return for." But Pope cites Ugaritic to show that taḥaṭ can mean "among criminals" (cf. KJV). The unbalanced line has prompted wild emendation (Dhorme, Kissane et al.). Once again we have a case of complimentary parallelism, the middle element—"he punishes (strikes)"—applying equally to both sides of the line.

Verses 29–33 are extremely difficult. Dozens of emendations are suggested, and some critics even leave blank spaces in their translations. The NIV attempts to stay reasonably close to the MT. Below we suggest some readings that will improve the NIV. The LXX omits these verses.

29 The RSV's use of dashes to indicate a parenthesis for this verse does not help. The verse apparently means there is no response to the cries of the needy in v.28. The NIV opts for the Qal (BHS one MS, "be quiet, inactive"). Gordis (*Job*, in loc.) makes a strained attempt to find a root in Arabic for yaršiaʿ ("condemn") that could mean "stir up" without accepting the metathesis yarʿiš ("stir up"). Otherwise Elihu has some reason to think Job has condemned God for his silence (cf. 24:12c).

וְעַל־גּוֹי וְעַל־אָדָם יָחַד (wᵉʿal-gôy wᵉʿal-ʾāḏām yāḥaḏ, "Yet he is over man and nation alike") fits the context much better if we see in yāḥaḏ ("alike") the third masculine singular of the root ḥḏh II (KB; Holladay, *Concise Lexicon*, s.v.), meaning "to see" (Aram.). We see this root in 3:6 (Notes). Thus: "He watches over each nation and each man to keep a godless man from ruling, etc."

31 The NIV's rendering of כִּי־אֶל־אֵל הֶאָמַר (kî-'el-'ēl he'āmar) as "Suppose a man says to God" is based on reading kî-'el-'elōah 'āmar ("If [suppose] to God one says").

Concerning נָשָׂאתִי לֹא אֶחְבֹּל (nāśā'tî lō' 'ehbōl, "I am guilty I will offend no more"), the idiom nś' 'wn ("bear guilt") is what the NIV has in mind with ellipsis of 'wn, because the idiom is common. Dhorme, Pope et al. repoint the text rendering niśśē'tî ("I have been led astray"). The words "no more" could be based on the frequentative use of the imperfect; but considering the unbalanced line, Dhorme (pp. 525–26; cf. Pope) takes the first two letters (bl) of the next verse as dittography and ends this line with 'adê ("still"). With the negative this yields the meaning "no more." He also sees haplography here and so begins the next line with 'ōd ("until"). See below.

32 Concerning בִּלְעֲדֵי אֶחֱזֶה (bil'adê 'ehezeh, "what I cannot see"), Gordis (Job, in loc.) disagrees with Pope, who says bil'adê is meaningless here. It is a preposition with a clause as nomen regens (Gordis), reading literally "apart from what I see." Dhorme reads: "Until I see, do thou instruct me."

33 In הֲמֵעִמְּךָ יְשַׁלְמֶנָּה (hamē'immekā yešalmennāh, "reward you on your terms"), the use of 'im ("with") in 10:13 and 27:11, where "with you" suggests what is in the mind of someone, what he thinks, permits the meaning "in your opinion" or "on your terms" (Dhorme). But "you" in "reward you" is not in the Hebrew. The person is hypothetical, "a man" (v.31) (though Job may be in mind), and the feminine suffix may refer to God's punishment (v.26). Thus read: "Should God make amends for it (his punishment) because you object?" Furthermore the end of the line does not have the word "repent." So if it is a call to repentance, it is being given in a very oblique way.

36 In עַל־תְּשֻׁבֹת בְּאַנְשֵׁי־אָוֶן ('al-tešubōt be'anšê-'āwen, "for answering with a wicked man"), it is not necessary to change the preposition b to k with the LXX and a few MSS (NIV, "like"). Job had been accused of keeping company with evil men (34:8) and so gave answers "with" their help.

---

5. The third speech

35:1–16

¹Then Elihu said:

²"Do you think this is just?
    You say, 'I will be cleared by God.'
³Yet you ask him, 'What profit is it to me,
    and what do I gain by not sinning?'

⁴"I would like to reply to you
    and to your friends with you.
⁵Look up at the heavens and see;
    gaze at the clouds so high above you.
⁶If you sin, how does that affect him?
    If your sins are many, what does that do to him?
⁷If you are righteous, what do you give to him,
    or what does he receive from your hand?
⁸Your wickedness affects only a man like yourself,
    and your righteousness only the sons of men.

⁹"Men cry out under a load of oppression;
    they plead for relief from the arm of the powerful.
¹⁰But no one says, 'Where is God my Maker,
    who gives songs in the night,
¹¹who teaches more to us than to the beasts of the earth
    and makes us wiser than the birds of the air?'

¹²He does not answer when men cry out
    because of the arrogance of the wicked.
¹³Indeed, God does not listen to their empty plea;
    the Almighty pays no attention to it.
¹⁴How much less, then, will he listen
    when you say that you do not see him,
that your case is before him
    and you must wait for him,
¹⁵and further, that his anger never punishes
    and he does not take the least notice of wickedness.
¹⁶So Job opens his mouth with empty talk;
    without knowledge he multiplies words."

Job had raised questions that really disturbed Elihu. In this speech he dealt with several very important issues that arose out of Job's problem about God's justice. Elihu began (vv. 1–3) by showing Job how inconsistent he was to claim in one breath God would vindicate him and then in another to complain he got no profit out of not sinning (cf. 34:9). In other words, if God is so unjust, why did Job want to be vindicated by him? A colloquial way of phrasing the question would be: What is the use of being good if God does not care? Elihu had missed Job's point, that he wanted to be vindicated because he did believe God was just. Of course Job, in his struggle to understand what God was doing, had sent out two signals, one of which Elihu, like the others, had not been able to hear.

In answer to Job's inconsistency (vv. 4–8), Elihu claimed it was God who got no benefit from Job whether he did right or not. God is far too transcendent for man to affect him by his little deeds. Job's righteousness or lack of it affected only people like himself (v. 8).

Another issue grows out of that last statement and centers around Job's concern over God's apparent indifference to the cries of the oppressed (cf. 24:1–12). Elihu maintained that God is not indifferent to people, but people are indifferent to God. People want God to save them; but they are not interested in honoring him as their Creator, Deliverer, and Source of wisdom (vv. 9–11). Human arrogance keeps God from responding to the empty cry for help (vv. 12–13). That is why God had not answered Job. The deafness from God derived from Job's complaints, questions, and challenges that reveal the same kind of arrogance (vv. 14–15). They are words without knowledge (v. 16).

Modern interpreters tend to find Elihu's advice shallow. Andersen (*Job*, pp. 257 –58) sees Elihu as a perfectionist with cruel advice. Should the oppressors in v. 9 arouse the anger of God no matter what the spirituality of those who call for help? Andersen thinks that Elihu was as mechanical in his theology as the counselors, with answers to prayer as well as God's judgments being automatic. And that to Elihu God was manageable and predictable while to Job God had sovereign freedom, but see 36:22–23. All this is a matter of theological balance. Any stress on God's justice at the expense of his grace or on his transcendence at the expense of his immanence is wrong.

No doubt there is a lack of balance in Elihu's advice, but there are also some commendable aspects if we are willing to allow him a margin of error in his overly zealous comments, as we allowed Job in his fits of rage. Zealots tend to be heartless; so we should not be surprised at Elihu's cold analysis of Job's complaints. Job had certainly minimized human responsibility in some of his remarks (7:20) and sounded arrogant enough in 31:35–37 to arouse the ire of a moralist like Elihu.

1–3 Job did not use these very words, but Elihu tried to reproduce two of Job's viewpoints. There is no doubting the first—Job was sure he would be vindicated (v.2; cf. 13:13–19). But where did Job say, "What do I gain by not sinning?" (v.3)? This is derived from his constant complaint that God treats the righteous and wicked alike, a major bone of contention with the wicked counselors. Job felt that, according to the principle of retribution, his suffering was not just. He was found guilty (9:28–29) without charges (10:2). So to Job a desire to be cleared made sense. But Elihu could only see in Job's words the accusation that God is unjust.

4–8 Many feel Elihu's answer is just a borrowing of material already said (but see Gordis, *Job*, pp. 546–53). Verse 4 along with chapter 32 make it clear that Elihu did not view this as a restatement. The relationship between divine transcendence and human behavior was often on Job's mind. Here also Job sounded inconsistent. He saw God as too attentive—the Watcher of men (7:17–20)—and yet so transcendent that he could say to God, "If I have sinned, what have I done to you?" (7:20). And Eliphaz had said, "Can a man be of benefit to God?" (22:2–3). To Elihu God was too transcendent to be either helped by righteousness (v.7) or hurt by sin (v.6). And this is further refined by alluding to two kinds of sin, omission (*ḥṭ'*) and commission (*pš '*), which can neither deprive God nor hurt him in any way.

There is no place in Elihu's theology for doing God's will out of love for him. Man affects only his fellow man by being good or bad (v.9). And though God may punish or reward man as Judge, there is no place for him in the role of a Father who can be hurt or pleased by man.

9–16 Job had devoted an entire speech to the subject of God's apparent indifference to his plight (ch. 23) and the plight of all who suffer and are oppressed (ch. 24). Elihu stated the issue in v.9 and then set about to give an answer. We must keep in mind what he has already said about God's purpose in human suffering. God uses it to teach (discipline) and warn (33:16–22). Or he may remain silent because he is using a tyrant as his instrument of punishment (34:29–30; cf. Isa 10:5–15). Or he may only be restraining his wrath in hope for repentance (33:29–30). It seems Elihu was not totally rigid in his moralistic justice since he allowed for the possibility of a mediating angel who could provide a ransom for the sinner and plead for grace (33:23–24). There is the possibility that those who cry for relief are also sinful and unwilling to bow before God as their Creator (v.10a) and Savior (v.10b). They cry only because of physical pain and not out of spiritual hunger (v.11; see Gordis, *Job*, p. 551).

The "songs in the night" of v.10 are most likely songs of praise as a result of deliverance (cf. "at night his song [*šîr*] is with me," Ps 42:8; but see Notes on *zᵉmirōt*). Verse 11 in the NIV (but see NIV mg. and Notes) refers to the capacity of the divine-image bearer (man) to hear the voice of God in contrast to brute beasts. As Elihu saw it, God does not listen to the cry of men when it comes to him as the empty sound of a brute beast (v.13).

Elihu felt that failure of suffering men to see that their Maker is also the author of wisdom and joy is a sign of arrogance on their part. The interpretation of v.12 is crucial. Are men crying because of the arrogance of the wicked? Or was he saying God does not answer because of the arrogance of the wicked? A comma after the first line of v.12 changes the meaning to the latter thought that continues in v.13.

Job might not be wicked, but he shared this arrogance and so got no answer (v.14). Elihu seems to have been offended by the very idea that Job should consider himself a litigant at God's court.

With his multiplicity of empty words, Job should not have expected to be heard (vv.14–16). Even worse was Job's rebellious spirit—chiding God for hiding his face (13:24; 23:3; cf. v.14) and seeking to march into his presence as an impatient litigant (13:15; 31:35–37). And now, with his case before God, Job dared to complain about waiting for an answer (30:20; cf. v.14c–d) and continued to accuse God of injustice (21:4; 24:1–12; cf. v.15, but see Notes).

Notes

2 The NIV's marginal reading is very unlikely as an option. Even though the preposition מִן (*min*) may express comparison, it is not used that way here in מֵאֵל (*mēʾēl*, "by God"). The MT says literally "my vindication (will be) from [*min*] God."

3 The NIV has rendered לָךְ (*lāk*, "to you") as "to me" because it views this first line in Hebrew as indirect discourse and the second as direct (cf. 19:28). So to make the translation smooth, both are made direct. Some take it all direct and understand the "to you" as a reference to God, which, it is felt, would fit Elihu's response in vv.6–7 better (cf. Driver-Gray, pp. 304–5).

The preposition מִן (*min*) in מֵחַטָּאתִי (*mēḥaṭṭāʾtî*, "by not sinning") is partitive (separative), hence "by not."

6 The verbs תַּעֲשֶׂה־לּוֹ . . . תִּפְעָל־בּוֹ (*tipʿāl-bô . . . taʿᵃśeh-lô*, "that affect him . . . that do to him") may be either second or third person (cf. RSV, "what do you do to him?").

10 Pope renders זְמִרוֹת (*zᵉmirôt*, "songs") "strength" based on the use of *ḏmr* ("mighty") in Arabic and in Ugaritic as an epithet of Baal as "the mighty one." The word also appears in OT proper names like Zimri (Pope, p. 264). No doubt it fits as an epithet of Yahweh in Exod 15:2; Ps 118:14; and Isa 12:2; but there is room for doubt here.

11 In מַלְּפֵנוּ מִבַּהֲמוֹת (*mallᵉpēnû mibbahᵃmôt*, "he teaches more to us than to the beasts"), the verb as Piel participle of *ʾlp* is no problem, though the consonant aleph has contracted. Again the meaning of the preposition *min* is in question. The two NIV margin notes on v.11 present a possible alternate. The meaning would be that God teaches man from (by) nature (cf. Pope). But keeping the comparative force of *min* does not necessarily yield the banal meaning suggested by Pope. That man is wiser than the beasts and birds could mean he alone can hear the voice of God.

12 For the usual local sense "there" for שָׁם (*šām*, untr. in NIV), see the RSV; but some see a temporal sense like the Arabic *tumma* ("then"; Driver-Gray, p. 268; Gordis, *Job*, p. 402). Dahood (*Psalms*, 16:81) suggests from an Amarna gloss *šumma*, "behold."

13 Since שָׁוְא (*šāwᵉ*, "empty [plea]") is masculine, the feminine suffix on לֹא יְשׁוּרֶנָּה (*lōʾ yᵉšûrennāh*, "pays no attention to it") translated "it" refers to all the pleading in the preceding verse (cf. Dhorme, "a pure waste of words"). Gordis's translation (*Job*, p. 402)—"But it is not true that God does not hear"—seems unlikely.

15 For בַּפַּשׁ (*bappaš*), NIV's "of wickedness" follows the ancient versions (see mg.), reading פֶּשַׁע (*pešaʿ*, "transgression"). Gordis (*Job*, pp. 391, 403) has made a good case for occasional elision of ayin in biblical orthography. A few clear cases are in Amos 8:8, where *nišqᵉāh* (Kethiv) stands for *nešqᵉʿāh* (Qere) and Hos 7:6, where *yāšēn* stands for *yaʿᵃšēn*.

6. *The fourth speech*

36:1–37:24

¹Elihu continued:

²"Bear with me a little longer and I will show you
    that there is more to be said in God's behalf.
³I get my knowledge from afar;
    I will ascribe justice to my Maker.
⁴Be assured that my words are not false;
    one perfect in knowledge is with you.

⁵"God is mighty, but does not despise men;
    he is mighty, and firm in his purpose.
⁶He does not keep the wicked alive
    but gives the afflicted their rights.
⁷He does not take his eyes off the righteous;
    he enthrones them with kings
    and exalts them forever.
⁸But if men are bound in chains,
    held fast by cords of affliction,
⁹he tells them what they have done—
    that they have sinned arrogantly.
¹⁰He makes them listen to correction
    and commands them to repent of their evil.
¹¹If they obey and serve him,
    they will spend the rest of their days in prosperity
    and their years in contentment.
¹²But if they do not listen,
    they will perish by the sword
    and die without knowledge.

¹³"The godless in heart harbor resentment;
    even when he fetters them, they do not cry for help.
¹⁴They die in their youth,
    among male prostitutes of the shrines.
¹⁵But those who suffer he delivers in their suffering;
    he speaks to them in their affliction.

¹⁶"He is wooing you from the jaws of distress
    to a spacious place free from restriction,
    to the comfort of your table laden with choice food.
¹⁷But now you are laden with the judgment due the wicked;
    judgment and justice have taken hold of you.
¹⁸Be careful that no one entices you by riches;
    do not let a large bribe turn you aside.
¹⁹Would your wealth
    or even all your mighty efforts
    sustain you so you would not be in distress?
²⁰Do not long for the night,
    to drag people away from their homes.
²¹Beware of turning to evil,
    which you seem to prefer to affliction.

²²"God is exalted in his power.
    Who is a teacher like him?
²³Who has prescribed his ways for him,
    or said to him, 'You have done wrong'?
²⁴Remember to extol his work,
    which men have praised in song.

²⁵ All mankind has seen it;
    men gaze on it from afar.
²⁶ How great is God—beyond our understanding!
    The number of his years is past finding out.

²⁷ "He draws up the drops of water,
    which distill as rain to the streams;
²⁸ the clouds pour down their moisture
    and abundant showers fall on mankind.
²⁹ Who can understand how he spreads out the clouds,
    how he thunders from his pavilion?
³⁰ See how he scatters his lightning about him,
    bathing the depths of the sea.
³¹ This is the way he governs the nations
    and provides food in abundance.
³² He fills his hands with lightning
    and commands it to strike its mark.
³³ His thunder announces the coming storm;
    even the cattle make known its approach.

^{37:1} At this my heart pounds
    and leaps from its place.
² Listen! Listen to the roar of his voice,
    to the rumbling that comes from his mouth.
³ He unleashes his lightning beneath the whole heaven
    and sends it to the ends of the earth.
⁴ After that comes the sound of his roar;
    he thunders with his majestic voice.
  When his voice resounds,
    he holds nothing back.
⁵ God's voice thunders in marvelous ways;
    he does great things beyond our understanding.
⁶ He says to the snow, 'Fall on the earth,'
    and to the rain shower, 'Be a mighty downpour.'
⁷ So that all men he has made may know his work,
    he stops every man from his labor.
⁸ The animals take cover;
    they remain in their dens.
⁹ The tempest comes out from its chamber,
    the cold from the driving winds.
¹⁰ The breath of God produces ice,
    and the broad waters become frozen.
¹¹ He loads the clouds with moisture;
    he scatters his lightning through them.
¹² At his direction they swirl around
    over the face of the whole earth
    to do whatever he commands them.
¹³ He brings the clouds to punish men,
    or to water his earth and show his love.

¹⁴ "Listen to this, Job;
    stop and consider God's wonders.
¹⁵ Do you know how God controls the clouds
    and makes his lightning flash?
¹⁶ Do you know how the clouds hang poised,
    those wonders of him who is perfect in knowledge?
¹⁷ You who swelter in your clothes
    when the land lies hushed under the south wind,
¹⁸ can you join him in spreading out the skies,
    hard as a mirror of cast bronze?

19 "Tell us what we should say to him;
　we cannot draw up our case because of our darkness.
20 Should he be told that I want to speak?
　Would any man ask to be swallowed up?
21 Now no one can look at the sun,
　bright as it is in the skies
　after the wind has swept them clean.
22 Out of the north he comes in golden splendor;
　God comes in awesome majesty.
23 The Almighty is beyond our reach and exalted in power;
　in his justice and great righteousness, he does not oppress.
24 Therefore, men revere him,
　for does he not have regard for all the wise in heart?"

Elihu needed a little more time to develop fully his defense of God's justice. His earlier apology had been designed to disarm Job by a spirit of self-abnegation (32:1 –33:7). Here, still full of words, he wanted Job to become aware of his credentials as God's messenger (vv.1–4).

First Elihu presented his premise that God is mighty and firm of purpose (v.5). That purpose is stated—God will not grant life to the wicked but always grants the rights of those who are wronged (v.6). He then proceeded to tell how that purpose is carried out (vv.6–10). No matter what life may bring, whether chains or affliction, God never takes his eyes off the righteous but uses their troubles for disciplinary instruction and to call them to repentance (vv.7–10). Responding to his call determines the course of a person's life and his fate—obey and live under his blessing; disobey and die in bitter resentment (vv.11–14).

A new stanza begins in v.15 (or possibly v.16) in which Elihu applied his message to Job. Having forsaken his condemnatory spirit (35:14–16), Elihu sought to comfort Job with the possibility of deliverance (v.15a). It was time Job saw the hand of God in his suffering. God uses affliction to amplify his voice and thus obtain man's attention (v.15). Job must understand that God was wooing him from the jaws of adversity, from slavery and oppression to freedom and comfort (vv.16–17).

Verses 18–21 are a further warning to Job probably about the dangers of prosperity and of turning to evil. But the translation of vv.18–20 is very uncertain (see NIV mg. and Notes below).

In v.22 Elihu completed his theme on God's purpose in human suffering by returning to his original premise: the greatness of God's power and the uniqueness of his ways (vv.22–23). Indeed his power guarantees his purposes, for in his sovereign freedom he has no one to whom he must give an account (v.23). He is also the perfect teacher who makes no mistakes. Job would do well to sit at the Master's feet and learn that his hand never does wrong. Then Job would be prepared to extol God and his work (vv.24, 26). Elihu, at this point, was so overwhelmed by the greatness of God that he burst forth into a hymn of praise. Its theme is the mystery of God's ways in nature. But Elihu's real purpose was to impress Job with the mystery of God's ways in providence. The two sometimes coincide (37:13).

The hymn extols the work of God in the autumnal rain. It is his hand that distills the drops, pours out the moisture on earth, and thus provides for the needs of man (vv.27–28). With flashing lightning and the crash of his thunder, God ushers in the winter season with its drenching rain and driving winds, its ice and snow, so that man and all God's creatures see his power on display (vv.29–30).

After this hymn Elihu asked Job a series of humbling questions about the mysteries of nature (37:14–18). If Job could not understand how God performs these marvels much less assist him, how then could he understand the far less obvious mysteries of God's providence (vv.19–20).

A final lesson from nature captured Elihu's imagination. When the winter is past and the skies are swept of clouds, the sun reigns supreme, and so does God in his golden splendor (vv.21–22). With this suggestion of divine theophany, Elihu returned again to his original premise about God's power and good purpose for man (v.23) as the reason for us to worship him (v.24).

Elihu's fourth speech was clearly designed as a preparation for the theophany that follows. Critics maintain it was written later and borrows from the divine speeches. Even if that is the case (cf. Gordis, who says the same author wrote this later in life), the material is still an integral part of the book consciously performing a literary purpose that appears to be twofold: to give another human perspective free from the heat of the debate and to prepare the reader (and Job) for the theophany.

1–4 Elihu was a little apologetic over the fact that he had even more to say in defense of God (v.1). Had he not claimed, however, to be bursting with words (32:15–20)? Interpreters have generally misunderstood the claim he was making for himself here (v.4). In 37:16 Elihu described God as "perfect in knowledge." That he should so describe himself (v.4b) has elicited the remark from Rowley that "Elihu is a stranger to modesty."

Kline (WBC, p. 485) suggests the words "one perfect in knowledge" (v.4b) possibly refers to God, as similar terminology does in 37:16. It is certainly unlikely Elihu would claim for himself the same perfection he attributes to God. Habel (*Job*, 1985, p. 494) uses the word "reasoning" instead of "knowledge" here and uses "mind" in 32:6, 10, and 17. But H.L. Ginsburg long ago suggested that the word used here and in 32:6, 10 comes from a cognate root that limits Elihu's perfection to his speech (Arab. *d'w*, "to call"; cf. Pope, p. 243, on H.L. Ginsberg and the Qumran Targum). That meaning is strengthened here by the feminine plural *millāy* ("my words") in v.4a paralleling the feminine plural *dē'ôt* ("utterances") in v.4b. On this basis Elihu was claiming to be one "perfect of utterance" because his speech derived from God (see Notes on v.3) who is the source of perfect words.

It is interesting that in 37:16, where he was speaking of God's perfect knowledge (words are not the subject), Elihu used the masculine plural (of majesty) as a divine appellative. Here, however, he used the feminine plural in agreement with "my words" (*millāy*) in v.4a.

5–14 Everything Elihu said from here on rests on the affirmation in v.5. See the Notes below for the reasons for a slightly different translation that reads: "God is mighty, he does not despair (faint);/ he is mighty and firm in his purpose."

God's power assures the fulfillment of his purpose. In this purpose God will never grant life to the wicked but will always see that those who are afflicted receive justice. Verses 6–7 must be understood as God's ultimate purpose since vv.8–12 are conditional. Elihu was making room for Job's complaints about the suffering of the righteous and the prosperity of the wicked. He was also answering Job's frustration over God's surveillance (7:17–21). God never takes his eyes off the righteous. But in order to eventually enthrone them, he must discipline them for their own good.

The key word in this passage is *mûsār* ("correction") in v.10. As a wisdom word used often in the Proverbs, it includes all that God does to teach human beings his wisdom by means of his commandments (v.10b) or by circumstances (v.8). God's unfainting purpose is to reach the hearts of people, if necessary by "cords of afflic-tion" (v.8b). In v.10 he makes them listen (Heb., "uncovers their ears") "to correc-tion," or perhaps "by the correction," that is, he gets their attention and then calls for repentance.

Once attention is gained, obedience leads to life (v.11) and disobedience leads to death (v.12). These verses sound like a message of prosperity and doom not signifi-cantly different than that of the counselors. But that might be an unfair judgment because Elihu was emphasizing the fact that the righteous are afflicted, a point mentioned by Eliphaz (5:17–18) but abandoned especially with reference to Job.

15–21 Elihu disapproved Job's contention that the wicked prosper; and even though he agreed that the righteous suffer, it was only because of their waywardness, which needs correction. So there was hope for Job. Elihu did not really face the issue of the suffering of the innocent. He assumed in v.9 that the afflicted always had done something for which they were being punished. Job, however, could be rescued by (v.15a; NIV has "in," but the preposition *b* could also mean "from") his suffering if he heard the voice of God wooing him away from the jaws of distress (v.16).

There are few verses in the entire OT that are more difficult to translate than 17 –20 in this chapter. The difficulty does not arise from the meaning of individual words but from the fact that they are so difficult to put together. The text may be disturbed, but more likely it is the rare meaning of key words that escapes us. The translations vary greatly. Most make it a sharp rebuke of Job (Pope, JB, TEV) for being unjust and for misuse of his power and wealth.

The following translation of vv.17–21 varies somewhat with the NIV by softening the tone without emending the Hebrew text. Explanations may be found in the Notes below.

> 17"Since you have had your fill of judgment due the wicked,
>   since judgment and justice have taken hold (of you),
> 18beware that no one entice you to want riches again.
>   Do not let the great price you are paying mislead you.
> 19Of what value was your wealth apart from affliction?
>   And of what value are all your mighty efforts?
> 20Do not long for the night,
>   when peoples will vanish from their place.
> 21Beware of turning to evil,
>   for that is why you are tested by affliction."

Elihu was admonishing Job to learn the lesson God was trying to teach him through his suffering. He warned Job not to allow his suffering to influence his judgment (v.17). Job would someday realize his affliction was of more value to him than his wealth and all his efforts to justify himself (v.18). He should not have longed for the tribunal of the terrible Judge (the night) but learned the lesson of submission God was teaching him through affliction (vv.20–21).

22–26 In a real sense these verses are both the climax of the preceding section and the first stanza of a hymn of praise. Elihu returned to the theme he began with—the power of God. The stanza has an introverted pattern:

> a God is great in power and a sovereign teacher (v.22).
>   b Man cannot prescribe his ways or judge his purpose (v.23).
>   c Therefore praise him in song (v.24).

b' Man sees his power from afar (v.25).
a' God is great, beyond understanding (v.26).

Elihu considered God's power and wisdom as the themes Job should dwell on rather than God's justice. The wisdom of the great Teacher (cf. 34:32; 35:11) assures the justice of his actions, and his power makes certain his wise purposes will be fulfilled. God's ways derive from his sovereign freedom (v.23a). This rules out man's right to question God's moral conduct (v.23b). Because man sees God's work at a great distance, he cannot understand it completely; so he who is wise will look on it with delight and praise (v.24). Elihu was here preparing the way for the theophany when Job would finally see his sovereign Lord and learn about his dominion. In v.26 Elihu was not saying we cannot know God (NEB, RSV) but that we cannot fully understand his greatness.

From 36:27 to 37:13 the hymn continues by extolling God's power in the elements. Having admonished Job about praising God for his work (v.24), Elihu here illustrated God's work in nature. The highly anthropomorphic terms are typical of this poetic genre (cf. Ps 18:7–15). Following the hymn Elihu closed his speech with admonitions to Job based on its contents (37:14–24).

27–33 Here we see God's active greatness in his creation as demonstrated by the rain cycle. Rain in the OT world was considered one of the most needed and obvious blessings of God. The phenomenon of condensation (v.27b) and precipitation (v.28), while not technically understood, was certainly observable. But evaporation (v.27) is not. Duhm therefore considered this proof that the Elihu speeches came a few centuries later than the divine speeches since such meteorological knowledge would have been obtained from the Greeks (cf. Driver-Gray, p. 315). Pope sees in Genesis 2:6 and in the Flood account a belief in cosmic reservoirs—above and below the earth—that rain comes from. But Pope's translation (pp. 267, 273) does not seem to fit completely with that notion: "He draws the waterdrops that distill from the flood." Elihu did not need a knowledge of physics since God is the one who does this (an idea even we who know the physics can still affirm), but he may have known more about the phenomenon than Pope is willing to admit (see Notes).

The Hebrew word for "his pavilion" (v.29) is rendered "his canopy" in Psalm 18:11, which the parallel line in the psalm clearly defines as "the dark rain clouds of the sky." In v.30 "bathing the depths of the sea" might be rendered "lights up the depths of the sea" since "to cover (bathe)" with lightning is equivalent to lighting up. See Notes on "the depths of the sea" (v.30). Verse 31 can be understood in context if we allow the speaker the privilege to use a parenthesis; so there is no need to move the verse (NEB, Pope). Verses 29–30, as descriptive of the storm, form such a parenthesis; and v.31 refers back to the showers of v.28. The NIV margin (v.31) suggests the reading: "by them [the showers] he nourishes the nations" rather than "governs" (see Notes). If the latter meaning is chosen, it would be better rendered "to judge or punish" since the word rarely (if ever) means "govern." Judging or punishing by the storm is conceivable in terms of God's use of lightning. The parallelism in v.31 favors the rarer meaning of the margin, but v.32 would favor the text.

Kline's comment on v.32 (WBC, p. 486) makes the anthropomorphism even more vivid. The Hebrew carefully uses the dual for hands (optional even for clapping, cf. 2 Kings 11:12). The use of "both hands" produces the figure of "expertly hurled missiles of warriors in the elite ambidextrous corps (36:32; cf. *Iliad* 21:183; I Chr 12:2)"(ibid.). So when the lightning performs God's purpose in striking its mark, it is against those he chooses to punish (37:13).

Verse 33 is very difficult. Many interpretations are given. The NIV text has sought to follow the Masoretic vocalization but even so had to make an arbitrary choice for the precise meaning. "The coming storm" (lit., "concerning it [or] him") could mean God's approach (cf. NIV mg.). But the margin rendering requires a different set of vowels for the second line (see Notes).

37:1–13 Andersen (*Job,* in loc.) sees a unit in vv.1–5 formed by two bicola (vv.1, 5) and two tricola (vv.2, 4) centered about a single line about lightning (v.3b). But notice how the hymn moves from precipitation in 36:27–28 to lightning in 36:29–32 then to thunder in 36:33–37:5 and back to precipitation in 37:6. The stanza on thunder (36:33–37:5) has an introverted pattern: ABCB'A'. Verse 36:33 (A) forms an inclusion with 37:5 (A'). The two quatrains (vv.1–2 [B] and 4 [B'] NIV) that stress how terrifying the sound is flank a bicolon about lightning (v.3) (C).

Elihu was impressed with God's voice as his word of dominion and power. By fiat he controls the snow and rain (v.6), and thunder is nothing less than the roar of his voice—a typical OT metaphor (cf. Ps 29). Elihu's heart pounded as God put on an awesome display of his power. The passage continues to reveal a keen observation of atmospheric conditions and their effects. Possibly evaporation and clearly the distillation of rain water was mentioned in 36:27. The clouds are reservoirs of moisture (v.11a) and arenas of lightning (v.11b). In their cyclonic movement (v.12), the clouds are subject to God's commands and perform his will. Elihu saw a direct relationship between God's rule over nature and his dominion over the affairs of man (v.13). He had already begun to anticipate the reasoning in the divine speeches. Critics claim this is evidence of the plagiarism of a later author. Others find it in keeping with what is evident all through the dialogue (Andersen, *Job,* p. 266, n. 2). Still others see Elihu's role as a divinely sent forerunner preparing the way for the theophany— a motif most notably expressed in Isaiah 40:3–5 and Malachi 4:5–6.

Verse 13 is a thematic climax that lists ways God may use the storm. Elihu wanted to do more than impress Job with God's power in nature. Here he showed how the mystery of God's ways in nature coincide with the mystery of his ways in providence. When God's purpose is corrective, as punishment for the wicked (Ps 18:11 –19), the storm is often connected with the deliverance of his people, thus demonstrating his covenant love (Josh 10:11; 1 Sam 7:10–11; Ps 105:32–33). God may also, however, demonstrate his covenant love by sending the rain in season (Deut 11:13 –17). The opposite (drought) is in view in vv.17–18 and that has prompted the NIV to insert the word "water" into the phrase "to his earth" (v.13). The addition is not needed, for there appear to be three totally different purposes for the storm in v.13: to punish, to show his love, and for his own pleasure (*le'arṣô;* see Notes on v.13). The last anticipates a concept limited to the divine speeches (cf. 38:26); one that could be missed without careful attention. Some things that God does have no other explanation than that they please him. Having arrived at this amazing point, Elihu was prepared to apply this truth to Job's situation.

14–20 The questioning format anticipates the divine method in the upcoming speeches. Job needed to stop and think of how absurd his position was. He was asked to supply knowledge he obviously did not have and was chided for his abysmal ignorance in the light of God's perfect knowledge (vv. 15–16). Verses 17–18 go together. Sweltering in the heat of the dry season with the sky like a brazen mirror, Job sat helpless. He could not do anything about the weather but endure it. How then can a mere creature, so lacking in knowledge and strength, expect to understand God's justice (vv. 19–20)? Elihu's switch to the first person in vv. 19–20 may be an attempt to soften the blow on Job's ego. Had Job not drawn up his case, affixed his signature, and called for an audience with God?

21–24 Elihu shifted his attention from his moral application back to a contemplation of the elements. But it was only to make an even more forceful moral application. After the storm, with the clearing skies (v. 21), comes the sun in its brilliance; likewise in golden splendor and awesome majesty God comes from his heavenly abode (ṣāpôn, "the north," v. 22; cf. 26:7 and Introduction). Elihu admonished Job that he needed to see God as God, almighty and morally perfect (v. 23), and prove he was wise in heart by worshiping (fearing) him (see Notes on v. 24).

Notes

36:3 Concerning אֶשָּׂא דֵעִי (ʾeśśāʾ dēʿî, "I get my knowledge"), it was noted above in the comments on vv. 1–4 that in v. 4 "speech" is preferred over "knowledge." But "knowledge" or "opinion" is more likely here.

5 Most emend וְלֹא יִמְאָס (welōʾ yimʾās, "but he does not despise"). Dhorme, Pope, Gordis, Driver-Gray et al. complain of the lack of balance in the line and emend the second כַּבִּיר (kabbîr, "mighty") to בְּבַר (bebar, "pure") and drop or transfer כֹּחַ (kōaḥ, "firm," "strong"), reading: "He does not despise the pure in heart." A major reason given for the emendation is the lack of an object for yimʾās. NIV's "men" is not in the text (cf. RSV, "any"). For a solution to this difficulty see 7:5, where the byform of mss ("melt") is spelled mʾs. Compare the same in Ps 58:8: "the wicked melt like water." This word (root) "melt" is used figuratively meaning "faint" or "despair" in 6:14 and 9:23. That meaning fits this text beautifully: "God is mighty, he does not despair (faint);/ he is mighty and firm in his purpose."

6 It is better to render לֹא־יְחַיֶּה (lōʾ-yeḥayyeh, "he does not keep . . . alive") "he does (or will) not grant life" with the parallel "he grants (or will grant) justice." The tense is open. The same openness is true in v. 7. The converted waws at the end of v. 7 and in vv. 9–10 have no tense significance.

12 For בְּשֶׁלַח (bešelaḥ, "by the sword"), the NIV margin—*"will cross the River"*—is preferred (cf. 33:18 Notes).

14 בַּקְּדֵשִׁים (baqqedēšîm, "among male prostitutes of the shrines") points to one of the horrors of the OT world, the temple prostitution tied to the fertility cult. No doubt children committed for ritual prostitution died young. In Deut 23:17–18 (cf. P.C. Craigie, *The Book of Deuteronomy* [Grand Rapids: Eerdmans, 1976], p. 301) the practice is forbidden in Israel (cf. 1 Kings 14:24; 15:12; 22:46; 2 Kings 23:7).

17 Concerning מָלֵאתָ (mālēʾtā, "But now you are laden"), Elihu's purpose was not to condemn Job but to try to get him to see the disciplinary value of God's use of judgment. We have therefore softened this verse by making it concessive and using the English perfect tense (see comments above, p. 1024).

18 כִּי־חֵמָה (kî-ḥēmāh) literally reads "For anger." The NIV reads this as an imperative hᵃmēh ("see"), an Aramaism from the root ḥmy, hence "Be careful" (cf. Pope).

The NIV aligns בְסָפֶק (besāpeq, "by riches") with śepeq ("riches," "plenty") in 20:22 and not as rendered in 27:23, where the same spelling means "clap," whence RSV gets "scoffing."

The NIV renders וְרַב־כֹּפֶר (weʾrāb̠-kōper) as "a large bribe"; but the word kōper is never used as "a bribe." It is usually "a ransom," "a price," whether ritual or otherwise.

19 For הֲיַעֲרֹךְ שׁוּעֲךָ (haʾyaʿaʾrōk̠ šûʿak̠ā), NIV arrives at "Would your wealth . . . sustain you" by an inference from the common meaning "set in battle array" and therefore "protect." From this the translators arrived at "sustains." But this seems far-fetched and requires another "you" that is not in the text. The verb also means "to evaluate" (Hiphil), hence our "of what value was your wealth" (see comments).

For לֹא בְצָר (lōʾ b̠eʾṣār), the NIV has again inserted more into the translation ("so you would not be in distress") than the Hebrew warrants. For the meaning "apart from" (lōʾ + b̠), cf. 4:21; 34:20 (see our translation above).

20 Concerning לַעֲלוֹת עַמִּים (laʿaʾlôt̠ ʿammîm, "to drag people away"), in Ps 102:24 (NIV) this verb clearly means in the Hiphil "to take away one's life." But since ʿammîm ("peoples") usually refers to nations, Job was being warned about a great catastrophe such as war or a plague.

21 בָּחַרְתָּ (bāharṭā, "you seem to prefer") includes the idea of making a choice by testing (cf. 34:4; Prov 10:20; Isa 48:10).

27 גָּרַע (gāraʿ) in the Qal means "to hinder" (15:4), "to limit" (15:8), and "take away" (36:7). Here the Piel—יְגָרַע (yeʾgāraʿ, "he draws up")—seems to mean "withdraw" as in v.7. Andersen (Job, in loc.; cf. also Driver-Gray, p. 282) suggests the possibility that נִטְפֵי־מָיִם (niṭpê-māyim, "drops of water") be read יָם נֹטְפִים (niṭpîm yām, "drops [from] the sea"), which is even more descriptive of evaporation.

The NIV translation of לְאֵדוֹ (leʾēd̠ô) as "to the streams") is in part based on the same interpretation of this rare word in Gen 2:6. Pope (p. 273) ties the word to the subterranean flood of Akkadian mythology. He explains the suffix as modification of the vocalic ending on the Akkadian (Sumerian) word edû. The mythological imagery need not be carried as far as Pope does, who posits two cosmic reservoirs, one above and one below the earth. Pope renders the line "that distill rain from the flood"; "from" being a rare possibility for the Hebrew ל (l) based on Ugaritic. The usual meaning for ʾēd̠ ("mist"; KJV, RSV, NIV mg.), unfortunately, has no philological support according to E.A. Speiser (Genesis, AB, vol. 1 [New York: Doubleday, 1964], pp. 14, 16).

28 The NIV takes the antecedent of the relative pronoun אֲשֶׁר (aʾšer) to be "the drops" in v.27a and for clarity supplies "their moisture." The verb is usually intransitive; so it may be better to read "which pour down from the clouds."

Concerning אָדָם רָב (ʾādām rāb̠, "abundant showers on mankind"), the meaning "showers" for rāb̠ (cf. reʾb̠îb̠îm, Deut 32:2) is proven by the parallel pair rb ("showers") and ar ("lightning") in Ugaritic (Fisher, Ras Shamra, 1:79). אוֹרוֹ (ʾôrô, "his lightning") in v.30 is an example of distant parallelism. Repointing ʾādām ("mankind") to aʾdāmāh ("the ground") (Dahood, Pope) is possible but not necessary.

29 אַף אִם־יָבִין (ʾap ʾim-yāb̠în, "Who can understand") is more literally, "Indeed, can one understand?" But that means "Who can?" Emending to מִי (mî, "who") is unwarranted (cf. BHS).

30 Concerning וְשָׁרְשֵׁי הַיָּם (weʾšoršê hayyām, "the depth of the sea"), many feel "he covers the roots of the sea" (with lightning) does not make sense. So many emendations are proposed, none of which are worth repeating. Pope's attempt to mythologize the verse by seeing the preposition עָלָיו (ʿālāyw, "about him") as Aliy, a Ugaritic epithet for the weather god, seems misguided in a book so dedicated to monotheism. Pope repoints כִּסָּה (kissāh, "he covers") to כִּסְאוֹ (kisseʾô, "his throne") and reads "the roots of the sea are his throne." But the idea in this text is not far-fetched. In Hab 3:3 God's "majesty covers" (kissāh) the heavens; so why should not his lightning flashes cover the roots (depths) of the sea?

31 The NIV renders בָּם יָדִין (b̠ām yād̠în) "This is the way he governs." If, according to Pope, the roots of the sea are *Aliy's* throne, why does he not govern the nations from them? Instead Pope moves v.31 to follow v.28 so that the nations can be "nourished" (*yādîn* is taken as a dialectical form of *yāzîn*, "nourish") from the drops of rain (v.27). We see no problem with the dialectical form meaning "he nourishes" (cf. NIV mg.), with *bām* ("by them") referring to the clouds of rain.

32 For עַל־כַּפַּיִם כִּסָּה־אוֹר (*'al-kappayim kissāh-'ôr*, "He fills his hands with lightning"), Gordis's resort (*Job*, p. 422) to Mishnaic Hebrew ("the double arch of heaven" for *kappayim*) to avoid the mythological imagery is just as misguided as Pope's attempt (p. 276) to turn the text into mythic literature ("lightning . . . may seem . . . to prance in the palms of the storm-god"). For the imagery compare Ps 18:14: "He shot his arrows . . . great bolts of lightning." Again the verb *kissāh* ("he fills" ["covers"]) has caused some consternation. Dhorme emends to *niśśa'* ("he lifts") and Pope to *nassāh* ("it flickers, prances"). The "covering of both hands (dual) with lightning" is like the prophet's words—"rays flashed from his hand, where his power was hidden" (Hab 3:4)—but here the figure is probably drawn from the ambidextrous corps mentioned in 1 Chron 12:2 as noted above.

33 The NIV (text) understands עָלָיו (*'ālāyw*, "concerning it") to be "the storm"; but the margin, which reads "announces his coming—/ the One zealous against evil," understands the antecedent as God. In this reading the second line requires *miqneh* ("cattle") be pointed *maqneh* (or *meqanneh*), "One zealous," and *'ôleh* ("[its] approach") becomes ' *awlāh* ("evil"). Gordis (*Job*, p. 424) makes a case on the basis of analogy, not direct usage, that *miqneh 'āp* means "the wrath of indignation." He follows Perles in taking *'al-'ôleh* ("concerning what rises") as the Aramaic *'il 'olāh* ("whirlwind"), yielding: "His thunder-clap proclaims his presence; his mighty wrath, the storm." This is an attractive possibility since it requires only slight vocalic change, but it is difficult to be dogmatic about a line with so many pitfalls.

37:2 The plural imperative with the infinitive שִׁמְעוּ שָׁמוֹעַ (*šime'û šāmôa'*, "Listen, listen") may be a stylistic trait. Since it occurred in 13:17 and 21:2, Gordis (*Job*, p. 425) thinks it points to single authorship. That it is plural rather than singular should not be stressed, for that is part of the idiom with the implied subject being indefinite.

3 The verb יִשְׁרֵהוּ (*yišrēhû*, "he unleashes him") is usually taken as an Aramaic *šrh* ("to let loose"; cf. Dan 5:16). The NIV substitutes "lightning" for the suffix "him." Gordis's *yōšer* ("strength") (*Job*, p. 425), while phonologically acceptable, must be rejected since it is not clearly attested; and Ugaritic uses this verb in the same way—*šrh larṣ brqm* ("he flashes lightning to the earth") (cf. Pope, p. 280). But whether it means "flashes" or "lets loose" is a moot question.

4 The problem with וְלֹא יְעַקְּבֵם (*welō' ye'aqqebēm*, "he holds nothing back") is the suffix *ēm*. It is not the pronoun "them" ("the lightnings," cf. RSV) since in v.3 that is singular. The NIV agrees with Pope that it is an enclitic particle but disagrees with his changing the subject from God to men. Pope has "men stay not when his voice is heard."

6 Concerning הֱוֵא (*hewē'*, "Fall"), BDB (p. 217, *hwh,* and p. 224, *hyh*) notes the full meaning of the verb that includes "fall out," hence "to happen." But in Arabic the root simply means "to fall down, descend," which would be the meaning here. The observation of Rowley that it is found only here in the OT will need revision if we are correct in seeing it in 24:18 (q.v. Notes).

7 In rendering בְּיַד־כָּל־אָדָם יַחְתּוֹם (*beyad-kol-'ādām yaḥtôm*) "he stops every man from his labor," the NIV is translating *ad sensum* from the literal: "he sets a seal on the hand of all mankind." Gordis (*Job*, p. 426; id., "A Note on yad," JBL 62 [1942]: 341–44) cites 9:7, where this verb (*ḥtm*) is used with the preposition *be'ad* (cf. Gen 7:16), and the Tell El-Amarna Canaanite glosses to prove *beyad* here is a divergent form of *be'ad*. The line then should be rendered "he shuts up (seals up) all mankind." Like the animals in the next verse, the snow and rain also shut man in.

For לָדַעַת כָּל־אַנְשֵׁי מַעֲשֵׂהוּ (*lāda'at kol-'anšê ma'aśēhû*), the NIV's "So that all men he has made may know his work" has a double reading of the Hebrew. It reads either "he has made" or "his work." The MT's "men of his work" means "whom he has made," but this leaves *lāḏaʿaṯ* without an object. The NEB dug up an unknown meaning for *daʿaṯ* ("stand idle"); others emend to *ʾenōš* ("[every] man") or *ʾanāšîm* ("[all] men"), reading "that all men may know his work."

11 The most popular modern emendation of בְּרִי (*berî*, "with moisture") to *bārāq* ("thunderbolt") or *bārāḏ* ("hail") (Beer, Budde, Gray, Dhorme, Pope) is phonologically unnecessary. Driver-Gray (2:291) noted the regular contraction *ri* from *rewi* ("saturation") from the root *rwh*, as *ʾi, ki, ʾi* are from *ʾwh, kwh, and ʿwh*. The emendation to *bārāq* is based on the parallelism, but every parallel is not synonymous, as is evident in the next verse. See Gordis (*Job*, p. 428) on the meaning of the verb *ṭrḥ* ("to load").

13 In the NIV's rendering of אִם־לְאַרְצוֹ (*ʾim-leʾarṣô*) as "or to water his earth," the words "to water" are supplied. The MT reads "whether for the rod, or for his earth (land) or for (his) love." Many have suggested the verb here is *rṣh* ("be pleased with") with prefixed aleph as in *ʾaḥawāṯî* ("my declaration") in 13:17 (cf. Pope, p. 283) and Dahood ("Job," p. 72). The translation would be "he brings the clouds for correction, or for his own good pleasure, or to show his love." It seems reasonable here to assume Elihu anticipated an important idea found in the divine speeches—that some things God does because it pleases him, and no other explanation need be given (cf. Andersen, *Job*, p. 266, esp. n. 2). The NIV margin assumes the same root but uses the nuance "to find favor" and makes the singular pronoun a collective for "men": "or to favor them and show his love."

15 For בְּשׂוּם (*beśûm*, "controls"), the idiom is (*śûm* + ʿ *al*: "put (a command) upon" (cf. Exod 5:8). The object is understood. The idiom is not unlike the use of *śim* with ellipsis of the object *lēḇ* ("mind"; cf. 4:20; 23:6; 24:12; 34:23).

16 On תְּמִים דֵּעִים (*temîm dēʿîm*, "who is perfect in knowledge"), compare the note on 36:4; but here the context is different. As an epithet of deity it is not so clear that *dēʿîm* means "speech" here. There is no parallel with "words" as in 36:4. The context is about "deeds," but compare Pope's references (p. 285) to Akkadian divine epithets regarding the perfection of divine speech. God does his deeds by fiat (v.15a).

22 Concerning מִצָּפוֹן זָהָב (*miṣṣāpôn zāhāḇ*, "out of the north . . . in golden splendor"), Dhorme defends the translation "golden splendor" or "rays" as the full meaning of *zāhāḇ* ("gold"). The supposed problem that the sun's rays do not come from the north neglects two matters. First, Elihu was here speaking of God, not the sun (cf. NIV); and, second, the word *ṣāpôn* is not here "the north" but God's heavenly abode (Isa 14:13–14), as we have noted in the Notes on 26:7 and in the Introduction (p. 871). Pope gives the Ugaritic parallels to Baal's abode, but his literal interpretation of "gold" as the gold in Baal's palace on Mount Zaphon is hardly necessary. Gordis (*Job*, in loc.) follows the LXX, which has "the clouds shining like gold," but this leaves the other side of the line dangling.

In עַל־אֱלוֹהַּ (*ʿal-ʾelôah*, "God comes"), the *ʿal* is usually taken as the preposition "upon," thus "upon God is" becomes in the RSV "God is clothed." Blommerde's treatment of *ʿal* as the divine epithet *ʾēl* ("The Most High") is likely. It is not clear whether the NIV is repeating the "comes" from the first colon or interprets *ʿal* as a verb or takes it as a preposition without inserting the word "clothed."

24 Turning לֹא־יִרְאֶה (*lōʾ-yirʾeh*) into a question ("for does he not have regard for") is the NIV's way of handling a difficult problem. The NIV margin is hardly justifiable (cf. RSV). The idea that the truly wise of heart are beneath God's notice is contrary to all wisdom thinking. Andersen (*Job*, p. 268) sees the line as an example of a repeated word where the second spelling was left defective (cf. id., "Orthography in Repetitive Parallelism," JBL 89 [1970]: 343–44), making it look like the verb *rʾh* ("see") instead of *yrʾ* ("fear"). The full spelling would be *yirʾuhû* ("they [all the wise of heart] fear him"). The *lōʾ* may be either the assertative *lʾ* ("surely") (Andersen) or a negative question as in NIV.

C. The Theophany (38:1–42:6)

Some modern interpreters of the Book of Job see in the divine speeches a God parading his power and void of all moral responsibility. Indeed some maintain the author of the book has created a brilliant caricature of the kind of god represented by those pedants, the counselors, who themselves are being caricatured by the author. The only hero is Job, who predicted in chapter 9 how God would act . J.W. Whedbee ("Studies in the Book of Job," *Semeia* 7 [1977]: 23–24) takes issue with D. Robertson's contention that God acted in this way. Robertson maintains God's rhetoric in the theophany fulfills the prediction that he is a god of power and skill but one who cannot govern with justice. Even God's claim to put down wickedness in 40:9–14 is said to be only a parody of God's prerogatives, and Job's repentance is tongue-in-cheek. So the poet is like "a medicine man" who has developed a strategy for curing man's fear of the unknown by "ridiculing the object feared" (see Robertson).

Others have held it is immoral by any human standards that there should be a game between the Almighty and Satan using as their pawn the soul of Job. Such a view overlooks the possibility we have already mentioned, that God does not meaninglessly allow Job to be tormented. On the contrary, he is honoring Job by putting his full confidence in the genuineness of Job's faith, which Satan has questioned. Tsevat ("Book of Job," pp. 73–106) suggests that in the divine speeches God is above human concepts of morality. As Tsevat says, "He who speaks to man in the book of Job is neither a just nor an unjust god but God" (ibid., p. 105). Rowley (pp. 167–207) says God cannot be above morality. He maintains that the Book of Job is concerned less with theology than with religion.

God offers to Job no theological explanation of the mystery of his suffering. The reader is told why Job was suffering in the Prologue, but that is to show that Job was innocent. Job was never told this; had he been told, the book would have immediately lost its message to all other sufferers. So the book is teaching us through the divine theophany that there is something more fundamental than an intellectual solution to the mystery of innocent suffering. Though the message reaches Job through his intellect, it is for his spirit. Job's greatest anguish in the Dialogue-Dispute was over the thought that he was separated from God. But why? Normally sin is the reason, as the counselors perceived. But Job learned through the theophany that God had not abandoned him. And it gradually dawned on Job that without knowing why he was suffering he could face it, so long as he was assured that God was his friend. Indeed the reader comes to learn that it was not only Job who was to be vindicated, but God's trust in him was also vindicated. Job's past experience with God was nothing compared with the experience that he found through the theophany. It was like hearing about God compared with the joy of seeing him (42:5), by which he meant something not literal but of the heart.

We differ with those who see in the divine theophany a God who is indifferent, cold, and aloof and almost making fun of Job. Irony is used, but the irony of God's questions are to instruct Job, not to humiliate him. Job had the high privilege here of sitting at the feet of the Lord. Had the Lord wanted to humiliate Job, he might have taken up his errors point for point like Elihu. No, Job needed to learn something about the character of God by walking through all creation with him and contemplating his natural marvels. Far from being crushed Job was being made wonderfully aware of who God is in a universe full of paradoxes for man and yet filled with joy and wonder. In this way Job learned to take God at his word without understanding hardly any of the mysteries of his universe much less the reason why he was suffering. Andersen (*Job*, p. 271) has a marvelous statement:

> Job is vindicated in a faith in God's goodness that has survived a terrible depriva-
> tion and, indeed, grown in scope, unsupported by Israel's historical creed of the
> mighty acts of God, unsupported by life in the covenant community, unsupport-
> ed by cult institutions, unsupported by revealed knowledge from the prophets,
> unsupported by tradition and contradicted by experience. Next to Jesus, Job
> must surely be the greatest believer in the whole Bible.

Gray (Driver-Gray, in loc.), in speaking about the relationship of Yahweh speeches to the purpose of the Book of Job, notes that what these speeches do not contain is almost as important as what they do. The speeches do not reverse the Lord's judgment in the Prologue about Job. Satan was wrong in impugning Job's inner reasons for being righteous, and the friends were wrong about Job's outward conduct as a reason for his suffering. God's rebuke of Job in 38:2 was for what he said during his intense suffering, not for earlier sins. The latter would have proved that the purely penal theory of suffering was correct. The friends by their theory implied they knew completely God's ways. One of the purposes of the Lord's speeches is to show that neither the counselors nor Job possessed such complete knowledge.

Indeed the speeches show how very limited man's knowledge is. On the surface it would appear that the speeches concentrate only on the natural world, but careful reading reveals something else. In the first speech (chs. 38–39) God's works in the natural creation are in view. He introduces this with the words "Who is this that darkens my counsel with words without knowledge?" (38:2). Then follow two chapters of proof that Job knew little of God's world, something modern man has learned much more of only to discover how much more lies beyond him. Job was humbled. He then agreed that his words were based on ignorance: "I put my hand over my mouth. . . . I will say no more" (40:4–5).

The second speech begins on an entirely different note. The introduction to the second speech in 40:8–14 tells about God's power and ability to crush the wicked and to look on every proud one and humble him and bring him low. The purpose here goes beyond showing Job that God is creator and sustainer of the natural world. It is to convince Job that God is Lord also of the moral order, and appropriately Job's response this time was repentance (42:1–6).

G.K. Chesterton, in a chapter entitled "Man Is Most Comforted by Paradoxes" (in Glatzer, pp. 228–37), enlightens us considerably on why he believes God appears to Job with a battery of questions rather than answers. Chesterton was convinced that a trivial poet would have had God appear and give answers. By these questions God himself takes up the role of a skeptic and turns Job's rationalism (e.g., his doubts about God's justice) against itself. God ironically accepted a kind of equality with Job as he called on Job to gird up his loins for a fair intellectual duel. Job had asked God to come into court with him and present a bill of indictment. God was willing but asked the right to cross-examine.

Both Socrates and Jesus used the methodology of asking questions of those who came with their questions (Luke 14:1–5; 20:1–8, 27–44). The method is to ply the doubter with questions until he doubts his doubts. Job was simply overwhelmed with mysteries and paradoxes for which he had no answers; but in the midst of it all he came to understand what was too good to be told, that God knows what he is doing in his universe. Job had many questions to put to God, as do we all. Instead of God's trying to prove that it is an explainable world, however, he insisted that it is stranger than Job had ever imagined. Yet in all the strangeness there is brightness and joy and opposition to evil and wrong; and the reader comes to understand that in a world of such paradoxes Job was suffering, not because he was the worst of men, but because he was one of the best. Indeed he was a grand type. In all his wounds he prefigured the wounds of that one who was the only truly holy man ever to live, Christ the Lord!

1. God's first discourse

38:1–40:2

¹Then the LORD answered Job out of the storm. He said:

² "Who is this that darkens my counsel
   with words without knowledge?
³ Brace yourself like a man;
   I will question you,
   and you shall answer me.

⁴ "Where were you when I laid the earth's foundation?
   Tell me, if you understand.
⁵ Who marked off its dimensions? Surely you know!
   Who stretched a measuring line across it?
⁶ On what were its footings set,
   or who laid its cornerstone—
⁷ while the morning stars sang together
   and all the angels shouted for joy?

⁸ "Who shut up the sea behind doors
   when it burst forth from the womb,
⁹ when I made the clouds its garment
   and wrapped it in thick darkness,
¹⁰ when I fixed limits for it
   and set its doors and bars in place,
¹¹ when I said, 'This far you may come and no farther;
   here is where your proud waves halt'?

¹² "Have you ever given orders to the morning,
   or shown the dawn its place,
¹³ that it might take the earth by the edges
   and shake the wicked out of it?
¹⁴ The earth takes shape like clay under a seal;
   its features stand out like those of a garment.
¹⁵ The wicked are denied their light,
   and their upraised arm is broken.

¹⁶ "Have you journeyed to the springs of the sea
   or walked in the recesses of the deep?
¹⁷ Have the gates of death been shown to you?
   Have you seen the gates of the shadow of death?
¹⁸ Have you comprehended the vast expanses of the earth?
   Tell me, if you know all this.

¹⁹ "What is the way to the abode of light?
   And where does darkness reside?

²⁰ Can you take them to their places?
　　Do you know the paths to their dwellings?
²¹ Surely you know, for you were already born!
　　You have lived so many years!

²² "Have you entered the storehouses of the snow
　　or seen the storehouses of the hail,
²³ which I reserve for times of trouble,
　　for days of war and battle?
²⁴ What is the way to the place where the lightning is dispersed,
　　or the place where the east winds are scattered over the earth?
²⁵ Who cuts a channel for the torrents of rain,
　　and a path for the thunderstorm,
²⁶ to water a land where no man lives,
　　a desert with no one in it,
²⁷ to satisfy a desolate wasteland
　　and make it sprout with grass?
²⁸ Does the rain have a father?
　　Who fathers the drops of dew?
²⁹ From whose womb comes the ice?
　　Who gives birth to the frost from the heavens
³⁰ when the waters become hard as stone,
　　when the surface of the deep is frozen?

³¹ "Can you bind the beautiful Pleiades?
　　Can you loose the cords of Orion?
³² Can you bring forth the constellations in their seasons
　　or lead out the Bear with its cubs?
³³ Do you know the laws of the heavens?
　　Can you set up ｛God's｝ dominion over the earth?

³⁴ "Can you raise your voice to the clouds
　　and cover yourself with a flood of water?
³⁵ Do you send the lightning bolts on their way?
　　Do they report to you, 'Here we are'?
³⁶ Who endowed the heart with wisdom
　　or gave understanding to the mind?
³⁷ Who has the wisdom to count the clouds?
　　Who can tip over the water jars of the heavens
³⁸ when the dust becomes hard
　　and the clods of earth stick together?

³⁹ "Do you hunt the prey for the lioness
　　and satisfy the hunger of the lions
⁴⁰ when they crouch in their dens
　　or lie in wait in a thicket?
⁴¹ Who provides food for the raven
　　when its young cry out to God
　　and wander about for lack of food?

^{39:1} Do you know when the mountain goats give birth?
　　Do you watch when the doe bears her fawn?
² Do you count the months till they bear?
　　Do you know the time they give birth?
³ They crouch down and bring forth their young;
　　their labor pains are ended.
⁴ Their young thrive and grow strong in the wilds;
　　they leave and do not return.

⁵ "Who let the wild donkey go free?
　　Who untied his ropes?
⁶ I gave him the wasteland as his home,
　　the salt flats as his habitat.

⁷He laughs at the commotion in the town;
    he does not hear a driver's shout.
⁸He ranges the hills for his pasture
    and searches for any green thing.

⁹"Will the wild ox consent to serve you?
    Will he stay by your manger at night?
¹⁰Can you hold him to the furrow with a harness?
    Will he till the valleys behind you?
¹¹Will you rely on him for his great strength?
    Will you leave your heavy work to him?
¹²Can you trust him to bring in your grain
    and gather it to your threshing floor?

¹³"The wings of the ostrich flap joyfully,
    but they cannot compare with the pinions and feathers of the
    stork.
¹⁴She lays her eggs on the ground
    and lets them warm in the sand,
¹⁵unmindful that a foot may crush them,
    that some wild animal may trample them.
¹⁶She treats her young harshly, as if they were not hers;
    she cares not that her labor was in vain,
¹⁷for God did not endow her with wisdom
    or give her a share of good sense.
¹⁸Yet when she spreads her feathers to run,
    she laughs at horse and rider.

¹⁹"Do you give the horse his strength
    or clothe his neck with a flowing mane?
²⁰Do you make him leap like a locust,
    striking terror with his proud snorting?
²¹He paws fiercely, rejoicing in his strength,
    and charges into the fray.
²²He laughs at fear, afraid of nothing;
    he does not shy away from the sword.
²³The quiver rattles against his side,
    along with the flashing spear and lance.
²⁴In frenzied excitement he eats up the ground;
    he cannot stand still when the trumpet sounds.
²⁵At the blast of the trumpet he snorts, 'Aha!'
    He catches the scent of battle from afar,
    the shout of commanders and the battle cry.

²⁶"Does the hawk take flight by your wisdom
    and spread his wings toward the south?
²⁷Does the eagle soar at your command
    and build his nest on high?
²⁸He dwells on a cliff and stays there at night;
    a rocky crag is his stronghold.
²⁹From there he seeks out his food;
    his eyes detect it from afar.
³⁰His young ones feast on blood,
    and where the slain are, there is he."

⁴⁰:¹The Lᴏʀᴅ said to Job:

²"Will the one who contends with the Almighty correct him?
    Let him who accuses God answer him!"

The broad structure of the divine speeches do not reveal the same drive toward symmetry found in some earlier speeches in Job. Although this first discourse opens and closes with a rebuke and challenge to Job, both really stand outside the discourse itself (38:2–3; 40:1–2). The following outline may help the reader find his way through the material.

Introductory Rebuke Challenge (38:2–3)

Subject: The Lord of Nature

    I. The Creator (38:4–15)
        A. of the earth (vv.4–7)
        B. of the sea (vv.8–11)
        C. of day and night (vv.12–15)

    II. The Ruler of Inanimate Nature (38:16–38)
        A. the depths and expanses (vv.16–18)
        B. light and darkness (vv.19–21)
        C. weather (vv.22–30)
        D. the stars (vv.31–33)
        E. floods (vv.34–38)

    III. The Ruler of Animate Nature (38:39–39:30)
        A. nourishment (vv.39–41)
        B. procreation (vv.39:1–4)
        C. wild freedom (vv.5–8)
        D. intractible strength (vv.9–12)
        E. incongruous speed (vv.13–18)
        F. fearsome strength (vv.19–25)
        G. flight of the predator (vv.26–30)

Closing Rebuke and Challenge (40:1–2)

38:1 Job saw no "golden splendor" or even the "awesome majesty" imagined by Elihu (37:22). Indeed it seems he saw nothing but the storm from which he heard the voice of Yahweh. This Israelite covenant name for God appears in the Prologue, in the Divine speeches, and in the Epilogue; but "the men of the east" do not know God by this name. The only use of Yahweh in chapters 3–37 is in 12:9, where MS evidence may point to an original text with Elohim (God), not Yahweh (LORD). The reason, of course, is that the Israelite author was in those chapters preserving the authentic vocabulary of that earlier generation or at least a non-Israelite society.

2–3 How did Job darken (obscure) God's counsel (v.2)? There can be no doubt that this refers to the extreme language of Job during his moments of poetic rage when he struggled with concepts of a deity who was his enemy—a phantom deity, one his own mind created. Here he needed to brace himself and wrestle with God as he really was (v.3). The format God had chosen was to ply Job with questions; but strangely he said nothing about Job's suffering, nor did he address the problem of theodicy. Job did not get the bill of indictment or verdict of innocence he wanted. But neither was he humiliated with a list of the sins he had committed for which he was being punished. The latter would have been the case if the counselors had been right. So by implication Job's innocence was established, and later it was directly affirmed (42:7–8).

It was important for Job to know that God was not his enemy as he had imagined. This encounter with the Lord to learn the lesson that God is God was Job's assurance that all was well. Job did not learn why he was suffering; but he did learn to accept God by faith as his Creator, Sustainer, and Friend. To learn this lesson he needed to get rid of his ignorant fantasies, his words without knowledge, brace himself like a man, and learn who God really was. This he was about to do by walking with God through his created universe and being questioned about his limitations as a creature in comparison with God's power and wisdom in creating and sustaining the universe. The speeches, then, succeeded in bringing Job to complete faith in God's goodness without receiving a direct answer to his questions concerning the justice of God.

4–7 The irony in the Lord's words "Surely you know" (v.5; cf. v.21) is sharp and purposeful. Job had dared to criticize God's management of the universe. Had he been present at the Creation (an obvious absurdity), he might have known something about God's management of its vast expanses (vv.4–6). But even the angels who were there could only shout for joy over the Creator's deeds (v.7). And here Job, an earth-bound man, has lost sight of who this Creator is. As a man full of words often questioning what the Lord was doing, he was told of the celestial chorus that celebrated God's creative activity, which was beyond any mere creature's ability to improve on by comment. That Job was learning this lesson we may infer from his response in 40:4–5.

For personification of the stars (v.7) in parallel with "the sons of God," see Psalm 104:4, where the winds are God's messengers (angels) and the lightning bolts his servants (cf. Heb 1:7).

8–11 Those who literalize the "house-building" figure of vv.4–6 to fabricate an ancient cosmography must also literalize the figure of the sea's "coming forth from the womb" (v.8); but v.9 quickly moves from figurative to literal making that impossible.

In the ancient Semitic world, control of the boisterous sea was a unique symbol of divine power and authority. The Lord controls the sea by his spoken word (v.11). In Luke 8:24–25 Jesus' ability to do the same identified him as God—as equal in power to Yahweh. That message is conveyed in vv.10–11, where the "doors" are the bounds the Lord sets for the sea. But the "doors" of v.8 are not the same. The meaning of the first verb in v.8 is seriously disputed (see Notes). Andersen (*Job*, in loc.) presents an attractive approach to the verse, tying it with the use of the same verb in the same gestation figure in Psalm 139:13, translating: "Who constructed the sea within the doors?/ Who delivered [it] when it burst from the womb?" The double doors here are the labia of the birth canal (cf. "the doors of the womb," 3:10), and God is the Creator of the sea as well as the midwife attending its birth. Although this calls for shifting the vowels in the verb translated "delivered" to make it causative (see Notes), the advantage to the context is enormous.

12–15 The morning and dawn (v.12) are personified. Surely Job did not give orders that caused these servants of the Lord to rise and seize "the earth by its edges and shake the wicked out of it" (v.13). The figure is based on the idea that daylight catches the wicked in the act and disperses them like one who shakes dirt from a blanket. The dawn flashes across the earth from east to west; and this, in the figure, is like seizing it by its edges and shaking it out. Verse 14 pictures the long, deep shadows of early morning when the earth reminds us of clay taking the shape of the seal pressed into it or of the folds of a garment. Daylight deprives the wicked of the kind of "light" they need. Here we have a subtle figure (v.15), for "the light" the wicked are denied is certainly "the darkness" that is their element, indeed, "deep darkness is their morning" (24:17). The wicked "put darkness for light and light for darkness" (Isa 5:20). With the same powerful figure, Jesus warned, "See to it, then, that the light within you is not darkness" (Luke 11:35).

16–18 In vv.4–15 God questioned Job about his knowledge of the origin and function of the world. Here he turned to mysteries of created things not visible to the human eye. Note the progression: journeying (v.16), then seeing (v.17), and then understanding what you see (v.18). Each step in this progression is increasingly impossible for Job. We see here that Yahweh's control over this unseen nether world is just as real as his control over the sea or the land of the living (cf. 26:5–6). If the names of various deities to whom the myths imputed control of these domains is here as an overtone (cf. Tsevat, "Book of Job," n. 29), it is to suggest that neither they nor Job but only Yahweh really understands and controls "all this" (v.18). What did Job know about those realms where no living human being had ever been?

19–21 What did Job know about the mystery of light and darkness? Again personification creates a vivid figure of God's cosmic control. The irony of v.21 that focuses on Job's creatural nature gives the clue to one of the purposes of the divine speeches —to show Job that God is God. To have been born before Creation in order to know all this is a patent absurdity (v.21). But that is what makes the irony poignant. In 15:7 Eliphaz similarly chided Job for assuming he had a knowledge older than the hills.

22–30 Again Yahweh questioned Job about his ability to journey to those inaccessible places (cf. vv.16–17) where he could see the sources of nature's rich supply (v.22). The term "storehouses" (*ōṣᵉrôt*) is used in Jeremiah 50:25 as a place for storing weapons (armory). In this case the arsenal figure carries out the thought that snow or hail are often God's weapons (v.23; Pss 78:47–48; 148:8; Isa 30:30). Sometimes with them he controls the destiny of nations.

Ignorance of the mystery of God's control of nature was one of Elihu's themes (37:14–18). Here, however, the questions point to something more basic—it was the Lord's world, not Job's! The Lord was taking Job for an imaginary walk through the cosmic sphere (and later through the earth) to impress on him the grandeur and mystery, the order and complexity of his world. Some of the teachings are direct, others analogical, by way of similitude (*māšāl*). The lesson Job needed to learn is the most important one in the universe—God is God.

After querying Job about these cosmic mysteries, the Lord made a statement in vv.25–26 that sounds trite on the surface but demands the attention of every human being. Elihu spoke of God's use of the elements to punish or bless (37:13), and there (assuming our interpretation is correct) he hinted at the point that the Lord made here—that he has the right to display his power in nature for no other reason than his own good pleasure. When he "waters a land where no man lives," God demonstrates that man is not the measure of all things. He waters the desert only because it pleases him to do so.

Could Job give the Lord realistic answers to questions Job's contemporaries had simplistically answered? Does the rain have a father or the ice a mother (vv. 28–29)? The standard myths viewed the rain as the semen of the storm god. But the rhetorical question is there to impress on Job that these apparent male and female aspects of inanimate nature are God's doing and his alone.

In v. 30 the freezing of the surface of the deep was a phenomenon unknown by common experience in and around the lands of the Bible. This is hardly a reason to reject the usual meaning for $t^eh\hat{o}m$ ("the deep") as the ocean. Like other passages in Job (cf. 26:7–10), this text reveals an expanded knowledge of natural phenomena.

31–33 Job had moved with the Lord, in his mind's eye, from the "recesses of the deep" and "gates of death" (vv. 16–17) to heavenly constellations. The terminology draws on the interpretation of those fanciful figures the ancients saw in the celestial constellations. Our language in this space age still uses the same terms. The antithesis of binding and loosening the imagined fetters that hold together the cluster of stars called Pleiades or the belt of the hunter Orion rests on poetic license and literary convention. The message is about God's cosmic dominion of these stars as they seasonally move across the sky (see Notes on vv. 31–32).

Verse 31 in the KJV reads, "the sweet influences of Pleiades." S.R. Driver (Driver-Gray, 2:307) doubted this was a reference to astrology. In v. 33 the astrological approach, while accepted by a few interpreters (cf. Rowley but see Notes), is not philologically or contextually necessary. There is a philological problem, however, with NIV's "dominion" since this would be the only place $mi\check{s}\underline{t}\bar{a}r$ has that meaning. As our Notes indicate, we prefer seeing here a pure antithesis. Job understood neither the laws of the heavenly bodies nor God's "inscription [signature]" ($mi\check{s}\underline{t}\bar{a}r$) in the earth, and that is exactly what Yahweh was talking to Job about. In Psalm 19 the psalmist honors Yahweh as Lord of the heavens that "declare [his] glory"; and in Psalm 8 he sings, "O LORD, our Lord, how majestic is your name [signature] in all the earth!"

34–38 These verses all refer to meteorological phenomena and related matters. The difference between them and vv. 22–30 seems to be the time, place, and purpose of the weather. Verse 38 indicates that the seasonal rain is in view—after the long months of the dry season, Yahweh is the one who orders the clouds to release their moisture (v. 34). Job and all mankind can only raise their voices in prayer to him who controls the former and the latter rain, that extension of the rainy season that provides a greater harvest.

The language used here has a playful humor. Imagine Job, if he were able, giving the clouds an order and suddenly being inundated with water (v. 34b). Or Job might decide to dispatch the lightning bolts, if he could, and they would report like lackeys to him and say, "Here we are" (v. 35). So even these seasonal rains are the result of Yahweh's bidding, who numbers every cloud and measures every jarful of rain (v. 37).

In v. 36 there are two words in Hebrew (one rendered "heart" in the NIV and the other "mind") whose meanings have been lost in antiquity. We can only guess at their meaning (see Notes). It is difficult to see how the words "heart" and "mind" have any relationship to this cosmic context. The NIV is based on $\underline{t}uh\hat{o}\underline{t}$ as used in Psalm 51:6 [8 MT] where the same spelling is rendered "inner parts" (see Notes). The word "mind" for $\acute{s}ekw\hat{\imath}$ is a pure guess since it is used only here. Of the many interpretations offered in the commentaries, all are tenuous. Some see here two birds reputed to have meteorological wisdom—the ibis (thought to be wise about the flooding of the Nile, the most important seasonal event in Egypt) and the cock (thought by the rabbis to forecast rain). See Dhorme for more details on this interpretation and the Notes for other opinions.

39–41 These verses really begin a new aspect of Yahweh's control over nature. From 38:39 to 40:30 the focus is on creatures of the animal world that are objects of curiosity and wonder to man. The choice is somewhat random, as if Yahweh is saying, "Here are only a few specimens of all my creatures, great and small, winged and earthbound, wild and tamed—but all are under my care and dominion." It has never crossed Job's mind to hunt prey for lions (v.39) or to stuff food into the outstretched gullets of the raven's nestlings (v.41). But are not their growls and squawks cries to God, on whom all these creatures ultimately depend?

39:1–4 Through the wild kingdom and its rich variety of creatures, God informs Job of his creative and sustaining activity. He provides for each species its own gestation period and ability to bear young in the field—without assistance and with a divinely ordered wisdom to provide for themselves and their young. The offspring of an ibex doe, unlike human infants that need years of care, can stand within minutes of birth and soon gambol off to thrive in the wild.

5–8 The selection is only representative of familiar creatures; otherwise the words about them would have little significance. One of the most admired animals of the OT world was the wild donkey. It was a compliment and a promise of an enviable freedom when the angel declared that Ishmael (Gen 16:12) would become "a wild donkey of a man." The creature was admired for both its freedom and its ability to survive under the harshest conditions. There is also a touch of humor in this passage. While its relative the domesticated donkey suffers the noise pollution of the crowded cities and the abuse of animal drivers (v.7), the wild donkey can laugh at that and somehow find green morsels in places humans cannot survive (v.8)—the salt flats and the barren leeward hills (v.6).

9–12 There was an implied contrast between the wild donkey and the tame donkey in vv.5–8. Here there is an explicit contrast between the wild ox and the tame ox. This animal (Heb. *rêm*; KJV, "unicorn"; Vul., "rhinoceros") is believed to be the now-extinct aurochs (*Bos primigenius*). Next to the elephant and rhino, it was the largest and most powerful land animal of the Bible world. Most of the nine OT occurrences of the word make reference to it as a symbol of strength (cf. Num 23:22; 24:8; Deut 33:17; Ps 29:6 et al.). It was already rare in Palestine in the time of Moses. Thutmose III tells of traveling far to hunt one, and the Assyrians hunted them often in the Lebanon mountains (see Assyrian relief in B. Mazar, *Views of the Biblical World* [Chicago: Jordan, 1959], iv:129). Once again it is a bit of divine humor to even mention the possibility of this fearsome creature harnessed to Job's plow, working his fields, or tethered in his barn. For information on all the animals in this chapter, the reader can refer to G.S. Cansdale's *Animals of Bible Lands* (Exeter: Paternoster, 1970).

13–18 The question format is now dropped, and the stanza speaks of God in the third person. Moreover these verses are missing in the LXX. Some, therefore, see them as an interpolation. But considering the penchant of the LXX for omitting sections where the Hebrew is difficult, this omission should not be considered determinative (see Notes). The question format was used to impress on Job his impotence in performing deeds that take divine power and wisdom. But since the ostrich appears to be ridiculous in its behavior (v.17), it simply wasn't appropriate to ask Job whether he could match God's strength or wisdom because neither is in view.

The ostrich has a tiny brain but is well programmed with instincts that assure its survival. It does not forsake its eggs (v.14, cf. KJV). The verb in this verse means "lay," though a homonym does mean "forsake" (cf. M. Dahood, "The Root עזב in Job" JBL 78 [1959]: 303–9). The seeming cruelty to her young (v.16; cf. Lam 4:3) derives from the practice of driving off the yearlings when mating season arrives. The ostrich has exceptional eyesight—the largest of any land animal with 360 degree vision. But the text concentrates on the bird's most incongruous feature: tremendous legs. One kick can tear open a lion or a man.

The lesson is that God can and does make creatures that appear odd and crazy to us if that pleases him. Imagine a bird that can't fly. Though it has wings it can run faster than a horse (v.18). Job could not understand what God was doing in his life, and God was telling him the created world is just as difficult to rationalize.

19–25 The horse is the only animal in this poem that is domestic. This unexpected feature still serves the Lord's purpose, for only one kind of horse is viewed—the charger, the war-horse. The creatures of the wild in their proud freedom and curious behavior are obviously beyond Job's control, but even a creature that man has tamed can display fearsome behavior that excites our imagination. The lines burst with the literary energy needed to do justice to the performance of this amazing creature during the height of the frenzy of battle. Our increased lexical knowledge has enhanced the vividness of these lines. The reader need only compare the clarity of the NIV with the KJV to appreciate this. For example in v.19 ra'māh means "a flowing mane," not "thunder" (KJV) or "strength" (RSV). In v.20 the horse is not made "afraid" but to "leap like a locust." And in v.21 he paws "fiercely," not "in the valley" (see Notes).

26–30 In v.26 the marvel for Job to contemplate is one we still view with amazement—the migratory instincts of birds. Our knowledge that some birds fly thousands of miles each year (cf. the arctic tern, which flies from the Arctic to the Antarctic) serves to validate this particular choice of God's faunal wonders. The two words used in vv.26–27 are the Hebrew generic names that include several species. The first (v.26) appears to be the sparrow hawk (nēṣ), a bird not resident to the Holy Land but known because it stops off there each year in its migration (Kline, WBC, p. 86). In v.27 the griffon vulture (nešer) is the largest bird of the area. The same word is used for the true eagle (NIV), but here a carrion eater is in mind. Several interesting characteristics of this bird are mentioned: its soaring ability, its aerie (nest) high on the crags, and its phenomenal eyesight.

40:1–2 These two verses conclude the first speech. Some omit v.1 (cf. LXX); others assume the Lord paused to see whether Job had a reply and then hearing none went on (Rowley, p. 235). Since Job has said nothing, a small problem arises because "the

LORD answered Job and said" (v.1, lit. Heb.). This expression was formulaic throughout the Dialogue-Dispute, where we might expect it, but also in the monologue of Elihu, where no one was answering (cf. 34:1; 35:1). Here it announces a hortatory line (v.2). In 38:1 the same formula had introduced this speech (though Job had not been speaking), and there also it was followed by words of exhortation; thus we find a kind of *inclusio* that ties together the entire first speech. Understanding the formulaic nature of the expression weakens the contention of those who say 38:1 should follow immediately after 31:40 (cf. W.A. Irwin, "The Elihu Speeches in the Criticism of the Book of Job," JR 17 [1937]: 37–47). The beginning of each Yahweh speech is designated by adding to this formula the words "out of the storm" (cf. 38:1; 40:6).

Here, then, in 40:2, the Lord gets to the point. Job had set himself up arbitrarily as God's accuser. How could Job assume such a lofty position in the light of who God is? After this front-row seat surveying the marvels and mysteries of God's created universe, was Job still ready to make his proud insinuations and accusations about the nature of God's lordship over all things? It was Job's turn to speak again. But there would be no long speeches, no more rage, no more challenging his Creator.

Notes

38:3 The figure חֲלָצֶיךָ ... אֱזָר־נָא (*ʾezār-nāʾ ... ḥalāṣeykā*, "Brace yourself") may be the ancient belt-wrestler. The hero girded his loins with a warrior's belt that would be snatched from him as a trophy if vanquished (cf. Pritchard, *Ancient Pictures,* fig. 219; C.H. Gordon, "Belt Wrestling in the Bible World," HUCA 23, part 1 [1950–51]: 136). But it may be more general (1 Kings 18:46; Isa 5:27).

8 The question וַיָּסֶךְ (*wayyāsek,* "Who shut up") is not explicit in Hebrew but must surely be carried over from what precedes. But there are two questions that precede: "Where were you?" (v.4) and "Who?" (v.5). Driver-Gray prefer the former question, and Blommerde following this translates this verb "to pour out" (*nsk*). Thus: "(Where were you) when the sea poured out of the two doors and went forth, erupting from the womb." There is no problem in ascribing the meaning "from" for *b* (cf. Blommerde, p. 19). But Andersen's solution (*Job,* in loc.) may be better: "Who constructed the sea within the doors?" This handles the verb as in Ps 139:13 ("knit together in the womb," cf. BDB, p. 651). He also suggests we revocalize the verb יֵצֵא (*yēṣēʾ,* "burst forth") to Hiphil *yôṣîʾ* (written defectively) and read "Who delivered it?" This certainly strengthens the context by making God creator as in v.4, not just an observer of the sea's birth.

9 For חֲתֻלָּתוֹ (*ḥᵃtullātô,* "wrapped it"), the RSV has "its swaddling band." The word is used only here, but the verb is used in Ezek 30:21 of putting on a bandage.

10 It is obvious that the usual meaning "I broke" for וָאֶשְׁבֹּר (*wāʾešbōr*) does not fit the context. NIV's "when I fixed" follows the RV, RSV et al., who probably connected the root with the Arabic *sbr* ("prescribe boundaries"). Pope (p. 294) shows how the Qumran Targum also understood the verb as "set (bounds)." Gordis (*Job,* in loc.) uses semantic correspondence to show *šbr* can mean "decree," "decide"; but there are no other OT examples for this meaning. Gaster, Guilleaume, and Dahood relate it to *špr* ("to measure") as in Ps 16:6 (cf. Blommerde, p. 133).

11 Gordis (*Job,* in loc.) wisely notes וָאֹמַר (*wāʾōmar,* "when I said") as anacrusis—an introductory word outside the poetic balance.

Delitzsch (2:316) sees יָשִׁית (yāšît) as a logical passive with an indefinite subject and with a typical ellipsis of the direct object, probably חֹק (ḥōq, "limit"; cf. 10:20; 14:13 and Notes on 4:20 for ellipsis with śîm, "put"). The NIV's lucid word "halt" may be considered a way of handling the logical passive "(a limit) is set." BHS wants to borrow the preposition from the word גָּאוֹן (ge'ôn, "proud") and metathesize it to get šbt ("to cease"), reading "here your proud waves cease."

13 The raised ayin in רְשָׁעִים (rešā'îm, "the wicked") represents a proto-Masoretic correction that was faithfully preserved (cf. also v.15; Judg 18:30; Ps 80:14). G.R. Driver's interpretation ("Two Astronomical Passages in the Old Testament," JTS, NS 4 [1953]: 208–12; cf. NEB) that these are the "evil stars" (e.g., the Dog Star if one rearranges the letters) is not likely since they are shaken out of the earth, not the heavens.

The verb נָעַר (nā'ar II) means "to shake, shake out or off." Its use in Ps 109:23 is instructive for this passage: "I fade away like an evening shadow;/ I am shaken off like a locust." Note how similar the figures of speech are to vv.13–14.

14 The NIV's rendering of וְיִתְיַצְּבוּ (weyityaṣṣebû) as "its features stand out" has "its features" inserted to account for the plural verb, which has only the "wicked" in v.13 as a reference. Scholars emend it to a feminine singular of ṣb' ("to tint or dye"). The RSV's "dyed like a garment" might refer to the color of the earth at dawn. As it stands the text might mean "they stand forth (in the light) like (the folds of) a garment." If "they" are the wicked, that is the reason they can be shaken off (v.13). Such an idea leads into v.15, where the wicked are denied their kind of light (i.e., darkness; cf. 24:17) by the coming of true light of day.

16 On נִבְכֵי־יָם (nibkê-yām, "the springs of the sea"), compare 28:11, where the MT's mibbekî (mibbekê) reflects the Ugaritic nbk (npk) "(water) source" (UT, p. 441). S.R. Driver (Driver-Gray, 2:303) said the etymology was unknown, but see G.M. Landes ("The Fountain at Jazer," BASOR 144 [1956]: 31–32) and M. Mansoor ("The Thanksgiving Hymns and the Massoretic Text," RQ 3 [1961–62]: 392–93).

17 צַלְמָוֶת (ṣalmāwet, "the shadow of death") appears in some contexts meaning "darkness," as its use in extrabiblical documents proves. But even in biblical times its meaning as derived from the two words "shadow" and "death" was recognized and used as this passage seems to confirm by using it in parallel with māwet ("death"). Of the ten times the word appears in Job, this is the only place the NIV renders it "shadow of death." It supports the same reading for Ps 23:4.

18 In כֻלָּה . . . אֶרֶץ ('āreṣ . . . kullāh, "the earth . . . all this") it may be better to take 'āreṣ ("land") and kullāh ("all of it") both to refer to the land of the shadow of death. Even though Akkadian and Ugaritic use 'āreṣ for the domain of the dead, it is at best rare in the OT. See Michel (pp. 70–72) for passages in Job where he thinks 'āreṣ might be translated "the underworld (netherworld)." Out of fourteen passages, including this one, only one is certain (10:21) and one other is possible but not probable (28:24).

24 Because of the parallel with קָדִים (qādîm, "[hot] east winds"), critics suggest various emendations for 'ôr ("lightning") in יֵחָלֶק אוֹר (yeḥāleq 'ôr, "lightning is dispersed"). The NEB translation "the heat spread abroad" (cf. Driver-Gray; see Rowley, p. 313) makes sense since in 41:18 (10 MT) 'ôr is the "hot breath of Leviathan." Some may feel "lightning" is appropriate in 41:18 also. In Isa 44:16 and 47:14, 'ûr is fire that people kindle to warm themselves.

25 See 28:26.

27 The NIV took מֹצָא (môṣā' [no equivalent in NIV]) to mean "the place or act of going forth" (BDB, p. 425; cf. 28:1). The meaning then is tautological: "to make sprout, the going forth of grass." The translation omits the repetition. Others see it as simple metathesis from ṣāmē', reading "the thirsty (land)," yielding "to make the thirsty land sprout grass."

31–33 See Amos 5:8 and Notes on 9:9. KJV's "sweet influences of Pleiades" for מַעֲדַנּוֹת כִּימָה (ma'adannôt kîmāh, "the beautiful Pleiades") comes from the earlier EV that got it from Jewish sources in the Middle Ages (Nachmanides et al.). Driver (Driver-Gray, 2:306–7), after citing a note in the Geneva Bible, maintained no astrological meaning was intended (cf. Pope, p. 300), only that the heliacal rising of Pleiades coincides with the beginning of spring that is the time when flowers, etc. ("sweet delights") are stimulated. But all this is wide of the mark. Like the KJV, the NIV's "beautiful" is based on the root ʿdn ("luxury," "delight," "dainty"); but the root with this meaning is always used in the masculine, not the feminine. The NIV margin suggests two out of a number of other possible alternates: "the twinkling" that is based on מָעַד (māʿad, "to quiver, tremble"; at least Jerome thought it meant "twinkle" in the Vul.); another is "the chains or bonds of," which requires a metathesis coming from ʿnd ("to bind") (31:36). The only other use of maʿaḏannōṯ in 1 Sam 15:32 presents the same problem. According to some translations the resigned Agag comes to be slain "delicately" (KJV), "cheerfully" (RSV), or "confidently" (NIV). All these are based on a semantic stretch of the root עדן (ʿdn). The NIV margin—"him trembling, yet"—is based on mʿd (cf. Beck). Pope, citing S.R. Driver's *Notes on the Hebrew Text and the Topography of the Books of Samuel* (2d ed. [London: Oxford University Press, 1966]), accepts the metathesis in both passages; so Agag comes "in fetters." But G.R. Driver ("Two Astronomical Passages in the Old Testament," JTS, NS 7 [1956]: 1–11) rejects "fetters" in 38:31, claiming support from Ugaritic and Arabic to show the word should be translated "company," "group" (cf. NEB, "cluster"). The words "Can you bind the cluster . . . and loose the cords" make excellent sense. Driver (ibid., p. 4) thinks the cords are Orion's belt.

32 On מַזָּרוֹת (mazzārôṯ, "the constellations"), compare mazzālôṯ ("constellations," 2 Kings 23:5). The two are usually identified on the basis of the interchange between *l* and *r* in Semitic dialects (Pope, p. 301). Both G.R. Driver ("Astronomical Passages," pp. 6–8) and Dhorme (pp. 589–90) question the identification. Driver sees the zodiacal constellations here in Job but the planets in 2 Kings 23:5. Dhorme (p. 590), stressing etymology (nēzer, "crown"), finds this to be the Corona Borealis.

For עַל (ʿal, "with") meaning "along with," cf. Gen 32:12; 1 Sam 14:32.

33 The root šṭr never appears as a verb and is found only here as מִשְׁטָרוֹ (mišṭārô, "God's dominion"; cf. šōṭēr, "official"). The root has to do with writing in Akkadian, Arabic, and Aramaic. On this nuance of the Hebrew root, see BDB, p. 1009.

Friedrich Delitzsch (cited in Dhorme, p. 591) was the first to point to the Assyrian šiṭir šamāmi ("the writing of the sky") meaning the stars (cf. also mašṭāru, "inscription"). Both the NIV and Pope think it means "God's dominion" here. But Gordis (*Job*, p. 451) finds a hidden plural (inscribed decrees = "order") making the verse antithetic: "Do you know the laws of heaven; can you establish order on the earth?" N.H. Tur-Sinai ("šiṭir šamê: din Himmelsschrift," *Archiv Orientální* 17, 2 [1949]: 419–33) ties the verse to Ps 19 and sees the "language of heaven going out into all the earth." Rowley (p. 245) makes it purely astrological—the heavenly writing is the stars. Pope (p. 290) understands it as God's rule on earth.

The verb could be śîm elliptical lēḇ (cf. 4:20; 23:6; 24:12; 34:23) giving the meaning "Have you considered his inscription in the earth?" i.e., God writes (reveals himself) not only in the heavens (Ps 19), but "in all the earth" (Ps 8:1). The evidence of God's hand in the earth is precisely what he took up throughout the rest of this speech.

36 בַּטֻּחוֹת (baṭṭuḥôṯ, "the heart") and לַשֶּׂכְוִי (laśśekwî, "the mind") have had a long history of attempts to interpret them, and there is still no consensus. Gordis (*Job*, pp. 452–53) lists four major views and gives reasons for eliminating three, and a case could be made for eliminating the fourth. One of the three is NIV's "heart" and "mind," which is essentially the same as KJV and RV and has the distinction of being the first presented by the Ibn Ezra. (The NIV mg. needs correction since it implies only one word is under consideration.) That ṭuḥôṯ means "the heart" is based on one other passage where the word is used: Ps 51:6 (8 MT). Here the parallel with śāṭum ("the inmost place") creates a reasonable assumption that, if this is from the same root, ṭuḥôṯ means something similar. But all attempts to arrive at a root in either case have been unsatisfactory. The same is true for śekwî, an OT *hapax legomenon*.

The second unsatisfactory explanation according to Gordis (*Job*, p. 453) is "clouds" and "mists" (cf. RSV, BDB). Here too the philological support is very weak (cf. Pope, p. 302) and the context's reference to wisdom is left unexplained.

The third view is that of many modern scholars and is summarized and supported by Pope (p. 256). Its philological base is an attempt to show that the words *tuḥôt* and *śekwî* sound like the names of two Egyptian gods: Thoth, the scribe-god and founder of knowledge, and Souchi, the Coptic name for the god Hermes-Mercury. This fits the wisdom concept; and though the name Thoth was popular among the Phoenicians and Neo-Babylonians in OT times, there is no evidence that the same is true for Souchi. Gordis (*Job*, p. 453) is right in questioning the notion that so uncompromising a monotheist as we have here would describe God giving wisdom to pagan deities. How could such be considered one of the wonders of God's creation (Gordis, ibid.)?

So the only interpretation that seems to have some philological support and that fits the immediate and overall context—though it too must be considered tentative—is the view reflected in TEV's paraphrase: "Who tells the ibis when the Nile will flood, or who tells the rooster that rain will fall?" Both Gordis and Dhorme (p. 591) support this view. The word *tuḥôt* then refers to the ibis bird, the symbol for Thoth, the Egyptian god of wisdom. Since the ibis was thought to foretell the rising of the Nile, by allusion we have a reference to one of nature's great wonders, though the text does not say that.

The philological support for *śekwî* as "the cock" that was believed to forecast rain is based on rabbinic references that are far from convincing, but Gordis (*Job*, p. 453) seems to accept it. This view fits the context if the allusion to a "wisdom" these birds have that man lacks is correct. But this interpretation ignores Ps 51:6 (8 MT), the only bit of OT philological evidence available. There is no satisfactory solution to the problem this text poses.

39:3 The literal meaning of חֶבְלֵיהֶם תְּשַׁלַּחְנָה (*ḥeḇlêhem teṣallaḥnāh*, "their labor pains are ended") is "they cast off their pains." The "pains" need not be metonymy for what causes them (BDB, s.v.) since *ḥaḇal* means "fetus" in Arabic (Pope).

4 Seeing בַּבָּר (*baḇbār*, "in the wilds") as an Aramaism corrects the KJV's "with corn," which is based on a common Hebrew homonym meaning "grain." Pope wishes to move the word up to v.3 on the basis of the Qumran Targum, which has no equivalent in either verse. The LXX has an equivalent; and though it misunderstood the word, it supports the MT.

12 The NIV's "to bring in your grain" follows כִּי־יָשׁוּב זַרְעֶךָ (*kî-yāšiwḇ zar'ekā*), the MT Qere: the Hiphil with the object "your grain." BHS mg., wanting a balanced bicolon, prefers the Kethiv (Qal): יָשׁוּב (*yāšûḇ*, "that he will come back"). But this leaves the second half difficult to translate; so BHS wants to emend it. To dispel the mystery one need only see anacrusis, viz., there are three parts to the line with "Can you trust him" outside the balance and applying to both sides.

13 The obscurity of אִם־אֶבְרָה חֲסִידָה וְנֹצָה (*'im-'eḇrāh ḥasîdāh wenōṣāh*, "but they cannot compare with the pinions and feathers of the stork") disappears when *'im* is understood as a particle of wishing (BDB, p. 50). The bicolon has a twinkle of humor when translated literally: "When the wing of the ostrich flaps joyfully, would that it was a stork's pinion and feathers!"

13–18 On the omission of these lines in the LXX, Habel (*Job*, 1985, p. 524) suggests, "It is much easier to see why the LXX would omit this awkward verse than to understand why someone would insert it later." He sees it as "a deliberate feature of the poet's plan."

19 On רַעְמָה (*ra'māh*) as "flowing mane" (NIV), see KB (p. 901).

20 The NIV renders הַתַרְעִישֶׁנּוּ (*hetar'îšennû*) as "Do you make him leap." The Qumran Targum translates *r'š* as "leap," though it is not generally used this way. The common meaning "shake" or "quake" (cf. v.24) is used as in Isa 9:5 (4 MT) and refers to the noise of an army (NIV, "battle"), not to trembling in fear" (KJV). The war-horses' hoofs sound like the roar of locusts, but this is accomplished by running and jumping.

21 The NIV's rendering of בְּעֶמֶק (bā'ēmeq) as "fiercely" is supported by both Ugaritic and Akkadian, which attest to 'mq meaning "strength," used adverbially here (cf. UT, p. 457).

25 The MT vocalizes בְּדִי (beᵈê) as if this were the preposition b with the substantive day (construct dê) ("sufficiency"), the combination meaning "as often as" (RSV, "when"); but this combination appears only with the preposition min (BDB, p. 91). Here and in 11:3 the idiom is like the Ugaritic bd ("song") used adverbially, hence NIV's "at the blast [song] of."

30 The verb יַעְלְעוּ (yeᵉaleᵉû, "feast on") is treated as a Piel of ל', an unknown root. BHS suggests a reduplicated form of lûaᵉ ("swallow," "lap"; cf. BDB, p. 534), but this entails adding another lamed after the yod. Others want to drop or explain away the first ayin (Dhorme). Pope (pp. 314–15) claims he has an Arabic root meaning "to shake a thing (in order) to pull it out," which would be Aramaized in this way. But he gives no documentation.

40:2 The NIV understands יִסּוֹר (yissôr), a *hapax legomenon*, to be from ysr ("to correct"). This requires adding the pronoun object "him," which does not appear in Hebrew. Others make yissôr a rare noun: "Will the faultfinder [yissôr] contend with the Almighty?" (RSV). Most revocalize rōḇ to rāḇ, a participle ("the one who contends"), and make it the subject of the verb sûr, meaning "yield." So Dhorme has "Will he who argues with Shaddai yield?" (cf. Pope).

In rendering יַעֲנֶנָּה (yaᵉanennah) as "answer him," the NIV has not followed the feminine form of the pronoun suffix, which has to be translated "it" or "this" (cf. RSV). No doubt NIV has chosen to be somewhat paraphrastic since "it" means Yahweh's argument.

---

2. Job's humbling

40:3-5

³Then Job answered the LORD:

⁴"I am unworthy—how can I reply to you?
I put my hand over my mouth.
⁵I spoke once, but I have no answer—
twice, but I will say no more."

3-5 Job, the challenger, in a hand-over-mouth posture (v.4), realized how complex and mysterious God's ways were. In other words, the view of the things from God's perspective had chastened Job. His reply was based not so much on his unworthiness (NIV) as on his insignificance. God had not crushed Job. God had not done what the counselors wanted when they reduced Job to zero, but he had cured Job's presumption. The Hebrew verb translated "unworthy" means "to be light" or "lightly esteemed" and in that sense "contemptible." Job saw how contemptible it must have appeared to God when he said "like a prince I would approach him" (31:37).

Job had been so moved by this experience, so taken out of himself by his vision of God, that he was released from his problem—his concern to be vindicated. And yet God had given him no explanation of his sufferings. He would no longer alternate outbursts of rage and self-pity. But he was still on the rack; suffering had not abated. Job had gone beyond it to see and trust God as his friend. As a friend God had brought Job out of his bitterness to a full realization that he must reckon with God as God. And yet Job still did not know how God had put himself on trial when he allowed Job to be afflicted under Satan's instigation. So Job was humbled and thereby prepared for the Lord's second speech, which will pull together some important threads and bring the drama to a climax.

Notes

4 In הֵן קַלֹּתִי (*hēn qallōṭî*, "I am unworthy"), the particle *hen* can mean "if" as well as "lo." Dhorme takes the verb to mean "be light in speech or thought" rather than lightly esteemed (BDB, p. 886) and translates "If I have been thoughtless." JB is similar: "My words have been frivolous." Pope stresses the Arabic meaning and is more literal: "Lo, I am small, how can I answer you." But the idea of "being contemptible" fits the way this word is used as a Canaanite gloss in the Tell El Amarna tablets (cf. BDB, p. 886; Gesenius-Buhl, *Handwörterbuch*, p. 714) and in Gen 16:4 and 1 Sam 2:30.

יָדִי . . . לְמוֹ־פִי (*yādî . . . lᵉmô-pî*, "my hand . . . over my mouth") is a gesture of silence and submission that Job used twice before (21:5; 29:9; cf. Judg 18:19 [KJV]; Prov 30:32; Mic 7:16).

5 As a figure of speech the idiom אַחַת . . . וּשְׁתָּיִם (*'aḥat . . . ûšᵉttayim*, "once, . . . twice"), so common in Semitic tongues (cf. Amos 1:3, 6, 9 et al.), should not be pressed unduly. Nor should the words "but I will say no more" be taken too literally (cf. 42:2–6). Job meant he had no rebuttal.

3. God's second discourse

40:6–41:34

⁶Then the LORD spoke to Job out of the storm:

⁷"Brace yourself like a man;
    I will question you,
    and you shall answer me.

⁸"Would you discredit my justice?
    Would you condemn me to justify yourself?
⁹Do you have an arm like God's,
    and can your voice thunder like his?
¹⁰Then adorn yourself with glory and splendor,
    and clothe yourself in honor and majesty.
¹¹Unleash the fury of your wrath,
    look at every proud man and bring him low,
¹²look at every proud man and humble him,
    crush the wicked where they stand.
¹³Bury them all in the dust together;
    shroud their faces in the grave.
¹⁴Then I myself will admit to you
    that your own right hand can save you.

¹⁵"Look at the behemoth,
    which I made along with you
    and which feeds on grass like an ox.
¹⁶What strength he has in his loins,
    what power in the muscles of his belly!
¹⁷His tail sways like a cedar;
    the sinews of his thighs are close-knit.

¹⁸ His bones are tubes of bronze,
> his limbs like rods of iron.
¹⁹ He ranks first among the works of God,
> yet his Maker can approach him with his sword.
²⁰ The hills bring him their produce,
> and all the wild animals play nearby.
²¹ Under the lotus plants he lies,
> hidden among the reeds in the marsh.
²² The lotuses conceal him in their shadow;
> the poplars by the stream surround him.
²³ When the river rages, he is not alarmed;
> he is secure, though the Jordan should surge against his
> mouth.
²⁴ Can anyone capture him by the eyes,
> or trap him and pierce his nose?

^{41:1} Can you pull in the leviathan with a fishhook
> or tie down his tongue with a rope?
² Can you put a cord through his nose
> or pierce his jaw with a hook?
³ Will he keep begging you for mercy?
> Will he speak to you with gentle words?
⁴ Will he make an agreement with you
> for you to take him as your slave for life?
⁵ Can you make a pet of him like a bird
> or put him on a leash for your girls?
⁶ Will traders barter for him?
> Will they divide him up among the merchants?
⁷ Can you fill his hide with harpoons
> or his head with fishing spears?
⁸ If you lay a hand on him,
> you will remember the struggle and never do it again!
⁹ Any hope of subduing him is false;
> the mere sight of him is overpowering.
¹⁰ No one is fierce enough to rouse him.
> Who then is able to stand against me?
¹¹ Who has a claim against me that I must pay?
> Everything under heaven belongs to me.

¹² "I will not fail to speak of his limbs,
> his strength and his graceful form.
¹³ Who can strip off his outer coat?
> Who would approach him with a bridle?
¹⁴ Who dares open the doors of his mouth,
> ringed about with his fearsome teeth?
¹⁵ His back has rows of shields
> tightly sealed together;
¹⁶ each is so close to the next
> that no air can pass between.
¹⁷ They are joined fast to one another;
> they cling together and cannot be parted.
¹⁸ His snorting throws out flashes of light;
> his eyes are like the rays of dawn.
¹⁹ Firebrands stream from his mouth;
> sparks of fire shoot out.
²⁰ Smoke pours from his nostrils
> as from a boiling pot over a fire of reeds.
²¹ His breath sets coals ablaze,
> and flames dart from his mouth.
²² Strength resides in his neck;
> dismay goes before him.

23 The folds of his flesh are tightly joined;
   they are firm and immovable.
24 His chest is hard as rock,
   hard as a lower millstone.
25 When he rises up, the mighty are terrified;
   they retreat before his thrashing.
26 The sword that reaches him has no effect,
   nor does the spear or the dart or the javelin.
27 Iron he treats like straw
   and bronze like rotten wood.
28 Arrows do not make him flee;
   slingstones are like chaff to him.
29 A club seems to him but a piece of straw;
   he laughs at the rattling of the lance.
30 His undersides are jagged potsherds,
   leaving a trail in the mud like a threshing sledge.
31 He makes the depths churn like a boiling caldron
   and stirs up the sea like a pot of ointment.
32 Behind him he leaves a glistening wake;
   one would think the deep had white hair.
33 Nothing on earth is his equal—
   a creature without fear.
34 He looks down on all that are haughty;
   he is king over all that are proud."

Second Speech (40:7–41:34 [40:7–41:26 MT])
Introductory Challenge to Job (40:7)
  Subject: The Lord of History

    I. Prologue: Lord Over the Moral Order (40:8–14)
      A. Rebuke of Job (40:8)
      B. God's majestic wrath against all wickedness (40:9–14)

    II. The First Monster (40:15–23)
      A. His might—four bicola (40:15–18)
      B. A primordial creature under God's control—climax (40:19)
      C. His security—four bicola (40:20–23)

    III The Second Monster (40:24–41:34)
      A. Man (Job) and Leviathan (40:24–41:10)
      B. God and Leviathan (under God's control)—climax (41:11–12)
      C. Description of Leviathan (41:13–24)
      D. Other mighty beings and Leviathan (41:25–34)

The descriptions of Behemoth and Leviathan have been assailed by many who are doubtful of their authenticity. For example, Driver-Gray (1:351–52) see this section as out of balance with the animal descriptions of the first speech and present a list of reasons why this could not have been written by the author of the first speech: the beastly descriptions are longer; the question format is less frequent, which tends to lessen the vividness of this as God's words; the focus here is on the body parts of the beasts while there it was on their habits, activities, and tempers; Behemoth and Leviathan are said to be Egyptian (the hippopotamus and the crocodile) while the earlier animals were Palestinian, etc. But Gordis (*Job*, p. 567) has shown how Driver-Gray's view is much too mechanical and does not allow for poetic creativity.

R.B.Y. Scott (*The Way of Wisdom* [New York: Macmillan, 1971], p. 159 n.) claims

40:15–41:34 is an anticlimax and adds nothing to the challenge of 40:6–14. Such a view overlooks a number of important matters. First, it is reasonable to assume the author intended a lengthy new speech to begin at 40:6 parallel to chapters 38–39. This is confirmed by the fact that the formula in 38:1 and 3 is repeated in 40:6–7 just as the new formula used in 27:1 is repeated in 29:1. The words "I will question you" (v.7) would be out of place only if there were no questions in the Behemoth and Leviathan sections (see Westermann's comment below). Second, 40:8–14 serves as a prologue to the rest of the speech. And the message of this prologue gives us the clue to the correct interpretation of the descriptions of Behemoth and Leviathan.

The Lord, acting as his own defense attorney, moves to the very heart of his case: Job's misunderstanding of God's attitude toward wickedness. Verses 8–14 question the contention that the God of the Book of Job is amoral and that one purpose of the book is to set aside the old biblical doctrine of justice and retribution (cf. Tsevat, "Book of Job," pp. 102–5). Here God addressed himself to the moral question and rebuked Job for daring to question his justice (v.8). Job had been discrediting (*pā-rar*, "to frustrate") God's justice by suggesting he was guilty of failing to run the world in the way Job imagined it should be run (e.g., 9:21–24; 24:1–12). Job's preoccupation with his own vindication has obscured the real issue—God alone has the power and majesty it takes to combat evil and turn it into good.

The imperatives in vv.10–11 that call on Job to display the attributes of deity are obviously intended to prove to him how helpless he is against the reality of the forces of evil in this world. Verse 14 places the emphasis on salvation from evil. The message is that Job's right hand cannot save but God's can. Indeed, if Job could do what he had claimed God had failed to do, then he did not need God at all—a horrible implication since Job had never denied God was Sovereign. Job's problems stem from that very belief. Gordis's notion (*Job*, p. 475) that God was tacitly conceding he had not been able to achieve completely his goal of obliterating evil is just the opposite of what this speech is all about. God stated the fact that wickedness exists and that he alone had the power to uphold his own honor by crushing it. Deliverance from all evil rests with God, not with man (vv.9–14). Westermann (*Structure of Job*, p. 105) has noted that the imperatives in many of these verses really have questions behind them. The words "Then adorn yourself with glory and splendor" means "Are you so adorned?" God had already pressed Job's own creatureliness on him in the first speech. Job thus needed to acknowledge God not only as Creator but Savior (v.14b). It is precisely these two attributes of God that stand behind the Yahweh speeches.

This prologue in vv.8–14 shows how the lengthy descriptions of the two creatures Behemoth and Leviathan serve the purpose of the book in a subtle and yet forceful way. This time God would accomplish more than he had in the first speech, where he humbled Job by showing him how he was Creator and Sustainer of the natural world. Here God would convince Job that he was also Lord of the moral order; one whose justice Job could not discredit. And appropriately Job's response this time was repentance (42:1–6). The concentration on these two awesome creatures, placed as they are after the assertion of the Lord's justice and maintenance of moral order, lends weight to the contention that they are symbolic though their features are drawn from animals like the hippopotamus and crocodile. Both words are used often in the OT without symbolic significance (Pss 8:8; 50:10; 73:22; 104:26; Joel 1:20; 2:22; Hab 2:17 et al.). But Leviathan sometimes symbolizes evil political powers. In keeping with what was said above (Introduction: Mythopoeic Language), in

Psalm 74:12–14 mythopoeic language about the many-headed Leviathan is historicized and used metaphorically to describe the Lord's great victory in history at the
Red Sea. The monster here is Egypt.

> But you, O God, are my king from of old;
>   you bring salvation upon the earth.
> It was you who split open the sea by your power;
>   you broke the heads of the monster in the waters.
> It was you who crushed the heads of Leviathan
>   and gave him as food to the creatures of the desert.

The same is true of Isaiah 27:1, where again the mythic chaos-figure Leviathan is
historicized to represent the final evil power in the end time. It is important to
stress that this terminology in Mesopotamia and Canaanite myth is always tied to
natural phenomena, never to historical events. Here in Job it is not a particular
historical event; but as the poem's prologue in vv.8–14 suggests, the theme is God's
actions against all creatures who dare assert themselves against him. Most important
for this interpretation of Job 40–41 is Isaiah 26:21–27:1. Here the prophet says:

> See, the Lord is coming out of his dwelling
>   to punish the people of the earth for their sins.
> The earth will disclose the blood shed upon her;
>   she will conceal her slain no longer.
> In that day,
>   the Lord will punish with his sword,
>   his fierce, great and powerful sword,
>   Leviathan the gliding serpent,
>   Leviathan the coiling serpent;
>   he will slay the monster of the sea.

Genesis 1:3 and Isaiah 27:1 present the OT view of the beginning and the end of
the history of sin in the world. They mark a major ideological difference between
the OT view of the origin and disposition of evil and that of Canaanite myth. On the
other hand, the serpent imagery is a continuity between the two that cannot be
ignored (see ANET, pp. 137–38). Imagery similar to Job is found in Revelation 12
–13. There we see a beast (Behemoth) as well as a dragon (Leviathan), both of
whom only God can subdue. Revelation 12:9 says: "The great dragon was hurled
down—that ancient serpent called the devil or Satan, who leads the whole world
astray. He was hurled to the earth, and his angels with him." There is no apocalyp-
tic tone to this part of Job, merely a free use of the same Canaanite imagery Isaiah
and the Psalmist knew so well.

Those who regard these creatures as literal animals must admit that the description given here in Job is an exaggeration of the appearance and power of hip-
popotamuses and crocodiles. Gunkle, Cheyne, and Pope understood them as mythological creatures. The present writer claims only mythological terminology is used
to present graphic descriptions of the powers of evil such as the Satan in the Prologue. But the Accuser cannot be openly mentioned here without revealing to Job
information he must not know if he is to continue as a model to those who also must
suffer in ignorance of God's explicit purpose for their suffering.

Both creatures share two qualities. First is the open (on the surface) quality of a
beast with oversize bovine or crocodilian features. This meets the needs of the
uninformed (as to events of the Prologue) Job who was learning a lesson about the
Lord's omnipotence. Second is the hidden quality of a cosmic creature (the Accuser

of the Prologue) whose creation preceded (40:19) and whose power outranks (41:33) all other creatures.

6–14 Using the same formula of challenge (v.7), God presented to Job another barrage of questions designed to bring him back to reality. After all Job's last words were a challenge (31:35–37) that threw into question God's integrity by suggesting that any indictment God might bring against Job would prove to be false (v.8). But all such was hypothetical nonsense. It came straight from Job's imagination. God had no such indictment of Job in the first place; but Job's attitude had to be corrected, for he wrongly assumed that he had to be vindicated by God. To do this the LORD reminded Job of who he (God) was. Did Job have an arm like God's—was he almighty (v.9)? And where was Job's majesty and glory (v.10)? Job began to realize why God had in his first discourse taken him through his garden of natural wonders. Could Job by his power and glory create and sustain all that? Obviously not! So Job needed also to leave to his Creator supremacy in the moral realm: Job had no power to crush wickedness finally; so obviously he needed to leave that ultimate exercise of justice to God. He needed to let God be God. He needed to cease his agitation over what God was doing and trust him to do right.

These verses are presented as an aggressive challenge to Job. "Unleash your fury . . . Crush the wicked . . . then I myself will admit that your own right hand can save you" (see vv.11–12, 14). But they are lovingly designed to shake Job's spirit into realizing God is the only Creator and the only Savior there is. Job needed to and would learn to quietly and trustfully rest in that truth. To confirm this truth the Lord proceeded to paint the word pictures of these awesome creatures that defied God and man. Indeed the second is so awesome nothing on earth is his equal (41:33).

15–24 Only one other place in the OT uses the word *bᵉhēmôt* as a singular. The *ôt* ending normally marks the feminine plural when the word simply means beast. Here the ending has an intensive force meaning the beast par excellence; that is, the beast becomes a monster. The other passage (Ps 73:22) is clearly metaphorical. There the psalmist confesses to God: "I was a brute beast before you." But if Behemoth is a mere beast in Job 40, the language, apart from hyperbole, is difficult to understand. What could possibly be the reason for such hyperbole? In v.19a Behemoth is labeled the "first among the works of God." Pope (p. 272) translates the line "a primordial production of God." This fits Pope's purely mythological interpretation, but we suggest it is mythopoeic language (cf. Ps 74:13–14), intended as another way of referring to a unique cosmic creature such as the Accuser in the Prologue. He is beyond the pale of mere human strength, just as the Accuser was. But, as noted above, this information cannot be revealed to Job and that explains the extravagant language. The use of the two names Behemoth and Leviathan is a poetic repetition, just as Psalm 74 refers to the breaking of the heads of the monster (*tanninim*) and the heads of Leviathan, both referring to the power of Egypt at the Red Sea. In Ugaritic the goddess Anat conquered the seven-headed Leviathan along with a bovine creature called "El's *Bullock*" (ANET, p. 137, line 41). Since similar mythopoeic language is used for Leviathan (Ps 74:12–14), it is a small step to view the Behemoth figure in the same light.

41:1–34 Verses 1–9 develop the thought that Leviathan is far too powerful for man to handle. The first eight verses are addressed to Job; and they assert that any relationship Job may attempt to have with the Leviathan will be doomed to failure—whether by treaty or by force. Linguistic problems in vv.10 and 12 make it necessary to be careful about their interpretation (see Notes), but most are agreed that at this point God states that he alone has the power to control Leviathan; therefore he is the only Supreme Being. In these verses we reach the climax of the stanza. But this is not the original conclusion of the whole poem as Westermann claims (*Structure of Job*, p. 119). It is perfectly good Hebrew style to put such a climax in the middle of the poem.

Before this climax the stress was on human impotence before the Leviathan. After the climax (vv.12–34) the poem becomes a masterly description of this creature that goes beyond anything ascribable to a mere crocodile or whale. We translate beginning in 41:18:

> His snorting flashes forth lightning;
> > his eyes are like the glow of dawn.
> Flames stream from his mouth;
> > sparks of fire leap forth.
> From his nostrils pours smoke,
> > as from a pot heated by burning brushwood.
> His breath sets coals ablaze;
> > a flame pours from his mouth.

And v.25

> When he arises, the heavenly beings are afraid;
> > they are beside themselves because of the crashing.

Swords, javelins, arrows, clubs, slingstones—all are ineffective against him according to vv.26–29. And in v.33 we read:

> "On earth there is not his equal;
> > he was made without fear.
> He looks down on all that is lofty;
> > he is king over all proud beings."

Is this merely a crocodile or should it be understood in light of Isaiah 27:1, etc.?

By telling of his dominion over Behemoth and Leviathan, the Lord is illustrating what he has said in 40:8–14. He is celebrating his moral triumph over the forces of evil. Satan, the Accuser, has been proved wrong though Job does not know it. The author and the reader see the entire picture that Job and his friends never knew. No rational theory of suffering is substituted for the faulty one the friends proffered. The only answer given is the same as in Genesis. God permitted the Accuser to touch Job as part of his plan to humiliate Satan. But now that the contest is over, God still did not reveal his reason to Job. Job did not find out what the readers know. That is why Job could be restored without destroying the integrity of the account. To understand this is to understand why the forces of moral disorder are veiled underneath mythopoeic language about ferocious, uncontrollable creatures. Once again we emphasize that if the specific and ultimate reason for his suffering had been revealed to Job—even at this point—the value of the account as a comfort to others who must suffer in ignorance would have been diminished if not cancelled.

In 41:9 the Hebrew Bible begins a new chapter. No doubt the scribes responsible for putting the break here noticed how the questions put to Job reached a climax in v.8. We agree that a break exists here but would put it after v.9 or possibly after v.10 (see Notes on v.10). After the lead-in (v.7; cf. 38:2–3), this speech has the following structure:

			Leviathan	
	Behemoth		41:1–41:34	
Prologue	40:15–24			Apex	
40:8–14	Description (15b–23)	Relationship to Job (41:1–10)	Relationship to God: Yahweh controls (41:11–12)	Comparative Description (41:13–34)
Sets moral tone	Relationship to Job (15b, 24) Relationship to God (15b, 19)			Human impotence (13–14) Display of power (14–32) Greatest earthly power (33–34)

Notes

---

11 The phrase כָּל־גֵּאֶה (*kol-gē'eh,* "every proud man") here and in v. 12 need not be limited to men. "Proud one" is a tighter translation and allows for the interpretation that God alone can control the forces of evil whether human or otherwise. Those forces include all the "proud" and "haughty" beings mentioned in 41:34. The same idea should be applied to the word "wicked" in v. 12. Such an interpretation would include the Accuser of the Prologue whom God, for good reason, does not see fit ever to mention to Job.

15 Although בְּהֵמוֹת (*behēmôt,* "the behemoth") looks like a plural, the singular verbs in this context prove it was understood as the plural of majesty or intensive plural, which like אֱלֹהִים (*'elōhîm,* "God") is not plural at all. As Pope notes, it is the Beast par excellence. In contrast to OT use of Leviathan, the mythopoeic usage suggested above appears only here and not elsewhere in the OT when the plural form of *behēmāh* is used (cf. Pss 8:8; 50:10; 73:22; Joel 1:20; 2:22; Hab 2:17).

19 For רֵאשִׁית דַּרְכֵי־אֵל (*rē'šît darkê-'ēl,* "first among the works of God"), the KJV reads "chief of the ways of God." Dahood renders this line "the finest manifestation of God's power." He bases this on the possibility that the Ugaritic *drkt* can mean "dominion" or "power" (cf. Prov 31:3; Hos 10:13). See M.J. Dahood's "Ugaritic DRKT and Biblical DEREK," JTS 15 (1954): 627–31, and id., *Psalms,* 16:2. But see also our note on 26:14.

GKC (p. 358, n.1) calls הָעֹשׂוֹ (*hā'ōśô,* "his Maker") an anomaly "since a word determined by a genitive does not admit of being determined by the article." This problem dissolves if the pronoun suffix is logically conceived as the direct object of the verbal aspect of this participle, reading "the one making him."

20 Two interpretations of כִּי־בוּל הָרִים יִשְׂאוּ־לוֹ (*kî-bûl hārîm yiśe'û-lô,* "The hills bring him their produce") seem equally convincing. The NIV understands *bûl* as a short form of *yebûl* ("produce"), in which case the stress is on the great amount of pasture this beast can devour. Pope calls attention to the bovine monsters of Ugaritic called "Eaters" and "Devourers" and the Gilgamesh Epic's Bull of Heaven with its prodigious intake. A slightly different translation renders the verb as passive (by means of an indefinite subject): "The produce of the hills is brought to him."

The other interpretation follows Tur-Sinai (*Job,* in loc.) in his comparison of the Akkadian *bûl şeri* ("beast[s] of the steppe") with *bul hārîm* ("beast of the hills"). The strength of this lies in the parallelism with "the beast(s) of the field" in v.20b (NIV, "wild animals").

But it is not necessary to follow Pope's insistence on emending the verb *yiśeʾû* ("they lift up"), which may be understood as an elliptical expression meaning either "show respect" (with *pānîm*) or "rejoice" (with *qôl*) and thereby paralleling the verb *śḥq* ("play") in v.20b (cf. Gordis, *Job,* p. 478).

23 כִּי־יָגִיחַ יַרְדֵּן (*kî-yāgîaḥ yardēn,* "though the Jordan should surge")—here and in Ps 42:6 (7 MT) are the only two places in the OT where *yardēn* ("Jordan") is used without the article, though both contexts use the article—Ps 42:3 (4 MT): *hayyôm* ("the day"); Job 40:20: *haśśādeh* ("the wild"). So this involves something more than the poetic nature of these texts. We would also expect an article with the word "river" in v.23a unless it is an epithet. In Ugaritic "River" was an epithet of Yam, the sea god (cf. ANET, p. 129); and the same may be true of Jordan if its basic meaning is "river" (cf. E.B. Smick, *Archaeology of the Jordan Valley* [Grand Rapids: Baker, 1973], pp. 26–30; C.H. Gordon, *The World of the Old Testament,* [Garden City, N.Y.: Doubleday, 1958], p. 122, n. 19). So if "Jordan" and "River" are used as names in support of the mythopoeic overtone, this does not in the least deprive the text of the colorful literal figure of the surging Jordan. Rather it suggests that underlying that figure and all this language based on a terrestrial mammoth is a cosmic creature that even cosmic beings cannot perturb; indeed only his Maker can handle him (v.19).

24 Attempts to emend בְּעֵינָיו (*beʿênāyw,* "by the eyes") to read "in his lair" (Kissane) or "by hooks" (Driver-Gray) or "by double rings" (Gordis) or make it refer to "a spring" (NIV mg.) are all misguided since "eyes" and "nose," which open and close the couplet, are a parallel pair. Dhorme's citing of Herodotus on using plaster on a crocodile's eyes to control him has the merit of reasonably explaining the meaning, but it also means this line goes with what follows. Since 41:1 begins a whole series of questions about Leviathan and none have been asked regarding Behemoth, it seems appropriate to begin the questioning here. Simply counting syllables (7/7) refutes those critics who think that *mî hûʾ* ("Who is he?" = "Who indeed?") fell out of the first half of v.24 (cf. H.H. Rowley, "Job," NCB, p. 258).

41:9 [41:1 MT] Instead of הֶן־תֹּחַלְתּוֹ (*hēn-tōḥaltô,* "any hope of subduing him"), one MS says "your hope"; but that merely shows how that editor struggled with the line. The NIV's paraphrase is based on understanding the third person pronoun as dative—"hope regarding him"—rather than as possessive—"his hope" (cf. KJV).

For הֲגַם (*hᵃgam,* untr. in NIV), the NIV (cf. BHS mg.) considers *h* a dittograph and thinks the particle *gam* ("also") is not needed in English.

In rendering אֶל־מַרְאָיו יֻטָל (*ʾel-marʾāyw yuṭāl*) as "the mere sight of him is overpowering," NIV treats the line as it appears in the MT, making the subject of the verb indefinite (cf. KJV, which inserts a negative: "Shall not one be cast down"). Others (e.g., Pope) have followed a lead suggested by the Syriac and Symmachus, which read *ʾēl* ("god") for the preposition *ʾel.* Pope likens it to the consternation of the gods over the monsters that Tiamat created (Babylonian Creation Epic, ANET, p. 64) and following Cheyne emends to *ʾēlîm* ("gods"), which requires the verb also be made plural. Pope, influenced by the KJV, also inserts a negative, reading: "Were not the gods cast down . . .?" Since this use of the preposition *ʾel* with the verb *ṭûl* ("cast down") is unusual, *ʾēl* ("god" or "godlike being") may be correct as a reference, not to God or even El of the Ugaritic pantheon, but to a mighty being, angelic or human (cf. 41:25). The force of *gam* ("also," "even") then may be significant; thus: "Even a mighty being (angel) is cast down at the sight of him" (cf. Kissane).

10 Gray, Dhorme, and Pope all see לֹא־אַכְזָר (*lōʾ-ʾakzār,* "no one is fierce enough") as descriptive of Leviathan and make it a question: "Is he not fierce . . .?" KJV, RSV, NIV et al. stress a slightly different point. The verse could be a contrast between the two powerful beings introducing the climax of the poem. We read: "Is he not fierce when one arouses him?/ But who is it that can stand against me?"

Instead of לְפָנַי (*lepānay,* "against me"), many Hebrew MSS and the LXX read "him" for "me." Blommerde (p. 8) appeals to the use of the third person suffix yod (see Notes on

9:35). Using the third person would keep the emphasis on Leviathan. This verse would go with v.9, and vv.11–12 would form the climax of the poem (see comments above and below).

11 In מִי הִקְדִּימַנִי וַאֲשַׁלֵּם (*mî hiqdîmanî wa'ăšallēm*, "Who has a claim against me that I must repay?"), the first verb (*hiqdîmanî*) means "to confront." The NIV uses *šalam* ("to repay"), the second verb, to throw light on the first verb. Hence "confronting to claim a debt" or "confronting to give a gift" (cf. Deut 23:4) is the way it is construed. If Paul has this verse in mind in Rom 11:35, he is at best paraphrasing; for he follows neither the Hebrew nor the LXX fully. The LXX, which reads: "Who can resist me and remain (safe)?" may have understood the second verb as an Aramaism. The so-called aphel stem (cf. Jer 25:3) would account for the aleph that normally would indicate the first person imperfect (NIV). But even in the Piel, the verb (*šlm*) can mean "remain" or "make safe" (cf. 8:6) as well as "repay." We agree, however, with Habel (*Job*, 1985) who wants to keep the first person (p. 555) and render the line "Whoever confronts me I requite" (p. 551).

The questions raised by Pope, Gordis, Dhorme et al. against the way KJV, RSV, and NIV translate לִי־הוּא (*lî-hû'*, "belongs to men") are legitimate. The Hebrew of this line does not say "under heaven all is mine" but "under all the heaven he (it) is mine," which is a problem as to both translation and context. Without emending the text the words can mean "he is against me," based on a similar syntax that appears in Gen 13:13. The whole line would then read: "Underneath all the heavens he [Leviathan] is against me." As the apex and climax of the poem, Yahweh is asserting his supremacy over this creature who uniquely opposes him because nothing on earth is his equal (v.33). Understanding vv.11 –12 in this way ties the Leviathan picture to the important concept of Yahweh's supremacy in the Prologue (40:8–14). This climax is flanked first by questions about man's (Job's) ability to overpower Leviathan (40:24–41:9) and then by a detailed description of the fearsome creature who terrifies even the mighty (angels?) (41:13–34).

12 In the NIV the description of Leviathan begins here—בַּדָּיו וּדְבַר־גְּבוּרוֹת וְחִין עֶרְכּוֹ (*baddāyw ûdᵉbār-gᵉbûrôt wᵉhîn 'erkô*, "his limbs, his strength and his graceful form"). But is this verse about his strong and graceful body? Many feel it is about his boasting against Yahweh. Much depends on whether the word *baddāyw* ("his limbs") comes from a root meaning "a part," "member," "limb," as used in 18:13, or from a root that means "idle, vain talk," as used in 11:3 (cf. BDB, pp. 94–95). The last word in the line—*'erkô* ("his form")—can be used either way but is used often in Job for the arrangement (form) of words (13:18; 23:4; 32:14; 33:5; 37:19). As for *hîn*, rather than making it a byform of *hēn* ("grace"), which is inappropriate for the context, we prefer to see here the root *hnn* II ("be loathsome, stale") as used by Job in 19:17, or from *hana'* ("bend"), which appears in Arabic for anything "crooked" or "dubious" (cf. W.T. Wortabet, *Wortabet's Arabic-English Dictionary* [Beirut: Librairie du Liban, 1968], p. 121). Moreover the objection that an animal (crocodile?) cannot speak is refuted by v.3 where he is attributed the ability to speak. Having established that Leviathan is too fierce for any human being, Yahweh now reaches his climax (apex) in vv.11–12. We translate:

> Who can confront me and remain safe?
> When under all the heavens he dares oppose me
> will not I silence [cf. 11:3] his boastings,
> his powerful word and his dubious arguments?

22 It is not really clear whether דְּאָבָה (*dᵉʾābāh*) means "dismay" (NIV) or "faintness" from the Aramaic *dʾb* ("to waste away"). The LXX confuses it with *'bd* ("destruction"), which fits the context better, but not the root. The Qumran Targum renders it "vigor" (cf. Pope, p. 343), which tends to support F.M. Cross, Jr. ("Ugaritic *dbʾat* and Hebrew Cognates," VetTest 2 [1952]: 163f.), who saw here a metathesis of the word *dbʾh* ("power" in Ugar.) (cf. Deut 33:25 where it means "strength").

The NIV's "goes" is too weak for the Aramaism דּוּץ (*dûṣ*, "dance"). We read the line "his power leaps before him."

24 לִבּוֹ (*libbô,* "his chest") is literally "his heart." The NIV has unfortunately taken this as metonymy, losing the moral tone. If this creature can be "proud" (v.34), he certainly can be hard-hearted and so stubborn. See Ezekiel's contrast between the heart of stone and the heart of flesh (11:19; 36:26).

25 The NIV, like the BHS conjecture, translates אֵלִים (*'ēlîm,* "the mighty") as if spelled *'êlîm* from *'ayil* ("ram," "leader," "chief"). The MT's *'ēlîm* ("gods" or "heavenly beings") suggests again the cosmic (hidden) aspect of Leviathan.

D. *Job's Closing Contrition*

42:1–6

¹Then Job replied to the Lᴏʀᴅ:

²"I know that you can do all things;
no plan of yours can be thwarted.
³ ˌYou asked,ᵤ 'Who is this that obscures my counsel without knowledge?'
Surely I spoke of things I did not understand,
things too wonderful for me to know.

⁴ˌ"You said,ᵤ 'Listen now, and I will speak;
I will question you,
and you shall answer me.'
⁵My ears had heard of you
but now my eyes have seen you.
⁶Therefore I despise myself
and repent in dust and ashes."

1–2 Job's immediate response (v.1) shows that he understood clearly the thrust of the second divine speech. As we have noted in the opening comments on that speech, the prologue (40:8–14) sets the tone—that God is all-powerful, especially as Lord over the moral sphere. He alone puts down evil and brings to pass all his holy will. This, as we have tried to show, is the thought also of the climax (apex) of the Leviathan poem (cf. 41:11–12; see Notes). Job opened his mouth to tell God that he had gotten the message: God's purpose is all that counts, and since he is God he is able to bring it to pass (v.2). There is nothing else Job needed to know—only, perhaps, that this Sovereign of the universe was his friend (42:7–8).

3–4 There are two unannounced quotations in these verses (cf. the beginnings of v.3 and v.4 in the Heb.). In v.3 Job appropriately agreed with the quote from 38:2. He admitted that he did, indeed, obscure God's counsel through ignorance. Chastened thus by the wonders of God (v.3c), he quoted in v.4 the line God himself had seen fit to use twice on Job (38:3; 40:7, at the opening of each speech). The question is expressive of the nature of the divine discourses. God took the witness stand in his own behalf and cross-examined Job who now records the final effect of this proceeding.

5–6 Job had heard about God (v.5). Finally his often-requested prayer to come into his presence has been answered—the result: withdrawal of his rash statements when he fanticized about God's failure to be just and loving. The verb translated "I despise myself" (v.6) could be rendered "I reject what I said" (see Notes). A major interpretative issue centers on the meaning of the second verb in v.6, translated "and repent." Andersen (*Job*, in loc.) stresses the thought that Job "confesses no sins here," but that is true only in the sense that Job's integrity has been vindicated. Job did not need to repent over sins that brought on his suffering since his suffering was not the result of his sin.

One should not, however, assume that Job had nothing to be sorry for. His questioning of God's justice, for which God chided him in 38:2 (quoted in v.3), is enough to call forth a change of heart and mind. But the word *nāḥam* ("repent") has a breadth of meaning that includes not only "to be sorry, repent" but also "to console oneself" or "be comforted." So it may be that Job was saying that because he had had this encounter with God (v.5b)—since he has really "seen" God—he has been delivered of his fantasy about God. Job thus rejected (despised) what he had so recently said; for he now understood that God was his friend, not his enemy. So he was consoled and comforted though still suffering.

Notes

3–4 The NIV's insertion of "You asked" and "You said" as indicators of unannounced quotes may be compared to KJV, which leaves the text as is and thereby obscures the meaning, or to NEB, which drops the first line of v.3 and suppresses v.4 to a footnote, suggesting the Hebrew has mistakenly added it.

 6 Note the lack of an object on the verb עַל־כֵּן אֶמְאַס (*'al-kēn 'emʾas*, "Therefore I despise myself"). We learn from its use in 7:16 and 36:5 that this verb leaves the object implied, to be supplied according to the needs of the context. "I despise myself" therefore is only one possible interpretation. Since the root often means "reject," the implied object in the light of v.3 is what he spoke in ignorance.

V. The Epilogue (42:7–17)

Job has learned that man by himself cannot deduce the reason why anyone suffers. Still unknown to Job was the fact that his suffering had been used by God to vindicate God's trust in him over against the accusations of the Accuser. So without anger toward him, God allowed Job to suffer in order to humiliate the Accuser and provide support to countless sufferers who would follow in Job's footsteps. Once the purpose of the book had been fulfilled, Job's suffering could not continue without God's being capricious. We see here the heart of the difference between the suffering of the wicked as punishment and of the righteous to accomplish God's higher purpose. This lavish restoration (double all he had) is not based on Job's righteousness but on God's love for him as one who had suffered the loss of all things for God's sake and for no other reason. Here Job joined the Suffering Servant of Isaiah 53 who "after the suffering of his soul" sees "the light of life" and is given "a portion among the great" and "will divide the spoils with the strong" (Isa 53:11–12).

A. *The Verdict*

42:7–9

> ⁷After the LORD had said these things to Job, he said to Eliphaz the Temanite, "I am angry with you and your two friends, because you have not spoken of me what is right, as my servant Job has. ⁸So now take seven bulls and seven rams and go to my servant Job and sacrifice a burnt offering for yourselves. My servant Job will pray for you, and I will accept his prayer and not deal with you according to your folly. You have not spoken of me what is right, as my servant Job has." ⁹So Eliphaz the Temanite, Bildad the Shuhite and Zophar the Naamathite did what the LORD told them; and the LORD accepted Job's prayer.

7–9 Why did God commend Job for "speaking of him what is right" and condemn the counselors who had always taken God's side, often with beautiful creedal hymns (v.7)? Some interpreters have taken this apparent incongruity as proof that the writer has in mind only the Job of the Prologue and that part of the story is lost where the counselors give advice similar to that of Job's wife. Such a view simplifies God's rebuke. Fortunately that approach to the book has been largely abandoned, but the question is still there. God had just rebuked Job for many wrong words during his dispute with the counselors; in what sense, then, was he here commended for saying what was right? Pope (p. 350) claims it will not do to take the word *nᵉkônāh* ("right") to mean "sincerity" since such a meaning cannot be sustained from usage.

Nᵉkônāh is based on the root *kûn* ("be established, made firm"), which has an adjectival derivative: *kēn,* meaning "upright" or "honest" (Gen 42:11, 19 et al.). That meaning fits Y. Kaufmann's claim (*Religion of Israel,* p. 335) that Job felt a moral duty to speak honestly before God (see Introduction: Authorship and Unity). But the derivative *kēn* is not used here. Of the wicked the psalmist says, "No truth [*nᵉkônāh*] is in their mouth" (Ps 5:9, lit. tr.). In 1 Samuel 23:23 the word means "reliable information." The counselors certainly lacked the right information about why Job was suffering. Job spoke without understanding (v.3) and was often fiery and emotional in his remarks (15:12–13; 18:4). His opinions and feelings were often wrong, but his facts were right. He was not being punished for sins he had committed. But the friends were claiming to know for a certainty things they did not know and so were falsely accusing Job while mouthing beautiful words about God. Job rightly accused them of lying about him and trying to flatter God (13:4, 7–11).

Pope (p. 350) mildly suggests that it may not be the words of the Dialogue that are in mind but that if they are, v.7 is "as magnificent a vindication as Job could have hoped for, proving that God values the integrity of the impatient protester and abhors pious hypocrites who would heap accusations on a tormented soul to uphold their theological position."

In v.8 the counselors who are no longer with Job are ordered by God to go back to Job with sacrificial animals sufficient to atone for their transgressions. The sacrifice performed by Job was an integral part of the worship in which Job prayed for them. Praying for your enemy (Matt 5:43–44; Luke 6:27–28) was already taught and practiced in the OT (Ps 35:12–14; 109:4–5). And showing mercy to one's enemies was a faith principle clearly required in Exodus 23:4–5. In the Wisdom Literature such behavior was considered a mark of godliness (Prov 25:21–22). The psalmist believed that those who repaid him "evil for good, and hatred for . . . friendship" (Ps 109:5) were opposing God; so he uttered imprecations against them (Ps 109:6–20; cf. Job 27:7; Matt 23:13–36). The two patterns of behavior are considered a problem only by those who do not think rebellion against God is very serious. Since God had a high purpose for Job's suffering, the counselors made themselves enemies of God by accusing Job. The large sacrifice (v.8) shows how grave the Lord considered their sin. Grave as it was he accepted Job's intercession (lit., "lifted up Job's face"). Job who might have held a grudge did not fail to love those who had spitefully abused him when he was most helpless. This lofty and practical truth is a fitting theological finale to a book that calls forth a rigorous exercise of both soul and mind.

Notes

8 The NIV has taken the liberty of adding to עֲשׂוֹת עִמָּכֶם נְבָלָה (*ʾăśôṯ ʾimmākem nᵉḇālāh*, "deal with you according to your folly") the extra pronoun "your," which avoids the anthropopathism that God should do folly. Pope (p. 350) wants to keep the striking figure adding that *nᵉḇālāh* ("wanton sin," "folly") is almost always sexual. Dhorme's position seems better. He renders (in loc.) the line "inflict on you something disgraceful." This is in keeping with the Prologue where the Accuser is permitted by God to do just this to Job.

B. *The Restoration*

42:10–17

> ¹⁰After Job had prayed for his friends, the Lᴏʀᴅ made him prosperous again and gave him twice as much as he had before. ¹¹All his brothers and sisters and everyone who had known him before came and ate with him in his house. They comforted and consoled him over all the trouble the Lᴏʀᴅ had brought upon him, and each one gave him a piece of silver and a gold ring.
> ¹²The Lᴏʀᴅ blessed the latter part of Job's life more than the first. He had fourteen thousand sheep, six thousand camels, a thousand yoke of oxen and a thousand donkeys. ¹³And he also had seven sons and three daughters. ¹⁴The first daughter he named Jemimah, the second Keziah and the third Keren-Happuch. ¹⁵Nowhere in all the land were there found women as beautiful as Job's daughters, and their father granted them an inheritance along with their brothers.
> ¹⁶After this, Job lived a hundred and forty years; he saw his children and their children to the fourth generation. ¹⁷And so he died, old and full of years.

10 The restoration, it is claimed, contradicts the purpose of the book, which is to present an alternate to the counselors' orthodox view of suffering held as normative in so much of the OT. When Job received again his prosperity, righteousness was rewarded and his whole case defeated. But we would remind the reader that the purpose was not to contradict normative OT theology but to provide a balance of truth. All things being equal, sin brings suffering and righteousness blessing. Since Job had successfully endured the test and proved that his righteousness was not rooted in his own selfishness, there was no reason for Job to continue to be tested; his sufferings needed to cease. God created humans so that he might bless them, not curse them. Job had been declared innocent of all those false accusations; so he

could not continue to suffer as punishment. And God's higher purpose had been fulfilled; so there was no reason why Job should not be restored.

11 Job's relatives who had kept their distance from the suffering spectacle (19:13–15) here proved themselves to be fair-weather friends. Their comforting and consoling came a little late, but their presents were expensive (v.11): a "ring of gold" (for the nose [Gen 24:47; Isa 3:21] or the ears [Gen 35:4; Exod 32:2]) and a "piece of silver" (*qᵉśîṭāh*). The latter was not money in the sense of coinage but an early designation of weight like the shekel (see Notes).

12–15 Verses 12–13 highlight the twofold increase of Job's possessions as compared to the Prologue (1:3). Everything is twofold except Job's sons and daughters. But Dhorme translates v.13 "fourteen sons," seeing an old Semitic dual form of the word for "seven" (pp. 651–52, but see Notes). This would leave only Job's daughters unmultiplied twofold. Pope (p. 352) claims that fits the general cultural pattern that frowned on a surplus of daughters. Whether or not that is the reason, it is curious that the author ignores the sons and concentrates on Job's daughters (vv.14–15). The Ugaritic literature proves this prominence of women is in keeping with the social milieu of epic tradition (see Notes on v.13).

The daughters are named and granted an inheritance even when sons are available. Zelophehad's daughters in Numbers 36 were granted an inheritance only because he had no sons. The stress on the great beauty of Job's daughters is also characteristic of the epic tradition (Sarna, *Prose of Job*, p. 24). Their names are indicative of their beauty: Jemimah means "turtledove"; Keziah is probably an aromatic plant as in the name Cinnamon ("cassia" in Ps 45:8); and Keren-Happuch means "a jar (horn) of eye paint."

16–17 Job's longevity was in keeping with patriarchal tradition (possibly double the normal span of Ps 90:10). Certainly the wisdom ideal of seeing one's grandchildren is fulfilled twice over to the fourth generation (cf. Gen 50:23); and the patriarchal formula "old and full of years," expressive of a completely fulfilled life, is used (cf. Gen 25:8; 35:29).

Notes

10 Gesenius (GKC, par. 91k) takes the singular noun רֵעֵהוּ (*rēʿēhû*, "his friends") to be collective. But it is also possible the author uses the singular to state a principle: "after Job prayed for his neighbor." This deed proves Job was spiritually ready for restoration.

11 קְשִׂיטָה (*qᵉśîṭāh*, "piece of silver") is used only here and in Gen 33:19 and Josh 24:32, which indicates it was an early (patriarchal?) unit of exchange. Its value is unknown, but the LXX (and other versions except Symm.) says each one gave him a lamb. Rabbis Akiba and Qimchi confirm its monetary meaning, and Dhorme notes that the lamb was used as a basis for uniformity in exchange so that a weight of gold or silver corresponding to the price of a lamb might have been called a *qᵉśîṭāh*. Compare the oldest Roman coins with a picture of an ox, sheep, or pig and the Latin *pecunia* from *pecus* ("cattle").

13 Concerning שִׁבְעָנָה בָנִים (*šibʿānāh bānîm*, "seven sons"), Dhorme defends the unique ending on *šibʿāh* as an old Semitic dual (*ān*), thus doubling the number of sons (see

above). But Sarna ("Poetry of Job," p. 18) sees only an archaism here related to the Ugaritic *šb'ny*, claiming the sociology of the story mirrors an epic background that tends to exalt the female as in vv. 14–15. Even in the Prologue (1:4, 13) the daughters participated in the feasts. In Ugaritic, Baal has three daughters—*Pdry*, *Tly*, and *Arṣy*—and seven unnamed sons; and in the Epic of Kirtu the king's daughter shares her father's estate with her brothers (ibid., p. 24).